THE 1996 PRENTICE HALL GUIDE TO ECONOMICS FACULTY

Compiled by
James R. Hasselback
College of Business
Florida State University
Tallahassee, Florida

PRENTICE HALL, Upper Saddle River, NJ 07458

Production Editor: *Joseph F. Tomasso*
Associate Editor: *Kristen Kaiser*
Acquisitions Editor: *Leah B. Jewell*
Manufacturing Buyer: *Ken Clinton*

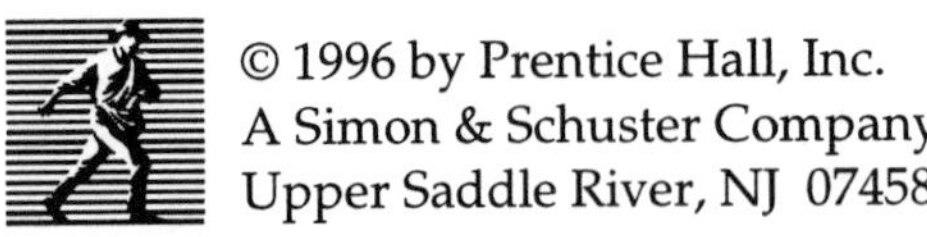

A Simon & Schuster Company
Upper Saddle River, NJ 07458

Printed in the United States of America

10 9 8 7 6 5 4 3 2 1

ISBN 0-13-253766-4

Prentice-Hall International (UK) Limited, *London*
Prentice-Hall of Australia Pty. Limited, *Sydney*
Prentice-Hall Canada Inc., *Toronto*
Prentice-Hall Hispanoamericana, S.A., *Mexico*
Prentice-Hall of India Private Limited, *New Delhi*
Prentice-Hall of Japan, Inc., *Tokyo*
Simon & Schuster Asia Pte. Ltd., *Singapore*
Editora Prentice-Hall do Brasil, Ltda., *Rio de Janeiro*

JAMES R. HASSELBACK

James R. Hasselback is a Professor of Taxation at Florida State University and has previously taught at Eastern Michigan University, the University of Florida, and Texas A&M University. He received his PhD in Accounting from Michigan State University. A member of the American Accounting Association and the American Taxation Association, he has published over 120 papers in professional and academic journals, including THE ACCOUNTING REVIEW, THE TAX ADVISER, FINANCIAL MANAGMENT, JOURNAL OF REAL ESTATE TAXATION, and the AMERICAN BUSINESS LAW JOURNAL.

Dr. Hasselback has presented papers at numerous national and regional professional meetings, and served as chairman at tax sessions of professional conferences. He regularly presents continuing education seminars for Certified Public Accountants. He is co-author on a two-volume introductory taxation textbook published by Commerce Clearing House, serving as technical editor on the second volume. Jim teaches in Florida State University's CPA Review Course.

Also, Jim is the editor of *Accounting Perspectives--The Journal*. The journal focuses on faculty issues such as research productivity, promotion, movement, and gender issues related to those topics.

Jim Hasselback has compiled an Accounting Faculty Directory published by Prentice Hall for the past twenty-one years. The Accounting Faculty Directory may be the most cited reference in the Accounting field. In addition to the Prentice Hall Guide to Economics Faculty, other Directories in the business field include: a Directory of Management Faculty, a Directory of Finance Faculty, a Directory of Marketing Faculty, and a Directory of Business Law Faculty. An Engineering Faculty Directory, published in November 1992, was his first venture in preparing a Directory outside of the business area. A Directory of Computer Science Faculty was published in March 1994. A Nursing Faculty Directory was published in January 1995. Work has begun on directories in other fields including Biology, Chemistry, Physics, Criminal Justice, and Mathematics.

TABLE OF CONTENTS

PRINCIPLES OF ECONOMICS

TWO-SEMESTER PRINCIPLES OF ECONOMICS

NEW EDITION

PRINCIPLES OF ECONOMICS
Fourth Edition

Karl E. Case
Wellesley College

Ray C. Fair
Yale University

Written by an award-winning educator and a highly respected macroeconomist, this best-selling introduction to economics demonstrates the relevance of economics in students' studies, lives, and the world. It shows them that economics is a powerful way of *thinking* and actually teaches them *how to think* like an economist and how to use economics to interpret world events.

This student-friendly, hands-on approach to economics provides a unified approach to economic theory, issues, and policies. A lively writing style, clear explanations, dynamic graphs, relevant examples, and an unparalleled supplements package keep students motivated throughout the course.

• *©1996, 1040 pp., Cloth (0-13-440488-2); (44048-7)*

Principles of Microeconomics
Fourth Edition

• *©1996, 650 pp., Paper (0-13-440918-3); (44091-7)*

Principles of Macroeconomics
Fourth Edition

• *©1996, 650 pp., Paper (0-13-440843-8); (44084-2)*

MODERN ECONOMICS
First Edition

Jan S. Hogendorn
Colby College

This exciting textbook provides complete coverage of the principles in a concise presentation without sacrificing rigor. Students' understanding of the material is strengthened with gripping examples, many international.

• *©1995, 832 pp., Cloth (0-13-103995-4); (10399-4)*

PRINCIPLES OF MICROECONOMICS

PRINCIPLES OF MICROECONOMICS
First Edition

Eugene Silberberg
University of Washington

This text is an uncluttered approach to economics with a strong emphasis on simple, social science methodology. All examples and analyses flow from a few basic assumptions, such as diminishing marginal values, the law of diminishing marginal product, and comparative advantage. Many nontraditional examples are used such as adoption markets, political markets, and changes in smoking habits.

• *©1995, 560 pp., Paper (0-13-103714-5); (10371-3)*

ECONOMIC ISSUES

ECONOMIC ISSUES: Rhetoric and Reality
First Edition

Michael Walden
North Carolina State University

This text provides a fresh and lively analysis of current "hot-button" economic issues — from income distribution and international competition, to health care, executive pay, and poverty. Throughout, it follows a consistent theme — i.e., that all is NOT bad with the economy, that markets work, and that problems facing the economy can best be solved by altering incentives.

• *©1995, 304 pp., Paper (0-13-300245-4); (30024-4)*

MACROECONOMICS

INTERMEDIATE MACROECONOMICS

NEW EDITION

MACROECONOMICS: Theories and Policies
Fifth Edition

Richard T. Froyen
University of North Carolina, Chapel Hill

The author explains the difference among macroeconomists on issues of theory and policy while comparing and contrasting modern macroeconomic theory.

• *©1996, 672 pp., Cloth (0-13-233867-X); (23386-6)*

NEW!

MACROECONOMY, THE: Private Choices, Public Actions, and Aggregate Outcomes
First Edition

Michael B. McElroy
North Carolina State University

By addressing the interests, needs, and abilities of students, this practical text prepares students for a lifetime of macroeconomic issues that will arise in their multiple roles of consumer, business decision-maker, voter, and opinion leader. The goal of the text is to help students reach a basic understanding of macroeconomics issues that will not evaporate soon after the final exam, but will become a part of an economic common sense to be drawn upon throughout their lives.

• *©1996, 496 pp., Cloth (0-02-378801-1); (U4539-5)*

INTERNATIONAL ECONOMICS

INTERNATIONAL ECONOMICS
Fifth Edition

Dominick Salvatore
Fordham University

The number one book in the market, this text presents all the principles and theories essential to an in-depth understanding of international economics (trade and finance). Making the study of international economics manageable for undergraduates, the chapters feature an intuitive approach with more rigorous proofs presented in chapter appendices.

Emphasizing the relevance of concepts and theories through numerous real-world examples and applications as well as over 60 actual case studies, this edition of this text is updated to reflect recent developments and still offers unfailingly evenhanded, unbiased coverage of policy and ideology issues.

- *©1995, 778 pp., Cloth (0-02-405381-3); (U6070-9)*

COMPARATIVE ECONOMICS

NEW EDITION

COMPARATIVE ECONOMICS
Second Edition

James Angresano
Univesity of Texas, Austin

The text maintains a unique interdisciplinary approach that emphasizes the fluid, evolutionary nature of economics, while presenting additional aspects of economies not usually addressed in similar books. While integrating economic thought with economic history, it provides an alternative for students and teachers who wish to explore the variations of "mixed market economy" across countries.

- *©1996, 612 pp., Cloth (0-13-381633-8); (38163-2)*

ECONOMICS OF POVERTY AND DISCRIMINATION

ECONOMICS OF POVERTY AND DISCRIMINATION, THE
Sixth Edition

Bradley R. Schiller
American University

This book was written to provide students with a broad overview of the dimensions of poverty and discrimination, the various explanations for these social ills, and the policy options for addressing them.

- *©1995, 288 pp., Paper (0-13-315136-0); (31513-5)*

POLITICAL ECONOMY

NEW!

READINGS IN INTERNATIONAL POLITICAL ECONOMY
First Edition

David Balaam
The University of Puget Sound

Michael Veseth
The University of Puget Sound

This interdisciplinary collection of readings helps lower-division students understand state-market relations. The text is designed to stand on its own or to supplement other IPE texts (such as Balaam and Veseth's *Introduction to International Political Economy*).

- *©1996, 416 pp., Paper (0-13-149600-X); (14960-9)*

INTRODUCTION TO INTERNATIONAL POLITICAL ECONOMY
First Edition

David Balaam
The University of Puget Sound

Michael Veseth
The University of Puget Sound

This comprehensive introduction to international political economy clearly shows lower-division students how politics and economics come together in today's global environment. The text shows how an understanding of IPE can help students make *sense* of global news, business investments, and government policies, by presenting the theories, institutions, and relationships found in IPE in simple ways that retain the complexity of the world issues and intellectual problems addressed.

• *©1996, 496 pp., Paper (0-13-149592-5); (14959-1)*

STATE IN THE AMERICAN POLITICAL ECONOMY, THE
First Edition

Marc Allan Eisner
Wesleyan University

This text presents a broad overview of the American political economy — focusing on changing patterns of state-economy relations in the United States over the course of the past century.

• *©1995, 416 pp., Cloth (0-13-294810-9); (29481-9)*

MANAGING WORLD ECONOMIC CHANGE: International Political Economy
Second Edition

Robert Allen Isaak
Pace University

Using a collective learning approach, this text utilizes the standard of *laissez faire* free market ideology as a springboard to analyze global economic change. The Second Edition focuses on how change is managed in the post-capitalist global economy of the '90s, stressing the human, strategic, and political dimensions.

• *©1995, 336 pp., Paper (0-13-181678-0); (18167-7)*

MICROECONOMICS

INTERMEDIATE MICROECONOMICS

MICROECONOMICS
Third Edition

B. Curtis Eaton
Simon Fraser University

Diane F. Eaton

This highly-regarded text teaches microeconomics as a way of looking at the world, using plenty of empirical data to focus the discussion. It is considered an upper mid-range text in its mathematical rigor while maintaining accessibility through examples and applications. Calculus is included in easy-to-refer-to footnotes. This is an entirely new and updated edition of *Microeconomics, Second Edition* that was previously published by Freeman.

• *©1995, 610 pp., Cloth (0-13-147331-X); (14733-0)*

MICROECONOMICS
Third Edition

Robert S. Pindyck
Massachusetts Institue of Technology

Daniel L. Rubinfeld
University of California, Berkeley

Written by two of the most distinguished authors in the field, the third edition of this popular and highly acclaimed text continues to present microeconomic theory in an accessible manner. Featuring examples of business and pubic policy applications in each chapter, this text demonstrates theory at work in real companies, industry, and government to give students a more relevant and engaging treatment of microeconomics. Conveying the very latest developments in the field through lucid exposition and always with a minimum of mathematics, this text is now full-color and has numerous graphs and illustrations to make it the clearest written, most current, and engaging microeconomics text available.

- *©1995, 699 pp., Cloth (0-02-395900-2); (U5534-5)*

MICROECONOMICS
First Edition

Robert L. Sexton
Pepperdine University

This concise and intuitive text is designed to give the student a feel for economic institutions and a sense of perspective in dealing with unsolved economic problems. The argument is essentially nonmathematical, but for those who use a more mathematical approach, calculus is included in the footnotes. It also bridges some of the differences between micro- and macro-economics.

- *©1995, 656 pp., Cloth (0-13-103672-6); (10367-1)*

MANAGERIAL ECONOMICS

NEW!

MANAGERIAL ECONOMICS AND ORGANIZATION
First Edition

Zoltan J. Acs

Daniel A. Gerlowski
both of University of Baltimore

Managerial Economics and Organization is the *first* text to integrate the economics of organization into undergraduate managerial economics. The text begins with the economics of exchange and systematically develops the theory of economic organization. The approach is designed to accurately reflect the changing business environment through examination of organizational issues from a historical, technical, and global perspective. Finally, *Managerial Economics and Organization* is more integrated with traditional business disciplines than other managerial economics texts.

- *©1996, 544 pp., Cloth (0-02-300292-1); (U0002-8)*

NEW EDITION

MANAGERIAL ECONOMICS: Economic Tools for Todays Decision Makers
Second Edition

Paul G. Keat
American Graduate School of International Management

Philip K.Y. Young
Pace University

One of the most distinctive features of this text is a running case study that traces the decision-making processes of a single firm. This creates a vivid, dynamic business setting for coverage of microeconomic theory and the tools of quantitative analysis used in management decision making.

Each chapter begins with a problem confronting the management of "Global Foods," a hypothetical corporation competing in the soft drink industry. With this case situation as a backdrop, students readily grasp how economic principles develop throughout the chapter and relate to everyday business activity. In addition, actual business examples from the popular press — including many international examples — are incorporated within chapters to reinforce the connection between economic concepts and business problems.

• *©1996, 640 pp., Cloth (0-02-362183-4); (U3722-8)*

PUBLIC FINANCE

PUBLIC BUDGETING IN AMERICA
Fourth Edition

Thomas D. Lynch
Florida Atlantic University

Authoritative, comprehensive, and practical, this text explores public budgeting and financial management from the public manager's perspective — offering a balanced blend of theory and nuts-and-bolts "how-to" information.

• *©1995, 400 pp., Cloth (0-13-735846-6); (73584-5)*

INDUSTRIAL ORGANIZATION

STRUCTURE OF AMERICAN INDUSTRY, THE
Ninth Edition

Walter Adams
Michigan State University

James W. Brock
Miami University, Ohio

The ninth edition of this widely used reader continues to offer the leading real-world survey of contemporary American industries. Providing a sound new treatment of the role of public policy in a free-enterprise economy, this text illustrates the broadest possible range of American market structures through a series of carefully chosen and well-developed case studies of specific industries, all written by leading authorities in their field.

• *©1995, 336 pp., Paper (0-02-300833-4); (U0019-2)*

GOVERNMENT AND BUSINESS (ECONOMICS EMPHASIS)

BUSINESS AND GOVERNMENT IN THE GLOBAL MARKETPLACE
Fifth Edition

Murray L. Weidenbaum
Washington University

Weidenbaum addresses the intricate relationship between the public sector and the private sector — why and how government intervenes in the economy and how business can respond. The Fifth Edition provides analyses from both perspectives, covering the ways in which government policy affects the activities of the modern corporation and the key responses on the part of business.

• *©1995, 592 pp., Cloth (0-13-305707-0); (30570-6)*

ENVIRONMENTAL/NATURAL RESOURCE ECONOMICS

ECONOMICS AND THE ENVIRONMENT
First Edition

Eban S. Goodstein
Skidmore College
(Formerly of Lewis & Clark College)

Lively and accessible in style — yet rigorous and comprehensive in content — this text explores environmental economics from the perspective of four basic questions: How much pollution is too much? Is government up to the job? How can we do better? How can we resolve global issues? It examines a broad range of topics applicable to today's policy debates, and presents not only the "standard analysis," but also full-length treatments of important issues at the cutting edge of environmental policy debates that are usually ignored by other texts. Timely examples are integrated throughout.

• *©1995, 544 pp., Cloth (0-13-088766-8); (08876-5)*

AGRICULTURAL ECONOMICS

NEW!

THE ECONOMICS OF AGRICULTURAL PRICES
First Edition

Peter Helmberger
University of Wisconsin, Madison

Jean-Paul Chavas
University of Wisconsin, Madison

By incorporating recent advances in economics that are indispensable to understanding how agricultural markets operate and how prices are determined, this text helps students learn to **think rigorously and analytically about real-life economic phenomena**, that is, to think like economist. It helps students gain a *holistic* and coherent understanding of the complexity, interdependency, and synthesis within the production/marketing/policy mix that is involved in agricultural pricing.

• *©1996, 320 pp., Cloth (0-13-372640-1); (37264-9)*

INTRODUCTION TO AGRICULTURAL ECONOMICS
First Edition

John B. Penson
Texas A&M University

Oral Capps
Texas A&M University

Parr C. Rosson
Texas A&M University

These authors provide beginning students in agriculture with a systematic introduction to the basic concepts and issues in economics as they relate to a major segment of the U.S. economy — the food and fiber industry. Their coverage traces the major microeconomic and macroeconomic forces influencing the decisions of producers and consumers of food and fiber products.

• *©1996, 512 pp., Cloth (0-13-102468-X); (10246-7)*

REAL ESTATE ECONOMICS

NEW!

URBAN ECONOMICS AND REAL ESTATE MARKETS
First Edition

Denise DiPasquale
Harvard University

William C. Wheaton
Massachusetts Institute of Technology

This up-to-date, highly-accessible text presents a unique combination of *both* economic theory *and* real estate applications, providing students with the tools and techniques needed to understand the operation of urban real estate markets. It examines residential and non-residential real estate markets — from the perspectives of both macro- and microeconomics — as well as the role of government in real estate markets.

• *©1996, 400 pp., Cloth (0-13-225244-9); (22524-3)*

QUANTITATIVE METHODS IN ECONOMICS

SECONDARY ECONOMETRICS

NEW EDITION

ECONOMETRIC MODELS, TECHNIQUES, AND APPRECIATIONS
Second Edition

Michael D. Intriligator
University of California, Los Angeles

Ronald G. Bodkin
University of Ottawa

Cheng Hsiao
University of California, Irvine

This text surveys the theories, techniques (model-building and data collection), and applications of econometrics. It focuses on those aspects of econometrics that are of major importance to students and researchers interested in performing, evaluating, or understanding econometric studies in a variety of areas.

• *©1996, 704 pp., Cloth (0-13-224775-5); (22477-4)*

ECONOMIC STATISTICS AND ECONOMETRICS
Third Edition

Thad W. Mirer
State University New York, Albany

Designed for courses in economic statistics and introductory econometrics that aim to mix the development of technique with its application to real economic analysis. The text emphasizes formulating and interpreting regression models in economics, rather than on deriving and presenting technical material. It covers only those statistical topics that constitute a foundation for basic econometrics, and treats regression models in detail.

- *©1995, 464 pp., Cloth (0-02-381831-X); (U4845-6)*

MATHEMATICAL ECONOMICS

MATHEMATICS FOR ECONOMIC ANALYSIS
First Edition

Knut Sydsaeter
University of Oslo

Peter I. Hammond
Stanford University

An introduction to those parts of mathematical analysis and linear algebra which are most important for economists.

- *©1995, 800 pp., Cloth (0-13-583600-X); (58360-9)*

ALABAMA
University of Alabama
U of Alabama at Birmingham
U of Alabama in Huntsville
Alabama A&M University
Alabama State University
Athens State College
Auburn University
Auburn U at Montgomery
Birmingham-Southern Coll
Jacksonville State Univ
University of Montevallo
University of North Alabama
Samford University
University of South Alabama
Troy State University
Tuskegee University
University of West Alabama
ALASKA
Univ of Alaska Anchorage
Univ of Alaska Southeast
Univ of Alaska Fairbanks
ARIZONA
University of Arizona
Arizona State University
Grand Canyon University
Northern Arizona University
ARKANSAS
Arkansas College
University of Arkansas
U of Arkansas at Little Rock
U of Arkansas at Pine Bluff
Arkansas State University
Arkansas Tech University
Univ of Central Arkansas
Harding University
Hendrix College
Southern Arkansas Univ
CALIFORNIA
Azusa Pacific University
Biola University
U of California-Berkeley
Univ of California-Davis
Univ of Calif-Irvine
Univ of Calif, Los Angeles
Univ of Calif, Riverside
Univ of Calif, San Diego
U of Calif, Santa Barbara
U of Calif, Santa Cruz
California Institute of Tech
California Lutheran Univ
Calif Polytechnic State U
Calif State Poly U-Pomona
Calif State U., Bakersfield
Calif State Univ, Chico
Calif St U-Dominguez Hills
Calif State Univ-Fresno
Calif State Univ, Fullerton
Calif State Univ, Hayward
Calif State Univ - Humboldt
Calif State Univ, Long Beach
Calif State U-Los Angeles
Calif State Univ, Northridge
Calif State Univ-Sacramento
Calif St U-San Bernardino
Calif State U - San Marcos
Calif State U, Stanislaus
Chapman College
Claremont McKenna College
John F. Kennedy University
La Sierra University
University of LaVerne
Loyola Marymount Univ
Mount St. Mary's College
Naval Postgraduate School
Occidental College
University of the Pacific
Pacific Union College
Pepperdine Univ-Malibu
Point Loma Nazarene College
University of Redlands
Saint Mary's College
University of San Diego
San Diego State University
University of San Francisco
San Francisco State Univ
San Jose State University
Santa Clara University
Sonoma State University
Univ of Southern California
Stanford University
Woodbury University
COLORADO
Adams State College
Colorado College
Univ of Colorado at Boulder
U of Colorado at Co Springs
Univ of Colorado at Denver
Colorado State University
University of Denver
Fort Lewis College
Mesa State College
Metropolitan State College
Univ of Northern Colorado
Regis College of Regis Univ
Univ of Southern Colorado
U.S. Air Force Academy
Western State College of CO
CONNECTICUT
University of Bridgeport
Central Connecticut St Univ
Connecticut College
University of Connecticut
Eastern Conn State Univ
Fairfield Universiy
University of Hartford
University of New Haven
Quinnipiac College
Sacred Heart University
Southern Connecticut St Un
Teikyo Post University
Wesleyan University
Western Conn State Univ
Yale University
DELAWARE
University of Delaware
Delaware State College
Wesley College
FLORIDA
Barry University
Bethune-Cookman College
Univ of Central Florida
Embry-Riddle Aeronautical U
University of Florida
Florida A&M University
Florida Atlantic Univ
Florida Institute of Tech
Florida International Univ
Florida Southern College
Florida State University
Jacksonville University
University of Miami
University of North Florida
Rollins College
St. Thomas University
University of South Florida
Stetson University
University of Tampa
University of West Florida
GEORGIA
Albany State College
Augusta College
Berry College
Clark Atlanta University
Clayton State College
Columbus College
Emory University
Fort Valley State College
Georgia College
University of Georgia
Georgia Institute Tech
Georgia Southern University
Georgia Southwestern Coll
Georgia State University
Kennesaw College
Mercer Univ-Atlanta
Mercer Univ-Macon
Morehouse College
Morris Brown College
North Georgia College
Oglethorpe University
Piedmont College
Valdosta State University
West Georgia College
HAWAII
Brigham Young Univ-Hawaii
Chaminade University
University of Hawaii at Hilo
Univ of Hawaii at Manoa
Hawaii Pacific University
IDAHO
Boise State University
University of Idaho
Idaho State University
ILLINOIS
Augustana College
Bradley University
University of Chicago
Chicago State University
DePaul University
Eastern Illinois Univ
Elmhurst College
University of Illinois
Univ of Illinois at Chicago
Illinois Benedictine College
Illinois Institute of Tech
Illinois State University
Illinois Wesleyan University
Lewis University
Loyola University of Chicago
Millikin University
North Central College
Northeastern Illinois Univ
Northern Illinois Univ
Northwestern University
Olivet Nazarene College
Roosevelt University
Sangamon State University
Southern Illinois Univ
So Illinois, Edwardsville
Western Illinois University
Wheaton College
INDIANA
Anderson University
Ball State University
Butler University
University of Evansville
DePauw University
Goshen College
Indiana University
Indiana Univ at Kokoma
Indiana Univ Northwest
Indiana Univ at South Bend
Indiana Univ Southeast
Indiana State University
Indiana Wesleyan University
University of Indianapolis
Marian College
University of Notre Dame
Purdue University
Purdue University at Calumet
Saint Marys College
Univ of Southern Indiana
Taylor University
Tri State University
Valparaiso University
IOWA
Buena Vista College
Central University of Iowa
Coe College
Drake University
Graceland College
Grinnell College
University of Iowa
Iowa State University
Loras College
Luther College
Morningside College
University of Northern Iowa
St. Ambrose University
Simpson College
Wartburg College
KANSAS
Emporia State University
Fort Hays State University
University of Kansas
Kansas State University
Kansas Wesleyan University
Pittsburg State University
Washburn Univ of Topeka
Wichita State University
KENTUCKY
Bellarmine College
Berea College
Brescia College
Centre College
Cumberland College
Eastern Kentucky University
University of Kentucky
Kentucky State University
University of Louisville
Morehead State University
Murray State University
Northern Kentucky Univ
Transylvania University
Western Kentucky University
LOUISIANA
Dillard University
Grambling State University
Louisiana State University
Louisiana St in Shreveport
Louisiana Tech University
Loyola Univ-New Orleans
Mc Neese State University
University of New Orleans
Nicholls State University
Northeast Louisiana Univ
Northwestern State U of LA
Southeastern Louisiana Univ
Southern University
U of Southwestern Louisiana
Tulane University
MAINE
Bates College
Bowdoin College
Colby College
Univ of Maine at Orono
Univ of Southern Maine
MARYLAND
University of Baltimore
Frostburg State University
Hood College
Johns Hopkins University
Loyola College in Maryland
University of Maryland
Univ Maryland-Baltimore Cnty
Morgan State University
Mount Saint Mary's College
Salisbury State University
Towson State University
United States Naval Academy
Western Maryland College
MASSACHUSETTS
American International Coll
Amherst College
Assumption College
Babson College
Bentley College
Boston College
Boston University
Brandeis University
Clark University
Fitchburg State College
Framingham State College
Harvard University
College of the Holy Cross
University of Massachusetts
U Massachusetts at Boston
U Massachusetts at Dartmouth
U Massachusetts at Lowell
Massachusetts Inst of Tech
Merrimack College
Mount Holyoke College
Nichols College
North Adams State College
Northeastern University
Regis College
Salem State College
Simmons College
Smith College
Stonehill College
Suffolk University
Tufts University
Wellesley College
Western New England College
Westfield State College
Wheaton College
Williams College
Worcester State College
MICHIGAN
Adrian College
Albion College
Alma College
Andrews University
Aquinas College
Calvin College
Central Michigan University
University of Detroit Mercy
Eastern Michigan University
Ferris State University
GMI Engineering & Mgt Inst
Grand Valley State Univ
Hillsdale College
Hope College
Kalamazoo College
Lake Superior State Univ
Lawrence Technological Univ
University of Michigan
Univ of Michigan-Dearborn
Univ of Michigan-Flint
Michigan State University
Michigan Technological Univ
Northern Michigan Univ
Northwood Institute
Oakland University
Olivet College
Saginaw Valley State Univ
Wayne State University
Western Michigan University
MINNESOTA
Gugsburg College
Bemidji State University
Bethel College
Carleton College
Concordia College MN
Gustavus Adolphus College
Hamline University
Macalister College
Mankato State University
University of Minnesota
U of Minnesota - Duluth
Moorhead State University
College of Saint Benedictine
College of St. Catherine
St. Cloud State University
St. Olaf College
College of St. Scholastica
University of St. Thomas-MN
Southwest State University
Winona State University
MISSISSIPPI
Alcorn State University
Belhaven College
Delta State University
Jackson State University
Millsaps College
Mississippi College
University of Mississippi
Mississippi State Univ
Mississippi Valley St Univ
U of Southern Mississippi
MISSOURI
Central Missouri State Univ
Drury College
Lincoln University
Lindenwood College
U of Missouri at Columbia
U Missouri--Kansas City
U Missouri at Rolla
U Missouri--St. Louis
Missouri Southern St Col
Missouri Western St College
Northeast Missouri State U
Northwest Missouri St Univ
Rockhurst College
Saint Louis University
Southeast Missouri St Univ
Southwest Baptist Univ
Southwest Missouri St Univ
Washington University
Webster University
William Jewell College
MONTANA
Eastern Montana College
University of Montana
Montana State University
NEBRASKA
Chadron State College
Creighton University
University of Nebraska
Univ of Nebraksa at Kearney
Univ of Nebraska at Omaha
Nebraksa Wesleyan Univ
Wayne State College
NEVADA
Univ of Nevada, Las Vegas
University of Nevada, Reno

NEW HAMPSHIRE
Dartmouth College
Keene State College
New Hampshire College
University of New Hampshire
Plymouth State College
Saint Anselm College
NEW JERSEY
Bloomfield College
Centenary College
Drew University
Fairleigh Dickinson-Madison
Fairleigh Dickinson-Teaneck
Jersey City State College
Kean College of New Jersey
Monmouth College
Montclair State College
New Jersey Inst Technology
Princeton University
Ramapo College of New Jersey
Rider College
Rowan College of New Jersey
Rutgers University-Camden
Rutgers University-Newark
Rutgers Univ-New Brunswick
Saint Peter's College
Seton Hall University
Stevens Institute of Tech
Stockton State College
Trenton State College
Upsala College
William Patterson College
NEW MEXICO
Eastern New Mexico Univ
University of New Mexico
New Mexico Highlands Univ
New Mexico State Univ
NEW YORK
Adelphi University
Alfred University
Barnard College
Canisius College
CUNY-Baruch College
CUNY-Brooklyn College
CUNY-Hunter College
CUNY-Lehman College
CUNY-Queens College
CUNY-Staten Island
Clarkson University
Colgate University
Columbia University
Cornell University
Dowling College
Elmira College
Fordham University
Hamilton College
Hartwick College
Hofstra University
Iona College
Ithaca College
LeMoyne College
Long Isl U, Brooklyn Campus
Long Island U-C.W. Post
Malloy College
Manhattan College
Marist College
Nazareth Col of Rochester
College of New Rochelle
New York University
New York Institute of Tech
Niagara University
Pace University
Rensselaer Poly Institute
University of Rochester
Rochester Inst of Technology
Russell Sage College
Saint Bonaventure Univ
St. Francis College
St. John Fisher College
St. John's University
St. Lawrence University
College of Saint Rose
Siena College
Skidmore College
SUNY College at Fredonia
State Un College at Geneseo
SUNY at Albany
SUNY at Binghamton
SUNY at Buffalo
SUNY at Cortland
SUNY - Empire State College
SUNY at New Paltz
SUNY at Old Westbury
SUNY College at Oneonta
SUNY at Oswego
SUNY at Plattsburgh
SUNY at Potsdam
SUNY College at Purchase
SUNY at Stony Brook
Syracuse University
Union College
United States Military Acad
Utica College
Vassar College
Wagner College
Yeshiva University
NORTH CAROLINA
Appalachian State Univ
Barton College
Campbell University
Catawba College
Davidson College
Duke University
East Carolina University
Elon College
Fayetteville State Univ
Gardner-Webb University
Greensboro College
Guilford College
Lenoir-Rhyn College
Meredith College
North Carolina at Ashville
University of North Carolina
North Carolina at Charlotte
North Carolina at Greensboro
North Carolina at Wilmington
North Carolina A&T State Un
North Carolina Central Univ
North Carolina State Univ
Pembroke State University
Pfeiffer College
Wake Forest University
Western Carolina University
Wingate College
Winston-Salem State Univ
NORTH DAKOTA
Jamestown College
University of Mary
Minot State University
University of North Dakota
North Dakota State Univ
OHIO
University of Akron
Ashland University
Baldwin-Wallace College
Bowling Green State Univ
Capital University
Case Western Reserve Univ
Cedarville College
Central State Univ-Ohio
University of Cincinnati
Cleveland State University
University of Dayton
Dennison University
University of Findley
Franklin University
Heidelberg College
John Carroll University
Kent State University
Kenyon College
Marietta College
Miami University
Oberlin College
Ohio University
Ohio Northern University
Ohio State University
Ohio Wesleyan University
Otterbein College
University of Rio Grande
University of Toledo
Wittenberg University
The College of Wooster
Wright State University
Xavier University
Youngstown State University
OKLAHOMA
Cameron University
Univ of Central Oklahoma
East Central University
Northeastern State Univ
University of Oklahoma
Oklahoma Baptist University
Oklahoma Christian U Sci/Art
Oklahoma City University
Oklahoma State University
Southern Nazarene Univ
Southeastern Oklahoma State
Southwestern Oklahoma St Un
University of Tulsa
OREGON
Eastern Oregon State College
Lewis & Clark College
Linfield College
University of Oregon
Oregon State University
University of Portland
Portland State University
Reed College
Southern Oregon St College
Western Oregon State College
Willamette University
PENNSYLVANIA
Albright College
Allegheny College
Beaver College
Bloomsburg University
Bryn Mawr College
Bucknell University
California Univ of Penn
Carnegie Mellon University
Cheyney University
Clarion University
Dickinson College
Drexel University
Duquesne University
East Stroudsburg University
Edinboro University of PA
Elizabethtown College
Franklin and Marshall Coll
Gannon University
Geneva College
Gettysburg College
Grove City College
Holy Family College
Immaculata College
Indiana U of Pennsylvania
King's College
Kutztown University of PA
Lafayette College
LaSalle University
Lehigh University
Lincoln University
Lock Haven University
Lycoming College
Mansfield University of PA
Marywood College
Millersville Univ of PA
Moravian College
Mulhenberg College
University of Pennsylvania
Penn State University
Penn State Univ-Erie
Penn State Univ-Harrisburg
University of Pittsburgh
U of Pittsburgh at Johnstown
Robert Morris College
Saint Joseph's University
Saint Vincent College
University of Scranton
Shippensburg University
Slippery Rock University
Susquehanna University
Temple University
Villanova University
Washington & Jefferson Coll
West Chester University
Westminster College of PA
Widener University
Wilkes University
York College of Pennsylvania
RHODE ISLAND
Brown University
Bryant College
Providence College
Rhode Island College
University of Rhode Island
Salve Regina University
SOUTH CAROLINA
Benedict College
College of Charleston
The Citadel
Clemson University
Converse College
Francis Marion College
Furman University
Lander University
Presbyterian College
Univ of South Carolina
Univ So Carolina at Aiken
U South Carolina at Spartanb
South Carolina St College
Winthrop University
Wofford College
SOUTH DAKOTA
Augustana College SD
Northern State University
University of South Dakota
South Dakota State Univ
TENNESSEE
Austin Peay State University
Belmont College
Carson-Newman College
Christian Brothers College
David Lipscomb University
East Tennessee State Univ
Fisk University
Freed Hardeman University
Memphis State University
Middle Tennessee State Univ
Rhodes College
University of the South
Southern Col of 7th Day Adv
University of Tennessee
Tennessee at Chattanooga
Univ of Tennessee at Martin
Tennessee State University
Tennessee Technological Un
Union University
Vanderbilt University
TEXAS
Amber University
Angelo State University
Baylor University
University of Dallas
Dallas Baptist University
East Texas State Univ
Hardin-Simmons University
University of Houston
Univ of Houston-Downtown
Univ of Houston-Clear Lake
Houston Baptist University
Howard Payne University
Lamar University
Univ of Mary Hardin-Baylor
McMurray University
Midwestern State University
University of North Texas
Prairie View A&M University
Rice University
St. Edward's University
St. Mary's University
University of St. Thomas-TX
Sam Houston State Univ
Southern Methodist Univ
Southwest Texas State Univ
Southwestern University
Stephen F. Austin St Univ
Tarleton State University
U of Texas at Arlington
Univ of Texas at Austin
Univ of Texas at Brownsville
Univ of Texas at Dallas
Univ of Texas at El Paso
Univ of Texas-Pan American
U of Texas of Permian Basin
Un of Texas at San Antonio
Univ of Texas at Tyler
Texas A&M University
Texas A&M - Corpus Christi
Texas A&M Univ-Kingsville
Texas A&M International Univ
Texas Christian University
Texas Lutheran College
Texas Southern University
Texas Tech University
Texas Wesleyan University
Texas Woman's University
Trinity University
West Texas A&M University
UTAH
Brigham Young University
Southern Utah University
University of Utah
Utah State University
Weber State University
Westminster U of Salt Lake C
VERMONT
Lyndon State College
Middlebury College
Norwich University
St. Michael's College
University of Vermont
VIRGINIA
Christopher Newport College
Emory and Henry College
George Mason University
Hampton University
James Madison University
Liberty University
Longwood College
Lynchburg College
Mary Baldwin College
Mary Washington College
Marymount University
Norfolk State University
Old Dominion University
Radford University
Regent University
University of Richmond
Roanoke College
Shenandoah University
University of Virginia
Virginia Commonwealth Univ
Virginia Military Institute
Virginia Poly Inst & St Un
Virginia State University
Washington and Lee Univ
College of William & Mary
WASHINGTON
Central Washington Univ
Eastern Washington Univ
Evergreen State College
Gonzaga University
Pacific Lutheran University
University of Puget Sound
Saint Martin's College
Seattle University
Seattle Pacific University
Walla Walla College
University of Washington
Washington State University
Western Washington Univ
Whitmore College
WASHINGTON DC
The American University
Catholic Univ of America
Univ of District of Columbia
Gallaudet University
George Washington Univ
Georgetown University
Howard University
WEST VIRGINIA
Alderson-Broaddus College
Fairmont State College
Shephard College
Marshall University
West Liberty State College
West Virginia University
West Virginia State College
WISCONSIN
Carroll College
Carthage College
Lakeland College
Marquette University
St. Norbert College
U of Wisconsin-Eau Claire
U of Wisconsin-Green Bay
U of Wisconsin-La Crosse
Univ of Wisconsin-Madison
Univ of Wisconsin-Milwaukee
Univ of Wisconsin-Oshkosh
Univ of Wisconsin-Parkside
U of Wisconsin-Platteville
U of Wisconsin-River Falls
U of Wisconsin-Stevens Point
Univ of Wisconsin-Superior
U of Wisconsin-Whitewater
WYOMING
University of Wyoming

THE 1994-95 PRENTICE HALL
GUIDE TO ECONOMICS FACULTY

Compiled by
James R. Hasselback
College of Business
Florida State University
Tallahassee, Florida 32306-1042
904-644-7884 Phone/Recorder
904-894-2244 Fax
E-Mail: JHASSEL@COB.FSU.EDU

This is the second DIRECTORY OF ECONOMICS FACULTY published by Prentice Hall, Inc. The Directory includes a listing of the Dean, Department Chairpersons, and full-time Economics faculty from almost 850 schools. It is compiled from information provided by the respective schools. The Directory is for the academic year 1995-96. Only United States schools plus four foreign schools were included in the survey. The Directory is expected to be published every two years.

Updated information is provided on over 97 percent of the schools. Typically at least three requests went to any school listed as not responding. Only that information received by July 17, 1995, is included in the Directory. Information taken from college catalogs may be provided on nonresponding departments.

The department phone number follows the area code in the first line of each school. The department secretary/administration assistant is included at the end of the first line. The fax number is shown in the second line. At the right side of the second line is the school's electronic-mail code.

The columns are as follows:

Name Rank School-Phone Electronic-Mail Area Degree Start

$ next to a Dean or Chairman indicates "Acting"

For the Chairperson, the title and rank are:

C	Chairman	D	Director	H	Head
Pr	Professor	Ac	Associate	As	Assistant

The electronic-mail column includes the individual's address. The individual address must be combined with the school electronic-mail address; for instance, jim@fsu. When an individual address includes an "@", that individual has a different school address from the school address listed in the second line of the school; the individual's complete electronic-mail address is included in the electronic-mail column. However, if an individual electronic-mail address ends with a "." then the school's address must be added to the individual address provided. Additional school addresses may be shown in a third line for the school. In some cases, an individual address was too long to fit in the column and was included in a line following the individual. Use the Super Computer to decipher this paragraph.

The degree column represents the highest earned degree or "all but dissertation," date received, and school.

The start column is for the year of beginning full-time employment at that school.

The teaching/research column is as follows:

A General Economics & Teaching
B Methodology & History of Econ Thought
C Mathematical & Quantitative Methods
D Microeconomics
E Macroeconomics & Monetary Economics
F International Economics
G Financial Economics
H Public Economics
I Health, Education, & Welfare
J Labor Economics
K Law & Economics
L Industrial Organization
M Business Adm & Business Economics
N Economic History
O Economic Development, Technological Change, & Growth
P Economic Systems
Q Agricultural & Natural Resource Economics
R Urban, Rural, & Regional Economics
T Demographic Economics

adapted from Journal of Economic Literature listing

In the second part of the Directory, individuals are listed in alphabetical order. The phone and electronic-mail columns are replaced with the individual's school.

Any mistakes in the Directory are my responsibility. However, some of the misinformation belongs to schools not providing complete information.

Any corrections, additional information, and new schools should be sent directly to me. If your school is not included, please send me a listing in a format similar to that provided in the Directory.

A special thanks goes to my Assistant, Sally Poyner, for her tireless effort in gathering the data for the Directory; particularly the numerous phone calls to turn nonresponding schools into responding schools.

James R. Hasselback

1995-96 PRENTICE HALL GUIDE TO ECONOMICS FACULTY
ALPHABETICAL BY SCHOOL

NAME	RANK	PHONE	E-MAIL	AREA	DEGREE			STRT
Abilene Christian Univ	Abilene, TX		79699-0001 (915) 674-2565				Darlene Mahaney	
Dept of Management Sciences	College of Business Adm Fax=674-2564							
Griggs, Jack	Dean	674-2245		Mgt	PHD	71	Tx-Austin	1-91
Reid, Brad	C-Pr	674-2053			JD	73	Tx-Austin	1975
Brister, Jozell	Assoc	674-2560			MS	73	North Tx	1980
Jackson, Don	Assoc	674-2634			DBA		Geo Wash	
Adams State College	Alamosa, CO		81102 (719) 589-7161				Ms. Dolly Maestas	
Department of Economics	School of Business Fax=589-7522							
Ellis, Theodore	Prof				PHD	72	Colo St	1967
Weston, Rafael R.	Prof				PHD	72	Harvard	1988
Adelphi University	Garden City, NY		11530 (516) 877-4970					
Department of Economics	Col of Arts & Sciences Fax=877-4191						ADELPHI.EDU	
Costello, Peter	Dean				PHD			
Gleicher, David	C-Ac			BJ	PHD	84	Columbia	1981
Machlis, David	Assoc			E	PHD	71	Rutgers	1968
Adrian College	Adrian, MI		49221-2575 (517) Ext 4432				Pat Husband	
Economics Faculty	Department of Economics Fax=264-3331							
phone: 265-5161								
Backman, William	C-Pr	265-5161		Mgt	ABD	73	Kentucky	8-81
Habib, Ahsan M.	Assoc	Ext 4330			PHD	80	McMaster	1981
University of Akron	Akron, OH		44325-1908 (216) 972-7546				Judy Major	
Department of Economics	Butchell Col Arts & Sci Fax=374-8795						UAKRON.EDU	
Moore, Randy	Dean	972-6030					UCLA	1993
Malhotra, Devinder	C-Pr	972-7937			PHD	79	Kansas St	1979
Byrne, Dennis	Prof	972-7939			PHD	75	Notre Dm	1975
Garofalo, Gasper A.	Prof	972-7548			PHD	74	Pittsburgh	1979
McGuire, Robert A.	Prof	972-7521			PHD	78	U Wash	1990
Parvin, Manoucher	Prof	972-7985			PHD	79	Columbia	1978
Erickson, Elizabeth L.	Assoc	972-7973			PHD	72	Illinois	1969
King, Randall H.	Assoc	972-7975			PHD	78	Ohio St	1978
Lin, Lung-Ho	Assoc	972-7974			PHD	74	Notre Dm	1978
Myers, Steven	Assoc	972-7421			PHD	80	Ohio St	1979
Sellers, Gary	Assoc	972-7938			PHD	77	Cincinnati	1976
Stratton, Richard	Assoc	972-7440	dickstratton	ADJ	PHD	77	Conn	1978
University of Alabama	Tuscaloosa, AL		35487-0224 (205) 348-7842				Sheila Smith, Prog Asst	
Dept Econ, Fnce & Legal Stds	Col Commerce & Bus Adm Fax=348-0590						ALSTON.CBA.UA.EDU	
Mason, J. Barry	Dean	348-7443	jbmason	Mktg	PHD	67	Alabama	1967
Russell Professor of Business Administration								
Helms, Billy P.	H-Pr	348-7842	bhelms	Fnce	PHD	73	Tennessee	1973
Cheng, David C.	Prof	348-7842	dcheng		PHD	73	Yale	1974
Evans, John S.	Prof	348-7842	jevans		PHD	71	Wisconsin	1968
Fish, Mary	Prof	348-7842	mfish		PHD	63	Oklahoma	1965
Formby, John P.	Prof	348-8667	jformby		PHD	65	Colorado	1982
Hayes Professor of Economics								
Gunther, William D.	Prof	348-8960	wgunther		PHD	69	Kentucky	1968
Associate Dean Research & Serv and Director, Ctr for Business & Econ Research								
Leathers, Charles G.	Prof	348-7842	clather		PHD	68	Oklahoma	1968
Misiolek, Walter S.	Prof	348-8980	wmisiole		PHD	76	Cornell	1975
Senior Associate Dean & Director of Graduate Programs								
Schlesinger, Harris	Prof	348-7842	hsclesi		PHD	80	Illinois	1987
VanHoose, David D.	Prof	348-7842	dvanhoos		PHD	84	N Carol	1990
Elder, Harold W.	Assoc	348-7842	helder		PHD	82	Va Tech	1981
Hooks, Donald L.	Assoc	348-7842	dhooks		PHD	71	Tx A&M	1971
Silver, J. Lew	Assoc	348-7842	jsilver		PHD	80	Duke	1990
Arce, M. Daniel	Asst	348-7842	darce		PHD	91	Illinois	1991
Cover, James P.	Asst	348-8977	jcover		PHD	82	Virginia	1982
Johnson, Mark	Asst	348-7842	mjohnson		PHD	86	Ca-SnDgo	1989
Kim, Myung J.	Asst	348-7842	mkim		PHD	89	U Wash	1989
Pecorino, Paul	Asst	348-0379	ppecorin		PHD	90	Duke	1994

U of Alabama at Birmingham Birmingham, AL 35294-4460 (205) 934-8830 Rose McCoy
Department of Economics School of Business Fax=975-6234 UABDPO.UAB.EDU
email: @1=anscube.asc.edu @2=dop.uab.edu

Name	Rank	Phone	Email	Fields	Degree	Yr	School	Year
Newport, M. Gene	Dean	934-8810		Mgt	PHD	63	Illinois	1971
Lee, Seung-Dong	C-Ac	934-8830	busf014	CDFQ	PHD	79	So Meth	1979
Lewis, David P.	Emer	934-8830		CER	PHD	68	Tennessee	1969
McCarl, Henry N.	Prof	934-8830	uabhnm01@1	AR	PHD	69	Penn St	1969
Ignatin, George	Assoc	934-8830		AJK	PHD	69	Tx-Austin	1969
Culver, Sarah	Asst	934-8830	busf058@2	CEFG	PHD	93	Houston	1993
Dasgupta, Manabendra	Asst	934-8830	busf082@2	CDHL	PHD	89	So Meth	1992
Sampson, Jon	Asst	934-8830		CEI	PHD	91	CUNY	1991

U of Alabama in Huntsville Huntsville, AL 35899 (205) Ms. Liz Patillo
Dept of Economic & Finance Col of Admin Science Fax=895-6328 UAH.EDU

Name	Rank	Phone	Email	Fields	Degree	Yr	School	Year
Billings, C. David	Dean	895-6735		H	PHD	69	Missouri	1981
Paul, Chris W.	C-Pr	895-6590		K	PHD	79	Tx A&M	1982
Schoening, Niles C.	Prof	895-6782		R	PHD	83	Tennessee	1983
Wilhite, Allen W.	Prof	895-6694		JK	PHD	81	Illinois	1988
Schnell, John F.	Assoc	895-6710		J	PHD	84	Illinois	1990
Allen, W. David	Asst	575-6105		J	PHD	94	Arkansas	1994

Alabama A&M University Normal, AL 35762 (205) 851-5294
Dept of Economics & Finance School of Business Fax=851-5839
phone: 851-5294

Name	Rank	Phone	Email	Fields	Degree	Yr	School	Year
Scott, Stanley V.	Dean	851-5485		Mktg	PHD		Ohio U	8-93
Rahimian, Eric N.	C-Ac	851-5294		ADOF	PHD	75	Indiana	1975
Alexander, James	Prof			EAOH	PHD		Tx-Austin	
Esensoy, Yilmaz	Prof			AOD	PHD	69	Ohio St	
Kim, Yang H.	Prof			AOE	PHD	67	Utah	1965
Salib, Anis B.	Prof			AI	PHD	72	Vanderbilt	1982
Elike, Uchenna I.	Asst			AOF	PHD	85	Alabama	1985
Ma, Yulong	Asst			GO	PHD		Tx-Austin	
Robbani, Mohammad	Asst			GO	PHD		Fla Intl	
Yousif, Salah A.	Asst			AJ	MA		Howard	
Karumanchi, V. R.	Inst			AO	MS		Ala A&M	

Alabama State University Montgomery, AL 36195-0271 (334) 293-4142 Ms. Jean Graham
Department of Business Adm Col of Business Admin Fax=265-9144

Name	Rank	Phone	Email	Fields	Degree	Yr	School	Year
Vaughn, Percy J. Jr.	Dean	293-4124		Mktg	DBA		Tx Tech	1974
Yeh, Chiou-Nan	C-Pr	293-4130			PHD	74	Mass	1974
Bakair, Saad T.	Assoc	293-6805			PHD			
Suwanakul, Sontachai	Assoc	293-4127			PHD	86	Arkansas	1989
Deprez, Johan	Asst	293-4128			PHD	87	Rutgers	
Slattery, Edward	Asst	293-4142			PHD	88	Colorado	1995
Wier, Thomas	Asst	293-4142			PHD	89	Tennessee	1995
Ezekannagha, Francine	Inst	293-6804			MS		Hendersn	1984

Univ of Alaska Anchorage Anchorage, AK 99508-8244 (907) 786-1770 Janet Burton
Department of Economics Sch of Public Affairs Fax=786-7739 ALASKA.EDU

Name	Rank	Phone	Email	Fields	Degree	Yr	School	Year
Tuck, Bradford H.	Dean	786-1915		CDL	PHD	73	Boston U	1977
Huskey, Lee	C-Pr	786-1905		AHJR	PHD	77	Wash St	1977
Goldsmith, O. Scott	Prof	786-7710		CH	PHD	76	Wisconsin	1985
Jackstadt, Stephen L.	Prof	786-1901		AEH	EDD	81	Indiana	1985
Knapp, Gunner P.	Prof	786-7717		QR	PHD	81	Yale	1981
Rohacek, Jerry K.	Prof	786-1662		DEN	MA	69	Ca-SnBarb	1973
Ross, Larry L.	Prof	786-1613		ADE	MS	71	Oregon	1971
Vercella, Kit J.	Prof	786-1620		ADEO	MA	72	Ca-SnDgo	1974
Hill, Pershing J.	Assoc	786-1763		EFH	PHD	76	Wash St	1975

Univ of Alaska Fairbanks Fairbanks, AK 99775-6080 (907) 474-7119 Burma Swan-Kincaid
Department of Economics School of Management Fax=474-5219 ALASKA.EDU

Name	Rank	Phone	Email	Fields	Degree	Yr	School	Year
Porter, David O.	Dean	474-7461	ffdop	Busi	PHD	70	Syracuse	1994
Criddle, Keith	Assoc	474-5995	ffkrc		PHD	89	Ca-Davis	1989
Goering, Gregory	Assoc	474-5572	ffgeg		PHD	90	Purdue	1990
Hermann, Mark	Assoc	474-7116	ffmlh		PHD	90	Wash St	1990
Logan, Robert	Assoc	474-6783	ffrrl		PHD	86	Iowa	1986
Read, Colin	Assoc	474-5975	ffclri		PHD	88	Queen's	1989
Boyce, John R.	Asst	474-5199	ffjrb		PHD	90	Ca-Davis	1988
Haney, Barbara	Asst	474-6520	ffbah		PHD	89	Notre Dm	1987
Pippenger, Michael	Asst	474-6530	ffmkp		PHD	90	Purdue	1991

Univ of Alaska Southeast Juneau, AK 99801 (907) 465-6417 Mary Elsner
Economics Faculty S of Edu, Lib Art & Sci Fax=465-6406 ALASKA.EDU

Name	Rank	Phone	Email	Fields	Degree	Yr	School	Year
Pugh, John R.	Dean	465-6417	jnjrp		MSSW		Tx-Austin	
Brown, William S.	Prof	465-6423	jfwsb		PHD	77	Colorado	1991

Albany State College — Albany, GA 31705 (912) 430-4770 — Carol Crayton
Economics Faculty — School of Business Adm Fax=430-5119

Name	Rank	Phone	Email	Fields	Degree	Yr	School	Since
Burgess, Walter J.	Dean	430-4772		Mgt	PHD	72	Geo St	
Kooti, John	Prof	430-4772			PHD	80	Mich St	1981
Ojemakindel, Abiodun	Assoc	430-4772			PHD	89	LSU	1989
Shah, Umanglal	Asst	430-4772			MS			

Albion College — Albion, MI 49224-1899 (517) 629-0419
Economics Faculty — Dept of Economics & Mgt Fax=629-0428 — ALBION

Name	Rank	Phone	Email	Fields	Degree	Yr	School	Since
McCarley, James F.	C-Pr	629-0294	jmccarley	J	PHD	70	Mich St	1965
Steinhauer, Larry	C-Pr	629-0423	lsteinauer		PHD	74	Chicago	1968
Christiansen, Daniel S.	Prof	629-0425	christiansen	CD	PHD	75	Stanford	1981
Bedient, John B.	Assoc	629-0343	jbedient		MBA	79	Indiana	1984
Cracraft, Scott	Assoc	629-0490			MS	60	Miss	1977
Saltzman, Gregory M.	Assoc	629-0422	gsaltzman		PHD	82	Wisconsin	1982
Hooks, Jon A.	Asst	629-0530	jhooks	G	PHD	89	Mich St	1989

Albright College — Reading, PA 19612-5234 (610) 921-7538 — Ms. Susan Miller
Economics Faculty — Dept of Econ & Business Fax=921-7530 — JOE.ALB.EDU

Name	Rank	Phone	Email	Fields	Degree	Yr	School	Since
Moyer, James T.	C-Pr	921-7781			PHD	76	Lehigh	9-68
Martin, David A.	Assoc	921-7888			DA	80	Lehigh	1983
Schwartz, David Lamar	Assoc	921-7782			MA	64	Mich St	1965
Lever, Jacqueline	Asst				PHD		Pittsburgh	
Saboori, Farhad	Asst	921-7884			PHD	85	Indiana	1986

Alcorn State University — Lorman, MS 39096 (601) 877-6411
Dept of Social Sciences — Div of Arts & Sciences Fax=877-6256

Name	Rank	Phone	Email	Fields	Degree	Yr	School	Since
Edney, Norris	D-Pr	877-6120			PHD		Mich St	
Director, Division of Graduate Studies								
Morris, Alpha	C-Ac	877-6411			PHD		Miss St	
Gau, Carolina	Prof	877-6416			PHD		Missouri	
Gau, Paul K.	Prof	877-6417			PHD	71	Illinois	1972
Coordinator, Economics								

Alderson-Broaddus College — Philippi, WV 26416 (304) 457-6259
Economics Faculty — Dept of Bus Adm & Econ Fax=457-6239 — AB.EDU
phone: 457-1700

Name	Rank	Phone	Email	Fields	Degree	Yr	School	Since
Heck, Charles R.	C-Ac	Ext 259		CDEF	EDD		Nova	8-93

Alfred University — Alfred, NY 14802 (607) 871-2124
Dept of Business Adm — College of Business Fax=871-2114
Did Not Respond--1994-95 Listing

Name	Rank	Phone	Email	Fields	Degree	Yr	School	Since
Szczerbacki, David	Dean	871-2124			PHD		SUNY-Buf	1981
Booker, James F.	Asst	871-2124			PHD	90	Colo St	1993

Allegheny College — Meadville, PA 16335 (814) 332-3358 — Ms. Sherry Proper
Economics Faculty — Department of Economics Fax=333-8180 — ALLEG.EDU

Name	Rank	Phone	Email	Fields	Degree	Yr	School	Since
Adams, Earl W. Jr.	C-Pr	332-3331	eadams	AEGH	PHD	71	MIT	1972
Andrew Wells Robertson Professor of Economics								
Cupper, Robert Dean	Prof	332-2881	bcupper	ACD	PHD	74	Pittsburgh	1977
Afrasiabi, Ahmad	Assoc	332-3334	bafrasia	BCQR	PHD	85	W Virginia	1985
Baskan, Asuman	Assoc	332-3336	abaskan	CDFE	PHD	88	Lehigh	1987
Casler, Stephen D.	Assoc	332-3337	scasler	ACEQ	PHD	83	Illinois	1988
Moskwa, Antoni	Assoc	332-3339	amoskwa	AFCP	PHD	75	Warsaw	1982
Gallet, Craig	Asst	332-3820	cgallet	CDL	PHD	94	Iowa St	1994
Golden, John M.	Asst	332-3338	jgolden	DIJN	PHD	89	Conn	1989
Goldstein, Donald	Asst	332-3340	dgoldste	ABG	PHD	91	Mass	1989

Alma College — Alma, MI 48801-1599 (517) 463-7149
Economics Faculty — Department of Economics Fax=463-7277 — ALMA.EDU

Name	Rank	Phone	Email	Fields	Degree	Yr	School	Since
Mueller, James V.	C-Ac	463-7183	mueller		ABD		Ca-Irvine	1976
Choksy, George Dorian	Assoc				PHD		Tennessee	1989
Johnson, Denise H.	Asst				PHD	93	Mass	1994

The American University — Washington, DC 20016-8029 (202) 885-3770
Department of Economics — Col of Arts & Sciences Fax=885-3790 — AMERICAN.EDU

Name	Rank	Phone	Email	Fields	Degree	Yr	School	Since
Bennett, Betty T.	Dean	885-2446	bbennett		PHD		NYU	1985
Sawers, Larry B.	C-Pr	885-3783	lsawers		PHD	69	Michigan	1969
Bergmann, Barbara R.	Prof	885-2725	bberg		PHD	59	Harvard	1988
Distinguished Professor								
Broder, Ivy E.	Prof	885-2125	ibroder		PHD	74	SUNY-SBr	1975

Epstein, Jose D.	Prof	885-2707	epstein		PHD	85	San Andres	
Director of Development Banking Program								
Hahnel, Robin E.	Prof	885-2712	rhahnel		PHD		American	1976
Lerman, Robert I.	Prof	885-3770	rlerman		PHD	70	MIT	1989
Muller, Ronald E.	Prof	527-0990			PHD		American	1970
Schydlowsky, Daniel M.	Prof	885-2521	dschyd		PHD	66	Harvard	1990
Thanh, Pham Chi	Prof	885-3777			PHD		NS Wales	1976
Wachtel, Howard M.	Prof	885-3784			PHD	69	Michigan	1969
Ayittey, George B. N.	VAsoc	885-3779			PHD	81	Manitoba	1994
Blecker, Robert A.	Assoc	885-3767	blecker		PHD	87	Stanford	1985
Feinberg, Robert M.	Assoc	885-3766	feinberg		PHD	76	Virginia	1989
Hazilla, Michael	Assoc	885-3148	hazilla		PHD	78	SUNY-Bin	1988
Husted, Thomas A.	Assoc	885-3773	husted		PHD	86	N Carol	1986
Isaac, Alan G.	Assoc	885-3785			PHD	86	Ca-Davis	1987
Lane, Julia I.	Assoc	885-3781	jilane		PHD	82	Missouri	1990
Willoughby, John A.	Assoc	885-3759	jwillou		PHD		Berkeley	1979
Wisman, Jon D.	Assoc	885-3158	jdwisma		PHD		American	1971
Floro, Maria Sagrario	Asst	885-3139	mfloro		PHD		Stanford	1988
Graham, Fred C.	Asst	885-3782	fgraham		PHD	85	Virginia	1988
Meurs, Mieke E.	Asst	885-3776	mmeurs		PHD	88	Mass	1989
Park, Walter G.	Asst	885-3774	wgp		PHD	91	Yale	1991

American International Coll	Springfield, MA		01109-3189	(413) 737-7000				
Department of Economics	School of Business Adm		Fax=737-2803					
Maher, Charles F.	Dean	747-6230			EDD	79	Mass	1978
Orcutt, Bonnie	C-As	737-7000		ADEI	PHD	94	Clark	1992
Smolowitz, Ira E.	Prof	747-6369			PHD	84	Rensselae	1988
Director, Center for Economic Education; Dean, Bureau of Business Research								

Amherst College	Amherst, MA		01002	(413) 542-2249			Jeanne E. Reinle	
Economics Faculty	Department of Economics		Fax=542-2090				AMHERST.EDU	
Barbezat, Daniel P.	C-Ac	542-7948	dpbarbezat	ANO	PHD	88	Illinois	1988
Beals, Ralph E.	Prof	542-2570	rebeals	ACO	PHD	70	MIT	1966
Clarence Francis Professor of Economics								
Kohler, Heinz	Prof	542-2083	hkohler	AP	PHD	61	Michigan	1961
Willard Long Thorp Professor of Economics								
Nicholson, Walter E.	Prof	542-2191	wenicholson	ACDJ	PHD	70	MIT	1968
Ward H. Patton, Jr. Professor of Economics								
Westhoff, Frank H.	Prof	542-2190	fwesthoff	ADH	PHD	74	Yale	1973
Woglom, Geoffrey R.	Prof	542-2433	grwoglom	AEG	PHD	74	Yale	1978
Yarbrough, Beth V.	Prof	542-2429	bvyarbrough	ADF	PHD	83	U Wash	1982
Rivkin, Steven G.	Asst	542-2106	sgrivkin	AIJ	PHD	91	UCLA	1993
Takeyama, Lisa N.	Asst	542-2271	lntakeyama	ADL	PHD	92	Stanford	1994
Xu, Xianonian	Asst	542-2230	xxu	AEO	PHD	91	Ca-Davis	1991

Anderson University	Anderson, IN		46012-3462	(317)				
Department of Business	Sch of Business & Econ		Fax=				ANDERSON.EDU	
Did Not Respond--1994-95 Listing								
Armstrong, Ken	Dean				PHD		Northwes	1990
Heberling, Gregory Dean	Assoc				MBA		Ball St	1978
Ritchey, Barry	Assoc	641-4357		DHR	PHD		Syracuse	1991

Andrews University	Berrien Spr, MI		49104-0024	(616) 471-3429				
Economics Department	School of Business		Fax=471-6158				ANDREWS.EDU	
Phillips, Harold	Dean	471-3102	phillips	Mgt	PHD		Florida	1990
Gibson, Ann	C-Pr	471-3118	gibson	Atg	PHD	92	Wash St	1992
Gashugi, Leonard K.	Prof	471-3581	gashugi	CF	PHD		Boston U	1979
Russell, Malcolm B.	Prof	471-3104	russell	EN	PHD	78	J Hopkins	1979
Swaine, David W.	Assoc	471-3105	swaine	CD	PHD		Notre Dm	1978
Bolin, Delynne	Asst	471-3429	bolin	EJ	PHD		Purdue	1995

Angelo State University	San Angelo, TX		76909	(915) 942-2046			Marilyn Baumann	
Dept Acct, Economics & Fnce	C of Professional Stds		Fax=942-2038					
Hegglund, Robert K.	Dean	942-2337		Mgt	PHD	72	Arkansas	1972
Dane, Andrew J.	H-Pr	942-2046			PHD	75	Oklahoma	1973
Maddox, D. Pat	Assoc	942-2076			PHD	82	Tx Tech	1982

Appalachian State Univ	Boone, NC		28608	(704) 262-2148				
Department of Economics	Walker College of Bus		Fax=262-2094				APPSTATE.EDU	
Peacock, Kenneth E.	Dean	262-2058		Atg	PHD	79	LSU	1983
Elledge, Barry	C-Pr	262-6121	elledgbw	IM	PHD	70	N Car St	1969
Combs, J. Paul	Prof	262-6161		MR	PHD	73	N Car St	1971
Courbois, Jean-Pierre	Prof	262-2117		F	PHD	68	American	1968
Durden, Gary C.	Prof	262-6077		H	PHD	71	Fla St	1982

Gaynor, Patricia Prof 262-6129 M PHD 74 Miami 1976
Guthrie, William G. III Prof 262-6126 BN PHD 80 N Carol 1980
Millsaps, Steven Prof 262-6080 M PHD 73 N Car St 1973
Perri, Timothy J. Prof 262-2251 DJ PHD 78 Ohio St 1980
Baik, Kyung H. Assoc 262-6128 DL PHD 89 Va Tech 1989
Ellis, Larry V. Assoc 262-6123 E PHD 78 Missouri 1978
Kirkpatrick, Rickey C. Assoc 262-6127 FM PHD 78 Tulane 1980
McRae, Larry T. Assoc 262-6125 M PHD 78 N Carol 1977
Schieren, George A. Assoc 262-4033 M PHD 75 N Carol 1977
Wallace, Frederick H. Assoc 262-6122 E PHD 87 Rice 1986
Shelley, Gary L. Asst 262-2927 EM PHD 90 Va Tech 1990
Milam, Richard Inst 262-6081 FM PHD 91 Va Tech 1991

Aquinas College Grand Rapids, MI 49506-1799 (616) Ext 4462
Economics Faculty Economics Department Fax=
phone: 459-8281
Beversluis, Eric H. C-Ac Ext 3602 PHD 70 Northwes 1988
Bennett, R. J. Prof Ext 3609 PHD St Louis 1969
Chaffee, Donald M. Jr. Prof 459-8281 PHD 70 Ca-Davis 1989
Robertson, Gary L. Assoc MA Detroit 1969
Yamazaki, Masato Asst Ext 4466 PHD 84 Duke 1987
Marin, Kenneth J. Adj MA Michigan 1988

University of Arizona Tucson, AZ 85721 (602) 621-6224 Lanna Greffet, Adm Asst
Department of Economics Col Business & Pub Adm Fax=621-7483 BPAVMS.BPA.ARIZONA.EDU
Smith, Kenneth R. Dean 621-2165 PHD 68 Northwes 1980
Isaac, R. Mark H-Pr 621-4831 misaac PHD 80 Cal Tech 1980
Block, Michael K. Prof 621-2854 PHD 72 Stanford 1981
Buehler, John E. Emer 621-6217 PHD 67 SUNY-Buf 1968
Cox, James C. Prof 621-6224 PHD 71 Harvard 1977
Fishback, Price V. Prof 621-4421 PHD 83 U Wash 1990
Herber, Bernard P. Prof 621-2431 PHD 69 U Wash 1957
Libecap, Gary D. Prof 621-2576 PHD 76 Penn 1984
Director Karl Eller Center
Marshall, Robert H. Prof 621-6219 PHD 57 Ohio St 1957
Oaxaca, Ronald L. Prof 621-4135 PHD 72 Princeton 1976
Reynolds, Stanley Prof 621-6224 PHD 83 Northwes 1982
Rieber, Michael Prof 621-4281
Smith, Vernon L. Prof 621-4747 PHD 55 Harvard 1975
Regents' Professor
Taylor, Lester D. Prof 621-6222 PHD 63 Harvard 1972
Tullock, Gordon Prof 621-2640 JD 47 Chicago 1987
Walker, Mark A. Prof 621-6155 PHD 70 Purdue 1990
Wells, Donald A. Prof 621-6240 PHD 61 Oregon 1969
Zajac, Edward E. Prof 621-2192 PHD 54 Stanford 1983
Drabicki, John Z. Assoc 621-4221 PHD 73 Purdue 1970
Heckerman, Donald G. Assoc 621-6224 PHD 67 MIT 1971
McBearty, James C. Assoc 621-1639 PHD 68 Illinois 1968
Sands, Barbara N. Assoc 621-2380 PHD 85 U Wash 1985
Swanson, Gerald Assoc 621-6220 PHD 72 Illinois 1970
Broseta, Bruno Asst 621-6238 PHD 94 Ca-SnDgo 1995
Ghose, Devajyoti Asst 621-6229 PHD 90 Ca-SnDgo 1990
Kantor, Shawn E. Asst 621-6230 PHD 90 Cal Tech 1990
Kroner, Kenneth F. Asst 621-6230 PHD 88 Ca-SnDgo 1988
Ratliff, James D. Asst 621-4560 PHD 93 Berkeley 1992
Stratton, Leslie A. Asst 621-6223 PHD 89 MIT 1988
Wooders, John C. Asst 621-6231 PHD 91 Cornell 1991
Billings, R. Bruce Lect 621-4436 PHD 69 Claremont 1965

Arizona State University Tempe, AZ 85287-3806 (602) 965-3531
Department of Economics College of Business Fax=965-0748 ASUACAD
Penley, Larry E. Dean 965-5516 iaclep Mgt PHD 76 Georgia 1985
Blakemore, Arthur E. C-Pr 965-3531 ieaeb PHD 77 S Illinois 1979
Boyes, William J. Prof 965-3531 icwjb PHD 74 Claremont 1969
Brada, Josef C. Prof 965-6524 atjcb PHD 71 Minnesota 1978
Burgess, Paul L. Prof 965-8432 icplb PHD 69 Colorado 1969
Faith, Roger L. Prof 965-3531 icrlf PHD 73 UCLA 1981
Gooding, Elmer R. Prof 965-5596 iaderg PHD 69 Kansas 1988
Happel, Stephen K. Prof 965-5001 icskh PHD 76 Duke 1975
Associate Dean Undergraduate Programs
Hoffman, Dennis L. Prof 965-3531 ifdlh PHD 78 Mich St 1979
Hogan, Timothy D. Prof 965-3961 ictdh PHD 71 Va Tech 1970
Jackson, Marvin R. Jr. Prof 965-3531 PHD 67 Berkeley 1962
Kingston, Jerry L. Prof 965-7457 iadjlk PHD 69 Penn St 1969
Knox, Robert L. Prof 965-3531 icrlk PHD 63 N Carol 1963
Low, Stuart A. Prof 965-5498 aosal PHD 79 Illinois 1979
McDowell, John M. Prof 965-7109 icjmd PHD 79 UCLA 1978

Name	Rank	Phone	E-mail	Field	Degree	Yr	School	Since
McPheters, Lee R.	Prof	965-3961	iaclrm		PHD	72	Va Tech	1976
Associate Dean, Graduate Program								
Melvin, Michael T.	Prof	965-6860	atmtm		PHD	80	UCLA	1980
Mendez, Jose A.	Prof	965-2723	atjym		PHD	80	So Meth	1980
Ormiston, Michael B.	Prof	965-7350	icmbo		PHD	77	J Hopkins	1984
DeSerpa, Allan C.	Assoc	965-3531	icacd		PHD	70	Ca-SnBarb	1975
Reffett, Kevin	Assoc	965-3531			PHD	90	Purdue	1995
Smith, Janet K.	Assoc	965-3531	iejks		PHD	80	UCLA	1981
Winkelman, Richard D.	Assoc	965-2128	atrzw		PHD	66	Illinois	1965
Ahn, Seung C.	Asst	965-6574	aasca		PHD	90	Mich St	1990
Datta, Manjira	Asst	965-3531			PHD	92	Cornell	1995
Schlee, Edward E.	Asst	965-5745	icees		PHD	88	Illinois	1990

University of Arkansas Fayetteville, AR 72701 (501) 575-ECON
Department of Economics College of Business Adm Fax=575-7687 COMP.UARK.EDU

Name	Rank	Phone	E-mail	Field	Degree	Yr	School	Since
Williams, Doyle Z.	Dean	575-5949		Atg	PHD	65	LSU	1993
Ziegler, Joseph A.	H-Pr	575-3266		R	PHD	71	Notre Dm	1980
Britton, Charles R.	Prof			E	PHD	71	Iowa	1978
Curington, William P.	Prof			J	PHD	79	Syracuse	1989
Dixon, Bruce	Prof			TQ	PHD		Ca-Davis	1986
Gay, David E.	Prof			H	PHD	73	Tx A&M	1983
Market, Donald R.	Prof			E	PHD	67	LSU	1975
McKinnon, Thomas	Prof			NA	PHD		Miss	1981
Murray, Tracy W.	Prof			F	PHD	69	Mich St	1978
Distinguished Professor & Chairholder, Phillips Petroleum Company Chair/IEB								
Tu, Yien-I	Prof			C	PHD	61	Iowa St	1981
White, Leonard A.	Prof			D	PHD	63	St Louis	1971
Ferrier, Gary D.	Assoc			DC	PHD	88	N Carol	1993
Sonstegaard, Miles H.	Assoc			H	PHD	58	Oregon	1969
Amin-Guttierez, De Pineres	Asst	575-6231		DE	PHD	92	Duke	1992
Durham, Yvonne	Asst			LD	PHD	94	Arizona	1994
Linvill, Carl	Asst			DC	PHD	93	N Carol	1993
Schulman, Craig	Asst			F	PHD	89	Tx A&M	1989

U of Arkansas at Little Rock Little Rock, AR 72204-1099 (501) 569-3354 Dixie Jordan 569-3354
Dept of Economics & Finance College of Business Adm Fax=569-8898 UALR

Name	Rank	Phone	E-mail	Field	Degree	Yr	School	Since
Vibhakar, Ashvin	Dean	569-3356		Fnce	PHD	80	Arkansas	8-81
Chisholm, Roger	C-Pr	569-8894			PHD	67	Chicago	1985
Adams, Jack E.	Prof	569-8879			PHD	75	Okla St	1980
Butler, James F.	Prof	569-8879			PHD	68	LSU	1963
Dorfman, Mark	Prof	569-8874			PHD	70	Illinois	1987
Ford, Richard	Prof	569-8876			PHD	79	Arkansas	1981
Galchus, Kenneth	Prof	569-8877			PHD	70	Wash U	1976
Lindeman, Bruce	Prof	569-8870			PHD		Duke	1975
Pickett, John C.	Prof	569-3354			PHD	70	Missouri	1986
Shull, Ralph	Prof	569-8857			PHD	72	Arkansas	1971
Martin, Charles	Assoc	569-8871			PHD	74	N Carol	1984
Terry, Andy	Assoc	569-8872			PHD	89	Michigan	1989
Holland, Larry C.	Asst	569-3354			PHD	94	Okla St	1995
Keller, Anita	Inst	569-8873			ABD			1991

U of Arkansas at Pine Bluff Pine Bluff, AR 71601 (501) 543-8575 Ruthie Johnson, Lula Smith
Department of Economics Sch of Business & Mgt Fax=543-8574

Name	Rank	Phone	E-mail	Field	Degree	Yr	School	Since
Fluker, John E.	Dean	543-8577		Quan	PHD		Houston	1989
Shahjahan, Mirza	Assoc	543-8575			PHD		Bonn	
Wu, Yeen-Kuen	Assoc	543-8575			MA		Atlanta	
Yang, Wei-Hsein	Assoc	543-8575			PHD		Nebraska	
Burkett, Evelyn	Asst	543-8575			MA		Houston	
Rucker, William	Asst	543-8575			ABD		Geo Wash	
Wang, William	Inst	543-8575			MBA		Atlanta	

Arkansas State University State Univ, AR 72467-0239 (501) 972-3416 Ms. Judy McCay
Dept of Economics & Dec Sys College of Business Fax=972-3868 CHEROKEE.ASTATE.EDU

Name	Rank	Phone	E-mail	Field	Degree	Yr	School	Since
Roderick, Roger D.	Dean	972-3035	roderick	Mgt	PHD	70	Illinois	1993
Brown, Christopher R.	C-Ac	972-3416	crbrown	AEKM	PHD	89	Tennessee	1990
Crawford, Jerry L.	Prof	972-3416	crawford	ADTM	PHD	69	Arkansas	1966
Dale, Lawrence Raymond	Prof	972-3810	dalex	ABPQ	PHD	89	Ohio U	1986
Kaminarides, John S.	Prof	972-3823	johnk	AFTO	PHD	68	Houston	1968
Director, Business Research								
Talbert, Lonnie E.	Prof	972-3416	letal	AQMT	PHD	64	N Car St	1966
Kesselring, Randall G.	Assoc	972-3416	randyk	ACJF	PHD	80	Oklahoma	1984
Latanich, Gary A.	Assoc	972-3416	latanich	AREM	PHD	78	Nebraska	1981
Marburger, Daniel R.	Assoc	972-3416	marburge	AJMD	PHD	89	Ariz St	1989

Arkansas Tech University — Russellville, AR 72801-2222 (501) 968-0354
Dept of Business & Economics — School of Business Fax=968-0677

Name	Rank	Phone	Email	Fields	Degree	Yr	School	Year
Tyler, Thomas P.	Dean	968-0490			PHD	80	Arkansas	1967
Smith, Richard S.	H-As	968-0492			PHD	74	Tx-Austin	1991
Cole, Raymond E.	Prof	968-0491			PHD	76	Arkansas	1970
Moore, Joseph L.	Prof	968-0688			PHD	75	Arkansas	1988

Ashland University — Ashland, OH 44805 (419) 289-5912 — Linda Braun
Department of Economics — Sch Bus Adm & Economics Fax=289-5949 — ASHLAND.EDU

Name	Rank	Phone	Email	Fields	Degree	Yr	School	Year
Rafeld, Frederick J.	Dean	289-5733			PHD	68	Ohio St	9-70
Nadler, Mark A.	C-Ac	289-5912			PHD		Iowa St	1989
A. L. Garber Family Chair of Economics								
Garcia, Javier	Assoc	289-5734			JD		Akron	1980
Rogers, Robert	Assoc	289-5739			PHD	83	Geo Wash	1993
Hanson, Phillip	Asst	289-5746			MA		Michigan	1988
Wasnich, Wendy	Asst	289-5735			MA		Ohio St	1985

Assumption College — Worcester, MA 01615-0005 (508) 767-7379 — Laurie Rochette
Economic Faculty — Dept Econ & Frgn Affair Fax=799-4502 — EVE.ASSUMPTION.EDU

Name	Rank	Phone	Email	Fields	Degree	Yr	School	Year
Hickey, Kevin L.	C-Ac	767-7296			MLA	76	Harvard	1972
Doyle, George A.	Prof	767-7579	gdoyle	FKOP	PHD	51	Fordham	1961
Kantarelis, Demetrius	Assoc	767-7557	dkantar	D	PHD	83	Clark	1983
Lynn, Stuart R.	Assoc	767-7565		ABFO	PHD	71	N Carol	1987
Fahy, Colleen A.	Asst	767-7558	cfahey	AHL	PHD	89	SUNY-Bin	1995
White, Thomas J.	Asst	767-7556	twhite	AEGQ	PHD	89	SUNY-Bin	1994
Pincince, Cecile M.	Lect	767-7004		AHJ	ABD		Clark	1980

Athens State College — Athens, AL 35611 (205) 233-8211 — Donna Thomas
Economics Faculty — School of Business Fax=233-8164 — AOL.COM

Name	Rank	Phone	Email	Fields	Degree	Yr	School	Year
Haynes, James F.	Dean	233-8116	aschaynes		PHD	80	Vanderbilt	1980
Erment, Gene	Prof	233-8120		A	EDD	65	North Tx	1968
Harper, Jeff	Asst	233-8234		CM	PHD	95	Auburn	1994
Newton, Dahlia	Asst	233-8175		A	MBA	81	W Carol	1987

Auburn University — Auburn, AL 36849-5242 (334) 844-4910 — Cathy Kruse 844-2901
Department of Economics — College of Business Fax=844-4615 — BUSINESS.AUBURN.EDU

Name	Rank	Phone	Email	Fields	Degree	Yr	School	Year
Alderman, C. Wayne	Dean	844-4030	walderman	Atg	DBA	77	Tennessee	4-77
Laband, David N.	H-Pr	844-2903	labandn		PHD	81	Va Tech	1994
Caudill, Steven B.	Prof	844-2907	scaudill		PHD	82	Florida	1981
Ekelund, Robert B. Jr.	Prof	844-2929	rekelund		PHD	67	LSU	1979
Lowder Eminent Scholar								
Hebert, Robert F.	Prof	844-2927	rhebert		PHD	70	LSU	1974
Russell Professor								
Jackson, John D.	Prof	844-2906	jjackson		PHD	77	Claremont	1984
Jones, Ethel B.	Prof	844-2916	ejones		PHD	61	Chicago	1975
Kaserman, David L.	Prof	844-2905			PHD	76	Florida	1986
Torchmark Professor								
Long, James E.	Prof	844-2911	jlong		PHD	74	Fla St	1974
Torchmark Professor								
Thompson, Henry L.	Prof	844-2910	hthompson		PHD	81	Houston	1987
Whitten, David O.	Prof	844-2928	dwhitten		PHD	70	Tulane	1968
Ault, Richard W.	Assoc	844-2919	rault		PHD	83	Virginia	1983
Barnett, Andy H.	Assoc	844-4980	abarnett		PHD	78	Virginia	1982
Beard, Thomas Randolph	Assoc	844-2918	rbeard		PHD	88	Vanderbilt	1988
Beil, Richard O.	Assoc	844-2921	rbeil		PHD	88	Tx A&M	1988
Garrison, Roger W.	Assoc	844-2920	rgarrisn		PHD	81	Virginia	1983
Gropper, Daniel M.	Assoc	844-2908	dgropper		PHD	89	Fla St	1988
Raymond, Jennie E.	Assoc	844-2923	jraymond		PHD	89	Vanderbilt	1989
Saba, Richard P.	Assoc	844-2922	rsaba		PHD	74	Tx A&M	1974
Thornton, Mark	Asst	844-4910			PHD	89	Auburn	
Wells, John M.	Asst	844-2902	jwells		PHD	94	Tx A&M	1994

Auburn U at Montgomery — Montgomery, AL 36117-3596 (205) 244-3454
Department of Economics — School of Business Fax=244-3792 — AUM.EDU

Name	Rank	Phone	Email	Fields	Degree	Yr	School	Year
Lake, Robert C.	Dean$	244-3478		Atg	DBA	77	La Tech	1971
Deravi, M. Keivan	Prof	244-3555		DFGJ	PHD	85	Okla St	1985
on leave; Director of Center for Government & Public Affairs								
Gregorowicz, Phillip	Prof	244-3575		EFGJ	PHD	82	N Illinois	1980
Hegji, Charles E.	Prof	244-3563		DFMJ	PHD	80	Wash U	1985
Lacy, Allen W.	Prof	244-3511		ETIH	PHD	71	Iowa St	1976
Moberly, H. Dean	Prof	244-3523		ADIQ	PHD	68	Tx A&M	1970
Chiles, Ted W.	Assoc	244-3512		ADJM	PHD	90	Penn St	1990
Clark, Joy	Assoc	244-3561		APQB	PHD	88	Tx A&M	1988
Sollars, David L.	Assoc	244-3486		KHAE	PHD	91	Fla St	1990

Augsburg College | Minneapolis, MN 55454 (612) 330-1149
Economics Faculty | Dept of Bus Adm & Econ Fax=

McNeff, Marie O.	Dean	330-1124			PHD		Nebraska	1968
Gupta, Satya P.	C-Pr	330-1149			PHD		S Illinois	1976
Sabella, Edward M.	Prof	330-1152			PHD		Minnesota	1961
Boeh, Jeanne	Asst	330-1760		I	PHD		Illinois	1990

Augusta College | Augusta, GA 30904-2200 (706) 737-1560 | Ms. Deloris Murray
Dept Acct, Econ, & Finance | School of Business Adm Fax=667-4064 | ADMIN.AC.EDU

Widener, Jack	Dean	737-1418			MBA			
Greene, Joseph	Assoc	737-1560	jgreene	AGI	MS		Georgia	1992
Brauer, Jurgen	Asst	737-1560	jbrauer	AFIT	PHD	89	Notre Dm	1991
Leightner, Jonathan E.	Asst	737-1560	jleightn	DTOP	PHD	89	N Carol	1989

Augustana College IL | Rock Island, IL 61201-2296 (309) 794-7457 | Melody Reid
Department of Economics | Div of Business & Educa Fax=794-7431 | AUGUSTANA.EDU

Nelson, Douglas	Prov	794-7312	adcdn		PHD	71	Iowa	1971
Ballman, Richard J. Jr.	C-Pr	794-7517	ecballman	ABDE	PHD	77	Iowa	1972
Conway, William B.	Prof	794-7267	ecconway	AFJK	PHD	69	Minnesota	1970
Marme, Christopher B.	Asst	794-7514	ecmarme	ACEO	PHD	94	Illinois	1988

Augustana College SD | Sioux Falls, SD 57197 (605) 336-5226
Department of Economics | Div of Social Sciences Fax=336-5229 | INST.AUGIE.EDU

Eggleston, Brian D.	C-Ac	336-5307	egglesto	ABQ	PHD	91	Wash St	1988
Carson, Leslie O.	Prof	336-5311	carson	ABM	MS	63	Colorado	1958
Whitney, Chet	Prof	336-4601	whitney	C	PHD	65	Kansas	1960
Nesiba, Reynold	Asst	336-5310	nesiba	EG	PHD	95	Notre Dm	1995

Austin Peay State University | Clarksville, TN 37044 (615) 648-7788 | Ms. Penny Howard
Department of Economics | College of Business Fax=648-5985 | LYNX.APSU.EDU

Reagan, Carmen C.	Dean	648-7674	reaganc	Mktg	DBA	83	Miss St	1988
Kim, Kil-Joong	C-Pr	648-7788	kimk	FO	PHD	80	Cincinnati	1980
Hutcheson, Aaron A.	Prof	648-7763	hutchesona	AQ	PHD		Clemson	1967
McMinn, Jim Thomas	Prof	648-7755	mcminnj	GM	DBA		Miss St	1977
Meadows, Tommy C.	Prof	648-7747	meadowst	HJ	PHD		Clemson	1977
Ukpolo, Victor	Assoc	648-6132	ukpolov	FO	PHD	85	American	1988

Azusa Pacific University | Azusa, CA 91702-7000 (818)
Economics Faculty | School of Bus & Mgt Fax= | APU.EDU

Lewis, Phillip V.	Dean	812-3090		Mgt	EDD	70	Houston	9-92
Conover, Roger	Asst	815-3823			MA		Ca-SnDgo	9-90
Verdugo, Paul	Asst	812-3091			MA		Ca Poly	9-80

Babson College | Babson Park, MA 02157-0901 (617) 239-4580 | Michele Wescott
Division of Economics | School of Management Fax=239-5239 | BABSON

Cohen, Allan R.	Dean	239-4316		Mgt	DBA	67	Harvard	
Marthinsen, John E.	C-Pr	239-4324			PHD	74	Conn	1974
Bayer, Arthur A.	Prof	239-4321			PHD	68	Mich St	1977
Casey, William L. Jr.	Prof	235-1200			PHD	63	Boston C	1964
Moss, Laurence S.	Prof	239-4580			PHD	71	Columbia	1977
Jones, Kent A.	Assoc	239-4477			PHD	81	Geneva	1982
McAuliffe, Robert E. Jr.	Assoc	235-1200			PHD	82	Virginia	1982
Axarloglou, Kostas	Asst	239-5512			PHD	93	Michigan	1994
Bonifaz, Roberto L.	Asst	239-4296			PHD		Boston U	
Polutnik, Lidija	Asst	239-4211					Geo St	1991
Ricciardi, Joseph M.	Asst	239-4530			PHD	85	Tx-Austin	1985

Baldwin-Wallace College | Berea, OH 44017-2088 (216) 826-2113 | Sandara Wojtolewicz
Department of Economics | Div of Social Sciences Fax=826-3868 | RS6000.BALDWIN.EDU

Rolleston, Barbara Sherman	C-Ac	826-2003	brolleston	HR	PHD		Cornell	1983
Ebert, Robert R.	Prof	826-2033	rebert	DFP	PHD	74	Case Wes	1967
Miller, Dennis D.	Assoc	826-2002	dmiller	OQ	PHD	85	Colorado	1987
Peart, Sandra Joan	Assoc	826-2120	speart	BD	PHD		Toronto	1989
Ross, Thomas A.	Assoc	826-2118	tross	CG	MA		Bowl Gr	
Sage, Lewis C.	Assoc	826-2119	lsage	CIJ	PHD	85	Maryland	1985
Heinicke, Craig W.	Asst	826-2419	cheinicke	NOE	PHD	91	Toronto	1991

Ball State University | Muncie, IN 47306-0340 (317) 285-5360 | Ms. Rita Disher
Department of Economics | College of Business Fax=285-8024 | BSUVC.BSU.EDU

Palomba, Neil A.	Dean	285-8192			PHD	66	Minnesota	8-84
Van Cott, T. Norman	C-Pr	285-5360			PHD	69	U Wash	1977
Bohanon, Cecil E.	Prof	285-5363			PHD	81	Va Tech	1980

Name	Rank	Phone	Email	Field	Degree	Yr	School	Year
Cheng, Chu-Yuan	Prof	285-5366			PHD	64	Geotown	1971
Coehlo, Philip R. P.	Prof	285-5376			PHD	69	U Wash	1986
Deitsch, Clarence R.	Prof	285-5368			PHD	74	N Hamp	1974
Flowers, Marilyn	Prof	285-5360			PHD	74	Va Tech	1990
Green, Jeffery	Prof	285-2056			PHD		Cornell	1972
Santoni, Gary J.	Prof	285-5365			PHD	72	New Mex	1988
Stone, Courtney C.	Prof	285-5378			PHD	73	UCLA	1991
Keil, Stanley R.	Assoc	285-5360			PHD	73	Oregon	1973
McClure, James Edward	Assoc	285-5375			PHD	83	Purdue	1982
Spector, Lee C.	Assoc	285-5360			PHD	85	Iowa	1985
Yoho, Devon L.	Assoc	285-8020			PHD	74	Missouri	1978
Director of Center for Economic Education								
Zegeye, Abera	Assoc	285-5379			PHD	77	Indiana	1974
Helland, Eric	Asst	285-5371			PHD		U Wash	1995
Horowitz, John B.	Asst	285-5360			PHD	88	Tx A&M	1989
Liu, Tung	Asst	285-3724			PHD	90	Ca-SnDgo	1990
Tabarrok, Alexander	Asst	285-5370			PHD		Geo Mason	1994

University of Baltimore — Baltimore, MD 21201-5779 (410) 837-4994 — Cindy Tannebaum
Dept of Economics & Finance — Merrick Sch of Business Fax=837-5722 — UBE.UB.UMD.EDU

Name	Rank	Phone	Email	Field	Degree	Yr	School	Year
Costello, Daniel E.	Dean	837-4955	daoa	SoPs	PHD	68	Mich St	6-90
Cebenoyan, A. Sinan	C-Ac	837-4928		Fnce	PHD		NYU	
Acs, Zoltan J.	Prof	837-5012			PHD	80	New Sch	1989
Conte, Michael A.	Prof	837-5029			PHD	79	Michigan	1989
Levy, David T.	Prof	837-5026			PHD		N Carol	
Sawhney, Bansi L.	Prof	837-5049			PHD	75	Geo Wash	1971
Stevens, David W.	Prof	837-4727			PHD	65	Colorado	
Executive Director of Jacob France Center								
Brownstein, Barry	Assoc	837-4960			PHD		Rutgers	
Geriowski, Daniel A.	Assoc	837-4987			PHD		Pittsburgh	

Barnard College — New York, NY 10027 (212) 854-3454 — Shirley Shum
Economics Faculty — Department of Economics Fax=854-8947

Name	Rank	Phone	Email	Field	Degree	Yr	School	Year
Burgstaller, Andre C.	C-Pr	854-3454			PHD	79	Columbia	1977
Foley, Duncan K.	Prof	854-3790			PHD	66	Yale	1977
Milenkovitch, Deborah D.	Prof	854-5140			PHD	66	Columbia	1965
Barrington, Linda	Asst	854-2082			PHD	91	Illinois	1991
Conrad, Cecilia A.	Asst	854-3333			PHD	82	Stanford	1975
Mehrling, Perry G.	Asst	854-4369			PHD	88	Harvard	1987

Barry University — Miami Shores, FL 33161-6695 (305)
Dept Economics & Finance — Andreas Sch of Business Fax=892-6412 — BARRYU

Name	Rank	Phone	Email	Field	Degree	Yr	School	Year
Lash, Lewis	Dean	899-3500		Mgt	DBA	81	Nova	9-97
Cruz, Robert D.	Assoc	899-3522			PHD	85	Penn	1993
Daghestani, Eddie	Assoc	899-3509			PHD	71	Colo St	1988
Duchatelet, Martine	Assoc	661-1622			PHD	77	Stanford	1989
Hervitz, Hugo M.	Assoc	758-3392			PHD	83	Indiana	1982
Morrell, Stephen O.	Assoc	899-3513			PHD	77	Va Tech	1990

Barton College — Wilson, NC 27893 (919) 399-6418 — Beth Jean Fitch
Economics Faculty — Dept of Business Prog Fax=

Name	Rank	Phone	Email	Field	Degree	Yr	School	Year
Davis, F. Mark	Dean	399-6343			PHD		Duke	8-78
Vice President for Academic Affairs								
Eggers, Ronald E.	C-As	399-6417		Busi	MBA		E Carol	8-78
Jaggi, Anand P.	Prof				PHD		Jabalpur	1971

Bates College — Lewiston, ME 04240 (207) 786-6085
Economics Faculty — Department of Economics Fax=786-6123 — ABACUS.BATES.EDU

Name	Rank	Phone	Email	Field	Degree	Yr	School	Year
Murray, Michael P.	C-Pr	786-6085	mmurray	R	PHD	74	Iowa St	1986
Phillips Professor of Economics								
Aschauer, David Alan	Prof			E	PHD		Rochester	1990
Elmer W. Campbell Professor of Economics								
Walther, Theodore	Prof	786-6088		FG	PHD	64	New Sch	1958
Williams, Anne D.	Prof	786-6091		O	PHD	76	Chicago	1981
Schwinn, Carl R.	Assoc	786-6090		IO	PHD	78	Cornell	1975
Hughes, James W.	Asst	786-6193		J	PHD	87	Michigan	1987
Maurer-Fazio, Margaret	Asst	786-6087			PHD		Pittsburgh	1985

Baylor University — Waco, TX 76798-8003 (817) 755-2263 — Susan Armstrong
Department of Economics — Hankamer Sch Busines Fax=755-1092 — BAYLOR.EDU

Name	Rank	Phone	Email	Field	Degree	Yr	School	Year
Scott, Richard C.	Dean	755-1211		Mgt	DBA	68	Indiana	1968
Truitt, W. James	C-Pr	755-2263			PHD	68	Illinois	1968
Herman W. Lay Prof Private Enterprise, & Director Cntr/Priv Entrp								
Gardner, H. Stephen	Prof	755-2263			PHD	78	Berkeley	1978
Herman Brown Professor of Economics								

Name	Rank	Phone	Email	Field	Degree	Yr	School	Year
Gilbreath, L. Kent	Prof	755-2263			PHD	71	Florida	1973
Stevens Professor of Private Enterprise								
Kelly, Thomas M.	Prof	755-2263			PHD	70	Okla St	1969
Director Center for Economic Analysis								
King, Arthur T.	Prof	755-2263			PHD	77	Colorado	1982
McKinney, Joseph A.	Prof	755-2263			PHD	70	Mich St	1976
Green, Steven L.	Assoc	755-2263			PHD	84	Brown	1986
Henderson, James W.	Assoc	755-2263			PHD		So Meth	1981
Ben H. Williams Professor of Economics								
Pisciotta, John L.	Assoc	755-2263			PHD		Tx-Austin	1980
Butler, Judy C.	Lect	755-2263			MS	74	Baylor	1974
Carmichael, Dodd	Lect	755-2263			MS	93	Baylor	1993
Johnson, Karen R.	Lect	755-2263			MIM		Baylor	1979
Odegaard, Thomas A.	Lect	755-2263			MA	70	Rice	1985

Beaver College — Glenside, PA 19038 (215)
Economics Faculty — Dept of Bus Adm & Econ Fax=

Name	Rank	Phone	Email	Field	Degree	Yr	School	Year
Biggs, William D.	C-Pr	572-2937		Mgt	PHD	74	Penn St	8-80
Morra, Wayne A.	Asst	572-2125			PHD	84	Temple	8-81

Belhaven College — Jackson, MS 39202-1789 (601) 968-5965
Economics Faculty — Div of Business Adm Fax=968-9998

Name	Rank	Phone	Email	Field	Degree	Yr	School	Year
Park, James W.	C-Pr	968-5965		AD	PHD	74	Alabama	1977
Penn, William M.	Prof	968-5966		AM	PHD	68	Duke	1981

Bellarmine College — Louisville, KY 40205-0671 (502) 452-8240 — Ms. Carol Huff
Department of Economics — Rubel Sch of Business Fax=452-8004

Name	Rank	Phone	Email	Field	Degree	Yr	School	Year
Popper, Edward T.	Dean	452-8240			PHD	78	Harvard	1994
Bethune, John J.	C-Ac	452-8240			PHD	87	Fla St	1984
Feltner, Richard L.	Prof	452-8240			PHD	65	N Car St	6-86
Slesnick, Frank	Prof	452-8240			PHD	72		1975
Hobbs, Bradley K.	Asst	452-8240			PHD	90	Fla St	1988
McCrickard, Myra J.	Asst	452-8240			PHD	89	N Car St	1989

Belmont University — Nashville, TN 37212-3757 (615) 385-6784
Economics Faculty — School of Business Fax=385-6455 — BELMONT.EDU

Name	Rank	Phone	Email	Field	Degree	Yr	School	Year
Eubanks, Clifford L.	Dean	386-4522		Mgt	PHD	67	Arkansas	1992
Hodgin, Gary L.	Assoc	385-6784			PHD	85	Tennessee	1983
Cochran, Howard H. Jr.	Asst	385-6477			DA		Mid Tenn	1994
Thompson, Mary M.	Asst	385-6784			MA		Notre Dm	1983

Bemidji State University — Bemidji, MN 56601-2699 (218) 755-2907 — Tammy Mayer
Department of Economics — Div of Social & Nat Sci Fax=755-4100 — BEMIDJI.MSUS.EDU

Name	Rank	Phone	Email	Field	Degree	Yr	School	Year
Lundberg, Kenneth R.	Dean$	755-2965		Chem	PHD		S Dakota	1968
Ley, Robert D.	C-Pr	755-2730			PHD		Wash St	1977
Johnson, Lowell E.	Prof	755-3709			PHD	75	Cornell	1976
Welle, Patrick G.	Prof	755-3873			PHD		Wisconsin	1982
Lehman, Eldon R.	Assoc				MA		W Tx St	1967

Benedict College — Columbia, SC 29204 (803) 253-5187
Business Adm Department — Division of Business Fax=253-5065
Did Not Respond--1994-95 Listing

Name	Rank	Phone	Email	Field	Degree	Yr	School	Year
Scott, Robert L.	C-Pr	253-5187		Mgt	EDD		S Carol	
Mahdi, Syed I.	Prof	253-5190			PHD	76	Mass	1975
Njoku, Anthanasius O.	Prof	253-5187			PHD		Illinois	

Bentley College — Waltham, MA 02154-4705 (617) 891-3183 — Terry Lesanto
Economics Faculty — College of Business Fax=891-2896 — BENTLEY.EDU

Name	Rank	Phone	Email	Field	Degree	Yr	School	Year
Schlorff, H. Lee	Dean	891-2113	hschlorff	Atg	PHD	73	Missouri	1978
Clarke, William A.	C-Ac	891-2143	wclarke	AD	PHD	73	Rutgers	1972
Grubaugh, Stephen G.	Prof	891-2539	sgrubaugh	CF	PHD	82	Chicago	1981
Rhodus, W. Gregory	Prof	891-3483		ACG	MA	75	Conn	1992
Zampieron, Alexander Alg	Prof	891-2126	azampieron	ABF	PHD	72	Fletcher	1965
Callan, Scott J.	Assoc	891-2024	scallan	CDQ	PHD	85	Tx A&M	1987
Kuntz, Dale F.	Assoc	891-2237	dkuntz	AEO	PHD	79	Conn	1975
Leeth, John D.	Assoc	891-2029	jleeth	GCJ	PHD	83	N Carol	1987
Mukerjee, Swati	Assoc	891-2956	smukerjee	DFI	PHD	86	Boston U	1989
Santerre, Rexford E.	Assoc	891-2938	rsanterre	DHI	PHD	83	Conn	1983
Stollar, Andrew J.	Assoc	891-2268	astollar	CFP	PHD	73	Boston C	1976
Sumner, Scott B.	Assoc	891-2945	ssumner	EN	PHD	84	Chicago	1982
Thomas, Janet M.	Assoc	891-2053	jthomas	DHQ	PHD	87	Boston C	1987
Gulley, O. David	Asst	891-2355	dgulley	EG	MA	89	Kentucky	1990
Meyer, Christine	Asst		cmeyer	EFH	PHD	95	MIT	1995
Stiroh, Kevin	Asst		kstiroh	EO	PHD	95	Harvard	1995

Berea College — Berea, KY 40404 (606) 986-9341 — Becky Grandgeorge
Economics Faculty — Dept of Business & Econ Fax=986-4506 — BEREA.EDU
phone: 986-9341

Name	Rank	Phone	Field	Degree	Yr	School	Year
Perkins, Alfred	Dean	Ext 5486	Hst	PHD		Harvard	1965
Tolliver, R. Wayne	C-Pr	Ext 6160		DBA	87	Kentucky	1975
Johnstone, Robert L.	Prof			PHD	61	Illinois	1964
Clarence M. Clark Professor of Mountain Agriculture and Economics							
Sowell, Clifford	Prof			PHD	78	Georgia	1981
Spears, Philip V.	Prof			PHD	71	Kentucky	1968
Stolte, William F.	Prof	986-9347		PHD	71	Syracuse	1970
Isaacs, Patricia	Assoc			DBA	94	Kentucky	1989
Kazura, Martie	Asst			MBA	90	Montana	1991
McCormack, Edward	Asst			MBA	80	E Kentuc	1985

Berry College — Mt. Berry, GA 30149 (706) 236-2233 — Sandy Briggs
Economics Faculty — School of Business Fax=295-2921 — BERRY.EDU
phone 232-5374

Name	Rank	Phone	Field	Degree	Yr	School	Year
Williams, Fred E.	Dean	236-2233	twilliams	PHD	70	Purdue	1995
Mixon, J. Wilson	Prof	Ext 2396		PHD	74	U Wash	1986
Shatto, Gloria M.	Prof	234-2707		PHD	66	Rice	1979
Sockwell, William D.	Assoc	Ext 2424		PHD	89	Vanderbilt	1988
Patrono, Michael Frank	Asst	Ext 2392		MS	88	Fla St	1989
Waggle, J. Douglas	Asst	Ext 2585		PHD		Alabama	1994

Bethel College-MN — St. Paul, MN 55112 (612) 638-6286 — Nikki Daniels
Economics Faculty — Business & Economics Fax=638-6001

Name	Rank	Phone	Field	Degree	Yr	School	Year
Danforth, David	C-Ac	638-6276		MBA	67	Harvard	1988
Essenburg, Timothy J.	Assoc	638-6296		PHD	91	Tennessee	1989
Abou-Zeid, Bassem	Asst	638-6293		PHD	90	Oklahoma	1990

Bethune-Cookman College — Daytona Bch, FL 32015 (904) Ext 339
Economics Faculty — Division of Business Fax=255-3989
phone 255-1401

Name	Rank	Phone	Field	Degree	Yr	School	Year
Long, Aubrey E.	C-Pr	Ext 355	Bus	PHD		Ohio St	1988
Williams, Mike M.	Prof			PHD		Ohio U	1991
Ziegler, William	Asst	Ext 406		ABD		Nova	1991

Biola University — LaMirada, CA 90639 (310) 903-4770 — Anne Saxton, K. Pedrick
Economics Faculty — School of Business Fax=903-4748

Name	Rank	Phone	Field	Degree	Yr	School	Year
Strand, Larry D.	Dean$	903-4770		MBA		S Calif	1986
Black, Michael	Assoc	903-4770	FNO	DBA		US Intl	1990
Buegler, Paul W.	Assoc	903-4770	DEK	JD		Wm Mitch	1978
Cooper, Ronald L.	Assoc	903-4770	CDEF	PHD		Berkeley	1994
Dill, Glenn V.	Assoc	903-4770	AD	MBA		Pepperdi	1990

Birmingham-Southern Coll — Birmingham AL 35254 (205)
Economics Faculty — Div of Econ & Bus Admin Fax=

Name	Rank	Phone	Field	Degree	Yr	School	Year
Gunter, Marjorie M.	C-Pr	226-4823	Atg	MBA	71	Samford	1978
Dale, Gary Thomas	Asst			MA	86	Alabama	1989
Sumner, Glenna L.	Asst			PHD	93	Oklahoma	1993

Bloomfield College — Bloomfield, NJ 07003 (201) Ext 339 — Monifa Mears Ext 339
Department of Economics — Divison of Business Fax=743-3998

Name	Rank	Phone	Field	Degree	Yr	School	Year
Powley, Ellen	C	Ext 414	Mktg	PHD		Pace	
Michailidis, Lazaros	Assoc	Ext 376		PHD		SUNY-Buf	1978
Gibson, Eleanor	Asst	Ext 378		MA		Columbia	1965

Bloomsburg Univ of Penn — Bloomsburg, PA 17815 (717) 389-4335
Department of Economics — College of Arts & Sci Fax=389-2094 — BLOOMU.EDU
Did Not Respond--1994-95 Listing

Name	Rank	Phone	Field	Degree	Yr	School	Year
Liu, Hsien-Tung	Dean	389-4410					
Lee, Woo Bong	C-Pr	389-4335		PHD	72	Rutgers	1977
Bawa, Ujagar S.	Prof	389-4340		PHD		Cornell	
Bohling, Peter H.	Prof	389-4343		PHD	77	Mass	1978
Kahn, Saleem M.	Prof	389-4681		PHD		J Gutenb	
Haririan, Mehdi	Assoc	389-4682		PHD	87	New Sch	1982
Mohindru, Rajesh K.	Assoc	389-4341		PHD		Penn	
Newson, Roosevelt	Assoc						
Obutelewicz, Robert S.	Assoc	389-4342		PHD		Mass	
Ross, Robert P.	Assoc	389-4335		MA	58	Wash U	1967
Bagi, Sukhwinder	Asst	389-4839		PHD		Vanderbilt	
Patch, Elizabeth P.	Asst	389-4737		PHD		Lehigh	

Boise State University	Boise, ID		83725	(208) 385-3351				
Department of Economics	College of Business		Fax=385-3637				COBFAC.IDBSU.EDU	
Ruud, William N.	Dean	385-1125	aburuud	Mgt	PHD		Nebraska	9-93
Twight, Charlotte	C-Pr	385-3351	rectwigh		PHD	83	U Wash	1986
Lichtenstein, Peter M.	Prof	385-1471	reclicht		PHD	74	Colorado	1975
Payne, Richard D.	Prof	385-3351	recpayne		PHD	70	S Calif	1970
Reynolds, R. Larry	Prof	335-3351	recreyno	BID	PHD	77	Wash St	1979
Skoro, Charles L.	Prof	385-3351	recskoro	JBI	PHD	77	Columbia	1982
Draayer, Gerald F.	Assoc	385-3351	reedraay		PHD		Ohio	1976
Director, Center for Economic Education								
Loucks, Christine	Assoc	385-3351	reclouck		PHD	83	Wash St	1989
Raha, Arun	Asst	385-3465	recraha	EFO	PHD	91	Wash St	1990

Boston College	Chestnut Hl, MA		02167-3808	(617) 552-3670			Kathy Tubman	
Department of Economics	College of Arts & Sci		Fax=552-2308				BCVMS.BC.EDU	
Barth, J. Robert	Dean	552-3271			PHD		Harvard	
Tresch, Richard W.	C-Ac	552-3670	tresch	H	PHD	73	MIT	1969
Anderson, James E.	Prof	552-3691		DF	PHD	69	Wisconsin	1969
Arnott, Richard J.	Prof	244-3674		DHR	PHD	75	Yale	1988
Belsley, David A.	Prof	552-3676		CD	PHD	65	MIT	1966
Cox, Donald C.	Prof	552-3677		DJ	PHD	80	Brown	1987
Gollop, Frank M.	Prof	552-3693		DO	PHD	74	Harvard	1979
Gottschalk, Peter	Prof	552-4517		CDIJ	PHD	73	Penn	1987
Hansen, Bruce	Prof	552-3678		CE	PHD	89	Yale	1994
Kraus, Marvin C.	Prof	552-3692		DR	PHD	73	Minnesota	1972
MacLeod, W. Bentley	Prof	552-3670		DJ	PHD	84	Brit Col	1995
Neenan, William B.	Prof	552-3262		HR	PHD	66	Michigan	1980
Academic Vice President and Dean of Faculties								
Peek, Joe	Prof	552-3686		E	PHD	79	Northwes	1978
Quinn, Joseph F.	Prof	552-4623	quinnj	DJ	PHD	75	MIT	1975
Richter, Donald K.	Prof	552-3678		DR	PHD	73	MIT	1977
Baum, Christopher F.	Assoc	552-3673		CE	PHD	77	Michigan	1977
McLaughlin, Francis M.	Assoc	552-3675		JN	PHD	64	MIT	1961
Assistant Chairperson, Department of Economics								
Murphy, Robert G.	Assoc	552-3688		EF	PHD	84	MIT	1984
Petersen, Harold A.	Assoc	552-4550		G	PHD	63	Brown	1960
Schiantarelli, Fabio	Assoc	552-3687		CEF	PHD	81	LondonEc	1992
Bai, Chong-en	Asst	552-3690		CD	PHD	93	Harvard	1992
Butcher, Kristin F.	Asst	552-3670		DJ	PHD	93	Princeton	1995
Canavan, Christopher	Asst	552-3689		EF	PHD	94	Columbia	1993
Marcouiller, Douglas	Asst	552-3685		FO	PHD	94	Tx-Austin	1994

Boston University	Boston, MA		02215	(617) 353-4389			Kate Buckley	
Department of Economics	College of Liberal Arts		Fax=353-4449				ACS.BU.EDU	
Berkey, Dennis	Dean			Math	PHD		Cincinnati	
Dean, Graduate School								
Miron, Jeffrey A.	C-Pr	353-4442	jmiron	EKN	PHD	84	MIT	1990
Chamley, Christophe	Prof	353-4250	chamley	HEO	PHD	77	Harvard	
Cooper, Russell W.	Prof	353-7082	rcooper	CDE	PHD	79	Penn	
Associate Chair								
Doeringer, Peter B.	Prof	353-4438		JL	PHD	66	Harvard	1974
Eaton, Jonathan	Prof	353-4142	eaton	FG	PHD	76	Yale	
Director of Graduate Studies								
Ellis, Randall P.	Prof	353-2741	ellisrp	CILQ	PHD	81	MIT	1981
Director, Undergraduate Studies								
Gale, Douglas	Prof	353-6675	gale	DEG	PHD	75	Cambridg	
Harris, John R.	Prof	353-8903	harrisjr	ER	PHD	67	Northwes	1975
Jones, Leroy P.	Prof	353-4123	jones	HLO	PHD	74	Harvard	1976
Director of Public Enterprise								
Kotlikoff, Laurence J.	Prof	353-4002	kotlikof	EH	PHD	77	Harvard	
Kyn, Oldrich	Prof	353-4539	okyn	CEP	PHD		Charles	1971
Lang, Kevin	Prof	353-5694	lang	JC	PHD	82	MIT	1987
Loury, Glenn C.	Prof	353-5662	gloury	DJ	PHD	76	MIT	1991
on sabbatical								
Lucas, Robert E. B.	Prof	353-4147	rlucas	CFJO	PHD	72	MIT	1976
on sabbatical								
Manove, Michael	Prof	353-3299	manove	D	PHD	70	MIT	1975
McGuire, Thomas G.	Prof	353-2995	tmcguire	HIL	PHD	76	Yale	1976
Mookherjee, Dilip M.	Prof	353-4392	dilipm	HLO	PHD	82	LondonEc	1995
Ray, Debraj	Prof	353-2417	debraj	COD	PHD	83	Cornell	1991
Director, Institute for Economic Development								
Riordan, Michael H.	Prof	353-5941	riordan	DL	PHD	81	Berkeley	1988
Director, Industry Studies Program								
Rosenthal, Robert W.	Prof	353-2742	rosentha	CD	PHD	71	Stanford	1987
Vogelsang, Ingo	Prof	353-2996	vogelsan	HL	PHD	69	Heidelbe	1981
on leave 2nd semester								
Weiss, Andrew M.	Prof	353-3086	aweiss	DGJ	PHD	76	Stanford	1987
Young, Alwyn	Prof	353-4534		O	PHD	90	Columbia	1995

Name	Rank	Phone	E-mail	Fields	Degree	Yr	School	Year
Beaudry, Paul	Assoc	353-4249	pbeaudry	EJL	PHD	89	Princeton	1990
leave of absence								
Fernandez, Raquel	Assoc	353-9583	raquel	DFL	PHD	88	Columbia	1992
leave of absence								
Ma, Ching-to Albert	Assoc	353-4010	ma	JL	PHD		LondonEc	
Tandon, Pankaj	Assoc	353-3089	ptandon	DO	PHD	79	Harvard	1978
Berman, Eli	Asst	353-6324	eli	CJ	PHD	93	Harvard	1993
Bui, Linda T.	Asst	353-4140	ltbui	HLQ	PHD	93	MIT	1993
leave of absence								
Donald, Stephen	Asst	353-4824	ocker	CE	PHD	90	Brit Col	1993
Gilchrist, Simon	Asst	353-6824	sgilchrist	C	PHD	90	Wisconsin	1995
Gonzalo, Jesus	Asst	353-6823	jgonzalo	CE	PHD	91	Ca-SnDgo	1991
on leave of absence								
Kortum, Sam	Asst	353-4822	kortum	ELO	PHD	92	Yale	1991
Minehart, Deborah	Asst	353-4436	minehart	CDL	PHD	94	Berkeley	1994
Munshi, Kaivan	Asst			LO	PHD	95	MIT	1995
Neeman, Zvika	Asst			CD	PHD	95	Northwes	1995
van Wincoop, Jan Eric	Asst	353-4535	vanwinco	EF	PHD	89	Harvard	1989

Bowdoin College — Brunswick, ME 04011 (207) 725-3340
Economic Faculty — Department of Economics Fax=725-3691 POLAR.BOWDOIN.EDU

Name	Rank	Phone	E-mail	Fields	Degree	Yr	School	Year
Fitzgerald, John M.	C-Ac	725-3593	jfitz	HC	PHD	83	Wisconsin	1983
Freeman, Albert Myrick III	Prof	725-3597	rfreeman	QD	PHD	65	U Wash	1965
William Shipman Professor of Economics								
Vail, David Jeremiah	Prof	725-3596	dvail	OQ	PHD		Yale	1970
Adams-Catlin Professor of Economics								
Connelly, Rachel E.	Assoc	725-3790	connelly	JT	PHD	85	Michigan	1985
DeCoster, Gregory Paul	Assoc	725-3726	gdecoste	ER	PHD	85	Tx-Austin	1985
Goldstein, Jonathan Paul	Assoc	725-3595	jgoldste	EC	PHD		Mass	1979
Jones, Michael	Assoc	725-3598	mjones	F	PHD		Yale	1987
McIntyre, Robert J.	VAsoc	725-3594	rmcintyre	NP	PHD		N Carol	
DeGraff, Deborah S.	Asst	725-3591	ddegraff	OT	PHD	89	Michigan	1991
Ortmann, Andreas	Asst	725-3592	aortmann	L	PHD	91	Tx A&M	1991

Bowling Green State Univ — Bowling Gr, OH 43403-0268 (419) 372-2646 Kelly M. Birr
Department of Economics — College of Business Fax=372-2875 CBA.BGSU.EDU

Name	Rank	Phone	E-mail	Fields	Degree	Yr	School	Year
Hoag, John H.	C-Pr	372-2831	jhoag		PHD	72	Kansas	1972
Browne, M. Neil	Prof	372-8060	nbrown2		PHD	69	Tx-Austin	1968
Distinguished Teaching Professor								
Chittle, Charles R.	Prof	372-8180	chittle		PHD	69	Purdue	1965
Haas, Paul F.	Prof	372-2649	phaas		PHD	70	Boston C	1967
Kim, Kyoo H.	Prof	372-2735	kkim		PHD	78	Wisconsin	1978
Reed, J. David	Prof	372-2647	dreed		PHD	70	Kansas St	1968
Douglas, Richard W. Jr.	Assoc	372-2648	rdougla		PHD		Iowa	1976
Benedict, Mary Ellen	Asst	372-8221	mbenedi@opie.		PHD	91	Car Mellon	1991
Fuerst, Timothy S.	Asst	372-6868	tfuerst		PHD	90	Chicago	1993
Haight, Alan D.	Asst	372-8111	ahaight		PHD	90	Wisconsin	1991
Quinn, J. Kevin	Asst	372-8652	kquinn		PHD		American	1990
Rosenberry, Lisa A.	Asst	372-8397	rosey		ABD		Va Tech	1995
Vanderhart, Peter G.	Asst	372-8070	pvander		PHD	91	Wisconsin	1991

Bradley University — Peoria, IL 61625 (309) 677-2296 Karen Olehy
Economic Faculty — College of Business Adm Fax=677-3374 BRADLEY

Name	Rank	Phone	E-mail	Fields	Degree	Yr	School	Year
Modianous, Doan	Dean$		dmod	Mgt	PHD	73	Tx Tech	1981
Wojcikewych, Raymond	C-Ac	677-2296			PHD	80	Penn St	1977
Goldberg, Kalman	Prof	677-2296			PHD	54	Cornell	1952
Scott, Robert C.	Prof	677-2297			PHD	75	Iowa	1975
Thorson, Douglas Y.	Prof	677-2298			PHD	62	Wisconsin	1960
Weinstein, Robert I.	Prof	677-2264			PHD	74	Tx-Austin	1980
Dean of the Graduate School								
Felder, Joseph	Assoc	677-2302			PHD	79	UCLA	1981
Highfill, Jannett K.	Assoc	677-2304			PHD	85	Kansas	1985
Sattler, Edward L.	Assoc	677-2303			PHD	79	Illinois	1977
O'Brien, Kevin M.	Asst	677-2299			PHD	88	Illinois	1992
Short, Deanne M.	Asst	677-2300			PHD	89	Purdue	1989

Brandeis University — Waltham, MA 02254 (617) 736-2240 Claire Cincotta
Department of Economics — College of Arts & Sci Fax=736-2263

Name	Rank	Phone	E-mail	Fields	Degree	Yr	School	Year
Miller, Robin F.	Dean	736-3451						
Dolbear, F. Treanery Jr.	C-Pr	736-2244			PHD	63	Yale	1968
Clinton S. Darling Professor of Economics								
Carter, Anne P.	Prof	736-2242			PHD	49	Harvard	1971
Fred C. Hecht Professor of Economics								
Evans, Robert Jr.	Prof	736-2261			PHD	59	Chicago	1967
Atran Professor of Labor Economics								
Lewbel, Arthur	Prof	736-2258			PHD	84	MIT	1984

Name	Rank	Phone	E-mail	Field	Degree	Yr	School	Hired
McCulloch, Rachel	Prof	736-2245			PHD	73	Chicago	1987
Petri, Peter A.	Prof	736-2256			PHD	76	Harvard	1974
Schhwalberg, Barney K.	Prof	736-2255			PHD		Harvard	
Jaffe, Adam B.	Assoc	736-2251			PHD	85	Harvard	
Jefferson, Gary H.	Assoc	736-2253			PHD	86	Yale	1984
Alexander, Barbara	Asst	736-2257						
Chakraborty, Atreyea	Asst	736-2247						
DeNicolo, Gianni	Asst	736-2249						
Plummer, Michael G.	Asst	736-2265			PHD	88	Mich St	1993
Click, Reid W.	Inst	736-2243			MBA	87	Chicago	

Brescia College — Owensboro, KY 42301 (502) 686-4217 — Nancy Rhodes
Economic Faculty — Division of Business Fax=686-4266

Name	Rank	Phone	E-mail	Field	Degree	Yr	School	Hired
Minks, Lawrence C.	C-Pr	686-4209			EDD	80	N Colo	8-88
Asefa, Sally Ann	Prof	686-4264			PHD	78	Iowa St	8-80

University of Bridgeport — Bridgeport, CT 06601-2449 (203) 576-4383
Dept of Business Economics — School of Business Fax=576-4388 — BRIDGEPORT.EDU

Name	Rank	Phone	E-mail	Field	Degree	Yr	School	Hired
Moriya, Frank E.	Dean	576-4384		Mktg	DBA	67	Geo Wash	1967
Chung, Hyung C.	C-Pr	576-4009			PHD	70	Columbia	1970
Katsimbris, George M.	Prof	576-4383			PHD	77	Conn	1978
Harvey Hubbell Professor of Economics and Finance								
Mullings, Llewellyn M.	Assoc	576-4363			PHD		Clark	
Gargalas, Vasilios	Asst	576-4370			PHD		NYU	1993
Kim, Gew-Rae	Asst	576-4372						

Brigham Young University — Provo, UT 84602 (801)
Department of Economics — Col Family,Home &SocSci Fax=378-2844 — BYU.EDU

Name	Rank	Phone	E-mail	Field	Degree	Yr	School	Hired
Pope, Clayne L.	Dean	378-2083			PHD	72	Chicago	1970
Jensen, Farrell	C-Pr	378-4057	fejensen		PHD	72	Kansas St	1982
Kearl, James R.	Prof	378-5812	jrkearl		PHD	75	MIT	1975
McDonald, James B.	Prof	378-5225	jim_mcdonald		PHD	70	Purdue	1972
Honors Office								
Park, William Laird	Prof	378-6037			PHD	63	Cornell	1977
Pope, C. Arden III	Prof	378-2157	popea		PHD	81	Iowa St	1984
Pope, Rulon D.	Prof	378-2327	rpope		PHD	76	Berkeley	1982
Spencer, David E.	Prof	378-7277	david_spencer		PHD	74	Tx A&M	1986
Wimmer, Larry T.	Prof	378-3354	wimmer		PHD	68	Chicago	1963
Lambson, Val E.	Assoc	378-7765	lambson		PHD	83	Rochester	1989
Ransom, Michael R.	Assoc	378-4736	ransom		PHD	83	Princeton	1988
Eide, Eric	Asst	378-5169	eide		PHD	93	Ca-SnBarb	1993
Manning, Richard L.	Asst	378-4740	rmanning		PHD	89	Chicago	1990
Pender, John	Asst	378-2037	pender		PHD	92	Stanford	1992
Phillips, Kerk	Asst	378-5928	kerk		PHD	91	Rochester	1992
Showalter, Mark	Asst	378-4645	showalter		PHD	91	MIT	1991
Snow, Karl N.	Asst				PHD	91	Chicago	1995
Thurston, Norman	Asst							1995
Timothy, Darren P.	Asst							1995

Brigham Young Univ-Hawaii — Laie, HI 96762-1294 (808) 293-3580
Economics Faculty — School of Business Fax=293-3582 — BYUH.EDU

Name	Rank	Phone	E-mail	Field	Degree	Yr	School	Hired
Neal, William G.	Dean	293-3580		Sys	EDD	77	Va Tech	1984
Haynes, C. Beth	Prof	293-3587		DG	PHD	81	Purdue	1994
Kimzey, Bruce W.	Prof	293-3585			PHD	70	Wash St	1989

Brown University — Providence, RI 02912 (401) 863-3836
Economic Faculty — Department of Economics Fax=863-1970 — BROWNVM.BROWN.EDU

Name	Rank	Phone	E-mail	Field	Degree	Yr	School	Hired
Henderson, J. Vernon	C-Pr	863-2886	j_henderson		PHD	72	Chicago	1974
Eastman Professor of Political Economy								
Borts, George H.	Prof	863-2458	george_borts		PHD	53	Chicago	1964
George S. and Nancy B. Parker Professor of Economics								
Galor, Oded	Prof	863-2117	oded		PHD	84	Columbia	1986
Garber, Peter M.	Prof	863-2145	peter_garber		PHD	77	Chicago	1985
Grossman, Herschel I.	Prof	863-2606	herschel		PHD	65	J Hopkins	1973
Merton P. Stolz Professor in the Social Sciences								
Lancaster, Anthony	Prof	863-2112	ec418000		PHD	65	StCathar	
Page, Talbot	Prof	863-1988	talbot_page		PHD	72	Cornell	
Pitt, Mark M.	Prof	963-2970	markp		PHD	77	Berkeley	
Poole, William	Prof	863-2697	wpoole		PHD	66	Chicago	1974
Herbert H. Goldberger Professor of Economics								
Putterman, Louis G.	Prof	863-3837	ec424000		PHD	80	Yale	1980
Ryder, Harl E.	Prof	863-2179	ec415000		PHD	67	Stanford	1965
Schupack, Mark B.	Prof	863-2887	ec40500		PHD	60	Princeton	1970
Stein, Jerome L.	Emer	863-2143	jls		PHD	55	Yale	1956
Eastman Professor of Political Economy - Emeritus								

Name	Rank	Phone	E-mail	Field	Degree	Yr	School	Since
Vohra, Rajiv	Prof	863-3030	rajiv_vohra		PHD	83	J Hopkins	
Cho, In-Koo	Assoc	863-3836			PHD	86	Princeton	1995
Feldman, Allan M.	Assoc	863-2415	allan_feldman		PHD	72	J Hopkins	1977
Serrano, Roberto	Assoc	863-2764	rserrano		PHD	92	Harvard	
Weil, David	Assoc	863-1754	dnweil		PHD	90	Harvard	
Driscoll, John	Asst	863-3836			PHD	95	Harvard	1995
Friedberg, Rachel	Asst	863-7578	rfried		PHD	93	MIT	
Gozalo, Pedro	Asst	863-3277	pg@pstc3.pstc		PHD	89	Ca-SnDgo	
Krishna, Pravin	Asst	863-3836			PHD	95	Columbia	1995
Sorensen, Bent	Asst	863-3807	bs@pstc3.pstc.		PHD	91	Copenhag	
Spagat, Michael	Asst	863-1978	mspagat		PHD	88	Harvard	
Yosha, Oved	Asst	863-2506	oved		PHD	92	Harvard	

Bryant College — Smithfield, RI 02917-1284 (401) 232-6338
Department of Economics — College of Business Fax=232-6319 RESEARCH1.BRYANT.EDU

Name	Rank	Phone	E-mail	Field	Degree	Yr	School	Since
Patterson, Michael	Dean	232-6060		Mgt	DBA	75	Geo Wash	8-86
Mirmirani, Sam	C-Ac	232-6338	smirmira	IMO	PHD	85	Clark	1982
Norton, R. D.	Prof	232-6307		FR	PHD	77	Princeton	1985
Sarkesian Professor of Business Economics								
Shaanan, Joseph	Prof	232-6340	jshaanan	FL	PHD	79	Cornell	
Sweeney, William B. Jr.	Prof	232-6097		AE	PHD	73	Sarasota	
Ilacqua, Joseph A.	Assoc	232-6098	jllacqua	AJ	EDD	93	Boston U	1968
Mini, Peter S.	Assoc	232-6226		BN	PHD		Tulane	
Bates, Laurie	Asst	232-6459	lbates	HD	PHD		Conn	
Elder, John	Asst	232-6338	jelder	CE	PHD		Virginia	
Han, Hsiang-Ling	Asst	232-6418	han	CE	PHD		Rochester	

Bryn Mawr College — Bryn Mawr, PA 19010 (610) 526-5038
Economics Faculty — Department of Economics Fax=526-7475
phone 526-5000

Name	Rank	Phone	E-mail	Field	Degree	Yr	School	Since
DuBoff, Richard B.	C-Pr	526-5178			PHD	64	Penn	1964
Farley, Noel J. J.	Prof	526-5176			PHD	65	Yale	
Ceglowski, Janet E.	Asst	526-5039			PHD	86	Berkeley	
Newburger, Harriet B.	Asst	526-5181			PHD	84	Wisconsin	1987
Rosalyn R. Schwartz Lectureship								
Ross, David R.	Asst	526-5076			PHD	84	Northwes	1992

Bucknell University — Lewisburg, PA 17837 (717) 524-1476 — Alice Vanbuskirk
Department of Economics — College of Arts & Sci Fax=524-3760 — BUCKNELL.EDU

Name	Rank	Phone	E-mail	Field	Degree	Yr	School	Since
Gerdes, Eugenia Proctor	Dean	524-3292			PHD		Duke	1974
Amott, Teresa Louise	C-Ac	524-1476			PHD		Boston C	1989
Anderson, John Whiting	Prof	524-1476			PHD		Penn	1961
Griffith, Winston Harold	Prof	524-1476			PHD		Howard	1987
Kresl, Peter K.	Prof	524-1478			PHD	70	Tx-Austin	1969
Shackelford, Jean A.	Prof	524-1476			PHD	74	Kentucky	1975
Krohn, Gregory A.	Assoc	524-3448			PHD	85	Wisconsin	1983
Moohr, Michael	Assoc	524-1476			PHD		Cambridg	1975
Sackrey, Charles Melvin	Assoc	524-1476			PHD		Tx-Austin	1980
White, Nancy E.	Assoc	524-1476			PHD	86	Colorado	1986
Ce, Wei	Asst	524-1476			PHD		Penn	
Kinnaman, Thomas	Asst	524-1476			PHD		Virginia	
Knoedler, Janet T.	Asst	524-1476			PHD		Tennessee	
Nega, Berhanu	Asst	524-1476			PHD		New Sch	1990

Buena Vista College — Storm Lake, IA 50588 (712)
Economics Faculty — School of Business Fax=749-2037 — BVC.EDU

Name	Rank	Phone	E-mail	Field	Degree	Yr	School	Since
Russell, Paul	Dean	749-2422			EDD	65	N Colo	9-67
Ullerich, Stan	Assoc	749-2419			PHD		Purdue	9-95

Butler University — Indianapolis, IN 46208 (317) 940-9221
Department of Economics — College of Business Adm Fax=940-9455 — BUTLER.EDU

Name	Rank	Phone	E-mail	Field	Degree	Yr	School	Since
Dahringer, Lee D.	Dean	940-9221	dahringer	Mktg	DBA	75	Colorado	1993
Main, Robert S.	C-Ac	940-9528	main	H	PHD	73	UCLA	1981
Horvath, Janos	Prof	940-9532	jhorvath	FE	PHD	67	Columbia	
John W. Arbuckle Professor of Economics								
Nichols, Archie J.	Prof	940-nich	ols	B	PHD	61	Penn	1957
Rieber, William J.	Prof	940-9846	rieber	F	PHD	79	Pittsburgh	1989
Fountain, Gwen A.	Assoc	940-foun	tain	A	PHD	72	Michigan	1976
Grossman, Peter Z.	Asst	940-9727	grossman	N	PHD	92	Wash U	1994
Efroymson Chair in Economics								

Calif Univ of Pennsylvania — California, PA 15419-1394 (412)
Dept of Business & Economics — Col of Science & Tech Fax=

Name	Rank	Phone	Degree	Yr	School	Year
Hart, Richard	Dean	938-4169	PHD		Minnesota	1978
Kopko, Robert J.	C-Ac	938-4371	MS		Penn St	1970
Chawdhry, M. Arshad	Prof	938-5990	PHD		Illinois	1976
Cole, Ismail	Prof		PHD		Pittsburgh	1984
Omarzal, Mahmood	Prof		PHD		Indiana	1979
Park, Young J.	Prof	938-4371	PHD	74	Temple	1977
Tarullo, P. Ronald	Prof		PHD		Pittsburgh	1978
Mongell, Susan	Assoc		PHD		Pittsburgh	1990

U of California at Berkeley — Berkeley, CA 94720 (510) 642-3581 — Michele Radford
Department of Economics — Col of Letters & Sci Fax=642-6615 — UCBCMSA

Name	Rank	Phone	Email	Degree	Yr	School	Year
Christ, Carol T.	Dean	642-1483					
Adelman, Irma	Prof	642-3345		PHD	55	Berkeley	1979
Akerlof, George A.	Prof	642-5837		PHD	66	MIT	1966
Anderson, Robert M.	Prof	642-0822		PHD		Yale	
Bardhan, Pranab K.	Prof	642-4527		PHD		Cambridg	
Brown, R. Clair	Prof	643-7090		PHD		Maryland	
Debreu, Gerard	Prof	642-7284		DSC	56	Paris	1962
DeVries, Jan	Prof	642-2813		PHD	70	Yale	
Eichengreen, Barry	Prof	642-2772		PHD	79	Yale	1987
Fishlow, Albert	Prof	642-4827		PHD	63	Harvard	1983
Frankel, Jeffrey A.	Prof	642-8084		PHD	78	MIT	1979
Gilbert, Richard J.	Prof	642-1507		PHD	76	Stanford	1976
Goldman, Steven M.	Prof	642-1955		PHD	66	Stanford	1979
Grossman, Gregory	Prof	642-0822		PHD	53	Harvard	1953
Katz, Michael on leave	Prof			PHD		Oxford	
Keeler, Theodore E.	Prof	642-4411		PHD	71	MIT	1977
Lee, Ronald D.	Prof	642-4535		PHD	71	Harvard	1979
McFadden, Daniel L.	Prof	643-8428		PHD	62	Minnesota	1963
Obstfeld, Maurice	Prof	643-9646		PHD	79	MIT	
Pierce, James L.	Prof	642-4321		PHD	64	Berkeley	1976
Quigley, John M.	Prof	642-7411	quigley	PHD	72	Harvard	1979
Reich, Michael	Prof	642-0822		PHD	74	Harvard	1974
Rogoff, Kenneth S.	Prof	642-0822		PHD	80	MIT	1989
Romer, Paul M.	Prof	643-8596		PHD	83	Chicago	
Rothenburg, Thomas J.	Prof	642-1955		PHD	66	MIT	1966
Rubinfeld, Daniel L.	Prof	642-1959		PHD	72	MIT	1983
Smale, Stephen	Prof	642-4367		PHD		Michigan	
Sutch, Richard C.	Prof	642-4159		PHD	68	MIT	1967
Tyson, Laura D.	Prof	642-6083		PHD	74	MIT	1977
Williamson, Oliver E.	Prof	642-8697		PHD	63	Car Mellon	1988
Craine, Roger	Assoc	642-3021		PHD	72	Maryland	1977
Dickens, William T.	Assoc	643-7074		PHD	81	MIT	1980
Farrell, Joseph V.	Assoc	642-9854		PHD	81	Oxford	
Romer, Christina D.	Assoc	642-1955		PHD	85	MIT	1988
Romer, David H.	Assoc	642-1955		PHD	85	MIT	1988
Ruud, Paul A.	Assoc	642-6709		PHD	81	MIT	1981
Hall, Bronwyn H.	Asst	642-3878		PHD	88	Stanford	1987
Hermalin, Benjamin E.	Asst	642-7575		PHD	88	MIT	1988
Rabin, Matthew	Asst	643-8622		PHD		MIT	

Univ of California, Davis — Davis, CA 95616-8578 (916) 752-0741 — Gerri Refsland
Department of Economics — Col of Letters & Sci Fax=752-9382 — UCDAVIS.EDU

Name	Rank	Phone	Email	Fields	Degree	Yr	School	Year
Quinzii, Martine	C-Pr	752-1567	mmquinzii	CDG	PHD	74	U Paris	1991
Borenstein, Severin	Prof	752-3033	sjborenstein		PHD	83	MIT	1989
Brzeski, Andrzej	Emer	752-0741		AP	PHD	64	Berkeley	1963
Feenstra, Robert	Prof	752-7022	refeenstra	F	PHD	81	MIT	1986
Kaneda, Hiromitsu	Emer	752-1581		AFOQ	PHD	64	Stanford	1973
Lindert, Peter H.	Prof	752-1983	phlinder	FN	PHD	67	Cornell	1978
Makowski, Louis	Prof	752-6142	lmakowski	DE	PHD	75	UCLA	1985
Mayer, Thomas	Emer	752-0741		BE	PHD	53	Columbia	1962
Olmstead, Alan L.	Prof	752-2043	alolmstead	HN	PHD	70	Wisconsin	1969
Roemer, John E.	Prof	752-3226	jeroemer	DP	PHD	74	Berkeley	1974
Sheffrin, Steven M.	Prof	752-1576	smsheffrin	EH	PHD	76	MIT	1976
Silvestre, Joaquim	Prof	752-1570	jbsilvestre	D	PHD	73	Minnesota	1983
Tuma, Elias H.	Emer	752-1572	chtuma	ANO	PHD	62	Berkeley	1967
Walton, Gary M.	Prof	757-4630		ADN	PHD	66	U Wash	1981
Wegge, Leon L.	Emer	752-1550	llwegge	F	PHD	63	MIT	1966
Woo, Wing T.	Prof	752-3035	wtwoo	EFOP	PHD	82	Harvard	1985
Bonanno, Giacomo F.	Assoc	752-1574	gfbonanno	CD	PHD	75	LondonEc	1987
Clark, Gregory	Assoc	752-9242	gclark	NO	PHD	85	Harvard	1990
Helms, L. Jay	Assoc	752-2094	ljhelms	DHI	PHD	79	MIT	1985
Hoover, Kevin D.	Assoc	752-2129	kdhoover	BE	DPHI	85	Oxford	1985
Nelson, Julie A.	Assoc	752-8396	janelson	BDH	PHD	86	Wisconsin	1988
Salyer, Kevin D.	Assoc	752-8359	kdsalyer	EG	PHD	85	Ca-SnBarb	1990

Name	Rank	Phone	Email	Field	Degree	Yr	School	Year
Triest, Robert K.	Assoc	752-1551	rtriest	HI	PHD	87	Wisconsin	1988
Cameron, Colin	Asst	752-0741	accameron	CIJ	PHD	88	Stanford	1989
Nehring, Klaus D.	Asst	752-3379	kdnehring	DG	PHD	91	Harvard	1992
Swenson, Deborah	Asst	752-1569	swenson@crete.	FH	PHD	91	MIT	1993
Gustafson, W. Eric	Emer	752-0741		AO	PHD	59	Harvard	1978

Univ of Calif, Irvine Irvine, CA 92717-5100 (714) 824-5788 R. Pellegrini/B. Atwell
Department of Economics Sch of Social Sciences Fax=824-2182 UCI.EDU

Name	Rank	Phone	Email	Field	Degree	Yr	School	Year
Schonfeld, William R.	Dean	824-6801	wrschonf	PolS	PHD		Princeton	
Glazer, Amihai	C-Pr	824-5974	aglazer		PHD	78	Yale	1978
Brownstone, David	Prof	824-6231	dbrownstone		PHD	80	Berkeley	1984
DeVany, Arthur S.	Prof	824-5269	asdevany		PHD	70	UCLA	1984
Fielding, Gordon J.	Prof	824-5448	gjfieldi		PHD	62	UCLA	1965
Johnston, John	Emer	824-5581	jjohnsto		PHD	57	Wales	1978
Kassouf, Sheen T.	Prof	824-7161	rpellegr		PHD	65	Columbia	1965
Lave, Charles	Prof	824-6502	calave		PHD	68	Stanford	1964
Lilien, David M.	Prof	824-6232	dmlilien		PHD	77	MIT	1984
Margolis, Julius	Emer	824-7003	jmargoli		PHD	49	Harvard	1976
McGuire, Martin C.	Prof	824-6190	mcmcguir		PHD	64	Harvard	1992
Small, Kenneth A.	Prof	824-5658	ksmall		PHD	76	Berkeley	1983
Bell, Duran	Assoc	824-7053	dbell		PHD	65	Berkeley	1965
Chew, Soo Hong	Assoc	824-5074	shchew		PHD	81	Brit Col	1991
Cohen, Linda	Assoc	824-5189	lrcohen		PHD	79	Cal Tech	1988
DiNardo, John	Asst	824-3191	jdinardo		PHD	90	Princeton	1991
Garfinkel, Michelle	Asst	824-3190	mgarfink		PHD	88	Brown	1991
Klein, Daniel B.	Asst	824-6363	dklein		PHD	87	NYU	1989
Lee, H. Hiro	Asst	824-6910	hlee		PHD	87	Berkeley	1987
Lee, Jaewoo	Asst	824-8529	jwlee		PHD	92	MIT	1992
Skaperdas, Stergios	Asst	824-4167	sskapero		PHD	88	J Hopkins	1988
Valletta, Robert G.	Asst	824-8126	rvallett		PHD	87	Harvard	1989

Univ of Calif, Los Angeles Los Angeles, CA 90024-1481 (310) 825-1011
Department of Economics Col of Letters & Sci Fax=206-2313 UCLA.EDU

Name	Rank	Phone	Degree	Yr	School	Year
Orbach, Raymond L.	Prov					
Riley, John G.	C-Pr	825-1541	PHD	72	MIT	1973
Aoki, Masanao	Prof	825-2360	PHD	65	Tokyo In	1983
Demsetz, Harold	Prof	825-3651	PHD	59	Northwes	1971
Arthur Andersen and Company Alumni Professor of Business Economics						
Edwards, Sebastian	Prof	825-1011	PHD	81	Chicago	1985
Ellickson, Bryan C.	Prof	825-4556	PHD	70	MIT	1973
Harberger, Arnold C.	Prof	825-7520	PHD	50	Chicago	
Intriligator, Michael D.	Prof	825-4144	PHD	63	MIT	1972
Klein, Benjamin	Prof	825-6547	PHD	70	Chicago	1978
Leamer, Edward E.	Prof	825-3557	PHD	70	Michigan	1975
Leijonhufvud, Axel S. B.	Prof	825-4126	PHD			
Levine, David K.	Prof	825-3810	PHD	81	MIT	1981
McCall, John J.	Prof	825-1849	PHD	59	Chicago	
Ostroy, Joseph M.	Prof	825-4627	PHD			
Shapley, Lloyd S.	Prof	825-3723	PHD			
Thompson, Earl A.	Prof	825-4387	PHD	61	Harvard	1965
Cameron, Trudy Ann	Assoc	825-3925	PHD	82	Princeton	1984
Farmer, Roger E. A.	Assoc	825-2523	PHD	82	W Ontario	1988
Murphy, George G. S.	Assoc	825-9397	PHD			
Sokoloff, Kenneth L.	Assoc	825-4249	PHD	82	Harvard	1980
Butz, David A.	Asst	825-6838	PHD	86	Northwes	1987
Currie, Janet	Asst	206-8380	PHD	88	Princeton	1988
Dick, Andrew R.	Asst	206-8408	PHD	89	Chicago	
Hansen, Gary D.	Asst	825-3847	PHD	86	Minnesota	1987
Ozler, Sule	Asst	825-2997	PHD	86	Stanford	1985
Potter, Simon M.	Asst	206-6732	PHD	90	Wisconsin	1990
Rosenthal, Jean-Laurent	Asst	825-2490	PHD	88	Cal Tech	1988
Ryu, Keungkwan	Asst	825-3466	PHD	90	Stanford	1990
Williams, Darrell L.	Asst	206-2794	PHD			

Univ of Calif, Riverside Riverside, CA 92521-0203 (909) Ext 1474 Karen Smith
Department of Economics Col of Human & Soc Sci Fax=787-5685 UCR.EDU
phone 787-5037

Name	Rank	Phone	Email	Field	Degree	Yr	School	Year
Velez-Iranez, Carlos	Dean	787-3594	carlos.velez		PHD	74	Ca-SnDgo	1994
Khan, Azizur Rahman	C-Pr	Ext 1470	azizur.khan	FOPR	PHD	66	Cambridge	1988
Carter, Susan B.	Prof	Ext 1589	susan.carter	AJNT	PHD	81	Stanford	1990
Chilcote, Ronald H.	Prof	Ext 1571	ronald.chilcote.	P	PHD	65	Stanford	1963
Gaffney, M. Mason	Prof	Ext 1574		AHR	PHD	56	Berkeley	1976
Griffin, Keith B.	Prof	787-4108		AOP	DPHI	65	Oxford	1988
Lippit, Victor D.	Prof	Ext 1582		AOP	PHD	71	Yale	1971
Pattanaik, Prasanta	Prof	Ext 1592	prasanta.pattana	AO	PHD	68	Delhi	1991
Pollin, Robert N.	Prof	Ext 1579	robert.pollin	AE	PHD	82	New Sch	1982
Russell, R. Robert	Prof	Ext 1585	robert.russell	ADH	PHD	65	Harvard	1986

Name	Rank	Phone	Email	Fields	Degree	Yr	School	Hired
Sherman, Howard J.	Prof	Ext 1576	howard.sherman	EK	PHD	60	S Calif	1966
Ullah, Aman	Prof	Ext 1591	aman.ullah	C	PHD	71	Delhi	1989
Cullenberg, Stephen E.	Assoc	Ext 1573	stephen.cullenbe	ABCP	PHD	87	Mass	1988
Dymski, Gary A.	Assoc	Ext 1570	gary.dymski	AEHP	PHD	87	Mass	1991
Chauvet, Marcelle	Asst	Ext 1587		AE	PHD	95	Penn	1995
Fairris, David H.	Asst	Ext 1578	david.fairris	AJP	PHD	84	Duke	1989
Felfand, Steven	Asst	Ext 1572		AOQ	PHD	94	Berkeley	1995
Gonzalez-Rivera, Gloria	Asst	Ext 1590	gloria.gonzalez	CG	PHD	91	Ca-SnDgo	1991
Guo, Jang-Ting	Asst	Ext 1588	jangting.guo	AC	PHD	93	UCLA	1993
Lee, Tae-Hwy	Asst			ACG	PHD	90	Ca-SnDgo	1995
Sengupta, Kunal	Asst	Ext 1583	kunal.sengupta	ADO	PHD	84	Cornell	1989

Univ of Calif, San Diego La Jolla, CA 92093-0508 (619) 534-3383 Beverly Applequiest
Department of Economics Thurgood Marshall Col Fax=534-7040 UCSD.EDU

Name	Rank	Phone	Email	Fields	Degree	Yr	School	Hired
Crawford, Vincent	C-Pr	534-1055	vcrawfor	D	PHD	76	MIT	1976
Attiyeh, Richard E.	Prof	534-6654		EI	PHD	66	Yale	1982
Vice Chancellor of Research and Dean, Graduate Studies								
Bear, Donald V. T.	Emer	534-4481		AE	PHD	63	Stanford	1965
Borjas, George J.	Prof	534-4828	gborjas	J	PHD	75	Columbia	1990
Conlisk, John	Prof	534-3832		ET	PHD	65	Stanford	1968
Engle, Robert F.	Prof	534-4553	rengle	CGR	PHD	66	Cornell	1975
Chancellor's Associates Chair in Econometrics								
Granger, Clive W. J.	Prof	534-3856	cgranger	C	PHD	74	Nottingh	1974
Chancellor's Associates Chair in Economics								
Groves, Theodore	Prof	534-2818	tgroves	DHM	PHD	70	Berkeley	1978
Hamilton, James D.	Prof	534-5986	jhamilto	D	PHD	83	Berkeley	1992
Heller, Walter P.	Prof	534-4692	wheller	DE	PHD	70	Stanford	1974
Machina, Mark J.	Prof	534-2391	mmachina	D	PHD	79	MIT	1979
Ramanathan, Ramu	Prof	534-6787	rramanat	CFO	PHD	67	Minnesota	1967
Sobel, Joel	Prof	534-4367	jsobel	D	PHD	78	Berkeley	1978
Starr, Ross	Prof	534-3879	rstarr	DE	PHD	72	Stanford	1980
White, Halbert L.	Prof	534-3502	hwhite	C	PHD	76	MIT	1979
Carson, Richard T.	Assoc	534-6319	rcarson	CQ	PHD	85	Berkeley	1985
Flavin, Marjorie A.	Assoc	534-4649	mflavin	E	PHD	81	MIT	1992
Guasch, Jose Luis	Assoc	534-4799	jguasch	DJO	PHD	76	Stanford	1978
Ramey, Garey	Assoc	534-5721	gramey	D	PHD	87	Stanford	1987
Ramey, Valerie	Assoc	543-2388	vramey	E	PHD	87	Stanford	1987
Rauch, James E.	Assoc	534-2405	jrauch	FO	PHD	85	Yale	1986
Betts, Julian R.	Asst	534-3369	jbetts	CJ	PHD	90	Queen's	1990
DenWaan, Wooten	Asst	543-0762	wdenhaas	AE	PHD	91	Car Mellon	1991
Elliott, Graham	Asst	534-3383	gelliott	CEF	PHD	94	Harvard	1994
Pereira, Alfredo M.	Asst	534-2988	apereira	H	PHD	88	Stanford	1987
on leave to William & Mary								
Raut, Lakshmi K.	Asst	534-2858	lraut	CO	PHD	85	Yale	1987
Timmerman, Allan	Asst	534-3383	atimmerm	CG	PHD	92	Cambridg	1994
Watson, Joel	Asst	534-3383	jwatson	CF	PHD	92	Stanford	1994

U of Calif, Santa Barbara Santa Barbara CA 93106-9210 (805) 893-3670 Julie Sears, Manager
Department of Economics Col of Letters & Sci Fax=893-8830 ECON.UCSB.EDU

Name	Rank	Phone	Email	Fields	Degree	Yr	School	Hired
Sonstelie, Jon C.	C-Pr	893-3670	jon	HR	PHD	75	Northwes	1977
Carrington-Crouch, Robert L.	Prof	893-2152	rlcc	A	PHD	67	Essex	1973
Comanor, William S.	Prof	893-2287		LD	PHD	64	Harvard	1975
Deacon, Robert T.	Prof	893-3679	deacon	QH	PHD	72	U Wash	1972
DeCanio, Stephen J.	Prof	893-3130	decanio	NCD	PHD	72	MIT	1978
Frech, H. E. III	Prof	893-3569	frech	LAI	PHD	74	UCLA	1973
Kolstad, Charles	Prof	893-2108	kolstad	QLD	PHD	82	Stanford	1992
Krouse, Clement G.	Prof	893-3804	krouse	D	PHD	69	UCLA	1979
Marshall, John M.	Prof	893-3670	marshall	A	PHD	69	MIT	1972
Mehra, Rajnish	Prof	893-3238	mehra	GF	PHD	78	Car Mellon	1988
Mercer, Lloyd J.	Prof	893-2895	mercer	ND	PHD	67	U Wash	1966
Morgan, W. Douglas	Prof	893-2653	dmorgan	HDE	PHD	69	Berkeley	1973
Phillips, Llad	Prof	893-2023	llad	JC	PHD	69	Harvard	1972
Sengupta, Jati K.	Prof	893-3797	sengupta	CO	PHD	62	Iowa St	1976
Shapiro, Perry	Prof	893-2253	pxshap	DH	PHD	67	Berkeley	1969
Stuart, Charles	Prof	893-3216	stuart	HKD	PHD	75	Lunds	1980
Bohn, Henning	Assoc	893-4532	bohn	EF	PHD	86	Stanford	1992
Grogger, Jeffrey T.	Assoc	893-4533	jeff	CE	PHD	87	Ca-SnDgo	1987
Trejo, Stephen J.	Assoc	893-3666	stevet	J	PHD	88	Chicago	1987
Funkhouser, Ed	Asst	893-3490	funkhous	OJ	PHD	90	Harvard	1992
Garratt, Rodney J.	Asst	893-2849	garratt	AEH	PHD	91	Cornell	1991
Hahm, Joon-Ho	Asst	893-2412	jhahm	EFGC	PHD	93	Columbia	1994
Qin, Cheng-Zhong	Asst	893-2753	qin	D	PHD	89	Iowa	1989
Steigerwald, Douglas G.	Asst	893-3151	doug	C	PHD	89	Berkeley	1988
Tesar, Linda L.	Asst	893-4333	linda	FGE	PHD	90	Rochester	1990
Nisbet, Mary	D	893-2284	nisbet	G	PHD	91	Glasgow	1991
Academic Coordinator								

Univ of Calif, Santa Cruz Santa Cruz, CA 95064 (408) 459-2743 Kim Tyler
Department of Economics Social Sciences Fax= UCSC.EDU

Name	Rank	Phone	E-mail	Fields	Degree	Yr	Institution	Since
Wittman, Donald A.	C-Pr	459-4445	wittman@cats.	KD	PHD	70	Berkeley	1969
Dooley, Michael	Prof	459-3662	mpd@cats.	F	PHD	71	Penn	1992
Friedman, Daniel	Prof	459-4981	dan@cash.	FG	PHD	77	Ca-SnCrz	1979
Grieson, Ronald E.	Prof	459-2968	grieson@cats.	RHD	PHD	72	Rochester	1980
Hutchison, Michael M.	Prof	459-4245	hutch@cats.	EFG	PHD	83	Oregon	1985
Ibister, John W.	Prof	459-2246	merrill@ucsco.	O	PHD	69	Princeton	1968
Provost Merrill College								
Kaun, David E.	Prof	459-2486	nuclear@cats.	J	PHD	64	Stanford	1966
Kletzer, Kenneth M.	Prof	459-3407	kkletzer@cats.	FDOH	PHD	82	Berkeley	1992
Singh, Nirvikar	Prof	459-4093	boxjenk@cats.	DLO	PHD	82	Berkeley	1982
Wah Wong, Christine Pui	Prof	459-4381	cwong@cats.	O	PHD	79	Berkeley	1986
Walsh, Carl E.	Prof	459-4082	walshc@cats.	E	PHD	76	Berkeley	1987
Cheung, Yin-Wong	Assoc	459-4247	cheung@cats.	C	PHD	90	Penn	1990
Elbaum, Bernard	Assoc	459-4248	elbaum@cats.	N	PHD	82	Harvard	1986
Fung, Kwok-Chiu	Assoc	459-3273	kcfung@cats.	F	PHD	70	Wisconsin	1989
Chinn, Menzie	Asst	459-2079	chinn@cats.	FCE	PHD	91	Berkeley	1991
Dresher, Katherine	Asst	459-4453	dresher@cats.	H	PHD	94	Wisconsin	1994
Fairlie, Robert	Asst	459-3332	rfairlie@cats.	J	PHD	94	Northwes	1994
Kletzer, Lori Gladstein	Asst	459-3596	lketzer@cats.	J	PHD	86	Berkeley	1993
Landesman, Miriam F.	Lect							
Shepherd, Robert J.	Lect							

California Institute of Tech Pasadena, CA 91125 (818) 395-4065 Susan G. Davis, Div Adm
Economics Faculty Div of Human & Soc Sci Fax=405-9841 CALTECH.EDU

Name	Rank	Phone	E-mail	Fields	Degree	Yr	Institution	Since
Ledyard, John O.	C-Pr	395-8482			PHD	67	Purdue	1985
Camerer, Colin	Prof	395-4054			PHD	81	Chicago	1994
Rea A. & Lela G. Axline Professor of Business Economics								
Davis, Lance E.	Prof	395-4092		N	PHD	56	J Hopkins	1968
Mary Stillman Harkness Professor of Social Science								
Grether, David M.	Prof	395-4068			PHD	69	Stanford	1970
Palfrey, Thomas R.	Prof	395-4088			PHD	81	Cal Tech	1986
Plott, Charles R.	Prof	395-4209			PHD	65	Virginia	1971
Edward S. Harkness Professor of Economics and Political Science								
Border, Kim Christian	Assoc	395-4062		C	PHD	79	Minnesota	1979
Bossaerts, Peter	Assoc	395-4028		G	PHD	86	UCLA	1990
Dubin, Jeffrey A.	Assoc	395-4059			PHD	82	MIT	1982
El-Gamal, Mahmoud A.	Asst	395-4422			PHD	88	Northwes	1989
Fohlin, Caroline	Asst	395-4401		NFL	PHD	94	Berkeley	1994
Ghirardato, Paolo	Asst			D	PHD	95	Berkeley	1995
Page, Scott	Asst	395-4216		H	PHD	93	Northwes	1993
Wilkie, Simon	Asst			L	PHD	90	Rochester	1995

California Lutheran Univ Thousand Oaks CA 91360-2787 (805) 493-3360
Economics Faculty School of Business Fax=493-3719 ROBLES.CALLUTHERAN.EDU

Name	Rank	Phone	E-mail	Fields	Degree	Yr	Institution	Since
Maxey, Charles	Dean	493-3358	maxey		PHD		Illinois	1991
Akbari, Ali	Prof	493-3379	akbari		PHD		S Calif	1984
Damooei, Jamshid	Assoc	493-3357	damooei		PHD		Surrey	1987

Cal Polytechnic State U-SLO S Luis Obispo CA 93407 (805) 756-2783 Eliane Yochum 756-2784
Economics Department School of Business Fax=756-1473 CYMBAL.CALPOL

Name	Rank	Phone	E-mail	Fields	Degree	Yr	Institution	Since
Boynton, William C.	Dean	756-2705		Atg	PHD	76	Mich St	9-85
Williamson, Daniel P.	H-Pr	756-1768			PHD	73	Ca-SnDgo	1970
Adams, John P.	Prof	756-2922			PHD	72	Claremont	1970
Beardsley, George L.	Prof	756-2356			PHD	74	Penn	1975
Kersten, Timothy W.	Prof	756-2555			PHD	73	Oregon	1971
Marlow, Michael L.	Prof	756-1764			PHD	78	Va Tech	1988
on leave to Florida Atlantic Univ								
Papakyriazis, Artemis	Prof	756-1765			PHD	82	Ca-River	1982
Papakyriazis, Panagiotis A.	Prof	756-7176			PHD	74	Ca-SnDgo	1971
Rice, Walter E.	Prof	756-2285			PHD	73	Claremont	1964
Associate Dean								
Fanchon, Phillip F.	Assoc	756-1766			PHD	82	Ca-SnBarb	
Shiers, Alden F.	Assoc	756-2564			PHD	77	Ca-SnBarb	1975
Villegas, Daniel J.	Asst	756-1767			PHD	79	Stanford	1987

Calif State Poly U-Pomona Pomona, CA 91768-4082 (909) 869-3842 Kelly Thompson
Economics Department College of Arts Fax=869-6987 CSUPOMONA.EDU

Name	Rank	Phone	E-mail	Fields	Degree	Yr	Institution	Since
Ho, Franklin Y. H.	C-Pr	869-3854			PHD	57	S Calif	1961
Al-Sabea, Taha H.	Prof	869-3855			PHD	68	S Calif	1968
Blumner, Sidney M.	Prof	869-3843	smblumner		PHD	68	Arizona	1967
Bray, Robert T.	Prof	869-3847			PHD	72	UCLA	1965
Burton, Maureen	Prof	869-3853	mburton		PHD	86	Ca-River	1988
Jaques, David G.	Prof	869-3851			PHD	73	Claremont	1965
Park, David J.	Prof	869-3844			PHD	62	S Calif	1965

Name	Rank	Phone	E-mail	Fields	Degree	Yr	School	Since
Shieh, John T.	Prof	869-3858			DBA	81	S Calif	1967
Sutton, James E.	Prof	869-3846			BS	55	Wisconsin	1964
Bresnock, Anne E.	Assoc	869-4593			PHD	81	Colorado	1990
Rush, Lynda M.	Assoc	869-3857			PHD	84	Ca-Davis	1986
Safarzadeh, Mohammad R.	Assoc	869-3852			PHD	84	Claremont	1987
Shute, Laurence	Assoc	869-3850	lshute		PHD	73	Columbia	1988
Ruiz, Nestor M.	Asst	869-3872			PHD	89	Ca-Davis	1990

Calif State U., Bakersfield — Bakersfield, CA 93311-1099 (805) 664-2460 — Sylvia O'Brien
Economics Department — Sch of Arts & Sciences Fax=664-2049 — CSUBAK.EDU

Name	Rank	Phone	E-mail	Fields	Degree	Yr	School	Since
Geigle, Ray	Dean	664-2221		PolS				
Evans, Mark O.	C-Pr	664-2460	mevans	AIQR	PHD	77	New Mex	1978
Falero, Frank Jr.	Prof	664-2462	ffalero	ADEG	PHD	67	Fla St	1972
Grammy, Abbas	Prof	664-2466	agrammy	ACOR	PHD	82	Colorado	1989
Malixi, Margaret M.	Prof	664-2464	mmalixi	ACFP	PHD	88	Wisconsin	1988
Oswald, Donald J.	Assoc	664-2465	doswald	ABKN	PHD	74	Wash St	1961

Calif State Univ, Chico — Chico, CA 95929-0430 (916) 898-6141 — Annette Schmidt
Department of Economics — Col of Behav & Soc Sci Fax=898-5901 — ECON.BERKELEY.EDU

Name	Rank	Phone	E-mail	Fields	Degree	Yr	School	Since
Shockley, Frederica	C-Pr	898-6141		HMOR	PHD	78	Geo St	1978
Adams, Ronald G.	Prof	898-6141		ACKR	PHD	75	Kansas St	1971
Eckalbar, John C.	Prof	898-5808			PHD	75	Colorado	1978
Fisher, Robert B.	Prof	895-5808			PHD		Oregon	1968
Francis, Gary E.	Prof	898-6141		ABGH	PHD	72	Colorado	1967
Gallo, David E.	Prof	898-5232		AEHQ	PHD		Oregon	1970
Hope, Barney F.	Prof	898-6141			PHD	79	Ca-River	1977
James, Robert G.	Prof	898-5997		EFG	PHD		Oregon	1981
Morlock, Mark J.	Prof	898-4784			PHD		Wash St	1980
O'Toole, James K.	Prof	898-5759			PHD		Va Tech	1984
Orr, John A.	Prof	898-5759			PHD		Wisconsin	1970
Perelman, Michael A.	Prof	898-5321			PHD	71	Berkeley	1971
Collidge, Catherine	Assoc	898-6141		AHKL	PHD		Va Tech	1984
Valentine, Ted	Assoc				PHD		Illinois	1990

Calif St U-Dominguez Hills — Carson, CA 90747 (310) 516-3446
Economics Department — Col of Arts & Sciences Fax= — CSUDH.EDU

Name	Rank	Phone	E-mail	Fields	Degree	Yr	School	Since
Palmer, Richard L.	Dean	516-3429		PolS	PHD	73	Claremont	1972
Billes, Frank V.	C-Pr	516-3446		AENP	PHD	74	UCLA	1972
Freed, Rodney Alan	Prof			ACR	PHD	77	Virginia	1979
Harris, James G.	Prof			AEDH	PHD	70	Oregon	1969
Kidane, Abraham Z.	Prof			AFOI	PHD	71	UCLA	1971
Moite, Leonard M.	Assoc			AEDJ	PHD	84	UCLA	1980

Calif State Univ-Fresno — Fresno, CA 93740-0020 (209) 278-3916 — Shirley Pennell
Department of Economics — Sch of Social Sciences Fax=278-7234 — CSUFRESNO.EDU

Name	Rank	Phone	E-mail	Fields	Degree	Yr	School	Since
Klassen, Peter J.	Dean	278-3013			PHD		S Calif	1966
Leet, Don R.	C-Pr	278-3916	don_leet		PHD	72	Penn	1969
Allison, Robert J.	Prof		robert_allison		PHD	66	Colorado	1967
Bush, Paul D.	Prof	278-4933	paul_bush		PHD	64	Claremont	1961
Cypher, James M.	Prof	278-4935	james_cypher		PHD	73	Ca-River	1967
Minick, Robert A.	Prof	278-4931	robert_minick		PHD		Tx-Austin	1962
Pisciottoli, Louis F.	Prof		louis_pisciottol		PHD	72	Duke	1967
Shaffer, Linda J.	Prof	278-4936	linda_shaffer		PHD	78	Northwes	1984
Shaw, John A. Jr.	Prof	278-2673	john_shaw		PHD	69	Purdue	1965
Fayazmanesh, Susan	Asst	278-2672			PHD	84	Ca-River	1990

Calif State Univ, Fullerton — Fullerton, CA 92634-9840 (714) 773-2228 — Shelley Drath
Department of Economics — School of Bus Adm & Ec Fax=773-3097 — FULLERTON.EDU

Name	Rank	Phone	E-mail	Fields	Degree	Yr	School	Since
Smith, Ephraim P.	Dean	773-2592		Atg	PHD	68	Illinois	8-90
Puri, Anil K.	C-Pr	773-2228			PHD	77	Minnesota	1977
Ayanian, Robert L.	Prof	773-2228			PHD	74	UCLA	1977
Chu, Kwang-Wen	Prof	773-3841			PHD	72	UCLA	1970
Dietz, James L.	Prof	773-2228			PHD	74	Ca-River	1973
Hall, Jane V.	Prof	773-2236			PHD	77	Berkeley	1981
Hettich, Walter	Prof	773-2228			PHD	67	Yale	1983
Long, Stewart L.	Prof	773-2228			PHD	74	Illinois	1973
Michaels, Robert J.	Prof	773-2228			PHD	72	UCLA	1968
Naish, Howard F.	Prof	773-2228			PHD		S Calif	1988
Rahmatian, Morteza Director, Center for Economic Education	Prof	773-2248			PHD		Wyoming	1988
Solberg, Eric J.	Prof	773-2228			PHD	74	Claremont	1973
Wolfson, Murray	Prof	773-2228			PHD	63	Wisconsin	1986
Brajer, Victor	Assoc	773-2228			PHD		New Mex	1987
Gill, Andrew M.	Assoc	773-3076			PHD	85	Wash St	1984
Wong, David C.	Assoc	773-2228			PHD		Ca-SnBarb	1981
Battacharya, Radha S.	Asst	773-2228			MA		Gokhale	1990
Dropsy, Vincent	Asst	773-2228			PHD		S Calif	1989
Purkayastha, Dipankar	Asst	773-3151			MA	81	India	1990

Calif State Univ, Hayward — Hayward, CA 94542-3067 (510) 885-3322
Department of Economics — Sch of Business & Econ Fax=885-2039 — CSUHAYWARD.EDU

Name	Rank	Phone	Email	Field	Degree	Yr	School	Since
Tontz, Jay L.	Dean	885-3291			PHD	66	N Carol	9-69
Ahiakpor, James C.	C-Pr	885-3330			PHD	81	Toronto	1991
Baird, Charles W.	Prof	885-3275			PHD	68	Berkeley	1972
Caassuto, Alexander E.	Prof	885-3922			PHD	73	UCLA	1971
Christiansen, Gregory B.	Prof	885-3301			PHD	81	Wisconsin	1983
Kamath, Shyam J.	Prof	885-4275			PHD	87	Simon Fr	1986
Leube, Kurt R.	Prof	885-3368			DLE	71	Salzburg	1985
Lima, Anthony K.	Prof	885-3889			PHD	80	Stanford	1979
Maxwell, Nan L.	Prof	885-3191	nmaxwell		PHD	83	Fla St	1985
Ozaki, Robert S.	Prof	885-3137			PHD	60	Harvard	1960
Paringer, Lynn C.	Prof	885-3986			PHD	78	Wisconsin	1981
Shmanske, Steven	Prof	885-3334			PHD	82	UCLA	1979
St. Clair, David J.	Prof	885-3327			PHD	79	Utah	1979
Lopus, Jane S.	Assoc	885-3140			MA	78	Ca-Haywd	1979
Kahane, Leo H.	Asst	885-3369			PHD	91	Columbia	1991

Humboldt State University — Arcata, CA 95521-8299 (707) 826-3224 — Patty Olson
Sch of Business & Economics — Col of Professional Std Fax=826-6666 — HUMBOLDT.EDU

Name	Rank	Phone	Email	Field	Degree	Yr	School	Since
Hines, Robert L.	C-Pr	826-3726	hinesr	Atg	PHD	78	Ariz St	1973
Grobey, John H.	Prof	826-3347			PHD	75	U Wash	1967
Hackett, Steven C.	Asst	826-3237			PHD	89	Tx A&M	1994
Yeager, Tim	Asst	826-3224			PHD	93	Wash U	1995

Calif State Univ, Long Beach — Long Beach, CA 90840-8504 (310) 985-5061
Department of Economics — Sch of Soc & Behav Sci Fax=985-5804 — CSULB.EDU

Name	Rank	Phone	Email	Field	Degree	Yr	School	Since
Abrahamse, Dorothy Z.	Dean	985-5381			PHD		Michigan	1967
Magaddino, Joseph P.	C-Pr	985-5061			PHD	72	Va Tech	1973
Anderson, Roy C.	Prof	985-5054			PHD		Tulane	1965
Beaumont, Marion S.	Prof	985-5076			PHD		Claremont	1967
Cole, Charles L.	Prof	985-5075			PHD		S Calif	1967
Crowther, Simeon J.	Prof	985-4634			PHD		Penn	1968
Edwards, Alejandra C.	Prof	985-5068			PHD	84	Chicago	1966
Farrell, Michael J.	Prof	985-5060			PHD	69	Stanford	1969
Glezakos, Constantine	Prof	985-5079			PHD	70	S Calif	1968
Hall, Darwin C.	Prof	985-5045			PHD	77	Berkeley	1986
Ishimine, Tomotaka	Prof	985-5065			PHD	71	Wisconsin	1967
Medoff, Marshall H.	Prof	985-5077			PHD	73	Berkeley	1979
Muraoka, Dennis D.	Prof	985-5078			PHD		Ca-SnBarb	1982
Roberts, Judith A.	Prof	985-5070			PHD	85	Michigan	1986
Rooney, Robert F.	Prof	985-5086			PHD		Stanford	1970
Singh, Davinder	Prof	985-5071			PHD		S Carol	1983
Skov, Iva L.	Prof	985-5087			PHD	76	S Calif	1972
Stern, Andrew	Prof	985-5083			PHD		Columbia	1967
Griffin, Peter B.	Assoc	985-4783			PHD		Ca-SnBarb	1990
Grobar, Lisa M.	Assoc	985-1652			PHD		Michigan	1969
Hou, Jack W.	Assoc	985-4710			PHD	89	Yale	1989

Calif State U, Los Angeles — Los Angeles, CA 90032-8121 (213) 343-2930 — Pat Tom
Dept of Economics & Stat — School of Bus & Econ Fax=343-2813 — CALSTATELA.EDU

Name	Rank	Phone	Email	Field	Degree	Yr	School	Since
Lemos, Ronald S.	Dean	343-2800		Bis	PHD	77	UCLA	6-93
Garston, Neil H.	C-Pr	343-2941			PHD	73	Brown	1975
Canarella, Giorgio	Prof	343-2933			PHD	73	Virginia	1973
Hammack, Judd	Prof	343-2935			PHD	69	U Wash	1970
Kim, Sun K.	Prof	343-2944			PHD	66	S Calif	1964
Ochoa, Eduardo M.	Prof	343-2930			PHD	84	New Sch	1984
Pollard, Stephen K.	Prof	343-2933			PHD	82	Ohio St	1982
Roseman, M. Richard	Prof	343-2935			PHD	69	Harvard	1970
Snyder, Donald on leave to Mt. St. Mary	Prof				PHD	71	Penn St	1975
Tomaska, John A.	Prof	343-2936			PHD	68	U Wash	1965
Wilson, Erika G.	Prof	343-2028			PHD	79	S Calif	1968
Carrington, Samantha	Assoc	343-2946			PHD	85	Ca-SnBarb	1986
Combs, Kathryn L.	Assoc	343-2946			PHD	88	Minnesota	1986
Jensen, George	Assoc	343-2934			PHD	68	U Wash	1962
Lai, Kon Sun	Assoc	343-2945			PHD	87	Penn	1987
Pulchritudoff, Nikolai	Assoc	343-2943			PHD	71	Ca-Davis	1972
Tran, Dang	Assoc	343-2949			PHD	77	Syracuse	1987
Finney, Miles	Asst	343-2937						
Hsieh, Edward T.	Asst	343-2950						
Larson, Tom Edward	Asst	343-2938			PHD	86	Berkeley	1987
Mohanty, Madhu	Asst	343-2949						
Sapra, Sunil	Asst	343-2941						
Vaidya, Ashish K.	Asst	343-2937			PHD	90	Ca-Davis	1991
Yoon, Mann	Asst	343-2943						

Calif State Univ, Northridge — Northridge, CA 91328-1280 (818) 885-2462 — Lucy Larson
Department of Economics — Sch of Bus Adm & Econ Fax=885-4903 — HUEY.CSUN.EDU

Name	Rank	Phone	E-mail	Field	Degree	Yr	Institution	Year
Hosek, William R.	Dean	885-2455			PHD	67	Ca-SnBarb	1988
Evans, Keith D.	C-Ac	885-2462			PHD	71	U Wash	1971
Anderson, Gary M.	Prof	885-2462		GLTR	PHD	87	Geo Mason	1987
Blake, Daniel R.	Prof	885-2462			PHD	71	Oregon	1971
Brown, William W.	Prof	885-2462			MA	66	UCLA	1975
Gifford, Adam Jr.	Prof	885 2462			PHD	72	Ca-SnDgo	1975
Johnson, Ivan C.	Prof	885-2462			PHD	71	W Ontario	1973
Krol, Robert	Prof	885-2462		FGT	PHD	82	S Illinois	1983
Lowenberg, Tony	Prof	885-2462		GH	PHD	84	Simon Fr	1984
Minisian, Jora	Prof	885-2462			PHD	60	Chicago	1972
Roberts, William W.	Prof	885-2462			PHD	74	Ca-SnDgo	1973
Saft, Lester F.	Prof	885-2462			PHD	76	UCLA	1971
Chapman, Kenneth S.	Assoc	885-2462		IG	PHD	86	Minnesota	1991
Friedman, Richard	Assoc	885-2462			ABD		CUNY	1961
Ng, Kenneth	Assoc	885-2462		N	PHD	88	Rochester	1986
Svorny, Shirley V.	Assoc	885-2462		IG	PHD	79	UCLA	1978
Yu, Ben T.	Assoc	885-2462			PHD	78	U Wash	1984
Halcoussis, Dennis	Asst	885-2462		C	PHD	92	Penn	1991
Tchakerian, Viken	Asst	885-2434		N	PHD	91	UCLA	1991
Virts, Nancy L.	Asst	885-2462		N	PHD	85	UCLA	1985

Calif State Univ, Sacramento — Sacramento, CA 95819-6088 (916) 278-6223 — Maryann T. Hewitt
Department of Economics — Sch of Arts & Sciences Fax=278-5768 — CSUS.EDU

Name	Rank	Phone	E-mail	Field	Degree	Yr	Institution	Year
Sullivan, William J.	Dean	278-6502						
Gutowsky, Albert R.	C-Pr	278-6223	arg		PHD	65	Oregon	1967
Curry, Robert L. Jr.	Prof	278-7254			PHD		Oregon	1966
Gambles, Glenn C.	Prof	278-6731			PHD		Maryland	1969
Henry, John F.	Prof	278-6193			PHD		McGill	1970
Kelly, Erwin L. Jr.	Prof	278-6194			AB	54	Berkeley	1971
Kerby, William C.	Prof	278-7112			PHD	71	Oregon	1967
Director, Economic Education Center								
Lund, Peter B.	Prof	278-7078			PHD		Berkeley	1970
McGowan, Susan	Prof	278-7079	mcgowans		PHD	77	Ca-Davis	1974
Polkinghorn, Bette A.	Prof	278-7080			PHD	72	Ca-Davis	1971
Ranlett, John G.	Prof	278-6099			PHD	56	Oregon	1957
Sander, Larry L.	Prof	278-7077			MS		Utah	1969
Scheel, Daniel Curtis	Prof	278-6919			PHD		Oregon	1969
Sexton, Terri A.	Prof	278-6484			PHD	81	Minnesota	1987
Yang, Yung Y.	Prof	278-6264			PHD	74	Oregon	1974
Dube, Smile W.	Assoc	278-7519			PHD		Tx-Austin	1989
Quade, Ane M.	Asst	278-7062			PHD	88	Illinois	1989

Calif St U, San Bernardino — S Bernardino, CA 92407-2397 (909) 880-5511 — Mary Schmidt
Department of Economics — Sch of Soc & Behave Sci Fax=880-7025 — CSUSB.EDU

Name	Rank	Phone	E-mail	Field	Degree	Yr	Institution	Year
Gruenbaum, Ellen R.	Dean$	880-5500	egruneba@wiley.	Anth	PHD	82	Conn	1986
Toruno, Mayo C.	C-Ac	880-5517	mtoruno		PHD	85	Ca-River	1983
Asheghian, Par	Prof	880-5499	pasheghi		PHD	80	Geo St	1991
Charkins, Ralph James	Prof	880-5518	rcharkin		PHD	70	N Carol	1976
Moss, Richard L.	Prof	880-5513	moss		PHD	73	New Mex	1973
Pierce, Thomas J.	Prof	880-5515	tpierce		PHD	76	Notre Dm	1976
Rose, Nancy E.	Prof	880-5516	nrose		PHD	85	Mass	1985
Konyar, Kazim	Asst	880-5514	kkonyar		PHD	85	Ca-River	1991
Nilsson, Eric A.	Asst	880-5564	enilsson		PHD	89	Mass	1989
Richer, Jerrell	Asst	880-5540	jricher		PHD	91	Ca-SnBarb	1991

Calif State U - San Marcos — San Marcos, CA 92069-1477 (619) 750-4103 — Catalina Huggins
Department of Economics — Col of Arts & Sciences Fax=750-4111 — SCUSM.EDU

Name	Rank	Phone	E-mail	Field	Degree	Yr	Institution	Year
Rocha, Victor	Dean	750-4200		BioS	PHD			
Arnold, Roger A.	D-Pr	750-4077			PHD		Va Tech	
Rider, Robert L.	Asst	750-4140			PHD	89	S Calif	1992
Ghiara, Ranjetta		750-4176			PHD			

Calif State U, Stanislaus — Turlock, CA 95380 (209) 667-3181 — Heidi Lofgren
Department of Economics — Col Arts, Letters & Sci Fax=667-3588 — CSUSTAN.EDU

Name	Rank	Phone	E-mail	Field	Degree	Yr	Institution	Year
Christofferson, Jay P.	Dean$			Biol	PHD		Hawaii	
Renning, H. Dieter	C-Pr	667-3327			DR	61	Freiburg	1970
Crist, William D.	Prof	667-3500			PHD	72	Nebraska	1969
Erickson, Edward C.	Prof	633-2181			PHD	70	S Calif	1970
Lee, Albert Yin-Po	Prof	667-3339			PHD	79	S Illinois	1970
White, Everett E. III	Asst	667-3182						

Calvin College — Grand Rapids, MI 49546 (616) 957-7191 — Jen Candler
Dept of Economics & Business — Division of Social Sci Fax=957-6501 — CALVIN.EDU

Name	Rank	Phone	E-mail	Field	Degree	Yr	School	Year
Roberts, Frank C.	Dean	957-6203	roberfr		PHD	73	Vanderbilt	1965
Van Der Heide, Evert M.	C-Pr	957-6099	evheide		PHD	82	Wayne St	1982
Monsma, George N. Jr.	Prof	957-6191	gmonsma		PHD	69	Princeton	1969
Tiemstra, John P.	Prof	957-6192	tmst		PHD	75	MIT	1975
Schaefer, Kurt C.	Assoc	957-6368	schk		PHD	84	Michigan	1987
DeVries, Rick	Asst	957-6247	redevrie		ABD	95	Notre Dm	1995
Vander Linde, Scott H.	Asst	957-6477	udls		PHD	89	Notre Dm	
VanderVeen, Tom	Asst				ABD	95	Brown	1995

Cameron University — Lawton, OK 73505-6377 (405)
Economics Faculty — School of Business Fax=581-2253 — CAMERON.EDU

Name	Rank	Phone	E-mail	Field	Degree	Yr	School	Year
McClung, Jacquetta J.	Dean	581-2267		Fnce	PHD	85	Oklahoma	8-90
Courington, John M.	Prof	581-2266			PHD		Okla St	1979
Horner, James	Prof	581-2269			PHD		Tx-Dallas	1976
Martinez, John	Prof	581-2270			PHD		Oklahoma	1973
Sukar, Abdul Hamid	Asst	581-2845			PHDT		Tx Tech	1987

Campbell University — Buies Creek, NC 27506 (910) 893-1390 — Sandra McLeod
Dept Bus Adm & Econ Box218 — Lundy-Fetterman Sch Bus Fax=893-1424

Name	Rank	Phone	E-mail	Field	Degree	Yr	School	Year
Folwell, Thomas H. Jr.	Dean				MA		Duke	1963
Mostashari, Shahriar	C-Pr				PHD		N Car St	1982
Norwood, Dwight Lamar	Assoc				PHD		Arkansas	1973
Raval, Vasant H.	Assoc				DBA		Newport	1986
Sikes, Ellen	Assoc				MS		N Carol	1966
Zinkhan, F. Christian	Assoc				DBA		Miss St	1987
George, Carolyn	Asst				PHD		Tennessee	1995
Hsiao, Yu-Mong	Asst				PHD	85	N Car St	1984
Overton, Bennie	Asst				PHD		N Car St	1995
Vaughan, Jo Ann	Asst				MA		N Car St	1988
Witherspoon, James E.	Asst				JD		Wake For	1983
Varma, Umesh C.	Inst				MS		Jackson	1988

Canisius College — Buffalo, NY 14208-1098 (716) 888-2670 — Donald I. Bossherdt
Dept of Economics & Finance — Wehle Sch of Business Fax=888-2525 — CANISIUS

Name	Rank	Phone	E-mail	Field	Degree	Yr	School	Year
Shick, Richard A.	Dean	888-2160		Fnce	PHD	73	SUNY-Buf	1978
Wilson, F. Scott	C-Ac	888-2674	wilson		PHD	76	Minnesota	1977
Hutton, Patricia A.	Prof	888-2673			PHD	80	Wisconsin	1981
Palumbo, George M.	Prof	888-2667			PHD	77	Syracuse	1978
Lichtenstein, Larry	Assoc	888-2677			PHD		SUNY	1981
Minet, Lawrence J.	Assoc	888-2681			PHD	53	Columbia	1958
Zaporowski, Mark P.	Assoc	888-2679			PHD	85	SUNY-Alb	1983
Eisenhauer, Joseph G.	Asst	888-2676			PHD	91	SUNY-Buf	1986

Capital University — Columbus, OH 43209-2394 (614) 236-6595
Dept of Business & Economics — College of Arts & Sci Fax=236-6540 — CAPITAL.EDU

Name	Rank	Phone	E-mail	Field	Degree	Yr	School	Year
McGary, Diana	Dean	236-6204			PHD		Union Gr	1979
Mittler, Dale	C-Ac	236-6595			MBA		Capital	1981
Baker, Stephen A.	Assoc	236-6136			PHD	82	York UK	1987
Rich, David	Inst	236-6138			MA		U Wash	1990

Carleton College — Northfield, MN 55057 (507) 663-4109 — Ms. Betty Kendall
Economics Faculty — Department of Economics Fax=663-4044 — CARLETON.EDU

Name	Rank	Phone	E-mail	Field	Degree	Yr	School	Year
Kanazawa, Mark T.	C-Ac	663-4106	mkanazaw		PHD	87	Stanford	1985
Lamson, George H. (Wadsworth W. Williams Professor of Economics)	Prof	663-4107	glamson		PHD	71	Northwes	1969
Lewis, Stephen R. Jr. (President)	Prof	663-4305			PHD	63	Stanford	1987
Paas, Martha W.	Prof	663-4103	mpaas		PHD	79	Bryn Maw	1975
Strand, Stephen H.	Prof	663-4104	sstrand		PHD	76	Vanderbilt	1981
Bierman, H. Scott	Assoc	663-4108	sbierman		PHD	85	Virginia	1982
Hemesath, Michael	Assoc	663-4105	mhemesat		PHD	88	Harvard	1989
Gibbons, Donna M.	Asst	663-5239	dgibbons		PHD	95	Brown	1993
Williams, E. Douglass	Asst	663-4007	ewilliam		PHD	89	Northwes	1989

Carnegie Mellon University — Pittsburgh, PA 15213-3890 (412) 268-2294 — Beverly Jones 268-3719
Department of Economics — Col of Human & Soc Sci Fax=268-7357 — ANDREW.CMU.EDU

Name	Rank	Phone	E-mail	Field	Degree	Yr	School	Year
Lirtzman, Sidney I.	Dean	802-6550		Mgt	PHD	55	Columbia	1973
Stearns, Peter N.	Dean			Hst	PHD		Harvard	1991
Spear, Stephen E.	H-Pr	268-8831	ss1f		PHD		Penn	1982
Cyert, Richard M.	Prof	268-8548			PHD	51	Columbia	1948
Epple, Dennis N.	Prof	578-2289			PHD	74	Princeton	1974
Klepper, Steven I.	Prof	268-3235			PHD	75	Cornell	1980

Name	Rank	Phone	Degree	Yr	School	Year
Kumar, Praveen	Prof		PHD		Stanford	1985
Kydland, Finn	Prof		PHD	73	Car Mellon	1977
Lave, Lester B.	Prof	268-8837	PHD	63	Harvard	1963
James H. Higgins Professor of Economics						
McCallum, Bennett T.	Prof	268-2347	PHD	69	Rice	1981
H. J. Heinz Professor of Economics						
Meltzer, Allan H.	Prof	268-2283	PHD	58	UCLA	1957
John M. Olin University Professor of Political Economy and Public Policy						
Poole, Keith T.	Prof		PHD		Rochester	1982
Spatt, Chester S.	Prof	268-8834	PHD	79	Penn	1979
Srivastava, Sanjay	Prof		PHD		MIT	1982
Miller, Robert A.	Assoc	268-3701	PHD	82	Chicago	1982
Seppi, Duane J.	Assoc		PHD		Chicago	1986
Shaw, Kathryn L.	Assoc	268-7586	PHD	81	Harvard	1981
Sowell, Fallaw B.	Assoc	268-3697	PHD	86	Duke	1988
Zin, Stanley E.	Assoc		PHD		Toronto	1988
Cameron, Lisa J.	Asst		PHD			
Telmer, Chris I.	Asst		PHD	92	Queen's	1992
Wang, Cheng	Asst		PHD		W Ontario	1994
Yaron, Amir	Asst		PHD		Chicago	1994
Zhang, Harold H.	Asst		PHD		Duke	1994
Dalton, W. Robert	Adj		PHD		Missouri	1985
Quinlivan, Gary M.	Adj		PHD	83	SUNY-Alb	1989

Carroll College — Waukesha, WI 53186 (414) 547-1211
Dept of Atg, Bus & Economics — College of Business Fax=524-7139 — CARROLL1.CC.EDU

Name	Rank	Phone	Degree	Yr	School	Year
Kader, Ahmad	C-Pr	524-7173	PHD		W Virginia	1974
Debrecht, Dennis M.	Assoc	524-7163	PHD	81	Iowa	1984
Kearns, Robert	Assoc	524-7160				

Carson-Newman College — Jefferson Cy, TN 37760 (615) 471-3316 — Crystle Bacon
Dept of Business & Economics — Division of Business Fax=471-3502

Name	Rank	Phone	Fields	Degree	Yr	School	Year
Russell, C. W. Jr.	C-Ac	471-3441	Mgt	JD		Tennessee	1991
Taylor, Millicent	Assoc	471-3433	DFC	PHD		Tennessee	8-95
Sellers, John R.	Asst	471-3318	ABEO	PHD	93	Tennessee	1991

Carthage College — Kenosha, WI 53141 (414) 551-5831 — Sandy Fredericks
Department of Economics — Social Sciences Div Fax=551-6208 — CNS.CARTHAGE.EDU

Name	Rank	Phone	Email	Fields	Degree	Yr	School	Year
Schlack, Robert F.	C-Pr	551-5831	rfs	FPR	PHD		Wayne St	1975
Matlsev, Yuri	Assoc		yuri	DFJP	PHD			1991
McClintock, Brent	Asst		btm	EFG	PHD		Colo St	1991

Case Western Reserve Univ — Cleveland, OH 44106-7206 (216) 368-4110 — Anne Soule'
Economics Department — Weatherhead Sch of Mgt Fax=368-5039 — PO.CWRU.EDU

Name	Rank	Phone	Email	Fields	Degree	Yr	School	Year
Cowen, Scott S.	Dean	368-2046		Atg	DBA	75	Geo Wash	9-76
Erdilek, Asim	C-Pr	368-4110	axe3	F	PHD	72	Harvard	1971
Carlsson, Bo A.	Prof	368-4112	bxc4	DFMO	PHD	72	Stanford	1984
William E. Umstattd Professor of Industrial Economics								
Fogarty, Michael S.	Prof	368-5535	msf3	RO	PHD	75	Pittsburgh	1986
Director, Center for Regional Economic Issues								
Peirce, William S.	Prof	368-4131	wsp	HOQ	PHD	66	Princeton	1966
Rosegger, Gerhard	Prof	368-4295	gxr2	OFND	DIUR	53	Austria	1965
Frank Tracy Carlton Professor of Economics								
Baird, Robert N.	Assoc	368-4185	rnb	A	PHD	65	Kentucky	1965
University Marshal								
Dor, Avi	Assoc	368-0208		I	PHD	86	CUNY	1995
John R. Mannix Blue Cross & Blue Shield Professor of Health Care Economics								
Dubin, Robin A.	Assoc	368-3981	rad4	RCD	PHD	82	J Hopkins	1988
Bogart, William T.	Asst	368-4296	wtb	HRDA	PHD	90	Princeton	1990
Hanchate, Amresh	Asst	368-2184	adh2	OQDC	PHD	92	Wisconsin	1992
Helper, Susan	Asst	368-5541	sxh23	ONM	PHD	87	Harvard	1990
Leete, Laura	Asst	368-5870	lbl2	IJ	PHD	92	Harvard	1991
Parkin, Richard J.	Asst	368-4294	rjp6	DJP	PHD	93	Mass	1992

Catawba College — Salisbury, NC 28144-2488 (704) 637-4405 — Dorothy Earle
Economic Faculty — Ketner School of Bus Fax=637-4422 — CATAWBA.EDU

Name	Rank	Phone	Fields	Degree	School	Year
Carter, J. Alvin	C-Ac	637-4406	Mgt	MBA	Geo St	1968
Tseng, S. C.	Prof	637-4407		PHD	Oklahoma	

Catholic Univ of America Washington, DC 20064 (202) 319-5236 Brenda Nichols
Dept of Economics & Business Sch of Arts & Sciences Fax=319-4426 CUA.EDU

Name	Rank	Phone	E-mail	Field	Degree	Yr	School	Since
Suziedelis, Antanas	Dean	319-5115		Psy	PHD			
Zampelli, Ernest M.	C-Pr	319-5236			PHD	82	Maryland	9-85
Bolino, August C.	Prof	681-8107			PHD	57	St Louis	
Boretsky, Michael	Prof	319-4797			PHD	64	Columbia	1980
Piedra, Alberto	Prof	319-5235			PHD			
Forbes, Kevin F.	Assoc	319-4794			PHD	82	Maryland	1983
Karake, Zeinab	Assoc	319-4796			PHD			
Agurirre, Sophia	Asst	319-4957			PHD			
Fettus, Sharon H.	Asst	319-6183			PHD			
Leon, Jean-Claude	Asst	319-5239			PHD	87	Geo Wash	1987
Saidi, Reza	Asst	319-4692			PHD			
Uppal, Jamshed Y.	Asst	319-4730			PHD			
Wikstrom, Joan E.	Lect	319-5236			MA			

Cedarville College Cedarville, OH 45314-0601 (513) 766-7910 Susan Terkelsen
Economic Faculty Dept of Business Admin Fax=766-2760 CEDARVILLE.EDU

Name	Rank	Phone	E-mail	Field	Degree	Yr	School	Since
Johnson, Sharon G.	C-Ac	766-7922	johns	Atg	DBA	78	Fla St	1993
Smith, Galen	Assoc	766-7923	smithg	ABFH	MS	68	Kansas St	1981
Wheeler, Bert	Assoc	766-7714	wheelerb	AFOP	PHD	85	Tennessee	1992

Centenary College Hackettstown, NJ 07840-9989 (908) 852-1400
Economics Faculty Division of Business Fax=813-1984

Name	Rank	Phone	E-mail	Field	Degree	Yr	School	Since
Quade, Robert	C-Ac	852-1400		Mktg	MBA		Iowa	8-86
Dunham, Heather	Assoc			ADEM	MBA		Rutgers	8-84
Nicholls, Grant	Inst			ADEM	MBA		Ins Bnkg	8-91

Univ of Central Arkansas Conway, AR 72032 (501) 450-3109 Barbara Hopp
Dept of Economics & Finance College of Business Adm Fax=327-9938 CCI.UCA.EDU

Name	Rank	Phone	E-mail	Field	Degree	Yr	School	Since
Lorenzi, Peter	Dean	450-3106		Mgt	PHD	78	Penn St	6-92
Cantrell, Pat	C-Ac	450-5333	patc		PHD	83	So Meth	8-84
Gufley, Loren	Prof				PHD		Arkansas	
Johnson, W. Clint	Prof				PHD	75	Tx Tech	1975
Kordsmeier, William F.	Assoc				PHD		Tx A&M	
Glenn, Kirsta	Asst				PHD	93	Vanderbilt	8-95
McGarrity, Joseph	Asst				PHD	94	Geo Mason	8-95
Seyfried, William L.	Asst				PHD	90	Purdue	8-90

Central Connecticut St Univ New Britain, CT 06050 (203) 832-2726
Department of Economics School of Arts & Sci Fax= CCSVA.CTSTATEU.EDU

Name	Rank	Phone	E-mail	Field	Degree	Yr	School	Since
Clarke, George A.	Dean				PHD		Penn St	1984
Pae, Ki-Tai	C-Pr	832-2726			PHD		Conn	1971
Altieri, Paul L.	Prof				PHD		Boston C	1975
Daigle, Ronald R.	Prof				PHD		Clark	1976
Kim, Ki Hoon	Prof				PHD	68	Conn	1967
Loughlin, James C.	Prof				PHD	65	Clark	1968
Papathanasis, Anastasios	Prof				PHD		Ca-Davis	1984
Zottola, Armand J.	Prof				PHD	70	Catholic	1970

Univ of Central Florida Orlando, FL 32816-1400 (407) 823-3266 Mrs. Mickey Mullen
Department of Economics College of Business Adm Fax=823-5741 PEGASUS.CC.UCF.EDU

Name	Rank	Phone	E-mail	Field	Degree	Yr	School	Since
Huseman, Richard C.	Dean	823-2181		Comm	PHD	65	Illinois	7-90
Hofler, Richard A.	C-Pr	823-2606	rhofler	CIJ	PHD	82	N Carol	1989
McHone, W. Warren	Prof	823-2629		R	PHD	80	Penn	1982
Raffa, Frederick A.	Prof	823-3266		E	PHD	69	Fla St	1969
Rungeling, Brian S.	Prof	275-2592		J	PHD	69	Kentucky	1981
Braun, Bradley M.	Assoc	823-2343		D	PHD		Tulane	1986
Day, A. Edward	Assoc	823-2620		D	PHD	76	Purdue	1983
Gibbs, W. Ernest	Assoc	823-5818		D	PHD		Rutgers	1987
Hosni, Djehane	Assoc	823-2069		O	PHD	78	Arkansas	1977
Martin, Thomas L.	Assoc	823-5681		B	PHD	81	Rice	1983
Pennington, Robert L.	Assoc	823-2886		D	PHD	77	Tx A&M	1983
Soskin, Mark D.	Assoc	823-3266		C	PHD	79	Penn St	1988
White, Kenneth R.	Assoc	823-5656		C	PHD	71	Oklahoma	1968
Xander, James A.	Assoc	823-5657		D	PHD	74	Georgia	1969
Agarwal, Rajshree	Asst			L	PHD	94	SUNY-Buf	1995
Kilbride, Wad[illegible] R.	Asst	823-3266		D	EDD		Fla Atl	1978
Otsuka, Yasu[illegible]	Asst	823-5628		D	PHD		Tennessee	1990
Euzent, Patricia	Inst	823-6075			MA		Clemson	1991

Central University of Iowa Pella, IA 50219 (515)
Economics Faculty Dept Econ, Atg & Mgt Fax= CENTRAL.EDU

Name	Rank	Phone	E-mail	Field	Degree	Yr	School	Since
Coombs, Virginia	Dean	628-5175	coombsv		PHD			1994
Freed, Jann E.	C-Ac	628-5168	freedj		PHD		Iowa St	1981
Glendening, Richard N.	Prof	628-5120	glendeningr	EFHO	PHD	93	Iowa St	1966
Wallace, Suzanne	Assoc	628-5318	wallaces	DJE	PHD	91	Georgia	1991

Central Michigan University Mt. Pleasant, MI 48859-2372 (517) 774-3870 Barb Sharp 774-3820
Department of Economics College of Arts & Sci Fax=774-2040 CMUVM

Name	Rank	Phone	Email	Field	Degree	Yr	School	Year
Pixon, Barbara	Dean$	774-3341		Musi	PHD			
Shields, Michael P.	C-Pr	774-6460	3zot2cf		PHD	75	Utah	
Zuberi, Habib A.	Prof	774-3372			PHD	71	S Illinois	1971
Bechtold, Brigitte	Assoc	774-3608			PHD	82	Penn	1982
Brunner, Lawrence P.	Assoc	774-3638			PHD	81	J Hopkins	1982
Clemmer, Richard B.	Assoc	774-3908			PHD	81	Chicago	1982
Falls, Gregory A.	Assoc	774-3655			PHD	82	Purdue	1981
Hill, James Richard	Assoc	774-3706			PHD	80	Kentucky	1981
Natke, Paul A.	Assoc	774-3653			PHD	82	Notre Dm	1981
Peterson, Thomas C.	Assoc	774-3222			PHD		UCLA	1972
Barbour, G. Jeffrey	Asst	774-3380			PHD		Fla St	1971
Basu, Bharati	Asst	774-3730	3niz5ld		PHD		Rochester	1990
Cecen, A. Aydin	Asst	774-3677	3ilzj6j		PHD		Indiana	1987
Chakraborty, Debasish	Asst	774-3678	3ro44vr		PHD		Pittsburgh	1988
Irwin, James R.	Asst	774-3697	32jmx6q		PHD	86	Rochester	1989
McDevitt, Catherine L.	Asst	774-3648			PHD	86	Rochester	1989
Zimmer, Basil G.	Asst	774-3600			PHD	72	Rutgers	1969

Central Missouri State Univ Warrensburg, MO 64093-5074 (816) 543-4246
Dept of Economics & Finance Col of Business & Econ Fax=543-8885 CMSU.EDU

Name	Rank	Phone	Email	Field	Degree	Yr	School	Year
Shaffer, Paul	Dean	543-4560		Mgt	PHD	74	Oklahoma	1986
Engelmann, Paul H.	C-Pr	543-4246			PHD	76	Okla St	1972
Brock, Baird A.	Prof	543-8614			PHD	77	Arkansas	1969
Karscig, Mark P.	Prof	543-4817			PHD	87	Pittsburgh	1981
Wilson, George W.	Prof	543-8597			PHD	76	Okla St	1972
Chambers, Catherine M.	Assoc	543-8605			PHD	90	Kentucky	1990
Chambers, Paul	Assoc	543-8610			PHD	89	Kentucky	1990
Swanson, James A.	Assoc	543-8580			PHD	87	Wash St	1986
McCoy, Kim	Asst	543-8576			PHD	94	Okla St	1990
Kugler, Penny L.	Inst	543-8570			MA	88	Cen Mo St	1988

Univ of Central Oklahoma Edmond, OK 73034-5209 (405) Ext 5843 Ofelia Tovar
Department of Economics College of Business Adm Fax=330-3821 AIXL.UCOK.EDU
phone: 341-2980

Name	Rank	Phone	Email	Field	Degree	Yr	School	Year
Metzger, Michael R.	C-Pr	341-2980	metzger		PHD	78	Stanford	1991
Caldwell, Jean	Prof				EDD	82	N Illinois	1981
Maxwell, Don P.	Prof	341-2980	maxwell		PHD	82	Okla St	1981
Shaaf, Mohammad	Prof		mshaaf		PHD	82	Tx Tech	1980
Smith, Paula	Assoc		psmith		PHD	84	Okla St	1987
De los Santos, Tomas	Asst				PHD	88	Clark	
Johnson, Joseph T.	Asst				PHD	80	Chicago	

Central State Univ-Ohio Wilberforce, OH 45384 (513) 376-6446
Department of Economics College of Business Fax=376-6206

Name	Rank	Phone	Email	Field	Degree	Yr	School	Year
Showell, Charles H. Jr.	Dean	376-6441		BAdm	PHD	75	Ohio St	9-88
Iwomi, Peter O.	C-Ac	376-6446			EDD		Cincinnati	1981
Vafaie, Massie	Asst	376-6441			PHD		Cincinnati	

Central Washington Univ Ellensburg, WA 98926 (509) 963-2664 Kathey Hatfield
Department of Economics Sch of Business & Econ Fax=963-1992 CWU.EDU

Name	Rank	Phone	Email	Field	Degree	Yr	School	Year
Dauwalder, David P.	Dean	963-1955			PHD	83	Ariz St	1993
Cocheba, Donald John	C-Pr	963-2411		QR	PHD	71	Wash St	1970
Distinguished Professor, Research (1992)								
Carbaugh, Robert John	Prof	963-3443		AFEK	PHD	74	Colo St	1985
Franz, Wolfgang W.	Prof	963-3420		HJK	PHD	70	Wash St	1969
Distinguished Professor, Public Service (1987)								
Mack, Richard Stanley	Prof	963-2663		RQP	PHD	72	Colo St	1972
Distinguished Professor, Research (1988)								
Saunders, Peter J.	Prof	963-1266		EHQ	PHD	81	Colorado	1988
Hedrick, David W.	Assoc	963-2664		AIO	PHD	84	Oregon	1987

Centre College Danville, KY 40422 (606) 238-5231 Patsy McAfee
Department of Economics Div of Social Studies Fax=236-7925 CENTRE.EDU

Name	Rank	Phone	Email	Field	Degree	Yr	School	Year
Brownlee, Robert J.	C-Pr	238-5245	brownlee	AER	PHD		Syracuse	1978
Campbell, Charles W. III	C-Pr	238-5239	campbelc	AEHF	PHD		Virginia	1968
Blazer Professor of Economics								
Johnson, Bruce K.	Assoc	238-5242	johnson	AJL	PHD	85	Virginia	1987
James Graham Brown Associate Professor of Economics								
Winrich, J. Steven	Assoc	238-5237	winrich	APN	PHD		Kentucky	1981
Anderson, David A.	Asst	238-5260	david	ACHK	PHD	92	Duke	1992

Chadron State College Chadron, NE 69337-2690 (308) 432-6365 Linda Nitsch
Department Business & Econ Sch Bus & Applied Sci Fax=432-6369

Name	Rank	Phone	Email	Field	Degree	Yr	Institution	Year
Crouse, Margaret	Dean	432-6365			PHD		Okla St	1979
Anderson, Tim	C-Pr	432-6290			EDD		Nebraska	1977
Afiat, Medhi	Prof	432-6290		MER	PHD		Kansas St	1985
Burke, Ronald L.	Prof	432-6290		MQE	PHD	70	Minnesota	1987

Chaminade University Honolulu, HI 96816-1578 (808) 735-6744 James Moses
Department of Economics College of Business Fax=735-4734

Name	Rank	Phone	Email	Field	Degree	Yr	Institution	Year
Steelquist, John	Dean	739-4600		Mgt	PHD		Tx A&M	1-84
Klauser, Jack E.	Prof	735-4711			PHD	77	NYU	1970
Street, Barbara P.	Prof	377-5865		ACEI	PHD	86	Virginia	1981
Director, Master of Business Adminstration Program								

Chapman University Orange, CA 92666 (714) 997-6684 Iris Fallon, Office Mgr
Economics Faculty School of Bus & Econ Fax=532-6081 NEXUS.CHAPMAN.EDU

Name	Rank	Phone	Email	Field	Degree	Yr	Institution	Year
McDowell, Richard L.	Dean	997-6684	mcdowell	Adm	PHD	74	Tufts	7-91
Adibi, Esmael	Prof	997-6693	adibi	AEFC	PHD	80	Claremont	1978
Director, Center for Economic Research								
Booth, Donald R.	Prof	997-6804	booth	AD	PHD	70	UCLA	1959
Doti, James L.	Prof	997-6611	doti	AEC	PHD	76	Chicago	1974
President of the University								
Pierson, Lynne M.	Prof	997-6805	pierson	NE	PHD	78	Ca-River	1972
Sfeir, Raymond	Assoc	997-6551	sfeir	AC	PHD	82	Ca-SnBarb	1985
Shabahang, Homa		997-6888	shabahan	F	PHD	83	Oklahoma	1991
Associate Dean								

College of Charleston Charleston, SC 29424-0001 (803) Ms. Barbara Green
Economic Faculty Sch of Business & Econ Fax= COFC.EDU

Name	Rank	Phone	Email	Field	Degree	Yr	Institution	Year
Rudd, Howard F.	Dean	953-5627			PHD	73	Tx Tech	1984
Morgan, J. Michael	C-Pr	953-8100	morganm		PHD		S Carol	1967
Clary, Betsy Jane	Prof	953-8107	claryb		PHD		Miss	1984
Condon, Clarence M. III	Assoc	953-8106	condonc		PHD		S Carol	1980
Jursa, Paul E.	Assoc	953-7836	jursap		PHD		Tx-Austin	1976
Hefner, Frank L.	Asst	953-8100	hefnerf		PHD	88	Kansas	1995

Cheyney U of Pennsylvania Cheyney, PA 19319 (610) 399-2368 Idella Boone 399-2368
Economics Faculty Dept of Business Adm Fax=399-2070

Name	Rank	Phone	Email	Field	Degree	Yr	Institution	Year
Williams, Edward E.	C-Pr	399-2430		MgtS	PHD		Drexel	1972
Sawyer, Juliet	Assoc	399-2382						
Songha, W. A.	Assoc	399-2433						
Chowdhury, Ma Monayem	Asst	399-2022			PHD	78	Temple	

University of Chicago Chicago, IL 60637-1561 (312) 702-8254 Marda J. Gross; Julie Less
Economics Faculty Department of Economics Fax=702-8490 CHICAGO.EDU

Name	Rank	Phone	Email	Field	Degree	Yr	Institution	Year
Lucas, Robert E. Jr.	D-Pr	702-8179			PHD	64	Chicago	1974
John Dewey Distinguished Service Professor								
Scheinkman, Jose	C-Pr	702-8192			PHD	74	Rochester	1973
Alvin H. Baum Professor								
Becker, Gary S.	Prof	702-8168			PHD	55	Chicago	1970
Bowman, Mary Jean	Emer	702-8161			PHD	38	Harvard	1958
Fogel, Robert W.	Prof	702-7709			PHD	63	J Hopkins	1981
Charles R. Walgreen Professor/Director, Center for Population Economics								
Galenson, David W.	Prof	702-8258			PHD	79	Harvard	1978
Hansen, Lars Peter	Prof	702-8170			PHD	78	Minnesota	1982
Homer J. Livingston Professor								
Harberger, Arnold C.	Emer				PHD	50	Chicago	1953
Gustavus F. and Ann M. Swift Distinguished Service Professor								
Heckman, James J.	Prof	702-0634			PHD	71	Princeton	1973
Henry Schultz Professor of Economics & Soc Sciences								
Mundlak, Yair	Prof	702-9811			PHD	57	Berkeley	1986
on leave 1995-96; Frederick Henry Prince Professor								
Rosen, Sherwin	Prof	702-8166			PHD	66	Chicago	1977
Edwin A. and Betty L. Bergman Professor of Economis & Social Sciences								
Sargent, Thomas	Prof	702-9014			PHD	68	Harvard	1991
David Rockefeller Profesor of Econ & Social Sci								
Sjaastad, Larry A.	Prof	702-8172			PHD	61	Chicago	1965
Sonnenschein, Hugo F.	Prof				PHD	64	Purdue	
President of University								
Stokey, Nancy	Prof	702-0915			PHD	78	Harvard	1990
Telser, Lester G.	Prof	702-8193			PHD	56	Chicago	1958
Tolley, George S.	Prof	702-8199			PHD	55	Chicago	1966
Townsend, Robert M.	Prof	702-8178			PHD	75	Minnesota	1985
Woodford, Michael	Prof	702-7147			PHD	83	MIT	1986

Name	Rank	Phone	E-mail	Field	Degree	Yr	School	Since
Cho, In-Koo	Assoc	702-9127			PHD	86	Princeton	1986
on leave to Brown University								
Cochrane, John H.	Assoc	702-3059			PHD	86	Berkeley	1985
Atkeson, Andrew G.	Asst	702-5841			PHD	88	Stanford	1988
Chen, Xiachong	Asst	702-9012			PHD	93	Ca-SnDgo	1993
Chwe, Michael	Asst	702-9015			PHD	91	Northwes	1992
Ichimura, Hidehiko	VAsst				PHD	87	MIT	1994
visiting from Minnesota								
Mulligan, Casey	Asst	702-9017			PHD	93	Chicago	1993
Neal, Derek A.	Asst	702-9013			PHD	92	Virginia	1991
Philipson, Tomas J.	Asst	702-9128			PHD	89	Penn	1989
Sanderson, Allen	SLect	702-7815			MA	70	Chicago	
Tsiang, Grace	SLect	702-3410			PHD	91	Chicago	1990

Chicago State University — Chicago, IL 60628-1598 (312) 995-2186 — Janie Davis
Department of Economics — Col of Arts & Sciences Fax=995-4482

Name	Rank	Phone	E-mail	Field	Degree	Yr	School	Since
Lindsey, Rachel L.	Dean	995-2105		Psyc	PHD		Chicago	1976
Blum, Fredrick	C-Pr	995-2187			MA			
Leach, Elroy M.	Assoc	995-2173			PHD	85	Il-Chicago	1985
Pingkaratwat, Nampeang	Assoc	995-2340			PHD		Il-Chicago	1982
Johnson, Mark	Asst	995-2310			PHD			
Kim, Shin	Inst				MS		Illinois	1987

Christian Brothers Univ — Memphis, TN 38104-5581 (901) 722-0489 — Ms. Carolyn Denegri
Dept of Economics & Finance — School of Business Fax=722-0494 — CBU.EDU

Name	Rank	Phone	E-mail	Field	Degree	Yr	School	Since
House, Ray S.	Dean	722-0316		Mktg	PHD	66	Miss	1985
Brittingham, Robert L.	H-Pr	722-0489		AD	PHD	73	St Louis	1989
Papachristou, Patricia T.	Prof	722-0301		TI	MBA	79	Memphis	1980
Kamery, Rob H.	Assoc	722-0414		ABJ	MS	81	Arkansas	1979

Christopher Newport Univ — Newport News VA 23606-2988 (804) 594-7176 — Ms. Iris Price
Dept of Economics & Finance — Col of Business & Econ Fax=594-7808 — POWHATAN.CC.CNU.EDU

Name	Rank	Phone	E-mail	Field	Degree	Yr	School	Since
Booker, H. Marshall	Prof	594-7174		AFMO	PHD		Virginia	1971
Park, Sang O.	Prof	594-7176		DFOR	PHD		N Carol	1982
Colonna, Carl M.	Assoc	594-7144		AEIR	MA		Old Dom	1970
Vachris, Michelle A.	Asst	594-7719		DFHK	PHD	92	Geo Mason	1994
Zestos, George K.	Asst	594-7067		CFHO	PHD		Indiana	1993
Brauer Professor								

University of Cincinnati — Cincinnati, OH 45221-0371 (513) 556-2600 — Susan Burns
Department of Economics — McMicken Col Arts & Sci Fax=556-2669 — UCBEH

Name	Rank	Phone	E-mail	Field	Degree	Yr	School	Since
Caruso, Joseph A.	Dean	556-5860		Chem	PHD	67	Mich St	
Gallo, Joseph C.	C-Pr	556-2605	gallojc	L	PHD	69	Missouri	
Berry, Charles A.	Prof	556-2624		O	PHD	68	Cincinnati	
Craycraft, Joseph L.	Prof	556-2614		L	PHD	64	Cincinnati	1962
Herman, E. Edward	Prof	556-2611		J	PHD	65	McGill	1966
Leftwich, Howard M.	Prof	556-2615		J	PHD	65	Illinois	
Mayer, Wolfgang	Prof	556-2618		FD	PHD	71	SUNY-Buf	1974
David Sinton Professor								
Vredeveld, George	Prof	556-2948			PHD	73	Indiana	1977
Wellington, Donald C.	Prof	556-2607		D	PHD	66	Chicago	
Whitmore, Harland W. Jr.	Prof	556-2622		E	PHD	69	Mich St	
Goddard, Haynes C.	Assoc	556-2621		H	PHD	70	Indiana	
Mourmouras, Alexandros	Assoc	556-2625		E	PHD	88	Minnesota	1988
Powers, John A.	Assoc	556-2616		C	PHD	66	Purdue	
Way, Philip K.	Assoc	556-2613		J	PHD	86	Warwick	
Zandvakili, Sourushe	Assoc	556-2629		J	PHD	87	Indiana	
Escoe, Jisela Meyer	Asst	556-3023		O	PHD		Ohio St	
Mills, Jeffrey A.	Asst	556-2619		C	PHD	89	Wash U	
Pal, Debashis	Asst	556-2630			PHD	90	Florida	
Shah, Sudhir	Asst	556-3024		DC	PHD		Princeton	
Williams, Nicolas	Asst	556-2390		J	PHD	89	Northwes	1990

The Citadel — Charleston, SC 29409-0215 (803) 953-5056 — Ms. Georgeann Pringle
Economics Faculty — Dept of Business Adm Fax=953-2212 — CITADEL.EDU

Name	Rank	Phone	E-mail	Field	Degree	Yr	School	Since
Bebensee, Mark A.	H-Ac	953-5056	bebensee		PHD	77	Duke	8-77
Silver, Stephen J.	Assoc	953-5163	silvers		PHD	83	Maryland	8-90
Sparks, Donald L.	Assoc	953-5159	sparksd		PHD	85	London	8-86
Woolsey, W. William	Assoc	953-5161	woolseyw		PHD	86	Geo Mason	8-86

CUNY-Baruch College New York, NY 10010 (212) 802-6350 Sylvia Clark/Evelyn Cohen
Dept of Economics & Finance School of Business Fax=802-6353 CUNYVM

Name	Rank	Phone	Degree	Yr	School	Since
Wolf, Avner	C-Ac	802-6354	PHD	83	Columbia	
Francis, Clark II	Prof	802-6359	PHD	66	Wash	
Lustgarten, Steven	Prof	802-6420	PHD	71	UCLA	
Marty, Alvin L.	Prof		PHD	55	Berkeley	1960
O'Neill, June E.	Prof		PHD	70	Columbia	1987
Director, Center for the Study of Business and Government						
Ross, Howard N.	Prof	802-6365	PHD	64	Columbia	1964
Stone, Irving	Prof	802-6369	PHD	62	Columbia	1962
Su, Vincent	Prof	802-6364	PHD	70	Rutgers	1971
Thomadakis, Stavros B.	Prof	802-6417	PHD	74	MIT	1974
Vora, Ashkok	Prof	802-6370	PHD	74	Northwes	1973
Allen, Linda	Assoc	802-6418	PHD	84	NYU	
Eytan, T. Hanan	Assoc	802-6416	PHD	85	Sloan	
Hessel, Christopher A.	Assoc	802-6415	PHD	78	NYU	
Katz, Steven	Assoc	802-6361	PHD	82	NYU	
Kleinberg, Norman L.	Assoc	802-6368	PHD	77	MIT	
Lee, Jae Won	Assoc	802-6360	PHD	69	CUNY	1972
Tandon, Kishore	Assoc	802-6355	PHD	80	Pittsburgh	
Weiss, Jeffrey H.	Assoc	802-6357	PHD	81	Wisconsin	1981
Ariel, Robert Andrew	Asst	802-6371	PHD	89	MIT	1986
Huckins, Larry E.	Asst	802-6381	PHD	83	Chicago	1980
Ma, Barry K.	Asst	802-6386	PHD	86	Stanford	1989
Mischel, Kenneth M.	Asst	802-6387	PHD	90	Columbia	
Webb, Gwendolyn P.	Asst	802-6374	PHD	88	NYU	1987
Tansey, Francis B.	Lect	802-6356	MBA	65	CUNY	

CUNY-Brooklyn College Brooklyn, NY 11210 (718) 951-5317 Alycen Bray
Department of Economics College of Liberal Arts Fax=951-4867 CUNYVM.CUNY.EDU

Name	Rank	Phone	Field	Degree	Yr	School	Since
Okun, Bernard	D-Pr	951-5217	CO	PHD	57	J Hopkins	1966
Zelcer, Moishe	C-Ac	951-5317	G	PHD	91	Baruch	1992
Bowers, Patricia F.	Prof	951-5317	G	PHD	65	NYU	1964
Friedman, Hershey	Prof	951-5119	M	PHD		CUNY	1986
Ginsburg, Helen	Prof	951-5101	J	PHD		New Sch	1977
Laibman, David	Prof	951-5317	AP	PHD		New Sch	1967
Lazarcik, Gregor	Prof	951-5317	O	PHD	60	Columbia	1985
Sardy, Hyman	Prof	951-5317	C	PHD	63	New Sch	1957
Arenberg, Yuri	Assoc	951-5317	D	PHD	86	NYU	1985
Bell, Robert	Assoc	951-5317	M	PHD		England	1986
Cherry, Robert D.	Assoc	951-5317	AJ	PHD	69	Kansas	1977
Goldberg, Paul A.	Assoc	951-5317	HP	PHD	84	Columbia	1978
Hughey, Alice M.	Assoc	951-5317	Q	PHD	84	Columbia	1986
Fox, Jerrald Mark	Asst	951-5317	J	PHD		Harvard	1988
Klein, Yehuda L.	Asst	951-5317	M	PHD		Berkeley	1985
Thorne, Emanuel D.	Asst	951-5317	A	PHD		Yale	1994

CUNY-Lehman College Bronx, NY 10468-1589 (718) 960-8297 Kim Pierce
Economics Faculty Dept of Economics & Atg Fax=960-1173

Name	Rank	Phone	Degree	Yr	School	Since
Shreiber, Chanoch	C-Pr	960-8297	PHD		Columbia	
Cirace, John	Prof	960-8388	PHD		Columbia	
Sharav, Itzhak	Prof	960-8388	PHD	71	CUNY	9-67
Kayaalp, Orhan	Assoc	960-8598	PHD		CUNY	1979
Alexanderson, Peter	Asst	960-8598	JD			
Brott, Alan	Asst	960-8388	MBA			
Bynoe, Ann	Asst	960-8159	PHD		NYU	
Cantor, Paul E.	Asst	960-8507	PHD	85	Ca-Davis	1984
Chatha, Jaspal	Asst	960-8461	PHD			
DiLiberto, Maryann	Asst	960-8461	PHD		Columbia	
Fields, Judith M.	Asst	960-8384	PHD	84	NYU	1984
Honig, Susan	Asst	960-8389	MS		Pace	
Kamen, Michele	Asst	960-8384	MBA		St Johns	
Kraus, James A.	Asst	960-8159	JD		Columbia	
Ratowsky, Henry	Asst	960-8507	PHD	76	CUNY	1988
Rios, Roberto J.	Asst	960-8461	PHD	87	Columbia	1979
Tauber, Linda	Asst	960-8389	MBA			
Chung, Kuk-Soo	Lect	960-8386	MA		Yale	
Rodriguez, Ada	Lect	960-8389	MBA			

CUNY-Hunter College New York, NY 10021 (212)
Department of Economics Div of Social Science Fax= CUNYVM.CUNY.EDU

Name	Rank	Phone	Email	Degree	Yr	School	Since
Lees, Susan	Dean$	772-5520		PHD		Michigan	
Honig, Marjorie	C-Pr	772-5400	mahhc	PHD	71	Columbia	
Agbeyegbe, Terence	Prof	772-5405					
Chernick, Howard	Prof	772-5400		PHD	76	Penn	1982
Randall, Laura	Prof	772-5430		PHD		Columbia	
Reimers, Cordella W.	Prof	772-5400		PHD	77	Columbia	1982

Name	Rank	Phone	E-mail	Fields	Degree	Yr	School	Since
Shull, Bernard Jr.	Prof	772-5437			PHD	57	Wisconsin	1970
Smith, Ronald G. E.	Prof	772-5431			DBA		LSU	
Filer, Randall K.	Assoc	772-5399			PHD	79	Princeton	1986
Golbe, Devra L.	Assoc	772-5408			PHD	79	NYU	1987
Goodspeed, Timothy J.	Assoc	772-5434			PHD	86	Maryland	9-94
Kabot, Alvin	Assoc	772-5393			LLM	63	NYU	9-67
McLaughlin, Kenneth J.	Assoc	772-5439			PHD	87	Chicago	9-94
George, Nashwa E.	Asst	772-5404			PHD	88	Baruch	9-85
Heyen, Keith A.	Asst	772-5395			MA	80	N Illinois	
Liveson, Avi	Asst	772-5394			LLM	75	NYU	9-86
Ryan, Huldah	Asst	772-5403						
Bergman, Lila	Lect	772-5436			MBA	79	Fordham	9-85

CUNY-Queens College — Flushing, NY 11367-0904 (718) 997-5440 — Ms. Barbara Crohia
Department of Economics — School of Gen Studies Fax=997-5535 — QCVAXA

Name	Rank	Phone	E-mail	Fields	Degree	Yr	School	Since
Edelstein, Michael	C-Pr	997-5440		NOF	PHD	70	Penn	1974
Edwards, Linda N. (Assistant Chair, Economics)	Prof	997-5464		JC	PHD	71	Columbia	1971
Franklin, Raymond S.	Prof	997-3070		JBP	PHD	66	Berkeley	1966
Gram, Harvey H.	Prof	997-5448		FCE	PHD	73	Wisconsin	1974
Hill, Melba A.	Prof	997-5455		JC	PHD	80	Duke	1989
Kaufmann, Hugo M.	Prof	997-5449	kaufmann	FE	PHD	68	Columbia	1967
Levenson, Albert M.	Prof	997-5444		DFC	PHD	59	Columbia	1961
Lipsey, Robert E. (Graduate Adviser)	Prof	997-5443		FC	PHD	61	Columbia	1967
Nelson, Ralph L.	Prof	997-5446		MG	PHD	55	Columbia	1964
Riskin, Carl A.	Prof	997-5454	riskin@qc.edu	POQ	PHD	69	Berkeley	1974
Roistacher, Elizabeth A.	Prof	997-5453		RH	PHD	72	Penn	1974
Tabb, William K.	Prof	997-5451		RO	PHD	68	Wisconsin	1971
Thurston, Thom B.	Prof	997-5457	thurston	EC	PHD	70	Berkeley	1971
Dohan, Michael R.	Assoc	997-5464		PQ	PHD	69	MIT	1971
Gabel, David J.	Assoc	997-5452		DNC	PHD	87	Wisconsin	1987
Solon, Babette S.	Assoc	997-5445		DJ	PHD	58	MIT	1961
Weiman, David F.	Assoc	997-5440		NOE	PHD	84	Stanford	1994
Feliciano, Zadia M.	Asst	997-5440		JC				1994
Field-Hendrey, Elizabeth	Asst	997-5456		NJC	PHD	85	Duke	1989
Nix, Joan	Asst	997-5447		DG	PHD	89	NYU	1988
Chiremba, Daniel S.	Lect	997-3142		O	MA	69	New Sch	1969

CUNY-Col of Staten Island — Staten Isl, NY 10314 (718) 982-2900
Economics Faculty — Dept Pol Sci,Econ &Phil Fax=982-2888

Name	Rank	Phone	E-mail	Fields	Degree	Yr	School	Since
Carey, Robin	C-Ac	982-2894		H	PHD	72	Conn	1976
Bressler, Barry	Prof	982-2905		CT	PHD	66	NYU	
Petratos, Vasilios	Assoc	982-2903		BF	PHD	70	NYU	1974
Schwarz, Samuel	Assoc	982-2897		KC	PHD	78	Columbia	1986
Meltzer, Yale L.	Asst	982-2897		EG	MBA	66	NYU	1983
Osakve, John U.	Asst	982-2898		FO	PHD	80	Nebraska	1991

Claremont McKenna College — Claremont, CA 91711-6400 (909) 621-2680
Economics Faculty — Department of Economics Fax=621-8249 — CLAREMONT.EDU
phone: 621-8555

Name	Rank	Phone	E-mail	Fields	Degree	Yr	School	Since
Fucaloro, Anthony	Dean	621-8117			PHD	69	Arizona	1974
Teeples, Ronald K. (Director, Institute of Government and Public Affairs)	C-Pr	607-2964	rteeples		PHD		UCLA	1969
Arndt, Sven W. (Charles M. Stone Professor of Money, Credit & Trade)	Prof	621-8012			PHD	64	Berkeley	1990
Bjork, Gordon C. (Jonathan B. Lovelace Professor)	Prof	607-3625			PHD		U Wash	1975
Stubblebine, William Craig	Prof	621-8012			PHD	63	Virginia	1966
Willett, Thomas D. (Horton Professor of Economics)	Prof	621-8012			PHD	67	Virginia	1977
Wright, Colin (Norwood and Frances Berger Professor of Business & Soc./Director,Lincoln Inst)	Prof	607-3003			PHD		Chicago	1977
Burdekin, Richard C. K.	Assoc	607-2884			PHD	85	Houston	1989
Eyrich, Gerald I.	Assoc	607-2654			PHD		Claremont	1967
Smith, Rodney T.	Assoc	607-2818			PHD	76	Chicago	1983
Keil, Manfred		607-3899						

Clarion Univ of Pennsylvania — Clarion, PA 16214-1232 (814) 226-2627 — Sharon Bauer
Department of Economics — College of Business Fax=226-1910 — VAXB.CLARION.EDU

Name	Rank	Phone	E-mail	Fields	Degree	Yr	School	Since
Grunenwald, Joseph P.	Dean	226-2600			DBA	81	Kent St	8-78
Balough, Robert S.	C-Pr	226-2627	balough		PHD	81	N Illinois	1981
Ross, William N.	Prof	226-1965			PHD	71	Kansas St	1972
Sanders, William V.	Prof	226-2623			PHD	81	Penn St	1981
Sohng, Soong Nark	Prof	226-2632			PHD	82	Wayne St	1981
Stine, William F.	Prof	226-2612			PHD	83	Fordham	1981

Vernon, Thomas T.	Prof	226-2619			PHD	71	Kansas St	1969
Yang, Chin-Wei	Prof	226-2609			PHD		W Virginia	1981
Haggerty, Mark E.	Assoc	226-2625			PHD		Wash St	1989
Smith, Lynn A.	Assoc	226-2633			PHD		Pittsburgh	1989
Raehsler, Rod D.	Asst	226-2630						

Clark University	Worcester, MA	01610-1477	(508) 793-7226				Ms. Peggy Moskowitz	
Economics Faculty	Department of Economics	Fax=793-7780					VAX.CLARKU.EDU	
Brown, John C.	C-Ac	793-7390	jbrown		PHD	86	Michigan	1986
Hsu, Robert C.	Prof	793-7281	rhsu		PHD	70	Berkeley	1971
Ott, Attiat F.	Prof	793-7447	aott		PHD	62	Michigan	1969
Director, Institute for Economic Studies								
Puffer, Frank W.	Prof	793-7228	fpuffer		PHD	68	Brown	1968
Veendorp, Emiel C.	Prof	793-7101			PHD	63	Rice	1976
Weinrobe, Maurice D.	Prof	793-7248	mweinrobe		PHD	69	Cornell	1976
Gray, Wayne B.	Assoc	793-7693	wgray		PHD	83	Harvard	1984
Bernhofen, Daniel	Asst	793-7359	dbernhofen		PHD	94	Syracuse	1989
Ferderer, J. Peter	Asst	793-7237			PHD	88	Wash U	1988

Clark Atlanta University	Atlanta, GA	30314-4391	(404) 880-6770				Gwen Donaway	
Department of Economics	School of Art & Science	Fax=880-6276						
Earvin, Larry	Dean	880-6770						
Bezuneh, Mesfin	C-Ac	880-8704			PHD		Va Tech	
Carter, Charlie	Assoc	880-8499			PHD		Illinois	
Nyomba, Ajamu	Asst	880-8481			PHD		Tx-Austin	

Clarkson University	Potsdam, NY	13699-5785	(315) 268-3998					
Dept of Economics & Finance	School of Business	Fax=268-3810						CLVM
Pease, Victor P.	Dean	268-2300			PHD	79	Arizona	
Mullen, John K.	C-Ac	268-4283		GHR	PHD	78	SUNY-Bin	1977
Menz, Fredric C.	Prof	268-6427		HQ	PHD	70	Virginia	1974
Atesoglu, H. Sonmez	Assoc	268-7981		EFO	PHD	72	Pittsburgh	1977
Baird, Philip	Asst	268-3870		GM	PHD	93	Tennessee	1992
Episcopos, Athanasius	Asst	268-6425		CDG	PHD	92	SUNY-Buf	1992
Frascatore, Mark	Asst	268-3850		DHL	PHD	94	Va Tech	1994
Vilasuso, Jon	Asst	268-6604		EFG	PHD	94	Conn	1994

Clayton State College	Morrow, GA	30260	(404) 961-3410					
Economics Faculty	School of Business	Fax=961-0801					CC.CSC.PEACHNET.EDU	
Hubbard, Charles W.	Dean$	961-3412		Mgt	PHD	70	Arkansas	1993
Wardrep, Bruce N.	C-Pr	961-3738	wardrep	Fnce	PHD	74	Geo St	9-91
Charles S. Conklin Professor of Finance								
Arjomand, Lari		961-3417			PHD			1980
Cash, Doris		961-3451			DBA			1975

Clemson University	Clemson, SC	29634-1309	(803) 656-3481				Cindy McIntire	
Department of Economics	College of Prof Studies	Fax=656-4192					CLEMSON	
Dougan, William R.	H-Pr$	656-4533		HDEL	PHD	81	Chicago	1988
Benjamin, Daniel K.	Prof	656-2956		DEGJ	PHD	75	UCLA	1985
Dwyer, Gerald P.	Prof	656-0384		CEG	PHD	79	Chicago	1989
Gordon, Donald F.	Prof	656-4534		DE	PHD	49	Cornell	1986
Abney Chair								
Lindsay, Cotton M.	Prof	656-3955		DHJK	PHD	68	Virginia	1984
J. Wilson Newman Professor								
Maloney, Michael T.	Prof	656-3430		DGKL	PHD	78	LSU	
McCormick, Robert E.	Prof	656-3441		DGKH	PHD	78	Tx A&M	
Shannon, Russell D.	Prof	656-3962		EFOP	PHD	66	Tulane	1966
Thompson, G. Richard	Prof	656-0946		HLM	PHD	72	Virginia	
Ulbrich, Holley H.	Prof	656-3968		HIR	PHD	69	Conn	1967
Alumni Professor								
Wallace, Myles S.	Prof	656-3965	myles	EFC	PHD	76	Colorado	1980
Warner, John T.	Prof	656-3967	jtwarne	DJE	PHD	76	N Car St	1980
Gordon, David	Assoc	656-3956		DE	PHD	94	Chicago	1992
Placone, Dennis L.	Assoc	656-3951		FPH	PHD	82	Pittsburgh	1976
Simon, Curtis J.	Asst	656-3966		JOR	PHD	85	SUNY-Bin	1985
Woo, Cheonsik	Asst	656-3964	wcheons		PHD	94	Columbia	1992

Cleveland State University	Cleveland, OH	44115	(216) 687-4520				Mrs. Karen Lee Scraga	
Department of Economics	College of Arts & Sci	Fax=687-9206					CSUOHIO.EDU	
Olson, Glending	Dean$	637-3660	g.olson		PHD	69	Stanford	1972
Bell, Edward B.	C-Ac	687-4519	e.bell	DHJ	PHD	73	Ohio St	1971
Mathur, Vijay K.	Prof	687-4526	v.mathur	DR	PHD	69	Wayne St	1968
Chang, Myong-Hun	Assoc	687-4523	m.chang	LDMN	PHD	89	J Hopkins	1988
Harford, Jon D.	Assoc	687-4524	j.harford	DHKQ	PHD	74	Stanford	1982

Stein, Sheldon H.	Assoc	687-4537	s.stein	CER	PHD	78	J Hopkins	1976
Stewart, Douglas O.	Assoc	687-4515	d.o.stewart	DH	PHD	74	Michigan	1972
Taub, Allan J.	Assoc	687-4528	a.taub	CD	PHD	73	Northwes	1971
Song, Frank M.	Asst	687-4525	f.song	EG	PHD	91	Ohio St	1991
Yerger, David B.	Asst	687-4535	d.yerger	DF	PHD	94	Penn St	1994

Coe College — Cedar Rapids, IA 52402 (319) 399-8714
Economics Faculty — Col of Bus Adm & Econ Fax=
Did Not Respond--1994-95 Listing

Spellman, William E.	C-Pr	399-8714			PHD	70	Kansas St	1970
George R. Baker Professor of Economics and Business Administration								
Sandberg, Michael L.	Prof				PHD	76	Iowa	1976
Vaitheswaran, Ramakrishna	Prof	399-8627			PHD	77	Iowa St	1973
Elnora H. and William B. Quarton Professor of Business Admin. and Economics								
Hansen, Dwight W.	Assoc				MA	76	Nebraska	1978
Larew, Barbara	Assoc				MA	81	Iowa	1981
Wu, Mickey Tai Chuen	Assoc				PHD	79	Kentucky	1979
Carstens, Pamela J.	Asst				MBA	85	Iowa	1985
McDonald, Michael	Asst				MA	81	Iowa	1981

Colby College — Waterville, ME 04901 (207) 872-3564 — Joyce Matthews
Economics Faculty — Economic Department Fax=872-3263 — COLBY.EDU

Reid, Clifford E.	C-Pr	872-3116	cereid	DCHR	PHD	73	Princeton	1987
Gemery, Henry A.	Prof	878-3137	hagemery	NAB	PHD	67	Penn	1961
Pugh Family Professor of Economics								
Hogendorn, Jan S.	Prof	872-3142	jshogend	FOA	PHD	66	London	1966
Grossman Professor of Economics								
Meehan, James W.	Prof	872-3136	jwmeehan	DM	PHD	67	Boston C	1973
Herbert E. Wadsworth Professor of Economics								
Nelson, Randy A.	Prof	872-3567	ranelson	GM	PHD	79	Illinois	1987
Douglas Professor of Economics								
Tietenberg, Thomas H.	Prof	872-3143	thtieten	QK	PHD	71	Wisconsin	1977
Mitchell Family Professor of Economics								
Barbezat, Debra A.	Assoc	872-3154	dabarbez	JIA	PHD	85	Michigan	1992
Findlay, David W.	Assoc	872-3153	dwfindla	EGA	PHD	86	Purdue	1985
Franko, Patrice	Assoc	872-3347	pmfranko	FAO	PHD	86	Notre Dm	1986
Donihue, Michael R.	Asst	872-3115	mrdonihu	CEA	PHD	89	Michigan	1989
Thornton, Saranna	Asst	872-3563	s_robins	FEA	PHD	89	Car Mellon	1989

Colgate University — Hamilton, NY 13346 (315) 824-7533 — Mrs. Kate McNitt
Economics Faculty — Economics Department Fax=824-7726 — CENTER.COLGATE.EDU

Turner, Robert W.	C-Ac	824-7529	rturner	CH	PHD	84	MIT	1983
Haines, Michael R.	Prof	824-7536	mhaines	TN	PHD	71	Penn	1990
Banfi Vintners Professor of Economics								
Mandle, Jay R.	Prof	824-7540	jmandle	ON	PHD	69	Penn	
W. Bradford Wiley Professor of Economics								
Pinchin, Hugh M.	Prof	824-7539	hpinchin	F	PHD	70	Yale	1965
Waldman, Don E.	Prof	824-7535	dwaldman	L	PHD	76	Cornell	1981
Baldani, Jeffrey P.	Assoc	824-7519	jbaldani	CD	PHD	83	Cornell	1982
Kato, Takao	Assoc	824-7562	tkato	J	PHD	86	Queen's	1986
Michl, Thomas R.	Assoc	824-7526	tmichl	EJ	PHD	84	New Sch	1983
Rao, Milind	Assoc	824-7991	mrao	EO	PHD	89	Columbia	1988
Grapard, Ulla A.	Asst	824-7538	ugrapard	AB	PHD	90	Cornell	1985
Jin, Fuchun	Asst	824-7537	fjin	E	PHD	93	Ohio St	1993
Khanna, Jyoti	Asst	824-7527	jkhanna	H	PHD	90	Iowa	1992
Rask, Kevin N.	Asst	824-7524	krask	QI	PHD	91	Duke	1991
Sturges, David M.	Asst		dsturges	EG	PHD	94	Yale	1995
Tiefenthaler, Jill M.	Asst	824-7523	tiefenthaler	TO	PHD	91	Duke	1991
Grove, Wayne A.	Inst	824-7991	wgrove	N	ABD		Illinois	1995

The Colorado College — Colorado Spr, CO 80903 (719) 389-6407
Economics Department — School of Business Fax=389-6927 — CC.COLORADO.EDU

Laux, Judith A.	C-Ac	389-6414	jlaux		PHD	90	Colorado	1979
Barton, William E.	Prof	389-6418			PHD	70	Missouri	1958
Becker, William S.	Prof	389-6416			PHD	70	LSU	1970
Bird, Michael C.	Prof	389-6445	mbird		PHD	68	Colorado	1968
Griffiths, L. Christopher	Prof	389-6417	cgriffiths		PHD	70	Colorado	1967
Hecox, Walter E.	Prof	389-6413	whecox		PHD	69	Syracuse	1970
Johnson, James A.	Prof	389-6614			MA	59	Stanford	1956
Weida, William J.	Prof	389-6409			DBA	75	Colorado	1985
Kapuria-Foreman, Vibha	Assoc	389-6419	vkapuria		PHD	87	Pittsburgh	1989
Redmount, Esther R.	Assoc	389-6412	eredmount		PHD	85	Virginia	1987
Rittenberg, Libby T.	Assoc	389-6410	lrittenberg		PHD	80	Rutgers	1989
Smith, Mark Griffin	Assoc	389-6411	msmith		PHD	87	Duke	1988

Univ of Colorado at Boulder Boulder, CO 80309-0256 (303) 492-6394 Sue Stortz 492-5168
Department of Economics College of Arts & Sci Fax=492-8960 COLORADO.EDU

Name	Rank	Phone	Email	Field	Degree	Yr	School	Hired
Middleton, Charles R.	Dean	492-7294	charles.middleto		PHD		Duke	
Kaempfer, William H.	C-Pr	492-4486	william.kaempfer		PHD	79	Duke	1981
Alm, James R.	Prof	492-8291	alm		PHD	80	Wisconsin	1983
Carlos, Ann M.	Prof	492-8737	ann.carlos		PHD	80	W Ontario	1990
Glahe, Fred R.	Prof	492-5186			PHD	64	Purdue	1965
Greenwood, Michael J.	Prof	492-7413			PHD	67	Northwes	1980
Director, Center for Economic Analysis								
Howe, Charles W.	Prof	492-7245	charles.howe		PHD	59	Stanford	1970
Director, Program for Environment and Behavior								
Hsiao, Frank S. T.	Prof	492-7908	frank.hsiao		PHD	67	Rochester	1975
Markusen, James R.	Prof	492-0748	james.markusen		PHD	73	Boston C	1990
Maskus, Keith E.	Prof	492-7588	keith.maskus		PHD	81	Michigan	1981
Director, Carl McGuire Center for International Studies								
McNown, Robert F.	Prof	492-8295	mcnown		PHD	71	Ca-SnDgo	1971
Morey, Edward R.	Prof	492-6898	edwarad.morey		PHD	78	Brit Col	1980
Poulson, Barry W.	Prof	492-7414	barry.poulson		PHD	65	Ohio St	1965
Roper, Don E.	Prof	492-7466	donald.roper		PHD	70	Chicago	1985
Singell, Larry D.	Prof	492-1809	larry.singell		PHD	65	Wayne St	1968
Udis, Bernard	Prof	492-8872			PHD	59	Princeton	1965
Lillydahl, Jane H.	Assoc	492-4599	jane.lillydahl		PHD	76	Duke	1976
Waldman, Donald M.	Assoc	492-6781	donald.waldman		PHD	79	Wisconsin	1984
Zax, Jeffrey S.	Assoc	492-8268	jeffrey.zax		PHD	84	Harvard	1990
Alberini, Anna	Asst	492-6653			PHD	92	Ca-SnDgo	1995
Beauchemin, Kenneth	Asst	492-2651			PHD	95	Iowa	1995
Cronshaw, Mark B.	Asst	492-6310	mark.cronshaw		PHD	89	Stanford	1989
De Bartolome, Charles	Asst	492-4464	charles.debartol		PHD	85	Penn	1993
Feeney, Joanne	Asst	492-5923	jo.feeney		MA	91	Rochster	1990
Flores, Nicholas E.	Asst	492-8145			PHD	95	Ca-SnDgo	1995
Kruse, Jamie I.	Asst	492-8736	jamie.kruse		PHD	88	Arizona	1987
Lee, Byong-Joo	Asst	492-2108	bj.lee		PHD	88	Wisconsin	1988
Rutherford, Thomas F.	Asst	492-5169			PHD	87	Stanford	1995

U of Colorado at Co Springs Colorado Spr, CO 80933-7150 (719) 593-3199
Economic Faculty Department of Economics Fax=593-3023 COLOSPGS

Name	Rank	Phone	Email	Field	Degree	Yr	School	Hired
Null, James A.	Dean	593-3122		PolS	PHD	70	Arizona	1970
Eubanks, Larry S.	C-Ac	593-3502		DHQ	PHD	80	Wyoming	1986
Ballantyne, A. Paul	Prof	593-3162		ABEO	PHD	65	Stanford	1967
Tregarthen, Timothy D.	Prof	593-3692		DEHR	PHD	72	Ca-Davis	1971
Greenwood, Daphne T.	Assoc	593-3508		HJT	PHD	80	Oklahoma	1980
DeBoer, Dale	Asst	593-3180		DFO	PHD	93	Ca-Davis	1993

Univ of Colorado at Denver Denver, CO 80217-3364 (303) 556-4413 Lynn Ferguson, Adm Asst
Department of Economics Col Liberal Arts & Sci Fax=556-3547 CUDNVR.DENVER.COLORADO

Name	Rank	Phone	Email	Field	Degree	Yr	School	Hired
Loflin, Marvin D.	Dean	556-2557		Engl	PHD		Indiana	
Medema, Steven G.	C-Ac	556-8511	smedema	HDK	PHD	89	Mich St	1989
Helburn, Suzanne W.	Emer	556-4413	shelburn	B	PHD	63	Indiana	1970
Johnson, Byron L.	Emer	556-2753			PHD	47	Wisconsin	1947
Morris, John R. Jr.	Prof	556-2570	jrmorris	D	PHD	66	Purdue	1970
Smith, W. James	Prof	556-4354	jsmith	E	PHD	76	Colorado	1989
Bramhall, David F.	Emer	556-4413			PHD		Penn	
Hsiao, Mei-Chu W.	Assoc	556-8322	mhsiao	OC	PHD	67	Rochester	1981
Argys, Laura M.	Asst	556-3949	largys	J	PHD		Colorado	
Beckman, Steven R.	Asst	556-3048		F	PHD	82	Ca-Davis	1988
Mocan, Naci H.	Asst	556-8540	nmocan	CJI	PHD	89	CUNY	1990
Polavarapu, Ramana V.	Asst	556-3950		IOCD	PHD	93	Ca-Davis	1993
email: rpolavar@carbon.denver.colorado.edu								
Rees, Daniel I.	Asst	556-3348	direes	J	PHD		Cornell	
Zheng, Buhong	Asst	556-4413			PHD	93	W Virginia	1995

Colorado State University Fort Collins, CO 80523 (970) 491-6566 Barbara Alldredge
Department of Economics Col of Liberal Arts Fax=491-2925 COLOSTATE.EDU

Name	Rank	Phone	Email	Field	Degree	Yr	School	Hired
Crabtree, Loren W.	Dean				PHD		Minnesota	
Revier, Charles F.	C-Pr	491-6566	crevier	EH	PHD	78	MIT	1974
Cochrane, Harold	Prof	491-6493	hcochrane	EA	PHD	75	Colorado	1975
Fan, Chuen-mei	Prof	491-5438	cmfan	HD	PHD	72	Minnesota	1978
Fan, Liang-Shing	Prof	491-5336	lsfan	AOF	PHD	65	Minnesota	1968
Keller, Robert R.	Prof	491-5421		EN	PHD	71	Wisconsin	1974
Associate Dean								
Ozawa, Terutomo	Prof	491-6076	tozawa	FO	PHD	66	Columbia	1974
Phillips, Ronnie J.	Prof	491-6079	rphillips	GB	PHD	80	Tx-Austin	1983
Rhodes, George F.	Prof	491-6657	grhodes	LC	PHD	74	Tx A&M	1978
Shulman, Steven J.	Prof	491-6940	sshulman	JKEI	PHD	84	Mass	1984
Stanfield, James Ronald	Prof	491-6891	rstanfield	BA	PHD	72	Oklahoma	1976
Cutler, Harvey	Assoc	491-5704	hcutler	EC	PHD	85	U Wash	1980
Kling, Robert W.	Assoc	491-6653	rkling	DQ	PHD	85	Kansas	1984
Bernasek, Alexandra	Asst	491-6856	abernasek	DA	PHD	92	Michigan	1992
Jianakoplos, Nancy A.	Asst	491-6537	njianakoplos	CE	PHD	83	Ohio St	1990

Columbia University	New York, NY 10027-6989 (212) 854-8057					Leslie Ann Poole	
Div of Finance & Economics	School of Business Fax=316-9355					COLUMBIA.EDU	
Feldberg, Meyer	Dean	854-6083		PHD	69	Capetown	1989
Edwards, Franklin R.	C-Pr	854-4202		PHD	64	Harvard	1980
Arthur F. Burns Professor of Free and Competitive Enterprise							
Adler, Michael	Prof	854-4682		DBA	68	Harvard	1968
Arzac, Enrique R.	Prof	854-4401		PHD	68	Columbia	1971
Bartel, Ann	Prof	854-4419		PHD	74	Columbia	1976
Beim, David O.	Prof	854-3484		PHL	66	Oxford	1991
Donaldson, John B.	Prof	854-4436		PHD	76	Car Mellon	1977
Freeman, James	Prof	854-4225		MBA	70	Penn	1991
Greenwald, Bruce C. N.	Prof	854-3491		PHD	78	MIT	1991
Heal, Geoffrey M.	Prof	854-6084		PHD	68	Cambridg	1983
Hubbard, R. Glenn	Prof	854-3493		PHD	83	Harvard	1988
Leff, Nathaniel H.	Prof	854-4223		PHD	66	MIT	1967
Mishkin, Frederic S.	Prof	854-8057		PHD	76	MIT	1983
on leave							
Nelson, Richard R.	Prof	854-8720		PHD	56	Yale	1986
Henry R. Luce Professor of International Political Economy							
Noam, Eli	Prof	854-4596		PHD	75	Harvard	1976
Director of Columbia Institute for Tele-Information							
Patrick, Hugh T.	Prof	854-3497		PHD	60	Michigan	1984
Director of the Center on Japanese Economy and Business							
Wilkinson, Maurice	Prof	854-4481		PHD	65	Harvard	1965
Giovannini, Alberto	Assoc	854-3471		PHD	83	MIT	1983
on leave							
Lichtenberg, Frank R.	Assoc	854-4408		PHD	82	Penn	1983
Sicherman, Nachum	Assoc	854-4464		PHD	87	Columbia	1991
Chemmanur, Thomas J.	Asst	854-4109		PHD	90	NYU	1989
Harrison, Ann	Asst	854-8057					
Lehr, William H.	Asst	854-4426		ABD	91	Stanford	1991
Siconolfi, Paolo	Asst	854-3474		PHD	87	Penn	1989
Wang, Albert	Asst	854-8057					
Willard, Kristen L.	Asst	854-8057				Princeton	

Columbus College	Columbus, GA 31907-5645 (706) 568-2280					Martha Daniel	
Dept of Business Adm	Turner School of Bus Fax=568-2184					USCN.BITNET	
Johnson, Robert S.	Dean	568-2044		PHD	64	Virginia	1993
Bill Heard Chair of Business Administration							
Embry, Olice H.	C-Pr	568-2284	Mgt	PHD	70	Geo St	1973
Daniels, Michael J.	Prof			PHD		Geo St	1980
Assistant Dean; Director, Center for Regional Economic Studies							
McCollum, James B.	Prof			PHD	68	Tulane	1976
Arno, Elsie R.	Assoc			MS		Auburn	1976

Concordia College MN	Moorhead, MN 56562 (218) 299-4411					Laura Klomstad	
Economics Faculty	Dept of Econ & Bus Adm Fax=299-3947						
Spilde, Roger H.	C-Pr	299-3070		MA	58	Iowa	1958
Harrison, Clifford E.	Prof	299-3476		EDD		Farleigh	1986
Heimarck, Theodore	Prof	299-3477		JD		Chicago	1961
Hiestand, Thomas W.	Assoc	299-3483		PHD		Kansas St	1972
Moewes, David S.	Assoc	299-3488		PHD		Utah	1968
Petree, Daniel L.	Assoc	299-3115		PHD		Kansas	1995
Anderson, Daniel	Asst	299-3950		MBA		N Dakota	1993
Dietz, Donna K.	Asst	299-3951		BS		N Dak St	1990
Foss, Robert K.	Asst	299-3486		MS		N Dakota	1988
Kroeten, Terrence	Asst	299-3489		PHD		Nebraska	1992
Mendes, Sergio A.	Asst	299-3199		MA		Va Tech	1992
Stuart, Iris C.	Asst	299-3478		PHD		Iowa	1990
Twedt, Ronald	Asst	299-3484		MBT		Minnesota	1991

Connecticut College	New London, CT 06320 (203) 439-2248						
Economics Faculty	Department of Economics Fax=439-5332						
McKenna, Edward J.	C-Ac			PHD		SUNY-SBr	
Pack, Spencer J.	Prof			PHD	83	N Hamp	1981
Peppard, Donald M. Jr.	Prof			PHD	75	Mich St	
Visgilio, Gerald R.	Prof			PHD		RhodeIsl	
Howes, Candance	Assoc		DF	PHD	91	Berkeley	1995
Jensen, Rolf W.	Assoc			PHD		Mass	
Cruz-Saco, Maria A.	Asst			PHD		Pittsburgh	
Ferdnance, Tyrone	Asst			PHD		Notre Dm	

University of Connecticut Storrs, CT 06269-1063 (203) 486-3022 Madeline Nasansky
Department of Economics Col of Lib Arts & Scien Fax=486-4463 UCONNVM.UCONN.EDU

Name	Rank	Phone	E-mail	Field	Degree	Yr	Institution	Year
Romano, Antonio	Dean	486-2713			PHD			
Miller, Stephen M.	H-Pr	486-3853	smiller	EF	PHD	72	SUNY-Buf	1970
Allen, Polly R.	Prof	486-3955	pallen	FE	PHD	70	Brown	1976
Barth, Peter S.	Prof	486-3023		J	PHD	65	Michigan	1973
Hallwood, Paul C.	Prof	445-3478		F	PHD	88	Aberdeen	1986
Heffley, Dennis R.	Prof	486-4669	dheffley	RI	PHD	75	Ca-SnBarb	193
Langlois, Richard N.	Prof	486-3472	langlois	B	PHD	81	Stanford	1983
McEachern, William A.	Prof	486-3272	mceacher	H	PHD	75	Virginia	1978
Ray, Subhash C.	Prof	486-3967	ray	CD	PHD	81	Ca-SnBarb	1982
Sacks, Stephen R.	Prof	486-4859	sacks	H	PHD	71	Berkeley	1971
Wright, Arthur W.	Prof	486-3773		KD	PHD	69	MIT	1979
Ahking, Francis W.	Assoc	486-3026	anking	EF	PHD	81	Va Tech	1980
Alpert, William T.	Assoc	322-3466	alpert	J	PHD	79	Columbia	1983
Carstensen, Fred V.	Assoc	486-0614	carsten	N	PHD	76	Yale	1982
Dua, Pami	Assoc	322-3466	dua	E	PHD	85	London	1987
Harmon, Oskar R.	Assoc	322-3466	oharm	H	PHD	80	Rutgers	1982
Hatzipanayoutou, Panos	Assoc	486-4762	hatzipa	F	PHD	85	SUNY-SBr	1985
Kimenyi, Samson M.	Assoc	486-3027	kimenyi	HI	PHD	86	Geo Mason	1991
Landau, Daniel L.	Assoc	596-4080		O	PHD	74	Chicago	1981
Lott, William F.	Assoc	486-3885	wlott	C	PHD	69	N Car St	1969
Miceli, Thomas J.	Assoc	486-5810	miceli	KR	PHD	88	Brown	1987
Sazama, Gerald W.	Assoc	486-3366	shazam	H	PHD	67	Wisconsin	1966
Segerson, Kathleen	Assoc	486-4567	segerson	QD	PHD	84	Cornell	1986
Chattopadhyay, Sajal	Asst	241-4860		I	PHD	90	Conn	1991
Cosgel, Metin M.	Asst	486-4662	cosgel	N	PHD	89	Iowa	1989
Cunningham, Steven R.	Asst	486-3550	cunning	EB	PHD	89	Fla St	1989
Kung, James	Asst				PHD	91	Cambridge	1995
Minkler, Alanson P.	Asst	486-4070		DK	PHD	88	Ca-Davis	1989
Omori, Yoshiaki	Asst	486-5267	omori	J	PHD	90	SUNY-SBr	1991
Randolph, Susan M.	Asst	486-4171	randolph	O	PHD	83	Cornell	1984
Ross, Stephen	Asst	486-3533	ross	R	PHD	94	Syracuse	1994

Converse College Spartanburg, SC 29302 (803) 596-9603
Dept of Economics & Business Col of Arts & Sciences Fax=583-9158

Name	Rank	Phone	E-mail	Field	Degree	Yr	Institution	Year
McDaniel, Thomas R.	Dean			Educ	PHD		J Hopkins	1980
Vice President for Academic Affairs & Provost								
Hughes, Woodrow W. Jr.	C-As	596-9089			PHD	89	S Carol	1986
Young, Madelyn V.	Asst	596-909			PHD	91	Geo St	1991

Cornell University Ithaca, NY 14853-7601 (607) 255-4254
Department of Economics Col of Arts & Sciences Fax=255-2818 CORNELLA.CUEDU

Name	Rank	Phone	E-mail	Field	Degree	Yr	Institution	Year
Mitra, Tapan	C-Pr	255-4062			PHD		Rochester	
Basu, Kaushik	Prof	255-2525			PHD		LondonEc	
Blume, Lawrence E.	Prof	255-9530			PHD		Berkeley	
Davis, Tom E.	Prof	255-5007			PHD		J Hopkins	
Easley, David	Prof	255-6253			PHD		Northwes	
Ehrenberg, Ronald G.	Prof	225-3026			PHD	70	Northwes	1985
Frank, Robert H.	Prof	256-4254			PHD	72	Berkeley	1972
Hay, George A.	Prof	256-3378		Law	PHD	69	Northwes	1979
Kiefer, Nicholas M.	Prof	255-6315			PHD	76	Princeton	1980
Majumdar, Mukul K.	Prof	255-3640			PHD		Berkeley	
H. T. Warshow and Robert Irving Warshow Professor								
Masson, Robert T.	Prof	255-6288			PHD	69	Berkeley	1976
McClelland, Peter D.	Prof	256-6285			PHD	67	Harvard	1968
Possen, Uri M.	Prof	255-6367			PHD	71	Yale	1971
Schuler, Richard E.	Prof	255-7579		Engr	PHD	72	Brown	1972
Shell, Karl	Prof	255-5277			PHD	65	Stanford	1986
Robert Julius Thorne Professor								
Smith, Bruce D.	Prof	255-6209			PHD	81	MIT	
Staller, George J.	Prof	255-4955			PHD	59	Cornell	1960
Thorbecke, Erik	Prof	255-2066			PHD	57	Berkeley	1974
H. Edward Babcock Professor of Economics and Food Economics								
Vanek, Jaroslav	Prof	255-4867			PHD		MIT	
Carl Marks Professor of International Studies								
Wan, Henry Y. Jr.	Prof	255-6211			PHD		MIT	
Lyons, Thomas P.	Assoc	255-9534			PHD	83	Cornell	1988
Conlin, Michael	Asst	255-6254			PHD		Wisconsin	
Hong, Youngmaio	Asst	255-5130			PHD		Ca-SnDgo	
Legros, Patrick A.	Asst	255-6287			PHD	89	Cal Tech	1989
Mitchell, Janet L.	Asst	255-5617			PHD	86	Northwes	1989
Subramanin, Shankar	Asst	255-2355			PHD		Berkeley	
Veracierto, Marcelo	Asst	255-4254			PHD		Minnesota	
Vogelsang, Tim	Asst	255-5108			PHD		Princeton	

Creighton University — Omaha, NE 68178-0130 (402) 280-2612 — Ms. Shirley Gust
Dept of Economics & Finance — Col of Business Admin Fax=280-2172 — CREIGHTON.EDU

Name	Rank	Phone	Email	Field	Degree	Yr	School	Year
Reznicek, Bernard	Dean	280-2852			MBA	59	Nebraska	1994
Allen, Robert F.	C-Pr	280-2612		DKL	PHD	69	Mich St	1986
Goss, Ernest P.	Prof	280-4757		RC	PHD	83	Tennessee	1992
MacMister Chair								
Murthy, N. R. Vasudeva	Prof	280-2128		CDH	PHD	75	SUNY-Bin	1979
Nitsch, Thomas O.	Prof	280-2887		ENP	PHD	63	Ohio St	1969
Fitzsimmons, Edward L.	Assoc	280-2170		AD	PHD	84	Nebraska	1984
Funk, Herbert J.	Emer			AC	PHD	64	Iowa St	1967
Phillips, Joseph M. Jr.	Assoc	280-2610		EO	PHD	82	Notre Dm	1988
Stockhausers, Gerard L. S.J.	Assoc	280-2614		DF	PHD	85	Michigan	1985
Cahill, Neil S.J.	Asst	280-2686		AN	PHL	47	St Louis	1962
Knudsen, James J.	Asst	280-2281		CHJ	PHD	89	Iowa St	1989

Cumberland College — Williamsburg, KY 40769-7984 (606)
Economics Faculty — Dept of Business Admin Fax= — CC.CUMBER.EDU
phone 549-2200

Name	Rank	Phone	Email	Field	Degree	Yr	School	Year
Hubbard, Harold F.	C-Pr	Ext 4254	hhubbard	BAdm	MBA	60	Kentucky	7-60
Tan, Chin	Assoc	Ext 4457			MBA	88	Tn Tech	1988

University of Dallas — Irving, TX 75062-4799 (214) 721-5308 — Kate Hohlt
Department of Economics — Constantin C of Lib Art Fax=721-5372 — ACAD.UDALLAS.EDU

Name	Rank	Phone	Email	Field	Degree	Yr	School	Year
Thurow, Glenn E.	Dean$	721-5242		PolS	PHD		Harvard	1974
Bostaph, Samuel H.	C-Ac	721-5308		BNP	PHD	76	S Illinois	1981
Doyle, William	Asst	721-5054		GN	PHD	91	Tennessee	1991
Weston, Samuel C.	Asst	721-5238		B	PHD	87	Pittsburgh	1987

Dallas Baptist University — Dallas, TX 75211 (214)
Department of Economics — College of Business Fax= — DBU.EDU

Name	Rank	Phone	Email	Field	Degree	Yr	School	Year
Nelson, Mary Jane	Dean	333-5244	maryjane	Mgt	PHD		Oklahoma	1992
Ellis, Charles M.	Prof				PHD	73	Alabama	

Dartmouth College — Hanover, NH 03755-1798 (603) 646-2617 — F. Bergeron, G. Wheatley
Department of Economics — Col of Arts & Sciences Fax=646-2122 — DARTMOUTH.EDU

Name	Rank	Phone	Email	Field	Degree	Yr	School	Year
Wright, James	Dean	646-3999		Hist	PHD	59	MIT	
Marion, Nancy P.	C-Pr	646-2511			PHD	77	Princeton	1976
Aizenmann, Joshua	Prof	646-2531			PHD	81	Chicago	1990
Baldwin, William Lee	Prof	646-2534			PHD	58	Princeton	1956
John French Professor								
Blancheflower, David Graham	Prof	646-2536			PHD	85	London	1989
Clement, Meredith Owen	Prof	646-2945			PHD	58	Berkeley	1956
Fischel, William Alan	Prof	646-2940			PHD	73	Princeton	1973
Gustman, Alan Leslie	Prof	646-2641			PHD	69	Michigan	1969
Loren M. Berry Professor								
Kohn, Meir G.	Prof	646-2648			PHD	73	MIT	1978
Menge, John A.	Prof	646-2529			PHD	59	MIT	1956
Scott, John T.	Prof	646-2941			PHD	76	Harvard	1977
Skinner, Jonathan	Prof	646-2942			PHD	83	UCLA	1995
Venti, Steven F.	Prof	646-2526			PHD	82	Harvard	1982
Knetter, Michael M.	Assoc	646-2121			PHD	88	Stanford	1988
Anderson, Patricia Mary	Asst	646-2532			PHD	91	Princeton	1991
Engelhardt, Gary	Asst	646-2537			PHD	93	MIT	1993
Hooker, Mark Allan	Asst	646-2934			PHD	90	Stanford	1990
Lusardi, Annamaria	Asst	646-2099			PHD	92	Princeton	1993
Samwick, Andrew A.	Asst	646-2893			PHD	93	MIT	1994
Slaughter, Matthew J.	Asst	646-2939			PHD	94	MIT	1994
Yi, Sang-Seung	Asst	646-2944			PHD	93	Harvard	1993
Klecan, Lindsey O.	VInst	646-2533			BA	87	Duke	
visiting from MIT								

David Lipscomb University — Nashville, TN 37204-3951 (615)
Economics Faculty — Dept of Business Adm Fax= — DLU.EDU
phone 269-1000

Name	Rank	Phone	Email	Field	Degree	Yr	School	Year
Boulware, George W.	C-Pr	Ext 2478	gboulwar	Mktg	PHD	76	S Carol	1982
Purity Dairies Distinguished Professor of Business Administration								
Ingram, William C.	H-Pr				PHD	73	W Virginia	9-74

Davidson College — Davidson, NC 28036 (704) 892-2398 — Barbara Carmack, Dept Asst
Department of Economics — Economics Fax=892-2005

Name	Rank	Phone	Email	Field	Degree	Yr	School	Year
Ross, Clark G.	C-Pr	892-2264		P	PHD	76	Boston C	1979
Frontis Johnston Professor of Economics								
Appleyard, Dennis R.	Prof	892-2456		F	PHD	66	Michigan	1990
James B. Duke Professor of International Studies								

Hess, Peter N.	Prof	892-2249		OT	PHD	82	N Carol	1980
Lindsey, Glenn C.	Prof	892-2284		G	MBA	56	Georgia	1957
Kumar, Vikram	Assoc	892-2265		E	PHD	87	Vanderbilt	1986
Martin, David W.	Assoc	892-2253		GQ	PHD	84	Illinois	1984
Simpson, Murray S.	Asst	892-2454		O	PHD	94	Illinois	1993
Wellington, Alison J.	Asst	892-2078		J	PHD	90	Michigan	1990

University of Dayton — Dayton, OH 45469-2240 (513) 229-2416 — Ms. Sandy Murphy
Dept of Economics & Finance — School of Business Adm Fax=229-2477 — DAYTON.EDU

Gould, Sam B.	Dean	229-3731	gould	Mgt	PHD	75	Mich St	1985
Frasca, Ralph R.	C-Ac	229-2405	frasca	A	PHD	75	Indiana	1972
Beladi, Hamid	Prof	229-2407	beladi		PHD	83	Utah St	1988
Weiler, John E.	Prof	229-2453	weiler	H	PHD	73	Cincinnati	1967
Gustafson, Elizabeth F.	Assoc	229-2406	gustafso	C	PHD	74	N Carol	1983
Hadley, Lawrence H.	Assoc	229-2403	hadleyla	J	PHD	75	Conn	1977
Pace, Richard R.	Asst	229-2568	pace	E	PHD	94	Rochester	1993
Ruggiero, John	Asst	229-2550	ruggiero	R	PHD	95	Syracuse	1995

University of Delaware — Newark, DE 19716 (302) 831-2563 — Sara Poultney
Department of Economics — Col of Business & Econ Fax=831-6968 — BE.COLLEGE.UDEL.EDU

Biederman, Kenneth R.	Dean	831-2551	biedermk	G	PHD	75	Purdue	1990
Latham, William R. III	C-Ac	831-2563	lathamw	RC	PHD	73	Illinois	1971
Abrams, Burton A.	Prof	831-1900	abramsb	EH	PHD	74	Ohio St	1974
Anderson, Lee G.	Prof	831-2650		Q	PHD	70	U Wash	1974
Professor, College of Marine Studies								
Butkiewicz, James L.	Prof	831-2551	butkiewj	E	PHD	77	Virginia	1984
Associate Dean								
Grubb, Farley	Prof	831-1905	grubbf	N	PHD	84	Chicago	1983
Hoffman, Saul D.	Prof	831-1907	hoffmans	TJ	PHD	77	Michigan	1977
Koford, Kenneth	Prof	831-1909	kofordk	H	PHD	77	UCLA	1979
Lewis, Kenneth A.	Prof	831-1912	lewisk	CE	PHD	69	Princeton	1973
Associate Chair, Economics								
Link, Charles R.	Prof	831-1921	linkc	J	PHD	71	Wisconsin	1981
Miller, Jeffrey B.	Prof	831-1911	millerj	EP	PHD	76	Penn	1981
Mulligan, James G.	Prof	831-1918	mulligaj	L	PHD	80	Minnesota	1980
O'Neill, James B.	Prof	831-2559	oneillj	A	PHD	71	Purdue	1971
Director, Center for Economic Education								
Seidman, Laurence S.	Prof	831-1917	seidmanl	H	PHD	74	Berkeley	1982
Settle, Russell F.	Prof	831-1914	settler	H	PHD	74	Wisconsin	1974
Agnello, Richard J.	Assoc	831-1901	agnellor	C	PHD	70	J Hopkins	1968
Black, David E.	Assoc	831-1902	blackd	HO	PHD	69	MIT	1975
Craig, Eleanor D.	Assoc	831-1904	craige	H	MA	61	Penn	1962
Associate Chair								
Donnelley, Lawrence P.	Assoc	831-2652		O	PHD	70	Brown	1968
Associate Provost, International Programs and Special Sessions								
Falaris, Evangelos M.	Assoc	831-1768	falarise	O	PHD	79	Minnesota	1986
Thornton, James R.	Assoc	831-1919	thorntoj	P	PHD	74	Cornell	1973
Ying, John S.	Assoc	831-1903	yingj	L	PHD	87	Berkeley	1987
Arnold, Michael	Asst	831-1916	arnoldm	LD	PHD	92	UCLA	1992
Beck, Stacie E.	Asst	831-1915	becks	GEF	PHD	87	Penn	1986
Parsons, George R.	Asst	831-6792		Q	PHD	85	Wisconsin	1985
College of Marine Studies								
Smith, Pamela	Asst	831-1903	smithp	F	PHD	92	Wisconsin	1993
Whited, Toni	Asst	831-2563	whitedt	GE	PHD	90	Princeton	1994

Delaware State University — Dover, DE 19901-2277 (302)
Department of Economics — School of Bus & Econ Fax=

Williams, James L.	Dean	739-3521			PHD		Georgia	1994
Ikein, Augustine	C-Ac				PHD		Atlanta	
Bieker, Richard F.	Prof				PHD		Kentucky	
Christopher, Jan	Asst				PHD		Howard	
Deeney, John	Asst				MS		Delaware	
Jamison, Lawrence	Asst				LLM		Geo Wash	
Panda, Dandeson	Asst				MBA		Atlanta	
Peppard, William	Asst				MS		S Eastrn	
Sheith, Kishor	Asst				MBA		Atlanta	
Stith, John	Asst				PHD		Union	
Townsend, Lizzie Waller	Asst				MBA		Atlanta	
Williamson, Joan	Asst				MA		NYU	

Delta State University — Cleveland, MS 38733 (601) 846-4185
Division of Econ & Finance — School of Business Fax=

Moore, Roy N.	Dean	846-4200		Mgt	PHD	71	Alabama	8-88
Moore, B. C.	C-As	846-4209		AG	MBA			8-86
Hinton, William Valentine	Prof	846-4196			PHD		Arkansas	
Wood, Clinton F.	Prof	846-4185			JD	80	Miss	8-84
Braddock, Dave	Asst	846-4189		ADEO	PHD	84	N Illinois	8-92
Eduardo, Marcelo	Asst	846-4198		AG	MBA			8-86
Sridharan, K. P.	Asst	846-4196		ACFG	PHD	92	Miss	8-92

Denison University Granville, OH 43023 (614) 587-6245 Judy Thompson
Economics Faculty Department of Economics Fax=587-6348 CC.DENISON.EDU

LaRoe, Ross M.	C-Ac	587-6473	laroe		PHD	82	American	1985
Bartlett, Robin L.	Prof	587-6574	barlett		PHD	74	Mich St	1973
King, Paul G. John Harris Chair	Prof	587-6314	king		PHD	71	Illinois	1967
Lucier, Richard L.	Prof	587-6462	lucier		PHD	72	Claremont	1971
Miller, Timothy I.	Prof	587-6403	millert		PHD	79	S Illinois	1978
Behdad, Sohrab	Assoc	587-6404	behdad		PHD	73	Mich St	1985
Boyd, David W.	Asst	587-6317	boyd		PHD	91	Ohio St	1991
Boyd, Laura A.	Asst	587-6316	boydl		PHD	91	Ohio St	1991
Burczak, Ted A.	Asst	587-6245	burczak		PHD	94	Mass	1995
Pascal, Nina S.	Asst	587-6245	pascal		PHD	79	CUNY	1995
Wells, David R.	Asst	587-6245			PHD	94	USC	1995

University of Denver Denver, CO 80208-0233 (303) 871-2569 Janet Moder
Department of Economics Social Sci, Arts & Hum Fax=871-2605 DU.EDU

Griesemer, James R.	Dean	871-3411	jgriesemer		DPA	88	Colorado	1994
Burford, William E.	C-As	871-2685			PHD		Ohio St	
Ellis, Gene	Assoc	871-2146			PHD	72	Tennessee	1978
Freeman, Katherine	Assoc	871-2151			PHD		Fla St	
Niehoff, Peter	Assoc	871-2152			PHD		Nebraska	
Ho, Peter S. W.	Asst	871-2259			PHD	89	Stanford	1989
Mott, Tracy L.	Asst	871-2569			PHD	82	Stanford	1991
Urquhart, Robert	Asst	871-2258			PHD		New Sch	
Wray, L. Randall	Asst	871-2245			PHD	88	Wash U	

DePaul University Chicago, IL 60604-2287 (312) 362-8781 Sue Schoeben
Department of Economics Col Arts & Sci/Cl Comm Fax=362-5452 DEPAUL.EDU

Mezey, Michael	Dean	362-8629		PolS	PHD			
Patten, Ronald J.	Dean	362-6783		Atg	PHD	63	Alabama	7-89
Oppenheimer, Margaret M.	C-Pr	362-8651			PHD	74	Northwes	
Batavia, Bala	Prof	362-8781			PHD	74	N Car St	1976
Brown, Francis	Emer							
Ciecka, James E.	Prof	362-8781			PHD	70	Purdue	1970
Diamond, James J.	Emer				PHD	62	Northwes	
Ghoshal, Animesh	Prof	362-8008			PHD	74	Michigan	1981
Krautmann, Anthony C.	Prof	362-6176			PHD	85	Iowa	1985
Mark, Adolph E.	Emer				PHD	63	Illinois	
Thornton, Richard M.	Emer				PHD	76	N Illinois	1974
Waters, William	Emer							
Wiltgen, Richard J.	Prof	362-8016			PHD	74	Illinois	1973
Miller, Michael S.	Assoc	362-8477			PHD	80	Pittsburgh	1980
Mondschean, Thomas H.	Assoc	362-5210			PHD	89	Wisconsin	1987
Sander, William III	Assoc	362-5240			PHD	78	Cornell	1989
Berdell, John	Asst	362-8781			PHD		Cambridg	
Bucci, Gabriella A.	Asst	362-6787			PHD	88	J Hopkins	1989
Choi, Jin	Asst	362-8842			PHD		Iowa St	
Dill, Floyd R.	Asst	362-8309			PHD		Cornell	
Donley, Thomas D.	Asst	362-8887			MS	87	Wisconsin	
Epstein, Seth	Asst	362-8112			PHD		Arizona	
Owen, Laura J.	Asst	362-8771			PHD	91	Yale	1990
Hayes, William	Emer							

DePauw University Greencastle, IN 46135-0037 (317)
Dept of Economics & Mgt College of Liberal Arts Fax= DEPAUW

Wachter, Daniel R.	C-Ac	658-4879			PHD	82	Purdue	1979
Catanese, Anthony V.	Prof	658-4884			PHD	72	S Illinois	1979
Field, William Joseph	Prof	658-4886			PHD	80	Michigan	1979
English, Mary P. Associate Dean of Academic Affairs	Assoc	658-4355			PHD	89	So Meth	1988

University of Detroit Mercy Detroit, MI 48219-0900 (313) 993-1238
Department of Economics Col of Liberal Arts Fax=993-1166 UDMERCY

Lowe, William J.	Dean	993-1287		Hist				
Byrne, Donald R.	C-Ac	993-3391			PHD	71	Notre Dm	1966
Shen, Raphael	Prof	993-1148			PHD	75	Mich St	1977
Song, Yoon K.	Prof	993-1095			PHD	69	Illinois	1969
Brorby, Bruce M.	Asst	993-1200			MA	67	Detroit	1971
Mosby, James B.	Asst	993-1096			MA	70	Detroit	1972
Pemberton, Donald K.	Asst	993-1097			PHD	70	Kansas	1969

Dickinson College
Economics Faculty — Carlisle, PA 17013 (717) 245-1381 — Isabel L. Houston
Department of Economics Fax= — DICKINSON.EDU

Name	Rank	Phone	E-mail	Fields	Degree	Yr	School	Year
Koont, Sinan	C-As			CFE	PHD	87	Mass	1986
Barone, Charles A.	Assoc			AO	PHD	78	American	1975
Bergsten, Gordon S.	Assoc	245-1529		NDE	PHD	77	Berkeley	1984
Bellinger, William K.	Asst	245-1358	bellinger_w	JE	PHD	85	Northwes	1981
Erfle, Stephen E.	Asst			LKD	PHD	83	Harvard	1989
Fratantuono, Michael J.	Asst			E	PHD	88	Wash	1988
Ramoo, Ratha	Asst	245-1596		DQI	PHD	92	Ca-SnBarb	1994

Dillard University
Economics Faculty — New Orleans, LA 70122 (504) 286-4699 — Helen Bougere 286-4698
Division of Business Fax=286-4851

Name	Rank	Phone	E-mail	Fields	Degree	Yr	School	Year
Chase, Edgar L. III	C-Pr	286-4697		Atg	JD		Loyola	
Mengistu, Tadessa	Assoc	286-4698			PHD		Indiana	
Osei, Anthony A.	Assoc	286-4698			PHD		Howard	
Fugar, Christian	Asst	286-4699			PHD			
Sheriff, Mohamed A.	Asst	286-4698			PHD		Howard	

Univ of District of Columbia
Dept Atg, Fnce, & Economics — Washington, DC 20008 (202) 282-3723 Sherron Woods/Laverne Harris
C of Professional Stds Fax=282-3706 — UDCVAX.BITNET

Name	Rank	Phone	E-mail	Fields	Degree	Yr	School	Year
Brach, Philip L.	Dean	282-3701			PHD		Catholic	1968
Quigley, Herbert G.	C-Pr	282-3726			DBA	77	Geo Wash	1969
Ezeani, Eboh	Prof	282-3723		O	PHD	76	American	1976
Tannen, Michael B.	Prof	282-3753		JIEA	PHD	74	Brown	1982
Boland, Dennis	Assoc	282-3723		BA	PHD		Illinois	1976
Lara, Vito B.	Assoc				PHD		Howard	
Omar, Hanai	Assoc	282-3750		AH	MS		Maryland	1976
Samhan, Muhammad	Assoc	282-2723		OP	PHD	76	American	1976
Siegmund, Frederick	Assoc	282-3723		LI	PHD		Okla St	1976
Vittal, Mallappa	Asst	282-3723		A	LLB		India	1975

Dowling College
Department of Economics — Oakdale, NY 11769-1999 (516) 244-3155 — Ms. Nancy Brandenstein
Sch of Arts & Sciences Fax=589-6644

Name	Rank	Phone	E-mail	Fields	Degree	Yr	School	Year
Caraway, James E.	Dean	244-3232			EDD		Tennessee	
Raji, Seyed	Prof	244-3118			PHD		NYU	
Sonny, Jacob	Assoc	244-3117			PHD		New Sch	
Greer, Mark	Asst	244-3239			PHD		Michigan	1994

Drake University
Department of Economics — Des Moines, IA 50311-4505 (515) 271-3122 — Nancy A. Smith
College of Arts & Sci Fax=271-3977 — DRAKE

Name	Rank	Phone	E-mail	Fields	Degree	Yr	School	Year
Troyer, Ron University Professor	Dean				PHD		W Michigan	1980
Berry, Dale A.	C-Pr	271-2895	db6831r		PHD	66	Indiana	1962
Hosseinzadeh, Esmail	Prof	271-4026	eh2991r		PHD	87	New Sch	1988
Newkirk, Wayne	Prof	271-3127	wn1431r		PHD	65	LSU	1967
Hewett, Roger S.	Assoc	271-3834	rh7291r		PHD	84	Illinois	1981
Weaver, Janice E.	Assoc	271-2898	jw9021r		PHD	76	Illinois	1983
Boal, William M.	Asst	271-2039			PHD	85	Stanford	1995

Drew University
Department of Economics — Madison, NJ 07940-4037 (201) 408-3434 — Lydia Feldman
College of Liberal Arts Fax=408-3143 — DREW.DREW.EDU

Name	Rank	Phone	E-mail	Fields	Degree	Yr	School	Year
Cucchi, Paolo M.	Dean				PHD	72	Princeton	1984
Curtis, Fred	C-Pr	408-3432		BJO	PHD	83	Mass	1978
Cole, Donald P.	Prof	408-3429		AH	PHD	68	Ohio St	1966
Seneca, Rosalind S.	Prof	408-3433		DL	PHD	71	Penn	1981
Isenberg, Dorene L.	Assoc	408-3435		E	PHD	86	Ca-River	
Smith, Bernard	Assoc	408-3595		HOP	PHD	82	Yale	1986
Colton, Nora Ann	Asst	408-3665		FPT	DPHL	92	Oxford	1994

Drexel University
Economics Department — Philadelphia, PA 19104-2875 (215) 895-2123
College of Business Adm Fax=895-6975 — DUVM.OCS.DREXEL.EDU

Name	Rank	Phone	E-mail	Fields	Degree	Yr	School	Year
Baer, Art	Dean	895-2110			MBA		Columbia	1993
Koziara, Edward C.	H-Pr	895-6994	koziarec		PHD	65		1966
McCain, Roger A. III	Prof	895-2176			PHD	71	LSU	1988
Yan, Chiou-shuang	Prof	895-6972			PHD	66	Purdue	1967
Hammoudeh, Shawka M.	Assoc	895-6673			PHD	80	Kansas	1990
Lester, Bijou	Assoc	895-2146			PHD	81	Penn	1988
Madan, Vibhas	Assoc	895-6970			PHD	89	Mich St	1989
Jeon, Bang Nam	Asst	895-2125			PHD	87	Indiana	1988

Drury College
Economics Faculty — Springfield, MO 65802 (417)
Breech S Bus Adm & Econ Fax=

Name	Rank	Phone	E-mail	Fields	Degree	Yr	School	Year
Strube, W. Curtis	D-Pr	865-8731			PHD	72	Arkansas	1969
Rohlf, William D. Jr.	Prof	865-8731			PHD	72	Kansas St	1972
Mullins, Steven	Assoc				PHD	83	Okla St	1982

Duke University — Durham, NC 27708-0097 (919) 660-1800 — Peggy East 660-1852
Economics Department — College of Arts & Sci Fax=684-8974 — ECON.DUKE.EDU

Name	Rank	Phone	E-mail	Degree	Yr	School	Year
Weintraub, E. Roy	Dean$		erw	PHE	69	Penn	1970
McElroy, Marjorie B.	C-Pr$	660-1840	mcelroy	PHD	69	Northwes	1976
DeMarchi, Neil B.	Prof	660-1815	demarchi	PHD	70	AustralN	1983
Goodwin, Crauford	Prof	684-3936	goodwin				
James D. Duke Professor							
Grabowski, Henry G.	Prof	660-1839	grabow	PHD	67	Princeton	1972
Graham, D. A.	Prof	660-1802	dag	PHD	69	Duke	1969
Havrilesky, Thomas	Prof	600-1824		PHD	66	Illinois	1969
Kelley, Allen C.	Prof	660-1825	kelley	PHD	64	Stanford	1972
James D. Duke Professor							
Moulin, Herve	Prof	660-1816	moulin				
James D. Duke Professor							
Sloan, Frank A.	Prof	660-1820	fsloan	PHD	69	Harvard	1993
Alexander McMahon Professor							
Tauchen, George	Prof	660-1812	get	PHD	78	Minnesota	1977
Tower, Edward	Prof	660-1818	tower	PHD	71	Harvard	1974
Director, Undergraduate Studies							
Treml, Vladimir G.	Prof	660-1841	treml	PHD	63	N Carol	1967
Vernon, John M.	Prof	660-1829	vernon	PHD	66	MIT	1969
Viscusi, W. Kip	Prof	660-1833	viscusi	PHD	76	Harvard	1980
George C. Allen Professor							
Wallace, T. Dudley	Emer	660-1855	wallace				
James D. Duke Professor							
Yohe, William P.	Prof	660-1835	yoke	PHD	59	Michigan	1958
Kimbrough, Kent P.	Assoc	660-1811	kent	PHD	80	Chicago	1980
An, Mark	Asst	660-1808	man	PHD	93	Cornell	1993
Gentry, William M.	Asst	660-1804	gentry	PHD	91	Princeton	1990
Peretto, Pietro	Asst	660-1800	peretto				1994
Yang, Dennis	Asst	660-1821	yang	PHD	93	Chicago	1992

Duquesne University — Pittsburgh, PA 15282-0104 (412) 396-5831 — Cathy Hramika
Economic Sciences Division — School of Bus & Admin Fax=396-4764 — DUQ.EDU

Name	Rank	Phone	Degree	Yr	School	Year
Murrin, Thomas J.	Dean	396-5157	DMS		Duquesne	1991
Bober, Stanley	Prof	396-6263	PHD	62	NYU	1964
Rethwisch, Kurt	Prof	396-6258	PHD	69	Maryland	1967
Bond, Richard E.	Assoc	396-6262	PHD	69	Maryland	1969
Marlin, Matthew R.	Assoc	396-6250	PHD	81	Fla St	1987
Harter, Cynthia L.	Asst	395-5831	ABD		Purdue	1995

East Carolina University — Greenville, NC 27858-4353 (919) 328-6006 — Mrs. Ellen Combs
Department of Economics — College of Arts & Sci Fax=328-6006 — ECUVM1

Name	Rank	Phone	E-mail	Degree	Yr	School	Year
Sparrow, Keats	Dean						
Bays, Carson W.	C-Pr	328-6006	ecbays	PHD	74	Michigan	1982
Baldwin, Marjorie L.	Assoc	328-6383	ecbaldwi	PHD	88	Syracuse	1989
Bishop, John A.	Assoc	328-6756	ecbishop	PHD	87	Alabama	1988
Parker, Randall E.	Assoc	328-6755	ecparker	PHD	86	Kentucky	1986
Whitehead, John C.	Assoc	328-6821	ecwhiteh	PHD	89	Kentucky	1989
Zeager, Lester A.	Assoc	328-6408	eczeager	PHD	87	Pittsburgh	1986
Ghent, Linda	VAsst	328-6751	ecghent	PHD	92	N Car St	1993
Haab, Timothy C.	Asst	328-6006	echaab	PHD	95	Maryland	1995
Huang, Ju-Chin	Asst	328-6742	echuang	PHD	94	N Car St	1993
Ross, Leola	Asst	328-6006	ecross	PHD	94	So Meth	1994
Rothman, Philip	Asst	328-6151	ecrothma	PHD	90	NYU	1992
Schumacher, Edward	Asst	328-6006	ecschuma	PHD	94	Fla St	1994

East Central University — Ada, OK 74820-6899 (405) Ext 274
Dept of Business Admin — School of Business Fax= — ECOK.EDU
phone: 332-8000

Name	Rank	Phone	Field	Degree	Yr	School	Year
Cowan, Mickey W.	Dean$	Ext 649	Atg	ABD		Okla St	9-74
Gaster, Walter D.	C-Pr	Ext 525	Mktg	DBA	82	La Tech	1970
Steger, Eric K.	Prof	Ext 267		PHD	80	La Tech	1970

East Stroudsburg University — E Stroudsburg PA 18301 (717) 424-3251 — Melanie Deuerlein
Department of Economics — Sch of Arts & Sciences Fax=424-3777 — ESU.EDU

Name	Rank	Phone	Field	Degree	Yr	School	Year
Neumann, Bonnie	Dean	424-3494					
Hartman, Harrison G.	C-Pr	424-3251	J	PHD	76	NYU	1964
Bunjun, Seewoonundun	Prof	424-3240	D	PHD	79	Penn St	1979
Christofides, Constantinos A	Prof	424-3329	CRT	PHD	77	Lehigh	1971
Kidman, Peter N.	Prof	424-3830	K	PHD	71	W Virginia	1977
DeCosmo, Michael C.	Assoc	424-3108		MBA	84	Lehigh	1984
Kane, Mamadou	Assoc	424-3279	EFN	MA	72	NYU	1973
Kercsmar, John	Assoc	424-3829	M	PHD	85	Houston	
Nyamwange, Richard	Assoc	424-3404	D	MBA	82	Long Isl	1987
Behr, Todd	Asst	424-3831	EH	MBA	78	Lehigh	1989
Neelakantan, P.	Asst	424-3823	D	PHD	92	SUNY-Buf	1992

East Tennessee State Univ — Johnson City, TN 37614-0686 (615) 929-4202 — Ms. Nancy Symes
Dept of Economics & Finance — College of Business Fax=929-5274 — ETSU.EAST-TENN-ST.EDU

Name	Rank	Phone	Email	Field	Degree	Yr	School	Year
Spritzer, Allan D.	Dean	929-5489	i64sprit	Mgt	PHD	71	Cornell	1981
Smith, Jon L.	C-Ac	929-4202			PHD	82	S Carol	1980
Bartell, H. Robert	Prof	929-4402			PHD	63	Columbia	1989
Director, Center of Banking								
Garrison, Sharon H.	Prof	929-4202			PHD	83	Tx-Arlin	1986
Granger, George L.	Prof	929-4202			PHD	71	Penn	1961
Hippie, F. Steb	Prof	929-4202			PHD	72	So Meth	1982
Alavi, Jafar	Assoc	929-4202			PHD	86	Tennessee	1985
Dotterweich, Douglas P.	Assoc	929-4202			PHD	78	Delaware	1984
Everett, Michael David	Assoc	929-4202			PHD	67	Wash U	1977
Mackara, W. Frederick	Assoc	929-4202			PHD	76	Tx A&M	1975
Mason, W. Joe Jr.	Assoc	929-4202			PHD	87	S Carol	1984
Russo, Daniel M.	Assoc	929-4202			BA	61	Rutgers	1967
Warren, J. Harold	Assoc	929-4202			PHD	69	Okla St	1969
Jennings, Donna	Asst	929-4202			PHD	95	Vanderbilt	1994

East Texas State Univ — Commerce, TX 75429 (903) 886-5681
Dept of Economics & Finance — College of Business Fax=886-5601

Name	Rank	Phone	Email	Field	Degree	Yr	School	Year
Edwards, Wendell E.	Dean$	886-5189		Atg	PHD	72	North Tx	1969
Avard, Stephen L.	C-Ac$			GFDE	PHD		North Tx	
Funderburk, Dale R.	Prof	886-5675		IDEF	PHD	71	Okla St	1968
Kersey, Bruce L.	Prof			DEG	PHD		LSU	
Shwiff, Steven S.	Assoc			CDRO	PHD		Tx A&M	
Carter, Shawn	Asst			DEFC	ABD		Tx A&M	

Eastern Conn State Univ — Willimantic, CT 06226-2295 (203) 465-5239 — Ms. Jean Stencil
Economics Faculty — Department of Economics Fax=456-2231 — ECSU.CT.STATEU.EDU

Name	Rank	Phone	Email	Field	Degree	Yr	School	Year
Horrocks, Robert	Dean	456-5293						
Parzych, Kenneth M.	C-Pr	456-5239	parzych		PHD		Conn	
Lombard, John	Prof				PHD		Conn	
Free, Rhona C.	Assoc	456-2231			PHD	83	Notre Dm	1983
Mann, Prem S.	Assoc	456-5216			PHD	88	UCLA	1986
Pachis, Dimitrios S.	Assoc				PHD		Mass	
Associate Vice President for Academic Affairs								
Roy, Tapan K.	Assoc	456-5502			PHD		Temple	1977
Zak, Gail	Asst				PHD		Tx A&M	

Eastern Illinois Univ — Charleston, IL 61920-3099 (217) 581-2719 — Lois Luallen
Department of Economics — College of Sciences Fax= — UXI.CTS.EIU.EDU

Name	Rank	Phone	Email	Field	Degree	Yr	School	Year
Wall, Lida	Dean	581-3328		Comm	PHD		Ohio St	1995
Karbassioon, Ebrahim	C-Pr	581-5429	karbassi		PHD	81	Nebraska	1980
Corley, Edward M.	Prof	581-2378			PHD	64	Okla St	1967
Lenihan, Patrick M.	Prof	581-6330			PHD	68	Wisconsin	1967
Nordin, Harold D.	Prof	581-6331			PHD	76	Illinois	1967
Sidwell, Richard J.	Prof	581-3812			PHD	72	Utah	1970
Smith, Allen W.	Prof	581-5312			PHD	70	Indiana	1970
Thompson, William F.	Prof	581-6327			PHD	79	Arkansas	1981
Bates, Lawrence W.	Assoc	581-2710			PHD	75	Tx-Austin	1970
Dao, Minh Quang	Assoc	581-6329			PHD	87	Illinois	1987
Fahy, Paul R.	Assoc	581-6332			PHD	76	Conn	1976
Mason, Timothy I.	Assoc	581-6966			PHD	87	Indiana	1989
Moshtagh, Ali R.	Assoc	581-6967			PHD	88	Arkansas	1987
Weber, William V.	Assoc	581-6328			PHD	85	Kansas	1988
Brodsky, Noel	Asst	581-6334			PHD	88	Illinois	1988
Bruehler, James	Asst	581-2719			PHD	93	Illinois	1993
Champlin, Dell	Asst	581-2719			PHD	90	Utah	1995
McPherson, Natalie	Asst	581-2719			PHD	87	Maryland	1994
Weisbrot, Mark	Asst	581-2719			PHD	93	Michigan	1990

Eastern Kentucky University — Richmond, KY 40475-3111 (606) 622-1769 — Mrs. Laura A. Weitkamp
Department of Economics — College of Business Fax=622-2359 — EKU.BITNET

Name	Rank	Phone	Email	Field	Degree	Yr	School	Year
Patrick, Alfred	Dean	622-1409			EDD	65	Tennessee	
O'Connor, J. Francis	C-Pr	622-1769	ecooconnor		PHD	74	Minnesota	1989
Engle, Fred A. Jr.	Prof	622-1118			EDD	66	Kentucky	1959
Karns, James M.	Prof	622-1776			PHD	75	Oklahoma	1975
Morrow, William R.	Prof	622-1773			PHD	68	Tennessee	1968
Sharp, Robert R.	Prof	622-1772			PHD	69	Kentucky	1969
Wright, Virginia B.	Prof	622-1390			PHD	71	Geo Wash	1982
Dickey, Steven W.	Assoc	622-4987			PHD	85	S Illinois	1983
Payne, James E.	Assoc	622-1771			PHD	89	Fla St	1992
Watkins, Thomas G.	Assoc	622-4980			PHD	79	Iowa St	1984
Wuilleumier, Rudolph B.	Asst	622-1118			BS	67	E Kentuc	1971

Eastern Michigan University Ypsilanti, MI 48197 (313) 487-3395 Ms. Deborah Wright
Department of Economics Col of Arts & Science Fax=481-3240 EMUVAX.EMICH.EDU
Internet location: http://www.emich.edu; email @1=emich.edu

Name	Rank	Phone	Email	Field	Degree	Yr	School	Year
Fish, Barry A.	Dean	487-4345	barry.fish@1		PHD	71	Wayne St	1970
Hanna, Raouf S.	H-Pr	487-3395	raouf.hanna@1		PHD	73	Indiana	1977
Chung, Young-Iob	Prof	487-6833	eco_chung		PHD	65	Columbia	1966
Moreland, Kemper W.	Prof	487-0279	eco_moreland		PHD	80	Wisconsin	1980
Pearson, Donald W.	Prof	487-0008	eco_pearson		PHD	70	Tx-Austin	1969
Vogt, Michael G.	Prof	487-0006	eco_vogt		PHD	76	Wisconsin	1978
Woodland, Bill M.	Prof	487-0269	eco_woodland		PHD	81	Purdue	1981
Abdullah, Dewan A.	Assoc	487-0072	eco_abdullah		PHD	84	Kentucky	1988
Edgren, John A.	Assoc	487-3068	eco_edgren		PHD	79	Michigan	1979
Erenburg, Sharon J.	Assoc	487-0385	eco_erenburg		PHD	86	Illinois	1987
Esposto, Alfredo G.	Assoc	487-0004	eco_esposto		PHD	83	Temple	1990
Figart, Deborah M.	Assoc	487-0279	eco_figart		PHD	86	American	1990
Hayworth, Steve	Assoc	487-0009	eco_hayworth		PHD	87	MIT	1977
Thornton, James	Assoc	487-0080	eco_thornton		PHD	91	Oregon	1991
Crary, David B.	Asst	487-0001	eco_crary		PHD	82	Maryland	1980
Multasuo, Eija	Asst	487-0007	eco_multasuo		PHD	89	Purdue	1989

Eastern New Mexico Univ Portales, NM 88130 (505)
Department of Economics College of Business Fax=562-2252 EMAIL.EMU.EDU

Name	Rank	Phone	Email	Field	Degree	Yr	School	Year
Martin, Dolores	Dean	562-2343			PHD	76	Va Tech	1993
Elston, Frank	C	562-2365	elstonf	GK	PHD	79	Virginia	1988

Eastern Oregon State College LaGrange, OR 97850-2899 (503) 962-3816 Theresa Ketchum
Department of Economics School of Adm Studies Fax=962-3428 EOSC.OSSHE.EDU

Name	Rank	Phone	Email	Field	Degree	Yr	School	Year
Larison, Robert	Dean	962-3558		Bus	PHD	95	Oregon	
Workman, William	Assoc	962-3371			PHD	78	Utah St	
Johnson, Colleen	Asst	962-3340			PHD	88	Wash St	

Eastern Washington Univ Cheney, WA 99004-2415 (509) 359-2281 Nancy Millard
Department of Economics Ltrs, Art & Soc Science Fax=359-6732

Name	Rank	Phone	Email	Field	Degree	Yr	School	Year
Yarwood, Edmund	Dean$	359-2287		Lang	PHD		N Carol	
Young, Shik C.	C-Pr	359-2281			PHD		Wash St	1966
Bonsor, Thomas W.	Prof	359-2428			MA	55	Tufts	1958
Bunting, David C.	Prof	359-7947			PHD	72	Oregon	1971
Karier, Thomas M.	Prof	359-6517			PHD		Berkeley	1981
Kiser, Larry L.	Prof	359-2422			PHD	73	Rutgers	1971
Liu, Tsung-Hua	Prof	359-2430			PHD		Toronto	1970
Neils, Allan E.	Prof	359-7044			JD		Gonzaga	1969
Trulove, William T.	Prof	359-2212			PHD		Oregon	1969
Brown, Lisa Jo	Assoc	359-2838			PHD		Colorado	1981
Orr, Douglas V.	Asst	359-2424			PHD	82	Colorado	1991

Edinboro University of PA Edinboro, PA 16444 (814) Ms. Gail Glenn
Dept of Business Adm & Econ Sch of Sci, Mgt & Tech Fax= VAX.EDINBORO.EDU

Name	Rank	Phone	Email	Field	Degree	Yr	School	Year
Mogavero, Michael A.	Dean	732-2400			PHD	79	Conn	1995
Dunn, James R.	C-Pr	732-2407	dunn		PHD	71	SUNY-Bin	
Min, An-Sik	Prof	732-2907			PHD	75	Iowa	1975
Adams, Robert J.	Assoc	732-2895			PHD	71	Penn St	1977
Hannan, Michael J.	Assoc	732-2407			PHD	88	W Virginia	1988
Hannes, Lance E.	Assoc	732-2707			MBA	87	Buffalo	1978
Meehan, James P.	Asst	732-2907			MA	61	Notre Dm	

Elizabethtown College Elizabethtown PA 17022-2298 (717) 361-1270 Ms. Eunice Ginder
Economics Faculty Department of Business Fax=361-1487 ETOWN.EDU
phone: 361-1000

Name	Rank	Phone	Email	Field	Degree	Yr	School	Year
Trostle, Randolph L.	C-Ac	Ext 1270			PHD	83	Lehigh	9-72
Evans, Hugh G. Jr.	Assoc	Ext 1276			MA		Penn St	1968
Hoppie, Maurice R.	Assoc	Ext 1277			PHD		Tennessee	1980
Stone, Richard G.	Assoc	Ext 1284			PHD		Temple	1987

Elmhurst College Elmhurst, IL 60126-3296 (708) 617-3122
Center for Bus & Economics Div of Social Sciences Fax=617-3742

Name	Rank	Phone	Email	Field	Degree	Yr	School	Year
Heiney, Joseph N.	D-Pr	279-4100			PHD	83	Chicago	1977
Coleman Foundation Distinguished Chair in Business								
Thoma, George A. Jr.	Prof	617-3098			PHD	73	N Illinois	1970
Schmitz, Suzanne	Asst	617-3115			PHD		Kentucky	1990
Wan, Siaw-Peng	Asst	617-3112			PHD		Illinois	

Elmira College Elmire, NY 14901 (607) 735-4930 Dawn Haupt
Economics Faculty Department of Economics Fax=735-1758 ELMIRA.EDU

Name	Rank	Phone	Email	Field	Degree	Yr	School	Year
Hoffman, Naphtali	C-Ac	735-1942			PHD	80	Case Wes	1976
Kasper, Victor Jr.	Asst				PHD	83	Rutgers	1990

Elon College — Elon College, NC 27244-2020 (910) 584-2566 — Ms. Janice Walker
Department of Economics — Love School of Business Fax=538-2643 — VAX1.ELON.EDU

Name	Rank	Phone	E-mail	Field	Degree	Yr	School	Since
Behrman, Richard H.	Dean$	584-2566		Mktg	MBA	54	NYU	1987
Barbour, James L.	C-Ac	584-2106	barbour	AB	PHD	87	Kentucky	1990
Tiemann, Thomas K.	Prof	584-2558	tiemann	RC	PHD	75	Vanderbilt	1984
Holt, Richard P. F.	Asst	584-2560	holtri	NJE	PHD	87	Utah	1991
Lilly, Gregory A.	Asst	584-2700	lillyg	CDA	PHD	88	Duke	1990
Redington, Douglas B.	Asst	584-2105			PHD	89	Wyoming	1995

Embry-Riddle Aeronautical U — Daytona Bch, FL 32114-3900 (904) 226-6694
Economics Faculty — Aviation Bus Adm Fax=226-6696 — BART.DB.ERAU.EDU

Name	Rank	Phone	E-mail	Field	Degree	Yr	School	Since
Harraf, Abe	C-Pr	226-6694			PHD	84	Utah St	
Tacker, Thomas L.		226-6701			PHD		N Carol	
Vasigh, Bijan		226-6722			PHD		NYU	

Emory University — Atlanta, GA 30322-2240 (404) 727-6364 — Erin Davis, Susan Lee
Economics Faculty — Department of Economics Fax=727-4639 — EMORY.EDU

Name	Rank	Phone	E-mail	Field	Degree	Yr	School	Since
Bright, David	Dean	727-6062						
Aranson, Peter H.	C-Pr	727-6648		KL	PHD	72	Rochester	1981
Bailey, Martin J.	Prof	727-6650		E	PHD	56	J Hopkins	1989
Benston, George J.	Prof	727-7831			PHD	63	Chicago	9-87
John H. Harland Professor of Finance, Economics, and Accounting								
Kafoglis, Milton Z.	Prof	727-7833	mkafogl	LI	PHD	58	Ohio St	1979
George Woodruff Professor of Economics								
McChesney, Fred	Prof	727-5791			PHD	82	Virginia	1983
Muth, Richard F.	Prof	727-0328		DR	PHD	58	Chicago	1983
Fuller E. Callaway Professor of Economics								
Rubin, Paul	Prof	727-6365	prubin	K	PHD	70	Purdue	1991
Schaffer, Beverly K.	Prof	727-6361		K	PHD	67	Duke	1965
Carlson, Leonard	Assoc	727-6375	econlac	DJN	PHD	77	Stanford	1975
Chirinko, Robert	Assoc	727-6645	rchirin	EG	PHD	82	Northwes	1994
Curran, Christopher	Assoc	727-6355	econcc	CDK	PHD	72	Purdue	1970
Carpenter, Robert	Asst	727-7834	econrc	EL	PHD	92	Wash U	1992
Dezhbakhsh, Hashem	Asst	727-4679		CG	PHD	89	Ohio St	1992
Levy, Daniel	Asst	727-2941	econdl	EC	PHD	90	Ca-Irvine	1992
Schrag, Joel	Asst	727-6363	jschrag	DKL	PHD	93	Berkeley	1993
Somanathan, E.	Asst	727-6387			ABD		Harvard	1995

Emory and Henry College — Emory, VA 24327 (540) 944-4121
Economics Faculty — Dept of Econ & Business Fax=944-4438

Name	Rank	Phone	E-mail	Field	Degree	Yr	School	Since
Love, Barry A.	C-Ac	944-4121			PHD		Virginia	1984
Holbert L. Harris Professorship in Free Enterprise								
Frost, Maria J.	VAsst	944-6194			PHD		London	
Wimmer, Bradley	Asst	944-4121			PHD	92	Kentucky	1992

Emporia State University — Emporia, KS 66801-5087 (316) 341-5347 — Ginger Tabares
Div Mgmt, Mktg, Fin & Econ — School of Business Fax=341-5418

Name	Rank	Phone	E-mail	Field	Degree	Yr	School	Since
Hashmi, Sajjad A.	Dean	341-5274			PHD	66	Penn	8-83
Jones Distinguished Professor								
Titus, Varkey K.	C-Ac	341-5347			PHD	80	Wash St	8-79
Pettengill, Glenn N.	Assoc	341-5389			PHD		Arkansas	1989
Catlett, Robert B.	Asst	341-5678			MA	75	Nebraska	1976
Janssen, Arthur J.	Asst	341-5401			MA		Missouri	1976

University of Evansville — Evansville, IN 47722 (812) 479-2851 — Anna Pitchers
Department of Economics — School of Business Adm Fax=479-2872 — EVANSVILLE.EDU

Name	Rank	Phone	E-mail	Field	Degree	Yr	School	Since
Mullins, Terry W.	Dean	479-2851	mullins	Mgt	PHD	78	Houston	1993
Tsai, Mau-Sung	Prof	479-2870	mt4		PHD	66	S Illinois	1964
Zimmer, Michael A.	Prof	479-2864	mz3		PHD		Tennessee	1976
Blalock, M. Gale	Assoc	479-2868	gb3		PHD		Okla St	1977

Evergreen State College — Olympia, WA 98505 (360) Ext 6513
Economics Faculty — Pol Economy & Soc Chg Fax=
Did Not Respond--Information Taken from College Catalog; phone 866-6000

Name	Rank	Phone	E-mail	Field	Degree	Yr	School	Since
Hahn, Jeanne	C			PolS	ABD	68	Chicago	1972
Bohmer, Peter G.		866-6000			PHD	85	Mass	1987
Bowerman, Priscilla V.		866-6000			MPHI	71	Yale	1973
Academic Dean								
Bruner, Bill					BA	67	W Wash	1981
Lidman, Russell M.					PHD	72	Wisconsin	1974
Nasser, Alan								
Nisbet, Charles T.					PHD	67	Oregon	1971
Weeks, Gregory C.		866-6000			PHD	78	Wash St	1981
Wommeldorf, Thomas					PHD	89	American	1989

Fairfield Universiy — Fairfield, CT 06430-7524 (203) Ext 2866 — Sally Williams
Department of Economics — Col of Arts & Sciences Fax=254-4119 — FAIRI.FAIRFIELD.EDU
phone: 254-4000

Grossman, Orin L.	Dean	254-4000	olgrossman	Musi	PHD		Yale	1993
Deak, Edward J.	C-Pr	254-4000	deak	LRK	PHD		Conn	1970
Walters, Joan G.	Prof	254-4000	walters	EF	PHD		Radcliff	1963
Buss, James A.	Assoc	254-4000	jabuss	EOP	PHD		Conn	1975
Earnhart, Dietrich	Assoc	254-4000	earnhart	QK	PHD	95	Wisconsin	1995
Lane, Philip J.	Assoc	254-4000	lane	EGR	PHD	83	Tufts	1981
LeClair, Mark S.	Assoc	254-4000	mleclair	FGC	PHD	87	Rutgers	1988
Miner, Laurence A.	Assoc	254-4000	miners	CIJA	PHD	79	N Carol	1981
Nantz, Kathryn A.	Assoc	254-4000	nantz	JDPA	PHD	87	Purdue	1986
Kelly, Robert A.	Asst	254-4000	rakelly	HKC	PHD		Geotown	1978
Peterson, G. Paul	VAsst	254-4000	gppeterson	NB	PHD		Colo St	1992

Fairleigh Dickinson Univ — Madison, NJ 07940 (201) 539-8830 — Doris Owen
Dept of Social Sci & Econ — Becton C of Arts & Sci Fax=
Did Not Respond--1994-95 Listing

Gora, JoAnn M.	Dean			Soci	PHD		Rutgers	
Bogan, Elizabeth C.	Prof	593-8830			PHD	71	Columbia	1971
Green, Kenneth R.	Prof			PolS	PHD		Mich St	
Lee, Eric Y.	Prof				PHD	73	Columbia	

Fairleigh Dickinson Univ — Teaneck, NJ 07666-1914 (201) 692-7215 — Mrs. Eileen Kerrigan
Dept Atg, Tax, Law, Econ, Fn — Silbermann Col of Bus Fax=

Angkatavanich, Virote	C-Pr	692-7215			PHD	67	New Sch	1963
Cassimatis, Peter J.	Prof	692-7294			PHD	67	New Sch	1964
Djimopoulos, Evangelos	Prof	692-7292			PHD	69	Columbia	
Toporovsky, Rinaldo	Prof	692-7296			PHD	72	Columbia	1969
Kessler, Adam	Assoc	692-7214			PHD		NYU	
Oseghale, Braimoh	Assoc	692-7267			PHD	89	Temple	1994
Kiernan, Joseph J.	Asst	692-7298			PHD		Fordham	
Kjetsaa, Richard W.	Asst	692-7295			PHD		Fordham	
Strait, Roger H.	Asst	692-2292			STB		Harvard	

Fairmont State College — Fairmont, WV 26554 (304) 367-4261 — Betty Cinalli
Department of Economics — Div of Business & Econ Fax=366-4870

Schaupp, Rebecca	C-Pr				EDD		W Virginia	
Hoyer-Swanson, Judith Y.	Assoc				MS		Va Tech	1973
Khalil, Mohamad	Assoc				PHD		W Virginia	
Laughlin, William	Assoc				MA		Cincinnati	
Potter, William Economics Coordinator	Assoc				MA		Memphis	

Fayetteville State Univ — Fayetteville, NC 28301-4298 (910) 486-1617 — Mrs. Judy Fish
Dept of Economics & Finance — Sch of Business & Econ Fax=486-1033 — HUGO.FSUFAY.EDU

Davis, Charles	Dean	486-1267	prcdavis	Mktg	PHD	81	Tennessee	1993
Nijhawan, Inder P.	Prof	486-1617			PHD		N Carol	
Okpala, Amon O.	Assoc	486-1594			PHD	84	LSU	1984
Roayaei, Abbas J.	Assoc	486-1592			PHD	84	Fla St	
Hasan, Tanwee	Asst	486-1985			PHD	93	Houston	
Jonsson, Petur	Asst	486-1984			PHD	86	Penn St	

Ferris State University — Big Rapids, MI 49307-2284 (616) 592-2735 — Barb Larie
Department of Economics — Col of Arts & Sciences Fax= — MUSIC.FERRIS.EDU

Hammersmith, Sue K.	Dean	592-3667			PHD		Indiana	1987
Thorp, John	H-Pr	592-2735	jthorp	Anth	PHD	78	Chicago	1989
Moffett, Russell E.	Prof	592-2765	rmoffett		PHD		Calif	1965
Teferra, Daniel	Prof	592-2767	dteferra		PHD	79	Wisconsin	1980
Afifi, Ashraf S.	Assoc	592-2766	aafifi		PHD	83	Kansas	1980
Ferdowsi, Abdollah	Assoc	592-2738	aferdowski		PHD	82	Mich St	1984
Olson, Dennis D.	Asst	592-2765	dolson		MA		Michigan	1979

University of Findlay — Findlay, OH 45840-3695 (419) 424-4539 — Ms. Kathy Bradford
Economics Faculty — Col Professional Stdys Fax=424-4822 — LUCY.FINDLAY.EDU

Gupta, Shiv K.	D-Pr	424-4548		AJ	DBA		London	1983
Gamba, Maria V.	Asst	424-4718		AD	MS		Wright St	1988
Tompkins, Daniel L.	Asst	424-5307	tompkins	G	PHD		Kentucky	1994

Fisk University — Nashville, TN 37208-3051 (615) 329-8570 — Mrs. Eula Black
Economics Faculty — Div of Business Admin Fax=329-8758

Smith, Solomon S.	D-Pr	329-8573		EGM	PHD	82	S Illinois	1988
Ponder, Henry President of the University/ Eratus Milo Cravath Professor of Economics	Prof	329-8555		Q	PHD	63	Ohio St	1984
Cambronero, Alfredo	Asst	329-8698		DOE	PHD	92	Vanderbilt	1992

Fitchburg State College	Fitchburg, MA	01420-2697	(508) 665-3397					
Economics Faculty	Department of Economics	Fax=665-3693						
Miccichi, Pasquale	C-Pr	665-3429		Hst	PHD		Boston U	1969
Murphy, Caroline	Prof	665-3253			PHD		Clark	1971
Wiegersma, Nancy A.	Prof	665-3088			PHD	76	Maryland	1979
Turk, Michael	Assoc	665-3731			PHD		Harvard	1982
Lwamugira, Pirudas L.	Asst	665-3281			PHD	90	Temple	1991
McKeon, John	Asst	665-3091			MS		S Illinois	1979

University of Florida	Gainesville, FL	32611	(904) 392-0151				Dian Studstill	
Department of Economics	College of Business Adm	Fax=392-7860					DALE.CBA.UFL.EDU	
Kraft, John L.	Dean	392-2397	kraftj		PHD	71	Pittsburgh	1990
Kenny, Lawrence W.	C-Pr	392-0151	kenny	DHJ	PHD	77	Chicago	1975
Adams, James D.	Prof	392-0124	adams	OJ	PHD	76	Chicago	1979
Berg, Sanford V.	Prof	392-0132	berg	T	PHD	70	Yale	1971
Exec Dir Public Utility Research Ctr;Public Utilities & Distinguished Serv Pr								
Blair, Roger Duncan	Prof	392-0179	rblair	KT	PHD	68	Mich St	1970
Huber Hurst Professor of Business and Legal Studies								
Denslow, David A. Jr.	Prof	392-0171	denslow	EH	PHD	74	Yale	1970
Distinguished Service Professor								
Dinopoulos, Elias	Prof	392-8150	dinopoe	FO	PHD	85	Columbia	1988
Lanzillotti, Robert F.	Prof	392-2397	lanz	T	PHD	53	Berkeley	1969
Dir Public Pol Resr Center; American Econ Int Free Enterprise Eminent Scholar								
Lewis, Tracy R.	Prof	392-7489		TDQ	PHD	75	Ca-SnDgo	1991
James Walter Eminent Scholar in Economics								
Romano, Richard E.	Prof	392-4812	romano	THOD	PHD	82	Pittsburgh	1982
Rush, Mark	Prof	392-0318	rush	EF	PHD	82	Rochester	1982
Sappington, David A.	Prof	392-3904	sapping	TD	PHD	80	Princeton	1989
Lanzillotti-McKethan Eminent Scholar								
Slutsky, Steven M.	Prof	392-8106	slutsky	DH	PHD	75	Yale	1984
Smith, Stanley K.	Prof	392-0171	stans	J	PHD	76	Michigan	1976
Director, Bureau of Economic and Business Research								
Vernon, Jack R.	Prof	392-6612	vernon	E	PHD	61	Northwes	1967
West, Carol Taylor	Prof		carolw	RQC	PHD	74	Michigan	1989
Director, Forcasting Program Bureau of Economics and Business Research								
Woodruff, William D.	Prof	392-0382	woodruff	N	PHD	52	Nottnghm	1966
Zabel, Edward	Prof	392-0147		D	PHD	56	Princeton	1981
Matherly Professor								
Bomberger, William A.	Assoc	392-0135	billb		PHD	73	Brown	1977
Goddard, Frederick O.	Assoc	392-0972	fgoddard		PHD	67	Duke	1966
Hamilton, Johnathan H.	Assoc	392-2999	hamilton	HRD	PHD	82	MIT	1984
Horowitz, Ann R.	Assoc	392-0198	horowitz		PHD	66	Indiana	1972
Toda, Yasushi	Assoc	392-0112	toda	RP	PHD	69	Harvard	1974
Waldo, Douglas G.	Assoc	392-1370	waldo	EFO	PHD	80	N Carol	1981
Ai, Chunrong	Asst	392-7859	aic	CT	PHD	90	MIT	1994
Costello, Donna M.	Asst	392-0383	dcos	EF	PHD	90	Rochester	1990
Werner, Megan	Asst	392-0475	wernermj	CHQ	PHD	94	Ca-SnDgo	1994
Xu, Bin	Asst			FO	PHD	95	Columbia	1995

Florida A&M University	Tallahassee, FL	32307	(904) 599-3138				Mrs. Pamela H. Leonard	
Department of Economics	College of Arts & Scien	Fax=561-2290						
Perry, Aubrey	Dean	599-3430		Psyc				
Taylor, Addis C.	C-Ac	599-3138		JM	PHD	83	Fla St	1976
Burggraf, Shirley	Prof	599-3126		CE	PHD	68	Case Wes	1968
Daniels, Rudolph	Prof	561-2052		DJQ	PHD	80	Fla St	1977
Oguledo, Victor I.	Assoc	561-2053		FL	PHD	89	Nebraska	1990
Auzenne, George R.	Lect	561-2057		LM	MS	63	Boston	1976

Florida Atlantic Univ	Boca Raton, FL	33431-0991	(407) 367-3220				Maryjane Noyes	
Department of Economics	Col of Social Sciences	Fax=367-2850					FAUVAX	
Marlow, Michael L.	C-Pr	367-3222			PHD	78	Va Tech	1995
Hung, Chao-shun	Prof	367-3223			PHD	82	Tx A&M	1982
Stronge, William B.	Prof	367-2833	strongew		PHD	71	Iowa St	1971
Bosshardt, William D.	Assoc			F	PHD	91	Purdue	1995
Director of Center for Economic Education								
Manage, Neela D.	Assoc	367-3226	manage		PHD	81	Geo Wash	1981
Yuhn, Ky-Hyan	Assoc	367-3224						

Florida Institute of Tech	Melbourne, FL	32901	(407) Ext 7167				S. Farinella	
Dept of Economics	School of Business	Fax=Ext 8896					WINNIE.FIT.EDU	
phone: 768-8000								
Hollingsworth, A. Thomas	Dean	Ext 7327	hollins	Mgt	PHD	69	Mich St	
Callahan, J. P.	C-Ac	Ext 7167	callahan		EDD		Cen Fla	
Shnaider, E.	Asst	Ext 8088	shnaider		PHD		Fla St	

Florida International Univ — Miami, FL 33199 (305) 348-2316 — Emily Carreras
Department of Economics — College of Arts & Sci Fax=348-3605 — FIU.EDU

Herriott, Arthur	Dean	348-2866	Chem	PHD		Florida	1993
Liossatos, Panagis S.	C-Pr	348-2316	CODR	PHD	68	Penn	1981
Carvajal, Manuel J.	Prof	348-3290	JITQ	PHD	74	Florida	1981
De Alonso, Irma	Prof	348-2318	OCH	PHD		York-Eng	1981
Jorge, Antonio	Prof	348-2072	BPOA	PHD		Villanova	
Moncarz, Raul	Prof	348-2592	EOF	PHD	69	Fla St	1972
Salazar-Carrillo, Jorge	Prof	348-3283	OFA	PHD	67	Berkeley	
Director, Center of Economic Research & Education							
Wilkins, Mira	Prof	348-3352	NF	PHD	57	Cambridge	1974
Anbarci, Nejat M.	Assoc	348-2735	DC	PHD	88	Iowa	1995
Karayaicin, Ali Cem	Assoc	348-3285	EF	PHD	89	Columbia	1989
Lipner, Kenneth	Assoc		RJA	PHD		Rutgers	1981
Willumsen, Maria Jose	Assoc	348-2316	RO	PHD	84	Cornell	1984
Arvin-Rad, Hassan	Asst	348-3287	CD	PHD	90	Penn	1989
Butler, Alison	Asst	348-2682	FEO	PHD	89	Oregon	1995
Goodspeed, Timothy J.	Asst		HF	PHD	86	Maryland	1990
Kelley, Bruce R.	Asst	348-3286	OF	PHD	90	Mass	1990
Magnani, Elisabetta	Asst	348-2316	JEFC	ABD		Yale	1995
Gummerson, A.	Lect	348-2381	AEF	PHD	71	Wisconsin	1989

Florida Southern College — Lakeland, FL 33801-5698 (813)
Dept of Bus & Economics — Division of Bus Adm Fax=680-4126

Hopkins, Duane L.	C-As	680-4285		MBA		Harvard	1982
Brown, Carl C.	Prof	680-4290		PHD		Okla St	1980
William F. Chatlos Professorship in Business & Economics							
Buccino, Joan G.	Prof	680-4277		PHD	90	S Fla	1980
Dorotha Tanner Chair in Ethics in Business & Economics							
Lebrenz, Eugene R.	VProf	680-4274		EDD		N Illinois	1987
Bias, Peter V.	Asst	680-4282	Bus	PHD	89	Cincinnati	1988

Florida State University — Tallahassee, FL 32306-2045 (904) 644-5001 — Fran Loeb 644-7089
Department of Economics — College of Soc Sciences Fax=644-4535 — COSS.FSU.EDU
email @1=garnet.acns.fsu.edu

Cnudde, Charles F.	Dean	644-5470		PolS	PHD	67	N Carol	1987
Laird, William E.	C-Pr	644-4557	wlaird		PHD	62	Virginia	1960
Bell, Frederick W.	Prof	644-7092			PHD	64	Wayne St	
Benson, Bruce L.	Prof	644-7094	bbenson		PHD	78	Tx A&M	1987
Canterbery, E. Ray	Prof	644-7209	canterbery		PHD	66	Wash U	1970
Cobbe, James H.	Prof	644-7091	jcobbe		PHD	77	Yale	1976
Director of Graduate Studies								
Downing, Paul B.	Prof	644-7648			PHD	67	Wisconsin	1980
Gapinski, James H.	Prof	644-7081			PHD	71	SUNY-Buf	1979
Gwartney, James D.	Prof	644-7645	ljgwartne		PHD	69	U Wash	1968
Hirsch, Barry T.	Prof	644-7207	bhirsch		PHD	77	Virginia	1990
Research Associate, Pepper Institute on Aging & Public Policy								
Holcombe, Randall G.	Prof	644-7095	holcomb		PHD	76	Va Tech	1988
Macesich, George	Prof	644-5465			PHD	58	Chicago	1959
Newell, Barbara W.	Prof	644-7096			PHD	58	Wisconsin	1987
Regents' Professor; email bnewell@mailer.fsu.edu								
Rasmussen, David W.	Prof	644-7641			PHD	69	Wash U	1968
Research Associate, Policy Sciences Program								
Rockwood, Charles E.	Prof	644-7088			PHD	63	Indiana	1960
Serow, William J.	Prof	644-1762	wserow		PHD	72	Duke	1981
Director, Center for Study of Population								
Sliger, Bernard F.	Prof	644-5001			PHD	55	Mich St	1972
Sorensen, Phillip E.	Prof	644-7093			PHD	66	Berkeley	1971
Beaumont, Paul M.	Assoc	644-5792			PHD	84	Penn	1988
Fournier, Gary M.	Assoc	644-7080	gfournie		PHD	81	Virginia	1980
Macpherson, David A.	Assoc	644-3586	dmacpher		PHD	87	Penn St	1992
Research Associate, Pepper Institute on Aging & Public Policy								
Marquis, Milton H.	Assoc	644-7204			PHD	85	Indiana	1986
McCaleb, Thomas S.	Assoc	644-7079			PHD	75	N Carol	1980
Associate Vice President, Academic Affairs								
Zuehlke, Thomas W.	Assoc	644-7208			PHD	83	Florida	1983
Norrbin, Stefan C.	Asst	644-7206	snorrbin@1		PHD	86	Ariz St	1990
Prasad, Kislaya	Asst	644-7083			PHD	88	Syracuse	1988
Sass, Tim R.	Asst	644-7087	tsass		PHD	84	U Wash	1990
Schmertmann, Carl P.	Asst	644-7100	schmertmann		PHD	88	Berkeley	1990

Fordham University — New York, NY 10458 (718) 817-4048 — Angela Bates
Department of Economics — Col of Arts & Sciences Fax=817-4925 — LARS.FORDHAM.EDU

Himmelberg, Robert	Dean		PHD			
Salvatore, Dominick	C-Pr	817-4048	PHD	71	CUNY	1970
Cammarosano, Joseph R.	Prof	817-4057	PHD	56	Fordham	1955
Dowling, Edward T.	Prof	817-4062	PHD	73	Cornell	1973

Heilbrun, James	Prof	817-4053			PHD	64	Columbia	1970
Vinod, Hrishinesh D.	Prof	817-4065			PHD	65	Harvard	1982
Basu, Parantap	Assoc	817-4061			PHD	85	Ca-SnBarb	1988
Brent, Robert J.	Assoc	817-4058			PHD	76	Manchest	1980
Diulio, Eugene A.	Assoc	817-4055			PHD	66	Columbia	1963
Assistant Chair, Undergraduate Education								
Leighton, Linda S.	Assoc	817-4054			PHD	78	Columbia	1979
Champ, Bruce	Asst	817-4056			PHD	90	Minnesota	1994
Geddes, Raymond R.	Asst	817-4049			PHD	91	Chicago	1991
Horning, Bruce C.	Asst	817-4066			PHD	88	Minnesota	1993
Kwiatkowski, Denis E.	Asst	817-4060			PHD	90	Mich St	1992
McLeod, Darryl L.	Asst	817-4064			PHD	82	Berkeley	1984
Redding, Lee S.	Asst	817-4061			ABD		Princeton	1993
Schwalbenberg, Henry M.	Asst	817-4059			PHD	88	Columbia	1988
Assistant Chair, Graduate Education								

Fort Hays State University	Hays, KS		67601-4099 (913) 628-5805				Linda Leiker	
Dept of Economics & Finance	College of Business		Fax=628-5398				FHSUVM.FHSU.EDU	
McCullick, Jack J.	Dean	628-5339			PHD	70	Kansas St	1966
Gamble, Ralph C. Jr.	C-Pr	628-5805	ecrg	AEG	PHD	89	Okla St	1984
Parker, Carl D.	Prof	628-5805		DIJM	PHD	71	Okla St	1976
Director, Employee Relations								
Rickman, Bill D.	Prof	628-5318		DEJ	PHD	82	Okla St	1972
Rupp, Daniel G.	Prof	628-4418		AFH	PHD	81	Kansas St	1968
Gilson, Preston	Asst	628-4107			PHD	93	St Louis	1988
Haag, Jerry	Asst			G	PHD	95	Tx-Austin	1995
Johansen, Thomas C.	Asst	628-5867			PHD	90	Okla St	1989
Lee, Jimmy	Asst	628-5868		EK	PHD	91	Penn St	1989

Fort Lewis College	Durango, CO		81301-3999 (970) 247-7294				Iris Mobley	
Department of Economics	School of Business Adm		Fax=247-7623				FLC	
Cave, John E. Jr.	Dean	247-7294		BusA	PHD	67	Minnesota	1990
Atencio, Leonard D.	Prof	247-7589			PHD	69	Kansas St	1968
Clay, James P.	Prof	247-7591			PHD	74	Kansas St	1982
Lynch, Vernon E. Jr.	Prof	247-7404			PHD	76	Arizona	1972
Lehman, Dale E.	Assoc	247-7494	lehmanm		PHD	81	Rochester	1983
Hai, Wen	Asst	247-7494			PHD	91	Ca-Davis	1992

Fort Valley State College	Fort Valley, GA		31030 (912) 825-6270				Khaleelah Muhammad	
Dept of Business Adm & Econ	Sch of Arts & Sciences		Fax=825-6319					
Crumbly, Isaac	Dean	825-6454		Biol	PHD			
Wilson, Richard	H-Pr	825-6270			PHD	82	Missouri	9-91
Yasin, Jehad	Assoc	825-6270						
Hatchett, Paul	Asst	825-6270			JD	93	Widener	9-92

Framingham State College	Framingham, MA		01701 (508) 626-4850				Marie Dinallo	
Economics Faculty	Dept of Econ & Bus Adm		Fax=626-4040					
Meaney, Martha M.	C-As	626-4889			MA		Boston C	
Anderson, Thomas	Prof	626-4857			PHD			
Barr, Joseph E.	Prof	626-4852			PHD		Boston C	
Krier, Donald F.	Prof	626-4884			PHD	69	Boston C	1973
Dunne, Maureen E.	Assoc	626-4861			MBA		Detroit	
McKinney, Marie M.	Assoc	626-4853			PHD	83	SUNY-Bin	1985
Wallace, Robert	Assoc	626-4888			PHD		Northwes	
White, Charles	Assoc	626-4892			PHD		Chicago	
Devine, Robert	Asst	626-4882			MA		Northeas	
Doyle-Burke, Christine	Asst	626-4886			MA		Boston C	
Farina, Louis	Asst	626-4885			MBA		Babson	
MacRitchie, Donald R.	Asst	626-4881			MA	85	Boston C	1987
Rogers, Mary T.	Asst	626-4858			PHD		Mass	
Ryan, Peter C.	Asst	626-4844			PHD		Mass	
Soriano, Beverly	Asst	626-4856			MS		Bentley	
Speros, Jonathan A.	Asst	626-4855						

Francis Marion University	Florence, SC		29501-0547 (803) 661-1419				Mary Greene	
Economics Faculty	School of Business		Fax=661-1165					
Fenton, James W. Jr.	Dean$	661-1422		Mgt	PHD	81	Iowa	1-89
Forrest Williams Professor of Entrepreneurship & Human								
Rinehart, James R.	Prof				PHD	62	Virginia	
Kyer, Ben L.	Assoc				PHD	84	W Virginia	
O'Brien, M. Barry	Assoc				PHD		S Carol	
Pompe, Jeffrey	Asst				PHD	90	Fla St	

Franklin University Columbus, OH 43215-5399 (614) 341-6330
Div of Atg, Econ & Fnce — Col of Business & Tech Fax=228-8478 — FRANKLIN.EDU

Name	Rank	Phone	Email	Field	Degree	Yr	School	Year
Schiavo, Richard G.	Dean	341-6316			PHD		Brandeis	1976
Newton, James E.	C	341-6330			MS		Wright St	
Clendenon, Irel D.	Prof	341-6314			MBA	83	Xavier	1970
Assistant Dean								
Moore, Margaret D.		341-6324			PHD		Ohio St	

Franklin and Marshall Coll Lancaster, PA 17604-3003 (717) 291-3916 Jill Simeral
Economics Faculty — Department of Economics Fax=291-3969 — ACAD.FANDM.EDU

Name	Rank	Phone	Email	Field	Degree	Yr	School	Year
Callari, Antonino	C-Pr	291-3947	a_callari		PHD	81	Mass	1979
Caniglia, Alan S.	Prof	291-3945	a_caniglia		PHD	83	Virginia	1982
Whitesell, William E.	Prof	291-3938	w_whitesell		PHD	63	Tx-Austin	1965
Henry P. & Mary B. Stager Professor of Economics								
Flaherty, Sean	Assoc	291-3940	s_flaherty	J	PHD	81	Berkeley	1980
Jaggi, Arvind	Asst	291-3920	a_jaggi		PHD	91	Illinois	1989
Rossetti, Jane	Asst	291-3906	j_rossetti		PHD	90	Duke	1992
Zein-Elabdin, Eiman	Asst	291-3916	e_zein-elabdin		PHD	93	Tennessee	1995
Charusheela, S.	Inst	291-3916	s_charusheela		ABD		Mass	1995

Freed Hardeman University Henderson, TN 38340-2399 (901) 989-6091 Mrs. Estelle Maxwell
Economics Faculty — School of Business Fax=989-6065

Name	Rank	Phone	Email	Field	Degree	Yr	School	Year
Wilson, Dwayne H.	Dean	989-6091		Mgt	PHD	91	Miss	8-75
Director of the Free Enterprise Center								
Anderson, Edwin L.	Asst	989-6098		CDEQ	PHD	90	Tennessee	8-91
Brooks, Rickey A.	Inst	989-6054		DEF	MBA	91	Miss	8-92

Frostburg State University Frostburg, MD 21532-1099 (301) 687-4386 Ms. Yvonne R. Gillespie
Department of Economics — School of Business Fax=687-4760

Name	Rank	Phone	Email	Field	Degree	Yr	School	Year
Wilkinson, Steven P.	Dean	687-4089			PHD	77	S Illinois	8-87
Dalton, Margaret M.	C-As	687-4386			PHD		W Virginia	
Burton, Robert C.	Prof	687-4390			PHD		Virginia	
Mizak, Daniel A.	Assoc	687-1096			PHD	84	Pittsburgh	1977
Neral, John A.	Assoc	687-4265			PHD	89	Pittsburgh	1986
McLellan, Jacquelynne W.	Asst	687-4394			PHD	93	Wayne St	1994
Rossi, Armond A.	Asst	687-4407			PHD		W Virginia	
Stair, Anthony G.	Asst	687-4788			PHD		W Virginia	

Furman University Greenville, SC 29613 (803) 294-2132 Brenda Chandler
Economics Faculty — Dept of Econ & Bus Adm Fax= — FRNMVAX1

Name	Rank	Phone	Email	Field	Degree	Yr	School	Year
Roe, R. David	C-Pr	294-3320			PHD	78	Duke	1977
Horney, Mary Jean	Prof	294-3315			PHD	77	Duke	1979
Frederick W. Symmes Professor of Economics								
Stanford, Richard A.	Prof	294-3322			PHD	71	Georgia	1968
David C Garrett Jr. Professor of Economics								
Gorman, Mary Jane	Assoc	294-3321			PHD	80	N Carol	1982
Khandke, Kailash	Asst				PHD	93	Ca-Davis	1995
Peterson, Kenneth D.	Asst	294-3043			PHD	91	SUNY	1990

Gallaudet University Washington DC 20002-3695 (202) 651-5040
Dept of Economics & Finance — School of Management Fax=651-5516 — GALLAUDET.GALLUA.EDU

Name	Rank	Phone	Email	Field	Degree	Yr	School	Year
Speegle, James R.	Dean	651-5312			PHD		Syracuse	1987
Chaikind, Stephen B.	C-Pr	651-5040			PHD	78	CUNY	1989

Gannon University Erie, PA 16541-001 (814) 871-7585
Dept of Economics & Finance — C of Bus, Educ, & Human Fax=871-7210 — CLUSTER.GANNON.EDU

Name	Rank	Phone	Email	Field	Degree	Yr	School	Year
Bennett, Charles A.	C-Ac	871-7585	bennett	A	MA	68	Fordham	1968
Director, Center for Economic Education								
Aburachis, Abdelrahman E.	Prof	871-7584		G	PHD	72	Pittsburgh	
Brooker, Robert F.	Assoc	871-7586		C	PHD	85	N Car St	1982
Mahan, Gary P.	Assoc	871-7588			PHD	78	N Car St	1977
Susa, Robert	Assoc				MA		Catholic	
Director, Honors Program								
Jay, Nancy	Asst				PHD			
Pryce, Priscilla	Asst				MBA		Columbia	
Wallace, Robert	Asst				PHD			
Wolfe, Mike	Lect				MBA		Gannon	

Gardner-Webb University Boiling Spr, NC 28017 (704)
Economics Faculty — Broyhill Sch of Mgt Fax=

Name	Rank	Phone	Email	Field	Degree	Yr	School	Year
Griggs, F. Keith	C-Pr	434-2361		BAdm	EDD	87	Va Tech	1965
Bottoms, I. Glenn	Prof				PHD		Geo St	1983
Negbenebor, Anthony I.	Assoc				PHD		Miss St	1989

GMI Engineering & Mgt Inst — Flint, MI 48504-4898 (810)
Economics Faculty — Management Department Fax=

Name	Rank	Phone	Email	Field	Degree	Yr	School	Since
Kangas, J. Eugene	H-Pr	762-7959		Mgt	PHD	65	Cincinnati	1990
Ioannatos, Petros	Asst				PHD	89	Wayne St	
Wing, Martin M.	Asst				PHD	89	Wayne St	

Geneva College — Beaver Falls, PA 15010-3599 (412) 847-6615 — B. Dawson
Economics Faculty — Dept of Bus, Atg & Mgt Fax=847-6696

Name	Rank	Phone	Email	Field	Degree	Yr	School	Since
Nutter, J. Randall	C-Pr	847-6613		Mgt	DSC	91	Nova	1992
Thomas, Mark	Asst	847-6615		ABN	ABD	95	Mich St	8-94

George Mason University — Fairfax, VA 22030-4444 (703) 993-1130
Department of Economics — College of Arts & Sci Fax=993-1133 — GMUVAX

Name	Rank	Phone	Email	Field	Degree	Yr	School	Since
Potter, David L.	Dean	993-8715						
Williams, Walter E.	C-Pr	993-1148			PHD	72	UCLA	1981
John M. Olin Distinguished Professor of Economics								
Bennett, James T.	Prof	993-1158			PHD	70	Case Wes	1975
William P. Snavely Professor of Economics								
Bloch, Howard Ruben	Prof	993-1157			PHD	64	Princeton	
Buchanan, James M.	Prof	993-2327			PHD	48	Chicago	1983
University Professor of Economics								
Congleton, Roger D.	Prof	993-2328			PHD	78	Va Tech	1988
Cowen, Tyler	Prof	993-1136			PHD	87	Harvard	
Crain, W. Mark	Prof	993-2325			PHD	76	Tx A&M	
Heiner, Ronald A.	Prof	993-2322			PHD	75	UCLA	1989
Phillips, Samuel H. Jr.	Prof	993-1149			PHD	66	Virginia	
Rowley, Charles K.	Prof	993-4026			PHD	64	Nottnghm	1984
Tollison, Robert	Prof	993-2315			PHD	69	Virginia	
Duncan Black Professor of Economics								
Vaughn, Karen I.	Prof	993-1146			PHD	71	Duke	1978
Wagner, Richard E.	Prof	993-2324			PHD	66	Virginia	1988
Holbert I. Harris Professor of Economics								
Chung, Jae Wan	Assoc	993-1156			PHD	72	NYU	
Levy, David M.	Assoc	993-2319			PHD	79	Chicago	1983
Reid, Joseph D.	Assoc	993-1159			PHD	74	Chicago	1983
Roback, Jennifer A.	Assoc	993-2326			PHD	80	Rochester	1985
Wiest, Philip Ray	Assoc	993-1131			PHD	76	Pittsburgh	
Meyer, Carrie A.	Asst	993-1143			PHD	88	Illinois	1988
Palmer, Harvey	Asst	993-1138						
Ramirez, Carlos	Asst	993-1145						
Thorbecke, Willem	Asst	993-1150			PHD	88	Berkeley	

George Washington Univ — Washington, DC 20052 (202) 994-6150 — Claudia St. Clair
Department of Economics — Columbian C Arts & Sci Fax=994-6147 — GWUVM.GWU.EDU
email: @1=gwis2.circ.gwu.edu @2=unix1.circ.gwu.edu

Name	Rank	Phone	Email	Field	Degree	Yr	School	Since
Salamon, Linda B.	Dean	994-6210			PHD	71	Bryn Mawr	
Cordes, Joseph J.	C-Pr	994-6151	jjcordes	H	PHD	77	Wisconsin	1975
Aschheim, Joseph	Prof	994-6153		E	PHD	54	Harvard	1964
Boulier, Bryan L.	Prof	994-8088	mortal	JT	PHD	74	Princeton	1981
Bradley, Michael D.	Prof	994-8089	bradley	E	PHD	82	N Carol	1987
Brock, Gerald W.	VProf				PHD	73	Harvard	
Dunn, Robert M. Jr.	Prof	994-7379		F	PHD	67	Stanford	1978
Goldfarb, Robert S.	Prof	994-7581		BJ	PHD	68	Yale	1980
Holman, Mary A.	Prof	994-6156		L	PHD	63	Geo Wash	
Kwoka, John E. Jr.	Prof	994-6922		L	PHD	72	Penn	1981
Pelzman, Joseph	Prof	994-7108	jpzg	F	PHD	76	Boston C	1980
Solomon, Elinor H.	Prof	994-6581		E	PHD	48	Harvard	1982
Solomon, Henry	Prof	994-4249		I	PHD	59	NYU	
Trost, Robert P.	Prof	994-9011		C	PHD	77	Florida	1981
Yezer, Anthony M.	Prof	994-6755			PHD	74	MIT	1972
Joutz, Frederick L.	Assoc	994-4899	fjoutz	EC	PHD	87	U Wash	1988
Malik, Arun	Assoc	994-5471	amalik@1	Q	PHD	84	J Hopkins	
Moore, Michael Owen	Assoc	994-6157	mom@2	F	PHD	88	Wisconsin	1988
Phillips, Robert F.	Assoc	994-8619		C	PHD	85	Columbia	1985
Smith, Stephen C.	Assoc	994-8086	scsmith	O	PHD	83	Cornell	1983
Suranovic, Steven M.	Assoc	994-7579	smsuan	F	PHD	87	Cornell	1988
Watson, Harry S.	Assoc	994-6685		H	PHD	81	Indiana	
Feasel, Edward	Asst	994-6686	feasel@1	E	PHD	94	Berkeley	1994
Fon, Vincy	Asst	994-7580	vfon@1	CD	PHD	81	Kansas	1979
Jain, Sanjay	Asst	994-8087	sjain@1	O				1994
Joshi, Sumit	Asst	994-6154	sumjos	CD	PHD	91	Indiana	1992
Reeves, Silke	Asst	994-0192	sfabian@2	E	PHD	93	UCLA	1993
Snyder, Christopher	Asst	994-6581	csnyder@1	L	PHD	94	MIT	1994
Vonortas, Nicholas S.	Asst	994-6458	vonortas	OL	PHD	89	NYU	
Zhao, Anna	Asst	994-0194	yzhao	O	PHD	93	Chicago	1993
Bailey, Mary Ann	Adj	676-4261		I	PHD	74	MIT	

Georgetown University Washington, DC 20057 (202) 687-5830
Department of Economics College of Arts & Sci Fax=687-6102 GUVAX

Name	Rank	Phone	Degree	Yr	School	Year
Lawton, Robert B.	Dean	687-4043	PHD			
Albrecht, James W.	Prof	687-6105	PHD	76	Berkeley	1992
Briefs, Henry W.	Emer	687-5830	PHD	54	Geotown	1973
Canzoneri, Matthew B.	Prof	687-5911	PHD	75	Minnesota	1985
Cuddington, John T.	Prof	687-6103	PHD	78	Wisconsin	
McElroy, F. William	Prof	687-5571	PHD	67	Geotown	1968
McNelis, Paul D.	Prof	687-5573	PHD	74	J Hopkins	1977
Schwartz, Marius	Prof	687-6112	PHD	82	UCLA	1982
Tybout, James R.	Prof	687-6066	PHD	80	Wisconsin	1980
Viksnins, George J.	Prof	687-5890	PHD	64	Geotown	1968
Vroman, Susan	Prof	687-6024	PHD	77	J Hopkins	1978
Brown, Douglas M.	Assoc	687-5772	PHD	69	W Virginia	1972
Collins, Susan M.	Assoc	687-5781	PHD	84	MIT	1992
Diba, Behzad T.	Assoc	687-5682	PHD		Brown	
Harris, William G.	Assoc	687-6104	PHD	67	Oregon	
Oweiss, Ibrahim M.	Assoc	687-5582	PHD	69	Minnesota	1967
Poirier, J. Eugene	Assoc	687-6104	PHD		Yale	
Rogers, Carol Ann	Assoc	687-5816	PHD	83	Princeton	1984
Tryon, Joseph L.	Assoc	687-5692	PHD		Harvard	
Feyzioglu, Tarhan	Asst	687-7144	PHD	90	Penn	
Moresi, Serge X.	Asst	687-5118	PHD	91	MIT	1991
Westbrook, M. Daniel	Asst	687-5880	PHD	78	Ohio St	1978
Kazmer, Daniel R.	Lect		PHD	73	MIT	

University of Georgia Athens, GA 30602-6252 (706) 542-1311 Judy A. Griffin
Economics Department Terry College of Bus Fax=542-3376 RIGEL.ECON.UGA.EDU

Name	Rank	Phone	Email	Fields	Degree	Yr	School	Year
Niemi, Albert W. Jr.	Dean	542-8100		N	PHD	69	Conn	1968
Bateman, Fred	H-Pr	542-3692	bateman	N	PHD	65	Tulane	1991
Nicholas A. Beadles Professor								
Atkinson, Scott E.	Prof	542-3691	atknsn	CQK	PHD	72	Colorado	1985
Danielsen, Albert L.	Prof	542-3807	daniel	MH	PHD	66	Duke	1963
DeLorme, Charles D. Jr.	Prof	542-3682	delorme	EH	PHD	66	LSU	1968
Kamerschen, David R.	Prof	542-3681		DK	PHD	64	Mich St	1974
Jasper N. Dorsey Professor								
Keenan, Donald C.	Prof	542-3668	keenan	CHR	DSC	78	Wash U	1978
Knapp, Charles B.	Prof	542-1214		J	PHD	72	Wisconsin	1987
President								
Lee, Dwight R.	Prof	542-3970	lee	DHM	PHD	72	Ca-SnDgo	1985
Bernard B. & Eugenia A. Ramsey Professor								
Lovell, Knox	Prof	542-3689	knox	D	PHD	66	Duke	1994
Herman & Mary Virginia Terry Professor								
Allsbrook, Ogden O.	Assoc	542-3698		E	PHD	66	Virginia	1968
Cornwell, Christopher M.	Assoc	542-3670	cornwl	CHJ	PHD	85	Mich St	1988
Lastrapes, William D.	Assoc	542-3569	last	CEF	PHD	86	N Carol	1990
Naqvi, Nadeem	Assoc	542-3667	naqvi	F	PHD	84	So Meth	1987
Selgin, George A.	Assoc	542-2734	selgin	EN	PHD	86	NYU	1989
Snow, Arthur	Assoc	542-3752	snow	DH	PHD	79	Wisconsin	1989
Trandel, Gregory A.	Assoc	542-3673	trandel	GK	PHD	92	Princeton	1989
Warren, Ronald S.	Assoc	542-3693	warren	JC	PHD	76	N Carol	1985
White, Lawrence H.	Assoc	542-3696	lwhite	ENB	PHD	82	UCLA	1988
Chandra, Vandana	Asst	542-3494	chandra	F	PHD	91	J Hopkins	1991
Klein, Peter G.	Asst	542-1311	klein	L	PHD	95	Berkeley	1995

Georgia College Milledgeville GA 31061 (912) 453-4210 Janis Zarkowsky
Dept of Economics & Finance School of Business Fax=453-5249 GAC.PEACHNET.EDU

Name	Rank	Phone	Fields	Degree	Yr	School	Year
Jones, Jo Ann	Dean	453-5497		PHD	77	La Tech	1976
Wolfenbarger, J. Larry	C-Pr	453-4210	ABPE	PHD	74	Tennessee	1987
Jones, Kenneth D.	Prof	471-2063		PHD	77	La Tech	1987
Dean, Graduate School							
Samprone, Joseph C. Jr.	Prof	454-2587	AD	PHD		Calif	1983
Speir, Edwin G.	Prof	453-4444		PHD		Denver	1981
President of the College							
Farr, William Kendrick	Assoc	454-2591	ADQ	PHD		Georgia	1985
Scott, Gerald E.	Assoc			PHD	87	Maryland	1994

Georgia Institute Tech Atlanta, GA 30332-0615 (404) 894-4919 Maria Barrett, Adm Asst
School of Economics Allen Col Mgt, Plcy & I Fax=894-1890 ECON.GATECH.EDU

Name	Rank	Phone	Email	Fields	Degree	Yr	School	Year
Hawkins, Robert G.	Dean	894-2601			PHD	66	NYU	1993
email: robert.hawkins@iac.gatech.edu								
Schaffer, William A.	D-Pr$	894-4915	william.schaffer	R	PHD	63	Duke	1963
Biven, W. Carl	Prof	894-1885	carl.biven	EB	PHD	56	St Louis	1958
Boston, Thomas D.	Prof	894-5020	thomas.boston	JN	PHD	76	Cornell	1985
Cebula, Richard J.	Prof	894-4914	richard.cebula	EDR	PHD	71	Geo St	1992
Chu, Kong	Prof	894-1886	kong.chu	OC	PHD	64	Tulane	1968
Moore, Mack A.	Prof	894-4363	mack.moore	J	PHD	63	Wisconsin	1963

Tarpley, Fred A. Jr.	Prof		fred.tarpley	D	PHD	67	Tulane	1962
Belton, Willie J. Jr.	Assoc	894-4388	willie.belton	E	PHD	86	Penn St	1987
McCarty, Marilu H.	Assoc	894-2621	marilu.mccarty	EH	PHD	72	Geo St	1972
Novus, Ian E.	Assoc	894-3542	ian.novus	D	PHD	85	Penn	1992
Sassone, Peter G.	Assoc	894-4912	peter.sassone	DH	PHD	73	Purdue	1972
Shaban, Radwan Ali	Assoc	894-4909	radwan.shaban	DO	PHD	85	Stanford	1991
Chou, Ray Yeu-Tien	Asst	894-4903	ray.chou	G	PHD	88	Ca-SnDgo	1988
Mrozek, Janusz R.	Asst	894-0353	janusz.mrozek	DQ	PHD	95	Stanford	1993

Georgia Southern University Statesboro, GA 30460-8151 (912) 681-5161 Vicki Guy/Carol McGovern
Dept of Finance & Economics College of Business Adm Fax=681-0292 GSVMS2.CC.GASOU.EDU

Gooding, Carl W.	Dean	681-5106		Mgt	PHD	76	Georgia	1986
Whitaker, William M.	C-Pr	681-5161			PHD	68	Kentucky	1989
Coston, Robert D.	Prof	681-5162			PHD	73	Arkansas	1970
Davis, Elynor G.	Assoc	681-5020			PHD	78	Tx A&M	1979
Jones, Marcia Noreen	Assoc	681-0404			PHD	86	Illinois	1986
Levernier, William B.	Assoc	681-5227			PHD	88	W Virginia	1989
Rickman, Dan S.	Assoc	681-0213			PHD	87	Wyoming	1993
Smith, William Robert	Assoc	681-5432			MBA	72	Ga South	1973
Brown, John H.	Asst	681-0896			PHD	89	Mich St	1994

Georgia Southwestern Coll Americus, GA 31709-4693 (912) 931-2079
Economic Faculty Div of History & Pol Sc Fax=

Baringer, Richard L.	C-Pr	931-2079		Hst	PHD		G Peabody	
Huddleston, Kenneth M.	Asst	931-2079			MBA		Geo St	

Georgia State University Atlanta, GA 30303-3083 (404) 651-2626 Barbara Sykes 651-3784
Department of Economics College of Business Adm Fax=651-2804 GSUVM1.GSU.EDU

Hogan, John D.	Dean	651-2604		MO	PHD	52	Syracuse	6-91
Rushing, Francis W.	C-Pr	651-3782		ANP	PHD	67	N Carol	1974
Holder of the Eugenia A. and Bernard B. Ramsey Chair of Private Enterprise								
Bahl, Roy W. Jr.	Prof	651-3993		HR	PHD	65	Kentucky	1988
Director of the Policy Research Center								
Cheng, Juei Ming	Prof	651-2769		CO	PHD	68	Purdue	1968
Cummings, Ronald G.	Prof	651-1888		Q	PHD	68	Kansas	1993
Noah Langdale Jr. Eminent Scholar Chair of Environmental Policy								
Ihlanfeldt, Keith R.	Prof	651-3968		HR	PHD	78	Wash U	1981
Kaufman, Bruce E.	Prof	651-2922		J	PHD	78	Wisconsin	1977
Martinez, Jorge L.	Prof	651-3989		DF	PHD	78	Wash U	1977
Ratajczak, Donald	Prof	651-3282		MN	PHD	72	MIT	1973
Director of the Economic Forecasting Center								
Saposnik, Rubin	Prof	651-3969		D	PHD	59	Minnesota	1970
Schreiber, Arthur F.	Prof	651-3773		R	DBA	69	Indiana	1969
Associate Dean								
Sjoquist, David L.	Prof	651-3995		DR	PHD	71	Minnesota	1970
Skogstad, Samuel J.	VProf	651-4967		EFO	PHD	65	Wash U	1994
Stephan, Paula E.	Prof	651-3988		JO	PHD	71	Michigan	1981
Ulveling, Edwin F.	Prof	651-2774		AO	PHD	81	Iowa St	1967
Farnham, Paul G.	Assoc	651-2624		DHI	PHD	78	Berkeley	1977
Long, C. Richard	Assoc	651-3788		BE	PHD	68	Vanderbilt	1968
Seaman, Bruce A.	Assoc	651-2775		D	PHD	78	Chicago	1978
Yip, Chong Kee	Assoc	651-2780		EF	PHD	88	Penn St	1988
Banerjee, Samiran	Asst	651-1919		CD	PHD	92	Minnesota	1992
Bollinger, Christopher R.	Asst	651-1917		CDJ	PHD	93	Wisconsin	1993
Brewer, Paul	Asst	651-4963		CDL	PHD	95	Cal Tech	1994
Hotchkiss, Julie L.	Asst	651-3986		CJ	PHD	89	Cornell	1989
Moore, Robert E.	Asst	651-3756		FO	PHD	88	Cornell	1989
Osborne, Laura L.	Asst	651-2873		C	PHD	94	Duke	1994
Walker, Mary Beth	Asst	651-3751		D	PHD	86	Rice	1991
Wallace, Sally	Asst	651-3959		GH	PHD	88	Syracuse	1991
Terrebonne, Peter	Inst	651-4379		A	PHD	92	Emory	1992

Gettysburg College Gettysburg, PA 17325-1486 (717) 337-6670 Ms. Betty Smith
Economics Faculty Department of Economics Fax=337-6251 CC.GETTYSBURG.EDU

Gondwe, Derrick K.	C-Pr	337-6673	dgondwe	ABEO	PHD	78	Manitoba	1977
Fender, Ann Harper	Prof	337-6671	fendera	ADNL	PHD	76	J Hopkins	1978
Railing, William F.	Prof	337-6678	wrailing	AHP	PHD	58	Cornell	1964
Fletcher, Jean W.	Assoc	337-6674	fletcher	AJD	PHD	83	Wash U	1986
Gemmill, Robert M.	Assoc	337-6672	rgemmill	AEG	ABD		Northwes	1958
Nirro, Katsuyuki	Assoc	337-6676	niirok	AC	PHD		Pittsburgh	1972
Stillwaggon, Eileen	Asst	337-6675	estillwa	AFQ	PHD	79	America	1995
Forstater, Mathew B.	Inst	337-6668	mforstat	ABF	ABD		New Sch	1992

Gonzaga University — Spokane, WA 99258-0001 (509) Ext 3403 — Jane Cruse
Department of Economics — Sch of Business Adm Fax=484-5811 — JEPSON.GONZAGA.EDU
phone: 328-4220

Name	Rank	Phone	Email	Fields	Degree	Yr	School	Date
Barnes, Clarence H.	Dean	Ext 3402			PHD	73	Tennessee	9-73
Beck, John H.	D-Ac	Ext 3429	beck	BHC	PHD	76	Mich St	1988
Wiseman, A. Clark	Prof	Ext 3432	wiseman	AF	PHD	68	U Wash	1981
Bennett, Randall W.	Assoc	Ext 3411	bennett	HL	PHD	84	Mich St	1988

Goshen College — Goshen, IN 46526 (219)
Economics Faculty — Dept of Atg, Bus & Econ Fax=535-7660 — GOSHEN.EDU

Name	Rank	Phone	Email	Fields	Degree	Yr	School	Date
Nyce, John D.	Dean	535-7503	johndn		MAT	66	Detroit	8-66
Geiser, Leonard	C-Pr	535-7451	lenrg		MBA		Chicago	1983
Good, Delmar	Prof	535-7452	delgg	AH	PHD	70	Illinois	2-67
Gunden, Randal G.	Asst	535-7454	randygg	EIO	ABD		Notre Dm	1984

Graceland College — Lamoni, IA 50140-1699 (515)
Economics Faculty — Division of Soc Sc-Econ Fax=

Name	Rank	Phone	Email	Fields	Degree	Yr	School	Date
Anders, Steven L.	C-Pr	784-5175		ARD	PHD	88	Kansas St	1978
Beck, Paul	Asst	784-5176		AFJE	PHD	94	Mo-Ks Cty	1992

Grambling State University — Grambling, LA 71245 (318) 274-2789 — Ms. Ollie Pruitt
Applied Economics Dept — College of Business Fax=274-2191 — GRAM.EDU

Name	Rank	Phone	Email	Fields	Degree	Yr	School	Date
Dhanani, Karim	Dean	274-2275		Atg	DBA	86	La Tech	9-77
Abraham, Girmai	H-Ac$	274-2781			PHD	81	Ohio St	9-82
Cadet, Marc	Assoc	274-2794			PHD		Kansas St	9-68
Ghebreyohannes, Keleta	Assoc	274-2795			PHD		Colo St	9-81
Hopusch, Edgar	Assoc	274-2780			PHD		Colorado	
Suliman, Osman	Assoc	274-2780			PHD	84	Indiana	1988
on leave to Millersville								
Bashir, Abdel Hamid	Asst	274-2744			PHD		Wisconsin	1990
Ghebreyesus, Ghirmay	Asst	274-2779			PHD		Strathcl	1990
Melancon, Melissa	Asst	274-3825			ABD		La Tech	
Larrymore, Norris	Inst	274-2464			MS		Penn	1988

Grand Canyon University — Phoenix, AZ 85017 (602) 589-2867 — Carol Greenwalt
Department of Economics — College of Business Fax=589-2532 — ENET.NET

Name	Rank	Phone	Email	Fields	Degree	Yr	School	Date
Sheriff, Don	Dean$	589-2820	cob					
Proffitt, Dennis	Prof	589-2822		GD	PHD	84	St Louis	1987

Grand Valley State Univ — Allendale, MI 49401 (616) 895-2535 — Thelma Cathey
Department of Economics — Seidman Sch Bus & Adm Fax=895-3286 — GVSU.EDU

Name	Rank	Phone	Email	Fields	Degree	Yr	School	Date
Turner, Emery C.	Dean	895-2163	turnere	Atg	DBA	66	Wash U	1994
Singh, Harinder	C-Pr	895-2545			PHD	85	Il-Chicago	1995
Gonce, Richard A.	Prof	895-2540		ABDK	PHD	66	Wisconsin	1972
Reifel, John W.	Prof	895-2541	reifelj	AHOR	PHD	72	Mich St	1971
Sicilian, Paul	Asst	895-2542		ACDJ	PHD	91	Illinois	1987
Simons, Gerald P.	Asst	895-2538			PHD	95	Kansas	1995
Thorsnes, Paul E.	Asst	895-2539			PHD	94	Oregon	1995

Greensboro College — Greensboro, NC 27401-1875 (910)
Economics Faculty — Div of Business Adm Fax=
phone 272-7102

Name	Rank	Phone	Email	Fields	Degree	Yr	School	Date
Jones, Thomas O. Jr.	C-Pr	272-7102		BAdm	DBA	72	Geo Wash	1986
Fred L. Proctor Sr. Professor of Business Administration								
Oerther, Frederick J.	Asst	272-7102			PHD	89	Geo Mason	1990

Grinnell College — Grinnell, IA 50112 (515)
Economics Faculty — Div of Social Studies Fax=269-3408

Name	Rank	Phone	Email	Fields	Degree	Yr	School	Date
Montgomery, Mark	C-Ac	269-3146		JQH	PHD	82	Wisconsin	1989
Mutti, John	Prof	269-3143		FHQ	PHD	74	Wisconsin	1987
Sydney Meyer Professor of International Economics								
Bateman, Bradley W.	Assoc	269-3145		B	PHD	84	Kentucky	1987
Ferguson, William D.	Assoc	269-3132		JE	PHD	89	Mass	1989
Munyon, Paul G.	Assoc	269-3142		L	PHD	75	Harvard	1982
Powell, Irene	Assoc	269-3125		IL	PHD	85	Wisconsin	1989
Seiz, Janet A.	Assoc	269-4868		BO	PHD	85	Duke	1989

Grove City College — Grove City, PA 16127-2104 (412) 458-2056
Economics Faculty — Department of Economics Fax=458-3852

Name	Rank	Phone	Email	Fields	Degree	Yr	School	Date
Sparks, John A.	C-Pr	458-2056			JD		Michigan	
Guiler, Charles J.	Assoc				MED		Ind St	
Mateer, Dirk	Assoc	458-2056			PHD	91	Fla St	1993
Miller, Tracy	Assoc	458-2000			PHD		Chicago	
Stitt, Kenneth	Inst	458-3364			MA		W Virginia	

Guilford College Greensboro, NC 27410 (910) 316-2267
Economics Faculty Department of Economics Fax=
Did Not Respond--1994-95 Listing

Clark, Carol M.	C-Ac	316-2267		Q	PHD	79	Michigan	1981
Williams, Robert G.	Prof	316-2282		F	PHD	78	Stanford	1978
Williams, Robert B.	Assoc	316-2218		R	PHD	84	N Carol	1987

Gustavus Adolphus College Saint Peter, MN 56082-1498 (507) 933-7414 Connie Baum
Economics Faculty Dept of Economics & Mgt Fax=933-7041

Wohl, Lawrence A.	C-Ac	933-7453			PHD	86	Wash St	1983
Jones, Ellis J.	Prof	933-7420			EDD	65	N Dakota	1958
McRostie, Clair	Prof				PHD	64	Wisconsin	1957
Ogden and Elizabeth Confer Professorship in Entrepreneurship								
Bungum, John L.	Assoc	933-7406			PHD	77	Nebraska	1979
Gersich, Frank	Assoc	933-7410			EDD	93	N Illinois	1984
Johnson, Bruce H.	Assoc	933-7011			PHD	79	Houston	1986
Reese, David A.	Assoc	933-7405			PHD	80	Virginia	1979
Thomas, William	Assoc	933-7409			PHD	85	N Carol	1991
Estenson, Paul	Asst	933-7408			PHD	86	Nebraska	1986
Johnston, Lewis	Asst	933-6273			PHD	90	Berkeley	1993

Hamilton College Clinton, NY 13323 (315) 859-4450 Dawn Woodward
Economics Faculty Department of Economics Fax=859-4632 ITSMAIL1.HAMILTON.EDU

Jensen, Elizabeth J.	C-Ac	859-4437	ejensen	LN	PHD	84	MIT	1983
Bradfield, James	Prof	859-4190	jbradfie	GD	PHD	73	Rochester	1976
Jones, Derek C.	Prof	859-4381	djones	PJ	PHD	74	Cornell	1972
Balkan, Erol M.	Assoc	859-4180	ebalkan	OF	PHD	88	Binghamt	1987
Pliskin, Jeffrey L.	Assoc	859-4143	jpliskin	CF	PHD	85	Michigan	1982
Georges, Christophre	Asst	859-4472	cgeorges	EJB	PHD	89	Michigan	1989
Hagstrom, Paul Alan	Asst	859-4146	phagstro	JHI	PHD	91	Wisconsin	1991
Kayser, Hilke A.	Asst	859-4234	hkayser	HIQ	PHD	94	Wisconsin	1993
Warner, Elizabeth J.	Asst	859-4419	ewarner	EH	PHD	89	Michigan	1989
Lutzker, Adam	Inst		alutzker	EB	ABD		Michigan	1995

Hamline University St. Paul, MN 55104-1284 (612) 641-2377 Kathryn Marron 641-2295
Economics Faculty Dept of Mgmt and Econ Fax=641-2956 HAMLIN.EDU

Bochnak, Mary	C	641-2377		M	PHD	82	Minnesota	1990
Jessup, Paul F.	Prof	641-2261	pjessup@seq.	G	PHD	66	Northwes	1988
William Kahlert Professor								
Gunderson, Elizabeth W.	Assoc	641-2263		C	PHD	91	Union In	1980
Akhavi-Pour, Hossein	Asst	641-2223		F	PHD	79	Kansas	1988
Aziz, Fahima	Asst	641-2262		DQ	PHD	95	Minnesota	1994
Boylston-Herndon, Jill	Asst	641-2436	jhbhernd@piper.	D	PHD	94	Florida	1994

Hampton University Hampton, VA 23668 (804) 727-5865 Kimberly Hyatt
Department of Economics School of Business Fax=727-5048 UNIXVAX.HAMPTON.EDU

Adeyiga, Janet A.	Dean$	727-5361		Atg	PHD	80	Missouri	1985
Sarki, Ayuba J.	C-Ac	727-5860			PHD	84	Georgia	1982
Babalola, Banji	Asst	727-5863			PHD	87	Howard	1987
Bills, Angela	Asst	727-5866			PHD	93	Michigan	1993
Grant, Lauria	Asst	727-5868			ABD		Syracuse	1991
Noel, Cuthbert	Asst	727-5861			PHD		Howard	1986
Omotoye, Richard	Asst	727-5862			PHD		Russia	1994

Hardin-Simmons University Abilene, TX 79698 (915)
Dept of Accounting & Finance School of Business Fax=670-1523

Gillette, Lynn	Dean	670-1356			PHD	80	Tx A&M	1994
Waldrup, Bob	C-Pr	670-1357		Atg	PHD	95	Miss	1995
Monhollon, Jimmie	Prof	670-1508			PHD			
Warren, Russell	Prof	670-1363			PHD			
Curtis, William	Assoc	670-1364			ABD	76	Tx-Austin	1976

Harding University Searcy, AR 72143-5590 (501) 279-4470 Helen Floyd
Economics Faculty School of Business Fax=279-4195 ACS.HARDING.EDU

McLeod, Randall J.	Dean	279-4201		Mktg	JD	74	Memphis	
Diffine, Donald P.	Prof	279-4470			PHD		Miss	1971
Robertson, Marvin	Prof	279-4307						

University of Hartford W Hartford, CT 06117-0395 (203) 768-4581 Linda Amirault
Department of Economics Barney Sch Bus & P Adm Fax=768-4198 HARTFORD

Libassi, Peter	Dean	768-4243			LLB		Yale	
Kolluri, Bharat R.	C-Pr	768-4581			PHD	77	SUNY-Buf	1976

Name	Rank	Phone			Degree	Yr	Institution	Since
Armentano, Dominick T.	Prof	768-4835			PHD	66	Conn	1966
on sabbatical								
Giannoros, Demetrios	Prof	768-4799			PHD	81	Boston U	
Panik, Michael J.	Prof	768-4836			PHD	70	Boston C	1968
Sullivan, John J.	Prof	768-4834			PHD	67	Conn	
Martin, Linda R.	Assoc	768-4185			PHD	81	S Carol	1986
Associate Dean								
Singamsetti, Nageswara Rao	Assoc	768-4779			PHD		SUNY-Buf	
Gullason, Edward T.	Asst	768-4864			PHD	86	Penn	1987
Rassekh, Farhad	Asst	768-5007			PHD	83	Houston	1989

Hartwick College Oneonta, NY 13820 (607) 431-4940
Department of Economics Div Social & Behav Sci Fax=431-4954 HARTWICK.EDU

Name	Rank	Phone	Email	Code	Degree	Yr	Institution	Since
Gotsch-Thompson, Susan	Dean							
Gaty, Lewis R. II	C-Pr	431-4950	gaty.l	ADEQ	MS		Stanford	1975
Stuligross, John D.	Prof			AEGR	PHD	71	Oklahoma	1980
Malone, Laurence J.	Assoc			ABFJ	PHD		New Sch	1986
Kigner, Brent M.	Asst			ACOP	PHD	90	Minnesota	1990

Harvard University Boston, MA 02163 (617)
Department of Economics Faculty of Arts & Sci Fax= HARVARD.EDU

Name	Rank	Phone	Degree	Yr	Institution	Since
Knowles, Jeremy R.	Dean					
Jorgenson, Dale W.	C-Pr	495-4661	PHD	59	Harvard	1969
Frederick E. Abbe Professor of Economics						
Alesina, Alberto F.	Prof	495-8388	PHD	86	Harvard	1988
Paul Sack Associate Professor of Political Economy						
Barro, Robert J.	Prof	495-3203	PHD	70	Harvard	1987
Campbell, John	Prof	496-6448				
Caves, Richard E.	Prof	495-2127	PHD	58	Harvard	1962
George Gund Professor of Economics & Business Administration						
Chamberlain, Gary	Prof	495-1869	PHD	75	Harvard	1987
Cooper, Richard N.	Prof	495-5076	PHD	62	Harvard	1981
Maurits C. Boas Professor ofInternational Economics						
Feldstein, Martin S.	Prof	495-5034	DPHL	67	Oxford	1969
George F. Baker Professor of Economics						
Freeman, Richard B.	Prof	868-3900				
Herbert S. Ascherman Professor of Economics						
Friedman, Benjamin M.	Prof	495-4246	PHD	71	Harvard	1972
William Joseph Maier Professor of Political Economy						
Fudenberg, Drew D.	Prof	496-5895	PHD	81	MIT	1987
Goldin, Claudia D.	Prof	495-3934	PHD	72	Chicago	1990
Green, Jerry R.	Prof	495-3950	PHD	70	Rochester	1973
David A. Wells Professor of Political Economy						
Griliches, Zvi	Prof	495-2181	PHD	57	Chicago	1969
Paul M. Warburg Professor of Economics						
Hart, Oliver D'Arcy	Prof	495-2144	PHD	74	Princeton	1993
Houthakker, Hendrick S.	Prof	495-2442	ECD	49	Amsterda	
Henry Lee Professor of Economics						
Kain, John F.	Prof	496-6174	PHD	61	Berkeley	1964
Katz, Lawrence F.	Prof	495-5148	PHD	85	MIT	1986
Kornai, Janos	Prof	495-1236	DSC	66	Hungaria	1986
Landes, David S.	Prof	495-4849				
Coolidge Professor of History and Economics						
Mankiw, N. Gregory	Prof	495-4301	PHD	84	MIT	1985
Director of Graduate Studies						
Marglin, Stephen A.	Prof	495-3759	PHD	65	Harvard	
Walter S. Barker Prof of Econ and Frank W. Taussig Research Prof of Economics						
Mas-Colell, Andreu	Prof	495-2146	PHD	72	Minnesota	1981
Louis Bergman Professor of Economics						
Maskin, Eric S.	Prof	495-4167				
Medoff, James L.	Prof	495-4209				
Meyer Kestnbaum Professor of Labor & Industry						
Perkins, Dwight H.	Prof	495-2164	PHD	64	Harvard	1963
Harold Hitchings Burbank Professor of Political Economy						
Rosovsky, Henry	Prof	495-4151	PHD	59	Harvard	1965
Lewis P. and Linda L. Geyser University Professor						
Sachs, Jeffrey D.	Prof	495-4112	PHD	80	Harvard	1983
Galen L. Stone Professor of International Trade						
Sen, Amartya K.	Prof	495-1871	PHD	59	Cambridg	1988
Lamont University Professor						
Shleifer, Andrei	Prof	495-5046	PHD	86	MIT	1991
Timmer, C. Peter	Prof	495-9778	PHD	69	Harvard	1980
Thomas D. Cabot Professor of Development Studies						
Weitzman, Martin L.	Prof	495-5103	PHD	67	MIT	1989
Ernest E. Monrad Professor of Economics						
Whinston, Michael D.	Prof	253-3361				
Williamson, Jeffrey G.	Prof	495-2438	PHD	61	Stanford	1983
Laird Bell Professor of Economics						

Cutler, David M.	Assoc	868-3900				MIT	
DeLong, J. Bradford	Assoc						
Imbens, Guido W.	Assoc	495-4129					
Leahy, John V.	Assoc	495-9592		PHD	90	Princeton	1990
Mandler, Michael A.	Assoc	495-0586		PHD	87	Yale	
Morduch, Jonathan J.	Assoc	495-0353		PHD	91	Harvard	1991
Sjostrom, J. Tomas	Assoc	495-8823					
Weinstein, David E.	Assoc	495-4690		PHD	92	Michigan	1991
Davis, Donald R.	Asst	496-6416		PHD	92	Columbia	1992
Glaeser, Edward	Asst						
Hall, Brian J.	Asst	495-2167		PHD	83	Harvard	1993
Laibson, David	Asst	496-3402					
Metrick, Andrew P.	Asst	496-7081					
Head Tutor							
Minter-Hoxby, Caroline	Asst	496-3588					
Tornell, Aaron	Asst	496-6284					
Roemer, Michael	SLect	495-4324		PHD	68	MIT	1974
Schor, Juliet B.	SLect	495-0588		PHD	82	Mass	1984
Wolowitz, Jeffrey	SLect	495-2109					
Jenkins, Glenn P.	Lect	495-4274		PHD	72	Chicago	1972

University of Hawaii-Hilo — Hilo, HI 96720-4091 (808) 933-3470 Mitzi Hennessey
Bus Adm & Economics Div — Col of Arts & Sciences Fax=933-3685 UHUNIX.UHCC.HAWAII.EDU

Hammes, David L.	H-Ac	Ext 400	hammes	PHD	85	Simon Fr	1988
Cauley, Jon	Prof	Ext 386		PHD	71	Colorado	
Hahn, Youngki	Prof	Ext 767		PHD	71	Ca-River	
Im, Eric I.	Prof	Ext 462		PHD	82	Hi-Manoa	
Sakai, Marcia	Assoc	Ext 457		PHD	85	Hi-Manoa	

Univ of Hawaii at Manoa — Honolulu, HI 96822 (808) 956-8496 Juliet M. Pila; Pat Nishita
Department of Economics — Col of Social Sciences Fax=956-4347 HAWAII.EDU

Dubanoski, Richard A.	Dean		Psyc	PHD	66	Minnesota	
Moncur, James E. T.	C-Pr$	956-8730		PHD	71	Wash St	1969
La Croix, Sumner J.	Prof	956-7061		PHD	81	U Wash	1981
Lee, Chung H.	Prof	956-8427		PHD	66	Berkeley	1980
Mak, James	Prof	956-8280		PHD	70	Purdue	1970
Mason, Andrew	Prof	956-8068		PHD	75	Michigan	1975
Naya, Seiji	Prof	586-2355		PHD	66	Wisconsin	1961
Peterson, Richard E.	Prof	956-7563		PHD	72	Berkeley	
Rose, Louis	Prof	956-8118		PHD	70	UCLA	1969
Roumasset, James A.	Prof	956-7496		PHD	73	Wisconsin	1976
Snow, Marcellus S.	Prof	956-7521		PHD	74	Berkeley	1974
Williams, Raburn M.	Prof	956-8615		PHD	70	Chicago	1969
Yeh, Yeong-Her	Prof	956-7749		PHD	66	Minnesota	1965
Bonham, Carl S.	Assoc	956-7605		PHD	89	Tx-Austin	1989
Ermini, Luigi	Assoc	956-8590		PHD	87	Ca-SnDgo	1990
James, William E.	Assoc			PHD	79	Hawaii	1984
on leave							
Raut, Lakshmi K.	Assoc	956-8496		PHD	85	Yale	1995
Bauer, John G.	Asst	944-7713		PHD	84	Michigan	1985
on leave							
Cheong, Kwang-Soo	Asst	956-7653		PHD	94	Stanford	1994
Gangnes, Byron S.	Asst	956-7285		PHD	90	Penn	1990
Konan, Denise	Asst	956-6310		PHD	93	Colorado	1993
Russo, Gerard G.	Asst	956-7065		PHD	89	Northwes	1987
Wiemer, Calla J.	Asst	956-7721		PHD	84	Wisconsin	1984

Hawaii Pacific University — Honolulu, HI 96813 (808)
Economics Faculty — Department of Economics Fax=

Romig, Rodney	Dean	544-0283		PHD	75	Nebraska	8-87
Ghosh, Stanley	Prof			PHD		Indiana	
Jackson, Dale	Assoc			PHD		SFran St	
Mardfin, Ward	Assoc			PHD		Hawaii	
Scholland, Ken	Assoc		MLFB	MSFB		Geotown	
Drabkin, Eric	Asst			PHD		UCLA	

Heidelberg College — Tiffin, OH 44883 (419)
Economics Faculty — Dept of Bus Adm & Econ Fax=448-2124 HEIDELBERG.EDU

Wickham, William T.	C-Pr	448-2280	Mgt	PHD	56	Case Wes	1977
Rennie, Henry	Prof	448-2221	AFO	PHD	73	Ohio St	1993
Chudzinski, James	Assoc	448-2109		PHD	88	Tx Tech	1988
Kirklin, Wayne	Assoc			MBA		NYU	1978
Cook, John	Asst	448-2280	AG	PHD	94	Kentucky	1995
Keener, Gary	Asst	448-2280	AH	PHD	93	Kentucky	1991

Hendrix College Conway, AR 72032-3080 (501)
Economics Faculty Dept of Econ & Business Fax=
Did Not Respond--1994-95 Listing
Kerr, Stephen W. C-Ac 450-1305 MBA 77 So Meth 1979
Berry, Stanley Keith Assoc 450-1233 PHD 79 Vanderbilt 1989
Rupert, Lyle M. Assoc 450-1237 MBA 85 Chicago 1987
Scott, Ralph D. Assoc 450-1306 PHD 83 Tulane 1979
Stanley, Tom D. Assoc 450-1276 PHD 82 Purdue 1986
Cotham, Ralph Asst 450-1259 JD Vanderbilt 1991

Hillsdale College Hillsdale, MI 49242-1298 (517)
Economics Faculty Dept Econ, Bus Adm, Atg Fax=437-3923
phone: 437-7341
VanEaton, Charles D. D-Pr Ext 2412 PHD 74 Tulane 1978
McCabe/UPS Professor
Ebeling, Richard M. Assoc MA 80 Rutgers 1988
Ludwig von Mises Chair
Paas, David Assoc PHD Nebraska 1993
Wolfram, Gary Assoc PHD Berkeley 1989
Coppock, Lee Asst PHD Geo Mason1994

Hofstra University Hempstead, NY 11550 (516) Stephanie CoPace
Dept Economics & Geography Col Liberal Arts & Sci Fax= HOFSTRA.EDU
Vogt, Robert C. Dean 463-5441 lasrcv PolS PHD 75 SUNY-Buf
Tenenbaum, Marcel C-Ac 560-5593 ecomzt PHD 69 Columbia 1964
DeFreitas, Gregory E. Assoc 560-5040 ecoged J PHD 79 Columbia
Guttmann, Robert P. Assoc 560-5602 F PHD 79 London
Moghadam, Fatemeh Assoc 560-5598 ecofzm NOQ PHD 79 Oxford
Christensen, Paul P. Asst 560-6024 ecoppc B PHD 76 Wisconsin
Kozlov, Nicholas N. Asst 560-6954 econnk P PHD 88 N Hamp

College of the Holy Cross Worcester, MA 01610-2395 (508) 793-3362 Mrs. Beverly Bylund
Economics Faculty Department of Economics Fax=793-3708 HOLYCROSS.EDU
Kosicki, George C-Ac 793-2689 kosicki ADJL PHD 85 Cornell 9-85
Carter, John R. Prof 793-2676 CDL PHD 76 Cornell 1976
O'Connell, John F. Prof 793-2680 CDIJ PHD 70 Wisconsin 1974
Schap, David J. Prof 793-2688 CDK PHD 82 Wash U 1981
Anderton, Charles H. Assoc 793-3441 ACDF PHD 86 Cornell 1986
Block, Walter Assoc 793-2743 DQR PHD 72 Columbia 1991
Gottschang, Thomas R. Assoc 793-2678 AOP PHD 82 Michigan 1979
Sanchez, Nicolas Assoc 793-3362 DENO PHD 72 S Calif 1977
Buffum, David R. Asst 793-3455 CDHJ PHD 92 Penn 1989
Cahill, Miles B. Asst 793-2682 AEJ PHD 95 Purdue 1995
Rask, Kolleen J. Asst 626-1305 EFOP PHD 89 Yale 1989

Holy Family College Philadelphia, PA 19114 (215) Ext 415 Mrs. Lucille Sliwa
Economics Faculty Business Adm Division Fax=637-1621
phone: 637-7700
Brady, Teresa H Ext 415 JD 89 Temple
Tokar, Bette L. Assoc 637-7700 EDD 93 Temple
Bilt, Mildred Lect MBA LaSalle

Hood College Frederick, MD 21701 (301) 696-3685 Colette Cooney
Economics Faculty Dept of Economics & Mgt Fax=694-7653 NIMUE.HOOD.EDU
Dahms, Joseph E. C-Ac 696-3687 dahms PHD 83 American 1978
Banks, Nina 696-3685
Obar, Ruth I. 696-3685

Hope College Holland, MI 49422-9000 (616) Joy Forgwe
Economics Faculty Dept of Econ & Bus Adm Fax=395-7922 HOPE.CIT.HOPE.EDU
Heisler, James B. C-Pr 395-7915 PD PHD 75 Nebraska 1981
Lunn, John E. Prof 395-7931 LD PHD 80 UCLA 1992
Gentenaar, Robert Assoc 395-7579 EC PHD 77 Mich St 1977
Klay, Robin Assoc 395-7581 BO PHD 73 Princeton 1979
Steen, Todd P. Assoc 395-7582 JT PHD 93 Harvard 1988

University of Houston Houston, TX 77204-5582 (713) 743-3800 Amber Papuga
Department of Economics Col of Social Science Fax=743-3709 UHUPVM1.UH.EDU
Rozelle, Richard Dean 743-4000
Mayor, Thomas H. C-Pr 743-3801 AK PHD 65 Maryland 1969
Bhargava, Alok Prof 743-3837 PHD 82 London 1989
DeGregori, Thomas R. Prof 743-3838 econ1m PHD 65 Tx-Austin 1967
Gregory, Paul R. Prof 743-3828 PHD 69 Harvard 1972

Levin, Dan	Prof	743-3841	econit	MI	PHD	82	MIT	1982
on leave to Ohio State University								
Ruffin, Roy J.	Prof	743-3827			PHD	67	Northwes	1976
Smith, Barton A.	Prof	743-3834		ADR	PHD	74	Chicago	1973
Smith, James L.	Prof	743-3797		DQ	PHD	77	Harvard	1983
Steele, Henry B.	Prof	743-3835			PHD		MIT	
Antel, John J.	Assoc	743-3808			PHD	82	UCLA	1981
Bean, Richard N.	Assoc	743-3831			PHD	71	U Wash	1970
Collier, Irwin L.	Assoc	743-3836			PHD	84	MIT	1981
Craig, Steven C.	Assoc	743-3812	econ30	HR	PHD	81	Penn	1989
Dechert, W. Davis	Assoc	743-3800			PHD		Cornell	
Kohlhase, Janet E.	Assoc	743-3799		RHD	PHD	80	Penn	1983
Papell, David H.	Assoc	743-3807	econh		PHD	81	Columbia	1984
Stern, Louis H.	Assoc	743-3839		R	PHD	64	UCLA	1967
Austin, Andrew	Asst	743-3832	econd0	HC	PHD		Penn	1991
Ben-Gad, Michael	Asst	743-3800			PHD	95	Chicago	1995
Guler, Kemal	Asst	743-3811			PHD	90	Cal Tech	1990
Juhn, Chinhui	Asst	743-3823			PHD	91	Chicago	1992
Loewy, Michael	Asst	743-3815		EG	PHD	86	Minnesota	1991
Ng, Pin T.	Asst	743-3810	pin@uh.edu		PHD	89	Illinois	1990
Palumbo, Michael G.	Asst	743-3824			PHD	92	Virginia	1992
Wilcox, Nathaniel	Asst	743-3840			PHD		Chicago	1991

Univ of Houston-Clear Lake — Houston, TX 77058-1098 (713) 283-3185 — Noel Turner
Economics, Fnce, Mktg & DSci — Sch of Bus & Public Adm Fax=283-3951 — UHCLZ

Staples, William A.	Dean	283-3100	Mktg	PHD	78	Houston	9-79
Perdue, D. Grady	C-Pr	283-3213	Fnce	PHD	85	Alabama	9-84
Cloninger, Dale O.	Prof	283-3210		DBA	73	Fla St	9-74
Hodgin, Robert F.	Assoc	283-3211		DA	80	Illin St	9-81
Weed, Norman L.	Assoc	283-3208		PHD	68	Tulane	9-94

Univ of Houston-Downtown — Houston, TX 77002 (713) 221-8017 — Ms. Marie Cepeda
Finance, Atg, & Comp Inf Sys — College of Business Fax=226-5238 — DT3.DT.UH.EDU

Bizzell, Bobby G.	Dean	221-8179	Mgt	PHD	71	Tx-Austin	1989
Leavins, John	C-Pr	221-8017	Atg	PHD	87	Houston	1978
Islam, Anisul	Assoc			PHD	84	Alberta	1990
Marvasti, Akbar B.	Assoc			PHD	85	LSU	1990
Nazemzadah, Asghar	Assoc			PHD	83	Fla St	1989

Houston Baptist University — Houston, TX 77074-3298 (713)
Economics Area — Col of Business & Econ Fax=995-3408

Garrison, R. Bruce	Dean	995-3325	Mgt	PHD	75	N Colo	1983
Herman Brown Chair of Business and Economics							
Matthews, Warren T.	Assoc			PHD	72	Tx A&M	1995

Howard University — Washington, DC 20059 (202)
Economics Department — College of Arts & Sci — HOWARD.EDU
–College of Arts & Sciences — Phone 806-6717 Fax 806-5262

Lee, Clarence	Dean			PHD			
Betsey, Charles L.	C-Pr			PHD		Michigan	
Chandler, Clevelend	Prof			PHD		Maryland	
Green, Rodney D.	Prof			PHD	80	American	1977
Huang, Lien-fu	Prof			PHD		Rochester	
Hung, Gregory	Prof			PHD		Virginia	
Kwack, Sung Y.	Prof			PHD	68	Berkeley	
McDonald, Vincent R.	Prof			PHD	68	Maryland	
Palmer, Ransford W.	Prof			PHD	66	Clark	1973
Wadhawan, Satish C.	Prof			PHD		Nehru	
Black, Emily	Assoc			PHD		Boston C	
Dompere, Kofi	Assoc			PHD		Temple	
Lee, Byung	Assoc			PHD		Wayne St	
Perkins, Mary	Assoc			PHD		American	
Graves, Janet R.	Asst			PHD		Tx-Austin	
Meepagaia, Gaminie	Asst			PHD	86	SUNY-Alb	1988

–College of Business — Phone 806-1545 Fax 797-6393

Harvey, Barron H.	Dean	806-1507	Atg	PHD	77	Nebraska	1982
Chargois, Josephine A.	C-Ac	806-1545	BusC	PHD		Indiana	
Ekanem, Frank	Asst	806-1500		PHD			
Hull, Everson	Asst	806-1500		PHD			
Lindsey, Debra A.	Asst	806-1638		PHD		Howard	
Aiyegoro, Ademois	Lect	806-1658		PHD		Geo Mason	
Straight, Ronald L.	Lect	806-1531		DBA	79	Geo Wash	1988

Howard Payne University — Brownwood, TX 76801 (915) 649-8704 — Mary Hill
Dept of Business Adm — School of Business Adm Fax=

Turner, Jeff	Dean$						
Spraberry, Hubert O.	Prof	649-8704		PHD	85	Tx Tech	1986

University of Idaho — Moscow, ID 83844-3172 (208) 885-6294 — Karen L. Gillespie
Department of Economics — Col of Business & Econ Fax=885-8939 — UIDAHO.EDU

Name	Rank	Phone	Email	Field	Degree	Yr	School	Year
Dangerfield, Byron J.	Dean$	885-6478		Mgt	PHD	85	U Wash	1987
Ghazanfar, Shaikh M.	H-Pr	885-7144	ghazi	HO	PHD	69	Wash St	1968
DiNoto, Michael J.	Prof	885-7148	dnt@crow.csrv.	JR	PHD	73	SUNY-Buf	1970
Miller, Jon R.	Prof	885-7506	jrmecon	BQ	PHD	74	Wash U	1989
Wenders, John T.	Prof	882-3696	jwenders	DL	PHD	67	Northwes	1981
Coffman, Richard B.	Assoc	885-7155	richardc	DL	PHD	72	U Wash	1978
Knudsen, John W.	Assoc	885-7147	jkudsen	EP	PHD	70	Minnesota	1972
Lyman, R. Ashley	Assoc	885-7145	alyman	DC	PHD	72	Northwes	1976
Kwan, Felix	Asst	885-7143	fkwan	EF	PHD	92	Wash U	1994

Idaho State University — Pocatello, ID 83209-0009 (208)
Department of Economics — Col of Arts & Sciences Fax=

Name	Rank	Phone	Email	Field	Degree	Yr	School	Year
Hjelm, Victor S.	Dean	236-3204		PolS	PHD	66	Colorado	1968
Hofman, Cornelius A.	C-Pr	236-2655			PHD	64	Utah	1960
Norman, Lee	Assoc	236-2385			PHD	80	Utah	1981
Benson, C. Scott	Asst	236-2860			PHD	88	Ca-Davis	1990
Stegner, Tesa	Asst	236-2393			PHD	89	Wash St	1992
Tokle, Robert J.	Asst	236-3835			PHD	86	Iowa St	1986
Vrooman, John	Asst	236-2943			PHD	76	Tx-Austin	1995

University of Illinois — Champaign, IL 61820 (217) 333-0120
Department of Economics — Col of Comm & Bus Admin Fax=244-6678 — UIUC.EDU
email: @1=vmd.cso.uiuc.edu @2=commerce.cba.uiuc.edu @3=uiucvmd

Name	Rank	Phone	Email	Degree	Yr	School	Year
Leuthold, Jane H.	H-Pr$	333-0102	leuthold@1	PHD	68	Wisconsin	1967
Arnould, Richard J.	Prof	244-0533	rarnould	PHD	68	Iowa St	1967
Baer, Werner	Prof	333-8388	baer@uxl.cso.	PHD	58	Harvard	1974
Bera, Anil K.	Prof	333-4596	paschimc@uxh.cso	PHD	83	Aust Na	1983
Brueckner, Jan K.	Prof	333-4557	jkbr@1	PHD	76	Stanford	1976
Ferber, Marianne A.	Emer	333-0142		PHD	54	Chicago	1956
Giertz, J. Fred	Prof	244-4822	fredg@igpa.	PHD	70	Northwes	1980
Gillespie, Robert W.	Emer	333-4586	rgillespie@2	PHD	61	MIT	1960
Gottheil, Fred	Prof			PHD		Duke	
Grinols, Earl L.	Prof	333-4595	egrinols@2	PHD	77	MIT	1984
Heins, A. James	Emer	333-2417		PHD	61	Wisconsin	1960
Hendricks, Wallace E.	Prof	333-6028	wally@uxl.cso.	PHD	73	Berkeley	1973
Kahn, Charles M.	Prof	333-2813	c-kahn	PHD	81	Harvard	1988
Koenker, Roger	Prof	333-4558		PHD	74	Michigan	1983
Lee, Alston on leave Colorado	Prof			PHD	78	Wash	1988
McMahon, Walter W.	Emer	333-4579	mcmahon@1	PHD	57	Iowa	1957
Neal, Larry	Prof	333-4678	neall1986@1	PHD	68	Berkeley	1967
Newbold, Paul on leave Nottingham	Prof			PHD	70	Wisconsin	1979
Orr, Daniel	Prof	333-4508	danorr	PHD	60	Princeton	1989
Rahsid, Salim	Prof	333-7388	salmrash@1	PHD	76	Yale	1981
Resek, Robert W.	Prof	244-4827	rresek@igpa.	PHD	61	Harvard	1961
Schran, Peter	Prof	333-4580		PHD	61	Berkeley	1965
Shafer, Wayne	Prof	333-0645		PHD	72	Ca-SnBarb	1990
Shupp, Franklin R.	Prof	244-6437	fshupp@2	PHD	59	Princeton	1960
Sprenkle, Case	Prof	333-4536		PHD	60	Yale	1960
Taira, Koji	Prof	333-1483		PHD	61	Stanford	1970
Ulen, Thomas	Prof	333-4593	tulen@law.	PHD	79	Stanford	1977
Yannelis, Nicholas C.	Prof	333-4584	nyannelis@2	PHD	83	Rochester	1988
Arvan, Lanny D.	Assoc	333-4587	larvan@uxl.cso.	PHD	81	Northwes	1980
DeBrock, Lawrence	Assoc	333-4553	ldebrock	PHD	80	Cornell	1979
Esfahani, Hadi S. on leave World Bank	Assoc			PHD	84	Berkeley	1984
Husby, Ralph D.	Assoc	333-6865		PHD	69	Cornell	1967
Steinkamp, Stanley W.	Emer	333-7300		PHD	58	Michigan	1958
Taub, Bart	Assoc	333-3467	btaub@uxh.cso.	PHD	81	Chicago	1989
Villamil, Anne P.	Assoc	244-6330	avillamil@2	PHD	88	Minnesota	1988
Williams, Steven R.	Assoc	333-4516		PHD	82	Northwes	1992
Williamson, H. F. Jr.	Assoc	333-4511	billw@vmd.cso.	PHD	69	Yale	1964
Conley, John	Asst	333-4590	jconley@2	PHD	90	Rochester	1989
Deltas, George M.	Asst			PHD		Yale	1995
Graziano, Paulette	Asst	333-4588	pgraz@vmd.cso.	MS	65	Illinois	1984
Greenstein, Shane on leave to Stanford University	Asst			PHD	89	Stanford	1990
Hallock, Kevin F.	Asst			PHD		Princeton	1995
Huggett, Mark	Asst	244-0488	huggett@uxh.cso.	PHD	91	Minnesota	1990
Krasa, Stefan	Asst	333-7698	krasa@3	PHD	87	Vienna	1990
Krebs, Tom	Asst			PHD		Columbia	1995
Kuan, Chung-Ming on leave	Asst			PHD	89	Ca-SnDgo	1989
Maloney, William on leave World Bank	Asst			PHD	90	Berkeley	1990

Univ of Illinois at Chicago — Chicago, IL 60607-7121 (312) 996-2684 — Ms. Lynn Lacey
Department of Economics — Col of Business Admin Fax=996-3344 — UICVM.UIC.EDU

Name	Rank	Phone	Email	Fields	Degree	Yr	School	Year
Uselding, Paul J.	Dean	996-2671	u59382	N	PHD	70	Northwes	1992
Chiswick, Barry R.	H-Pr	864-2684	u16020	J	PHD	67	Columbia	1978
Ayal, Eliezer B.	Prof	413-2361		O	PHD	61	Cornell	1972
Bassett, Gilbert W.	Prof	996-5777	u09006	C	PHD	73	Michigan	1973
Camacho, Antonio	Prof	996-8651	u09006	D	PHD	65	Minnesota	1968
Chiswick, Carmel U.	Prof	996-8721	u13914	T	PHD	72	Columbia	1978
Kosobud, Richard F.	Prof	996-2266	u17253	D	PHD	63	Penn	
Lehrer, Evelyn L.	Prof	996-2363	u28082	T	PHD	78	Northwes	
Director, Undergraduate Studies								
McDonald, John F.	Prof	996-2362	u08589	R	PHD	71	Yale	1981
Miller, Oscar	Prof	996-5247		A	AM	46	Chicago	1948
Officer, Lawrence H.	Prof	996-0689	u22093	F	PHD	65	Harvard	1987
Persky, Joseph J.	Prof	996-2687	u09102	R	PHD	71	Harvard	
Stokes, Houston H.	Prof	996-0971	u09080	D	PHD	69	Chicago	1968
Tam, Mo-Yin S.	Prof	413-2360	u08950	P	PHD	74	SUNY-SBr	1974
White, William D.	Prof	996-2267	u09019	I	PHD	75	Harvard	1975
Chaloupka, Frank J. IV	Assoc	413-2367	u35678	I	PHD	88	CUNY	1988
Peck, Richard M.	Assoc	996-2365	u29211	D	PHD	83	Princeton	1981
Pieper, Paul J.	Assoc	996-5214	u32808	E	PHD	84	Northwes	1982
Director of Graduate Studies								
Stanford, William G.	Assoc	996-0970	u27455	C	PHD	84	Northwes	
Ierulli, Kathryn	Asst	996-3913		D	PHD	94	Chicago	
Karras, Georgios	Asst	996-2321	u47633	E	PHD	90	Ohio St	
Moses, Ronald P.	Asst	996-2599		F	PHD		Chicago	

Univ Illinois at Springfield — Springfield, IL 62794-9243 (217) 786-7174 — Marilynn Mooney
Department of Economics — Sch of Business & Mgt Fax=786-7188

Name	Rank	Phone	Email	Fields	Degree	Yr	School	Year
Munkirs, John R.	Dean	786-6355		BN	PHD	73	Oklahoma	1972
Ayers, Michael	C-Ac	786-7405		OR	PHD	74	Oklahoma	1971
Mouhamed, Adil	Assoc	786-7174		FP	PHD	85	Nebraska	1988
Siddiquee, Baker A.	Assoc	786-7174		DEH	PHD	88	Manitoba	1987

Illinois Benedictine College — Lisle, IL 60532-0900 (708) Ext 7003 — Ms. Sara Scheiner
Dept of Business & Econ — Div of Social Science Fax=960-1126
phone: 960-1500

Name	Rank	Phone	Email	Fields	Degree	Yr	School	Year
Eber, John E.	Dean	Ext 4850		M	EDD	83	N Illinois	1976
Lee, Soyon	C-Pr	Ext 7003		FO	PHD	77	N Illinois	1974
Gahala, Charles L.	Prof	Ext 7008		MG	EDD	83	N Illinois	1984
Roth, Margarete P.	Prof	Ext 7005		FA	PHD	67	Cologne	1970
Meister, Charles G.	Assoc	Ext 7015		M	MBA	75	Northwes	1984
Quick, Lawrence	Assoc	Ext 7011		M	PHD	84	Northwes	1987
Eschbach, Doris	Asst	Ext 7014		M	ABD		St Louis	1993

Illinois Institute of Tech — Chicago, IL 60661 (312) 906-6500
Department of Business Adm — Stuart Sch of Business Fax=906-6549 — IITVAX

Name	Rank	Phone	Email	Fields	Degree	Yr	School	Year
Hassan, M. Zia	Dean	906-6515		Mgt	PHD	65	Ill Tech	1960
Chung, Joseph Sang-Hoon	Prof				PHD	64	Wayne St	1964
Hall, W. Clayton	Assoc				PHD		Illinois	
Tourk, Khairy A.	Assoc				PHD		Berkeley	

Illinois State University — Normal, IL 61790-4200 (309) 438-8625 — Janice Pritchett
Dept of Economics Box 4200 — Col of Arts & Sciences Fax=438-5228 — ILSTU.EDU

Name	Rank	Phone	Email	Fields	Degree	Yr	School	Year
Ramsey, David D.	C-Ac	438-8625	ddramsey	DEH	PHD	67	Minnesota	1973
Chizmar, John F.	Prof	438-7301	jfchizmar	CM	PHD	71	Boston C	1971
Nelson, Michael A.	Prof	438-8720	manelson	G	PHD	80	Purdue	1981
Ostrosky, Anthony L. Jr.	Prof	438-7071	alostros	ADEC	PHD	73	Pittsburgh	1973
Owen, Virginia L.	Prof	438-3765	vlowen	DA	PHD	69	Illinois	1964
Ram, Rati	Prof	438-8625	ratiram		PHD	76	Chicago	1982
Distinguished Professor								
Singh, Ram Das	Prof	438-3005	rdsingh		PHD	70	N Delhi	1981
Cohn, Raymond L.	Assoc	438-7892	rlcohn	DN	PHD	77	Oregon	1983
Goel, Rajeev Kumar	Assoc	438-2060	rkgoel	CO	PHD	87	Houston	1989
Hiebert, L. Dean	Assoc	438-8300	dhieber	ADE	PHD	72	Wisconsin	1973
Morey, Mathew James	Assoc	438-3765	mjmorey	CM	PHD		Illinois	
Norton, Seth	Assoc	438-2996	swnorton	M	PHD	82	Chicago	1992
on leave to Wheaton College, Illinois								
Rich, Daniel P.	Assoc	438-8528	dprich	DJ	PHD	87	Houston	1987
Skaggs, Neil T.	Assoc	438-7204	ntskaggs	BDE	PHD	80	Duke	1979
Walbert, Mark S.	Assoc	438-8625	mswalber	CDE	PHD	84	New Mex	1984
Abdalla, Adil	Asst	438-8495	aabdall	F	PHD	88	Iowa	1988
Carlson, J. Lon	Asst	438-8625	lcarlson	PQ	PHD	84	Illinois	1986
Cobb-Clark, Deborah	Asst	438-8428	dcclark	DJ	PHD	90	Michigan	1991
Hasan, Nazmul	Asst	438-3747		G	PHD	93	Illinois	1993
email hasan@ysidro.econ.uiuc.edu								
Mohammadi, Hassan	Asst	438-7777	hmohamma	E	PHD	88	Wash St	1988

Illinois Wesleyan University — Bloomington, IL 61702-2900 (309) 556-3184 — Jean Lage
Department of Economics — Business & Econ Div Fax=556-3411 — TITAN.IWU.EDU

Name	Rank	Phone	Field	Degree	Yr	School	Since
Gardner, Mona J.	D-Pr	556-3171	Fnce	PHD		Cincinnati	1988
Rust Professor of Insurance/Finance; Dir of Div of Business & Economics							
Seeborg, Michael C.	H-Pr	556-3184	J	PHD	76	Utah	1989
Robert S. Eckley Distinguished Professor of Economics							
Chapman, Margaret L.	Assoc	556-3191	L	PHD	77	Illinois	1977
Leekley, Robert M.	Assoc	556-3178		PHD	74	Mich St	1974
Lowry, Pamela	Asst	556-3489	F	PHD	92	Maryland	1992

Immaculata College — Immaculata, PA 19345 (610) Ext 3472
Economics Faculty — Dept of Econ, Atg & Bus Fax=251-1668
phone: 647-4400

Name	Rank	Phone	Degree	School	Since
Kokat, Robert G.	C-Ac	Ext 3472	DBA	Indiana	1990
Coyle, Sister Ann	Assoc	Ext 3470	MA	Temple	
Sumpta, Sister Virginia A.	Assoc	Ext 3147	MA	Catholic	
Pilotte, Sheree	Asst	Ext 3464	PHD	Indiana	

Indiana University — Bloomington, IN 47405-6601 (812) 855-1021 — Linda Baker
Department of Economics — Col of Arts & Sciences Fax=855-3736 — INDIANA.EDU

Name	Rank	Phone	E-mail	Degree	Yr	School	Since
Lowengrub, Morton	Dean	855-2392	lowengru	PHD			
Wilson, John D.	C-Ac	855-8035	wilsonj	PHD	79	MIT	1985
Becker, Robert	Prof	855-3014	becker	PHD	78	Rochester	1978
Becker, William	Prof	855-3577	beckerw	PHD	73	Pittsburgh	1979
Gardner, Roy J.	Prof	855-2146	gardner	PHD	75	Cornell	1983
Kiesling, Herbert J.	Prof	855-5817	kiesling	PHD	65	Harvard	1965
Kniesner, Thomas J.	Prof	855-7256	kniesne	PHD	76	Ohio St	1988
Kuznets, Paul W.	Prof	855-3213	kuznets	PHD	64	Yale	1964
Morrison, Clarence C.	Prof	855-7791	morrison	PHD	64	N Carol	1970
Orr, Lloyd D.	Prof	855-6897	orr	PHD	64	Northwes	1964
Saunders, Phillip	Prof	855-4050	saunders	PHD	64	MIT	1970
Schmidt, David R.	Prof	855-2543	drschmid	PHD	94	CIT	1993
Trivedi, Pravin K.	Prof	855-3567	trivedi	PHD	70	LondonEc	1987
von Furstenberg, George	Prof	855-4764	vonfurst	PHD	66	Princeton	1970
Rudy Professor of Economics							
Walker, James M.	Prof	855-2760	walkerj	PHD	78	Tx A&M	1984
Waller, Christopher J.	Prof	885-2383	waller	PHD	85	Wash St	1986
Williams, Arlington W.	Prof	855-4564	williama	PHD	78	Arizona	1979
Alexeev, Michael	Assoc	855-7103	malexeev	PHD	84	Duke	1992
Buffie, Edward F.	Assoc	855-9566	ebuffie	PHD	82	Yale	1992
Chang, Fwu-Ranq	Assoc	855-6070	changf	PHD	85	Chicago	1983
Rotella, Elyce J.	Assoc	885-7858	rotella	PHD	77	Penn	1981
Witte, Willard E.	Assoc	855-2080	witte	PHD	75	Wisconsin	1981
Kaganovich, M.	Asst	855-6967	mkaganov	PHD	85	USSR	1991
Leeper, Eric M.	Asst	855-9157		PHD	89	Minnesota	1995
Ming, Xing	Asst	855-1021		PHD	95	Rice	1995
Pedroni, Peter	Asst	855-7925	ppedroni	PHD	93	Columbia	1993
Raff, Horst	Asst	855-7928	hraff	PHD	91	W Ontario	1993
Burdick, Clark	Lect	855-4850	caburdic	ABD			1993
Janeba, Eckhard	Lect	855-1021		ABD		Bonn	1994

Indiana Univ at Kokomo — Kokomo, IN 46904-9003 (317)
Economics Faculty — Div of Business & Econ Fax=

Name	Rank	Phone	Field	Degree	Yr	School	Since
Von der Embse, Thomas J.	Dean	455-9446	Mgt	PHD	68	Ohio St	1990
Pendse, Dilip C.	Assoc	455-9279		PHD	71	Oreg St	
Pulikonda, Naga	Assoc	455-9282		PHD	77	Illinois	
Parkison, Kathy	Asst	455-9462		PHD	83	Purdue	1993

Indiana Univ South Bend — South Bend, IN 46634 (219) — IUSB
Economics Faculty — Div of Business & Econ Fax=237-4599

Name	Rank	Phone	Degree	Yr	School	Since
Patti, Charles	Dean					
Agbetsiafa, Douglas K.	Prof	237-4208	PHD	80	Notre Dm	1980
Bartholomew, A. Wayne	Prof		PHD	68	Cornell	1968
Herschede, Alfred J.	Prof	237-4303	PHD	76	Illinois	1976
Joray, Paul A.	Prof	237-4227	PHD		Illinois	1971
Kochanowski, Paul S.	Prof		DBA		Indiana	1972
Peck, John E.	Prof		PHD		Notre Dm	1969
Director of Bureau of Business and Economic Research						

Indiana Univ Northwest — Gary, IN 46408-1197 (219)
Economics Faculty — Div of Business & Econ Fax=980-6579

Name	Rank	Phone	Field	Degree	Yr	School	Since
Vasquez, Marilyn E.	Dean	980-6633	BuAd	JD	88	Valparis	1979
Lynch, G.	Prof	980-6907	RTE	PHD	63	Wash St	1981
Singer, L.	Prof	980-6913	RTE	PHD	58	Indiana	1969
Bhatia, Shyam L.	Assoc	980-6634	F	PHD	76	Indiana	1976
Coffin, Donald A.	Assoc	438-3005	JNO	PHD	79	W Virginia	
Olmsted, George M.	Asst	980-6646	HG	PHD	84	Northwes	1987

Indiana Univ Southeast — New Albany, IN 47150 (812) 941-2362 — Mrs. Carol Goins
Department of Economics — Div of Business & Econ Fax=941-2672 — IUSMAIL.IUS.INDIANA.ED

Name	Rank	Phone	Email	Field	Degree	Yr	School	Year
Greckel, Fay E.	Dean	941-2325	fgreckel	OJR	PHD	69	Indiana	1967
Altmann, James L.	Prof	941-2307	jaltmann	DM	PHD	78	Wisconsin	1978
Felton, Marianne V.	Prof	941-2324	mfelton	ZIEC	PHD	79	Indiana	1976
Alse, Jahardhanan	Asst	941-2520	jalse	FE	PHD	93	Wisconsin	1992
Schansberg, D. Eric	Asst	941-2527	dshansb	HJC	PHD	91	Tx A&M	1992

Indiana U of Pennsylvania — Indiana, PA 15705-1087 (412) 357-2640 — Ms. Debbie D. Mahan
Economics Faculty — Humanities & Social Sci Fax=357-6485 — GROVE.IUP.EDU

Name	Rank	Phone	Email	Field	Degree	Yr	School	Year
Carter, Brenda	Dean	357-2280	brenda_carter		PHD			
Walker, Donald A.	C	357-2640	dawalker	BD	PHD	61	Harvard	1969
Agyei Asamoah, Yaw	Prof	357-2641	osebo	FO	PHD	85	Wash U	1984
Dyal, James A.	Prof	357-4856	jimdyal	JR	PHD	75	Illinois	1977
Garvin, Alexander	Prof	357-4827		CE	PHD	73	Tennessee	1969
Karatjas, Nicholas	Prof	357-4855	karatjas	CDI	PHD	76	SUNY-SBr	1978
Martel, Arthur H.	Prof	357-4775	arthur_martel	JK	PHD	74	Mass	1970
Radell, Willard W.	Prof	357-4776	willard_radell	NP	PHD	80	Illinois	1981
Stonebraker, Robert J.	Prof	357-4770	bobstone	EK	PHD	73	Princeton	1971
Cross, John W.	Assoc	357-4781		EG	MA	68	Mass	1969
Holt, Harry G.	Assoc	357-2642	harry_holt	IP	MS	61	Bucknell	1968
Huff, Marvin	Assoc	357-4774		JK	MA	68	Illinois	1969
Radakovic, George	Assoc	357-4826	george_radakovic	JR	PHD	79	Pittsburgh	1986
Ware, Stephen B.	Assoc	357-4771		BE	BA	61	Ohio Wes	1969

Indiana State University — Terre Haute, IN 47809 (812) 237-2160 — Carolyn Greenwalt
Department of Economics — College of Arts & Sci Fax=237-4349 — SCIFAC.INDSTATE.EDU

Name	Rank	Phone	Email	Field	Degree	Yr	School	Year
Weixlmann, Joseph	Dean	237-2788	asceix@amber.	Engl	PHD	73	Kansas	1976
Kyle, James T.	C-Ac	237-2159	eckyle	J	ABD	63	Indiana	1963
Burkett, Paul G.	Prof	237-2164	ecburke	EO	PHD	84	Syracuse	1991
Conant, John L.	Prof	237-2163	econjlc	DJB	PHD	84	Tennessee	1981
Fischbaum, Marvin N.	Prof	237-2171	ecfisch	DP	PHD	65	Columbia	1965
Parks, Terrance C.	Prof	237-2173	ecparks	OED	PHD	74	Illinois	1966
Richards, Donald G.	Assoc	237-2179	ecparmi	FO	PHD	83	Conn	1985
Sorensen, Duane L.	Assoc	237-2166		R	MS	61	Iowa St	1968
Chen, Aimin	Asst	237-2175	ecchen	PD	PHD	90	Penn St	1991
Guell, Robert	Asst	237-2169	ecguell	HC	PHD	91	Syracuse	1991
Lotspeich, Richard	Asst	237-2176	eclotsp	PQ	PHD	86	New Mex	1990

Indiana Wesleyan — Marion, IN 46953 (317) 677-2303 — Linda MacKay 677-2289
Dept of Atg, Business & Econ — Division of Social Sci Fax=677-2284 — INDWES.EDU

Name	Rank	Phone	Email	Field	Degree	Yr	School	Year
Martin, Glenn R.	C-Pr	677-2300		Hist	PHD	73	Ball St	1967
Showalter, Jerry	C-Ac	677-2289		Atg	MACC			
Pongracic, Ivan	Asst	677-2145			MA	68	Zagreb	1987

University of Indianapolis — Indianapolis, IN 46227-3697 (317) 788-3378
Department of Economics — School of Business Fax=788-3300 — GANDLF.UINDY.EDU

Name	Rank	Phone	Email	Field	Degree	Yr	School	Year
Livesay, Robin R. (O. T. Fitzwater Professor of Business)	Dean	788-3370		Mgt	PHD	74	Ohio St	1979
Gurtunca, Esen Z. (Donald W. Tanselle Professor of Economics)	Prof	788-3287			PHD	73	Purdue	1974
Conrad, James M.	Assoc	788-3232			PHD	70	Kentucky	1979
Foust, James D.	Assoc	788-3495			PHD	68	N Carol	1985

Iona College — New Rochelle, NY 10801-1890 (914) 633-2216
Dept of Economics — Col of Arts & Science Fax=633-2608 — IONA.BITNET

Name	Rank	Phone	Email	Field	Degree	Yr	School	Year
Rosenberg, Warren	Dean			Bio	PHD	82	NYU	1981
Acker, Mary H.	C-Ac	633-2215		FG	PHD	82	Fordham	1982
Holland, John J. Jr.	Emer	636-2216		EN	PHD	72	NYU	1963
Jantzen, Robert H.	Assoc	637-2731	rhj1	CIJ	PHD	82	Northeas	1982
Pescatrice, Donn	Assoc	637-2729			PHD	75	Purdue	1983
Spagnolo, John A.	Assoc	637-2730		R	PHD	82	Fordham	1978

University of Iowa — Iowa City, IA 52242-1323 (319) 335-0829 — Margaret Jesse, Adm Asst
Department of Economics — College of Business Adm Fax=335-1956 — UIOWA.EDU
email: @1=scout-po.biz.uiowa.edu

Name	Rank	Phone	Email	Field	Degree	Yr	School	Year
Fethke, Gary C.	Dean	335-0868	gary-fethke		PHD	68	Iowa	1974
Riezman, Raymond G.	C-Pr	335-0829			PHD	77	Minnesota	
Albrecht, William P.	Prof	335-3125	william-albrecht		PHD	65	Yale	1965
Fethke, Carol	Prof	335-0504	carol-fethke		PHD	71	Iowa	1975
Forsythe, Robert (Associate Dean)	Prof	335-0865	robert_forsythe		PHD	75	Car Mellon	1981
Fuller, John W.	Prof	335-0038			PHD	68	Wash St	1979

Name	Rank	Phone	Email	Degree	Yr	School	Year
Horowtiz, Joel	Prof	335-0844	joel-horowitz	PHD	67	Cornell	1982
Joseph, Hyman	Prof	335-0837	hyman-joseph	PHD	69	Northwes	1966
McCloskey, Donald N.	Prof	335-2290	donald-mccloskey	PHD	70	Harvard	1980
Nelson, Forrest D.	Prof	335-0854	forrest-nelson	PHD	75	Rochester	1980
Neumann, George R.	Prof	335-0850	george-neumann	PHD	74	Northwes	1984
Nordquist, Gerald L.	Prof	335-0833	gerald-nordquist	PHD	60	Iowa	1968
Pogue, Thomas F.	Prof	335-0843	thomas-pogue	PHD	68	Yale	1965
Savin, Nathan E.	Prof	335-0855	gene-savin	PHD	69	Berkeley	1986
Sgontz, Larry G.	Prof	335-0852	larry-sgontz	PHD	64	Illinois	1964
Siebert, Calvin D.	Prof	335-0851	calvin-siebert	PHD	66	Berkeley	1965
Whiteman, Charles H.	Prof	335-0834	charles-whiteman	PHD	81	Minnesota	1980
Wu, Shih-Yen	Prof	335-0846	swh@1	PHD	60	Northwes	1964
Balch, Michael S.	Assoc	335-0847	michael-balch	PHD	65	NYU	1971
Blume, Andreas	Assoc	335-0931	andreas-blume	PHD	89	Ca-SnDgo	1989
Corbae, P. Dean	Assoc	335-0962	p-corbae	PHD	90	Yale	1989
Ingram, Marlynne B. F.	Assoc	335-0897	beth-ingram	PHD	86	Iowa	1988
Kocherlakota, Narayana	Assoc	335-0936		PHD	87	Chicago	1990
email: nkocherl@scout-po.biz.uiowa.edu							
Solow, John L.	Assoc	335-0845	john-solow	PHD	83	Stanford	1981
Kim, Yong-Gwan	Asst	335-3810	ykim@1	PHD	90	Ca-SnDgo	1990
Lobato, Ignacio	Asst	335-0958	ilobato@1	PHD	94	London	1994
McCutcheon, Barbara	Asst	335-0932	barbara-mccutcho	PHD	91	Chicago	1990
Tamura, Robert F.	Asst	335-0961	robert-tamura	PHD	88	Chicago	1988

Iowa State University Ames, IA 50011-1070 (515) 294-6740 Diana McLaughlin
Department of Economics Col Liberal Arts & Sci Fax=294-0221 IASTATE.EDU

Name	Rank	Phone	Email	Field	Degree	Yr	School	Year
Hoffman, Elizabeth	Dean	294-7740	ehoffma		PHD	79	Cal Tech	1993
Miranowski, John A.	C-Pr	294-6741	jmirski	Q	PHD	75	Harvard	1995
Adams, Jean W.	Prof	294-5886	jwadams	L	PHD	73	Illinois	1972
Adams, Roy Dean	Prof	294-5886	radams	HE	PHD	72	Illinois	1972
Fletcher, Lehman B.	Prof	294-5820	lbf	O	PHD	69	Berkeley	1960
Harl, Neil E.	Prof	294-6354	harl	QK	PHD	65	Iowa St	1964
Huffman, Wallace E.	Prof	294-6359	whuffman	J	PHD	72	Chicago	1974
Lapan, Harvey E.	Prof	294-5917	hlapan	DF	PHD	71	MIT	1972
Luckett, Dudley G.	Prof	294-2701	dluckett	EN	PHD	58	Tx-Austin	1957
Mattila, John Peter	Prof	294-5813		J	PHD	69	Wisconsin	1973
Merrill, William C.	Prof	294-6846	wmerrill	O	PHD	64	Berkeley	1964
Meyer, Charles W.	Prof	294-5887	cmeyer	G	PHD	61	J Hopkins	1961
Orazem, Peter F.	Prof	294-5827	pfo	J	PHD	83	Yale	1982
Prescott, James R.	Prof	294-5860		R	PHD	64	Harvard	1973
Sandler, Todd M.	Prof	294-5783	tsandler	HD	PHD	71	SUNY-Bin	1986
Starleaf, Dennis R.	Prof	294-5811	dstar	E	PHD	67	Vanderbilt	1963
Tesfatsion, Leigh S.	Prof	294-0138	tesfatsi	E	PHD	75	Minnesota	1990
Vandewetering, Hylke	Prof	294-5888	hivdw	O	PHD	64	Iowa St	1964
Falk, Barry L.	Assoc	294-5875	bfalk	E	PHD	82	Minnesota	1980
Quirmbach, Herman C.	Assoc	294-6221	hcqbach	L	PHD	83	Princeton	1990
Schroeter, John R.	Assoc	294-5876	johns	L	PHD	81	Minnesota	1983
Athanasoulis, Stefano	Asst				PHD	95	Yale	1995
Bilias, Yannis G.	Asst				PHD	95	Illinois	1995
de Fontnouvelle, Patrick	Asst				PHD	95	Wisconsin	1995

Ithaca College Ithaca, NY 14850 (607) 274-3200 Tina Bennett
Department of Economics Sch of Humanities & Sci Fax=274-3474 ITHACA

Name	Rank	Phone	Field	Degree	Yr	School	Year
Erlich, Howard	Dean			PHD			
Musgrave, Frank W.	C-Pr$	274-3200	IJ	PHD	68	Rutgers	1968
Mieczkowski, Bogdan	Prof		AF	PHD		Illinois	1954
Hinderliter, Roger H.	Assoc		BE	PHD	70	Wash U	1970
Kacapyr, Elia W.	Assoc	274-3200	AG	PHD	85	Geo St	1985
Kolberg, William	Assoc		AQ	PHD		Rhode Isl	1984
Monroe, Michael C.	Asst		AIR	PHD		Cornell	1988
Wetchler, Sherry J.	Asst		AJHI	PHD	92	Maryland	1990

Jackson State University Jackson, MS 39217-0560 (601) 968-2531 Deborah Mihchalls
Dept Econ, Finance & Gen Bus School of Business Fax=968-2690 JSUMS.EDU
Box 17760

Name	Rank	Phone	Field	Degree	Yr	School	Year
Glover, Glenda	Dean	968-2411	Atg	PHD	90	Geo Wash	1994
Hurley, John F.	C-Ac	968-2531		PHD	71	Illinois	1972
Chao, Ching Y.	Prof	968-2451		PHD	64	Iowa St	1972
Alexander, McKinley	Assoc	982-6315		PHD	86	Illinois	1975
Bowling, James	Assoc	968-2606		PHD	85	Miss	1975
Grass, R. Gail	Assoc	968-2028		PHD	89	Harvard	1989
Assad, Jean-Claud	Asst	968-2604		PHD	87	Howard	1991
Jeffries, Christopher N.	Asst	968-2607		PHD	88	Fla St	1992
McGill-Tillman, Patricia	Inst	968-2605		MA	65	Atlanta	1968

Jacksonville University — Jacksonville, FL 32211 (904) — Ms. Bess Meyers
Div Atg, Econ & Finance — College of Business Fax=745-7467

Name	Rank	Phone			Degree	Yr	School	Year
Pordeli, Hassan	Dean$	Ext 7431			PHD	83	Nebraska	1983
Brady, James J.	Prof				PHD	69	Notre Dm	
Jessie Ball duPont Professor of Economics								
Borg, J. Rody	Assoc	744-3950			PHD	86	N Carol	1984
Buck, John	Asst	745-7431			PHD	89	Wisconsin	1994
Hoover, Gary	Asst	745-7431			PHD	95	Kent	1995
Perry, Mark	Asst	744-3950			PHD	93	Geo Mason	1993

Jacksonville State Univ — Jacksonville, AL 36265-9982 (205) 782-5776 — Ms. Kelly Roberts
Dept of Econ & Finance/Stat — Col Commerce & Bus Adm Fax=782-5312

Name	Rank	Phone			Degree	Yr	School	Year
Fielding, William	C-Pr	782-5771			PHD		S Carol	1968
Cypert, Clifford L.	Prof	782-5505			PHD		Oklahoma	1974
Paxton, Donald	Prof	782-5799			PHD		Tulane	1977
Thompson, Paul	Prof	782-5392			PHD		Duke	1974
Bennett, Doris S.	Assoc	782-5514			PHD		Alabama	1986
McCarty, Cynthia S.	Asst	782-5777			PHD		N Carol	1990

James Madison University — Harrisonburg, VA 22807 (540) 568-3216 — Mrs. Loretta Grunewald
Department of Economics — College of Business Fax=568-3010 — VAX1.ACS.JMU.EDU

Name	Rank	Phone	Email	Fields	Degree	Yr	School	Year
Fields, T. Windsor	H-Pr	568-3216	fieldstw	EC	PHD	78	Virginia	1990
Carrier, Ronald E.	Prof	568-6241		A	PHD	60	Illinois	1971
President								
Horn, Robert N.	Prof	568-3219	hornrn	JD	PHD	78	N Hamp	1978
Kipps, Paul H.	Prof	568-3252	kippsph	A	PHD	68	Cornell	1968
Associate Dean								
Kohen, Andrew I.	Prof	568-3220	kohenai	JD	PHD	73	Ohio St	1976
Rosser, J. Barkley Jr.	Prof	568-3094	rosserjb	R	PHD	76	Wisconsin	1977
Varghese, K. Thomas	Prof	568-3206	varghekt	E	PHD	71	Wayne St	1970
Wood, William C.	Prof	568-3243	woodwc	DA	PHD	80	Virginia	1989
Director, Center for Economic Education								
Ahmed, Ehsan	Assoc	586-3214	ahmedex	EC	PHD	83	Mich St	1984
Director Office of Economic Services								
Jerome, Robert T. Jr.	Assoc	568-3029	jeromert	DF	PHD	82	Virginia	1981
Kreutzer, David W.	Assoc	568-3218	kreutzdw	FH	PHD	84	Geo Mason	1984
Milliman, Scott R.	Assoc	568-3213	millimsr	DQ	PHD	85	Wisconsin	1986
Rosser, Marina V.	Assoc	568-3094	rossermv	FP	PHD	79	MoscowSt	1987
Smith, Vardaman Russell	Assoc	568-3221	smithvr	B	PHD	80	Penn St	1979
Brunton, Bruce G.	Asst	581-3211	bruntobg	FNO	PHD	89	Utah	1984
Doyle, Joanne M.	Asst	568-3030	doylejm	DC	PHD	93	Boston C	1993
Elwood, S. Kirk	Asst	568-3098	elwoodsk	EFC	PHD	93	Ca-Davis	1992
Dobkins, Linda H.	Inst	568-3099	dobkinlh	RFE	PHD	95	Va Tech	1995

Jamestown College — Jamestown, ND 58045 (701) Ext 2481
Economics Faculty — Business Adm & Econ Dpt Fax=253-4318 — ACC.JC.EDU
phone 252-3467

Name	Rank	Phone	Email	Fields	Degree	Yr	School	Year
Gash, Dennis N.	C-Ac	Ext 2481	gash	ADEF	ABD	78	Northwes	1993

Jersey City State College — Jersey City, NJ 07305-1597 (201) 200-3230 — Ms. Rita Lange
Economics Department — Sch of Arts & Science Fax=200-2072

Name	Rank	Phone		Fields	Degree	Yr	School	Year
Hordon, Harris	C-Pr	200-3230		AG	PHD		NYU	
Ghebrat, Ezra	Assoc	300-3390		AD	PHD		New Sch	
Anderson, Richard T.	Asst	200-2285		AI	PHD		CUNY	
Steinberg, Ivan	Asst	200-3462		LA	MA		New Sch	
Vohra, Rubina A.	Asst	200-3074		AJ	PHD		Northeas	

John Carroll University — Cleveland, OH 44118 (216) 397-4508 — Barbara Lovequist
Dept of Economics & Finance — School of Business Fax=397-1728 — JCVAXA.JCU.EDU

Name	Rank	Phone	Email	Fields	Degree	Yr	School	Year
Navratil, Frank J.	Dean	397-4521	navratil	G	PHD	74	Notre Dm	1973
Zlatoper, Thomas J.	C-Ac	397-4583	zlatoper	ACD	PHD	80	Northwes	1984
Bombelles, Joseph T.	Prof	397-4655		ABOP	PHD	65	Case Wes	1963
Soper, John C.	Prof	397-3027	jsoper	ENA	PHD	70	Mass	1982
Calkins, Lindsay Noble	Assoc	397-4467	calkins	ADH	PHD	86	Michigan	1986
Cima, Lawrence R.	Assoc	397-4534	lrcima	ADEF	PHD	82	W Virginia	1971
Emanuele, Rosemarie	Asst	397-4182	emanuele	JDH	PHD	92	Boston C	1990
Jeon, B. Philip	Asst	397-4616	jeon	CEJT	PHD	90	Kentucky	1991
Simmons, Walter O.	VAsst			JKNO	PHD	94	Wayne St	1995
Welki, Andrew M.	Asst	397-4550	welki	HR	PHD	83	Penn St	1982
Dunbar, Donald J. S.J.	VInst			A	MA	91	Michigan	1995

John F. Kennedy University — Walnut Creek CA 94596 (510) 295-0600
Economics Faculty — School of Management Fax=295-0604
no full-time Economics faculty

Name	Rank	Phone		Fields	Degree	Yr	School	Year
Carroll, Frank J.	Dean	295-0600		Mgt	MBA	81	St Mary's	1-85

Johns Hopkins University — Baltimore, MD 21218 (410) 516-7601 — Donna Althoff 516-7677
Department of Economics — Sch of Arts & Sciences Fax=516-7600 — JHU.EDU

Name	Rank	Phone	Email	Field	Degree	Yr	School	Year
Knapp, Steven	Dean	516-8212			PHD			1994
Maccini, Louis J.	C-Pr	516-7607			PHD	70	Northwes	1969
Ball, Laurence M.	Prof	516-7605			PHD		MIT	1994
Gersovitz, Mark	Prof	516-7612			PHD	75	Yale	1994
Hamilton, Bruce W.	Prof	516-7613			PHD	72	Princeton	1973
Karni, Edi	Prof	516-7608			PHD	71	Chicago	1981
Khan, M. Ali	Prof	516-545			PHD		Yale	1988
Moffitt, Robert A.	Prof				PHD	75	Brown	1995
Young, H. Peyton	Prof	516-6118			PHD	70	Michigan	1994
Harrington, Joseph E.	Assoc	516-7615			PHD	84	Duke	1983
Carrington, William J.	Asst	516-7760			PHD	89	Chicago	1989
Carroll, Christopher D.	Asst				PHD	90	MIT	1995
de Lima, Pedro F.	Asst	516-7610			PHD	92	Wisconsin	1993
Velde, Francois R.	Asst	516-5564			PHD	92	Stanford	1993

Kalamazoo College — Kalamazoo, MI 49006 (616) 337-7028 — Esther Cleason 337-7028
Dept of Economics & Business — Liberal Arts Education Fax=337-7251 — KZOO.EDU

Name	Rank	Phone	Email	Field	Degree	Yr	School	Year
Hussen, Ahmed M.	C-Ac	337-7025	hussen	DQ	PHD	78	Oreg St	1985
Thomas, Philip S.	Prof	337-7023	thomas	FO	PHD	61	Michigan	1965
Athey, Michael J.	Assoc	337-7026	mathey	EO	PHD	91	Wash U	1995
McKinney, Hannah J.	Asst	337-7024	mckinney	HJR	PHD	84	Penn	1988
Moffit, Tim	Asst	337-7031	moffit	M	MBA	84	Dartmouth	1994
Reinert, Kenneth	Asst	337-7027	reinert	FDE	PHD	88	Maryland	1993

University of Kansas — Lawrence, KS 66045-2113 (913) 864-3501 — Leanea Wales
Department of Economics — Col Liberal Arts & Sci Fax=864-5270 — UKANVM

Name	Rank	Phone	Email	Field	Degree	Yr	School	Year
Muyskens, James L.	Dean			Phil	PHD		Michigan	1971
Sicilian, Joseph M.	C-Ac	864-3501			PHD	77	Purdue	1977
El-Hodiri, Mohamed A.	Prof	864-3501			PHD	66	Minnesota	1966
Lien, Da-Hsiang D.	Prof	864-3501			PDD	86	Cal Tech	1986
Weiss, Thomas J.	Prof	864-3501			PHD		N Carol	1967
Wu, De-Min	Prof	864-3501			PHD	63	Wisconsin	1964
Bhattacharya, Gautam	Assoc	864-3501			PHD	80	Rochester	1980
Burns, Malcolm R.	Assoc	864-3501			PHD	75	Minnesota	1975
Comolli, Paul M.	Assoc	864-3501			PHD		Iowa	1972
Faurot, David J.	Assoc	864-3501			PHD	75	Northwes	1975
Frevert, Peter	Assoc	864-3501			PHD		Purdue	1964
Iwata, Shigeru	Assoc	864-3501			PHD		UCLA	1988
Mitsui, Toshihide	Assoc	864-3501			PHD		Minnesota	1981
Rosenbloom, Joshua L.	Assoc	864-3501			PHD	88	Stanford	1988
Hess, Gregory	Asst	864-3501			PHD	89	J Hopkins	1993
Larudee, Mehrene	Asst	864-3501			ABD		Mass	1984
Shin, Kwanho	Asst	864-3501			ABD		UCLA	1984
Zhang, Jianbo	Asst	864-3501			PHD	90	Penn St	1990

Kansas State University — Manhattan, KS 66506-4001 (913) 532-7357 — Velda Deutsch
Department of Economics — Col of Arts & Sciences Fax=532-6919 — KSUVM.KSU.EDU

Name	Rank	Phone	Email	Field	Degree	Yr	School	Year
Nicholls, Peter	Dean	532-6900		Math	PHD		Cambridg	1991
Ragan, James F. Jr.	H-Pr	532-7357	jfrjr	JA	PHD	75	Wash U	1977
Babcock, Michael W.	Prof	532-4571		RQ	PHD	73	Illinois	1972
Emerson, M. Jarvin	Prof	532-4574	jarv	RQ	PHD	63	Iowa	1962
Nafziger, E. Wayne	Prof	532-4579	nafwayne	OPF	PHD	67	Illinois	1966
Thomas, Lloyd R. Jr.	Prof	532-4584	lbt	EA	PHD	70	Northwes	1968
Akkina, Krishna Rao	Assoc	532-4570	krishna	ECO	PHD	72	Minnesota	1972
Chang, Yang-Ming	Assoc	532-4573		DCF	PHD	84	SUNY-Buf	1984
Gormely, Patrick J.	Assoc	532-4576	gormely	OF	PHD	67	Duke	1967
McNulty, Mark S.	Assoc	532-4578	mmcnulty	CD	PHD	86	Iowa St	1985
Oldfather, Michael	Assoc	532-4580		E	PHD	80	Ohio	1983
Olson, Edwin G.	Assoc	532-4581	ekokbo	HBM	PHD	71	U Wash	1968
Bratsberg, Bernt	Asst	532-4572	bernt	JD	PHD	91	Ca-SnBarb	1991
Fisher, Walter	Asst	532-4575		EFC	PHD	90	U Wash	1992
Terrell, Milton	Asst	532-4583	dalvik	CEH	PHD	91	Duke	1991
Weisman, Dennis	Asst	532-4588	weisman	KD	PHD	93	Florida	1993
Trenary, Roger C.	Inst	532-4585	trenary	A	MA	72	Wayne St	1977

Kansas Wesleyan University — Salina, KS 67401-6196 (913)
Dept Bus, Atg & Economics — Div of Social Sciences Fax=827-0927
phone: 827-5541

Name	Rank	Phone	Email	Field	Degree	Yr	School	Year
Hull, Karen	C-As	Ext 255		Atg	MACC			

Kean College of New Jersey	Union, NJ	07083	(908) 527-2238				Elaine Mahon	
Dept Econ, Fnce & Geography	Sch Bus, Govt & Tech		Fax=354-2883				KEAN.EDU	
Anderson, Charles E.	Dean	527-2531			PHD	75	Stanford	7-88
Kempey, William M.	C-Pr	527-2390			PHD	70	NYU	9-78
Kim, Youn Suk	Prof	527-2489			PHD	73	New Sch	9-74
Saffer, Henry	Assoc	527-2400			PHD		CUNY	9-85
Schumacher, Howard	Assoc	527-2428			MA		Columbia	9-56
Carreno, Eufronio	Asst	527-2374			PHD		Rutgers	9-88
Condon, Carol M.	Asst	527-2391			PHD	78	Columbia	9-85

Keene State College	Keene, NH	03431-4183	(603) 358-2544					
Department of Economics	Sciences & Soc Sciences		Fax=358-2257					
Leversee, Gordon J.	Dean				PHD		Duke	1981
Duston, Thomas E.	Assoc				PHD		Brown	1984
Sherry, Robert L.	Assoc				PHD	79	Yale	1984
Dolenc, Patrick V	Asst				PHD		Utah	1991

Kennesaw State College	Marietta, GA	30061-0444	(404) 423-6091	Yvonne Bryant/Julee Childre				
Dept of Economics & Finance	Coles Sch of Business		Fax=423-6539	KSCMAIL.KENNESAW.EDU				
Mescon, Timothy S.	Dean	423-6342	tmescon	JM	PHD	79	Georgia	1990
Curley, Michael D.	C-Pr	423-6091	mcurley	ADMG	PHD	74	Kentucky	1984
Anderson, Thomas C.	Assoc	423-6111	tanderson	ADM	PHD	72	Berkeley	1985
Brothman, Billie Ann	Assoc	423-6496	bbrothman	AGIM	PHD	78	Notre Dm	1989
Gilliam, Kenneth P.	Assoc	423-6319	kgilliam	ACD	PHD	76	Lehigh	1984
Goodwin, Randall B.	Assoc	423-6101	rgoodwin	ADM	PHD	82	Georgia	1982
Park, Jong-Heum	Assoc	423-6429	jpark	ADFO	PHD	74	Okla St	1988
Prime, Penelope B.	Assoc	423-6579	pprime	ADFO	PHD	87	Michigan	1991
Tiwari, Kashi N.	Assoc	423-6086	ktiwari	CEG	PHD	81	So Meth	1988
Bumbarner, Mary	Asst	423-6341	mbumbarner	AERH	PHD	84	Geo St	1985
Reibman, Spencer S.	Asst	423-6720	sreibman	ADF	MBA	76	Chicago	1991
Sabbarese, Donald M.	Asst	423-6094	dSabbarese	AEM	PHD	84	Geo St	1978
Tutterow, Roger C.	Asst	423-6144	rtutterow	ACDM	PHD	90	Geo St	1991
Mirza, Faisal K.	Inst	423-6092	fmirza	AD	MBA	76	Indiana	1981

Kent State University	Kent, OH	44242-0001	(216) 672-2366	Diane Williams Ext 221				
Dept Economics PO Box 5190 phone 672-2366	College of Business Adm		Fax=672-2448				KENTVM	
Stevens, George E.	Dean	672-2772	gstevens	ADMS	DBA	79	Kent St	1995
Williams, Donald R.	C-Pr$	Ext 399	dwilliam	J	PHD	84	Northwes	1983
Bennett, Richard E.	Prof	Ext 361	rbennett	C	PHD	70	Ohio St	1968
Casper, Cheryl A.	Prof	672-2366	ccasper	D	PHD	75	Case Wes	1973
McKee, David L.	Prof	Ext 214	dmckee	OR	PHD	66	Notre Dm	1967
Mount, Randall I.	Prof	Ext 327	rmount	CD	PHD	69	Purdue	1966
Raymond, Richard D.	Emer	Ext 395		DR	PHD	63	Brown	1970
Upton, Charles W.	Prof	Ext 311	cupton	EQ	PHD	69	Car Mellon	8-89
Williams, Harold R. Associate Dean	Prof	Ext 222	hwilliam	EF	PHD	65	Nebraska	1966
Kent, Richard J.	Assoc	Ext 216	rkent	E	PHD	76	Berkeley	1983
Woudenberg, Henry W. Jr.	Assoc	Ext 234	hwoudenb	E	PHD	68	Mich St	1967
Ellis, Michael A.	Asst	Ext 211	mellis	EF	PHD	91	Tx A&M	1990

University of Kentucky	Lexington, KY	40506-0034	(606)					
Department of Economics	Col of Bus & Economics		Fax=257-8938				UKCC.EDU	
Furst, Richard W.	Dean	257-8939		Fnce	DBA	68	Wash U	1981
Webb, Michael A.	C-Pr	257-1166	ecowebb	FO	PHD	80	Illinois	1980
Ali, Mukhtar M.	Prof	257-7636	eco131	C	PHD	69	Wisconsin	1969
Berger, Mark C.	Prof	257-1282	eco171	J	PHD	81	Ohio St	1981
Black, Dan A.	Prof	257-7641	eco145	DJI	PHD	83	Purdue	1983
Blomquist, Glenn C.	Prof	257-3924	eco167	HQR	PHD	77	Chicago	1980
Fackler, James S.	Prof	257-7649	eco134	E	PHD	77	Indiana	1982
Garen, John E.	Prof	257-3581	eco157	J	PHD	82	Ohio St	1982
Gift, Richard E.	Prof	257-7640	regift01	FB	PHD	65	Duke	1965
Harvey, Curtis E.	Prof	257-3626		P	PHD	63	S Calif	1963
Hultman, Charles W.	Prof	257-7651		F	PHD	60	Iowa	1969
Jensen, Richard A.	Prof	257-1266	eco189	D	PHD	80	Northwes	1980
Krislov, Joseph	Prof	257-3057	eco192	JN	PHD	54	Wisconsin	1954
McGee, L. Randolph	Prof	257-1119	ecolrm	MG	PHD	63	Tulane	1963
Scott, Frank A. Jr.	Prof	257-7643	eco135	GH	PHD	79	Virginia	1979
Stober, William J.	Prof	257-1048	stober	D	PHD	65	Duke	1965
Toma, Eugenia F.	Prof	257-1156	pub702	H	PHD	77	Va Tech	1977
Gillette, Robert	Assoc	257-1411	jrgill01	A	PHD	86	Tx A&M	1994
Hoyt, William H.	Assoc	257-2518	eco183	RHG	PHD	86	Iowa	1969
Kim, Yoonbai	Assoc	257-2838	ykim01	EFG	PHD	87	Stanford	1991
Madden, John L.	Assoc	257-4811	jlmadden	N	PHD	68	Kansas St	1968
Toma, Mark	Assoc	268-4966	eco204	E	PHD	51	Va Tech	1989
Dickert, Stacy	Asst	257-3626		GHJ	PHD	95	Wisconsin	1995
Hoyt, Gail Mitchell	Asst	257-2517	eco211	A	PHD	92	Kentucky	1994
Stoker, James	Asst	257-3626		E	PHD	95	Chicago	1995
Wang, Weiren	Asst	257-4149	eco110	M	PHD	90	S Calif	1990

Kentucky State University	Frankfort, KY 40601 (502) 227-6708						Christy Roberts
Dept of Bus Admin-Economics	School of Business Fax=227-6404						
Lee, Dae Sung	Dean 227-6714		ADEC	PHD	69	Mass	1969
Assibey-Mensah, Albert	Asst 227-6284		AG	PHD	94	Cincinnati	1994
Park, Chaewon	Asst 227-6921		ACJ	PHD		Indiana	1992
Sokoloff, Joel J.	Asst 227-6914		ACE	MA	67	Mass	1974

Kenyon College	Gambier, OH 43022-9623 (614)						
Economics Faculty	Department of Economics Fax=						KENYON.EDU
Did Not Respond--1994-95 Listing							
Keeler, James	C-Ac 427-5285	keeler		PHD	81	Indiana	1984
Brehm, Carl T.	Prof 427-2244			PHD	58	Indiana	1963
Gensemer, Bruce L.	Prof 427-5283			PHD	66	Michigan	
Trethewey, Richard L.	Assoc			PHD	71	U Wash	1969
Harrington, David E.	Asst 427-5328			PHD	87	Wisconsin	1986
Himmelright Assistant Professor in Economics							
Kynski, Kathy	Asst			PHD		Wisconsin	
Himmelright Assistant Professor of Economics							

King's College	Wilkes-Barre, PA 18711 (717) Ext 5696						Janet Meade
Department of Economics	McGowan Sch of Business Fax=826-5989						KINGS.EDU
phone 826-5000							
Schoen, Edward J.	Dean 826-5932	ejschoen	Law	JD	68	Geotown	9-72
John S. Davis Distinguished Service Professor in Business							
Hosseini, Hamid S.	C-Ac 826-5900			PHD	77	Oregon	9-86
Arnold, Thomas R.	Prof 826-5900	trarnold		PHD	70	Syracuse	6-60
Herve A. LeBlanc Distinguished Service Professor in Liberal Arts							
Rose, Margarita M.	Asst 826-5900	mmrose		PHD	89	Notre Dm	9-90
Singer, Russell	Asst 826-5900	rjsinger		BS	58	Wilkes	9-67
Director of International Business Program							

Kutztown University of PA	Kutztown, PA 19530 (610) 683-4584						Mrs. Tracy Acker
Department of Economics	College of Business Fax=683-4573						KUTZTOWN.EDU
Hartz, Theodore A.	Dean 683-4575	jartz	Fnce	MBA		Lehigh	1977
Hvidding, James M.	C-Pr 683-4593	hvidding	EB	PHD	76	Maryland	1986
Daneshyar, Arifeen M.	Prof 683-4592	daneshya	AE	PHD	76	S Illinois	1984
Margolis, H. Albert	Prof 683-1372	margolis	NC	PHD	69	Purdue	1976
Luizer, James C.	Assoc 683-4595		JC	PHD	84	Lehigh	1984
Sraiheen, Abdulwahab	Assoc 683-4597	sraiheen	CM	PHD	86	Penn St	1990
Zelleke, Girma	Assoc 683-4598	zelleke	FO	PHD	84	Colorado	1986

Lafayette College	Easton, PA 18042 (610)						
Economics Faculty	Dept of Econ & Business Fax=						LAFAYETTE.EDU
Bukics, Rose Marie	C-Pr			MBA		Lehigh	1980
Chambers, Donald	Prof 250-5303			PHD		N Carol	
Hochman, Harold M.	Prof 250-5315			PHD	65	Yale	1992
Wm. E. Simon Professor of Political Economics							
Seifried, Edmond J.	Prof			PHD		W Virginia	1978
Ahene, Rexford A.	Assoc 250-5305			PHD	83	Wisconsin	1982
Bruggink, Thomas H.	Assoc 250-5307			PHD	79	Illinois	1978
Heavey, Jerome F.	Assoc			PHD		Penn St	1973
Averett, Susan	Asst 250-5307			PHD	91	Colorado	1991
Beckman, Mary P.	Asst			PHD		Notre Dm	1985
Bodenhorn, Howard	Asst 250-5308			PHD	90	Rutgers	1993
Burton, Mark L.	Asst 250-5308			PHD	91	Tennessee	1990
DeVault, James M.	Asst			PHD	90	Wisconsin	1989
Engle, Ruth	Asst 250-5311						
Gamber, Edward N.	Asst 250-5310			PHD	86	Va Tech	
Hutchinson, Gladstone	Asst 250-5304			PHD	90	Clark	1992
Kushner, Roland	Asst 250-5309						

Lake Superior State Univ	Sault S Marie MI 49783-1699 (906) 635-2426						Ms. Laurine Kelly
Economics Faculty	School of Business Fax=635-2111						
Harger, Bruce T.	Dean 635-2421		A	PHD	91	Mich St	9-67
Erikkila, John	C-Ac 635-2108		ADEF	PHD	87	W Ontario	9-90
Gaertner, Robert C.	Assoc 635-2177		DM	MBA	65	Norte Dm	1-70
Meiser, Charles W.	Assoc 635-2473		C	MS	66	Purdue	9-68

Lakeland College	Sheboygan, WI 53082-0359 (414) 565-1543						
Economics Faculty	Dept of Business Admin Fax=565-1206						
Schilcutt, J. Garland	C-Pr 565-1271		M	LLD		Marian	1958
Kudek, James F.	Assoc 565-1273		ABCD	MBA		Wi-Milw	1982
Qastin, Abdul Masesh	Assoc 565-1269		DGNP	MBA		Minnesota	1985
Schwartz, Adina Tzur	Assoc 565-1296		AEFG	MA		Wisc-Mil	1986
Botana, Joseph D.	Asst 565-1336		AFND	MBA		Roosevelt	1990

Lamar University — Beaumont, TX 77710 (409) 880-8647 — Mrs. Cloris Moser
Dept of Economics & Finance — College of Business Fax=880-1752 — LAMAR.EDU

Name	Rank	Phone	Email	Field	Degree	Yr	School	Year
Swerdlow, Robert A.	Dean$	880-8603		Mktg	PHD	76	Arkansas	1978
Hawkins, Charles F.	C-Pr	880-8647		RK	PHD		LSU	1966
Regents' Professor of Economics								
Allen, Charles L.	Prof	880-8656		RC	PHD		Arkansas	1979
Parigi, Sam F.	Prof	880-8652		J	PHD	64	Tx-Austin	1961
Regents' Professor of Economics								
Choi, Jai-Young	Assoc	880-8062		DF	PHD		Oklahoma	1982
Montano, Carl B.	Assoc	880-8651		OQ	PHD	82	Mich St	1981
Price, Donald I.	Assoc	880-8655		MO	PHD	80	Arkansas	1981
Allen, Joel L.	Asst	880-8657		B	MS	60	Baylor	1960

Lander University — Greenwood, SC 29649 (803) 229-8232 — Joyce Shelton
Economic Faculty — School of Business Adm Fax=229-8890

Name	Rank	Phone	Email	Field	Degree	Yr	School	Year
Molander, J. Dale	Dean	229-8232		Mktg	PHD	66	U Wash	1989
Dumont, David A.	Prof	229-8354		ADJR	PHD	77	SUNY-Alb	1972
Caines, W. Royce	Assoc	229-8355		ALPQ	PHD	88	Clemson	1988

LaSalle University — Philadelphia, PA 19141 (215)
Department of Economics — College of Arts & Sci Fax= — LASALLE.EDU
Did Not Respond--1994-95 Listing

Name	Rank	Phone	Email	Field	Degree	Yr	School	Year
Geruson, Richard T.	C-Ac	951-1178		TR	PHD	73	Penn	1958
Kane, Joseph A.	Prof	951-1040			PHD		Temple	1961
Duffy, John A.	Assoc	951-1180			PHD	71	Boston C	1964
George, David L.	Assoc	951-1175		ABN	PHD	84	Temple	1979
Grady, John	Assoc	951-1360			MA		Temple	1960
Robison, H. David	Assoc	951-1184		QC	PHD	83	Maryland	1988
Cairo, Joseph P.	Asst	951-1177			MA		Penn	1963
Mshomba, Richard	Asst	951-1116		FO	PHD	92	Illinois	1991
Paulin, Elizabeth	Asst	951-1181		J	PHD		Tx-Austin	1988
Ratkus, Mark	Asst	951-1183			PHD	76	Notre Dm	1973

La Sierra University — Riverside, CA 92515-8247 (909) 785-2064 — Vernell Kaufholtz
Economics Faculty — Sch of Business & Mgt Fax=785-2700 — LASIERRA.EDU

Name	Rank	Phone	Email	Field	Degree	Yr	School	Year
Felder, Henry E.	Dean	785-2064	hfelder	Mtg	PHD	75	Stanford	7-95
Selivanoff, George A.	C-Pr	785-2313	gselivan	AF	PHD	64	American	1984
Thomas, Johnny	Asst	785-2085	jthomas	C	MBA	88	LomaLinda	1989

University of LaVerne — LaVerne, CA 91750 (909) 593-3337 — Barbara Buchanan
School of Bus & Economics — College of Grad & Prof Fax=596-8990 — ULVACS.ULAVERNE.EDU

Name	Rank	Phone	Email	Field	Degree	Yr	School	Year
Ispahani, Ahmed S.	Prof	593-4208	ispahani		PHD		S Calif	1964
Thakur, Rita	Prof	593-4206			MBA		NW Mo St	1978

Lawrence Technological Univ — Southfield, MI 48075-1058 (810) 204-3250 — Joyce McKissen
Dept of Humanities — Col of Arts & Sciences Fax=204-3518 — LTUVAX
phone 356-0200

Name	Rank	Phone	Email	Field	Degree	Yr	School	Year
Rodgers, James	Dean	204-3500		Engl	PHD	79	E Anglia	
Hotelling, Harold	C-Ac	204-3520			PHD	82	Duke	

Lehigh University — Bethlehem, PA 18015 (610) 758-3420 — Diane Oechsle
Department of Economics — College of Bus & Econ Fax=758-4499 — LEHIGH.EDU

Name	Rank	Phone	Email	Field	Degree	Yr	School	Year
Schmotter, James W.	Dean	758-3402	jws4	Mgt	PHD	73	Northwes	1994
Munley, Vincent G.	C-Pr	758-3428	vgm0	HI	PHD	79	SUNY-Bin	1980
Aronson, J. Richard	Prof	758-3411	jra1	HG	PHD	64	Clark	1965
William L. Clayton Professor of Business and Economics								
Cohen, Alvin	Prof	758-3414	ac05	FO	PHD	62	Florida	1970
Director of International Careers								
Hyclak, Thomas J.	Prof	758-3425	tjh7	JR	PHD	76	Notre Dm	1979
Innes, Jon T.	Prof	758-3417	jti1	EB	PHD	67	Oregon	1987
King, Arthur E.	Prof	758-4451	aek0	FP	PHD	76	Ohio St	1976
McNamara, John R.	Prof	758-3415	njm1	MO	PHD	71	Rensselae	1973
Lee Iacocca Professor of Business & Economics								
Thornton, Robert J.	Prof	758-3460	rjt1	JI	PHD	70	Illinois	1970
Charles W. MacFarlane Professor of Economics								
Callahan, Colleen M.	Assoc	758-3445	cmc1	FN	PHD	87	N Carol	1984
Dearden, James A.	Assoc	758-5129	jad8	DH	PHD	87	Penn St	1989
Deily, Mary E.	Assoc	758-4951	med4	LQ	PHD	85	Harvard	1991
Gunter, Frank R.	Assoc	758-4540	frg2	FK	PHD	85	J Hopkins	1984
O'Brien, Anthony P.	Assoc	758-3442	ao01	NE	PHD	86	Berkeley	1987
Taylor, Larry W.	Assoc	758-3416	lwt0	CE	PHD	84	N Carol	1984
Chisholm, Darlene C.	Asst	758-3422	dcc0	LD	PHD	91	U Wash	1991
McDonald, Judith Ann	Asst	758-5345	djm0	FE	PHD	86	Princeton	1990
Watkins, Todd A.	Asst	758-4954	taw4	LO	PHD	95	Harvard	1992

LeMoyne College Syracuse, NY 13214-1399 (315) 445-4465
Economics Faculty Department of Economics Fax=445-4540 MAPLE.LEMOYNE
Barnett, William R. Dean 445-4310 Rel PHD Chicago 1977
Blackley, Paul R. C-Pr 445-4465 black_p HR PHD 82 Syracuse 1982
Arora, Harjit K. Assoc 445-4437 arora EFH PHD 84 Wi-Milw 1987
Blackley, Dixie M. Assoc 445-4437 black_d DRC PHD 84 Syracuse 1982
Conger, Darius J. Assoc 445-4671 conger JTP PHD 73 Oklahoma 1981
Shepard, Edward M. Assoc 445-4341 shepard HJL PHD 87 Boston C 1990

Lenoir-Rhyne College Hickory, NC 28603 (704) 328-7225 Dottie Crafton
Dept of Economics & Pol Sci Div of Social & Beh Sci Fax= LRC.EDU
Boatmon, Ellis G. C-Pr 328-7230 Hist PHD S Carol 1966
Ashman, H. Lowell C-Pr 328-7213 PHD Utah 1975
Mauney, William M. Prof 328-7218 MA 76 Appalach 1967
Centennial Professor of Economics - Director Broyhill Institute
Wright, Jeffrey J. Asst 328-7217 PHD 87 Conn 1989

Lewis University Romeoville, IL 60441 (815) Ext 531
Department of Economics College of Business Fax=Ext 3330
phone 838-0500
Perrone, James Dean Ext 360 Ecol
Hill, Lawrence G. C-Pr Ext 377 PHD 76 N Illinois 1968
Marker, William Inst Ext 260 MA 85 N Illinois 1988

Lewis & Clark College Portland, OR 97219 (503) 768-7606 Sharon Barnes
Department of Economics Col of Arts & Sciences Fax=768-7379 LCLARK.EDU
Hart-Landsberg, Martin C-Pr 768-7624 marty POFA PHD 74 Wisconsin 1978
Grant, James H. C-As 768-7623 grant CDJA PHD 79 Mich St 1987
Mattersdorff, Guenter H. Prof 768-7622 GHAR PHD 58 Harvard 1963

Liberty University Lynchburg, VA 24506-8001 (804) 582-2338 Angela Peterson
Dept of Economics & Finance School of Bus & Govt Fax=582-2470
Atkins, Robert T. Dean 582-2480 Mktg PHD 77 Arkansas 1991
Mateer, Robert N. C-Pr 582-2338 MBA Tulane 1984
Synn, Kyung-Hi Prof 582-2338 PHD Ohio St 1989
Zaffke, Maurice Prof 582-2338
Lai, Tsung Assoc 582-2338 PHD

Lincoln University-MO Jefferson Cty MO 65101 (314)
Department of Economics College of Business Fax=681-6074
Hirst, Richard Dean 681-5488 PHD Missouri 7-91
LePage, James Assoc 681-6081 PHD Kansas 1984
Arabian, Ghodratollah Asst 681-6077 PHD Indiana 1984

Lincoln University-PA Lincoln Univ, PA 19352 (610) Ext 3394 Melanie Murray Ext 3394
Dept of Economics & Bus Adm Div of Social Sciences Fax=
phone 932-8300
Dadson, William C Ext 6191 PHD
Ramdas, Ganga P. Asst Ext 3376 PHD Temple

Lindenwood College St. Charles, MO 63301-1695 (314) 949-4952 Marilyn Leach
Economics Faculty Div Management & LCIE Fax=949-4910 LC.LINDENWOOD.EDU
Taich, Arlene Prov 949-4952 ataich PHD St Louis 8-80
Ezvan, Kazimiera Prof 949-4952 PHD S Illinois 8-81
Hagan, Oliver Prof 949-4936 hagan MS Baylor 9-90
Hafer, Gail Assoc 949-4930 hafer PHD S Illinois 9-93
Kemper, Daniel Assoc 949-4957 dkemper MBA Lindenwd 1-88

Linfield College McMinnville, OR 97128-6894 (503) 434-2405 Joyce Anderson
Economics Faculty Dept of Economics & Bus Fax=434-2566 LINFIELD.EDU
Emery, Richard F. C-As 434-2298 rfemery Atg MBA E N Mex 1986
Hansen, David Prof 434-2253 dhansen MS Portland 1969
Chambers, Scott Assoc 434-2401 schamb PHD 88 Ca-Davis 1990
Grant, Randy R. Asst 434-2402 rgrant PHD Nebraska 1993
Summers, Jeffrey A. Asst 434-2297 jsummer PHD 87 Purdue 1992

Lock Haven University Lock Haven, PA 17745 (717) 893-2163 Gale Spangler
Dept of Hist, Pol Sci, Econ College of Arts & Sci Fax=893-2432
Gross, Janet S. Dean Engl PHD N Carol 1989
DeLavan, Nelson C 893-2646 Hst
Carroll, Richard R. Prof PHD 73 Kentucky 1977
Chatterton, R. Edward Prof 893-2222 PHD 80 Wash St 1982
Perna, Francis M. Prof PHD Cornell 1981
Wion, Douglas A. Assoc 893-2447 PHD 80 Penn St 1980

Long Isl U, Brooklyn Campus Brooklyn, NY 11201-5372 (718) 488-1025 Ms. Mina Pacheco
Department of Economics Conolly C Liberal A & S Fax=488-1125

Name	Rank	Phone	Email	Field	Degree	Yr	School	Year
Cohen, David	Dean			Biol	PHD		NYU	
Varma, Ranbir	C-Pr	834-6000		AFOP	PHD	57	New Sch	1959
Lombardi, Waldo J.	Prof			ACD	PHD		Columbia	
Zewail, Amin A.	Assoc			AEHR	PHD		Fordham	
Sherer, George	Inst			ABD	MPHI		Columbia	

Long Island U.-C.W. Post Brookville, NY 11548-0570 (516) 299-2321 Rhonda Pereira
Department of Economics College of Liberal Arts Fax=299-4169

Name	Rank	Phone	Email	Field	Degree	Yr	School	Year
Schmidt-Raghavan, Malthili	Dean	299-2235		Phil	PHD		Michigan	
Gafar, John S.	C-Pr	299-2371			PHD	79	W Indies	1980
Solar, Donald	Prof	299-2321			PHD	63	Columbia	1965
Mourdoukoutas, Panos	Assoc	299-2322			PHD	83	SUNY-SBr	1984
Zeineldin, Aly	Assoc	299-2370			PHD		NYU	
Lu, Laura	Asst	299-2369			PHD	89	SUNY-SBr	
Roy, Udayan	Asst	299-2405			PHD		SUNY-SBr	

Longwood College Farmville, VA 23909 (804) 395-2042 Ms. Janet Evans
Dept of Economics & Finance School of Bus & Econ Fax=395-2203 LWCNET.LWC.EDU

Name	Rank	Phone	Email	Field	Degree	Yr	School	Year
Farmer, Berkwood M.	Dean	395-2045	bfarmer	Q	PHD	70	N Car St	1991
Brastow, Raymond T.	C-As	395-2370	rbrastow	J	PHD	87	U Wash	1987
Shaw, Sue O.	Assoc	395-2371	sshaw		PHD		Harvard	1986
Adusei, Edward O.	Asst	395-2459	eadusei		PHD	88	Va Tech	1992
Marks, Melanie B.	Asst	395-2372	mmerrell		PHD	93	Tx A&M	1993

Loras College Dubuque, IA 52004-0178 (319)
Department of Economics Div Soc Sci & Beh Stds Fax=
Did Not Respond--Information Taken from College Catalog

Name	Rank	Phone	Email	Field	Degree	Yr	School	Year
Naumann, Rev. John J.	C-Ac			Psyc	PHD	88	Fordham	1975
O'Connor, Dennis A.	C-Ac	588-7519			PHD	84	Notre Dm	1983
Giannakouros, George	Prof				PHD	74	Iowa	1966
Sula, Laddie J.	Prof	588-7507			PHD	76	Geo St	1983
Simon, Peter J.	Asst				PHD	89	N Illinois	1989

Louisiana State University Baton Rouge, LA 70803-6306 (504) 388-5211 Mary Jo Neathery
Department of Economics College of Business Adm Fax=388-3807 LSUVM.SNCC.LSU.EDU

Name	Rank	Phone	Email	Field	Degree	Yr	School	Year
Clark, Thomas D. Jr.	Dean	338-3211			DBA	77	Fla St	8-95
Scott, Loren C.	C-Pr	388-3779		J	PHD	69	Okla St	1969
Thomas J. Singletary Distinguished Professor of Business Administration								
Beard, Thomas R.	Prof	388-3787		E	PHD	63	Duke	1961
LSU Alumni Professor								
Campbell, William F.	Prof	388-3780		N	PHD	66	Virginia	
Culbertson, W. Patton Jr.	Prof	388-3783	eoculb	F	PHD	72	Tx-Austin	
Hill, R. Carter	Prof	388-1490	eohill	C	PHD	75	Missouri	
Mack H. Hornbeak Business Partnership Professor								
Johnson, David B.	Prof	388-3796		H	PHD	68	Virginia	
email eojohneconomicssumus.								
Jones, Lamar B.	Prof	388-8891		J	PHD	65	Tx-Austin	1967
Director of MBA								
Koray, Faik A.	Prof	388-3801	eoroka	EF	PHD	84	Duke	1984
McMillin, W. Douglas	Prof	388-3798	eodoug	E	PHD	79	LSU	1985
South Central Bell Business Partnership Professor								
Moore, William J.	Prof	388-3792	eomoore	IJ	PHD	70	Tx-Austin	
Gulf Coast Coca Cola Business Partnership Professor								
Newman, Robert J.	Prof	388-3794		IJ	PHD	80	UCLA	1983
South Central Bell Business Partnership Professor; Director, Graduate Studies								
Rice, G. Randolph	Prof	388-3799		C	PHD	70	Kentucky	1969
Richardson, James A.	Prof	388-6743	parich	H	PHD	71	Michigan	1970
Alumni Professor of Economics; Director Public Administration Institute								
Smyth, David J.	Prof	388-3803		E	PHD	68	Birmgham	1987
LSU Foundation Professor of Economics								
Turnbull, Geoffrey K.	Prof	388-3795	eoturn	DH	PHD	83	Wi-Milw	1984
CJ Brown Distinguished Professor of Real Estate								
Bigelow, John P.	Assoc	388-3793	jbigelo	CD	PHD	81	Penn	7-94
Kleit, Andrew N.	Assoc	388-3790	eokleit	HK	PHD	87	Yale	1992
Miyagiwa, Kaz	VAsoc	388-3782		FO	PHD	85	Tx-Austin	8-95
Palivos, Theodore	Asst	388-3791	eopali	F	PHD	92	Penn St	1992

Louisiana St in Shreveport Shreveport, LA 71115-2399 (318) 797-5241 Donna Carney
Dept of Economics & Finance College of Business Adm Fax=797-5208

Name	Rank	Phone	Email	Field	Degree	Yr	School	Year
Goetz, Joe F. Jr.	Dean	797-5383		Atg	PHD	74	Nebraska	1995
Casperson, Luvonia J.	C-Pr	797-5241			PHD	74	Oklahoma	1975
Austin, John A.	Prof	797-5022			PHD		Ariz St	1983
Brendler, Michael D.	Prof	797-5024			PHD		Tx A&M	1977

Name	Rank	Phone	E-mail	Field	Degree	Yr	School	Since
Harju, Melvin W.	Prof	797-5241			PHD	72	Florida	1977
Jones, Charlotte	Prof	797-5383			DBA		La Tech	1984
Merkle, Paul E.	Prof	797-5241			PHD	77	La Tech	1976
Hsieh, Eric	Assoc	797-5145			PHD		LSU	1989
Vines, Timothy	Assoc	797-5016			PHD		Tennessee	1989

Louisiana Tech University Ruston, LA 71272-0001 (318) 257-4149 Brenda Sanderson
Dept of Economics & Finance College of Admin & Bus Fax=257-4253 VM.CC.LATECH.EDU

Name	Rank	Phone	E-mail	Field	Degree	Yr	School	Since
Emery, John T.	Dean	257-4526	emery	Fnce	PHD	69	U Wash	1994
Sale, Tom S. III	H-Pr$	624-1414	tomsale	GE	PHD	72	LSU	1965
Darrat, Ali F.	Prof	257-3874			PHD	81	Indiana	1987
Gilley, Otis W.	Prof	257-3768	gilley		PHD	79	Purdue	1988
Smith, Lawrence C.	Prof	257-2112			PHD	68	Miss	1970
Fincher, Phillip E.	Assoc	257-2241			PHD		Miss	1964
Mangum, James M.	Assoc	257-2509			PHD	72	Okla St	1970
O'Boyle, Edward John	Assoc	257-3701			PHD		St Louis	1977
Chopin, Marc	Asst	257-4464	chopin@cab.	L	PHD	92	Tx A&M	1992

University of Louisville Louisville, KY 40292-0001 (502) 852-7832
Sch of Econ & Urban Affairs Col Business & Pub Adm Fax=852-7557 ULKYVM

Name	Rank	Phone	E-mail	Field	Degree	Yr	School	Since
Taylor, Robert L.	Dean	852-7684	rltaylo1	Mgt	DBA	72	Indiana	8-84
Nelson, John P.	D-Pr	852-4857	jpnelso01		PHD	68	Kentucky	
Meyer, Peter	Prof	852-6626	pbmeye02		PHD	70	Wisconsin	
Nahata, Babu L.	Prof	852-4864	b0naha01		PHD	77	N Illinois	8-78
Chou, Nan-Ting	Assoc	852-4840	ntchou01		PHD	86	Ohio St	1991
Coomes, Paul A.	Assoc	852-4841	pacoom01		PHD	85	Tx-Austin	1985
Gliderbloom, John	Assoc	852-6626	j1gild01		PHD	83	Ca-SnBarb	
Gohmann, Stephan F.	Assoc	852-4844	sfgohm01		PHD	84	N Car St	1988
Olson, Dennis O.	Assoc	852-4858	doolso01		PHD	82	Wyoming	1987
Vahaly, John	Assoc	852-4863	j0vaha01		PHD	75	Vanderbilt	1975
Davidson, Audrey	Asst	852-4839	abdavi01		PHD	93	Auburn	1993
Hawroth, Barry	Asst		bmhawo01		PHD	94	Ca-Davis	1995

Loyola College in Maryland Baltimore, MD 21210-2699 (410) 617-2357 Bonnie Nauman
Department of Economics Sellinger Sch Bus & Mgt Fax=617-2118 LOYOLA.EDU

Name	Rank	Phone	E-mail	Field	Degree	Yr	School	Since
Anton, Ronald J. S.J.	Dean	617-2301		Mgt	PHD	89	Northwes	1989
Walters, Stephen J. K.	C-Pr	617-2213	sjkw	KL	PHD	82	UCLA	1981
Derrick, Frederick W.	Prof	617-2712	fwd	CI	PHD	76	N Car St	1982
DiLorenzo, Thomas J.	Prof	617-2755		KLH	PHD	80	Va Tech	1992
Larson, John C.	Prof	617-2476	jcl	E	PHD	77	Minnesota	1974
Scott, Charles E.	Prof	617-2618	ces	MJH	PHD	79	Vanderbilt	1985
Bell, Arleigh T. Jr.	Assoc	617-2470	bell	FD	PHD	71	New Sch	1970
Jordan, John M.	Assoc	617-2477	JMJ	C	PHD	70	Purdue	1964
Meador, Mark W.	Assoc	617-2723	meador	EG	PHD	80	U Wash	1980
Williams, Nancy A.	Assoc	617-2825	naw	QH	PHD	84	Berkeley	1987

Loyola University - Chicago Chicago, IL 60611 (312) 915-6062 Miegan Lesher
Department of Economics School of Business Adm Fax=915-8508 LUCCPUA

Name	Rank	Phone	E-mail	Field	Degree	Yr	School	Since
Bryan, William R.	Dean	915-6113		Fnce	PHD	61	Wisconsin	1995
Mirza, David B.	C-Ac	915-6062			PHD	73	Northwes	1969
Cain, Louis P.	Prof	915-6075			PHD	69	Northwes	1968
Cinar, E. Mine	Assoc	915-6066			PHD		Tx A&M	1983
Gobin, Roy T.	Assoc	915-6074			PHD		Illinois	1978
Vanderporten, Bruce S.	Assoc	915-6076			PHD	73	Wayne St	1978
Gabriel, Paul E.	Asst	915-6070			PHD	87	Kentucky	1990
Hayford, Marc D.	Asst	915-6073			PHD	87	Brown	1986
Merriman, David F.	Asst	915-6071			PHD	83	Wisconsin	1987
Surdam, David	Asst	915-6067			PHD	94	Chicago	1994
Bailey BVM, Mary P. F.	Inst	508-8487			MA	69	Notre Dm	1991

Loyola Univ-New Orleans New Orleans, LA 70118 (504) 865-3544
Department of Economics College of Business Adm Fax=865-3496

Name	Rank	Phone	E-mail	Field	Degree	Yr	School	Since
O'Brien, J. Patrick	Dean	865-3544		AEHR	PHD	77	Okla St	1995
Walker, Deborah L.	C-Ac	865-3924		ABDJ	PHD	87	Geo Mason	1987
Dauterive, Jerry W. Associate Dean	Prof	865-3545		ADH	PHD	76	Tx Tech	1979
Barnett, William	Assoc	865-2165		DEFK	PHD	74	Mich St	1974
Mundell, Cyril Lee	Assoc	865-2549		AC	PHD	76	N Carol	1981
Saliba, Michael T.	Assoc	865-2681		ADM	PHD	72	Oklahoma	1973
Wood, J. Stuart	Assoc	865-2171		GM	PHD	80	NYU	1984

Loyola Marymount Univ — Los Angeles, CA 90045-2699 (310) 338-7373 — M. Edwards/B. Bernard
Department of Economics — College of Liberal Arts Fax=338-1950 — LMUMAIL.LMU.EDU

Name	Rank	Phone	E-mail	Fields	Degree	Yr	Institution	Since
Milligan, Mary R.S.H.M.	Dean	338-2716	mmilliga	Theo	DHL			1990
Singleton, Robert	C-As	338-7373	rsinglet	AJR	PHD	83	UCLA	1982
Devine, James N.	Assoc	338-2948	jdevine	AEJN	PHD	81	Berkeley	1985
Earley, Joseph E.	Assoc	338-4572	jearley	AC	PHD	74	Fordham	1974
Shoukry, Kamal	Assoc	338-8215	kshoukry	ABCE	PHD	72	S Calif	1980
Thimester, Renate	Assoc	338-2817	rthimest	ABKM	PHD	67	Alabama	1971
Zekavat, Seid M.	Assoc	338-7372	szekavat	ACG	PHD	64	S Calif	1964
Eusufzai, Zaki	Asst	338-2822	zeusufza	ACFD	PHD	94	UCLA	1989
Fuentes, Gabriel	Asst	338-5956	gfuentes	DLO	PHD	94	Berkeley	1994
Konow, James D.	Asst	338-2956	jkonow	ACD	PHD	93	UCLA	1989

Luther College — Decorah, IA 52101-1045 (319) 387-1340 — Jeri Laursen
Dept of Economics & Business — Div of Social Sciences Fax=387-1088

Name	Rank	Phone	E-mail	Fields	Degree	Yr	Institution	Since
Kaschins, Edward A.	H-Pr	387-1130			PHD	73	Iowa	1961
Lund, Mark	Prof				PHD		Iowa St	1978
Leake, Richard S.	Assoc				MBA		Wisconsin	1975
Gomersall, C. Nicholas	Asst				PHD	91	Cornell	1991

Lycoming College — Williamsport, PA 17701 (717) 321-4000 — Mrs. Carole Thompson
Economics Faculty — Dept of Economics Fax=321-4090 — LYCOMING.EDU

Name	Rank	Phone	E-mail	Fields	Degree	Yr	Institution	Since
Madresehee, Mehrdad	C-Ac	321-4179	madreseh	FHKL	PHD	85	Wash St	1986
Opdahl, Roger W.	Prof	321-4173	opdahl	AENR	DED	70	Penn St	1962
Shangraw Professor of Economics								
Sprunger, Philip W.	Asst	321-7657	sprunger	AJQ	PHD	93	Indiana	1993

Lynchburg College — Lynchburg, VA 24501-3199 (804) 544-8464 — Anne Pingstock
Dept of Economics — Sch of Business & Econ Fax=544-8499 — LYNCHBURG.EDU

Name	Rank	Phone	E-mail	Fields	Degree	Yr	Institution	Since
Husted, Stewart W.	Dean	522-8621		Mgt	PHD	77	MSU	9-89
Messerschmidt, Daniel C.	C-Pr	522-8458			PHD	84	Iowa St	1985
Director, Center for Economics Education								
Prinzinger, Joseph M.	Prof	522-8329			PHD	74	Geo St	1984
Savoian, Roy T.	Prof	522-8256			PHD	79	Ca-SnBarb	1984
Turek, Joseph H.	Assoc	522-8542			PHD	87	SUNY-Alb	1986

Lyndon State College — Lyndonville, VT 05851 (802) 626-9371
Economic Faculty — Business Adm Department Fax=626-9770 — QUEEN.LSC.VSC.EDU

Name	Rank	Phone	E-mail	Fields	Degree	Yr	Institution	Since
Myers, Rex C.	Dean	626-9371		Hst	PHD	72	Montana	9-91
Academic Affairs								
Siegel, Rachel S.	C-Ac	626-9371	siegelr	CGQN	MBA	89	Yale	9-90

Lyon College — Batesville, AR 72501 (501) 698-4258 — Peggy Weaver
Department of Economics — Business & Econ Div Fax=698-4622 — SHIRE.AC.ARKNET.EDU

Name	Rank	Phone	E-mail	Fields	Degree	Yr	Institution	Since
Cooper, Thomas E.	C-Ac	698-4364	tcooper	DGHL	PHD	84	Princeton	1987
Anne J. Stewart Professor of Economics								
Hine, Steven C.	Asst	698-1740			PHD	86	Wash St	1994
Morong, Cyril J.	Asst	698-4271			PHD		Wash St	1989

Macalester College — St. Paul, MN 55105 (612) 696-6227 — Nancy H. Jones
Economics Faculty — Dept of Economics Fax= — MAC.CC.MACALSTR.EDU

Name	Rank	Phone	E-mail	Fields	Degree	Yr	Institution	Since
Simler, Norman J.	C-Pr	696-6739		AE	PHD	59	Minnesota	1991
Egge, Karl A.	Prof	696-6227	egge	AGM	PHD	73	Ohio St	1970
F. R. Bigelow Professor of Economics								
Asianian, Paul J.	Assoc				MBA	67	U Wash	1967
Sukhatme, Vasant A.	Assoc	696-6744	sukhatme	ADO	PHD	77	Chicago	1978
Edward John Noble Associate Professor of Economics								
Bunn, Julie A.	Asst	696-6776	bunn	AFQ	PHD	93	Stanford	1992
Krueger, Gary J.	Asst	696-6222		ACP	PHD	89	Wisconsin	1989
Moe, Karine S.	Asst	696-6227	moe	AJ	ABD	95	Minnesota	1995

Univ of Maine — Orono, ME 04469-5774 (207) 581-1850 — Ms. Debra A. Perro
Department of Economics — Col of Social & Beh Sci Fax=581-1953 — MAINE.MAINE.EDU

Name	Rank	Phone	E-mail	Fields	Degree	Yr	Institution	Since
Wihry, David F.	C-Ac	581-1850	dwihry	HIA	PHD	72	Syracuse	1969
Burke, Melvin	Prof	581-1853		O	PHD	67	Pittsburgh	1966
Clark, David H.	Prof	581-1862		JOA	PHD	62	Wisconsin	1963
Coupe, John D.	Prof	581-1852	rec385	ACD	PHD	60	Clark	1962
Duchesneau, Thomas D.	Prof	581-1858	rec360	AO	PHD	69	Boston C	1967
Hunt, Gary	Prof	581-1861	garyhunt	AR	PHD	84	Colorado	1993
Lutz, Mark A.	Prof	581-1859		AB	PHD	72	Berkeley	1970
Morici, Peter G.	Prof	581-1850		F	PHD	74	SUNY-Alb	1988
Townsend, Ralph E.	Prof	581-1854	rec359	CHQA	PHD	83	Wisconsin	1980
Breece, James H.	Assoc	581-1863	breece	AEF	PHD	82	Boston C	1983
Montgomery, Michael	Asst	581-1857	rec365	AE	PHD	88	Florida	1991
Prasch, Robert E.	Asst	581-1864		AB	PHD	92	Berkeley	1990

Manhattan College Riverdale, NY 10471 (718) 920-0141
Dept of Economics & Finance School of Business Fax=884-0255 MANVAX
Did Not Respond--Information Taken from College Catalog

Name	Rank	Phone	Degree		School	Year
Suarez, James M.	Dean	920-0239	PHD	72	Columbia	1984
Shojai, Siamack	C-Ac		PHD		Fordham	1989
Sun, Emily M.	Prof	920-0463	PHD	57	Michigan	1964
Abdulahad, Faraj	Assoc		PHD	68	Boston C	1970
Geisst, Charles R.	Assoc		PHD		London	1985
Gidwani, Sushila J.	Assoc		PHD	64	Minnesota	1965
Rao, Polavarapu M.	VAsoc		PHD	72	NYU	1990
Tomer, John F.	Assoc	920-0462	PHD	73	Rutgers	1983
Wheeler, Herbert E.	Assoc		PHD		Fordham	1978
Elias, Carlos G.	Asst	920-0462	PHD	89	NYU	1990
MacLachlan, Fiona C.	Asst		PHD		NYU	1992
Topyan, Kudret	Asst		PHD		CUNY	1991
Winczewski, Greg A.	Asst		PHD		Fordham	1993

Mankato State University Mankato, MN 56001-8400 (507) 389-2969 Barbara Lutz
Dept Economics & Intl Bus College of Business Fax=389-5497 MANKATO.MSUS.EDU

Name	Rank	Phone	Email	Fields	Degree		School	Year
Abouelenein, Gaber A.	Dean	389-5420		M	PHD	69	Illinois	1968
Abel, David R.	C-Pr	389-2969	david_abel@ms1.	AE	ABD		Minnesota	1969
Askalani, Mohamed H.	Prof	389-5328	askalāni1@vax1.	AC	PHD	70	Iowa St	1969
Chowdhury, Ashok K.	Prof	389-6614	chowdhury@vax1.	AC	PHD	80	Iowa St	1980
Hickerson, Steven	Prof	389-5330		ABK	PHD		Nebraska	1980
Kesler, Jason J.	Prof	389-5331	kesler@vax1.	AJ	DA		Idaho	1980
Lee, Joseph S.	Prof	389-2713		JK	PHD	70	Mass	1970
Renner, Donald E.	Prof	389-5249	renner@vax1.	ACHR	PHD		Cincinnati	1979
Schiming, Richard C.	Prof	389-5323		AE	PHD	74	Ohio St	1981
Sharma, Ved P.	Prof	389-2711	sharma@vax1.	CDT	PHD	77	Wash U	1976
Simonson, Robert D.	Prof	389-5324	simonson@vax1.	AJ	PHD		Nebraska	1981
Skorr, Arlen J.	Prof	389-2712	skorr@vax1.	AE	PHD	70	Nebraska	1965
Smith, Gerald A.	Prof	389-5325	smith@vax1.	AOQ	PHD	79	LSU	1979
Thompson, Paul J.	Prof	389-5326	thompson@vax1.	AI	PHD	68	Iowa	1963
Wells, Arnold R.	Prof	389-5248		ADM	PHD	66	Minnesota	1966
Tix, Paul	Asst	389-2711		AC	MS		N Dak St	1984

Mansfield University of PA Mansfield, PA 16933 (717) 662-4760
Economics Faculty Politics & Econ Dept Fax=662-4113 MNSFLD.EDU

Name	Rank	Phone	Email	Degree		School	Year
Dalmolen, Albert	C-As	662-4760	vmhostl	PHD	71	American	1987
Yacovissi, William A.	Prof	662-4764		PHD	89	SUNY-Bin	1976
Carpenter, Bruce E.	Assoc	662-4761		PHD	90	Conn	1987

Marian College Indianapolis, IN 46222-1997 (317) 929-0269
Economics Faculty Business Fax=929-0263

Name	Rank	Phone	Degree		School	Year
Merle, Jill A.	C	929-0269	MBA	89	Indiana	1989
Schuttler, Robert D.	Inst	929-0269	MBA	80	Evansville	1985

Marietta College Marietta, OH 45750-3031 (614) 376-4633 Darlene Bonnette
Brachman Dp Econ, Mgt & Atg College of Business Fax=376-7501

Name	Rank	Phone	Fields	Degree		School	Year
MacHaffie, Fraser	C-Ac	376-4633	Atg	MBA		Cleve St	1982
Delemeester, Gregory	Assoc	376-4630	AD	PHD	89	Tx A&M	1986
Milton Friedman Chair in Economics							
Khorassani, Jacqueline	Asst	376-4621	AEFH	ABD	92	W Virginia	1994

Marist College Poughkeepsie, NY 12601-1387 (914) 575-3225 Jean Talbot
Economic Faculty School of Management Fax=575-3640

Name	Rank	Phone	Fields	Degree		School	Year
Kelly, John C.	Dean	575-3225		PHD		Boston C	1962
Hamilton, Gregory L.	Assoc	575-3000		PHD		Okla St	1990
Black, Geoffrey	Asst	575-3000	H	PHD		U Wash	1995
Davis, Ann E.	Asst	575-3000		PHD	83	Boston C	1981
Morley, John	Asst	575-3000		PHD	87	Yale	1995

Marquette University Milwaukee, WI 53201-1881 (414) 288-7377 Louisa E. Eastman
Department of Economics College of Business Adm Fax=288-1660 MUCSD

Name	Rank	Phone	Fields	Degree		School	Year
Mandell, Lewis	Dean	288-7141	Fnce	PHD	70	Tx-Austin	1995
Hunter, William J.	C-Ac	288-1449		PHD	79	Va Tech	1982
Brush, Brian C.	Prof	288-5152		PHD	73	N Carol	1968
Associate Dean College of Business Administration							
Smiley, William G.	Prof	288-5664		PHD	73	Iowa	1973
Booth, Douglas E.	Assoc	288-7310		PHD		U Wash	
Breeden, Charles H.	Assoc	288-3370		PHD	77	Va Tech	1979
Chowdhury, Abdur R.	Assoc	288-3417		PHD	83	Kentucky	1989
Clark, David E.	Assoc	288-3339		PHD	86	SUNY-Bin	1985
Crane, Steven E.	Assoc	288-1450		PHD	81	Colorado	1980

Davis, John B.	Assoc	288-5438			PHD	85	Mich St	
McGibany, James M.	Assoc	288-7187			PHD	83	Mich St	1983
Nourzad, Farrokh	Assoc	288-3570			PHD	82	Kansas	1981
Toumanoff, Peter	Assoc	288-7523						1995
Daniels, Joseph P.	Asst	288-3368			PHD	92	Indiana	1989
Fraedrich, Ann I.	Asst	288-1452			PHD	90	Purdue	1989

Marshall University Huntington, WV 25755-2360 (304) 696-6492
Department of Economics College of Business Fax=696-4344 MARSHALL.EDU

Kent, Calvin A.	Dean	696-2614			PHD	67	Missouri	1993
Adkins, Roger L.	C-Pr	696-2609			PHD	81	Kansas St	1981
Akkihal, Ramchandra G.	Prof	696-2613			PHD	69	Tennessee	1970
Kontos, Nicholas C.	Assoc	696-2606			MA	58	Indiana	1961
Wilkins, Allen J.	Assoc	696-3351			PHD	84	Wisconsin	1985
Shuklian, Steve	Asst	696-2605			PHD	88	Utah	1988
Sweetser, Wendell E. Jr.	Asst	676-6498			PHD	79	Va Tech	1977
Thompson, Mark	Asst	696-2382			PHD	94	Geo St	1994
Zapalska, Alina	Asst	696-3234			PHD	91	Kentucky	1991

University of Mary Bismarck, ND 58504-9652 (701)
Economics Faculty Division of Business Fax=255-7687
phone 255-7500

Borgelt, Marvin	C-Ac	Ext 439		Mgt	MBA	82	Maryland	9-82
Boor, Randy	Assoc	Ext 438						

Mary Baldwin College Staunton, VA 24401 (703) 887-7053
Economics Faculty Department of Economics Fax= CIT.MBC.EDU

Klein, Judy C.	C-Ac	887-7053	jklein	BC	PHD	86	London P	1982
McCormick, Amy	Asst	887-7114		J	PHD	95	Harvard	1995

Univ of Mary Hardin-Baylor Belton, TX 76513 (817) 939-4644
Dept Atg, Economics & Fnce School of Business Fax=939-4535

Baldwin, Lee E.	Dean	939-4644		Mgt	PHD	80	North Tx	1992
Fabritius, Michael	Prof	939-4655		ABDE	PHD	87	Tx-Austin	1987

Claude McBryde Professor of Finance-Economics

Mary Washington College FredericksburgVA 22401-5358 (703) 654-1483 Jane Clark 654-1066
Economics Faculty Department of Economics Fax=654-1074 MWU.EDU

Greenlaw, Steven A.	C-Ac	654-1483	greenla	EFA	PHD	87	SUNY-Bin	1982
Rycroft, Robert S.	Prof	654-1500	rrycroft	CHJG	PHD	78	Maryland	1977
Stageberg, Stephen P.	Assoc	654-1486	sstagebe	CFN	PHD	84	Geotown	1982
Ray, Margaret A.	Asst	654-1485	mray	LQRA	PHD	88	Tennessee	

Univ Maryland-Baltimore Co Baltimore, MD 21228 (410) 455-2137 Iris Bachelor
Department of Economics Col of Arts & Sciences Fax=

Burchard, Robert	Dean$	455-2386		Biol	PHD			
Sorkin, Alan L.	C-Pr	455-2173			PHD	66	J Hopkins	1974
Bradley, Michael E.	Prof	455-2170			PHD	67		
Goldfarb, Marsha G.	Prof	455-2171			PHD	68	Northwes	1973
Lord, William A.	Assoc	455-2498			PHD	84	Indiana	1987
McConnell, Virginia D.	Assoc	455-2068			PHD	78	Maryland	
Mitch, David F.	Assoc	455-2157			PHD	82	Chicago	1983
Peake, Charles F.	Assoc	455-2168			PHD	68	Maryland	1967
Takacs, Wendy E.	Assoc	455-2174			PHD	76	J Hopkins	1981
Wu, Roland Y.	Assoc	455-2176			PHD	71		
Carroll, Kathleen A.	Asst	455-2169			PHD	76	J Hopkins	1980
Gindling, Thomas	Asst	455-3629			PHD	87		
Knapp, Kimberly	Asst	455-3243			PHD	88		
Lamdin, Douglas J.	Asst	455-2672			PHD	91	Maryland	1989
Humphreys, Brad	Inst	455-2177						
Davis, Mary	Lect	455-3177			MBA	78	Maryland	
Kingerski, Angie	Lect	455-3644						

University of Maryland College Park, MD 20742-7215 (301) 405-3266 Martha Best 405-3506
Department of Economics Col Behav & Social Sci Fax=405-3542 UMDD

Goldstein, Irwin	Dean	405-1679			PHD	64	Maryland	1991
Straszheim, Mahlon R.	C-Pr	405-3266			PHD	66	Harvard	
Abraham, Katherine G. (on leave)	Prof				PHD	82	Harvard	1988
Almon, Clopper Jr.	Prof	405-4604			PHD	62	Harvard	1966
Ausubel, Lawrence M.	Prof	405-3495			PHD	84	Stanford	1992
Baily, Martin N.	Prof				PHD	72	MIT	1987
Betancourt, Roger R.	Prof	405-3479			PHD	69	Wisconsin	1980

Brechling, Frank P.	Prof	454-6305	405-3480		PHD	55	Trinity	1979
Calvo, Guillermo	Prof	405-3553			PHD	74	Yale	1994
Clague, Chirstopher K.	Prof	405-3064			PHD	66	Harvard	1979
Cropper, Maureen L.	Prof	405-3266			PHD	73	Cornell	1980
Dardis, Rachel	Prof	405-6645			PHD	65	Minnesota	1992
Dorsey, John W.	Prof	405-3501			PHD	65	Harvard	1989
Drazen, Allen	Prof	405-3477			PHD	76	MIT	1990
Haltiwanger, John C.	Prof	405-3490			PHD	81	J Hopkins	1987
Hulten, Charles R.	Prof	405-3549			PHD	73	Berkeley	1985
Kelejian, Harry	Prof	405-3492			PHD	68	Wisconsin	1968
Montgomery, Edward B.	Prof	405-3498			PHD	82	Harvard	1990
Murrell, Peter	Prof	405-3476			PHD	77	Penn	1977
Oates, Wallace	Prof	405-3496			PHD	65	Stanford	1979
Olson, Mancur	Prof	405-3497			PHD	60	Harvard	1969
Panagariya, Arvind	Prof	405-3546			PHD	78	Princeton	1978
Prucha, Ingmar R.	Prof	405-3499			PHD	77	Viena	1981
Schelling, Thomas	Prof	405-3494			PHD	51	Harvard	1991
Schwab, Robert M.	Prof	405-3478			PHD	80	J Hopkins	1980
Bennett, Robert L.	Assoc	405-3515			PHD	63	Tx-Austin	1966
Coughlin, Peter J.	Assoc	405-3482			PHD	76	SUNY	1982
Cramton, Peter C.	Assoc	405-6987			PHD	84	Stanford	1993
Evans, William N.	Assoc	405-3486			PHD	87	Duke	1987
Meyer, Paul A.	Assoc	405-3491			PHD	66	Stanford	1965
Wallis, John J.	Assoc	405-3552			PHD	81	U Wash	1983
Weinstein, Paul A.	Assoc	405-4534			PHD	61	Northwes	1965
Binder, Michael	Asst	405-3466			PHD	95	Penn	1995
Chao, John	Asst	405-4366			PHD	95	Yale	1995
Fikkert, Brian	Asst	405-3481			PHD	94	Yale	1994
Hoff, Karla	Asst	405-3490			PHD	89	Princeton	
Kranton, Rachel E.	Asst	405-3487			PHD	93	Berkeley	1993
Lyon, Andrew B.	Asst	405-3493			PHD	86	Princeton	1987
Sakellaris, Plutarchos	Asst	405-3509			PHD	92	Harvard	1992
Sen, Arijet	Asst	405-3512			PHD	93	Princeton	1993
Swamy, Anand V.	Asst	405-3489			PHD	93	Northwes	1993

Marymount University	Arlington, VA	22207-4299 (703) 284-5910					Sara Caltrider	
Economics Faculty	School of Business Adm	Fax=527-3830						
Sigethy, Robert	Dean	284-5910		Mgt	PHD		American	1983
Long, Teresa M.	Prof	284-5918			PHD	80	Iowa St	1981
Marshall, Louise	Assoc	284-5932			PHD	89	Maryland	1976

Marywood College	Scranton, PA	18509-1598 (717)						
Economics Faculty	Bus & Mgr Science Prog	Fax=						
Dagher, Sam P.	D-Pr	348-6274		Fnce	PHD	74	Ohio St	
Fagal, Frederick F. Jr.	Assoc				PHD	81	Syracuse	1987

University of Massachusetts	Amherst, MA	01003 (413) 545-2590					Judy Dietel UMASS	
Faculty Soc & Behav Sci&Econ	Col of Arts & Science	Fax=545-2921						
Boyce, James K.	C-Pr	545-3815			PHD	85	Oxford	1985
Bowles, Samuel S.	Prof	545-1373			PHD	65	Harvard	1973
Brimmer, Andrew F.	VProf				PHD	57	Harvard	
Costrell, Robert M.	Prof	545-1374			PHD	78	Harvard	1978
Crotty, James R.	Prof	545-2768			PHD	73	Car Mellon	1974
Deere, Carmen D.	Prof	545-0455			PHD	78	Berkeley	1977
Folbre, Nancy	Prof	545-3283			PHD	79	Mass	1985
Gintis, Herbert M.	Prof	545-6363			PHD	69	Harvard	1975
Katzner, Donald W.	Prof	545-6350			PHD	65	Minnesota	1975
Kindahl, James K.	Prof	545-0954			PHD	58	Chicago	1967
Kotz, David M.	Prof	545-4536			PHD	75	Berkeley	
Resnick, Stephen A.	Prof	545-0947			PHD	64	MIT	
Rottenberg, Simon	Prof	545-0421			PHD	50	Harvard	1971
Shepherd, William G.	Prof	545-0443			PHD	63	Yale	1986
Wolff, Richard D.	Prof	545-6351			PHD	69		
Bausor, Randall S.	Assoc	545-0595			PHD	78	Duke	1979
Epstein, Gerald A.	Assoc	545-6355			PHD	81	Princeton	1987
Flaherty, Diane P.	Assoc	545-4703			PHD	78		
Friedman, Gerald	Assoc	545-6357			PHD	86	Harvard	1984
Heim, Carol E.	Assoc	545-0854			PHD	82		
Rao, J. Mohan	Assoc	545-4808			PHD	82	Harvard	1989
Ballou, Dale	Asst	545-6358			PHD	89	Yale	
Olney, Martha L.	Asst	545-6359			PHD	85	Berkeley	1984
Saunders, Lisa F.	Asst	545-0546			PHD	87	Berkeley	1987

U Massachusetts at Boston Boston, MA 02125-3393 (617) 287-6950 Ms. Yvonne Ceurvels
Department of Economics Col of Arts & Sciences Fax= UMBSKY.CC.UMB.EDU

Name	Rank	Phone	E-mail	Fields	Degree	Yr	School	Year
Terkla, David G.	C-Pr	287-6952	terkla	QRHL	PHD	79	Berkeley	1987
Chiong, Winston R.	Prof	287-6957	chiong	E	PHD	74	Boston C	1982
Esposito, Louis	Prof	287-5600	esposito	L	PHD	68	Boston C	1968
Ferleger, Louis	Prof	287-6964	ferleger	N	PHD	78	Temple	1978
Gershenberg, Irving	Prof	287-6954	gershenberg	O	PHD	67	Berkeley	1982
MacEwan, Arthur	Prof	287-6956	macewan	FOI	PHD	69	Harvard	1975
Wolozin, Harold	Prof	287-6961	wolozin	B	PHD	55	Columbia	1966
Albelda, Randy P.	Assoc	287-6971	albelda	JI	PHD	83	Mass	1988
Campen, James T.	Assoc	287-6962	campen	EG	PHD	76	Harvard	1976
Cotton, Jeremiah	Assoc	287-6965	cotton	IJ	PHD	83	Michigan	1985
Lynde, Catherine	Assoc	287-6959	lynde	EF	PHD	85	Ca-Davis	1983
Stevenson, Mary H.	Assoc	287-6958	stevenson	JI	PHD	74	Michigan	1972
Brown, Paul	Asst	287-6953	brown	QE	PHD	90	Wisconsin	1990
Kapler, Janis	Asst	287-6955	kapler	FL	PHD	93	American	1993
Trost, Alice	Asst	287-6960	trost	R	PHD	94	SUNY-Bin	1992

U Massachusetts-Dartmouth No Dartmouth MA 02747 (508) 999-8280
Department of Economics Col of Arts & Sciences Fax= UMASSD.EDU

Name	Rank	Phone	E-mail	Fields	Degree	Yr	School	Year
Buckley, Suzann	Dean	999-8268						
Esposito, Frances F.	C-Pr	999-8280	fesposito		PHD	67	Boston C	1967
Berger, David E.	Prof	999-8256	dberger	IJOR	PHD	72	Wash U	1972
Georgianna, Daniel L.	Prof	999-8414	dgeorgianna		PHD	77	Mass	1977
Hogan, William V.	Prof	999-8257	whogan		PHD	76	Cornell	1976
Ohly, John H.	Assoc	999-8518		A	PHD	76	Boston U	1977
Shadbegian, Ronald	Asst	999-8337	rshadbegian	HKQ	PHD	91	Clark	1993
Walgreen, Sonia	VLect	999-8337			MA	63	Boston C	1984

U of Massachusetts at Lowell Lowell, MA 01854-2881 (508) 934-2780 Judy 934-2821
Department of Economics Col of Arts & Sciences Fax=934-3071 WOODS.UML.EDU

Name	Rank	Phone	E-mail	Fields	Degree	Yr	School	Year
Shirvani, Hamid	Dean	934-3847		Arch	PHD		Princeton	
Sanz, Ernesto	C-Ac	934-2782	sanze	FNP	PHD		Boston C	
Cederlund, Albert M.	Prof	934-2783		HL	PHD	75	Clark	
MacBeth, Thomas G.	Prof	934-2790		AC	PHD	62	S Calif	
McDonough, Carol C.	Prof	934-2784		DN	PHD	69	Boston C	1970
Sihag, Balbir S.	Prof	934-2786		CI	PHD	78	MIT	1980
Carter, Michael J.	Assoc	934-2794		CEQ	PHD		Stanford	
Dery, George C.	Assoc	934-2788		CD	MA		Boston C	
Goodwin, Susan A. Vice Chancellor of Administration & Finance	Assoc	934-3450		G	PHD		Tufts	
Lahiri, Supriya	Assoc	934-2789	lahiris	CQ	PHD	75	Delhi	
Pyle, Jean L.	Assoc	934-2792	pyleje	JOR	PHD		Mass	
Snoonian, Paul E.	Assoc	934-2793		EQ	PHD	71	Mich St	

Massachusetts Inst of Tech Cambridge, MA 02139-4307 (617) 253-6666 K. Swan
Department of Economics Sch Humanities &Soc Sci Fax=258-7258 ATHENA.MIT.EDU

Name	Rank	Phone	E-mail	Fields	Degree	Yr	School	Year
Khoury, Phillip S.	Dean			Hist	PHD			
Joskow, Paul L. Mitsui Professor of Economics and Management; Associate Head	H-Pr	253-6664		O	PHD	72	Yale	1972
Blanchard, Olivier J. Class of 1941 Professor	Prof	253-8891		G	PHD	77	MIT	1985
Diamond, Peter A. John and Jennie S. MacDonald Professor of Economics	Prof	253-3363		E	PHD	63	MIT	1966
Dornbusch, Rudiger	Prof	253-3648		F	PHD	71	Chicago	
Eckaus, Richard S. Ford International Professor of Economics	Prof	253-3367		O	PHD	54	MIT	1965
Fischer, Stanley	Prof	253-6666	stanley	G	PHD	69	MIT	
Fisher, Franklin M.	Prof	253-3373		P	PHD	60	Harvard	1960
Hausman, Jerry A.	Prof	253-3644		C	DPHI	73	Oxford	1973
Holmstrom, Bengt	Prof				PHD	78	Stanford	1995
Modigliani, Franco	Emer	253-7153			PHD	44	New Sch	1960
Newey, Whitney K. David W. Skinner Professor of Political Economy	Prof	253-6420		C	PHD			
Piore, Michael J.	Prof	253-3377		J	PHD	66	Harvard	
Poterba, James M.	Prof	253-6673		H	DPHI	83	Oxford	
Rothenberg, Jerome	Prof	253-2674		R	PHD	54	Columbia	1966
Samuelson, Paul A.	Emer	253-3368		D	PHD	41	Harvard	1940
Schmalensee, Richard L. Goldon Y. Billard Professor Economics & Management	Prof	253-2957		O	PHD	70	MIT	1977
Siegel, Abraham J. Howard W. Johnson Professor of Management	Prof	253-7158			PHD			
Solow, Robert M. Institute Professor	Prof	253-5268		E	PHD	51	Harvard	1958
Temin, Peter Elish Gray II Professor	Prof	253-3126		N	PHD	64	MIT	1965

Thurow, Lester C.	Prof	253-2932		PHD	64	Harvard	1968
Gordon Y. Billard Professor of Economics and Mgt; on leave							
Tirole, Jean	VProf	253-5596	O	PHD	81	MIT	1984
Wheaton, William C.	Prof	253-1723	R	PHD	72	Penn	1972
Banerjee, Abhijit	Assoc	253-8855	G				
Caballero, Ricardo	Assoc	253-0489	E	PHD	88	MIT	1992
Harris, Jeffrey E.	Assoc	253-2677	I	PHD	75	Penn	1976
Acemoglu, Daron	Asst	253-1927	J	PHD	92	LondonEc	1993
Athey, Susan	Asst	253-6407	L	PHD	95	Stanford	1995
Bai, Jushan J.	Asst	253-6217	C				
Bernard, Andrew B.	Asst	253-3488	E	PHD	91	Stanford	1991
Costa, Dora L.	Asst	253-2989	B				
Genesove, David J.	Asst	253-8788	O	PHD	91	Princeton	1991
Gruber, Jonathan H.	Asst	253-8892	G	PHD	92	Harvard	1992
Kremer, Michael R.	Asst	253-3504	E	PHD	92	Harvard	1992
Piketty, Thomas	Asst	253-9647	T				
Pischke, Jorn-Steffen	Asst	253-1942	J	PHD	92	Princeton	1993
Smith, Lones A.	Asst	253-0914	D	PHD	91	Chicago	1991
Ventura, Jaume	Asst		E	PHD	95	Harvard	1995

McMurry University Abilene, TX 79697 (915)
Economic Faculty School of Business Fax=

Presley, Ronald W.	Dean	691-6396	PHD	75	Okla St	1994
Williams, Eugene	Prof		PHD	71	Arkansas	1988

McNeese State University Lake Charles, LA 70609-2135 (318) 475-5520
Dept of Business & Economics College of Business Fax=475-5510 UCSVM.MCNEESE.EDU

Mondy, R. Wayne	Dean	475-5514		DBA	74	La Tech	1986
Phelps, Lonnie D.	H-Pr	475-5520		DBA		La Tech	
Foshee, Andrew W.	Prof	475-5562		PHD	80	LSU	1978
Kurth, Michael M.	Prof	475-5558		PHD		Va Tech	1984
McNiel, Douglas W.	Prof	475-5560	dmcniel	PHD	77	Okla St	1984
Rahman, A. K. M. Matiur	Asst	475-5573		PHD		So Meth	1989

University of Memphis Memphis, TN 38152 (901) 678-2474 Nancy Wilson
Department of Economics Fogelman Col Bus & Econ Fax=678-5380 MEMSTVX1

Randall, Donna	Dean	678-2432	Mgt	PHD	82	Wash St	1995
Rubin, Rose M.	C-Pr	678-2474		PHD	68	Kansas St	
Chang, Cyril F.	Prof	678-2474		PHD	79	Virginia	1981
Ciscel, David H.	Prof	678-2534		PHD	71	Houston	1973
Acting Dean, Graduate School							
Daniel, Coldwell III	Prof	454-2475		PHD	68	Virginia	1970
Depperschmidt, Thomas O.	Prof	454-2474		PHD	65	Tx-Austin	1966
Evans, Richard D.	Prof	678-2474		PHD	70	Harvard	1978
Fung, Kwok-Kwan	Prof	678-4626		PHD	70	Harvard	1975
Gnuschke, John E.	Prof	678-2281		PHD	75	Missouri	1976
Director, Ctr for Manpower Studies and Bureau of Business & Economic Research							
Gootzeit, Michael J.	Prof	678-4625		PHD	66	Purdue	1975
Okunade, Albert A.	Prof	678-2474		PHD	86	Arkansas	1987
Wells, Donald R.	Prof	454-2409		PHD	65	S Calif	1967
White-Means, Shelley L.	Prof	678-2456		PHD	83	Northwes	1988
Heath, Julia A.	Assoc	678-2474		PHD	86	S Carol	1986
Reid, John Joseph	Assoc	678-4627		PHD	62	Virginia	1966
Bose, Pinaki	Asst			PHD	90	NYU	9-95
Rogers, John E.	Asst	678-4657		PHD	88	N Carol	1993
Smith, William	Asst	678-3675		PHD	87	Virginia	1993

Mercer University-Atlanta Atlanta, GA 30341-4415 (404) 986-3199
Economics Faculty Stetson Sch Bus & Econ Fax=986-3337

Joiner, W. Carl	Dean	986-3235	PHD	78	Alabama	1974
Johnson, Victoria	Prof		DPA		Georgia	1985
Associate Dean						
Biegeleisen, J. Alan	Assoc	986-3338	PHD		Geo St	1982
Yu, Tie-Liu	Assoc	986-3368	PHD		Miss St	1990

Mercer University-Macon Macon, GA 31207-0001 (912)
Economic Faculty Stetson Sch Bus & Econ Fax=752-2635

Joiner, William Carl	Dean	752-2832	Mgt	PHD	78	Alabama	1974
Andrews, Charles Haynes	Prof	752-2832		PHD	67	Vanderbilt	1973
Stetson Professor of Economics							
Mounts, William S. Jr.	Prof	752-2832		PHD	77	Georgia	1978
Barber, G. Russell Jr.	Assoc	752-2162		PHD	90	Miss	1973

Meredith College	Raleigh, NC	27607-5298 (919) 829-8470						
Economic Faculty	Dept Business & Econ	Fax=829-2828						
Oatsvall, Rebecca S.	H-Pr	829-8470			PHD	78	S Carol	1984
Johnson, James	Prof				PHD		Duke	1980
Chappell, Glenn	Assoc				PHD		Tennessee	1991
Spencer, Theresa	Assoc				PHD		N Car St	1987
Wakeman, Douglas	Assoc				PHD		N Carol	1987

Merrimack College	North Andover MA 01845	(508) Ext 4245					LInda Trimble	
Dept of Economics	Div of Liberal Arts	Fax=837-5078					MERRIMACK.EDU	
phone 837-5000								
DeCiccio, Albert C.	Dean	837-5244		Engl	PHD		Ariz St	
Laramie, Anthony J.	C-Ac	837-5246			PHD		Clark	
Amariglio, Jack	Assoc	Ext 4313			PHD		Mass	
Charos, Evangelos N.	Assoc	Ext 4247			PHD	84	N Hamp	1983
Donovan, Elaine M.	Assoc	837-5447			PHD		Houston	
Looney, Lawrence J.	Assoc	Ext 4245			MA		Boston C	
Tontar, Charles F.	Assoc	Ext 4165			MA		New Sch	

Mesa State College	Grand JunctionCO 81502	(303) 248-1696					Teresa Holman	248-1696
Dept of Social Sciences	Sch Humanities & Beh Sc	Fax=248-1934						
Arosteguy, Daniel J.	Dean	248-1230			PHD		Colo St	1976
Schultz, Steven	C-Ac	248-1418		Hst	PHD			
Rees, David M.	Assoc				PHD		Oregon	1983
Herr, Elizabeth	Asst	248-1751			PHD		Colorado	

Metropolitan St Coll Denver	Denver, CO	80217-3362 (303) 556-3217						
Department of Economics	School of Business	Fax=556-3966						
Brown, Michael	Dean$	556-3245			PHD		Colorado	
Kulkarni, Kishore G.	C-Pr	556-2675			PHD	82	Pittsburgh	
Akacern, Mohammed	Prof	556-4649						
Call, Stephen T.	Prof	556-3916			PHD	77	Indiana	1979
Erickson, Erick Lee	Prof	556-3038			PHD		New Mex	
Pasternak, Richard E.	Prof	556-4935			PHD		Alabama	
Stone, Gerald W. Jr.	Emer	556-3218			PHD		Rice	
Fleisher, Arthur A. III	Assoc	556-4079			PHD	87	Geo Mason	1990
Gilliam, Lynde O.	Assoc	556-3037			PHD		Colo St	
Cochran, John	Asst	556-3218			PHD	85	Colorado	

University of Miami	Coral Gables, FL	33124-6550 (305) 284-5540					Ms. Denise Eutsey	
Department of Economics	Sch of Business Admin	Fax=284-2985			UMIAMIVM.IR.MIAMI.EDU			
Sugrue, Paul K.	Dean	284-4643		Mas	PHD	77	Mass	1977
Robins, Philip K.	C-Pr	284-5540	pkrobins	IJ	PHD	72	Wisconsin	1982
Connolly, Michael B.	Prof	284-5540		F	PHD	69	Chicago	1987
DeAlessi, Louis	Prof	284-5540	ldealessi	DK	PHD	61	UCLA	1975
Fishe, Raymond P. H.	Prof	284-5540	rfishe	CD	PHD	79	Florida	1981
Holtmann, Alphonse G.	Prof	284-5440	hholtmann	DI	PHD	63	Wash U	1981
Wallace, Neil	Prof	284-5540	nwallace	E	PHD	64	Chicago	1994
Barnett Banks Chair of Money and Banking								
Devereux, John J.	Assoc	284-5540	jdevereaux	FH	PHD	88	Chicago	1988
Foley, James W.	Assoc	284-4641		O	PHD	69	Mich St	1968
Locay, Luis	Assoc	284-5540	llocay	DO	PHD	83	Chicago	1989
Price, Hollis F. Jr.	Assoc	284-5540	hprice	R	PHD	72	Colorado	1971
Streeter, Lanny E.	Assoc	284-5540	lstreeter	C	PHD	70	Illinois	1967
Carey, Kevin	Asst	284-5540	carey	E	PHD	94	Princeton	1994
Liu, Peter C.	Asst	284-5540	pliu	C	PHD	89	Florida	1990
Lombard, Karen	Asst	284-5540	klombard		PHD	93	Chicago	1993
Roberts, Bryan	Asst	284-5540	broberts	ED	PHD	93	MIT	1993
Taber, Alex	Asst	284-5540	ataber	CE	ABD		Chicago	1994
Tanner, Evan C.	Asst	284-5540	etanner	FE	PHD	88	UCLA	1989

Miami University	Oxford, OH	45056-1675 (513) 529-2836					Sandra richardson	
Department of Economics	R.T. Farmer Sch Bus Adm	Fax=529-6992			SBA-LAWS.SBA.MUOHIO.ED			
Short, Daniel G.	Dean	529-3631	dshort	Atg	PHD	77	Michigan	7-95
Erekson, O. Homer	C-Pr	529-2836	herekson	HR	PHD	80	N Carol	1978
Brock, James W.	Prof	529-2846	jbrock	AK	PHD	81	Mich St	1979
Bill R. Moeckel Professor of Business								
Dunlevy, James A.	Prof	529-5333	jdunlevy	JF	PHD	74	Northwes	1980
Director, Program in International Studies								
Even, William E.	Prof	529-2865	beven	JC	PHD	84	Iowa	1983
Ferguson, John D.	Prof	529-3136	dfergus	EF	PHD	74	Brown	1970
Flueckiger, Gerald E.	Prof	529-2852	gflueck	CD	PHD	70	Purdue	1968
Hall, Thomas E.	Prof	529-2862	thall	EC	PHD	82	Ca-SnBarb	1982
Director of Graduate Studies								
Hart, William R.	Prof	529-4352	rhart	EA	PHD	76	Wash U	1974

Name	Rank	Phone	E-mail	Field	Degree	Yr	School	Year
Hutchinson, William K.	Prof	529-2856	whutchen	EF	PHD	75	Iowa	1972
McBride, Mark E.	Prof	529-2864	mcbride		PHD	79	Wash U	1983
Miller, Norman C.	Prof	529-2854	nmiller	EF	PHD	66	Pittsburgh	1985
Julian G. Lange Professor of Economics & American Enterprise								
Noble, Nicholas R.	Prof	529-6288	nnoble	EC	PHD	78	Cincinnati	1976
Seiver, Daniel A.	Prof	529-2863	dseiver	TG	PHD	74	Yale	1978
Sullivan, Dennis H.	Prof	529-2859	dsulliv	HI	PHD	75	Princeton	1973
Williamson, Samuel H.	Prof	529-2851	swilliam	NI	PHD	68	Purdue	1983
Curme, Michael A.	Assoc	529-6215	mcurme	JD	PHD	89	Illinois	1988
Davis, George K.	Assoc	529-2842	gdavis	EO	PHD	84	So Meth	1985
Mehdizadeh, Mostafa	Assoc	529-4936		A	PHD	80	Oklahoma	1982
Raynold, Prosper	Assoc	529-4348	praynold	EG	PHD	89	LSU	1989
Ziegert, Andrea	VAsoc	529-2486	aziegert	HI	PHD	85	N Carol	1992
Briggs, Hugh	Asst	529-2845	hbriggs	CD	PHD	89	Wisconsin	1990
Ghosal, Vivek	Asst	529-6668	vghosal	DE	PHD	88	Florida	1990
Granderson, Gerald	Asst	529-2841	ggrander	DG	PHD	93	N Carol	1993
Gupta, Barnali	Asst	529-4116	bgupta	DR	PHD	90	Florida	1993
Lage, Maureen	Asst	529-2840	mlage	AE	PHD	91	Penn St	1990
Li, Elizabeth	Asst	863-8833		AF	PHD	82	Cornell	1990
Ligeralde, Antonio	Asst	529-4932	tligeral	CE	PHD	89	Rice	1991
Lyons, John S.	Asst	529-2853	jlyons	NO	PHD	77	Berkeley	1985
Platt, Glenn	Asst	529-2869	gplatt	CR	PHD	93	Car Mellon	1993
Treglia, Michael	Asst	529-2858	mtreglia	CD	PHD	89	Penn St	1991
Miller, Gerald M.	SInst	529-2838	jmiller	DC	MA	73	Brown	1971
Assistant Chairperson								

University of Michigan	Ann Arbor, MI	48109-1220 (313) 764-2355			Susan Moulton
Department of Economics	Col Lit,Science, & Arts	Fax=764-2769			UM.CC.UMICH.EDU
Goldenberg, Edie	Dean	764-0322		PHD			
Courant, Paul N.	C-Pr	763-2499		PHD	74	Princeton	1973
Adams, William James	Prof	764-5273		PHD	73	Harvard	1973
Bergstrom, Theodore C.	Prof	764-2367		PHD	67	Stanford	1975
Brown, Charles C.	Prof	763-6867		PHD	74	Harvard	1985
Cross, John D.	Prof	763-3479		PHD	65	Princeton	1965
Deardorff, Alan V.	Prof	764-6817	deardorff	PHD	71	Cornell	1970
Gramlich, Edward M.	Prof	764-3490		PHD	65	Yale	1976
Holbrook, Robert S.	Prof	763-1282		PHD	65	Berkeley	1965
Howrey, E. Philip	Prof	763-1087					
Hymans, Saul H.	Prof	764-3299		PHD	64	Berkeley	1964
Johnson, George	Prof	764-2374					
Juster, F. Thomas	Prof	764-4207		PHD	56	Columbia	1973
Laitner, John	Prof	763-9620		PHD	76	Harvard	1975
Lee, Lung-Fei	Prof	764-2363		PHD	77	Rochester	1991
Porter, Richard C.	Prof	764-2355		PHD	57	Yale	1964
Salant, Stephen W.	Prof	764-2355		PHD	73	Penn	1981
Saxonhouse, Gary R.	Prof	764-3296		PHD	71	Yale	1970
Shapiro, Matthew D.	Prof	764-2355		PHD	84	MIT	1989
Simon, Carl	Prof	763-3074					
Slemrod, Joel B.	Prof	936-3914		PHD	80	Harvard	1987
Solon, Gary R.	Prof	763-1306		PHD	83	Princeton	1983
Stafford, Frank P.	Prof	764-2355		PHD	68	Chicago	1974
Stern, Robert M.	Prof	764-2373		PHD	58	Columbia	1961
Varian, Hal R.	Prof	764-2364		PHD	73	Berkeley	1977
Weisskopf, Thomas E.	Prof	763-3037		PHD	66	MIT	1972
White, Michelle J.	Prof	763-3096		PHD	73	Princeton	1984
Barsky, Robert	Assoc	764-9476					
Bound, John	Assoc	747-2319					
Kimball, Miles S.	Assoc	764-2375		PHD	87	Harvard	1987
Lam, David A.	Assoc	764-2355		PHD	83	Berkeley	1983
Levinsohn, James A.	Assoc	763-2319		PHD	88	Princeton	1987
Mackie-Mason, Jeffrey K.	Assoc	764-7438		PHD	86	MIT	1986
Stachetti, Ennio	Assoc	764-8022		PHD	83	Wisconsin	1992
Whatley, Warren	Assoc	764-5256					
Basu, Susanto	Asst	764-5359		PHD	92	Harvard	1992
Charles, Kerwin	Asst			PHD	95		1995
Chen, Yan	Asst	764-2355		PHD	94	Cal Tech	1994
Kossoudji, Sherrie A.	Asst	764-2381		PHD	84	Michigan	1987
Levenstein, Margaret C.	Asst	764-5274		PHD	91	Yale	1990
Li, David	Asst	763-9561		PHD	92	Harvard	1992
Oppers, Stefan	Asst	764-2368		PHD	93	Harvard	1993
Roth, David	Asst	763-5317		PHD	93	Yale	1992
Shaffer, Greg	Asst	763-5319		PHD	89	Princeton	
Sonmez, Tayfon	Asst			PHD	95		1995
Gerson, Janet	Lect						
Thompson, Frank W.	Lect			PHD	73	Harvard	1990
Wolfe, Janet C.	Lect	763-2392		MPP	80	Michigan	1987

Univ of Michigan-Dearborn — Dearborn, MI 48128-1491 (313) 593-5096 — Kathleen M. Endlein
Dept of Social Science — Col of Arts, Sci & Ltrs Fax=593-5552 — UMICH.EDU

Presley, John W.	Dean	593-5490			PHD		S Illinois	1992
Hull, Brooks B.	C-Ac	593-5096	bhull@ca.f1.umd.	ADLQ	PHD	82	U Wash	1981
Roehl, Richard Associate Dean	Prof	593-5490	rroehl	ABDN	PHD	68	Berkeley	1976
Twomey, Michael J.	Prof	593-5176	mwomey	AEFO	PHD	73	Cornell	1977
Crowell, Elizabeth	Assoc	436-9183	ecrowell		PHD	71	Indiana	1978
Smith, Patricia	Assoc	593-5205	psmith	ACDH	PHD	86	Va Tech	1988
Ellis, Steffany G.	Asst	436-9180	sellis	AEFO	PHD	93	NC-Charl	1992
Pietrykowski, Bruce	Asst	593-9970	bpietrk	AJPR	PHD	90	New Sch	1988
Reaves, Natalie	Asst	593-5147	nreaves	AIL	PHD	95	Wayne St	1994
Shah, Parth	Asst	436-9171	pshah	APE	PHD	90	Auburn	1991

Univ of Michigan-Flint — Flint, MI 48502-2186 (810) 762-3280 — Judy J. Bedore
Department of Economics — Col of Arts & Sciences Fax=762-3687 — CROB.FLINT.UMICH.EDU

Zeff, Jacqueline L.	Dean	762-3234	zeff_j	Engl	PHD		Pittsburgh	1991
Reddy, Nallapu N.	C-Pr	762-3280	reddy_n		PHD	67	Penn St	1974
Kowal, Lubomyr M.	Prof	762-3280	kowal_l		PHD	65	Illinois	1966
Nas, Tevfik F.	Prof	762-3280	nas_t		PHD	77	Fla St	1982
Weber, Charles T.	Assoc	762-3280	weber_c		PHD	77	Wayne St	1977
Johnston, Charles W.	Asst	762-3280	johnston_c		PHD	88	Tx-Austin	1988
Matcheck, Dale C.	Asst	762-3280	matchek_d		PHD	93	Cornell	1990
Olmstead, Jennifer C.	Asst	762-3280	olmstead_j		PHD	94	Ca-Davis	1993

Michigan State University — East Lansing, MI 48824-1121 (517) 355-7583 — Terie Snyder 355-5238
Department of Economics — College of Business Fax=432-1068 — BANYAN.MSU.EDU

Henry, James B.	Dean	355-8378		Fnce	PHD	70	Syracuse	7-94
Menchik, Paul L.	C-Pr	355-5238	paul.menchik		PHD	76	Penn	1979
Allen, Bruce T.	Prof	355-7739			PHD	65	Cornell	
Ballard, Charles L.	Prof	353-2961			PHD	83	Stanford	1983
Ballie, Richard	Prof	355-1864			PHD		London	
Boyer, Kenneth D.	Prof	353-9088			PHD	75	Michigan	1984
Brown, Byron W.	Prof	355-2364			PHD	66	J Hopkins	1978
Davidson, Carl	Prof	355-7756			PHD	87	Boston U	1982
Fisher, Ronald C.	Prof	353-4582			PHD	77	Brown	1976
Goddeeris, John H.	Prof	353-6466			PHD	80	Wisconsin	1980
Holzer, Harry J.	Prof	355-8320			PHD	83	Harvard	1983
Kannappan, Subbiah	Prof	355-1816			PHD		Tufts	
Kreinin, Mordechai E.	Prof	355-6579			PHD	52	Michigan	1959
Ladenson, Mark L.	Prof	353-3007			PHD	70	Northwes	1984
Liedholm, Carl E.	Prof	355-1812			PHD	65	Michigan	1967
Mackey, M. Cecil	Prof	355-7583			PHD		Illinois	
Meyer, Jack	Prof	355-7749			PHD	74	Stanford	1983
Neumark, David B.	Prof	353-7275			PHD	87	Harvard	1995
Obst, Norman P.	Prof	353-5252			PHD	70	Purdue	1973
Rasche, Robert H.	Prof	355-7755			PHD	66	Michigan	1975
Samuels, Warren J.	Prof	355-1860			PHD	57	Wisconsin	1968
Schmidt, Peter J.	Prof	355-8381			PHD	70	Mich St	1977
Strassmann, W. Paul	Emer	355-7583			PHD	56	Maryland	
Strauss, John	Prof	355-1863			PHD	81	Mich St	1992
Woodbury, Stephen A.	Prof	355-4587			PHD	81	Wisconsin	1982
Wooldridge, Jeff	Prof	353-5972			PHD			
Amsler, Christine E.	Assoc	355-3774			PHD	80	Penn	
Biddle, Jeff E.	Assoc	353-7862			PHD	85	Duke	1985
Cookingham, Mary E.	Assoc	355-0293			PHD		Berkeley	
Glomm, Gerhard	Assoc	355-7349			PHD	88	Minnesota	1995
Irvine, F. Owen	Assoc	355-4667			PHD	76	MIT	1982
LaLonde, Robert J.	Assoc	355-7583			PHD	85	Princeton	1995
Martin, Lawrence W.	Assoc	353-3528			PHD		Maryland	
Matusz, Steven J.	Assoc	353-8719			PHD	83	Penn	1983
Pecchenino, Rowena A.	Assoc	353-6621			PHD	85	Wisconsin	1985
Segerstrom, Paul S.	Assoc	355-9647			PHD	84	Rochester	1984
Chung, Ching-fan	Asst	353-9933			PHD	87	Wisconsin	1988
Creane, Anthony J.	Asst	355-4667			PHD	91	Virginia	1990
Herrero, Maria Jose	Asst	353-9916			PHD		London	1995
Krupp, Corinne M.	Asst	353-7281			PHD	90	Penn	1989
Mullin, Wallace P.	Asst	353-9934			PHD	92	MIT	1992
Papke, Leslie E.	Asst	355-3773			PHD	87	MIT	1990

Michigan Technological Univ — Houghton, MI 49931-1295 (906)
Economics Faculty — School of Bus & Eng Adm Fax= — MTU.EDU

Klippel, R. Eugene	Dean	487-2669	gklippel	Mktg	PHD	91	Penn St	1994
Campbell, Gary A.	Prof	487-2803	gcampbe	Q	PHD	82	Penn St	1982
Gale, James R.	Prof	487-2674	jrbale	E	PHD	72	Iowa	1971
Joyce, B. Patrick	Prof	487-2677	pjoyce	D	PHD	74	Missouri	1972

Monson, Terry D. Prof 487-3124 tmonson F PHD 72 Minnesota 1977
Associate Dean
Merz, Thomas E. Assoc 487-2805 temerz PHD 80 Pittsburgh 1980
Nelson, Paul A. Assoc 487-2809 pnelson M PHD 74 Wisconsin 1972
Roberts, Mark C. Assoc 487-2771 mroberts PHD 85 Arizona 1985
Davutyan, Nurhan Asst 487-3081 ndavutya C PHD 88 Ca-SnBarb 1990

Middle Tennessee State Univ Murfreesboro, TN 37132 (615) 898-2520 Christie Pickel,ThenartisEllis
Dept of Economics & Finance College of Business Fax=898-5538 MTSU.EDU
Haskew, Barbara S. Dean 898-2764 PHD 69 Tennessee 1988
Lee, John T. C-Pr 898-2520 PHD 77 Georgia 1984
Balch, Billy W. Prof 898-2381 PHD 68 Alabama 1964
DePrince, Albert E. Jr. Prof 898-5995 PHD 78 NYU 1991
Fayissa, Bichaka Prof 898-2385 PHD 82 Tennessee 1980
Ford, William s. Prof 898-2889 PHD 66 Michigan 1991
Weatherford Chair
Graddy, Duane B. Prof 898-2525 PHD 74 Lehigh 1972
Hannah, Richard Prof 898-2228 PHD 81 Utah 1992
Hollman, Kenneth W. Prof 898-2673 PHD 70 Alabama 1982
Martin Chair of Insurance
Homalfar, Ghassem Prof 898-2384 PHD 82 Alabama 1982
Kawahito, Kiyoshi Prof 898-5751 PHD 71 Maryland 1971
Kitrell, Frederick J. Prof 898-2364 PHD 70 Miss 1971
Kyle, Reuben Prof 898-5617 PHD 72 Tennessee 1972
Director, Bureau of Business & Economic Research
Newsome, Bobby A. Prof 898-5618 PHD 85 Georgia 1989
Rogers, Walter B. Prof 898-2527 PHD 69 Okla St 1981
Zietz, Joachim Prof 898-5619 PHD 81 Gottingen 1989
Evans, Boyd Assoc 898-5473 MA 64 Auburn 1965
James, John B. Assoc 898-2383 PHD 70 Tx A&M 1969
Nguyen, Nghiep H. Assoc 898-5117 PHD 81 Tennessee 1981
Strickland, Thomas H. Assoc 898-2931 PHD 79 Oklahoma 1988
Deme, Mamit Asst 898-5750 PHD 90 Tx-Austin 1990
Eff, E. Anthon Asst 898-2387 PHD 89 Tx-Austin 1990
Feller, James F. Asst 898-2365 PHD 79 Florida 1984
Norman, Emily Asst 898-5497 PHD 94 Fla St 1993
Sarver, Lee Asst 898-5919 PHD 87 Tennessee 1991

Middlebury College Middlebury, VT 05753 (802) Ext 5327 Sheila Cassin
Economics Faculty Department of Economics Fax=388-8637
phone: 388-3711
Sommers, Paul M. C-Pr Ext 5325 PHD 76 Ca-SnDgo 1976
Claudon, Michael Paul Prof Ext 5324 PHD 71 J Hopkins 1970
Colander, David C. Prof Ext 5302 PHD 76 Columbia 1982
Christian A. Johnson Distinguished Professor of Economics
Cornwall, Richard R. Prof Ext 5326 PHD 68 Berkeley 1977
Horlacher, David E. Prof Ext 3141 PHD 73 Penn St 1992
A. Barton Hepburn Professor of Economics
Wonnacott, Paul Prof Ext 5540 PHD 59 Princeton 1994
Alan R. Holmes Visiting Professor in Monetary Economics
Wunnava, Phanindra V. Assoc Ext 5024 PHD 86 SUNY-Bin 1985
Carr, Thomas A. Asst Ext 5787 PHD 88 Colorado 1990
Ramaswamy, Sunder Asst Ext 5322 PHD 90 Purdue 1990
Slay, Benjamin Harlow Asst Ext 5112 PHD 89 Indiana 1994
Stephenson, Kevin M. Asst Ext 5917 PHD 92 Cornell 1992
Dighe, Ranjit S. Inst ABD Yale 1995
Matthews, Peter H. Inst ABD Yale 1995

Midwestern State University Wichita Falls TX 76308-2099 (817)
Department of Economics Div of Business Admin Fax=
Fukasawa, Yoshikazu Dean 689-4360 EF PHD 79 Kansas St 1978
Director, Bureau of Business & Government Research
Krienke, Albert B. Prof 689-4722 DP PHD Tx A&M 1965
Rodriguez, Louis J. Prof 689-4211 EF PHD LSU 1981
President
Welch, Robert G. Prof 689-4290 DG PHD Oreg St 1966
Harmel, Robert Assoc 689-4365 DL PHD Iowa St 1989

Millersville Univ of PA Millersville, PA 17551 (717) 872-3679 Mrs. Joan D. Haigh
Dept of Economics Sch of Human & Soc Sci Fax=871-2003 MILLERSV.EDU
Clark-Newman, Linda Dean 872-3553 PHD 68 N Carol 1994
Suliman, Osman C-Pr 872-3679 PHD 84 Indiana 1993
Hamid, M. Khalil Prof 872-3560 PHD 66 Iowa 1968
Hau, Jong-Chol Prof 872-3582 PHD 67 St Louis 1969
Leela, Secunderabad N. Assoc 872-3576 PHD 65 Bombay 1969
Margolis, Marvin S. Assoc 872-3561 PHD 69 Purdue 1981

Millikin University Decatur, IL 62522 (217)
Dept of Economics & Finance — Tabor Sch of Business Fax=424-3993 — MAIL.MILLIKIN.EDU
Did Not Respong - 1994-95 Listing

Name	Rank	Phone	Email	Field	Degree	Yr	School	Year
Mannweiler, Richard A.	Dean	424-6284	rmannwei	Mgt	MSIR		Purdue	1979
Watson, James O.	C-Ac	424-6380	jwatson		PHD	76	Purdue	1979
Liberatore, Anthony F.	Assoc	546-6446	aliberat		PHD		Conn	1984
Cohn, Cheryl L. area code (309)	Asst	827-8478	ccohn		DA	85	Ill St	1984

Millsaps College Jackson, MS 39210-0001 (601) 974-1274 — Ms. Carol Heatherly
Economic Faculty — Esle Sch of Management Fax=974-1260 — OKRA.MILLSAPS.EDU

Name	Rank	Phone	Email	Field	Degree	Yr	School	Year
Parker, Hugh J.	Dean	974-1250		Atg	PHD	82	Okla St	1987
Taylor, Patrick A. Director of BBA Program	C-Ac	974-1274	taylorpa	AD	PHD	84	Alabama	1984
Brooking, Carl G.	Prof	974-1261	brookcg	CDK	PHD	74	Penn	1981
Taylor, Susan W.	Asst	974-1278	taylorsw	AFH	PHD	89	LSU	1992

University of Minnesota Minneapolis, MN 55455-0413 (612) 625-6353 — Sara Shuford
Department of Economics — College of Liberal Arts Fax=624-0209 — ATLAS.SOCSCI.UMN.EDU

Name	Rank	Phone	Email	Field	Degree	Yr	School	Year
Davis, Julia M.	Dean			Audi	PHD		S Miss	
Swan, Craig E.	C-Pr	625-6353	econdept		PHD	70	Yale	1969
Allen, Beth Elaine	Prof	625-8213			PHD	78	Berkeley	1992
Chipman, John S. Regents' Professor	Prof	625-2816			PHD	51	J Hopkins	1955
Coen, Edward	Emer				PHD	53	London	
Feldman, Roger D.	Prof	624-5669			PHD	76	Rochester	1985
Foster, Edward M. Director Graduate Studies	Prof	373-4393			PHD	61	MIT	1983
Geweke, John F.	Prof				PHD	75	Minnesota	1990
Hurwicz, Leo	Prof	625-5808			LLM	38	Warsaw	1951
Jordan, James S.	Prof	625-8526	jjordan		PHD	75	Northwes	1976
Kareken, John H.	Prof				PHD		MIT	1958
Kehoe, Timothy J.	Prof	625-1589			PHD	79	Yale	1987
LeRoy, Stephen F.	Prof				PHD	71	Penn	
Mohring, Herbert D.	Emer	373-5268			PHD	59	MIT	1961
Prescott, Edward C.	Prof	373-0350			PHD	67	Car Mellon	1980
Richter, Marcel K.	Prof	625-7832			PHD	59	MIT	1959
Ruttan, Vernon W. Regents' Professor	Prof	376-3560			PHD	52	Chicago	1976
Schuh, G. Edward	Prof	373-0945			PHD	61	Chicago	1979
Smith, Harlan	Emer				PHD		Chicago	
Holmes, Thomas J.	Assoc				PHD	85	Northwes	1995
Kiyotaki, Nobuhiro	Assoc				PHD		Harvard	1991
McLennan, Andrew M.	Assoc	256-6339			PHD	82	Princeton	1987
Rogerson, Richard D.	Assoc				PHD		Minnesota	1991
Werner, Jan	Assoc				PHD		Bonn	1987
Gownsaukaran, Gautam	Asst				PHD	95	Yale	1995
Ichimura, Hidehiko	Asst				PHD	87	MIT	1987
Keane, Michael P.	Asst	624-0840			PHD	89	Brown	1988
Kehoe, Patrick J.	Asst				PHD	86	Harvard	1984
Kitamura, Yuichi	Asst				PHD	93	Yale	1993
Merlo, Antonio	Asst				PHD	92	NYU	1992
Ohanian, Lee E.	Asst				PHD	93	Rochester	1995

U of Minnesota - Duluth Duluth, MN 55812-2496 (218) 726-7284 — Becky Skurla
Department of Economics — Sch of Business & Econ Fax=726-6509 — UB.D.UMN.EDU

Name	Rank	Phone	Email	Field	Degree	Yr	School	Year
Lievano, R. J.	Dean	726-7251	rlievano		PHD	75	Houston	1994
Jesswein, Wayne A.	H-Pr	726-7297	wjesswei	F	PHD	69	Illinois	1974
Anderson, Curtis L.	Prof	726-7568	canderso	QA	PHD	81	Wyoming	1980
Junk, Paul E.	Prof	726-6140		E	PHD	62	Northwes	1979
Lichty, Richard W.	Prof	726-7219	rlichty	R	PHD	71	Kansas St	1971
Peterson, Jerrold M.	Prof	726-7256	jpeterson	HE	PHD	70	Illinois	1969
Raab, Raymond L.	Prof	726-8508	rraab1	L	PHD	71	Colo St	1985
Steinnes, Donald N.	Prof	726-8243	dsteinne	C	PHD	72	Northwes	1981
Nelson, Dennis L.	Assoc	726-8383		A	PHD	70	Minnesota	1964
O'Brien, A. Maureen	Assoc	726-7981	mobrien	J	PHD	83	West Va	1982
Vose, David	Assoc	726-8756	dvose	Q	PHD	66	Wisconsin	1966
Hoffman, Robert	Asst	726-7284		E	PHD	92	Boston C	1995

Minot State University Minot, ND 58702-5002 (701) 857-3130 — Mrs. Robyn Miller
Div Social Sci-Dept of Econ — Col of Arts & Sciences Fax=839-6933 — WARP6.CS.MISU.NODAK.EDU

Name	Rank	Phone	Email	Field	Degree	Yr	School	Year
Elhardt, Dale G.	Dean	857-3159		Soci	PHD		Colo St	1970
Wagner, Jonathan M.	C	857-3130		Hst	PHD		Wisconsin	1984
King, Clay B.	Assoc	857-3133		A	PHD		Wash St	1975
Huenneke, Steve	Asst	857-3035		AR	PHD		Kansas St	1991
Xia, Feng Lei	Asst	857-3130		AF	PHD		Kansas St	1994

Mississippi College Clinton, MS 39058 (601) 925-3214 Shea Elkins
Dept Business Adm-Economics Sch of Business Admin Fax=925-3804

Roberts, Lloyd	Dean	925-3419			PHD	74	Miss	1982
Hood, Frank	Prof	925-3413			PHD	72		1972
Lee, Gerald R.	Prof	925-3220			PHD	73	Miss	1970

University of Mississippi University, MS 38677 (601) 232-7076 Ms. Sue Hodge
Dept of Economics & Finance School of Business Adm Fax=232-5821 BUS.OLEMISS.EDU

Boxx, Randy	Dean	232-5820		Mgt	PHD	71	Arkansas	1971
Womer, N. Keith	C-Pr	232-7076			PHD	70	Penn St	1986
Belongia, Michael T.	Prof	232-7785		E	PHD	82	N Car St	1993
Shughart, William F. II	Prof	232-7076			PHD	78	Tx A&M	1988
Self Chair of Free Enterprise Holder								
Smith, Lewis	Prof	232-5924		E	PHD	71	Tennessee	1971
Wood, Edgar	Prof	232-5830			PHD	67	LSU	1967
Director of Center of Economic Education								
Chappell, William	Assoc	232-5708			PHD	83	S Carol	1987
Conlon, John	Assoc	232-5708			PHD	78	Chicago	1987
Dorsey, Robert	Assoc	232-7575		ED	PHD	89	Arizona	1989
Mayer, Walt	Assoc	232-5980		E	PHD	86	Florida	1987
Tosh, Dennis S.	Assoc	232-5101			PHD	80	Geo St	1980
Boose, Mary Ann	Asst	232-7291			PHD	88	Wash U	1988
Graham, A. Steven	Asst	232-5845			PHD	90	Queen's	1990
Kildegaard, Arne C.	Asst	232-7530			PHD		Tx-Austin	1993
Moen, Jon R.	Asst	232-5467			PHD	87	Chicago	1990
Razzolini, Laura	Asst	232-7530		D	PHD	94	So Meth	1994
VanBoening, Mark V.	Asst	232-5841			PHD		Arizona	1990

Mississippi State Univ Miss St, MS 39762-6135 (601)
Dept Finance & Economics Col of Business & Indus Fax=325-2410 COBILAN.MSSTATE.EDU

Lewis, Harvey S.	Dean	325-2580		Fnce	PHD	66	Arkansas	6-92
Register, Charles A.	C-Pr	325-3241			PHD	84	Okla St	1993
Awh, Robert Y.	Prof	325-2341			PHD	60	Florida	1968
Chressanthis, George A.	Prof	325-2561			PHD	83	Purdue	1987
Eatherly, Billy Jack	Prof				PHD	64	So Meth	
Grimes, Paul W.	Prof	325-1987			PHD	84	Okla St	1987
Campbell, Charles A.	Assoc	325-7477	ccampell		PHD	85	Tennessee	1985
Sanderson, Patricia L.	Assoc	325-1970			PHD	77	Oklahoma	1979
Tsiritakes, Emmuanuel	Assoc				PHD	87	Va Tech	1986
Verrall, George	Assoc	325-1978			DBA	72	Miss St	1965

Mississippi Valley St Univ Itta Bena, MS 38941-1400 (601) 254-3601 Mrs. Mary Carter
Economics Faculty Business Adm Department Fax=

Williams, Cliff F.	C-Pr	254-3601		BuEd	EDD		Houston	1960
Chowdhury, Farhad	Prof	254-3606			PHD		Miss St	1993
Kim, Juho	Prof	254-3604			PHD		Oklahoma	1973
Rajanikauth, N.	Inst	254-3609			MBA		Miss St	1987
Warner, Rickey	Inst				MA		Atlanta	1988

U of Missouri - Columbia Columbia, MO 65211 (314) 882-4574 Sheila Akers Adm Asst
Department of Economics Col of Arts & Sciences Fax=882-2697 MIZZOU1.MISSOURI.EDU

Clark, Larry	Dean	882-4421		Thea	PHD	63	Illinois	1966
Podgursky, Michael J.	C-Pr	882-4575			PHD	80	Wisconsin	1995
Hicks, W. Whitney	Prof	882-3483	econwh	O	PHD	65	Stanford	1965
Lee, Maw Lin	Prof	882-2777	econmll	C	PHD	61	Wisconsin	1968
Loschky, David J.	Prof	882-7282	econ0844	TN	PHD	62	Harvard	1967
Menezes, Carmen F.	Prof	882-6094	econcfm	DF	PHD	66	Northwes	1965
Ratti, Ronald A.	Prof	882-6474	econrr	EFG	PHD	75	So Meth	1975
Wallace, Richard L.	Prof	882-1154			PHD	65	Vanderbilt	1967
Vice President for Academic Affairs								
Geiss, Charles G.	Assoc	882-6073	econcg	C	PHD	74	N Carol	1972
Johnson, Walter L.	Assoc	882-3871	econwj	AEGH	PHD	63	Duke	1965
Mandy, David M.	Assoc	882-1763	econdm	CD	PHD	87	Illinois	1994
Mueser, Peter R.	Assoc	882-6427	econprm	DJT	PHD	83	Chicago	1985
Raymon, Neil A.	Assoc	882-3072	econnr	CDEF	PHD	77	Colorado	1983
Schilling, Donald J.	Assoc	882-6878	econdon	EF	PHD	67	N Carol	1964
Chesser, David	Asst	882-5572	econdc	FE	PHD	95	Virginia	1993
Cheung, Kowk Hung (Francis)	Asst	882-9925	econfran	DJR	PHD	89	Mich St	1989
Dickhaus, Elizabeth	Asst	882-4164		IN	PHD	74	Missouri	1974
Lee, Kiseok	Asst	882-4229	econklee	C	PHD	90	Chicago	1987
Lin, Chyi-Ing	Asst	882-0429	econclin	FO	PHD	93	Michigan	1993
Ni, Xiagoguang	Asst	882-6878	econni@umc	EH	PHD	91	Minnesota	1990
Wang, Xinghe	Asst	882-4954	econwang	CDO	PHD	90	Iowa	1990

U Missouri--Kansas City Kansas City, MO 64110-2499 (816) 235-1314 Ms. Sheila Steverson
Department of Economics Col of Arts & Sciences Fax=235-5263 VAX1.UMKC.EDU

Durig, James	Dean	235-2538		Chem	PHD		MIT	1993
Ward, John O.	C-Pr	235-1309	wardj	KIO	PHD	70	Oklahoma	1969
Brazelton, W. Robert	Prof	235-2831		EP	PHD	61	Oklahoma	1963
Hubbell, L. Kenneth	Prof	235-2835		GHM	PHD		Nebraska	1968
Olson, Gerald W.	Prof	235-1317		CGH	PHD		Rutgers	1971
Shepherd, A. Ross	Prof	235-2836		DF	PHD	63	Syracuse	1967
Wagner, F. Eugene	Prof	235-2840		AJO	PHD	67	Syracuse	1967
Eaton, Peter J.	Assoc	235-2832		CI	PHD	76	Florida	1979
Sturgeon, James I.	Assoc	235-3837		BO	PHD	74	Oklahoma	1977
Vorst, Karen S.	Assoc	235-2838		EC	PHD	80	Indiana	1980
Young, Ben	Lect	235-1314		A	PHD	73	Oklahoma	1993

University Missouri - Rolla Rolla, MO 65401-0249 (314) 341-4800 Mary Wieland
Department of Economics Col of Arts & Sciences Fax=341-4866 UMR.EDU

Johnson, Walter D.	C-Pr	341-4809	c8029wj@umrvmb.		PHD		Oklahoma	1988
Hentzel, David	Prof	341-4827	hentzel		PHD		S Illinois	1969
Bryant, Richard R.	Assoc	341-4823	rrbryant		PHD	84	Ca-Davis	1977
Gelles, Gregory	Assoc	341-4825	gelles		PHD		W Virginia	1989
Manning, Linda M.	Assoc	341-4828	lindam		PHD	90	Il-Chicago	1989
Thompson, Philip B.	VAsst	341-4893	philthom		PHD	88	Arizona	1994

U Missouri--St. Louis St. Louis, MO 63121-4499 (314) Gloria Axe
Department of Economics Col of Arts & Sciences Fax= UMSLVMA

Jones, E. Terrence	Dean				PHD			
Levin, Sharon G.	C-Pr	516-5560	c4876	DJ	PHD	73	Michigan	1974
Feigenbaum, Susan K.	Prof	516-5554		DHKP	PHD	80	Wisconsin	1988
Mitchell, William E.	Prof	516-5550		EG	PHD	67	Duke	1965
Phares, Donald	Prof	516-5551		HR	PHD	70	Syracuse	1969
Sorensen, Robert L.	Prof	516-5562	cit52	KMAO	PHD	71	Va Tech	1970
Undergraduate Coordinator								
Ireland, Thomas R.	Assoc	516-5558			PHD	68	Virginia	1972
Rose, David C.	Assoc	516-5307		CDIJ	PHD	87	Virginia	1985
Graduate Coordinator								
Bowen, J. Ray II	Asst	516-5557	sjrbowe	FOP	PHD	92	Michigan	1990
Greene, Clinton	Asst	516-5351		CE	PHD	92	Ca-Davis	1994
Kridel, Donald	Asst	516-5553		CD	PHD	87	Arizona	1993
McBride, Timothy	Asst	516-5530	stomcbr	IH	PHD	87	Wisconsin	1991
McCorkle, Sarapage	Asst	516-5248		A	EDD	87	Mo-St Lo	1970
Director, Center for Economic Education								
Winkler, Anne E.	Asst	516-5563	c4934	JT	PHD	89	Illinois	1989
Allison, Michael	Lect	516-5306	smallis	CE	ABD		Virginia	1993
Phares, Kathleen	Lect	516-5570		A	MA	76	Mo-St Lo	1977
Sulter, Mary	Lect	516-5248		A	MIEE		Delaware	
Associate Director, Center for Economic Education								

Missouri Southern St Col Joplin, MO 64801-1595 (417) 625-9319
Department of Economics Sch of Business Admin Fax=625-9604

Gray, James W.	Dean	625-9319	MBA	69	Arkansas	1969
Eberhardt, Duane	Prof	625-9536	PHD		S Calif	1986
Jaswal, Jasbir S.	Prof	625-9551	PHD		Missouri	1977
La Near, Richard E.	Prof	625-9530	PHD		Miss	1987
Dr. J. R. Kuhn Chair of Business Administration						
Miller, Robert J.	Assoc	625-9345	MA		Cen MoSt	1968
Rawlins, Richard	Asst	625-9716	MS		Okla St	1988
Larson, Marvin L.	Inst	625-9723	MA		Mo-St Lo	1990

Missouri Western St College Saint Joseph, MO 64507-2294 (816) 271-4338
Dept of Business & Economics Div of Professional Std Fax= ACAD.MWSC.EDU

Perkins, Charles A.	Dean	271-4205	perkins	Fnce	PHD		Geo Wash	1991
Lawson, Larry	C-Ac	271-4251	lawson	Fnce	PHD		Colorado	1993
Hamzaee, Reza G.	Prof	271-4262	hamzaee	E	PHD	85	Ariz St	1984
McMurry, Patrick H.	Prof	271-4276	mcmurray	J	PHD		Arkansas	1978
Vargha, Nader	Assoc	271-4339	vargha	B	MA		Oklahoma	1980
Lawson, Catherine L.	Asst	271-4338		EB	PHD		Colorado	1995

Molloy College Rockville Cn, NY 11570 (516) Ext 275
Economics Faculty Dept Bus, Acct, & Econ Fax=Ext 7295
phone 678-5000

Butler, Sister Agnes	C-As	Ext 275	ABD		Indiana	
Talmers, William N.	Adj	Ext 275	PHD	54	MIT	1979

Monmouth College - NJ W Lg Branch NJ 07764 (908) 571-3430
Dept of Economics & Finance Sch of Business Admin Fax=571-3523

Name	Rank	Phone		Field	Degree	Yr	School	Since
Dempsey, William A.	Dean	571-3423		Mktg	DBA	73	Maryland	1-89
Bolton, John	C-Ac	571-3667			MBA		Adelphi	
Pressman, Steven	Prof	571-3658			PHD	83	New Sch	1981
Weber, Richard E.	Prof	571-3661			PHD		Rutgers	
Aslanbeigui, Nahid	Assoc	571-3642			PHD	84	Michigan	1988
Feist, William R.	Assoc	571-3430			PHD		Temple	
Mahajan, Y. Lal	Assoc	571-3647			PHD		N Illinois	
Moliver, Donald M.	Assoc	571-3660			PHD		Va Tech	

University of Montana Missoula, MT 59812-1216 (406) 243-2925 Becky Hanway
Department of Economics Col of Arts & Sciences Fax=243-4076 UMT.EDU

Name	Rank	Phone		Field	Degree	Yr	School	Since
Flightner, James A.	Dean	243-2632			PHD			
Power, Thomas M.	C	243-4586		HQR	PHD		Princeton	
Barrett, Richard	Prof	243-4497		EOJQ	PHD		Wisconsin	
Duffield, John W.	Prof	243-2925		Q	PHD	74	Yale	1974
Dulaney, Ronald A.	Prof	243-4667		DJ	PHD		Columbia	
O'Donnell, Dennis J.	Prof	243-2926		OJR	PHD		Penn St	
Photiades, John G.	Prof	243-5612		BOH	PHD		Illinois	
Unger, Kay C.	Prof	243-4655		IDEC	PHD		J Hopkins	
Wicks, John H.	Prof	243-4122		DH	PHD		Illinois	
Dalenberg, Douglas R.	Assoc	243-4406		CRL	PHD	87	Oregon	1990
Kupilik, Michael H.	Assoc	243-4575		PHBN	PHD	76	Colorado	1976

Montana State University Bozeman, MT 59717-0292 (406) 994-3701 Renee' Cook, Adm Asst
Department of Economics Col of Letters & Sci Fax=994-4838 MSU.OSCS.MONTANA.EDU

Name	Rank	Phone		Field	Degree	Yr	School	Since
Drumheller, John E.	Dean	994-4405		Phys	PHD	62	Colorado	1964
Greer, Clyde	H	994-3701			PHD	70	Minnesota	1970
Anderson, Terry L.	Prof	994-3701			PHD	72	U Wash	1972
Antle, John M.	Prof	994-3701			PHD	80	Chicago	1987
Johnson, Ronald N.	Prof	994-3701			PHD	77	U Wash	1981
Stroup, Richard L.	Prof	994-3701			PHD	70	U Wash	1969
Young, Douglas J.	Prof	994-3701			PHD	78	Wisconsin	1977
Rucker, Randal R.	Assoc	994-3701			PHD	84	U Wash	1991
Stratmann, Thomas	Asst	994-3701			PHD	90	Maryland	1990

Montana State Univ-Billings Billings, MT 59101-0298 (406)
Dept of Management & Econ Sch of Business & Econ Fax=657-2051

Name	Rank	Phone		Field	Degree	Yr	School	Since
Kerby, Joe Kent	Dean	657-2295		Mktg	PHD	66	Columbia	1992
Graham, Reginald A.	C-Pr	657-1610		Mktg	PHD	70	Case Wes	1991
Farsio, Farzad	Assoc	657-2033			PHD	89	Claremont	1987
Harris, R. Scott	Assoc	657-1653			PHD	85	Calif	1988

Montclair State College U Montclair, NJ 07043 (201) 655-5255 Ms. Ida S. Fazzo
Department of Economics Sch of Business Admin Fax=655-5455 SATURN.MONTCLAIR.EDU

Name	Rank	Phone	Email	Field	Degree	Yr	School	Since
LeBel, Phillip	Dean$	655-4304	lebel	DOQH	PHD	77	Boston U	1981
Leveen, Serpil Sisik	C-Pr$	655-7402	leveen	ADEG	PHD	73	NYU	1974
Desai, Suresh	Prof	655-4370			PHD		UCLA	
Flint, Harold	Prof	655-7403		AEGP	PHD	72	S Illinois	1971
Chakraborty, Chandana	Assoc	655-4125		ACDO	PHD		Rensselae	
Honig, Solomon	Assoc	655-5255		ADKR	PHD	76	Columbia	1981
Rawlins, Glenville W.	Assoc	655-4339		AGOQ	PHD		NYU	
Rezvani, Farahmand	Assoc	655-7568		ACGH	PHD		CUNY	
Baytas, Ahmet	Asst	655-7633			PHD		Illinois	
Pirouz, Kamrouz	Asst	655-5124		ADGN	PHD		Hawaii	
Praveen, John	Asst	655-7075		ADGN	PHD		Berkeley	
Zamanian, Zaman	Asst	655-7399		ACEF	PHD		Indiana	
Scher, Frances	Inst	655-4135		AHIT	MA		Columbia	

University of Montevallo Montevallo, AL 35115 (205) 665-6540 Penny Cummings
Economics Faculty College of Business Fax=665-6560 UM.MONTEVALLO.EDU

Name	Rank	Phone	Email	Field	Degree	Yr	School	Since
Word, William R.	Dean	665-6540	word		PHD	70	Tennessee	1979
Shinn, Earl W. III	C-Ac	655-6536	shinn		PHD	92		1988
Blevins, Dallas	Prof	665-6542	blevins		DBA	76	Fla St	1983
MacPherson, Rod	Assoc	665-6535	macpherson		DBA		Miss St	

Moorhead State University Moorhead, MN 56563 (218) 236-2842 Cynthia Funk
Economics Department Business & Industry Fax=236-2168 MHD1.MOORHEAD.MSUS.EDU

Name	Rank	Phone		Field	Degree	Yr	School	Since
Crockett, David J.	Dean	236-2076		Fnce	PHD		Iowa	1993
Cooper, John M.	C-As	236-4030			MA	75	Oregon	1972
Dobis, Vernon J.	C-Ac	236-4029			PHD	94	Manitoba	1981
Greenley, Douglas A.	Prof	236-4031			PHD	79	Colo St	1978
Knighton, Daniel R.	Prof	236-4027			PHD	73	N Carol	1970
Sun, Li-teh	Prof	236-4026			PHD	72	Okla St	1982
Flores, Oscar	Assoc	236-3499			PHD	90	Cincinnati	1989
Farooque, Golam	Asst	236-2599			PHD	91	Northeas	1991

Moravian College	Bethlehem, PA	18018	(610) 861-1381				Mrs. Mayann Weaver	
Economic Faculty	Dept Economics & Bus		Fax=861-1466				MORAVIAN.EDU	
West, James P.	C-Pr				PHD		Lehigh	1989
Parkinson, Thomas L.	Prof				PHD		Mass	1985
Ravelle, James J.	Prof			UB	DA		Lehigh	1978
Brower, George D.	Assoc				PHD	85	SUNY-Buf	1989
Collins, May N.	Asst				PHD	92	S Calif	1993
Ravelle, Linda J.	Asst				PHD		Lehigh	1989
Von Allmen, Peter	Asst	861-1413			PHD	90	Temple	1990

Morehead State University	Morehead, KY	40351-1689	(606) 783-2152				Mary Lykins	
Department of Economics	Sch of Business & Econ		Fax=783-5025				MOREKYVM	
Carrell, Michael R.	Dean	783-2174		Mgt	DBA	76	Kentucky	1995
Buck, Roland	Prof	783-2722			PHD	79	Tx A&M	1983
Miller, Green	Prof	783-2721			PHD	85	Kentucky	1979
Ahmadig, S. Ali	Asst	783-2797			EDD	87	Houston	1995
Yasin, Mesghena	Asst	783-2758			PHD	86	Cincinnati	1986
Ryan, Anne-Marie	Inst	783-5288			MS	93	Wisconsin	1991

Morehouse College	Atlanta, GA	30314	(404) 215-2618	Mrs. Patricia Allen/Jackson				
Economics Faculty	Dept Economics & Bus Ad		Fax=215-2719					
Sheftall, Willis B.	C-Pr	681-2800			PHD	81	Geo St	1986
Charles E. Merrill Professor of Economics								
Handy, John	Prof				PHD		Geo St	1978
Eagan, J. Vincent	Assoc				PHD		Geo St	1993
Gissy, William G.	Asst				PHD		Geo St	1988
Green, Sam	Asst				PHD		Northwes	1993
Morman, Martin R.	Asst				PHD		Geo St	1990
Oriyomi, Abi	Asst				PHD			
Winstead, Richard E.	Asst				BA		Fisk	1975

Morgan State University	Baltimore, MD	21239	(410) 319-3438				Jo Ann McCready	
Department of Economics	Col of Arts & Sciences		Fax=319-3358					
Hollis, Burney	Dean	319-3090						
Fessiehatzen, Tekie	C-Pr	319-3438			PHD		Pittsburgh	
Favor, Homer	Prof	319-3558			PHD		Pittsburgh	
Whittaker, Victor A.	Prof	319-3440			PHD	71	Illinois	1974
Amegbe, Annan	Assoc	319-3531			PHD	77	Catholic	1978
Evans, Bernice	Asst	319-3446			MBA		CUNY-Bar	
Karangu, Mwangi	Asst	319-3440			PHD		Walden	
Bagheri, Rashid	Inst	319-3099			MA		Howard	
Kimani, Joseph	Inst	319-3099			MBA		Atlanta	

Morningside College	Sioux City, IA	51106-1751	(712) 274-5131				Deb Protexter	
Economics Faculty	Dept of Economics		Fax=274-5101		CHIEF.MORNINGSIDE.EDU			
Gilsdorf, Keith F.	C-As	274-5289	kgooo1	LJ	PHD	90	Nebraska	1994

Morris Brown College	Atlanta, GA	30314-4140	(404) 220-3735				Rudine Avery	
Economics Faculty	Dept of Econ & Bus Adm		Fax=688-5985					
phone 222-0270								
Coleman, Cyiata D.	Dir	Ext 3735		FGOR	PHD	86	S Illinois	8-89

Mount Holyoke College	South Hadley, MA	01075	(413) 538-2432					
Economics Faculty	Department of Economics		Fax=538-2512				MTHOLYOKE.EDU	
Montgomery, Sarah S.	Dean	538-2432			PHD	60	Wisconsin	1956
Paus, Eva	C-Ac	538-2518			PHD	83	Pittsburgh	1987
Moseley, Fred B.	Prof	538-2517	fmoseley		PHD	82	Mass	1989
Rapoport, John	Prof	538-2752			PHD	70	Penn	1970
Dean of Studies								
Robertson, Robert L. Jr.	Prof	538-2432			PHD	60	Wisconsin	1962
Christiansen, Jens	Assoc	538-2750			PHD		Stanford	
Robinson, Michael D.	Assoc	538-2215			PHD	87	Tx-Austin	1988
Desser, Arna S.	Asst	538-2261			PHD		Maryland	
Gabriel, Satyananda Jordan	Asst	538-2043			PHD		Mass	
Hartley, James E.	Asst	538-2566			PHD		Ca-Davis	1994

Mount Saint Mary's College	Los Angeles, CA	90049	(310) 471-9517					
Economics Faculty	Dept Business & Econ		Fax=476-9296					
Chalon Campus								
Geranios, John W.	C	471-9517			PHD		S Calif	
Whitman, Katherine	Asst	471-9517						

Muhlenberg College	Allentown, PA	18104-5586 (610) 821-3278					Anitra Witkowski	
Economics Faculty	Department of Economics Fax=821-3536						MAX.MUHLENBERG.EDU	
Heitmann, George Jr.	C-Pr	821-3278	heitmann		PHD	63	Princeton	1-94
Marshall, James N.	Prof	821-3284			PHD	82	Lehigh	1975
Sinha, Rohini P.	Prof	821-3282			PHD	65	New Sch	1965
Kish-Goodling, Donna M.	Asst	821-3479			PHD	92	Lehigh	1990
Raymond, Arthur J.	Asst	821-3278			PHD	90	Tufts	1991

Murray State University	Murray, KY	42071-3304 (502) 762-4188					Marion Elkins	
Dept of Economics & Finance	Col Bus & Public Affair Fax=762-3482						MSUMUSIK.MURSUKY.EDU	
Harrison, Dannie	Dean	762-4181	dannie	AEP	PHD	74	S Illinois	1969
Mathis, Gilbert L.	C-Pr	762-4283		DFQ	PHD	66	Ohio St	1966
Brasfield, David	Assoc	762-4324	a00936f	EG	PHD	89	N Carol	1986
McCoy, James	Assoc	762-4274	a18015f	DF	PHD	86	N Carol	1985
Milkman, Martin	Assoc	762-4282	a08138f	CJH	PHD	89	Oregon	1988
Hassan, Seid	Asst	762-4284	a56044f	E	PHD	93	Tx A&M	1992
Brown, Barry	Lect	762-4277	a06723f	E	MS	77	Murray St	1991

Naval Postgraduate School	Monterey, CA	93943-5104 (408) 656-2161					Sonja Johnson 656-2777	
Economics Faculty	Dept of Systems Mgt Fax=656-3407						NPS.NAVY.MIL	
Harris, Reuben T.	C-Pr	656-2768	harris	Mgt	PHD	75	Stanford	7-78
Boger, Dan C.	Prof	656-2607			PHD	79	Berkeley	1979
Jones, Carl R.	Prof	656-2995			PHD	65	Claremont	1965
LaCivita, Charles J.	Prof	656-2445			PHD	81	Ca-SnBarb	1985
Looney, Robert	Prof	656-3484			PHD	69	Berkeley	1977
Mehay, Stephen L.	Prof	656-2643			PHD	73	UCLA	1985
Melese, Francois	Assoc	656-2009			PHD	82	Belgium	1987
Webb, Natalie J.	Asst	656-2013			PHD	92	Duke	1992
Wellington, Alison J.	Asst	656-2912		J	PHD	90	Michigan	1995
on leave from Davidson College								
Blandin, Jim		656-3497						
Boynton, Robert		656-2310						
Frederiksen, Peter		656-2661						
Gates, William R.		656-2754			PHD	74	Yale	1988
Groshek, Gerald		656-2468						
Henderson, David R.		656-2524			PHD	76	UCLA	1984
Hildebrandt, Gregory		656-2767						
Parker, Pat		656-2097						
Stroup, Mike		656-3669						
Terasawa, Katchan		656-2463			PHD	72	Kansas	1972
Thomas, George		656-2741						

Nazareth Coll of Rochester	Rochester, NY	14618 (716) Ext 558					Joan Van du Zer	
Economics Faculty	Dept Bus, Econ, & Mgt Fax=586-2452							
phone 586-2525								
Zappia, Gerard	C-Ac	Ext 561			MSED		Nazareth	
Aerni, April Laskey	Assoc	Ext 549			PHD		Cincinnati	
DaBoll-Lavoie, Joseph T.	Assoc	Ext 592			PHD		SUNY-Bin	
Maley, Leonard A.	Assoc	Ext 550			MBA	62	Cincinnati	
Schroeder, Edward A.	Assoc				PHD	80	UCLA	1988

University of Nebraska	Lincoln, NE	68588-0489 (402) 472-2319					Carol Nelson	
Department of Economics	College of Business Adm Fax=472-9777						UNLINFO.UNL.EDU	
Goebel, Jack	Dean	472-9500			MA	68	Nebraska	1994
MacPhee, Craig R.	C-Pr	472-2319	cmacphee	F	PHD	70	Mich St	1969
Paul C. Burnmeister College Professor								
Anderson, John E.	Prof	472-1190	janderson	H	PHD	77	Claremont	1991
Director of Graduate Program								
Hayden, F. Gregory	Prof	472-2332	ghayden	HQI	PHD	68	Tx-Austin	1967
Lamphear, F. Charles	Prof	472-7928		O	PHD	67	Kansas St	1966
Director, Bureau of Business Research								
Petr, Jerry L.	Prof	472-3003	jpetr	P	PHD	67	Indiana	1966
C. Wheaton Battey Professor of Economics								
Rejda, George E.	Prof	472-2319			PHD	61	Penn	1963
V. J. Skutt Professor of Economics								
Riefler, Roger F.	Prof	472-2327	rriefler	R	PHD	66	U Wash	1973
Schmidt, James R.	Prof	472-2315	jschmidt		PHD	78	Rice	1977
Thompson, Gerald E.	Prof	472-3372			PHD	53	Iowa	1954
Walstad, William B.	Prof	472-2333		I	PHD	78	Minnesota	1982
State Farm Professorship								
Cushing, Matthew J.	Assoc	472-2323	mcushing	EJ	PHD	85	Virginia	1992
Fuess, Scott M.	Assoc	472-6281		J	PHD	86	Purdue	1986
Gupta, Harish C.	Assoc	472-2129		FO	PHD	69	Tennessee	1969
Kim, Benjamin J. C.	Assoc	472-3083	kimjc	F	PHD	83	UCLA	1983
May, Ann Mari	Assoc	472-3369	amay	BE	PHD	87	Colo St	1987
McGarvey, Mary G.	Assoc	472-9415	mcgarvey	E	PHD	83	Virginia	1992
Rosenbaum, David I.	Assoc	472-2318	dir		PHD	85	Wisconsin	1985
Jans, Ivette	Asst	472-3367	ijans	DF	PHD	89	Cantrbry	1989
Van den Berg, Hendrik F.	Asst	472-3004		F	PHD	89	Wisconsin	1989

Univ of Nebraska at Kearney — Kearney, NE 68849-0517 (308) — Connie J. Fie
Department of Economics — Sch of Business & Tech Fax=865-8669

Name	Rank	Phone	Email	Field	Degree	Yr	School	Since
Hadley, Galen D.	Dean	865-8342		Atg	PHD	75	Nebraska	8-91
Sechtem, Everett A.	C-Pr				PHD	86	Nebraska	1970
Blake, Gordon	Prof				PHD		Nebraska	1963
Kotcherlokota, V. V.	Assoc				PHD		India	1986
Marxsen, Craig S.	Assoc				PHD		Geo St	1987
Eshleman, Tom	Asst				PHD		Okla St	1993
Hillburn, Chris I.	Asst				PHD		Iowa St	1990
Jenkins, Allan	Asst				PHD		Nebraska	1987

Univ of Nebraska at Omaha — Omaha, NE 68182-3747 (402) 554-2570 — Scott Hays
Department of Economics — Col of Business Admin Fax=554-3747 CBAFACULTY.UNOMAHA.EDU

Name	Rank	Phone	Email	Field	Degree	Yr	School	Since
Sosin, H. Kim	C-Pr	554-2570	sosin@unomaha	ECO	PHD	70	Nebraska	1970
Lee, Bun Song (on leave 1995-96)	Prof	554-2785	blee	FO	PHD	73	So Meth	1982
Nielsen, Donald A.	Prof	554-2453	dnielsen	AR	PHD	70	Syracuse	1972
Sindt, Roger	Prof	554-2570	rsindt	AR	PHD	72	Tx-Austin	1979
Turner, Keith K.	Prof	554-2803	kturner	EM	PHD	68	Nebraska	1969
Wohar, Mark	Prof	554-2803	mwohar	ECGF	PHD	85	Illinois	1988
Zahn, Frank	Prof	554-2257	fzahn	E	PHD	69	Ca-SnBarb	1979
Baum, Donald N.	Assoc	334-8003	dbaum	HD	PHD	79	Claremont	1987
Corcoran, William J.	Assoc	554-2915	wcorcora	LQD	PHD	75	Rutgers	1980
Diamond, Arthur M.	Assoc	554-3657	adiamond	BJ	PHD	78	Chicago	1986
Connell, Donald R.	Asst	554-2570	dconnell	AF	MS	58	FtHaysSt	1965
Lin, Shuanglin	Asst	554-2818	slin	CDEO	PHD	89	Purdue	1989
West, Janet Mason	Asst	554-2570	jwest	AJ	MA	64	Mich St	1967

Nebraska Wesleyan Univ — Lincoln, NE 68504-2796 (402) 465-2041 — Arleine Kobza
Div Economics-Social Science — Dept Bus Admin & Econ Fax=465-2179

Name	Rank	Phone	Field	Degree	Yr	School	Since
Hudson, Thomas K.	C-Ac	465-2205	BAdm	PHD	91	Nebraska	1988
Fairchild, Loretta	Prof	465-2204		PHD	72	Cornell	1975
Gleason, Joyce G. (on leave)	Asst	465-2444		PHD	86	Nebraska	

Univ of Nevada, Las Vegas — Las Vegas, NV 89154-6005 (702) 895-3776 — Judy Feliz
Department of Economics — Col of Business & Econ Fax=895-1354

Name	Rank	Phone	Degree	Yr	School	Since
Cummings, Wm. Theodore	Dean$	895-3362	PHD	78	Ariz St	1980
Daneshvary, Nasser	C-Pr	895-3194	PHD	84	Tennessee	1990
Carroll, Thomas M.	Prof	895-3652	PHD	73	Syracuse	1986
Hoppe, Hans Hermann	Prof	895-3227	PHD		Goethe	1986
Malamud, Bernard	Prof	895-3294	PHD	71	New Sch	1968
Ray, Clarence G.	Prof	895-0817	PHD	72	S Carol	1971
Schwer, Keith	Prof	895-3191	PHD	73	Maryland	1986
Karstensson, Lewis	Assoc	895-3653	PHD	75	Ohio	1979
Ridgway, Terry R.	Assoc	895-3016	PHD	74	Arizona	1968
Waddoups, C. Jeffrey	Assoc	895-3497	PHD	89	Utah	1989
Assane, Djeto	Asst	895-3284	PHD	88	Colorado	1988
Blair, Benjamin	Asst	895-3376	PHD	92	Florida	1994
Chen, Lein-Lein	Asst	895-3950	PHD	92	U Miami	1993
Cronovich, Ron	Asst	895-3015	PHD	95	Michigan	1994
Gazel, Richard	Asst	895-3191	PHD	93	Illinois	1993
Neill, Helen	Asst	895-4892	PHD	92	New Mex	1992
Robinson, William J.	Asst	895-3769	PHD	83	Colorado	1980

University of Nevada, Reno — Reno, NV 89557-0016 (702) 784-6850 — Theresa E. Moser
Department of Economics — Col of Business Admin Fax=784-4728 UNR.EDU

Name	Rank	Phone	Email	Degree	Yr	School	Since
Reed, Howard M.	Dean	784-4912	cioreed@equinox.	PHD	75	Utah	1972
Chu, Shih-Fan	C-Pr	784-6850	sfchu@unssun.	PHD	68	Illinois	1967
Atkinson, Glendel W.	Prof	784-6678		PHD	68	Oklahoma	1967
Cargill, Thomas F.	Prof	784-6812		PHD	68	Ca-Davis	1973
Eadington, William R.	Prof	784-6887		PHD	73	Claremont	1969
Raffiee, Kambiz	Prof	784-6864		PHD	83	Oregon	1983
Dobra, John L.	Assoc	784-6859		PHD	80	Va Tech	1980
Metts, Robert Lyle	Assoc	784-1115		PHD	85	Berkeley	1984
Wendel, Jeanne L.	Assoc	784-6695	wendel@scs.	PHD	77	So Meth	1985
Mitchell, Mike	Asst	784-1112		PHD	88	Oregon	1988
Parker, Elliott	Asst	784-6408		PHD	92	U Wash	1992
Pingle, Mark	Asst	784-6634	pingle@equinox.	PHD	88	S Calif	1990
Song, Shunfeng	Asst	784-6860		PHD	92	Ca-Irvine	1992

University of New Hampshire Durham, NH 03824-3593 (603) 862-3457 Sinthy Kounlasa
Department of Economics Whittemore Sch Bus & Ec Fax=862-4468 CHRISTA.UNH.EDU

Goodridge, Lyndon E.	Dean	862-1983			PHD	71	Purdue	1990
England, Richard W.	C-Pr	662-3335	rwe	OQ	PHD	74	Michigan	1976
Puth, Robert C.	Prof	862-3373		N	PHD	67	Northwes	1967
Simos, Evangelos O.	Prof	862-3363		EF	PHD	77	N Illinois	1977
Conway, Karen Smith	Assoc	862-3386		HJ	PHD	87	N Carol	1990
Elmslie, Bruce T.	Assoc	862-3347		BF	PHD	88	Utah	1989
Herold, Marc W.	Assoc	862-3375		O	PHD	77	Berkeley	1975
Mills, Richard L.	Assoc	862-3350		CD	PHD	67	Indiana	1967
Niman, Neil B.	Assoc	862-3336		BL	PHD	85	Tx-Austin	1987
Schmidt, Torsten	Assoc	862-3349		DL	PHD	90	Florida	1988
Thompson, Allen R.	Assoc	862-2771		GM	PHD	73	Tx-Austin	1974
Wible, James R.	Assoc	862-3324		BE	PHD	80	Penn St	1984
Graduate Program Coordinator								
Bradford, David	Asst	862-3279		DI	PHD	91	LSU	1991
Goldberg, Michael	Asst	862-3385		EF	PHD	91	NYU	1991
Sedo, Stan	Asst	862-3357		CJ	PHD	91	Michigan	1992

New Hampshire College Manchester, NH 03104-1394 (603) 668-2211 Carol Charest Ext 2269
Economic & Finance Dept School of Business Fax=645-9665

Doucette, Francis G.	Dean	668-2211		EDD	78	Vanderbilt	8-94
Widener, Steven	C-Ac	668-2211		PHD		N Hamp	
Hall, Yvonne C.	Prof			PHD		Colo St	
Johnson, R. Larry	Prof			DBA	82	Geo Wash	
Hassan, Mahboubul	Assoc			MAPE	82	Boston U	
White, Charles V. A.	Assoc			PHD		Ohio St	

University of New Haven West Haven, CT 06516-1999 (203) 932-7355 Marie Pietrandrea
Department of Economics School of Business Fax=932-1469

Allen, Jerry L.	Dean$	932-7115	Mktg	PHD		S Illinois	9-90
Woodruff, Mary Martha	C-Ac	932-7361		DED		Bridgprt	
Kaplan, Phillip	Prof	932-7419		PHD	64	J Hopkins	
Parker, Joseph A.	Prof	932-7349		PHD		Oklahoma	
Shapiro, Steven J.	Assoc	932-7496		PHD	88	Geotown	1987
Suster, Zeljan	Assoc	932-7494		PHD		Yugoslav	
Theilman, Ward	Assoc	932-7356		PHD		Illinois	

New Jersey Inst Technology Newark, NJ 07102 (201) 596-3248 Essie Richardson
Economics Faculty Sch of Industrial Mgt Fax=596-3074 NJIT.EDU

Chakrabarti, Alok K.	Dean	596-3256	Mgt	PHD	72	Northwes	1989
Distinguished Professor of Management; Sponsored Chair in Management of Tech							
Anyanwu, Lenard	Asst	596-6426		PHD			
Bonitsis, Theologos H.	Asst	596-3263		PHD	84	CUNY	1990
Datta-Gupta, Nabanita	Asst			PHD	90	Cornell	1990

University of New Mexico Albuquerque, NM 87131-1101 (505) 277-5304 Dixie Lee Prowell
Department of Economics Col of Arts & Sciences Fax=277-9445 UNM.EDU

Gordon, William C.	Dean	277-3046	wgordon		PHD	73	Rutgers	1978
Brookshire, David S.	C-Pr	277-5304	brookshire	QR	PHD	76	New Mex	1989
Burness, H. Stuart	Prof	277-1952		ACDQ	PHD	70	Kansas	1978
Gisser, Micha	Prof	277-2420		ADLQ	PHD	62	Chicago	1973
Pham, Chung	Prof	277-3145		CEGO	PHD	62	Penn	1963
Bohara, Alok	Assoc	277-5903	bohara	CIQ	PHD	86	Colorado	1987
Davila, Alberto	Assoc	277-5560	davila	EJTR	PHD	82	Iowa St	1989
Ganderton, Philip	Assoc	277-1962	gandini	CHIQ	PHD	89	Ca-SnBarb	1989
McKee, Michael	Assoc	277-1960	mckee	HKQL	PHD	85	Carleton	1991
Santos, Richard	Assoc	277-2107	santos	IJ	PHD	77	Mich St	1989
Sauer, Christine	Assoc	277-1963	sauer	AEF	PHD	87	Brown	1985
Tailby, Don	Assoc	277-5226		ABNO	PHD	61	Rutgers	1967
Berrens, Robert	Asst	277-9004	rberrens	DHQ	PHD	93	Oreg St	1994
Binder, Melissa	Asst	277-5304		FJ	PHD	95	Columbia	1995
Chermak, Janie	Asst	277-5304		DQ	PHD	91	Co Mines	1995
Gawande, Kishore	Asst	277-1965	gawande	CEFP	PHD	91	UCLA	1991

New Mexico Highlands Univ Las Vegas, NM 87701-4211 (505) 454-3579
Economics Faculty School of Prof Studies Fax= MERLIN.NMHU.EDU

Sanchez, Lorenzo	D-As	454-3522		Atg	MBA	77	North Tx	1991
Ferran, Manuel A.	Assoc	454-3575	m_ferran	ADEG	PHD	69	Oklahoma	1993

New Mexico State Univ — Las Cruces, NM 88003-0001 (505) 646-2113 — Stella Barrio
Dept of Econ & Internl Bus — Col Business Adm & Econ Fax=646-1915 — NMSU.EDU

Name	Rank	Phone	Email	Field	Degree	Yr	School	Year
Arnold, Daniel R.	Dean	646-4083	darnold		DBA	76	La Tech	7-94
Nowotny, Kenneth	H-Pr	646-2113	knowotny		PHD	77	Tx-Austin	1976
Ellis, Michael	Prof	646-4101	mellis		PHD	75	Ca-River	1973
Nordyke, James W.	Emer	646-5688			PHD	59	Princeton	1964
Orton, Eliot S.	Emer	646-3800	econ020		PHD	71	Cornell	1970
Peach, James T.	Prof	646-3113	jpeach		PHD	78	Tx-Austin	1980
Smith, David	Prof	646-5879			PHD	71	Nebraska	1970
Willman, Elliott	Prof	646-1005			PHD	77	Indiana	1979
Brook, Kathleen	Assoc	646-4905			PHD	76	Tx-Austin	1980
Cabe, Richard	Assoc	646-5909	rcabe		PHD	83	Wyoming	1988
Enomoto, Carl E.	Assoc	646-1992	econ012		PHD	82	Tx A&M	1983
Gegax, Douglas A.	Assoc	646-1903			PHD	84	Wyoming	1984
Ghosh, Soumendra	Assoc	646-2340			PHD	87	Utah St	1988
Matta, Benjamin N.	Assoc	646-4085	econ011		PHD	79	Tx-Austin	1972
McGuckin, J. T.	Assoc	646-6302			PHD	90	Wisconsin	1989
Popp, Anthony V.	Assoc	646-5198	apopp		PHD	80	N Illinois	1981
Tanski, Janet M.	Assoc	646-1905	jtanski		PHD	91	SUNY-Buf	1989
Adrisson, Rick	Asst	646-4988			ABD	94	Nebraska	8-94
Erickson, Christopher A.	Asst	646-5715	chericks		PHD	89	Ariz St	1987
Mora, Marie T.	Asst				ABD	95	Tx A&M	8-95

University of New Orleans — New Orleans, LA 70148 (504) 286-6485 — Marie Radosti 286-6487
Dept of Economics & Finance — College of Business Adm Fax=286-6397 — UNO

Name	Rank	Phone	Email	Field	Degree	Yr	School	Year
Ryan, Timothy P.	Dean	286-6241			PHD	78	Ohio St	1978
Hibernia Professor of Economics								
Mukherjee, Tarun K.	C-Pr	286-7146		Fnce	DBA	77	Tx Tech	
Altazan, John E.	Prof	286-6434			PHD	54	Illinois	1958
Davis, J. Ronnie	Prof	286-7148			PHD	67	Virginia	1989
Hartley, Michael J.	Prof	286-6904			PHD		Penn	
Jeffress, Philip W.	Prof	286-6899			PHD	69	Kentucky	1995
Larson, David A.	Prof	286-6902			PHD	68	Maryland	
Mercuro, Nicholas	Prof	286-6270			PHD	77	Mich St	1977
Miller, Edward M.	Prof	286-6913			PHD	70	MIT	1984
Saussy, Gordon A.	Prof	286-7147			PHD	72	Yale	1970
Whitney, Gerald A.	Prof	286-6903			PHD	77	Tulane	
Abdel-Rahman, Hersham M.	Assoc	286-7343			PHD	87	Penn	1987
Brite, Robert L.	Assoc	286-6897			PHD	69	Rutgers	1970
Lane, Walter J.	Assoc	286-7145			PHD	78	Ca-SnDgo	1986
Lopez, Franklin A.	Assoc	286-6914			PHD		Tulane	
McLain, James J.	Assoc	286-6907			PHD	72	Pittsburgh	1972
Naka, Atsuyuki	Assoc	286-6896			PHD	89	Arizona	1989
Speyrer, Janet F.	Assoc	286-6981			PHD	82	J Hopkins	1987
Director, Division of Business & Economic Research								
Turunen-Red, Arja H.	Assoc	286-6912			PHD	85	Brit Col	1995
Wolfson, Melville Z.	Assoc	286-6917			PHD		Illinois	
Bakshi, Gurdip S.	Asst	286-6096			PHD		Wisconsin	
Tufte, David R.	Asst	286-7094			PHD	92	SUNY-Buf	1992

College of New Rochelle — New Rochelle, NY 10805 (914) 654-5582
Div of Social Science-Econ — Sch of Arts & Sciences Fax=

Name	Rank	Phone	Email	Field	Degree	Yr	School	Year
Bailey, Joan	Dean				PHD		Yale	
Ong, Bruce Nelson	C-Ac			PolS	PHD		Virginia	
Malloy, Mary	Asst			AHJO	PHD			

New York University — New York, NY 10003 (212)
Department of Economics — Faculty Arts & Sciences — FASECON.ECON.NYU.EDU
email: @2=stern.nyu.edu
–Faculty Arts & Sciences — Phone 998-8900 Fax 995-4186

Name	Rank	Phone	Email	Field	Degree	Yr	School	Year
Benhabib, Jess	C-Pr	998-8909			PHD	76	Columbia	1980
Gately, Dermot	Prof	998-8955			PHD	71	Princeton	1973
Leontief, Wassily W.	Prof	998-7484			PHD	28	Berlin	
Nadiri, M. Ishaq	Prof	998-8968			PHD	65	Berkeley	1971
Ordover, Janusz A.	Prof	998-8956			PHD	73	Columbia	1982
Ramsey, James B.	Prof	998-8947			PHD	68	Wisconsin	
Schotter, Andrew	Prof	998-8952			PHD	73	NYU	1985
Stein, Bruno	Prof	998-8916	bstein		PHD	59	NYU	1959
Tirzner, Israel M.	Prof	998-8914			PHD	57	NYU	
Wilson, Charles A.	Prof	998-8954			PHD	76	Rochester	1983
Wolff, Edward N.	Prof	998-8917			PHD	74	Yale	1974
Benoit, Jean Pierre	Assoc	998-8934			PHD	83	Stanford	
Flinn, Christopher	Assoc	998-8925			PHD	84	Chicago	
Frydman, Roman	Assoc	998-8967			PHD	78	Columbia	1983
Nyarko, Yaw	Assoc	998-8928			PHD	86	Cornell	1988
Prager, Jonas	Assoc	998-8911			PHD	64	Columbia	1964
Rizzo, Mario J.	Assoc	998-8932			PHD	77	Chicago	1979

Name	Rank	Phone	E-mail	Fields	Degree	Yr	Institution	Year
Vanderklaauw, H. Wilbert	Assoc	998-8951			PHD	92	Brown	1992
Wasow, Bernard M.	Assoc	998-8944			PHD	76	Stanford	1975
Boettke, Peter J.	Asst	998-8959			PHD	89	Geo Mason	1990
Olley, G. Steven	Asst	998-8907			PHD	92	Wisconsin	1991
Velasco, Andres	Asst	998-8958			PHD	88	Columbia	
–Stern School of Business	Phone	998-0860	Fax 995-4218				Ms. Diane Belleville	
Daly, George G.	Dean	998-0900	gdale@2	D	PHD	67	Northwes	1993
Wachtel, Paul A.	C-Pr	998-0874	pwachtel@2	EG	PHD	71	Rochester	1972
Research Professor								
Backus, David	Prof	998-0873	dbackus@2	EFG	PHD	81	Yale	1990
Diamond, Daniel E.	Prof	998-4010	ddiamond@2	DEN	PHD	58	NYU	1958
Greene, William H.	Prof	998-0876	wgreene@2	CDE	PHD	76	Wisconsin	1982
Guilfoll, John D.	Prof	998-4015	jguilfoi@2	DKN	PHD	64	NYU	1964
Katz, Barbara G.	Prof	998-0865	bkatz@2	CDP	PHD	73	Penn	1974
Kavesh, Robert A.	Prof	998-0863	rkavesh@2	B	PHD	54	Harvard	1958
Marcus Nadler Professor of Finance & Economics								
Pugel, Thomas A.	Prof	998-0907	tpugel@2	DEF	PHD	78	Harvard	1978
Ramachandran, Rama	Prof	998-0759	rramacha@2	DEH	PHD	75	Brown	1987
Sato, Ryuzo	Prof	998-0757	rsato@2	CO	PHD	62	J Hopkins	1985
C. V. Starr Professor of Economics								
Smith, George	Prof	998--878	gsmith@2	N	PHD	76	Harvard	1988
Sylla, Richard	Prof	998-0869	rsylla@2	DN	PHD	69	Harvard	1990
Henry Kaufman Professor of the History of Financial Institutions & Markets								
Walter, Ingo	Prof	998-0707	iwalter@2	FG	PHD	66	NYU	1970
Charles Simon Professor of Applied Financial Economics								
White, Lawrence	Prof	998-0880	lwhite@2	DGKL	PHD	69	Harvard	1976
Arthur E. Imperitore Professor of Economics								
Campa, Jose	Assoc	998-0429	jcampa@2	DF	PHD	91	Harvard	1991
on leave 1995-96								
Economides, Nicholas S.	Assoc	0864	neconomi@2	DKL	PHD	81	Berkeley	1990
Evans, Martin D. D.	Assoc	998-0875	mevans@2	EFG	PHD	87	Princeton	1982
Roubini, Nouriel	Assoc	998-0860	nroubini@2	EF	PHD	88	Harvard	1995
Crucini, Mario J.	Asst	998-0860	mcrunini	E	PHD	91	Rochester	1991
visiting from Ohio State Univ 1995-96								
Flyer, Frederick A.	Asst	998-0877	fflyer@2	DJ	PHD	93	Chicago	1993
Green, Gordon R.	Asst	998-0860	ggreen@2	D	PHD	93	Northwes	1995
visiting 1995-96								
Himmelberg, Charles	Asst	998-0870	chimmelb@2	DEL	PHD	90	Northwes	1990
on leave 1995-96								
Lopomo, Giuseppe	Asst	998-0859	glopomo@2	CD	PHD	94	Stanford	1994
Simard, Dominique	Asst	998-0400	dsimard@2	EF	PHD	92	Queen's	1995
visiting from Rutgers-New Brunswick 1995-96								
Wolf, Holger C.	Asst	998-0088	hwolf@2	EFO	PHD	92	MIT	1992

New York Institute of Tech — New York, NY 11568 (516) 686-7754 — Trudy Waser
Department of Economics — School of Management Fax=484-8328 — STUDENT.NYIT.EDU
261- exchange have 212 area code

Name	Rank	Phone	E-mail	Fields	Degree	Yr	Institution	Year
Poczter, Abram	Dean	686-7554		Mktg	PHD	79	Columbia	1980
Kliman, Andrew J.	C-As	686-7709	akliman	B	PHD		Utah	1989
Chandrasekar, Krishnamurti	Prof	261-1602			PHD	69	New Sch	1969
Lee, Molly K. S.	Prof	686-7708			PHD		NYU	1970
Schwartz, Carol H.	Prof	686-7739			PHD	63	Columbia	1987
Kutasovic, Paul R.	Assoc	686-7709			PHD	83	Rutgers	1988
Afxentiou, Diamando	Asst	348-3065	afxentiou:jl		PHD	90	W Virginia	1990

Niagara University — Niagara Univ, NY 14109 (716) 286-8160
Dept of Commerce-Economics — Col of Business Admin Fax= — NIAGARA.EDU

Name	Rank	Phone	E-mail	Fields	Degree	Yr	Institution	Year
Miller, Keith T.	Dean	286-8050		Mgt	PHD		Arizona	1994
Scherer, Philip M.	C-Pr	286-8165			PHD	72	Missouri	1980
Lee, Tenpao	Prof		286-8177		PHD		Iowa St	1987
Neimanis, George J.	Prof	286-8169			MA	65	NYU	1970
Warren, Stanton A.	Prof	286-8173			PHD	73	SUNY-Buf	1981
Peek, William A.	Assoc	286-8171			PHD	85	Syracuse	1980
Praetzel, Gary D.	Assoc	286-8182			PHD	80	SUNY-Buf	1981

Nicholls State University — Thibodaux, LA 70310 (504) 448-4232 — Bobbie Taylor
Dept of Economics & Finance — Col of Business Admin Fax=448-4922 — CENAC.NICH.EDU

Name	Rank	Phone	E-mail	Fields	Degree	Yr	Institution	Year
Gros, Ridley J. Jr.	Dean	448-4170	grosr		PHD	71	LSU	1971
McManis, Bruce L.	H-Pr	448-4188	mcmanisb	G	PHD	81	LSU	1978
Boyet, Wayne E.	Prof	448-4231	boyetw	G	PHD	65	N Car St	1985
Chotigeat, Tosporn	Prof	448-4189	chotigeatt	FO	PHD	78	S Illinois	1988
Field, William P. Jr.	Prof	448-4193	fieldw	E	PHD	71	N Carol	1973
Kooros, Syrous	Prof	448-4407	kooross	EFO	PHD	80	Rensselae	1991
Coats, R. Morris	Assoc	448-4237	coatsm	HIRQ	PHD	83	Va Tech	1985
Lee, Sang	Asst	448-4235	lees	GF	PHD	90	N Orleans	1991

Nichols College
Department of Economics
phone: 943-1560

Dudley, MA 01571-5000 (508) Ext 102
College of Business Adm Fax=

Name	Rank	Phone	Field	Degree	Yr	School	Year
Warren, Edward G.	Dean	Ext 201		PHD	79	Brown	1974
Olive, Frank	C-Ac	Ext 253	Atg	MBA	80	Maryland	1982
Corkum, Keith H.	Prof	Ext 256		PHD	76	Lehigh	1972
Nordstrom, Louise	Prof	Ext 259		PHD			

Norfolk State University
Dept of Political Sci & Econ

Norfolk, VA 23504 (804) 683-8999
Sch of Social Sciences Fax=683-9413

Name	Rank	Phone	Degree	Yr	School	Year
Gordon, Rudolph T.	Dean	683-8566	PHD		NYU	1963
Barnes, Elsie M.	H-Ac	683-8999	DA		Lehigh	1973
Frazier, Patricia A.	Prof	683-9578	PHD		Clemson	1994
Liang-Rong, Shiau	Prof	683-9581	PHD		Arkansas	1972
Bembridge, Neville G.	Assoc	683-8268	PHD		Manitoba	1975
Bowen, Freddie R. Jr.	Asst	623-8790	MA	70	Wash U	1970

North Adams State College
Economics Faculty

North Adams, MA 01247 (413) 662-5311
Business Adm & Econ Pgm Fax=662-5306

Barbara P. Sunskis
MECN.MASS.EDU

Name	Rank	Phone	Degree	School
Kahn, Abraham	H-Ac	Ext 5306	MA	SUNY-Alb
Grant, Stephen K.	Assoc	Ext 5268	PHD	Clark
Hajizadeh, Avaz	Assoc	Ext 5329	PHD	Rensselae
Kendall, Elizabeth A.	Assoc	Ext 5269	MLS	Mass
Ovitsky, Nancy L.	Asst	Ext 5307	PHD	Illinois
Zomorrodian, Reza	Asst	Ext 5303	EDD	Mass

University of North Alabama
Dept of Economics & Finance

Florence, AL 35632-0001 (205) 760-4270
School of Business Fax=760-4234

Debbie Westmoreland

Name	Rank	Phone	Field	Degree	Yr	School	Year
Stewart, William S.	Dean	760-4261	Mgt	PHD	77	Miss	1960
Morris, Barry K.	C-Pr	760-4411		PHD	74	Arkansas	1974
Butler, Michael W.	Prof	760-4270		PHD	74	Arkansas	1973
Copeland, Joe B.	Prof	760-4270		PHD	74	Arkansas	1983
Free, Veronica	Prof	760-4675		PHD	70	Miss St	1984
Rychtanek, Leonard E.	Prof	760-4301		PHD	79	Fla St	1983
Gordon, Bruce	Assoc	760-4415		PHD	93	North Tx	1986
Couch, Jim	Asst	760-4412		MAS	85	Al-Huntsv	1991
Foster, Mark	Inst	760-4417		MA	91	Alabama	1992
Thomas, Regina	Inst	760-4371		MA	92	Alabama	1992

North Carolina at Asheville
Economics Faculty

Asheville, NC 28804-3299 (704) 251-6550
Department of Economics Fax=251-6614

Ms. Kim Moore
UNCA

Name	Rank	Phone	Degree	Yr	School	Year
Browning, Shirley C.	C-Pr	251-6550	PHD	71	Conn	1970
Sulock, Joseph M.	Prof	251-6568	PHD	76	Virginia	1975
Larson, Bruce D.	Assoc	251-6562	PHD	83	N Carol	1983
Nickless, Pamela J.	Assoc	251-6563	PHD	76	Purdue	1983
Bell, Christopher Ross	Asst	251-6552	PHD	87	Penn	1989
Dickens, Edwin T.	Asst	251-6552	PHD		New Sch	
Bumgarner, Sarah J.	Lect	251-6569	MBA		Appalach	

University of North Carolina
Div Soc Sci-Dept Economics

Chapel Hill, NC 27599-3305 (919) 966-2383
Col of Arts & Sciences Fax=966-4986

Mrs. Page LoRe'
MHS.UNC.EDU

Name	Rank	Phone	Email	Degree	Yr	School	Year
Birdsall, Stephen S.	Dean	962-3082		PHD			
Guilkey, David K.	C-Pr	966-2385		PHD	73	N Carol	1983
email dguilkey.plore.econ@mhs.unc.edu							
Akin, John S.	Prof	966-5334	jakin.econ	PHD	71	Michigan	1973
Benavie, Arthur	Prof	966-5326	sthomas.econ	PHD	63	Michigan	1967
Black, Stanley W.	Prof	966-5926	sblack.econ	PHD	65	Yale	1983
Lurcy Professor							
Blau, David M.	Prof	966-3962	dblau.econ	PHD	80	Wisconsin	1992
Norman L. Johnson Professor							
Conway, Patrick	Prof	966-5376	conway.econ	PHD	84	Princeton	
Darity, William A. Jr.	Prof	966-5392	smason.econ	PHD	78	MIT	1983
Boshamer Professor							
Field, Alfred J.	Prof	966-5347	afield.econ	PHD	67	Iowa St	1967
Director of Graduate Studies							
Friedman, James W.	Prof	966-3669	friedman.econ	PHD	63	Yale	1985
Kenan Professor							
Froyen, Richard T.	Prof	966-5375	sthomas.econ	PHD	72	Maryland	1971
Gallant, A. Ronald	Prof	966-5338	arg.econ	PHD			
Latane' Professor							
Gallman, Robert E.	Prof	966-2355	bgallman.econ	PHD	56	Penn	1962
Kenan Professor							
Ingram, James C.	Emer	966-5327		PHD	52	Cornell	1952
McFarland, David	Prof	966-5342	sgarner.econ	PHD			

Murphy, James L.	Prof	966-5346	sgarner.econ		PHD	64	Purdue	1964
Dean, UNC Summer School								
Pfouts, William	Emer	966-2383			PHD	52	N Carol	1947
Rosefielde, Steven	Prof	966-5371	sthomas.econ		PHD	72	Harvard	1970
Salemi, Michael K.	Prof	966-5391	msalemi.econ		PHD	76	Minnesota	1976
Zachary Smith Professor								
Stewart, John F.	Prof	966-5345	jstewart.econ		PHD	76	Wisconsin	1975
Tarascio, Vincent J.	Prof	966-5374	sthomas.econ		PHD	66	Rice	1964
Editor, "Southern Economic Journal"								
Tauchen, Helen	Prof	966-5394	htauchen.econ		PHD	77	Minnesota	1977
Waud, Roger N.	Prof	966-5332	smason.econ		PHD	65	Berkeley	1969
Biglaiser, Gary	Assoc	966-4884	gb.econ		PHD	88	Berkeley	1988
Mezzetti, Claudio	Assoc	966-5377	sgarner.econ		PHD	88	Oxford	1990
Mroz, Thomas A.	Assoc	966-5395	mroz.econ		PHD	84	Stanford	1989
Orsagh, Thomas	Assoc	966-5373	sthomas.econ		PHD	64	Penn	1965
Parke, William	Assoc	966-5393	bparke.econ		PHD	80	Yale	1988
Turchi, Boone A.	Assoc	966-5348	bturchi.econ		PHD	73	Michigan	1971
Wilde, James A.	Assoc	966-2383	csimnad.econ		PHD	68	Princeton	1965
Associate Chairperson; Director, Undergraduate Studies								
Hagiwara, Miwako	Asst	966-5343	mhagiwar.econ		PHD	90	Calif	1990
Herce, Miguel A.	Asst	966-3682	mherce.econ		PHD	90	Ca-SnDgo	1990
Rapaport, Carol	Asst	966-5336	cjr.econ		PHD	89	Stanford	1988
Rhode, Paul	Asst	966-3250	prhode.econ		PHD	90	Stanford	1990
Strumpf, Koleman	Asst	966-2383	csimnad.econ		PHD	95	MIT	1995
Willis, Rachel A.	Lect	966-3710	rwillis.econ		PHD	90	Northwes	1982

North Carolina at Charlotte — Charlotte, NC 28223 (704) 547-2186 Jackie Harper, Salra Reece — UNCC.EDU
Department of Economics — Col of Business Admin Fax=547-3123

Mazze, Edward M.	Dean	547-2165	Mktg	PHD	66	Penn St	1993
Davis, William Young Jr.	C-Pr	547-2187		PHD	70	Georgia	1970
Connaughton, John E.	Prof	547-4134		PHD	81	Northeas	1978
Director, UNC-Charlotte Economic "Forecast"							
Madsen, Ron	Prof	547-4127					
Neel, Richard E.	Prof	547-4122		PHD	60	Ohio St	1969
Schwarz, Peter M.	Prof	547-4126		PHD	80	Ohio St	1978
Zuber, Richard A.	Prof	547-4129		PHD	78	Kentucky	1978
Amato, Louis	Assoc	547-4130		PHD	80	S Carol	1980
Gandar, John Maxim	Assoc	547-4133		PHD		Missouri	1982
Liner, Gaines Howard	Assoc	547-4128		PHD	71	Clemson	1971
Russo, Benjamin	Assoc	547-4137		PHD	85	Iowa	1984
Tseng, Hui-Kuan	Assoc	547-4123		PHD	88	Illinois	1988
Tucker, Irvin Burchard III	Assoc	547-4136		PHD		S Carol	1981
Dole, Carol	Asst	547-4171		PHD	92	Florida	
Lin, Hwan-Chyang	Asst	547-3796		PHD		Illinois	
McGregor, Rob R.	Asst	547-4121		PHD		S Carol	
Miller, Ellen Marie	Asst	547-4132		PHD	83	Florida	1982
Tori, Cynthia R.	Asst	547-4428		PHD	93	Kentucky	1993

North Carolina at Greensboro — Greensboro, NC 27412-5001 (910) 334-5463 — IRIS.UNCG.EDU
Department of Economics — Bryan Sch of Bus & Econ Fax=334-5580

Weeks, James K.	Dean	334-5338	weeksjk	Mgt	PHD	74	S Carol	1976
Allen, Stuart D.	H-Pr	334-5463	allen		PHD	77	Virginia	1976
Caldwell, Bruce J.	Prof	334-5463	caldwell		PHD	79	N Carol	1978
Link, Albert N.	Prof	334-5146	linkan		PHD	76	Tulane	1982
Ruhm, Christopher J.	Prof	334-5463	ruhmcj		PHD	84	Berkeley	1991
Seaks, Terry G.	Prof	334-5463	tgseaks		PHD	72	Duke	1972
Leyden, Dennis P.	Assoc	334-5463	leyden		PHD	87	Car Mellon	1984
McCrickard, Donald L.	Assoc	334-5463	mccrickd		PHD	76	N Carol	1975
Neufeld, John L.	Assoc	334-5463	neufeld		PHD	75	Michigan	1974
Snowden, Kenneth A.	Assoc	334-5463	snowden		PHD	83	Wisconsin	1983
Brod, Andrew C.	Asst	334-5463	broadac		PHD	92	Minnesota	1989
Shivakuma, Ram	Asst	334-5463	shivakum		PHD	92	Indiana	1993
Shobe, William	Asst	334-5463	shobew		PHD	91	Minnesota	1989

North Carolina at Wilmington — Wilmington, NC 28403-3297 (910) — ECN.UNCWIL.EDU
Dept of Economics & Finance — Cameron Sch of Bus Adm Fax=

Rockness, Howard O.	Dean	395-3501	csba@notech	Atg	PHD	73	U Wash	8-93
Farrell, Claude H. III	C-Pr	395-3510	farrell	EGR	PHD	74	N Car St	
Hall, William Woodward Jr.	Prof		hallw	QR	PHD	72	Clemson	
Director, Center for Business & Economics Services								
Hill, Roger Post	Prof		hillr	G	PHD	68	Mich St	
Carter, Denis G.	Assoc		carterd	F	PHD		Florida	
Howell, Kristen K.	Assoc		howellk	F	PHD	89	Kentucky	
Lawson, Luther Drew	Assoc		lawsonl	AJL	PHD		Tennessee	
Wadman, William Morgan	Assoc		wadmanw	CDH	PHD		Claremont	
Morgan, John E. Jr.	Asst		morganj	AC	PHD		Georgia	
Robinson, Ned Stephen	Asst		robinsonn	A	PHD		Oklahoma	
Ross, Kevin L.	Asst		rossk	FG	PHD		Fla St	

North Carolina A&T State Un — Greensboro, NC 27411 (910) 334-7746 — Ms. Cathy Dalton
Department of Economics — Sch of Business & Econ Fax=334-7093 — ATSUVAX1
phone 334-7744

Name	Rank	Phone	Email	Field	Degree	Yr	School	Date
Craig, Quiester	Dean	334-7632		Atg	PHD	72	Missouri	8-72
Simmons, Michael	C-As	Ext 2000			PHD	79	Wash St	
Benjamin, Julian	Prof	Ext 2020			PHD		SUNY-Buf	
Coley, Basil G.	Prof	334-7744			PHD	71	Illinois	1966
Khan, Anwar S.	Prof	Ext 2007			PHD	72	Wisconsin	
Obeng, Kofi UPS Chair	Prof	Ext 2018			PHD	81	Penn	1982
Addus, Abdussalam A.	Assoc	Ext 2009			PHD	82	Penn St	1980
Chen, David Y.	Assoc	Ext 2014			PHD	71	Wisconsin	
Jeong, Dong K.	Assoc	Ext 2013			PHD	74	Wayne St	
King, Vereda J.	Assoc	Ext 2008			PHD		Duke	
Morse, Lawrence B.	Assoc	Ext 2003			PHD	68	Minnesota	1976
Assar, Nasia	Asst	Ext 2010			PHD		W Virginia	
Azam, Abul	Asst	Ext 2016			PHD		Duke	
Grainger, Maury	Asst	Ext 2001						
Price, Gregory N.	Asst	Ext 2011			PHD		Wi-Milwa	
Sakano, Ryoich	Asst	Ext 2015			PHD	90	Alabama	1992
Simkins, Scott P.	Asst	Ext 2001			PHD	88	Iowa	
Sink, Harry	Adj	Ext 4014						

North Carolina Central Univ — Durham, NC 27707 (919) 560-6127
Department of Economic — School of Business Fax=560-6163 — NCCU1.ACC.NCCU.EDU

Name	Rank	Phone	Email	Field	Degree	Yr	School	Date
Fleming, Sundar W.	Dean	560-6458	fleming	Mktg	PHD	77	Duke	1987
Balfour, B. Burton	C-Ac	560-6127	bbb		PHD	74	N Car St	1973
Burnim, Mickey L. Vice Chancellor Academic Affairs & Provost	Prof	560-6230			PHD	77	Wisconsin	1986
Amoateng, Kofi	Assoc	560-6554			PHD	86	Tx-Austin	1990
Dutton, Marilyn	Asst	560-6546			PHD	89	Duke	1991
Maafo, E. Victor	Asst	560-6005						

North Carolina State Univ — Raleigh, NC 27695-8110 (919) 515-3274 — Jo Todd, Adm Asst
Department of Economics — College of Management Fax=515-7873 — NCSU.EDU

Name	Rank	Phone	Email	Field	Degree	Yr	School	Date
Lewis, Richard J.	Dean	515-5560	richard_lewis	Mktg	DBA	64	Mich St	7-93
Palmquist, Raymond B.	C-Pr	515-3274	palmquist	QDR	PHD	78	U Wash	1979
Allen, Steven G.	Prof	515-6941	steve_allen	JD	PHD	78	Harvard	1978
Clark, Robert	Prof	515-4568	robert_clark	JD	PHD	74	Duke	1975
Erickson, Edward W.	Prof	515-3201	ed_erickson	LQD	PHD	86	Vanderbilt	1965
Fearn, Robert M.	Prof	515-4616	fearn	JDP	PHD	68	Chicago	1965
Fisher, Douglas	Prof	515-2887	doug_fisher	EN	PHD	65	Chicago	1977
Flath, David	Prof	515-2472	david_flath	LDP	PHD	76	UCLA	1976
Grennes, Thomas	Prof	515-3274	tom_grennes	FD	MA	65	Wisconsin	1968
Hall, Alastair R.	Prof	515-2887	alastair_hall	C	PHD		Warwick	1985
Holthausen, Duncan M. Jr.	Prof	515-7680	duncan_holthanse	DC	PHD	76	Northwes	1974
Hyman, David Neil	Prof	515-2472	hyman_david	HA	PHD	69	Princeton	1969
Knoeber, Charles R.	Prof	515-7680	charles_knoeber	LKDG	PHD	76	UCLA	1976
Margolis, Stephen E.	Prof	515-3274	steve_margolis	LKD	PHD	78	UCLA	1982
Pearce, Douglas K.	Prof	515-2472	doug_pearce	EG	PHD	74	Wisconsin	1985
Seater, John J.	Prof	515-2472	john_seater	EH	PHD	75	Brown	1981
Thurman, Walter N.	Prof	515-4545	wally_thurman	QCD	PHD	84	Chicago	1984
Ball, David Stafford	Assoc	515-3274	david_bell	FND	PHD	67	N Carol	1966
Craig, Lee A.	Assoc	515-2887	lee_craig	NJD	PHD	89	Indiana	1989
Headen, Alvin E.	Assoc	515-2887	al_headen	IJD	PHD	81	MIT	1986
Lapp, John S.	Assoc	515-7680	john_lapp	EGF	PHD	74	Princeton	1974
McElroy, Michael B.	Assoc	515-7680	mike_mcelroy	E	PHD	70	Northwes	1970
Newmark, Craig M.	Assoc	515-7680	craig_newmark	LD	PHD	84	UCLA	1984
Wessels, Walter J.	Assoc	515-2472	walt_wessels	JD	PHD	76	Chicago	1975
Tsoulouhas, Theofanis	Asst	515-7680	fanis_tsoulouhas	CD	PHD	93	Illinois	1993

North Central College — Naperville, IL 60566-7063 (708) 420-3409
Economic Department — Div Economic & Bus Adm Fax=420-4234

Name	Rank	Phone	Email	Field	Degree	Yr	School	Date
Love, Thomas M.	C-Pr	420-3409						
Vander Meulen, Allen Jr.	Prof	420-6294			PHD	67	Wisconsin	1972
Bogart, Marti S.	Assoc	420-6213			PHD	75	Brown	1978
Whitaker, Andrew L.	Assoc	420-6218			PHD	86	Purdue	1982
Barger, Peter S.	Asst	420-6215			PHD	88	Illinois	1988
Hotopp, Susan	Asst	420-6294			PHD	89	Illinois	1989
					PHD	89	Illinois	1991

University of North Dakota — Grand Forks, ND 58202-8369 (701) 777-2637 — Ruth Holweger
Department of Economics — Col of Bus & Pub Admin Fax=777-5099 — BADLANDS.NODAK.EDU

Name	Rank	Phone	Email	Field	Degree	Yr	School	Date
Lawrence, W. Fred	Dean	777-2135		Mgt	PHD	80	Geo St	8-76
Winer, Jane Louise	Dean	742-3833		Psy	PHD	75	Ohio St	1975
Ramsett, David E.	C-Pr	777-3349			PHD	68	Oklahoma	1968
Blackwell, J. Lloyd III	Prof	777-3357			PHD	73	Geo St	1980

Name	Rank	Phone	E-mail	Field	Degree	Yr	Institution	Year
Ceyhun, Fikret	Prof	777-3348			PHD	72	Wayne St	1970
Korbach, Robert J.	Prof	777-3356			PHD	73	Maryland	1970
O'Neill, Patrick B.	Assoc	777-3358			PHD	87	Boston C	1987
Stradley, Scot A.	Assoc	777-3353			PHD		Utah	
Bagheri, Fatoah	Asst	777-3350			PHD		Penn	1978
Biederman, Daniel K.	Asst	777-3347			PHD		Kansas	1987

North Dakota State Univ — Fargo, ND 58105-5075 (701) 231-8567 — Jill Blazek, Adm Asst
Department of Economics — Col Humanities & Soc Sc Fax=231-1047

Name	Rank	Phone	E-mail	Field	Degree	Yr	Institution	Year
Bovard, Richard	Dean	231-7857		Engl	PHD			1995
O'Relly, Z. Edward	C-Pr	231-8819		AFOP	PHD	72	Tennessee	1969
Dobitz, Clifford P.	Prof	231-8653		ABDK	PHD	71	Colo St	1970
Gerdes, William D.	Prof	231-8813		CEG	PHD	78	Nebraska	1978
Herren, R. Stanley	Assoc	231-7698		ABE	PHD	75	Duke	1985
Lindgren, Jon G.	Assoc	231-8809		AGH	PHD	68	Missouri	1968

University of North Florida — Jacksonville, FL 32224-2645 (904) 646-2640 — UNF1VM
Department of Economics — Col of Business Admin Fax=646-2594

Name	Rank	Phone	E-mail	Field	Degree	Yr	Institution	Year
Traynham, Earle C. Jr.	Dean	646-2590	traynham		PHD	73	S Carol	1973
Borg, Mary O.	Prof	646-2640	mborg	HT	PHD	85	N Carol	1984
Director of University Scholar Programs								
Mason, Paul M.	Prof	646-2641	pmason	HE	PHD	84	Tx-Austin	1985
Perry, Joseph M.	Prof	646-2640	jperry	NOR	PHD	66	Northwes	1971
Shapiro, Stephen L.	Assoc	646-2641	sshapiro	AH	PHD	72	S Carol	1972
Director, Center for Economic Education								
Woods, Louis A.	Assoc	646-2641		OQR	PHD	72	N Carol	1972
Steagall, Jeffrey W.	Asst	646-260j	steagal		PHD	90	Wisconsin	1990

North Georgia College — Dahlonega, GA 30597 (706) 864-1607
Economic Faculty — Dept of Business Admin Fax=864-1562

Name	Rank	Phone	E-mail	Field	Degree	Yr	Institution	Year
Dennis, H. Lawrence	H-Pr	864-1610		Atg	DBA	76	Kentucky	1968
Grant, Clayton	Prof	864-1610			PHD	71	Clemson	1986
Dillard Munford Professor of Business								
Pearce, John F.	Prof				PHD		Alabama	1970
Fuller E. Callaway Professor of Economics								
Amerson, H. S.	Assoc	864-1610			PHD	93	Am U-Lon	1983
DeBerry, Thomas	Assoc				PHD	94	Tx Tech	1995
Schneider, Lynn	Asst				PHD	95	Houston	1995

University of North Texas — Denton, TX 76203-3677 (817) 565-2573 — Nancy L. Boyd Adm Asst
Department of Economics — Col of Arts & Sciences Fax=565-4426

Name	Rank	Phone	E-mail	Field	Degree	Yr	Institution	Year
Bell, Nora K.	Dean			BioE	PHD		N Carol	
Abernathy, Lewis M.	Prof	565-2251		J	PHD	67	Oklahoma	1963
Director, Labor & Industrial Relations Institute								
Cobb, Steven Lee	Assoc	565-2184		O	PHD	87	N Carol	1987
Molina, David Jude	Assoc	565-4543		C	PHD	83	Tx A&M	1985
Nieswiadomy, Michael L.	Assoc	565-2573			PHD	83	Tx A&M	1985
Brown, Robert W.	Asst	565-2254			PHD	91	Ca-SnBarb	1991
Greene, Michael	Asst	565-4544			PHD	89	N Hamp	1990
Koelln, Kenneth	Asst	565-4542			PHD	91	Florida	1991
McPherson, Michael	Asst	565-2270			PHD	92	Mich St	1992
Redfearn, Michael	Asst	565-2220			PHD	92	Mich St	1992
Tieslau, Margie	Asst	565-3442			PHD	92	Mich St	1992
Battaglia, Kari L.	Lect	565-4541			MA		North Tx	1987
Ellis, Harry Jr.	Lect	565-2246			MA		Mich St	1990
Lynch, Karla	Lect	565-3186			MS		North Tx	1993

Northeast Louisiana Univ — Monroe, LA 71209-0110 (318) 342-1150 — Juanita Hyatt — ALPHA.NLU.EDU
Dept of Economics & Finance — College of Business Adm Fax=342-1209

Name	Rank	Phone	E-mail	Field	Degree	Yr	Institution	Year
Short, Larry E.	Dean	342-1100	dbashort	Mgt	DBA	71	Colorado	1994
Moser, Ernest R.	H-Ac	342-1150	ecmoser	BM	PHD	73	Tx A&M	1972
Fox, Eugene H.	Prof	342-1164			PHD	62	Alabama	1965
Coordinator of Special Projects								
Nelson, Paul S.	Assoc	342-1157	ecnelson	DL	PHD	85	Tx A&M	1989
Scott, John L.	Assoc	342-1160	ecscott	DC	PHD	90	S Carol	1989
Eisenstadt, Robert C.	Asst	342-1162	eceisenstadt	J	PHD		Geo St	
Futayyeh, Mohamed-Amin	Asst	342-1163			PHD		Oklahoma	
Kogut, Carl A.	Asst	342-1154	eckogut	DL	PHD	84	Tx A&M	1992
Lee, Tommy R.	Inst	342-1169			MBA		NE La	

Northeast Missouri State U — Kirksville, MO 63501-4221 (816) 785-4636 — Sandra Schneider
Department of Economics — Div of Social Science Fax=785-4181

Name	Rank	Phone	E-mail	Field	Degree	Yr	Institution	Year
Lyons, James J.	H-Pr	785-4636		Psyc	PHD		Ohio St	1972
Patterson, Seymour	Prof	785-4360			PHD		Oklahoma	1980

Sublette, Werner Johann	Prof	785-4651			PHD		Arizona	1974
Nnadozie, Emmanuel U.	Assoc	785-4099			PHD	87	Sorbonne	1989
Sawani, Mustafa A.	Assoc	785-4659			PHD		Missouri	1985
Sung, Jane C.	Assoc	785-4658			PHD	85	Wayne St	1987
Gillette, David H.	Asst	785-4334			PHD		Wash St	1990
Murray, Charles	Asst	785-4324			BA		Iowa St	1991
Olson, Terry L.	Asst	785-4503			PHD	86	Illinois	1990

Northeastern University — Boston, MA 02115 (617) 373-2882
Department of Economics — Col of Arts & Sciences Fax=373-3640 — LYNX.NEU.EDU

Adams, John	C-Pr	373-2872	jadams		PHD	68	Tx-Austin	1990
Alam, M. Shahid	Prof	373-2849			PHD	79	W Ontario	1988
Fraumeni, Barbara M.	Prof	373-2252			PHD	80	Boston C	1982
Goldstein, Harold M.	Prof	373-2884			PHD	61	Clark	1961
Herrnstadt, Irwin L.	Prof	373-3650			PHD	64	MIT	1960
Kim, Sungwoo	Prof	373-2893			PHD	57	Berkeley	1972
Morrison, Steven A.	Prof	373-3646			PHD	79	Berkeley	1982
Schachter, Gustav	Prof	373-2886			PHD	62	NYU	1965
Sum, Andrew M.	Prof	373-2242			MA	71	MIT	1971
Alper, Neil O.	Assoc	373-2839			PHD	77	Pittsburgh	1979
Bolnick, Bruce R.	Assoc	373-5097			PHD	72	Yale	1983
Brookins, Oscar T.	Assoc	373-2251			PHD	76	SUNY-Buf	1983
Dadkhah, Kamran N.	Assoc	373-2297			PHD	75	Indiana	1981
Dyer, Alan W.	Assoc	373-2610			PHD	82	Maryland	1983
Wassall, Gregory H. Graduate Director	Assoc	373-2196			PHD	78	Rutgers	1979
Chowdhury-Bose, Gopa	Asst	373-2316			PHD	84	London	1988
Haughton, Jonathan H.	Asst	373-4520			PHD	83	Harvard	1987
Keil, Katherine A.	Asst	373-2874			PHD	89	Ca-SnDgo	1990
Keil, Manfred W.	Asst	373-3645			PHD	85	London	1988
Parente, Stephen	Asst	373-2879			PHD	90	Minnesota	1991
Plesko, George A.	Asst	373-2890			PHD	85	Wisconsin	1989

Northeastern Illinois Univ — Chicago, IL 60625-4699 (312) 794-2638 — Ginger Veugeler
Department of Economics — Col of Arts & Sciences Fax=794-6243
phone 583-4050

Boni, John	Dean	Ext 4023		Engl	PHD		Denver	
Winston, Barbara	C-Pr	794-2609			PHD		Northwes	1974
Freiberg, Lewis	Prof	794-2581			PHD	72	Kentucky	1982
Bergan, Daniel J.	Assoc	794-2577			PHD		Tx Tech	
Brewton, Audie R.	Assoc	794-2552			PHD	80	Utah	1984
Sthman, Diane L.	Assoc	794-2579			PHD		Il-Chicago	
Stuart, Edward F.	Assoc	794-2574			PHD	78	Oklahoma	1986
Collum, Thomas E.	Asst	794-2573			MA	75	Northwes	1977
Rothstein, Sheldon H.	Asst	794-2578			MA		Chicago	

Northeastern State Univ — Tahlequah, OK 74464-2399 (918) 458-2091 — Toni Wofford
Dept of Econ, Mgt & Mktg — Col of Business & Indus Fax=458-2337
phone: 456-5511

Williams, Earl R.	Dean	458-2091		DMN	PHD	68	Tennessee	1968
Hileman, A. Eugene	C-Pr	456-5511		Mgt	PHD	88	Tennessee	1970
Greubel, Robert T.	Prof			AEF	PHD		Arkansas	1965

Northern Arizona University — Flagstaff, AZ 86011-5066 (520) 523-3657 — Michele Allen
Dept of Business Admin-Econ — Col of Business Admin Fax=523-7331 — NAUVAX.UCC.NAU.EDU

Walka, Joseph J.	Dean	523-7345	jjw@al.ucc.nau.e	HI	PHD	69	Harvard	1986
Gunderson, Ronald J.	Prof	523-7358	rong	DR	PHD	77	Nebraska	1977
Hildred, William M.	Prof	523-7365	wmh	HA	PHD	64	Colo St	1988
Pinto, James V.	Prof	523-7356	pinto	DC	PHD	75	Oklahoma	1981
Brown, Doug	Assoc	523-7394		OP	PHD	85	Colo St	1985
Campione, Wendy A.	Assoc	523-7360		HJ	PHD	84	Illinois	1981
Duncan, Wallace H.	Assoc	523-7366		EA	PHD	76	Wyoming	1978
Jerrell, Max E.	Assoc	523-7405	jerrell	EC	PHD	84	Ariz St	1981
Smith, Dean G.	Assoc	523-7396	dsmith	RH	PHD	85	Tx A&M	1989
Leachman, Lori	Asst	523-7340	lll	EF	PHD	87	S Carol	1993
Eastwood, John D.	Lect	523-7353	jde	CD	MS	80	Wyoming	1990

Univ of Northern Colorado — Greeley, CO 80639 (970) 351-2739 — Linda Jack
Department of Economics — Col of Arts & Sciences Fax=351-1571 — BENTLEY.UNIVNORTHCO.EDU

Kovar, Roger A.	Dean	351-2707		Chem	PHD		Wyoming	1970
Livingston, Marie L.	C-Pr	351-2739	mllivin	FHOQ	PHD	84	Colo St	1985
Garrison, Ann J.	Assoc	351-1560		HITR	MA		N Colo	1966
Green, John W.	Assoc	351-1558		CTQR	PHD	76	Penn	1985
Kallon, Kelfala M.	Assoc	351-2134	kmkallo	EFHO	PHD	83	Virginia	1993
Aske, David	Asst	351-1564		AITR	PHD		Nebraska	1992
Graham, Patricia E.	Asst	351-1559		IJOQ	PHD		Colo St	1988
McDaniel, Bruce	Asst	351-1163		CGMQ	PHD		Colo St	1992

Northern Illinois Univ — Dekalb, IL 60115-2854 (815) 753-1031 — Ms. Bonny St. John
Department of Economics — Col Liberal Arts & Sci Fax=753-6302 — CORN.CSO.NIU.EDU
email @1=mvs.cso.niu.edu

Name	Rank	Phone	Email	Degree	Yr	School	Year
Kitterle, Frederick	Dean	753-1061					7-95
Scaperlanda, Anthony E.	C-Pr	753-6970	taoaes1	PHD	64	Tx-Austin	1964
Dalal, Ardeshir J.	Prof	753-6971	taoajd1	PHD		Iowa	
Gherity, James A.	Prof	753-6964		PHD	58	Illinois	1964
Kim, Young Chin	Prof	753-6972	taoyck1	PHD	68	Columbia	1970
Kwon, Jene K.	Prof	753-6977		PHD	68	Iowa	1968
La Tourette, John E. President	Prof	753-9500		PHD	62	Rutgers	
Levy, Lester S.	Prof	753-6982		PHD	56	Cornell	
Mallela, Parthasaradhi	Prof	753-6974		PHD		Rochester	
Martellaro, Joseph A.	Emer	753-6966		PHD		Notre Dm	
Mohabbat, Khan A.	Prof	753-6973	taokam1	PHD		SUNY	
Nord, Steven	Prof	753-6976		PHD		Illinois	
Skeels, Jack W.	Prof	753-6981		PHD	57	Wisconsin	1963
Williams, Martin	Prof	753-6960		PHD		SUNY	
Bechdolt, Burley V. Assistant Chairperson	Assoc	753-6959		PHD	70	S Calif	1970
Karlson, Stephen	Assoc	753-6980	taoshk1@1	PHD		Wisconsin	
Porter-Hudak, Susan	Assoc	753-6983		PHD		Wisconsin	
Graeser, Paul	Asst	753-6963		PHD		Columbia	
Renshaw, Robert H.	Asst	753-6968		PHD	64	Mich St	1965
Skidmore, Mark	Asst	753-6967	taomls1	PHD	94	Colorado	1994
Temple, Judy A.	Asst	753-6962		PHD	90	Mich St	
Van Buer, Franklin D.	Asst	753-1098		PHD	68	Illinois	1983
Wilcox-Gok, Virginia L.	Asst	753-6957	taovlw1	PHD	84	Wash U	1994

University of Northern Iowa — Cedar Falls, IA 50614-0129 (319) 273-2412
Department of Economics — Col of Business Admin Fax=273-2922 — UNI.EDU

Name	Rank	Phone	Email	Degree	Yr	School	Year
Abraham, Fred J.	H-Pr	273-6172	abrahamf	PHD	73	Oregon	1973
Anderson, B. Wylie	Prof	273-2951	andersonbw	PHD	73	Iowa	1966
McCormick, Kenneth J.	Prof	273-6051	mccormick	PHD	82	Iowa St	1982
Rives, Janet M.	Prof	273-6368	rives	PHD	71	Duke	1984
Yousefi, Mahmood	Prof	273-6722	yousefi	PHD	74	Ca-SnBarb	1981
Hakes, David R.	Assoc	273-3597	hakes	PHD	85	Iowa St	1992
Krieg, Randall G.	Assoc	273-2126	krieg	PHD	87	Colorado	1987
Raiklin, Ernest G.	Assoc	273-6380	raiklin	PHD	84	New Sch	1986
Strein, Charles T.	Assoc	273-2592	strein	PHD	77	Illinois	1970
Uyar, Bulent	Assoc	273-6343	uyar	PHD	77	Pittsburgh	1991
Brown, Ken	Asst	273-2956	brownk	PHD	94	Illinois	1994
Cummings, Donald G.	Asst	273-2637		PHD	75	Tulane	1963
Johnson, Donn M.	Asst	273-2103	johnsond	PHD	89	Colo St	1989
Mardis, Barbara K.	Inst	273-3062	mardis	MBA	81	N Iowa	1981

Northern Kentucky Univ — Highland Hght KY 41099-0503 (606) 572-6581 — Edith Hill
Economics, Fnce & Info Sys — College of Business Fax=572-6177 — NKU.EDU

Name	Rank	Phone	Field	Degree	Yr	School	Year
Comte, Thomas E.	Dean	572-5551	Mgt	PHD	78	Missouri	7-91
Adams, David R.	C-Pr	572-6581		EDD	75	Kentucky	1980
Clayton, Gary E.	Prof	572-6542		PHD	74	Utah	1980
Giesbrecht, Martin G.	Prof	572-5153		PHD	58	Munich	1987
Cate, Thomas H.	Assoc	572-5799		PHD	79	Fla St	1975
Lang, Nancy A. Director Center for Economic Education	Assoc	572-5155		EDD	83	Georgia	1983
Noyd, Louis E.	Assoc	572-5160		PHD	73	Oregon	1972
Snyder, Richard S.	Asst	572-5651		PHD	76	Indiana	1978

Northern Michigan Univ — Marquette, MI 49855 (906) 227-2220 — Alice McKinney
Department of Economics — Liberal Studies Program Fax=227-2229 — NMU.EDU

Name	Rank	Phone	Field	Degree	Yr	School	Year
Swaine, Howard R.	H-Pr	227-1214	AKDH	PHD	65	UCLA	1966
Aho, Arnold A.	Prof	227-1217	AJ	MA		Lehigh	1969
Carlson, David L.	Prof	227-1218	AEN	BA		N Mich	1961
Holmstrom, Thomas K.	Prof	227-1216	AEF	PHD		Okla St	1966
Zaki, Mokhlis Y.	Prof	227-1215	ACDO	PHD	69	Berkeley	1969

Northern State University — Aberdeen, SD 57401-7198 (605) 626-2400
Dept of Business & Economics — Sch of Business & Tech Fax=626-3022

Name	Rank	Phone	Degree	Yr	School	Year
Arnold, Clyde L.	Dean	626-2400	PHD	82	Oklahoma	1988
Trierweiler, John	C-Pr	626-2576	PHD	70	Nebraska	1985
Neumann, Hillar Jr.	Assoc	626-7719	PHD		Rutgers	1983
Christe-David, Rohn	Asst	626-3002	PHD	94	S Carol	1994
Xiang, Ping Qui	Asst	626-3001	PHD	93	Iowa	1993
Peterson, John	Inst	626-2434	ABD		Kansas	1992

Northwest Missouri St Univ Maryville, MO 64468-6001 (816) 562-1836 Alise Meyer
Department of Economics Col Bus, Govt & Cpt Sci Fax=562-1484 NORTHWEST.MISSOURI.EDU

Name	Rank	Phone	ID	Field	Degree	Yr	School	Year
DeYoung, Ronald C.	Dean	582-7682	0700037	BEd	EDD	71	N Illinois	1984
McLaughlin, Patrick	C	562-1291	0100141	F	JD		Mo-Ks Cty	1978
Jelavich, Mark S.	Prof	562-1763	0100232	FR	PHD	80	J Hopkins	1981
Kharadia, Virabhai C.	Prof	562-1284	0100250	AED	PHD	73	Illinois	1973
Collier, Ben	Assoc	562-1762	0100063	ARE	PHD	81	Purdue	1981
Shanklin, James T.	Asst	562-1764	0100437	AD	MS	66	S Illinois	1966

Northwestern University Evanston, IL 60208-2600 (708) 491-5140 Ethel McKay King
Department of Economics Col of Arts & Sciences Fax=491-7001 NWU.EDU

Name	Rank	Phone	Email	Field	Degree	Yr	School	Year
Dumas, Lawrence B.	Dean			Biol	PHD		Wisconsin	
Gordon, Robert J.	C-Pr	491-5697	rjg		PHD	67	MIT	1973
Stanley G. Harris Professor of the Social Sciences								
Alexis, Marcus	Prof	467-1318	m-alexis		PHD	59	Minnesota	1985
Daniel F. and Ada L. Rice Professor of Economics								
Altonji, Joseph G.	Prof	491-8218			PHD	81	Princeton	1990
Blank, Rebecca M.	Prof	491-3784	rblank		PHD	83	MIT	1989
Braeutigam, Ronald R.	Prof	491-8243	braeutigam		PHD	76	Stanford	1975
Harvey Kapnick Professor of Business Institutions & Transportation Center								
Christiano, Lawrence	Prof	491-8231			PHD	82	Columbia	
Coen, Robert M.	Prof	491-8207	rcoen		PHD	67	Northwes	1971
Dekel, Eddie	Prof	491-4414	dekel		PHD	86	Harvard	
Eichenbaum, Martin	Prof	491-8232	eich		PHD	81	Minnesota	1988
Eisner, Robert	Emer	491-5394			PHD	51	J Hopkins	1952
William R. Kenan Professor Emeritus								
Kamien, Morton I.	Prof	491-5167			PHD	64	Purdue	1970
Matthews, Steven A.	Prof	491-3527	s-matthews		PHD	78	Cal Tech	1980
Matzkin, Rosa L.	Prof	491-8220			PHD	86	Minnesota	
Mokyr, Joel	Prof	491-5693	j-mokyr		PHD	74	Yale	1974
Robert H. Strotz Professor of Arts & Sciences								
Mortensen, Dale T.	Prof	491-8230	d-mortensen		PHD	67	Car Mellon	1965
Ida C. Cook Professor of Consumer Economics								
Moses, Leon N.	Prof	491-8209	leon1		PHD	52	Harvard	1959
Myerson, Roger B.	Prof	491-3729	jpanzar		PHD	76	Harvard	1976
Panzar, John C.	Prof	491-8242	jpanzar		PHD	75	Stanford	1983
Louis W. Menk Professor								
Porter, Robert H.	Prof	491-3491	r-porter		PHD	81	Princeton	1987
William R. Kenan Jr. Professor								
Reiter, Stanley	Prof	491-3527			PHD	55	Chicago	
Charles E. and Emma H. Morrison Professor of Economics								
Rogerson, William P.	Prof	491-8484	wrogerson		PHD		Cal Tech	
Saari, Donald G.	Prof	491-5580			PHD		Purdue	
Satterthwaite, Mark A.	Prof	491-5482			PHD	73	Wisconsin	1973
Weisbrod, Burton A.	Prof	491-8704	b-weisbrod		PHD	58	Northwes	
John Evans Professor of Economic, Director,Ctr for Urban Affairs & Policy Rec								
Wolinsky, Asher	Prof	491-4415	wolinsky		PHD		Stanford	
Domowitz, Ian	Assoc	491-8228	domowitz		PHD		Ca-SnDgo	
Household International Corporation Research Professor								
Matsuyama, Kiminori	Assoc	491-8490	kmatsu		PHD		Harvard	
Meyer, Bruce	Assoc	491-8226	bmeyer		PHD	87	MIT	1987
Bagwell, Kyle W.	Asst	491-2535			PHD	86	Stanford	1986
Conley, Timothy	Asst	491-8266			PHD	95	Chicago	1995
Ferrie, Joseph	Asst	491-8210	j-ferrie		PHD	92	Chicago	
Hellerstein, Judith	Asst	491-8224	jkhstein		PHD	94	Harvard	
Montgomery, James D.	Asst	491-8223	jdm		PHD	89	MIT	1989
Pesendorfer, Wolfgang	Asst	491-2529	wpes		PHD	92	UCLA	
Taber, Christopher	Asst	491-8229			PHD	95	Chicago	1995
Taylor, Alan	Asst	491-8234	amt		PHD	93	Harvard	
Trejos, Alberto	Asst	491-5395	ajt623		PHD	94	Penn	
Udry, Christopher R.	Asst	491-8235	udry		PHD	91	Yale	1990
Valimaki, Juuso	Asst	491-8227			PHD	95	Penn	1995
Savage, Ian P.	SLect	491-5140	ipsavage		PHD	84	Leeds	
Assistant Chairperson								

Northwestern State U of LA Natchitoches, LA 71497 (318) 357-5161 Deborah Powell
Economics Faculty Division of Business Fax=357-5990

Name	Rank	Phone	Email	Field	Degree	Yr	School	Year
Smiley, Barry A	D-Pr	357-5163			DBA	75	La Tech	
Bacdayan, Andrew W.	Prof	357-5698			PHD	73	Utah St	
Elliott, Steven	Assoc	357-5700			PHD		La Tech	
Jones, Robert C. III	Asst	357-4581			PHD	91	UCLA	
Prince, Steven	Asst	357-5179			PHD		Utah	

Northwood University Midland, MI 48640-2398 (517)
Economics Faculty Business Fax=

Name	Rank	Phone	Email	Field	Degree	Yr	School	Year
Chen, Catherine W.	Dean	837-4371			PHD		Minnesota	1974
Amin, R. John	H-Pr	837-4431			PHD			
Haywood, Dale M.	Prof	837-4291			PHD			
Luptowski, Thomas S.	Prof	837-4263			BS			

Norwich University | Northfield, VT 05663 (802) 485-2212
Dept of Economics & Finance | Div of Business & Mgt Fax=485-2580

Vanecek, Frank T.	H-Pr	485-2212		Mis	DBA	82	Kent St	1974
Hurd, John II	Prof	485-2217			PHD	69	Penn	1978
Mohaghegh, Mehdi	Assoc				PHD	86	Clark	1986
Murtaugh, Frank M. Jr.	Assoc	485-2216			PHD	81	Emory	1982

University of Notre Dame | Notre Dame, IN 46556 (219) 631-6335 | Ms. Juli Tate
Department of Economics | Col of Arts & Sciences Fax=631-8809 | ND.EDU

Dutt, Amitava K.	C-Pr	631-6335	amitava.k.dutt	EFOC	PHD	83	MIT	1988
Bartell, Ernest J.	Prof	631-6580	ernest.j.bartell	O	PHD	66	Princeton	1977
Craypo, Charles	Prof	631-7585	charles.craypo	J	PHD	66	Mich St	1978
Goulet, Denis A.	Prof	631-5250	denis.a.goulet	O	PHD	63	SaoPaula	1979
Jarsulic, Marc W.	Prof	631-7570	marc.w.jarsulie	EC	PHD	78	Penn	1985
Kim, Kwan S.	Prof	631-5179	kwan.s.kim	OF	PHD	67	Minnesota	1975
Leahy, William H.	Prof	631-7238	william.h.leahy	JR	PHD		Notre Dm	1963
Mirowski, Philip E.	Prof	631-7580	philip.e.mirowsk	B	PHD	79	Michigan	1990
Ros, Jaime	Prof	631-7009	jaime.ros	OE	PHD	78	Cambridg	1990
Skurski, Roger B.	Prof	631-7016	roger.b.skurski	P	PHD	70	Wisconsin	1974
Swartz, Thomas R.	Prof	631-7737	thomas.r.swartz	HA	PHD	65	Indiana	1965
Wilber, Charles K.	Prof	631-6335	charles.k.wilber	BOP	PHD	66	Maryland	1975
Betson, David M.	Assoc	631-5068	david.m.betson	HI	PHD	80	Wisconsin	1979
Bonello, Frank J.	Assoc	631-7229	frank.j.bonello	EA	PHD	68	Mich St	1968
Ghilarducci, Teresa	Assoc	631-7581	teresa.ghilarduc	J	PHD	84	Berkeley	1983
Lorenz, Edward H.	Assoc	631-7590	edward.h.lorenz	J	PHD	93	Cambridg	1986
Marsh, Lawrence C.	Assoc	631-6210	lawrence.c.marsh	CD	PHD	76	Mich St	1975
Rakowski, James J.	Assoc	631-6644	james.j.rakowski	DF	PHD	68	Minnesota	1967
Rath, Kali P.	Assoc	631-6954	kali.p.rath	CD	PHD	92	J Hopkins	1990
Ruccio, David F.	Assoc	631-6434	david.f.ruccio	BO	PHD	84	Mass	1982
Warlick, Jennifer L.	Assoc	631-7531	jennifer.l.warli	HI	PHD	79	Wisconsin	1981
Howes, Candance	Asst		candace.howes	DF	PHD	91	Berkeley	1991
Sent, Esther-Mirjam	Asst	631-6979	esther-mirjamsen	BE	PHD	94	Stanford	1994
Wolfson, Martin H.	Asst	631-8093	martin.h.wolfson	EG	PHD	84	American	1990
You, Jong-Il	Asst	631-6979	jong-il.you	OFCE	PHD	91	Harvard	1990

Oakland University | Rochester, MI 48309-4401 (810) 370-3294 Brenda Paxton 370-3283
Department of Economics | School of Business Adm Fax=370-4275 | OAKLAND

Murphy, Kevin J.	C-Ac	370-3294	murphy	JC	PHD	81	Mich St	1985
Botsas, Eleftherios N.	Prof	370-3289	botsas	FA	PHD	65	Wayne St	1976
Fosu, Augustin K.	Prof	370-3523	fosu	JOC	PHD	79	Northwes	1979
Izraeli, Oded	Prof	370-3524	izraeli	RHA	PHD	73	Chicago	1978
Stano, Miron	Prof	370-3291	stano	IL	PHD	71	Cornell	1977
Folland, Sherman T.	Assoc	370-4086	folland	IB	PHD	74	Iowa	1986
Sahu, Anandi P.	Assoc	370-3537	sahu	EG	PHD	85	Wash U	1985
Tracy, Ronald L.	Assoc	370-3514	tracy	CE	PHD	75	Mich St	1983
Coppin, Addington M.	Asst	370-3541	coppin	FO	PHD	87	W Indies	1989
Mobley, Lee	Asst	370-3277	mobley	LI	PHD	89	Ca-SnBarb	1991
Mukheyi, Nivedita	Asst	370-4087	mukheyi	EF	PHD	92	Va Tech	1992

Oberlin College | Oberlin, OH 44074 (216) 775-8483 | Che Gonzalez
Department of Economics | Col of Arts & Sciences Fax=775-6978 | QMGATE.CC.OBERLIN.EDU

Feinleib, Mary Ella	Dean	775-8410	feinleib	Biol	PHD	66	Harvard	1995
Zinser, James E.	C-Pr	775-8484	james_zinser	KLO	PHD	67	Oregon	1967
Cleeton, David L.	Prof	775-8449	david_cleeton	DGIM	PHD	80	Wash U	1980
Kasper, Hirshel	Prof	775-8489	hirschel_kasper	DJ	PHD	63	Minnesota	1963
Montiel, Peter J.	Prof	775-8592	peter_montiel	EF	PHD	78	MIT	1990
Danforth-Lewis Professor								
Piron, Robert	Prof	775-8485	robert_piron	BD	PHD	66	Northwes	1961
Craig, Barbara	Assoc	775-8766	barbara_craig	CFQ	PHD	88	Minnesota	1989
Fernandez, Luis	Assoc	775-8486	luis_fernandez	CDGL	PHD	83	Berkeley	1980
Sheppard, Stephen C.	Assoc	775-8657	stephen_sheppard	CR	PHD	84	Wash U	1990
Tharp, Charles	Lect	775-8176	charles_tharp	M	MA	80	Oxford	1989

Occidental College | Los Angeles, CA 90041 (213) 259-2775 | Betty Tracy
Economics Faculty | Department of Economics Fax=341-4990

Studenmund, A. H.	C-Pr	259-2776	C	PHD	70	Cornell	1970
Richard W. Millar Professor of Economics & Director of Institutional Research							
Halstead, James F.	Prof	259-2778	A	PHD	72	Stanford	1977
Moore, Robert L.	Prof	259-2779	J	PHD	77	Harvard	1978
Whitney, James D.	Prof	259-2750	F	PHD	83	Wisconsin	1982
Hirschfeld, Mary L.	Assoc	259-2932	N	PHD	89	Harvard	1988
Pastor, Manuel Jr.	Assoc	259-2849	O	PHD	84	Mass	1984
Hamilton, Jean	Inst	259-2971	J	MA	92	Berkeley	1994

Oglethorpe University Atlanta, GA 30319 (404)
Department of Economics Div Economics & Bus Adm Fax=364-8500

Name	Rank	Phone	E-mail	Fields	Degree	Yr	School	Since
Tucker, Dean	C-Ac	261-1441		HMQ	PHD	79	Mich St	1-88
Rikard Chaired Professor								
Hetherington, Bruce W.	Prof	261-1441		NE	PHD	82	Va Tech	1980
Shropshire, William O.	Prof	262-1441		EO	PHD	63	Duke	1979
Callaway Professor of Economics								

Ohio University Athens, OH 45701-2979 (614) 593-2040
Department of Economics Col of Arts & Sciences Fax=593-0181 OHIOU.EDU

Name	Rank	Phone	E-mail	Fields	Degree	Yr	School	Since
Palmer, Jan S.	C-Ac	593-2032		A	PHD	74	Mich St	1979
Adie, Douglas K.	Prof	260-2033		BGM	PHD	68	Chicago	1968
Boyd, Roy G.	Prof	593-2050		QH	PHD	81	Duke	1984
Doroodian, Khosrow	Prof	593-2046		QAF	PHD		Oregon	
Gallaway, Lowell	Prof	593-2036			PHD	59	Ohio St	1967
Distinguished Professor								
Ghazalah, Ismail A.	Prof	593-2034		DFHI	PHD	69	Berkeley	1969
Klingaman, David C.	Prof	593-2047		DE	PHD	67	Virginia	1967
Koshal, Rajindar K.	Prof	593-2038		TACQ	PHD	68	Rochester	1970
Shukla, Vishwa S.	Prof	593-2039			PHD	72	Wisconsin	1966
Vedder, Richard K.	Prof	593-2037			PHD	65	Illinois	1965
Distinguished Professor								
Jung, Chulho	Assoc	593-2041		CDFQ	PHD	89	Michigan	1989
Rossiter, Rosemary D.	Assoc	593-2043			PHD	80	Wi-Milw	1983
Caporale, Tony	Asst	593-2051			PHD		Geo Mason	
Marshall, Kathryn G.	Asst	593-2042		HQ	PHD		Berkeley	
McKiernan, Barbara	Asst	593-2049		EGN	PHD	94	Geo Mason	1994
Winter, Harold	Asst	593-2048		KL	PHD	90	Rochester	

Ohio Northern University Ada, OH 45810 (419) 772-2082 Diane Thede 772-2082
Department of Economics Col of Business Admin Fax=772-1932 MILTON.ONU.EDU

Name	Rank	Phone	E-mail	Fields	Degree	Yr	School	Since
Maris, Terry L.	Dean	772-2070	tmaris	Mgt	PHD	79	Nebraska	1990
Goldberg, Roger H.	Prof	772-2076	rgoldberg		PHD	81	Indiana	1969
Meininger, Richard P.	Assoc	772-2083	rreininger		PHD	87	Ohio U	1973
Assistant Dean								
Meenakshi, Rishi	Asst	772-2026	mrishi		PHD	93	Mass	1993

Ohio State University Columbus, OH 43210-1172 (614) 292-6701
Department of Economics Col of Social & Beh Sci Fax= OSU.EDU

Name	Rank	Phone	E-mail	Fields	Degree	Yr	School	Since
Hashimoto, Masanori	C-Pr	292-4196	hashimoto.1	J	PHD	71	Columbia	1987
Cosslett, Stephen R.	Prof	292-4106	cosslett.1		PHD	79	Berkeley	1987
Director of Graduate Studies								
Dunn, Lucia	Prof	292-8071	dunn.4	J	PHD	74	Berkeley	
Evans, Paul D.	Prof	292-0072	evens.21	E	PHD	76	Chicago	1987
Fleisher, Belton M.	Prof	292-6429	fleisher.1	J	PHD	61	Stanford	1965
Gonzalez-Vega, Claudio	Prof	292-0387	gonzalez.4	O	PHD	76	Stanford	
Gouke, Cecil G.	Prof	292-2170	gouke.1	M	PHD	67	NYU	1973
Haurin, Donald R.	Prof	292-8448	haurin.2	R	PHD	78	Chicago	1975
Associate Dean								
Ichiishi, Tatsuro	Prof	292-0762	ichiishi.1	C	PHD	74	Berkeley	1987
Levin, Dan	Prof			MI	PHD	82	MIT	1995
Maddala, G. S.	Prof	292-4812	maddala.1		PHD	63	Chicago	1975
Eminent Scholar								
Marvel, Howard P.	Prof	422-1020	marvel.2	L	PHD	75	Chicago	1973
McCafferty, Stephen A.	Prof	292-7122	mccafferty.1	EF	PHD	77	Brown	1982
McCulloch, J. Houston	Prof	292-0382	mcculloch.2		PHD	73	Chicago	1979
Miyazaki, Hajime	Prof	292-7939	miyazaki.1	LJ	PHD	77	Berkeley	1984
Olsen, Randall J.	Prof	292-5654	olsen.6	J	PHD	77	Chicago	
Director Center for Human Resource Research								
Parsons, Donald O.	Prof	292-2670	parsons.1	J	PHD	70	Chicago	1970
Ray, Edward J.	Prof	292-5881	ray.1	F	PHD	71	Stanford	
Senior Vice Provost								
Sandberg, Lars G.	Prof	292-2070	sandberg.1	NO	PHD	64	Harvard	
Schmeidler, David	Prof	292-1148	schmeidler.1		PHD	69	Hebrew	
Steckel, Richard H.	Prof	422-5008	steckel.1	N	PHD	77	Chicago	1977
Baack, Bennett D.	Assoc	292-2489	baack.1	N	PHD	72	U Wash	1988
Koizumi, Tetsunori	Assoc	292-7313	kiozumi.2	E	PHD	70	Brown	1970
Lam, Pok-sang	Assoc	292-6567	lam.1	E	PHD	86	Harvard	1985
Mark, Nelson C.	Assoc	292-0413	mark.1	FG	PHD	83	Chicago	1983
Mumy, Gene E.	Assoc	292-0376	mumy.1	D	PHD	74	J Hopkins	1978
Peck, James D.	Assoc	292-0182	peck.33	D	PHD	85	Penn	1992
Reagan, Patricia B.	Assoc	292-0192	reagan.3	LJ	PHD	80	MIT	
Campbell, Colin	Asst				PHD		Northwes	1995
Chipty, Tasneem	Asst	292-2051	chipty.1	L	PHD	93	MIT	
Choi, In	Asst	292-0387	choi.1		PHD	90	Yale	1989
Crucini, Mario J.	Asst	292-6482	crucini.1	E	PHD	91	Rochester	1991
on leave to New York University 1995-96								

Name	Rank	Phone	Email	Field	Degree	Yr	School	Year
Fisher, Eric O.	Asst	292-2009	fisher.244	F	PHD	85	Berkeley	1993
Glass, Amy J.	Asst	292-1149	glass.29	F	PHD	93	Penn	1993
Light, Audrey	Asst		light.20		PHD	87	UCLA	1995
Reitman, David	Asst	292-4194	reitman.1	L	PHD	87	Stanford	1986
Viard, Alan D.	Asst	292-4192	viard.1		PHD	90	Harvard	1990
Zhao, Jingang	Asst	292-6523	zhao.18	CD	PHD	92	Yale	
McCulloch, Laurence		292-5528	mcculloch.1					

Ohio Wesleyan University — Delaware, OH 43015 (614) — Pat Masters
Economics Faculty — Department of Economics Fax=369-0810 — OWU.COMMCN

Name	Rank	Phone	Field	Degree	Yr	School	Year
Cook, Clifford G.	C-Ac	368-3539	Atg	MBA	76	Drexel	1984
Gharrity, Norman J.	Prof			PHD	66	J Hopkins	1962
Gitter, Robert J.	Prof	368-3536		PHD	78	Wisconsin	1976
Harvey, Joann P.	Assoc			MBA		Ohio St	1981
Simon, Alice E.	Assoc			PHD		Ohio St	1985
Alexander, Peter	Asst	368-3538		PHD	90	Mass	1990

University of Oklahoma — Norman, OK 73019-0450 (405) 325-2861 — Tami Kinsey
Department of Economics — Col of Arts & Sciences Fax=325-5842

Name	Rank	Phone	Field	Degree	Yr	School	Year
Young, David	Dean	325-2077					
Dauffenbach, Robert C.	Prof	744-5125	J	PHD	73	Illinois	
Huetter, David A.	Prof	325-2931	L	PHD	72	Case Wes	1974
Kondonassis, Alexander J.	Prof	325-5234	NO	PHD	61	Indiana	1979
David Ross Boyd Professor of Economics							
Murry, Donald A.	Prof		L	PHD	66	Missouri	
Clark, William M.	Assoc		O	PHD		Virginia	
Hartigan, James C.	Assoc	325-2358	FL	PHD	79	Duke	1988
Holmes, Alexander B.	Assoc		RD	PHD	74	SUNY-Bin	
Reed, Robert	Assoc	325-2861	JD	PHD	85	Northwes	1992
Cunningham, Elizabeth	Asst	325-2861	J	PHD	91	Cornell	1991
Dunne, Stephanie	Asst	325-3861	DJL	PHD	92	Va Tech	1992
Dunne, Timothy	Asst	325-2861	DLJ	PHD	87	Penn St	1992
Ju, Jiandong	Asst	325-2861	D	PHD	95	Penn St	1995
Kasturia, Sangeeta	Asst	325-2861	D	PHD	95	Ca-San Cr	1995

Oklahoma Baptist University — Shawnee, OK 74801-2590 (405) 878-3254
Economics Faculty — Dickinson Sch Business Fax=878-3253
phone 878-3254

Name	Rank	Phone	Field	Degree	Yr	School	Year
Babb, Robert M.	Dean	Ext 3254		EDD	89	Kentucky	8-89
Lloyd Minter Professor of Business							
Brattin, Max Alan	Assoc	Ext 3273		MBA		LSU	1966
Reeder, Danny	Asst	Ext 3281		PHD		Okla St	1991

Oklahoma Christian U Sci/Art — Oklahoma Cy OK 73136-1100 (405) 425-5560 — Wanda Neel
Economics Faculty — College of Business Fax=425-5574

Name	Rank	Phone	Field	Degree	Yr	School	Year
Skaggs, W. Jack	Dean	425-5567		EDD	87	Okla St	
Leftwich, Howard D.	C-Pr	425-5561	Atg	DBA	70	Oklahoma	6-67

Oklahoma City University — Oklahoma City OK 73106 (405)
Economics Faculty — Meinders Sch Business Fax=521-5098

Name	Rank	Phone	Field	Degree	Yr	School	Year
Carmichael, David	Dean	521-5276		PHD	94	Oklahoma	8-94
Craig, George	C-Pr	521-5095		PHD		Illinois	1982
Fitzgerald, Patrick W.	Prof	521-5168		PHD	79	Tx-Austin	1982
Alli, Ali M.	Assoc	521-5132		PHD		Okla St	1985
Moini, Mostafa	Assoc	521-5357		PHD		Oklahoma	1965
Shandiz, Mohmood	Assoc	521-5130		PHD	81	Okla St	1985
Associate Dean							
Willner, Jonathan	Asst		FO	PHD	94	Purdue	1995

Oklahoma State University — Stillwater, OK 74078-0555 (405) 744-5195 — Judy Willis
Department of Economics — Col of Business Admin Fax=744-5180

Name	Rank	Phone	Field	Degree	Yr	School	Year
Trennepohl, Gary L.	Dean	744-5075	Fnce	PHD	76	Tx Tech	1995
Jadlow, Joseph M. Jr.	H-Pr	744-5195		PHD	70	Virginia	1968
Amos, Orley M. Jr.	Prof	744-8657		PHD	79	Iowa St	1979
Applegate, Michael J.	Prof	744-5197		PHD	73	Iowa St	1974
Edgmand, Michael R.	Prof	744-5109		PHD	68	Mich St	1983
Lage, Gerald M.	Prof	744-6256		PHD	67	Minnesota	1966
Moomaw, Ronald L.	Prof	744-7359		PHD	76	Princeton	1972
CBA Associates Chair							
Olson, Kent W.	Prof	744-8655		PHD	69	Oregon	1974
Steindl, Frank G.	Prof	744-5091		PHD	63	Iowa	1962
Regents' Professor and Ardmore Chair							
Warner, Larkin B.	Prof	744-5108		PHD	61	Indiana	1960
Regents' Professor							

Name	Rank	Phone	Email	Field	Degree	Yr	School	Hired
Willett, Keith D.	Prof	744-8656			PHD	82	New Mex	1981
Adkins, Lee C.	Assoc	744-8637			PHD	88	LSU	1988
Currier, Kevin M.	Assoc	744-8658			PHD	85	SUNY-Alb	1984
Fain, James R.	Assoc	744-8651			PHD	86	Purdue	1986
Gade, Mary N.	Assoc	744-8652			PHD	86	Mich St	1986
Price, Edward O. III	Assoc	744-7669			PHD	80	Tx A&M	1979
Savvides, Andreas	Assoc	744-5110			PHD	83	Florida	1985

Old Dominion University Norfolk, VA 23529-0229 (804) 683-3567 Vicky Curtis
Department of Economics Col of Bus & Pub Admin Fax=683-5639 ODUVM

Name	Rank	Phone	Email	Field	Degree	Yr	School	Hired
Sims, J. Taylor	Dean	683-3521		Mktg	PHD	70	Illinois	7-94
Yochum, Gilbert R.	C-Pr	683-3535			PHD	74	W Virginia	1975
Agarwal, Vinod	Prof	683-3526			PHD	86	Ca-SnBarb	
Graduate Program Director								
Henry, Louis H.	Prof	683-4865			PHD	70	Notre Dm	1970
Director, Academic Honors Program								
Koch, James V.	Prof	683-3159			PHD	68	Northwes	1990
President								
Mullin, Gail	Prof	683-3574			PHD	83	Indiana	
Qureski, Usman	Prof	683-3571			PHD	79	Houston	
Strangways, Raymond S.	Prof	683-4986			PHD	66	Tulane	1962
Talley, Wayne K.	Prof	683-3534			PHD	72	Kentucky	1972
Eminent Professor								
Colburn, Christopher B.	Assoc	683-4341			PHD		Tx A&M	1987
Schwarz-Miller, Ann V.	Assoc	683-3572			PHD		Northwes	1978
Turner, Charlie G.	Assoc	683-3576			PHD	81	Harvard	1984
Anderson, Eric E.	Asst	683-3512			PHD		U Wash	1984

Olivet College Olivet, MI 49076 (616)
Economics Faculty Dept of Bus Adm & Econ Fax=749-7650

Name	Rank	Phone	Email	Field	Degree	Yr	School	Hired
Kiebala, Susan	C-As	749-7610			MBA	77	W Mich	1989
Homer, John S.	Assoc				MA	69	Hawaii	1979
Johnson, Kirk	Asst				MA	90	Wayne St	1990

Olivet Nazarene University Kankakee, IL 60901 (815) 939-5133 Kay Zoltani
Economics Faculty Business Department Fax=939-0416 OLIVET.EDU
Did Not Respond--1994-95 Listing

Name	Rank	Phone	Email	Field	Degree	Yr	School	Hired
Rewerts, Glen	C-As$	939-5133			JD	87	S Illinois	1993
Koch, Paul R.	Assoc	939-5100	pkoch	ABHP	ABD		Ill St	1992

University of Oregon Eugene, OR 97403-1285 (503) 346-6027 Linda M. Steller 346-1263
Department of Economics Col of Arts & Sciences Fax=346-5026 OREGON.UOREGON.EDU

Name	Rank	Phone	Email	Field	Degree	Yr	School	Hired
Palm, Risa I.	Dean	346-3902						
Gray, Jo Anna	H-Pr	346-1266	jgray	E	PHD	76	Chicago	1989
Evans, George	Prof	346-6027	gevans	E	PHD	80	Berkeley	1994
John B. Hamacher Professor of Economics								
Goldstein, Henry	Prof	346-4670		F	PHD	67	J Hopkins	1967
Haynes, Stephen E.	Prof	346-4665	shaynes	FE	PHD	76	Ca-SnBarb	1978
Khang, Chulsoon	Prof	346-4660		FEO	PHD	65	Minnesota	1966
Stone, Joe A.	Prof	346-4663	jstone	JFE	PHD	77	Mich St	1970
W. E. Miner Professor of Economics								
Ellis, Christopher J.	Assoc	346-4657	cjellis	E	PHD	83	Warwick	1983
Kolpin, Van W.	Assoc	346-3011	vkolpin	C	PHD	86	Iowa	1986
Singell, Larry D. Jr.	Assoc	346-4672	lsingell	J	PHD	88	Ca-SnBarb	1988
Thoma, Mark A.	Assoc	346-4673	mthoma	E	PHD	85	Wash St	1987
Wilson, Wesley W.	Assoc	346-4631	wilson	CD	PHD	86	Wash St	1989
Blonigen, Bruce A.	Asst			FL	PHD	95	Ca-Davis	1995
Figlio, David N.	Asst			HR	PHD	95	Wisconsin	1995
Harbaugh, William T.	Asst			HQ	PHD	95	Wisconsin	
Silva, Emilson	Asst	346-4671	esilva	OH	PHD	93	Illinois	1993
Ziliak, James P.	Asst	346-4681	jziliak	J	PHD	93	Indiana	1993

Oregon State University Corvallis, OR 97331-3612 (503) 737-2321 Rod Johnson
Department of Economics College of Liberal Arts Fax=737-5917 CCMAIL.ORSTM.EDU

Name	Rank	Phone	Email	Field	Degree	Yr	School	Hired
Wilkins, Bill H.	Dean				PHD	62	Tx-Austin	1961
Tremblay, Victor J.	C-Pr	737-2321	tremblav	DLC	PHD	83	Wash St	9-90
Farrell, John P.	Prof	737-1479	farrellj	BO	PHD	73	Wisconsin	9-72
McMullen, B. Starr	Prof	737-1480	mcmullenb	LE	PHD	79	Berkeley	9-80
Vars, R. Charles Jr.	Prof	737-1472		HO	PHD	69	Berkeley	9-66
Chao, Chi-Chur	Assoc	737-1481	chaoc	EF	PHD	87	S Illinois	9-90
Fraundorf, Martha	Assoc	737-1477	fraundom	J	PHD	76	Cornell	9-76
Kerkvliet, Joe R.	Assoc	737-1482	kerkvlij	L	PHD	86	Wyoming	9-88
O'Sullivan, Arthur M.	Assoc	737-2508		DR	PHD	81	Princeton	9-92
Baek, Dae-Hyun	Asst	737-1475	baekd	EF	PHD	90	Ohio St	9-91
Connelly, Laura	Asst	737-3025		HL	ABD		Northwes	9-94
Martins, Carlos	Asst	737-1476		DCL	PHD	92	Tennessee	9-92
Ohno, Yuka	Asst	737-3019		FL	PHD	93	U Wash	9-94
Tremblay, Carol	Asst	737-1468	tremblac	CJ	PHD	84	Wash St	9-92

Otterbein College — Westerville, OH 43081 (614) 823-1481
Economics Faculty — Dept Bus, Atg & Econ Fax=898-1014 — IM.BATTELLE.ORG

Name	Rank	Phone	Email	Field	Degree	Yr	School	Year
Abdallah, Kamel	C-Ac	823-1892	kaabdallah	Mgt	PHD	91	Ohio St	1990
Lewis, J. Patrick	Prof	823-1460			PHD	74	Ohio St	1974
Aristotelous, Kyriacos	Asst	823-1611			PHD	93	Ohio St	1993

Pace University — New York, NY 10038-1502 (212) 346-1469
Department of Economics — Dyson Col of Arts & Sci Fax= — PACEVM

Name	Rank	Phone	Email	Field	Degree	Yr	School	Year
Masiello, Charles	Dean	346-1710			PHD		CUNY	
Schaake, Richard A.	C-As	346-1467			MBA		NYU	1966
Hurmozi, Farroh	Prof	346-1464			PHD		New Sch	
Swift, William J.	Prof	346-1468			PHD	69	Wash U	1966
Lutt, Elizabeth	Assoc	346-1465			PHD		Columbia	
O'Brien, Peter A. Jr.	Assoc	346-1466			MBA	57	Rutgers	1964

University of the Pacific — Stockton, CA 95211 (209) 946-2258 — Suzanne B. Westphal
Department of Economics — College of the Pacific Fax=946-2257 — UOP.EDU

Name	Rank	Phone	Email	Field	Degree	Yr	School	Year
Benedetti, Robert R.	Dean			PolS	PHD	75		
Flynn, Dennis O.	C-Pr		dopflynn	DENO	PHD	77	Utah	1979
Herrin, William E.	Assoc			R	PHD	85	SUNY-Bin	1985
Keefe, David E.	Assoc	946-2258		FT	PHD	80	Berkeley	1978
Meyer, Peter J.	Assoc	946-2258		BJL	PHD	79	Berkeley	1985
Opiela, Timothy P.	Assoc			E	PHD	87	Tx A&M	1986
Warner, Lori	Assoc			BEN	PHD	86	Utah	1987
Ordovensky, J. Farley	Asst			HJ	PHD	92	Duke	1993

Pacific Lutheran University — Tacoma, WA 98447-0004 (206) 535-7598 — Ms. Peggy Jobe
Department of Economics — Div of Social Sciences Fax=535-8305 — PLU.EDU

Name	Rank	Phone	Email	Field	Degree	Yr	School	Year
Smith, Earl	Dean			Soci	PHD			
Nugent, Rachel A.	C-As	535-7684	nugentra	DFQH	PHD	94	Geo Wash	1991
Brue, Stanley L.	Prof	535-7634		ABJ	PHD	71	Nebraska	1971
Miller, Marlen F.	Prof	535-8746			PHD	62	Minnesota	1970
Peterson, Norris A.	Prof	535-7645	petersna	J	PHD	81	Minnesota	1981
Vinje, David L.	Prof	535-7144		O	PHD	64	Wisconsin	1970
Wentworth, Donald R.	Prof	535-7644		A	PHD	65	Minnesota	1972
Jensen, Robert J.	Assoc	535-7594	jensenrj		MA	67	Nebraska	1968
Reiman, Mark A.	Assoc	535-8875		FPQ	PHD	88	U Wash	1988
Travis, Karen	Lect	535-8307		CFI	ABD		U Wash	1995

Pacific Union College — Angwin, CA 94508-9797 (707) 965-6238
Economics Faculty — Dept of Bus Adm & Econ Fax=965-6237 — PUC.EDU

Name	Rank	Phone	Email	Field	Degree	Yr	School	Year
Kopitzke, Henry	C-Pr	965-6526		Law	JD	80	Idaho	1973

Pembroke State University — Pembroke, NC 28372-1510 (910) 521-6214 — Rena Hill
Economics Faculty — Dept of Business & Econ Fax=521-6162

Name	Rank	Phone	Email	Field	Degree	Yr	School	Year
Mattox, Bruce W. Sr.	Prof	521-6464			PHD		Oreg St	1988
Director of Economic Development								
Frederick, James R.	Asst	521-6592			PHD	83	Wayne St	1988

University of Pennsylvania — Philadelphia, PA 19104-6297 (215) 898-7701
Department of Economics — Sch of Arts & Sciences Fax=573-2057 — ECON.SAS.UPENN.EDU
emai: @1=penndrls.upenn.edu

Name	Rank	Phone	Email	Field	Degree	Yr	School	Year
Bloomfield, Arthur I.	Emer				PHD	42	Chicago	1958
Stevens, Rosemary	Dean	898-2327						
Postlewaite, Andrew W.	C-Pr	898-7515	apostlew	DH	PHD	74	Northwes	1980
Pacific Term Professor in the Social Studies								
Adams, F. Gerard	Prof	898-7725	adams		PHD	56	Michigan	1961
Ando, Albert K.	Prof	898-7712	aando		PHD	59	Car Mellon	1963
Behrman, Jere R.	Prof	898-7704	jbehrman	OJL	PHD	66	MIT	1965
William R. Kenan Jr. Professor of Economics; Acting Graduate Group Chair								
Cass, David	Prof	898-5735	dcass	DCG	PHD	65	Stanford	1974
Paul F. & E. Warren Shafer Miller Professor of Economics								
Cooley, Thomas F.	Prof	898-6880		E	PHD	71	Penn	1995
Ethier, Wilfred J.	Prof	898-5105	jjohns@1	F	PHD	70	Rochester	1969
Hess, Arleigh P. Jr.	Emer	898-8473			PHD	49	Penn	1949
Associate Undergraduate Chair for Advising								
Klein, Lawrence R.	Emer	898-7713			PHD	44	MIT	1958
Benjamin Franklin Professor of Economics & Finance								
Levine, Herbert S.	Prof	898-7706	hlevine	P	PHD	61	Harvard	1960
Malenbaum, Wilfred	Emer				PHD	41	Harvard	1959
Mansfield, Edwin	Prof	898-7788			PHD	55	Duke	1963
Mariano, Roberto S.	Prof	898-6771	mariano		PHD	70	Stanford	1971
Matsui, Akihiko	Prof	898-7749	amatsui	CDE	PHD	90	Northwes	1990
William P. Carey Term Assistant Professor of Economics								

Phillips, Almarin	Emer				PHD	53	Harvard	1953
Rob, Rafael	Prof	898-6775	rrob		PHD	81	UCLA	1984
Rosenzweig, Mark R.	Prof	898-7408		OJL	PHD	73	Columbia	1990
email markr@markr2.pop.upenn.edu								
Summers, Robert	Emer	898-7717			PHD	56	Stanford	1959
Wachter, Michael L.	Prof	898-6804		KJ	PHD	70	Harvard	1969
William B. Johnson Professor of Law & Econ; email mwachter@oyez.law.upenn.edu								
Wolpin, Kenneth I.	Prof	898-8484			PHD	74	CUNY	1995
Wright, Randall	Prof	898-7194	rwright	JE	PHD	86	Minnesota	1987
Diebold, Francis X.	Assoc	898-1507	diebold		PHD	86	Penn	1989
Undergraduate Chair								
Kehoe, Patrick J.	Assoc	898-7409	pkehoe	POF	PHD	86	Harvard	1992
Ronald S. Lauder Term Associate Professor of Economics								
Mailath, George J.	Assoc	898-7908	gmailath	CDH	PHD	85	Princeton	1985
Atkeson, Andrew G.	Asst	898-7712	aatkeson	PF	PHD	88	Stanford	1993
Kei Mori Fellow of the Institute for Economic Research								
Corradi, Valentina	Asst	898-1505	corradi		PHD	94	Ca-SnDgo	1994
Cres, Herve	Asst	898-6260	hres		PHD	94	Geneve	1994
Gouveia, Miguel	Asst	898-8486	mgouveia	JH	PHD	91	Rochester	1991
Hahn, Jinyong	Asst	898-5652	jajm		PHD	93	Harvard	1993
William P. Carey Term Assistant Professor of Economics								
Hanes, Christopher L.	Asst	898-7733	chanes	NJE	PHD	90	Harvard	1990
Kajii, Atsushi	Asst	898-1875	akajii	G	PHD	91	Harvard	1991
Morris, Stephen	Asst	898-6356	smorris	CD	PHD	91	Yale	1991
Benjamin V. Schlein Term Assistant Professor of Economics								
Ohanian, Lee E.	Asst	898-6880	lohanian	E	PHD	93	Rochester	1992
Lawrence R. Klein Fellow of the Institute for Econ Research; on leave U Minn								
Perli, Roberto	Asst	898-1504		E	PHD	95	NYU	1995
Rios-Rull, Jose-Victor	Asst	898-7767		O	PHD	90	Minnesota	1992
Simon Kuznets Term Assistant Profess of Econ; email vr0j@anaga.sas.upenn.edu								
Zhou, Ruilin	Asst	898-6774		FDE	PHD	93	Pittsburgh	1993
Milton C. Denbo Term Assistant Prof Econ; email ruilin@ysidro.sas.upenn.edu								
Jovanovic, Boyan	Prof	898-4084	jovanovi	EL	PHD	78	Chicago	1995

Penn State University	Univ Park, PA		16802 (814) 865-1456 Linda Spangler/Anna McMullin					
Department of Economics	College of Liberal Arts Fax=863-4775						PSUVM.BITNET	
Marshall, Robert C.	H-Pr	865-1456			PHD	83	Ca-SnDgo	1995
Baye, Michael R.	Prof	865-6050	mrb12	DIO	PHD	83	Purdue	1991
Bond, Eric W.	Prof	863-0315	ewb1	F	PHD	79	Rochester	1981
Crocker, Keith J.	Prof	863-1294	ist	KD	PHD	81	Car Mellon	1986
Feller, Irwin	Prof	865-9561	iqf	O	PHD	66	Minnesota	1963
Fox, Thomas G.	Prof	863-2650	tgf	A	PHD	66	Syracuse	1966
Klein, Philip A.	Prof	865-5781	pak11	E	PHD	58	Berkeley	1955
Krishna, Kala	Prof	865-1106	kmk4	F	PHD	84	Princeton	1993
Lombra, Raymond E.	Prof	865-5452	rl3	E	PHD	71	Penn St	1969
Nelson, Jon P.	Prof	865-8871	jpn	QD	PHD	70	Wisconsin	1969
Roberts, Mark J.	Prof	863-1535	m7r	D	PHD	80	Wisconsin	1980
Rodgers, James D.	Prof	863-2876	jdr	HK	PHD	70	Virginia	1969
Welsh, Arthur	Prof	863-1295	alw3	A	PHD	63	Illinois	1986
Coulson, N. Edward	Assoc	863-0625	fyj	R	PHD	83	Ca-SnDgo	1984
Gresik, Thomas A.	Assoc	863-8007	txg8	D	PHD	87	Northwes	1991
Ickes, Barry W.	Assoc	863-2652	io4	P	PHD	84	Berkeley	1983
Krishna, Vijay	Assoc	863-8543	vxk5	D	PHD	83	Princeton	1993
Roberts, Bee-Yan	Assoc	863-1996	byr	O	PHD	80	Wisconsin	1981
Rosenberg, Richard	Assoc	865-2201	rxr1	A	PHD	69	Minnesota	1965
Sharpiro, David	Assoc	863-1533	d89	J	PHD	72	Princeton	1980
Terza, Joseph V.	Assoc	863-3743	jvt	C	PHD	81	Pittsburgh	1986
Wang, Ping	Assoc	865-1525	pxw4	E	PHD	87	Rochester	1987
Laing, Derek	Asst	863-2656	dxl8	E	PHD	89	Essex	1989
Li, Victor	Asst	863-8544	vxl3	E	PHD	92	Northwes	1992
Ribar, David	Asst	863-7417	dcr7	J	PHD	90	Brown	1990
Rogers, Diane	Asst	863-0771	dlr9	H	PHD	91	Virginia	1989
Rogers, John H.	Asst	863-0084	jrh5	E	PHD	89	Virginia	1989
Syropoulos, C.	Asst	865-4921	cxs19	F	PHD	89	Yale	1988
Wilhelm, Mark	Asst	863-7416	mxw10	I	PHD	90	NYU	1990
Schlow, David	Lect	863-8542	d14	A	PHD	84	Penn St	1991

Penn State - Erie	Erie, PA		16563-1400 (814) 898-6107					
School of Business	Behrend College		Fax=898-6223				PSUVM.PSU.EDU	
Magenau, John M. III	D-Ac	898-6173	jqm1	JM	PHD	88	SUNY-Buf	1985
Weller, Barry R.	H-Ac	898-6326	brw	ACE	PHD	71	Penn St	1971
Fizel, John L.	Assoc	898-6266	fzk	L	PHD	81	Mich St	1985
Kurre, James A.	Assoc	898-6266	k12	RA	PHD	82	Penn St	1977
Louie, Kenneth K. T.	Assoc	898-6265	obr	FJ	PHD	87	Penn St	1984

Penn State Univ-Harrisburg Middleton, PA 17057-4898 (717) 948-6141 Becky Dolan
Department of Economics School of Business Fax=948-6456
Dhir, Krishna S. Dir 948-6141 Atg PHD 75 Colorado 1991
Murti, Vedula N. C-As 948-6164 PHD 66 Penn 1969
DeRooy, Jacob Assoc 948-6155 PHD 69 Rutgers 1975

Pepperdine Univ-Malibu Malibu, CA 90263 (310) 456-4372
Social Science Division Seaver College Fax=456-4314 PEPPERDINE.EDU
Wilson, John F. Dean 456-4281 Rel PHD 67 Iowa 1983
Fagan, Ronald C-Pr 456-4818 rfagan Soci PHD Wash St 1978
Batchelder, Ronald W. Prof 456-4544 rbatch DEFK PHD 75 UCLA 1984
Sexton, Robert L. Prof 456-4345 rsexton ADNQ PHD 80 Colorado 1979
Galles, Gary M. Assoc 456-4250 ggalles AHLR PHD 88 UCLA 1982

Pfeiffer College Misenheimer, NC 28109 (704)
Department of Economics Div of Business & Econ Fax=463-2046
Bleau, Barbara Lee H-Pr 463-1360 PHD 80 Penn St 8-86
Jefferson-Pilot Professor of Management Science
Jozsa, Frank Assoc PHD 77 Geo St 1991
Poplin, Toby L. Assoc MA 68 Appalach 1976
Coordinator of the Div of Business & Economics

Piedmont College Demorest, GA 30535-0010 (706) Ext 250 Tammy Riddle
Economics Faculty Division of Business Fax=776-2811
phone: 778-8500
Elger, John F. C Ext 250
Gardner, Mark L. Prof Ext 250 PHD 85 Geo St 1979

Pittsburg State University Pittsburg, KS 66762 (316) 235-4547 Mrs. Kriss Hess
Dept Econ, Finance & Banking Kelch Sch of Bus & Econ Fax=232-7515 MAIL.PITTSTATE.EDU
Mendelhall, Terry L. Dean 235-4598 Mgt PHD 81 Kansas St 1964
Fischer, Charles C. C-Pr 235-4547 BJ PHD 75 Wash St 1974
Smith, Kenneth L. Prof 235-4547 G PHD Ca-River
Cortes, Bienvenido S. Assoc 235-4547 F PHD Okla St
Crough, B. Jane Lect 235-4547 A MBA Pittsburgh
Lal, Anil K. Lect 235-4547 A PHD Wash St

University of Pittsburgh Pittsburgh, PA 15260 (412) 648-1760 Irene Petrovich/Della Sinclair
Department of Economics Col of Arts & Sciences Fax=648-1793 VMS.CIS.PITT.EDU
Koehler, Peter F. M. Dean 624-6090 pfkt@pitt.edu PHD Rochester
Giarratani, Frank C-Pr 648-1742 frankg R PHD 75 W Virginia 1979
Cassing, James H. Prof 648-8746 jcassing F PHD 75 Iowa 1985
Gruver, Gene W. Prof 648-1731 gruver O PHD 72 Iowa St 1970
Ham, John Prof 648-1762 johnham J PHD 80 Princeton 1991
Husted, Steven L. Prof 648-1757 husted1 F PHD 80 Mich St 1980
Kagel, John H. Prof 648-1753 kagel D PHD 70 Purdue 1988
Katz, Arnold M. Prof 648-1752 akatz J PHD 61 Yale
Maeshiro, Asatoshi Prof 648-1756 aiueo C PHD 65 Michigan 1979
Mesa-Lago, Carmelo Prof 648-2828 P PHD 68 Cornell 1968
Distinguished Service Professor of Economics and Latin American Studies
Ochs, Jack N. Prof 624-5711 jochs H PHD 66 Indiana 1968
Rawski, Thomas G. Prof 648-7062 tgrawski O PHD 72 Harvard 1985
Richard, Jean Francois Prof 648-1750 fantin C PHD 73 Louvain 1991
Roth, Alvin E. Prof 648-1735 alroth PHD 74 Stanford 1982
Mellon Professor
Svejnar, Jan Prof 648-2826 jan1 J PHD 79 Princeton 1987
Wells, Jerome C. Prof 648-1749 wells01 O PHD 64 Michigan 1964
Beeson, Patricia E. Assoc 648-1754 beeson R PHD 83 Oregon 1983
Chesler, Herbert Assoc 648-1706 chesler J PHD 64 MIT 1963
DeJong, David Assoc 648-2242 dejong E PHD 89 Iowa 1989
Kenkel, James L. Assoc 648-1767 kenkel C PHD 69 Purdue 1969
Sontheimer, Kevin C. Assoc 648-7071 sontheim D PHD 69 Minnesota 1979
Wichers, C. Robert Assoc 648-1794 wichers C PHD 68 Amdersta 1976
Aoyagi, Masaki Asst 648-1737 maoyagi D PHD 92 Princeton 1992
Berkowitz, Daniel Asst 64807072 dmberk GH PHD 88 Columbia 1992
Cooper, David Asst 64801748 dcooper G PHD 92 Princeton 1992
Duffy, John Asst 648-1733 jduffy E PHD 92 UCLA 1992
Harrigan, James Asst 648-2243 harrigan F PHD 91 UCLA 1989
Boerio, Eileen Lect 648-1760 boerio D MA 77 Pittsburgh 1977
Cassing, Shirley Lect 648-1729 cassing R PHD 76 Iowa 1985

U of Pittsburgh at Johnstown Johnstown, PA 15904 (814) 269-2990
Div of Social Sci-Economics Col of Arts & Sciences Fax=269-7255 VMS.CIS.PITT.EDU

McGahagan, Thomas A.	C-As	269-2985	mgahagan	FN	PHD	76	Penn	1982
Yates, Michael Daniel	Prof	269-2986	mikey	JP	PHD	76	Pittsburgh	1969
Berger, George	Assoc	269-2982	berger	EJK	PHD	87	Ca-Davis	1989
Long, Stanley G.	Assoc	269-2990	sglong	ADR	PHD	69	Iowa	1973
retires 12-95								
Strausser, Clark W.	Assoc	269-2980		CG	PHD	70	Minnesota	1973
Lavine, Jeffrey A.	Asst	269-7000	jlavine		MA	68	Pittsburgh	1970
Director of Administration and Budget								

Plymouth State College Plymouth, NH 03264 (603) 535-2610
Economics Faculty Department of Business Fax=535-2711 PLYMOUTH.EDU

Beniot, William R.	C-Pr	535-2610			MS	80	S Calif	
Couvillion, L. Michael	Assoc	536-2205		I	PHD	82	La Tech	1980
Jang, Soo M.	Assoc	535-2413		E	PHD	78	Cincinnati	1983
Brickley, Colleen	Inst	535-2278		D	ABD	78	N Hamp	1993

Point Loma Nazarene College San Diego, CA 92106 (619) 221-2305
Economics Faculty Dept of Bus & Economics Fax=221-2691

Havens, Rebecca A.	C-As				PHD		Ca-SnDgo	1990
Campbell, Everett	Prof				PHD		Temple	1989
McEliece, James H.	Assoc				PHD		Co Mines	1994
Anderson, Mark A.	Asst				MBA		Ca-SanBer	1988
on leave Univ Kentucky								

University of Portland Portland, OR 97203-5798 (503) 283-7224 Connie Tamashiro
Economics Faculty School of Business Adm Fax=283-7399 UOFPORT.EDU

Robertson, James W.	Dean	283-7224		Atg	PHD	63	U Wash	1987
Adrangi, Bahram	Prof	283-7220	adrangi	CDFR	PHD	82	Oregon	1982
Higgins, Neal O.	Prof	283-7226	higgins	RH	PHD	74	Nebraska	1976
Allender, Mary E.	Assoc	283-7154		L	PHD	90	Oregon	1985
Easton, Todd E.	Assoc	283-7209	easton	J	PHD	84	Berkeley	1981
Seal, James W.	Assoc	283-7272		HRE	PHD	77	Illinois	1977

Portland State University Portland, OR 97207-0751 (503) 725-3915 Rita Spears
Department of Economics Col Liberal Arts & Sci Fax=725-4882 CH2.CH.PDX.EDU
home page eclab.ch.pdx.edu

Kaiser, Marvin	Dean	725-3514			PHD			1993
Youngelson-Neal, Helen L.	C-Pr	725-3929	hahya		PHD	66	Columbia	1967
Brinkman, Richard L.	Prof	725-3938	brinkman		PHD	65	Rutgers	1961
Burgess, Giles H.	Prof	725-3942	giles		PHD	73	Oregon	1969
Crick, Nelson B.	Prof	725-3930	nelson		PHD	67	Colorado	1967
Hall, John B.	Prof	725-3939	johnh		PHD	84	New Sch	1985
Lin, Kuan-Pin	Prof	725-3931	kuan-pin		PHD	77	SUNY-SBr	1979
Palm, Thomas	Prof	725-3933	tomp		PHD	67	Michigan	1967
Potiowsky, Thomas P.	Prof	725-3935	thomasp		PHD	81	Colorado	1982
Qayum, Abdul	Prof	725-3936	abdul		DSC	59	Netherld	1970
Tuchscherer, Thomas H.	Prof	725-3940	tuchscherer		PHD	73	Northwes	1966
Walker, John F.	Prof	725-3934	johnw		PHD	72	Utah	1966
King, Mary C.	Asst	725-3944	maryw		PHD	91	Berkeley	1992

Prairie View A&M University Prairie View, TX 77446-0951 (409) 857-2122 Virgie L. Holmes
Dept of Economics & Finance College of Business Fax=857-2797

Jones, Barbara A. P.	Dean	857-4310			PHD	73	Geo St	1987
Song, Kean P.	H-As	857-2122			PHD	93	Houston	1988
Khan, Moosa	Prof	857-2122			PHD	86	Simon Fr	1989
Soliman, Mostafa A.	Assoc	857-2122			PHD	67	Iowa St	1971
Thiagarajan, Kuttalam R.	Asst	857-2122			MA	55	Annamali	1967

Presbyterian College Clinton, SC 29325 (803) 833-8370 Myra Templeton
Economics Faculty Dept of Econ & Bus Adm Fax=833-8481 CS1.PRESBY.EDU

Howell, Samuel Lide	C-Ac	833-8370	slhowell		MACC		S Carol	1980
Slice, Jerry Kibler	Assoc	833-8274	jkslice		PHD		Miss St	1989
Lipford, Jody W.	Asst	833-8353	jlipford	H	PHD		Clemson	1991

Princeton University Princeton, NJ 08544-1021 (609)
Economics Faculty Department of Economics Fax= PUCC

Rosen, Harvey S.	C-Pr	258-4000	g5994		PHD	74	Harvard	1974
Asenfelter, Orley C.	Prof	452-4040			PHD	70	Princeton	1968
Bernanke, Ben S.	Prof	258-5635			PHD	79	MIT	1985
Blinder, Alan S.	Prof	258-4000			PHD	71	MIT	1971
Bradford, David F.	Prof	258-4842			PHD	66	Stanford	1966

Name	Rank	Phone	Degree	Yr	School	Year
Branson, William H.	Prof	258-4828	PHD	67	MIT	1967
Card, David E.	Prof	258-4045	PHD	83	Princeton	1983
Chow, Gregory C.	Prof					
Deaton, Angus S.	Prof	258-5967	PHD	74	Cambridg	1983
Dixit, Avinash K.	Prof	258-4013	PHD	68	MIT	1981
Farber, Henry S.	Prof		PHD	77	Princeton	
Goldfeld, Stephen M.	Prof	258-4031	PHD	63	MIT	1969
Grossman, Gene M.	Prof	258-4823	PHD	80	MIT	1980
Gul, Faruk	Prof	258-4000	PHD		Princeton	1995
Kenen, Peter B.	Prof	258-4051	PHD	58	Harvard	1971
Walker Professor Economics & International Finance						
Kuenne, Robert E.	Prof	258-4002	PHD	53	Harvard	1969
Malkiel, Burton G.	Prof	258-4000	PHD	64	Princeton	1966
Powell, James L.	Prof		PHD	82	Stanford	
Quandt, Richard E.	Prof	258-4005	PHD	57	Harvard	1959
Reinhardt, Uwe E.	Prof		PHD	70	Yale	1967
Rubinstein, Ariel	Prof		PHD	79	Hebrew	
Shapiro, Harold T.	Prof	258-6100	PHD	64	Princeton	1988
Trussell, T. James	Prof					
Willig, Robert D.	Prof	258-4843	PHD	73	Stanford	1978
Paxson, Christina H.	Assoc	258-6474	PHD	86	Columbia	1986
Case, Anne C.	Asst	258-2177	PHD	88	Princeton	1991
Jones, Charles	Asst	258-4000	PHD	94	Michigan	1994
Krueger, Alan B.	Asst					
Lizzeri, Alessandro	Asst	258-4000	PHD	95	Northwes	1995
Metcalf, Gilbert E.	Asst	258-4017	PHD	88	Harvard	1988
Van Zandt, Timothy	Asst					
Lumsdaine, Robin	Inst					
Pesenti, Paolo	Inst					

Providence College — Providence, RI 02918-0001 (401) 865-2194 — Norma Collins

Department of Economics — Economics — Fax=865-2057 — PROVIDENCE.EDU

Name	Rank	Phone	Fields	Degree	Yr	School	Year
Lenon, Mary Jane	C-As	865-2566	REI	PHD	89	Conn	1986
O'Brien, Francis T.	C-Ac	865-2156	JK	MA	57	Boston C	1958
Kessler, Alan L.	Assoc	865-2248	DH	PHD	84	Boston C	1985
Latif-Zuman, Nazma	Assoc	865-2572	OFC	PHD		Northeas	
Simeone, William J.	Assoc	865-2567	JEI	PHD	85	Boston C	1959
Jain, Vandana	Asst	865-2571	CO	PHD	89	India	1990
Mulligan, Robert M.	Asst	865-2565	EK	MA	61	Boston C	1965
Sawdy, George F.	Asst	865-2570	QEH	PHD		Brown	
Kaparakis, Emanuel	Inst	865-2568	EGF	ABD		Conn	1990
Palumbo, Edwin P.	Inst	865-2189	RJ	MA		Boston C	

University of Puget Sound — Tacoma, WA 98416-0140 (206) 756-3136 — Reggie Tison

Economics Faculty — Department of Economics Fax=756-3500 — UPS.EDU

Name	Rank	Phone	Email	Fields	Degree	Yr	School	Year
Stirling, Kathleen J.	C-Ac	756-3590	stirling	AEIT	PHD	87	Notre Dm	
Combs, Ernest F.	Prof	756-3595	combs	AOQ	PHD	71	U Wash	1967
Goodman, Douglas	Prof	756-3596	goodman	AE	PHD	78	Illinois	1977
Hands, Wade	Prof	756-3592	hands	ABC	PHD	65	U Wash	
Mann, Bruce D.	Prof	756-3593	mann	ADJK	PHD	76	Indiana	1975
Singleton, Ross	Prof	756-3591	singleton	ADKO	PHD	77	Oregon	
Veseth, Michael	Prof	756-3720	veseth	AFH	PHD	76	Purdue	1975
Nunn, Elizabeth	Asst	756-3553	nunn	AEN	PHD	89	Wash U	
on leave Fall 1995								

Purdue University — W Lafayette, IN 47907-1310 (317) 494-4449 — Marsha Lowery

Economics Program — Krannert Grad Sch Mgt Fax=494-9658 — MGT.PURDUE.EDU

Name	Rank	Phone	Email	Fields	Degree	Yr	School	Year
Weidenaar, Dennis J.	Dean	494-4366	weidend	Mgt	PHD	69	Purdue	1966
Thursby, Jerry G.	H-Pr	494-4462	jgt		PHD	75	N Carol	1988
Barron, John M.	Prof	494-4451	barron		PHD	76	Brown	1976
Carlson, John A.	Prof	494-4450	carlson		PHD	61	J Hopkins	1962
Loeb Professor of Economics								
Harrington, Peter V.	Prof	494-8545	peterh		MAT	68	Purdue	1971
Horwich, George	Prof	494-4443	ghorwich		PHD	54	Chicago	1956
Hu, Sheng C.	Prof	494-4461	sch		PHD	70	Rochester	1968
Kadiyala, K. Rao	Prof	494-4476	kadiyala		PHD	66	Wisconsin	1970
Kovenock, Dan J.	Prof	494-4468	kovenock		PHD	83	Wisconsin	1983
Moore, James C.	Prof	494-4430	duke		PHD	68	Minnesota	1969
Papke, James A.	Prof	494-4442	papke		PHD	59	Cornell	1962
Thursby, Marie C.	Prof	494-4463	mct		PHD	74	N Carol	1988
Burton D. Morgan Chair of Private Enterprise								
Umbeck, John R.	Prof	494-4447	umbeck		PHD	76	U Wash	1975
Watts, Michael W.	Prof	494-8543	bfp		PHD	78	LSU	1981
Hueckel, Glenn R.	Assoc	494-4402	hueckel		PHD	72	Wisconsin	1972
Lynch, Gerald J.	Assoc	494-4388	lynch		PHD	75	Kentucky	1983
McCarthy, Patrick S.	Assoc	494-4460	mccarthy		PHD	76	Claremont	1978
Novshek, William	Assoc	494-4418	novshek		PHD	79	Northwes	1986

Pomery, John D. Assoc 494-4515 pomery PHD 77 Rochester 1982
Haveman, Jon Asst 494-4449 hvemanj PHD 92 Michigan 1992
Matheny, Ken Asst 494-4449 kmatheny PHD 92 UCLA 1992
Mehta, Shailendra Asst 494-5703 mehta PHD 90 Harvard 1990
Netz, Janet Asst 494-4452 netz PHD 92 Michigan 1994
Noussair, Charles Asst 494-4416 noussair PHD 93 Cal Tech 1994

Purdue University-Calumet Hammond, IN 46323 (219) 989-2388
Department of Management Sch of Professional Std Fax=989-2750 CALUMET.PURDUE.EDU
Silver, Gerald Dean 989-2468 Mgt EDD 74 Columbia 1989
Sil, Shomir H-Ac PHD
Das, Bhaskar Assoc 988-2313 PHD 91 Miss 1991
Jennings, E. James Assoc 989-2381 PHD 79 1978
McGrath, Paul T. Assoc 989-2425 PHD 88 N Illinois 1986

Quinnipiac College Hamden, CT 06518-1908 (203) 281-8720
Department of Economics School of Business Fax=281-8664
Strang, Roger A. Dean 281-8720 Mgt DBA Harvard
Martie, Charles W. C-Ac 281-5202 PHD Conn 1991
DeAndrea, Vincent F. Prof PHD 72 Mass 1968
Driscoll, Vincent R. Prof 281-8788 PHD New Sch 1969
Gius, Mark P. Asst PHD 91 Penn St 1994
Kelly, Tricia Asst PHD Mass 1995
Pace, William Asst PHD Conn 1995

Radford University Radford, VA 24142 (703) 831-5100 Ms. Teresa Grubb
Dept of Economics Col of Business & Econ Fax=831-6209
Blaylock, Bruce K. Dean 831-5300 Mgt PHD 80 Geo St 1994
Beeson, Bennie E. Jr. Prof 831-5891 PHD 71 Tennessee
Hashemzadeh, Nozar Prof 831-5888 PHD Va Tech
Wooley, Douglas C. Prof 831-5885 PHD Conn
Birecree, Adrieene M. Assoc 831-5887 PHD Notre Dm
Hayes, Michael N. Assoc 529-2836 PHD 86 Ca-Davis
Kasturi, Prahlad Assoc 831-5892 PHD Hawaii
Roufagalas, John Assoc 831-5999 PHD 86 Florida 1985
Santopietro, George D. Assoc 831-5889 PHD 86 Va Tech 1987
Wilson, Loretta S. Asst 831-5100 PHD 86 Mass

Ramapo Coll of New Jersey Mahwah, NJ 07430-1680 (201)
Economics Faculty School Adm & Business Fax=529-7508
Did Not Respond--Information Taken from College Catalog
Bond, Richard D-Pr 529-7500 PHD 72 Yale
McLewin, Phillip J. Assoc 529-7630 PHD 70 Cornell 1974

University of Redlands Redland, CA 92373 (909)
Department of Economics Business & Management Fax=
Segur, W. Hubbard C-Pr 335-4068 Busi PHD Ca-Davis 1989
Halvorsen, Marcia L. Prof 793-2121 PHD 78 Geo St 1975
Bandzak, Ruth Anne Asst MA Notre Dm 1988
Fazeli, Rafat R. Asst 793-2121 PHD 92 New Sch 1989
Makgetla, Neva S. Asst PHD Berlin 1987

Reed College Portland, OR 97202 (503) 771-1112 Lois Hobbs
Department of Economics Div History & Soc Sci Fax=777-7776 REED.EDU
Parker, Jeffrey A. C-Pr 771-1112 parker AECF PHD 81 Stanford 1988
George Hay Professor of Economics
Foley, Michael Asst 771-1112 mfoley ANQ ABD Michigan 1992
Hare, Denise Asst 771-1112 dhare AJOD PHD 92 Stanford 1992
Netusil, Noelwah R. Asst 771-1112 netusil AQDH PHD 92 Illinois 1990
Zygmont, Zenon X. Asst 771-1112 zzygmont APLF PHD 94 Geo Mason 1993

Regent University Virginia Bch, VA 23464-9850 (804) 579-4302 Mrs. Barbara Bilyk
Economics Faculty Robertson Sch of Govt Fax=579-4595 BEACON.REGENT.EDU
Munday, John C. Jr. Dean$ 579-4302 jmunday PHD Illinois 1983
Bom, Philip C. Prof 579-4303 philbom PHD Free 1983

Regis College - MA Weston, MA 02193 (617)
Economics Program Div of Social Sciences Fax=899-4725
phone: 893-1820
Oates, Sister Mary J. C-Pr Ext 2628 PHD 69 Yale 1970
Hewins, Dana C. Assoc Ext 2073 PHD 74 Illinois
Coiner, H. Michael Asst Ext 2073 PHD Yale

Regis College of Regis Univ	Denver, CO		80221 (303) 458-4170					
Economics Program	Div of Business		Fax=964-5485					
Valentine, Martha	D-As	458-4170						
Richard, James S.	Assoc	458-4185			PHD	80	Tx-Austin	1979
Seidenstricker, Kenneth C.	Assoc	458-4182			MA		Marquette	

Rensselaer Poly Institute	Troy, NY		12180-3590 (518) 276-6387				Betty Jean Kaufmann	
Department of Economics	Sch of Human & Soc Sci		Fax=276-4871					
Phelan, Thomas	Dean	276-6575		Hist	STL		Catholic	
Vitallano, Donald F.	C-Ac	276-8093			PHD		CUNY	
Diwan, Romesh K.	Prof	276-6386			PHD	65	Birmingh	
Gowdy, John M.	Prof	473-0769			PHD	80	W Virginia	1983
Hohenberg, Paul M.	Prof	276-8092			PHD	63	MIT	1977
MacDonald, James M.	Prof	276-8095			PHD	83	SUNY-Buf	1987
Norsworthy, J. Randolph	Prof	763-2337			PHD	66	Virginia	
O'Hara, Sabine	Asst				PHD		Goetting	
Stodder, James P.	Asst	276-4773			PHD		Yale	1990

University of Rhode Island	Kingston, RI		02881-0808 (401)					
Department of Economics	Col of Arts & Sciences		Fax=				URIACC.URI.EDU	
Rogers, Steffen H.	Dean			Soci	PHD	68	Vanderbilt	1991
Barnett, Harold C.	C-Pr	792-2070	hbarnett		PHD	73	MIT	1970
Burkett, John P.	Prof	792-4122			PHD	81	Berkeley	1981
Ramsay, Glenworth A.	Prof	792-4129			PHD	74	Boston C	1973
Ramstad, Yngve	Prof	792-4113			PHD	81	Berkeley	1982
Ramstad, Yngve	Prof	792-4113			PHD	81	Berkeley	1982
Starkey, James L.	Prof	792-2212			PHD	71	Boston C	1967
Larado, Leonard P.	Assoc	792-4128			PHD	79	Indiana	1981
McIntyre, Richard	Assoc	792-4126			PHD	89	Mass	1989
Mead, Arthur C.	Assoc	792-4123			PHD	78	Boston C	1976
Miller, Carole F.	Assoc	792-4111			PHD	88	Syracuse	1986
Sharif, Mohammed	Assoc	792-4119			PHD	83	Boston U	1984
Suzawa, Gilbert S.	Assoc	792-4125			PHD	73	Brown	1971
Latos, Charles	Asst	277-3830			PHD	77	Brown	1969

Rhode Island College	Providence RI		02908 (401) 456-8036				Norma Briere	
Dept of Econ & Management	Center for Mgt & Tech		Fax=456-8379				RIC.EDU	
Costa, Crist	C-Pr	456-8036			PHD			
Sahba, Nazanin	D	456-8283		Tech	PHD			
Moore, Peter R.	Prof	456-8037			PHD		Illinois	
Blais, Jeffrey	Assoc	456-8037			PHD	75	Pittsburgh	1986
Copur, Halil	Assoc	456-8036			PHD		Cornell	
on sabbatical 1995-96								
Kazemi, Abbas A.	Assoc	456-9557			PHD		SUNY-SBr	
Marks, Peter A.	Assoc	456-9529			PHD		N Carol	
Stecker, Albert	Assoc	456-9521			DBA		Indiana	
Karim, Aleman	Asst	456-9538			PHD		Boston U	

Rhodes College	Memphis, TN		38112-1690 (901) 726-3853				Jean Minmeir	
Dept of Economics & Bus Adm	Div Social Sciences		Fax=726-3718				VAX.RHODES.EDU	
Planchon, John M.	C-Ac	726-3978		Mktg	PHD		Alabama	
Bolch, Ben W.	Prof	726-3995			PHD	66	N Carol	1987
Iskander, Wasfy B.	Prof	726-3983			PHD		Indiana	
McMahon, Marshall E.	Prof	726-3795			PHD	72	Vanderbilt	1972
Orvis, Charles C.	Assoc	726-3922			PHD	75	Minnesota	1973
Rollosson, Michael	Inst	726-3566			ABD			1993

Rice University	Houston, TX		77005-1892 (713) 527-4875				Patsy Williams	
Economics Faculty	Department of Economics		Fax=285-5278				RICE.EDU	
Pomerantz, James	Dean	527-8101		Psyc				
Zodrow, George R.	C-Pr	527-4875	econ		PHD	80	Princeton	1979
Brito, Dagobert L.	Prof	527-4875			PHD	70	Rice	1984
George A. Peterkin Professor of Political Economy								
Brown, Bryan W.	Prof	527-8101	bwbwn		PHD	77	Penn	1983
Hargrove Professor of Economics								
Brown, James	Prof	527-8101						
Bryant, John B.	Prof	527-4875			PHD	75	Car Mellon	1981
Henry S. Fox, Sr. Professor of Economics								
Gillis, Malcolm	Prof	527-8101						
President								
Hartley, Peter R.	Prof	527-8101			PHD	80	Chicago	1986
Mieszkowski, Peter	Prof	527-8101			PHD	63	J Hopkins	1981
Cline Professor of Economics & Finance								
Sickles, Robin C.	Prof	527-8101			PHD	76	N Carol	1985
Smith, Gordon W.	Prof	527-8101			PHD	66	Harvard	1968

Name	Rank	Phone	Email	Field	Degree	Yr	School	Year
Soligo, Ronald	Prof	527-4843			PHD	64	Yale	1967
Chae, Suchan	Asst	527-8101			PHD	85	Penn	1985
Chang, Yoosoon	Asst	527-4875			PHD	95	Yale	1995
Dudey, Marc Peter	Asst	527-8101			PHD	84	Princeton	1990
Kim, Dae-il	Asst	527-8101			PHD	92	Chicago	1992
Merz, Monika	Asst	527-8101			PHD	94	Northwes	1994
Vella, Francis G. M.	Asst				PHD	90	Rochester	1990
Yi, Kei-Mu	Asst	527-8101			PHD	89	Chicago	1990

University of Richmond — Richmond, VA 23173 (804) 289-8587 — Angela McGrath
Department of Economics — E.C. Robins Sch of Bus Fax=289-8878 — URVAX

Name	Rank	Phone	Email	Field	Degree	Yr	School	Year
New, J. Randolph	Dean	289-8550		Mgt	PHD	78	Ariz St	1994
Cook, Robert W. Jr.	C-Ac	289-8561			PHD	81	Va Tech	1980
Edwards, N. Faye	Prof	289-8590			PHD	68	Kentucky	1968
Dolan, Robert C.	Assoc	289-8562			PHD	82	Rutgers	1980
Nicholson, Robert H.	Assoc	298-8565			PHD	72	N Carol	1972
Raines, J. Patrick	Assoc	289-8566			PHD		Alabama	1982
Schmidt, Robert M.	Assoc	289-8569			PHD	81	Duke	1981
Whitaker, David A.	Assoc	289-8560			PHD	71	Florida	1969
Wight, Jonathan B.	Assoc	289-8570			PHD	82	Vanderbilt	1982
Craft, Erik D.	Asst	287-6573			PHD	95	Chicago	1994
Dean, David H.	Asst	289-8559			PHD		Rutgers	1987
McGoldrick, Kim Marie	Asst	289-8575			PHD	93	SUNY-Bin	1992

Rider University — Lawrenceville NJ 08648-3099 (609)
Department of Economics — College of Business Adm Fax=896-5304 — RIDER

Name	Rank	Phone	Email	Field	Degree	Yr	School	Year
Sandberg, Mark E.	Dean	896-5152		Mgt	PHD	71	Cornell	1970
McCall, Charles W.	C-Ac	895-5562		EJ	PHD	82	Temple	1979
Corman, Hope	Prof	895-5559		IJKT	PHD	78	CUNY	1988
Gishlick, Herbert E.	Prof	895-5564		ER	PHD	73	Penn	1964
Talarico, Joseph F.	Prof	896-5126		F	PHD	58	Rutgers	1967
Bentley, Jerome T.	Assoc	895-5563			PHD		Pittsburgh	
Taga, Leonore S.	Assoc	895-5531			PHD	79	Berkeley	1986
Kaestner, Robert J.	Asst	895-5523		IJT	PHD	88	CUNY	1989

University of Rio Grande — Rio Grande, OH 45674 (614) 245-7267 — Carolyn Jolly
Department of Economics — E.E. Evans Col Bus Mgt Fax=245-7123

Name	Rank	Phone	Email	Field	Degree	Yr	School	Year
Kool, Krishna L.	Dean$	245-7268			PHD	76	Tennessee	1970
Kilby, C. Robert	Asst	245-7269			PHD	93	Cincinnati	1993
Straub, Paul	Asst	245-7388			PHD	91	Illinois	1995

Roanoke College — Salem, VA 24153-3794 (703) 375-2426 — Cathy Hoover
Economics Faculty — Dept of Bus Adm & Econ Fax=375-2426 — ACC.ROANOKE.EDU

Name	Rank	Phone	Email	Field	Degree	Yr	School	Year
Garren, Kenneth	Dean	375-2203		Math	PHD	68	Va Tech	1967
Lynch, Larry A.	C-Pr	375-2413	llynch	Mgt	PHD	87	Va Tech	1978
Fleming, Garry A.	Assoc	375-2509			PHD	87	Kentucky	
Lowry, Darryl W.	Assoc	375-2428			PHD	81	Berkeley	1981
Stauffer, Robert F.	Assoc	375-2427			PHD	78	Va Tech	

Robert Morris College — Coraopolis, PA 15108-1189 (412) 227-6859
Dept of Social Science — Sch of Appl Sci & Educ Fax=391-3329 — ROBERT-MORRIS.EDU

Name	Rank	Phone	Email	Field	Degree	Yr	School	Year
Shank, Jon	Dean	262-8279			EDD		Pittsburgh	
Norberg, Robert W.	C-As	227-6859			MA		Ind-Penn	1968
Litzinger, Patrick J.	Prof	262-8438			PHD	75	Pittsburgh	1977
Eschenfelder, Mark J.	Assoc				PHD	93	W Illin	
Lynch, James W.	Assoc				MA	72	Pittsburgh	1974
Reiland, Ralph R.	Assoc				MBA		Duquesne	
Zeman, Allan H.	Assoc	227-6844			PHD	78	Pittsburgh	1964
De Los Santos, Adora	Asst				PHD		Penn St	

University of Rochester — Rochester, NY 14627-0156 (716) 275-7221 — Janet Wood
Department of Economics — Col of Arts & Science Fax=256-2309 — CC.ROCHESTER.EDU

Name	Rank	Phone	Email	Field	Degree	Yr	School	Year
Aslin, Richard N.	Dean				PHD		Minnesota	
Stockman, Alan C.	C-Pr	275-7221	stoc@troi.		PHD	78	Chicago	1979
Wilson Professor of Economics								
Banks, Jeffrey S.	Prof	275-2954	bnks@troi.		PHD	86	Cal Tech	
Engerman, Stanley L.	Prof	275-3165	enge@dbv.		PHD	62	J Hopkins	1963
John Munro Professor of Economics								
France, Robert R.	Prof				PHD		Princeton	
Greenwood, Jeremy	Prof	275-1871	gree@db1.	D	PHD	83	Rochester	1992
Hanushek, Eric A.	Prof	275-5059	hanu@troi.		PHD	68	MIT	1978
Director, W.A. Wallis Institute of Political Economy								
Jones, Ronald W.	Prof	275-2688	jonr@troi.		PHD	56	MIT	1958
Xerox Professor of Economics								

Name	Rank	Phone	Email	Field	Degree	Yr	School	Year
McKenzie, Lionel W.	Emer	275-3096			PHD	42	Princeton	1957
Oi, Walter Y.	Prof	275-4991	oiwa@troi.		PHD	61	Chicago	1967
Elmer B. Milliman Professor of Economics								
Phelps, Charles E.	Prof	275-5149			PHD	73	Chicago	1984
Provost								
Plosser, Charles I.	Prof	275-3754			PHD	76	Chicago	1978
John M. Olin Distinguished Professor of Economics								
Thomson, William L.	Prof	275-2236	wth2@db1.		PHD		Stanford	
Bils, Mark	Assoc	275-0488	bils@db1.	D	PHD		MIT	
Boyd, John	Assoc	275-4239	boyj@troi.cc.		PHD		Indiana	
Hopenhayn, Hugo	Assoc	275-4081	huho@trio.		PHD		Minnesota	
Kahn, James A.	Assoc	275-5781			PHD	86	MIT	1986
Rebelo, Sergio	Assoc	275-4320	stre@troi.	D	PHD		Rochester	
Alononso, Irasema	Asst	275-4980	iral@trio.		PHD		Minnesota	
Campbell, Jeff	Asst	275-7307	jyrc@troi.		PHD		Northwes	1994
Hodgson, Doug	Asst	275-5782			PHD		Yale	
Jacoby, Hanan	Asst	275-0093	hanj@troi.		PHD	89	Chicago	1989
Krusell, Per	Asst	275-4903	pekr@troi.	O	PHD	92	Minnesota	1994
Leung, Siu Fai	Asst	275-5273	sfle@uordbv		PHD	87	Chicago	1988
Sundaram, Rangarajan K.	Asst	275-4196	rsdr@troi.		PHD		Cornell	
Wolkoff, Michael	Lect	275-5279	wolk@troi.		PHD		Michigan	
Deputy Chairperson, Department of Economics								

Rochester Inst of Technology Rochester, NY 14623-5604 (716)
Div Soc Sci-Dept of Econ Col of Liberal Arts Fax=475-7120 RITVAX.ISC.RIT.EDU

Name	Rank	Phone	Email	Field	Degree	Yr	School	Year
Daniels, William	Dean				PHD			
Vernarelli, Michael J.	C-Pr	475-2455			PHD	78	SUNY-Bin	1976
Hopkins, Thomas D.	Prof	475-6648	tdhgsm	DHK	PHD	71	Yale	1988
Arthur J. Gosnell Professor of Economics								
Humphries, John	Prof	475-6464			PHD	67	Syracuse	1962
Lee, Hoyoung	Prof	475-2406		ABDE	PHD		Maryland	1970
Dumangane, Constantino Sr.	Assoc	475-2807	econ.dwelop	GLDM	PHD		SUNY-Buf	1986
Mitchell, Jeannette C.	Asst	475-6077	jcmgsm	FOB	ABD		Utah	1985

Rockhurst College Kansas City, MO 64110-2508 (816)
Department of Economics School of Management Fax=926-4666 VAX1.ROCKHURST.EDU

Name	Rank	Phone	Degree	Yr	School	Year
Clark, Robert M.	Dean	926-4200	PHD	88	Syracuse	1991
McClelland, Patrick C.	VProf		PHD	81	American	1985
Tansey, Michael M.	Prof	273-3061	PHD	78	Wisconsin	1982
Arthur, E. Eugene	Assoc		DBA	75		1968
Miller, Gerald	Assoc		PHD		Notre Dm	1982
Stellern, Michael J.	Asst		PHD	83	Arizona	1979
Pirner, James	Lect		MA	67		1983
Rabbitt, Michael T.	Lect		MA	75	Wash U	1988

Rollins College Winter Park, FL 32789-4499 (407) 646-2569 Sharon Miller
Economics Faculty Department of Economics Fax=646-2600 ROLLINS

Name	Rank	Phone	Field	Degree	Yr	School	Year
Schutz, Eric A.	C-Ac	646-2509		PHD	82	N Carol	1987
Rock, Charles Patrick	Prof	646-2152		PHD	86	Cornell	1984
Hales, Waynes D.	Assoc	646-2407		PHD	74	Okla St	1971
Kypralos, Harry N.	Assoc	646-2510		PHD	87	Virginia	1983
Skelley, A. Chris	Assoc	646-2489		PHD	85	Brown	1987
Steen, Robert C.	Assoc	646-2614	RHN	PHD	82	Princeton	1987
Taylor, Kenna C.	Assoc	646-2312		PHD	79	Florida	1974

Roosevelt University Chicago, IL 60605-1394 (312) 341-3695
Dept Econ/Sch Policy Studies Col of Arts & Sciences Fax=341-3680 ROOSEVELT.EDU

Name	Rank	Phone	Degree	Yr	School	Year
Tallman, Ronald	Dean	341-3670				
Langer, Gary F.	D-Ac	341-3692	PHD	80	Mass	1983
Rosenberg, Sam	Prof	341-3697	PHD	75	Berkeley	1982
Balkin, Steven M.	Assoc	341-3696	PHD	76	Wayne St	1984
Lapidus, June	Assoc	341-3765	PHD	88	Mass	1990
Stein, Howard	Assoc	341-3692	PHD	83	Ca-River	1983
Baiman, Ron	Asst	341-3879	PHD	89	New Sch	1994

Rowan Col of New Jersey Glassboro, NJ 08028-1748 (609) 256-4060 Patricia Jenkins
Department of Economics School of Liberal Arts Fax= ELAN.ROWAN.EDU
phone 256-4500

Name	Rank	Phone	Email	Field	Degree	Yr	School	Year
Bartelt, Pearl	Dean	256-4850		Soci	PHD		Ohio State	1972
Hitchner, Benjamin	C-As	256-4061	hitchner		MS		Penn	1964
Hamer, Thomas P.	Prof	256-4062	hame7090		PHD	75	Claremont	1974
Jam, Habib O. E.	Assoc	Ext 3320			PHD		S Illinois	1979
Kressler, Peter	Assoc	Ext 3321			PHD		Penn	1972
Mukhoti, Bela	Assoc	Ext 3322			PHD	64	London	1974

Russell Sage College Troy, NY 12180-4115 (518) 270-2245 Mary Ghent
Economics Faculty Dept of Economics & Bus Fax=271-4545 SAGENET.EDU

Name	Rank	Phone	Email	Fields	Degree	Yr	School	Since
Dalton, Robert H.	C-As	270-2245			MBA	83	Syracuse	9-85
Melero, Francisco	Assoc				PHD		Rensselae	
Sabi, Manijeh	Assoc	270-2397			PHD	86	Northeas	1988
Tribble, John A.	Assoc	270-2296			PHD	75	Utah St	1976
Adamou, Nikolaos	Asst	270-2067			PHD	88	Rensselae	9-89

Rutgers University-Camden Camden, NJ 08102 (609) 225-6136 Pennie Prete
Department of Economics Col of Arts & Sciences Fax=225-6495 ZODIAC

Name	Rank	Phone	Email	Fields	Degree	Yr	School	Since
Catlin, Robert A.	Dean				PHD			
Seplaki, Les	C-Pr	225-6319			PHD	70	Ca-River	
Yamada, Tetsuji	Assoc	225-6025			PHD	87	CUNY	1987
Chen, Baolin	Asst	225-6025			PHD			
Na, Jinpeng	Asst	225-6025			PHD		SUNY-SBr	

Rutgers University-Newark Newark, NJ 07102 (201) 648-5259 Marilyn Johnson
Department of Economics Col of Arts & Sciences Fax=648-5819 DRACO.RUTGERS.EDU

Name	Rank	Phone	Email	Fields	Degree	Yr	School	Since
Hosford, David	Dean	648-5213		Hst	PHD			
Loeb, Peter D.	C-Pr	648-5259			PHD	73	Rutgers	1973
Coate, Douglas C.	Prof	648-5164			PHD	74	CUNY	1971
Cullity, John P.	Emer	648-5473			PHD	63	Columbia	1977
Troy, Leo	Prof	648-5529			PHD	58	Columbia	
Graham, John W. III	Assoc	648-5354			PHD	78	Northwes	1986
Seiglie, Carlos C.	Assoc	648-5914			PHD	91	Chicago	1986
VanderHoff, James H.	Assoc	648-5256			PHD	79	N Carol	1980
Cagliessi, Gabriella	Asst	648-5350			PHD		Penn	

Rutgers Univ-New Brunswick New BrunswickNJ 08903 (908) 932-7363
Department of Economics Faculty of Arts & Sci Fax=942-7416 ZODIAC.RUTGERS.EDU

Name	Rank	Phone	Email	Fields	Degree	Yr	School	Since
Foley, Richard F.	Dean	932-7896						
White, Eugene N.	C-Pr	932-7486	white	N	PHD	80	Illinois	1980
Blair, Douglas H.	Prof	932-7858	blair	D	PHD	76	Yale	1981
Bordo, Michael D.	Prof	932-7069	bordo	N	PHD	72	Chicago	1989
Dutta, Manoranjan	Prof	932-7054	dutta	E	PHD	62	Penn	1989
Gigliotti, Gary A.	Prof	932-7466	gigliott	D	PHD	78	Columbia	1978
Killingworth, Mark R.	Prof	932-7794		J	DPHI	77	Oxford	1978
Klein, Roger W.	Prof	932-7543	rogklein	C	PHD	70	Yale	1995
Marcus, Matityahu	Prof	932-7344		G	PHD	63	Brown	1962
McLean, Richard P.	Prof	932-7709	mclean	D	PHD	79	SUNY-SBr	1986
Perry, Martin K.	Prof	932-7850	mperry	L	PHD	76	Stanford	1989
Rockoff, Hugh T.	Prof	932-7857	rockoff	N	PHD	72	Chicago	1971
Rubin, Jeffrey I.	Prof	932-7452	jrubin	H	PHD	75	Duke	1973
Russell, Louise B.	Prof	932-6507	lrussell	I	PHD	71	Harvard	1987
Sato, Kazuo	Prof	932-7077		E	PHD	60	Yale	1984
Seneca, Joseph J.	Prof	932-7265		H	PHD	68	Penn	1976
Stuart, Robert C.	Prof	49708841	stuart	P	PHD	69	Wisconsin	1968
Tangri, Shanti S.	Prof	932-7460		O	PHD	61	Berkeley	1970
Taussig, Michael K.	Prof	932-7382	taussig	H	PHD	66	MIT	1967
Tsurumi, Hiroki	Prof	932-7932	tsurumi	C	PHD	67	Penn	1974
Gang, Ira N.	Assoc	932-7405	gang	O	PHD	83	Cornell	1986
Hartline, Jessie C.	Assoc	932-7951		G	PHD	68	Rutgers	1968
Hughes, Joseph P.	Assoc	932-7517		D	PHD	74	N Carol	1975
Prusa, Thomas	Assoc	932-8271	prusa	F	PHD	88	Stanford	1994
Sheflin, Neil	Assoc	932-7834	sheflin	C	PHD	79	Rutgers	1975
Sopher, Barry	Assoc	932-7197	sopher	D	PHD	88	Iowa	1987
Altshuler, Rosanne	Asst	932-7783	altshuler	H	PHD	88	Penn	1992
Chan, Sewin	Asst			H	PHD	95	Columbia	1995
Kim, Chulsoo	Asst	932-7080	chkim	E	PHD	90	Stanford	1990
Logan, John W. III	Asst	932-7469	jlogan	L	PHD	87	Cornell	1987
Mizrach, Bruce	Asst	932-8261	mizrach	E	PHD	87	Penn	1995
Moon, Choon-Geol	Asst	932-8259	moon	C	PHD	87	Stanford	1987
Moore, Bartholomew J.	Asst	932-7797	moore	E	PHD	90	Columbia	1990
Pietra, Tito	Asst	932-8108		D	PHD	89	Penn	1988
Romeo, Charles J.	Asst	932-8260		C	PHD	89	Duke	1990
Simard, Dominique	Asst	932-7491	simard	E	PHD	92	Queen's	1991

on leave to New York University 1995-96

Sacred Heart University Fairfield, CT 06432 (203) 371-7953
Economics Program Fac Fin Stds,Govt & Law Fax=365-7538 SHU.SACREDHEART.EDU

Name	Rank	Phone	Email	Fields	Degree	Yr	School	Since
Corrigan, Tom D.	C-Ac				PHD		Maryland	
Orlowski, Lucjan T.	Prof		orlowski	EFGP	PHD	79	Poland	1983
Frangul, Ramzi N.	Assoc				PHD		NYU	
Lim, Ralph	Assoc		lim	GLM	MBA		Penn	
Yatrakis, Pan G.	Assoc		yatr_pan	DEFI	PHD		NYU	
Mangiero, Susan M.	Asst		mangiero	ACDG	ABD		Conn	

Saginaw Valley State Univ — Univ Center, MI 48710 (517)
Department of Economics — Col of Business & Mgt Fax=790-7656 — SVSU.EDU

Name	Rank	Phone	Email	Field	Degree	Yr	School	Year
Carlson, Severin C.	Dean	790-4064		Fnce	DBA	79	Indiana	1994
Novey, Donald F.	C-Pr	790-4352			MS		S Dak St	1969
Kanthi, Mahendra S.	Prof	790-4379			PHD		Kentucky	1984
Park, Hong Youl	Prof	790-4084			PHD	75	Utah St	1975
Sarkar, Shyamalendu S.	Prof	790-4367			PHD	69	Mich St	1969
Welch, William P.	Assoc	790-5605			PHD	86	U Wash	1986

St. Ambrose University — Davenport, IA 52803 (319) 383-5985 — Caryl S. Catlin
Dept of Econ & Bus Admin — College of Business Fax=328-6409 — SAUNIX.SAU.EDU

Name	Rank	Phone	Email	Field	Degree	Yr	School	Year
Jensen, James O.	Dean	383-8759	jjensen	Mgt	PHD	69	Iowa	1980
Harris, Ralph	C-Pr	383-8962	rharris	Stat	PHD	73	Iowa	1993
Begin, Floyd C.	Prof	383-8701	fbegin		PHD	74	Iowa	1985
Chohan, Ray V.	Prof	383-8738	rchohan		PHD	75	Port St	1978
Kabis, Zeinhom M.	Prof	383-8739	zkabis		PHD	68	Illinois	1973
Oberle, Wayne H.	Prof	383-8719	woberle		PHD		Missouri	1977
Woodruff, Theodore S.	Prof	383-5985	twoodruf		PHD		Columbia	1995
Hall, Phillip	Assoc	phall			PHD		Nebraska	1995
Lee, Christopher	Assoc		clee		PHD	90	Geo Mason	1995
Lynn, Billy	Assoc	383-5490	blynn		PHD	94	Illinois	1994
Mullins, James E.	Assoc	383-8714	jmullins		MA	65	Marquette	1969
Tracy, William T.	Assoc	383-8756	wtracy		EDD		Marquette	1979
Bereskin, C. Gregory	Asst	383-8867	gbereskn		PHD	83	Missouri	1991
Hammermeister, John	Asst	383-8922	jhammerr		MBA		Oregon	
Lindemann, Bonnie L.	Asst	383-8750	blindemn		PHD	93	Iowa	1984
Shovlain, Raymond J.	Asst	383-8773	rshovlan		MBA	80	StAmbros	1982
Byrne, John	Inst	328-6406	jbyrne		MBA		Notre Dm	

Saint Anselm College — Manchester, NH 03102-1310 (603)
Economics Faculty — Dept of Economics & Bus Fax=641-7116

Name	Rank	Phone	Email	Field	Degree	Yr	School	Year
Romps, John F.	C-Ac	641-7140		ABEH	MA	68	Fordham	1968
Kenison, Arthur M.	Prof	641-7138		ACG	PHD	80	Boston U	1980
Kenison, Jeanne H.	Assoc	669-1030		C	EDD	86	Vanderbilt	1988
Minor, Frank	Assoc	641-7125			PHD			
Moses, Anthony T.	Assoc	641-7139			PHD			
Becker, Gilbert B.	Asst	641-7134		AD	PHD	83	Boston C	1987

College of Saint Benedict — St Joseph, MN 56374 (612) 363-5383
Economics Faculty — Department of Economics Fax=363-3298 — CSBSJU.EDU
share faculty with Saint John's Univ, Collegeville MN

Name	Rank	Phone	Email	Field	Degree	Yr	School	Year
Rambeck, Charles	C-Ac	363-3524						
Friedrich, Joseph	Prof				MA	70	Wisconsin	1967
Diedrich, Ernest R.	Assoc				PHD	83	Colo St	
Finn, Daniel Rush	Assoc				PHD	77	Chicago	1977
Clemens Chair in Economics and the Liberal Arts-Dean, School of Theology								
Litterst, Laurence J.	Assoc	363-5917			PHD	81	N Illinois	1979
Olson, John F.	Assoc	363-5406			PHD	84	Rochester	1985
Lewis, Margaret	Asst	363-5977			PHD	89	Maryland	1989

Saint Bonaventure Univ — S Bonaventure NY 14778 (716)
Economics Faculty — Sch of Business Admin Fax=375-2191 — SBU.EDU

Name	Rank	Phone	Email	Field	Degree	Yr	School	Year
Burns, John H.	Dean	375-2200		Fnce	PHD	70	Mich St	1991
Kirk, Eugene F.	Asst	375-2069		G	PHD	74	Boston C	1972

College of St. Catherine — St Paul, MN 55105 (612) 690-8717
Economics Faculty — Department of Economics Fax=690-6024 — ALEX.STKATE.EDU

Name	Rank	Phone	Email	Field	Degree	Yr	School	Year
Ashley, James R.	C-Ac	690-6852	jrashley	AL	PHD	84	Wisconsin	1984
Jewell, Nasrin	Prof	690-6830		OA	PHD	81	Wisconsin	1981
Shikha, Deep	Asst	690-6577		FA	PHD	77	LSU	1985

St. Cloud State University — Saint Cloud, MN 56301-4498 (612) 255-2227
Department of Economics — Col of Social Sciences Fax=654-5198 — STCLOUD.MSUS.EDU

Name	Rank	Phone	Email	Field	Degree	Yr	School	Year
Merritt, Raymond	Dean	255-4790			PHD	68	Minnesota	1985
Luksetich, William A.	C-Pr	255-4291	a00001		PHD	73	N Illinois	1972
Edwards, Mary E.	Prof	255-3742	edwards		PHD	88	Tx A&M	1985
Gallagher, Daniel J.	Prof	255-3051	s00008		PHD	76	Maryland	1982
Gleisner, Richard F.	Prof	255-3052	b00001		PHD	72	Geotown	1968
Larkin, L. Andrew	Prof	255-2298	larkin		PHD	82	Nebraska	1982
Lofgreen, Harold A.	Prof	255-4250	lofgreen		PHD	72	Iowa	1972
Director, Social Science Research Institute								
Moghaddam, Masoud	Prof	255-4209	masoud		PHD	82	Iowa St	1983
White, Michael D.	Prof	255-3163	mdwhite		PHD	78	Tx Tech	1978
Banaian, King	Assoc	255-2209	a00050		PHD	86	Claremont	1984

Name	Rank	Phone	Email	Field	Degree	Yr	School	Year
Bodvarsson, Orn B.	Assoc	255-2968	i00042		PHD	86	Simon Fr	1988
Hampton, Nathan E.	Assoc	255-3825	h00003		PHD	89	Ca-SnBarb	1987
Masih, Nolin	Assoc	255-3051			PHD	88	Kansas	1964
Kang, Eungmin B.	Asst	654-5223	kang		PHD	90	Geo St	1990
MacDonald, Richard A.	Asst	255-4781	macdonald		PHD	92	SUNY-Buf	1989
Director, Center for Economic Education								
Nold-Hughes, Patricia A.	Asst	255-2076	nold		PHD	91	Ca-SnBarb	1988
Patridge, Mark	Asst				PHD	91	Illinois	1995

St. Edward's University Austin, TX 78704-6489 (512) 448-8550
Department of Economics Sch of Behav & Soc Sci Fax=448-8492

Name	Rank	Phone	Email	Field	Degree	Yr	School	Year
Hopper, Marianne F.	Dean			CrJu	PHD	79		1977
Koch, James C.	C-Ac	448-8453			MSIR	59	Loyola-C	1960
Tombe, Wani Luan	Asst	448-8599			PHD	85	Tx-Austin	1990

St. Francis College-NY Brooklyn Hght NY 11201 (718) Ext 266
Economics Faculty Economics Department Fax=522-1274
phone: 522-2300

Name	Rank	Phone	Email	Field	Degree	Yr	School	Year
Quick, Paddy	C-Pr	Ext 266		ABN	PHD	75	Harvard	9-85
Santiago, Aida E.	Asst	Ext 266		ABJO	MA		New Sch	9-85

St. John Fisher College Rochester, NY 14618 (716)
Economics Faculty Department of Economics Fax= SJFC.EDU

Name	Rank	Phone	Email	Field	Degree	Yr	School	Year
Pate, David S.	C-Ac	385-8120	dp1518	J	PHD	85	Iowa St	1987
Maley, Jean E.	Prof	385-8097			PHD	72	Rochester	1968
Linsley, Colin A.	Assoc	385-8099		N	PHD	86	Essex	1987
Maggs, Gary E.	Assoc	385-8432		E	PHD	86	W Virginia	1986
Roche, John T.	Assoc	385-8119			PHD	81	Mass	1981
Filson, Darren	VInst	385-8161		L	ABD		Rochester	1995

St. John's University Jamaica, NY 11439 (718)
Dept of Economics & Finance Col of Business Admin Fax=591-8784 STJOHNS.EDU

Name	Rank	Phone	Email	Field	Degree	Yr	School	Year
Mauer, Laurence J.	Dean	990-6477			PHD	67	Tennessee	1983
Associate Vice President								
Angelini, Anthony L. P.	C-Ac	990-6420			MA	51	Temple	
Carvounis, Christos C.	Prof				PHD		New Sch	
Eng, Maximo	Prof	990-6161			PHD	66	NYU	1985
Distinguished Professor								
Jain, Chaman Lal	Prof				PHD		American	
Lawson, Stanley J.	Prof	990-6161			PHD	73	NYU	1978
Lees, Francis A.	Prof	990-6161			PHD	61	NYU	1961
Marshall, John F.	Prof				PHD		SUNY-SBr	
Rider, Christine	Prof	969-8000			PHD	79	New Sch	1976
Simunek, Vladimir J.	Prof				PHD		Charles	
Bansal, Vipul	Assoc							
Buechner, M. Northup	Assoc	990-6161			PHD	71	Virginia	1970
Chen, Thomas P.	Assoc	990-7347			PHD		CUNY	
Choi, Young Back	Assoc	876-3101			PHD	86	Michigan	
Clark, Charles	Assoc	990-7343			PHD	90	New Sch	1985
Conhaim, Louis E.	Assoc	990-6161			PHD	60	Columbia	1979
Ellis, Mary Elizabeth	Assoc				PHD		S Carol	
Englander, Valerie	Assoc	390-4545			PHD	75	Rutgers	1982
Flowers, Edward B.	Assoc				PHD		Geo St	
Furfero, Arlene J.	Assoc				PHD		Rutgers	
Giacalone, Joseph A.	Assoc	990-6161			PHD	71	Columbia	1985
Gokturk, S. Sadik	Assoc				PHD		Columbia	
Gordon, Sara L.	Assoc	969-6161			PHD	71	Stanford	1978
Liaw, K. Thomas	Assoc	990-6161	liawt		PHD	88	Northwes	9-88
Little, Charles H.	Assoc				PHD		Calif	
Associate Director & Managing Editor, Business Research Institute								
Maran, Michael J.	Assoc				PHD		Penn	
Pappas, Anthony	Assoc							
Shapiro, Aharon H.	Assoc	969-8000			PHD	66	New Sch	1967
Tomic, Igor M.	Assoc				PHD		CUNY	
Haye, Eric M.	Asst				PHD	90	SUNY-Bin	1990
Moy, Ronald L.	Asst				PHD	90	Rutgers	
Terregrossa, Ralph A.	Asst				PHD		SUNY-Bin	
Wong, Kwok-Fai Matthew	Asst				PHD		Manitoba	
Yuyuenwomjgwatana, Robert	Asst							
Pizzigno, Gregory D.	Adj				MBA		St Johns	
Assistant Dean & Director of Graduate Program								

Saint Joseph's University	Philadelphia, PA 19131-1395 (215) 660-1593					Mrs. Dori Pappas	
Department of Economics	Col of Arts & Sciences Fax=473-0001					SJU.EDU	
McCarthy, Vincent A.	Dean		Phil	PHD	74	Stanford	1989
Provost							
Prendergast, George A.	C-Pr	660-1592		PHD	72	Penn	1956
Bookman, Milica Zarkovic	Assoc	660-1590		PHD	83	Temple	1983
Dragonette, Joseph E.	Assoc	660-1594		PHD	74	Penn	1967
Pryor, Zora P.	VAsoc	660-1593		PHD	69	Harvard	1984
Fox, Nancy R.	Asst	660-1596		PHD	89	Penn	1986

St. Lawrence University	Canton, NY 13617 (315) 386-5430						Karen Pcolar	
Economics Faculty	Department of Economics Fax=386-5819						MVSCI.STLAWU.EDU	
Richardson, David H.	C-Pr	379-5431	dric	CJEF	PHD	63	Purdue	1979
Charles A. Dana Professor of Economics								
Young, Jeffrey T.	Prof	379-5427	jyou	BQ	PHD	75	Colorado	1980
Blewett, Robert Allan	Assoc	379-5429	rble	OHR	PHD	80	Va Tech	1983
FitzRandolph, Peter Winfield	Assoc	379-5425	pfit	FN	PHD	79	Tufts	1973
Stevens, Sarah Allen	Assoc	379-5969	sste	FE	PHD	88	J Hopkins	1984
Vrooman, David H. Jr.	Assoc	379-5428		GE	PHD	76	SUNY-Alb	1965
Deitz, Richard	VAsst			RHL	ABD	95	SUNY-Bin	1995
Horwitz, Steven G.	Asst		shor	EPB	PHD	90	Geo Mason	1989
Rudolph, Linda	Asst			QKL	ABD	95	Conn	1995

Saint Louis University	St. Louis, MO 63108 (314) 977-3848					Audrey Reilly	
Department of Economics	Sch of Business Admin Fax=977-3897					SLUVCA.SLU.EDU	
Seitz, Neil E.	Dean	977-3833	Fnce	PHD	73	Ohio St	1975
Welch, Patrick J.	C-Pr	977-3848		PHD	73	Pittsburgh	1983
Grossman, Leroy J.	Prof	977-3830		PHD	63	Vanderbilt	1964
Stevenson, Thomas M. Jr.	Prof	977-3845		PHD	64	Illinois	1965
Roman, Paul D.	Assoc	977-3844		PHD	67	St Louis	1966
Chaney, Rick L.	Asst	977-3862		PHD	84	Illinois	1986
Dean St Louis-Madrid							
Cremers, Emily T.	Asst	977-7154		PHD	91	Minnesota	1992
Islam, Muhammad Q.	Asst	977-3822		PHD		Indiana	1988
Strauss, Jack K.	Asst	977-3813		PHD		Duke	

Saint Martin's College	Lacey, WA 98503-1297 (360) 438-4512				Linda Newman	
Economics Faculty	Div Business & Econ Fax=438-4522					
Knutson, Jerry L.	Dean	438-4512	MBA	83	Puget Sd	1987
Wallace, Don	Asst	438-4329	PHD	63	U Wash	

Saint Mary's College-CA	Moraga, CA 94575-4230 (510) 631-4607							
Economics Faculty	Sch of Econ & Bus Adm Fax=326-4027						STMARYS-CA.EDU	
Epstein, Edwin M.	Dean	631-4604	eepstein	BLaw	LLD	61	Yale	1994
Bodily, Jerry J.	C-Pr	631-4607	jbodily		PHD		Purdue	1978
Chase, Kristine L.	Prof	631-4590	kchase		PHD	87	Maryland	1985
Lee, William C.	Prof	631-4589	wlee		PHD	77	Ca-SnBarb	1982
Allen, Roy E.	Assoc	631-4595	rallen		PHD		Berkeley	1985
Hannon, Joan U.	Assoc	631-4588	jhannon		PHD	78	Wisconsin	1987
Moseldjord, Asbjorn	Assoc	631-4596	amoseidj		PHD		Ca-SnBarb	1991
Wingate, Stanley R.	Asst	631-4061	swingate		PHD		Oregon	1988

Saint Marys College-IN	Notre Dame, IN 46556-5001 (219)							
Economics Faculty	Dept Bus Admin & Econ Fax=284-4716						SAINTMARYS.EDU	
McElroy, Jerome L.	C-Pr	284-4488	jmcelroy	AEFO	PHD	71	Colorado	8-82
Measell, Richard F.	Asst	284-4525		ADHJ	PHD	85	Maryland	8-83

St. Mary's University-TX	San Antonio, TX 78284 (210) 436-3112						
Department of Economics	Sch of Human & Soc Sci Fax=436-3500						
Miller, Charles H.	Dean		Theo	STD	73	Rome	
Robbins, Roy E.	C-As			MA	75	St Marys	
Manuel, David P.	Prof			PHD	75	Miss	
Velez, Alejandro	Prof			PHD	77	Florida	
Scott, Gary J.	Asst	436-3111		PHD	93	Notre Dm	1994

Saint Michael's College	Colchester, VT 05439-0125 (802) 654-2298							
Economics Faculty	Department of Economics Fax=655-3680						SMCVAX.SMVT.EDUC	
Versteeg, Jennie G.	C-Pr	654-2298	versteeg	ANFO	PHD	74	Clark	1980
Kessel, Herbert	Prof	654-2460	kessel	AJDC	PHD	81	Boston U	1977
Carvellas, John N.	Assoc	654-2365	carvellas	ACER	PHD	81	Syracuse	1974
Ramazani, M. Reza	Asst	654-2360	ramazani	AFEC	PHD	90	Colorado	1986

St. Norbert College — DePere, WI 54115-2099 (414)
Department of Economics — Div of Social Sciences Fax=337-4098

Name	Rank	Phone	Email	Field	Degree	Yr	School	Year
King, Elizabeth G.	C-Ac			PolS	PHD		Missouri	1973
Mammen, Thampy	C-Pr	337-3230			PHD	67	Penn	1968
Manion, Thomas A. President	Prof				PHD		Clark	1983
Odorzynski, Sandra J.	Assoc	337-3224			PHD	76	Purdue	1978
Paul, Sanjay	Asst	337-3889			PHD	92	SUNY-Buf	1992
Quinn, Kevin G.	Asst	337-3447			PHD		Il-Chicago	

St. Olaf College — Northfield, MN 55057-1098 (507) 646-3149 — Lauretta Anderson
Economics Faculty — Department of Economics Fax=646-3523 — STOLAF.EDU

Name	Rank	Phone	Email	Field	Degree	Yr	School	Year
Schodt, David W.	C-Pr	646-3156	schodt	OAH	PHD	80	Wisconsin	1977
Carlson, William L.	Prof	646-3152	carlson	C	PHD		Michigan	1973
Dalgaard, Bruce R. Husby-Johnson Professor in Business & Ecnonmics	Prof	646-3567	dalgaard	EPA	PHD	76	Illinois	1992
Emery, E. David	Prof	646-3139	emeryd	DIA	PHD	69	Minnesota	1969
Gery, Frank W.	Prof	646-3150	gery		PHD	57	Boston U	1962
Becker, Anthony D.	Assoc	437-2882	becker	DLC	PHD		Duke	1987
Chadwick, Kathy	Assoc	646-3154	chadwick	M	PHD		Northwes	1985
Emery, Mary Ann	Assoc	646-3139	emerym	M	MA	65	Minnesota	1969
Judge, Rebecca P.	Assoc	646-3151	judge	ADQ	PHD	76	Duke	1987
Soderlind, Steven D.	Assoc	646-3153	soderlin	RA	PHD	80	Mass	1982
Wahl, Jenny Bourne	Assoc	646-3639	wahl	ADH	PHD	85	Chicago	1988
Ashman, James G. Director, Paul & Anne Finstad Center for Entrepreneurial Studies	Asst	646-3814		M	MA		Minnesota	1993
Geodde, Richard	Asst	646-3126	goedde	M	MBA		Wisconsin	1988
Ophaug, John	Asst	646-3149			JD		Minnesota	1978
Pernecky, Mark L.	Asst	646-3432	pernecky	EJA	PHD	90	Notre Dm	1990
Pomponio, Xun	Asst	646-3151	pomponio	FP	PHD		Penn St	1991
Wojick, Paul P.	Asst	646-3152	wojick	AE	PHD	89	Colorado	1988
Evans, Shirley	Inst	646-3154	evanssh	M	MBT		Minnesota	1985

Saint Peter's College — Jersey City, NJ 07306 (201) 915-9250 — Nancy Carbone
Economics Faculty — Department of Economics Fax=

Name	Rank	Phone	Email	Field	Degree	Yr	School	Year
D'Amico, Thomas F.	C-Ac				PHD	83	NYU	1982
Maher, William F. X.	Prof				PHD		Boston C	1965
Manna, Rolando N.	Inst				MA		NYU	1988
Packer, Stephen B.	Lect				MA		Chicago	1989

College of Saint Rose — Albany, NY 12203 (518) 458-5272 — Lisa DeMase
Economics Faculty — School of Business Fax=458-5449

Name	Rank	Phone	Email	Field	Degree	Yr	School	Year
Hurley, Michael W.	AcDn	458-5465		HumR	PHD			
Mehtabdin, Khalid R.	Assoc	458-5467			PHD	79	Pittsburgh	1986
Sung, Simona	Asst	458-5269			PHD			

College of St. Scholastica — Duluth, MN 55811-4199 (218)
Economic Faculty — Dept of Management Fax= — CSS1.CSS.EDU

Name	Rank	Phone	Email	Field	Degree	Yr	School	Year
Edwards, Barbara	C-As	723-6150			PHD		Minnesota	8-94
Kotamraju, Pradeep	Asst	723-6715			PHD	89	Illinois	1995
Barrett, Anthony		723-6471			PHD			

St. Thomas University-FL — Miami, FL 33054 (305)
Economic Faculty/Dept of Mgt — School of Business Adm Fax=

Name	Rank	Phone	Email	Field	Degree	Yr	School	Year
Kalogeras, Gus	Dean	628-6776		Fnce	PHD	74	Baruch	1993
Bradley, John H.	C-Pr	628-6598		Mgt	DCS	78	Georgia	1978
Carrillo, Raul J.	Assoc				DA		U Miami	1972
Flax, Stanley	Asst				MBA		NYU	1986

University of St. Thomas-MN — St. Paul, MN 55105-1096 (612) 962-5675 — Christine Igielski
Economics Faculty — Div of Social Sciences Fax=962-6360 — STTHOMAS.EDU
phone 962-5000

Name	Rank	Phone	Email	Field	Degree	Yr	School	Year
Carroci, Noreen	Dean	962-5000						
Fairchild, Daniel R.	C-Ac	962-5676	drfairchild	F	PHD	78	St Louis	1976
Jones, David D.	Prof	962-5675		E	PHD	75	Indiana	1972
Alexander, Susan L.	Assoc	962-5677	slalexander	F	PHD	77	So Meth	1981
Blumenthal, Marsha A.	Assoc	962-5678	mablumenthal	JH	PHD	85	Minnesota	1984
Garhart, Robert E. Jr.	Assoc	962-5679	regarhart	R	PHD	82	Pittsburgh	1981
Gray, Charles M.	Assoc	962-4301	cmgray	K	PHD	78	Wash U	1976
Kreitzer, Joseph L.	Assoc	962-5683	jlkreitzer	C	PHD		Iowa	1981
Langan, Terence G.	Assoc	962-5684	t9langan	L	PHD	88	Minnesota	
Marcott, Craig S.	Assoc	962-5685	csmarcott	C	PHD		Purdue	1982
Selim, Mohamed Ali	Assoc	962-5180	maselim	A	PHD		Minnesota	1959
Vincent, James W.	Assoc	962-5689	jwvincent	Q	PHD	82	Wisconsin	1988
Walsh, William J.	Assoc	962-5690	wjwalsh	E	PHD		Notre Dm	1970
Papagapitos, Agapipos	Asst	962-5686	a9papagapitos	OP	PHD		Ohio St	
Riley, Robert	Asst	962-5687	rjriley	F	PHD		Wisconsin	
Supel, Mary R.	Asst	962-5688	m9supel	L	BA		Denison	1976

University of St. Thomas-TX Houston, TX 77006-4696 (713) 525-2100
Department of Economics Cameron Sch of Business Fax=525-2110

Name	Rank	Phone	Email	Field	Degree	Yr	School	Since
Ho, Yhi-Min	Dean	522-7911		OQ	PHD	65	Vanderbilt	8-70
Hugh Roy and Lillie Cullen Professor of Economics								
Wilbratte, Barry J.	C-Pr	522-7911		FG	PHD	71	Tulane	1971
Morefield, Roger D.	Assoc	522-7911		I	PHD	77	Duke	1980
Shirvani, Hassan M.	Assoc	522-7911		FG	PHD	79	Harvard	1986
Yazdi, Khalil	Assoc	522-7911		M	PHD	87	Houston	1990
Canac, Pierre	Asst	522-7911		F	PHD	87	Houston	1990

Saint Vincent College Latrobe, PA 15650-2690 (412) 539-9761
Economics Faculty Department of Economics Fax=537-4554

Name	Rank	Phone	Email	Field	Degree	Yr	School	Since
Quinlivan, Gary M.	C-Pr			F	PHD	83	SUNY-Alb	1981
Weissert, Lee J.	Asst				MA		Pittsburgh	1988

Salem State College Salem, MA 01970-4589 (508)
Department of Economics Sch of Business & Econ Fax=741-6027

Name	Rank	Phone	Email	Field	Degree	Yr	School	Since
Burton, Wayne M.	Dean	741-6640			EDD	91	Vanderbilt	
Wesolowski, Karl A.	C-Ac	741-6636			MA		Boston C	
Calabro, Eugene A.	Prof	741-6653			MA		Boston C	
Lucas, Henry A. Jr.	Assoc	741-6683			JD		Suffolk	
Crofts, Robert D.	Asst	741-6615			MA		Northeas	
Pawlak, Andrew T.	Asst	741-6682			MA		Tufts	
Siden, Dorothy R.	Asst	741-6681			PHD	90	Northeas	

Salisbury State University Salisbury, MD 21801-6860 (410)
Department of Economics Perdue Sch of Business Fax=543-6068 SAE.SSU.UMD.EDU

Name	Rank	Phone	Email	Field	Degree	Yr	School	Since
Bebee, Richard F.	Dean	543-6316	rfbebee	Atg	PHD	71	Colorado	7-91
Greene, Benjamin B. Jr.	Assoc	543-6315	bbgreene		PHD	74	Boston C	8-78
Kraft, Evan	Asst	543-6315	evkraft		PHD	90	New Sch	8-90
Ralston, Scott N.	Asst	543-6315	sxralston		PHD	88	Tennessee	8-88
Upadhyaya, Kamal	Lect	543-6315	kxupadhaya		PHD	93	Auburn	1993

Salve Regina University Newport, RI 02840-4192 (401) 847-6650
Economics Faculty Department of Economics Fax=

Name	Rank	Phone	Email	Field	Degree	Yr	School	Since
Lawber, Harold E. Jr.	C-Ac	847-6650		ABEN	PHD	89	Conn	1988
Tang, Gloria	Assoc	847-6650		COT	PHD	94	Walden	1986
Tonn, Victor Lux	Assoc	847-6650		CFGO	PHD	84	Utah St	1984
Coughlan, Carmel	Asst	847-6650			MBA	90	Salve Rg	1990

Sam Houston State Univ Huntsville, TX 77341 (409) 294-1265 Ms. Sally Kundig
Dept of Econ & Bus Analysis Col of Business Admin Fax=294-3612 SHSU.EDU

Name	Rank	Phone	Email	Field	Degree	Yr	School	Since
Gilmore, James E.	Dean	294-1254	gba.jeg	Fnce	EDD	69	Houston	1956
Green, William B.	C-Pr	294-1265	eco_wbg		PHD	74	LSU	1974
Samuels, George E.	Prof	294-1269	eco_ges		PHD	72	Oregon	1975
Sweeney, Vernon E.	Prof	294-1273	eco_ves		PHD	68	Tx-Austin	1971
Townsend, David C.	Prof	294-1264	eco_dct		PHD	53	LSU	1982
Bumpass, Donald L.	Assoc	294-1268	eco_dlb		PHD	76	Okla St	1992
Beaty, Valerie P.	Asst	294-3712	eco_vxb		ABD		Tx A&M	1993
Greenwade, George D.	Asst	294-1266	eco_gdg		PHD	88	Tx Tech	1986
Muehsam, Mitchell J.	Asst	294-1243	eco_mjm		PHD	89	Tx A&M	1989

Samford University Birmingham, AL 35229 (205) 870-2367 Lu Dennis
Economics Faculty School of Business Fax=870-2464

Name	Rank	Phone	Email	Field	Degree	Yr	School	Since
Clark, William	Dean$	870-2308			PHD		Arkansas	1994
Hendon, Fred N.	Prof	870-2549			PHD	68	Alabama	1968
Marshall, Jennings B.	Prof	870-2539			PHD		Kentucky	1986

University of San Diego San Diego, CA 92110-2492 (619)
Department of Economics Sch of Business Admin Fax=260-4891 ACUSD.EDU

Name	Rank	Phone	Email	Field	Degree	Yr	School	Since
Burns, James M.	Dean	260-4886		Mgt	DBA	68	Harvard	1974
Anderson, Joan B.	Prof	260-4857			PHD	71	Ca-SnDgo	1981
O'Neil, Robert F.	Prof				PHD	75	Fordham	
Yandell, Dirk	Prof				PHD	81	Purdue	1981
Allen, Andrew T.	Assoc	260-4832			PHD	83	Illinois	1984
Dimon, Denise	Assoc	260-4836			PHD	86	Illinois	1983
Gin, Alan	Assoc	260-4883			PHD	87	Ca-SnBarb	1988
Holt, Charles F.	Assoc	291-6480			PHD	70	Purdue	1973
Narwold, Andrew	Assoc	260-4875			PHD	91	Ca-SnBarb	1991
Sandy, Jonathan G.	Assoc	260-4880			PHD	86	Ca-SnBarb	1986

San Diego State University	San Diego, CA 92182-4485 (619) 594-1675					Marie Butler 594-5530		
Department of Economics	Col of Arts & Letters Fax=594-5062					SDSU.EDU		
Strand, Paul J.	Dean				PHD		Ohio St	1977
Boddy, Raford D.	C-Pr	594-5530			PHD	68	Michigan	1980
Adler, Ranatte K.	Prof	594-1662			PHD		New Mex	1982
Clement, Norris C.	Prof	594-5860			PHD		Colorado	1968
Frantz, Roger S.	Prof	594-3718			PHD		Wash St	1978
Green, Louis C.	Prof	594-5680			PHD		Berkeley	1976
Grossbard-Shechtman, Shoshan	Prof	594-5468			PHD	78	Chicago	1981
Kartman, Arthur E.	Prof	594-5539			PHD	69	U Wash	1968
Madhaven, Murugappa C.	Prof	594-5492			PHD	69	Wisconsin	1968
Nam, Woo Hyun	Prof	594-5478			PHD		U Wash	1968
Stewart, Douglas B.	Prof	594-5502			PHD	70	Oregon	1971
Thayer, Mark A.	Prof	594-5510			PHD		New Mex	1981
Venieris, Yiannis P.	Prof	594-5503			PHD		Oregon	1967
Gerber, James B.	Assoc	594-5532			PHD	86	Ca-Davis	1985
Hambleton, John W.	Assoc	594-5458			PHD	71	Wisconsin	1969
Steinberg, Danny	Assoc	594-1670			PHD	82	Harvard	1987
Dazimi, Camilla	Asst	594-1675			PHD	95	Ca-Irvine	1995

University of San Francisco	San Francisco CA 94117-1080 (415) 666-6671							
Department of Economics	Col of Arts & Sciences Fax=666-2346					USFCA.EDU		
Nel, Stanley D.	Dean	666-6172		Fnce	PHD	80	Cape Twn	1983
Veitch, John	C-Ac	666-6271			PHD	85	Northwes	1985
Fischer, Hartmut	Prof	666-6453			PHD	73	Berkeley	1970
Koti, Tetteh A.	Prof	666-6670			PHD	70	Berkeley	1981
Lehmann, Michael B.	Prof	666-6631	lehmannm		PHD	69	Cornell	1966
N'Chu-Oguie, Charles	Assoc	666-6189			PHD	84	Stanford	1984
Lau, Man-Lui	Asst	666-6730			PHD	86	Cornell	1992

San Francisco State Univ	San Francisco CA 94132 (415) 338-1839					Alex Katz		
Department of Economics	Col of Behav & Soc Sci Fax=338-1057					SFSU.EDU		
Julian, Joseph	Dean	338-1846		Soci	PHD	64	U Wash	1986
Schweitzer, Robert N.	C-Pr	338-1839			PHD	63	Berkeley	1962
Anspach, Ralph	Prof	338-7513			PHD	63	Berkeley	1963
Spring Semester only								
Blecha, Betty J.	Prof	338-1447			PHD	76	Iowa	1983
Gemello, John M.	Prof	338-1839			PHD	74	Stanford	1975
Associate Vice President for Academic Resources								
Mason, William J.	Prof	338-7513			PHD	58	Iowa	1958
Moss, Joanna	Prof	338-3026			PHD	78	New Sch	1981
Osman, Jack W.	Prof	338-1116			PHD	66	Rutgers	1967
Shen, Ruth R.	Prof	338-1009			PHD	61	J Hopkins	1964
Sisk, David E.	Prof	338-1715			PHD	76	UCLA	1978
Vencill, C. Daniel	Prof	338-7514			PHD	71	Stanford	1974
King, Philip G.	Assoc	338-2108			PHD	87	Cornell	1987
Mar, Donald W.	Assoc	338-2499			PHD	85	Berkeley	1987
Potepan, Michael	Assoc	338-2648			PHD	85	Ca-Davis	1991
Xu, Peng	Asst	338-7512			PHD	94	Iowa	1994

San Jose State University	San Jose, CA 95192-0114 (408) 924-5400					Janice Fister		
Department of Economics	Sch of Social Sciences Fax=924-5406					SJSU.EDU		
Walsh, James P.	Dean	924-5300		Hist	PHD	70	Berkeley	1966
Willis, James F.	C-Pr	924-5400			PHD	66	So Meth	1966
Cheng, Doris	Prof	924-5423			PHD	76	Notre Dm	1988
Chu, Betty Y.	Prof	924-5419			PHD	73	Notre Dm	1974
Folsom, Roger Nils	Prof	924-5418			PHD	73	Claremont	1976
Garnel, Donald	Prof	924-5407			PHD	66	Berkeley	1958
Gonzalez, Rodolfo	Prof	924-5416			PHD	90	Ca-Davis	1990
Greer, Douglas F.	Prof	924-5409			PHD	68	Cornell	1975
Leigh, J. Paul	Prof	924-1368			PHD	79	Wisconsin	1981
Nunn, Geoffrey E.	Prof	924-5410			PHD	73	Virginia	1974
Primack, Martin L.	Prof	924-5412			PHD	63	N Carol	1966
Shieh, Yeung-Nan	Prof	924-5413			PHD	80	Tx A&M	1989
Snowbarger, Marvin R.	Prof	924-5422			PHD	66	Michigan	1966
Watkins, Thayer H.	Prof	924-5420			PHD	65	Colorado	1957
Johnson, William B.	Assoc	924-5421			MA	54	Stanford	1960
Means, Tom S.	Assoc	924-5414			PHD	83	UCLA	1986
Pogodzinski, Joseph Michael	Assoc	924-5421			PHD	80	SUNY-SBr	1987
Saurman, David	Assoc	924-1371			PHD	79	Tx A&M	1991
Ortega, Lydia	Asst	924-1369			PHD	87	Geo Mason	1989

Santa Clara University Santa Clara, CA 95053 (408) 554-4341 Sharon Squyres
Department of Economics Leavey Sch of Bus & Adm Fax=554-2331 SCUACC.SCU.EDU

Name	Rank	Phone	E-mail	Field	Degree	Yr	School	Year
Koch, James L.	Dean	554-4523	jkoch	Mgt	PHD	72	UCLA	1990
Demmert, Henry G.	C-Ac	554-4344	hdemmert		PHD	72	Stanford	1968
Belotti, Mario L.	Prof	554-4086	mbelotti		PHD	69	Tx-Austin	1959
W. M. Keck Foundation Professor-Director, Institute of Agribusiness								
Donnelly, William F.	Prof	554-4948			PHD	69	NYU	1969
Field, Alexander J.	Prof	554-4348	afield		PHD	74	Berkeley	1982
Associate Dean Graduate Studies								
Heineke, John M.	Prof	554-4346	jheineke		PHD	68	Iowa	1968
Whalen, Thaddeus J. Jr.	Prof	554-4791			PHD	64	Berkeley	1962
Associate Dean Undergraduate Studies								
Iannaccone, Laurence R.	Assoc	554-4345	liannaccone		PHD	84	Chicago	1982
Kamas, Linda	Assoc	554-6950	lkamas		PHD	82	Berkeley	1988
Russell, Thomas R.	Assoc	554-6953	trussell		PHD	73	Cambridg	1978
Sundstrom, William A.	Assoc	554-6892	wsundstrom		PHD	86	Stanford	1987
Kevane, Michael	Asst		mkevane		PHD	94	Berkeley	1995
Page, Marianne E.	Asst		mpage		PHD	95	Michigan	1995
Popper, Helen A.	Asst	554-6952	hpopper		PHD	90	Berkeley	1991

University of Scranton Scranton, PA 18510-4602 (717) 941-4048 Susan Moir
Dept of Economics & Finance School of Management Fax=941-4342 SCRANTON

Name	Rank	Phone	E-mail	Field	Degree	Yr	School	Year
Horton, Joseph J.	Dean	941-4208	jh446		PHD	68	So Meth	1986
Ghosh, Satyajit P.	C-Ac	941-6197			PHD	86	SUNY-Buf	1986
Bose, Mrigen	Assoc	941-7727			PHD		Utah	1968
Corcione, Frank P.	Assoc	941-7760			PHD		Lehigh	1978
Grambo, Ralph W. Jr.	Assoc	941-7417			PHD		Penn	1973
Hussain, Riaz	Assoc	941-7497			PHD		J Hopkins	1967
Murli, Rajan	Assoc	941-6240			PHD		Temple	1989
Nguyen, Hong V.	Assoc	941-7475			PHD	81	SUNY-Bin	1979
Scahill, Edward M.	Assoc	941-4187			PHD	83	SUNY-Bin	1989
Trussler, Susan	Assoc	941-6122			PHD		Penn St	1985
Kallianiotis, John	Asst	941-7577			PHD		CUNY	1990

Seattle University Seattle, WA 98122-4460 (206) 296-2540 Ms. Peggy Allende
Dept of Economics & Finance Albers Sch Bus & Econ Fax=296-2486 SEATTLEU.EDU

Name	Rank	Phone	E-mail	Field	Degree	Yr	School	Year
Viscione, Jerry A.	Dean	296-5700			PHD	73	Boston U	1988
Genevieve Albers Chair in Business Administration								
Yates, Barbara M.	C-Pr	296-2540	byates	AEGH	PHD	69	Michigan	1970
Rivers, Mary J.	Assoc	296-5717	rivers	CDM	PHD	82	Pittsburgh	1978
Hiedemann, Bridget	Asst	296-2803	bgh	DJT	PHD	92	Duke	1994
Nickerson, Peter H.	Asst	296-5737	phn	Q	PHD	85	U Wash	1984
Peterson, Dean J.	Asst	296-2538	dean	B	PHD	94	Illinois	1991
Sorenson, Timothy L.	Asst	296-5738	tsore	MDF	PHD	91	Harvard	1991
Weber, Christian E.	Asst	296-5725	cweber	EO	PHD	92	Duke	1993
West, James E.	Asst	296-2805	jwest	AD	PHD	94	Michigan	1994
Wilamoski, Peter R.	Asst	296-2536	pwilamos	F	PHD	91	Oregon	1992

Seattle Pacific University Seattle, WA 98119 (206) 281-2700 Ruth Myers
Department of Economics Sch of Business & Econ Fax=281-2733 SPU.EDU

Name	Rank	Phone	E-mail	Field	Degree	Yr	School	Year
Hill, Alec	Dean$	281-2992	adhill	Ethi	JD	80	U Wash	9-79
Downing, Douglas A.	C-Ac	281-2890	ddowing	ACH	PHD	87	Yale	1983
Deming, Jonathan C.	Assoc	281-2181	jdeming	BR	PHD	79	Oregon	1977
Poznanska, Joanna K.	Assoc	281-2935		F	PHD	76	Warsaw	1988
Surdyk, Lisa	Asst	281-2709	l_surdyk	G	PHD	81	U Wash	1981

Seton Hall University South Orange, NJ 07079-2692 (201) 761-7723 Mrs. Carol Flynn
Department of Economics Stillman School of Bus Fax=761-9217 LANMAIL.SHU.EDU

Name	Rank	Phone	E-mail	Field	Degree	Yr	School	Year
Kelly, Frederick J.	Dean	761-9013		Fnce	PHD	74	Columbia	1988
Tzannetakis, George	C-Pr	761-9211	tzanneta		PHD	64	NYU	
Dall, John J. Jr.	Prof	761-9356	dall		PHD	68	Penn	
Jordan, W. John	Prof	761-9236	jordan		PHD	77	SUNY-Alb	1977
Ketkar, Kusum	Prof	761-9102	ketkar		PHD	80	Vanderbilt	
Tinari, Frank D.	Prof	761-9125	tinari		PHD	76	Fordham	
Ikpoh, Andrew	Assoc	761-9799	ikpoh		PHD	88	Columbia	
Kant, Chander	Assoc	761-9281	kant		PHD	80	So Meth	
Grivoyannis, Elias C.	Asst	761-9565	grivoyan		PHD	89	NYU	
Loviscek, Anthony	Asst	761-9127	loviscek		PHD	80	W Virginia	
Noulas, Athanasios	Asst	761-9259	noulas		PHD	89	Conn	

Shenandoah University Winchester, VA 22601-5195 (703)
Economics Faculty Byrd School of Business Fax= SU.EDU

Name	Rank	Phone	E-mail	Field	Degree	Yr	School	Year
Pavsek, Daniel A.	Dean	665-4526	dpavsek		PHD	81	Case Wes	1992

Shepherd College — Shepherdstwn WV 25443-1569 (304) 876-5241 — Ms. Brenda Baker
Department of Economics — Sch Professional Stds Fax= — SCVAX.WUNET.EDU

Name	Rank	Phone	E-mail	Field	Degree	Yr	School	Year
Reid, Kathleen A.	C-Ac	876-5306	kreid		PHD	86	Penn St	1983
Johnson, E. William	Prof	876-5432			PHD	74	Virginia	1971
Phillips, Edward S.	Prof	876-5353			PHD	70	Colorado	1974
Kinney, Kinney	Assoc	876-5434			PHD		Maryland	1994
Schultz, John A.	Assoc	876-5352			PHD	85	S Carol	1988

Shippensburg University — Shippensburg, PA 17257 (717) 532-1437 — Karen Kelley
Department of Economics — College of Business Fax=530-4003

Name	Rank	Phone	E-mail	Field	Degree	Yr	School	Year
Pope, James A.	Dean	532-1435		Mgt	PHD	78	N Carol	1992
Finucane, Brendan P.	C-Pr	532-1437			PHD		Pittsburgh	1982
Bastin, Hamid	Prof	532-1679			PHD	89	Geo St	1989
Bej, Emil	Prof	532-1291			DR	70	Ukranian	1969
Eggleston, Robert C.	Prof	531-1675			PHD		Pittsburgh	1965
Hunt, Joseph W.	Prof	532-1139			PHD	66	Indiana	1980
Lee, Daniel Y.	Prof	532-1556			PHD	86	Pittsburgh	1986
Mathis, Stephen A.	Prof	532-1696			PHD	79	Iowa St	1979
Posatko, Robert C.	Prof	532-1138			PHD	75	Penn St	1981
Reinwald, Thomas P.	Prof	532-1437			PHD	73	Illinois	1974
Koscianski, Janet	Assoc	532-1174			PHD	90	S Illinois	1990

Siena College — Loundonville, NY 12211-1462 (518) 783-2398
Department of Economics — Business Division Fax=783-4293 — SIENA

Name	Rank	Phone	E-mail	Field	Degree	Yr	School	Year
Sanders, Patricia	Dean	783-2321	sanders		PHD	80	Conn	9-93
Shirey, Richard L.	C-Ac	783-2398			PHD		SUNY-Alb	
Howe, Edward T.	Prof				PHD	73	SUNY-Alb	
Reinhart, Blaise F.	Prof				PHD		Catholic	
Ajluni, Salem S.	Asst	783-2929			PHD	92	Utah	1991
Trees, W. Scott	Asst				PHD		Notre Dm	

Simmons College — Boston, MA 02115-5898 (617) 521-2595 — Rita Oriani
Economics Faculty — Department of Economics Fax=521-3198 — VMSVAX.SIMMONS.EDU

Name	Rank	Phone	E-mail	Field	Degree	Yr	School	Year
Biewener, Carole	C-Ac	521-2583	cbiewener	FB	PHD	89	Mass	1987
Basch, Donald L.	Prof	521-2584		D	PHD	77	Yale	1980
Tolpin, Harriet G.	Prof	521-2652		I	PHD	73	Boston C	1974
Dean of Graduate School for Health Studies								
Kenyon, Daphne A.	Assoc	521-2587		HI	PHD	80	Michigan	1989
Sawtelle, Barbara A.	Assoc	521-2582		E	PHD	76	MIT	
Sjogren, Jane O.	VAsoc	521-2581		HJ	PHD	81	Stanford	
Aoki, Masato	Asst	521-2580			PHD	95	Mass	1994

Simpson College — Indianola, IA 50125 (515) 961-1513 — Cindy Hamilton
Dept Mgt, Atg & Economics — Div of Policy Studies Fax=961-1498 — STORM.SIMPSON.EDU

Name	Rank	Phone	E-mail	Field	Degree	Yr	School	Year
Chezum, Brian	H-Pr				PHD	92	Kentucky	1995
Colella, Francis J.	H-Pr				PHD	73	Fordham	1977

Skidmore College — Saratoga Sprg NY 12866-1632 (518) Ext 2197 — Gina Swift
Economics Faculty — Department of Economics Fax=584-3023 — SCOTT.SKIDMORE.EDU

Name	Rank	Phone	E-mail	Field	Degree	Yr	School	Year
Baum, Sandra R.	C-Pr	584-5000	sbaum		PHD	81	Columbia	1987
Rotheim, Roy J.	Prof	584-5000	rrotheim		PHD	77	Rutgers	1980
Goodstein, Eban	Assoc	584-5000	eban		PHD	89	Michigan	1989
Jones, Robert J.	Assoc	584-5000	rjones		PHD	78	Columbia	1973
Koechlin, Tim	Assoc	584-5000	tkoechli		PHD	89	Mass	1988
Lee, Kie Bok	Assoc	584-5000	klee		PHD	67	Virginia	1963
Odekon, Mehmet A.	Assoc	584-5000	modekon		PHD	77	SUNY-Alb	1983

Slippery Rock University — Slippery Rock PA 16057-1326 (412) 738-2039 — Leigh McGuirk
Dept of Economics & Finance — Col Info Sci & Bus Adm Fax=738-2959 — SRU

Name	Rank	Phone	E-mail	Field	Degree	Yr	School	Year
Mastrianna, Frank V.	Dean	738-2008	un3600		PHD	68	Cincinnati	3-87
Tannery, Frederick J.	C-Ac	738-2579	fjt		PHD	80	Pittsburgh	1981
Baroutsis, A. Paul	Prof	738-2575			PHD	72	Purdue	1972
Mamoozadeh, G. Abbas	Assoc	738-2578			PHD			
Noorbakhsh, Abbas	Assoc	738-2576	axn		PHD	89	Kansas St	1990
Culp, David B.	Asst	738-2971			MA			
Valencia, Jesus M.	Asst	738-2577			PHD	88	Pittsburgh	1983

Smith College — Northampton, MA 01063 (413) 585-3600 — Judy Fountain
Department of Economics — Economics Fax=585-3389 — SMITH.SMITH.EDU

Name	Rank	Phone	E-mail	Field	Degree	Yr	School	Year
Pfeifer, Karen	C-Ac	585-3623	kpfeifer	BNOP	PHD	81	American	1979
Aldrich, Mark	Prof	585-3603	maldrich	JLN	PHD	69	Tx-Austin	1968
Averitt, Robert T.	Prof	585-3604	raveritt	ABE	PHD	61	Tx-Austin	1961
Bartlett, Randall	Prof	585-3605	rbartlett	AHR	PHD	71	Stanford	1977

Name	Rank	Phone	Email	Field	Degree	Yr	School	Since
Buchele, Robert	Prof	585-3607	rbuchele	CEJP	PHD	76	Harvard	1977
Kaufman, Roger T.	Prof	585-3612	rtkaufman	CEJP	PHD	78	MIT	1983
Leonard, Frederick	Prof	585-3614	fleonard	AEG	PHD		Michigan	
Morris, Cynthia T.	Prof	585-3619	cmorris	BNOP	PHD	59	Yale	1983
Zimbalist, Andrew	Prof	585-3622	zimbalist	CJLP	PHD	74	Harvard	1974
Haas-Wilson, Deborah	Assoc	585-3636	dhwilson	DIL	PHD	83	Berkeley	1984
Mahdavi, Mahnaz	Assoc	585-3629	mmahdavi	FGM	PHD	86	Michigan	1985
Reinhardt, Nola	Assoc	585-3617	nreinhar	OPQ	PHD	81	Berkeley	1981
Riddell, Thomas A.	Assoc	585-4910	triddell	HNPQ	PHD	75	American	1980
Savoca, Elizabeth A.	Assoc	585-3615	esavoca	CEIT	PHD	82	Berekely	1982
Staelin, Charles P.	Assoc	585-3621	cstaelin	ACDK	PHD	71	Michigan	1981
Browning, Cynthia M.	Asst	585-3606	cbrownin	BCE	PHD	89	Michigan	1993

Sonoma State University Rohnert Park, CA 94928-3609 (707) 664-2377
Department of Economics Sch of Business & Econ Fax=664-4009 SONOMA.EDU

Name	Rank	Phone	Email	Field	Degree	Yr	School	Since
Clark, Lawrence S.	Dean	644-2220		Law	LLM	80	DePaul	1994
Benito, Carlos	C-Pr	664-2366			PHD	73	Ca-Davis	1990
Ben-Zion, Barry	Prof				PHD	73	Oregon	1969
Garlin, Victor A.	Prof				PHD	65	Berkeley	1970
Hayes, Sue E.	Prof				PHD	75	Berkeley	1974
Lewis, Stephen D.	Prof	664-2549			PHD	69	Ca-SnBarb	1982

University of the South Sewanee, TN 37383-1000 (615)
Department of Economics Col of Arts & Sciences Fax=598-1145
phone 598-1000

Name	Rank	Phone	Email	Field	Degree	Yr	School	Since
Keele, Robert	Dean	598-1248	bkeele	PolS	PHD			
Ingles, Jerry Lee	C-Pr	598-1235	jingles		PHD		Cornell	
Schaefer, Arthur McCluny	Prof	598-1146	aschaefer		PHD		Penn	
Gottfried, Robert Richard	Assoc	598-1243	rgottri		PHD		N Carol	
Hendrickson, Jill K.	Assoc	598-1805	jhenddric		PHD		Notre Dm	1995
Mohiuddin, Yasmeen	Asst	598-1462	ymohiudd		PHD		Vanderbilt	
Nickols, Mark W.	Asst	598-1160	mnickols		PHD		Fla St	1995

University of South Alabama Mobile, AL 36688-0002 (334) 460-7171 Ms. Lissa Williams
Department of Economics C of Bus & Mgt Studies Fax=460-6529 USOUTHAL.EDU

Name	Rank	Phone	Email	Field	Degree	Yr	School	Since
Moore, Carl C.	Dean	460-6102		Mgt	PHD	71	Alabama	1973
Swofford, James L.	C-Pr	460-6705	jswoffor@jaguar1	E	PHD	81	Florida	1984
Barakeh, A. K.	Prof	460-6711		F	PHD	68	Indiana	1968
Bobo, James R.	Emer				PHD	61	LSU	1978
Chang, Semoon	Prof	460-6156		M	PHD	71	Fla St	1972
Forbus, Philip R.	Assoc			AD	PHD	78	Arkansas	1978
Stutsman, A. Douglas	Emer	460-6706		AB	PHD	70	Miss	1968
Ashley, Terry	Asst	460-6731			PHD	91	Auburn	1991

Univ So Carolina at Aiken Aiken, SC 29801 (803) 641-3340
Economics Faculty School Bus Adm & Econ Fax=641-3445
phone 648-6851

Name	Rank	Phone	Email	Field	Degree	Yr	School	Since
Vyas, Niren M.	H-Ac	648-6851		Mktg	PHD	81	S Carol	1981
Shelburn, Marsha	Prof	648-6851			PHD	80	N Carol	1980
Folsom, Davis	Assoc	648-6851			PHD	79	Conn	1979

Univ of South Carolina Columbia, SC 29208 (803) 777-7400 Georgene Dance
Department of Economics Col of Business Admin Fax=777-6876 DARLA.BADM.SCAROLINA

Name	Rank	Phone	Email	Field	Degree	Yr	School	Since
Shrock, David L.	Dean	777-3176		Tran	DBA	74	Indiana	1994
Wilder, Ronald P.	C-Pr	777-7400			PHD	69	Vanderbilt	1987
Addison, John T.	Prof	777-4608			PHD	71	London	
Breger, Gerald E.	Emer	777-4780			PHD	64	Arkansas	
Carlsson, Robert J.	Prof	777-6044			PHD	64	Rutgers	
Clower, Robert W.	Prof	777-5919			DLIT	78	Oxford	1986
Hugh C. Lane Professor of Economics								
Cohn, Elchanan	Prof	777-2714			PHD	68	Iowa St	
Harrison, Glenn W.	Prof	777-4943			PHD	82	UCLA	
Dewey H. Johnson Professor of Economics								
Kiker, B. F.	Prof	777-4904			PHD	65	Tulane	1971
Jeff B. Bates Professor of Public Administration & Finance								
Liles, W. Pierce	Prof	777-2306			PHD	72	S Carol	
Martin, Randolph C.	Prof	777-2510			PHD	71	Wash U	1970
Director of the Research Division								
Putnam, William F.	Emer	777-7602			MS	57	S Carol	
Senior Associate Dean								
Chappell, Henry W.	Assoc	777-4940			PHD	79	Yale	1980
McDermott, John H.	Assoc	777-4939			PHD	79	Brown	1983
Phillips, William H.	Assoc	777-4930			PHD	80	MIT	1979
Director Undergraduate Studies								
Rawson, William S.	Assoc	777-3865			PHD	67	Duke	1967

Name	Rank	Phone	Email	Field	Degree	Yr	School	Hired
Blackburn, McKinley L.	Asst	777-4931			PHD	87	Harvard	1987
Boucher-Breuer, Janice L.	Asst	777-7419			PHD	87	N Carol	1987
Chilton, John B.	Asst	777-6087			PHD	89	Brown	1988
Leung, Sui-ki	Asst	777-2875			DPHI	88	UCLA	
Rutstrom, Lisa	Asst	777-4932						
Woodward, Doug P.	Asst	777-2510			PHD	86	Tx-Austin	
Research Economist, Division of Research								
Balch, Donald C.	Lect	777-6828						
Broadley, James P. Jr.	DLect	777-2786						

U South Carolina at Spartanb	Spartanburg, SC 29303	(803) 599-2581						Elda Rattie
Department of Economics	Sch of Bus Admin & Econ	Fax=599-2598						
Bennett, Jerome V.	Dean	599-2593		Atg	PHD	76	S Carol	1986
Bailey, Duncan	Prof	599-2301		AEOR	PHD		Va Tech	1984
Jilling, Michael	Prof	599-2586		ACMF	PHD		S Carol	1975
Reese, James W.	Assoc	599-2585		AFPH	PHD		Tennessee	1982
Rook, Sarah P.	Assoc	599-2584		ADTN	PHD		N Car St	1980
Jolly, Eric S.	Asst	599-2288		A	MA		Ohio U	1968
Connelly, Robert A. Jr.	Inst	599-2230		A	MA		Appalach	1972

South Carolina St University	Orangeburg, SC 29117	(803) 536-8070						Ms. Patricia McDonald
Dept Agribusiness & Econ	School of Business	Fax=536-8066						
Adams, Barbara L.	Dean$	536-8980		Atg	PHD	81	Tx A&M	1990
Modeste, Nelson	C-Ac	536-8076			PHD			1994
Londhe, Suresh R.	Prof	536-8449			PHD	65	LSU	1969
Onunkwo, Emmanuel N.	Prof	536-8843			PHD	73	Geotown	1978
Kyereme, Stephen	Assoc	536-8448			PHD	84	Cornell	1984
Mustafa, Muhammad	Assoc	536-8459			PHD	88	Wayne St	1989
Selassie, Haile G.	Assoc	536-8456			PHD	83	Okla St	1984
Sureshwaran, S.	Asst	536-8452			PHD	89	Clemson	1990
Brown, Lloyd	Inst	536-7136			ABD		S Carol	1994

University of South Dakota	Vermillion, SD 57069-2390	(605) 677-5455						Ann Ward
Department of Economics	School of Business	Fax=677-5427						USD.EDU
Johnson, Jerry W.	Dean	677-5287	jerryj@sunbird.		PHD	71	Iowa St	1967
Brown, Ralph J.	Prof	677-5620			PHD	70	Colorado	1977
Johnson, Dennis A.	Prof	677-5552			PHD	72	Iowa	1964
Ring, Raymond J. Jr.	Prof	677-5319	rring@charlie.		PHD	73	Kansas	1978
Wymar, Benno	Prof	677-5550			PHD	73	Nebraska	1968
Reinke, Robert W.	Assoc	677-5540			PHD	82	Minnesota	1987
Sasser, Sue Lynn	Asst	677-5559	ssassar@sunflowr		PHD	83	Tx Womans	
Waldron, Randall	Asst	677-6643	rwaldron@charlie		PHD	94	Vanderbilt	1994

South Dakota State Univ	Brookings, SD 57007	(605) 688-4141						June Larkin
Economics Department	Col of Agri & Biol Sci	Fax=688-6386						
Bryant, David A.	Dean	688-4148			PHD	71	Arizona	1987
Lundeen, Ardelle A.	H-Pr	688-4141		Q	PHD	76	Iowa St	1976
Dobbs, Thomas L.	Prof	688-4874		Q	PHD	69	Maryland	1978
Gilbert, Howard A.	Prof	688-4844		A	PHD	67	Oreg St	1966
Greenbaum, Harry	Prof	688-4846		E	PHD	61	Ohio St	1961
Janssen, Larry L.	Prof	688-4871		Q	PHD	78	Nebraska	1978
Kamps, William E.	Prof	688-4845		E	PHD	74	Wash St	1972
Kim, Han J.	Prof	688-4848		C	PHD	69	Oreg St	1967
Lamberton, Charles E.	Prof	688-4865		G	PHD	75	Iowa St	1974
Lyons, Patrick A.	Prof	688-4842		M	JD	74	S Dakota	1975
Murra, Gene E.	Prof	688-4864		Q	PHD	63	Ohio St	1959
O'Brien, Jamie L.	Prof	688-4144		K	MPA	84	S Dakota	1984
Peterson, Donald L.	Prof	688-4859	ec24	Q	PHD	73	Nebraska	1974
Shane, Richard C.	Prof	688-4862		Q	PHD	78	Wash St	1977
Taylor, Donald C.	Prof	688-4872		O	PHD	65	Minnesota	1980
Beutler, Martin K.	Assoc	394-2236	sdsu01	Q	PHD	86	Purdue	1986
Feuz, Dillon M.	Assoc	688-4105		Q	PHD	90	Colo St	1990
Franklin, Douglas R.	Assoc	688-4861		Q	PHD	82	Utah	1988
Pflueger, Burton W.	Assoc	688-4141	ex16	Q	PHD	85	Illinois	1985
Adamson, Dwight W.	Asst	688-4847		E	PHD	88	Wash St	1989
Fausti, Scott W.	Asst	688-4868		F	PHD	91	Illinois	1991
Qasmi, Bashir A.	Asst	688-4870		Q	PHD	86	Iowa St	1987
Sondey, John A.	Asst	688-4873	ec35	H	PHD	89	Wash St	1990
Cumber, Carol J.	Inst	688-4849	ec21	M	PHD	94	S Dak St	1990
Danielson, Joan G.	Inst	688-4851		A	ABD		Auburn	1994
Ellingson, Wayne D.	Inst	688-4869		C	BS	70	Iowa St	1980
Fredrickson, Trygve G.	Inst	688-4866		M	MBA	89	S Dakota	1990
Gustafson, Curtis O.	Inst	688-4850		M	MPA	86	S Dakota	1989
Rasmussen, Chris H.	Inst	688-4145		M	BA	75	SW State	1978

University of South Florida Tampa, FL 33620-5500 (813) 974-4252 Mary Bennett
Department of Economics Col of Business Admin Fax=974-3030 BSNOI.BSN.USF.EDU

Name	Rank	Phone	E-mail	Fields	Degree	Yr	School	Year
Anderson, Robert	Dean$	974-3262			PHD	70	North Tx	
Rowe, John W.	C-Pr	974-6543	jrowe	D	PHD	66	Illinois	1979
Bellante, Donald M.	Prof	974-6386	dbellant	J	PHD	71	Fla St	1985
Curtis, Thomas D.	Prof	974-6525		B	PHD	65	Indiana	1974
Desalvo, Joseph S.	Prof	974-6388	jdesalvo	R	PHD	68	Northwes	1983
Gyimah-Brempong, Kwabena	Prof	974-6520	kgyimah	O	PHD	81	Wayne St	1994
Herander, Mark G.	Prof	974-6540	mherande	F	PHD	80	N Carol	1979
Herman, Walter J.	Prof	974-6526		E	PHD	65	Florida	1980
Porter, Philip	Prof	974-6539	pporer	H	PHD	78	Tx A&M	1985
Shows, E. Warren	Prof	974-6535	wshows	L	PHD	68	Geo St	1964
Cooke, John P.	Assoc	974-6504		H	PHD	67	Colorado	1968
Ford, Edward J. Jr.	Assoc	974-6559	eford	R	PHD	71	Boston C	1971
Green, Carole A.	Assoc	974-6521	cgreen	B	PHD	82	Illinois	1982
Shannon, Robert F.	Assoc	974-6532			PHD	66	Illinois	1966
Spence, James G.	Assoc	432-5524			PHD	79	Oklahoma	1975
Thomas, Christopher R.	Assoc	974-6546	cthomas	L	PHD	80	Tx A&M	1982
Wilson, R. Mark	Assoc	974-6514	mwilson	I	PHD	77	Northwes	1978
Kamp, Bradley	Asst	974-6549	bkamp	L	PHD	93	Ca-SnDgo	1992
Lee, San-Sub	Asst	974-6554	slee	H	PHD	91	N Carol	1990
Picone, Gabriel	Asst	974-6537	gpicone	C	PHD	93	Vanderbilt	1993
Racine, Jeff	Asst	974-6555	jracine	C	PHD	91	W Ontario	1993
Swinton, John	Asst			Q	ABD		Wisconsin	1995
Bartlett, Sue	Lect	974-6547	sbartlet		MA	93	S Fla	1994
Brandmeyer, Sunne	Lect	974-6509	sbeandme		MA	78	S Fla	1985
Grigg, Vernon H.	Lect	359-4339			PHD	54	MIT	1981

Southeast Missouri St Univ C Girardeau, MO 63701-4799 (314) 651-2181 Ms. Donna Masterson
Department of Economics Harrison Coll Business Fax=651-2200 SEMOVM

Name	Rank	Phone	E-mail	Fields	Degree	Yr	School	Year
McDougall, Gerald S.	Dean	651-2112	c476bux	HL	PHD	74	Claremont	1993
Summary, Rebecca M.	C-Pr	651-2945	c694sse	FA	PHD	83	Illinois	1983
Domazlicky, Bruce R.	Prof	651-2013	c819sse	A	PHD	76	Wyoming	1986
Eubank, Wayne F.	Prof	651-2014	c847bue		PHD		Kentucky	1964
Fox, Pauline H.	Prof	651-2181	c858sse		PHD	75	Okla St	1978
Fulton, Betty	Prof	651-2950	c646bue	P	PHD		Missouri	1968
Kerr, Peter M.	Prof	651-2012	c446ssb	AEBF	PHD	79	Kansas	1980
Park, Kang Hoon	Prof	651-2942	c382bue	CF	PHD	81	S Illinois	1979
Sutton, Terry	Prof	651-2944	c721bue		PHD		Kansas St	1972
Weber, William L.	Assoc	651-2946	c645sse	GHI	PHD	86	S Illinois	1986
Primont, Diane F.	Asst	651-2819	c794sse	JD	PHD	87	N Carol	1990

Southeastern Louisiana Univ Hammond, LA 70402 (504) 549-2086 Lou Salisbury
Dept of Economics & Bus Res College of Business Fax=549-2881 SELU.EDU

Name	Rank	Phone	E-mail	Fields	Degree	Yr	School	Year
Miller, Joseph H. Jr.	Dean	549-2258			PHD	77	Miss	9-76
Hsing, Yu	H-Pr	549-2086	yhsing	EJOR	PHD	83	Tennessee	1987
Brar, Jagjit S.	Prof	549-3084		EF	PHD	72	Oreg St	1973
Lange, Ralph W.	Prof	549-2081		AF	PHD	74	LSU	
Gibson, Jo Anne	Assoc	549-3098		EF	PHD		Miss	
Pedersen, William E.	Asst	549-2855		AGH	PHD	95	N Orleans	1994
Sundar, Cuddalore S.	Asst	549-5929	sundar	ADGI	PHD	93	N Orleans	1993
Thomasson, Henry E.	Asst	549-3068		AJ	MS		LSU	

Southeastern Oklahoma State Durant, OK 74701-0609 (405) Ext 2713
Dept of Economics & Finance School of Business Fax=920-7479
phone 924-0121

Name	Rank	Phone	E-mail	Fields	Degree	Yr	School	Year
Chinn, Kenneth	C-Ac	924-0121		EC	PHD	91	Colo St	1982
Jenkins, Sidney L.	Asst			AQ	MS	59	Okla St	1968
Stuart, Edwin	Asst			AG	JD	67	Florida	1992

Southern Col of 7th Day Adv Collegedale, TN 37315-0370 (615)
Economics Faculty Dept of Bus & Office Ad Fax=

Name	Rank	Phone	E-mail	Fields	Degree	Yr	School	Year
VandeVere, Wayne E.	C-Pr	238-2750		Atg	PHD	67	Mich St	1956
Erickson, Richard	Assoc	238-2755		A	MBA	81	Austin Pea	1984

Southern University Baton Rouge, LA 70813-9723 (504) 771-2992
Department of Economics College of Business Fax=771-5262

Name	Rank	Phone	E-mail	Fields	Degree	Yr	School	Year
Birkett, Brenda S.	Dean	771-5641		Atg	PHD	80	LSU	8-80
Jindia, Jaswant R.	C-Pr	771-2992			PHD	70	Illinois	1970
Andrews, Donald R.	Prof			QR	PHD	80	Tx A&M	1995
Cheng, Benjamin S.	Prof	771-5642			PHD	71	Oklahoma	1971
Yigletu, Ashagre	Assoc				PHD		Belgrade	1972
Agnihotri, Krisna	Asst				MA		Punjab	1969
Lokhande, Vineeta	Asst				PHD		LSU	1994
Osagie, Emmanuel I.	Asst				PHD		LSU	1985
Smyser, Michael	Asst				PHD		Fla Intl	1991

Southern Arkansas Univ Magnolia, AR 71753 (501) 235-5146 Pam Nunley
Dept of Economics & Finance Sch of Business Admin Fax=235-4800 SAUMAG.EDU

Name	Rank	Phone	Email	Field	Degree	Yr	School	Year
Rankin, David F.	Dean	235-4300	dfrankin	Fnce	PHD	70	Miss	1968
Ashby, David J.	C	235-4304	jdasby	G	MBA		Miss	1992
Bellamy, Scott	Asst	235-5162	scbellamy	I	MBA		Kentucky	1993

Univ of Southern California Los Angeles, CA 90089-1421 (213) 740-8335 Lisa Rayburn
Div Soc Sci&Comm-Dept Econ Col of Ltrs, Arts & Sci Fax=740-8543 USC.EDU

Name	Rank	Phone	Email	Field	Degree	Yr	School	Year
Schapiro, Morton Owen	Dean	740-8218	schapiro@almaak.		PHD	79	Penn	1991
Kuran, Timur	C-Pr	740-7432	kuran@rcf.		PHD	82	Stanford	1982
Day, Richard H.	Prof	740-2432			PHD	61	Harvard	1976
Easterlin, Richard A.	Prof	743-6993			PHD	53	Penn	1982
Elliott, John E.	Prof	740-3510			PHD	56	Harvard	1966
Gordon, Peter	Prof	743-2770	pgordon@almaak.		PHD	71	Penn	1971
Kalaba, Robert E.	Prof	740-2109			PHD	58	NYU	1969
Magill, Michael J. P.	Prof	740-2104			PHD	70	Brown	1979
Nugent, Jeffrey B.	Prof	740-2107	nugent@almaak.		PHD	65	New Sch	1973
Richardson, Harry W.	Prof	740-3954			MA	61	Manchester	1975
Vuong, Quang	Prof	740-3528	qvuong@mizar		PHD	82	Northwes	1982
Yett, Donald E.	Prof	740-3514			PHD	68	Berkeley	1966
Cheng, Harrison C.	Assoc	740-2105	hacheng@mizar.		PHD	77	Berkeley	1978
DePrano, Michael E.	Assoc	740-3525	deprano@rcf.		PHD	63	Illinois	1963
Weiss, Andrew	Assoc	740-8842	aweiss@almaak.		PHD	84	Sydney	1984
Betts, Caroline	Asst	740-2430	cbetts@rcf.		PHD	94	Brit Col	1994
Cason, Timothy	Asst	740-3511	cason@almaak.		PHD	91	Berkeley	1991
Mui, Vai-Lam	Asst	740-2108	vailam@almaak.		PHD	92	Berkeley	1992
Neumeyer, Pablo	Asst	740-2110	pablo@almaak.		PHD	92	Columbia	1991
Robinson, James A.	Asst				PHD	93	Yale	1995
Rosendorff, Peter	Asst	740-3529	bpeter@almaak.		PHD	93	Columbia	1992
Kamrany, Nake M.	SLect	740-6997			PHD	62	S Calif	1976

Univ of Southern Colorado Pueblo, CO 81001-4901 (719) 549-2142
Bus Admin & Economics Dept School of Business Fax=549-2909 USCOLO.EDU

Name	Rank	Phone	Email	Field	Degree	Yr	School	Year
Ward, Bart H.	Dean	549-2142		Atg	PHD	73	Northwes	1994
Billington, Peter J.	C-Pr	549-2880			PHD	83	Cornell	1989
Duncan, Kevin C.	Asst	549-2228		JR	PHD	87	Utah	1994
Ribal, John L.	Asst	549-2129		HF	PHD		Notre Dm	1988

Southern Connecticut St Un New Haven, CT 06515 (203) 392-5629 Mrs. Karen A. Jordan
Dept of Economics & Finance School of Business Fax=392-5863 SCSUD

Name	Rank	Phone	Email	Field	Degree	Yr	School	Year
Leader, Alan H.	Dean	392-5631		Mgt	DBA	63	Indiana	1985
Crakes, Gary M.	C-Pr	392-5619			PHD	84	Conn	1980
Buck, Donald T.	Prof	392-5618			MA	61	N Hamp	1965
Hsu, Yu-Chu	Prof	392-5622			PHD		Cornell	
Morgan, Alfred D.	Prof	392-5624			PHD		Harvard	
Andoh, Samuel K.	Assoc	392-5616			PHD	86	NYU	
Eldridge, Robert M.	Assoc	392-5628			DBA	87	Geo Wash	
Gebremariam, Yilma	Assoc	392-5620			PHD	89	S Calif	1990
Mostaghimi, Mehdi	Assoc	392-5625			PHD		Virginia	
Bodo, Peter	Asst	392-5617			PHD		Conn	
Mills, Judith W.	Asst	392-5623			PHD		SUNY-SBr	1991
Savage, Deborah A.	Asst	392-5627			PHD		Conn	
Thorson, James A.	Asst	392-5626			PHD	91	Il-Chicago	1992

Southern Illinois Univ Carbondale, IL 62901-4631 (618) 536-7746 Mrs. Nancy Mallett
Department of Economics College of Liberal Arts Fax=453-2717 SIUCVMB.SIU.EDU

Name	Rank	Phone	Email	Field	Degree	Yr	School	Year
Jackson, John S. III	Dean	453-2466			PHD	72	Vanderbilt	
Primont, Daniel A.	C-Pr	453-5082	primo	DC	PHD	70	Ca-SnBarb	1978
Fare, Rolf	Prof	453-5065	ga1322	CD	DOC	76	Lund	1978
Grabowski, Richard L.	Prof	453-5067	ga1571	OF	PHD	77	Utah	1979
Grosskopf, Shawna	Prof	453-5068	ga1304	CHJ	PHD	77	Syracuse	1977
Laumas, G. S.	Prof	453-5740	ga3956	EC	PHD	66	Wayne St	1990
Myers, John G.	Emer	453-5073			PHD	61	Columbia	1977
Sharma, Subhash	Prof	453-5070	sharma	C	PHD	83	Kentucky	1983
Takayama, Akira	Prof	453-2827		FEDC	PHD	62	Rochester	1983
Vandeveer Chair of Economics								
Trescott, Paul B.	Prof	453-5095		EB	PHD	54	Princeton	1976
Ellis, Robert J. Jr.	Emer	453-5063			PHD	66	Virginia	1965
Foran, Terry G.	Assoc	453-5066		J	PHD	71	Penn St	1970
Mitchell, Thomas M.	Assoc	453-5072	ga1700	DC	PHD	84	Brown	1983
Chau, Nancy	Asst			FO	PHD	95	J Hopkins	1995
Cribari-Neto, Francisco	Asst	453-5062		E	PHD	94	Illinois	1994
email cribari@c22s.c-wham.siu.edu								
Dibooglu, Selhattin	Asst	453-5346	sdibo	F	PHD	93	Iowa St	1993
Jensen, Mark	Asst	453-5347		EC	PHD	94	Wash U	1994

So Illinois, Edwardsville	Edwardsville, IL	62026-1102 (618) 692-2542					Sally Moonier	
Department of Economics	School of Business	Fax=692-3047					ENIAC.AC.SIUE.EDU	
Ault, David E.	Dean	692-3823	dault		PHD	69	Illinois	1969
Elliott, Donald S. Jr.	C-Pr	692-2542			PHD	76	Minnesota	1976
email: delliot@daisy.ac.siue.edu								
Haver, Rik W.	Prof	692-2747	haferr		PHD	79	Va Tech	
Levin, Stanford L.	Prof	692-2542	levins		PHD	74	Michigan	1972
Lin, An-Yhi (Steven)	Prof	692-2580		CDFO	PHD	67	Iowa St	1968
Meisel, John B.	Prof	692-2581	meiselj		PHD	78	Boston C	1977
Rutman, Gilbert L.	Prof	692-2571			PHD	65	Duke	1969
Turay, Abdul M.	Prof	692-3010			PHD	78	Oklahoma	1995
Edmonds, Radcliff G. Jr.	Assoc	692-2598	edmondsr		PHD	79	Michigan	1977
Pettit, Mary Ann	Inst	692-2583			MA	77	Tennessee	1989
Sullivan, Timothy	Inst	692-3469			ABD	95	Maryland	1995
Wolff, Laura	Inst	692-2875			MS	88	Missouri	1990

Univ of Southern Indiana	Evansvillle, IN	47712-3597 (812) 464-1979						
Dept of Economics & Finance	School of Business	Fax=464-1960					SMTP.USI.EDU	
Fisher, Philip C.	Dean	464-1718		Mgt	PHD	79	Stanford	1991
Cox, Steven R.	C-Pr	464-1983	scox.ucs		PHD	71	Michigan	1989
Quddus, Munir	Prof	464-1745	mqudus.ucs		PHD	85	Vanderbilt	1984
Schibik, Timothy J.	Assoc	464-1880	tschibik.ucs		PHD	89	W Virginia	1988
Chasel-Cordo, Peter	Asst	465-1033	cashel.ucs		PHD	88	Houston	1994
Khayum, Mohammed	Asst	464-7034	mkhayum.ucs		PHD	90	Temple	1991
Mahoney, Timothy B.	Inst	464-1947	tmahoney.ucs		MS	65	Illinois	1987

Univ of Southern Maine	Portland, ME	04103-4899 (207) 780-4020						
Department of Economics	School of Business	Fax=780-4662					USM.MAINE.EDU	
Gutmann, Jean	Dean	780-4020			MBA	74	Maine	
Bay, John W.	Prof	780-4445	jbay	E	PHD	66	Boston C	1965
Executive Director Off Campus Instruction								
Durgin, Frank A. Jr.	Prof	780-4306		NPQ	DRD	56	France	1964
McMahon, Robert C.	Assoc	780-4308	mcmahon	R	PHD	70	Lehigh	1969
Medley, Joseph E.	Assoc	780-4293	medley	BO	PHD	81	Mass	1983
Phillips, William A.	Assoc	780-4313	phillips	ACDF	PHD	79	Fla St	1980
Goldstein, Nance	Asst	780-4602	nance	IJ	PHD	88	Kentucky	1987
Hillard, Michael	Asst	780-4416		EJ	PHD	88	Mass	1987

Southern Methodist Univ	Dallas, TX	75275-0496 (214) 768-2694				Pontip Vattaka	
Department of Economics	Dedman College	Fax=768-1821				CIS.SMU.EDU	
Jones, James F. Jr.	Dean	768-3212		PHD			
Weber, Shlomo	C-Pr	768-3577	sweber@sun.	PHD	79	Hebrew	1993
Robert H. & Nancy Dedman Research Fellow							
Batra, Raveendra N.	Prof	768-2707		PHD	69	S Illinois	1973
Bierens, Herman	Prof	768-3856	hbierens@sun.	PHD	80	Amsterdm	1990
Robert H. and Nancy Dedman Tustee Professor							
Maasoumi, Esfandiar	Prof	768-4298	emaaso@sun.	PHD	77	London	1989
Robert H. & Nancy Dedman Professor							
Russell, William R.	Prof	768-2715		PHD		Wash	1971
Balke, Nathan S.	Assoc	768-2693	hrqr0006@vm.	PHD	86	Northwes	1986
Deb, Rajat	Assoc	768-3556		PHD	75	London	1976
Fomby, Thomas	Assoc	768-2559	h2br1001@vm.	PHD	75	Missouri	1975
Hayes, Kathy J.	Assoc	768-2714		PHD	80	Syracuse	1989
Huffman, Gregory	Assoc	768-3344	huffman@sun.	PHD	83	Minnesota	1992
Seo, Tae Kun	Assoc	768-3547		PHD	73	Tx A&M	1973
Slottje, Daniel J.	Assoc	768-3555	h2cr1001@vm.	PHD	83	Tx A&M	1989
Davis, Michael L.	Asst	768-3394		PHD	83	So Meth	1991
Dolmas, James	Asst	768-3806	jdolmas@sun.	PHD	93	Rochester	1993
Ginther, Donna	Asst			PHD	95	Wisconsin	1995
Konishi, Hideo	Asst	768-4398	hkonishi@sun.	PHD	94	Rochester	1994
Lin, Ping	Asst	768-3288	plin@sun.	PHD	93	Minnesota	1993
Osang, Thomas	Asst	768-3269	tosand@sun.	PHD	94	Ca-SnDgo	1994
Saggi, Kamal	Asst			PHD	95	Penn	1995

U of Southern Mississippi	Hattiesburg, MS	39406-5072 (601) 266-4648				Ms. Janet McKee	
Dept Economics & Intl Bus	Col of Business Adm	Fax=266-4920					
Black, Tyrone	Dean	266-4659	E	PHD	70	Tulane	1969
Carter, George H. III	C-Ac	266-4648	R	PHD	77	Tx A&M	1979
Lewis, Eddie Miley Jr.	Prof	266-4652	F	DBA	74	Miss St	1970
Nissan, Edward	Prof	266-4656	R	PHD	69	Tx A&M	1969
Sawyer, W. Charles	Prof	266-4489	F	PHD	83	Arkansas	1983
Klinedinst, Mark A.	Assoc	266-4649	P	PHD	87	Cornell	1986
Niroomand, Farhang	Assoc	266-5028	F	PHD	83	Mich St	1984
Whitesell, Frank Cook	Assoc	266-4366	A	PHD	71	Tulane	1968
Dickie, Mark T.	Asst	266-4648	Q	PHD	89	Wyoming	1994
Goffe, William L.	Asst	266-4484	C	PHD	90	N Carol	1993
Green, Trellis Garnett	Asst	266-4662	Q	PHD	84	Fla St	1983
McQuiston, James M. Jr.	Asst	266-4234		BS	56	So Miss	1960
Mixon, Frank	Asst	266-4648	J	PHD	92	Auburn	1994

Southern Nazarene Univ	Bethany, OK		73008	(405) 491-6359				
Economics Faculty	School of Business			Fax=491-6384			NOV.SNU.EDU	
Mills, Larry W.	C-Pr	491-6392	lmills	Mgt	PHD	78	Oklahoma	1969
Seyfert, Jeff	Asst	491-6671	jseyfert		MBA	89	Tulsa	1990
Southern Oregon St College	Ashland, OR		97520-5022	(503) 552-6431				
Department of Economics	Social Science Area			Fax=552-6439			SOSC1.SOSC.OSSHE.EDU	
Pirasteh, Hassan	Prof	552-6434	pirasteh	CEG	PHD	85	Oregon	1982
Rubenson, Daniel L.	Prof	482-6437	drube	CEK	PHD	85	Car Mellon	1986
3/4 time administration								
Young, Linda W.	Assoc		lwyoung	JEOF	PHD	87	Berkeley	1994
Southern Utah University	Cedar City, UT		84720	(801) 865-8167				
Dept of Businss-Economics	Sch of Bus, Tech & Comm			Fax=586-5493				
Salmon, Robert O.	Dean	586-5401		Mgt	MS	78	Ariz St	1991
Horgesheimer, Jerry	C-Ac	586-5407			PHD	73	Ariz St	1992
Bowman, Rhead S.	Assoc	586-5412			PHD	75	Utah	1978
Porter, Arthur L.	Assoc	586-5404			MBA	70	Stanford	1987
Groesbeck, John D.	Asst	586-7784			PHD	93	Utah St	1993
Southwest Baptist Univ	Bolivar, MO		65613-2496	(417) 326-1951				
Business Administration	College of Business			Fax=326-1887				
Middleton, Kenneth A.	Dean	326-1752		Mgt	PHD		Ariz St	1991
DeBauche, Susan	C-As	326-1951		Bus	EDD		Arkansas	1985
Jones, James G.	Asst	326-1757		ECO	MBA		Arkansas	1988
Southwest Missouri St Univ	Springfield, MO		65804-0094	(417) 836-5516			Ms. Annette Havens	
Department of Economics	Col Humanity & Pub Aff			Fax=836-8972			VMA.SMSU.EDU	
Warren, Bernice S.	Dean	836-5529		Engl	PHD	67	Missouri	1969
Hoftyzer, John	H-Pr	836-5347	joh689f		PHD	74	Indiana	1987
Bell, Joe A.	Prof	836-5140	jab856f		PHD	80	Okla St	1971
Hoppes, Robert B.	Prof	836-5352	rbh018f		PHD	75	Nebraska	1980
Lages, John David	Prof	836-5515	jdl934f		PHD	67	Iowa St	1963
Stone, Allan D.	Prof	836-5350			PHD	73	Oklahoma	1972
Wasson, E. Dale	Prof	836-5349	edw389f		PHD	80	Okla St	1969
Wyrick, Thomas L.	Prof	836-5060	tlw918f		PHD	79	Va Tech	1978
Olsen, Reed N.	Assoc	836-5379	rno174f		PHD	89	Illinois	1990
Sheets, Doris Files	Assoc	836-5351	def230f		PHD	81	Missouri	1974
Barari, Mahua	Asst	836-5171	mab953f		PHD	92	Iowa St	1993
Cox, Larry G.	Asst	836-5551			MA	70	Kansas St	1970
Topping, Elizabeth E.	Asst	836-5615	eet326f		PHD	85	Missouri	1979
Geile, Gerald L.	Inst	836-5740	gig138f		MA	91	St Louis	1991
Southwest State University	Marshall, MN		56258	(507)				
Economics Faculty	Dept of Business Adm			Fax=537-6577				
Ramos, Melba	Dean	537-6218		Anth	PHD		Mass	1993
Mitchell, George	C-Pr	537-6223		Mgt	ABD			
Blistein, Allen	Prof				PHD		Minnesota	1976
Cameron, John	Assoc				PHD		Nebraska	1986
Southwest Texas State Univ	San Marcos, TX		78666-4616	(512) 245-2547				
Dept Finance & Economics	School of Business			Fax=245-3089				
Gowens, Paul R.	Dean	245-2311			PHD	73	Miss	1980
Sanders, Don	C-Ac	245-2547			JD	77	Tx-Austin	1979
Blankmeyer, Eric	Prof	245-2547			PHD	71	Princeton	1982
Flammang, Robert A.	Prof	245-2547			PHD	62	Iowa	1991
Morgan, Celia A.	Prof	245-2547			PHD	71	Houston	1971
Savage, Vernon H.	Prof	245-2547			PHD		Tx-Austin	
Mogab, John William	Assoc	245-2547			PHD		Tennessee	
Yeargan, Howard Reig	Assoc	245-2547			MS		Tx A&M	
Charles, Joni S.	Asst	245-2547			PHD	87	Purdue	1984
Kishan, Ruby Pandey	Asst	245-2547			PHD	86	Tx A&M	
McClung, Bruce Alan	Asst	245-2547			PHD	88	Tx A&M	1988
Murphy, Edward V.	Asst	245-2547			PHD		Geo Mason	1992
Showalter, Dean	Asst	245-2547			PHD	94	Kentucky	1995
Southwestern University	Georgetown, TX		78627-0770	(512) 863-1574			Kathy Buchhorn	
Economic & Business Dept	Brown Col of Arts & Sci			Fax=863-5788			RALPH.TXSWU.EDU	
Rosenthal, Michael R.	Dean	863-1567	rosenthm	Chem	PHD		Illinois	1989
Provost								
Sellers, Fred E.	C-Ac	863-1574	sellerf	Atg	PHD	84	Kansas	1987
Northrop, Emily M.	Assoc	863-1591	northroe	ENQR	PHD	88	Tx-Austin	1994
Roberts, Kenneth D.	Assoc	863-1993	robertsk	GFOT	PHD	80	Wisconsin	1981
Young, Mary E.	Assoc	863-1994	youngm	CEJQ	PHD	89	Tx-Austin	1990
Early, Dirk W.	Asst	863-1592	earlyd	DFHR	PHD	95	Virginia	1994

U of Southwestern Louisiana Lafayette, LA 70504-4570 (318) 231-6662 Sheila Beasley
Dept of Economics & Finance Col of Business Admin Fax=231-6195 USL.EDU

Name	Rank	Phone		Field	Degree	Yr	School	Since
Duggar, Jan W.	Dean	231-6491			PHD	67	Fla St	1989
Payne, Bruce	C-Pr	231-6662		Fnce				
Greco, Anthony	Prof	231-6669						
O'Donnell, Margaret	Prof	231-6665						
Gale, Louis	Asst	231-6663			PHD	94	Ariz St	1995
Heath, W. Cary	Asst	231-5728			PHD	82	LSU	
La Point, James	Asst	231-6671						
McLean, Roy L.	Asst	231-6047			PHD	94	S Calif	1995
Ressler, Rand	Asst	231-6666						
Waters, Melissa	Asst	231-6082						
Watson, J. Keith	Asst	231-5727			PHD	83	Tx A&M	
Rumore, Nancy C.	Inst	231-6667			MS	80	LSU	

Southwestern Oklahoma St U Weatherford, OK 73096-3098 (405) 774-3066 Nancy Grammer
Dept Economics & Bus Adm School of Business Fax=774-3795

Name	Rank	Phone		Field	Degree	Yr	School	Since
Kaufman, Jerry M.	Dean	774-3282		Atg	PHD	74	Okla St	1992
Rhee, Anthony	C-Pr	774-3049			PHD	79	Kent St	1994
Jawahar, Jim	Prof	774-3045						
Nowka, Harry E.	Prof	774-3754			EDD		Okla St	1963
Russell, R. K.	Prof	774-3081			PHD		Okla St	1973
Sehorn, Annette	Prof	774-3040						
Hankins, Marvin	Asst	774-3750			EDD		Okla St	1979
Sanders, Kenneth K.	Asst	774-3706			PHD	90	Utah St	1990

Stanford University Stanford, CA 94305-6072 (415) 725-3266 Jennifer Cairns 723-3713
Department of Economics Sch of Humanities & Sci Fax=725-5702 LELAND

Name	Rank	Phone		Field	Degree	Yr	School	Since
Shoven, John B.	Dean	723-3273			PHD	73	Yale	1978
Starrett, David A.	C-Pr	723-3712	dstar		PHD	68	Stanford	1973
Amemiya, Takeshi	Prof	723-3986			PHD	64	J Hopkins	1968
Aoki, Masahiko	Prof	723-3975			PHD	67	Minnesota	1984
Bernheim, B. Douglas	Prof	725-8732			PHD	82	MIT	1994
Boskin, Michael J.	Prof	723-3864			PHD	71	Berkeley	1970
Bresnahan, Timothy F.	Prof	723-9471			PHD	80	Princeton	1979
Brown, Donald J.	Prof	725-2726			PHD	69	Stevens	1988
David, Paul A.	Prof	723-3710			PHD	73	Harvard	1969
Fuchs, Victor R.	Emer	326-7639			PHD	55	Columbia	1974
Hall, Robert E.	Prof	723-2215			PHD	67	MIT	1978
Hammond, Peter J.	Prof	723-3987			PHD	74	Cambridge	1979
Harris, Donald J.	Prof	723-3028			PHD	66	Berkeley	1972
Hickman, Bert G.	Emer	723-3417			PHD	51	Berkeley	1966
Krueger, Anne	Prof	723-0188			PHD	58	Wisconsin	
Krugman, Paul R.	Prof	723-7359		F	PHD	77	MIT	1994
Kurz, Mordecai	Prof	723-2220			PHD	61	Yale	1966
Lau, Lawrence J.	Prof	723-3708			PHD	69	Berkeley	1966
MaCurdy, Thomas E.	Prof	723-3983			PHD	78	Chicago	1983
McKinnon, Ronald I.	Prof	723-3721			PHD	61	Minnesota	1961
Milgrom, Paul R.	Prof	723-3397			PHD	79	Stanford	1987
Noll, Roger G.	Prof	723-2297			PHD	67	Harvard	1984
Pencavel, John H.	Prof	723-3981			PHD	69	Princeton	1979
Associate Chair								
Rosenberg, Nathan	Prof	723-1902			PHD	55	Wisconsin	
Stiglitz, Joseph E.	Prof	723-9309			PHD	86	MIT	
on leave to Council of Economic Advisers								
Taylor, John B.	Prof	723-9677			PHD	73	Stanford	
Wright, Gavin	Prof	723-3837			PHD	69	Yale	1982
Greif, Avner	Assoc	725-8936			PHD	89	Northwes	1993
Wolak, Frank A.	Assoc	723-3944			PHD	85	Harvard	1986
Horvath, Michael	Asst	723-4116			PHD	94	Northwes	1994
Jones, Chad	Asst	723-9276			PHD	93	MIT	1993
Kochar, Anjini	Asst	723-9766			PHD	91	Chicago	1990
Litwack, John M.	Asst	723-2296			PHD	88	Penn	1988
McClellan, Mark	Asst				PHD	93	Harvard	9-95
Nechyba, Thomas	Asst	723-5962			PHD	94	Rochester	1994
Qian, Yingyi	Asst	723-3984			PHD	90	Harvard	1990
Royalty, Anne	Asst	723-2298			PHD	93	Yale	1993
Schaffner, Julie L.	Asst	723-3978			PHD	86	Yale	

SUNY at Fredonia Fredonia, NY 14063-1198 (716) 673-3509 Dorothy Radloff
Economics Faculty Department of Economics Fax=673-3332 JANE.CS.FREDONIA.EDU

Name	Rank	Phone	Email	Field	Degree	Yr	School	Since
Hansen, John A.	C-Pr	673-3509	hansen	LD	PHD	80	Yale	1984
El Nasser, Marwan M.	Prof	673-3509	elnasser	EG	PHD	70	Ohio St	1970
Foeller, William H.	Prof	673-3509	foeller	AJ	PHD	72	Iowa St	1984
Parai, Amar K.	Prof	673-3522	parai	AF	PHD	79	So Meth	1988
Choudhary, Munir A. S.	Assoc	673-3522	choudhary	CE	PHD	85	Fla St	1987
Peterson, Janice L.	Assoc	673-3403	peterson	BA	PHD	87	Nebraska	1990
Sarkar, Amin U.	Assoc	673-3403	sarkar	OQ	PHD	88	Berkeley	1989
El-Mofty, Samar M.	Asst	673-3403	elmofty	IJ	PHD	83	Illinois	1989

SUNY Col at Cortland Cortland, NY 13045 (607) 753-4109 Denise Riley
Department of Economics College of Arts & Sci Fax=

Name	Rank	Phone		Degree	Yr	School	Year
Phillips, Timothy P.	C-As	753-2440		MBA		Clarkson	
Doane, Donna L.	Assoc	753-2439		PHD			
Prus, Mark J.	Assoc	753-5758		PHD		Utah	
Surette, Gerald M.	Assoc	753-2434		BA			
Wickman, Kenneth P.	Assoc	753-2436		PHD	62	Syracuse	1968
Botwinick, Howard I.	Asst	753-2435		PHD		New Sch	
Choudhury, Sharmila	Asst	753-2441		BA	80	Calcutta	1989
Krall, Mary Elyse	Asst	753-2438					
Lynch, Robert	Asst	753-2440		PHD			
Polley, Susanne M.	Asst	753-2469					
Asuzu, Mark	Lect	753-2213					
Avery, Emerson R.	Lect	753-4109					
Berardi, Peter A.	Lect	753-5782		MBA			
Chase, Larry	Lect	753-4109					
Graham, Katherine	Lect	753-4110		MS		Cornell	
Shirley, John	Lect	753-2190					
VonDonsel, Richard	Lect	753-2469					

State Un College at Geneseo Geneseo, NY 14454-1401 (716) 245-5367
Department of Economics Jones Sch of Business Fax=245-5467

Name	Rank	Phone	Field	Degree	Yr	School	Year
Moore, Gary A.	H-Pr	245-5367	JK	PHD	74	Nebraska	9-74
Martin, David A.	Prof	245-5372	BA	PHD	64	Syracuse	1966
Strang, Daniel R.	Prof	245-5365	CQ	PHD	75	Cornell	1992
Morse, Kenneth O.	Asst	245-5466	FA	PHD	94	Denver	1992
Stone, Leonie L.	Asst	245-4365	OD	PHD	93	Ohio St	1993

SUNY at Old Westbury Old Westbury, NY 11568 (516)
Economics Faculty Dept of Bus Econ & Fnce Fax=876-3209 SNYOLDVA

Name	Rank	Phone		Degree	Yr	School	Year
O'Sullivan, Patrick	C-Pr			PHD		Fordham	
Forti, Annette	Prof			PHD		Fordham	
Geyikdogi, Yasar	Prof			PHD		Bath	
Leon, Hyglus	Assoc			PHD		S Hamptn	
Mickens, Alvin D.	Assoc	876-3331		PHD	72	NYU	1978
Tabriztchi, Sireusse	Assoc			PHD		Columbia	

SUNY College at Oneonta Oneonta, NY 13820 (607) 436-3458 Ms. Dawn Sanzone
Dept of Economics & Business Liberal Arts & Business Fax=436-2543

Name	Rank	Phone	Field	Degree	Yr	School	Year
Maguire, Margaret S.	Dean$	436-3694	M	PHD		Penn	1995
Lubell, Alfred M.	C-Pr	436-3458	ADF	PHD	74	NYU	1974
Ring, David W.	Assoc	436-2127	DEPR	PHD	82	SUNY-SBr	1981
Thomas, Wade L.	Assoc	436-2116	DE	PHD	82	Nebraska	1989
Beck, Edward J.	Asst	436-3695	DE	MBA	82	Syracuse	1977
Ingalls, Carolyn A.	Asst	436-3519	M	MBA		SUNY-Bin	
Krug, Ronald W.	Asst	436-2448	M	MBA		SUNY-Alb	
Majestic, Paulette R.	Asst	436-3381	M	MBA		Pittsburgh	
Matukonis, Michael	Asst	436-2544	M	MBA		Idaho	
O'Dea, William P.	Asst	436-2127	DEP	PHD	88	SUNY-Alb	1979
Puritz, Frederick A.	Asst	436-3509	M	MBA		Harvard	
Sessions, Lynne	Asst	436-3184	M	MBA		Pittsburgh	
Walsh, Stephen M.	Asst	436-3213	M	PHD		Ca-River	

SUNY College at Oswego Oswego, NY 13126 (315) 341-2137 Betty Bennett
Economics Faculty Col of Arts & Sciences Fax=341-5444 OSWEGO.OSWEGO.EDU

Name	Rank	Phone		Degree	Yr	School	Year
Kane, John C.	C-Ac$	341-3479		PHD	86	SUNY-SBr	1983
Jhun, U-Jin	Prof	341-3486		PHD	73	SUNY-Alb	1972
Spizman, Lawrence	Prof	341-3485		PHD	77	SUNY-Alb	1977
Atri, Said	Assoc	341-2175		PHD	82	SUNY-Alb	1981
Miller, Jack	Assoc	341-3484		PHD	84	W Virginia	1981
Prychitko, David	Assoc	341-3417		PHD	88	Geo Mason	1989
Dunne, Elizabeth A.	Asst	341-3488		ABD		Iowa	1990
Graham, Glenn	Asst	341-3482		PHD	95	SUNY-Bin	
Hornig, Ellen	Asst	341-3480		PHD	87	Cornell	1984
Shiman, Daniel R.	Asst	341-3487		PHD	86	Northwes	1990

SUNY at Stony Brook Stony Brook, NY 11794-4384 (516) 632-7550 Ruth Ben-Zvi, 632-7527
Economics Faculty Department of Economics Fax=632-7516 DATALAB2.SBS.SUNYSB.EDU

Name	Rank	Phone	Email	Degree	Yr	School	Year
Muench, Thomas	C-Pr	632-7560	tmuench	PHD	65	Purdue	1975
Dubey, Pradeep	Prof	632-7549		PHD	75	Cornell	1989
Hause, John C.	Prof	632-7530	jhause	PHD	62	Chicago	1978
Hool, Bryce	Prof	632-7012		PHD	74	Berkeley	1979
Hurd, Michael	Prof	632-7551	mhurd	PHD	71	Berkeley	1978
Neuberger, Egon	Prof	632-7545		PHD	58	Harvard	1967
Director of Graduate Studies							
Neyman, Abraham	Prof	632-7546		PHD	77	Hebrew U	1989
Sanderson, Warren	Prof	632-7552	wsanderson	PHD	74	Stanford	1989

Name	Rank	Phone	E-mail	Field	Degree	Yr	Institution	Year
Tauman, Yair	Prof	632-7557			PHD	79	Hebrew U	1989
Zschock, Dieter	Prof	632-7553	ozschock		PHD	67	Tufts	1966
Zweig, Michael	Prof	632-7536	mzweig		PHD	67	Michigan	1967
Mittnik, Stefan	Assoc	632-7532	smittnik		PHD	87	Wash U	1987
Montgomery, Mark	Assoc	632-7523	mmontgomery		PHD	82	Michigan	1988
Prusa, Thomas	Assoc	632-7563	tprusa		PHD	88	Stanford	
Aoki, Reiko	Asst	632-7558	raoki		PHD	87	Stanford	1990
Cassou, Steven P.	Asst	632-7559	scassou		PHD	89	Minnesota	1988
Hillas, John	Asst	632-7562	jhillas		PHD	87	Stanford	1990
Kamihigashi, Takashi	Asst	632-7548	tkamihigashi		PHD	94	Wisconsin	1994
Dawes, William	Lect	632-7534	wdawes		PHD	72	Purdue	1969
Director of Undergraduate Studies								
Univ at Albany, SUNY	Albany, NY		12222	(518) 442-4735			Sue Phillips	
Department of Economics	Col of Arts & Sciences		Fax=442-4736				ALBANY.EDU	
Gillespie, Judith	Dean	442-4654	dean@cas.					
Lahiri, Kajal	C-Pr	442-4758	kl758@cnsibm.	E	PHD	75	Rochester	1977
Daniel, Betty C.	Prof	442-4747	bd892@cnsvax.	EF	PHD	76	N Carol	1983
Kinal, Terrance	Prof	442-4744	twk58@cnsibm.		PHD	76	Minnesota	1980
Renshaw, Edward F.	Prof	442-4756	renshaw@cnsibm.		H	PHD		
Chicago								
Santiago, Carlos E.	Prof	442-4890	ces95@cnsvax.	OJ	PHD	82	Cornell	1988
Sattinger, Michael	Prof	442-4761	ms339@cnsibm.	J	PHD	73	Car Mellon	1981
Uppal, Joginder S.	Prof	442-4748	jsull@cnsvax.	OH	PHD		Minnesota	
Walker, Franklin V.	Prof	442-4749	fwalker@cnsibm.	FE	PHD	58	Harvard	1966
Dieffenbach, Bruce C.	Assoc	442-4750	bd455@cnsvax.	E	PHD	72	Harvard	1978
Jerison, Michael	Assoc	442-4287	mi770@cnsvax.	DC	PHD		Wisconsin	
Kalish, Richard J.	Assoc	442-4760	rkalish@cnsvax.	N	PHD	63	Colorado	1969
Lankford, R. Hamilton	Assoc	442-4743	rh104@cnsvax.	HD	PHD	81	N Carol	1981
Lee, Pong S.	Assoc	442-4759	plee@cnsvax.	OE	PHD		Yale	
Mirer, Thad W.	Assoc	442-4755	mirer@cnsibm.	H	PHD	71	Yale	1973
Reeb, Donald J.	Assoc	442-4738	dreeb@cnsvax.	RG	PHD	63	Syracuse	1965
Yun, Kwan Koo	Assoc	442-4741	ky948@cnsvax.	CD	PHD		Stanford	
Chaudhuri, Anita	Asst	442-4139	ac256@cnsvax.	IJ	PHD		Rutgers	
Joh, Sung-Wook	Asst	442-4737	joh@cnsvax.		PHD		Harvard	
Kim, Jae-Young	Asst	442-4926	jykim@cnsunix.		PHD		Minnesota	
Sanjak, Jolyne	Asst	442-4751	jss82@cnsvax.	QF	PHD		Wisconsin	
SUNY at Binghamton	Binghamton, NY		13902-6000	(607) 777-2572			Joanne F. Ardune	
Div Soc Sci - Dept Economics	Harpur Col Arts & Sci		Fax=777-2681				BINGVMB.BITNET	
Brehm, Sharon S.	Dean			Psyc	PHD		Duke	
Polachek, Solomon W.	C-Pr	777-2572	bg2776		PHD	73	Columbia	1983
Basmann, Robert L.	Prof	777-2228			PHD	66	Iowa St	1988
Bischoff, Charles W.	Prof	777-2647			PHD	68	MIT	1977
Director of Graduate Studies								
Britto, Ronald	Prof	777-2660			PHD	66	Brown	1974
Clark, Clifford D.	Prof	777-4351			PHD	53	Chicago	1973
Cowing, Thomas G.	Prof		bg1894		PHD	70	Berkeley	1969
Greene, Kenneth V.	Prof	777-2944			PHD	68	Virginia	1968
Masters, Stanley H.	Prof	777-2660			PHD	65	Princeton	1981
Nelson, Phillip J.	Prof	777-2228			PHD	67	Columbia	1969
Eapen, A. Thomas	Assoc	777-2339			PHD	61	Michigan	1966
Kern, Clifford R.	Assoc	777-2228			PHD	74	Harvard	1971
Kokkelenberg, Edward C.	Assoc	777-2550			PHD	81	Northwes	1980
Leighton, Richard I.	Assoc	777-2339			PHD	61	Duke	1964
Liu, Jung-Chao	Assoc	777-2689			PHD	60	Michigan	1970
Lovejoy, Robert M.	Assoc	777-2944			PHD	63	Michigan	1965
Ofek, Haim	Assoc	777-4351			PHD	71	Columbia	1981
Seiglie, Carlos	Assoc				PHD	91	Chicago	1994
Yoon, Bong J.	Assoc	777-2689			PHD	78	Illinois	1983
Kang, Inbong	Asst				PHD	93	Rochester	1995
SUNY at Buffalo	Buffalo, NY		14260-1520	(716) 645-2121				
Department of Economics	Fac of Social Science		Fax=645-2127				UBVM	
Mackinnon, Ross D.	Dean	636-3101		Geog	PHD		NYU	
Michaels, Albert	C $	645-2121						
Anas, Alex	Prof	645-2121	ecoalex	DR	PHD	75	Penn	1991
Chang, Winston W.	Prof	645-2121	ecochang	DF	PHD	68	Rochester	1967
Gort, Michael	Prof	645-2121	ecogort	O	PHD	54	Columbia	1964
Revankar, Nagesh S.	Prof	645-2121	ecorevan	DC	PHD	67	Wisconsin	1967
Zarembka, Paul	Prof	645-2121	ecopaulz	BO	PHD	67	Wisconsin	1976
Harwitz, Mitchell	Assoc	645-2121	ecohar	COTR	PHD	59	MIT	1958
Holmes, James M.	Assoc	645-2121		EF	PHD	67	Chicago	1967
Morgan, Peter B.	Assoc	645-2121	ecopetem	D	PHD	78	Canterbu	1989
Romans, Thomas J.	Assoc	645-2121	ecoroman	HR	PHD	63	Brown	1967
Barnett, Richard	Asst	645-2121	ecobarn	EF	PHD	89	Minnesota	1989
Geide-Stevenson, Doris	Asst	645-2121		DF	PHD	95	SUNY-Buf	1995
Ljungqvist, Lars	Asst	645-2121	ljung	EF	PHD	88	Minnesota	1994
Yin, Yong	Asst	645-2121		CDE	PHD	95	Ohio St	1995

SUNY Empire State College Saratoga Spr, NY 12866-4391 (518) 587-2100
Economic Faculty Business Mgt & Econ Fax=587-5448 SESCVA.ESC.EDU
area codes 598=(212) 587=(518) 358&948=(914) 360&997=(516) 394&886&244=(716)

Name	Phone	Email	Fields	Degree	School	Year
Angiello, Joseph	358-3990	jangiello	A	PHD	Tx-Austin	1983
DuBois, David	244-3884	ddubois	M	PHD	Union In	1976
Fortunato, Michael	587-2100	mfortuna	OMF	PHD	Harvard	1990
Giordano, Justin	598-0640	jgiordan	M	MBA	St Johns	1992
Herdendorf, Phyllis	886-8020	pherdend	F	PHD	SUNY	1987
Jarvis, Leslie	997-4700	ljarvis	A	PHD	New Sch	1986
Jones, Otolorin	587-2100	ojones	A	PHD	Ohio U	1985
Lill, Lloyd	394-1110	llill	BO	PHD	Walden	1973
Musoke, Moses	948-6206	mmusoke	NM	PHD	Wisconsin	1985
Pauszek, Ruffin	587-2100	rpauszek	A	MBA	SUNY-Buf	1992
Sussman, Jeffrey	997-4700	jsussman	G	PHD	CUNY	1975
Todd, Edward	360-1215		A	PHD	Chicago	1985
Weiss, Jeffrey	948-6206	jweiss	A	PHD	Harvard	1986

SUNY at New Paltz New Paltz, NY 12561-2499 (914) 257-2969 Jannette Carcich
Department of Economics Economics Fax=257-2947 NPVM.NEWPALTZ.EDU

Name	Rank	Phone	Email	Fields	Degree		School	Year
Bloom, Jay D.	C-Ac	257-2944	bloomj	ADJ	MA	58	Chicago	1965
Garlick, Peter C.	Prof	257-2944		BEHN	PHD	72	London	1969
Sebestyen, Zoltan H.	Assoc	257-3566		DFA	PHD	68	Columbia	1969
Seshu, Chigurupati R.	Assoc	257-3559		AEO	PHD	60	New Sch	1967
Mozayeni, Simin B.	Asst	257-2919		ALH	PHD	53	Columbia	1990

SUNY, Col at Plattsburgh Plattsburgh, NY 12901-2697 (518) 564-3184 Beverly Cross
Department of Economics Sch of Business & Econ Fax=564-3183 SPLAVA.CC.PLATTSBURGH.

Name	Rank	Phone	Email	Fields	Degree		School	Year
Gandhi, Prem P.	Dean	564-3184	gandhipp	FO	PHD	73	New Sch	9-66
Dixon, Warren R.	C-Pr	564-4196	dixonwr	BP	PHD	71	Colorado	1968
Jang, Young S.	Prof	564-4193	jangys	CD	PHD	69	SUNY-Alb	1968
Page, Walter	Prof	564-3182	pagewp	DE	PHD	68	Kansas	1983
Stoller, Michael A.	Prof	564-4195	stollema	MK	PHD	77	Wash U	1975
Withington, Robert P.	Assoc	564-2226	withinpr	NJ	PHD	76	Penn	1972
Christopherson, Robert L.	Asst	564-4218	christrl	GH	PHD	90	Wayne St	1990
Duffy, Neal E.	Asst	564-4194	duffyne	CR	PHD	82	W Virginia	1982
Fitzpatrick, Ellen	Asst	564-3184	fitzpae	FOQ	PHD	94	Mich St	1994

SUNY Col at Potsdam Potsdam, NY 13676-2294 (315) 267-2206 Margaret Nicola
Department of Economics Sch of Arts & Sciences Fax=267-2797

Name	Rank	Phone	Degree		School	Year
Pletcher, Galen K.	Dean	267-2231	PHD		Michigan	
Baktari, Paul	C-Ac	267-2204	PHD		W Virginia	
Chugh, Ram L.	Prof	267-2206	PHD	70	Wayne St	1970
Wightman, James W.	Prof	267-2200	PHD		Clark	
Cliff, Lee	Assoc	267-2295	MBA		Clarkson	
Nuwer, Michael J.	Assoc	267-2077	PHD	85	Utah	1986
Shu, Florence P.	Assoc	267-2221	PHD	86	Mich St	1986
Portugal, Edwin	Asst	267-2212	PHD		SUNY-Alb	
Rezelman, John R.	Asst	267-2202	MA		Indiana	
Zwerling, Harris T.	Asst		PHD	79	Wisconsin	1988

SUNY College at Purchase Purchase, NY 10577-1400 (914) 251-6600 Joan Mazzari
Division of Social Science Coll Arts & Letters Fax=

Name	Rank	Phone	Degree		School	Year
Hunt, Alfred	Dean	251-6480				
Christensen, Kimberly	C-Ac	251-6622	PHD	86	Mass	1985
O'Cleiracain, Seamus	Prof	251-6600	PHD	71	Michigan	1974
Bell, Peter	Assoc	251-6633	PHD	68	Wisconsin	1971
Ikeda, Sanford	Asst	251-6614	PHD	88	NYU	1990

Stephen F. Austin St Univ Nacogdoches, TX 75962-3009 (409) 468-4301 Barbara Roos
Dept of Economics & Finance College of Business Fax=468-1447

Name	Rank	Phone	Fields	Degree		School	Year
Young, Marlin C.	Dean	468-3101	BEd	EDD	74	Ariz St	1967
Jones, Clifton T.	C-Pr	468-4301	CD	PHD	85	Tx A&M	1995
Hunter, Thomas Kenneth	Prof	468-4301		PHD	68	Tennessee	1968
Key, Euell Dwyane	Prof	468-4301		PHD	70	S Illinois	1970
Murdock, E. Wayne	Prof	468-4301		PHD	71	Oklahoma	1972
Howard, James E.	Assoc	468-4301		PHD		Georgia	1976
Stewart, Milton D. Jr.	Assoc	468-4301		PHD	72	Tx-Austin	1966
Dumas, Rocky N.	Lect	468-4301		MBA		SF Austi	1985

Stetson University Deland, FL 32720-3756 (904) 822-7570 Robin Carter
Department of Economics Col of Arts & Sciences Fax=822-7569 SUVAX1.STETSON.EDU

Name	Rank	Phone	Email	Fields	Degree		School	Year
Maris, Gary L.	Dean	822-7515		PolS	PHD		Duke	1986
Wood, Richard H. Jr.	C-Pr	822-7570	wood	AFO	PHD	72	Wisconsin	1970
Long, Neal B.	Prof	822-7571		ACP	PHD	64	Indiana	1974
Thaver, Ranjini L.	Asst	822-7573		AHP	PHD	95	Notre Dm	1992

Richard Stockton College Hoboken, NJ 08240 (609) 652-1776
Department of Economics Social & Behavioral Sci Fax=748-5509 STOCKTON.EDU

Carr, David	Dean	652-1776			PHD		SUNY-Bin	1978
Ghorashi, Gholam-Reza	C-Ac	652-1776			PHD		Fordham	1981
Elmore, Elizabeth A.	Prof	652-1776			PHD		Notre Dm	1972
Harrison, Kenneth	Assoc	652-1776	laprod2556		PHD		SUNY-Alb	1976
Lakew, Melaku	Assoc	652-1776			PHD		Ca-River	1982
Alpan, Erkan	Asst	652-1776			PHD		Ca-River	1980

Stonehill College North Easton, MA 02357 (508) 230-1276
Economics Faculty Dept of Economics Fax=238-9253 LCC.STONEHILL.EDU

Kazemi, Hossein S.	C-Ac	230-1276		EF	PHD		Clark	1982
Pepin, Raymond A.	Prof	238-1270		AD	PHD	71	Clark	1969
Rosenthal, Robert A.	Prof	230-1200		AL	PHD	78	Boston U	1975
Kienzle, Edward C.	Assoc	238-1382		HC	PHD	76	Boston C	1980
Motomura, Akira	Assoc	238-1081		KN	PHD	85	Northwes	1995
Hammerle, Nancy E.	Asst	230-1257		A	MA		Temple	1980
McKinsey, James W.	Asst	230-1080		A	ABD		Yale	1986

Suffolk University Boston, MA 02108-2770 (617) 573-8259 Mary K. Anooshian
Department of Economics Col Liberal Arts & Sci Fax=720-4272 SUFFOLK.EDU

Ronayne, Michael R.	Dean				PHD		Notre Dm	
Tuerck, David G.	C-Pr	573-8259			PHD	66	Virginia	1982
Mohtadi, Shahruz	Assoc				PHD	84	LSU	1983
Sawhney, Saroj	Assoc				PHD		Northeas	
Shannon, John C.	Assoc				MA		Boston C	
Baek, In-Mee	VAsst				PHD		Indiana	
Jaggia, Sanjiv	Asst				PHD	90	Indiana	
Kelly, Alison	Asst				PHD		Boston C	

Susquehanna University Selinsgrove, PA 17870-1001 (717) 372-4186
Department of Economics Weis Sch of Business Fax=372-4491

Bellas, Carl J.	Dean	372-4455		Mgt	PHD	69	Oregon	9-83
Fisher, Warren L.	H-Pr	372-4186		ABQ	PHD	73	Conn	1988
Rusek, Antonin	Assoc	372-4182		EFP	PHD	84	SUNY-SBr	1986
Zadeh, Ali Haji-Mohamad	Assoc	372-4189		CEGO	PHD	82	Mich St	1987
Onafowora, Olugbenga A.	Asst	372-4187		CDOQ	PHD	89	W Virginia	1989

Swarthmore College Swarthmore, PA 19081-1397 (610) 328-8125 Rose Maio/M. A. Stewart
Department of Economics Div of Social Sciences Fax=328-7352 SWARTHMORE.EDU

Golub, Stephen S.	C-Pr	328-8103	sgolub1	AE	PHD	83	Yale	1981
Hollister, Robinson G. Jr.	Prof	328-8105	rhollis1	IJ	PHD	65	Stanford	1971
Joseph Wharton Professor of Economics								
Kuperberg, Mark J.	Prof	328-8123	mkuperb1	EK	PHD	81	MIT	1977
Pryor, Frederic	Prof	328-8130	fpryor1	OP	PHD	57	Yale	1972
Saffran, Bernard	Prof	328-8124	bsaffra1	AH	PHD	63	Minnesota	1973
Franklin and Betty Barr Professor of Economics								
Westphal, Larry E.	Prof	328-8096	lwestph1	DO	PHD	69	Harvard	1985
Caskey, John P.	Assoc	328-8128	jcaskey1	EG	PHD	84	Stanford	1988
Magenheim, Ellen B.	Assoc	328-8140	emagen1	DI	PHD	86	Maryland	1986
O'Connell, Stephen A.	Assoc	328-8107	soconne1	EO	PHD	86	MIT	1990
Bayer, Amanda	Asst	328-7821	abayer1	DJ	ABD		Yale	1992

Syracuse University Syracuse, NY 13244-1090 (315) 443-3843 Dee Ficarro 443-3414
Department of Economics Maxwell S Citznship &PA Fax=443-9082 SUVM.SYR.EDU
email @1=maxwell.syr.edu

Palmer, John L.	Dean	443-2252			PHD	70	Stanford	1988
Wasylenko, Michael J.	C-Pr	443-3612	mwasylanico@1		PHD	75	Syracuse	1989
Burkhauser, Richard V.	Prof	443-3114	burkhaus		PHD	76	Chicago	1990
Follain, James R.	Prof	443-2414			PHD	76	Ca-Davis	1988
Greytak, David	Prof	443-9055	dgreytak@1		PHD	68	Wash U	
Kelly, Jerry S.	Prof	443-2345	jskelly		PHD	69	Harvard	
Miner, Jerry	Prof	443-9065	jminer@1		PHD	58	Michigan	
Richardson, J. David	Prof	443-4339	jdrichardson@1		PHD	70	Michigan	
Smeeding, Timothy M.	Prof	443-9045	smeeding		PHD	75	Wisconsin	
Tussing, A. Dale	Prof	443-2642	tussing		PHD	64	Syracuse	1966
Yinger, John M.	Prof	443-9062			PHD	74	Princeton	1986
Dutkowsky, Donald H.	Assoc	443-1918	dutkow		PHD	82	SUNY-Buf	1985
Gensemer, Susan H.	Assoc	443-2294	gensemer		PHD	84	Purdue	
Holtz-Eakin, Douglas	Assoc	443-9050	djheakin		PHD	85	Princeton	
Ondrich, Jan Ivar	Assoc	443-9052			PHD	83	Wisconsin	
Couch, Kenneth A.	Asst	443-5067	kacouch		PHD	92	Northwes	
Crews, Amy D.	Asst				PHD	94	Virginia	
Dunn, Thomas	Asst	443-5053	tadunn		PHD	92	Northwes	
Evensky, Jerry	Asst	443-5863	noze		PHD	84	Syracuse	1985

Greaney, Theresa M. Asst PHD 94 Michigan
Hong, Lu Asst 443-1746 PHD 91 Minnesota
Kao, C. H. Asst 443-3233 cdkao PHD 83 SUNY-SBr
Lovely, Mary E. Asst 443-9048 mel PHD 89 Michigan 1988
Ozlu, Elvan Asst 443-4079 PHD 93 Ariz St

University of Tampa Tampa, FL 33606-1490 (813) Ext 3336
Department of Economics College of Business Fax=258-7408
phone: 253-6222
Stumpf, Steven Dean 253-6221 Mgt PHD 78 NYU 1993
Truscott, Michael Hugh C-Pr 253-6222 AEF PHD 71 LSU 1971
Fesmire, James M. Prof 253-6222 DKL PHD 73 Florida 1973
Dana Professor of Economics
Hoke, Leon R. Jr. Prof 253-6222 ADJ PHD 79 Pittsburgh 1981
Brust, Peter J. Assoc 253-6222 EF PHD 80 Indiana 1981
LeClair, Daniel R. Asst 253-6222 ADL PHD 88 Florida 1989

Tarleton State University Stephenville, TX 76402 (817) 968-9141 Rosiene Robertson968-9021
Dept of Social Sciences Col of Arts & Sciences Fax=968-9784
Johanson, Lamar Dean 968-9141 BioS PHD 67 Tx A&M 1961
Koestler, Fred H-Ac 968-9021 PHD
Atkinson, William Eugene Assoc 968-9021 Hst PHD 78 Tx Chr 1967
Zelman, Patricia G. Assoc 968-9629 N PHD 80 Ohio St 1982
Beaty, William L. Asst 968-9622 ADR MS 73 Utah St 1985
Jafri, Syed Hussain Ali Asst 968-9633 AFG PHD 86 Wisconsin 1989

Taylor University Upland, IN 46989-1001 (317) 998-5135 Nancy Gillespie
Dept of Business, Atg & Econ Division of Business Fax= TAYLORU.EDU
Bennett, Christopher P. C-Ac 998-5318 chbennett MBA 74 UCLA 1988
Associate Dean
Erickson, Lee E. Prof 998-5138 leerickso PHD 75 Michigan 1979
Mitchell, Hadley T. Asst 998-5135 PHD 85 Tennessee 1993

Teikyo Post University Waterbury, CT 06723-2540 (203) 596-4652 Vivian H. Adomaitis
Economic Faculty School of Business Adm Fax=575-9691
Hartman, Frederic C. Dean 596-4651 MBA 56 Penn 1987
Philippides, Andreas Assoc 596-4661 PHD 94 Conn 1988

Temple University Philadelphia, PA 19122 (215) 204-8880 Ms. Karen Robinson
Department of Economics Sch of Business & Mgt Fax=204-8173 TEMPLEVM
Buck, Andrew J. C-Pr 204-1985 C PHD 77 Illinois 1977
Bandera, Vladimir N. Prof 204-5039 FP PHD 60 Berkeley 1972
Blackstone, Erwin A. Prof 204-5027 L PHD 68 Michigan 1976
Dunkelberg, William C. Prof 204-6810 M PHD 69 Michigan 1987
Hakim, Simon Prof 204-5037 R PHD 76 Penn 1976
Kushnirsky, Fyodor I. Prof 204-5021 P PHD 68 Moscow 1980
Raphaelson, Arnold H. Prof 204-8165 H PHD 60 Clark 1970
Rima, Ingrid H. Prof 204-8190 B PHD 51 Penn 1946
Stull, William J. Prof 204-5022 IR PHD 72 MIT 1976
Bernstein, Richard E. Assoc 204-8182 MG PHD 73 Brown 1972
Bowman, Gary W. Assoc 204-5026 D PHD 71 Car Mellon 1973
Diamantaras, Dimitrios Assoc 204-8169 CD PHD 88 Rochester 1988
Fardmanesh, Mohsen Assoc 204-5043 OF PHD 85 Yale 1985
Goetz, Michael Assoc 204-1762 MH PHD 77 Minnesota 1978
Holmes, William L. Assoc 204-8175 CD PHD 66 Illinois 1966
Klotz, Benjamin P. Assoc 204-8452 E PHD 69 Minnesota 1975
Lady, George Assoc 204-8174 CD PHD 67 J Hopkins 1981
Leeds, Michael A. Assoc 204-8030 J PHD 82 Princeton 1982
Phelps, Charlotte D. Assoc 204-1677 TI PHD 61 Yale 1967
Rappoport, Paul N. Assoc 204-5025 C PHD 74 Ohio St 1977
Seidenstat, Paul Assoc 204-8893 H PHD 64 Northwes 1967
Sorrentino, John A. Jr. Assoc 204-8164 Q PHD 73 Purdue 1979
Weintraub, Andrew R. Assoc 787-1919 A PHD 66 Rutgers 1973
Weiss, Merle Assoc 204-5029 IJ PHD 67 Columbia 1972
Bognanno, Michael Asst 204-1680 J PHD 90 Cornell 1990
Ryan, Daniel Asst PL PHD 90 Berkeley 1990
Swanson, Charles Asst 204-8168 E PHD 91 Minnesota 1993
Thomas, Ravi Asst 204-1615 H PHD 88 Berkeley 1989
Westbrook, Jilleen Asst 204-8180 FI PHD 93 Claremont 1993
Wolcott, Susan Asst 204-8887 FN PHD 88 Stanford 1990

University of Tennessee	Knoxville, TN	37996-0550 (615) 974-3303		Donna Kemper 974-1697				
Department of Economics	Col of Business Admin	Fax=974-4601		UTKVM1.UTK.EDU				
Neel, C. Warren	Dean	974-5061		Mgt	PHD	69	Alabama	9-69
Fox, William F.	C-Pr	974-1697	pa11178		PHD	75	Ohio St	1979
Bohm, Robert A.	Prof	974-1687			PHD	71	Wash U	1968
Bowlby, Roger L.	Prof	974-1694			PHD	58	Tx-Austin	1965
Chang, Hui-Shyong	Prof	974-1692			PHD	73	Vanderbilt	1971
Clark, Don P.	Prof	974-1706			PHD	78	Mich St	1978
Cole, William E.	Prof	974-1690			PHD	65	Tx-Austin	1965
Davidson, Paul	Prof	974-4221			PHD	59	Penn	1987
J. Fred Holly Professor of Political Economy								
Garrison, Charles B.	Prof	974-1691			PHD	68	Kentucky	
Herzog, Henry W. Jr.	Prof	974-1701			PHD	74	Maryland	1974
Lee, Feng-Yao	Prof	974-1696			PHD	65	Mich St	
Mayhew, Anne	Prof	974-1689	pa10781		PHD	66	Tx-Austin	1968
Mayo, John W.	Prof	974-6081	pa80898		PHD		Wash U	
Schlottmann, Alan M.	Prof	974-1700			PHD	75	Wash U	1975
Gauger, Jean A.	Assoc	974-1702			PHD	84	Iowa St	1985
Glustoff, E.	Assoc	974-1705			PHD		Stanford	
Kahn, James R.	Assoc	974-1699			PHD	81	Maryland	
Murray, Matthew N.	Assoc	974-5441			PHD	86	Syracuse	1986
Bearse, Peter	Asst	974-3303			PHD	95	Virginia	1995
Farmer, Amy F.	Asst	974-1704			PHD	91	Duke	1992
Rubin, Jonathan D.	Asst	974-1710			PHD		Ca-Davis	1993

Tennessee at Chattanooga	Chattanooga, TN	37403-2598 (615) 755-4360						
Department of Economics	Col of Arts & Sciences	Fax=755-5255				UTCVM.UTC.EDU		
Summerlin, Tim	Dean	755-4635	tsummerlin	Engl	PHD	73	Yale	1994
Hutchinson, E. Bruce	H	755-4180	bhutchin	DFLR	PHD	79	Virginia	1982
Clark, J. R.	Prof	755-4118	jclark	M	PHD	70	Va Tech	1993
Probasco Chair in Free Enterprise								
Giffin, Phillip E.	Prof	755-4129		DBLN	PHD	72	Tennessee	1977
Keilany, Ziad	Prof	755-4116		EO	PHD	68	Indiana	1968
Guerry Professor								
Pratt, Leila J.	Prof	755-4138	lpratt	DC	PHD	75	Va Tech	1974
Hart Professor								
Rabin, Alan	Prof	755-4154		E	PHD	77	Virginia	1977
UC Foundation Professor								
Efaw, Fritz W.	Assoc	755-4688		CJ	PHD	87	Rutgers	1988
Garrett, John R.	Assoc	755-4080		EFG	PHD	85	Mass	1984
UC Foundation Associate Professor								

Univ of Tennessee at Martin	Martin, TN	38238-5015 (901) 587-7226				Tammy McWherter		
Department of Econ & Finance	Sch of Business Admin	Fax=587-7241						
Young, Gary F.	Dean	587-7225			PHD	77	La Tech	
Figgins, Bob G.	C-Pr	587-7232			PHD	73	Arkansas	1973
Barr, Saul Z.	Prof	587-7239			EDD		Florida	
Cashdollar, Parker D.	Prof	587-7242			PHD	71	Tennessee	
Davis, William L.	Assoc	587-7228			PHD		Okla St	

Tennessee State University	Nashville, TN	37203-3401 (615)						
Dept of Economics & Finance	School of Business	Fax=						
Curry, Tilden J.	Dean	963-7124		Plan	PHD	78	Fla St	1976
Hartmann, G. Bruce	H-Pr	963-7146			PHD	74	SUNY-Alb	1974
MBA Coordinator								
Hasty, John M. Jr.	Prof				PHD	73	Geo State	
Holbrook, Selah Thomas	Prof				PHD	74	Georgia	
Masten, John T.	Prof				PHD	67	S Illinois	
Vowels, Robert C.	Prof				PHD	64	American	
Wahid, Abu	VProf				PHD		Manitoba	
Weis, Charles E.	Prof				DBA	74	Ariz St	
Chevin, Stanley	Asst				PHD	75	Tennessee	

Tennessee Technological Un	Cookeville, TN	38505 (615)				TNTECH		
Dept of Economics & Finance	Col of Business Admin	Fax=372-6112						
Bell, Robert R.	Dean	372-3372		Mgt	PHD	70	Florida	1976
Williams, Norman C.	C-Ac	372-3745			PHD	72	Arkansas	1972
Cho, Whewon	Prof	528-3160			PHD	71	Vanderbilt	1983
Throckmorton, H. Bruce	Prof				PHD	72	Arkansas	1971
Isbell, Steven	Assoc				PHD	85	Miss	1985
Rappi, Magdalena	Assoc				PHD	85	S Carol	1985
Stephens, Mark A.	Assoc	528-3368			PHD	85	Tennessee	1980
Jonokin, Jon	Asst	372-3767			PHD	94	Tennessee	1989

U of Texas at Arlington Arlington, TX 76019-0479 (817) 273-3061 Barbara Seller, Adm Asst
Department of Economics College of Business Adm Fax=273-3145 WILLARD.UTA.EDU

Name	Rank	Phone	Email	Field	Degree	Yr	School	Since
Petersen, Russell J.	Dean	273-2881		Atg	PHD	71	U Wash	8-94
Martin, Robert E.	C-Pr	273-3061	bmart	CD	PHD	79	So Meth	1991
Amacher, Ryan C.	Prof	273-3061		FH	PHD	71	Virginia	1992
Carney, Kim	Prof	273-3064		I	PHD	68	So Meth	1967
Furubotn, Eirik G.	Prof	273-3396		DNB	PHD	59	Columbia	1982
Eunice & James L. West Chair								
Gramm, Wendy L.	Prof	273-3061		K	PHD	71	Northwes	1993
Hayashi, Paul M.	Prof	273-3257		D	PHD	69	So Meth	1965
Holland, Thomas E.	Prof	273-3061		D	PHD	63	Duke	1970
Meiners, Roger E.	Prof	273-3116		KJ	PHD	76	Va Tech	1993
Miller, Roger F.	Prof	273-3061		K	PHD	68	Chicago	1993
Mullendore, Walter	Prof	273-3397		R	PHD	68	Iowa St	1969
Zeigler, Lawrence F.	Prof	273-3384	ziegler	M	PHD	69	Iowa	1969
Cardenas, Jill	Assoc	273-3849		I	PHD	89	North Tx	1990
Duwaji, Ghazi	Assoc	273-3148		F	PHD	66	Duke	1966
Himarios, Daniel D.	Assoc	273-3278		FE	PHD	84	Va Tech	1983
McCall, John B.	Assoc	273-3283		OQ	PHD	68	Okla St	1964
Nehman, Gerlad	Assoc	273-3287		Q	PHD	73	Ohio St	1993
Crowder, William J.	Asst	273-3147		EF	PHD	93	Arizona	1992
Fleissig, Adrian R.	Asst	273-3284		O	PHD	93	N Carol	1993
Smythe, Donald J.	Asst	273-3090		BR	PHD	93	Yale	1992
Wilson, Richard C.	Asst	273-3383		AH	MA	66	Georgia	1966
Himarios, Jane	Lect	273-3293			PHD	83	Va Tech	1986
Liggett, Ron	Lect	273-2635			MBA	89	Tx-Arlin	1989
McCraw, Jessica	Lect	273-3286			MA	78	DePaul	1990
Okello, Paul F.	Lect				MA	89	Tx-Arlin	1990
Wilson, Linda	Lect	273-3282			MS	92	North Tx	1993

Univ of Texas at Austin Austin, TX 78712-1172 (512) 471-3211 Kathy Slade, Exec Asst
Department of Economics College of Liberal Arts Fax=471-3510 MUNDO.ECO.UTEXAS.EDU

Name	Rank	Phone	Field	Degree	Yr	School	Since
Ekland-Olson, Sheldon	Dean		Soci	PHD	71	Wash	9-71
Dusansky, Richard	C-Pr	471-3211	DH	PHD	69	Brown	9-89
Richard J. Gonzales Regents Chair Professor							
Dacy, Douglas C.	Prof	471-3211	EO	PHD	64	Harvard	1-65
Fullerton, Don	Prof	471-3211	HQ	PHD	78	Berkeley	9-94
Addison Baker Duncan Centennial Professor of Economics							
Geraci, Vincent J.	Prof	471-3211	CI	PHD	74	Wisconsin	9-73
Glade, William P. Jr.	Prof	471-3211	OR	PHD	55	Tx-Austin	9-70
Senior Scholar Latin American Program							
Hamermesh, Daniel S.	Prof	471-3211	J	PHD	69	Yale	9-73
E.E. Hale Centennial Professor & Director Center for Applied Research in Econ							
Hansen, Niles M.	Prof	471-3211	RP	PHD	63	Indiana	1-63
Leroy G. Denmann, Jr. Regents Professor in Economics							
Jannuzi, F. Tomasson	Prof	471-3211	OR	PHD	58	LondonEc	9-68
Associate Chair							
Kendrick, David A.	Prof	471-3211	CE	PHD	66	MIT	7-70
Ralph W. Yarborough Centennial Professor of Liberal Arts							
McAfee, R. Preston	Prof	471-3211	D	PHD	80	Purdue	9-90
Rex G. Baker, Jr. Professor of Political Economy							
McDonald, Stephen L.	Prof	471-3211	HQ	PHD	51	Tx-Austin	9-61
Addison Baker Duncan Centennial Professor in Economics							
Morgan, Daniel C. Jr.	Prof	471-3211	H	PHD	62	Wisconsin	7-76
Norman, Alfred L.	Prof	471-3211	C	PHD	71	Minnesota	7-72
Sibley, David S.	Prof	471-3211	D	PHD	73	Yale	1-91
John Michael Stuart Centennial Professor of Ecnomics							
Slesnick, Daniel T.	Prof	471-3211	CH	PHD	82	Harvard	9-82
Stahl, Dale O.	Prof	471-3211	DC	PHD	81	Berkeley	7-88
Bronars, Stephen G.	Assoc	471-3211	JD	PHD	83	Chicago	9-92
Cleaver, Harry	Assoc	471-3211	P	PHD	75	Stanford	9-76
Conroy, Michael E.	Assoc	471-3211	OR	PHD	72	Illinois	9-71
Freeman, Scott	Assoc	471-3211	E	PHD	83	Minnesota	9-91
Kumbhakar, Subal C.	Assoc	471-3211	CD	PHD	86	S Calif	9-86
Stinchcombe, Maxwell B.	Assoc	471-3211	DC	PHD	86	Berkeley	1-94
Wilson, Paul W.	Assoc	471-3211	RC	PHD	86	Brown	9-90
Burke, Jonathan L.	Asst	471-3211	D	PHD	85	MIT	7-90
Conklin, James A.	Asst	471-3211	EN	PHD	93	Stanford	1-94
Hanson, Gordon H.	Asst	471-3211	FO	PHD	92	MIT	9-92
Hickenbottom, Wayne R.	Asst	471-3211	HJ	PHD	92	Minnesota	9-91
Oettinger, Gerald	Asst	471-3211	JC	PHD	93	MIT	9-92
Scoones, W. David	Asst	471-3211	D	PHD	91	Queen's	9-93
Wilcoxen, Peter J.	Asst	471-3211	QD	PHD	89	Harvard	9-91
Zheng, Xu John	Asst	471-3211	CO	PHD	92	Princeton	9-92

Univ Texas at Brownsville	Brownsville, TX	78520	(210) 544-8267				Molly Delgado	
Business Adm Department	School of Business	Fax=982-0159					UTB.EDU	
Boze, Betsy V.	Dean	982-0231	bboze	Mktg	PHD	84	Arkansas	1994
Florey, Randall	C-Ac	982-0230		Mktg	PHD	82	North Tx	1990
Buettgen, Elise	Assoc	982-0232		AFG	PHD	53	Kiel	1979
Lackey, Charles	Assoc			AFL	PHD	84	S Carol	1995
McCorkle, Gary	Asst	544-8991		ABM	MS	71	E Tx St	1989

Univ of Texas at Dallas	Richardson, TX	75083-0688	(214) 883-2920				Mary Jane Tate	
Dept of Economics & Finance	Sch of Social Sciences	Fax=883-2735					UTDALLAS.EDU	
Hanson, Royce	Dean	883-2935	royce		PHD	63	American	1963
Beron, Kurt J.	H-Ac	883-2929	kberon		PHD	85	N Carol	1985
Associate Dean								
Berry, Brian J. L.	Prof	883-2041	berry		PHD	58	Wash	
L. V. Berkner Professor								
Dumas, Lloyd J.	Prof	883-2010	ljdumas		PHD	72	Columbia	1979
Hicks, Donald A.	Prof	883-2733	dahicks		PHD	76	N Carol	
Hoch, Irving J.	Prof	883-2928	hoch		PHD	57	Chicago	1985
Redlinger, Lawrence J.	Prof	883-2350			PHD	69	Northwes	
Dean School of General Studies								
Fass, Simon M.	Assoc	883-2938	fass		PHD	78	UCLA	
Murdoch, James	Assoc	883-2280	murdoch		PHD	82	Wyoming	
Seldon, Barry	Assoc	883-2043	seldon		PHD	85	Duke	
Vijverberg, Wim P. M.	Assoc	883-2042	vijver		PHD	81	Pittsburgh	1986
Jargowky, Paul	Asst	883-2992	jargo		PHD	91	Harvard	
MacNair, Elizabeth	Asst	883-2994	macnair		PHD	93	Houston	

Univ of Texas at El Paso	El Paso, TX	79968-0543	(915) 747-5245				Gloria Armistead	
Dept of Economics & Finance	Col of Business Admin	Fax=747-6282						
Hoy, Frank	Dean	747-5241		Mgt	PHD	79	Tx A&M	9-91
Roth, Timothy P.	C-Pr	747-5245			PHD	70	Tx A&M	1970
A.B. Templeton Professor								
Herbst, Anthony F.	Prof	747-5245			PHD		Purdue	1987
Herendeen, James B.	Prof	747-5245			PHD	63	Penn St	1992
James, Dilmus Delano	Prof	747-5245			PHD	70	Mich St	1958
Brannon, Jeffery T.	Assoc	747-5245			PHD		Alabama	1982
Holcomb, James H. Jr.	Assoc	747-5245			PHD	85	Tx A&M	1985
Associate Dean								
Johnson, Steve A.	Assoc	747-5245			PHD	88	Alabama	1987
Schauer, David A.	Assoc	747-5245			PHD	75	Notre Dm	1975
Smith, William Doyle	Assoc	747-5245			PHD	81	Tx Tech	1981
Sprinkle, Richard L.	Assoc	747-5245			PHD	82	Arkansas	1982
Tollen, Robert D.	Assoc	747-5245			PHD		Tx-Austin	1972
Smith, Charles L.	Asst	747-5245			PHD		Tx Tech	1991

Univ of Texas-Pan American	Edinburg, TX	78539-2999	(210) 381-3354					
Dept of Accounting & Econ	Col of Business Admin	Fax=381-3312						
McCallister, Linda	Dean	381-5087		Comm	PHD	81	Purdue	1995
Ellard, Charles J.	C-Pr	381-3391			PHD	74	Houston	1976
Cardenas, Gilbert	Prof	381-3369			PHD	77	Illinois	1975
Crews, Mike	Assoc	381-3353			PHD			
Taube, Paul M.	Assoc	381-2579			PHD	86	SUNY-Alb	1988
Vento, Edward	Assoc	381-3362			PHD	72	Tx A&M	1982
Asgary, Nader	Lect	381-3395			PHD			

U of Texas of Permian Basin	Odessa, TX	79762-8301	(915) 552-2171					
Dept of Economics	Div of Business Admin	Fax=552-2374					UTPB	
Klein, Gary	Dean	552-2194		Mis	PHD	81	Purdue	
Hodges, Paul E.	Prof	552-2193			PHD	74	Stanford	

Un of Texas at San Antonio	San Antonio, TX	78249-0633	(210) 691-4315					
Div of Economics & Finance	College of Business	Fax=691-5837					UTSA.EDU	
email: @1=lonestar.jpl.utsa.edu	@2=pclan.utsa.edu							
Gaertner, James F.	Dean	691-4313		Atg	PHD	77	Tx A&M	1983
Flory-Truett, Lila J.	D-Pr	691-4315		DFMO	PHD	72	Iowa	1975
de la Vina, Lynda	Prof	691-4317			PHD	82	Rice	1979
Associate Dean								
Hollas, Daniel R.	Prof	691-4313			PHD	77	Illinois	1988
Associate Vice President for Academic Affairs								
Truett, Dale B.	Prof	691-5313	dtruett@2	DFMO	PHD	67	Tx-Austin	1973
Ayers, Ronald M.	Assoc	691-5302	rayers@1	GJM	PHD	78	Tulane	1979
Collinge, Robert A.	Assoc	691-5312	rcolling@1	FHKQ	PHD	83	Maryland	1987
Firoozi, Fathall K.	Assoc	691-5395	ffiroozi@2	CF	PHD	87	Oklahoma	1988
Mahdavi, Saeid	Assoc	691-5301	smahdavi@2	EFO	PHD	85	Ca-SnBarb	1984
Merrifield, John D.	Assoc	691-5310	jmerrifi@2	HQR	PHD	84	Wyoming	1987
Weiher, Kenneth E.	Assoc	691-5315	kweither@2	BEN	PHD	75	Indiana	1975
Zhou, Su	Asst	691-5398	szhou@1	CEFP	PHD	91	Ariz St	1991

Univ of Texas at Tyler — Tyler, TX 75799 (903) 566-7371 — Dixie Schaitberger
Economics Faculty — School of Liberal Arts Fax=566-7377

Name	Rank	Phone	Email	Field	Degree	Yr	School	Since
Lefevre, Stephen	Dean	566-7368		PolS	PHD	75	Ca-River	1975
Kane, Tim D.	Prof	566-7430			PHD	72	Tx-Austin	1981

Texas A&M University — Coll Station, TX 77843-4228 (409) 845-7351 — Carolyn Teeter
Department of Economics — College of Business Adm Fax=847-8757 — TAMU.EDU

Name	Rank	Phone	Email	Field	Degree	Yr	School	Since
Jones, Woodrow	Dean$	845-5141		PolS	PHD	74	Oregon	1988
Gronberg, Timothy J.	H-Pr	845-7358	tjg@zeus.		PHD	78	Northwes	1977
Allen, John William	Prof	845-7398			PHD	67	Illinois	1967
Anderson, Richard K.	Prof	845-4547	rka3591@acs.		PHD	76	Purdue	1975
Auernheimer, Leonardo	Prof	845-7302	leonardo@econ4.		PHD	73		1973
Baltagi, Badi H. — George Summey Professorship	Prof	845-7380	e304bb@tamvmi.		PHD	79	Penn	1988
Battalio, Ray — Currie Professorship in Liberal Arts	Prof	845-7340			PHD	69	Purdue	1969
Browning, Edgar K. — Al Chalk Professor of Economics	Prof	845-7355			PHD	71	Princeton	1984
Greenhut, Melvin L. — Distinguished Professor of Economics-G.T.& G.H.Abell Professor of Liberl Arts	Emer	845-7351			PHD	51	Wash U	1966
Griffin, James M. — Cullen Professorship	Prof	845-9950			PHD	70	Penn	1982
Hanson, John R. II	Prof	845-4593	jrh4503@zeus.		PHD	72	Penn	1974
Hwang, Hae-Shin	Prof	845-7301			PHD	76	Minnesota	1977
Jansen, Dennis W.	Prof	845-7351	dwj3887@zeus.		PHD	83	N Carol	1983
Maurice, S. Charles	Prof	845-7531			PHD	67	Georgia	1967
Moroney, John R.	Prof	845-7351			PHD	64	Duke	1981
Pejovich, Svetozar	Prof	845-7722			PHD	63	Geotown	1975
Reynolds, Morgan O. — email 74157,2764@compulerv.com	Prof	845-7307			PHD	71	Wisconsin	1974
Saving, Thomas R. — Director Private Enterprise Research Center; Distinguished Prof of Economics	Prof	845-7358	trs9019@tam2000.		PHD	60	Chicago	1968
Tian, Guoqiang	Prof	845-7393	gqt7885@venus.		PHD	87	Minnesota	1987
Welch, Finis R. — Abell Professor	Prof	847-8648	bbc@econ1.		PHD	66	Chicago	1991
Wiggins, Steven N. — George R. Jordan Professorship	Prof	845-7383	snw@econ4.		PHD	79	MIT	1979
Deere, Donald R.	Assoc	845-7351	bbc@econ1.		PHD	83	MIT	1983
Gilbert, Roy F.	Assoc	845-7357			PHD	69	Mich St	1970
Neilson, William S.	Assoc	845-9954	wsn@econ4.		PHD	88	Ca-SnDgo	1988
Ureta, Manuelita	Assoc	847-9449	manuelita-ureta		PHD	87	Berkeley	1991
Van Huyck, John B.	Assoc	845-7351	jvh@econ4.		PHD	86	Brown	1985
Cho, Dongchal	Asst	845-7353	d0c374a@tamvm1.		PHD	86	Wisconsin	1991
McCue, Kristen	Asst	845-7348	kmc@econ0.		PHD	90	Chicago	1989
Pierce, Brooks	Asst	845-7339	brp@econ0.		PHD	90	Chicago	1989
Sarin, Rajiv	Asst	845-7382	rajiv@econ4.		PHD			9-94
Taylor, Curtis	Asst	845-7354	crt@econ0.		PHD	92	Yale	1992
Vahid, Farshid	Asst	845-7351	fv@econ0.		PHD	93		1993

Texas A&M - Corpus Christi — Corpus Chr, TX 78412 (512) 994-2665
FEDS — College of Business Fax=994-2725 — TAMUCC.EDU

Name	Rank	Phone	Email	Field	Degree	Yr	School	Since
Abdelsamad, Moustafa H.	Dean	994-2655		Fnce	DBA	70	Geo Wash	7-91
McMinn, Robert D.	C-Pr	994-2665	rmcminn	A	PHD	73	Oklahoma	9-74
Nzeogwu, Okeleke	Assoc	994-5831	onzeogwu	AO	PHD	88	Missouri	9-93

Texas A&M Univ-Kingsville — Kingsville, TX 78363 (512)
Economics Faculty — Cl Business Adm Box 184 Fax= — TAIU.EDU

Name	Rank	Phone	Email	Field	Degree	Yr	School	Since
Bigbee, Delton L.	Dean	595-3801	dbigbee	Fnce	DBA	81	Tx Tech	1985
Nash, Robert T.	Prof	595-2355	s-nash		PHD		Tx A&M	1971
Rossman, Joseph E.	Assoc	595-2506	j-rossman		PHD		Iowa St	1976
Nemec, Richard W.	Asst	595-2507	r-nemec		MBA		Tx A&M-Kg	1981

Texas A&M International Univ — Laredo, TX 78040-9960 (210) 724-6429 — Araceli Chapa/Linda Solano
Dept of Economics & Finance — College of Business Adm Fax=725-3348 — TAIMVS1

Name	Rank	Phone	Email	Field	Degree	Yr	School	Since
Fatemi, Khosrow	Dean	722-8001	lfsxr00	Mgt	PHD	72	S Calif	8-82
Patrick, J. Michael	C-Pr				PHD	77	Mich St	
Berg-Andreassen, Jan	Assoc				PHD		Houston	
Islam, Muhammad	Assoc				PHD		Vanderbilt	
Carr, Barry	Asst	724-9784			PHD		Oklahoma	

Texas Christian University — Fort Worth, TX 76129 (817) 921-7230 — Ms. Christina Ho
Department of Economics — AddRan Col/Arts & Sci Fax=

Name	Rank	Phone	Email	Field	Degree	Yr	School	Since
McCracken, Michael D.	Dean	921-7160		Biol	PHD	69	Indiana	1971
McNertney, Edward M.	C-Ac	921-7230			PHD	77	Mass	1977
Becker, Charles McVey	Assoc	921-7230			PHD	66	Arizona	1967

Name	Rank	Phone		Degree	Yr	School	Year
Butler, Michael R.	Assoc	921-7230		PHD	86	N Carol	1986
Harvey, John T.	Assoc	921-7230		PHD	87	Tennessee	1987
Elliott, Dawn Richards	Asst	921-7230		PHD	94	New Sch	1995
Moore, Myra	Asst	921-7230		PHD	94	Georgia	1994
Quinn, Stephen F.	Asst	921-7230		PHD	94	Illinois	1995

Texas Lutheran College Seguin, TX 78155-5999 (210) 372-6070
Economics Faculty Dept of Econ & Pol Sci Fax=372-8096

Name	Rank	Phone		Degree	Yr	School	Year
Giesber, Frank W.	C-Pr	379-6071	A	PHD	78	Tx-Austin	1966
Citzler, Annette	Prof	372-6072	A	PHD	85	Tx A&M	1977

Texas Southern University Houston, TX 77004 (713) 527-7210 TSU.EDU
Dept Hst, Geography & Econ College of Arts & Sci Fax=

Name	Rank	Phone	Degree	School
Sapp, John	Dean			
Akalou, Woldie-Michael	H	527-7429	PHD	UCLA
Horwitz, Sigmund	Prof	527-7735	PHD	Houston
Keleta, Ethiopia	Assoc	527-7702	PHD	Rice
Norman, Emlyn A.	Asst	527-7892	AM	Harvard
Norris, Hodge	Asst	527-7814	MS	Tx A&I
Batie, Clarence	Inst	527-7815	MA	PrairieV

Texas Tech University Lubbock, TX 79409-1014 (806) 742-2201 Karen Davis
Department of Economics Col of Arts & Sciences Fax=742-1137

Name	Rank	Phone	Degree	Yr	School	Year
Hill, Lewis E.	C-Pr	742-2201	PHD	57	Tx-Austin	1967
Butler, Charles Edward	Prof	742-2201	PHD	66	Harvard	1971
Gilliam, John Charles	Prof	742-2201	PHD	59	Iowa	1962
Jonish, James E.	Prof	742-2201	PHD	69	Michigan	1973
Steinmeier, Thomas L.	Prof	742-2201	PHD	75	Yale	1982
Troub, Roger M.	Prof	742-2201	PHD	68	Oklahoma	1967
Gilbert, Ronald D.	Assoc	742-2201	PHD	70	Okla St	1977
Becker, Klaus G.	Asst	742-2201	PHD	87	Kansas	1989
McComb, Robert P.	Asst	742-2201	PHD	89	Illinois	1991
Brown, Robert K.			MA	85	Houston	
Chengalath, Gopal		742-2201	PHD			
Hudgins, David		742-2201	PHD			
Rouse, Robert		742-2201	PHD			
Von Ende, Terry		742-2201	PHD		Kansas	1990

Texas Wesleyan University Fort Worth, TX 76105-1536 (817) 531-4840 JoAnn Moore
Economics Faculty School of Business Fax=531-4268

Name	Rank	Phone	Field	Degree	Yr	School	Year
Hart, Sandra Hile	Dean$	531-4840	Mktg	PHD	84	Tx A&M	1985
Klaasen, Thomas Albert	Prof			PHD	69	Mich St	1989
Ellis, Charles Michael	Assoc			PHD	73	Alabama	1983
McLain, Louis P.	Assoc			MBA	74	So Meth	1976

Texas Woman's University Denton, TX 76204 (817) 898-2111 Ms. Laurie Hammett
Dept of Business & Economics Col of Arts & Sciences Fax=898-2120

Name	Rank	Phone	Field	Degree	Yr	School	Year
Collier, Robert E.	Dean	898-3326	Biol	PHD		Illinois	
Bulls, Derrell W.	C-Pr	898-2102		PHD	71	Tx Tech	1977
Hersh-Cochran, Mona S.	Prof			PHD		So Meth	
Conaro Professor of Business and Economics							
Green, Ralph T.	VAsoc			PHD		Duke	
Adler, Kathleen S.	VAsst	898-2111		PHD	93	So Meth	1995

University of Toledo Toledo, OH 43606-3390 (419) 537-2572 Wanda Clark
Department of Economics Col of Arts & Sciences Fax=537-7844 ECON.UTOLEDO.EDU
email: @1=uoft02.utoledo.edu

Name	Rank	Phone	Email	Field	Degree	Yr	School	Year
Muraco, William	Dean$	573-2641		Geog	PHD			
Magura, Michael	C-Pr	537-4631	mm@mm.		PHD	72	Boston C	1969
Gylys, Julius A.	Emer	537-4135			PHD		Wayne St	1967
Lesage, James P.	Prof	537-4754	jpl@jpl.		PHD	83	Boston C	1988
Roy, Raj	Prof	537-4430			PHD	68	Wayne St	1963
Weiss, Steven J.	Prof	537-4124	sweiss@1		PHD	71	Colorado	1968
Chang, Hsin	Assoc	537-4677			PHD		Michigan	1989
Dowd, Michael R.	Assoc	537-4603	mrd@mrd.		PHD	90	SUNY-Buf	1989
Tank, Frederick E.	Assoc	537-2562	fet@fet.		PHD		Wayne St	1970
Black, David C.	Asst	537-4153	dcb@dcb.		PHD	92	SUNY-Buf	1990
Keith, Kristen	Asst	537-4132	kkeith@1		PHD		Ohio St	1994
Murray, John E.	Asst	537-4148	jmurray@1		PHD	92	Ohio St	1994
Bracy, Paula M.	Adj	537-4148			MA		Toledo	1984

Towson State University | Towson, MD 21204-7097 (410) 830-2959 | C. F. Eifert
Department of Economics | Sch of Business & Econ Fax=830-3424 | TOWSONVX

Name	Rank	Phone		Degree		School	Year
Leberknight, Alan	Dean	830-3342		MBA		Loyola	1995
Fenstermaker, J. Van	C-Pr	830-2145		PHD	63	Illinois	1988
Dorn, James A.	Prof	830-2956		PHD	76	Virginia	1973
Georgiou, George C.	Prof	830-2146		PHD	79	Geo Wash	1980
Kong, Chang Min	Prof	830-2191		PHD	77	Wi-Milw	1978
Paul, Harvey	Prof	830-2954		PHD	72	SUNY-Buf	1966
Shin, Bong Ju	Prof	830-2951		PHD	69	Ohio St	1966
Egger, John B.	Assoc	830-3576		PHD	85	NYU	1987
Weintraub, Irvin	Assoc	830-2952		MS	51	Columbia	1966
Woroby, Tamara	Assoc	830-3575		PHD	81	Queens	1978
Laurence, Louise	Asst	830-3275		PHD	87	Maryland	1987
Lee, Kangoh	Asst	830-3551		PHD	87	Illinois	1990
Li, Ling	Asst	830-2675		PHD	94	Pittsburgh	1994
Sullivan, Timothy	Asst	830-2338		PHD	87	Illinois	1989

Transylvania University | Lexington, KY 40508 (606) 233-8104
Economics Faculty | Div of Bus Adm & Econ Fax=233-8749

Name	Rank	Phone		Degree		School	Year
Pepper, Michael R.	C-Pr	233-8249		MS		N Hamp	1989
Lynch, Lawrence K.	Prof	233-8157		PHD	66	Kentucky	1979
Erfani, G. Rod	Assoc	233-8196		PHD	84	Fla St	1986

Trenton State College | Trenton, NJ 08650-4700 (609) 771-3496
Economics Program | School of Business Fax=771-2845

Name	Rank	Phone		Degree		School	Year
Robinson, James W.	Dean	771-3050		PHD	67	Duke	1992
Samanta, Subarna K.	C-Ac	771-3496		PHD	85	So Meth	1987
Breslin, Thomas	Prof			PHD		W Virginia	
Liu, Chao-Nan	Prof			PHD		Tx A&M	
Naples, Michele I.	Assoc	771-2896		PHD	82	Mass	
Leven, Bozen	Asst			PHD		Cornell	
Vandegrift, Donald	Asst			PHD	93	Conn	

Tri-State University | Angola, IN 46703-0307 (219) 665-4243
Dept of Social Sciences | Sch of Arts & Sciences Fax=665-4292 | TRISTATE.EDU

Name	Rank	Phone	Field	Degree		School	Year
Tichenor, Delores	Dean	665-4242					
Morin, John E.	C-Pr	665-4206	SocS	MS		Ind St	1966
Zimmer, Donald T.	Prof	665-4199		PHD		Indiana	1973
Moore, Derald L.	Assoc	665-4207		MA		Mich St	1968
Scheffer, Ronald E.	Assoc	665-4202		MA		Ohio	1967

Trinity University | San Antonio, TX 78212-7200 (210) 736-7221 | Susie DuBose
Department of Economics | Div of Behav & Adm Stds Fax=736-7255 | TRINITY.EDU

Name	Rank	Phone	Email	Field	Degree		School	Year
Stefl, Mary	Dean	736-7521		Hlth				
Huston, John H.	C-Ac	736-8471	jhouston		PHD	83	Wisconsin	1983
Breit, William L.	Prof	736-8492	wbreit		PHD	61	Mich St	1982
E. M. Stevens Distinguished Professor of Economics								
Butler, Richard V.	Prof	736-7256	rbutler		PHD	77	MIT	1982
Calgaard, Ronald K.	Prof				PHD		Iowa	1979
President								
Salvucci, Richard	Prof	736-8494	rsalvucc					
Spencer, Roger W.	Prof	736-7222	rspencer		PHD	69	Virginia	1980
Davis, Joe C.	Assoc	736-7226	jdavis		PHD	71	Tx-Austin	1969
Gonzalez, Jorge G.	Asst	736-7224	jgonzali		PHD	89	Mich St	1989
Kamdar, Nipoli	Asst	736-7441	nkamdar		PHD	93	Syracuse	1993
Patterson, Debra Moore	Asst	736-7223	dpatters		PHD	94	Virginia	1994

Troy State University | Troy, AL 36082 (334) 670-3459
Dept Mktg, Mgt & Economics | Sorrell Col of Business Fax=670-3599 | ASNTSU.ASN.NET

Name	Rank	Phone	Email	Degree		School	Year
Curtis, Wayne C.	Dean$	670-3137		PHD	71	Miss St	1967
Kirkland, Jack	Assoc	670-3579		PHD	82	Wash St	1995
Merkel, Edward T.	Assoc	670-3194		PHD	74	N Illinois	1978
Assistant Dean							
Thompson, Charles L.	Asst	670-3195	tsuclt01	MS	82	Auburn	1984
Uze, Barry A.		670-3153		MA	85	Miss	1989
Director, Center for Economic Education							

Tufts University | Medford, MA 02155 (617) 627-3560 | Valerie A. Ricciardone
Department of Economics | Col of Liberal Arts Fax=627-3917 | PEARL.TUFTS.EDU
phone: 628-5000

Name	Rank	Phone	Email	Field	Degree		School	Year
Glater, Marilyn	Dean	627-3864	mglater	PolS	PHD			
Garman, David M.	C-Ac$	Ext 2683	dgarman		PHD	89	Michigan	1983
Fortune, Peter	Prof	627-3138	pfortune		PHD	72	Harvard	1977
on leave								

Name	Rank	Phone	Email	Field	Degree	Yr	School	Year
Ioannides, Yannis M.	Prof	627-3294		E	PHD	74	Stanford	1995
Morrison, Catherine	Prof	627-3663	cmorriso		PHD	82	Brit Col	1982
on leave								
Bianconi, Marcello	Assoc	Ext 2677	mbiancon		PHD	88	Illinois	1989
Brown, Drusilla K.	Assoc	627-3096	dbrown		PHD	84	Michigan	1983
Dapice, David O.	Assoc	Ext 5947			PHD	73	Harvard	1973
Loury, Linda D.	Assoc	627-3348	ldatcher		PHD	78	MIT	1978
Pepall, Lynne	Assoc	627-3560	lpepall		PHD	83	Cambridg	1987
Richards, Daniel J.	Assoc	Ext 2679	drichard		PHD	81	Yale	1985
Chin, Judith	Asst	627-3137	jchin		PHD	93	Princeton	1992
on leave								
Downes, Thomas A.	Asst	Ext 2687	tdownes		PHD	88	Stanford	1994
Metcalf, Gilbert	Asst	627-3685	gmetcalf		PHD	88	Harvard	1994
Milyo, Jeffrey	Asst	627-3662	jmilyo		PHD	94	Stanford	1992
Zabel, Jeffrey	Asst	Ext 2318	jzabel		PHD	87	Ca-SnDgo	1989
Tulane University	New Orleans, LA	70118-5698	(504) 865-5321					
Department of Economics	Col of Arts & Sciences		Fax=865-5869					
Avery-Peck, Alan J.	Dean$	865-5720			PHD		Brown	
Oakland, William H.	C-Pr	862-8343			PHD	65	MIT	1979
Freudenberger, Herman	Prof	865-5321			PHD	57	Columbia	
Grier, Kevin B.	Prof	865-5317			PHD	84	Wash U	1994
Horiba, Yutaka	Prof	862-8346			PHD	69	Purdue	1971
Kelly, Eamon M.	Prof	865-5001			PHD	65	Columiba	1981
President								
McMillen, Daniel P.	Prof	862-8358			PHD	87	Northwes	1994
Tanner, J. Ernest	Prof	862-8355			PHD	68	Brown	1971
Edwards, John H.	Assoc	862-8357			PHD	85	Maryland	1985
Gaston, Noel G.	Assoc	862-8344			PHD	88	Cornell	
Malueg, David A.	Assoc	862-8356			PHD	83	Northwes	
Pritchett, Jonathan B.	Assoc	862-8359			PHD	86	Chicago	1985
Lee, Hahn S.	Asst	862-8347			PHD	90	Ca-SnDgo	
Morrison, Andrew R.	Asst	862-8354			PHD	89	Vanderbilt	1988
Semenick Alam, Ila	Asst	862-8532			PHD	94	Rice	1994
Taylor, Leon E.	Asst	862-8340			PHD		Maryland	
University of Tulsa	Tulsa, OK	74104-3189	(918) 631-2219				Kimberly Crowther	
Department of Economics	Col of Business Admin		Fax=631-2142				VAX1.UTULSA.EDU	
Mabry, Rodney H.	Dean	631-2213		Fnce	PHD	75	N Carol	6-94
Ray, Cadwell L.	C-Ac	631-2221			PHD		Tx-Austin	
Dugger, William M.	Prof	631-2951			PHD	74	Tx-Austin	
Steib, Steve B.	Prof	631-2219			PHD	72	Iowa St	1972
Horn, Bobbie L.	Assoc	631-2219			PHD		Iowa St	
KariKari, John A.	Assoc	631-3157						
Soltow, Allen R.	Assoc	631-2335			PHD	69	Iowa St	1973
Tuskegee University	Tuskegee, AL	36088	(334) 727-8116				Kim Raudenbush	
Dept of Economics	School of Business		Fax=727-8604					
Newhouse, Benjamin	Dean	727-8286		Atg	PHD	82	Michigan	1-84
Sara, Tejinder S.	H-Ac	727-8707	tsara		PHD		Mass	
Cheng, William	Assoc	727-6307			PHD	90	SUNY-Bin	1990
Duncan, Jerome	Assoc	727-2673			PHD		Florida	1991
Lieu, George	Assoc	727-8733			PHD			
Upchurch, Leo	Assoc	727-8732			PHD	82	Michigan	1990
Olowolayemo, Suryudeen	Asst	727-8712			PHD		Auburn	1994
Shalishali, Kasazi	Asst				PHD	93	Auburn	1993
Solomon, Hassana	Asst	727-6307			PHD		Auburn	1993
Union College-NY	Schenectady, NY	12308-2311	(518) 388-6200				Sandra Geraci	
Department of Economics	Div of Social Sciences		Fax=388-6656				GAR.UNION.EDU	
Klein, J. Douglass	C-Ac	388-6056	kleind	LQD	PHD	75	Wisconsin	1979
Prosper, Peter A. Jr.	Prof	388-6219	prosperp	JA	PHD	70	Cornell	1964
Reynolds, Bruce L.	Prof	388-6217	reynoldb	ODP	PHD	75	Michigan	1974
Fried, Harold O.	Assoc	388-6368	friedh	CIL	PHD	78	N Carol	1983
Kenney, James M.	Assoc	388-6018	kennyj	QDMG	PHD	72	Stanford	1972
Lewis, Bradley G.	Assoc	388-6232	lewisb	GMN	PHD	83	Chicago	1979
McCarty, Therese A.	Assoc	388-6045	mccartyt	GI	PHD	87	Michigan	1987
Schmidt, Shelton S.	Assoc	388-6218	schmidts	LCA	PHD	77	Virginia	1974
Motahar, Eshragh	Asst	388-6065	motahare	EFG	PHD	89	J Hopkins	1984
Schmidt, Stephen J.	Asst	388-6200	schmids2	LCD	PHD	95	Stanford	1994
Yalsawarng, Suthathip	Asst	388-6606	yaisawas	CD	PHD	89	S Illinois	1989
Mukherjee, Joya	VInst	388-6200	mukherjj	CO	ABD		Rice	1994
Union University	Jackson, TN	38305-3697	(901) 661-5360				Judy Leforgee	
Department of Economics	Sch of Business Admin		Fax=661-5366					
Myatt, Sam	C	661-5370			EDD		Memphis	
Padelford, Walton M.	Prof	661-5362		ABFO	PHD	75	LSU	1980

U.S. Air Force Academy Colorado Spr, CO 80840-6238 (719) 472-3080
Department of Economics Social Science Division Fax=472-2945 DFAMIL2.USAFA.AF.MIL

Name	Rank	Phone	Email		Degree	Yr	School	Year
Franck, Raymond	H	472-3080	franckre		PHD		Harvard	
on sabbatical 1994-96								
Vliet, Laurence C.	H-As$	470-3080	vlietlc		MA		Pittsburgh	
Roth, R. Theodore	Prof		rothrt		PHD		MIT	
Taylor, Peter M.	Prof	472-3080	taylorpm		PHD		Maryland	
Durchholz, Matthew L.	Assoc		durcholzml		PHD		So Meth	
Linster, Bruce G.	Assoc	472-3080	linsterbg		PHD	90	Michigan	1990
Cook, Jeffrey J.	Asst	472-3080	cookjj		MA		Indiana	
Coop, Lindsay	Asst	472-3080	coopla		MA			
Fullerton, Richard L.	Asst	472-3080	fullertonrl		PHD		Tx-Austin	
Hoekstra, Merrill C.	Asst	472-3080	hoekstramc		MA		Ca-SnBarb	
Lucchesi, Michael S.	Asst		lucchesims		MA		U Wash	
Ludke, Jerry A.	Asst		ludkeja		MA		Stanford	
McGarrity, John P.	Asst	472-3080	mcgarrityjp		MA		Tx-Austin	
Slate, Stephen T.	Asst		slatest		PHD		Colorado	
Tenney, Curtis G.	Asst	472-3080	tenneycg		ABD		Okla St	
Vernon, Rodney G.	Asst	472-3080	vernonrg		MS		AF Inst	
Gorney, Anne L.	Inst	472-3080	gorneyal		MS		AF Inst	
Neel, Stewart D.	Inst	472-3080	neelsd		ABD		Rochester	

U.S. Military Academy West Point, NY 10996 (914) 938-3795
Economics Faculty Dept of Social Sciences Fax=938-4563 USMA.EDU

Name	Rank	Phone	Email		Degree	Yr	School	Year
Golden, James R.	H-Pr	938-2800	jj9125		PHD	72	Harvard	1975
Gujarati, Damodar N.	Prof				PHD	65	Chicago	1990
Scribner, Barry L.	Assoc				PHD		Harvard	1988
Dudley, Dean	Asst				PHD		Indiana	1993
Lofgren, Stephanie	Asst				PHD		Northwes	1995

U.S. Naval Academy Annapolis, MD 21402-5042 (410) 293-6880
Economics Department Div of Human & Soc Sci Fax=293-6899 NADN.USNA.NAVY.MILL

Name	Rank	Phone	Email		Degree	Yr	School	Year
Fredland, John E.	C-Pr	293-6880	fredland		PHD	70	Michigan	1974
Bowman, William R.	Prof	293-6897	bowman		PHD	79	Maryland	1980
Goodman, Rae Jean B.	Prof	293-6891	goodman		PHD	76	Wash U	1973
Little, Roger D.	Prof	293-6889	little		PHD	70	Houston	1970
Morris, Clair E. Jr.	Prof	293-6893	morris		PHD	72	Wisconsin	1966
Gibb, Arthur Jr.	Assoc	293-6886	gibb		PHD		Michigan	1974
Whitaker, A. Royal	Assoc	293-6885	whitaker		PHD	65	Penn	1965
Zak, Thomas A.	Assoc	293-6895	zakt		PHD	80	Vanderbilt	1981
Getter, Darryl	Asst	293-6888	getter		PHD	94	Wash U	1994
Thierfelder, Karen	Asst	293-6894	thier		PHD	92	Wisconsin	1992

Upsala College East Orange, NJ 07019-1186 (201) 266-7000
Economics Faculty Department of Economics Fax=
Did Not Respond--1994-95 Listing

Name	Rank	Phone	Email	Field	Degree	Yr	School	Year
Lee, E. Yong	C-Ac			CD	PHD	75	Rutgers	1975
Olson, William	Assoc			EN	PHD		Mass	1983
Zamani, Amir	Asst			F	PHD		Columbia	1991

University of Utah Salt Lake CY, UT 84112 (801) 581-7481 Ginger Head Adm Officer
Department of Economics Col of Soc & Behav Sci Fax=585-5649 ECON.SBS.UTAH.EDU

Name	Rank	Phone	Email	Field	Degree	Yr	School	Year
Gelfand, Donna M.	Dean	581-8620		Psyc	PHD	61	Stanford	1964
Hunt, E. K.	C-Pr	581-7656	hunt		PHD	68	Utah	1978
Gander, James P.	Prof	581-5670	gander		PHD	66	Berkeley	1965
Girton, Lance	Prof	581-7622	girton		PHD	76	Chicago	1978
Glick, Mark	Prof	581-7464	glick		PHD	85	New Sch	1985
Jameson, Kenneth P.	Prof	581-8620	jameson		PHD	70	Wisconsin	1989
Lieberman, Sima	Prof	581-7704	liberman		PHD	67	Berkeley	1967
Mangum, Garth L.	Prof	581-6127	mangum		PHD	60	Harvard	1969
Phillips, Peter W.	Prof	585-6465	phillips		PHD	80	Stanford	1978
Rock, James M.	Prof	581-7481	rock		PHD	66	Northwes	1967
Sievers, Allen M.	Prof	581-7456	sievers		PHD	48	Columbia	1968
Blattenberger, Gail R.	Assoc	581-7591	gail		PHD	77	Michigan	1981
Carlisle, William T.	Assoc	581-8511	carlisle		PHD	75	Cornell	1971
Fowles, Richard G.	Assoc	581-4577	fowles		PHD	85	Utah	1990
Kiefer, David M.	Assoc	581-4308	kiefer		PHD	74	Michigan	1981
Reynolds, Stephen E.	Assoc	581-7603	reynolds		PHD	69	Wisconsin	1969
Waltzman, Norman J.	Assoc	581-7600	waltzman		PHD	88	American	1988
Berik, Gunseli	Asst	581-7435	berik		PHD	86	Mass	1994
Cagatay, Nilufer	Asst	581-7667	cagatay		PHD	86	Stanford	1991
Ehrbar, Hans G.	Asst	581-7797	ehrbar		PHD	85	Michigan	1986
Erturk, Korkut	Asst	581-4576	korkut		PHD	92	New Sch	
Lozada, Gabriel A.	Asst	581-7650	lazada		PHD	87	Stanford	1993
Maloney, Tom	Asst	581-7697	maloney		PHD	93	Michigan	
Merva, Mary	Asst	581-7435	merva		PHD	89	Rutgers	1990

Utah State University — Logan, UT 84322-3530 (801) 797-2310 Suzette Alder, Adm Asst
Department of Economics — College of Business Fax=797-2701 B202.USU.EDU

Name	Rank	Phone	E-mail	Field	Degree	Yr	School	Since
Stephens, David B.	Dean	797-2272	dstephens	Mgt	PHD	75	Tx-Austin	6-87
Snyder, Donald L.	H-Pr	797-2305	dsnyder	CQ	PHD	79	Utah St	1981
Bailey, DeeVon	Prof	797-2316	dbailey	Q	PHD	83	Tx A&M	1983
Biswas, Basudeb	Prof	797-2304	biswas	CFO	PHD	76	Chicago	1976
Durtschi, Reed R.	Prof	797-2300	rdurtschi	AE	PHD	67	U Wash	1958
Fullerton, Herbert H.	Prof	797-2324	hfullerton	OQR	PHD	71	Iowa St	1969
Glover, Terrence F.	Prof	797-2297	tglover	DCQ	PHD	71	Purdue	1974
Godfrey, E. Bruce	Prof	797-2294	bruceg	Q	PHD	71	Oreg St	1977
Hansen, Gary B.	Prof	797-2287	garyh	J	PHD	71	Cornell	1967
Director Business & Economic Development Services								
Keith, John E.	Prof	797-2303	jkeith	DEQR	PHD	73	Utah St	1972
Lewis, W. Cris	Prof	797-2327	clewis	MCR	PHD	69	Iowa St	1972
Lyon, Kenneth S.	Prof	797-2292	klyon	CDEQ	PHD	70	Chicago	1966
Nielsen, Darwin B.	Prof	797-2321	dnielsen	Q	PHD	64	Oreg St	1965
Petersen, Harold Craig	Prof	797-1170	cpeterson	GM	PHD	73	Stanford	1973
Whitaker, Morris D.	Prof	797-1840		FO	PHD	70	Purdue	1970
Director of International Program								
Bond, Larry Keith	Assoc	797-2320	lbond	Q	PHD	72	Utah St	1972
Fawson, Christopher	Assoc	797-2296	cfawson	CGMO	PHD	86	Tx A&M	1990
Israelsen, L. Dwight	Assoc	797-2298	disraelsen	ABDE	PHD	73	MIT	1980
Barrett, Christopher	Asst	797-2306	cbarrett	OQF	PHD	93	Wisconsin	1995
Batabyal, Amitrajeet	Asst			FOQ	PHD	94	Berkeley	1995
Reinhorn, Les	Asst	797-2317	lreinhorn	AEH	PHD	94	Stanford	1994
Thilmany, Dawn	Asst	797-2322	dthilmany	FGOQ	PHD	94	Ca-Davis	1994
Weninger, Quinn	Asst			CQ	PHD	95	Maryland	1995
Bowles, Tyler	Lect	797-2378	tbowles	AF	PHD	91	N Carol	1994
Mohapatra, Sarita	Lect			ADF	PHD	95	Utah St	1995
Bentley, Marion	ExtSp	797-2284		H	MPA	70	NYU	1975

Utica College — Utica, NY 13502-4892 (315) 792-3113
Economics Program — Div of Business Admin Fax=792-3173

Name	Rank	Phone	E-mail	Field	Degree	Yr	School	Since
Blanchfield, William C.	Dean				PHD		SUNY-Alb	1966
Neun, Stephen P.	C-Ac	792-3113			PHD		Conn	1982
Fenner, Richard G.	Asst				PHD	92	Syracuse	1989

Valdosta State University — Valdosta, GA 31698-0075 (912) 245-2234 Barbara Cape
Dept of Mktg & Economics — Sch of Business Admin Fax=245-6498 GRITS.VALDOSTA.PEACHNET.E

Name	Rank	Phone	E-mail	Field	Degree	Yr	School	Since
Stanley, Kenneth L.	Dean	333-5991		Fnce	PHD	78	Purdue	1984
Allen, Ralph C.	Prof			F	PHD	81	Geo St	1981
Love, Jim L.	Prof	245-3824		R	PHD	83	Okla St	1983
Plumly, L. Wayne Jr.	Prof	245-3815		J	PHD	83	Geo St	1983
Kushner, Joseph W.	Assoc	245-2249			PHD	69	Tennessee	1969
Saltz, Ira	Assoc			F	PHD		Berkeley	1989

Valparaiso University — Valparaiso, IN 46383 (219) 464-5696 Kay Mooney
Department of Economics — Col of Arts & Sciences Fax=464-5381 EXODUS.VALPO.EDU

Name	Rank	Phone	E-mail	Field	Degree	Yr	School	Since
Gilbertson, Philip N.	Dean	464-5314	pgilbertson	Engl	PHD		Kentucky	
Henderson, James P.	C-Pr	464-5404	jhenderson	NBA	PHD	77	N Illinois	1975
Bernard, James A. Jr.	Assoc	464-5045		AOP	PHD	72	Notre Dm	
Burnette, Joyce	Asst	464-6814	jburnette	NJF	PHD	94	Northwes	1995
Shingleton, Virginia	Asst	464-5405	vshingleton	CJIA	PHD	94	Notre Dm	1992

Vanderbilt University — Nashville, TN 37235 (615) 322-2871 Edda Leithner
Dept of Econ & Business Adm — Col of Arts & Sciences Fax=343-8495 CTRVAX.VANDERBILT.EDU

Name	Rank	Phone	E-mail	Field	Degree	Yr	School	Since
Goodman, Madeleine	Dean	322-2851		Biol	PHD	73	Hawaii	1994
Damon, William W.	C-Pr	322-2871	damonww	DGM	PHD	70	Cornell	1976
Atack, Jeremy	Prof	343-2467	atackj	N	PHD	76	Indiana	1993
Bell, Clive L. G.	Prof	322-2937		OG	PHD	75	Sussex	1986
Daughety, Andrew F.	Prof	322-2871		LK	PHD	72	Case Wes	1995
Driskill, Robert A.	Prof	343-1516		EFM	PHD	78	J Hopkins	1992
Finegan, T. Aldrich	Prof	322-3445		J	PHD	60	Chicago	1970
Foster, James E.	Prof	322-2192	fosterje	DG	PHD	82	Cornell	1990
Huang, Cliff J.	Prof	322-3796	huangxcj	C	PHD	68	N Carol	1969
Margo, Robert A.	Prof	322-2189	margora	NJ	PHD	82	Harvard	1989
Reinganum, Jennifer F.	Prof	322-2871		LK	PHD	79	Northwes	1995
Russell, Clifford S.	Prof	322-8506		HQ	PHD	68	Harvard	1986
Director, Institute for Public Policy Studies								
Siegfried, John J.	Prof	322-2429	siegfrjj	LJ	PHD	72	Wisconsin	1972
Westfield, Fred M.	Prof	322-2388		D	PHD	57	MIT	1965
Wildasin, David E.	Prof	343-2468	wildasin	G	PHD	76	Iowa	1993
Anderson, Kathryn H.	Assoc	322-0263	anderskh	JO	PHD	78	N Car St	1980
Dir Graduate Pgm in Econ Devel; Senior Fellow, Inst for Public Policy Studies								
Butler, John Scott	Assoc	322-3237	butlerjs	GC	PHD	82	Cornell	1982
Senior Fellow, Institute for Public Policy Studies								

Getz, Malcolm	Assoc	322-3425	getz	HR	PHD	73	Yale	1973
Hinshaw, C. Elton	Assoc	322-3453		N	PHD	66	Vanderbilt	1966
Maneschi, Andrea	Assoc	322-2993		FO	PHD	64	J Hopkins	1969
Sweeney, George H. Associate Dean	Assoc	322-2845		DL	PHD	77	Northwes	1976
Bell, Anne M.	Asst	322-2871		EN	PHD	95	Wisconsin	1995
Horowitz, Andrew W.	Asst	322-2196	horowita	OL	PHD	89	Wisconsin	1989
Lai, Edwin	Asst	322-2482	laiel	FOL	PHD	91	Stanford	1991
Lee, Junsoo	Asst	322-3582	leej	E	PHD	91	Mich St	1991
Rousseau, Peter L.	Asst	322-2871		EM	PHD	95	Stern Sch	1995
Slotsve, George A.	Asst	322-2920	slotsvga	JD	PHD	89	Wisconsin	1988
Song, E. Young	Asst	322-0716		FE	PHD	90	Harvard	1990
Watts, Alison	Asst	322-3425	wattsa	DHG	PHD	93	Duke	1993
Weinhold, Diana	Asst	322-2466	weinhold	FO	PHD	94	Ca-SnDgo	1994

Vassar College Poughkeepsie, NY 12601 (914) 437-7395 Susan M. Conger
Department of Economics Economics Fax=437-7187 VASSAR

Jehle, Geoffrey A.	C-Pr	437-5210	jehle	D	PHD	83	Princeton	1981
Kennett, David A.	Prof	437-7000	kennett	F	PHD	76	Columbia	1976
Thompson, Alexander M.	Prof	437-5257	thompson	BH	PHD	79	Stanford	1977
Herbst, Lawrence A.	Assoc	437-7398		N	PHD	74	Penn	1970
Johnson, Shirley B.	Assoc	437-5214	sjlans	I	PHD		Columbia	1967
Lunt, William E.	Assoc	437-7396	lunt	C	PHD		Stanford	1974
Bellemore, Fred A.	Asst	437-7393	frbellemore	H	PHD		MIT	1992
Johnson, Paul A.	Asst	437-7000	pajohnson	E	PHD	89	Stanford	1995
Kilby, Christopher P.	Asst	437-5212	chkilby	O	PHD		Stanford	1993
Knoblauch, Vicki I.	Asst	437-7000		DL	PHD	91	Wi-Milw	1995
Smith, John Z.	Asst	437-5207	josmith	J	PHD		MIT	1993
Leonard, Thomas E.	Inst	437-7000		BEK	ABD		Geo Wash	1995

University of Vermont Burlington, VT 05405-0078 (802)
Department of Economics Col of Arts & Sciences Fax= UNV.EDU

Ball, Howard	Dean	656-3166		PolS	PHD	70	Rutgers	1989
Thomson, Ross	C-Ac	656-3064	ross.thomson	NDB	PHD	76	Yale	1991
Alnasrawi, Abbas	Prof	656-3064		FOQ	PHD	65	Harvard	1963
email aalnasrawi@moose.								
Campagna, Anthony S.	Prof	656-3064	acampagna@moose.	EH	PHD			66
Rutgers								1965
Chase, Richard X.	Prof	656-3064	rchase@moose.	BE	PHD	66	Maryland	1966
Gibson, William A.	Prof	656-3064		CFOQ	PHD	77	Berkeley	1986
email: gibson@econs.umass.edu								
Boyd, Michael L.	Assoc	656-3064	mboyd@moose.	NOQP	PHD	84	Stanford	1984
Gedeon, Shirley J.	Assoc	656-0188		EP	PHD	82	Mass	1981
Knodell, Jane E.	Assoc	656-3064		EN	PHD	84	Stanford	1986
McCrate, Elaine D.	Assoc	656-3064	emccrate@uvmvm.	JIT	PHD			85
Mass								1985
Rizvi, Saiyid A.	Assoc	656-3064	srizvi@moose.	BDF	PHD	90	New Sch	1987
Woolf, Arthur G.	Assoc	656-3064	awoolf@moose.	HNR	PHD	80	Wisconsin	1980
Brooks, Nancy	Asst	656-0183	nbrooks@moose.	DHQR	PHD	94	Penn	1994
Seguino, Stephanie	Asst			EFOP	PHD	94	American	1995
Sethi, Rajiv	Asst	656-3064	rajiv.sethi	BCGQ	PHD	93	New Sch	1993

Villanova University Villanova, PA 19085-1678 (610) 519-4370 Kathleen Brown 519-6924
Department of Economics Col of Commerce & Fnce Fax=519-7864 VUUAXCOM

Taylor, Kenneth B.	C-As	519-4370	PHD	80	SUNY-SBr	1985
Mathis, Edward J.	Prof	519-4387	PHD	71	SUNY-Buf	1966
Thanawala, Kishor H.	Prof	519-4385	PHD	61	Bombay	1967
Zech, Charles E.	Prof	519-4371	PHD	73	Notre Dm	1974
DeFina, Robert H.	Assoc	519-6431	PHD	79	Wash U	1989
Donziger, Alan J.	Assoc	519-4315	PHD	72	ByrnMawr	1967
Kroch, Eugene A.	Assoc	519-6428	PHD	78	Harvard	1991
Wolnicki, Miron J.	Assoc	519-4384	PHD	80	Lodz	1984
Zaleski, Peter A.	Assoc	519-4378	PHD	88	Maryland	1987
Alexandrin, Glen	Asst	519-6101	PHD	67	Clark	1970
Asher, Cheryl	Asst	519-4159	PHD	81	Penn	1984
Asher, Martin A.	Asst	519-6427	PHD	86	Penn	1984
Casario, Michelle	Asst	519-4362	PHD		Northeas	1991
Clain, Suzanne H.	Asst	519-6556	PHD	84	Princeton	1987
Farrell, Rev. John	Asst	519-4324	PHD	72	Catholic	1993
Giordano, James N.	Asst	519-4167	PHD	82	Indiana	1983
Mao, Wen	Asst	519-4370	PHD	94	Va Tech	1995
Matthews, John O.	Asst	519-4357	PHD	85	Temple	1986
Walsh, C. Gerald	Asst	519-4165	MA	60	Detroit	1960
Wasson, Renya Reed	Asst	519-6995	PHD	92	Brown	1992
Webster, Elaine	Asst	519-4364	MED	70	Rutgers	1986

University of Virginia Charlottesvil VA 22903-3288 (804) 924-3177 Peggy Pasternak
J. Wilson Dept of Economics Grad Sch of Arts & Sci Fax=982-2904 VIRGINIA.EDU

Name	Rank	Phone	E-mail	Field	Degree	Yr	School	Year
Plog, Stephen E.	Dean	924-3437	sep6n		PHD	77	Michigan	1978
Olsen, Edgar O.	C-Pr	924-3443	eoo	HI	PHD	68	Rice	1983
Baxter, Marianne	Prof	924-3997	mb6s	FE	PHD	84	Chicago	1993
Elzinga, Kenneth G.	Prof	924-6752	kge8z	L	PHD	67	Mich St	1967
Epps, Thomas W.	Prof	924-7947	twe	GC	PHD	69	Duke	1972
Undergraduate Director								
Holt, Charles A.	Prof	924-7894	cah2k	CDL	PHD	77	Car Mellon	1989
James, John A.	Prof	924-3525	jaj8y	NO	PHD	74	MIT	1978
Johnson, William R.	Prof	924-3251	wrj8y	DJ	PHD	75	MIT	1974
King, Robert G.	Prof	924-3994	rgk4m	EG	PHD	80	Brown	1993
A. Willis Robertson Professor of Economics								
Mills, David E.	Prof	924-3061	dem9j	LD	PHD	75	Stanford	1975
Mirman, Leonard J.	Prof	924-6756	lm8h	ACDQ	PHD	70	Rochester	1986
Paul Goodloe McIntire Professor of Economics								
Sherman, Roger	Prof	924-6746	rs5w	LD	PHD	66	Car Mellon	1971
Brown-Forman Professor of Economics								
Whitaker, John K.	Prof	924-3459	jw9s	BC	PHD	62	Cambridg	1969
Georgia S. Bankard Porfessor of Economics								
Anderson, Simon P.	Assoc	924-3861	sa9w	LDR	PHD	85	Queen's	1987
Balasubrahmanian, Ravikumar	Assoc	924-3402	rb8s	EO	PHD	89	Iowa	1989
Engers, Maxim P.	Assoc	924-3130	mpe2m	ACD	PHD	84	UCLA	1982
Michener, Ronald W.	Assoc	924-6753	rwm3n	EN	PHD	81	Chicago	1979
Graduate Director								
Stern, Steven N.	Assoc	924-6754	sns5r	JCI	PHD	85	Yale	1985
Brien, Michael	Asst	924-6750	brien	JT	PHD	91	Chicago	1993
Gurmu, Shiferaw	Asst	924-3660	sg2m	CF	PHD	92	Indiana	1992
John, A. Andrew	Asst	924-6747	aaj9w	AE	PHD	88	Yale	1993
Khan, Aubhik	Asst	924-7581	ak2g	EO	PHD	93	Penn	1993
Kreider, Brent	Asst	924-3177	bk5x	HI	PHD	94	Wisconsin	1994

Virginia Commonwealth Univ Richmond, VA 23284-4000 (804) 828-1717 Susan Ross, Jackie Mayo
Department of Economics School of Business Fax=828-8884

Name	Rank	Phone	Degree	Yr	School	Year
Tuckman, Howard P.	Dean	828-1595	PHD	70	Wisconsin	1993
Bowman, John H.	C-Pr	828-7141	PHD	73	Ohio St	1981
Hoffer, George E.	Prof	828-7089	PHD	72	Virginia	1970
Beall, Larry G.	Assoc	828-7140	PHD	63	Duke	1970
Harrison, William B. III	Assoc	828-7142	PHD	72	Maryland	1972
O'Toole, Dennis M.	Assoc	828-3185	PHD	71	Ohio U	1967
Pratt, Michael D.	Assoc	828-1717	PHD		Kansas	1979
Reilly, Robert J.	Assoc	828-3184	PHD	78	Tennessee	1978
Schaefer, Kurt C.	Assoc	828-7147	PHD	84	Michigan	
Wetzel, James N.	Assoc	828-7145	PHD	74	N Carol	1974
Davis, Douglas D.	Asst	828-7187	PHD	84	Indiana	1987
Harless, David W.	Asst	828-7190	PHD	88	Indiana	
Mitchell, Shannon K.	Asst	828-7148	PHD	89	Virginia	1990
Perez, Stephen J.	Asst	828-7141	PHD		Ca-Davis	
Peterson, Steven P.	Asst	828-3186	PHD	89	Indiana	1989

Virginia Military Institute Lexington, VA 24450-0304 (703) 464-7234 Beverly Clements
Dept of Economics & Business Liberal Arts Division Fax=464-7677

Name	Rank	Phone	Degree	Yr	School	Year
Badgett, Lee D.	Dean	464-7212	PHD	71	Yale	1990
Reclam, Michael	H-Ac	464-7234	PHD	84	Ca-River	1986
Claiborn, Edward Lee	Prof	464-7234	PHD	64	Princeton	1981
Daley, Edward Vincent	Prof	464-7234	PHD		Missouri	1981
Duncan, Floyd Harold	Prof	464-7234	PHD		S Carol	1978
Bush, Howard Francis	Assoc	464-7234	PHD		Florida	1994
Sexton, Edwin A.	Assoc	464-7234	PHD	87	Illinois	1992
O'Connor, Roy John	Inst	464-7234	MBA		Hartford	1992
Woundy, Douglas Stanley	Inst	464-7234	ABD		Va Comm	1989

Virginia Poly Inst & St Un Blacksburg, VA 24061-0316 (540) 231-5688 Mrs. Sherry Williams
Department of Economics Col of Arts & Sciences Fax=231-5097 VTVM1.CC.VT.EDU

Name	Rank	Phone	E-mail	Field	Degree	Yr	School	Year
Bates, Robert C.	Dean	231-5421	bates					
Salehi-Isfahani, Djavad	C-Ac$	231-7697	salehi	O	PHD	77	Harvard	1984
Feltenstein, Andrew	Prof	231-7958	andrew	D	PHD	76	Yale	1993
Kats, Amoz	Prof	231-6289	amoz	D	PHD	72	Minnesota	1974
Meiselman, David I.	Prof		ecstu2	D	PHD	61	Chicago	1971
Nova Campus; Director of Graduate Program								
Tideman, T. Nicolaus	Prof	231-7592	ntideman	H	PHD	69	Chicago	1975
Ashley, Richard A.	Assoc	231-6220	ashley	E	PHD	82	Ca-SnDgo	1981
Cothren, Richard D.	Assoc	231-6980	cothren	E	PHD	81	N Carol	1985
Eckel, Catherine C.	Assoc	231-7707	utill	P	PHD	83	Virginia	1983
Sibert, Anne C.	Assoc	231-4431	asibert	FE	PHD	82	Car Mellon	1993
Ahn, Hyungtaik	Asst	231-7590	ahn	D	PHD	91	Wisconsin	1991
Ball, Sheryl B.	Asst	231-4349	sball	M	PHD	91	Northwes	1992

Gilles, Robert P.	Asst	231-4069	gilles	D	PHD	90	Tilburg	1991
Grossman, Philip J.	Vasst	231-7654		P	PHD	84	Virginia	1995
visiting from Wayne State Univ								
Haller, Hans H.	Asst	231-7591	haller	D	PHD	78	Bonn U	1985
Lagunoff, Roger D.	Asst	231-7981			PHD	89	Minnesota	1995
Lutz, Nancy A.	Asst	231-7353	lutz	L	PHD	87	Stanford	1992
Michalopoulos, Charles	Asst	231-5942	cmich	J	PHD	94	Wisconsin	1992
Nuxoll, Daniel A.	Asst	231-7474	nuxoll	F	PHD	92	Brown	1991
Parigi, Bruno M.	Asst	231-4537	parigi		PHD	90	Rutgers	1990
Snyder, Susan	Asst	231-4378		H				1995
Verbrugge, Randal	VAsst	231-4348		F				1995
Vriend, Nicholas	VAsst	231-5442		F	PHD	93	Florence	1995
Wang, Yong	Asst	231-5764	ywang	E	PHD	90	Brown	1990
Cremer, Jacques	Adj				PHD	78	MIT	1983
Virginia State University	Petersburg, VA	23806	(804) 524-5335				Mrs. Shirley Lewis	
Dept of Economics & Finance	School of Business	Fax=524-5541					VSU.EDU	
Gregory, Sadie R.	Dean	524-5166	sgregory		PHD	87	Howard	1-79
Khan, Agha Nisar	Prof	524-5872	akhan		PHD	70	Va Tech	1972
Meeks, Thomas J.	Prof	524-5364	tmeeks		PHD	71	Duke	1969
Whyte, Charles D.	Prof	524-5978	cwhyte		PHD	69	Ohio St	1974
Badu, Yaw Agyeman	Assoc	524-5324	abadu		PHD	80	S Carol	1984
Bawuah, Kwado	Assoc	524-5881	kbawuah		PHD	83	Va Tech	1987
Eseonu, Maxwell O.	Assoc	524-5882	meseonu		PHD	83	Howard	1982
Boese, Alan Ervin	Asst	524-5070	aboese		MA	70	S Illinois	1971
Wagner College	Staten Island,NY	10301	(718) 390-3122				Camille Cook	
Economics Faculty	Business Administration	Fax=390-3467						
Michael, James	H-Ac	390-3122		Fnce	PHD			
Wake Forest University	Winston-SalemNC	27109	(910) 759-5334				Faith W. Kisel	
Department of Economics	7505 Reynolda Station	Fax=759-4809					WFU.EDU	
Hammond, Claire Holton	C-Ac	759-5292	hammonc		PHD	82	Virginia	1978
Brown, David G.	Prof	759-4878			PHD	61	Princeton	1990
email david_brown@mail.mba.wfu.edu								
Frey, Donald E.	Prof	759-5618	frey		PHD	72	Princeton	1972
Hammond, J. Daniel	Prof	759-5335	hammond		PHD	79	Virginia	1978
Moorhouse, John C.	Prof	759-5130	moorhous		PHD	69	Northwes	1969
Wood, John H.	Prof	759-5250	jw		PHD	64	Purdue	1985
Reynolds Professor of Economics								
Lawlor, Michael S.	Assoc	759-5174	lawlor		PHD	86	Iowa St	1986
Patterson, Perry L.	Assoc	759-5528	patterso		PHD	86	Northwes	1986
Cottrell, Allin F.	Asst	759-5762	cottrell		PHD	81	Edinbrgh	1989
Huck, Paul F.	Asst	759-5923	huck		PHD	93	Northwes	1989
Whaples, Robert M.	Asst	759-4916	whaples		PHD	90	Penn	1991
Yates, Andrew J.	Asst	759-5231	yates		PHD	92	Stanford	1993
Walla Walla College	College Place,WA	99362	(509) 527-2951				Ms. Cheri Windemuth	
Economics Faculty	Department of Business	Fax=527-2253					WWC.EDU	
Anderson, Norman	C-Pr	527-2096	andeno		JD		So Meth	1987
Chuah, Kim Liang	Assoc	527-2652	chuaki	ACEG	PHD	92	Wash St	1991
Wartburg College	Waverly, IA	50677-1003	(319) 352-8415					
Economics Faculty	Dept of Bus Adm & Econ	Fax=352-8514					WARTBURG.EDU	
Magnall, Paul	C-Ac	352-8428	magnall	Atg	MBA	82	N Iowa	1983
Kramer, Melvin L.	Prof	352-8452			PHD	66	Iowa	1956
Shipman, William A.	Prof	352-8315			PHD	77	Pittsburgh	1972
Campbell, Gloria L.	Assoc				MBA	84	N Iowa	1979
Yee, Janice G.	Asst	352-8485			PHD	90	Clark	1991
Washburn Univ of Topeka	Topeka, KS	66621	(913) Ext 1308				Phyllis Sanderson	
Department of Economics	Col of Arts & Sciences	Fax=231-1063					ACC.WUACC.EDU	
phone: 231-1010 Ext 1309								
McKibbin, Lawrence	Dean	231-1010	zzmiki	L	PHD	68	Stanford	1991
Gustavson, Robert L.	Prof	231-1010	zzgust		PHD	76	Colorado	1976
Olson, Richard	Prof	231-1010	zzolso		PHD	65	Nebraska	1980
Kerchner, Robert B.	Assoc	231-1010	zzkerc		PHD	73	Missouri	1976
Smith, Russell E.	Assoc	231-1010	zzsmith		PHD	84	Illinois	1984
Woolf, Linda L.	Assoc	231-1010	zzwool		PHD	70	Kansas St	1969
Dickes, Allen L.	Inst				MA	70	Toledo	1978
Director, Institutional Research								

University of Washington	Seattle, WA 98195 (206)					
Dept of Finance & Bus Econ	Sch of Business Adm					UWACDC
–School of Business Adm	Phone 543-4773 Fax 685-9392					Jennifer Raines
Bradford, William D.	Dean 543-4752		PHD	72	Ohio St	1994
Schall, Lawrence D.	C-Pr 543-7689		PHD	69	Chicago	1967
Alberts, William W.	Prof 543-6579		PHD	61	Chicago	1987
Ferson, Wayne	Prof 543-1843		PHD	82	Stanford	1992
Frost, Peter S.	Prof 543-0992		PHD	66	UCLA	1969
Haley, Charles	Prof 543-7697		PHD	68	Stanford	1966
Hess, Alan C.	Prof 543-4579		PHD	69	Car Mellon	1967
Higgins, Robert C.	Prof 543-4379		PHD	69	Stanford	1967
Karpoff, Jonathan M.	Prof 685-4954		PHD	82	UCLA	1983
Roley, V. Vance	Prof 543-7476		PHD	77	Harvard	1983
Siegel, Andrew F.	Prof 543-4476		PHD	83	MIT	1990
Kamara, Avraham	Assoc 543-0652		PHD	86	Columbia	1984
Malatesta, Paul H.	Assoc 685-1987		PHD	81	Rochester	1980
Rice, Edward M.	Assoc 543-4480		PHD	78	UCLA	1979
Koski, Jennifer L.	Asst 543-7975 jkoski		PHD	91	Stanford	1991
Novaes, Walter	Asst 543-4435		PHD	93	MIT	1993
Pontiff, Jeffrey	Asst 543-3021		PHD	94	Rochester	1992
Hadjimichalakis, Karma	SLect 685-8044		PHD	74	Rochester	1970
Tarhouni, Ali	SLect 543-4577		PHD	84	Mich St	1985
–Col of Arts & Sciences						
Norman, Joe G. Jr.	Dean	Chem	PHD	72	MIT	1972
Turnovsky, Stephen J.	C-Pr 543-5955		PHD	68	Harvard	1987
Barzel, Yoram	Prof		PHD	61	Chicago	1961
Brown, Gardner	Prof		PHD	64	Berkeley	1965
Bruce, Neil	Prof		PHD	75	Chicago	1990
Halvorsen, Robert F.	Prof		PHD	73	Harvard	1972
Hartman, Richard C.	Prof		PHD	71	Berkeley	1971
Nelson, Charles R.	Prof		PHD	65	Wisconsin	1975
Parks, Richard	Prof		PHD	66	Berkeley	1970
Siberberg, Eugene	Prof		PHD	64	Purdue	1967
Startz, Richard	Prof		PHD	78	MIT	1984
Thornton, Judith Ann	Prof		PHD	66	Radcliff	1961
Deolalikar, Anil B.	Assoc		PHD	81	Stanford	1989
Engel, Charles M.	Assoc		PHD	83	Berkeley	1991
Hadjimichalakis, Michael	Assoc		PHD	69	Rochester	1969
Kochin, Levis A.	Assoc		PHD	75	Chicago	1972
Leffier, Keith B.	Assoc		PHD	77	UCLA	1978
Lundberg, Shelly J.	Assoc		PHD	81	Northwes	1984
Rao, Potluri M.	Assoc		PHD	69	Chicago	1973
Thomas, Robert P.	Assoc		PHD	64	Northwes	1968
Wong, Kar-Yiu	Assoc		PHD	83	Columbia	1983
Eicher, Theo S.	Asst		PHD	94	Columbia	1994
Ellis, Gregory M.	Asst		PHD	92	Berkeley	1988
Khalil, Fahad A.	Asst		PHD	71	Va Tech	1991
Lawaree, Jacques P.	Asst		PHD	90	Berkeley	1990
Rose, Elaina	Asst		PHD	93	Penn	1993
Zwot, Eric W.	Asst		PHD	92	Yale	1993
Heyne, Paull Theodore	SLect		PHD	63	Chicago	1976
Salehi-Esfahani, Haideh	SLect		PHD	85	Penn	1990
Turnovsky, Michelle H. L.	SLect		PHD	78	Aust Nat	1987
Director, Undergraduate Studies						

Washington University	St. Louis, MO 63130-4899 (314) 935-5670					Karen Rensing
Department of Economics	Col of Arts & Sciences Fax=935-4156					WUSTL.EDU
email: @1=wuecon.wustl.edu @2=wuecona.wustl.edu						
Macias, Edward	Dan		PHD	70	MIT	1970
Neuefeind, Wilhelm	C-Pr 935-5632	wilhelm@neuefein	PHD	72	Bonn	1978
Barnett, William A.	Prof 935-4236	barnett@1	PHD	74	Car Mellon	1990
Benham, Lee K.	Prof 935-4535	benham@1	PHD	70	Stanford	1974
Berliant, Marcus C.	Prof	berliant@2	PHD	82	Berkeley	1994
Felix, David	Emer 935-5639	felix@1	PHD	55	Berkeley	1964
Greenberg, Edward	Prof 935-5641	edg@2	PHD	61	Wisconsin	1963
Leven, Charles L.	Emer 935-5836		PHD	58	Northwes	1964
Meyer, Laurence H.	Prof 935-5648		PHD	70	MIT	1969
North, Douglass C.	Prof 935-5809		PHD	52	Berkeley	1983
Henry R. Luce Prof of Law & Liberty; 1993 Nobel Prize in Econ; leave 1995-96						
Pollak, Robert A.	Prof		PHD	64	MIT	1995
Hernreich Distinguished Professor of Economics						
Schofield, Norman J.	Prof 935-4774	schofld@1	PHD	85	Essex	1986
William Taussig Professor						
Weidenbaum, Murray L.	Prof 935-5662		PHD	58	Princeton	1961
Edward Mallinckrodt Distinguished University Professor						
Fazzari, Steven M.	Assoc 935-5693	fazz@2	PHD	82	Stanford	1982
Nye, John V. C.	Assoc 935-6736	nye@1	PHD	85	Northwes	1985
Parks, Robert P.	Assoc 935-5665	bparks@2	PHD	71	Purdue	1971
Petersen, Bruce C.	Assoc 935-5643	petersen@2	PHD	81	Harvard	1991

Name	Rank	Phone	Email	Field	Degree	Yr	School	Year
Raines, Fredric Q.	Assoc	935-5636	raines@1		PHD	67	Wisconsin	1964
Rothstein, Paul	Assoc	935-4352	rstein@2		PHD	88	Berkeley	1988
Winter, Eyal	Assoc	935-5809			PHD	88	Hebrew	1995
Keating, John W.	Asst	935-7335	keating@1		PHD	89	Northwes	1989
Kim, Sukkoo	Asst	935-4961	soks@2		PHD	93	UCLA	1993
Nachbar, John	Asst	935-5612	nachbar@1		PHD	88	Harvard	1990
Olson, Mary K.	Asst	935-4437	olson@1		PHD	91	Stanford	1990

Washington & Jefferson Col Washington, PA 15301 (412)
Economics Faculty Dept of Economics & Bus Fax=223-5271

Name	Rank	Phone	Email	Field	Degree	Yr	School	Year
Gregor, John J.	C-Pr	223-6150			PHD	76	Penn St	1989
Siren, Raymond L.	Prof	223-6154			PHD		Pittsburgh	1975
Boyles, William B.	Assoc	229-5126			MBA		Oklahoma	1977
Herbener, Jeffrey M.	Assoc	223-6151			PHD		Okla St	1986
Stifflemire, Paul F. Jr.	Asst	229-5125			MBA		Suffolk	1986
Swint, Kenneth J.	Asst	223-6156			PHD	89	Pittsburgh	1988
Lyon, William R.	Inst	223-6516			MBA		Morehead	1988

Washington and Lee Univ Lexington, VA 24450 (703) 463-8604 Carol Ruley
Department of Economics Sch Comm, Econ & Pol Fax=463-8639 FS.COMMERCE.WLU.EDU

Name	Rank	Phone	Email	Field	Degree	Yr	School	Year
Peppers, Larry C.	Dean	463-8602	peppers.l.c		PHD		Vanderbilt	1986
Herrick, Bruce H.	C-Pr	463-8615	herrick.b.h	OP	PHD	64	MIT	1980
John F. Hendon Professor of Economics								
Cline, Philip L.	Prof	463-8622	cline.p.l	C	PHD	75	Okla St	1975
Lewis Whitabker Adams Professor of Economics								
Gunn, John McKenzie	Emer	463-8616	gunn.j.m	E	MA	54	Princeton	1957
Lewis Whitaker Adams Professor of Economics Emeritus								
Kaiser, Carl P.	Prof	463-8617	kaiser.c.p	JC	PHD	80	Wash U	1979
Lowry, Stanley T.	Prof	463-8614	lowry.s.t	BK	PHD	58	LSU	1959
Phillips, Charles F. Jr.	Prof	463-8618	phillips.c.f	L	PHD	60	Harvard	1959
Robert C. Brown Professor of Economics								
Winfrey, John C.	Prof	463-8606	winfrey.j.c	DH	PHD	65	Duke	1965
Anderson, Michael A.	Assoc	463-8971	anderson.m.a	F	PHD	90	Wisconsin	1990
Goldsmith, Arthur H.	Assoc	463-8970	goldsmith.a.h	E	PHD	79	Illinois	1990
Hooks, Linda M.	Assoc	463-8621	hooks.l.m	E	PHD	91	UCLA	1993
Smitka, Michael J.	Assoc	463-8625	smitka.m.j.	FL	PHD	89	Yale	1986
Holliday, A. J.	Asst	463-8628	holliday.a.j.	K	PHD		Virginia	1993
Konz, Jeffery M.	Asst	463-8970		E	PHD		N Carol	1994

Washington State University Pullman, WA 99164-4741 (509) 335-6651 Ms. Frankie Harvey
Department of Economics Col of Business & Econ Fax=335-4362 WSUVM1

Name	Rank	Phone	Email	Field	Degree	Yr	School	Year
Leigh, Duane E.	C-Pr	335-4441			PHD	69	Mich St	1968
Berney, Robert E.	Prof	335-5141			PHD	63	Wisconsin	1966
Joerding, Wayne H.	Prof	335-6468			PHD	79	Northwes	1979
Krautkraemer, Jeffrey A.	Prof	335-3420			PHD	82	Stanford	1981
Lowinger, Thomas C.	Prof	335-4913			PHD	70	Mich St	1978
Schaefer, Donald F.	Prof	335-6737			PHD	67	N Carol	1982
Stromsdorfer, Ernst W.	Prof	335-4471			PHD	62	Wash U	1983
Associate Dean								
Batina, Raymond	Assoc	335-8057			PHD	85	Minnesota	1985
Clark, Carolyn	Assoc	335-6651			PHD	70	Berkeley	1973
Fort, Rodney D.	Assoc	335-6468			PHD	85	Cal Tech	1984
Hallagan, William S.	Assoc	335-6651			PHD	77	Ca-Davis	1984
Inaba, Frederick S.	Assoc	335-6651			PHD	74	Berkeley	1977
Nziramasanga, Mudziviri T.	Assoc	335-6651			PHD	74	Stanford	1973
Roseman, Robert E.	Assoc	335-1193			PHD	82	Minnesota	1983
Smith, D. Stanton	Assoc	335-5314			PHD	69	Tx-Austin	1968
Cardell, N. Scott	Asst				PHD	89	Harvard	1989

Wayne State College Wayne, NE 68787 (402) 375-7292 Donna Stutheit
Department of Economics Div of Social Sciences Fax=375-7204 WSCGATE.WSC.EDU

Name	Rank	Phone	Email	Field	Degree	Yr	School	Year
Karlen, Jean	H-Pr	375-7292		Soci	PHD		Nebraska	1976
Dalal, Meenakshi N.	Prof	375-7509		OE	PHD	84	Northeas	1985
on leave								
Parker, Charles	Asst		cparker	AEK	PHD	94	Ohio St	8-95

Wayne State University Detroit, MI 48202 (313) 577-3345 Donna Hill/Delores Tennille
Department of Economics Col of Liberal Arts Fax=577-0149 WAYNEST1

Name	Rank	Phone	Email	Field	Degree	Yr	School	Year
Goodman, Allen C.	C-Pr	577-3344	agoodman		PHD	76	Yale	1986
Finn, Thomas J. Jr.	Prof	577-3232			PHD	59	Harvard	1963
Lee, Li Way	Prof	577-0070			PHD	76	Columbia	1981
Levin, Jay H.	Prof	577-3345			PHD	68	Michigan	1976
Owen, John D.	Prof	577-2846			PHD	64	Columbia	1975
Rossana, Robert J.	Prof	577-3760			PHD	80	J Hopkins	1991
Braid, Ralph M.	Assoc	577-2540			PHD	79	MIT	1988

Jensen, Gail A.	Assoc	577-3345			PHD	86	Minnesota	1989
Bekdache, Basma	Asst	577-3231			PHD	94	Boston	1994
Cotter, Kevin D.	Asst	577-3233			PHD		Minnesota	1989
Durkin, John T.	Asst	577-2693			PHD		Chicago	1991
Grossman, Philip J.	Asst	577-3236			PHD	84	Virginia	1990
on leave to Virginia Tech Univ								
Hunsaker, Julie	Asst	577-0603			PHD	93	Purdue	1993
Mavros, Panagiotis	Asst	577-3355			PHD	93	Cornell	1992
Spurr, Stephen J.	Asst	577-3232			PHD		Chicago	1987
Wassmer, Robert W.	Asst	577-3235			PHD	89	Mich St	1989
Yoon, Gawon	Asst	577-3349			PHD	94	Ca-SnDgo	1994

Weber State University — Ogden, UT 84408-3807 (801) 626-6066 — Leanna Griffin
Department of Economics — Col of Business & Econ Fax=626-7423 — COBE.WEBER.EDU

Vaughan, Michael B.	Dean	626-6084		AMK	PHD	80	Nebraska	1981
Alston, Richard M.	C-Pr	626-6061	ralston	ABNQ	PHD	70	Cornell	1969
Chi, Wan Fu	Prof	626-6792	wchi	AC	PHD	69	S Illinois	1969
Cloward, Dix W.	Prof	626-7177	dcloward	A	EDD	70	Utah St	1963
Fuller, Dan A.	Prof	626-6794	dfuller	ADH	PHD	82	N Carol	1981
Mbaku, John M.	Prof	626-7442	jmbaku	AHOP	PHD	85	Georgia	1991
Nowell, Clifford	Assoc	626-6488	cnowell	ADQ	PHD	88	Wyoming	1988
Tinkler, Sarah E.	Assoc	626-7101	stinkler	AF	PHD	89	Oregon	1988
Crone, Lisa	Asst	626-7428	lcrone	AQ	PHD	94	Wyoming	1993

Webster University — St. Louis, MO 63119-3194 (314) 968-7021 — Lois Pollard
Business Department — Sch of Business & Mgt Fax=968-7077

Miles, Wilford G.	Dean	968-7561		Mgt	PHD	68	Arkansas	1995
Berry, Lucille	C			Fnce	PHD	87	St Louis	1984
Beuttenmuller, Doris Henle	Prof	968-7021		AIJN	PHD		St Louis	1974
Westerfield, Donald	Prof	968-7021		DIMC	PHD		St Louis	1984
Hinson, Steve Y.	Asst	968-7021		AFDH	PHD		Kentucky	1993
Groetsch, James A.		968-6908			PHD		St Louis	
Associate Dean European Campuses								

Wellesley College — Wellesley, MA 02181 (617) 283-2154 — Helen Graham
Economics Faculty — Department of Economics Fax=283-2177

Joyce, Joseph P.	C-Ac	283-2160			PHD	84	Boston U	1982
Case, Karl E.	Prof	283-2178			PHD	77	Harvard	1987
Goldman, Marshall I.	Prof	283-2161			PHD	61	Harvard	1958
Lindauer, David	Prof	283-2159			PHD	79	Harvard	1981
Matthaei, Julie Ann	Prof	283-2181			PHD	78	Yale	1978
Morrison, Rodney J.	Prof	283-2182			PHD	65	Wisconsin	
Witte, Ann D.	Prof	283-2163			PHD	71	N Car St	1985
Andrews, Marcellus	Assoc	283-2179			PHD	86	Yale	1986
Kauffman, Kyle	Assoc	283-2153			PHD	93	Illinois	1993
Blomberg, Brock	Asst				PHD	94	J Hopkins	1995
Chang, Pamela	Asst	283-2164			PHD	93	Stanford	1992
Hansen, Korinna	Asst	283-2158			PHD	92	Rochester	1994
Levine, Philip	Asst	283-2493			PHD	91	Princeton	1990
Skeath, Susan E.	Asst	283-2180			PHD	89	Princeton	1989
Velenchik, Ann D.	Asst	283-2183			PHD	89	Stanford	1989

Wesley College — Dover, DE 19901-9912 (302) 736-2514
Economics Faculty — Division of Business Fax=736-2301
no full-time Economics faculty

Jacobs, Kathleen C.	C-Pr	736-2519		Mgt	EDD	87	Temple	1988

Wesleyan University — Middletown, CT 06459-6067 (203) 685-2340 — Mary Leighton Wood
Economics Faculty — Department of Economics Fax=685-2781 — EAGLE.WESLEYAN.EDU

Lovell, Michael C.	C-Pr	685-2355	mlovell	E	PHD	59	Harvard	1969
Chester D. Hubbard Professor of Economics & Social Science								
Adelstein, Richard P.	Prof	685-2366	radelstein	K	PHD	75	Penn	1975
Barber, William J.	Emer	685-2362	wbarber	B	DPHI	57	Oxford	1957
Andrews Professor of Economics								
Bonin, John P.	Prof	685-2353	jbonin	P	PHD	73	Rochester	1970
Kilby, Peter	Prof	685-2365	pkilby	O	DPHI	67	Oxford	1965
Lebergott, Stanley	Emer	685-2364	slebergott	N	MA	39	Michigan	1962
University Professor								
Miller, Richard A.	Prof	685-2354	ramiller	L	PHD	62	Yale	1960
Andrews Professor of Economics								
Moore, Basil J.	Prof	685-2363	bmoore	E	PHD	58	J Hopkins	1958
Mueller, Marnie	VProf			I	PHD	65	Yale	
Whitin, Thomson M.	Emer	685-2347	twhitin	C	PHD	52	Princeton	1963
Hubbard Professor								
Yohe, Gary W.	Prof	685-3658	gyohe	D	PHD	75	Yale	1977

Blass, Asher A.	VAsoc			L	PHD	88	Harvard	
Ramirez, Miguel	VAsoc				PHD	84	Illinois	
Rayack, Wendy	Assoc	685-2358	wrayack	J	PHD	84	Wisconsin	1983
Grossman, Richard	Asst	685-2356	rgrossman	N	PHD	88	Harvard	1990
Jacobsen, Joyce P.	Asst	685-2357	jjacobson	J	PHD	91	Stanford	1993
Selover, David D.	Asst	685-2352	dselover	F	PHD	91	Ca-SnDgo	1990
Skillman, Gilbert L.	Asst	685-2359	gskillman	D	PHD	85	Michigan	1993

University of West Alabama — Livingston, AL 35470 (205) Ext 260 — Nettie Foy
Dept of General Business — College of Bus & Comm Fax=652-9318
phone: 652-9661

Stennis, Earl A.	Dean	652-9661		AgEc	PHD		Miss St	9-94
Carr, Linda	Prof				EDD		Alabama	1962
Akpom, Uchenna N.	Asst				PHD	89	Kentucky	1992

West Chester Univ of PA — West Chester, PA 19383 (610) 436-3460 — Pat Mareci
Department of Economics — Sch of Bus & Public Aff Fax=436-3170 — WCUPA.EDU

Fiorentino, Christopher M.	Dean	436-2930	cfiorentino	DQ	PHD	89	Temple	9-85
Bove, Roger E.	C-Ac	436-2134	rbove	FP	PHD	73	Harvard	1984
Benzing, Cynthia D.	Prof	436-2217	cbenzing	AEG	PHD	87	Drexel	1988
Naggar, Tahany	Prof	436-2834	tnaggar	ADTN	PHD	76	Oklahoma	1977
Sylvester, Patrick J.	Prof	436-2964			PHD	73	Bryn Mawr	
DeMoss, Philip M.	Assoc	436-2964	pdemoss	AGM	PHD	69	Kansas St	1973
Mohan, Daniel	Assoc	436-3468	dmohan	GM	PHD	75	Rutgers	1980
Dunleavy, Kevin C.	Asst	436-3422	kdunleavy	ACE	PHD	79	Duke	1979
Tolin, Thomas	Asst	436-1082	ttolin	JD	PHD	92	Houston	1992

University of West Florida — Pensacola, FL 32514-5752 (904) 474-2659 — Mary McBride
Dept of Finance & Economics — College of Business Fax=474-2716 — UWF

Carper, William B.	Dean	474-2349			PHD	79	Va Tech	1995
Huth, William L.	C-Pr	474-2652		AMG	PHD	80	Arkansas	1989
Ashraf, Javed	Assoc	474-2664		AJ	PHD	86	N Illinois	1990
Arguea, Nestor M.	Asst	474-3071		ACD	PHD	90	S Calif	1990
Harper, Richard K.	Asst	474-3072		AFM	PHD	89	Duke	1989

West Georgia College — Carrollton, GA 30118 (404) 836-6477 — Ms. Elizabeth Key
Department of Economics — School of Business Fax=836-6774 — SBF.BUS.WESTGA.EDU

Hovey, David Hiram	Dean	836-6467	dhovey	Mgt	PHD	78	LSU	8-84
Fryman, Richard F.	C-Pr	836-6477	rfryman	AH	PHD	67	Illinois	1986
Gustafson, Leland Verne	Prof	836-6477	lgustaf	AC	PHD	74	Fla St	
Guynn, Richard Dickson	Prof	836-6477	rguynn	JA	PHD		Alabama	
Scott, Carole Elizabeth	Prof	836-6477	escott	NO	PHD		Geo St	
Schaniel, William C.	Assoc	836-6477	wschani	BP	PHD	85	Tennessee	
Boldt, David John	Asst	836-6477	dboldt	AR	PHD	87	New Mex	1988
Dutt, Swarna D.	Asst	836-6477	sdutt	F	PHD	93	Wayne St	1994
Raper, Michael Dennis	Asst	836-6477	mraper	AR	PHD		Geo St	

Sewell Chair of Private Enterprise

West Liberty State College — West Liberty, WV 26074 (304) 336-8053 — Sharon Rinderer
Dept of Atg & Economics — School of Business Adm Fax=336-8582

McCollough, John P.	Dean	336-8053		Mgt	PHD	71	N Dakota	1971
Reuther, Carol	C-As	336-8156			MS	73	Fla St	1991
Hatzopoulos, Sydma	Assoc	336-8153			MA	80	Va Tech	1990
Mullin, Marian V.	Assoc	336-8054			MS	85	R Morris	1975
Rosenberg, Allan B.	Assoc	336-8068			MS	57	Illinois	1982

Coordinator of Regents BA Program

West Texas A&M University — Canyon, TX 79016-0187 (806) 656-2525 — Betsey Bavousett
Dept of Atg, Econ & Finance — Pickens Col of Business Fax=656-2927

Miller, Jerry D.	Dean	656-2530		Fnce	PHD	70	LSU	1993
Duman, Barry L.	H-Pr	656-2519		BDP	PHD	71	S Calif	1969
Kelso, Patrick R.	Assoc			EHN	PHD	68	Tx-Austin	1967
Rosa, Duane J.	Assoc			EOQ	PHD	89	Tx Tech	1984
Smith, Evelyn K.	Asst			ABJO	PHD	75	Tx A&M	1990

Director of Economic Education

West Virginia University — Morgantown, WV 26506-6025 (304) 293-7859 — Tammy Scroggs
Department of Economics — Col of Business & Econ Fax=293-7061 — WVBE1.BE.WVU.EDU
email: @1=WVNVM.WVNET.EDU

Stern, Sydney V.	Dean	293-7800	stern	Engr	PHD	62	Ga Tech	1994
Trumbull, William N.	C-Ac	293-7860	trumbull	HKD	PHD	85	N Carol	1983
Adams, Donald R. Jr.	Prof	293-7861	adams	N	PHD	67	Penn	1981
Anselin, Luc	Prof	293-8546	u41bc@1	RC	PHD	80	Corning	1993

Britt, Robert D.	Prof	293-7862	britt	BN	PHD	66	Colorado	1968
Hawley, Clifford B.	Prof	293-7865	hawley	JD	PHD	77	Duke	1978
Hwang, Ming-jeng	Prof	293-7866	hwang	DRC	PHD	73	Tx A&M	1974
Isseman, Andrew W.	Prof	293-4101	wlabys@1	R	PHD	75	Penn	1984
Kymn, Kern O.	Prof	293-7867	kymn	EC	PHD	64	Chicago	1976
Labys, Walter C.	Prof	293-6253	u24c4@1	Q	PHD	68	Nottnghm	1975
Mann, Patrick C.	Prof	293-7872	mann	DH	PHD	67	Indiana	1967
Mitchell, Douglas W.	Prof	293-7868	mitchell	E	PHD	78	Princeton	1984
Norton, Virgil	Prof	293-6253		QI	PHD	64	Oreg St	1986
Reece, William S.	Prof	293-4092	reece	CH	PHD	75	Wash U	1990
Associate Dean								
Witt, Tom S.	Prof	293-7835	witt	CR	PHD	74	Wash U	1970
Balvers, Ronald J.	Assoc	293-7880	balvers	EG	PHD	84	Pittsburgh	1991
Cushing, Brian J.	Assoc	293-7881	cushing	RCH	PHD	81	Maryland	1981
Fletcher, Jerald J.	Assoc	293-6253	jfletch@1	Q	PHD	82	Berkeley	1989
Phipps, Tim	Assoc	293-6353	u55e@1	Q	PHD	82	Berkeley	1989
Bandyopadhyay, Sudeshna	Asst	293-7869	bandys	J	PHD	92	Maryland	1992
Chow, C. Victor	Asst	293-7888	chow	G	PHD	89	Alabama	1989
Douglas, Stratford M.	Asst	293-7863	douglas	CHD	PHD	87	N Carol	990
Park, Eun-Soo	Asst	293-7875	park	D	PHD	93	Northwes	1992
Sobel, Russell S.	Asst	293-7864	sobel	H	PHD	94	Fla St	1994
Wall, Howard J.	Asst	293-7871	wall	FD	PHD	89	SUNY-Buf	1988
Watts, Royce J.	Asst	293-5695		C	MS	61	W Virginia	1955
Wu, Yangru	Asst	293-7859	wu	F	PHD	93	Ohio St	1995
Yangru, Wu	Asst	293-7859	wu	F	PHD	93	Ohio St	1995

West Virginia State College	Institute, WV		25112-1000 (304) 766-3065				Norma Bukovac	
Department of Economics	Div of Bus Admin & Econ		Fax=766-4127					
Did Not Respond--1994-95 Listing								
Henderson, Sandra R.	C-Ac	766-3064		AFR	MA	60	Pittsburgh	1968
Hunyadi, Csilla	Asst	766-3054		AGM	PHD	86	Budapest	1989
Swanke, Thomas A.	Asst	766-3062		AEJO	PHD	93	Colorado	1993

Western Carolina University	Cullowhee, NC		28723-9033 (704) Ext 226				Kathy Brashear	
Dept of Economics & Finance	School of Business		Fax=227-7414				WCUVAX1.WCU.EDU	
Schreiber, Max M.	C-Ac	227-7401	schreibr		PHD	78	S Carol	1977
Jones, Royal Maurice	Prof	227-7401			PHD	67	Maryland	1971
Spencer, Austin Harvey	Prof	227-7401			PHD	72	Indiana	1980
White, Harry Ruff	Prof	227-7401			PHD	66	Kentucky	1968
Hays, Patrick Allen	Assoc	227-7401			PHD	77	N Carol	1985
Jarrell, Stephen B.	Assoc	227-7401			PHD	78	Purdue	1988
McMahan, Ralph Stephen	Assoc	227-7401			PHD	74	Arkansas	1970
Tye, Duncan Rene	Assoc	227-7401			PHD	74	Tulane	1977
Wade, John	Assoc	227-7401			PHD	82	Purdue	1977
Alen, Grace	Asst	227-7401			PHD	91	S Carol	1992
Kask, Susan B.	Asst	227-7401			PHD	88	Wyoming	1993

Western Conn State Univ	Danbury, CT		06810 (203) 837-8484					
Div of Social Sciences	Sch of Arts & Sciences		Fax=837-8525				WCSUB.CTSTATEU.EDU	
Hawkes, Carol A.	Dean				PHD		Columbia	
Bannister, Jerry	C-Ac	837-8454		Soci	MA		Syracuse	
Skinner, Steven P.	Prof	837-8457			PHD		Conn	
Owoye, Oluwole	Assoc	837-8456			PHD	89	N Illinois	
Pan, Zuohong	Asst				PHD		Mich St	

Western Illinois University	Macomb, IL		61455-1396 (309) 298-1153				Mary Sherwood	
Department of Economics	College of Business		Fax=298-1020				CCMAIL.WIU.BGU.EDU	
Walzer, Norman C.	D-Pr	298-1031	nwalzer	AHR	PHD	70	Illinois	1970
Director, Illinois Institute for Rural Affairs								
Jones, Warren	C-Ac	298-1477	wjones	AEHN	PHD	82	Iowa	1983
Hattwick, Richard E.	Prof	298-1594	rhattwick	AM	PHD	65	Vanderbilt	1969
Director Center for Business & Economic Research								
Marx, Karl B.	Prof	298-1734	kmarx	ADH	PHD	61	Illinois	1961
Pledge, Michael T.	Prof	298-1637	mpledge	AEG	PHD	68	Houston	1968
Rao, Vaman	Prof	298-1321	vrao	ACEO	PHD	73	Missouri	1979
Yunker, James A.	Prof	298-1639	jyunker	ACDP	PHD	71	Northwes	1968
Andrianacos, Dimitri	Assoc	298-2331	dandrianacos	ACE	PHD	89	Chicago	1990
Fosu, Joseph	Assoc	298-2265	jfosu	AEO	PHD	87	Iowa St	1987
Rock, Steven M.	Assoc	298-1343	srock	AJ	PHD	75	Northwes	1990
Stratton, Peter J.	Assoc	298-1638	pstratton	AD	PHD	70	N Illinois	1970
Straub, LaVonne	Assoc	298-1413	lstraub	AIJR	PHD	83	Utah	1982
Kleiner, William C.	Asst	298-1032	wkleiner	AEF	PHD	74	Mich St	1971

Western Kentucky University | Bowling Green KY 42101-3576 (502) 745-2249 | Karen Braun
Department of Economics | Col of Business Admin Fax=745-3893 | WKYUVM

Name	Rank	Phone	Field	Degree	Yr	School	Year
Brown, J. Michael	Dean	745-3893	G	PHD	71	Kentucky	1988
Wassom, John C.	H-Pr	745-2249	G	PHD	70	Indiana	1971
Borland, Melvin V.	Prof	745-3112	BDA	PHD	72	Wash U	1978
Kim, Hak Youn	Prof	745-3187	CDO	PHD	82	Cincinnati	1983
Lile, Stephen E.	Prof	745-3115	H	PHD	72	Kentucky	1973
Pulsinelli, Robert W.	Prof	745-3118	DK	PHD	74	Rutgers	1967
Ramey, James Vice President of Administration	Prof	745-2434	GH	PHD	80	Kentucky	1992
Wisley, Thomas O.	Prof	745-3127	GHK	PHD	79	Purdue	1985
Cantrell, Richard P.	Assoc	745-3146	C	MA	63	S Illinois	1967
Davis, William W.	Assoc	745-3123	F	PHD	65	Kenucky	1970
Goff, Brian L.	Assoc	745-3855	GHK	PHD	86	Geo Mason	1986
Howsen, Roy M.	Assoc	745-3172	D	PHD	80	Arkansas	1981
Myers, Daniel A.	Assoc	745-384	R	PHD	86	Vanderbilt	1986
Noser, Thomas C.	Assoc	745-3642	CA	PHD	86	Alabama	1984
Roberts, Charles A.	Assoc	745-3105	BN	PHD	79	Georgia	1969
Valinezhad, Moosa	Assoc	745-3111	FE	PHD	88	Geo St	1988
Carey, Cathrine	Asst	745-6401	F	PHD	92	Kentucky	1992

Western Maryland College | Westminster, MD 21157 (410) 857-2450 | Pat Holford
Economics Faculty | Dept of Econ & Bus Adm Fax=857-2729

Name	Rank	Phone	Degree	Yr	School	Year
Law, Alton D.	C-Pr	848-7000	PHD	68	Rutgers	1966
Olsh, John Lindsay	Prof	848-7000	PHD		Ca-Davis	1980
Seidel, Ethan A.	Prof	848-7000	PHD	77	J Hopkins	1969
Claycombe, Richard J.	Assoc	848-7000	PHD	80	Geo Wash	1981
Milstein, Susan Matz	Assoc	848-7000	MBA		MtStMary	1983
Singer, Diana Sue	Assoc	848-7000	MBA		Loyola	1983

Western Michigan University | Kalamazoo, MI 49008-5023 (616) 387-5535 | Mrs. Becky Ryder
Department of Economics | Col of Arts & Sciences Fax=387-3999 | WMICH.EDU

Name	Rank	Phone	E-mail	Field	Degree	Yr	School	Year
Ferraro, Douglas P.	Dean	387-4350	douglas.ferraro	Psyc	PHD	65	Columbia	1990
Sichel, Werner	C-Pr	387-5539	werner.sichel	D	PHD	64	Northwes	1960
Barrett, Nancy S. Provost	Prof	387-2380	nancy.barrett	E	PHD	68	Harvard	1991
Gardner, Wayland D.	Prof	387-5542	wayland.gardner	H	PHD	58	Wisconsin	1964
Hoffman, Emily P.	Prof	387-5546	emily.hoffman	J	PHD	75	Mass	1981
Pozo, Susan	Prof	387-5553	susan.pozo	F	PHD	80	Mich St	1982
Thistle, Paul D.	Prof	387-5528	paul.thistle	D	PHD	83	Tx A&M	1992
Alexander, Donald L.	Assoc	387-5526	donald.alexander	D	PHD	83	Penn St	9900
Asefa, Sisay	Assoc	387-5540	sisay.asefa	O	PHD	80	Iowa St	1980
Caruso, Phillip P.	Assoc	383-1704	pillip.caruso	E	PHD	77	Mich St	1967
Harik, Bassam	Assoc	387-5554	bassam.harik	E	PHD	78	Wayne St	1979
Harik, Salim	Assoc	387-5544	salim.harik	F	PHD	75	Wayne St	1976
Huang, Wei-Chiao	Assoc	387-5547	wei-chiao.huang	J	PHD	84	Ca-SnBarb	1985
Kern, William	Assoc	387-5549	william.kern	B	PHD	82	Colo St	1987
Meyer, Donald J.	Assoc	387-5531	donald.meyer	D	PHD	83	Tx A&M	1991
Neill, Jon R.	Assoc	387-5551	jon.neill	H	PHD	83	Pittsburgh	1980
Wheeler, Mark V.	Assoc	387-5563	mark.wheeler	E	PHD	85	Kentucky	1990
Zhou, Huizhong	Assoc	387-5550	huizhong.zhou	C	PHD	86	Northwes	1990
Alvi, Eskander	Asst	387-5547	eskander.alvi	E	PHD	85	J Hopkins	1994
Higgins, Matthew L.	Asst	387-5543	matthew.higgins	C	PHD	89	Illinois	1995

Western New England Coll | Springfield, MA 01119-2684 (413) 782-1480 | Donna Utter
Department of Economics | Col of Arts & Sciences Fax=782-1746

Name	Rank	Phone	Field	Degree	Yr	School	Year
Porter, Burton F.	Dean	782-1218	Phil	PHD		StAndrews	
Skillman, Richard K.	C-Ac	782-1602		MALD		Tufts	
Andrulis, John A.	Prof	782-1601		PHD	75	Purdue	1981
Meeropol, Michael A.	Prof	782-1252		PHD		Wisconsin	
Eskot, Herbert J.	Asst	782-1743		PHD	84	Tufts	1984

Western Oregon State Col | Monmouth, OR 97361 (503) 838-8226 | Dianna Hewett
Div of Business & Economics | Sch Liberal Arts & Sci Fax=838-8474 | -

Name	Rank	Phone	Degree	Yr	School	Year
Minahan, John P.	Dean		PHD	69	Geotown	1986
Bahari-Kashani, Hamid	C-Ac	838-8722	PHD	83	Wash St	1988
Finster, Ronald D.	Prof	838-8410	PHD	70	Arizona	1971
Singh, Ajmer	Prof	838-8244	PHD	64	Oreg St	1965
Leadley, John C.	Asst	838-8719	PHD		Wisconsin	

Western State College of CO | Gunnison, CO 81231 (970) 943-7011
Economics Faculty | Dept Econ, Hst & PolSci Fax=943-3380 | WSC.COLORADO.EDU

Name	Rank	Phone	Degree	Yr	School	Year
Stewart, Jim	C	943-7011				
Axelson, David J.	Assoc	943-3081	EDD	76	Colorado	1982
Reyn, Stephanie	Assoc		PHD	92		

Western Washington Univ Bellingham, WA 98225-9074 (360) 650-3910
Department of Economics Col of Business & Econ Fax=650-4844 WWU.EDU

Name	Rank	Phone	Fields	Degree	Yr	School	Year
Murphy, Dennis R.	Dean	650-3896	FM	PHD	74	Indiana	1979
Nelson, David M.	C-Ac	650-4804	EGI	PHD	75	Oregon	1977
Harder, K. Peter	Prof	650-3920	BNP	PHD	68	Nebraska	1970
Merrifield, David E.	Prof	650-3909	M	PHD	82	Claremont	1983
Hagen, Daniel A.	Assoc	650-3964	JEFQ	PHD	83	Berkeley	1988
Hansen, Julia L.	Assoc	650-3204	DR	PHD	84	Berkeley	1988
Henson, Steven E.	Assoc	650-4843	QD	PHD	82	Oregon	1985
Sleeman, Allan G.	Assoc	650-3910 -	CD	PHD	83	Simon Fr	1977
Weymark, Diana N.	Asst	650-2867	EF	PHD	90	Brit Col	1988
Hendryson, Mary Ann	Lect	650-4799	DOF	ABD		Wash St	1989
Whalley, Pamela	Lect	650-4823	DG	ABD		Indiana	1989

Westfield State College Westfield, MA 01086 (413) 572-5590 Helen Lent
Economics Faculty Dept of Econ & Bus Mgt Fax=562-3613 RCN

Name	Rank	Phone	Fields	Degree	Yr	School	Year
Ettman, Philip	C-Ac	572-5695	Mgt	JD		Boston U	1982
Bellico, Russell P.	Prof	572-5312		EDD		Mass	1970
Darrow, John J.	Prof	572-5715		PHD		Conn	1971
Paquette, Laurence R.	Prof	572-5742		PHD	85	Mass	1987
Pellegrino, Kathleen B.	Prof	572-5329		MBA	76	W NewEng	1978
Gural, Michael L.	Assoc	572-5591		MA		Rutgers	1982
Kotzen, Nancy	Assoc	572-5313		MBA		W NewEng	1981
Wagner, John R.	Assoc	572-5697		PHD	77	Temple	1986
Daniel, Cornelia M.	Asst	572-5696		PHD		Mass	1990
Healy, Gerald	Asst	572-5693		MBA		American	1981
Knipes, Bradford	Asst	572-5574		PHD		Mass	1988
McFarlin, Thomas	Asst	572-5314		MBA		W NewEng	1978
Merlo, Gary E.	Asst	572-5694		MBA		W NewEng	1983
Sullivan, Kathryn	Asst	572-5592		PHD		Mass	1992
Thomas, Oommen	Asst	572-5725		MBA		W NewEng	1980

Westminster College-PA NewWilmingtonPA 16172 (412) 946-7160 Mrs. Kathleen A. Proctor
Economics Faculty Dept of Business & Econ Fax=946-7171 WESTMINSTER.EDU

Name	Rank	Phone	Fields	Degree	Yr	School	Year
Miller, Gail L.	C-Pr	946-7160	Bus	DBA		Kentucky	1983
Fischmar, Daniel E.	Prof	946-7162		PHD		S Illinois	1975
Carter, Kent	Assoc	946-7164		PHD		Mass	1991
Captain William McKee Chair of Economics & Business							
Groothuis, Peter A.	Assoc	946-7163		PHD	89	Kentucky	1989
Rosengarth, Tom E.	Assoc	946-7169		MS		Bowl Grn	1979
Fong, Tat P.	Asst	946-7166		PHD		Pittsburgh	1993
Corrado, Marilyn S.	Inst	946-7165		MBA		Youngstn	1990

Westminster Cl of Salt Lk Ct Salt Lk City, UT 84105 (801) 488-4220
Economics Program Gore School of Business Fax=466-6916 WHITEWATER.WCSLC.EDU

Name	Rank	Phone	Email	Fields	Degree	Yr	School	Year
Seidelman, James E.	Dean	488-4222	c.seidelman		PHD	86	Utah	1980
Ehin, Charles	D-Pr	488-1611	c.ehin	M	PHD	72	Oklahoma	1983
Chapman, Richard	Assoc	488-4228	d-chapman	JNB	PHD	92	Utah	1985
Hansen, Ann	Assoc	488-4146	a-hansen	CHL	PHD	81	Utah	1990
Watkins, John P.	Assoc	488-4221	j-watkin	BNQ	PHD	85	Utah	1984
Wrotniak, Maria	Assoc	488-4155	m-wrotni	BCO	PHD	80	Lodz	1989

Wheaton College-IL Wheaton, IL 60187 (708)
Economics Faculty Dept of Business & Econ Fax= DAVID.WHEATON.EDU

Name	Rank	Phone	Email	Fields	Degree	Yr	School	Year
Howard, Bruce	C-Ac	752-5313	bhoward	ABM	PHD		N Illinois	1980
Halteman, James	Prof	752-5312	haltman	AB	PHD	74	Penn St	1979
Hill, Peter J.	Prof	260-5033		ANPQ	PHD	70	Chicago	1986
George F. Bennett Professor of Economics								
Ewert, Norman J.	Assoc			AF	PHD		S Illinois	1973
Norton, Seth	Assoc			GJLM	PHD	82	Chicago	1995
Aldeen Chair								
Tomal, Anette	Asst			AIM	PHD		Illinois	1995

Wheaton College-MA Norton, MA 02766 (508) 285-8200
Economics Faculty Department of Economics Fax= WHEATONMA.EDU

Name	Rank	Phone	Email	Fields	Degree	Yr	School	Year
Weil, Gordon	C-Pr	Ext 5350	gordon_weil	FOP	PHD	81	Tufts	1981
Walgreen, John A.	Prof	Ext 5354			PHD	65	Boston C	1967
Gildea, John A.	Assoc	Ext 5346	john_gildea	EG	PHD	85	Duke	1985
Miller, John A.	Assoc	Ext 5351			PHD	82	Pittsburgh	1979
Wyss, Brenda	Asst	Ext 5349	brenda_wyss	JTO	PHD	95	Mass	1992

Whitworth College Spokane, WA 99251 (509) 466-3282 Patricia Parker
Economics Faculty Dept of Economics & Bus Fax=466-3720

Name	Rank	Phone	Fields	Degree	Yr	School	Year
LaShaw, Margie N.	C-As	466-3283	Atg	MACC		Wash St	1988
McKinney, Charles W.	Assoc	466-3283		PHD		Wash St	1985
Schatz, Richard E.	Assoc	466-3283		PHD		Hawaii	1989
Hergenrather, Richard A.	Asst	466-3283		PHD		P Drucker	1994

Wichita State University Wichita, KS 67260-0078 (316) 689-3220 Mrs. Julia Carter
Department of Economics Barton Sch of Business Fax=689-3845 TWSUVM.UC.TWSU.EDU

Graham, Gerald H.	Dean	689-3200		Mgt	PHD	68	LSU	1967
Haydon, Randall B.	C-Pr	689-3220			PHD	62	Illinois	1970
Cho, Dong Woo	Prof	689-3220	dwcho		PHD	73	Illinois	1972
Perline, Martin M.	Prof	689-3220			PHD	65	Ohio St	1965
Skaggs, Jimmy M.	Prof	689-3220	skaggs		PHD	70	Tx Tech	1970
Webb, Samuel C.	Prof	689-3220			PHD	68	Kansas	1966
Cheng, Jen-Chi	Assoc	689-3220	cheng		PHD	89	Vanderbilt	1989
Clark, James E.	Assoc	689-3220	jeclark		PHD	77	Northwes	1976
Director Center for Economic Education								
Duell, Dennis	Assoc	689-3220	duell		PHD	69	Illinois	1967
Hersch, Philip L.	Assoc	689-3220	plhersch		PHD	82	Ohio St	1983
Pfannestiel, Maurice	Assoc	689-3220	pfannest		PHD	67	Okla St	1966
Terrell, William T.	Assoc	689-3220			PHD	70	Vanderbilt	1967
Li, Qing	Asst	689-3220			PHD	95	Houston	1995
Decker, Terence N.	Inst	689-3220			ABD	93	Wichita St	1990
Dimmen, Janet L.	Inst	689-3220			ABD	78	Ohio St	1981

Widener University Chester, PA 19013-5792 (610) 499-4306 Mrs. Kay Veacock
Department of Economics School of Management Fax=499-4614

DiAngelo, Joseph A. Jr.	Dean	499-4301		Mgt	EDD	87	Temple	1980
Saltzman, Cynthia J.	C-Ac	499-4326		EFGO	PHD	86	Maryland	1980
Duggal, Vijaya G.	Prof	499-1176		CEDQ	PHD	67	Harvard	1983
Fuhr, Joseph P.	Prof	499-1172		DIKQ	PHD	81	Temple	1979
Waldauer, Charles	Prof	499-4329		DEHR	PHD	69	Syracuse	1968
Zahka, William J.	Prof	499-4477		ABNO	ABD		Bryn Maw	1959
Leppel, Karen	Assoc	499-1170		JCT	PHD	80	Princeton	1985
Williams, Mary L.	Assoc	499-4324		BOMQ	PHD	84	Temple	1982
Zangeneh, Hamid	Assoc	499-1140		EFGP	PHD	84	Missouri	1985
Armstrong, Thomas O.	Asst	499-1142		HKQD	PHD	89	Temple	1989

Wilkes University Wilkes-Barre, PA 18766 (717) 831-4225 Ms. Sandra L. Rybak
Dept of Business & Economics Sch Bus,Society &PubPol Fax=831-4917 WILKES1.WILKES.EDU'

Giamartino, Gary A.	Dean	831-4704	ggiamar	M	PHD	79	Vanderbilt	7-93
Raspen, Richard G.	C-Ac	831-4702	rraspen	M	PHD	91	Penn	7-67
Taylor, Wagiha A.	Prof	831-4712		EF	PHD	66	Clark	1969
Seeley, Robert D.	Assoc	831-4717		AIJ	PHD	86	Maryland	9-89
Latzko, David	Asst	831-4718	dlatzko	DEF	PHD		Maryland	9-93

Willamette University Salem, OR 97301 (503)
Department of Economics College of Liberal Arts Fax=375-5398 WILLAMETTE.EDU

Cress, Lawrence	Dean	370-6285		Hst	PHD		Virginia	
Frew, James R.	C-Ac	370-6232			PHD	79	Purdue	1984
Archer, Stephen H.	Prof	370-6224			PHD	58	Minnesota	1973
Guy F. Atkinson Porfessor of Economics & Finance								
Beaton, C. Russell	Prof	370-6306			PHD		Claremont	1971
Choate, G. Marc	Prof	370-6224			PHD		U Wash	1974
Hanson, James S.	Prof	370-6316			PHD	71	Stanford	1976
Hibbard, Thomas H.	Prof	370-6317			PHD	67	Claremont	1973
Gray, Jerry	Assoc	370-6307			PHD		Utah	1990
Whiting, Cathleen L.	Assoc	370-6075			PHD	86	U Wash	1986
Negri, Donald H.	Asst	370-6326			PHD		Michigan	1988

College of William & Mary Williamsburg, VA 23187 (804) Mary Ferraro
Department of Economics Faculty Arts & Sciences Fax= MAIL.WM.EDU

Lutzer, David J.	Dean			Math	PHD		U Wash	1987
Hausman, William J.	C-Pr	221-2381	wjhaus		PHD	76	Illinois	1981
Archibald, Robert B.	Prof	221-2366	rbarch		PHD	74	Purdue	1976
Baker, Samuel H. III	Prof	221-2371	shbake		PHD	70	Virginia	1969
Campbell, Donald E.	Prof	221-2383	decamp		PHD	72	Princeton	1989
CSX Professor of Economics Public Policy								
Finifter, David H.	Prof	221-2370	dhfini		PHD	74	Pittsburgh	1973
Garrett, Martin A.	Prof	221-2375	mcgarr		PHD	66	Vanderbilt	1963
Haulman, Clyde A.	Prof	221-1276	ahaul		PHD	69	Fla St	1969
Moody, Carlisle E.	Prof	221-2373	cemood		PHD	70	Conn	1970
Percira, Alfredo M.	Prof				PHD	88	Stanford	1995
Schifrin, Leonard	Prof	221-2382	lgschi		PHD	64	Michigan	1964
Chancellor Professor								
Abegaz, Berhanu	Assoc	221-2379	bxabeg		PHD	82	Penn	1982
Feldman, David H.	Assoc	221-2372	dhfeld		PHD	82	Duke	1988
Jensen, Eric R.	Assoc	221-2365	erjens		PHD	82	Michigan	1982
Roberts, Bruce B.	Assoc	221-2377	bcrobe		PHD	81	Mass	1979
Jilani, Saleha	Asst				PHD	94	J Hopkins	1992
Kiesling, Lynne	Asst	221-2374	lxkies		PHD	93	Northwes	1992
McGrath, Richard	Asst	221-2387			MA		Virginia	1993

Name	Rank	Phone	Email	Field	Degree	Yr	School	Since
Mushinski, David	Asst				MA	94	Wisconsin	1995
Owen, Diane	Asst	221-2380	dsowe1		MA	86	Yale	1992
Rodgers, William	Asst	221-2398	wmrodg		PHD	93	Harvard	1993
Rodgers, Yana	Asst	221-1276	yvrodg		PHD	93	Harvard	1993
Weise, Charles	Asst	221-2432	clweis		PHD	93	Wisconsin	1993
Xu, Zhenhui	Asst	221-2378	zhenxu		PHD	93	Virginia	1993
Canfield, Michelle	Inst				MA	91	Virginia	1995
Wegge, Simone	Inst				MA	89	Northwes	1995

William Jewell College Liberty, MO 64068-9988 (816) 781-7700
Economics Faculty Dept of Bus Adm & Econ Fax=781-3164
phone 781-7700

Name	Rank	Phone	Field	Degree	Yr	School	Since
Cook, Michael T.	C-Pr	Ext 5699	EF	PHD	83	Vanderbilt	1978
John W. Boatwright Professor of Economics							
Miller, Otis E.	Prof	Ext 5703		PHD	62	Missouri	1978
Jacobsen, Lowell R. Jr.	Assoc	Ext 5693	DM	PHD	86	Edinburg	1981

Wm Patterson Coll of NJ Wayne, NJ 07470 (201) 595-2434 Mrs. Angela Mazza
Dept of Economics & Finance Sch Human, Mgt &Soc Sci Fax=595-2955

Name	Rank	Phone	Degree	Yr	School	Since
Gardiner, Elaine	Dean		PHD		Ohio U	1992
Leung, Cho Kin	C-Pr	595-2434	PHD	68	NYU	1974
Dorai, Gopal C.	Prof		PHD	67	Wayne St	1974
Eapen, Ana N.	Prof		PHD	62	Michigan	1973
Haroian, Berch	Prof		PHD	72	NYU	1978
Laurence, Martin M.	Prof		PHD		NYU	1970
Ghosh, Arabinda	Assoc	595-2221	PHD	72	CUNY	1984
Liddicost, Clifton	Assoc		MA		Temple	1966
Swanson, Paul	Assoc		PHD		Columbia	1982
Cai, Francis	Asst		PHD		CUNY	1993
Ramin, Taghi	Asst		PHD		NYU	1984

Williams College Williamstown, MA 01267 (413) 597-2476 Joanne Thornton
Economics Faculty Department of Economics Fax=597-4045

Name	Rank	Phone	Degree	Yr	School	Since
Winston, Gordon C.	C-Pr	597-2254	PHD	64	Stanford	1963
Orrin Sage Professor of Political Science						
Bolton, Roger E.	Prof	597-2393	PHD	64	Harvard	1966
Edward Door Griffin Professor of Economics						
Bradburd, Ralph M.	Prof	597-2300	PHD	76	Columbia	1976
Bruton, Henry J.	Emer	597-2357	PHD	52	Harvard	1962
John J. Gibson Professor of Econ,Resident Fellow of the Cntr for Human&SocSci						
Hill, Catharine Bond	Prof	597-3143	PHD	85	Yale	1985
McFarland, Earl L. Jr.	Prof	597-3184	PHD	73	Columbia	1968
McPherson, Michael S.	Prof	597-4351	PHD	74	Chicago	1974
Herbert H. Lehman Professor of Economics						
Sabot, Richard	Prof	597-3082	DPHI		Oxford	
Chair of the Center for Development Economics						
Husbands, Kaye G.	Assoc	597-2469	PHD	90	Harvard	
Macunovich, Diane J.	Assoc	597-2471	PHD	89	S Calif	1989
Banerji, Arup	Asst		PHD	91	Penn	1990
Constantine, Jill M.	Asst	597-2995	PHD	94	Penn	
Corbett, David J.	Asst	597-2408	PHD	91	Harvard	
Honderich, Kiaran A.	Asst		PHD	91	Mass	
on leave						
Jaeger, William K.	Asst	597-3213	PHD	85	Stanford	
Rao, Vijayendra	Asst	597-2144	PHD	90	Penn	
Samson, Mike	Asst	597-2325	PHD	94	Stanford	
Schulz, Eric	Asst	597-2101	PHD	93	Northwes	
Zimmerman, David J.	Asst	597-3184	PHD	92	Princeton	1991

Wingate College Wingate, NC 28174 (704) 233-8148 Ms. Kathryn Rowe
Economics Program Div Business & Econ Fax=
Did Not Respond--1994-95 Listing

Name	Rank	Phone	Field	Degree	Yr	School	Since
Palmer, Charles F.	Dean	233-8147	AH	PHD			1993
Doss, Veda	C-Pr	233-8144	BDJF	PHD	69	Syracuse	1984

Winona State University Winona, MN 55987-0838 (507) 457-5014 Jan Tollefson
Dept of Economics & Finance College of Business Fax=457-5697

Name	Rank	Phone	Field	Degree	Yr	School	Since
Gorman, Ken	Dean	457-5014	BusE	EDD		N Illinois	1980
Kauffman, Daniel E.	C-Pr	457-5195		PHD		Nebraska	1983
Gieske, Michael	Prof	457-5171		BS		Iowa St	1972
Manrique, Gabriel G.	Prof	457-5193		PHD	82	Notre Dm	1989
Salyards, Donald M.	Prof	457-5622		PHD		Kansas St	1975
Gallegos, Alejandro	Assoc	457-5469		PHD	86	Wi-Milw	1988
Hyle, Matthew R.	Assoc	457-5496		PHD	85	Maryland	1988
Pevas, Mary Ann	Asst	457-5014		PHD		Notre Dm	1990
on leave 1995-96							

Winston-Salem State Univ — Winston-SalemNC 27110 (910) 750-2334 — Sandra L. McCracken
Economics Faculty — Div of Business & Econ Fax=750-2335

Name	Rank	Phone	Email	Field	Degree	Yr	School	Since
Johnson, George A.	D-As$	750-2330		Atg	PHD	90	Va Tech	8-92
Okonkwo, Valentine	C-Ac	750-2334			PHD		Fla St	4-85
Elassar, Sammy E.	Prof	750-2339			PHD	68	Maryland	1968

Winthrop University — Rock Hill, SC 29733 (803) 323-2186
Dept Atg, Fnce & Econ — School of Business Adm Fax=323-3960 — ACAD.WINTHROP.EDU

Name	Rank	Phone	Email	Field	Degree	Yr	School	Since
Padgett, Jerry H.	Dean	323-2185			PHD	68	Purdue	9-72
Bond, James G.	C-Pr	323-2186		Atg	PHD	77	S Carol	9-79
Cooper, Robert	Prof				PHD	67	Virginia	9-64
Parker, Darrell F.	Prof				PHD	84	Purdue	9-85
Grier Professor of Business Administration-Economics								
Stone, Gary L.	Prof				PHD	80	N Carol	9-75
Vo, Han X.	Assoc				PHD	79	Tennessee	9-79

U of Wisconsin-Eau Claire — Eau Claire, WI 54702-4004 (715) 836-5743
Department of Economics — Sch of Arts & Sciences Fax=836-2944 — UWEC

Name	Rank	Phone	Email	Field	Degree	Yr	School	Since
Reynolds, Donald F.	Dean	836-2542	reynolds	Math	PHD		Tx Chr	1992
Young, Edward G.	C-Pr	836-5743	youngeg		PHD	77	Wash St	1977
Egan, James P.	Prof	836-3242	eganjp		PHD	82	Syracuse	1970
Hansen, Jan M.	Prof	836-2150	hansenjm		PHD	74	Missouri	1985
Kolb, Fredric	Prof	836-3518	kolbfr		PHD	71	Utah	1971
Leitner, Keith R.	Prof	836-3254	leitnerkr		PHD	74	Kansas St	1974
Oyen, Duane B.	Prof	836-3507	oyend		PHD	73	Iowa	1976
Wassink, Darwin	Prof	836-3513	wassind	FO	PHD	68	Stanford	1976
Avin, Rose Marie	Assoc	836-4513	avinr		PHD	86	Maryland	1987
Carroll, Wayne D.	Assoc	836-3388	carrolwd		PHD	84	Minnesota	1986
DaCosta, Maria N.	Assoc	836-4511	dacostmn		PHD	87	Northeas	1989
Benesh, Diann	Lect	836-3527	beneshdg		MS		Va Tech	1976
Jasek-Rysdahl, Kelvin	Lect	836-4104	jasekrkd		ABD		Colo St	1994

Univ of Wisconsin-Green Bay — Green Bay, WI 54311-7001 (414) 465-2355
Economics Faculty — Department of Economics Fax=465-2791

Name	Rank	Phone	Email	Field	Degree	Yr	School	Since
Pollis, Carol	Dean				PHD		Okla St	
Shariff, Ismail	C-Pr				PHD		Wisconsin	
Murray, James M.	Prof	465-2426			PHD	62	Oregon	1969
Stoll, John R.	Prof				PHD	80	Kentucky	
Kangayappan, Kumaraswamy	Assoc				PHD		Wisconsin	
Smith, Larry J.	Assoc				PHD		Chicago	
Troyer, Michael D.	Assoc				PHD		Duke	
Jennings, Ann	Asst				PHD		Utah	

U of Wisconsin-La Crosse — La Crosse, WI 54601 (608) 785-8099 — Diane Dobbs, Prog Asst
Department of Economics — College of Business Fax=785-6700 — MAIL.UWLAX.EDU

Name	Rank	Phone	Email	Field	Degree	Yr	School	Since
Fuller, Rex D.	Dean	785-8090	fuller	JM	PHD	82	Utah	1981
Daellenbach, Lawrence A.	C-Pr	785-8108	daell_la	ADR	PHD	69	Iowa St	1969
Clark, Barry S.	Prof	785-6860	clark_bs	BHOP	PHD	80	Mass	1978
Khandker, A. Wahhab	Prof	785-6862	khandker	ACF	PHD	80	So Meth	1983
Knowles, Glenn J.	Prof	785-6861	knowles	CQR	PHD	80	Minnesota	1985
Sherony, Deith R.	Prof	785-8101	sherony	ACE	PHD	82	Wi-Milw	1983
Hampton, Mary B.	Assoc	785-6867	hampton	GHIJ	PHD	91	Wi-Milw	1991
Haupert, Michael J.	Assoc	785-6863	haupert	AEN	PHD	89	Wash U	1989
Anderson, Donna M.	Asst	785-6864	ander_dm	DIJ	PHD	93	Mich St	1994
Nyatepe-Coo, Akorlie A.	Asst	785-6865	nyatepec	FHO	PHD	89	N Illinois	1989

Univ of Wisconsin-Madison — Madison, WI 53706-1397 (608) 263-2989 — Mary Anne Clarke
Economics Program — Col of Letters & Sci Fax=262-2033 — WISC.EDU
email: @1=facstaff.wisc.edu @2=ae.agecon.wisc.edu @3=cournot.econ.wisc.edu

Name	Rank	Phone	Email	Field	Degree	Yr	School	Since
Certain, Phillip	Dean	262-2644		Chem				
Haveman, Robert H.	C-Pr	263-2326	haveman		PHD	63	Vanderbilt	1970
John Bascom Professor of Economics								
Baldwin, Robert E.	Prof	263-7397	rebaldwi@1		PHD	50	Harvard	1964
Taussig & Hilldale Professor of Economics								
Brock, William Allen	Prof	263-6665	brock		PHD	69	Berkeley	1981
F. P. Ramsey Professor of Economics								
Chao, Kang	Prof	263-3861			PHD	62	Michigan	1967
David, Martin H.	Prof	262-3281	david@ssc.		PHD	60	Michigan	1962
Deneckere, Raymond	Prof	263-6724	rdenecke		PHD	83	Wisconsin	1993
Feige, Edgar L.	Prof	231-3330	feige		PHD	63	Chicago	1963
Goldberger, Arthur S.	Prof	263-3876	asgoldbe@1		PHD	58	Michigan	1960
Harold M. Groves & Vilas Professor of Economics								
Hansen, W. Lee	Prof	263-3869	hansenwlee		PHD	58	J Hopkins	1965
Hester, Donald D.	Prof	263-3879	ddhester		PHD	61	Yale	1968
Kennan, John F.	Prof	262-5393	jkennan		PHD	73	Northwes	1992

Name	Rank	Phone	Email	Field	Degree	Yr	School	Year
Lyall, Katharine C.	Prof	262-4048			PHD	69	Cornell	1982
President								
Manski, Charles F.	Prof	263-3880	manski@ssc.		PHD	73	MIT	1983
Romnes & WARF Professor of Economics								
Nichols, Donald A.	Prof	263-2327	nichols@2		PHD	68	Yale	1983
Rust, John P.	Prof	262-0485	jrust@thor.econ.		PHD	83	MIT	
Samuelson, Larry W.	Prof	263-7791	larrysam@3		PHD	78	Illinois	
Strasma, John D.	Prof	262-6974	strasma@2		PHD	60	Harvard	1966
Voos, Paula B.	Prof	263-3866	voospb		PHD	82	Harvard	1981
West, Kenneth D.	Prof	262-0033	west		PHD	83	MIT	1988
Wolfe, Barbara L.	Prof	262-6358	wolfe@ssc.		PHD	73	Penn	1976
Andreoni, James R.	Assoc	263-3863	james		PHD	86	Michigan	1986
Che, Yeon-Koo	Assoc	262-2819	yche		PHD	91	Stanford	1991
Durlauf, Steven N.	Assoc	263-3859	durlauf		PHD	86	Yale	1993
Dutta, Prajit	Assoc	262-6723	pkdutta		PHD	87	Cornell	1993
LeBaron, Blake	Assoc	263-2516	blakel		PHD	88	Chicago	1988
Manuelli, Rodolfo	Assoc	263-3877	manuelli		PHD	86	Minnesota	1993
Scholz, J. Karl	Assoc	262-5380	scholz		PHD	88	Stanford	1988
Staiger, Robert W.	Assoc	262-2265	staiger		PHD	85	Michigan	1993
Walker, James R.	Assoc	263-3863	walker@ssc.		PHD	86	Chicago	1987
Keller, Wolfgang	Asst				PHD	95	Yale	1995
Levinson, Arik	Asst	262-9890	arikl		PHD	93	Columbia	1993
Shea, John	Asst		johnshea		PHD	90	MIT	1990

Name	Rank	Phone	Email	Field	Degree	Yr	School	Year
Univ of Wisconsin-Milwaukee	Milwaukee, WI		53201 (414) 229-4811					
Department of Economics	Col of Letters & Sci		Fax=229-3860					
Halloran, William F.	Dean	229-4654		Engl	PHD		Duke	
Bahmani-Oskooee, Mohsen	C-Pr	229-6493			PHD	81	Mich St	1981
Heywood, John S.	Prof	229-4437			PHD	86	Michigan	1986
Lee, Tong Hun	Prof	229-4429			PHD	61	Wisconsin	1967
Mamalakis, Markos J.	Prof	229-4449			PHD	62	Berkeley	1967
Perlman, Richard W.	Prof	229-4212			PHD	53	Columbia	1964
Pesek, Boris P.	Emer	963-4680			PHD	56	Chicago	1967
Schenker, Eric	Prof	229-4235			PHD	57	Florida	1959
Schur, Leon M.	Emer	963-4678			PHD	55	Wisconsin	1964
Arora, Swarnjit S.	Assoc	229-6617			PHD	71	SUNY-Buf	1978
Belman, Dale	Assoc	229-4374			PHD		Wisconsin	1985
Drago, Robert W.	Assoc	229-6494			PHD	83	Mass	1983
Holahan, William L.	Assoc	963-5759			PHD	74	Brown	1972
Kandil, Magda	Assoc	229-6146			PHD	88	Wash St	1992
Kim, Sunwoong	Assoc	229-6924			PHD	85	MIT	1989
Meadows, G. Richard	Assoc	229-5883			PHD	72	Wash U	1971
Mohtadi, Hamid	Assoc	229-5334			PHD	82	Michigan	1983
Niho, Yoshio	Assoc	229-4811			PHD	73	Brown	1970
Peoples, James A.	Assoc	229-4482			PHD	84	Berkeley	1990
Hyatt, Douglas E.	Asst	229-4680			PHD	92	Toronto	1992
Wolfson, Paul J.	Asst	229-4338			PHD		Yale	1988

Name	Rank	Phone	Email	Field	Degree	Yr	School	Year
Univ of Wisconsin-Oshkosh	Oshkosh, WI		54901-8676 (414) 424-1441					
Department of Economics	Col Letters & Sciences		Fax=		VAXA.CIS.UWOSH.EDU			
Zimmerman, Michael	Dean	424-1210		Biol	PHD			1992
McGee, M. Kevin	C-Ac	424-7155	mcgee	H	PHD	83	Ohio St	1982
Grunloh, James J.	Prof	424-2441	grunloh	A	PHD	79	Wash U	1969
Gunderson, Ralph O.	Prof	424-1473		OR	PHD	78	Arkansas	1987
Lee, Hy Sang	Prof	424-7150		O	PHD	65	Wisconsin	1962
Voelker, Keith E.	Prof	424-1222		J	PHD	69	Wisconsin	1970
Associate Dean								
Hussain, Syed Bashir	Assoc	424-7149		F	PHD	83	Calif	1982
Vanscyoc, Lee	Assoc	424-7153		AL	PHD	87	Nebraska	1987
Brannon, J. Isaac	Asst	424-7154	brannon	J	PHD	93	Indiana	1994
Burnett, Nancy J.	Asst	424-1471	burnett	E	PHD	88	UCLA	1994
Mitchell, Milt	Asst	424-1473		Q	MA	65	Wisconsin	1967
Robson, Denise A.	Asst	424-7152		AF	PHD	93	Nebraska	1994

Name	Rank	Phone	Email	Field	Degree	Yr	School	Year
Univ of Wisconsin-Parkside	Kenosha, WI		53141-2000 (414) 595-2316				Josephine McCool	
Department of Economics	School of Liberal Arts		Fax=595-2265				UWP.EDU	
Pavalko, Ronald	Dean$	595-2384	pavalko@it.	Soci	PHD	63	UCLA	1979
Duetsch, Larry L.	C-Pr	595-2377	lduetsch@vm.	DKL	PHD	70	Wisconsin	1970
Keehn, Richard	Prof	595-2259		EGN	PHD	72	Wisconsin	1970
Cloutier, Norman R.	Assoc	595-2572		DJR	PHD	81	W Virginia	1981
Kaufman, Dennis A.	Assoc	595-2192	kaufman@cs.	CH	PHD	87	Kansas	1987
Rosenberg, Richard E.	Assoc	595-2268	rosenbe1@cs.	FOP	PHD	70	Wisconsin	1970
Khan, Farida C.	Asst	595-2662	fkhan@vm.	FO	PHD	90	Maryland	1990

U of Wisconsin-Platteville — Platteville, WI 53818-3099 (608) — Jan Schultz
Department of Economics — C of Liberal Arts & Edu Fax= — UWPLATT.EDU

Name	Rank	Phone	Email	Field	Degree	Yr	School	Year
Stevenson, G.	Dean$	342-1547						
Liska, Terrence L.	C-Ac	342-1550	liska		PHD	82	Wisconsin	1980
Al Yasiri, Kahtan A.	Prof	342-1822			PHD		Iowa St	1965
Simonson, John C.	Prof	342-1560			PHD		Wisconsin	1966
Soofi, Abdollah S.	Assoc	342-1570			PHD	81	Ca-River	1980
Al Yasiri, Ann M.	Asst	342-1822			MA		Wisconsin	1979
Dehghan, Farhad	Asst	342-1564			PHD		Illinois	1985
Ifediora, John O.	Asst	342-1564			PHD		Il-Chicago	1988
Peckham, Brian W.	Asst	342-1570			PHD	79	Wisconsin	1987

U of Wisconsin-River Falls — River Falls, WI 54022-5001 (715)
Department of Economics — Col of Arts & Sciences Fax= — UWRF.EDU

Name	Rank	Phone	Email	Field	Degree	Yr	School	Year
Prochnow, Neal H.	Dean	425-3366		Phys	PHD		Duke	9-64
Potts, Glenn T.	C-Pr	425-3991			PHD	76	Iowa St	1976
Cowen, Janna L.	Prof	425-3519			PHD	79	Nebraska	1979
Schultz, Brian L.	Prof	425-3125			PHD	80	Notre Dm	1979
Brux, Jacqueline M.	Assoc	425-3125			PHD	83	Michigan	1986
Eftekhari, Hossein	Assoc	425-3519			PHD	85	Nebraska	1985
Ngoboka, Pascal	Asst	425-3158			PHD	87	Wi-Milwa	1990
Tabesh, Hamid	Asst	425-3158			PHD	87	Iowa St	1988
Walker, John	Asst	425-3125			PHD	89	Utah	1990

U of Wisconsin-Stevens Point — Stevens Point WI 54481-3897 (715) 346-2728 — J. Cayo
Div of Business & Economics — Col Letters & Sciences Fax=346-4215

Name	Rank	Phone	Email	Field	Degree	Yr	School	Year
Paul, Justus F.	Dean	346-4224		Hist	PHD		Nebraska	1966
Cray, Randy F.	C-Ac	346-2537			PHD		Kansas St	1986
Weiser, Lawrence A.	Prof	346-3310			PHD	67	Wisconsin	1972
Christie, Darrell A.	Assoc	346-2018			MS		Illinois	1964
Palmini, Dennis J.	Assoc	346-3875			PHD	75	Illinois	1980
Jacobsen, Clifford C.	Asst	346-4576			MA		Ca-River	1969
Wang, Jin	Asst	346-4358			PHD		Kansas St	1990

Univ of Wisconsin-Superior — Superior, WI 54880-2898 (715) 394-8206 — Sharon McCuster
Dept Atg, Fnce & Econ — Cl Professional Studies Fax= — UWSUPER.EDU

Name	Rank	Phone	Email	Field	Degree	Yr	School	Year
Bahnick, Karen K.	Dean	394-8207	kbahnick	Mgt	PHD		Iowa	1966
Trudeau, Gregory P.	H-Ac	394-8209		Atg	MBA		StThomas	1988
Abrahamsson, Bernhard J.	Prof	394-8262			PHD	66	Wisconsin	1989
Beam, Robert D.	Assoc	394-8302			PHD		Cincinnati	1980

U of Wisconsin-Whitewater — Whitewater, WI 53190-1790 (414) 472-1361 — Christie Kornhoff
Department of Economics — Col of Business & Econ Fax=472-4863

Name	Rank	Phone	Email	Field	Degree	Yr	School	Year
Domitrz, Joseph S.	Dean	472-1343			PHD	71	S Illinois	1976
Kim, Kirk Y.	C-Pr	472-5576			PHD	70	Utah	1969
Bhargava, Ashok	Prof	472-4704			PHD	75	Wisconsin	1970
Dominguez, John R.	Prof	472-5586			PHD		MIT	1988
Laurent, Jerome K.	Prof	472-4715			PHD	73	Indiana	1965
Rich, Stuart	Prof	472-1776			PHD		Indiana	1959
Silva, Donald H.	Prof	472-1355			PHD		Missouri	1964
Snow, Sandra L.	Prof	472-1361			PHD	76	Missouri	1981
Weston, Gerald A.	Prof	472-5583			PHD	65	Wash St	1968
Zarinnia, Abdullah	Prof	472-5585			PHD		Nebraska	1967
Marks, Denton	Assoc	472-5576			PHD	81	Princeton	1990
Parks, Susan	Assoc	472-1747			PHD		Purdue	1980
Glosser, Stuart M.	Asst	472-5580			PHD	85	Tx-Austin	1985
Schweigert, Thomas E.	Asst	472-5582			PHD	90	Wisconsin	1984
Dunbar, Ronald	Lect	472-1354			PHD	95	Wisconsin	1995
Guthrie, Robert	Lect	472-5582			PHD		Indiana	1994

Wittenberg University — Springfield, OH 45501 (513) 327-7928 — Norma Kettler
Economics Faculty — Department of Economics Fax=327-6340 — WITTENBG
Did Not Respond--1994-95 Listing

Name	Rank	Phone	Email	Field	Degree	Yr	School	Year
Ankrom, Jeff A.	C-Ac	327-7930	jfank		PHD	82	Notre Dm	1982
Cheema, Balwir Singh	Assoc	327-7931			PHD		American	1966
Goulet, Janet C.	Assoc	327-7929			PHD	75	Notre Dm	1975
Wishart, David M.	Assoc	327-7303			PHD	85	Illinois	1983
Gwinn, Larry	Asst	327-7934			PHD		Kansas	1988
Tiffany, Frederick G.	Asst	327-7933			PHD	88	Penn	1987

Wofford College — Spartanburg, SC 29303-3663 (803) 597-4588
Economics Faculty — Dept of Econ & Atg Fax=597-4019

Name	Rank	Phone	Email	Field	Degree	Yr	School	Year
Stephenson, Matthew A.	C-Pr	597-4570			PHD	65	Tulane	1970
T. B. Stackhouse Professor of Economics								
Wallace, Richard M.	Assoc	597-4572			PHD	81	S Carol	1982
Machovec, Frank M.	Asst	597-4586			PHD	86	NYU	1988
McArthur, John R.	Asst	597-4571			PHD	91	Claremont	1990

Woodbury University Burbank, CA 91510-7846 (818) 767-0888 Rebecca Cruz
Economics Faculty Sch of Business & Mgt Fax=504-9320

Name	Rank	Phone	Email	Field	Degree	Yr	School	Year
Richman, Marvin	Dean	767-0888		Busi	MBA		Chicago	-93
Chan, Anthony K.	Assoc	767-0888		DF	PHD		Claremont	9-89
Gendel, Eugene B.	Assoc	767-0888		J	PHD	79	Boston U	7-94

The College of Wooster Wooster, OH 44691 (216)
Economics Faculty Department of Economics Fax=
Did Not Respond--Information Taken from College Catalog

Name	Rank	Phone	Email	Field	Degree	Yr	School	Year
Pollock, Gene Edward	C-Pr	263-2407			PHD	71	Ohio St	1961
Baird, William M.	Prof				PHD	68	Ohio St	1968
Galster, George C.	Prof	263-2409			PHD	74	MIT	1974
Reimer, Richard D.	Prof	263-2309			PHD	62	Mich St	1962
Hoge Professor of Economics								
Burnell, Barbara S.	Assoc	263-2417			PHD	77	Illinois	1977
Burnell, James D.	Assoc	263-2308			PHD	77	Illinois	1977
Sell, John W.	Assoc	263-2383			PHD	81	UCLA	1981
Sheppard, Katharine P.	Asst	263-2439			PHD	84	Maryland	1988

Worcester State College Worcester, MA 01602-2597 (508) 793-8091 Esther Golub 793-8091
Economics Faculty Dept of Bus Adm & Econ Fax=793-8048

Name	Rank	Phone	Email	Field	Degree	Yr	School	Year
Stefanini, Maureen	C-Pr	793-8091			EDD		Boston U	7-93
Hartwig, Robert J.	C-Pr				PHD		Wisconsin	1970
Kelley, George T.	Prof				PHD		Clark	1969
Gross, Lorna S.	Assoc				PHD	87	Clark	1995
Lee, Wei Pang	Assoc	793-8101			PHD			
Trimby, F. Stephen	Assoc				MA	69	Clark	1970

Wright State University Dayton, OH 45435 (513) 873-3070 Penny Stacy
Department of Economics Col of Business & Admin Fax=873-3545 DESIRE.WRIGHT.EDU

Name	Rank	Phone	Email	Field	Degree	Yr	School	Year
Kumar, Rishi	Dean	873-4859			PHD	72	Wayne St	1974
Premus, Robert	C-Pr	873-3070			PHD	75	Lehigh	1975
Blair, John	Prof	873-3484			PHD		W Virginia	
Fichtenbaum, Rudy H.	Prof	873-3085			PHD	80	Missouri	1980
Renas, Stephen M.	Prof	873-3030			PHD	71	Geo St	
Sav, Thomas G.	Prof	873-2405			PHD	81	Geo Wash	1985
Swaney, James A.	Prof	813-2769			PHD	79	Colo St	
Dung, Tran H.	Assoc	873-2295			PHD	78	Syracuse	1982
Olson, Paulette I.	Assoc	873-2409			PHD	89	Utah	1988
Traynor, Thomas L.	Assoc	873-2025			PHD	88	Purdue	1988
Hopkins, Barbara	Asst	873-2080			PHD		Maryland	1995
Osborne, Evan	Asst	873-4599			PHD		UCLA	1995
Endres, Carole R.	Inst	813-2823			MS	87	Wright St	
Lowry, Kathleen	Inst	873-3643			MS	77	Ohio St	
Staley, Samuel R.	Inst	813-3643			MS	87	Wright St	
Sylvester, Roger A.	Inst	873-2115			MS	87	Wright St	
Director, MS Program In Social & Applied Economics								

University of Wyoming Laramie, WY 82071 (307) 766-2178
Dept of Economics & Finance College of Business Fax=766-5090 UWYO

Name	Rank	Phone	Email	Field	Degree	Yr	School	Year
Forster, Bruce A.	Dean	766-4194	bforster	EQ	PHD	74	Austrlia	1987
Phillips, Owen R.	C-Ac	766-6669	exper	DK	PHD	80	Stanford	1985
Birch, John W.	Prof	766-4215	birch	RC	PHD	62	J Hopkins	1964
Cramer, Curtis A.	Prof	766-3384		BK	PHD	66	Maryland	1966
Crocker, Thomas D.	Prof	766-6423	crocker	Q	PHD	67	Missouri	1975
D'Arge, Ralph C.	Prof	766-6425		QO	PHD	69	Cornell	1975
Gerking, Shelby D.	Prof	766-4890	sgerking	RC	PHD	75	Indiana	1978
Morgan, William E.	Prof	766-6315		H	PHD	64	Colorado	1968
Shogren, Jason F.	Prof	766-2178		Q	PHD	86	Wyoming	1995
Tschirhart, John T.	Prof	766-2356	dddfh	DK	PHD	75	Purdue	1985
Hersch, Joni	Assoc	766-2358	jhersch	CJ	PHD	81	Northwes	1989
Mason, Charles F.	Assoc	766-5336	ceccm1a	DK	PHD	83	Berkeley	1982
Sterbenz, Frederic P.	Assoc	766-2201	sterbenz	EG	PHD	81	Penn	1981
Del Rossi, Alison	Asst	766-6424	delrossi	HK	PHD	92	Penn	1992
Wang, Lih-Jau	Asst	766-3143	lwang	F	PHD	90	Ca-SnDgo	1990

Xavier University Cincinnati, OH 45207-3212 (513) 745-3051 Ms. Izola White
Dpt Econ & Human Resources Col of Business Admin Fax=745-2929 XAVIER

Name	Rank	Phone	Email	Field	Degree	Yr	School	Year
Geeding, Daniel W.	Dean	745-3528		Mgt	PHD	72	Cincinnati	1969
Director of Institutional Research, Records & Registration								
Zimmerman, Robert O.	C-Pr	745-3075		ADEF	PHD	69	SUNY-Buf	1970
Bryant, Harold L.	Prof	745-3051		AF	PHD	67	Cincinnati	1967
Donnelly, Lawrence I.	Prof	745-3054		AJM	PHD	64	Cincinnati	1956
Marmo, Michael	Prof	745-3056		J	PHD	71	Illinois	1970
Bertaux, Nancy E.	Assoc	745-2930		ABJN	PHD	87	Michigan	1985
Blackwell, Melanie A.	Assoc	745-2037		ACQ	PHD	88	Kentucky	1987
Cobb, Steven A.	Assoc	745-3053		AEHR	PHD	74	Brown	1984
Rankin, Carol A.	Assoc	745-2932		ADJ	PHD	80	Houston	1984
Weinberg, David R.	Assoc	745-3052		ARP	PHD	73	Berkeley	1980

Name	Rank	Phone	Dept	Degree	Yr	Institution	Year
Gerring, Lori F.	Asst	745-2931	ACEM	PHD	84	Cincinnati	1989
Rashed, Jamal A.	Asst	745-2938	ACFO	PHD	88	So Meth	1989

Yale University New Haven, CT 06520-8268 (203) 432-3576 Pam Warner
Economics Faculty Department of Economics Fax=432-6249

Name	Rank	Phone	Dept	Degree	Yr	Institution	Year
Brainard, William C.	C-Pr	432-3571		PHD	63	Yale	1981
Abreu, Dilip	Prof	432-3587					
Andrews, Donald W. K.	Prof	432-0684		PHD	82	Berkeley	1982
Bewley, Truman F.	Prof	432-3719		PHD	70	Berkeley	1983
Director of Graduate Studies							
Broude, Henry W.	Prof	432-2550		PHD	54	Harvard	1978
Brown, Donald	Prof	432-3580					
Evenson, Robert E.	Prof	432-3626		PHD	68	Chicago	1977
Fair, Ray C.	Prof	432-3715		PHD	68	MIT	1974
Geanakoplos, John	Prof	432-3397					
Hamada, Koichi	Prof	432-3610		PHD	65	Yale	1986
Jaynes, Gerald	Prof	432-1170					
Klevorick, Alvin K.	Prof	432-3705		PHD	67	Princeton	1975
Levin, Richard C.	Prof	432-2550		PHD	74	Yale	1974
President Yale University							
Mendelsohn, Robert	Prof	432-5128		PHD	78	Yale	1984
Montias, J. Michael	Prof	432-3247		PHD	58	Columbia	1963
Nalebuff, Barry J.	Prof	432-5968		DPH	82	Nuffield	1989
Nordhaus, William D.	Prof	432-3576		PHD	67	MIT	1967
Pakes, Ariel	Prof	432-3560		PHD	79	Harvard	
Pearce, David	Prof	432-3587					
Peck, Merton J.	Prof	432-3550		PHD	54	Harvard	1978
Director of Undergraduate Studies							
Phillips, Peter	Prof	432-3695					
Ranis, Gustav	Prof	432-3632		PHD	56	Yale	1960
Ross, Stephen A.	Prof	432-6016		PHD	69	Harvard	1977
Sterling Professor of Economics & Finance							
Scarf, Herbert E.	Prof	432-3693		PHD	54	Princeton	1963
Schultz, T. Paul	Prof	432-3620		PHD	66	MIT	1975
Shiller, Robert J.	Prof	432-3708		PHD	72	MIT	1982
Shubik, Martin	Prof	432-3704		PHD	53	Princeton	
Sims, Christopher A.	Prof	432-3550		PHD	68	Harvard	
Srinivasan, T. N.	Prof	436-8418		PHD	62	Yale	1980
Berry, Steven T.	Assoc	432-3556		PHD	89	Wisconsin	1988
Sala-i-Martin, Xavier	Assoc	432-3695		PHD	90	Harvard	
Waldfogel, Joel	Assoc	432-3562		PHD	90	Stanford	1990
Zhou, Lin	Assoc	432-3716		PHD	89	Princeton	1989
Bergemann, Dirk	Asst	432-3592		PHD		Penn	
Boozer, Michael	Asst	432-3623		MA	90	Princeton	1993
Buchinsky, Moshe	Asst	432-3566					
Guinnane, Timothy J.	Asst	432-3616		PHD	89	Berkeley	
Hunt, Jennifer A.	Asst	432-3714		PHD	92	Harvard	1992
Lanjouw, Jean	Asst	432-3568					
Levy, Philip	Asst	432-3638					
Linton, Oliver	Asst	432-3717					
Pesendorfer, Martin	Asst	432-3592					
Polak, Benjamin	Asst	432-3590		PHD	92	Harvard	

Yeshiva University New York, NY 10033-3299 (212) 960-5214 Cecil Levinson
Department of Economics Yeshiva College Fax=960-5245

Name	Rank	Phone	Dept	Degree	Yr	Institution	Year
Adler, Norman	Dean	960-5214	Psyc	PHD			
Levine, Aaron	C-Pr	960-5214		PHD		NYU	
Samson and Halina Bitensky Professor of Economics							
Kanovsky, Eliyahu	Prof	960-5214		PHD			
Ludwig Jesselson Chair in Economics; spring only							
Skoorka, Bruce	Prof	960-5214		PHD	92	NYU	
Horowitz, Avery M.	Assoc	960-5214		PHD	84	CUNY	1986
Assistant Dean							
Weissman, Seth		960-5214					

York College of Pennsylvania York, PA 17405-7199 (717) 846-7788 Julie Sterner
Economic Faculty Dept of Business Adm Fax=849-1607 YORKCOL.EDU

Name	Rank	Phone	Dept	Degree	Yr	Institution	Year
Meisenhelter, Mary C.	C-As		Mgt	ABD		Geo Wash	1985
Landis, Brook	Assoc			PHD		Cornell	
Scalet, Kenneth G.	Assoc			MBA		St Johns	1970
Azad, Hamid	Asst			PHD		Utah St	
Molz, Ferdinand	Adj			PHD		Catholic	

Youngstown State University Youngstown, OH 44555-0001 (216) Dena Kay Crissman
Department of Economics Col of Arts & Sciences Fax= YSUB

Name	Rank	Phone	Dept	Degree	Yr	Institution	Year
Brothers, Barbara	Dean		Engl	PHD	73	Kent St	
Stocks, Anthony H.	C-Pr	742-3428		PHD	63	SUNY-Buf	1968

Bee, Richard H.	Prof	742-1677			DBA	76	Kent St	
Kermani, Taghi T.	Prof	742-3430			PHD	59	Nebraska	
Koss, Joseph J.	Prof	742-3433			EDD	87	Akron	
Liu, Yih-Wu	Prof	742-1674			PHD	68	S Illinois	
Mehra, Jadish C.	Prof	742-1681			PHD	68	SUNY-Buf	1965
Milley, Donald J.	Prof	742-1676			PHD	74	SUNY-Buf	
Porter, Tod	Prof	742-3431			PHD	84	Syracuse	1984
Ronaghy, Hassan A.	Prof	742-3432			PHD	69	Wisconsin	
Morris, Clyde D.	Assoc	742-3434			PHD	87	Case Wes	
Petruska, Dennis A.	Assoc	742-1679			PHD	84	Ohio St	1984
Riley, Teresa M.	Assoc	742-1675			PHD	84	Syracuse	1984
Usip, Ebenge E.	Assoc	742-1682			PHD	84	Conn	1985

Foreign Schools

McMaster University — Hamilton Canada ON L8S 4M4 (905) Ext24630 — Ms. Kathy Matthews
Finance & Bus Econ Area — DeGroote Sch of Bus Fax=521-8995 — MCMASTER.CA
phone: 525-9140

Kwan, Clarence C. Y.	C-Pr	Ext23797	kwanc	G	PHD	79	Toronto	1979
Chan, M. W. Luke	Prof	Ext29648	chanmwl	DE	PHD	78	Mcmaster	1981
Cheung, C. Sherman	Prof	Ext23968	cheungs	G	PHD	91	Illinois	1981
Krinsky, Itzhak	Prof	Ext23984	krinsky	G	PHD	83	McMaster	1982
Mountain, Dean C.	Prof	Ext23988	mountaind	CD	PHD	79	W Ontario	1987
Chamberlain, Trevor W.	Assoc	Ext23980	chambert	G	PHD	86	Toronto	1985
Deaves, Richard W.	Assoc	Ext23976	deaves	EG	PHD	87	Toronto	1987
Lee, Jason	Asst	Ext23987	leej	G	PHD	91	Alberta	1990
Thomas, Hugh A.	Asst	Ext23983	thomash	G	PHD	91	NYU	1991

INSEAD 77305 — Fontainebleau France 33-1 60724212
Economics Area — Business Fax=60724242 — INSEAD.FR

Borges, Antonio	Dean	60726221	borges		PHD	80	Stanford	9-93
Gabel, Landis	C-Pr		gabel	D	PHD	77	Penn	9-82
Ayres, Robert	Prof	60724011	ayres		PHD	58	London	9-92
Michaud, Claude	Prof	64224805	michaud		D		Bordeaux	8-70
Rob, Rafael	Prof	60724393	rob					
Story, Jonathan	Prof	60724328	story		PHD	73	J Hopkins	7-74
Wyplosz, Charles	Prof	60724212	wyplosz	FE	PHD	78	Harvard	9-72
Burda, Michael C. on leave	Assoc	60724251			PHD	87	Harvard	9-87
Roller, Lars-Hendrik on leave	Assoc	60724251			PHD	87	Penn	9-87
Cadot, Olivier	Asst	60724393	cadot		PHD	89	Princeton	9-89
Fatas, Antonio	Asst	60724251	antonio		PHD	93	Harvard	1-94
Kende, Michael	Asst	60724328	kende		PHD	92	MIT	9-92
Webber, Douglas	Asst	60724328	webber		PHD	85	Essex	1-91

University of Lancaster — LancasterLA1 4YX England 01524
Economics — The Management School Fax=

Watson, S. R.	Dean		
Sapsford, David	H-Pr	PHD	Leeds
Balasubramanyam, V. N.	Prof	PHD	Illinois
Taylor, James	Prof	PHD	Lancaster
Kirby, Maurice W.	Read	PHD	Sheffield
Armstrong, Harvey W.	SLect	MSC	London
Johnes, Geraint	SLect	PHD	Lancaster
Rose, Mary B.	SLect	PHD	Manchest
Rothschild, Robert	SLect	MA	Cape Town
Snowden, Peter N.	SLect	PHD	Leeds
Westall, Oliver M.	SLect	BSC	London
Bradley, Steven	Lect	PHD	Lancaster
Corless, Neil	Lect	MA	Lancaster
Ferguson, Paul R.	Lect	BA	Lancaster
Izadi, Hooshang	Lect	PHD	Essex
Read, Robert A.	Lect	PHD	Reading
Steele, Gerald R.	Lect	MA	Sheffield

Manchester Inst Sci & Tech — Manchester, UK M60 1QD 44-61 200-3455
Economics Faculty — School of Management Fax=200-3505 — U2.SM.UMIST.AC.UK
Did Not Respond--1994-95 Listing

Robertson, Ivan T.	C-Pr	200-3443	robertson	Mgt	PHD	Open	1981
Bosworth, Derek L.	Prof	200-3438	bosworth		PHD	Warwick	1992
Ingham, Hilary C.	SLect	200-3481	ingham		PHD	Glasgow	1987
Bowe, Michael A.	Lect	200-3407	bowe		PHD	Carleton	1993
Duffy, Martyn H.	Lect	200-3483	duffy		MS	Bristol	1972
Eliot, Stuart J.	Lect	200-3480	eliot		MA	Manchest	1974
Jones, Trefor T.	Lect	200-3484	jones		PHD	Dundee	1976
Simpson, Paul	Lect	200-3485	simpson		MA	Newcastl	1984
Sachinides, Philip	Fell	200-3425	sachinides		MA	New York	1991
Simms, Jonathon	Fell	200-3417	simms		MSC	Southamp	1993

ALPHABETICAL BY INDIVIDUAL

Name	Rank	Location	Area	Degree			Start
Abdalla, Adil	Asst	Illinois St	F	PHD	88	Iowa	1988
Abdel-Rahman, Hersham M.	Assoc	New Orleans		PHD	87	Penn	1987
Abdulahad, Faraj	Assoc	Manhattan		PHD	68	Boston C	1970
Abdullah, Dewan A.	Assoc	E Michigan		PHD	84	Kentucky	1988
Abegaz, Berhanu	Assoc	Wm & Mary		PHD	82	Penn	1982
Abel, David R.	C-Pr	Mankato St	AE	ABD		Minnesota	1969
Abernathy, Lewis M.	Prof	North Texas	J	PHD	67	Oklahoma	1963
Abou-Zeid, Bassem	Asst	Bethel-MN		PHD	90	Oklahoma	1990
Abouelenein, Gaber A.	Dean	Mankato St	M	PHD	69	Illinois	1968
Abraham, Fred J.	H-Pr	No Iowa		PHD	73	Oregon	1973
Abraham, Girmai	H-Ac$	Grambling St		PHD	81	Ohio St	9-82
Abraham, Katherine G.	Prof	Maryland		PHD	82	Harvard	1988
Abrahamse, Dorothy Z.	Dean	CS-Long Bch		PHD		Michigan	1967
Abrahamsson, Bernhard J.	Prof	Wis-Superior		PHD	66	Wisconsin	1989
Abrams, Burton A.	Prof	Delaware	EH	PHD	74	Ohio St	1974
Abreu, Dilip	Prof	Yale					
Aburachis, Abdelrahman E.	Prof	Gannon	G	PHD	72	Pittsburgh	
Acemoglu, Daron	Asst	MIT	J	PHD	92	LondonEc	1993
Acker, Mary H.	C-Ac	Iona	FG	PHD	82	Fordham	1982
Acs, Zoltan J.	Prof	Baltimore		PHD	80	New Sch	1989
Adamou, Nikolaos	Asst	Russell Sage		PHD	88	Rensselae	9-89
Adams, David R.	C-Pr	No Kentucky		PHD			
Adams, Donald R. Jr.	Prof	W Virginia	N	PHD	67	Penn	1981
Adams, Earl W. Jr.	C-Pr	Allegheny	AEGH	PHD	71	MIT	1972
Andrew Wells Robertson Professor of Economics							
Adams, F. Gerard	Prof	Pennsylvania		PHD	56	Michigan	1961
Adams, Jack E.	Prof	Ark-Ltl Rock		PHD	75	Okla St	1980
Adams, James D.	Prof	Florida	OJ	PHD	76	Chicago	1979
Adams, Jean W.	Prof	Iowa State	L	PHD	73	Illinois	1972
Adams, John	C-Pr	Northeastern		PHD	68	Tx-Austin	1990
Adams, John P.	Prof	Cal Poly-SLO		PHD	72	Claremont	1970
Adams, Robert J.	Assoc	Edinboro		PHD	71	Penn St	1977
Adams, Ronald G.	Prof	CS-Chico	ACKR	PHD	75	Kansas St	1971
Adams, Roy Dean	Prof	Iowa State	HE	PHD	72	Illinois	1972
Adams, Walter	Retir	Michigan St		PHD	47	Yale	1947
Distinguished Professor; President Emeritus							
Adams, William James	Prof	Michigan		PHD	73	Harvard	1973
Adamson, Dwight W.	Asst	So Dakota St	E	PHD	88	Wash St	1989
Addison, John T.	Prof	So Carolina		PHD	71	London	
Addus, Abdussalam A.	Assoc	N Carol A&T		PHD	82	Penn St	1980
Adelman, Irma	Prof	Cal-Berkeley		PHD	55	Berkeley	1979
Adelstein, Richard P.	Prof	Wesleyan-CT	K	PHD	75	Penn	1975
Adibi, Esmael	Prof	Chapman	AEFC	PHD	80	Claremont	1978
Adie, Douglas K.	Prof	Ohio Univ	BGM	PHD	68	Chicago	1968
Adkins, Lee C.	Assoc	Oklahoma St		PHD	88	LSU	1988
Adkins, Roger L.	C-Pr	Marshall		PHD	81	Kansas St	1981
Adler, Kathleen S.	VAsst	Txs Woman's		PHD	93	So Meth	1995
Adler, Michael	Prof	Columbia		DBA	68	Harvard	1968
Adler, Ranatte K.	Prof	San Diego St		PHD		New Mex	1982
Adrangi, Bahram	Prof	Portland	CDFR	PHD	82	Oregon	1982
Adrisson, Rick	Asst	New Mex St		ABD	94	Nebraska	8-94
Aduddell, Robert M.	Retir	Loyola-Chicg		PHD	71	Northwes	1965
Adusei, Edward O.	Asst	Longwood		PHD	88	Va Tech	1992
Aerni, April Laskey	Assoc	Nazareth		PHD		Cincinnati	
Afiat, Medhi	Prof	Chadron St	MER	PHD		Kansas St	1985
Afifi, Ashraf S.	Assoc	Ferris State		PHD	83	Kansas	1980
Afrasiabi, Ahmad	Assoc	Allegheny	BCQR	PHD	85	W Virginia	1985
Afxentiou, Diamando	Asst	NY Inst Tech		PHD	90	W Virginia	1990
Agarwal, Rajshree	Asst	Cen Florida	L	PHD	94	SUNY-Buf	1995
Agarwal, Vinod	Prof	Old Dominion		PHD	86	Ca-SnBarb	
Agbetsiafa, Douglas K.	Prof	Ind-So Bend		PHD	80	Notre Dm	1980
Agbeyegbe, Terence	Prof	CUNY-Hunter					
Agnello, Richard J.	Assoc	Delaware	C	PHD	70	J Hopkins	1968
Agnihotri, Krisna	Asst	Southern		MA		Punjab	1969
Agurirre, Sophia	Asst	Catholic		PHD			
Agyei Asamoah, Yaw	Prof	Indiana U-PA	FO	PHD	85	Wash U	1984
Ahene, Rexford A.	Assoc	Lafayette		PHD	83	Wisconsin	1982
Ahking, Francis W.	Assoc	Connecticut	EF	PHD	81	Va Tech	1980
Ahmadig, S. Ali	Asst	Morehead St		EDD	87	Houston	1995
Ahmed, Ehsan	Assoc	Jms Madison	EC	PHD	83	Mich St	1984
Ahn, Hyungtaik	Asst	Virg Tech	D	PHD	91	Wisconsin	1991
Ahn, Seung C.	Asst	Arizona St		PHD	90	Mich St	1990
Aho, Arnold A.	Prof	No Michigan	AJ	MA		Lehigh	1969
Ai, Chunrong	Asst	Florida	CT	PHD	90	MIT	1994
Aitken, Hugh G. J.	Retir	Amherst		PHD	51	Harvard	1965
Aiyegoro, Ademois	Lect	Howard		PHD		Geo Mason	

Name	Rank	Institution	Fields	Degree	Yr	Degree School	Year
Aizenmann, Joshua	Prof	Dartmouth		PHD	81	Chicago	1990
Ajluni, Salem S.	Asst	Siena		PHD	92	Utah	1991
Akacern, Mohammed	Prof	Metro St-CO					
Akalou, Woldie-Michael	H	Txs Southern		PHD		UCLA	
Akbari, Ali	Prof	Calif Luther		PHD		S Calif	1984
Akerlof, George A.	Prof	Cal-Berkeley		PHD	66	MIT	1966
Akhavi-Pour, Hossein	Asst	Hamline	F	PHD	79	Kansas	1988
Akin, John S.	Prof	No Carolina		PHD	71	Michigan	1973
Akkihal, Ramchandra G.	Prof	Marshall		PHD	69	Tennessee	1970
Akkina, Krishna Rao	Assoc	Kansas State	ECO	PHD	72	Minnesota	1972
Akpom, Uchenna N.	Asst	West Alabama		PHD	89	Kentucky	1992
Al Yasiri, Ann M.	Asst	Wis-Plattev		MA		Wisconsin	1979
Al Yasiri, Kahtan A.	Prof	Wis-Plattev		PHD		Iowa St	1965
Al-Sabea, Taha H.	Prof	CS-Pomona		PHD	68	S Calif	1968
Alam, M. Shahid	Prof	Northeastern		PHD	79	W Ontario	1988
Alavi, Jafar	Assoc	East Tenn St		PHD	86	Tennessee	1985
Albelda, Randy P.	Assoc	Mass-Boston	JI	PHD	83	Mass	1988
Alberini, Anna	Asst	Colorado		PHD	92	Ca-SnDgo	1995
Alberts, William W.	Prof	U Washington		PHD	61	Chicago	1987
Albrecht, James W.	Prof	Georgetown		PHD	76	Berkeley	1992
Albrecht, William P.	Prof	Iowa		PHD	65	Yale	1965
Aldrich, Mark	Prof	Smith	JLN	PHD	69	Tx-Austin	1968
Alen, Grace	Asst	W Carolina		PHD	91	S Carol	1992
Alesina, Alberto F.	Prof	Harvard		PHD	86	Harvard	1988
Paul Sack Associate Professor of Political Economy							
Alexander, Barbara	Asst	Brandeis					
Alexander, Donald L.	Assoc	W Michigan	D	PHD	83	Penn St	9900
Alexander, James	Prof	Alabama A&M	EAOH	PHD		Tx-Austin	
Alexander, McKinley	Assoc	Jackson St		PHD	86	Illinois	1975
Alexander, Peter	Asst	Ohio Wesley		PHD	90	Mass	1990
Alexander, Susan L.	Assoc	St Thomas-MN	F	PHD	77	So Meth	1981
Alexanderson, Peter	Asst	CUNY-Lehman		JD			
Alexandrin, Glen	Asst	Villanova		PHD	67	Clark	1970
Alexeev, Michael	Assoc	Indiana		PHD	84	Duke	1992
Alexis, Marcus	Prof	Northwestern		PHD	59	Minnesota	1985
Daniel F. and Ada L. Rice Professor of Economics							
Ali, Mukhtar M.	Prof	Kentucky	C	PHD	69	Wisconsin	1969
Allen, Andrew T.	Assoc	San Diego		PHD	83	Illinois	1984
Allen, Beth Elaine	Prof	Minnesota		PHD	78	Berkeley	1992
Allen, Bruce T.	Prof	Michigan St		PHD	65	Cornell	
Allen, Charles L.	Prof	Lamar	RC	PHD		Arkansas	1979
Allen, Joel L.	Asst	Lamar	B	MS	60	Baylor	1960
Allen, John William	Prof	Texas A&M		PHD	67	Illinois	1967
Allen, Linda	Assoc	CUNY-Baruch		PHD	84	NYU	
Allen, Polly R.	Prof	Connecticut	FE	PHD	70	Brown	1976
Allen, Ralph C.	Prof	Valdosta St	F	PHD	81	Geo St	1981
Allen, Robert F.	C-Pr	Creighton	DKL	PHD	69	Mich St	1986
Allen, Roy E.	Assoc	St Marys-Cal		PHD		Berkeley	1985
Allen, Steven G.	Prof	N Carol St	JD	PHD	78	Harvard	1978
Allen, Stuart D.	H-Pr	N Car-Greens		PHD	77	Virginia	1976
Allen, W. David	Asst	Alabama-Hunt	J	PHD	94	Arkansas	1994
Allender, Mary E.	Assoc	Portland	L	PHD	90	Oregon	1985
Alli, Ali M.	Assoc	Okla City		PHD		Okla St	1985
Allison, Michael	Lect	Mo-St Louis	CE	ABD		Virginia	1993
Allison, Robert J.	Prof	CS-Fresno		PHD	66	Colorado	1967
Allsbrook, Ogden O.	Assoc	Georgia	E	PHD	66	Virginia	1968
Alm, James R.	Prof	Colorado		PHD	80	Wisconsin	1983
Almon, Clopper Jr.	Prof	Maryland		PHD	62	Harvard	1966
Alnasrawi, Abbas	Prof	Vermont	FOQ	PHD	65	Harvard	1963
Alononso, Irasema	Asst	Rochester		PHD		Minnesota	
Alpan, Erkan	Asst	R Stockton		PHD		Ca-River	1980
Alper, Neil O.	Assoc	Northeastern		PHD	77	Pittsburgh	1979
Alpert, William T.	Assoc	Connecticut	J	PHD	79	Columbia	1983
Alse, Jahardhanan	Asst	Indiana SE	FE	PHD	93	Wisconsin	1992
Alston, Richard M.	C-Pr	Weber State	ABNQ	PHD	70	Cornell	1969
Altazan, John E.	Prof	New Orleans		PHD	54	Illinois	1958
Altieri, Paul L.	Prof	Central Conn		PHD		Boston C	1975
Altmann, James L.	Prof	Indiana SE	DM	PHD	78	Wisconsin	1978
Altonji, Joseph G.	Prof	Northwestern		PHD	81	Princeton	1990
Altshuler, Rosanne	Asst	Rutgers-N Br	H	PHD	88	Penn	1992
Alvi, Eskander	Asst	W Michigan	E	PHD	85	J Hopkins	1994
Amacher, Ryan C.	Prof	Tx-Arlington	FH	PHD	71	Virginia	1992
Amariglio, Jack	Assoc	Merrimack		PHD		Mass	
Amato, Louis	Assoc	N Car-Charl		PHD	80	S Carol	1980
Amegbe, Annan	Assoc	Morgan State		PHD	77	Catholic	1978
Amemiya, Takeshi	Prof	Stanford		PHD	64	J Hopkins	1968
Amerson, H. S.	Assoc	No Georgia		PHD	93	Am U-Lon	1983
Amin, R. John	H-Pr	Northwood		PHD			
Amin-Guttierez, De Pineres	Asst	Arkansas	DE	PHD	92	Duke	1992
Amoateng, Kofi	Assoc	N Carol Cen		PHD	86	Tx-Austin	1990

Name	Rank	Institution	Fields	Degree	Yr	Degree School	Year
Amos, Orley M. Jr.	Prof	Oklahoma St		PHD	79	Iowa St	1979
Amott, Teresa Louise	C-Ac	Bucknell		PHD		Boston C	1989
Amrhein, Joseph	Retir	St Michael's		PHD	58	NYU	
Amsler, Christine E.	Assoc	Michigan St		PHD	80	Penn	
An, Mark	Asst	Duke		PHD	93	Cornell	1993
Anas, Alex	Prof	SUNY-Buffalo	DR	PHD	75	Penn	1991
Anbarci, Nejat M.	Assoc	Fla Internat	DC	PHD	88	Iowa	1995
Anders, Steven L.	C-Pr	Graceland	ARD	PHD	88	Kansas St	1978
Anderson, B. Wylie	Prof	No Iowa		PHD	73	Iowa	1966
Anderson, Charles E.	Dean	Kean		PHD	75	Stanford	7-88
Anderson, Curtis L.	Prof	Minn-Duluth	QA	PHD	81	Wyoming	1980
Anderson, Daniel	Asst	Concordia C		MBA		N Dakota	1993
Anderson, David A.	Asst	Centre	ACHK	PHD	92	Duke	1992
Anderson, Donna M.	Asst	Wis-La Cross	DIJ	PHD	93	Mich St	1994
Anderson, Edwin L.	Asst	Freed Hardem	CDEQ	PHD	90	Tennessee	8-91
Anderson, Eric E.	Asst	Old Dominion		PHD		U Wash	1984
Anderson, Gary M.	Prof	CS-Northrdge	GLTR	PHD	87	Geo Mason	1987
Anderson, James E.	Prof	Boston Coll	DF	PHD	69	Wisconsin	1969
Anderson, Joan B.	Prof	San Diego		PHD	71	Ca-SnDgo	1981
Anderson, John E.	Prof	Nebraska	H	PHD	77	Claremont	1991
Anderson, John Whiting	Prof	Bucknell		PHD		Penn	1961
Anderson, Kathryn H.	Assoc	Vanderbilt	JO	PHD	78	N Car St	1980
Anderson, Lee G.	Prof	Delaware	Q	PHD	70	U Wash	1974
Anderson, Mark A.	Asst	Pt Loma Naz		MBA		Ca-SanBer	1988
Anderson, Michael A.	Assoc	Wash & Lee	F	PHD	90	Wisconsin	1990
Anderson, Patricia Mary	Asst	Dartmouth		PHD	91	Princeton	1991
Anderson, Richard K.	Prof	Texas A&M		PHD	76	Purdue	1975
Anderson, Richard T.	Asst	Jersey City	AI	PHD		CUNY	
Anderson, Robert M.	Prof	Cal-Berkeley		PHD		Yale	
Anderson, Roy C.	Prof	CS-Long Bch		PHD		Tulane	1965
Anderson, Simon P.	Assoc	Virginia	LDR	PHD	85	Queen's	1987
Anderson, Terry L.	Prof	Montana St		PHD	72	U Wash	1972
Anderson, Thomas	Prof	Framingham		PHD			
Anderson, Thomas C.	Assoc	Kennesaw St	ADM	PHD	72	Berkeley	1985
Anderton, Charles H.	Assoc	Holy Cross	ACDF	PHD	86	Cornell	1986
Ando, Albert K.	Prof	Pennsylvania		PHD	59	Car Mellon	1963
Andoh, Samuel K.	Assoc	So Conn St		PHD	86	NYU	
Andreoni, James R.	Assoc	Wisconsin		PHD	86	Michigan	1986
Andrews, Charles Haynes Stetson Professor of Economics	Prof	Mercer-Macon		PHD	67	Vanderbilt	1973
Andrews, Donald R.	Prof	Southern	QR	PHD	80	Tx A&M	1995
Andrews, Donald W. K.	Prof	Yale		PHD	82	Berkeley	1982
Andrews, Marcellus	Assoc	Wellesley		PHD	86	Yale	1986
Andrianacos, Dimitri	Assoc	W Illinois	ACE	PHD	89	Chicago	1990
Andrulis, John A.	Prof	W New Eng		PHD	75	Purdue	1981
Angelini, Anthony L. P.	C-Ac	St John's		MA	51	Temple	
Angiello, Joseph		SUNY-Empire	A	PHD		Tx-Austin	1983
Angkatavanich, Virote	C-Pr	F Dick-Teane		PHD	67	New Sch	1963
Angrist, Joshua D.	SLect	Hebrew Univ		PHD	89	Princeton	1991
Ankrom, Jeff A.	C-Ac	Wittenberg		PHD	82	Notre Dm	1982
Anselin, Luc	Prof	W Virginia	RC	PHD	80	Corning	1993
Anspach, Ralph	Prof	San Fran St		PHD	63	Berkeley	1963
Antel, John J.	Assoc	Houston		PHD	82	UCLA	1981
Antle, John M.	Prof	Montana St		PHD	80	Chicago	1987
Anyanwu, Lenard	Asst	NJ Inst Tech		PHD			
Aoki, Masahiko	Prof	Stanford		PHD	67	Minnesota	1984
Aoki, Masanao	Prof	UCLA		PHD	65	Tokyo In	1983
Aoki, Masato	Asst	Simmons		PHD	95	Mass	1994
Aoki, Reiko	Asst	SUNY-Stony B		PHD	87	Stanford	1990
Aoyagi, Masaki	Asst	Pittsburgh	D	PHD	92	Princeton	1992
Applegate, Michael J.	Prof	Oklahoma St		PHD	73	Iowa St	1974
Appleyard, Dennis R. James B. Duke Professor of International Studies	Prof	Davidson	F	PHD	66	Michigan	1990
Arabian, Ghodratollah	Asst	Lincoln-MO		PHD		Indiana	1984
Aranson, Peter H.	C-Pr	Emory	KL	PHD	72	Rochester	1981
Arce, M. Daniel	Asst	Alabama		PHD	91	Illinois	1991
Archer, Stephen H. Guy F. Atkinson Porfessor of Economics & Finance	Prof	Willamette		PHD	58	Minnesota	1973
Archibald, Robert B.	Prof	Wm & Mary		PHD	74	Purdue	1976
Arenberg, Yuri	Assoc	CUNY-Brookly	D	PHD	86	NYU	1985
Arguea, Nestor M.	Asst	West Florida	ACD	PHD	90	S Calif	1990
Ariel, Robert Andrew	Asst	CUNY-Baruch		PHD	89	MIT	1986
Aristotelous, Kyriacos	Asst	Otterbein		PHD	93	Ohio St	1993
Arjomand, Lari		Clayton St		PHD			1980
Armentano, Dominick T.	Prof	Hartford		PHD	66	Conn	1966
Armstrong, Harvey W.	SLect	U Lancaster		MSC		London	
Armstrong, Ken	Dean	Anderson U		PHD		Northwes	1990
Armstrong, Thomas O.	Asst	Widener	HKQD	PHD	89	Temple	1989
Arndt, Sven W. Charles M. Stone Professor of Money, Credit & Trade	Prof	Claremont		PHD	64	Berkeley	1990

Arno, Elsie R.	Assoc	Columbus		MS		Auburn	1976
Arnold, Clyde L.	Dean	Northern St		PHD	82	Oklahoma	1988
Arnold, Michael	Asst	Delaware	LD	PHD	92	UCLA	1992
Arnold, Roger A.	D-Pr	CS-S Marcos		PHD		Va Tech	
Arnold, Thomas R.	Prof	King's Col		PHD	70	Syracuse	6-60
Herve A. LeBlanc Distinguished Service Professor in Liberal Arts							
Arnott, Richard J.	Prof	Boston Coll	DHR	PHD	75	Yale	1988
Arnould, Richard J.	Prof	Illinois		PHD	68	Iowa St	1967
Aronson, J. Richard	Prof	Lehigh	HG	PHD	64	Clark	1965
William L. Clayton Professor of Business and Economics							
Arora, Harjit K.	Assoc	LeMoyne	EFH	PHD	84	Wi-Milw	1987
Arora, Swarnjit S.	Assoc	Wis-Milwauke		PHD	71	SUNY-Buf	1978
Arosteguy, Daniel J.	Dean	Mesa State		PHD		Colo St	1976
Arthur, E. Eugene	Assoc	Rockhurst		DBA	75		1968
Arvan, Lanny D.	Assoc	Illinois		PHD	81	Northwes	1980
Arvin-Rad, Hassan	Asst	Fla Internat	CD	PHD	90	Penn	1989
Arzac, Enrique R.	Prof	Columbia		PHD	68	Columbia	1971
Aschauer, David Alan	Prof	Bates	E	PHD		Rochester	1990
Elmer W. Campbell Professor of Economics							
Aschheim, Joseph	Prof	George Wash	E	PHD	54	Harvard	1964
Asefa, Sally Ann	Prof	Brescia		PHD	78	Iowa St	8-80
Asefa, Sisay	Assoc	W Michigan	O	PHD	80	Iowa St	1980
Asenfelter, Orley C.	Prof	Princeton		PHD	70	Princeton	1968
Asgary, Nader	Lect	Tx-Pan Amer		PHD			
Ashby, David J.	C	Southern Ark	G	MBA		Miss	1992
Asheghian, Par	Prof	CS-San Bern		PHD	80	Geo St	1991
Asher, Cheryl	Asst	Villanova		PHD	81	Penn	1984
Asher, Martin A.	Asst	Villanova		PHD	86	Penn	1984
Ashley, James R.	C-Ac	St Catherine	AL	PHD	84	Wisconsin	1984
Ashley, Richard A.	Assoc	Virg Tech	E	PHD	82	Ca-SnDgo	1981
Ashley, Terry	Asst	So Alabama		PHD	91	Auburn	1991
Ashman, H. Lowell	C-Pr	Lenoir-Rhyne		PHD		Utah	1975
Ashman, James G.	Asst	St Olaf	M	MA		Minnesota	1993
Ashraf, Javed	Assoc	West Florida	AJ	PHD	86	N Illinois	1990
Asianian, Paul J.	Assoc	Macalester		MBA	67	U Wash	1967
Askalani, Mohamed H.	Prof	Mankato St	AC	PHD	70	Iowa St	1969
Aske, David	Asst	No Colorado	AITR	PHD		Nebraska	1992
Aslanbeigui, Nahid	Assoc	Monmouth		PHD	84	Michigan	1988
Assad, Jean-Claud	Asst	Jackson St		PHD	87	Howard	1991
Assane, Djeto	Asst	Nev-L Vegas		PHD	88	Colorado	1988
Assar, Nasia	Asst	N Carol A&T		PHD		W Virginia	
Assibey-Mensah, Albert	Asst	Kentucky St	AG	PHD	94	Cincinnati	1994
Asuzu, Mark	Lect	SUNY-Cortlan					
Atack, Jeremy	Prof	Vanderbilt	N	PHD	76	Indiana	1993
Atencio, Leonard D.	Prof	Fort Lewis		PHD	69	Kansas St	1968
Atesoglu, H. Sonmez	Assoc	Clarkson	EFO	PHD	72	Pittsburgh	1977
Athanasoulis, Stefano	Asst	Iowa State		PHD	95	Yale	1995
Athey, Michael J.	Assoc	Kalamazoo	EO	PHD	91	Wash U	1995
Athey, Susan	Asst	MIT	L	PHD	95	Stanford	1995
Atkeson, Andrew G.	Asst	Chicago		PHD	88	Stanford	1988
Atkeson, Andrew G.	Asst	Pennsylvania	PF	PHD	88	Stanford	1993
Kei Mori Fellow of the Institute for Economic Research							
Atkinson, Glendel W.	Prof	Nevada-Reno		PHD	68	Oklahoma	1967
Atkinson, Scott E.	Prof	Georgia	CQK	PHD	72	Colorado	1985
Atri, Said	Assoc	SUNY Oswego		PHD	82	SUNY-Alb	1981
Attiyeh, Richard E.	Prof	Ca-San Diego	EI	PHD	66	Yale	1982
Atwood, Edward Charles Jr.	Retir	Wash & Lee		PHD	59	Princeton	1969
Auernheimer, Leonardo	Prof	Texas A&M		PHD	73		1973
Ault, David E.	Dean	S Ill-Edward		PHD	69	Illinois	1969
Ault, Richard W.	Assoc	Auburn		PHD	83	Virginia	1983
Austin, Andrew	Asst	Houston	HC	PHD		Penn	1991
Austin, Ellis T.	Deces			PHD	55	Mich St	
Austin, John A.	Prof	La St-Shreve		PHD		Ariz St	1983
Ausubel, Lawrence M.	Prof	Maryland		PHD	84	Stanford	1992
Auzenne, George R.	Lect	Florida A&M	LM	MS	63	Boston	1976
Avard, Stephen L.	C-Ac$	East Txs St	GFDE	PHD		North Tx	
Averett, Susan	Asst	Lafayette		PHD	91	Colorado	1991
Averitt, Robert T.	Prof	Smith	ABE	PHD	61	Tx-Austin	1961
Avery, Emerson R.	Lect	SUNY-Cortlan					
Avin, Rose Marie	Assoc	Wis-Eau Clar		PHD	86	Maryland	1987
Awh, Robert Y.	Prof	Miss State		PHD	60	Florida	1968
Axarloglou, Kostas	Asst	Babson		PHD	93	Michigan	1994
Axelson, David J.	Assoc	Western St		EDD	76	Colorado	1982
Ayal, Eliezer B.	Prof	Ill-Chicago	O	PHD	61	Cornell	1972
Ayanian, Robert L.	Prof	CS-Fullerton		PHD	74	UCLA	1977
Ayers, Michael	C-Ac	Il-Springfld	OR	PHD	74	Oklahoma	1971
Ayers, Ronald M.	Assoc	Tx-S Antonio	GJM	PHD	78	Tulane	1979
Ayittey, George B. N.	VAsoc	American U		PHD	81	Manitoba	1994
Ayres, Robert	Prof	INSEAD		PHD	58	London	9-92
Azad, Hamid	Asst	York-Penn		PHD		Utah St	

Azam, Abul	Asst	N Carol A&T		PHD		Duke	
Aziz, Fahima	Asst	Hamline	DQ	PHD	95	Minnesota	1994
Baack, Bennett D.	Assoc	Ohio State	N	PHD	72	U Wash	1988
Babalola, Banji	Asst	Hampton		PHD	87	Howard	1987
Babcock, Michael W.	Prof	Kansas State	RQ	PHD	73	Illinois	1972
Babilot, George	Retir	San Diego St		PHD	58	Oregon	1956
Bacdayan, Andrew W.	Prof	NW St of LA		PHD	73	Utah St	
Backus, David	Prof	New York U	EFG	PHD	81	Yale	1990
Badgett, Lee D.	Dean	Va Military		PHD	71	Yale	1990
Badu, Yaw Agyeman	Assoc	Virginia St		PHD	80	S Carol	1984
Baek, Dae-Hyun	Asst	Oregon State	EF	PHD	90	Ohio St	9-91
Baek, In-Mee	VAsst	Suffolk		PHD		Indiana	
Baer, Werner	Prof	Illinois		PHD	58	Harvard	1974
Bagheri, Fatoah	Asst	North Dakota		PHD		Penn	1978
Bagheri, Rashid	Inst	Morgan State		MA		Howard	
Bagi, Sukhwinder	Asst	Bloomsburg		PHD		Vanderbilt	
Bagwell, Kyle W.	Asst	Northwestern		PHD	86	Stanford	1986
Bahari-Kashani, Hamid	C-Ac	W Oregon St		PHD	83	Wash St	1988
Bahatiuk, Nicholas G.	Retir	LeMoyne		PHD		Ukranian	1962
Bahl, Roy W. Jr.	Prof	Georgia St	HR	PHD	65	Kentucky	1988
Bahmani-Oskooee, Mohsen	C-Pr	Wis-Milwauke		PHD	81	Mich St	1981
Bahnick, Karen K.	Dean	Wis-Superior	Mgt	PHD		Iowa	1966
Bai, Chong-en	Asst	Boston Coll	CD	PHD	93	Harvard	1992
Bai, Jushan J.	Asst	MIT	C				
Baik, Kyung H.	Assoc	Appalach St	DL	PHD	89	Va Tech	1989
Bailey BVM, Mary P. F.	Inst	Loyola-Chicg		MA	69	Notre Dm	1991
Bailey, DeeVon	Prof	Utah State	Q	PHD	83	Tx A&M	1983
Bailey, Duncan	Prof	SC-Spartanbu	AEOR	PHD		Va Tech	1984
Bailey, Martin J.	Prof	Emory	E	PHD	56	J Hopkins	1989
Bailey, Mary Ann	Adj	George Wash	I	PHD	74	MIT	
Baily, Martin N.	Prof	Maryland		PHD	72	MIT	1987
Baiman, Ron	Asst	Roosevelt		PHD	89	New Sch	1994
Baird, Charles W.	Prof	CS-Hayward		PHD	68	Berkeley	1972
Baird, Philip	Asst	Clarkson	GM	PHD	93	Tennessee	1992
Baird, Robert N.	Assoc	Case Western	A	PHD	65	Kentucky	1965
Baird, William M.	Prof	Wooster		PHD	68	Ohio St	1968
Bakair, Saad T.	Assoc	Alabama St		PHD			
Baker, Samuel H. III	Prof	Wm & Mary		PHD	70	Virginia	1969
Baker, Stephen A.	Assoc	Capital		PHD	82	York UK	1987
Bakkal, Ilter	Assoc	Central Iowa	BNCQ	PHD		N Illinois	1986
Bakshi, Gurdip S.	Asst	New Orleans		PHD		Wisconsin	
Baktari, Paul	C-Ac	SUNY-Potsdam		PHD		W Virginia	
Balabkins, Nicholas W.	Retir	Lehigh		PHD	56	Rutgers	1966
Balasubrahmanian, Ravikumar	Assoc	Virginia	EO	PHD	89	Iowa	1989
Balasubramanyam, V. N.	Prof	U Lancaster		PHD		Illinois	
Balch, Billy W.	Prof	Mid Tenn St		PHD	68	Alabama	1964
Balch, Donald C.	Lect	So Carolina					
Balch, Michael S.	Assoc	Iowa		PHD	65	NYU	1971
Baldani, Jeffrey P.	Assoc	Colgate	CD	PHD	83	Cornell	1982
Baldwin, Marjorie L.	Assoc	East Carol		PHD	88	Syracuse	1989
Baldwin, Robert E.	Prof	Wisconsin		PHD	50	Harvard	1964
Taussig & Hilldale Professor of Economics							
Baldwin, William Lee	Prof	Dartmouth		PHD	58	Princeton	1956
John French Professor							
Balfour, B. Burton	C-Ac	N Carol Cen		PHD	74	N Car St	1973
Balkan, Erol M.	Assoc	Hamilton	OF	PHD	88	Binghamt	1987
Balke, Nathan S.	Assoc	So Methodist		PHD	86	Northwes	1986
Balkin, Steven M.	Assoc	Roosevelt		PHD	76	Wayne St	1984
Ball, David Stafford	Assoc	N Carol St	FND	PHD	67	N Carol	1966
Ball, Laurence M.	Prof	J Hopkins		PHD		MIT	1994
Ball, Sheryl B.	Asst	Virg Tech	M	PHD	91	Northwes	1992
Ballantyne, A. Paul	Prof	Colorado Spr	ABEO	PHD	65	Stanford	1967
Ballard, Charles L.	Prof	Michigan St		PHD	83	Stanford	1983
Ballie, Richard	Prof	Michigan St		PHD		London	
Ballman, Richard J. Jr.	C-Pr	Augustana IL	ABDE	PHD	77	Iowa	1972
Ballou, Dale	Asst	Massachusett		PHD	89	Yale	
Balough, Robert S.	C-Pr	Clarion		PHD	81	N Illinois	1981
Baltagi, Badi H.	Prof	Texas A&M		PHD	79	Penn	1988
George Summey Professorship							
Balvers, Ronald J.	Assoc	W Virginia	EG	PHD	84	Pittsburgh	1991
Banaian, King	Assoc	St Cloud St		PHD	86	Claremont	1984
Bandera, Vladimir N.	Prof	Temple	FP	PHD	60	Berkeley	1972
Bandyopadhyay, Sudeshna	Asst	W Virginia	J	PHD	92	Maryland	1992
Bandzak, Ruth Anne	Asst	Redlands		MA		Notre Dm	1988
Banerjee, Abhijit	Assoc	MIT	G				
Banerjee, Samiran	Asst	Georgia St	CD	PHD	92	Minnesota	1992
Banerji, Arup	Asst	Williams		PHD	91	Penn	1990
Banks, Jeffrey S.	Prof	Rochester		PHD	86	Cal Tech	
Banks, Nina		Hood					
Bansal, Vipul	Assoc	St John's					

Baqir, Ghalib M.	Retir	Alabama St	1995	PHD	67	St Louis	1973
Barakeh, A. K.	Prof	So Alabama	F	PHD	68	Indiana	1968
Barari, Mahua	Asst	SW Missouri		PHD	92	Iowa St	1993
Barber, G. Russell Jr.	Assoc	Mercer-Macon		PHD	90	Miss	1973
Barber, William J.	Emer	Wesleyan-CT	B	DPHI	57	Oxford	1957
Andrews Professor of Economics							
Barbezat, Daniel P.	C-Ac	Amherst	ANO	PHD	88	Illinois	1988
Barbezat, Debra A.	Assoc	Colby	JIA	PHD	85	Michigan	1992
Barbour, G. Jeffrey	Asst	Cen Michigan		PHD		Fla St	1971
Barbour, James L.	C-Ac	Elon	AB	PHD	87	Kentucky	1990
Bardhan, Pranab K.	Prof	Cal-Berkeley		PHD		Cambridg	
Barger, Peter S.	Asst	No Central		PHD	89	Illinois	1989
Barnes, Clarence H.	Dean	Gonzaga		PHD	73	Tennessee	9-73
Barnes, Elsie M.	H-Ac	Norfolk St		DA		Lehigh	1973
Barnes, Robert R.	Retir	Millersville		MA	67	Penn	1963
Barnett, Andy H.	Assoc	Auburn		PHD	78	Virginia	1982
Barnett, Harold C.	C-Pr	Rhode Island		PHD	73	MIT	1970
Barnett, Richard	Asst	SUNY-Buffalo	EF	PHD	89	Minnesota	1989
Barnett, William	Assoc	Loyola-N Orl	DEFK	PHD	74	Mich St	1974
Barnett, William A.	Prof	Wash Univ		PHD	74	Car Mellon	1990
Barone, Charles A.	Assoc	Dickinson Cl	AO	PHD	78	American	1975
Baroutsis, A. Paul	Prof	Slippery Roc		PHD	72	Purdue	1972
Barr, Joseph E.	Prof	Framingham		PHD		Boston C	
Barr, Saul Z.	Prof	Tenn-Martin		EDD		Florida	
Barrett, Anthony		St Scholasti		PHD			
Barrett, Christopher	Asst	Utah State	OQF	PHD	93	Wisconsin	1995
Barrett, Nancy S.	Prof	W Michigan	E	PHD	68	Harvard	1991
Barrett, Richard	Prof	Montana	EOJQ	PHD		Wisconsin	
Barrington, Linda	Asst	Barnard		PHD	91	Illinois	1991
Barro, Robert J.	Prof	Harvard		PHD	70	Harvard	1987
Barron, John M.	Prof	Purdue		PHD	76	Brown	1976
Barsky, Robert	Assoc	Michigan					
Bartel, Ann	Prof	Columbia		PHD	74	Columbia	1976
Bartell, Ernest J.	Prof	Notre Dame	O	PHD	66	Princeton	1977
Bartell, H. Robert	Prof	East Tenn St		PHD	63	Columbia	1989
Barth, J. Robert	Dean	Boston Coll		PHD		Harvard	
Barth, Peter S.	Prof	Connecticut	J	PHD	65	Michigan	1973
Bartholomew, A. Wayne	Prof	Ind-So Bend		PHD	68	Cornell	1968
Bartlett, Randall	Prof	Smith	AHR	PHD	71	Stanford	1977
Bartlett, Robin L.	Prof	Denison		PHD	74	Mich St	1973
Bartlett, Sue	Lect	South Fla		MA	93	S Fla	1994
Barton, William E.	Prof	Colorado Col		PHD	70	Missouri	1958
Barzel, Yoram	Prof	U Washington		PHD	61	Chicago	1961
Basch, Donald L.	Prof	Simmons	D	PHD	77	Yale	1980
Bashir, Abdel Hamid	Asst	Grambling St		PHD		Wisconsin	1990
Baskan, Asuman	Assoc	Allegheny	CDFE	PHD	88	Lehigh	1987
Basmann, Robert L.	Prof	SUNY-Bingham		PHD	66	Iowa St	1988
Bassett, Gilbert W.	Prof	Ill-Chicago	C	PHD	73	Michigan	1973
Bastin, Hamid	Prof	Shippensburg		PHD	89	Geo St	1989
Basu, Bharati	Asst	Cen Michigan		PHD		Rochester	1990
Basu, Kaushik	Prof	Cornell		PHD		LondonEc	
Basu, Parantap	Assoc	Fordham		PHD	85	Ca-SnBarb	1988
Basu, Susanto	Asst	Michigan		PHD	92	Harvard	1992
Batabyal, Amitrajeet	Asst	Utah State	FOQ	PHD	94	Berkeley	1995
Batavia, Bala	Prof	DePaul		PHD	74	N Car St	1976
Batchelder, Ronald W.	Prof	Pepper-Malib	DEFK	PHD	75	UCLA	1984
Bateman, Bradley W.	Assoc	Grinnell	B	PHD	84	Kentucky	1987
Bateman, Fred	H-Pr	Georgia	N	PHD	65	Tulane	1991
Nicholas A. Beadles Professor							
Bates, Laurie	Asst	Bryant	HD	PHD		Conn	
Bates, Lawrence W.	Assoc	E Illinois		PHD	75	Tx-Austin	1970
Batie, Clarence	Inst	Txs Southern		MA		PrairieV	
Batina, Raymond	Assoc	Wash State		PHD	85	Minnesota	1985
Batra, Raveendra N.	Prof	So Methodist		PHD	69	S Illinois	1973
Battacharya, Radha S.	Asst	CS-Fullerton		MA		Gokhale	1990
Battaglia, Kari L.	Lect	North Texas		MA		North Tx	1987
Battalio, Ray	Prof	Texas A&M		PHD	69	Purdue	1969
Currie Professorship in Liberal Arts							
Bauer, John G.	Asst	Hawaii-Manoa		PHD	84	Michigan	1985
Baum, Christopher F.	Assoc	Boston Coll	CE	PHD	77	Michigan	1977
Baum, Donald N.	Assoc	Neb-Omaha	HD	PHD	79	Claremont	1987
Baum, Sandra R.	C-Pr	Skidmore		PHD	81	Columbia	1987
Bausor, Randall S.	Assoc	Massachusett		PHD	78	Duke	1979
Bawa, Ujagar S.	Prof	Bloomsburg		PHD		Cornell	
Bawuah, Kwado	Assoc	Virginia St		PHD	83	Va Tech	1987
Baxter, Marianne	Prof	Virginia	FE	PHD	84	Chicago	1993
Bay, John W.	Prof	So Maine	E	PHD	66	Boston C	1965
Baye, Michael R.	Prof	Penn State	DIO	PHD	83	Purdue	1991
Bayer, Amanda	Asst	Swarthmore	DJ	ABD		Yale	1992
Bayer, Arthur A.	Prof	Babson		PHD	68	Mich St	1977

Name	Rank	Institution	Fields	Degree	Yr	Degree School	Year
Bays, Carson W.	C-Pr	East Carol		PHD	74	Michigan	1982
Baytas, Ahmet	Asst	Montclair St		PHD		Illinois	
Beall, Larry G.	Assoc	Virg Comm		PHD	63	Duke	1970
Beals, Ralph E.	Prof	Amherst	ACO	PHD	70	MIT	1966
Clarence Francis Professor of Economics							
Beam, Robert D.	Assoc	Wis-Superior		PHD		Cincinnati	1980
Bean, Richard N.	Assoc	Houston		PHD	71	U Wash	1970
Bear, Donald V. T.	Emer	Ca-San Diego	AE	PHD	63	Stanford	1965
Beard, Thomas R.	Prof	Louisiana St	E	PHD	63	Duke	1961
LSU Alumni Professor							
Beard, Thomas Randolph	Assoc	Auburn		PHD	88	Vanderbilt	1988
Beardsley, George L.	Prof	Cal Poly-SLO		PHD	74	Penn	1975
Bearse, Peter	Asst	Tennessee		PHD	95	Virginia	1995
Beasley, Christine Daughtry	Retir	Campbell		MA		E Carol	1969
Beaton, C. Russell	Prof	Willamette		PHD		Claremont	1971
Beaty, Valerie P.	Asst	Sam Houston		ABD		Tx A&M	1993
Beaty, William L.	Asst	Tarleton St	ADR	MS	73	Utah St	1985
Beauchemin, Kenneth	Asst	Colorado		PHD	95	Iowa	1995
Beaudry, Paul	Assoc	Boston Univ	EJL	PHD	89	Princeton	1990
Beaumont, Marion S.	Prof	CS-Long Bch		PHD		Claremont	1967
Beaumont, Paul M.	Assoc	Florida St		PHD	84	Penn	1988
Bechdolt, Burley V.	Assoc	No Illinois		PHD	70	S Calif	1970
Bechtold, Brigitte	Assoc	Cen Michigan		PHD	82	Penn	1982
Beck, Edward J.	Asst	SUNY-Oneonta	DE	MBA	82	Syracuse	1977
Beck, John H.	D-Ac	Gonzaga	BHC	PHD	76	Mich St	1988
Beck, Paul	Asst	Graceland	AFJE	PHD	94	Mo-Ks Cty	1992
Beck, Stacie E.	Asst	Delaware	GEF	PHD	87	Penn	1986
Beck, William C. II	Retir	USAF Academy		MA		Michigan	
Becker, Anthony D.	Assoc	St Olaf	DLC	PHD		Duke	1987
Becker, Charles McVey	Assoc	Tx Christian		PHD	66	Arizona	1967
Becker, Gary S.	Prof	Chicago		PHD	55	Chicago	1970
Becker, Gilbert B.	Asst	St Anselm	AD	PHD	83	Boston C	1987
Becker, Klaus G.	Asst	Texas Tech		PHD	87	Kansas	1989
Becker, Robert	Prof	Indiana		PHD	78	Rochester	1978
Becker, William	Prof	Indiana		PHD	73	Pittsburgh	1979
Becker, William S.	Prof	Colorado Col		PHD	70	LSU	1970
Beckman, Mary P.	Asst	Lafayette		PHD		Notre Dm	1985
Beckman, Steven R.	Asst	Colo-Denver	F	PHD	82	Ca-Davis	1988
Bedient, John B.	Assoc	Albion		MBA	79	Indiana	1984
Bee, Richard H.	Prof	Youngstown		DBA	76	Kent St	
Beeson, Bennie E. Jr.	Prof	Radford		PHD	71	Tennessee	
Beeson, Patricia E.	Assoc	Pittsburgh	R	PHD	83	Oregon	1983
Begin, Floyd C.	Prof	St Ambrose		PHD	74	Iowa	1985
Behdad, Sohrab	Assoc	Denison		PHD	73	Mich St	1985
Behr, Todd	Asst	E Stroudsbur	EH	MBA	78	Lehigh	1989
Behrman, Jere R.	Prof	Pennsylvania	OJL	PHD	66	MIT	1965
William R. Kenan Jr. Professor of Economics; Acting Graduate Group Chair							
Beil, Richard O.	Assoc	Auburn		PHD	88	Tx A&M	1988
Beim, David O.	Prof	Columbia		PHL	66	Oxford	1991
Bej, Emil	Prof	Shippensburg		DR	70	Ukranian	1969
Bekdache, Basma	Asst	Wayne State		PHD	94	Boston	1994
Beladi, Hamid	Prof	Dayton		PHD	83	Utah St	1988
Bell, Anne M.	Asst	Vanderbilt	EN	PHD	95	Wisconsin	1995
Bell, Arleigh T. Jr.	Assoc	Loyola-Maryl	FD	PHD	71	New Sch	1970
Bell, Christopher Ross	Asst	N Car-Ashvil		PHD	87	Penn	1989
Bell, Clive L. G.	Prof	Vanderbilt	OG	PHD	75	Sussex	1986
Bell, Duran	Assoc	Calif-Irvine		PHD	65	Berkeley	1965
Bell, Edward B.	C-Ac	Cleveland St	DHJ	PHD	73	Ohio St	1971
Bell, Frederick W.	Prof	Florida St		PHD	64	Wayne St	
Bell, Joe A.	Prof	SW Missouri		PHD	80	Okla St	1971
Bell, Peter	Assoc	SUNY-Purchas		PHD	68	Wisconsin	1971
Bell, Robert	Assoc	CUNY-Brookly	M	PHD		England	1986
Bellamy, Scott	Asst	Southern Ark	I	MBA		Kentucky	1993
Bellante, Donald M.	Prof	South Fla	J	PHD	71	Fla St	1985
Bellemore, Fred A.	Asst	Vassar	H	PHD		MIT	1992
Bellico, Russell P.	Prof	Westfield St		EDD		Mass	1970
Bellinger, William K.	Asst	Dickinson Cl	JE	PHD	85	Northwes	1981
Belman, Dale	Assoc	Wis-Milwauke		PHD		Wisconsin	1985
Belongia, Michael T.	Prof	Mississippi	E	PHD	82	N Car St	1993
Belotti, Mario L.	Prof	Santa Clara		PHD	69	Tx-Austin	1959
W. M. Keck Foundation Professor-Director, Institute of Agribusiness							
Belsley, David A.	Prof	Boston Coll	CD	PHD	65	MIT	1966
Belton, Willie J. Jr.	Assoc	Georgia Tech	E	PHD	86	Penn St	1987
Bembridge, Neville G.	Assoc	Norfolk St		PHD		Manitoba	1975
Ben-Gad, Michael	Asst	Houston		PHD	95	Chicago	1995
Ben-Zion, Barry	Prof	Sonoma State		PHD	73	Oregon	1969
Benavie, Arthur	Prof	No Carolina		PHD	63	Michigan	1967
Benedict, Mary Ellen	Asst	Bowling Gr		PHD	91	Car Mellon	1991
Benesh, Diann	Lect	Wis-Eau Clar		MS		Va Tech	1976
Benhabib, Jess	C-Pr	New York U		PHD	76	Columbia	1980

Benham, Lee K.	Prof	Wash Univ		PHD	70	Stanford	1974
Benito, Carlos	C-Pr	Sonoma State		PHD	73	Ca-Davis	1990
Benjamin, Daniel K.	Prof	Clemson	DEGJ	PHD	75	UCLA	1985
Benjamin, Julian	Prof	N Carol A&T		PHD		SUNY-Buf	
Bennett, Charles A.	C-Ac	Gannon	A	MA	68	Fordham	1968
Bennett, Doris S.	Assoc	Jacksonvl St		PHD		Alabama	1986
Bennett, James T.	Prof	George Mason		PHD	70	Case Wes	1975
William P. Snavely Professor of Economics							
Bennett, R. J.	Prof	Aquinas		PHD		St Louis	1969
Bennett, Randall W.	Assoc	Gonzaga	HL	PHD	84	Mich St	1988
Bennett, Richard E.	Prof	Kent State	C	PHD	70	Ohio St	1968
Bennett, Robert L.	Assoc	Maryland		PHD	63	Tx-Austin	1966
Benolt, Jean Pierre	Assoc	New York U		PHD	83	Stanford	
Benson, Bruce L.	Prof	Florida St		PHD	78	Tx A&M	1987
Benson, C. Scott	Asst	Idaho State		PHD	88	Ca-Davis	1990
Benston, George J.	Prof	Emory		PHD	63	Chicago	9-87
John H. Harland Professor of Finance, Economics, and Accounting							
Bentley, Jerome T.	Assoc	Rider		PHD		Pittsburgh	
Bentley, Marion	ExtSp	Utah State	H	MPA	70	NYU	1975
Benz, George A.	Retir	St Marys-Txs		PHD	69	Oklahoma	1985
Benzing, Cynthia D.	Prof	West Chester	AEG	PHD	87	Drexel	1988
Bera, Anil K.	Prof	Illinois		PHD	83	Austr Na	1983
Berardi, Peter A.	Lect	SUNY-Cortlan		MBA			
Berdell, John	Asst	DePaul		PHD		Cambridg	
Bereskin, C. Gregory	Asst	St Ambrose		PHD	83	Missouri	1991
Berg, Sanford V.	Prof	Florida	T	PHD	70	Yale	1971
Exec Dir Public Utility Research Ctr;Public Utilities & Distinguished Serv Pr							
Berg-Andreassen, Jan	Assoc	Tx A&M Intl		PHD		Houston	
Bergan, Daniel J.	Assoc	NE Illinois		PHD		Tx Tech	
Bergemann, Dirk	Asst	Yale		PHD		Penn	
Berger, David E.	Prof	Mass-Dartmou	IJOR	PHD	72	Wash U	1972
Berger, George	Assoc	Pitts-Johnst	EJK	PHD	87	Ca-Davis	1989
Berger, Mark C.	Prof	Kentucky	J	PHD	81	Ohio St	1981
Bergman, Lila	Lect	CUNY-Hunter		MBA	79	Fordham	9-85
Bergmann, Barbara R.	Prof	American U		PHD	59	Harvard	1988
Distinguished Professor							
Bergsten, Gordon S.	Assoc	Dickinson Cl	NDE	PHD	77	Berkeley	1984
Bergstrom, Theodore C.	Prof	Michigan		PHD	67	Stanford	1975
Berik, Gunseli	Asst	Utah		PHD	86	Mass	1994
Berkowitz, Daniel	Asst	Pittsburgh	GH	PHD	88	Columbia	1992
Berliant, Marcus C.	Prof	Wash Univ		PHD	82	Berkeley	1994
Berman, Eli	Asst	Boston Univ	CJ	PHD	93	Harvard	1993
Bernanke, Ben S.	Prof	Princeton		PHD	79	MIT	1985
Bernard, Andrew B.	Asst	MIT	E	PHD	91	Stanford	1991
Bernard, James A. Jr.	Assoc	Valparaiso	AOP	PHD	72	Notre Dm	
Bernasek, Alexandra	Asst	Colorado St	DA	PHD	92	Michigan	1992
Berney, Robert E.	Prof	Wash State		PHD	63	Wisconsin	1966
Bernheim, B. Douglas	Prof	Stanford		PHD	82	MIT	1994
Bernhofen, Daniel	Asst	Clark		PHD	94	Syracuse	1989
Bernstein, Richard E.	Assoc	Temple	MG	PHD	73	Brown	1972
Beron, Kurt J.	H-Ac	Texas-Dallas		PHD	85	N Carol	1985
Berrens, Robert	Asst	New Mexico	DHQ	PHD	93	Oreg St	1994
Berry, Brian J. L.	Prof	Texas-Dallas		PHD	58	Wash	
L. V. Berkner Professor							
Berry, Charles A.	Prof	Cincinnati	O	PHD	68	Cincinnati	
Berry, Dale A.	C-Pr	Drake		PHD	66	Indiana	1962
Berry, Stanley Keith	Assoc	Hendrix		PHD	79	Vanderbilt	1989
Berry, Steven T.	Assoc	Yale		PHD	89	Wisconsin	1988
Bertaux, Nancy E.	Assoc	Xavier	ABJN	PHD	87	Michigan	1985
Betancourt, Roger R.	Prof	Maryland		PHD	69	Wisconsin	1980
Bethune, John J.	C-Ac	Bellarmine		PHD	87	Fla St	1984
Betsey, Charles L.	C-Pr	Howard		PHD		Michigan	
Betson, David M.	Assoc	Notre Dame	HI	PHD	80	Wisconsin	1979
Betts, Caroline	Asst	So Calif		PHD	94	Brit Col	1994
Betts, Julian R.	Asst	Ca-San Diego	CJ	PHD	90	Queen's	1990
Beutler, Martin K.	Assoc	So Dakota St	Q	PHD	86	Purdue	1986
Beuttenmuller, Doris Henle	Prof	Webster	AIJN	PHD		St Louis	1974
Beversluis, Eric H.	C-Ac	Aquinas		PHD	70	Northwes	1988
Bewley, Truman F.	Prof	Yale		PHD	70	Berkeley	1983
Bezuneh, Mesfin	C-Ac	Clark Atlant		PHD		Va Tech	
Bhargava, Alok	Prof	Houston		PHD	82	London	1989
Bhargava, Ashok	Prof	Wis-Whitewat		PHD	75	Wisconsin	1970
Bhatia, Shyam L.	Assoc	Indiana NW	F	PHD	76	Indiana	1976
Bhattacharya, Gautam	Assoc	Kansas		PHD	80	Rochester	1980
Bianconi, Marcello	Assoc	Tufts		PHD	88	Illinois	1989
Biddle, Jeff E.	Assoc	Michigan St		PHD	85	Duke	1985
Biederman, Daniel K.	Asst	North Dakota		PHD		Kansas	1987
Biederman, Kenneth R.	Dean	Delaware	G	PHD	75	Purdue	1990
Biegeleisen, J. Alan	Assoc	Mercer-Atlan		PHD		Geo St	1982
Bieker, Richard F.	Prof	Delaware St		PHD		Kentucky	

Bierens, Herman	Prof	So Methodist		PHD	80	Amsterdm	1990
Robert H. and Nancy Dedman Tustee Professor							
Bierman, H. Scott	Assoc	Carleton		PHD	85	Virginia	1982
Biewener, Carole	C-Ac	Simmons	FB	PHD	89	Mass	1987
Bigelow, John P.	Assoc	Louisiana St	CD	PHD	81	Penn	7-94
Biglaiser, Gary	Assoc	No Carolina		PHD	88	Berkeley	1988
Bilias, Yannis G.	Asst	Iowa State		PHD	95	Illinois	1995
Billes, Frank V.	C-Pr	CS-Dominguez	AENP	PHD	74	UCLA	1972
Billings, C. David	Dean	Alabama-Hunt	H	PHD	69	Missouri	1981
Billings, R. Bruce	Lect	Arizona		PHD	69	Claremont	1965
Billington, Peter J.	C-Pr	So Colorado		PHD	83	Cornell	1989
Bills, Angela	Asst	Hampton		PHD	93	Michigan	1993
Bils, Mark	Assoc	Rochester	D	PHD		MIT	
Bilt, Mildred	Lect	Holy Family		MBA		LaSalle	
Binder, Melissa	Asst	New Mexico	FJ	PHD	95	Columbia	1995
Binder, Michael	Asst	Maryland		PHD	95	Penn	1995
Birch, John W.	Prof	Wyoming	RC	PHD	62	J Hopkins	1964
Birckmayer, H. Peter	Retir	SUNY-Empire	O	MBA	56	Cornell	1983
Bird, Michael C.	Prof	Colorado Col		PHD	68	Colorado	1968
Birecree, Adrieene M.	Assoc	Radford		PHD		Notre Dm	
Bischoff, Charles W.	Prof	SUNY-Bingham		PHD	68	MIT	1977
Bishop, John A.	Assoc	East Carol		PHD	87	Alabama	1988
Biswas, Basudeb	Prof	Utah State	CFO	PHD	76	Chicago	1976
Biven, W. Carl	Prof	Georgia Tech	EB	PHD	56	St Louis	1958
Bjork, Gordon C.	Prof	Claremont		PHD		U Wash	1975
Jonathan B. Lovelace Professor							
Black, Dan A.	Prof	Kentucky	DJI	PHD	83	Purdue	1983
Black, David C.	Asst	Toledo		PHD	92	SUNY-Buf	1990
Black, David E.	Assoc	Delaware	HO	PHD	69	MIT	1975
Black, Emily	Assoc	Howard		PHD		Boston C	
Black, Fischer		Goldman Sach		PHD	64	Harvard	1984
Goldman Sachs; 85 Broad 29th Fl; New York NY 10004; 212-902-8859							
Black, Geoffrey	Asst	Marist	H	PHD		U Wash	1995
Black, Michael	Assoc	Biola	FNO	DBA		US Intl	1990
Black, Stanley W.	Prof	No Carolina		PHD	65	Yale	1983
Lurcy Professor							
Black, Tyrone	Dean	So Miss	E	PHD	70	Tulane	1969
Blackburn, McKinley L.	Asst	So Carolina		PHD	87	Harvard	1987
Blackley, Dixie M.	Assoc	LeMoyne	DRC	PHD	84	Syracuse	1982
Blackley, Paul R.	C-Pr	LeMoyne	HR	PHD	82	Syracuse	1982
Blackstone, Erwin A.	Prof	Temple	L	PHD	68	Michigan	1976
Blackwell, J. Lloyd III	Prof	North Dakota		PHD	73	Geo St	1980
Blackwell, Melanie A.	Assoc	Xavier	ACQ	PHD	88	Kentucky	1987
Blair, Benjamin	Asst	Nev-L Vegas		PHD	92	Florida	1994
Blair, Douglas H.	Prof	Rutgers-N Br	D	PHD	76	Yale	1981
Blair, John	Prof	Wright State		PHD		W Virginia	
Blair, Roger Duncan	Prof	Florida	KT	PHD	68	Mich St	1970
Huber Hurst Professor of Business and Legal Studies							
Blais, Jeffrey	Assoc	Rhode Isl Cl		PHD	75	Pittsburgh	1986
Blake, Daniel R.	Prof	CS-Northrdge		PHD	71	Oregon	1971
Blake, Gordon	Prof	Neb-Kearney		PHD		Nebraska	1963
Blakemore, Arthur E.	C-Pr	Arizona St		PHD	77	S Illinois	1979
Blalock, M. Gale	Assoc	Evansville		PHD		Okla St	1977
Blanchard, Olivier J.	Prof	MIT	G	PHD	77	MIT	1985
Class of 1941 Professor							
Blanchflower, David Graham	Prof	Dartmouth		PHD	85	London	1989
Blanchfield, William C.	Dean	Utica		PHD		SUNY-Alb	1966
Blandin, Jim		Naval Postgr					
Blank, Rebecca M.	Prof	Northwestern		PHD	83	MIT	1989
Blankmeyer, Eric	Prof	SW Texas St		PHD	71	Princeton	1982
Blass, Asher A.	VAsoc	Wesleyan-CT	L	PHD	88	Harvard	
Blattenberger, Gail R.	Assoc	Utah		PHD	77	Michigan	1981
Blau, David M.	Prof	No Carolina		PHD	80	Wisconsin	1992
Norman L. Johnson Professor							
Bleau, Barbara Lee	H-Pr	Pfeiffer		PHD	80	Penn St	8-86
Jefferson-Pilot Professor of Management Science							
Blecha, Betty J.	Prof	San Fran St		PHD	76	Iowa	1983
Blecker, Robert A.	Assoc	American U		PHD	87	Stanford	1985
Blevins, Dallas	Prof	Montevallo		DBA	76	Fla St	1983
Blewett, Robert Allan	Assoc	St Lawrence	OHR	PHD	80	Va Tech	1983
Blinder, Alan S.	Prof	Princeton		PHD	71	MIT	1971
Blistein, Allen	Prof	SW State		PHD		Minnesota	1976
Bloch, Howard Ruben	Prof	George Mason		PHD	64	Princeton	
Block, Michael K.	Prof	Arizona		PHD	72	Stanford	1981
Block, Walter	Assoc	Holy Cross	DQR	PHD	72	Columbia	1991
Blomberg, Brock	Asst	Wellesley		PHD	94	J Hopkins	1995
Blomquist, Glenn C.	Prof	Kentucky	HQR	PHD	77	Chicago	1980
Blonigen, Bruce A.	Asst	Oregon	FL	PHD	95	Ca-Davis	1995
Bloom, Jay D.	C-Ac	SUNY-N Paltz	ADJ	MA	58	Chicago	1965
Bloomfield, Arthur I.	Emer	Pennsylvania		PHD	42	Chicago	1958

Bloss, Richard J.	Retir	Chicago St		PHD		Penn	1968
Blum, Fredrick	C-Pr	Chicago St		MA			
Blume, Andreas	Assoc	Iowa		PHD	89	Ca-SnDgo	1989
Blume, Lawrence E.	Prof	Cornell		PHD		Berkeley	
Blumenthal, Marsha A.	Assoc	St Thomas-MN	JH	PHD	85	Minnesota	1984
Blumner, Sidney M.	Prof	CS-Pomona		PHD	68	Arizona	1967
Blush, Lawrence D.	Retir	West Liberty		MA	59	Ohio St	1963
Boal, William M.	Asst	Drake		PHD	85	Stanford	1995
Bober, Stanley	Prof	Duquesne		PHD	62	NYU	1964
Bobo, James R.	Emer	So Alabama		PHD	61	LSU	1978
Boddy, Raford D.	C-Pr	San Diego St		PHD	68	Michigan	1980
Bodenhorn, Howard	Asst	Lafayette		PHD	90	Rutgers	1993
Bodily, Jerry J.	C-Pr	St Marys-Cal		PHD		Purdue	1978
Bodo, Peter	Asst	So Conn St		PHD		Conn	
Bodvarsson, Orn B.	Assoc	St Cloud St		PHD	86	Simon Fr	1988
Boeh, Jeanne	Asst	Augsburg	I	PHD		Illinois	1990
Boerio, Eileen	Lect	Pittsburgh	D	MA	77	Pittsburgh	1977
Boese, Alan Ervin	Asst	Virginia St		MA	70	S Illinois	1971
Boettke, Peter J.	Asst	New York U		PHD	89	Geo Mason	1990
Bogan, Elizabeth C.	Prof	F Dick-Madis		PHD	71	Columbia	1971
Bogart, Marti S.	Assoc	No Central		PHD	86	Purdue	1982
Bogart, William T.	Asst	Case Western	HRDA	PHD	90	Princeton	1990
Boger, Dan C.	Prof	Naval Postgr		PHD	79	Berkeley	1979
Bognanno, Michael	Asst	Temple	J	PHD	90	Cornell	1990
Bohanon, Cecil E.	Prof	Ball State		PHD	81	Va Tech	1980
Bohara, Alok	Assoc	New Mexico	CIQ	PHD	86	Colorado	1987
Bohling, Peter H.	Prof	Bloomsburg		PHD	77	Mass	1978
Bohm, Robert A.	Prof	Tennessee		PHD	71	Wash U	1968
Bohmer, Peter G.		Evergreen St		PHD	85	Mass	1987
Bohn, Henning	Assoc	Cal-Santa Br	EF	PHD	86	Stanford	1992
Boland, Dennis	Assoc	Univ of D C	BA	PHD		Illinois	1976
Bolch, Ben W.	Prof	Rhodes		PHD	66	N Carol	1987
Boldt, David John	Asst	West Georgia	AR	PHD	87	New Mex	1988
Bolin, Delynne	Asst	Andrews	EJ	PHD		Purdue	1995
Bolino, August C.	Prof	Catholic		PHD	57	St Louis	
Bollinger, Christopher R.	Asst	Georgia St	CDJ	PHD	93	Wisconsin	1993
Bolnick, Bruce R.	Assoc	Northeastern		PHD	72	Yale	1983
Bolton, John	C-Ac	Monmouth		MBA		Adelphi	
Bolton, Roger E.	Prof	Williams		PHD	64	Harvard	1966
Edward Door Griffin Professor of Economics							
Bom, Philip C.	Prof	Regent		PHD		Free	1983
Bombelles, Joseph T.	Prof	John Carroll	ABOP	PHD	65	Case Wes	1963
Bomberger, William A.	Assoc	Florida		PHD	73	Brown	1977
Bonanno, Giacomo F.	Assoc	Cal-Davis	CD	PHD	75	LondonEc	1987
Bond, Eric W.	Prof	Penn State	F	PHD	79	Rochester	1981
Bond, Larry Keith	Assoc	Utah State	Q	PHD	72	Utah St	1972
Bond, Richard E.	Assoc	Duquesne		PHD	69	Maryland	1969
Bonello, Frank J.	Assoc	Notre Dame	EA	PHD	68	Mich St	1968
Bonham, Carl S.	Assoc	Hawaii-Manoa		PHD	89	Tx-Austin	1989
Bonhan, John M.	Retir	Tulsa		PHD	65	Okla St	
Bonifaz, Roberto L.	Asst	Babson		PHD		Boston U	
Bonin, John P.	Prof	Wesleyan-CT	P	PHD	73	Rochester	1970
Bonitsis, Theologos H.	Asst	NJ Inst Tech		PHD	84	CUNY	1990
Bonsor, Thomas W.	Prof	East Wash		MA	55	Tufts	1958
Bonutti, Karl	Retir	Cleveland St		PHD		Fribourg	1965
Booker, H. Marshall	Prof	Chris Newpor	AFMO	PHD		Virginia	1971
Booker, James F.	Asst	Alfred		PHD	90	Colo St	1993
Bookman, Milica Zarkovic	Assoc	St Joseph		PHD	83	Temple	1983
Boor, Randy	Assoc	Mary					
Boose, Mary Ann	Asst	Mississippi		PHD	88	Wash U	1988
Booth, Donald R.	Prof	Chapman	AD	PHD	70	UCLA	1959
Booth, Douglas E.	Assoc	Marquette		PHD		U Wash	
Booth, John M.	Retir	Stetson		PHD		Penn	1973
Boozer, Michael	Asst	Yale		MA	90	Princeton	1993
Border, Kim Christian	Assoc	Cal Tech	C	PHD	79	Minnesota	1979
Bordo, Michael D.	Prof	Rutgers-N Br	N	PHD	72	Chicago	1989
Borenstein, Severin	Prof	Cal-Davis		PHD	83	MIT	1989
Boretsky, Michael	Prof	Catholic		PHD	64	Columbia	1980
Borg, J. Rody	Assoc	Jacksonvil U		PHD	86	N Carol	1984
Borg, Mary O.	Prof	North Fla	HT	PHD	85	N Carol	1984
Borges, Antonio	Dean	INSEAD		PHD	80	Stanford	9-93
Borjas, George J.	Prof	Ca-San Diego	J	PHD	75	Columbia	1990
Borland, Melvin V.	Prof	W Kentucky	BDA	PHD	72	Wash U	1978
Borts, George H.	Prof	Brown		PHD	53	Chicago	1964
George S. and Nancy B. Parker Professor of Economics							
Bose, Mrigen	Assoc	Scranton		PHD		Utah	1968
Bose, Pinaki	Asst	Memphis		PHD	90	NYU	9-95
Boskin, Michael J.	Prof	Stanford		PHD	71	Berkeley	1970
Bossaerts, Peter	Assoc	Cal Tech	G	PHD	86	UCLA	1990
Bosshardt, William D.	Assoc	Fla Atlantic	F	PHD	91	Purdue	1995

Bostaph, Samuel H.	C-Ac	Dallas	BNP	PHD	76	S Illinois	1981
Boston, Thomas D.	Prof	Georgia Tech	JN	PHD	76	Cornell	1985
Bosworth, Derek L.	Prof	Manches Inst		PHD		Warwick	1992
Botana, Joseph D.	Asst	Lakeland	AFND	MBA		Roosevelt	1990
Botsas, Eleftherios N.	Prof	Oakland	FA	PHD	65	Wayne St	1976
Bottoms, I. Glenn	Prof	Gardner-Webb		PHD		Geo St	1983
Botwinick, Howard I.	Asst	SUNY-Cortlan		PHD		New Sch	
Boucher-Breuer, Janice L.	Asst	So Carolina		PHD	87	N Carol	1987
Boulier, Bryan L.	Prof	George Wash	JT	PHD	74	Princeton	1981
Bound, John	Assoc	Michigan					
Bourque, Philip J.	Retir	U Washington		PHD	56	Penn	1957
Bove, Roger E.	C-Ac	West Chester	FP	PHD	73	Harvard	1984
Bowe, Michael A.	Lect	Manches Inst		PHD		Carleton	1993
Bowen, Freddie R. Jr.	Asst	Norfolk St		MA	70	Wash U	1970
Bowen, J. Ray II	Asst	Mo-St Louis	FOP	PHD	92	Michigan	1990
Bowerman, Priscilla V.		Evergreen St		MPHI	71	Yale	1973
Bowers, Patricia F.	Prof	CUNY-Brookly	G	PHD	65	NYU	1964
Bowlby, Roger L.	Prof	Tennessee		PHD	58	Tx-Austin	1965
Bowles, Samuel S.	Prof	Massachusett		PHD	65	Harvard	1973
Bowles, Tyler	Lect	Utah State	AF	PHD	91	N Carol	1994
Bowles, W. Donald	Retir	American U	1994	PHD	58	Columbia	1957
Bowling, James	Assoc	Jackson St		PHD	85	Miss	1975
Bowman, Gary W.	Assoc	Temple	D	PHD	71	Car Mellon	1973
Bowman, John H.	C-Pr	Virg Comm		PHD	73	Ohio St	1981
Bowman, Mary Jean	Emer	Chicago		PHD	38	Harvard	1958
Bowman, Rhead S.	Assoc	So Utah		PHD	75	Utah	1978
Bowman, William R.	Prof	USN Academy		PHD	79	Maryland	1980
Boyce, James K.	C-Pr	Massachusett		PHD	85	Oxford	1985
Boyce, John R.	Asst	Alaska-Fairb		PHD	90	Ca-Davis	1988
Boyd, David W.	Asst	Denison		PHD	91	Ohio St	1991
Boyd, John	Assoc	Rochester		PHD		Indiana	
Boyd, Laura A.	Asst	Denison		PHD	91	Ohio St	1991
Boyd, Michael L.	Assoc	Vermont	NOQP	PHD	84	Stanford	1984
Boyd, Roy G.	Prof	Ohio Univ	QH	PHD	81	Duke	1984
Boyer, Kenneth D.	Prof	Michigan St		PHD	75	Michigan	1984
Boyes, William J.	Prof	Arizona St		PHD	74	Claremont	1969
Boyet, Wayne E.	Prof	Nicholls St	G	PHD	65	N Car St	1985
Boyles, William B.	Assoc	Wash & Jeff		MBA		Oklahoma	1977
Boylston-Herndon, Jill	Asst	Hamline	D	PHD	94	Florida	1994
Boynton, Robert		Naval Postgr					
Bracy, Paula M.	Adj	Toledo		MA		Toledo	1984
Brada, Josef C.	Prof	Arizona St		PHD	71	Minnesota	1978
Bradburd, Ralph M.	Prof	Williams		PHD	76	Columbia	1976
Braddock, Dave	Asst	Delta State	ADEO	PHD	84	N Illinois	8-92
Bradfield, James	Prof	Hamilton	GD	PHD	73	Rochester	1976
Bradford, David	Asst	New Hampshir	DI	PHD	91	LSU	1991
Bradford, David F.	Prof	Princeton		PHD	66	Stanford	1966
Bradley, Michael D.	Prof	George Wash	E	PHD	82	N Carol	1987
Bradley, Michael E.	Prof	MD-Baltim Co		PHD	67		
Bradley, Steven	Lect	U Lancaster		PHD		Lancaster	
Brady, James J.	Prof	Jacksonvil U		PHD	69	Notre Dm	
Jessie Ball duPont Professor of Economics							
Brady, Teresa	H	Holy Family		JD	89	Temple	
Braeutigam, Ronald R.	Prof	Northwestern		PHD	76	Stanford	1975
Harvey Kapnick Professor of Business Institutions & Transportation Center							
Braid, Ralph M.	Assoc	Wayne State		PHD	79	MIT	1988
Brainard, William C.	C-Pr	Yale		PHD	63	Yale	1981
Brajer, Victor	Assoc	CS-Fullerton		PHD		New Mex	1987
Bramhall, David F.	Emer	Colo-Denver		PHD		Penn	
Brandmeyer, Sunne	Lect	South Fla		MA	78	S Fla	1985
Brannon, J. Isaac	Asst	Wis-Oshkosh	J	PHD	93	Indiana	1994
Brannon, Jeffery T.	Assoc	Txs-El Paso		PHD		Alabama	1982
Branson, William H.	Prof	Princeton		PHD	67	MIT	1967
Brar, Jagjit S.	Prof	SE Louisiana	EF	PHD	72	Oreg St	1973
Brasfield, David	Assoc	Murray State	EG	PHD	89	N Carol	1986
Brastow, Raymond T.	C-As	Longwood	J	PHD	87	U Wash	1987
Bratsberg, Bernt	Asst	Kansas State	JD	PHD	91	Ca-SnBarb	1991
Brattin, Max Alan	Assoc	Okla Baptist		MBA		LSU	1966
Brauer, Jurgen	Asst	Augusta	AFIT	PHD	89	Notre Dm	1991
Braun, Bradley M.	Assoc	Cen Florida	D	PHD		Tulane	1986
Bray, Robert T.	Prof	CS-Pomona		PHD	72	UCLA	1965
Brazelton, W. Robert	Prof	Mo-Kansas Ct	EP	PHD	61	Oklahoma	1963
Brechling, Frank P.	Prof	Maryland		PHD	55	Trinity	1979
Breece, James H.	Assoc	Maine	AEF	PHD	82	Boston C	1983
Breeden, Charles H.	Assoc	Marquette		PHD	77	Va Tech	1979
Breger, Gerald E.	Emer	So Carolina		PHD	64	Arkansas	
Brehm, Carl T.	Prof	Kenyon		PHD	58	Indiana	1963
Breit, William L.	Prof	Trinity		PHD	61	Mich St	1982
E. M. Stevens Distinguished Professor of Economics							
Brendler, Michael D.	Prof	La St-Shreve		PHD		Tx A&M	1977

Name	Rank	Institution	Fields	Degree	Yr	School	Year
Brennan, Michael J.	Retir	Wesleyan-CT	J	PHD	56	Chicago	1974
Brent, Robert J.	Assoc	Fordham		PHD	76	Manchest	1980
Breslin, Thomas	Prof	Trenton St		PHD		W Virginia	
Bresnahan, Timothy F.	Prof	Stanford		PHD	80	Princeton	1979
Bresnock, Anne E.	Assoc	CS-Pomona		PHD	81	Colorado	1990
Bressler, Barry	Prof	CUNY-Stn Isl	CT	PHD	66	NYU	
Brewer, Paul	Asst	Georgia St	CDL	PHD	95	Cal Tech	1994
Brewton, Audie R.	Assoc	NE Illinois		PHD	80	Utah	1984
Brickley, Colleen	Inst	Plymouth St	D	ABD	78	N Hamp	1993
Briefs, Henry W.	Emer	Georgetown		PHD	54	Geotown	1973
Brien, Michael	Asst	Virginia	JT	PHD	91	Chicago	1993
Briggs, Hugh	Asst	Miami U-Ohio	CD	PHD	89	Wisconsin	1990
Brimmer, Andrew F.	VProf	Massachusett		PHD	57	Harvard	
Brinkman, Richard L.	Prof	Portland St		PHD	65	Rutgers	1961
Brister, Jozell	Assoc	Abilene Chr		MS	73	North Tx	1980
Brite, Robert L.	Assoc	New Orleans		PHD	69	Rutgers	1970
Brito, Dagobert L.	Prof	Rice		PHD	70	Rice	1984
George A. Peterkin Professor of Political Economy							
Britt, Robert D.	Prof	W Virginia	BN	PHD	66	Colorado	1968
Brittingham, Robert L.	H-Pr	Christian Br	AD	PHD	73	St Louis	1989
Britto, Ronald	Prof	SUNY-Bingham		PHD	66	Brown	1974
Britton, Charles R.	Prof	Arkansas	E	PHD	71	Iowa	1978
Broadley, James P. Jr.	DLect	So Carolina					
Brock, Baird A.	Prof	Cen Missouri		PHD	77	Arkansas	1969
Brock, Gerald W.	VProf	George Wash		PHD	73	Harvard	
Brock, James W.	Prof	Miami U-Ohio	AK	PHD	81	Mich St	1979
Bill R. Moeckel Professor of Business							
Brock, John R. Jr.	Retir	USAF Academy		PHD	88	Cornell	1982
Brock, William Allen	Prof	Wisconsin		PHD	69	Berkeley	1981
F. P. Ramsey Professor of Economics							
Brod, Andrew C.	Asst	N Car-Greens		PHD	92	Minnesota	1989
Broder, Ivy E.	Prof	American U		PHD	74	SUNY-SBr	1975
Brodsky, Noel	Asst	E Illinois		PHD	88	Illinois	1988
Bronars, Stephen G.	Assoc	Texas	JD	PHD	83	Chicago	9-92
Brook, Kathleen	Assoc	New Mex St		PHD	76	Tx-Austin	1980
Brooker, Robert F.	Assoc	Gannon	C	PHD	85	N Car St	1982
Brooking, Carl G.	Prof	Millsaps	CDK	PHD	74	Penn	1981
Brookins, Oscar T.	Assoc	Northeastern		PHD	76	SUNY-Buf	1983
Brooks, Nancy	Asst	Vermont	DHQR	PHD	94	Penn	1994
Brooks, Rickey A.	Inst	Freed Hardem	DEF	MBA	91	Miss	8-92
Brooks, Samuel W. III	Deces	Valdosta St		MBA		Georgia	1965
Brookshire, David S.	C-Pr	New Mexico	QR	PHD	76	New Mex	1989
Brorby, Bruce M.	Asst	Detroit Merc		MA	67	Detroit	1971
Broseta, Bruno	Asst	Arizona		PHD	94	Ca-SnDgo	1995
Brothman, Billie Ann	Assoc	Kennesaw St	AGIM	PHD	78	Notre Dm	1989
Brott, Alan	Asst	CUNY-Lehman		MBA			
Broude, Henry W.	Prof	Yale		PHD	54	Harvard	1978
Brower, George D.	Assoc	Moravian		PHD	85	SUNY-Buf	1989
Brown, Barry	Lect	Murray State	E	MS	77	Murray St	1991
Brown, Bryan W.	Prof	Rice		PHD	77	Penn	1983
Hargrove Professor of Economics							
Brown, Byron B.	Retir	So Oregon St	FNOP	PHD	64	Houston	1968
Brown, Byron W.	Prof	Michigan St		PHD	66	J Hopkins	1978
Brown, Carl C.	Prof	Fla Southern		PHD		Okla St	1980
William F. Chatlos Professorship in Business & Economics							
Brown, Charles C.	Prof	Michigan		PHD	74	Harvard	1985
Brown, Christopher R.	C-Ac	Arkansas St	AEKM	PHD	89	Tennessee	1990
Brown, David G.	Prof	Wake Forest		PHD	61	Princeton	1990
Brown, Donald	Prof	Yale					
Brown, Donald J.	Prof	Stanford		PHD	69	Stevens	1988
Brown, Doug	Assoc	No Arizona	OP	PHD	85	Colo St	1985
Brown, Douglas M.	Assoc	Georgetown		PHD	69	W Virginia	1972
Brown, Drusilla K.	Assoc	Tufts		PHD	84	Michigan	1983
Brown, Francis	Emer	DePaul					
Brown, Gardner	Prof	U Washington		PHD	64	Berkeley	1965
Brown, J. Michael	Dean	W Kentucky	G	PHD	71	Kentucky	1988
Brown, James	Prof	Rice					
Brown, James D.	Retir	So Conn St		PHD		Wisconsin	
Brown, John C.	C-Ac	Clark		PHD	86	Michigan	1986
Brown, John H.	Asst	Geo Southern		PHD	89	Mich St	1994
Brown, Ken	Asst	No Iowa		PHD	94	Illinois	1994
Brown, Lisa Jo	Assoc	East Wash		PHD		Colorado	1981
Brown, Lloyd	Inst	So Carol St		ABD		S Carol	1994
Brown, Michael	Dean$	Metro St-CO		PHD		Colorado	
Brown, Murray	Retir	SUNY-Buffalo	CD	PHD	56	New Sch	1967
Brown, Paul	Asst	Mass-Boston	QE	PHD	90	Wisconsin	1990
Brown, R. Clair	Prof	Cal-Berkeley		PHD		Maryland	
Brown, Ralph J.	Prof	South Dakota		PHD	70	Colorado	1977
Brown, Robert E.	Deces	NW Missouri	1994	MA	56	Tx A&I	1971
Brown, Robert K.		Texas Tech		MA	85	Houston	

Name	Rank	Institution	Fields	Degree	Yr	School	Year
Brown, Robert W.	Asst	North Texas		PHD	91	Ca-SnBarb	1991
Brown, William S.	Prof	Alaska SE		PHD	77	Colorado	1991
Brown, William W.	Prof	CS-Northrdge		MA	66	UCLA	1975
Browne, M. Neil	Prof	Bowling Gr		PHD	69	Tx-Austin	1968
Distinguished Teaching Professor							
Browning, Cynthia M.	Asst	Smith	BCE	PHD	89	Michigan	1993
Browning, Edgar K.	Prof	Texas A&M		PHD	71	Princeton	1984
Al Chalk Professor of Economics							
Browning, Shirley C.	C-Pr	N Car-Ashvil		PHD	71	Conn	1970
Brownlee, Robert J.	C-Pr	Centre	AER	PHD		Syracuse	1978
Brownstein, Barry	Assoc	Baltimore		PHD		Rutgers	
Brownstone, David	Prof	Calif-Irvine		PHD	80	Berkeley	1984
Bruce, Neil	Prof	U Washington		PHD	75	Chicago	1990
Brue, Stanley L.	Prof	Pacific Luth	ABJ	PHD	71	Nebraska	1971
Brueckner, Jan K.	Prof	Illinois		PHD	76	Stanford	1976
Bruehler, James	Asst	E Illinois		PHD	93	Illinois	1993
Bruggink, Thomas H.	Assoc	Lafayette		PHD	79	Illinois	1978
Bruner, Bill		Evergreen St		BA	67	W Wash	1981
Brunner, Lawrence P.	Assoc	Cen Michigan		PHD	81	J Hopkins	1982
Brunton, Bruce G.	Asst	Jms Madison	FNO	PHD	89	Utah	1984
Bruschke, Heinrich H.	Retir	St Louis		MA	63	Minnesota	1973
Brush, Brian C.	Prof	Marquette		PHD	73	N Carol	1968
Brust, Peter J.	Assoc	Tampa	EF	PHD	80	Indiana	1981
Bruton, Henry J.	Emer	Williams		PHD	52	Harvard	1962
John J. Gibson Professor of Econ,Resident Fellow of the Cntr for Human&SocSci							
Brux, Jacqueline M.	Assoc	Wis-Rvr Fall		PHD	83	Michigan	1986
Bryant, Harold L.	Prof	Xavier	AF	PHD	67	Cincinnati	1967
Bryant, John B.	Prof	Rice		PHD	75	Car Mellon	1981
Henry S. Fox, Sr. Professor of Economics							
Bryant, Richard R.	Assoc	Mo-Rolla		PHD	84	Ca-Davis	1977
Brzeski, Andrzej	Emer	Cal-Davis	AP	PHD	64	Berkeley	1963
Bucci, Gabriella A.	Asst	DePaul		PHD	88	J Hopkins	1989
Buccino, Joan G.	Prof	Fla Southern		PHD	90	S Fla	1980
Dorotha Tanner Chair in Ethics in Business & Economics							
Buchanan, James M.	Prof	George Mason		PHD	48	Chicago	1983
University Professor of Economics							
Buchele, Robert	Prof	Smith	CEJP	PHD	76	Harvard	1977
Buchinsky, Moshe	Asst	Yale					
Buck, Andrew J.	C-Pr	Temple	C	PHD	77	Illinois	1977
Buck, Donald T.	Prof	So Conn St		MA	61	N Hamp	1965
Buck, John	Asst	Jacksonvil U		PHD	89	Wisconsin	1994
Buck, Roland	Prof	Morehead St		PHD	79	Tx A&M	1983
Buechner, M. Northup	Assoc	St John's		PHD	71	Virginia	1970
Buegler, Paul W.	Assoc	Biola	DEK	JD		Wm Mitch	1978
Buehler, John E.	Emer	Arizona		PHD	67	SUNY-Buf	1968
Buettgen, Elise	Assoc	Tx-Brownsvil	AFG	PHD	53	Kiel	1979
Buffie, Edward F.	Assoc	Indiana		PHD	82	Yale	1992
Buffum, David R.	Asst	Holy Cross	CDHJ	PHD	92	Penn	1989
Bui, Linda T.	Asst	Boston Univ	HLQ	PHD	93	MIT	1993
Bukics, Rose Marie	C-Pr	Lafayette		MBA		Lehigh	1980
Bulls, Derrell W.	C-Pr	Txs Woman's		PHD	71	Tx Tech	1977
Bumbarner, Mary	Asst	Kennesaw St	AERH	PHD	84	Geo St	1985
Bumgarner, Sarah J.	Lect	N Car-Ashvil		MBA		Appalach	
Bumpass, Donald L.	Assoc	Sam Houston		PHD	76	Okla St	1992
Bungum, John L.	Assoc	Gustavus Ado		PHD	77	Nebraska	1979
Bunjun, Seewoonundun	Prof	E Stroudsbur	D	PHD	79	Penn St	1979
Bunn, Julie A.	Asst	Macalester	AFQ	PHD	93	Stanford	1992
Bunting, David C.	Prof	East Wash		PHD	72	Oregon	1971
Burczak, Ted A.	Asst	Denison		PHD	94	Mass	1995
Burda, Michael C.	Assoc	INSEAD		PHD	87	Harvard	9-87
Burdekin, Richard C. K.	Assoc	Claremont		PHD	85	Houston	1989
Burdick, Clark	Lect	Indiana		ABD			1993
Burford, William E.	C-As	Denver		PHD		Ohio St	
Burgess, Giles H.	Prof	Portland St		PHD	73	Oregon	1969
Burgess, Paul L.	Prof	Arizona St		PHD	69	Colorado	1969
Burggraf, Shirley	Prof	Florida A&M	CE	PHD	68	Case Wes	1968
Burgstaller, Andre C.	C-Pr	Barnard		PHD	79	Columbia	1977
Burke, John F. Jr.	Retir	Cleveland St		PHD		Notre Dm	1967
Burke, John T.	Retir	W Michigan	Atg	PHD	58	Mich St	1962
Burke, Jonathan L.	Asst	Texas	D	PHD	85	MIT	7-90
Burke, Melvin	Prof	Maine	O	PHD	67	Pittsburgh	1966
Burke, Ronald L.	Prof	Chadron St	MQE	PHD	70	Minnesota	1987
Burkett, Evelyn	Asst	Ark-Pine Blf		MA		Houston	
Burkett, John P.	Prof	Rhode Island		PHD	81	Berkeley	1981
Burkett, Paul G.	Prof	Indiana St	EO	PHD	84	Syracuse	1991
Burkhauser, Richard V.	Prof	Syracuse		PHD	76	Chicago	1990
Burnell, Barbara S.	Assoc	Wooster		PHD	77	Illinois	1977
Burness, H. Stuart	Prof	New Mexico	ACDQ	PHD	70	Kansas	1978
Burnett, Nancy J.	Asst	Wis-Oshkosh	E	PHD	88	UCLA	1994
Burnette, Joyce	Asst	Valparaiso	NJF	PHD	94	Northwes	1995

Burnim, Mickey L.	Prof	N Carol Cen		PHD	77	Wisconsin	1986
Burns, Malcolm R.	Assoc	Kansas		PHD	75	Minnesota	1975
Burnside, A. Craig	Retir	Pittsburgh	4-95	PHD	91	Northwes	1992
Burton, Mark L.	Asst	Lafayette		PHD	91	Tennessee	1990
Burton, Maureen	Prof	CS-Pomona		PHD	86	Ca-River	1988
Burton, Robert C.	Prof	Frostburg St		PHD		Virginia	
Bush, Howard Francis	Assoc	Va Military		PHD		Florida	1994
Bush, Paul D.	Prof	CS-Fresno		PHD	64	Claremont	1961
Buss, James A.	Assoc	Fairfield	EOP	PHD		Conn	1975
Butcher, Kristin F.	Asst	Boston Coll	DJ	PHD	93	Princeton	1995
Butkiewicz, James L.	Prof	Delaware	E	PHD	77	Virginia	1984
Butler, Alison	Asst	Fla Internat	FEO	PHD	89	Oregon	1995
Butler, Charles Edward	Prof	Texas Tech		PHD	66	Harvard	1971
Butler, Donald T.	Retir	Central Iowa		PHD	60	Wisconsin	1953
Butler, James F.	Prof	Ark-Ltl Rock		PHD	68	LSU	1963
Butler, John Scott	Assoc	Vanderbilt	GC	PHD	82	Cornell	1982
Butler, Judy C.	Lect	Baylor		MS	74	Baylor	1974
Butler, Michael R.	Assoc	Tx Christian		PHD	86	N Carol	1986
Butler, Michael W.	Prof	No Alabama		PHD	74	Arkansas	1973
Butler, Richard V.	Prof	Trinity		PHD	77	MIT	1982
Butler, Sister Agnes	C-As	Molloy		ABD		Indiana	
Butz, David A.	Asst	UCLA		PHD	86	Northwes	1987
Bynoe, Ann	Asst	CUNY-Lehman		PHD		NYU	
Byrne, Dennis	Prof	Akron		PHD	75	Notre Dm	1975
Byrne, Donald R.	C-Ac	Detroit Merc		PHD	71	Notre Dm	1966
Byrne, John	Inst	St Ambrose		MBA		Notre Dm	
Caassuto, Alexander E.	Prof	CS-Hayward		PHD	73	UCLA	1971
Caballero, Ricardo	Assoc	MIT	E	PHD	88	MIT	1992
Cabe, Richard	Assoc	New Mex St		PHD	83	Wyoming	1988
Cadet, Marc	Assoc	Grambling St		PHD		Kansas St	9-68
Cadot, Olivier	Asst	INSEAD		PHD	89	Princeton	9-89
Cagatay, Nilufer	Asst	Utah		PHD	86	Stanford	1991
Cagliessi, Gabriella	Asst	Rutgers-Newk		PHD		Penn	
Cahill, Miles B.	Asst	Holy Cross	AEJ	PHD	95	Purdue	1995
Cahill, Neil S.J.	Asst	Creighton	AN	PHL	47	St Louis	1962
Cai, Francis	Asst	Wm Patterson		PHD		CUNY	1993
Cain, Louis P.	Prof	Loyola-Chicg		PHD	69	Northwes	1968
Caines, W. Royce	Assoc	Lander	ALPQ	PHD	88	Clemson	1988
Cairo, Joseph P.	Asst	LaSalle		MA		Penn	1963
Calabro, Eugene A.	Prof	Salem State		MA		Boston C	
Caldwell, Bruce J.	Prof	N Car-Greens		PHD	79	N Carol	1978
Caldwell, Jean	Prof	Central Okla		EDD	82	N Illinois	1981
Calgaard, Ronald K.	Prof	Trinity		PHD		Iowa	1979
Calkins, Lindsay Noble	Assoc	John Carroll	ADH	PHD	86	Michigan	1986
Call, Stephen T.	Prof	Metro St-CO		PHD	77	Indiana	1979
Callahan, Colleen M.	Assoc	Lehigh	FN	PHD	87	N Carol	1984
Callahan, J. P.	C-Ac	Fla Inst Tec		EDD		Cen Fla	
Callan, Scott J.	Assoc	Bentley	CDQ	PHD	85	Tx A&M	1987
Callari, Antonino	C-Pr	Frank & Mars		PHD	81	Mass	1979
Calvo, Guillermo	Prof	Maryland		PHD	74	Yale	1994
Camacho, Antonio	Prof	Ill-Chicago	D	PHD	65	Minnesota	1968
Cambronero, Alfredo	Asst	Fisk	DOE	PHD	92	Vanderbilt	1992
Camerer, Colin	Prof	Cal Tech		PHD	81	Chicago	1994
Rea A. & Lela G. Axline Professor of Business Economics							
Cameron, Colin	Asst	Cal-Davis	CIJ	PHD	88	Stanford	1989
Cameron, John	Assoc	SW State		PHD		Nebraska	1986
Cameron, Lisa J.	Asst	Carnegie Mel		PHD			
Cameron, Ottamise C. W.	Retir	So Miss	F	DBA	69	Indiana	1962
Cameron, Rondo	Retir	Emory		PHD	52	Chicago	
Cameron, Trudy Ann	Assoc	UCLA		PHD	82	Princeton	1984
Cammarosano, Joseph R.	Prof	Fordham		PHD	56	Fordham	1955
Campa, Jose	Assoc	New York U	DF	PHD	91	Harvard	1991
Campagna, Anthony S.	Prof	Vermont	EH	PHD	66	Rutgers	1965
Campbell, Burnham O.	Retir	Hawaii-Manoa		PHD	61	Stanford	1967
Campbell, Charles A.	Assoc	Miss State		PHD	85	Tennessee	1985
Campbell, Charles W. III	C-Pr	Centre	AEHF	PHD		Virginia	1968
Blazer Professor of Economics							
Campbell, Colin	Asst	Ohio State		PHD		Northwes	1995
Campbell, Donald E.	Prof	Wm & Mary		PHD	72	Princeton	1989
CSX Professor of Economics Public Policy							
Campbell, Everett	Prof	Pt Loma Naz		PHD		Temple	1989
Campbell, Gary A.	Prof	Mich Tech	Q	PHD	82	Penn St	1982
Campbell, Gloria L.	Assoc	Wartburg		MBA	84	N Iowa	1979
Campbell, Jeff	Asst	Rochester		PHD		Northwes	1994
Campbell, John	Prof	Harvard					
Campbell, Thomas C.	Retir	Virg Comm		PHD	47	Pittsburgh	1980
Campbell, William F.	Prof	Louisiana St	N	PHD	66	Virginia	
Campen, James T.	Assoc	Mass-Boston	EG	PHD	76	Harvard	1976
Campione, Wendy A.	Assoc	No Arizona	HJ	PHD	84	Illinois	1981
Canac, Pierre	Asst	St Thomas-TX	F	PHD	87	Houston	1990

Canarella, Giorgio	Prof	CS-L Angeles		PHD	73	Virginia	1973
Canavan, Christopher	Asst	Boston Coll	EF	PHD	94	Columbia	1993
Canfield, Michelle	Inst	Wm & Mary		MA	91	Virginia	1995
Caniglia, Alan S.	Prof	Frank & Mars		PHD	83	Virginia	1982
Canterbery, E. Ray	Prof	Florida St		PHD	66	Wash U	1970
Cantor, Paul E.	Asst	CUNY-Lehman		PHD	85	Ca-Davis	1984
Cantrell, Pat	C-Ac	Cen Arkansas		PHD	83	So Meth	8-84
Cantrell, Richard P.	Assoc	W Kentucky	C	MA	63	S Illinois	1967
Canzoneri, Matthew B.	Prof	Georgetown		PHD	75	Minnesota	1985
Caporale, Tony	Asst	Ohio Univ		PHD		Geo Mason	
Carbaugh, Robert John	Prof	Central Wash	AFEK	PHD	74	Colo St	1985
Card, David E.	Prof	Princeton		PHD	83	Princeton	1983
Cardell, N. Scott	Asst	Wash State		PHD	89	Harvard	1989
Cardenas, Gilbert	Prof	Tx-Pan Amer		PHD	77	Illinois	1975
Cardenas, Jill	Assoc	Tx-Arlington	I	PHD	89	North Tx	1990
Carey, Cathrine	Asst	W Kentucky	F	PHD	92	Kentucky	1992
Carey, Kevin	Asst	U Miami	E	PHD	94	Princeton	1994
Carey, Robin	C-Ac	CUNY-Stn Isl	H	PHD	72	Conn	1976
Cargill, Thomas F.	Prof	Nevada-Reno		PHD	68	Ca-Davis	1973
Carlisle, William T.	Assoc	Utah		PHD	75	Cornell	1971
Carlos, Ann M.	Prof	Colorado		PHD	80	W Ontario	1990
Carlson, David L.	Prof	No Michigan	AEN	BA		N Mich	1961
Carlson, J. Lon	Asst	Illinois St	PQ	PHD	84	Illinois	1986
Carlson, John A.	Prof	Purdue		PHD	61	J Hopkins	1962
Loeb Professor of Economics							
Carlson, Leonard	Assoc	Emory	DJN	PHD	77	Stanford	1975
Carlson, William L.	Prof	St Olaf	C	PHD		Michigan	1973
Carlsson, Bo A.	Prof	Case Western	DFMO	PHD	72	Stanford	1984
William E. Umstattd Professor of Industrial Economics							
Carlsson, Robert J.	Prof	So Carolina		PHD	64	Rutgers	
Carmichael, Dodd	Lect	Baylor		MS	93	Baylor	1993
Carney, Kim	Prof	Tx-Arlington	I	PHD	68	So Meth	1967
Carpenter, Bruce E.	Assoc	Mansfield		PHD	90	Conn	1987
Carpenter, Robert	Asst	Emory	EL	PHD	92	Wash U	1992
Carr, Barry	Asst	Tx A&M Intl		PHD		Oklahoma	
Carr, Linda	Prof	West Alabama		EDD		Alabama	1962
Carr, Thomas A.	Asst	Middlebury		PHD	88	Colorado	1990
Carreno, Eufronio	Asst	Kean		PHD		Rutgers	9-88
Carrier, Ronald E.	Prof	Jms Madison	A	PHD	60	Illinois	1971
Carrillo, Raul J.	Assoc	St Thomas-FL		DA		U Miami	1972
Carrington, Samantha	Assoc	CS-L Angeles		PHD	85	Ca-SnBarb	1986
Carrington, William J.	Asst	J Hopkins		PHD	89	Chicago	1989
Carrington-Crouch, Robert L.	Prof	Cal-Santa Br	A	PHD	67	Essex	1973
Carroll, Christopher D.	Asst	J Hopkins		PHD	90	MIT	1995
Carroll, Kathleen A.	Asst	MD-Baltim Co		PHD	76	J Hopkins	1980
Carroll, Richard R.	Prof	Lock Haven		PHD	73	Kentucky	1977
Carroll, Thomas M.	Prof	Nev-L Vegas		PHD	73	Syracuse	1986
Carroll, Wayne D.	Assoc	Wis-Eau Clar		PHD	84	Minnesota	1986
Carson, Leslie O.	Prof	Augustana SD	ABM	MS	63	Colorado	1958
Carson, Richard T.	Assoc	Ca-San Diego	CQ	PHD	85	Berkeley	1985
Carstens, Pamela J.	Asst	Coe		MBA	85	Iowa	1985
Carstensen, Fred V.	Assoc	Connecticut	N	PHD	76	Yale	1982
Carter, Anne P.	Prof	Brandeis		PHD	49	Harvard	1971
Fred C. Hecht Professor of Economics							
Carter, Charlie	Assoc	Clark Atlant		PHD		Illinois	
Carter, Denis G.	Assoc	N Car-Wilmin	F	PHD		Florida	
Carter, George H. III	C-Ac	So Miss	R	PHD	77	Tx A&M	1979
Carter, John R.	Prof	Holy Cross	CDL	PHD	76	Cornell	1976
Carter, Kent	Assoc	Westminst-PA		PHD		Mass	1991
Captain William McKee Chair of Economics & Business							
Carter, Michael J.	Assoc	Mass-Lowell	CEQ	PHD		Stanford	
Carter, Shawn	Asst	East Txs St	DEFC	ABD		Tx A&M	
Carter, Susan B.	Prof	Cal-Riversid	AJNT	PHD	81	Stanford	1990
Caruso, Phillip P.	Assoc	W Michigan	E	PHD	77	Mich St	1967
Carvajal, Manuel J.	Prof	Fla Internat	JITQ	PHD	74	Florida	1981
Carvellas, John N.	Assoc	St Michael's	ACER	PHD	81	Syracuse	1974
Carvounis, Christos C.	Prof	St John's		PHD		New Sch	
Casario, Michelle	Asst	Villanova		PHD		Northeas	1991
Case, Anne C.	Asst	Princeton		PHD	88	Princeton	1991
Case, Karl E.	Prof	Wellesley		PHD	77	Harvard	1987
Casey, William L. Jr.	Prof	Babson		PHD	63	Boston C	1964
Cash, Doris		Clayton St		DBA			1975
Cashdollar, Parker D.	Prof	Tenn-Martin		PHD	71	Tennessee	
Caskey, John P.	Assoc	Swarthmore	EG	PHD	84	Stanford	1988
Casler, Stephen D.	Assoc	Allegheny	ACEQ	PHD	83	Illinois	1988
Cason, Timothy	Asst	So Calif		PHD	91	Berkeley	1991
Casper, Cheryl A.	Prof	Kent State	D	PHD	75	Case Wes	1973
Casperson, Luvonia J.	C-Pr	La St-Shreve		PHD	74	Oklahoma	1975
Cass, David	Prof	Pennsylvania	DCG	PHD	65	Stanford	1974
Paul F. & E. Warren Shafer Miller Professor of Economics							

Cassimatis, Peter J.	Prof	F Dick-Teane		PHD	67	New Sch	1964
Cassing, James H.	Prof	Pittsburgh	F	PHD	75	Iowa	1985
Cassing, Shirley	Lect	Pittsburgh	R	PHD	76	Iowa	1985
Cassou, Steven P.	Asst	SUNY-Stony B		PHD	89	Minnesota	1988
Catanese, Anthony V.	Prof	DePauw		PHD	72	S Illinois	1979
Cate, Thomas H.	Assoc	No Kentucky		PHD	79	Fla St	1975
Catlett, Robert B.	Asst	Emporia St		MA	75	Nebraska	1976
Caudill, Steven B.	Prof	Auburn		PHD	82	Florida	1981
Cauley, Jon	Prof	Hawaii-Hilo		PHD	71	Colorado	
Caves, Richard E.	Prof	Harvard		PHD	58	Harvard	1962
George Gund Professor of Economics & Business Administration							
Ce, Wei	Asst	Bucknell		PHD		Penn	
Cebula, Richard J.	Prof	Georgia Tech	EDR	PHD	71	Geo St	1992
Cecen, A. Aydin	Asst	Cen Michigan		PHD		Indiana	1987
Cederlund, Albert M.	Prof	Mass-Lowell	HL	PHD	75	Clark	
Ceglowski, Janet E.	Asst	Bryn Mawr		PHD	86	Berkeley	
Ceyhun, Fikret	Prof	North Dakota		PHD	72	Wayne St	1970
Chadwick, Kathy	Assoc	St Olaf	M	PHD		Northwes	1985
Chae, Suchan	Asst	Rice		PHD	85	Penn	1985
Chaffee, Donald M. Jr.	Prof	Aquinas		PHD	70	Ca-Davis	1989
Chaikind, Stephen B.	C-Pr	Gallaudet		PHD	78	CUNY	1989
Chaing, Alpha C.	Retir	Connecticut		PHD			
Chakraborty, Atreyea	Asst	Brandeis					
Chakraborty, Chandana	Assoc	Montclair St	ACDO	PHD		Rensselae	
Chakraborty, Debasish	Asst	Cen Michigan		PHD		Pittsburgh	1988
Chaloupka, Frank J. IV	Assoc	Ill-Chicago	I	PHD	88	CUNY	1988
Chamberlain, Gary	Prof	Harvard		PHD	75	Harvard	1987
Chamberlain, Trevor W.	Assoc	McMaster U	G	PHD	86	Toronto	1985
Chambers, Catherine M.	Assoc	Cen Missouri		PHD	90	Kentucky	1990
Chambers, Donald	Prof	Lafayette		PHD		N Carol	
Chambers, Paul	Assoc	Cen Missouri		PHD	89	Kentucky	1990
Chambers, Scott	Assoc	Linfield		PHD	88	Ca-Davis	1990
Chamley, Christophe	Prof	Boston Univ	HEO	PHD	77	Harvard	
Champ, Bruce	Asst	Fordham		PHD	90	Minnesota	1994
Champlin, Dell	Asst	E Illinois		PHD	90	Utah	1995
Chan, Anthony K.	Assoc	Woodbury	DF	PHD		Claremont	9-89
Chan, M. W. Luke	Prof	McMaster U	DE	PHD	78	Mcmaster	1981
Chan, Sewin	Asst	Rutgers-N Br	H	PHD	95	Columbia	1995
Chandler, Clevelend	Prof	Howard		PHD		Maryland	
Chandra, Vandana	Asst	Georgia	F	PHD	91	J Hopkins	1991
Chandrasekar, Krishnamurti	Prof	NY Inst Tech		PHD	69	New Sch	1969
Chaney, Rick L.	Asst	St Louis		PHD	84	Illinois	1986
Chang, Cyril F.	Prof	Memphis		PHD	79	Virginia	1981
Chang, Fwu-Ranq	Assoc	Indiana		PHD	85	Chicago	1983
Chang, Hsin	Assoc	Toledo		PHD		Michigan	1989
Chang, Hui-Shyong	Prof	Tennessee		PHD	73	Vanderbilt	1971
Chang, Myong-Hun	Assoc	Cleveland St	LDMN	PHD	89	J Hopkins	1988
Chang, Pamela	Asst	Wellesley		PHD	93	Stanford	1992
Chang, Semoon	Prof	So Alabama	M	PHD	71	Fla St	1972
Chang, Winston W.	Prof	SUNY-Buffalo	DF	PHD	68	Rochester	1967
Chang, Yang-Ming	Assoc	Kansas State	DCF	PHD	84	SUNY-Buf	1984
Chang, Yoosoon	Asst	Rice		PHD	95	Yale	1995
Chao, Chi-Chur	Assoc	Oregon State	EF	PHD	87	S Illinois	9-90
Chao, Ching Y.	Prof	Jackson St		PHD	64	Iowa St	1972
Chao, John	Asst	Maryland		PHD	95	Yale	1995
Chao, Kang	Prof	Wisconsin		PHD	62	Michigan	1967
Chapman, Janet G.	Retir	Pittsburgh		PHD	63	Columbia	1964
Chapman, Kenneth S.	Assoc	CS-Northrdge	IG	PHD	86	Minnesota	1991
Chapman, Margaret L.	Assoc	Ill Wesleyan	L	PHD	77	Illinois	1977
Chapman, Richard	Assoc	Westminst-UT	JNB	PHD	92	Utah	1985
Chappell, Glenn	Assoc	Meredith		PHD		Tennessee	1991
Chappell, Henry W.	Assoc	So Carolina		PHD	79	Yale	1980
Chappell, William	Assoc	Mississippi		PHD	83	S Carol	1987
Charkins, Ralph James	Prof	CS-San Bern		PHD	70	N Carol	1976
Charle, Edwin G.	Retir	Ohio Univ		PHD	58	Indiana	
Charles, Joni S.	Asst	SW Texas St		PHD	87	Purdue	1984
Charles, Kerwin	Asst	Michigan		PHD	95		1995
Charos, Evangelos N.	Assoc	Merrimack		PHD	84	N Hamp	1983
Charusheela, S.	Inst	Frank & Mars		ABD		Mass	1995
Chase, Kristine L.	Prof	St Marys-Cal		PHD	87	Maryland	1985
Chase, Larry	Lect	SUNY-Cortlan					
Chase, Richard X.	Prof	Vermont	BE	PHD	66	Maryland	1966
Chasel-Cordo, Peter	Asst	So Indiana		PHD	88	Houston	1994
Chatha, Jaspal	Asst	CUNY-Lehman		PHD			
Chatterton, R. Edward	Prof	Lock Haven		PHD	80	Wash St	1982
Chattopadhyay, Sajal	Asst	Connecticut	I	PHD	90	Conn	1991
Chau, Nancy	Asst	So Illinois	FO	PHD	95	J Hopkins	1995
Chaudhuri, Anita	Asst	SUNY-Albany	IJ	PHD		Rutgers	
Chauvet, Marcelle	Asst	Cal-Riversid	AE	PHD	95	Penn	1995
Chawdhry, M. Arshad	Prof	Calif U-Penn		PHD		Illinois	1976

Che, Yeon-Koo	Assoc	Wisconsin		PHD	91	Stanford	1991
Cheema, Balwir Singh	Assoc	Wittenberg		PHD		American	1966
Chemmanur, Thomas J.	Asst	Columbia		PHD	90	NYU	1989
Chen, Aimin	Asst	Indiana St	PD	PHD	90	Penn St	1991
Chen, Baolin	Asst	Rutgers-Camd		PHD			
Chen, David Y.	Assoc	N Carol A&T		PHD	71	Wisconsin	
Chen, Lein-Lein	Asst	Nev-L Vegas		PHD	92	U Miami	1993
Chen, Thomas P.	Assoc	St John's		PHD		CUNY	
Chen, Xiachong	Asst	Chicago		PHD	93	Ca-SnDgo	1993
Chen, Yan	Asst	Michigan		PHD	94	Cal Tech	1994
Cheng, Benjamin S.	Prof	Southern		PHD	71	Oklahoma	1971
Cheng, Chu-Yuan	Prof	Ball State		PHD	64	Geotown	1971
Cheng, David C.	Prof	Alabama		PHD	73	Yale	1974
Cheng, Doris	Prof	San Jose St		PHD	76	Notre Dm	1988
Cheng, Harrison C.	Assoc	So Calif		PHD	77	Berkeley	1978
Cheng, Jen-Chi	Assoc	Wichita St		PHD	89	Vanderbilt	1989
Cheng, Juei Ming	Prof	Georgia St	CO	PHD	68	Purdue	1968
Cheng, William	Assoc	Tuskegee		PHD	90	SUNY-Bin	1990
Chengalath, Gopal		Texas Tech		PHD			
Cheong, Kwang-Soo	Asst	Hawaii-Manoa		PHD	94	Stanford	1994
Chermak, Janie	Asst	New Mexico	DQ	PHD	91	Co Mines	1995
Chernick, Howard	Prof	CUNY-Hunter		PHD	76	Penn	1982
Cherry, Robert D.	Assoc	CUNY-Brookly	AJ	PHD	69	Kansas	1977
Chesler, Herbert	Assoc	Pittsburgh	J	PHD	64	MIT	1963
Chesser, David	Asst	Missouri	FE	PHD	95	Virginia	1993
Cheung, C. Sherman	Prof	McMaster U	G	PHD	91	Illinois	1981
Cheung, Kowk Hung (Francis)	Asst	Missouri	DJR	PHD	89	Mich St	1989
Cheung, Yin-Wong	Assoc	Ca-Santa Crz	C	PHD	90	Penn	1990
Chevin, Stanley	Asst	Tenn State		PHD	75	Tennessee	
Chew, Soo Hong	Assoc	Calif-Irvine		PHD	81	Brit Col	1991
Chezum, Brian	H-Pr	Simpson		PHD	92	Kentucky	1995
Chhikara, Rajkumar	Retir	Iowa State		PHD	86	Illinois	1986
Chi, Wan Fu	Prof	Weber State	AC	PHD	69	S Illinois	1969
Chilcote, Ronald H.	Prof	Cal-Riversid	P	PHD	65	Stanford	1963
Chiles, Ted W.	Assoc	Auburn-Montg	ADJM	PHD	90	Penn St	1990
Chilton, John B.	Asst	So Carolina		PHD	89	Brown	1988
Chin, Judith	Asst	Tufts		PHD	93	Princeton	1992
Chinn, Kenneth	C-Ac	SE Okla St	EC	PHD	91	Colo St	1982
Chinn, Menzie	Asst	Ca-Santa Crz	FCE	PHD	91	Berkeley	1991
Chiong, Winston R.	Prof	Mass-Boston	E	PHD	74	Boston C	1982
Chipman, John S.	Prof	Minnesota		PHD	51	J Hopkins	1955
Regents' Professor							
Chipty, Tasneem	Asst	Ohio State	L	PHD	93	MIT	
Chiremba, Daniel S.	Lect	CUNY-Queens	O	MA	69	New Sch	1969
Chirinko, Robert	Assoc	Emory	EG	PHD	82	Northwes	1994
Chisholm, Darlene C.	Asst	Lehigh	LD	PHD	91	U Wash	1991
Chisholm, Roger	C-Pr	Ark-Ltl Rock		PHD	67	Chicago	1985
Chiswick, Barry R.	H-Pr	Ill-Chicago	J	PHD	67	Columbia	1978
Chiswick, Carmel U.	Prof	Ill-Chicago	T	PHD	72	Columbia	1978
Chittle, Charles R.	Prof	Bowling Gr		PHD	69	Purdue	1965
Chizmar, John F.	Prof	Illinois St	CM	PHD	71	Boston C	1971
Cho, Dong Woo	Prof	Wichita St		PHD	73	Illinois	1972
Cho, Dongchal	Asst	Texas A&M		PHD	86	Wisconsin	1991
Cho, In-Koo	Assoc	Chicago		PHD	86	Princeton	1986
on leave to Brown University							
Cho, Whewon	Prof	Tenn Tech		PHD	71	Vanderbilt	1983
Choate, G. Marc	Prof	Willamette		PHD		U Wash	1974
Chohan, Ray V.	Prof	St Ambrose		PHD	75	Port St	1978
Choi, In	Asst	Ohio State		PHD	90	Yale	1989
Choi, Jai-Young	Assoc	Lamar	DF	PHD		Oklahoma	1982
Choi, Jin	Asst	DePaul		PHD		Iowa St	
Choi, Kee	Retir	Worcester St		PHD		Harvard	1970
Choi, Young Back	Assoc	St John's		PHD	86	Michigan	
Choksy, George Dorian	Assoc	Alma		PHD		Tennessee	1989
Chopin, Marc	Asst	Louisiana Te	L	PHD	92	Tx A&M	1992
Chotigeat, Tosporn	Prof	Nicholls St	FO	PHD	78	S Illinois	1988
Chou, Nan-Ting	Assoc	Louisville		PHD	86	Ohio St	1991
Chou, Ray Yeu-Tien	Asst	Georgia Tech	G	PHD	88	Ca-SnDgo	1988
Choudhary, Munir A. S.	Assoc	SUNY-Fredoni	CE	PHD	85	Fla St	1987
Choudhury, Sharmila	Asst	SUNY-Cortlan		BA	80	Calcutta	1989
Chow, C. Victor	Asst	W Virginia	G	PHD	89	Alabama	1989
Chow, Gregory C.	Prof	Princeton					
Chowdhury, Abdur R.	Assoc	Marquette		PHD	83	Kentucky	1989
Chowdhury, Ashok K.	Prof	Mankato St	AC	PHD	80	Iowa St	1980
Chowdhury, Farhad	Prof	Miss Vall St		PHD		Miss St	1993
Chowdhury, Ma Monayem	Asst	Cheyney		PHD	78	Temple	
Chowdhury-Bose, Gopa	Asst	Northeastern		PHD	84	London	1988
Chressanthis, George A.	Prof	Miss State		PHD	83	Purdue	1987
Christ, Carol T.	Dean	Cal-Berkeley					
Christe-David, Rohn	Asst	Northern St		PHD	94	S Carol	1994

Christensen, Kimberly	C-Ac	SUNY-Purchas		PHD	86	Mass	1985
Christensen, Paul P.	Asst	Hofstra	B	PHD	76	Wisconsin	
Christiano, Lawrence	Prof	Northwestern		PHD	82	Columbia	
Christiansen, Daniel S.	Prof	Albion	CD	PHD	75	Stanford	1981
Christiansen, Gregory B.	Prof	CS-Hayward		PHD	81	Wisconsin	1983
Christiansen, Jens	Assoc	Mt Holyoke		PHD		Stanford	
Christie, Darrell A.	Assoc	Wis-Stev Pt		MS		Illinois	1964
Christofides, Constantinos A	Prof	E Stroudsbur	CRT	PHD	77	Lehigh	1971
Christopher, Jan	Asst	Delaware St		PHD		Howard	
Christopherson, Robert L.	Asst	SUNY-Plattsb	GH	PHD	90	Wayne St	1990
Chu, Betty Y.	Prof	San Jose St		PHD	73	Notre Dm	1974
Chu, Kong	Prof	Georgia Tech	OC	PHD	64	Tulane	1968
Chu, Kwang-Wen	Prof	CS-Fullerton		PHD	72	UCLA	1970
Chu, Shih-Fan	C-Pr	Nevada-Reno		PHD	68	Illinois	1967
Chuah, Kim Liang	Assoc	Walla Walla	ACEG	PHD	92	Wash St	1991
Chudzinski, James	Assoc	Heidelberg		PHD	88	Tx Tech	1988
Chugh, Ram L.	Prof	SUNY-Potsdam		PHD	70	Wayne St	1970
Chung, Ching-fan	Asst	Michigan St		PHD	87	Wisconsin	1988
Chung, Hyung C.	C-Pr	Bridgeport		PHD	70	Columbia	1970
Chung, Jae Wan	Assoc	George Mason		PHD	72	NYU	
Chung, Joseph Sang-Hoon	Prof	Illinois Tch		PHD	64	Wayne St	1964
Chung, Kuk-Soo	Lect	CUNY-Lehman		MA		Yale	
Chung, Nae Hoon	Deces			PHD	63	Mich St	
Chung, Young-Iob	Prof	E Michigan		PHD	65	Columbia	1966
Chwe, Michael	Asst	Chicago		PHD	91	Northwes	1992
Ciecka, James E.	Prof	DePaul		PHD	70	Purdue	1970
Cima, Lawrence R.	Assoc	John Carroll	ADEF	PHD	82	W Virginia	1971
Cinar, E. Mine	Assoc	Loyola-Chicg		PHD		Tx A&M	1983
Cirace, John	Prof	CUNY-Lehman		PHD		Columbia	
Ciscel, David H.	Prof	Memphis		PHD	71	Houston	1973
Citzler, Annette	Prof	Tx Lutheran	A	PHD	85	Tx A&M	1977
Clague, Chirstopher K.	Prof	Maryland		PHD	66	Harvard	1979
Claiborn, Edward Lee	Prof	Va Military		PHD	64	Princeton	1981
Clain, Suzanne H.	Asst	Villanova		PHD	84	Princeton	1987
Clark, Barry S.	Prof	Wis-La Cross	BHOP	PHD	80	Mass	1978
Clark, Carol M.	C-Ac	Guilford	Q	PHD	79	Michigan	1981
Clark, Carolyn	Assoc	Wash State		PHD	70	Berkeley	1973
Clark, Charles	Assoc	St John's		PHD	90	New Sch	1985
Clark, Clifford D.	Prof	SUNY-Bingham		PHD	53	Chicago	1973
Clark, David E.	Assoc	Marquette		PHD	86	SUNY-Bin	1985
Clark, David H.	Prof	Maine	JOA	PHD	62	Wisconsin	1963
Clark, Don P.	Prof	Tennessee		PHD	78	Mich St	1978
Clark, Gregory	Assoc	Cal-Davis	NO	PHD	85	Harvard	1990
Clark, J. R.	Prof	Tenn-Chattan	M	PHD	70	Va Tech	1993
Probasco Chair in Free Enterprise							
Clark, James E.	Assoc	Wichita St		PHD	77	Northwes	1976
Clark, Joy	Assoc	Auburn-Montg	APQB	PHD	88	Tx A&M	1988
Clark, Robert	Prof	N Carol St	JD	PHD	74	Duke	1975
Clark, Wayne Walter	Retir	Brigham Yg		PHD	60	Tx A&M	1962
Clark, William M.	Assoc	Oklahoma	O	PHD		Virginia	
Clarke, George A.	Dean	Central Conn		PHD		Penn St	1984
Clarke, Jere W.	Retir	So Conn St		PHD		Virginia	
Clarke, William A.	C-Ac	Bentley	AD	PHD	73	Rutgers	1972
Clary, Betsy Jane	Prof	Charleston		PHD		Miss	1984
Claudon, Michael Paul	Prof	Middlebury		PHD	71	J Hopkins	1970
Clay, James P.	Prof	Fort Lewis		PHD	74	Kansas St	1982
Claycombe, Richard J.	Assoc	W Maryland		PHD	80	Geo Wash	1981
Clayton, Gary E.	Prof	No Kentucky		PHD	74	Utah	1980
Cleaver, Harry	Assoc	Texas	P	PHD	75	Stanford	9-76
Cleeton, David L.	Prof	Oberlin	DGIM	PHD	80	Wash U	1980
Clement, Meredith Owen	Prof	Dartmouth		PHD	58	Berkeley	1956
Clement, Norris C.	Prof	San Diego St		PHD		Colorado	1968
Clemmer, Richard B.	Assoc	Cen Michigan		PHD	81	Chicago	1982
Clendenon, Irel D.	Prof	Franklin		MBA	83	Xavier	1970
Click, Reid W.	Inst	Brandeis		MBA	87	Chicago	
Cliff, Lee	Assoc	SUNY-Potsdam		MBA		Clarkson	
Cline, Philip L.	Prof	Wash & Lee	C	PHD	75	Okla St	1975
Lewis Whitabker Adams Professor of Economics							
Cloninger, Dale O.	Prof	Houston-Cl L		DBA	73	Fla St	9-74
Cloutier, Norman R.	Assoc	Wis-Parkside	DJR	PHD	81	W Virginia	1981
Cloward, Dix W.	Prof	Weber State	A	EDD	70	Utah St	1963
Clower, Robert W.	Prof	So Carolina		DLIT	78	Oxford	1986
Hugh C. Lane Professor of Economics							
Coate, Douglas C.	Prof	Rutgers-Newk		PHD	74	CUNY	1971
Coats, R. Morris	Assoc	Nicholls St	HIRQ	PHD	83	Va Tech	1985
Cobb, Steven A.	Assoc	Xavier	AEHR	PHD	74	Brown	1984
Cobb, Steven Lee	Assoc	North Texas	O	PHD	87	N Carol	1987
Cobb-Clark, Deborah	Asst	Illinois St	DJ	PHD	90	Michigan	1991
Cobbe, James H.	Prof	Florida St		PHD	77	Yale	1976

Name	Rank	Institution	Fields	Degree	Yr	Degree School	Since
Cocheba, Donald John	C-Pr	Central Wash	QR	PHD	71	Wash St	1970
Distinguished Professor, Research (1992)							
Cochran, Howard H. Jr.	Asst	Belmont		DA		Mid Tenn	1994
Cochran, John	Asst	Metro St-CO		PHD	85	Colorado	
Cochrane, Harold	Prof	Colorado St	EA	PHD	75	Colorado	1975
Cochrane, John H.	Assoc	Chicago		PHD	86	Berkeley	1985
Coehlo, Philip R. P.	Prof	Ball State		PHD	69	U Wash	1986
Coen, Edward	Emer	Minnesota		PHD	53	London	
Coen, Robert M.	Prof	Northwestern		PHD	67	Northwes	1971
Coffin, Donald A.	Assoc	Indiana NW	JNO	PHD	79	W Virginia	
Coffman, Richard B.	Assoc	Idaho	DL	PHD	72	U Wash	1978
Cohen, Alvin	Prof	Lehigh	FO	PHD	62	Florida	1970
Cohen, Linda	Assoc	Calif-Irvine		PHD	79	Cal Tech	1988
Cohn, Cheryl L.	Asst	Millikin		DA	85	Ill St	1984
Cohn, Elchanan	Prof	So Carolina		PHD	68	Iowa St	
Cohn, Raymond L.	Assoc	Illinois St	DN	PHD	77	Oregon	1983
Coiner, H. Michael	Asst	Regis-MA		PHD		Yale	
Colander, David C.	Prof	Middlebury		PHD	76	Columbia	1982
Christian A. Johnson Distinguished Professor of Economics							
Colburn, Christopher B.	Assoc	Old Dominion		PHD		Tx A&M	1987
Cole, Charles L.	Prof	CS-Long Bch		PHD		S Calif	1967
Cole, Donald P.	Prof	Drew	AH	PHD	68	Ohio St	1966
Cole, Ismail	Prof	Calif U-Penn		PHD		Pittsburgh	1984
Cole, Raymond E.	Prof	Ark Tech		PHD	76	Arkansas	1970
Cole, William E.	Prof	Tennessee		PHD	65	Tx-Austin	1965
Colella, Francis J.	H-Pr	Simpson		PHD	73	Fordham	1977
Coleman, Cyiata D.	Dir	Morris Brown	FGOR	PHD	86	S Illinois	8-89
Coley, Basil G.	Prof	N Carol A&T		PHD	71	Illinois	1966
Collidge, Catherine	Assoc	CS-Chico	AHKL	PHD		Va Tech	1984
Collier, Ben	Assoc	NW Missouri	ARE	PHD	81	Purdue	1981
Collier, George A. Jr.	Retir	SE Okla St	ARM	PHD	78	Okla St	1972
Collier, Irwin L.	Assoc	Houston		PHD	84	MIT	1981
Collinge, Robert A.	Assoc	Tx-S Antonio	FHKQ	PHD	83	Maryland	1987
Collins, May N.	Asst	Moravian		PHD	92	S Calif	1993
Collins, Susan M.	Assoc	Georgetown		PHD	84	MIT	1992
Collum, Thomas E.	Asst	NE Illinois		MA	75	Northwes	1977
Colonna, Carl M.	Assoc	Chris Newpor	AEIR	MA		Old Dom	1970
Colton, Nora Ann	Asst	Drew	FPT	DPHL	92	Oxford	1994
Comanor, William S.	Prof	Cal-Santa Br	LD	PHD	64	Harvard	1975
Combs, Ernest F.	Prof	Puget Sound	AOQ	PHD	71	U Wash	1967
Combs, J. Paul	Prof	Appalach St	MR	PHD	73	N Car St	1971
Combs, Kathryn L.	Assoc	CS-L Angeles		PHD	88	Minnesota	1986
Comolli, Paul M.	Assoc	Kansas		PHD		Iowa	1972
Conant, John L.	Prof	Indiana St	DJB	PHD	84	Tennessee	1981
Condon, Carol M.	Asst	Kean		PHD	78	Columbia	9-85
Condon, Clarence M. III	Assoc	Charleston		PHD		S Carol	1980
Conger, Darius J.	Assoc	LeMoyne	JTP	PHD	73	Oklahoma	1981
Congleton, Roger D.	Prof	George Mason		PHD	78	Va Tech	1988
Conhaim, Louis E.	Assoc	St John's		PHD	60	Columbia	1979
Conklin, James A.	Asst	Texas	EN	PHD	93	Stanford	1-94
Conley, John	Asst	Illinois		PHD	90	Rochester	1989
Conley, Timothy	Asst	Northwestern		PHD	95	Chicago	1995
Conlin, Michael	Asst	Cornell		PHD		Wisconsin	
Conlisk, John	Prof	Ca-San Diego	ET	PHD	65	Stanford	1968
Conlon, John	Assoc	Mississippi		PHD	78	Chicago	1987
Connaughton, John E.	Prof	N Car-Charl		PHD	81	Northeas	1978
Connell, Donald R.	Asst	Neb-Omaha	AF	MS	58	FtHaysSt	1965
Connelly, Laura	Asst	Oregon State	HL	ABD		Northwes	9-94
Connelly, Rachel E.	Assoc	Bowdoin	JT	PHD	85	Michigan	1985
Connelly, Robert A. Jr.	Inst	SC-Spartanbu	A	MA		Appalach	1972
Connolly, Michael B.	Prof	U Miami	F	PHD	69	Chicago	1987
Conover, Roger	Asst	Azusa Pacif		MA		Ca-SnDgo	9-90
Conrad, Cecilia A.	Asst	Barnard		PHD	82	Stanford	1975
Conrad, James M.	Assoc	Indianapolis		PHD	70	Kentucky	1979
Conroy, Michael E.	Assoc	Texas	OR	PHD	72	Illinois	9-71
Constantine, Jill M.	Asst	Williams		PHD	94	Penn	
Conte, Michael A.	Prof	Baltimore		PHD	79	Michigan	1989
Conway, Karen Smith	Assoc	New Hampshir	HJ	PHD	87	N Carol	1990
Conway, Patrick	Prof	No Carolina		PHD	84	Princeton	
Conway, William B.	Prof	Augustana IL	AFJK	PHD	69	Minnesota	1970
Cook, Jeffrey J.	Asst	USAF Academy		MA		Indiana	
Cook, John	Asst	Heidelberg	AG	PHD	94	Kentucky	1995
Cook, Michael T.	C-Pr	Wm Jewell	EF	PHD	83	Vanderbilt	1978
John W. Boatwright Professor of Economics							
Cook, Robert W. Jr.	C-Ac	Richmond		PHD	81	Va Tech	1980
Cooke, John P.	Assoc	South Fla	H	PHD	67	Colorado	1968
Cookingham, Mary E.	Assoc	Michigan St		PHD		Berkeley	
Cooley, Thomas F.	Prof	Pennsylvania	E	PHD	71	Penn	1995
Coomes, Paul A.	Assoc	Louisville		PHD	85	Tx-Austin	1985
Coop, Lindsay	Asst	USAF Academy		MA			

Cooper, David	Asst	Pittsburgh	G	PHD	92	Princeton	1992
Cooper, John M.	C-As	Moorhead St		MA	75	Oregon	1972
Cooper, Richard N.	Prof	Harvard		PHD	62	Harvard	1981
Maurits C. Boas Professor ofInternational Economics							
Cooper, Robert	Prof	Winthrop		PHD	67	Virginia	9-64
Cooper, Ronald L.	Assoc	Biola	CDEF	PHD		Berkeley	1994
Cooper, Russell W.	Prof	Boston Univ	CDE	PHD	79	Penn	
Cooper, Thomas E.	C-Ac	Lyon College	DGHL	PHD	84	Princeton	1987
Anne J. Stewart Professor of Economics							
Copeland, Joe B.	Prof	No Alabama		PHD	74	Arkansas	1983
Coppin, Addington M.	Asst	Oakland	FO	PHD	87	W Indies	1989
Coppock, Lee	Asst	Hillsdale		PHD		Geo Mason	1994
Copur, Halil	Assoc	Rhode Isl Cl		PHD		Cornell	
Corbae, P. Dean	Assoc	Iowa		PHD	90	Yale	1989
Corbett, David J.	Asst	Williams		PHD	91	Harvard	
Corcione, Frank P.	Assoc	Scranton		PHD		Lehigh	1978
Corcoran, William J.	Assoc	Neb-Omaha	LQD	PHD	75	Rutgers	1980
Cordes, Joseph J.	C-Pr	George Wash	H	PHD	77	Wisconsin	1975
Corkum, Keith H.	Prof	Nichols Col		PHD	76	Lehigh	1972
Corless, Neil	Lect	U Lancaster		MA		Lancaster	
Corley, Edward M.	Prof	E Illinois		PHD	64	Okla St	1967
Corman, Hope	Prof	Rider	IJKT	PHD	78	CUNY	1988
Cornwall, Richard R.	Prof	Middlebury		PHD	68	Berkeley	1977
Cornwell, Christopher M.	Assoc	Georgia	CHJ	PHD	85	Mich St	1988
Corradi, Valentina	Asst	Pennsylvania		PHD	94	Ca-SnDgo	1994
Corrado, Marilyn S.	Inst	Westminst-PA		MBA		Youngstn	1990
Corrigan, Tom D.	C-Ac	Sacred Heart		PHD		Maryland	
Cortes, Bienvenido S.	Assoc	Pittsburg St	F	PHD		Okla St	
Cosgel, Metin M.	Asst	Connecticut	N	PHD	89	Iowa	1989
Cosslett, Stephen R.	Prof	Ohio State		PHD	79	Berkeley	1987
Costa, Crist	C-Pr	Rhode Isl Cl		PHD			
Costa, Dora L.	Asst	MIT	B				
Costello, Donna M.	Asst	Florida	EF	PHD	90	Rochester	1990
Coston, Robert D.	Prof	Geo Southern		PHD	73	Arkansas	1970
Costrell, Robert M.	Prof	Massachusett		PHD	78	Harvard	1978
Cotham, Ralph	Asst	Hendrix		JD		Vanderbilt	1991
Cothren, Richard D.	Assoc	Virg Tech	E	PHD	81	N Carol	1985
Cotter, Kevin D.	Asst	Wayne State		PHD		Minnesota	1989
Cotton, Jeremiah	Assoc	Mass-Boston	IJ	PHD	83	Michigan	1985
Cottrell, Allin F.	Asst	Wake Forest		PHD	81	Edinbrgh	1989
Couch, Jim	Asst	No Alabama		MAS	85	Al-Huntsv	1991
Couch, Kenneth A.	Asst	Syracuse		PHD	92	Northwes	
Coughlan, Carmel	Asst	Salve Regina		MBA	90	Salve Rg	1990
Coughlin, Peter J.	Assoc	Maryland		PHD	76	SUNY	1982
Coulson, N. Edward	Assoc	Penn State	R	PHD	83	Ca-SnDgo	1984
Coupe, John D.	Prof	Maine	ACD	PHD	60	Clark	1962
Courant, Paul N.	C-Pr	Michigan		PHD	74	Princeton	1973
Courbois, Jean-Pierre	Prof	Appalach St	F	PHD	68	American	1968
Courington, John M.	Prof	Cameron		PHD		Okla St	1979
Couvillion, L. Michael	Assoc	Plymouth St	I	PHD	82	La Tech	1980
Cover, James P.	Asst	Alabama		PHD	82	Virginia	1982
Cowen, Janna L.	Prof	Wis-Rvr Fall		PHD	79	Nebraska	1979
Cowen, Tyler	Prof	George Mason		PHD	87	Harvard	
Cowing, Thomas G.	Prof	SUNY-Bingham		PHD	70	Berkeley	1969
Cox, Donald C.	Prof	Boston Coll	DJ	PHD	80	Brown	1987
Cox, James C.	Prof	Arizona		PHD	71	Harvard	1977
Cox, Larry G.	Asst	SW Missouri		MA	70	Kansas St	1970
Cox, Steven R.	C-Pr	So Indiana		PHD	71	Michigan	1989
Coyle, Sister Ann	Assoc	Immaculata		MA		Temple	
Crabtree, Loren W.	Dean	Colorado St		PHD		Minnesota	
Cracraft, Scott	Assoc	Albion		MS	60	Miss	1977
Craft, Erik D.	Asst	Richmond		PHD	95	Chicago	1994
Craig, Barbara	Assoc	Oberlin	CFQ	PHD	88	Minnesota	1989
Craig, Eleanor D.	Assoc	Delaware	H	MA	61	Penn	1962
Craig, George	C-Pr	Okla City		PHD		Illinois	1982
Craig, Lee A.	Assoc	N Carol St	NJD	PHD	89	Indiana	1989
Craig, Steven C.	Assoc	Houston	HR	PHD	81	Penn	1989
Crain, W. Mark	Prof	George Mason		PHD	76	Tx A&M	
Craine, Roger	Assoc	Cal-Berkeley		PHD	72	Maryland	1977
Crakes, Gary M.	C-Pr	So Conn St		PHD	84	Conn	1980
Cramer, Curtis A.	Prof	Wyoming	BK	PHD	66	Maryland	1966
Cramton, Peter C.	Assoc	Maryland		PHD	84	Stanford	1993
Crane, Steven E.	Assoc	Marquette		PHD	81	Colorado	1980
Crary, David B.	Asst	E Michigan		PHD	82	Maryland	1980
Crawford, Jerry L.	Prof	Arkansas St	ADTM	PHD	69	Arkansas	1966
Crawford, Vincent	C-Pr	Ca-San Diego	D	PHD	76	MIT	1976
Cray, Randy F.	C-Ac	Wis-Stev Pt		PHD		Kansas St	1986
Craycraft, Joseph L.	Prof	Cincinnati	L	PHD	64	Cincinnati	1962
Craypo, Charles	Prof	Notre Dame	J	PHD	66	Mich St	1978
Creane, Anthony J.	Asst	Michigan St		PHD	91	Virginia	1990

Cremer, Jacques	Adj	Virg Tech		PHD	78	MIT	1983
Cremers, Emily T.	Asst	St Louis		PHD	91	Minnesota	1992
Cres, Herve	Asst	Pennsylvania		PHD	94	Geneve	1994
Crews, Amy D.	Asst	Syracuse		PHD	94	Virginia	
Crews, Mike	Assoc	Tx-Pan Amer		PHD			
Cribari-Neto, Francisco	Asst	So Illinois	E	PHD	94	Illinois	1994
Crick, Nelson B.	Prof	Portland St		PHD	67	Colorado	1967
Criddle, Keith	Assoc	Alaska-Fairb		PHD	89	Ca-Davis	1989
Crist, William D.	Prof	CS-Stanislau		PHD	72	Nebraska	1969
Crocker, Keith J.	Prof	Penn State	KD	PHD	81	Car Mellon	1986
Crocker, Thomas D.	Prof	Wyoming	Q	PHD	67	Missouri	1975
Crofts, Robert D.	Asst	Salem State		MA		Northeas	
Cron, William R.	Prof	Cen Mich	Atg	PHD	73	Mich St	1982
Crone, Lisa	Asst	Weber State	AQ	PHD	94	Wyoming	1993
Cronovich, Ron	Asst	Nev-L Vegas		PHD	95	Michigan	1994
Cronshaw, Mark B.	Asst	Colorado		PHD	89	Stanford	1989
Cropper, Maureen L.	Prof	Maryland		PHD	73	Cornell	1980
Cross, John D.	Prof	Michigan		PHD	65	Princeton	1965
Cross, John W.	Assoc	Indiana U-PA	EG	MA	68	Mass	1969
Crotty, James R.	Prof	Massachusett		PHD	73	Car Mellon	1974
Crough, B. Jane	Lect	Pittsburg St	A	MBA		Pittsburgh	
Crowder, William J.	Asst	Tx-Arlington	EF	PHD	93	Arizona	1992
Crowell, Elizabeth	Assoc	Mich-Dearbor		PHD	71	Indiana	1978
Crowther, Simeon J.	Prof	CS-Long Bch		PHD		Penn	1968
Crucini, Mario J.	Asst	Ohio State	E	PHD	91	Rochester	1991
on leave to New York University 1995-96							
Cruz, Robert D.	Assoc	Barry		PHD	85	Penn	1993
Cruz-Saco, Maria A.	Asst	Conn Coll		PHD		Pittsburgh	
Cuddington, John T.	Prof	Georgetown		PHD	78	Wisconsin	
Culbertson, W. Patton Jr.	Prof	Louisiana St	F	PHD	72	Tx-Austin	
Cullenberg, Stephen E.	Assoc	Cal-Riversid	ABCP	PHD	87	Mass	1988
Cullity, John P.	Emer	Rutgers-Newk		PHD	63	Columbia	1977
Culp, David B.	Asst	Slippery Roc		MA			
Culver, Sarah	Asst	Alabama-Birm	CEFG	PHD	93	Houston	1993
Cumber, Carol J.	Inst	So Dakota St	M	PHD	94	S Dak St	1990
Cummings, Donald G.	Asst	No Iowa		PHD	75	Tulane	1963
Cummings, Ronald G.	Prof	Georgia St	Q	PHD	68	Kansas	1993
Noah Langdale Jr. Eminent Scholar Chair of Environmental Policy							
Cunningham, Elizabeth	Asst	Oklahoma	J	PHD	91	Cornell	1991
Cunningham, Steven R.	Asst	Connecticut	EB	PHD	89	Fla St	1989
Cupper, Robert Dean	Prof	Allegheny	ACD	PHD	74	Pittsburgh	1977
Curington, William P.	Prof	Arkansas	J	PHD	79	Syracuse	1989
Curley, Michael D.	C-Pr	Kennesaw St	ADMG	PHD	74	Kentucky	1984
Curme, Michael A.	Assoc	Miami U-Ohio	JD	PHD	89	Illinois	1988
Curran, Christopher	Assoc	Emory	CDK	PHD	72	Purdue	1970
Currie, Janet	Asst	UCLA		PHD	88	Princeton	1988
Currier, Kevin M.	Assoc	Oklahoma St		PHD	85	SUNY-Alb	1984
Curry, Robert L. Jr.	Prof	CS-Sacrament		PHD		Oregon	1966
Curtis, Fred	C-Pr	Drew	BJO	PHD	83	Mass	1978
Curtis, Thomas D.	Prof	South Fla	B	PHD	65	Indiana	1974
Curtis, Wayne C.	Dean$	Troy State		PHD	71	Miss St	1967
Curtis, William	Assoc	Hardin-Simm		ABD	76	Tx-Austin	1976
Cushing, Brian J.	Assoc	W Virginia	RCH	PHD	81	Maryland	1981
Cushing, Matthew J.	Assoc	Nebraska	EJ	PHD	85	Virginia	1992
Cutler, David M.	Assoc	Harvard				MIT	
Cutler, Harvey	Assoc	Colorado St	EC	PHD	85	U Wash	1980
Cyert, Richard M.	Prof	Carnegie Mel		PHD	51	Columbia	1948
Cypert, Clifford L.	Prof	Jacksonvl St		PHD		Oklahoma	1974
Cypher, James M.	Prof	CS-Fresno		PHD	73	Ca-River	1967
D'Ambrosio, Charles A.	Retir	U Washington		PHD	82	Illinois	1980
D'Amico, Thomas F.	C-Ac	St Peters		PHD	83	NYU	1982
D'Arge, Ralph C.	Prof	Wyoming	QO	PHD	69	Cornell	1975
DaBoll-Lavoie, Joseph T.	Assoc	Nazareth		PHD		SUNY-Bin	
DaCosta, Maria N.	Assoc	Wis-Eau Clar		PHD	87	Northeas	1989
Dacy, Douglas C.	Prof	Texas	EO	PHD	64	Harvard	1-65
Dadkhah, Kamran N.	Assoc	Northeastern		PHD	75	Indiana	1981
Daellenbach, Lawrence A.	C-Pr	Wis-La Cross	ADR	PHD	69	Iowa St	1969
Daghestani, Eddie	Assoc	Barry		PHD	71	Colo St	1988
Dahms, Joseph E.	C-Ac	Hood		PHD	83	American	1978
Daigle, Ronald R.	Prof	Central Conn		PHD		Clark	1976
Dalal, Ardeshir J.	Prof	No Illinois		PHD		Iowa	
Dalal, Meenakshi N.	Prof	Wayne St Col	OE	PHD	84	Northeas	1985
Dale, Gary Thomas	Asst	Birminghm So		MA	86	Alabama	1989
Dale, Lawrence Raymond	Prof	Arkansas St	ABPQ	PHD	89	Ohio U	1986
Dalenberg, Douglas R.	Assoc	Montana	CRL	PHD	87	Oregon	1990
Daley, Edward Vincent	Prof	Va Military		PHD		Missouri	1981
Dalgaard, Bruce R.	Prof	St Olaf	EPA	PHD	76	Illinois	1992
Husby-Johnson Professor in Business & Ecnonmics							
Dall, John J. Jr.	Prof	Seton Hall		PHD	68	Penn	
Dalmolen, Albert	C-As	Mansfield		PHD	71	American	1987

Name	Rank	Institution	Fields	Degree	Yr	Degree School	Year
Dalton, George	Deces	Northwestern		PHD		Oregon	
Dalton, Margaret M.	C-As	Frostburg St		PHD		W Virginia	
Dalton, W. Robert	Adj	Carnegie Mel		PHD		Missouri	1985
Daly, George G.	Dean	New York U	D	PHD	67	Northwes	1993
Damon, William W.	C-Pr	Vanderbilt	DGM	PHD	70	Cornell	1976
Damooei, Jamshid	Assoc	Calif Luther		PHD		Surrey	1987
Dane, Andrew J.	H-Pr	Angelo State		PHD	75	Oklahoma	1973
Daneshvary, Nasser	C-Pr	Nev-L Vegas		PHD	84	Tennessee	1990
Daneshyar, Arifeen M.	Prof	Kutztown	AE	PHD	76	S Illinois	1984
Danforth, David	C-Ac	Bethel-MN		MBA	67	Harvard	1988
Daniel, Betty C.	Prof	SUNY-Albany	EF	PHD	76	N Carol	1983
Daniel, Coldwell III	Prof	Memphis		PHD	68	Virginia	1970
Daniel, Cornelia M.	Asst	Westfield St		PHD		Mass	1990
Daniels, Joseph P.	Asst	Marquette		PHD	92	Indiana	1989
Daniels, Michael J.	Prof	Columbus		PHD		Geo St	1980
Daniels, Rudolph	Prof	Florida A&M	DJQ	PHD	80	Fla St	1977
Danielsen, Albert L.	Prof	Georgia	MH	PHD	66	Duke	1963
Danielson, Joan G.	Inst	So Dakota St	A	ABD		Auburn	1994
Dao, Minh Quang	Assoc	E Illinois		PHD	87	Illinois	1987
Dapice, David O.	Assoc	Tufts		PHD	73	Harvard	1973
Dardis, Rachel	Prof	Maryland		PHD	65	Minnesota	1992
Darity, William A. Jr.	Prof	No Carolina		PHD	78	MIT	1983
Boshamer Professor							
Darrat, Ali F.	Prof	Louisiana Te		PHD	81	Indiana	1987
Darrow, John J.	Prof	Westfield St		PHD		Conn	1971
Das, Bhaskar	Assoc	Purdue-Calmu		PHD	91	Miss	1991
Dasgupta, Manabendra	Asst	Alabama-Birm	CDHL	PHD	89	So Meth	1992
Datta, Manjira	Asst	Arizona St		PHD	92	Cornell	1995
Datta-Gupta, Nabanita	Asst	NJ Inst Tech		PHD	90	Cornell	1990
Dauffenbach, Robert C.	Prof	Oklahoma	J	PHD	73	Illinois	
Daughety, Andrew F.	Prof	Vanderbilt	LK	PHD	72	Case Wes	1995
Dauterive, Jerry W.	Prof	Loyola-N Orl	ADH	PHD	76	Tx Tech	1979
David, Martin H.	Prof	Wisconsin		PHD	60	Michigan	1962
David, Paul A.	Prof	Stanford		PHD	73	Harvard	1969
Davidson, Audrey	Asst	Louisville		PHD	93	Auburn	1993
Davidson, Carl	Prof	Michigan St		PHD	87	Boston U	1982
Davidson, Paul	Prof	Tennessee		PHD	59	Penn	1987
J. Fred Holly Professor of Political Economy							
Davila, Alberto	Assoc	New Mexico	EJTR	PHD	82	Iowa St	1989
Davis, Ann E.	Asst	Marist		PHD	83	Boston C	1981
Davis, Donald R.	Asst	Harvard		PHD	92	Columbia	1992
Davis, Douglas D.	Asst	Virg Comm		PHD	84	Indiana	1987
Davis, Elynor G.	Assoc	Geo Southern		PHD	78	Tx A&M	1979
Davis, George K.	Assoc	Miami U-Ohio	EO	PHD	84	So Meth	1985
Davis, J. Ronnie	Prof	New Orleans		PHD	67	Virginia	1989
Davis, Joe C.	Assoc	Trinity		PHD	71	Tx-Austin	1969
Davis, John B.	Assoc	Marquette		PHD	85	Mich St	
Davis, Lance E.	Prof	Cal Tech	N	PHD	56	J Hopkins	1968
Mary Stillman Harkness Professor of Social Science							
Davis, Mary	Lect	MD-Baltim Co		MBA	78	Maryland	
Davis, Michael L.	Asst	So Methodist		PHD	83	So Meth	1991
Davis, Tom E.	Prof	Cornell		PHD		J Hopkins	
Davis, William L.	Assoc	Tenn-Martin		PHD		Okla St	
Davis, William W.	Assoc	W Kentucky	F	PHD	65	Kenucky	1970
Davis, William Young Jr.	C-Pr	N Car-Charl		PHD	70	Georgia	1970
Davutyan, Nurhan	Asst	Mich Tech	C	PHD	88	Ca-SnBarb	1990
Dawes, William	Lect	SUNY-Stony B		PHD	72	Purdue	1969
Dawson, John C.	Retir	Grinnell	1994	PHD	57	Cornell	1971
Day, A. Edward	Assoc	Cen Florida	D	PHD	76	Purdue	1983
Day, Richard H.	Prof	So Calif		PHD	61	Harvard	1976
Dazimi, Camilla	Asst	San Diego St		PHD	95	Ca-Irvine	1995
De Alonso, Irma	Prof	Fla Internat	OCH	PHD		York-Eng	1981
De Bartolome, Charles	Asst	Colorado		PHD	85	Penn	1993
de Fontnouvelle, Patrick	Asst	Iowa State		PHD	95	Wisconsin	1995
de la Vina, Lynda	Prof	Tx-S Antonio		PHD	82	Rice	1979
de Lima, Pedro F.	Asst	J Hopkins		PHD	92	Wisconsin	1993
De Los Santos, Adora	Asst	Robt Morris		PHD		Penn St	
De los Santos, Tomas	Asst	Central Okla		PHD	88	Clark	
Deacon, Robert T.	Prof	Cal-Santa Br	QH	PHD	72	U Wash	1972
Deak, Edward J.	C-Pr	Fairfield	LRK	PHD		Conn	1970
DeAlessi, Louis	Prof	U Miami	DK	PHD	61	UCLA	1975
Dean, David H.	Asst	Richmond		PHD		Rutgers	1987
DeAndrea, Vincent F.	Prof	Quinnipiac		PHD	72	Mass	1968
Dearden, James A.	Assoc	Lehigh	DH	PHD	87	Penn St	1989
Deardorff, Alan V.	Prof	Michigan		PHD	71	Cornell	1970
Deaton, Angus S.	Prof	Princeton		PHD	74	Cambridg	1983
Deaves, Richard W.	Assoc	McMaster U	EG	PHD	87	Toronto	1987
Deb, Rajat	Assoc	So Methodist		PHD	75	London	1976
DeBerry, Thomas	Assoc	No Georgia		PHD	94	Tx Tech	1995
DeBoer, Dale	Asst	Colorado Spr	DFO	PHD	93	Ca-Davis	1993

Debrecht, Dennis M.	Assoc	Carroll		PHD	81	Iowa	1984
Debreu, Gerard	Prof	Cal-Berkeley		DSC	56	Paris	1962
DeBrock, Lawrence	Assoc	Illinois		PHD	80	Cornell	1979
DeCanio, Stephen J.	Prof	Cal-Santa Br	NCD	PHD	72	MIT	1978
Dechert, W. Davis	Assoc	Houston		PHD		Cornell	
Decker, Terence N.	Inst	Wichita St		ABD	93	Wichita St	1990
DeCosmo, Michael C.	Assoc	E Stroudsbur		MBA	84	Lehigh	1984
DeCoster, Gregory Paul	Assoc	Bowdoin	ER	PHD	85	Tx-Austin	1985
Deeney, John	Asst	Delaware St		MS		Delaware	
Deere, Carmen D.	Prof	Massachusett		PHD	78	Berkeley	1977
Deere, Donald R.	Assoc	Texas A&M		PHD	83	MIT	1983
DeFina, Robert H.	Assoc	Villanova		PHD	79	Wash U	1989
DeFreitas, Gregory E.	Assoc	Hofstra	J	PHD	79	Columbia	
DeGraff, Deborah S.	Asst	Bowdoin	OT	PHD	89	Michigan	1991
DeGregori, Thomas R.	Prof	Houston		PHD	65	Tx-Austin	1967
Dehghan, Farhad	Asst	Wis-Plattev		PHD		Illinois	1985
Deily, Mary E.	Assoc	Lehigh	LQ	PHD	85	Harvard	1991
Deitsch, Clarence R.	Prof	Ball State		PHD	74	N Hamp	1974
Deitz, Richard	VAsst	St Lawrence	RHL	ABD	95	SUNY-Bin	1995
DeJong, David	Assoc	Pittsburgh	E	PHD	89	Iowa	1989
Dekel, Eddie	Prof	Northwestern		PHD	86	Harvard	
Del Rossi, Alison	Asst	Wyoming	HK	PHD	92	Penn	1992
Delemeester, Gregory	Assoc	Marietta	AD	PHD	89	Tx A&M	1986
Milton Friedman Chair in Economics							
DeLong, J. Bradford	Assoc	Harvard					
DeLorme, Charles D. Jr.	Prof	Georgia	EH	PHD	66	LSU	1968
Deltas, George M.	Asst	Illinois		PHD		Yale	1995
DeMarchi, Neil B.	Prof	Duke		PHD	70	AustralN	1983
Deme, Mamit	Asst	Mid Tenn St		PHD	90	Tx-Austin	1990
Deming, Jonathan C.	Assoc	Seattle Pac	BR	PHD	79	Oregon	1977
Demmert, Henry G.	C-Ac	Santa Clara		PHD	72	Stanford	1968
DeMoss, Philip M.	Assoc	West Chester	AGM	PHD	69	Kansas St	1973
Demsetz, Harold	Prof	UCLA		PHD	59	Northwes	1971
Arthur Andersen and Company Alumni Professor of Business Economics							
Deneckere, Raymond	Prof	Wisconsin		PHD	83	Wisconsin	1993
DeNicolo, Gianni	Asst	Brandeis					
Denslow, David A. Jr.	Prof	Florida	EH	PHD	74	Yale	1970
Distinguished Service Professor							
DenWaan, Wooten	Asst	Ca-San Diego	AE	PHD	91	Car Mellon	1991
Denzer, Thomas F.	Retir	Rockhurst	1994	STB	62		1957
Deolalikar, Anil B.	Assoc	U Washington		PHD	81	Stanford	1989
Depperschmidt, Thomas O.	Prof	Memphis		PHD	65	Tx-Austin	1966
DePrano, Michael E.	Assoc	So Calif		PHD	63	Illinois	1963
Deprez, Johan	Asst	Alabama St		PHD	87	Rutgers	
DePrince, Albert E. Jr.	Prof	Mid Tenn St		PHD	78	NYU	1991
Deravi, M. Keivan	Prof	Auburn-Montg	DFGJ	PHD	85	Okla St	1985
Dernburg, Thomas F.	Retir	American U		PHD	57	Yale	1975
DeRooy, Jacob	Assoc	Penn St-Harr		PHD	69	Rutgers	1975
Derrick, Frederick W.	Prof	Loyola-Maryl	CI	PHD	76	N Car St	1982
Dery, George C.	Assoc	Mass-Lowell	CD	MA		Boston C	
Desai, Suresh	Prof	Montclair St		PHD		UCLA	
Desalvo, Joseph S.	Prof	South Fla	R	PHD	68	Northwes	1983
DeSerpa, Allan C.	Assoc	Arizona St		PHD	70	Ca-SnBarb	1975
Desser, Arna S.	Asst	Mt Holyoke		PHD		Maryland	
DeVany, Arthur S.	Prof	Calif-Irvine		PHD	70	UCLA	1984
DeVault, James M.	Asst	Lafayette		PHD	90	Wisconsin	1989
Devereux, John J.	Assoc	U Miami	FH	PHD	88	Chicago	1988
Devine, James N.	Assoc	Loyola Marym	AEJN	PHD	81	Berkeley	1985
Devine, Robert	Asst	Framingham		MA		Northeas	
Devino, William S.	Retir	Maine		PHD	59	Mich St	1960
DeVries, Jan	Prof	Cal-Berkeley		PHD	70	Yale	
DeVries, Rick	Asst	Calvin		ABD	95	Notre Dm	1995
Dezhbakhsh, Hashem	Asst	Emory	CG	PHD	89	Ohio St	1992
Diamantaras, Dimitrios	Assoc	Temple	CD	PHD	88	Rochester	1988
Diamond, Arthur M.	Assoc	Neb-Omaha	BJ	PHD	78	Chicago	1986
Diamond, Daniel E.	Prof	New York U	DEN	PHD	58	NYU	1958
Diamond, James J.	Emer	DePaul		PHD	62	Northwes	
Diamond, Peter A.	Prof	MIT	E	PHD	63	MIT	1966
John and Jennie S. MacDonald Professor of Economics							
Diba, Behzad T.	Assoc	Georgetown		PHD		Brown	
Dibooglu, Selhattin	Asst	So Illinois	F	PHD	93	Iowa St	1993
Dick, Andrew R.	Asst	UCLA		PHD	89	Chicago	
Dickens, Edwin T.	Asst	N Car-Ashvil		PHD		New Sch	
Dickens, William T.	Assoc	Cal-Berkeley		PHD	81	MIT	1980
Dickert, Stacy	Asst	Kentucky	GHJ	PHD	95	Wisconsin	1995
Dickes, Allen L.	Inst	Washburn		MA	70	Toledo	1978
Dickey, Steven W.	Assoc	E Kentucky		PHD	85	S Illinois	1983
Dickhaus, Elizabeth	Asst	Missouri	IN	PHD	74	Missouri	1974
Dickie, Mark T.	Asst	So Miss	Q	PHD	89	Wyoming	1994
Diebold, Francis X.	Assoc	Pennsylvania		PHD	86	Penn	1989

Diedrich, Ernest R.	Assoc	St Benedict		PHD	83	Colo St	
Dieffenbach, Bruce C.	Assoc	SUNY-Albany	E	PHD	72	Harvard	1978
Dietz, Donna K.	Asst	Concordia C		BS		N Dak St	1990
Dietz, James L.	Prof	CS-Fullerton		PHD	74	Ca-River	1973
Diffine, Donald P.	Prof	Harding		PHD		Miss	1971
Dighe, Ranjit S.	Inst	Middlebury		ABD		Yale	1995
DiLiberto, Maryann	Asst	CUNY-Lehman		PHD		Columbia	
Dill, Floyd R.	Asst	DePaul		PHD		Cornell	
Dill, Glenn V.	Assoc	Biola	AD	MBA		Pepperdi	1990
DiLorenzo, Thomas J.	Prof	Loyola-Maryl	KLH	PHD	80	Va Tech	1992
Dimmen, Janet L.	Inst	Wichita St		ABD	78	Ohio St	1981
Dimon, Denise	Assoc	San Diego		PHD	86	Illinois	1983
DiNardo, John	Asst	Calif-Irvine		PHD	90	Princeton	1991
Dinopoulos, Elias	Prof	Florida	FO	PHD	85	Columbia	1988
DiNoto, Michael J.	Prof	Idaho	JR	PHD	73	SUNY-Buf	1970
Diulio, Eugene A.	Assoc	Fordham		PHD	66	Columbia	1963
Diwan, Romesh K.	Prof	Rensselaer		PHD	65	Birmingh	
Dixit, Avinash K.	Prof	Princeton		PHD	68	MIT	1981
Dixon, Bruce	Prof	Arkansas	TQ	PHD		Ca-Davis	1986
Dixon, Warren R.	C-Pr	SUNY-Plattsb	BP	PHD	71	Colorado	1968
Djimopoulos, Evangelos	Prof	F Dick-Teane		PHD	69	Columbia	
Doak, Paul D.	Retir	Iowa State	1994	PHD	65	Iowa St	1961
Doane, Donna L.	Assoc	SUNY-Cortlan		PHD			
Dobbs, Thomas L.	Prof	So Dakota St	Q	PHD	69	Maryland	1978
Dobis, Vernon J.	C-Ac	Moorhead St		PHD	94	Manitoba	1981
Dobitz, Clifford P.	Prof	N Dakota St	ABDK	PHD	71	Colo St	1970
Dobkins, Linda H.	Inst	Jms Madison	RFE	PHD	95	Va Tech	1995
Dobra, John L.	Assoc	Nevada-Reno		PHD	80	Va Tech	1980
Doeringer, Peter B.	Prof	Boston Univ	JL	PHD	66	Harvard	1974
Dohan, Michael R.	Assoc	CUNY-Queens	PQ	PHD	69	MIT	1971
Dolan, Robert C.	Assoc	Richmond		PHD	82	Rutgers	1980
Dolbear, F. Treanery Jr.	C-Pr	Brandeis		PHD	63	Yale	1968
Clinton S. Darling Professor of Economics							
Dole, Carol	Asst	N Car-Charl		PHD	92	Florida	
Dolenc, Patrick V	Asst	Keene State		PHD		Utah	1991
Dolmas, James	Asst	So Methodist		PHD	93	Rochester	1993
Domazlicky, Bruce R.	Prof	SE Missouri	A	PHD	76	Wyoming	1986
Dominguez, John R.	Prof	Wis-Whitewat		PHD		MIT	1988
Domitrz, Joseph S.	Dean	Wis-Whitewat		PHD	71	S Illinois	1976
Domowitz, Ian	Assoc	Northwestern		PHD		Ca-SnDgo	
Household International Corporation Research Professor							
Dompere, Kofi	Assoc	Howard		PHD		Temple	
Donald, Stephen	Asst	Boston Univ	CE	PHD	90	Brit Col	1993
Donaldson, John B.	Prof	Columbia		PHD	76	Car Mellon	1977
Donihue, Michael R.	Asst	Colby	CEA	PHD	89	Michigan	1989
Donley, Thomas D.	Asst	DePaul		MS	87	Wisconsin	
Donnelley, Lawrence P.	Assoc	Delaware	O	PHD	70	Brown	1968
Donnelly, Lawrence I.	Prof	Xavier	AJM	PHD	64	Cincinnati	1956
Donnelly, William F.	Prof	Santa Clara		PHD	69	NYU	1969
Donovan, Elaine M.	Assoc	Merrimack		PHD		Houston	
Donziger, Alan J.	Assoc	Villanova		PHD	72	ByrnMawr	1967
Dooley, Michael	Prof	Ca-Santa Crz	F	PHD	71	Penn	1992
Dor, Avi	Assoc	Case Western	I	PHD	86	CUNY	1995
John R. Mannix Blue Cross & Blue Shield Professor of Health Care Economics							
Dorai, Gopal C.	Prof	Wm Patterson		PHD	67	Wayne St	1974
Dorfman, Mark	Prof	Ark-Ltl Rock		PHD	70	Illinois	1987
Dorn, James A.	Prof	Towson State		PHD	76	Virginia	1973
Dornbusch, Rudiger	Prof	MIT	F	PHD	71	Chicago	
Doroodian, Khosrow	Prof	Ohio Univ	QAF	PHD		Oregon	
Dorsey, John W.	Prof	Maryland		PHD	65	Harvard	1989
Dorsey, Robert	Assoc	Mississippi	ED	PHD	89	Arizona	1989
Doss, Veda	C-Pr	Wingate	BDJF	PHD	69	Syracuse	1984
Doti, James L.	Prof	Chapman	AEC	PHD	76	Chicago	1974
Dotterweich, Douglas P.	Assoc	East Tenn St		PHD	78	Delaware	1984
Dougan, William R.	H-Pr$	Clemson	HDEL	PHD	81	Chicago	1988
Douglas, Richard W. Jr.	Assoc	Bowling Gr		PHD		Iowa	1976
Douglas, Stratford M.	Asst	W Virginia	CHD	PHD	87	N Carol	990
Dowd, Michael R.	Assoc	Toledo		PHD	90	SUNY-Buf	1989
Dowling, Edward T.	Prof	Fordham		PHD	73	Cornell	1973
Downes, Thomas A.	Asst	Tufts		PHD	88	Stanford	1994
Downing, Douglas A.	C-Ac	Seattle Pac	ACH	PHD	87	Yale	1983
Downing, Paul B.	Prof	Florida St		PHD	67	Wisconsin	1980
Doyle, George A.	Prof	Assumption	FKOP	PHD	51	Fordham	1961
Doyle, Joanne M.	Asst	Jms Madison	DC	PHD	93	Boston C	1993
Doyle, William	Asst	Dallas	GN	PHD	91	Tennessee	1991
Doyle-Burke, Christine	Asst	Framingham		MA		Boston C	
Draayer, Gerald F.	Assoc	Boise State		PHD		Ohio	1976
Drabicki, John Z.	Assoc	Arizona		PHD	73	Purdue	1970
Drabkin, Eric	Asst	Hawaii Pacif		PHD		UCLA	
Drago, Robert W.	Assoc	Wis-Milwauke		PHD	83	Mass	1983

Dragonette, Joseph E.	Assoc	St Joseph		PHD	74	Penn	1967
Drazen, Allen	Prof	Maryland		PHD	76	MIT	1990
Dresher, Katherine	Asst	Ca-Santa Crz	H	PHD	94	Wisconsin	1994
Driscoll, John	Asst	Brown		PHD	95	Harvard	1995
Driscoll, Vincent R.	Prof	Quinnipiac		PHD		New Sch	1969
Driskill, Robert A.	Prof	Vanderbilt	EFM	PHD	78	J Hopkins	1992
Dropsy, Vincent	Asst	CS-Fullerton		PHD		S Calif	1989
Dua, Pami	Assoc	Connecticut	E	PHD	85	London	1987
Dube, Smile W.	Assoc	CS-Sacrament		PHD		Tx-Austin	1989
Dubey, Pradeep	Prof	SUNY-Stony B		PHD	75	Cornell	1989
Dubin, Jeffrey A.	Assoc	Cal Tech		PHD	82	MIT	1982
Dubin, Robin A.	Assoc	Case Western	RCD	PHD	82	J Hopkins	1988
DuBoff, Richard B.	C-Pr	Bryn Mawr		PHD	64	Penn	1964
DuBois, David		SUNY-Empire	M	PHD		Union In	1976
Duchatelet, Martine	Assoc	Barry		PHD	77	Stanford	1989
Duchesneau, Thomas D.	Prof	Maine	AO	PHD	69	Boston C	1967
Dudey, Marc Peter	Asst	Rice		PHD	84	Princeton	1990
Dudley, Dean	Asst	USM Academy		PHD		Indiana	1993
Duell, Dennis	Assoc	Wichita St		PHD	69	Illinois	1967
Duetsch, Larry L.	C-Pr	Wis-Parkside	DKL	PHD	70	Wisconsin	1970
Duffield, John W.	Prof	Montana	Q	PHD	74	Yale	1974
Duffy, John	Asst	Pittsburgh	E	PHD	92	UCLA	1992
Duffy, John A.	Assoc	LaSalle		PHD	71	Boston C	1964
Duffy, Martyn H.	Lect	Manches Inst		MS		Bristol	1972
Duffy, Neal E.	Asst	SUNY-Plattsb	CR	PHD	82	W Virginia	1982
Duggal, Vijaya G.	Prof	Widener	CEDQ	PHD	67	Harvard	1983
Duggar, Jan W.	Dean	SW Louisiana		PHD	67	Fla St	1989
Dugger, William M.	Prof	Tulsa		PHD	74	Tx-Austin	
Dulaney, Ronald A.	Prof	Montana	DJ	PHD		Columbia	
Duman, Barry L.	H-Pr	West Tx A&M	BDP	PHD	71	S Calif	1969
Dumangane, Constantino Sr.	Assoc	Rochest Tech	GLDM	PHD		SUNY-Buf	1986
Dumas, Lloyd J.	Prof	Texas-Dallas		PHD	72	Columbia	1979
Dumas, Rocky N.	Lect	S F Austin		MBA		SF Austi	1985
Dumont, David A.	Prof	Lander	ADJR	PHD	77	SUNY-Alb	1972
Dunbar, Donald J. S.J.	VInst	John Carroll	A	MA	91	Michigan	1995
Dunbar, Ronald	Lect	Wis-Whitewat		PHD	95	Wisconsin	1995
Duncan, Floyd Harold	Prof	Va Military		PHD		S Carol	1978
Duncan, Jerome	Assoc	Tuskegee		PHD		Florida	1991
Duncan, Kevin C.	Asst	So Colorado	JR	PHD	87	Utah	1994
Duncan, Wallace H.	Assoc	No Arizona	EA	PHD	76	Wyoming	1978
Dung, Tran H.	Assoc	Wright State		PHD	78	Syracuse	1982
Dunham, Heather	Assoc	Centenary	ADEM	MBA		Rutgers	8-84
Dunkelberg, William C.	Prof	Temple	M	PHD	69	Michigan	1987
Dunleavy, Kevin C.	Asst	West Chester	ACE	PHD	79	Duke	1979
Dunlevy, James A.	Prof	Miami U-Ohio	JF	PHD	74	Northwes	1980
Dunn, James R.	C-Pr	Edinboro		PHD	71	SUNY-Bin	
Dunn, Lucia	Prof	Ohio State	J	PHD	74	Berkeley	
Dunn, Robert M. Jr.	Prof	George Wash	F	PHD	67	Stanford	1978
Dunn, Thomas	Asst	Syracuse		PHD	92	Northwes	
Dunne, Elizabeth A.	Asst	SUNY Oswego		ABD		Iowa	1990
Dunne, Maureen E.	Assoc	Framingham		MBA		Detroit	
Dunne, Stephanie	Asst	Oklahoma	DJL	PHD	92	Va Tech	1992
Dunne, Timothy	Asst	Oklahoma	DLJ	PHD	87	Penn St	1992
Durchholz, Matthew L.	Assoc	USAF Academy		PHD		So Meth	
Durden, Gary C.	Prof	Appalach St	H	PHD	71	Fla St	1982
Durgin, Frank A. Jr.	Prof	So Maine	NPQ	DRD	56	France	1964
Durham, Yvonne	Asst	Arkansas	LD	PHD	94	Arizona	1994
Durkin, John T.	Asst	Wayne State		PHD		Chicago	1991
Durlauf, Steven N.	Assoc	Wisconsin		PHD	86	Yale	1993
Durtschi, Reed R.	Prof	Utah State	AE	PHD	67	U Wash	1958
Dusansky, Richard	C-Pr	Texas	DH	PHD	69	Brown	9-89
Richard J. Gonzales Regents Chair Professor							
Duston, Thomas E.	Assoc	Keene State		PHD		Brown	1984
Dutkowsky, Donald H.	Assoc	Syracuse		PHD	82	SUNY-Buf	1985
Dutt, Amitava K.	C-Pr	Notre Dame	EFOC	PHD	83	MIT	1988
Dutt, Swarna D.	Asst	West Georgia	F	PHD	93	Wayne St	1994
Dutta, Manoranjan	Prof	Rutgers-N Br	E	PHD	62	Penn	1989
Dutta, Prajit	Assoc	Wisconsin		PHD	87	Cornell	1993
Dutton, Marilyn	Asst	N Carol Cen		PHD	89	Duke	1991
Duwaji, Ghazi	Assoc	Tx-Arlington	F	PHD	66	Duke	1966
Dvorak, Eldon J.	Retir	CS-Long Bch	1994	PHD	62	U Wash	1961
Dwyer, Gerald P.	Prof	Clemson	CEG	PHD	79	Chicago	1989
Dyal, James A.	Prof	Indiana U-PA	JR	PHD	75	Illinois	1977
Dye, Howard S.	Prof	0retirFla		PHD	49	Cornell	1973
Dyer, Alan W.	Assoc	Northeastern		PHD	82	Maryland	1983
Dymski, Gary A.	Assoc	Cal-Riversid	AEHP	PHD	87	Mass	1991
Eadington, William R.	Prof	Nevada-Reno		PHD	73	Claremont	1969
Eagan, J. Vincent	Assoc	Morehouse		PHD		Geo St	1993
Eapen, A. Thomas	Assoc	SUNY-Bingham		PHD	61	Michigan	1966
Eapen, Ana N.	Prof	Wm Patterson		PHD	62	Michigan	1973

Earley, Joseph E.	Assoc	Loyola Marym	AC	PHD	74	Fordham	1974
Early, Dirk W.	Asst	Southwestern	DFHR	PHD	95	Virginia	1994
Earnhart, Dietrich	Assoc	Fairfield	QK	PHD	95	Wisconsin	1995
Easley, David	Prof	Cornell		PHD		Northwes	
Easterlin, Richard A.	Prof	So Calif		PHD	53	Penn	1982
Eastham, George M.	Retir	Cal Poly-SLO		PHD	78	Claremont	1966
Easton, Todd E.	Assoc	Portland	J	PHD	84	Berkeley	1981
Eastwood, John D.	Lect	No Arizona	CD	MS	80	Wyoming	1990
Eatherly, Billy Jack	Prof	Miss State		PHD	64	So Meth	
Eaton, Jonathan	Prof	Boston Univ	FG	PHD	76	Yale	
Eaton, Peter J.	Assoc	Mo-Kansas Ct	CI	PHD	76	Florida	1979
Ebeling, Richard M.	Assoc	Hillsdale		MA	80	Rutgers	1988
Ludwig von Mises Chair							
Eber, John E.	Dean	Il Benedict	M	EDD	83	N Illinois	1976
Eberhardt, Duane	Prof	Missouri So		PHD		S Calif	1986
Ebert, Robert R.	Prof	Baldwin-Wal	DFP	PHD	74	Case Wes	1967
Eckalbar, John C.	Prof	CS-Chico		PHD	75	Colorado	1978
Eckaus, Richard S.	Prof	MIT	O	PHD	54	MIT	1965
Ford International Professor of Economics							
Eckel, Catherine C.	Assoc	Virg Tech	P	PHD	83	Virginia	1983
Economides, Nicholas S.	Assoc	New York U	DKL	PHD	81	Berkeley	1990
Edelstein, Michael	C-Pr	CUNY-Queens	NOF	PHD	70	Penn	1974
Edgmand, Michael R.	Prof	Oklahoma St		PHD	68	Mich St	1983
Edgren, John A.	Assoc	E Michigan		PHD	79	Michigan	1979
Edmonds, Radcliff G. Jr.	Assoc	S Ill-Edward		PHD	79	Michigan	1977
Eduardo, Marcelo	Asst	Delta State	AG	MBA			8-86
Edwards, Alejandra C.	Prof	CS-Long Bch		PHD	84	Chicago	1966
Edwards, Bruce E.	Retir	Bowling Gr		PHD		Michigan	1966
Edwards, Franklin R.	C-Pr	Columbia		PHD	64	Harvard	1980
Arthur F. Burns Professor of Free and Competitive Enterprise							
Edwards, John H.	Assoc	Tulane		PHD	85	Maryland	1985
Edwards, Linda N.	Prof	CUNY-Queens	JC	PHD	71	Columbia	1971
Edwards, Mary E.	Prof	St Cloud St		PHD	88	Tx A&M	1985
Edwards, N. Faye	Prof	Richmond		PHD	68	Kentucky	1968
Edwards, Sebastian	Prof	UCLA		PHD	81	Chicago	1985
Efaw, Fritz W.	Assoc	Tenn-Chattan	CJ	PHD	87	Rutgers	1988
Eff, E. Anthon	Asst	Mid Tenn St		PHD	89	Tx-Austin	1990
Eftekhari, Hossein	Assoc	Wis-Rvr Fall		PHD	85	Nebraska	1985
Egan, James P.	Prof	Wis-Eau Clar		PHD	82	Syracuse	1970
Egge, Karl A.	Prof	Macalester	AGM	PHD	73	Ohio St	1970
F. R. Bigelow Professor of Economics							
Egger, John B.	Assoc	Towson State		PHD	85	NYU	1987
Eggleston, Brian D.	C-Ac	Augustana SD	ABQ	PHD	91	Wash St	1988
Eggleston, Robert C.	Prof	Shippensburg		PHD		Pittsburgh	1965
Ehin, Charles	D-Pr	Westminst-UT	M	PHD	72	Oklahoma	1983
Ehrbar, Hans G.	Asst	Utah		PHD	85	Michigan	1986
Ehrenberg, Ronald G.	Prof	Cornell		PHD	70	Northwes	1985
Eichenbaum, Martin	Prof	Northwestern		PHD	81	Minnesota	1988
Eichengreen, Barry	Prof	Cal-Berkeley		PHD	79	Yale	1987
Eicher, Theo S.	Asst	U Washington		PHD	94	Columbia	1994
Eide, Eric	Asst	Brigham Yg		PHD	93	Ca-SnBarb	1993
Eisenhauer, Joseph G.	Asst	Canisius		PHD	91	SUNY-Buf	1986
Eisenstadt, Robert C.	Asst	NE Louisiana	J	PHD		Geo St	
Eisner, Robert	Emer	Northwestern		PHD	51	J Hopkins	1952
Ekanem, Frank	Asst	Howard		PHD			
Ekelund, Robert B. Jr.	Prof	Auburn		PHD	67	LSU	1979
Lowder Eminent Scholar							
El Nasser, Marwan M.	Prof	SUNY-Fredoni	EG	PHD	70	Ohio St	1970
El-Gamal, Mahmoud A.	Asst	Cal Tech		PHD	88	Northwes	1989
El-Hodiri, Mohamed A.	Prof	Kansas		PHD	66	Minnesota	1966
El-Mofty, Samar M.	Asst	SUNY-Fredoni	IJ	PHD	83	Illinois	1989
Elassar, Sammy E.	Prof	Winston-Sal		PHD	68	Maryland	1968
Elbaum, Bernard	Assoc	Ca-Santa Crz	N	PHD	82	Harvard	1986
Elder, Harold W.	Assoc	Alabama		PHD	82	Va Tech	1981
Elder, John	Asst	Bryant	CE	PHD		Virginia	
Eldridge, Robert M.	Assoc	So Conn St		DBA	87	Geo Wash	
Elias, Carlos G.	Asst	Manhattan		PHD	89	NYU	1990
Elike, Uchenna I.	Asst	Alabama A&M	AOF	PHD	85	Alabama	1985
Eliot, Stuart J.	Lect	Manches Inst		MA		Manchest	1974
Ellard, Charles J.	C-Pr	Tx-Pan Amer		PHD	74	Houston	1976
Elledge, Barry	C-Pr	Appalach St	IM	PHD	70	N Car St	1969
Ellickson, Bryan C.	Prof	UCLA		PHD	70	MIT	1973
Ellickson, Donald L.	Retir	Wis-Eau Clar		PHD	66	Wisconsin	1958
Ellingson, Wayne D.	Inst	So Dakota St	C	BS	70	Iowa St	1980
Elliott, Dawn Richards	Asst	Tx Christian		PHD	94	New Sch	1995
Elliott, Donald S. Jr.	C-Pr	S Ill-Edward		PHD	76	Minnesota	1976
Elliott, Graham	Asst	Ca-San Diego	CEF	PHD	94	Harvard	1994
Elliott, John E.	Prof	So Calif		PHD	56	Harvard	1966
Elliott, Steven	Assoc	NW St of LA		PHD		La Tech	
Ellis, Charles M.	Prof	Dallas Bapt		PHD	73	Alabama	

Ellis, Charles Michael	Assoc	Txs Wesleyan		PHD	73	Alabama	1983
Ellis, Christopher J.	Assoc	Oregon	E	PHD	83	Warwick	1983
Ellis, Gene	Assoc	Denver		PHD	72	Tennessee	1978
Ellis, Gregory M.	Asst	U Washington		PHD	92	Berkeley	1988
Ellis, Harry Jr.	Lect	North Texas		MA		Mich St	1990
Ellis, Larry V.	Assoc	Appalach St	E	PHD	78	Missouri	1978
Ellis, Mary Elizabeth	Assoc	St John's		PHD		S Carol	
Ellis, Michael	Prof	New Mex St		PHD	75	Ca-River	1973
Ellis, Michael A.	Asst	Kent State	EF	PHD	91	Tx A&M	1990
Ellis, Randall P.	Prof	Boston Univ	CILQ	PHD	81	MIT	1981
Ellis, Robert J. Jr.	Emer	So Illinois		PHD	66	Virginia	1965
Ellis, Steffany G.	Asst	Mich-Dearbor	AEFO	PHD	93	NC-Charl	1992
Ellis, Theodore	Prof	Adams State		PHD	72	Colo St	1967
Elmore, Elizabeth A.	Prof	R Stockton		PHD		Notre Dm	1972
Elmslie, Bruce T.	Assoc	New Hampshir	BF	PHD	88	Utah	1989
Elston, Frank	C	E New Mexico	GK	PHD	79	Virginia	1988
Elwood, S. Kirk	Asst	Jms Madison	EFC	PHD	93	Ca-Davis	1992
Elzinga, Kenneth G.	Prof	Virginia	L	PHD	67	Mich St	1967
Emanuele, Rosemarie	Asst	John Carroll	JDH	PHD	92	Boston C	1990
Emerson, M. Jarvin	Prof	Kansas State	RQ	PHD	63	Iowa	1962
Emery, E. David	Prof	St Olaf	DIA	PHD	69	Minnesota	1969
Emery, Mary Ann	Assoc	St Olaf	M	MA	65	Minnesota	1969
Endres, Carole R.	Inst	Wright State		MS	87	Wright St	
Eng, Maximo	Prof	St John's		PHD	66	NYU	1985
Distinguished Professor							
Engel, Charles M.	Assoc	U Washington		PHD	83	Berkeley	1991
Engelhardt, Gary	Asst	Dartmouth		PHD	93	MIT	1993
Engelmann, Paul H.	C-Pr	Cen Missouri		PHD	76	Okla St	1972
Engerman, Stanley L.	Prof	Rochester		PHD	62	J Hopkins	1963
John Munro Professor of Economics							
Engers, Maxim P.	Assoc	Virginia	ACD	PHD	84	UCLA	1982
England, Richard W.	C-Pr	New Hampshir	OQ	PHD	74	Michigan	1976
Englander, Valerie	Assoc	St John's		PHD	75	Rutgers	1982
Engle, Fred A. Jr.	Prof	E Kentucky		EDD	66	Kentucky	1959
Engle, Robert F.	Prof	Ca-San Diego	CGR	PHD	66	Cornell	1975
Chancellor's Associates Chair in Econometrics							
Engle, Ruth	Asst	Lafayette					
English, Mary P.	Assoc	DePauw		PHD	89	So Meth	1988
Enomoto, Carl E.	Assoc	New Mex St		PHD	82	Tx A&M	1983
Episcopos, Athanasius	Asst	Clarkson	CDG	PHD	92	SUNY-Buf	1992
Epple, Dennis N.	Prof	Carnegie Mel		PHD	74	Princeton	1974
Epps, Thomas W.	Prof	Virginia	GC	PHD	69	Duke	1972
Epstein, Gerald A.	Assoc	Massachusett		PHD	81	Princeton	1987
Epstein, Jose D.	Prof	American U		PHD	85	San Andres	
Epstein, Seth	Asst	DePaul		PHD		Arizona	
Erdilek, Asim	C-Pr	Case Western	F	PHD	72	Harvard	1971
Erekson, O. Homer	C-Pr	Miami U-Ohio	HR	PHD	80	N Carol	1978
Erenburg, Sharon J.	Assoc	E Michigan		PHD	86	Illinois	1987
Erfani, G. Rod	Assoc	Transylvania		PHD	84	Fla St	1986
Erfle, Stephen E.	Asst	Dickinson Cl	LKD	PHD	83	Harvard	1989
Erickson, Christopher A.	Asst	New Mex St		PHD	89	Ariz St	1987
Erickson, Edward C.	Prof	CS-Stanislau		PHD	70	S Calif	1970
Erickson, Edward W.	Prof	N Carol St	LQD	PHD	86	Vanderbilt	1965
Erickson, Elizabeth L.	Assoc	Akron		PHD	72	Illinois	1969
Erickson, Erick Lee	Prof	Metro St-CO		PHD		New Mex	
Erickson, Lee E.	Prof	Taylor		PHD	75	Michigan	1979
Erickson, Richard	Assoc	S Col 7th Dy	A	MBA	81	Austin Pea	1984
Erikkila, John	C-Ac	Lk Superior	ADEF	PHD	87	W Ontario	9-90
Erment, Gene	Prof	Athens State	A	EDD	65	North Tx	1968
Ermini, Luigi	Assoc	Hawaii-Manoa		PHD	87	Ca-SnDgo	1990
Erturk, Korkut	Asst	Utah		PHD	92	New Sch	
Eschbach, Doris	Asst	IL Benedict	M	ABD		St Louis	1993
Eschenfelder, Mark J.	Assoc	Robt Morris		PHD	93	W Illin	
Escoe, Jisela Meyer	Asst	Cincinnati	O	PHD		Ohio St	
Esensoy, Yilmaz	Prof	Alabama A&M	AOD	PHD	69	Ohio St	
Eseonu, Maxwell O.	Assoc	Virginia St		PHD	83	Howard	1982
Esfahani, Hadi S.	Assoc	Illinois		PHD	84	Berkeley	1984
Eshleman, Tom	Asst	Neb-Kearney		PHD		Okla St	1993
Eskot, Herbert J.	Asst	W New Eng		PHD	84	Tufts	1984
Esposito, Frances F.	C-Pr	Mass-Dartmou		PHD	67	Boston C	1967
Esposito, Louis	Prof	Mass-Boston	L	PHD	68	Boston C	1968
Esposto, Alfredo G.	Assoc	E Michigan		PHD	83	Temple	1990
Essenburg, Timothy J.	Assoc	Bethel-MN		PHD	91	Tennessee	1989
Estenson, Paul	Asst	Gustavus Ado		PHD	86	Nebraska	1986
Ethier, Wilfred J.	Prof	Pennsylvania	F	PHD	70	Rochester	1969
Eubank, Wayne F.	Prof	SE Missouri		PHD		Kentucky	1964
Eubanks, Larry S.	C-Ac	Colorado Spr	DHQ	PHD	80	Wyoming	1986
Eusufzai, Zaki	Asst	Loyola Marym	ACFD	PHD	94	UCLA	1989
Euzent, Patricia	Inst	Cen Florida		MA		Clemson	1991
Evans, Bernice	Asst	Morgan State		MBA		CUNY-Bar	

Name	Rank	Institution	Fields	Degree	Yr	Degree School	Year
Evans, Boyd	Assoc	Mid Tenn St		MA	64	Auburn	1965
Evans, George	Prof	Oregon	E	PHD	80	Berkeley	1994
John B. Hamacher Professor of Economics							
Evans, Hugh G. Jr.	Assoc	Elizabethtwn		MA		Penn St	1968
Evans, John S.	Prof	Alabama		PHD	71	Wisconsin	1968
Evans, Keith D.	C-Ac	CS-Northrdge		PHD	71	U Wash	1971
Evans, Mark O.	C-Pr	CS-Bakersf	AIQR	PHD	77	New Mex	1978
Evans, Martin D. D.	Assoc	New York U	EFG	PHD	87	Princeton	1982
Evans, Paul D.	Prof	Ohio State	E	PHD	76	Chicago	1987
Evans, Richard D.	Prof	Memphis		PHD	70	Harvard	1978
Evans, Robert Jr.	Prof	Brandeis		PHD	59	Chicago	1967
Atran Professor of Labor Economics							
Evans, Shirley	Inst	St Olaf	M	MBT		Minnesota	1985
Evans, William N.	Assoc	Maryland		PHD	87	Duke	1987
Even, William E.	Prof	Miami U-Ohio	JC	PHD	84	Iowa	1983
Evensky, Jerry	Asst	Syracuse		PHD	84	Syracuse	1985
Evenson, Robert E.	Prof	Yale		PHD	68	Chicago	1977
Everett, Michael David	Assoc	East Tenn St		PHD	67	Wash U	1977
Ewert, Norman J.	Assoc	Wheaton-IL	AF	PHD		S Illinois	1973
Eyrich, Gerald I.	Assoc	Claremont		PHD		Claremont	1967
Eytan, T. Hanan	Assoc	CUNY-Baruch		PHD	85	Sloan	
Ezeani, Eboh	Prof	Univ of D C	O	PHD	76	American	1976
Ezekannagha, Francine	Inst	Alabama St		MS		Hendersn	1984
Ezvan, Kazimiera	Prof	Lindenwood		PHD		S Illinois	8-81
Fabritius, Michael	Prof	Mary Hrdn-By	ABDE	PHD	87	Tx-Austin	1987
Claude McBryde Professor of Finance-Economics							
Fackler, James S.	Prof	Kentucky	E	PHD	77	Indiana	1982
Fagal, Frederick F. Jr.	Assoc	Marywood		PHD	81	Syracuse	1987
Fahy, Colleen A.	Asst	Assumption	AHL	PHD	89	SUNY-Bin	1995
Fahy, Paul R.	Assoc	E Illinois		PHD	76	Conn	1976
Fain, James R.	Assoc	Oklahoma St		PHD	86	Purdue	1986
Fair, Ray C.	Prof	Yale		PHD	68	MIT	1974
Fairchild, Daniel R.	C-Ac	St Thomas-MN	F	PHD	78	St Louis	1976
Fairchild, Loretta	Prof	Nebraska Wes		PHD	72	Cornell	1975
Fairlie, Robert	Asst	Ca-Santa Crz	J	PHD	94	Northwes	1994
Fairris, David H.	Asst	Cal-Riversid	AJP	PHD	84	Duke	1989
Faith, Roger L.	Prof	Arizona St		PHD	73	UCLA	1981
Falaris, Evangelos M.	Assoc	Delaware	O	PHD	79	Minnesota	1986
Falero, Frank Jr.	Prof	CS-Bakersf	ADEG	PHD	67	Fla St	1972
Falk, Barry L.	Assoc	Iowa State	E	PHD	82	Minnesota	1980
Falls, Gregory A.	Assoc	Cen Michigan		PHD	82	Purdue	1981
Fan, Chuen-mei	Prof	Colorado St	HD	PHD	72	Minnesota	1978
Fan, Liang-Shing	Prof	Colorado St	AOF	PHD	65	Minnesota	1968
Fanchon, Phillip F.	Assoc	Cal Poly-SLO		PHD	82	Ca-SnBarb	
Farber, Henry S.	Prof	Princeton		PHD	77	Princeton	
Fardmanesh, Mohsen	Assoc	Temple	OF	PHD	85	Yale	1985
Fare, Rolf	Prof	So Illinois	CD	DOC	76	Lund	1978
Farina, Louis	Asst	Framingham		MBA		Babson	
Farley, Noel J. J.	Prof	Bryn Mawr		PHD	65	Yale	
Farmer, Amy F.	Asst	Tennessee		PHD	91	Duke	1992
Farmer, Berkwood M.	Dean	Longwood	Q	PHD	70	N Car St	1991
Farmer, Roger E. A.	Assoc	UCLA		PHD	82	W Ontario	1988
Farnham, Paul G.	Assoc	Georgia St	DHI	PHD	78	Berkeley	1977
Farooque, Golam	Asst	Moorhead St		PHD	91	Northeas	1991
Farr, William Kendrick	Assoc	Georgia Col	ADQ	PHD		Georgia	1985
Farrell, Claude H. III	C-Pr	N Car-Wilmin	EGR	PHD	74	N Car St	1991
Farrell, John P.	Prof	Oregon State	BO	PHD	73	Wisconsin	9-72
Farrell, Joseph V.	Assoc	Cal-Berkeley		PHD	81	Oxford	
Farrell, Michael J.	Prof	CS-Long Bch		PHD	69	Stanford	1969
Farrell, Rev. John	Asst	Villanova		PHD	72	Catholic	1993
Farsio, Farzad	Assoc	Mont St-Bill		PHD	89	Claremont	1987
Fass, Simon M.	Assoc	Texas-Dallas		PHD	78	UCLA	
Fatas, Antonio	Asst	INSEAD		PHD	93	Harvard	1-94
Faurot, David J.	Assoc	Kansas		PHD	75	Northwes	1975
Fausti, Scott W.	Asst	So Dakota St	F	PHD	91	Illinois	1991
Favor, Homer	Prof	Morgan State		PHD		Pittsburgh	
Fawson, Christopher	Assoc	Utah State	CGMO	PHD	86	Tx A&M	1990
Fayazmanesh, Susan	Asst	CS-Fresno		PHD	84	Ca-River	1990
Fayissa, Bichaka	Prof	Mid Tenn St		PHD	82	Tennessee	1980
Fazeli, Rafat R.	Asst	Redlands		PHD	92	New Sch	1989
Fazzari, Steven M.	Assoc	Wash Univ		PHD	82	Stanford	1982
Fearn, Robert M.	Prof	N Carol St	JDP	PHD	68	Chicago	1965
Feasel, Edward	Asst	George Wash	E	PHD	94	Berkeley	1994
Feeney, Joanne	Asst	Colorado		MA	91	Rochster	1990
Feenstra, Robert	Prof	Cal-Davis	F	PHD	81	MIT	1986
Feige, Edgar L.	Prof	Wisconsin		PHD	63	Chicago	1963
Feigenbaum, Susan K.	Prof	Mo-St Louis	DHKP	PHD	80	Wisconsin	1988
Feinberg, Robert M.	Assoc	American U		PHD	76	Virginia	1989
Feist, William R.	Assoc	Monmouth		PHD		Temple	
Felder, Joseph	Assoc	Bradley		PHD	79	UCLA	1981

Feldman, Allan M.	Assoc	Brown		PHD	72	J Hopkins	1977
Feldman, David H.	Assoc	Wm & Mary		PHD	82	Duke	1988
Feldman, Roger D.	Prof	Minnesota		PHD	76	Rochester	1985
Feldstein, Martin S.	Prof	Harvard		DPHL	67	Oxford	1969
George F. Baker Professor of Economics							
Felfand, Steven	Asst	Cal-Riversid	AOQ	PHD	94	Berkeley	1995
Feliciano, Zadia M.	Asst	CUNY-Queens	JC				1994
Felix, David	Emer	Wash Univ		PHD	55	Berkeley	1964
Feller, Irwin	Prof	Penn State	O	PHD	66	Minnesota	1963
Feller, James F.	Asst	Mid Tenn St		PHD	79	Florida	1984
Feltenstein, Andrew	Prof	Virg Tech	D	PHD	76	Yale	1993
Feltner, Richard L.	Prof	Bellarmine		PHD	65	N Car St	6-86
Felton, Marianne V.	Prof	Indiana SE	ZIEC	PHD	79	Indiana	1976
Fender, Ann Harper	Prof	Gettysburg	ADNL	PHD	76	J Hopkins	1978
Fenner, Richard G.	Asst	Utica		PHD	92	Syracuse	1989
Fenstermaker, J. Van	C-Pr	Towson State		PHD	63	Illinois	1988
Fenton, Sister Helen M.	Retir	Regis-MA		PHD	73	Boston C	
Ferber, Marianne A.	Emer	Illinois		PHD	54	Chicago	1956
Ferderer, J. Peter	Asst	Clark		PHD	88	Wash U	1988
Ferdnance, Tyrone	Asst	Conn Coll		PHD		Notre Dm	
Ferdowsi, Abdollah	Assoc	Ferris State		PHD	82	Mich St	1984
Ferguson, John D.	Prof	Miami U-Ohio	EF	PHD	74	Brown	1970
Ferguson, Paul R.	Lect	U Lancaster		BA		Lancaster	
Ferguson, William D.	Assoc	Grinnell	JE	PHD	89	Mass	1989
Ferleger, Louis	Prof	Mass-Boston	N	PHD	78	Temple	1978
Fernandez, Luis	Assoc	Oberlin	CDGL	PHD	83	Berkeley	1980
Fernandez, Raquel	Assoc	Boston Univ	DFL	PHD	88	Columbia	1992
Ferran, Manuel A.	Assoc	New Mex High	ADEG	PHD	69	Oklahoma	1993
Ferrie, Joseph	Asst	Northwestern		PHD	92	Chicago	
Ferrier, Gary D.	Assoc	Arkansas	DC	PHD	88	N Carol	1993
Ferson, Wayne	Prof	U Washington		PHD	82	Stanford	1992
Fesmire, James M.	Prof	Tampa	DKL	PHD	73	Florida	1973
Dana Professor of Economics							
Fessiehatzen, Tekie	C-Pr	Morgan State		PHD		Pittsburgh	
Fethke, Carol	Prof	Iowa		PHD	71	Iowa	1975
Fethke, Gary C.	Dean	Iowa		PHD	68	Iowa	1974
Fettus, Sharon H.	Asst	Catholic		PHD			
Feuz, Dillon M.	Assoc	So Dakota St	Q	PHD	90	Colo St	1990
Feyzioglu, Tarhan	Asst	Georgetown		PHD	90	Penn	
Fichtenbaum, Rudy H.	Prof	Wright State		PHD	80	Missouri	1980
Field, Alexander J.	Prof	Santa Clara		PHD	74	Berkeley	1982
Field, Alfred J.	Prof	No Carolina		PHD	67	Iowa St	1967
Field, William Joseph	Prof	DePauw		PHD	80	Michigan	1979
Field, William P. Jr.	Prof	Nicholls St	E	PHD	71	N Carol	1973
Field-Hendrey, Elizabeth	Asst	CUNY-Queens	NJC	PHD	85	Duke	1989
Fielding, Gordon J.	Prof	Calif-Irvine		PHD	62	UCLA	1965
Fielding, William	C-Pr	Jacksonvl St		PHD		S Carol	1968
Fields, Judith M.	Asst	CUNY-Lehman		PHD	84	NYU	1984
Fields, T. Windsor	H-Pr	Jms Madison	EC	PHD	78	Virginia	1990
Figart, Deborah M.	Assoc	E Michigan		PHD	86	American	1990
Figgins, Bob G.	C-Pr	Tenn-Martin		PHD	73	Arkansas	1973
Figlio, David N.	Asst	Oregon	HR	PHD	95	Wisconsin	1995
Fikkert, Brian	Asst	Maryland		PHD	94	Yale	1994
Filer, Randall K.	Assoc	CUNY-Hunter		PHD	79	Princeton	1986
Filson, Darren	VInst	St John Fshr	L	ABD		Rochester	1995
Finch, Eugene B.	Retir	Kean		PHD		Syracuse	9-69
Fincher, Phillip E.	Assoc	Louisiana Te		PHD		Miss	1964
Findlay, David W.	Assoc	Colby	EGA	PHD	86	Purdue	1985
Finegan, T. Aldrich	Prof	Vanderbilt	J	PHD	60	Chicago	1970
Finifter, David H.	Prof	Wm & Mary		PHD	74	Pittsburgh	1973
Finley, Henry E.	Retir	Florida A&M		PHD		Indiana	1959
Finn, Daniel Rush	Assoc	St Benedict		PHD	77	Chicago	1977
Clemens Chair in Economics and the Liberal Arts-Dean, School of Theology							
Finn, Thomas J. Jr.	Prof	Wayne State		PHD	59	Harvard	1963
Finney, Miles	Asst	CS-L Angeles					
Finster, Ronald D.	Prof	W Oregon St		PHD	70	Arizona	1971
Finucane, Brendan P.	C-Pr	Shippensburg		PHD		Pittsburgh	1982
Fiorentino, Christopher M.	Dean	West Chester	DQ	PHD	89	Temple	9-85
Firoozi, Fathall K.	Assoc	Tx-S Antonio	CF	PHD	87	Oklahoma	1988
First, Ramona K.	Retir	San Fran St		PHD	49	Wisconsin	1956
Fischbaum, Marvin N.	Prof	Indiana St	DP	PHD	65	Columbia	1965
Fischel, William Alan	Prof	Dartmouth		PHD	73	Princeton	1973
Fischer, Charles C.	C-Pr	Pittsburg St	BJ	PHD	75	Wash St	1974
Fischer, Hartmut	Prof	San Francisc		PHD	73	Berkeley	1970
Fischer, Stanley	Prof	MIT	G	PHD	69	MIT	
Fischmar, Daniel E.	Prof	Westminst-PA		PHD		S Illinois	1975
Fish, Barry A.	Dean	E Michigan		PHD	71	Wayne St	1970
Fish, Mary	Prof	Alabama		PHD	63	Oklahoma	1965
Fishback, Price V.	Prof	Arizona		PHD	83	U Wash	1990
Fishbaugh, Charles P.	Retir	New Orleans	1995	PHD	66	Indiana	1967

Fishe, Raymond P. H.	Prof	U Miami	CD	PHD	79	Florida	1981
Fisher, Douglas	Prof	N Carol St	EN	PHD	65	Chicago	1977
Fisher, Eric O.	Asst	Ohio State	F	PHD	85	Berkeley	1993
Fisher, Franklin M.	Prof	MIT	P	PHD	60	Harvard	1960
Fisher, Robert B.	Prof	CS-Chico		PHD		Oregon	1968
Fisher, Ronald C.	Prof	Michigan St		PHD	77	Brown	1976
Fisher, Walter	Asst	Kansas State	EFC	PHD	90	U Wash	1992
Fisher, Warren L.	H-Pr	Susquehanna	ABQ	PHD	73	Conn	1988
Fishlow, Albert	Prof	Cal-Berkeley		PHD	63	Harvard	1983
Fitzgerald, John M.	C-Ac	Bowdoin	HC	PHD	83	Wisconsin	1983
Fitzgerald, Patrick W.	Prof	Okla City		PHD	79	Tx-Austin	1982
Fitzpatrick, Ellen	Asst	SUNY-Plattsb	FOQ	PHD	94	Mich St	1994
FitzRandolph, Peter Winfield	Assoc	St Lawrence	FN	PHD	79	Tufts	1973
Fitzsimmons, Edward L.	Assoc	Creighton	AD	PHD	84	Nebraska	1984
Fizel, John L.	Assoc	Penn St-Erie	L	PHD	81	Mich St	1985
Flaherty, Diane P.	Assoc	Massachusett		PHD	78		
Flaherty, Sean	Assoc	Frank & Mars	J	PHD	81	Berkeley	1980
Flammang, Robert A.	Prof	SW Texas St		PHD	62	Iowa	1991
Flanagan, Edward J.	Retir	Bradley		PHD	69	Mich St	1963
Flath, David	Prof	N Carol St	LDP	PHD	76	UCLA	1976
Flavin, Marjorie A.	Assoc	Ca-San Diego	E	PHD	81	MIT	1992
Flax, Stanley	Asst	St Thomas-FL		MBA		NYU	1986
Fleisher, Belton M.	Prof	Ohio State	J	PHD	61	Stanford	1965
Fleissig, Adrian R.	Asst	Tx-Arlington	O	PHD	93	N Carol	1993
Fleming, Garry A.	Assoc	Roanoke		PHD	87	Kentucky	
Fletcher, Daniel O.	Retir	Denison		PHD	60	Michigan	1966
Fletcher, Jean W.	Assoc	Gettysburg	AJD	PHD	83	Wash U	1986
Fletcher, Jerald J.	Assoc	W Virginia	Q	PHD	82	Berkeley	1989
Fletcher, Lehman B.	Prof	Iowa State	O	PHD	69	Berkeley	1960
Flinn, Christopher	Assoc	New York U		PHD	84	Chicago	
Flint, Harold	Prof	Montclair St	AEGP	PHD	72	S Illinois	1971
Flores, Nicholas E.	Asst	Colorado		PHD	95	Ca-SnDgo	1995
Flores, Oscar	Assoc	Moorhead St		PHD	90	Cincinnati	1989
Floro, Maria Sagrario	Asst	American U		PHD		Stanford	1988
Flory-Truett, Lila J.	D-Pr	Tx-S Antonio	DFMO	PHD	72	Iowa	1975
Flowers, Edward B.	Assoc	St John's		PHD		Geo St	
Flowers, Marilyn	Prof	Ball State		PHD	74	Va Tech	1990
Flueckiger, Gerald E.	Prof	Miami U-Ohio	CD	PHD	70	Purdue	1968
Flyer, Frederick A.	Asst	New York U	DJ	PHD	93	Chicago	1993
Flynn, Dennis O.	C-Pr	Pacific	DENO	PHD	77	Utah	1979
Foeller, William H.	Prof	SUNY-Fredoni	AJ	PHD	72	Iowa St	1984
Fogarty, Michael S.	Prof	Case Western	RO	PHD	75	Pittsburgh	1986
Fogel, Robert W.	Prof	Chicago		PHD	63	J Hopkins	1981
Charles R. Walgreen Professor/Director, Center for Population Economics							
Fohlin, Caroline	Asst	Cal Tech	NFL	PHD	94	Berkeley	1994
Folbre, Nancy	Prof	Massachusett		PHD	79	Mass	1985
Foley, Duncan K.	Prof	Barnard		PHD	66	Yale	1977
Foley, James W.	Assoc	U Miami	O	PHD	69	Mich St	1968
Foley, Michael	Asst	Reed	ANQ	ABD		Michigan	1992
Follain, James R.	Prof	Syracuse		PHD	76	Ca-Davis	1988
Folland, Sherman T.	Assoc	Oakland	IB	PHD	74	Iowa	1986
Folsom, Davis	Assoc	So Car-Aiken		PHD	79	Conn	1979
Folsom, Roger Nils	Prof	San Jose St		PHD	73	Claremont	1976
Fomby, Thomas	Assoc	So Methodist		PHD	75	Missouri	1975
Fon, Vincy	Asst	George Wash	CD	PHD	81	Kansas	1979
Fong, Tat P.	Asst	Westminst-PA		PHD		Pittsburgh	1993
Foran, Terry G.	Assoc	So Illinois	J	PHD	71	Penn St	1970
Forbes, Kevin F.	Assoc	Catholic		PHD	82	Maryland	1983
Forbus, Philip R.	Assoc	So Alabama	AD	PHD	78	Arkansas	1978
Ford, Edward J. Jr.	Assoc	South Fla	R	PHD	71	Boston C	1971
Ford, Richard	Prof	Ark-Ltl Rock		PHD	79	Arkansas	1981
Ford, William s.	Prof	Mid Tenn St		PHD	66	Michigan	1991
Weatherford Chair							
Formby, John P.	Prof	Alabama		PHD	65	Colorado	1982
Hayes Professor of Economics							
Forstater, Mathew B.	Inst	Gettysburg	ABF	ABD		New Sch	1992
Forster, Bruce A.	Dean	Wyoming	EQ	PHD	74	Austrlia	1987
Forsythe, Robert	Prof	Iowa		PHD	75	Car Mellon	1981
Fort, Rodney D.	Assoc	Wash State		PHD	85	Cal Tech	1984
Forti, Annette	Prof	SUNY Old Wes		PHD		Fordham	
Fortunato, Michael		SUNY-Empire	OMF	PHD		Harvard	1990
Fortune, Peter	Prof	Tufts		PHD	72	Harvard	1977
Foshee, Andrew W.	Prof	McNeese St		PHD	80	LSU	1978
Foss, Robert K.	Asst	Concordia C		MS		N Dakota	1988
Foster, Edward M.	Prof	Minnesota		PHD	61	MIT	1983
Foster, James E.	Prof	Vanderbilt	DG	PHD	82	Cornell	1990
Foster, Mark	Inst	No Alabama		MA	91	Alabama	1992
Fosu, Augustin K.	Prof	Oakland	JOC	PHD	79	Northwes	1979
Fosu, Joseph	Assoc	W Illinois	AEO	PHD	87	Iowa St	1987
Fountain, Gwen A.	Assoc	Butler	A	PHD	72	Michigan	1976

Name	Rank	Institution	Fields	Degree	Yr	Degree Inst	Yr
Fournier, Gary M.	Assoc	Florida St		PHD	81	Virginia	1980
Foust, James D.	Assoc	Indianapolis		PHD	68	N Carol	1985
Fowles, Richard G.	Assoc	Utah		PHD	85	Utah	1990
Fox, Eugene H.	Prof	NE Louisiana		PHD	62	Alabama	1965
Fox, Jerrald Mark	Asst	CUNY-Brookly	J	PHD		Harvard	1988
Fox, Nancy R.	Asst	St Joseph		PHD	89	Penn	1986
Fox, Pauline H.	Prof	SE Missouri		PHD	75	Okla St	1978
Fox, Thomas G.	Prof	Penn State	A	PHD	66	Syracuse	1966
Fox, William F.	C-Pr	Tennessee		PHD	75	Ohio St	1979
Fraedrich, Ann I.	Asst	Marquette		PHD	90	Purdue	1989
France, Robert R.	Prof	Rochester		PHD		Princeton	
Francis, Clark II	Prof	CUNY-Baruch		PHD	66	Wash	
Francis, Gary E.	Prof	CS-Chico	ABGH	PHD	72	Colorado	1967
Franck, Raymond	H	USAF Academy		PHD		Harvard	
Frangul, Ramzi N.	Assoc	Sacred Heart		PHD		NYU	
Frank, Robert H.	Prof	Cornell		PHD	72	Berkeley	1972
Frankel, Jeffrey A.	Prof	Cal-Berkeley		PHD	78	MIT	1979
Franklin, Douglas R.	Assoc	So Dakota St	Q	PHD	82	Utah	1988
Franklin, Raymond S.	Prof	CUNY-Queens	JBP	PHD	66	Berkeley	1966
Franko, Patrice	Assoc	Colby	FAO	PHD	86	Notre Dm	1986
Frantz, Roger S.	Prof	San Diego St		PHD		Wash St	1978
Franz, Wolfgang W.	Prof	Central Wash	HJK	PHD	70	Wash St	1969
Distinguished Professor, Public Service (1987)							
Frasca, Ralph R.	C-Ac	Dayton	A	PHD	75	Indiana	1972
Frascatore, Mark	Asst	Clarkson	DHL	PHD	94	Va Tech	1994
Fratantuono, Michael J.	Asst	Dickinson Cl	E	PHD	88	Wash	1988
Fraumeni, Barbara M.	Prof	Northeastern		PHD	80	Boston C	1982
Fraundorf, Martha	Assoc	Oregon State	J	PHD	76	Cornell	9-76
Frazier, Patricia A.	Prof	Norfolk St		PHD		Clemson	1994
Frech, H. E. III	Prof	Cal-Santa Br	LAI	PHD	74	UCLA	1973
Frederick, James R.	Asst	Pembroke St		PHD	83	Wayne St	1988
Frederiksen, Peter		Naval Postgr					
Fredland, John E.	C-Pr	USN Academy		PHD	70	Michigan	1974
Fredrickson, Trygve G.	Inst	So Dakota St	M	MBA	89	S Dakota	1990
Free, Rhona C.	Assoc	Eastern Conn		PHD	83	Notre Dm	1983
Free, Veronica	Prof	No Alabama		PHD	70	Miss St	1984
Freed, Jann E.	C-Ac	Central Iowa		PHD		Iowa St	1981
Freed, Rodney Alan	Prof	CS-Dominguez	ACR	PHD	77	Virginia	1979
Freeman, Albert Myrick III	Prof	Bowdoin	QD	PHD	65	U Wash	1965
William Shipman Professor of Economics							
Freeman, James	Prof	Columbia		MBA	70	Penn	1991
Freeman, Katherine	Assoc	Denver		PHD		Fla St	
Freeman, Richard B.	Prof	Harvard					
Herbert S. Ascherman Professor of Economics							
Freeman, Scott	Assoc	Texas	E	PHD	83	Minnesota	9-91
Freiberg, Lewis	Prof	NE Illinois		PHD	72	Kentucky	1982
Freudenberger, Herman	Prof	Tulane		PHD	57	Columbia	
Frevert, Peter	Assoc	Kansas		PHD		Purdue	1964
Frew, James R.	C-Ac	Willamette		PHD	79	Purdue	1984
Frey, Donald E.	Prof	Wake Forest		PHD	72	Princeton	1972
Fried, Harold O.	Assoc	Union	CIL	PHD	78	N Carol	1983
Friedberg, Rachel	Asst	Brown		PHD	93	MIT	
Friedman, Benjamin M.	Prof	Harvard		PHD	71	Harvard	1972
William Joseph Maier Professor of Political Economy							
Friedman, Daniel	Prof	Ca-Santa Crz	FG	PHD	77	Ca-SnCrz	1979
Friedman, Gerald	Assoc	Massachusett		PHD	86	Harvard	1984
Friedman, Hershey	Prof	CUNY-Brookly	M	PHD		CUNY	1986
Friedman, James W.	Prof	No Carolina		PHD	63	Yale	1985
Kenan Professor							
Friedman, Milton	Emer	Chicago		PHD	46	Columbia	1946
Friedman, Richard	Assoc	CS-Northrdge		ABD		CUNY	1961
Friedrich, Joseph	Prof	St Benedict		MA	70	Wisconsin	1967
Frost, Maria J.	VAsst	Emory Henry		PHD		London	
Frost, Peter S.	Prof	U Washington		PHD	66	UCLA	1969
Froyen, Richard T.	Prof	No Carolina		PHD	72	Maryland	1971
Frydman, Roman	Assoc	New York U		PHD	78	Columbia	1983
Fryman, Richard F.	C-Pr	West Georgia	AH	PHD	67	Illinois	1986
Fuchs, Victor R.	Emer	Stanford		PHD	55	Columbia	1974
Fudenberg, Drew D.	Prof	Harvard		PHD	81	MIT	1987
Fuentes, Gabriel	Asst	Loyola Marym	DLO	PHD	94	Berkeley	1994
Fuerst, Timothy S.	Asst	Bowling Gr		PHD	90	Chicago	1993
Fuess, Scott M.	Assoc	Nebraska	J	PHD	86	Purdue	1986
Fugar, Christian	Asst	Dillard		PHD			
Fuhr, Joseph P.	Prof	Widener	DIKQ	PHD	81	Temple	1979
Fujii, Edwin T.	Deces	Hawaii-Manoa		PHD	73	Stanford	
Fukasawa, Yoshikazu	Dean	Midwest St	EF	PHD	79	Kansas St	1978
Fuller, Dan A.	Prof	Weber State	ADH	PHD	82	N Carol	1981
Fuller, John W.	Prof	Iowa		PHD	68	Wash St	1979
Fuller, Rex D.	Dean	Wis-La Cross	JM	PHD	82	Utah	1981

Name	Rank	School	Fields	Degree	Yr	Degree School	Since
Fullerton, Don	Prof	Texas	HQ	PHD	78	Berkeley	9-94
Addison Baker Duncan Centennial Professor of Economics							
Fullerton, Herbert H.	Prof	Utah State	OQR	PHD	71	Iowa St	1969
Fullerton, Richard L.	Asst	USAF Academy		PHD		Tx-Austin	
Fulton, Betty	Prof	SE Missouri	P	PHD		Missouri	1968
Funderburk, Dale R.	Prof	East Txs St	IDEF	PHD	71	Okla St	1968
Fung, Kwok-Chiu	Assoc	Ca-Santa Crz	F	PHD	70	Wisconsin	1989
Fung, Kwok-Kwan	Prof	Memphis		PHD	70	Harvard	1975
Funk, Herbert J.	Emer	Creighton	AC	PHD	64	Iowa St	1967
Funkhouser, Ed	Asst	Cal-Santa Br	OJ	PHD	90	Harvard	1992
Furfero, Arlene J.	Assoc	St John's		PHD		Rutgers	
Furubotn, Eirik G.	Prof	Tx-Arlington	DNB	PHD	59	Columbia	1982
Eunice & James L. West Chair							
Futayyeh, Mohamed-Amin	Asst	NE Louisiana		PHD		Oklahoma	
Futrell, Gene Allen	Deces	Iowa State	1994	PHD	64	Ohio St	1964
Gabel, David J.	Assoc	CUNY-Queens	DNC	PHD	87	Wisconsin	1987
Gabel, Landis	C-Pr	INSEAD	D	PHD	77	Penn	9-82
Gabriel, Albert H.	Retir	SW Okla St		PHD	65	Mich St	1956
Gabriel, Paul E.	Asst	Loyola-Chicg		PHD	87	Kentucky	1990
Gabriel, Satyananda Jordan	Asst	Mt Holyoke		PHD		Mass	
Gade, Mary N.	Assoc	Oklahoma St		PHD	86	Mich St	1986
Gaertner, Robert C.	Assoc	Lk Superior	DM	MBA	65	Norte Dm	1-70
Gafar, John S.	C-Pr	Lg Isl-Post		PHD	79	W Indies	1980
Gaffney, M. Mason	Prof	Cal-Riversid	AHR	PHD	56	Berkeley	1976
Gahala, Charles L.	Prof	IL Benedict	MG	EDD	83	N Illinois	1984
Galbreath, George T.	Retir	CS-Pomona		MA	49	Stanford	1953
Galchus, Kenneth	Prof	Ark-Ltl Rock		PHD	70	Wash U	1976
Gale, Douglas	Prof	Boston Univ	DEG	PHD	75	Cambridg	
Gale, James R.	Prof	Mich Tech	E	PHD	72	Iowa	1971
Gale, Louis	Asst	SW Louisiana		PHD	94	Ariz St	1995
Galenson, David W.	Prof	Chicago		PHD	79	Harvard	1978
Gallagher, Daniel J.	Prof	St Cloud St		PHD	76	Maryland	1982
Gallant, A. Ronald	Prof	No Carolina		PHD			
Latane' Professor							
Gallaway, Lowell	Prof	Ohio Univ		PHD	59	Ohio St	1967
Distinguished Professor							
Gallegos, Alejandro	Assoc	Winona State		PHD	86	Wi-Milw	1988
Galles, Gary M.	Assoc	Pepper-Malib	AHLR	PHD	88	UCLA	1982
Gallet, Craig	Asst	Allegheny	CDL	PHD	94	Iowa St	1994
Gallman, Robert E.	Prof	No Carolina		PHD	56	Penn	1962
Kenan Professor							
Gallo, David E.	Prof	CS-Chico	AEHQ	PHD		Oregon	1970
Gallo, Joseph C.	C-Pr	Cincinnati	L	PHD	69	Missouri	
Gallup, Lanny W.	Retir	Okla City		MS	63	Okla St	1964
Galor, Oded	Prof	Brown		PHD	84	Columbia	1986
Galster, George C.	Prof	Wooster		PHD	74	MIT	1974
Gamba, Maria V.	Asst	Findlay	AD	MS		Wright St	1988
Gamber, Edward N.	Asst	Lafayette		PHD	86	Va Tech	
Gamble, Ralph C. Jr.	C-Pr	Fort Hays St	AEG	PHD	89	Okla St	1984
Gambles, Glenn C.	Prof	CS-Sacrament		PHD		Maryland	1969
Gandar, John Maxim	Assoc	N Car-Charl		PHD		Missouri	1982
Gander, James P.	Prof	Utah		PHD	66	Berkeley	1965
Ganderton, Philip	Assoc	New Mexico	CHIQ	PHD	89	Ca-SnBarb	1989
Gandhi, Prem P.	Dean	SUNY-Plattsb	FO	PHD	73	New Sch	9-66
Gang, Ira N.	Assoc	Rutgers-N Br	O	PHD	83	Cornell	1986
Gangnes, Byron S.	Asst	Hawaii-Manoa		PHD	90	Penn	1990
Gapinski, James H.	Prof	Florida St		PHD	71	SUNY-Buf	1979
Garber, Peter M.	Prof	Brown		PHD	77	Chicago	1985
Garcia, Javier	Assoc	Ashland		JD		Akron	1980
Gardner, B. Delworth	Retir	Brigham Yg		PHD	60	Chicago	1986
Gardner, H. Stephen	Prof	Baylor		PHD	78	Berkeley	1978
Herman Brown Professor of Economics							
Gardner, Mark L.	Prof	Piedmont		PHD	85	Geo St	1979
Gardner, Roy J.	Prof	Indiana		PHD	75	Cornell	1983
Gardner, Wayland D.	Prof	W Michigan	H	PHD	58	Wisconsin	1964
Garen, John E.	Prof	Kentucky	J	PHD	82	Ohio St	1982
Garfinkel, Michelle	Asst	Calif-Irvine		PHD	88	Brown	1991
Gargalas, Vasilios	Asst	Bridgeport		PHD		NYU	1993
Garhart, Robert E. Jr.	Assoc	St Thomas-MN	R	PHD	82	Pittsburgh	1981
Garlick, Peter C.	Prof	SUNY-N Paltz	BEHN	PHD	72	London	1969
Garlin, Victor A.	Prof	Sonoma State		PHD	65	Berkeley	1970
Garman, David M.	C-Ac$	Tufts		PHD	89	Michigan	1983
Garnel, Donald	Prof	San Jose St		PHD	66	Berkeley	1958
Garofalo, Gasper A.	Prof	Akron		PHD	74	Pittsburgh	1979
Garratt, Rodney J.	Asst	Cal-Santa Br	AEH	PHD	91	Cornell	1991
Garrett, John R.	Assoc	Tenn-Chattan	EFG	PHD	85	Mass	1984
UC Foundation Associate Professor							
Garrett, Martin A.	Prof	Wm & Mary		PHD	66	Vanderbilt	1963
Garrison, Ann J.	Assoc	No Colorado	HITR	MA		N Colo	1966
Garrison, Charles B.	Prof	Tennessee		PHD	68	Kentucky	

Garrison, Roger W.	Assoc	Auburn		PHD	81	Virginia	1983
Garrison, Sharon H.	Prof	East Tenn St		PHD	83	Tx-Arlin	1986
Garston, Neil H.	C-Pr	CS-L Angeles		PHD	73	Brown	1975
Garvin, Alexander	Prof	Indiana U-PA	CE	PHD	73	Tennessee	1969
Gashugi, Leonard K.	Prof	Andrews	CF	PHD		Boston U	1979
Gaston, Noel G.	Assoc	Tulane		PHD	88	Cornell	
Gately, Dermot	Prof	New York U		PHD	71	Princeton	1973
Gates, William R.		Naval Postgr		PHD	74	Yale	1988
Gaty, Lewis R. II	C-Pr	Hartwick	ADEQ	MS		Stanford	1975
Gau, Carolina	Prof	Alcorn State		PHD		Missouri	
Gau, Paul K.	Prof	Alcorn State		PHD	71	Illinois	1972
Gauger, Jean A.	Assoc	Tennessee		PHD	84	Iowa St	1985
Gawande, Kishore	Asst	New Mexico	CEFP	PHD	91	UCLA	1991
Gay, David E.	Prof	Arkansas	H	PHD	73	Tx A&M	1983
Gaynor, Patricia	Prof	Appalach St	M	PHD	74	Miami	1976
Gazel, Richard	Asst	Nev-L Vegas		PHD	93	Illinois	1993
Geanakoplos, John	Prof	Yale					
Gebremariam, Yilma	Assoc	So Conn St		PHD	89	S Calif	1990
Geddes, Raymond R.	Asst	Fordham		PHD	91	Chicago	1991
Gedeon, Shirley J.	Assoc	Vermont	EP	PHD	82	Mass	1981
Gegax, Douglas A.	Assoc	New Mex St		PHD	84	Wyoming	1984
Geide-Stevenson, Doris	Asst	SUNY-Buffalo	DF	PHD	95	SUNY-Buf	1995
Geile, Gerald L.	Inst	SW Missouri		MA	91	St Louis	1991
Geiss, Charles G.	Assoc	Missouri	C	PHD	74	N Carol	1972
Geisst, Charles R.	Assoc	Manhattan		PHD		London	1985
Gelles, Gregory	Assoc	Mo-Rolla		PHD		W Virginia	1989
Gemello, John M.	Prof	San Fran St		PHD	74	Stanford	1975
Gemery, Henry A.	Prof	Colby	NAB	PHD	67	Penn	1961
Pugh Family Professor of Economics							
Gemmill, Robert M.	Assoc	Gettysburg	AEG	ABD		Northwes	1958
Gendel, Eugene B.	Assoc	Woodbury	J	PHD	79	Boston U	7-94
Genesove, David J.	Asst	MIT	O	PHD	91	Princeton	1991
Gensemer, Bruce L.	Prof	Kenyon		PHD	66	Michigan	
Gensemer, Susan H.	Assoc	Syracuse		PHD	84	Purdue	
Gentenaar, Robert	Assoc	Hope	EC	PHD	77	Mich St	1977
Gentry, William M.	Asst	Duke		PHD	91	Princeton	1990
Geodde, Richard	Asst	St Olaf	M	MBA		Wisconsin	1988
George, Carolyn	Asst	Campbell		PHD		Tennessee	1995
George, David L.	Assoc	LaSalle	ABN	PHD	84	Temple	1979
George, Nashwa E.	Asst	CUNY-Hunter		PHD	88	Baruch	9-85
Georges, Christophre	Asst	Hamilton	EJB	PHD	89	Michigan	1989
Georgianna, Daniel L.	Prof	Mass-Dartmou		PHD	77	Mass	1977
Georgiou, George C.	Prof	Towson State		PHD	79	Geo Wash	1980
Geraci, Vincent J.	Prof	Texas	CI	PHD	74	Wisconsin	9-73
Gerber, James B.	Assoc	San Diego St		PHD	86	Ca-Davis	1985
Gerdes, Eugenia Proctor	Dean	Bucknell		PHD		Duke	1974
Gerdes, William D.	Prof	N Dakota St	CEG	PHD	78	Nebraska	1978
Geriowski, Daniel A.	Assoc	Baltimore		PHD		Pittsburgh	
Gerking, Shelby D.	Prof	Wyoming	RC	PHD	75	Indiana	1978
Gernant, Paul L.	Retir	Ferris State		PHD		Michigan	1979
Gerring, Lori F.	Asst	Xavier	ACEM	PHD	84	Cincinnati	1989
Gershenberg, Irving	Prof	Mass-Boston	O	PHD	67	Berkeley	1982
Gersich, Frank	Assoc	Gustavus Ado		EDD	93	N Illinois	1984
Gerson, Janet	Lect	Michigan					
Gersovitz, Mark	Prof	J Hopkins		PHD	75	Yale	1994
Geruson, Richard T.	C-Ac	LaSalle	TR	PHD	73	Penn	1958
Gery, Frank W.	Prof	St Olaf		PHD	57	Boston U	1962
Getter, Darryl	Asst	USN Academy		PHD	94	Wash U	1994
Getz, Malcolm	Assoc	Vanderbilt	HR	PHD	73	Yale	1973
Geweke, John F.	Prof	Minnesota		PHD	75	Minnesota	1990
Geyikdogi, Yasar	Prof	SUNY Old Wes		PHD		Bath	
Gharrity, Norman J.	Prof	Ohio Wesley		PHD	66	J Hopkins	1962
Ghazalah, Ismail A.	Prof	Ohio Univ	DFHI	PHD	69	Berkeley	1969
Ghazanfar, Shaikh M.	H-Pr	Idaho	HO	PHD	69	Wash St	1968
Ghebrat, Ezra	Assoc	Jersey City	AD	PHD		New Sch	
Ghebreyesus, Ghirmay	Asst	Grambling St		PHD		Strathcl	1990
Ghebreyohannes, Keleta	Assoc	Grambling St		PHD		Colo St	9-81
Ghent, Linda	VAsst	East Carol		PHD	92	N Car St	1993
Gherity, James A.	Prof	No Illinois		PHD	58	Illinois	1964
Ghiara, Ranjetta		CS-S Marcos		PHD			
Ghilarducci, Teresa	Assoc	Notre Dame	J	PHD	84	Berkeley	1983
Ghirardato, Paolo	Asst	Cal Tech	D	PHD	95	Berkeley	1995
Ghorashi, Gholam-Reza	C-Ac	R Stockton		PHD		Fordham	1981
Ghosal, Vivek	Asst	Miami U-Ohio	DE	PHD	88	Florida	1990
Ghose, Devajyoti	Asst	Arizona		PHD	90	Ca-SnDgo	1990
Ghosh, Arabinda	Assoc	Wm Patterson		PHD	72	CUNY	1984
Ghosh, Satyajit P.	C-Ac	Scranton		PHD	86	SUNY-Buf	1986
Ghosh, Soumendra	Assoc	New Mex St		PHD	87	Utah St	1988
Ghosh, Stanley	Prof	Hawaii Pacif		PHD		Indiana	
Ghoshal, Animesh	Prof	DePaul		PHD	74	Michigan	1981

Giacalone, Joseph A.	Assoc	St John's		PHD	71	Columbia	1985
Giamartino, Gary A.	Dean	Wilkes	M	PHD	79	Vanderbilt	7-93
Giannakouros, George	Prof	Loras		PHD	74	Iowa	1966
Giannoros, Demetrios	Prof	Hartford		PHD	81	Boston U	
Giarratani, Frank	C-Pr	Pittsburgh	R	PHD	75	W Virginia	1979
Gibb, Arthur Jr.	Assoc	USN Academy		PHD		Michigan	1974
Gibbens, John M.	Retir	Wis-Whitewat		PHD	64	Iowa St	1961
Gibbons, Donna M.	Asst	Carleton		PHD	95	Brown	1993
Gibbs, W. Ernest	Assoc	Cen Florida	D	PHD		Rutgers	1987
Gibson, Eleanor	Asst	Bloomfield		MA		Columbia	1965
Gibson, Jo Anne	Assoc	SE Louisiana	EF	PHD		Miss	
Gibson, William A.	Prof	Vermont	CFOQ	PHD	77	Berkeley	1986
Gidwani, Sushila J.	Assoc	Manhattan		PHD	64	Minnesota	1965
Giertz, J. Fred	Prof	Illinois		PHD	70	Northwes	1980
Giesber, Frank W.	C-Pr	Tx Lutheran	A	PHD	78	Tx-Austin	1966
Giesbrecht, Martin G.	Prof	No Kentucky		PHD	58	Munich	1987
Giesecke, Leonard F.	Deces	Southwestern		PHD	75	Tx-Austin	1968
Gieske, Michael	Prof	Winona State		BS		Iowa St	1972
Giffin, Phillip E.	Prof	Tenn-Chattan	DBLN	PHD	72	Tennessee	1977
Gifford, Adam Jr.	Prof	CS-Northrdge		PHD	72	Ca-SnDgo	1975
Gift, Richard E.	Prof	Kentucky	FB	PHD	65	Duke	1965
Gigliotti, Gary A.	Prof	Rutgers-N Br	D	PHD	78	Columbia	1978
Gilbert, Howard A.	Prof	So Dakota St	A	PHD	67	Oreg St	1966
Gilbert, Richard J.	Prof	Cal-Berkeley		PHD	76	Stanford	1976
Gilbert, Ronald D.	Assoc	Texas Tech		PHD	70	Okla St	1977
Gilbert, Roy F.	Assoc	Texas A&M		PHD	69	Mich St	1970
Gilbreath, L. Kent	Prof	Baylor		PHD	71	Florida	1973
Stevens Professor of Private Enterprise							
Gilchrist, Simon	Asst	Boston Univ	C	PHD	90	Wisconsin	1995
Gildea, John A.	Assoc	Wheaton-MA	EG	PHD	85	Duke	1985
Gill, Andrew M.	Assoc	CS-Fullerton		PHD	85	Wash St	1984
Gilles, Robert P.	Asst	Virg Tech	D	PHD	90	Tilburg	1991
Gilles, William	Retir	Nebraska		EDE	73	Nebraska	1963
Gillespie, Judith	Dean	SUNY-Albany					
Gillespie, Robert W.	Emer	Illinois		PHD	61	MIT	1960
Gillette, David H.	Asst	NE Missouri		PHD		Wash St	1990
Gillette, Robert	Assoc	Kentucky	A	PHD	86	Tx A&M	1994
Gilley, Otis W.	Prof	Louisiana Te		PHD	79	Purdue	1988
Gilliam, John Charles	Prof	Texas Tech		PHD	59	Iowa	1962
Gilliam, Kenneth P.	Assoc	Kennesaw St	ACD	PHD	76	Lehigh	1984
Gilliam, Lynde O.	Assoc	Metro St-CO		PHD		Colo St	
Gillis, Malcolm	Prof	Rice					
Gilsdorf, Keith F.	C-As	Morningside	LJ	PHD	90	Nebraska	1994
Gilson, Preston	Asst	Fort Hays St		PHD	93	St Louis	1988
Gin, Alan	Assoc	San Diego		PHD	87	Ca-SnBarb	1988
Gindling, Thomas	Asst	MD-Baltim Co		PHD	87		
Ginsburg, Helen	Prof	CUNY-Brookly	J	PHD		New Sch	1977
Ginther, Donna	Asst	So Methodist		PHD	95	Wisconsin	1995
Gintis, Herbert M.	Prof	Massachusett		PHD	69	Harvard	1975
Giordano, James N.	Asst	Villanova		PHD	82	Indiana	1983
Giordano, Justin		SUNY-Empire	M	MBA		St Johns	1992
Giovannini, Alberto	Assoc	Columbia		PHD	83	MIT	1983
Girton, Lance	Prof	Utah		PHD	76	Chicago	1978
Gishlick, Herbert E.	Prof	Rider	ER	PHD	73	Penn	1964
Gisser, Micha	Prof	New Mexico	ADLQ	PHD	62	Chicago	1973
Gissy, William G.	Asst	Morehouse		PHD		Geo St	1988
Gitter, Robert J.	Prof	Ohio Wesley		PHD	78	Wisconsin	1976
Giunta, A. John	Retir	Scranton		PHD		Syracuse	1960
Gius, Mark P.	Asst	Quinnipiac		PHD	91	Penn St	1994
Glade, William P. Jr.	Prof	Texas	OR	PHD	55	Tx-Austin	9-70
Glaeser, Edward	Asst	Harvard					
Glahe, Fred R.	Prof	Colorado		PHD	64	Purdue	1965
Glass, Amy J.	Asst	Ohio State	F	PHD	93	Penn	1993
Glazer, Amihai	C-Pr	Calif-Irvine		PHD	78	Yale	1978
Gleason, Joyce G.	Asst	Nebraska Wes		PHD	86	Nebraska	
Gleicher, David	C-Ac	Adelphi	BJ	PHD	84	Columbia	1981
Gleisner, Richard F.	Prof	St Cloud St		PHD	72	Geotown	1968
Glendening, Richard N.	Prof	Central Iowa	EFHO	PHD	93	Iowa St	1966
Glenn, Kirsta	Asst	Cen Arkansas		PHD	93	Vanderbilt	8-95
Glezakos, Constantine	Prof	CS-Long Bch		PHD	70	S Calif	1968
Glick, Lee	Retir	Duquesne		PHD		Pittsburgh	
Glick, Mark	Prof	Utah		PHD	85	New Sch	1985
Gliderbloom, John	Assoc	Louisville		PHD	83	Ca-SnBarb	
Glomm, Gerhard	Assoc	Michigan St		PHD	88	Minnesota	1995
Glosser, Stuart M.	Asst	Wis-Whitewat		PHD	85	Tx-Austin	1985
Glover, Terrence F.	Prof	Utah State	DCQ	PHD	71	Purdue	1974
Glustoff, E.	Assoc	Tennessee		PHD		Stanford	
Gnuschke, John E.	Prof	Memphis		PHD	75	Missouri	1976
Gobin, Roy T.	Assoc	Loyola-Chicg		PHD		Illinois	1978
Goddard, Frederick O.	Assoc	Florida		PHD	67	Duke	1966

Goddard, Haynes C.	Assoc	Cincinnati	H	PHD	70	Indiana	
Goddeeris, John H.	Prof	Michigan St		PHD	80	Wisconsin	1980
Godfrey, E. Bruce	Prof	Utah State	Q	PHD	71	Oreg St	1977
Goel, Rajeev Kumar	Assoc	Illinois St	CO	PHD	87	Houston	1989
Goering, Gregory	Assoc	Alaska-Fairb		PHD	90	Purdue	1990
Goetz, Michael	Assoc	Temple	MH	PHD	77	Minnesota	1978
Goff, Brian L.	Assoc	W Kentucky	GHK	PHD	86	Geo Mason	1986
Goffe, William L.	Asst	So Miss	C	PHD	90	N Carol	1993
Gohmann, Stephan F.	Assoc	Louisville		PHD	84	N Car St	1988
Gokturk, S. Sadik	Assoc	St John's		PHD		Columbia	
Golbe, Devra L.	Assoc	CUNY-Hunter		PHD	79	NYU	1987
Goldberg, Kalman	Prof	Bradley		PHD	54	Cornell	1952
Goldberg, Michael	Asst	New Hampshir	EF	PHD	91	NYU	1991
Goldberg, Paul A.	Assoc	CUNY-Brookly	HP	PHD	84	Columbia	1978
Goldberg, Roger H.	Prof	Ohio Northrn		PHD	81	Indiana	1969
Goldberger, Arthur S.	Prof	Wisconsin		PHD	58	Michigan	1960
Harold M. Groves & Vilas Professor of Economics							
Golden, James R.	H-Pr	USM Academy		PHD	72	Harvard	1975
Golden, John M.	Asst	Allegheny	DIJN	PHD	89	Conn	1989
Goldfarb, Marsha G.	Prof	MD-Baltim Co		PHD	68	Northwes	1973
Goldfarb, Robert S.	Prof	George Wash	BJ	PHD	68	Yale	1980
Goldfeld, Stephen M.	Prof	Princeton		PHD	63	MIT	1969
Goldin, Claudia D.	Prof	Harvard		PHD	72	Chicago	1990
Goldman, Marshall I.	Prof	Wellesley		PHD	61	Harvard	1958
Goldman, Steven M.	Prof	Cal-Berkeley		PHD	66	Stanford	1979
Goldsmith, Arthur H.	Assoc	Wash & Lee	E	PHD	79	Illinois	1990
Goldsmith, O. Scott	Prof	Alaska-Ancho	CH	PHD	76	Wisconsin	1985
Goldstein, Donald	Asst	Allegheny	ABG	PHD	91	Mass	1989
Goldstein, Harold M.	Prof	Northeastern		PHD	61	Clark	1961
Goldstein, Henry	Prof	Oregon	F	PHD	67	J Hopkins	1967
Goldstein, Jonathan Paul	Assoc	Bowdoin	EC	PHD		Mass	1979
Goldstein, Nance	Asst	So Maine	IJ	PHD	88	Kentucky	1987
Gollop, Frank M.	Prof	Boston Coll	DO	PHD	74	Harvard	1979
Golub, Stephen S.	C-Pr	Swarthmore	AE	PHD	83	Yale	1981
Gomersall, C. Nicholas	Asst	Luther		PHD	91	Cornell	1991
Gonce, Richard A.	Prof	Grand Valley	ABDK	PHD	66	Wisconsin	1972
Gondwe, Derrick K.	C-Pr	Gettysburg	ABEO	PHD	78	Manitoba	1977
Gonzalez, Jorge G.	Asst	Trinity		PHD	89	Mich St	1989
Gonzalez, Rodolfo	Prof	San Jose St		PHD	90	Ca-Davis	1990
Gonzalez-Rivera, Gloria	Asst	Cal-Riversid	CG	PHD	91	Ca-SnDgo	1991
Gonzalez-Vega, Claudio	Prof	Ohio State	O	PHD	76	Stanford	
Gonzalo, Jesus	Asst	Boston Univ	CE	PHD	91	Ca-SnDgo	1991
Good, Delmar	Prof	Goshen	AH	PHD	70	Illinois	2-67
Gooding, Elmer R.	Prof	Arizona St		PHD	69	Kansas	1988
Goodman, Allen C.	C-Pr	Wayne State		PHD	76	Yale	1986
Goodman, Douglas	Prof	Puget Sound	AE	PHD	78	Illinois	1977
Goodman, Rae Jean B.	Prof	USN Academy		PHD	76	Wash U	1973
Goodridge, Lyndon E.	Dean	New Hampshir		PHD	71	Purdue	1990
Goodspeed, Timothy J.	Asst	Fla Internat	HF	PHD	86	Maryland	1990
Goodstein, Eban	Assoc	Skidmore		PHD	89	Michigan	1989
Goodwin, Crauford	Prof	Duke					
James D. Duke Professor							
Goodwin, Randall B.	Assoc	Kennesaw St	ADM	PHD	82	Georgia	1982
Goodwin, Susan A.	Assoc	Mass-Lowell	G	PHD		Tufts	
Gootzeit, Michael J.	Prof	Memphis		PHD	66	Purdue	1975
Gordon, Bruce	Assoc	No Alabama		PHD	93	North Tx	1986
Gordon, Brunhild	Retir	South Fla		PHD	57	S Calif	1960
Gordon, David	Assoc	Clemson	DE	PHD	94	Chicago	1992
Gordon, Donald F.	Prof	Clemson	DE	PHD	49	Cornell	1986
Abney Chair							
Gordon, Peter	Prof	So Calif		PHD	71	Penn	1971
Gordon, Robert J.	C-Pr	Northwestern		PHD	67	MIT	1973
Stanley G. Harris Professor of the Social Sciences							
Gordon, Sara L.	Assoc	St John's		PHD	71	Stanford	1978
Gorman, Mary Jane	Assoc	Furman		PHD	80	N Carol	1982
Gormely, Patrick J.	Assoc	Kansas State	OF	PHD	67	Duke	1967
Gorney, Anne L.	Inst	USAF Academy		MS		AF Inst	
Gort, Michael	Prof	SUNY-Buffalo	O	PHD	54	Columbia	1964
Goss, Ernest P.	Prof	Creighton	RC	PHD	83	Tennessee	1992
MacMister Chair							
Gottfried, Robert Richard	Assoc	Univ South		PHD		N Carol	
Gottheil, Fred	Prof	Illinois		PHD		Duke	
Gottschalk, Peter	Prof	Boston Coll	CDIJ	PHD	73	Penn	1987
Gottschang, Thomas R.	Assoc	Holy Cross	AOP	PHD	82	Michigan	1979
Gouke, Cecil G.	Prof	Ohio State	M	PHD	67	NYU	1973
Goulet, Denis A.	Prof	Notre Dame	O	PHD	63	SaoPaula	1979
Goulet, Janet C.	Assoc	Wittenberg		PHD	75	Notre Dm	1975
Gouveia, Miguel	Asst	Pennsylvania	JH	PHD	91	Rochester	1991
Gowdy, John M.	Prof	Rensselaer		PHD	80	W Virginia	1983
Gowens, Paul R.	Dean	SW Texas St		PHD	73	Miss	1980

Name	Rank	Institution	Fields	Degree	Yr	School	Since
Gownsaukaran, Gautam	Asst	Minnesota		PHD	95	Yale	1995
Gozalo, Pedro	Asst	Brown		PHD	89	Ca-SnDgo	
Grabowski, Henry G.	Prof	Duke		PHD	67	Princeton	1972
Grabowski, Richard L.	Prof	So Illinois	OF	PHD	77	Utah	1979
Graddy, Duane B.	Prof	Mid Tenn St		PHD	74	Lehigh	1972
Grady, John	Assoc	LaSalle		MA		Temple	1960
Graeser, Paul	Asst	No Illinois		PHD		Columbia	
Graham, A. Steven	Asst	Mississippi		PHD	90	Queen's	1990
Graham, D. A.	Prof	Duke		PHD	69	Duke	1969
Graham, Fred C.	Asst	American U		PHD	85	Virginia	1988
Graham, Glenn	Asst	SUNY Oswego		PHD	95	SUNY-Bin	
Graham, John W. III	Assoc	Rutgers-Newk		PHD	78	Northwes	1986
Graham, Katherine	Lect	SUNY-Cortlan		MS		Cornell	
Graham, Patricia E.	Asst	No Colorado	IJOQ	PHD		Colo St	1988
Graham, William R.	Retir	CS-L Angeles		PHD	69	Arizona	1969
Grainger, Maury	Asst	N Carol A&T					
Gram, Harvey H.	Prof	CUNY-Queens	FCE	PHD	73	Wisconsin	1974
Grambo, Ralph W. Jr.	Assoc	Scranton		PHD		Penn	1973
Gramlich, Edward M.	Prof	Michigan		PHD	65	Yale	1976
Gramm, Wendy L.	Prof	Tx-Arlington	K	PHD	71	Northwes	1993
Grammy, Abbas	Prof	CS-Bakersf	ACOR	PHD	82	Colorado	1989
Granderson, Gerald	Asst	Miami U-Ohio	DG	PHD	93	N Carol	1993
Granger, Clive W. J.	Prof	Ca-San Diego	C	PHD	74	Nottingh	1974
Chancellor's Associates Chair in Economics							
Granger, George L.	Prof	East Tenn St		PHD	71	Penn	1961
Grant, Clayton	Prof	No Georgia		PHD	71	Clemson	1986
Dillard Munford Professor of Business							
Grant, James H.	C-As	Lewis & Clrk	CDJA	PHD	79	Mich St	1987
Grant, Lauria	Asst	Hampton		ABD		Syracuse	1991
Grant, Randy R.	Asst	Linfield		PHD		Nebraska	1993
Grant, Stephen K.	Assoc	N Adams St		PHD		Clark	
Grapard, Ulla A.	Asst	Colgate	AB	PHD	90	Cornell	1985
Grass, R. Gail	Assoc	Jackson St		PHD	89	Harvard	1989
Graves, Janet R.	Asst	Howard		PHD		Tx-Austin	
Gray, Charles M.	Assoc	St Thomas-MN	K	PHD	78	Wash U	1976
Gray, Jerry	Assoc	Willamette		PHD		Utah	1990
Gray, Jo Anna	H-Pr	Oregon	E	PHD	76	Chicago	1989
Gray, Wayne B.	Assoc	Clark		PHD	83	Harvard	1984
Graziano, Paulette	Asst	Illinois		MS	65	Illinois	1984
Greaney, Theresa M.	Asst	Syracuse		PHD	94	Michigan	
Greckel, Fay E.	Dean	Indiana SE	OJR	PHD	69	Indiana	1967
Greco, Anthony	Prof	SW Louisiana					
Green, Carole A.	Assoc	South Fla	B	PHD	82	Illinois	1982
Green, Gordon R.	Asst	New York U	D	PHD	93	Northwes	1995
Green, Jeffery	Prof	Ball State		PHD		Cornell	1972
Green, Jerry R.	Prof	Harvard		PHD	70	Rochester	1973
David A. Wells Professor of Political Economy							
Green, John W.	Assoc	No Colorado	CTQR	PHD	76	Penn	1985
Green, Louis C.	Prof	San Diego St		PHD		Berkeley	1976
Green, Ralph T.	VAsoc	Txs Woman's		PHD		Duke	
Green, Rodney D.	Prof	Howard		PHD	80	American	1977
Green, Sam	Asst	Morehouse		PHD		Northwes	1993
Green, Steven L.	Assoc	Baylor		PHD	84	Brown	1986
Green, Trellis Garnett	Asst	So Miss	Q	PHD	84	Fla St	1983
Green, William B.	C-Pr	Sam Houston		PHD	74	LSU	1974
Greenbaum, Harry	Prof	So Dakota St	E	PHD	61	Ohio St	1961
Greenberg, Edward	Prof	Wash Univ		PHD	61	Wisconsin	1963
Greene, Benjamin B. Jr.	Assoc	Salisbury St		PHD	74	Boston C	8-78
Greene, Clinton	Asst	Mo-St Louis	CE	PHD	92	Ca-Davis	1994
Greene, Joseph	Assoc	Augusta	AGI	MS		Georgia	1992
Greene, Kenneth V.	Prof	SUNY-Bingham		PHD	68	Virginia	1968
Greene, Michael	Asst	North Texas		PHD	89	N Hamp	1990
Greene, William H.	Prof	New York U	CDE	PHD	76	Wisconsin	1982
Greenhut, Melvin L.	Emer	Texas A&M		PHD	51	Wash U	1966
Distinguished Professor of Economics-G.T.& G.H.Abell Professor of Liberl Arts							
Greenlaw, Steven A.	C-Ac	Mary Wash	EFA	PHD	87	SUNY-Bin	1982
Greenley, Douglas A.	Prof	Moorhead St		PHD	79	Colo St	1978
Greenstein, Shane	Asst	Illinois		PHD	89	Stanford	1990
Greenwade, George D.	Asst	Sam Houston		PHD	88	Tx Tech	1986
Greenwald, Bruce C. N.	Prof	Columbia		PHD	78	MIT	1991
Greenwood, Daphne T.	Assoc	Colorado Spr	HJT	PHD	80	Oklahoma	1980
Greenwood, Jeremy	Prof	Rochester	D	PHD	83	Rochester	1992
Greenwood, Michael J.	Prof	Colorado		PHD	67	Northwes	1980
Greer, Clyde	H	Montana St		PHD	70	Minnesota	1970
Greer, Douglas F.	Prof	San Jose St		PHD	68	Cornell	1975
Greer, Mark	Asst	Dowling		PHD		Michigan	1994
Gregor, John J.	C-Pr	Wash & Jeff		PHD	76	Penn St	1989
Gregorowicz, Phillip	Prof	Auburn-Montg	EFGJ	PHD	82	N Illinois	1980
Gregory, Paul R.	Prof	Houston		PHD	69	Harvard	1972
Gregory, Sadie R.	Dean	Virginia St		PHD	87	Howard	1-79

Name	Rank	Institution	Field	Degree	Yr	Degree Inst	Since
Greif, Avner	Assoc	Stanford		PHD	89	Northwes	1993
Grennes, Thomas	Prof	N Carol St	FD	MA	65	Wisconsin	1968
Gresik, Thomas A.	Assoc	Penn State	D	PHD	87	Northwes	1991
Grether, David M.	Prof	Cal Tech		PHD	69	Stanford	1970
Greubel, Robert T.	Prof	NE St-Okla	AEF	PHD		Arkansas	1965
Greytak, David	Prof	Syracuse		PHD	68	Wash U	
Grier, Kevin B.	Prof	Tulane		PHD	84	Wash U	1994
Grieson, Ronald E.	Prof	Ca-Santa Crz	RHD	PHD	72	Rochester	1980
Griffin, James M.	Prof	Texas A&M		PHD	70	Penn	1982
Cullen Professorship							
Griffin, Keith B.	Prof	Cal-Riversid	AOP	DPHI	65	Oxford	1988
Griffin, Peter B.	Assoc	CS-Long Bch		PHD		Ca-SnBarb	1990
Griffith, Winston Harold	Prof	Bucknell		PHD		Howard	1987
Griffiths, L. Christopher	Prof	Colorado Col		PHD	70	Colorado	1967
Grigg, Vernon H.	Lect	South Fla		PHD	54	MIT	1981
Griliches, Zvi	Prof	Harvard		PHD	57	Chicago	1969
Paul M. Warburg Professor of Economics							
Grimes, Paul W.	Prof	Miss State		PHD	84	Okla St	1987
Grinols, Earl L.	Prof	Illinois		PHD	77	MIT	1984
Grivoyannis, Elias C.	Asst	Seton Hall		PHD	89	NYU	
Grobar, Lisa M.	Assoc	CS-Long Bch		PHD		Michigan	1969
Grobey, John H.	Prof	CS-Humboldt		PHD	75	U Wash	1967
Groesbeck, John D.	Asst	So Utah		PHD	93	Utah St	1993
Grogger, Jeffrey T.	Assoc	Cal-Santa Br	CE	PHD	87	Ca-SnDgo	1987
Gronberg, Timothy J.	H-Pr	Texas A&M		PHD	78	Northwes	1977
Groothuis, Peter A.	Assoc	Westminst-PA		PHD	89	Kentucky	1989
Gropper, Daniel M.	Assoc	Auburn		PHD	89	Fla St	1988
Groshek, Gerald		Naval Postgr					
Gross, Lorna S.	Assoc	Worcester St		PHD	87	Clark	1995
Grossbard-Shechtman, Shoshan	Prof	San Diego St		PHD	78	Chicago	1981
Grosskopf, Shawna	Prof	So Illinois	CHJ	PHD	77	Syracuse	1977
Grossman, Gene M.	Prof	Princeton		PHD	80	MIT	1980
Grossman, Gregory	Prof	Cal-Berkeley		PHD	53	Harvard	1953
Grossman, Herschel I.	Prof	Brown		PHD	65	J Hopkins	1973
Merton P. Stolz Professor in the Social Sciences							
Grossman, Leroy J.	Prof	St Louis		PHD	63	Vanderbilt	1964
Grossman, Peter Z.	Asst	Butler	N	PHD	92	Wash U	1994
Efroymson Chair in Economics							
Grossman, Philip J.	Asst	Wayne State		PHD	84	Virginia	1990
on leave to Virginia Tech Univ							
Grossman, Richard	Asst	Wesleyan-CT	N	PHD	88	Harvard	1990
Grove, Wayne A.	Inst	Colgate	N	ABD		Illinois	1995
Groves, Theodore	Prof	Ca-San Diego	DHM	PHD	70	Berkeley	1978
Grubaugh, Stephen G.	Prof	Bentley	CF	PHD	82	Chicago	1981
Grubb, Farley	Prof	Delaware	N	PHD	84	Chicago	1983
Gruber, Jonathan H.	Asst	MIT	G	PHD	92	Harvard	1992
Grunloh, James J.	Prof	Wis-Oshkosh	A	PHD	79	Wash U	1969
Gruver, Gene W.	Prof	Pittsburgh	O	PHD	72	Iowa St	1970
Guasch, Jose Luis	Assoc	Ca-San Diego	DJO	PHD	76	Stanford	1978
Guell, Robert	Asst	Indiana St	HC	PHD	91	Syracuse	1991
Gufley, Loren	Prof	Cen Arkansas		PHD		Arkansas	
Guiler, Charles J.	Assoc	Grove City		MED		Ind St	
Guilfoll, John D.	Prof	New York U	DKN	PHD	64	NYU	1964
Guilkey, David K.	C-Pr	No Carolina		PHD	73	N Carol	1983
Guinnane, Timothy J.	Asst	Yale		PHD	89	Berkeley	
Gujarati, Damodar N.	Prof	USM Academy		PHD	65	Chicago	1990
Gul, Faruk	Prof	Princeton		PHD		Princeton	1995
Guler, Kemal	Asst	Houston		PHD	90	Cal Tech	1990
Gullason, Edward T.	Asst	Hartford		PHD	86	Penn	1987
Gulley, O. David	Asst	Bentley	EG	MA	89	Kentucky	1990
Gummerson, A.	Lect	Fla Internat	AEF	PHD	71	Wisconsin	1989
Gunden, Randal G.	Asst	Goshen	EIO	ABD		Notre Dm	1984
Gunderson, Elizabeth W.	Assoc	Hamline	C	PHD	91	Union In	1980
Gunderson, Ralph O.	Prof	Wis-Oshkosh	OR	PHD	78	Arkansas	1987
Gunderson, Ronald J.	Prof	No Arizona	DR	PHD	77	Nebraska	1977
Gunn, John McKenzie	Emer	Wash & Lee	E	MA	54	Princeton	1957
Lewis Whitaker Adams Professor of Economics Emeritus							
Gunter, Frank R.	Assoc	Lehigh	FK	PHD	85	J Hopkins	1984
Gunther, William D.	Prof	Alabama		PHD	69	Kentucky	1968
Guo, Jang-Ting	Asst	Cal-Riversid	AC	PHD	93	UCLA	1993
Gupta, Barnali	Asst	Miami U-Ohio	DR	PHD	90	Florida	1993
Gupta, Harish C.	Assoc	Nebraska	FO	PHD	69	Tennessee	1969
Gupta, Satya P.	C-Pr	Augsburg		PHD		S Illinois	1976
Gupta, Shiv K.	D-Pr	Findlay	AJ	DBA		London	1983
Gural, Michael L.	Assoc	Westfield St		MA		Rutgers	1982
Gurmu, Shiferaw	Asst	Virginia	CF	PHD	92	Indiana	1992
Gurtunca, Esen Z.	Prof	Indianapolis		PHD	73	Purdue	1974
Donald W. Tanselle Professor of Economics							
Gustafson, Curtis O.	Inst	So Dakota St	M	MPA	86	S Dakota	1989
Gustafson, Elizabeth F.	Assoc	Dayton	C	PHD	74	N Carol	1983

Gustafson, Leland Verne	Prof	West Georgia	AC	PHD	74	Fla St	
Gustafson, W. Eric	Emer	Cal-Davis	AO	PHD	59	Harvard	1978
Gustavson, Robert L.	Prof	Washburn		PHD	76	Colorado	1976
Gustman, Alan Leslie	Prof	Dartmouth		PHD	69	Michigan	1969
Loren M. Berry Professor							
Guthrie, Robert	Lect	Wis-Whitewat		PHD		Indiana	1994
Guthrie, William G. III	Prof	Appalach St	BN	PHD	80	N Carol	1980
Gutowsky, Albert R.	C-Pr	CS-Sacrament		PHD	65	Oregon	1967
Guttmann, Robert P.	Assoc	Hofstra	F	PHD	79	London	
Guynn, Richard Dickson	Prof	West Georgia	JA	PHD		Alabama	
Gwartney, James D.	Prof	Florida St		PHD	69	U Wash	1968
Gwinn, Larry	Asst	Wittenberg		PHD		Kansas	1988
Gyimah-Brempong, Kwabena	Prof	South Fla	O	PHD	81	Wayne St	1994
Gylys, Julius A.	Emer	Toledo		PHD		Wayne St	1967
Haab, Timothy C.	Asst	East Carol		PHD	95	Maryland	1995
Haag, Jerry	Asst	Fort Hays St	G	PHD	95	Tx-Austin	1995
Haas, Paul F.	Prof	Bowling Gr		PHD	70	Boston C	1967
Haas-Wilson, Deborah	Assoc	Smith	DIL	PHD	83	Berkeley	1984
Habib, Ahsan M.	Assoc	Adrian		PHD	80	McMaster	1981
Hackett, Steven C.	Asst	CS-Humboldt		PHD	89	Tx A&M	1994
Hadjimichalakis, Karma	SLect	U Washington		PHD	74	Rochester	1970
Hadjimichalakis, Michael	Assoc	U Washington		PHD	69	Rochester	1969
Hadley, Lawrence H.	Assoc	Dayton	J	PHD	75	Conn	1977
Hafer, Gail	Assoc	Lindenwood		PHD		S Illinois	9-93
Hagan, Oliver	Prof	Lindenwood		MS		Baylor	9-90
Hagen, Daniel A.	Assoc	Western Wash	JEFQ	PHD	83	Berkeley	1988
Haggerty, Mark E.	Assoc	Clarion		PHD		Wash St	1989
Hagiwara, Miwako	Asst	No Carolina		PHD	90	Calif	1990
Hagstrom, Paul Alan	Asst	Hamilton	JHI	PHD	91	Wisconsin	1991
Hahm, Joon-Ho	Asst	Cal-Santa Br	EFGC	PHD	93	Columbia	1994
Hahn, Jinyong	Asst	Pennsylvania		PHD	93	Harvard	1993
William P. Carey Term Assistant Professor of Economics							
Hahn, Youngki	Prof	Hawaii-Hilo		PHD	71	Ca-River	
Hahnel, Robin E.	Prof	American U		PHD		American	1976
Hai, Wen	Asst	Fort Lewis		PHD	91	Ca-Davis	1992
Haight, Alan D.	Asst	Bowling Gr		PHD	90	Wisconsin	1991
Hailstones, Thomas J.	Deces	South Fla		PHD	51	St Louis	1988
Haines, Michael R.	Prof	Colgate	TN	PHD	71	Penn	1990
Banfi Vintners Professor of Economics							
Hajizadeh, Avaz	Assoc	N Adams St		PHD		Rensselae	
Hakes, David R.	Assoc	No Iowa		PHD	85	Iowa St	1992
Hakim, Simon	Prof	Temple	R	PHD	76	Penn	1976
Halcoussis, Dennis	Asst	CS-Northrdge	C	PHD	92	Penn	1991
Hales, Waynes D.	Assoc	Rollins		PHD	74	Okla St	1971
Haley, Charles	Prof	U Washington		PHD	68	Stanford	1966
Hall, Alastair R.	Prof	N Carol St	C	PHD		Warwick	1985
Hall, Bernard	Retir	Kent State	BNH	PHD	55	Berkeley	1955
Hall, Brian J.	Asst	Harvard		PHD	83	Harvard	1993
Hall, Bronwyn H.	Asst	Cal-Berkeley		PHD	88	Stanford	1987
Hall, Darwin C.	Prof	CS-Long Bch		PHD	77	Berkeley	1986
Hall, Jane V.	Prof	CS-Fullerton		PHD	77	Berkeley	1981
Hall, John B.	Prof	Portland St		PHD	84	New Sch	1985
Hall, Phillip	Assoc	St Ambrose		PHD		Nebraska	1995
Hall, Robert E.	Prof	Stanford		PHD	67	MIT	1978
Hall, Thomas E.	Prof	Miami U-Ohio	EC	PHD	82	Ca-SnBarb	1982
Hall, W. Clayton	Assoc	Illinois Tch		PHD		Illinois	
Hall, William Woodward Jr.	Prof	N Car-Wilmin	QR	PHD	72	Clemson	
Hall, Yvonne C.	Prof	New Hamp Col		PHD		Colo St	
Hallagan, William S.	Assoc	Wash State		PHD	77	Ca-Davis	1984
Haller, Hans H.	Asst	Virg Tech	D	PHD	78	Bonn U	1985
Hallock, Kevin F.	Asst	Illinois		PHD		Princeton	1995
Hallwood, Paul C.	Prof	Connecticut	F	PHD	88	Aberdeen	1986
Halstead, James F.	Prof	Occidental	A	PHD	72	Stanford	1977
Halteman, James	Prof	Wheaton-IL	AB	PHD	74	Penn St	1979
Haltiwanger, John C.	Prof	Maryland		PHD	81	J Hopkins	1987
Halvorsen, Marcia L.	Prof	Redlands		PHD	78	Geo St	1975
Halvorsen, Robert F.	Prof	U Washington		PHD	73	Harvard	1972
Ham, C. L.	Retir	CS-Northrdge	8-94	PHD	72	S Calif	1963
Ham, John	Prof	Pittsburgh	J	PHD	80	Princeton	1991
Hamada, Koichi	Prof	Yale		PHD	65	Yale	1986
Hambleton, John W.	Assoc	San Diego St		PHD	71	Wisconsin	1969
Hamer, Thomas P.	Prof	Rowan Col-NJ		PHD	75	Claremont	1974
Hamermesh, Daniel S.	Prof	Texas	J	PHD	69	Yale	9-73
E.E. Hale Centennial Professor & Director Center for Applied Research in Econ							
Hamid, M. Khalil	Prof	Millersville		PHD	66	Iowa	1968
Hamilton, Bruce W.	Prof	J Hopkins		PHD	72	Princeton	1973
Hamilton, Gregory L.	Assoc	Marist		PHD		Okla St	1990
Hamilton, James D.	Prof	Ca-San Diego	D	PHD	83	Berkeley	1992
Hamilton, Jean	Inst	Occidental	J	MA	92	Berkeley	1994
Hamilton, Johnathan H.	Assoc	Florida	HRD	PHD	82	MIT	1984

Name	Rank	Institution	Fields	Degree	Yr	Degree School	Year
Hammack, Judd	Prof	CS-L Angeles		PHD	69	U Wash	1970
Hammerle, Nancy E.	Asst	Stonehill	A	MA		Temple	1980
Hammermeister, John	Asst	St Ambrose		MBA		Oregon	
Hammes, David L.	H-Ac	Hawaii-Hilo		PHD	85	Simon Fr	1988
Hammond, Claire Holton	C-Ac	Wake Forest		PHD	82	Virginia	1978
Hammond, J. Daniel	Prof	Wake Forest		PHD	79	Virginia	1978
Hammond, Peter J.	Prof	Stanford		PHD	74	Cambridge	1979
Hammoudeh, Shawka M.	Assoc	Drexel		PHD	80	Kansas	1990
Hampton, Mary B.	Assoc	Wis-La Cross	GHIJ	PHD	91	Wi-Milw	1991
Hampton, Nathan E.	Assoc	St Cloud St		PHD	89	Ca-SnBarb	1987
Hamzaee, Reza G.	Prof	Missouri Wes	E	PHD	85	Ariz St	1984
Han, Hsiang-Ling	Asst	Bryant	CE	PHD		Rochester	
Hanchate, Amresh	Asst	Case Western	OQDC	PHD	92	Wisconsin	1992
Hands, Wade	Prof	Puget Sound	ABC	PHD	65	U Wash	
Handy, John	Prof	Morehouse		PHD		Geo St	1978
Hanes, Christopher L.	Asst	Pennsylvania	NJE	PHD	90	Harvard	1990
Haney, Barbara	Asst	Alaska-Fairb		PHD	89	Notre Dm	1987
Hankins, Marvin	Asst	SW Okla St		EDD		Okla St	1979
Hanna, Raouf S.	H-Pr	E Michigan		PHD	73	Indiana	1977
Hannah, Richard	Prof	Mid Tenn St		PHD	81	Utah	1992
Hannan, Michael J.	Assoc	Edinboro		PHD	88	W Virginia	1988
Hannes, Lance E.	Assoc	Edinboro		MBA	87	Buffalo	1978
Hanni, Eila A.	Retir	South Fla		PHD	70	Yale	1970
Hannon, Joan U.	Assoc	St Marys-Cal		PHD	78	Wisconsin	1987
Hansen, Ann	Assoc	Westminst-UT	CHL	PHD	81	Utah	1990
Hansen, Bruce	Prof	Boston Coll	CE	PHD	89	Yale	1994
Hansen, David	Prof	Linfield		MS		Portland	1969
Hansen, Dwight W.	Assoc	Coe		MA	76	Nebraska	1978
Hansen, Gary B.	Prof	Utah State	J	PHD	71	Cornell	1967
Hansen, Gary D.	Asst	UCLA		PHD	86	Minnesota	1987
Hansen, Jan M.	Prof	Wis-Eau Clar		PHD	74	Missouri	1985
Hansen, John A.	C-Pr	SUNY-Fredoni	LD	PHD	80	Yale	1984
Hansen, Julia L.	Assoc	Western Wash	DR	PHD	84	Berkeley	1988
Hansen, Korinna	Asst	Wellesley		PHD	92	Rochester	1994
Hansen, Lars Peter	Prof	Chicago		PHD	78	Minnesota	1982
Homer J. Livingston Professor							
Hansen, Niles M.	Prof	Texas	RP	PHD	63	Indiana	1-63
Leroy G. Denmann, Jr. Regents Professor in Economics							
Hansen, W. Lee	Prof	Wisconsin		PHD	58	J Hopkins	1965
Hanson, Gordon H.	Asst	Texas	FO	PHD	92	MIT	9-92
Hanson, James S.	Prof	Willamette		PHD	71	Stanford	1976
Hanson, John R. II	Prof	Texas A&M		PHD	72	Penn	1974
Hanson, Phillip	Asst	Ashland		MA		Michigan	1988
Hanushek, Eric A.	Prof	Rochester		PHD	68	MIT	1978
Happel, Stephen K.	Prof	Arizona St		PHD	76	Duke	1975
Harbaugh, William T.	Asst	Oregon	HQ	PHD	95	Wisconsin	
Harberger, Arnold C.	Emer	Chicago		PHD	50	Chicago	1953
Gustavus F. and Ann M. Swift Distinguished Service Professor							
Harder, K. Peter	Prof	Western Wash	BNP	PHD	68	Nebraska	1970
Hare, Denise	Asst	Reed	AJOD	PHD	92	Stanford	1992
Harford, Jon D.	Assoc	Cleveland St	DHKQ	PHD	74	Stanford	1982
Harger, Bruce T.	Dean	Lk Superior	A	PHD	91	Mich St	9-67
Harik, Bassam	Assoc	W Michigan	E	PHD	78	Wayne St	1979
Harik, Salim	Assoc	W Michigan	F	PHD	75	Wayne St	1976
Haririan, Mehdi	Assoc	Bloomsburg		PHD	87	New Sch	1982
Harju, Melvin W.	Prof	La St-Shreve		PHD	72	Florida	1977
Harl, Neil E.	Prof	Iowa State	QK	PHD	65	Iowa St	1964
Harless, David W.	Asst	Virg Comm		PHD	88	Indiana	
Harmel, Robert	Assoc	Midwest St	DL	PHD		Iowa St	1989
Harmon, Oskar R.	Assoc	Connecticut	H	PHD	80	Rutgers	1982
Haroian, Berch	Prof	Wm Patterson		PHD	72	NYU	1978
Harper, Jeff	Asst	Athens State	CM	PHD	95	Auburn	1994
Harper, Richard K.	Asst	West Florida	AFM	PHD	89	Duke	1989
Harraf, Abe	C-Pr	Embry-Riddle		PHD	84	Utah St	
Harrigan, James	Asst	Pittsburgh	F	PHD	91	UCLA	1989
Harrington, David E.	Asst	Kenyon		PHD	87	Wisconsin	1986
Himmelright Assistant Professor in Economics							
Harrington, Joseph E.	Assoc	J Hopkins		PHD	84	Duke	1983
Harrington, Peter V.	Prof	Purdue		MAT	68	Purdue	1971
Harris, Donald J.	Prof	Stanford		PHD	66	Berkeley	1972
Harris, James G.	Prof	CS-Dominguez	AEDH	PHD	70	Oregon	1969
Harris, Jeffrey E.	Assoc	MIT	I	PHD	75	Penn	1976
Harris, John R.	Prof	Boston Univ	ER	PHD	67	Northwes	1975
Harris, R. Scott	Assoc	Mont St-Bill		PHD	85	Calif	1988
Harris, William G.	Assoc	Georgetown		PHD	67	Oregon	
Harrison, Ann	Asst	Columbia					
Harrison, Clifford E.	Prof	Concordia C		EDD		Farleigh	1986
Harrison, Dannie	Dean	Murray State	AEP	PHD	74	S Illinois	1969
Harrison, Glenn W.	Prof	So Carolina		PHD	82	UCLA	
Dewey H. Johnson Professor of Economics							

Harrison, Kenneth	Assoc	R Stockton		PHD		SUNY-Alb	1976
Harrison, William B. III	Assoc	Virg Comm		PHD	72	Maryland	1972
Hart, Oliver D'Arcy	Prof	Harvard		PHD	74	Princeton	1993
Hart, William R.	Prof	Miami U-Ohio	EA	PHD	76	Wash U	1974
Hart-Landsberg, Martin	C-Pr	Lewis & Clrk	POFA	PHD	74	Wisconsin	1978
Harter, Cynthia L.	Asst	Duquesne		ABD		Purdue	1995
Hartigan, James C.	Assoc	Oklahoma	FL	PHD	79	Duke	1988
Hartley, James E.	Asst	Mt Holyoke		PHD		Ca-Davis	1994
Hartley, Michael J.	Prof	New Orleans		PHD		Penn	
Hartley, Peter R.	Prof	Rice		PHD	80	Chicago	1986
Hartline, Jessie C.	Assoc	Rutgers-N Br	G	PHD	68	Rutgers	1968
Hartman, Harrison G.	C-Pr	E Stroudsbur	J	PHD	76	NYU	1964
Hartman, Richard C.	Prof	U Washington		PHD	71	Berkeley	1971
Hartmann, G. Bruce	H-Pr	Tenn State		PHD	74	SUNY-Alb	1974
Harvey, Curtis E.	Prof	Kentucky	P	PHD	63	S Calif	1963
Harvey, Joann P.	Assoc	Ohio Wesley		MBA		Ohio St	1981
Harvey, John T.	Assoc	Tx Christian		PHD	87	Tennessee	1987
Harwitz, Mitchell	Assoc	SUNY-Buffalo	COTR	PHD	59	MIT	1958
Hasan, Nazmul	Asst	Illinois St	G	PHD	93	Illinois	1993
Hasan, Tanwee	Asst	Fayetteville		PHD	93	Houston	
Hashemzadeh, Nozar	Prof	Radford		PHD		Va Tech	
Hashimoto, Masanori	C-Pr	Ohio State	J	PHD	71	Columbia	1987
Haskew, Barbara S.	Dean	Mid Tenn St		PHD	69	Tennessee	1988
Hassan, Mahboubul	Assoc	New Hamp Col		MAPE	82	Boston U	
Hassan, Seid	Asst	Murray State	E	PHD	93	Tx A&M	1992
Hasty, John M. Jr.	Prof	Tenn State		PHD	73	Geo State	
Hatchett, Paul	Asst	Ft Valley St		JD	93	Widener	9-92
Hattwick, Richard E.	Prof	W Illinois	AM	PHD	65	Vanderbilt	1969
Hatzipanayoutou, Panos	Assoc	Connecticut	F	PHD	85	SUNY-SBr	1985
Hatzopoulos, Sydma	Assoc	West Liberty		MA	80	Va Tech	1990
Hau, Jong-Chol	Prof	Millersville		PHD	67	St Louis	1969
Haughton, Jonathan H.	Asst	Northeastern		PHD	83	Harvard	1987
Haulman, Clyde A.	Prof	Wm & Mary		PHD	69	Fla St	1969
Haupert, Michael J.	Assoc	Wis-La Cross	AEN	PHD	89	Wash U	1989
Haurin, Donald R.	Prof	Ohio State	R	PHD	78	Chicago	1975
Hause, John C.	Prof	SUNY-Stony B		PHD	62	Chicago	1978
Hausman, Jerry A.	Prof	MIT	C	DPHI	73	Oxford	1973
Hausman, William J.	C-Pr	Wm & Mary		PHD	76	Illinois	1981
Haveman, Jon	Asst	Purdue		PHD	92	Michigan	1992
Haveman, Robert H.	C-Pr	Wisconsin		PHD	63	Vanderbilt	1970
John Bascom Professor of Economics							
Havens, Rebecca A.	C-As	Pt Loma Naz		PHD		Ca-SnDgo	1990
Haver, Rik W.	Prof	S Ill-Edward		PHD	79	Va Tech	
Havrilesky, Thomas	Prof	Duke		PHD	66	Illinois	1969
Hawkins, Charles F.	C-Pr	Lamar	RK	PHD		LSU	1966
Regents' Professor of Economics							
Hawkins, Robert G.	Dean	Georgia Tech		PHD	66	NYU	1993
Hawley, Clifford B.	Prof	W Virginia	JD	PHD	77	Duke	1978
Hawroth, Barry	Asst	Louisville		PHD	94	Ca-Davis	1995
Hayashi, Paul M.	Prof	Tx-Arlington	D	PHD	69	So Meth	1965
Hayden, F. Gregory	Prof	Nebraska	HQI	PHD	68	Tx-Austin	1967
Haydon, Randall B.	C-Pr	Wichita St		PHD	62	Illinois	1970
Haye, Eric M.	Asst	St John's		PHD	90	SUNY-Bin	1990
Hayes, Kathy J.	Assoc	So Methodist		PHD	80	Syracuse	1989
Hayes, Michael N.	Assoc	Radford		PHD	86	Ca-Davis	
Hayes, Sue E.	Prof	Sonoma State		PHD	75	Berkeley	1974
Hayes, William	Emer	DePaul					
Hayford, Marc D.	Asst	Loyola-Chicg		PHD	87	Brown	1986
Haynes, C. Beth	Prof	Brighm Yg-Hl	DG	PHD	81	Purdue	1994
Haynes, James F.	Dean	Athens State		PHD	80	Vanderbilt	1980
Haynes, Michael C.	Retir	So Oregon St	ADK	MS	64	Brig Yg	1964
Haynes, Stephen E.	Prof	Oregon	FE	PHD	76	Ca-SnBarb	1978
Hays, Patrick Allen	Assoc	W Carolina		PHD	77	N Carol	1985
Haywood, Dale M.	Prof	Northwood		PHD			
Hayworth, Steve	Assoc	E Michigan		PHD	87	MIT	1977
Hazilla, Michael	Assoc	American U		PHD	78	SUNY-Bin	1988
Headen, Alvin E.	Assoc	N Carol St	IJD	PHD	81	MIT	1986
Heal, Geoffrey M.	Prof	Columbia		PHD	68	Cambridg	1983
Healy, Gerald	Asst	Westfield St		MBA		American	1981
Heath, Julia A.	Assoc	Memphis		PHD	86	S Carol	1986
Heath, W. Cary	Asst	SW Louisiana		PHD	82	LSU	
Heavey, Jerome F.	Assoc	Lafayette		PHD		Penn St	1973
Heberling, Gregory Dean	Assoc	Anderson U		MBA		Ball St	1978
Hebert, Robert F.	Prof	Auburn		PHD	70	LSU	1974
Russell Professor							
Heckerman, Donald G.	Assoc	Arizona		PHD	67	MIT	1971
Heckman, James J.	Prof	Chicago		PHD	71	Princeton	1973
Henry Schultz Professor of Economics & Soc Sciences							
Hecox, Walter E.	Prof	Colorado Col		PHD	69	Syracuse	1970
Hedrick, David W.	Assoc	Central Wash	AIO	PHD	84	Oregon	1987

Name	Rank	Institution	Fields	Degree	Yr	Degree Inst	Year
Heffley, Dennis R.	Prof	Connecticut	RI	PHD	75	Ca-SnBarb	193
Hefner, Frank L.	Asst	Charleston		PHD	88	Kansas	1995
Hegji, Charles E.	Prof	Auburn-Montg	DFMJ	PHD	80	Wash U	1985
Heilbrun, James	Prof	Fordham		PHD	64	Columbia	1970
Heim, Carol E.	Assoc	Massachusett		PHD	82		
Heimarck, Theodore	Prof	Concordia C		JD		Chicago	1961
Heineke, John M.	Prof	Santa Clara		PHD	68	Iowa	1968
Heiner, Ronald A.	Prof	George Mason		PHD	75	UCLA	1989
Heiney, Joseph N.	D-Pr	Elmhurst		PHD	83	Chicago	1977
Coleman Foundation Distinguished Chair in Business							
Heinicke, Craig W.	Asst	Baldwin-Wal	NOE	PHD	91	Toronto	1991
Heins, A. James	Emer	Illinois		PHD	61	Wisconsin	1960
Heisler, James B.	C-Pr	Hope	PD	PHD	75	Nebraska	1981
Heitmann, George Jr.	C-Pr	Muhlenberg		PHD	63	Princeton	1-94
Helburn, Suzanne W.	Emer	Colo-Denver	B	PHD	63	Indiana	1970
Helland, Eric	Asst	Ball State		PHD		U Wash	1995
Heller, Walter P.	Prof	Ca-San Diego	DE	PHD	70	Stanford	1974
Hellerstein, Judith	Asst	Northwestern		PHD	94	Harvard	
Helms, L. Jay	Assoc	Cal-Davis	DHI	PHD	79	MIT	1985
Helper, Susan	Asst	Case Western	ONM	PHD	87	Harvard	1990
Hemesath, Michael	Assoc	Carleton		PHD	88	Harvard	1989
Henderson, David R.		Naval Postgr		PHD	76	UCLA	1984
Henderson, J. Vernon	C-Pr	Brown		PHD	72	Chicago	1974
Eastman Professor of Political Economy							
Henderson, James M.	Deces	Duke		PHD	55	Harvard	1986
Henderson, James P.	C-Pr	Valparaiso	NBA	PHD	77	N Illinois	1975
Henderson, James W.	Assoc	Baylor		PHD		So Meth	1981
Ben H. Williams Professor of Economics							
Henderson, Sandra R.	C-Ac	W Virg St	AFR	MA	60	Pittsburgh	1968
Henderson, Upton B.	Retir	Central Okla		PHD	65	Missouri	1971
Hendon, Fred N.	Prof	Samford		PHD	68	Alabama	1968
Hendricks, Wallace E.	Prof	Illinois		PHD	73	Berkeley	1973
Hendrickson, Jill K.	Assoc	Univ South		PHD		Notre Dm	1995
Hendryson, Mary Ann	Lect	Western Wash	DOF	ABD		Wash St	1989
Henry, John F.	Prof	CS-Sacrament		PHD		McGill	1970
Henry, Louis H.	Prof	Old Dominion		PHD	70	Notre Dm	1970
Henson, Steven E.	Assoc	Western Wash	QD	PHD	82	Oregon	1985
Hentzel, David	Prof	Mo-Rolla		PHD		S Illinois	1969
Herander, Mark G.	Prof	South Fla	F	PHD	80	N Carol	1979
Herbener, Jeffrey M.	Assoc	Wash & Jeff		PHD		Okla St	1986
Herber, Bernard P.	Prof	Arizona		PHD	69	U Wash	1957
Herbst, Anthony F.	Prof	Txs-El Paso		PHD		Purdue	1987
Herbst, Lawrence A.	Assoc	Vassar	N	PHD	74	Penn	1970
Herce, Miguel A.	Asst	No Carolina		PHD	90	Ca-SnDgo	1990
Herdendorf, Phyllis		SUNY-Empire	F	PHD		SUNY	1987
Herendeen, James B.	Prof	Txs-El Paso		PHD	63	Penn St	1992
Hergenrather, Richard A.	Asst	Whitworth		PHD		P Drucker	1994
Hermalin, Benjamin E.	Asst	Cal-Berkeley		PHD	88	MIT	1988
Herman, E. Edward	Prof	Cincinnati	J	PHD	65	McGill	1966
Herman, Walter J.	Prof	South Fla	E	PHD	65	Florida	1980
Hermann, Mark	Assoc	Alaska-Fairb		PHD	90	Wash St	1990
Herold, Marc W.	Assoc	New Hampshir	O	PHD	77	Berkeley	1975
Herr, Elizabeth	Asst	Mesa State		PHD		Colorado	
Herren, R. Stanley	Assoc	N Dakota St	ABE	PHD	75	Duke	1985
Herrero, Maria Jose	Asst	Michigan St		PHD		London	1995
Herrick, Bruce H.	C-Pr	Wash & Lee	OP	PHD	64	MIT	1980
John F. Hendon Professor of Economics							
Herrin, William E.	Assoc	Pacific	R	PHD	85	SUNY-Bin	1985
Herrnstadt, Irwin L.	Prof	Northeastern		PHD	64	MIT	1960
Hersch, Joni	Assoc	Wyoming	CJ	PHD	81	Northwes	1989
Hersch, Philip L.	Assoc	Wichita St		PHD	82	Ohio St	1983
Herschede, Alfred J.	Prof	Ind-So Bend		PHD	76	Illinois	1976
Hersh-Cochran, Mona S.	Prof	Txs Woman's		PHD		So Meth	
Conaro Professor of Business and Economics							
Hervitz, Hugo M.	Assoc	Barry		PHD	83	Indiana	1982
Herzog, Henry W. Jr.	Prof	Tennessee		PHD	74	Maryland	1974
Hess, Alan C.	Prof	U Washington		PHD	69	Car Mellon	1967
Hess, Arleigh P. Jr.	Emer	Pennsylvania		PHD	49	Penn	1949
Associate Undergraduate Chair for Advising							
Hess, Gregory	Asst	Kansas		PHD	89	J Hopkins	1993
Hess, Peter N.	Prof	Davidson	OT	PHD	82	N Carol	1980
Hessel, Christopher A.	Assoc	CUNY-Baruch		PHD	78	NYU	
Hester, Donald D.	Prof	Wisconsin		PHD	61	Yale	1968
Hetherington, Bruce W.	Prof	Ogelthorpe	NE	PHD	82	Va Tech	1980
Hettich, Walter	Prof	CS-Fullerton		PHD	67	Yale	1983
Hewett, Roger S.	Assoc	Drake		PHD	84	Illinois	1981
Hewins, Dana C.	Assoc	Regis-MA		PHD	74	Illinois	
Heyen, Keith A.	Asst	CUNY-Hunter		MA	80	N Illinois	
Heyne, Paull Theodore	SLect	U Washington		PHD	63	Chicago	1976
Heywood, John S.	Prof	Wis-Milwauke		PHD	86	Michigan	1986

Hibbard, Thomas H.	Prof	Willamette		PHD	67	Claremont	1973
Hickenbottom, Wayne R.	Asst	Texas	HJ	PHD	92	Minnesota	9-91
Hickerson, Steven	Prof	Mankato St	ABK	PHD		Nebraska	1980
Hickey, Kevin L.	C-Ac	Assumption		MLA	76	Harvard	1972
Hickman, Bert G.	Emer	Stanford		PHD	51	Berkeley	1966
Hicks, Donald A.	Prof	Texas-Dallas		PHD	76	N Carol	
Hicks, W. Whitney	Prof	Missouri	O	PHD	65	Stanford	1965
Hiebert, L. Dean	Assoc	Illinois St	ADE	PHD	72	Wisconsin	1973
Hiedemann, Bridget	Asst	Seattle	DJT	PHD	92	Duke	1994
Hiestand, Thomas W.	Assoc	Concordia C		PHD		Kansas St	1972
Higgins, Matthew L.	Asst	W Michigan	C	PHD	89	Illinois	1995
Higgins, Neal O.	Prof	Portland	RH	PHD	74	Nebraska	1976
Higgins, Robert C.	Prof	U Washington		PHD	69	Stanford	1967
Highfill, Jannett K.	Assoc	Bradley		PHD	85	Kansas	1985
Hildebrandt, Gregory		Naval Postgr					
Hildred, William M.	Prof	No Arizona	HA	PHD	64	Colo St	1988
Hill, Catharine Bond	Prof	Williams		PHD	85	Yale	1985
Hill, James Richard	Assoc	Cen Michigan		PHD	80	Kentucky	1981
Hill, Lawrence G.	C-Pr	Lewis		PHD	76	N Illinois	1968
Hill, Lewis E.	C-Pr	Texas Tech		PHD	57	Tx-Austin	1967
Hill, Melba A.	Prof	CUNY-Queens	JC	PHD	80	Duke	1989
Hill, Pershing J.	Assoc	Alaska-Ancho	EFH	PHD	76	Wash St	1975
Hill, Peter J.	Prof	Wheaton-IL	ANPQ	PHD	70	Chicago	1986
George F. Bennett Professor of Economics							
Hill, R. Carter	Prof	Louisiana St	C	PHD	75	Missouri	
Mack H. Hornbeak Business Partnership Professor							
Hill, Roger Post	Prof	N Car-Wilmin	G	PHD	68	Mich St	
Hillard, Michael	Asst	So Maine	EJ	PHD	88	Mass	1987
Hillas, John	Asst	SUNY-Stony B		PHD	87	Stanford	1990
Hillburn, Chris I.	Asst	Neb-Kearney		PHD		Iowa St	1990
Himarios, Daniel D.	Assoc	Tx-Arlington	FE	PHD	84	Va Tech	1983
Himarios, Jane	Lect	Tx-Arlington		PHD	83	Va Tech	1986
Himmelberg, Charles	Asst	New York U	DEL	PHD	90	Northwes	1990
Hinderliter, Roger H.	Assoc	Ithaca	BE	PHD	70	Wash U	1970
Hine, Steven C.	Asst	Lyon College		PHD	86	Wash St	1994
Hinshaw, C. Elton	Assoc	Vanderbilt	N	PHD	66	Vanderbilt	1966
Hinson, Steve Y.	Asst	Webster	AFDH	PHD		Kentucky	1993
Hinton, William Valentine	Prof	Delta State		PHD		Arkansas	
Hippie, F. Steb	Prof	East Tenn St		PHD	72	So Meth	1982
Hirsch, Barry T.	Prof	Florida St		PHD	77	Virginia	1990
Hirschfeld, Mary L.	Assoc	Occidental	N	PHD	89	Harvard	1988
Hitchner, Benjamin	C-As	Rowan Col-NJ		MS		Penn	1964
Ho, Franklin Y. H.	C-Pr	CS-Pomona		PHD	57	S Calif	1961
Ho, Peter S. W.	Asst	Denver		PHD	89	Stanford	1989
Ho, Yhi-Min	Dean	St Thomas-TX	OQ	PHD	65	Vanderbilt	8-70
Hugh Roy and Lillie Cullen Professor of Economics							
Hoag, John H.	C-Pr	Bowling Gr		PHD	72	Kansas	1972
Hobbs, Bradley K.	Asst	Bellarmine		PHD	90	Fla St	1988
Hoch, Irving J.	Prof	Texas-Dallas		PHD	57	Chicago	1985
Hochman, Harold M.	Prof	Lafayette		PHD	65	Yale	1992
Wm. E. Simon Professor of Political Economics							
Hodges, Paul E.	Prof	Txs-Perm Bas		PHD	74	Stanford	
Hodgin, Gary L.	Assoc	Belmont		PHD	85	Tennessee	1983
Hodgin, Robert F.	Assoc	Houston-Cl L		DA	80	Illin St	9-81
Hodgson, Doug	Asst	Rochester		PHD		Yale	
Hoekstra, Merrill C.	Asst	USAF Academy		MA		Ca-SnBarb	
Hoff, Karla	Asst	Maryland		PHD	89	Princeton	
Hoffer, George E.	Prof	Virg Comm		PHD	72	Virginia	1970
Hoffman, Dennis L.	Prof	Arizona St		PHD	78	Mich St	1979
Hoffman, Emily P.	Prof	W Michigan	J	PHD	75	Mass	1981
Hoffman, Naphtali	C-Ac	Elmira		PHD	80	Case Wes	1976
Hoffman, Robert	Asst	Minn-Duluth	E	PHD	92	Boston C	1995
Hoffman, Saul D.	Prof	Delaware	TJ	PHD	77	Michigan	1977
Hofler, Richard A.	C-Pr	Cen Florida	CIJ	PHD	82	N Carol	1989
Hofman, Cornelius A.	C-Pr	Idaho State		PHD	64	Utah	1960
Hoftyzer, John	H-Pr	SW Missouri		PHD	74	Indiana	1987
Hogan, John D.	Dean	Georgia St	MO	PHD	52	Syracuse	6-91
Hogan, Timothy D.	Prof	Arizona St		PHD	71	Va Tech	1970
Hogan, William V.	Prof	Mass-Dartmou		PHD	76	Cornell	1976
Hogendorn, Jan S.	Prof	Colby	FOA	PHD	66	London	1966
Grossman Professor of Economics							
Hohenberg, Paul M.	Prof	Rensselaer		PHD	63	MIT	1977
Hoke, Leon R. Jr.	Prof	Tampa	ADJ	PHD	79	Pittsburgh	1981
Holahan, William L.	Assoc	Wis-Milwauke		PHD	74	Brown	1972
Holbrook, Robert S.	Prof	Michigan		PHD	65	Berkeley	1965
Holbrook, Selah Thomas	Prof	Tenn State		PHD	74	Georgia	
Holcomb, James H. Jr.	Assoc	Txs-El Paso		PHD	85	Tx A&M	1985
Holcombe, Randall G.	Prof	Florida St		PHD	76	Va Tech	1988
Holland, John J. Jr.	Emer	Iona	EN	PHD	72	NYU	1963
Holland, Larry C.	Asst	Ark-Ltl Rock		PHD	94	Okla St	1995

Name	Rank	School	Fields	Degree	Yr	Institution	Since
Holland, Thomas E.	Prof	Tx-Arlington	D	PHD	63	Duke	1970
Hollas, Daniel R.	Prof	Tx-S Antonio		PHD	77	Illinois	1988
Holliday, A. J.	Asst	Wash & Lee	K	PHD		Virginia	1993
Hollister, Robinson G. Jr.	Prof	Swarthmore	IJ	PHD	65	Stanford	1971
Joseph Wharton Professor of Economics							
Hollman, Kenneth W.	Prof	Mid Tenn St		PHD	70	Alabama	1982
Martin Chair of Insurance							
Holman, Mary A.	Prof	George Wash	L	PHD	63	Geo Wash	
Holmes, Alexander B.	Assoc	Oklahoma	RD	PHD	74	SUNY-Bin	
Holmes, James M.	Assoc	SUNY-Buffalo	EF	PHD	67	Chicago	1967
Holmes, Thomas J.	Assoc	Minnesota		PHD	85	Northwes	1995
Holmes, William L.	Assoc	Temple	CD	PHD	66	Illinois	1966
Holmstrom, Bengt	Prof	MIT		PHD	78	Stanford	1995
Holmstrom, Thomas K.	Prof	No Michigan	AEF	PHD		Okla St	1966
Holt, Charles A.	Prof	Virginia	CDL	PHD	77	Car Mellon	1989
Holt, Charles F.	Assoc	San Diego		PHD	70	Purdue	1973
Holt, Harry G.	Assoc	Indiana U-PA	IP	MS	61	Bucknell	1968
Holt, Richard P. F.	Asst	Elon	NJE	PHD	87	Utah	1991
Holthausen, Duncan M. Jr.	Prof	N Carol St	DC	PHD	76	Northwes	1974
Holtmann, Alphonse G.	Prof	U Miami	DI	PHD	63	Wash U	1981
Holtz-Eakin, Douglas	Assoc	Syracuse		PHD	85	Princeton	
Holzer, Harry J.	Prof	Michigan St		PHD	83	Harvard	1983
Holzman, Franklyn Dunn	Retir	Tufts		PHD	52	Harvard	1961
Homalfar, Ghassem	Prof	Mid Tenn St		PHD	82	Alabama	1982
Homer, John S.	Assoc	Olivet		MA	69	Hawaii	1979
Honderich, Kiaran A.	Asst	Williams		PHD	91	Mass	
Hong, Lu	Asst	Syracuse		PHD	91	Minnesota	
Hong, Youngmaio	Asst	Cornell		PHD		Ca-SnDgo	
Honig, Marjorie	C-Pr	CUNY-Hunter		PHD	71	Columbia	
Honig, Solomon	Assoc	Montclair St	ADKR	PHD	76	Columbia	1981
Honig, Susan	Asst	CUNY-Lehman		MS		Pace	
Honkalehto, Oswald	Retir	Colgate	C	PHD	69	MIT	1962
Hood, Frank	Prof	Miss College		PHD	72		1972
Hooker, Mark Allan	Asst	Dartmouth		PHD	90	Stanford	1990
Hooks, Donald L.	Assoc	Alabama		PHD	71	Tx A&M	1971
Hooks, Jon A.	Asst	Albion	G	PHD	89	Mich St	1989
Hooks, Linda M.	Assoc	Wash & Lee	E	PHD	91	UCLA	1993
Hool, Bryce	Prof	SUNY-Stony B		PHD	74	Berkeley	1979
Hoover, Gary	Asst	Jacksonvil U		PHD	95	Kent	1995
Hoover, Kevin D.	Assoc	Cal-Davis	BE	DPHI	85	Oxford	1985
Hope, Barney F.	Prof	CS-Chico		PHD	79	Ca-River	1977
Hopenhayn, Hugo	Assoc	Rochester		PHD		Minnesota	
Hopkins, Barbara	Asst	Wright State		PHD		Maryland	1995
Hopkins, Duane L.	C-As	Fla Southern		MBA		Harvard	1982
Hopkins, Thomas D.	Prof	Rochest Tech	DHK	PHD	71	Yale	1988
Arthur J. Gosnell Professor of Economics							
Hoppe, Hans Hermann	Prof	Nev-L Vegas		PHD		Goethe	1986
Hoppes, Robert B.	Prof	SW Missouri		PHD	75	Nebraska	1980
Hoppie, Maurice R.	Assoc	Elizabethtwn		PHD		Tennessee	1980
Hopusch, Edgar	Assoc	Grambling St		PHD		Colorado	
Hordon, Harris	C-Pr	Jersey City	AG	PHD		NYU	
Horgesheimer, Jerry	C-Ac	So Utah		PHD	73	Ariz St	1992
Horiba, Yutaka	Prof	Tulane		PHD	69	Purdue	1971
Horlacher, David E.	Prof	Middlebury		PHD	73	Penn St	1992
A. Barton Hepburn Professor of Economics							
Horn, Bobbie L.	Assoc	Tulsa		PHD		Iowa St	
Horn, Robert N.	Prof	Jms Madison	JD	PHD	78	N Hamp	1978
Horner, James	Prof	Cameron		PHD		Tx-Dallas	1976
Horney, Mary Jean	Prof	Furman		PHD	77	Duke	1979
Frederick W. Symmes Professor of Economics							
Hornig, Ellen	Asst	SUNY Oswego		PHD	87	Cornell	1984
Horning, Bruce C.	Asst	Fordham		PHD	88	Minnesota	1993
Horowitz, Andrew W.	Asst	Vanderbilt	OL	PHD	89	Wisconsin	1989
Horowitz, Ann R.	Assoc	Florida		PHD	66	Indiana	1972
Horowitz, Avery M.	Assoc	Yeshiva		PHD	84	CUNY	1986
Horowitz, John B.	Asst	Ball State		PHD	88	Tx A&M	1989
Horowtiz, Joel	Prof	Iowa		PHD	67	Cornell	1982
Horton, Joseph J.	Dean	Scranton		PHD	68	So Meth	1986
Horvath, Janos	Prof	Butler	FE	PHD	67	Columbia	
John W. Arbuckle Professor of Economics							
Horvath, Michael	Asst	Stanford		PHD	94	Northwes	1994
Horwich, George	Prof	Purdue		PHD	54	Chicago	1956
Horwitz, Sigmund	Prof	Txs Southern		PHD		Houston	
Horwitz, Steven G.	Asst	St Lawrence	EPB	PHD	90	Geo Mason	1989
Hosek, William R.	Dean	CS-Northrdge		PHD	67	Ca-SnBarb	1988
Hoselitz, Bert F.	Emer	Chicago		JD	36	Vienna	1945
Hosni, Djehane	Assoc	Cen Florida	O	PHD	78	Arkansas	1977
Hosseini, Hamid S.	C-Ac	King's Col		PHD	77	Oregon	9-86
Hosseinzadeh, Esmail	Prof	Drake		PHD	87	New Sch	1988
Hotchkiss, Julie L.	Asst	Georgia St	CJ	PHD	89	Cornell	1989

Hotelling, Harold	C-Ac	Lawrence Tec		PHD	82	Duke	
Hotopp, Susan	Asst	No Central		PHD	89	Illinois	1991
Hou, Chi-Ming	Deces	Colgate	1994	PHD	54	Columbia	1956
Hou, Jack W.	Assoc	CS-Long Bch		PHD	89	Yale	1989
Houston, A. Craig	Retir	Dickinson Cl		PHD	62	Penn St	1956
Houthakker, Hendrick S.	Prof	Harvard		ECD	49	Amsterda	
Henry Lee Professor of Economics							
Howard, Bruce	C-Ac	Wheaton-IL	ABM	PHD		N Illinois	1980
Howard, James E.	Assoc	S F Austin		PHD		Georgia	1976
Howe, Charles W.	Prof	Colorado		PHD	59	Stanford	1970
Howe, Edward T.	Prof	Siena		PHD	73	SUNY-Alb	
Howell, Kristen K.	Assoc	N Car-Wilmin	F	PHD	89	Kentucky	
Howell, Samuel Lide	C-Ac	Presbyterian		MACC		S Carol	1980
Howes, Candance	Asst	Notre Dame	DF	PHD	91	Berkeley	1991
Howrey, E. Philip	Prof	Michigan					
Howsen, Roy M.	Assoc	W Kentucky	D	PHD	80	Arkansas	1981
Hoyer-Swanson, Judith Y.	Assoc	Fairmont St		MS		Va Tech	1973
Hoyt, Gail Mitchell	Asst	Kentucky	A	PHD	92	Kentucky	1994
Hoyt, William H.	Assoc	Kentucky	RHG	PHD	86	Iowa	1969
Hsia, Ke Ting	Retir	CS-L Angeles		PHD	66	Wisconsin	1963
Hsiao, Frank S. T.	Prof	Colorado		PHD	67	Rochester	1975
Hsiao, James C.	Retir	So Conn St		PHD		Conn	
Hsiao, Mei-Chu W.	Assoc	Colo-Denver	OC	PHD	67	Rochester	1981
Hsiao, Yu-Mong	Asst	Campbell		PHD	85	N Car St	1984
Hsieh, Edward T.	Asst	CS-L Angeles					
Hsieh, Eric	Assoc	La St-Shreve		PHD		LSU	1989
Hsing, Yu	H-Pr	SE Louisiana	EJOR	PHD	83	Tennessee	1987
Hsu, Robert C.	Prof	Clark		PHD	70	Berkeley	1971
Hsu, Yu-Chu	Prof	So Conn St		PHD		Cornell	
Hu, Sheng C.	Prof	Purdue		PHD	70	Rochester	1968
Huang, Cliff J.	Prof	Vanderbilt	C	PHD	68	N Carol	1969
Huang, Ju-Chin	Asst	East Carol		PHD	94	N Car St	1993
Huang, Lien-fu	Prof	Howard		PHD		Rochester	
Huang, Wei-Chiao	Assoc	W Michigan	J	PHD	84	Ca-SnBarb	1985
Hubbard, R. Glenn	Prof	Columbia		PHD	83	Harvard	1988
Hubbell, L. Kenneth	Prof	Mo-Kansas Ct	GHM	PHD		Nebraska	1968
Huck, Paul F.	Asst	Wake Forest		PHD	93	Northwes	1989
Huckins, Larry E.	Asst	CUNY-Baruch		PHD	83	Chicago	1980
Huddle, Donald L.	Retir	Rice		PHD	64	Vanderbilt	1964
Huddleston, Kenneth M.	Asst	Georgia SW		MBA		Geo St	
Hudgins, David		Texas Tech		PHD			
Hueckel, Glenn R.	Assoc	Purdue		PHD	72	Wisconsin	1972
Huenneke, Steve	Asst	Minot State	AR	PHD		Kansas St	1991
Huetter, David A.	Prof	Oklahoma	L	PHD	72	Case Wes	1974
Huff, Marvin	Assoc	Indiana U-PA	JK	MA	68	Illinois	1969
Huffman, Gregory	Assoc	So Methodist		PHD	83	Minnesota	1992
Huffman, Wallace E.	Prof	Iowa State	J	PHD	72	Chicago	1974
Huggett, Mark	Asst	Illinois		PHD	91	Minnesota	1990
Hughes, James W.	Asst	Bates	J	PHD	87	Michigan	1987
Hughes, Johnathan R. T.	Deces	Northwestern		PHIL		Oxford	
Hughes, Joseph P.	Assoc	Rutgers-N Br	D	PHD	74	N Carol	1975
Hughes, Woodrow W. Jr.	C-As	Converse		PHD	89	S Carol	1986
Hughey, Alice M.	Assoc	CUNY-Brookly	Q	PHD	84	Columbia	1986
Hull, Brooks B.	C-Ac	Mich-Dearbor	ADLQ	PHD	82	U Wash	1981
Hull, Everson	Asst	Howard		PHD			
Hulten, Charles R.	Prof	Maryland		PHD	73	Berkeley	1985
Hultman, Charles W.	Prof	Kentucky	F	PHD	60	Iowa	1969
Humphreys, Brad	Inst	MD-Baltim Co					
Humphries, John	Prof	Rochest Tech		PHD	67	Syracuse	1962
Hung, Chao-shun	Prof	Fla Atlantic		PHD	82	Tx A&M	1982
Hung, Gregory	Prof	Howard		PHD		Virginia	
Hunsaker, Julie	Asst	Wayne State		PHD	93	Purdue	1993
Hunt, E. K.	C-Pr	Utah		PHD	68	Utah	1978
Hunt, Gary	Prof	Maine	AR	PHD	84	Colorado	1993
Hunt, Jennifer A.	Asst	Yale		PHD	92	Harvard	1992
Hunt, Joseph W.	Prof	Shippensburg		PHD	66	Indiana	1980
Hunter, Thomas Kenneth	Prof	S F Austin		PHD	68	Tennessee	1968
Hunter, William J.	C-Ac	Marquette		PHD	79	Va Tech	1982
Hunyadi, Csilla	Asst	W Virg St	AGM	PHD	86	Budapest	1989
Hurd, John II	Prof	Norwich		PHD	69	Penn	1978
Hurd, Michael	Prof	SUNY-Stony B		PHD	71	Berkeley	1978
Hurley, John F.	C-Ac	Jackson St		PHD	71	Illinois	1972
Hurmozi, Farroh	Prof	Pace		PHD		New Sch	
Hurwicz, Leo	Prof	Minnesota		LLM	38	Warsaw	1951
Husbands, Kaye G.	Assoc	Williams		PHD	90	Harvard	
Husby, Ralph D.	Assoc	Illinois		PHD	69	Cornell	1967
Huskey, Lee	C-Pr	Alaska-Ancho	AHJR	PHD	77	Wash St	1977
Hussain, Riaz	Assoc	Scranton		PHD		J Hopkins	1967
Hussain, Syed Bashir	Assoc	Wis-Oshkosh	F	PHD	83	Calif	1982
Hussen, Ahmed M.	C-Ac	Kalamazoo	DQ	PHD	78	Oreg St	1985

Husted, Steven L.	Prof	Pittsburgh	F	PHD	80	Mich St	1980
Husted, Thomas A.	Assoc	American U		PHD	86	N Carol	1986
Huston, John H.	C-Ac	Trinity		PHD	83	Wisconsin	1983
Hutcheson, Aaron A.	Prof	Austin Peay	AQ	PHD		Clemson	1967
Hutchinson, E. Bruce	H	Tenn-Chattan	DFLR	PHD	79	Virginia	1982
Hutchinson, Gladstone	Asst	Lafayette		PHD	90	Clark	1992
Hutchinson, William K.	Prof	Miami U-Ohio	EF	PHD	75	Iowa	1972
Hutchison, Michael M.	Prof	Ca-Santa Crz	EFG	PHD	83	Oregon	1985
Huth, William L.	C-Pr	West Florida	AMG	PHD	80	Arkansas	1989
Huttman, John P.	Retir	San Fran St		PHD	69	London	1970
Hutton, Patricia A.	Prof	Canisius		PHD	80	Wisconsin	1981
Hvidding, James M.	C-Pr	Kutztown	EB	PHD	76	Maryland	1986
Hwang, Hae-Shin	Prof	Texas A&M		PHD	76	Minnesota	1977
Hwang, Ming-jeng	Prof	W Virginia	DRC	PHD	73	Tx A&M	1974
Hyatt, Douglas E.	Asst	Wis-Milwauke		PHD	92	Toronto	1992
Hyclak, Thomas J.	Prof	Lehigh	JR	PHD	76	Notre Dm	1979
Hyle, Matthew R.	Assoc	Winona State		PHD	85	Maryland	1988
Hyman, David Neil	Prof	N Carol St	HA	PHD	69	Princeton	1969
Hymans, Saul H.	Prof	Michigan		PHD	64	Berkeley	1964
Iannaccone, Laurence R.	Assoc	Santa Clara		PHD	84	Chicago	1982
Ibister, John W.	Prof	Ca-Santa Crz	O	PHD	69	Princeton	1968
Ichiishi, Tatsuro	Prof	Ohio State	C	PHD	74	Berkeley	1987
Ichimura, Hidehiko	Asst	Minnesota		PHD	87	MIT	1987
Ickes, Barry W.	Assoc	Penn State	P	PHD	84	Berkeley	1983
Ierulli, Kathryn	Asst	Ill-Chicago	D	PHD	94	Chicago	
Ifediora, John O.	Asst	Wis-Plattev		PHD		Il-Chicago	1988
Ignatin, George	Assoc	Alabama-Birm	AJK	PHD	69	Tx-Austin	1969
Ihlanfeldt, Keith R.	Prof	Georgia St	HR	PHD	78	Wash U	1981
Ikeda, Sanford	Asst	SUNY-Purchas		PHD	88	NYU	1990
Ikein, Augustine	C-Ac	Delaware St		PHD		Atlanta	
Ikpoh, Andrew	Assoc	Seton Hall		PHD	88	Columbia	
Ilacqua, Joseph A.	Assoc	Bryant	AJ	EDD	93	Boston U	1968
Im, Eric I.	Prof	Hawaii-Hilo		PHD	82	Hi-Manoa	
Imbens, Guido W.	Assoc	Harvard					
Inaba, Frederick S.	Assoc	Wash State		PHD	74	Berkeley	1977
Ingalls, Carolyn A.	Asst	SUNY-Oneonta	M	MBA		SUNY-Bin	
Ingham, Hilary C.	SLect	Manches Inst		PHD		Glasgow	1987
Ingles, Jerry Lee	C-Pr	Univ South		PHD		Cornell	
Ingram, James C.	Emer	No Carolina		PHD	52	Cornell	1952
Ingram, Marlynne B. F.	Assoc	Iowa		PHD	86	Iowa	1988
Innes, Jon T.	Prof	Lehigh	EB	PHD	67	Oregon	1987
Intriligator, Michael D.	Prof	UCLA		PHD	63	MIT	1972
Ioannatos, Petros	Asst	GMI		PHD	89	Wayne St	
Ioannides, Yannis M.	Prof	Tufts	E	PHD	74	Stanford	1995
Ireland, Thomas R.	Assoc	Mo-St Louis		PHD	68	Virginia	1972
Irvine, F. Owen	Assoc	Michigan St		PHD	76	MIT	1982
Irwin, James R.	Asst	Cen Michigan		PHD	86	Rochester	1989
Isaac, Alan G.	Assoc	American U		PHD	86	Ca-Davis	1987
Isaac, R. Mark	H-Pr	Arizona		PHD	80	Cal Tech	1980
Isaacs, Patricia	Assoc	Berea		DBA	94	Kentucky	1989
Isbell, Steven	Assoc	Tenn Tech		PHD	85	Miss	1985
Isenberg, Dorene L.	Assoc	Drew	E	PHD	86	Ca-River	
Ishimine, Tomotaka	Prof	CS-Long Bch		PHD	71	Wisconsin	1967
Iskander, Wasfy B.	Prof	Rhodes		PHD		Indiana	
Islam, Anisul	Assoc	Houston-Down		PHD	84	Alberta	1990
Islam, Muhammad	Assoc	Tx A&M Intl		PHD		Vanderbilt	
Islam, Muhammad Q.	Asst	St Louis		PHD		Indiana	1988
Ispahani, Ahmed S.	Prof	LaVerne		PHD		S Calif	1964
Israelsen, L. Dwight	Assoc	Utah State	ABDE	PHD	73	MIT	1980
Isseman, Andrew W.	Prof	W Virginia	R	PHD	75	Penn	1984
Iwand, Thomas	Retir	Nebraska	D	PHD	59	Oregon	1967
Iwata, Shigeru	Assoc	Kansas		PHD		UCLA	1988
Iwomi, Peter O.	C-Ac	Cen St-Ohio		EDD		Cincinnati	1981
Izadi, Hooshang	Lect	U Lancaster		PHD		Essex	
Izraeli, Oded	Prof	Oakland	RHA	PHD	73	Chicago	1978
Jackson, Dale	Assoc	Hawaii Pacif		PHD		SFran St	
Jackson, Don	Assoc	Abilene Chr		DBA		Geo Wash	
Jackson, John D.	Prof	Auburn		PHD	77	Claremont	1984
Jackson, Marvin R. Jr.	Prof	Arizona St		PHD	67	Berkeley	1962
Jackstadt, Stephen L.	Prof	Alaska-Ancho	AEH	EDD	81	Indiana	1985
Jacobsen, Clifford C.	Asst	Wis-Stev Pt		MA		Ca-River	1969
Jacobsen, Joyce P.	Asst	Wesleyan-CT	J	PHD	91	Stanford	1993
Jacobsen, Lowell R. Jr.	Assoc	Wm Jewell	DM	PHD	86	Edinburg	1981
Jacoby, Hanan	Asst	Rochester		PHD	89	Chicago	1989
Jadlow, Joseph M. Jr.	H-Pr	Oklahoma St		PHD	70	Virginia	1968
Jaeger, William K.	Asst	Williams		PHD	85	Stanford	
Jaffe, Adam B.	Assoc	Brandeis		PHD	85	Harvard	
Jafri, Syed Hussain Ali	Asst	Tarleton St	AFG	PHD	86	Wisconsin	1989
Jaggi, Anand P.	Prof	Barton		PHD		Jabalpur	1971
Jaggi, Arvind	Asst	Frank & Mars		PHD	91	Illinois	1989

Jaggia, Sanjiv	Asst	Suffolk		PHD	90	Indiana	
Jain, Chaman Lal	Prof	St John's		PHD		American	
Jain, Sanjay	Asst	George Wash	O				1994
Jain, Vandana	Asst	Providence	CO	PHD	89	India	1990
Jam, Habib O. E.	Assoc	Rowan Col-NJ		PHD		S Illinois	1979
James, Dilmus Delano	Prof	Txs-El Paso		PHD	70	Mich St	1958
James, John A.	Prof	Virginia	NO	PHD	74	MIT	1978
James, John B.	Assoc	Mid Tenn St		PHD	70	Tx A&M	1969
James, Robert G.	Prof	CS-Chico	EFG	PHD		Oregon	1981
James, William E.	Assoc	Hawaii-Manoa		PHD	79	Hawaii	1984
Jameson, Kenneth P.	Prof	Utah		PHD	70	Wisconsin	1989
Jamison, Lawrence	Asst	Delaware St		LLM		Geo Wash	
Janeba, Eckhard	Lect	Indiana		ABD		Bonn	1994
Jang, Soo M.	Assoc	Plymouth St	E	PHD	78	Cincinnati	1983
Jang, Young S.	Prof	SUNY-Plattsb	CD	PHD	69	SUNY-Alb	1968
Jannuzi, F. Tomasson	Prof	Texas	OR	PHD	58	LondonEc	9-68
Jans, Ivette	Asst	Nebraska	DF	PHD	89	Cantrbry	1989
Jansen, Dennis W.	Prof	Texas A&M		PHD	83	N Carol	1983
Janssen, Arthur J.	Asst	Emporia St		MA		Missouri	1976
Janssen, Larry L.	Prof	So Dakota St	Q	PHD	78	Nebraska	1978
Jantzen, Robert H.	Assoc	Iona	CIJ	PHD	82	Northeas	1982
Jaques, David G.	Prof	CS-Pomona		PHD	73	Claremont	1965
Jargowky, Paul	Asst	Texas-Dallas		PHD	91	Harvard	
Jarrell, Stephen B.	Assoc	W Carolina		PHD	78	Purdue	1988
Jarsulic, Marc W.	Prof	Notre Dame	EC	PHD	78	Penn	1985
Jarvis, Leslie		SUNY-Empire	A	PHD		New Sch	1986
Jasek-Rysdahl, Kelvin	Lect	Wis-Eau Clar		ABD		Colo St	1994
Jaswal, Jasbir S.	Prof	Missouri So		PHD		Missouri	1977
Jawahar, Jim	Prof	SW Okla St					
Jay, Nancy	Asst	Gannon		PHD			
Jaynes, Gerald	Prof	Yale					
Jeannero, Marshall J.	Retir	Bentley	AGP	PHD	69	Fletcher	1966
Jefferson, Gary H.	Assoc	Brandeis		PHD	86	Yale	1984
Jeffress, Philip W.	Prof	New Orleans		PHD	69	Kentucky	1995
Jeffries, Christopher N.	Asst	Jackson St		PHD	88	Fla St	1992
Jehle, Geoffrey A.	C-Pr	Vassar	D	PHD	83	Princeton	1981
Jelavich, Mark S.	Prof	NW Missouri	FR	PHD	80	J Hopkins	1981
Jenkins, Allan	Asst	Neb-Kearney		PHD		Nebraska	1987
Jenkins, Glenn P.	Lect	Harvard		PHD	72	Chicago	1972
Jenkins, Sidney L.	Asst	SE Okla St	AQ	MS	59	Okla St	1968
Jennings, Ann	Asst	WI-Green Bay		PHD		Utah	
Jennings, Donna	Asst	East Tenn St		PHD	95	Vanderbilt	1994
Jennings, E. James	Assoc	Purdue-Calmu		PHD	79		1978
Jensen, Elizabeth J.	C-Ac	Hamilton	LN	PHD	84	MIT	1983
Jensen, Eric R.	Assoc	Wm & Mary		PHD	82	Michigan	1982
Jensen, Farrell	C-Pr	Brigham Yg		PHD	72	Kansas St	1982
Jensen, Gail A.	Assoc	Wayne State		PHD	86	Minnesota	1989
Jensen, George	Assoc	CS-L Angeles		PHD	68	U Wash	1962
Jensen, Mark	Asst	So Illinois	EC	PHD	94	Wash U	1994
Jensen, Richard A.	Prof	Kentucky	D	PHD	80	Northwes	1980
Jensen, Robert J.	Assoc	Pacific Luth		MA	67	Nebraska	1968
Jensen, Rolf W.	Assoc	Conn Coll		PHD		Mass	
Jeon, B. Philip	Asst	John Carroll	CEJT	PHD	90	Kentucky	1991
Jeon, Bang Nam	Asst	Drexel		PHD	87	Indiana	1988
Jeong, Dong K.	Assoc	N Carol A&T		PHD	74	Wayne St	
Jerison, Michael	Assoc	SUNY-Albany	DC	PHD		Wisconsin	
Jerome, Robert T. Jr.	Assoc	Jms Madison	DF	PHD	82	Virginia	1981
Jerrell, Max E.	Assoc	No Arizona	EC	PHD	84	Ariz St	1981
Jessup, Paul F.	Prof	Hamline	G	PHD	66	Northwes	1988
William Kahlert Professor							
Jesswein, Wayne A.	H-Pr	Minn-Duluth	F	PHD	69	Illinois	1974
Jewell, Nasrin	Prof	St Catherine	OA	PHD	81	Wisconsin	1981
Jhun, U-Jin	Prof	SUNY Oswego		PHD	73	SUNY-Alb	1972
Jianakoplos, Nancy A.	Asst	Colorado St	CE	PHD	83	Ohio St	1990
Jilani, Saleha	Asst	Wm & Mary		PHD	94	J Hopkins	1992
Jilling, Michael	Prof	SC-Spartanbu	ACMF	PHD		S Carol	1975
Jin, Fuchun	Asst	Colgate	E	PHD	93	Ohio St	1993
Jindia, Jaswant R.	C-Pr	Southern		PHD	70	Illinois	1970
Joerdling, Wayne H.	Prof	Wash State		PHD	79	Northwes	1979
Joh, Sung-Wook	Asst	SUNY-Albany		PHD		Harvard	
Johansen, Thomas C.	Asst	Fort Hays St		PHD	90	Okla St	1989
John, A. Andrew	Asst	Virginia	AE	PHD	88	Yale	1993
Johnes, Geraint	SLect	U Lancaster		PHD		Lancaster	
Johnson, Bruce H.	Assoc	Gustavus Ado		PHD	79	Houston	1986
Johnson, Bruce K.	Assoc	Centre	AJL	PHD	85	Virginia	1987
James Graham Brown Associate Professor of Economics							
Johnson, Byron L.	Emer	Colo-Denver		PHD	47	Wisconsin	1947
Johnson, Colleen	Asst	E Oregon St		PHD	88	Wash St	
Johnson, D. Gale	Emer	Chicago		PHD	45	Iowa St	1944
Johnson, David B.	Prof	Louisiana St	H	PHD	68	Virginia	

Johnson, Denise H.	Asst	Alma		PHD	93	Mass	1994
Johnson, Dennis A.	Prof	South Dakota		PHD	72	Iowa	1964
Johnson, Donn M.	Asst	No Iowa		PHD	89	Colo St	1989
Johnson, Dudley W.	Retir	U Washington		PHD	57	Northwes	1960
Johnson, E. William	Prof	Shepherd		PHD	74	Virginia	1971
Johnson, George	Prof	Michigan					
Johnson, Ivan C.	Prof	CS-Northrdge		PHD	71	W Ontario	1973
Johnson, James	Prof	Meredith		PHD		Duke	1980
Johnson, James A.	Prof	Colorado Col		MA	59	Stanford	1956
Johnson, Joseph T.	Asst	Central Okla		PHD	80	Chicago	
Johnson, Karen R.	Lect	Baylor		MIM		Baylor	1979
Johnson, Kirk	Asst	Olivet		MA	90	Wayne St	1990
Johnson, Lowell E.	Prof	Bemidji St		PHD	75	Cornell	1976
Johnson, M. Bruce	Retir	Cal-Santa Br		PHD	62	Northwes	1968
Johnson, Mark	Asst	Alabama		PHD	86	Ca-SnDgo	1989
Johnson, Mark	Asst	Chicago St		PHD			
Johnson, Paul A.	Asst	Vassar	E	PHD	89	Stanford	1995
Johnson, R. Larry	Prof	New Hamp Col		DBA	82	Geo Wash	
Johnson, Robert S.	Dean	Columbus		PHD	64	Virginia	1993
Bill Heard Chair of Business Administration							
Johnson, Ronald N.	Prof	Montana St		PHD	77	U Wash	1981
Johnson, Shirley B.	Assoc	Vassar	I	PHD		Columbia	1967
Johnson, Steve A.	Assoc	Txs-El Paso		PHD	88	Alabama	1987
Johnson, Victoria	Prof	Mercer-Atlan		DPA		Georgia	1985
Johnson, W. Clint	Prof	Cen Arkansas		PHD	75	Tx Tech	1975
Johnson, Walter D.	C-Pr	Mo-Rolla		PHD		Oklahoma	1988
Johnson, Walter L.	Assoc	Missouri	AEGH	PHD	63	Duke	1965
Johnson, William B.	Assoc	San Jose St		MA	54	Stanford	1960
Johnson, William R.	Prof	Virginia	DJ	PHD	75	MIT	1974
Johnston, Charles W.	Asst	Mich-Flint		PHD	88	Tx-Austin	1988
Johnston, John	Emer	Calif-Irvine		PHD	57	Wales	1978
Johnston, Lewis	Asst	Gustavus Ado		PHD	90	Berkeley	1993
Johnstone, Robert L.	Prof	Berea		PHD	61	Illinois	1964
Clarence M. Clark Professor of Mountain Agriculture and Economics							
Jolly, Eric S.	Asst	SC-Spartanbu	A	MA		Ohio U	1968
Jones, Barbara A. P.	Dean	Prairie View		PHD	73	Geo St	1987
Jones, Bryce J.	Retir	Rockhurst	1994	PHD	55	St Louis	1964
Jones, Carl R.	Prof	Naval Postgr		PHD	65	Claremont	1965
Jones, Chad	Asst	Stanford		PHD	93	MIT	1993
Jones, Charles	Asst	Princeton		PHD	94	Michigan	1994
Jones, Charlotte	Prof	La St-Shreve		DBA		La Tech	1984
Jones, Clifton T.	C-Pr	S F Austin	CD	PHD	85	Tx A&M	1995
Jones, David D.	Prof	St Thomas-MN	E	PHD	75	Indiana	1972
Jones, Derek C.	Prof	Hamilton	PJ	PHD	74	Cornell	1972
Jones, Ellis J.	Prof	Gustavus Ado		EDD	65	N Dakota	1958
Jones, Ethel B.	Prof	Auburn		PHD	61	Chicago	1975
Jones, James G.	Asst	SW Baptist	ECO	MBA		Arkansas	1988
Jones, Kenneth D.	Prof	Georgia Col		PHD	77	La Tech	1987
Jones, Kent A.	Assoc	Babson		PHD	81	Geneva	1982
Jones, Lamar B.	Prof	Louisiana St	J	PHD	65	Tx-Austin	1967
Jones, Leroy P.	Prof	Boston Univ	HLO	PHD	74	Harvard	1976
Jones, Marcia Noreen	Assoc	Geo Southern		PHD	86	Illinois	1986
Jones, Michael	Assoc	Bowdoin	F	PHD		Yale	1987
Jones, Otolorin		SUNY-Empire	A	PHD		Ohio U	1985
Jones, Robert C. III	Asst	NW St of LA		PHD	91	UCLA	
Jones, Robert J.	Assoc	Skidmore		PHD	78	Columbia	1973
Jones, Ronald W.	Prof	Rochester		PHD	56	MIT	1958
Xerox Professor of Economics							
Jones, Royal Maurice	Prof	W Carolina		PHD	67	Maryland	1971
Jones, Trefor T.	Lect	Manches Inst		PHD		Dundee	1976
Jones, Warren	C-Ac	W Illinois	AEHN	PHD	82	Iowa	1983
Jonish, James E.	Prof	Texas Tech		PHD	69	Michigan	1973
Jonokin, Jon	Asst	Tenn Tech		PHD	94	Tennessee	1989
Jonsson, Petur	Asst	Fayetteville		PHD	86	Penn St	
Jordan, James S.	Prof	Minnesota		PHD	75	Northwes	1976
Jordan, John M.	Assoc	Loyola-Maryl	C	PHD	70	Purdue	1964
Jordan, W. John	Prof	Seton Hall		PHD	77	SUNY-Alb	1977
Jorge, Antonio	Prof	Fla Internat	BPOA	PHD		Villanova	
Jorgenson, Dale W.	C-Pr	Harvard		PHD	59	Harvard	1969
Frederick E. Abbe Professor of Economics							
Joseph, Hyman	Prof	Iowa		PHD	69	Northwes	1966
Joshi, Sumit	Asst	George Wash	CD	PHD	91	Indiana	1992
Joskow, Paul L.	H-Pr	MIT	O	PHD	72	Yale	1972
Mitsui Professor of Economics and Management; Associate Head							
Joutz, Frederick L.	Assoc	George Wash	EC	PHD	87	U Wash	1988
Jovanovic, Boyan	Prof	Pennsylvania	EL	PHD	78	Chicago	1995
Joyce, B. Patrick	Prof	Mich Tech	D	PHD	74	Missouri	1972
Joyce, Joseph P.	C-Ac	Wellesley		PHD	84	Boston U	1982
Jozsa, Frank	Assoc	Pfeiffer		PHD	77	Geo St	1991
Ju, Jiandong	Asst	Oklahoma	D	PHD	95	Penn St	1995

Name	Rank	School	Fields	Degree	Yr	Institution	Year
Judge, Rebecca P.	Assoc	St Olaf	ADQ	PHD	76	Duke	1987
Juhn, Chinhui	Asst	Houston		PHD	91	Chicago	1992
Jung, Chulho	Assoc	Ohio Univ	CDFQ	PHD	89	Michigan	1989
Junk, Paul E.	Prof	Minn-Duluth	E	PHD	62	Northwes	1979
Jursa, Paul E.	Assoc	Charleston		PHD		Tx-Austin	1976
Juster, F. Thomas	Prof	Michigan		PHD	56	Columbia	1973
Kabis, Zeinhom M.	Prof	St Ambrose		PHD	68	Illinois	1973
Kabot, Alvin	Assoc	CUNY-Hunter		LLM	63	NYU	9-67
Kacapyr, Elia W.	Assoc	Ithaca	AG	PHD	85	Geo St	1985
Kader, Ahmad	Prof	Carroll		PHD		W Virginia	1980
Kadiyala, K. Rao	Prof	Purdue		PHD	66	Wisconsin	1970
Kaempfer, William H.	C-Pr	Colorado		PHD	79	Duke	1981
Kaestner, Robert J.	Asst	Rider	IJT	PHD	88	CUNY	1989
Kafoglis, Milton Z.	Prof	Emory	LI	PHD	58	Ohio St	1979
George Woodruff Professor of Economics							
Kaganovich, M.	Asst	Indiana		PHD	85	USSR	1991
Kagel, John H.	Prof	Pittsburgh	D	PHD	70	Purdue	1988
Kahane, Leo H.	Asst	CS-Hayward		PHD	91	Columbia	1991
Kahn, Abraham	H-Ac	N Adams St		MA		SUNY-Alb	
Kahn, Charles M.	Prof	Illinois		PHD	81	Harvard	1988
Kahn, James A.	Assoc	Rochester		PHD	86	MIT	1986
Kahn, James R.	Assoc	Tennessee		PHD	81	Maryland	
Kahn, Saleem M.	Prof	Bloomsburg		PHD		J Gutenb	
Kain, John F.	Prof	Harvard		PHD	61	Berkeley	1964
Kaiser, Carl P.	Prof	Wash & Lee	JC	PHD	80	Wash U	1979
Kajii, Atsushi	Asst	Pennsylvania	G	PHD	91	Harvard	1991
Kalaba, Robert E.	Prof	So Calif		PHD	58	NYU	1969
Kalish, Richard J.	Assoc	SUNY-Albany	N	PHD	63	Colorado	1969
Kallianiotis, John	Asst	Scranton		PHD		CUNY	1990
Kallon, Kelfala M.	Assoc	No Colorado	EFHO	PHD	83	Virginia	1993
Kamara, Avraham	Assoc	U Washington		PHD	86	Columbia	1984
Kamas, Linda	Assoc	Santa Clara		PHD	82	Berkeley	1988
Kamath, Shyam J.	Prof	CS-Hayward		PHD	87	Simon Fr	1986
Kamdar, Nipoli	Asst	Trinity		PHD	93	Syracuse	1993
Kamen, Michele	Asst	CUNY-Lehman		MBA		St Johns	
Kamerschen, David R.	Prof	Georgia	DK	PHD	64	Mich St	1974
Jasper N. Dorsey Professor							
Kamery, Rob H.	Assoc	Christian Br	ABJ	MS	81	Arkansas	1979
Kamien, Morton I.	Prof	Northwestern		PHD	64	Purdue	1970
Kamihigashi, Takashi	Asst	SUNY-Stony B		PHD	94	Wisconsin	1994
Kaminarides, John S.	Prof	Arkansas St	AFTO	PHD	68	Houston	1968
Kamp, Bradley	Asst	South Fla	L	PHD	93	Ca-SnDgo	1992
Kamps, William E.	Prof	So Dakota St	E	PHD	74	Wash St	1972
Kamrany, Nake M.	SLect	So Calif		PHD	62	S Calif	1976
Kanazawa, Mark T.	C-Ac	Carleton		PHD	87	Stanford	1985
Kandil, Magda	Assoc	Wis-Milwauke		PHD	88	Wash St	1992
Kane, John C.	C-Ac$	SUNY Oswego		PHD	86	SUNY-SBr	1983
Kane, Joseph A.	Prof	LaSalle		PHD		Temple	1961
Kane, Mamadou	Assoc	E Stroudsbur	EFN	MA	72	NYU	1973
Kane, Tim D.	Prof	Texas-Tyler		PHD	72	Tx-Austin	1981
Kaneda, Hiromitsu	Emer	Cal-Davis	AFOQ	PHD	64	Stanford	1973
Kang, Eungmin B.	Asst	St Cloud St		PHD	90	Geo St	1990
Kang, Inbong	Asst	SUNY-Bingham		PHD	93	Rochester	1995
Kangayappan, Kumaraswamy	Assoc	WI-Green Bay		PHD		Wisconsin	
Kannappan, Subbiah	Prof	Michigan St		PHD		Tufts	
Kanovsky, Eliyahu	Prof	Yeshiva		PHD			
Ludwig Jesselson Chair in Economics; spring only							
Kant, Chander	Assoc	Seton Hall		PHD	80	So Meth	
Kantarelis, Demetrius	Assoc	Assumption	D	PHD	83	Clark	1983
Kanthi, Mahendra S.	Prof	Saginaw Vall		PHD		Kentucky	1984
Kantor, Shawn E.	Asst	Arizona		PHD	90	Cal Tech	1990
Kao, C. H.	Asst	Syracuse		PHD	83	SUNY-SBr	
Kaparakis, Emanuel	Inst	Providence	EGF	ABD		Conn	1990
Kaplan, Phillip	Prof	New Haven		PHD	64	J Hopkins	
Kapler, Janis	Asst	Mass-Boston	FL	PHD	93	American	1993
Kapuria-Foreman, Vibha	Assoc	Colorado Col		PHD	87	Pittsburgh	1989
Karake, Zeinab	Assoc	Catholic		PHD			
Karangu, Mwangi	Asst	Morgan State		PHD		Walden	
Karatjas, Nicholas	Prof	Indiana U-PA	CDI	PHD	76	SUNY-SBr	1978
Karayaicin, Ali Cem	Assoc	Fla Internat	EF	PHD	89	Columbia	1989
Karbassioon, Ebrahim	C-Pr	E Illinois		PHD	81	Nebraska	1980
Kareken, John H.	Prof	Minnesota		PHD		MIT	1958
Karier, Thomas M.	Prof	East Wash		PHD		Berkeley	1981
KariKari, John A.	Assoc	Tulsa					
Karim, Aleman	Asst	Rhode Isl Cl		PHD		Boston U	
Karlson, Stephen	Assoc	No Illinois		PHD		Wisconsin	
Karni, Edi	Prof	J Hopkins		PHD	71	Chicago	1981
Karns, James M.	Prof	E Kentucky		PHD	75	Oklahoma	1975
Karpoff, Jonathan M.	Prof	U Washington		PHD	82	UCLA	1983
Karras, Georgios	Asst	Ill-Chicago	E	PHD	90	Ohio St	

Karscig, Mark P.	Prof	Cen Missouri		PHD	87	Pittsburgh	1981
Karsten, Siegfried G.	Retir	West Georgia	8-94	PHD	70	Utah	1978
Karstensson, Lewis	Assoc	Nev-L Vegas		PHD	75	Ohio	1979
Kartman, Arthur E.	Prof	San Diego St		PHD	69	U Wash	1968
Karumanchi, V. R.	Inst	Alabama A&M	AO	MS		Ala A&M	
Kaschins, Edward A.	H-Pr	Luther		PHD	73	Iowa	1961
Kaserman, David L.	Prof	Auburn		PHD	76	Florida	1986
Torchmark Professor							
Kask, Susan B.	Asst	W Carolina		PHD	88	Wyoming	1993
Kasper, Hirshel	Prof	Oberlin	DJ	PHD	63	Minnesota	1963
Kasper, Victor Jr.	Asst	Elmira		PHD	83	Rutgers	1990
Kassouf, Sheen T.	Prof	Calif-Irvine		PHD	65	Columbia	1965
Kasturi, Prahlad	Assoc	Radford		PHD		Hawaii	
Kasturia, Sangeeta	Asst	Oklahoma	D	PHD	95	Ca-San Cr	1995
Kasun, Jacqueline R.	Retir	CS-Humboldt		PHD	56	Columbia	1969
Kato, Takao	Assoc	Colgate	J	PHD	86	Queen's	1986
Kats, Amoz	Prof	Virg Tech	D	PHD	72	Minnesota	1974
Katsimbris, George M.	Prof	Bridgeport		PHD	77	Conn	1978
Harvey Hubbell Professor of Economics and Finance							
Katz, Arnold M.	Prof	Pittsburgh	J	PHD	61	Yale	
Katz, Barbara G.	Prof	New York U	CDP	PHD	73	Penn	1974
Katz, Lawrence F.	Prof	Harvard		PHD	85	MIT	1986
Katz, Michael	Prof	Cal-Berkeley		PHD		Oxford	
Katz, Steven	Assoc	CUNY-Baruch		PHD	82	NYU	
Katzner, Donald W.	Prof	Massachusett		PHD	65	Minnesota	1975
Kauffman, Daniel E.	C-Pr	Winona State		PHD		Nebraska	1983
Kauffman, Kyle	Assoc	Wellesley		PHD	93	Illinois	1993
Kaufman, Bruce E.	Prof	Georgia St	J	PHD	78	Wisconsin	1977
Kaufman, Dennis A.	Assoc	Wis-Parkside	CH	PHD	87	Kansas	1987
Kaufman, Roger T.	Prof	Smith	CEJP	PHD	78	MIT	1983
Kaufmann, Hugo M.	Prof	CUNY-Queens	FE	PHD	68	Columbia	1967
Kaun, David E.	Prof	Ca-Santa Crz	J	PHD	64	Stanford	1966
Kavesh, Robert A.	Prof	New York U	B	PHD	54	Harvard	1958
Marcus Nadler Professor of Finance & Economics							
Kawahito, Kiyoshi	Prof	Mid Tenn St		PHD	71	Maryland	1971
Kayaalp, Orhan	Assoc	CUNY-Lehman		PHD		CUNY	1979
Kayser, Hilke A.	Asst	Hamilton	HIQ	PHD	94	Wisconsin	1993
Kazemi, Abbas A.	Assoc	Rhode Isl Cl		PHD		SUNY-SBr	
Kazemi, Hossein S.	C-Ac	Stonehill	EF	PHD		Clark	1982
Kazmer, Daniel R.	Lect	Georgetown		PHD	73	MIT	
Kazura, Martie	Asst	Berea		MBA	90	Montana	1991
Keane, Michael P.	Asst	Minnesota		PHD	89	Brown	1988
Kearl, James R.	Prof	Brigham Yg		PHD	75	MIT	1975
Kearns, Robert	Assoc	Carroll					
Keating, John W.	Asst	Wash Univ		PHD	89	Northwes	1989
Keefe, David E.	Assoc	Pacific	FT	PHD	80	Berkeley	1978
Keehn, Richard	Prof	Wis-Parkside	EGN	PHD	72	Wisconsin	1970
Keeler, James	C-Ac	Kenyon		PHD	81	Indiana	1984
Keeler, Theodore E.	Prof	Cal-Berkeley		PHD	71	MIT	1977
Keenan, Donald C.	Prof	Georgia	CHR	DSC	78	Wash U	1978
Keener, Gary	Asst	Heidelberg	AH	PHD	93	Kentucky	1991
Kehoe, Patrick J.	Asst	Minnesota		PHD	86	Harvard	1984
Kehoe, Patrick J.	Assoc	Pennsylvania	POF	PHD	86	Harvard	1992
Ronald S. Lauder Term Associate Professor of Economics							
Kehoe, Timothy J.	Prof	Minnesota		PHD	79	Yale	1987
Keil, Katherine A.	Asst	Northeastern		PHD	89	Ca-SnDgo	1990
Keil, Manfred		Claremont					
Keil, Manfred W.	Asst	Northeastern		PHD	85	London	1988
Keil, Stanley R.	Assoc	Ball State		PHD	73	Oregon	1973
Keilany, Ziad	Prof	Tenn-Chattan	EO	PHD	68	Indiana	1968
Guerry Professor							
Keith, John E.	Prof	Utah State	DEQR	PHD	73	Utah St	1972
Keith, Kristen	Asst	Toledo		PHD		Ohio St	1994
Kelejian, Harry	Prof	Maryland		PHD	68	Wisconsin	1968
Keleta, Ethiopia	Assoc	Txs Southern		PHD		Rice	
Keller, Anita	Inst	Ark-Ltl Rock		ABD			1991
Keller, Robert R.	Prof	Colorado St	EN	PHD	71	Wisconsin	1974
Keller, Wolfgang	Asst	Wisconsin		PHD	95	Yale	1995
Kelley, Allen C.	Prof	Duke		PHD	64	Stanford	1972
James D. Duke Professor							
Kelley, Bruce R.	Asst	Fla Internat	OF	PHD	90	Mass	1990
Kelley, George T.	Prof	Worcester St		PHD		Clark	1969
Kelly, Alison	Asst	Suffolk		PHD		Boston C	
Kelly, Eamon M.	Prof	Tulane		PHD	65	Columiba	1981
Kelly, Erwin L. Jr.	Prof	CS-Sacrament		AB	54	Berkeley	1971
Kelly, Jerry S.	Prof	Syracuse		PHD	69	Harvard	
Kelly, John C.	Dean	Marist		PHD		Boston C	1962
Kelly, Robert A.	Asst	Fairfield	HKC	PHD		Geotown	1978
Kelly, Thomas M.	Prof	Baylor		PHD	70	Okla St	1969
Kelly, Tricia	Asst	Quinnipiac		PHD		Mass	1995

Name	Rank	Institution	Field	Degree	Yr	Degree From	Since
Kelso, Patrick R.	Assoc	West Tx A&M	EHN	PHD	68	Tx-Austin	1967
Kemper, Daniel	Assoc	Lindenwood		MBA		Lindenwd	1-88
Kempey, William M.	C-Pr	Kean		PHD	70	NYU	9-78
Kendall, Elizabeth A.	Assoc	N Adams St		MLS		Mass	
Kende, Michael	Asst	INSEAD		PHD	92	MIT	9-92
Kendrick, David A.	Prof	Texas	CE	PHD	66	MIT	7-70
Ralph W. Yarborough Centennial Professor of Liberal Arts							
Kenen, Peter B.	Prof	Princeton		PHD	58	Harvard	1971
Walker Professor Economics & International Finance							
Kenison, Arthur M.	Prof	St Anselm	ACG	PHD	80	Boston U	1980
Kenison, Jeanne H.	Assoc	St Anselm	C	EDD	86	Vanderbilt	1988
Kenkel, James L.	Assoc	Pittsburgh	C	PHD	69	Purdue	1969
Kennett, David A.	Prof	Vassar	F	PHD	76	Columbia	1976
Kenney, James M.	Assoc	Union	QDMG	PHD	72	Stanford	1972
Kenny, Lawrence W.	C-Pr	Florida	DHJ	PHD	77	Chicago	1975
Kent, Calvin A.	Dean	Marshall		PHD	67	Missouri	1993
Kent, Richard J.	Assoc	Kent State	E	PHD	76	Berkeley	1983
Kenyon, Daphne A.	Assoc	Simmons	HI	PHD	80	Michigan	1989
Kerby, William C.	Prof	CS-Sacrament		PHD	71	Oregon	1967
Kerchner, Robert B.	Assoc	Washburn		PHD	73	Missouri	1976
Kercsmar, John	Assoc	E Stroudsbur	M	PHD	85	Houston	
Kerkvliet, Joe R.	Assoc	Oregon State	L	PHD	86	Wyoming	9-88
Kermani, Taghi T.	Prof	Youngstown		PHD	59	Nebraska	
Kern, Clifford R.	Assoc	SUNY-Bingham		PHD	74	Harvard	1971
Kern, William	Assoc	W Michigan	B	PHD	82	Colo St	1987
Kerr, Peter M.	Prof	SE Missouri	AEBF	PHD	79	Kansas	1980
Kerr, Stephen W.	C-Ac	Hendrix		MBA	77	So Meth	1979
Kersey, Bruce L.	Prof	East Txs St	DEG	PHD		LSU	
Kersten, Timothy W.	Prof	Cal Poly-SLO		PHD	73	Oregon	1971
Kesler, Jason J.	Prof	Mankato St	AJ	DA		Idaho	1980
Kessel, Herbert	Prof	St Michael's	AJDC	PHD	81	Boston U	1977
Kesselring, Randall G.	Assoc	Arkansas St	ACJF	PHD	80	Oklahoma	1984
Kessler, Adam	Assoc	F Dick-Teane		PHD		NYU	
Kessler, Alan L.	Assoc	Providence	DH	PHD	84	Boston C	1985
Ketkar, Kusum	Prof	Seton Hall		PHD	80	Vanderbilt	
Kevane, Michael	Asst	Santa Clara		PHD	94	Berkeley	1995
Key, Euell Dwyane	Prof	S F Austin		PHD	70	S Illinois	1970
Khalil, Fahad A.	Asst	U Washington		PHD	71	Va Tech	1991
Khalil, Mohamad	Assoc	Fairmont St		PHD		W Virginia	
Khan, Agha Nisar	Prof	Virginia St		PHD	70	Va Tech	1972
Khan, Anwar S.	Prof	N Carol A&T		PHD	72	Wisconsin	
Khan, Aubhik	Asst	Virginia	EO	PHD	93	Penn	1993
Khan, Azizur Rahman	C-Pr	Cal-Riversid	FOPR	PHD	66	Cambridge	1988
Khan, Farida C.	Asst	Wis-Parkside	FO	PHD	90	Maryland	1990
Khan, M. Ali	Prof	J Hopkins		PHD		Yale	1988
Khan, Moosa	Prof	Prairie View		PHD	86	Simon Fr	1989
Khandke, Kailash	Asst	Furman		PHD	93	Ca-Davis	1995
Khandker, A. Wahhab	Prof	Wis-La Cross	ACF	PHD	80	So Meth	1983
Khang, Chulsoon	Prof	Oregon	FEO	PHD	65	Minnesota	1966
Khanna, Jyoti	Asst	Colgate	H	PHD	90	Iowa	1992
Kharadia, Virabhai C.	Prof	NW Missouri	AED	PHD	73	Illinois	1973
Khayum, Mohammed	Asst	So Indiana		PHD	90	Temple	1991
Khorassani, Jacqueline	Asst	Marietta	AEFH	ABD	92	W Virginia	1994
Kidane, Abraham Z.	Prof	CS-Dominguez	AFOI	PHD	71	UCLA	1971
Kidman, Peter N.	Prof	E Stroudsbur	K	PHD	71	W Virginia	1977
Kiebala, Susan	C-As	Olivet		MBA	77	W Mich	1989
Kiefer, David M.	Assoc	Utah		PHD	74	Michigan	1981
Kiefer, Nicholas M.	Prof	Cornell		PHD	76	Princeton	1980
Kienzle, Edward C.	Assoc	Stonehill	HC	PHD	76	Boston C	1980
Kiernan, Joseph J.	Asst	F Dick-Teane		PHD		Fordham	
Kiesling, Herbert J.	Prof	Indiana		PHD	65	Harvard	1965
Kiesling, Lynne	Asst	Wm & Mary		PHD	93	Northwes	1992
Kigner, Brent M.	Asst	Hartwick	ACOP	PHD	90	Minnesota	1990
Kiker, B. F.	Prof	So Carolina		PHD	65	Tulane	1971
Jeff B. Bates Professor of Public Administration & Finance							
Kilbride, Wade R.	Asst	Cen Florida	D	EDD		Fla Atl	1978
Kilby, C. Robert	Asst	Rio Grande		PHD	93	Cincinnati	1993
Kilby, Christopher P.	Asst	Vassar	O	PHD		Stanford	1993
Kilby, Peter	Prof	Wesleyan-CT	O	DPHI	67	Oxford	1965
Kildegaard, Arne C.	Asst	Mississippi		PHD		Tx-Austin	1993
Killingworth, Mark R.	Prof	Rutgers-N Br	J	DPHI	77	Oxford	1978
Kim, Benjamin J. C.	Assoc	Nebraska	F	PHD	83	UCLA	1983
Kim, Chulsoo	Asst	Rutgers-N Br	E	PHD	90	Stanford	1990
Kim, Dae-il	Asst	Rice		PHD	92	Chicago	1992
Kim, Gew-Rae	Asst	Bridgeport					
Kim, Hak Youn	Prof	W Kentucky	CDO	PHD	82	Cincinnati	1983
Kim, Han J.	Prof	So Dakota St	C	PHD	69	Oreg St	1967
Kim, Jae-Young	Asst	SUNY-Albany		PHD		Minnesota	
Kim, Juho	Prof	Miss Vall St		PHD		Oklahoma	1973
Kim, Ki Hoon	Prof	Central Conn		PHD	68	Conn	1967

Kim, Kil-Joong	C-Pr	Austin Peay	FO	PHD	80	Cincinnati	1980
Kim, Kirk Y.	C-Pr	Wis-Whitewat		PHD	70	Utah	1969
Kim, Kwan S.	Prof	Notre Dame	OF	PHD	67	Minnesota	1975
Kim, Kyoo H.	Prof	Bowling Gr		PHD	78	Wisconsin	1978
Kim, Myung J.	Asst	Alabama		PHD	89	U Wash	1989
Kim, Shin	Inst	Chicago St		MS		Illinois	1987
Kim, Sukkoo	Asst	Wash Univ		PHD	93	UCLA	1993
Kim, Sun K.	Prof	CS-L Angeles		PHD	66	S Calif	1964
Kim, Sungwoo	Prof	Northeastern		PHD	57	Berkeley	1972
Kim, Sunwoong	Assoc	Wis-Milwauke		PHD	85	MIT	1989
Kim, Yang H.	Prof	Alabama A&M	AOE	PHD	67	Utah	1965
Kim, Yong-Gwan	Asst	Iowa		PHD	90	Ca-SnDgo	1990
Kim, Yoonbai	Assoc	Kentucky	EFG	PHD	87	Stanford	1991
Kim, Youn Suk	Prof	Kean		PHD	73	New Sch	9-74
Kim, Young Chin	Prof	No Illinois		PHD	68	Columbia	1970
Kimani, Joseph	Inst	Morgan State		MBA		Atlanta	
Kimball, Miles S.	Assoc	Michigan		PHD	87	Harvard	1987
Kimbrough, Kent P.	Assoc	Duke		PHD	80	Chicago	1980
Kimenyi, Samson M.	Assoc	Connecticut	HI	PHD	86	Geo Mason	1991
Kimzey, Bruce W.	Prof	Brighm Yg-HI		PHD	70	Wash St	1989
Kinal, Terrance	Prof	SUNY-Albany		PHD	76	Minnesota	1980
Kindahl, James K.	Prof	Massachusett		PHD	58	Chicago	1967
King, Arthur E.	Prof	Lehigh	FP	PHD	76	Ohio St	1976
King, Arthur T.	Prof	Baylor		PHD	77	Colorado	1982
King, Clay B.	Assoc	Minot State	A	PHD		Wash St	1975
King, Mary C.	Asst	Portland St		PHD	91	Berkeley	1992
King, Paul G.	Prof	Denison		PHD	71	Illinois	1967
John Harris Chair							
King, Philip G.	Assoc	San Fran St		PHD	87	Cornell	1987
King, Randall H.	Assoc	Akron		PHD	78	Ohio St	1978
King, Robert G.	Prof	Virginia	EG	PHD	80	Brown	1993
A. Willis Robertson Professor of Economics							
King, Vereda J.	Assoc	N Carol A&T		PHD		Duke	
Kingerski, Angie	Lect	MD-Baltim Co					
Kingston, Jerry L.	Prof	Arizona St		PHD	69	Penn St	1969
Kinnaman, Thomas	Asst	Bucknell		PHD		Virginia	
Kinney, Kinney	Assoc	Shepherd		PHD		Maryland	1994
Kipps, Paul H.	Prof	Jms Madison	A	PHD	68	Cornell	1968
Kirby, Maurice W.	Read	U Lancaster		PHD		Sheffield	
Kirk, Eugene F.	Asst	St Bonaventu	G	PHD	74	Boston C	1972
Kirkland, Jack	Assoc	Troy State		PHD	82	Wash St	1995
Kirklin, Wayne	Assoc	Heidelberg		MBA		NYU	1978
Kirkpatrick, Rickey C.	Assoc	Appalach St	FM	PHD	78	Tulane	1980
Kiser, Larry L.	Prof	East Wash		PHD	73	Rutgers	1971
Kish-Goodling, Donna M.	Asst	Muhlenberg		PHD	92	Lehigh	1990
Kishan, Ruby Pandey	Asst	SW Texas St		PHD	86	Tx A&M	
Kitamura, Yuichi	Asst	Minnesota		PHD	93	Yale	1993
Kitrell, Frederick J.	Prof	Mid Tenn St		PHD	70	Miss	1971
Kiyotaki, Nobuhiro	Assoc	Minnesota		PHD		Harvard	1991
Kjetsaa, Richard W.	Asst	F Dick-Teane		PHD		Fordham	
Klaasen, Thomas Albert	Prof	Txs Wesleyan		PHD	69	Mich St	1989
Klassen, Peter J.	Dean	CS-Fresno		PHD		S Calif	1966
Klauser, Jack E.	Prof	Chaminade		PHD	77	NYU	1970
Klay, Robin	Assoc	Hope	BO	PHD	73	Princeton	1979
Klecan, Lindsey O.	VInst	Dartmouth		BA	87	Duke	
Klein, Benjamin	Prof	UCLA		PHD	70	Chicago	1978
Klein, Daniel B.	Asst	Calif-Irvine		PHD	87	NYU	1989
Klein, J. Douglass	C-Ac	Union	LQD	PHD	75	Wisconsin	1979
Klein, Judy C.	C-Ac	Mary Baldwin	BC	PHD	86	London P	1982
Klein, Lawrence R.	Emer	Pennsylvania		PHD	44	MIT	1958
Benjamin Franklin Professor of Economics & Finance							
Klein, Peter G.	Asst	Georgia	L	PHD	95	Berkeley	1995
Klein, Philip A.	Prof	Penn State	E	PHD	58	Berkeley	1955
Klein, Roger W.	Prof	Rutgers-N Br	C	PHD	70	Yale	1995
Klein, Yehuda L.	Asst	CUNY-Brookly	M	PHD		Berkeley	1985
Kleinberg, Norman L.	Assoc	CUNY-Baruch		PHD	77	MIT	
Kleiner, William C.	Asst	W Illinois	AEF	PHD	74	Mich St	1971
Kleit, Andrew N.	Assoc	Louisiana St	HK	PHD	87	Yale	1992
Klepper, Steven I.	Prof	Carnegie Mel		PHD	75	Cornell	1980
Kletzer, Kenneth M.	Prof	Ca-Santa Crz	FDOH	PHD	82	Berkeley	1992
Kletzer, Lori Gladstein	Asst	Ca-Santa Crz	J	PHD	86	Berkeley	1993
Klevorick, Alvin K.	Prof	Yale		PHD	67	Princeton	1975
Kliman, Andrew J.	C-As	NY Inst Tech	B	PHD		Utah	1989
Klinedinst, Mark A.	Assoc	So Miss	P	PHD	87	Cornell	1986
Kling, Robert W.	Assoc	Colorado St	DQ	PHD	85	Kansas	1984
Klingaman, David C.	Prof	Ohio Univ	DE	PHD	67	Virginia	1967
Klotz, Benjamin P.	Assoc	Temple	E	PHD	69	Minnesota	1975
Knapp, Charles B.	Prof	Georgia	J	PHD	72	Wisconsin	1987
Knapp, Gunner P.	Prof	Alaska-Ancho	QR	PHD	81	Yale	1981
Knapp, Kimberly	Asst	MD-Baltim Co		PHD	88		

Knetter, Michael M.	Assoc	Dartmouth		PHD	88	Stanford	1988
Kniesner, Thomas J.	Prof	Indiana		PHD	76	Ohio St	1988
Knight, Robert E. L.	Retir	Maryland		PHD	58	Berkeley	1960
Knighton, Daniel R.	Prof	Moorhead St		PHD	73	N Carol	1970
Knipes, Bradford	Asst	Westfield St		PHD		Mass	1988
Knoblauch, Vicki I.	Asst	Vassar	DL	PHD	91	Wi-Milw	1995
Knodell, Jane E.	Assoc	Vermont	EN	PHD	84	Stanford	1986
Knoeber, Charles R.	Prof	N Carol St	LKDG	PHD	76	UCLA	1976
Knoedler, Janet T.	Asst	Bucknell		PHD		Tennessee	
Knowles, Glenn J.	Prof	Wis-La Cross	CQR	PHD	80	Minnesota	1985
Knowles, Jeremy R.	Dean	Harvard					
Knox, Robert L.	Prof	Arizona St		PHD	63	N Carol	1963
Knudsen, James J.	Asst	Creighton	CHJ	PHD	89	Iowa St	1989
Knudsen, John W.	Assoc	Idaho	EP	PHD	70	Minnesota	1972
Knusel, Jack L.	Retir	Wis-Whitewat		PHD		Colorado	1965
Koch, James C.	C-Ac	St Edwards		MSIR	59	Loyola-C	1960
Koch, James V.	Prof	Old Dominion		PHD	68	Northwes	1990
Koch, Paul D.	Prof	Kansas	Fnce	PHD	80	Mich St	1988
Koch, Paul R.	Assoc	Olivet Nazar	ABHP	ABD		Ill St	1992
Kochanowski, Paul S.	Prof	Ind-So Bend		DBA		Indiana	1972
Kochar, Anjini	Asst	Stanford		PHD	91	Chicago	1990
Kocherlakota, Narayana	Assoc	Iowa		PHD	87	Chicago	1990
Kochin, Levis A.	Assoc	U Washington		PHD	75	Chicago	1972
Koechlin, Tim	Assoc	Skidmore		PHD	89	Mass	1988
Koelln, Kenneth	Asst	North Texas		PHD	91	Florida	1991
Koenker, Roger	Prof	Illinois		PHD	74	Michigan	1983
Koford, Kenneth	Prof	Delaware	H	PHD	77	UCLA	1979
Kogut, Carl A.	Asst	NE Louisiana	DL	PHD	84	Tx A&M	1992
Kohen, Andrew I.	Prof	Jms Madison	JD	PHD	73	Ohio St	1976
Kohler, Heinz	Prof	Amherst	AP	PHD	61	Michigan	1961
Willard Long Thorp Professor of Economics							
Kohlhase, Janet E.	Assoc	Houston	RHD	PHD	80	Penn	1983
Kohn, Meir G.	Prof	Dartmouth		PHD	73	MIT	1978
Koizumi, Tetsunori	Assoc	Ohio State	E	PHD	70	Brown	1970
Kokat, Robert G.	C-Ac	Immaculata		DBA		Indiana	1990
Kokkelenberg, Edward C.	Assoc	SUNY-Bingham		PHD	81	Northwes	1980
Kolb, Fredric	Prof	Wis-Eau Clar		PHD	71	Utah	1971
Kolberg, William	Assoc	Ithaca	AQ	PHD		Rhode Isl	1984
Kolluri, Bharat R.	C-Pr	Hartford		PHD	77	SUNY-Buf	1976
Kolmer, Lee Roy	Retir	Iowa State	1994	PHD	54	Iowa St	1973
Kolpin, Van W.	Assoc	Oregon	C	PHD	86	Iowa	1986
Kolstad, Charles	Prof	Cal-Santa Br	QLD	PHD	82	Stanford	1992
Konan, Denise	Asst	Hawaii-Manoa		PHD	93	Colorado	1993
Kondonassis, Alexander J.	Prof	Oklahoma	NO	PHD	61	Indiana	1979
David Ross Boyd Professor of Economics							
Kong, Chang Min	Prof	Towson State		PHD	77	Wi-Milw	1978
Konishi, Hideo	Asst	So Methodist		PHD	94	Rochester	1994
Konow, James D.	Asst	Loyola Marym	ACD	PHD	93	UCLA	1989
Kontos, Nicholas C.	Assoc	Marshall		MA	58	Indiana	1961
Konyar, Kazim	Asst	CS-San Bern		PHD	85	Ca-River	1991
Konz, Jeffery M.	Asst	Wash & Lee	E	PHD		N Carol	1994
Koo, Anthony Y.	Retir	Michigan St		PHD	46	Harvard	
Kool, Krishna L.	Dean$	Rio Grande		PHD	76	Tennessee	1970
Koont, Sinan	C-As	Dickinson Cl	CFE	PHD	87	Mass	1986
Kooros, Syrous	Prof	Nicholls St	EFO	PHD	80	Rensselae	1991
Kooti, John	Prof	Albany State		PHD	80	Mich St	1981
Kopecky, Helen Pauline	Retir	Oklahoma St		PHD	72	Houston	1973
Kopko, Robert J.	C-Ac	Calif U-Penn		MS		Penn St	1970
Koray, Faik A.	Prof	Louisiana St	EF	PHD	84	Duke	1984
Korbach, Robert J.	Prof	North Dakota		PHD	73	Maryland	1970
Kordsmeier, William F.	Assoc	Cen Arkansas		PHD		Tx A&M	
Kornai, Janos	Prof	Harvard		DSC	66	Hungaria	1986
Kortum, Sam	Asst	Boston Univ	ELO	PHD	92	Yale	1991
Koscianski, Janet	Assoc	Shippensburg		PHD	90	S Illinois	1990
Koshal, Rajindar K.	Prof	Ohio Univ	TACQ	PHD	68	Rochester	1970
Kosicki, George	C-Ac	Holy Cross	ADJL	PHD	85	Cornell	9-85
Koski, Jennifer L.	Asst	U Washington		PHD	91	Stanford	1991
Kosobud, Richard F.	Prof	Ill-Chicago	D	PHD	63	Penn	
Koss, Joseph J.	Prof	Youngstown		EDD	87	Akron	
Kossoudji, Sherrie A.	Asst	Michigan		PHD	84	Michigan	1987
Kotamraju, Pradeep	Asst	St Scholasti		PHD	89	Illinois	1995
Kotcherlokota, V. V.	Assoc	Neb-Kearney		PHD		India	1986
Koti, Tetteh A.	Prof	San Francisc		PHD	70	Berkeley	1981
Kotlikoff, Laurence J.	Prof	Boston Univ	EH	PHD	77	Harvard	
Kotz, David M.	Prof	Massachusett		PHD	75	Berkeley	
Kotzen, Nancy	Assoc	Westfield St		MBA		W NewEng	1981
Kovenock, Dan J.	Prof	Purdue		PHD	83	Wisconsin	1983
Kowal, Lubomyr M.	Prof	Mich-Flint		PHD	65	Illinois	1966
Koziara, Edward C.	H-Pr	Drexel		PHD	65		1966
Kozlov, Nicholas N.	Asst	Hofstra	P	PHD	88	N Hamp	

Kozmetsky, George	Retir	Texas	O	PHD	57	Harvard	9-66
Kraft, Evan	Asst	Salisbury St		PHD	90	New Sch	8-90
Kraft, John L.	Dean	Florida		PHD	71	Pittsburgh	1990
Krall, Mary Elyse	Asst	SUNY-Cortlan					
Kramer, Melvin L.	Prof	Wartburg		PHD	66	Iowa	1956
Kranton, Rachel E.	Asst	Maryland		PHD	93	Berkeley	1993
Krasa, Stefan	Asst	Illinois		PHD	87	Vienna	1990
Kraus, James A.	Asst	CUNY-Lehman		JD		Columbia	
Kraus, Marvin C.	Prof	Boston Coll	DR	PHD	73	Minnesota	1972
Krautkraemer, Jeffrey A.	Prof	Wash State		PHD	82	Stanford	1981
Krautmann, Anthony C.	Prof	DePaul		PHD	85	Iowa	1985
Krebs, Tom	Asst	Illinois		PHD		Columbia	1995
Kreider, Brent	Asst	Virginia	HI	PHD	94	Wisconsin	1994
Kreinin, Mordechai E.	Prof	Michigan St		PHD	52	Michigan	1959
Kreitzer, Joseph L.	Assoc	St Thomas-MN	C	PHD		Iowa	1981
Kremer, Michael R.	Asst	MIT	E	PHD	92	Harvard	1992
Kresl, Peter K.	Prof	Bucknell		PHD	70	Tx-Austin	1969
Kressler, Peter	Assoc	Rowan Col-NJ		PHD		Penn	1972
Kreutzer, David W.	Assoc	Jms Madison	FH	PHD	84	Geo Mason	1984
Kridel, Donald	Asst	Mo-St Louis	CD	PHD	87	Arizona	1993
Krieg, Randall G.	Assoc	No Iowa		PHD	87	Colorado	1987
Krienke, Albert B.	Prof	Midwest St	DP	PHD		Tx A&M	1965
Krier, Donald F.	Prof	Framingham		PHD	69	Boston C	1973
Krinsky, Itzhak	Prof	McMaster U	G	PHD	83	McMaster	1982
Krishna, Kala	Prof	Penn State	F	PHD	84	Princeton	1993
Krishna, Pravin	Asst	Brown		PHD	95	Columbia	1995
Krishna, Vijay	Assoc	Penn State	D	PHD	83	Princeton	1993
Krishnan, V. N.	Retir	Bowling Gr		PHD	68	Mich St	1965
Krislov, Joseph	Prof	Kentucky	JN	PHD	54	Wisconsin	1954
Kroch, Eugene A.	Assoc	Villanova		PHD	78	Harvard	1991
Kroeten, Terrence	Asst	Concordia C		PHD		Nebraska	1992
Krohn, Gregory A.	Assoc	Bucknell		PHD	85	Wisconsin	1983
Krol, Robert	Prof	CS-Northrdge	FGT	PHD	82	S Illinois	1983
Kroner, Kenneth F.	Asst	Arizona		PHD	88	Ca-SnDgo	1988
Krouse, Clement G.	Prof	Cal-Santa Br	D	PHD	69	UCLA	1979
Krueger, Alan B.	Asst	Princeton					
Krueger, Anne	Prof	Stanford		PHD	58	Wisconsin	
Krueger, Gary J.	Asst	Macalester	ACP	PHD	89	Wisconsin	1989
Krug, Ronald W.	Asst	SUNY-Oneonta	M	MBA		SUNY-Alb	
Krugman, Paul R.	Prof	Stanford	F	PHD	77	MIT	1994
Krupp, Corinne M.	Asst	Michigan St		PHD	90	Penn	1989
Kruse, Jamie I.	Asst	Colorado		PHD	88	Arizona	1987
Krusell, Per	Asst	Rochester	O	PHD	92	Minnesota	1994
Kuan, Chen I.	Retir	SUNY-Albany	OF	PHD		Berkeley	
Kuan, Chung-Ming	Asst	Illinois		PHD	89	Ca-SnDgo	1989
Kudek, James F.	Assoc	Lakeland	ABCD	MBA		Wi-Milw	1982
Kuenne, Robert E.	Prof	Princeton		PHD	53	Harvard	1969
Kugler, Penny L.	Inst	Cen Missouri		MA	88	Cen Mo St	1988
Kulkarni, Kishore G.	C-Pr	Metro St-CO		PHD	82	Pittsburgh	
Kumar, Praveen	Prof	Carnegie Mel		PHD		Stanford	1985
Kumar, Rishi	Dean	Wright State		PHD	72	Wayne St	1974
Kumar, Vikram	Assoc	Davidson	E	PHD	87	Vanderbilt	1986
Kumbhakar, Subal C.	Assoc	Texas	CD	PHD	86	S Calif	9-86
Kung, James	Asst	Connecticut		PHD	91	Cambridge	1995
Kuntz, Dale F.	Assoc	Bentley	AEO	PHD	79	Conn	1975
Kuperberg, Mark J.	Prof	Swarthmore	EK	PHD	81	MIT	1977
Kupilik, Michael H.	Assoc	Montana	PHBN	PHD	76	Colorado	1976
Kuran, Timur	C-Pr	So Calif		PHD	82	Stanford	1982
Kurre, James A.	Assoc	Penn St-Erie	RA	PHD	82	Penn St	1977
Kurth, Michael M.	Prof	McNeese St		PHD		Va Tech	1984
Kurz, Mordecai	Prof	Stanford		PHD	61	Yale	1966
Kushner, Joseph W.	Assoc	Valdosta St		PHD	69	Tennessee	1969
Kushner, Roland	Asst	Lafayette					
Kushnirsky, Fyodor I.	Prof	Temple	P	PHD	68	Moscow	1980
Kutasovic, Paul R.	Assoc	NY Inst Tech		PHD	83	Rutgers	1988
Kuznets, Paul W.	Prof	Indiana		PHD	64	Yale	1964
Kwack, Sung Y.	Prof	Howard		PHD	68	Berkeley	
Kwan, Clarence C. Y.	C-Pr	McMaster U	G	PHD	79	Toronto	1979
Kwan, Felix	Asst	Idaho	EF	PHD	92	Wash U	1994
Kwiatkowski, Denis E.	Asst	Fordham		PHD	90	Mich St	1992
Kwoka, John E. Jr.	Prof	George Wash	L	PHD	72	Penn	1981
Kwon, Jene K.	Prof	No Illinois		PHD	68	Iowa	1968
Kydland, Finn	Prof	Carnegie Mel		PHD	73	Car Mellon	1977
Kyer, Ben L.	Assoc	Fran Marion		PHD	84	W Virginia	
Kyereme, Stephen	Assoc	So Carol St		PHD	84	Cornell	1984
Kyle, James T.	C-Ac	Indiana St	J	ABD	63	Indiana	1963
Kyle, Reuben	Prof	Mid Tenn St		PHD	72	Tennessee	1972
Kymn, Kern O.	Prof	W Virginia	EC	PHD	64	Chicago	1976
Kyn, Oldrich	Prof	Boston Univ	CEP	PHD		Charles	1971

Name	Rank	Institution	Fields	Degree	Year	Degree Institution	Year
Kynski, Kathy	Asst	Kenyon		PHD		Wisconsin	
Himmelright Assistant Professor of Economics							
Kypralos, Harry N.	Assoc	Rollins		PHD	87	Virginia	1983
La Croix, Sumner J.	Prof	Hawaii-Manoa		PHD	81	U Wash	1981
La Near, Richard E.	Prof	Missouri So		PHD		Miss	1987
Dr. J. R. Kuhn Chair of Business Administration							
La Point, James	Asst	SW Louisiana					
La Tourette, John E.	Prof	No Illinois		PHD	62	Rutgers	
Laband, David N.	H-Pr	Auburn		PHD	81	Va Tech	1994
Labys, Walter C.	Prof	W Virginia	Q	PHD	68	Nottnghm	1975
LaCivita, Charles J.	Prof	Naval Postgr		PHD	81	Ca-SnBarb	1985
Lackey, Charles	Assoc	Tx-Brownsvil	AFL	PHD	84	S Carol	1995
Lacy, Allen W.	Prof	Auburn-Montg	ETIH	PHD	71	Iowa St	1976
Ladd, George W.	Retir	Iowa State	1994	PHD	55	Illinois	1955
Ladenson, Mark L.	Prof	Michigan St		PHD	70	Northwes	1984
Lady, George	Assoc	Temple	CD	PHD	67	J Hopkins	1981
Lage, Gerald M.	Prof	Oklahoma St		PHD	67	Minnesota	1966
Lage, Maureen	Asst	Miami U-Ohio	AE	PHD	91	Penn St	1990
Lages, John David	Prof	SW Missouri		PHD	67	Iowa St	1963
Lagunoff, Roger D.	Asst	Virg Tech		PHD	89	Minnesota	1995
Lahiri, Kajal	C-Pr	SUNY-Albany	E	PHD	75	Rochester	1977
Lahiri, Supriya	Assoc	Mass-Lowell	CQ	PHD	75	Delhi	
Lai, Edwin	Asst	Vanderbilt	FOL	PHD	91	Stanford	1991
Lai, Kon Sun	Assoc	CS-L Angeles		PHD	87	Penn	1987
Lai, Tsung	Assoc	Liberty		PHD			
Laibman, David	Prof	CUNY-Brookly	AP	PHD		New Sch	1967
Laibson, David	Asst	Harvard					
Laing, Derek	Asst	Penn State	E	PHD	89	Essex	1989
Laird, William E.	C-Pr	Florida St		PHD	62	Virginia	1960
Laitner, John	Prof	Michigan		PHD	76	Harvard	1975
Lakew, Melaku	Assoc	R Stockton		PHD		Ca-River	1982
Lal, Anil K.	Lect	Pittsburg St	A	PHD		Wash St	
LaLonde, Robert J.	Assoc	Michigan St		PHD	85	Princeton	1995
Lam, David A.	Assoc	Michigan		PHD	83	Berkeley	1983
Lam, Pok-sang	Assoc	Ohio State	E	PHD	86	Harvard	1985
Lamberton, Charles E.	Prof	So Dakota St	G	PHD	75	Iowa St	1974
Lambson, Val E.	Assoc	Brigham Yg		PHD	83	Rochester	1989
Lamdin, Douglas J.	Asst	MD-Baltim Co		PHD	91	Maryland	1989
Lamphear, F. Charles	Prof	Nebraska	O	PHD	67	Kansas St	1966
Lamson, George H.	Prof	Carleton		PHD	71	Northwes	1969
Wadsworth W. Williams Professor of Economics							
Lancaster, Anthony	Prof	Brown		PHD	65	St Cathar	
Landau, Daniel L.	Assoc	Connecticut	O	PHD	74	Chicago	1981
Landes, David S.	Prof	Harvard					
Coolidge Professor of History and Economics							
Landesman, Miriam F.	Lect	Ca-Santa Crz					
Landis, Brook	Assoc	York-Penn		PHD		Cornell	
Lane, Julia I.	Assoc	American U		PHD	82	Missouri	1990
Lane, Philip J.	Assoc	Fairfield	EGR	PHD	83	Tufts	1981
Lane, Walter J.	Assoc	New Orleans		PHD	78	Ca-SnDgo	1986
Lang, Kevin	Prof	Boston Univ	JC	PHD	82	MIT	1987
Lang, Nancy A.	Assoc	No Kentucky		EDD	83	Georgia	1983
Langan, Terence G.	Assoc	St Thomas-MN	L	PHD	88	Minnesota	
Lange, Ralph W.	Prof	SE Louisiana	AF	PHD	74	LSU	
Langer, Gary F.	D-Ac	Roosevelt		PHD	80	Mass	1983
Langlois, Richard N.	Prof	Connecticut	B	PHD	81	Stanford	1983
Lanjouw, Jean	Asst	Yale					
Lankford, R. Hamilton	Assoc	SUNY-Albany	HD	PHD	81	N Carol	1981
Lanzillotti, Robert F.	Prof	Florida	T	PHD	53	Berkeley	1969
Dir Public Pol Resr Center; American Econ Int Free Enterprise Eminent Scholar							
Lapan, Harvey E.	Prof	Iowa State	DF	PHD	71	MIT	1972
Lapidus, June	Assoc	Roosevelt		PHD	88	Mass	1990
Lapp, John S.	Assoc	N Carol St	EGF	PHD	74	Princeton	1974
Lara, Vito B.	Assoc	Univ of D C		PHD		Howard	
Larado, Leonard P.	Assoc	Rhode Island		PHD	79	Indiana	1981
Laramie, Anthony J.	C-Ac	Merrimack		PHD		Clark	
Larew, Barbara	Assoc	Coe		MA	81	Iowa	1981
Larkin, L. Andrew	Prof	St Cloud St		PHD	82	Nebraska	1982
LaRoe, Ross M.	C-Ac	Denison		PHD	82	American	1985
Larrymore, Norris	Inst	Grambling St		MS		Penn	1988
Larson, Bruce D.	Assoc	N Car-Ashvil		PHD	83	N Carol	1983
Larson, David A.	Prof	New Orleans		PHD	68	Maryland	
Larson, John C.	Prof	Loyola-Maryl	E	PHD	77	Minnesota	1974
Larson, Marvin L.	Inst	Missouri So		MA		Mo-St Lo	1990
Larson, Tom Edward	Asst	CS-L Angeles		PHD	86	Berkeley	1987
Larudee, Mehrene	Asst	Kansas		ABD		Mass	1984
Lastrapes, William D.	Assoc	Georgia	CEF	PHD	86	N Carol	1990
Latanich, Gary A.	Assoc	Arkansas St	AREM	PHD	78	Nebraska	1981
Latham, William R. III	C-Ac	Delaware	RC	PHD	73	Illinois	1971
Latif-Zuman, Nazma	Assoc	Providence	OFC	PHD		Northeas	

Name	Rank	Institution	Fields	Degree	Yr	School	Year
Latos, Charles	Asst	Rhode Island		PHD	77	Brown	1969
Latzko, David	Asst	Wilkes	DEF	PHD		Maryland	9-93
Lau, Lawrence J.	Prof	Stanford		PHD	69	Berkeley	1966
Laughlin, William	Assoc	Fairmont St		MA		Cincinnati	
Laumas, G. S.	Prof	So Illinois	EC	PHD	66	Wayne St	1990
Laumas, Prem S.	Retir	No Illinois	1995	PHD	65	Wayne St	1971
Laurence, Louise	Asst	Towson State		PHD	87	Maryland	1987
Laurence, Martin M.	Prof	Wm Patterson		PHD		NYU	1970
Laurent, Jerome K.	Prof	Wis-Whitewat		PHD	73	Indiana	1965
Laux, Judith A.	C-Ac	Colorado Col		PHD	90	Colorado	1979
Lave, Charles	Prof	Calif-Irvine		PHD	68	Stanford	1964
Lave, Lester B.	Prof	Carnegie Mel		PHD	63	Harvard	1963
James H. Higgins Professor of Economics							
Lavine, Jeffrey A.	Asst	Pitts-Johnst		MA	68	Pittsburgh	1970
Law, Alton D.	C-Pr	W Maryland		PHD	68	Rutgers	1966
Lawaree, Jacques P.	Asst	U Washington		PHD	90	Berkeley	1990
Lawber, Harold E. Jr.	C-Ac	Salve Regina	ABEN	PHD	89	Conn	1988
Lawlor, Michael S.	Assoc	Wake Forest		PHD	86	Iowa St	1986
Lawson, Catherine L.	Asst	Missouri Wes	EB	PHD		Colorado	1995
Lawson, Luther Drew	Assoc	N Car-Wilmin	AJL	PHD		Tennessee	
Lawson, Robert L.	Retir	Ball State		PHD	67	Iowa	1963
Lawson, Stanley J.	Prof	St John's		PHD	73	NYU	1978
Lawton, Robert B.	Dean	Georgetown		PHD			
Lazarcik, Gregor	Prof	CUNY-Brookly	O	PHD	60	Columbia	1985
Lazonick, William H.	Retir	Barnard		PHD		Harvard	1985
Leach, Elroy M.	Assoc	Chicago St		PHD	85	Il-Chicago	1985
Leachman, Lori	Asst	No Arizona	EF	PHD	87	S Carol	1993
Leadley, John C.	Asst	W Oregon St		PHD		Wisconsin	
Leahy, John V.	Assoc	Harvard		PHD	90	Princeton	1990
Leahy, William H.	Prof	Notre Dame	JR	PHD		Notre Dm	1963
Leake, Richard S.	Assoc	Luther		MBA		Wisconsin	1975
Leamer, Edward E.	Prof	UCLA		PHD	70	Michigan	1975
Leathers, Charles G.	Prof	Alabama		PHD	68	Oklahoma	1968
LeBaron, Blake	Assoc	Wisconsin		PHD	88	Chicago	1988
LeBel, Phillip	Dean$	Montclair St	DOQH	PHD	77	Boston U	1981
Lebergott, Stanley	Emer	Wesleyan-CT	N	MA	39	Michigan	1962
University Professor							
Lebrenz, Eugene R.	VProf	Fla Southern		EDD		N Illinois	1987
LeClair, Daniel R.	Asst	Tampa	ADL	PHD	88	Florida	1989
LeClair, Mark S.	Assoc	Fairfield	FGC	PHD	87	Rutgers	1988
Ledyard, John O.	C-Pr	Cal Tech		PHD	67	Purdue	1985
Lee, Albert Yin-Po	Prof	CS-Stanislau		PHD	79	S Illinois	1970
Lee, Alston	Prof	Illinois		PHD	78	Wash	1988
Lee, Bun Song	Prof	Neb-Omaha	FO	PHD	73	So Meth	1982
Lee, Byong-Joo	Asst	Colorado		PHD	88	Wisconsin	1988
Lee, Byung	Assoc	Howard		PHD		Wayne St	
Lee, Christopher	Assoc	St Ambrose		PHD	90	Geo Mason	1995
Lee, Chung H.	Prof	Hawaii-Manoa		PHD	66	Berkeley	1980
Lee, Dae Sung	Dean	Kentucky St	ADEC	PHD	69	Mass	1969
Lee, Daniel Y.	Prof	Shippensburg		PHD	86	Pittsburgh	1986
Lee, Dwight R.	Prof	Georgia	DHM	PHD	72	Ca-SnDgo	1985
Bernard B. & Eugenia A. Ramsey Professor							
Lee, E. Yong	C-Ac	Upsala	CD	PHD	75	Rutgers	1975
Lee, Eric Y.	Prof	F Dick-Madis		PHD	73	Columbia	
Lee, Feng-Yao	Prof	Tennessee		PHD	65	Mich St	
Lee, Gerald R.	Prof	Miss College		PHD	73	Miss	1970
Lee, H. Hiro	Asst	Calif-Irvine		PHD	87	Berkeley	1987
Lee, Hahn S.	Asst	Tulane		PHD	90	Ca-SnDgo	
Lee, Hoyoung	Prof	Rochest Tech	ABDE	PHD		Maryland	1970
Lee, Hy Sang	Prof	Wis-Oshkosh	O	PHD	65	Wisconsin	1962
Lee, Jae Won	Assoc	CUNY-Baruch		PHD	69	CUNY	1972
Lee, Jaewoo	Asst	Calif-Irvine		PHD	92	MIT	1992
Lee, Jason	Asst	McMaster U	G	PHD	91	Alberta	1990
Lee, Jimmy	Asst	Fort Hays St	EK	PHD	91	Penn St	1989
Lee, Joe W.	Retir	Howard		DBA		Indiana	
Lee, John T.	C-Pr	Mid Tenn St		PHD	77	Georgia	1984
Lee, Joseph S.	Prof	Mankato St	JK	PHD	70	Mass	1970
Lee, Junsoo	Asst	Vanderbilt	E	PHD	91	Mich St	1991
Lee, Kangoh	Asst	Towson State		PHD	87	Illinois	1990
Lee, Kie Bok	Assoc	Skidmore		PHD	67	Virginia	1963
Lee, Kiseok	Asst	Missouri	C	PHD	90	Chicago	1987
Lee, Li Way	Prof	Wayne State		PHD	76	Columbia	1981
Lee, Lung-Fei	Prof	Michigan		PHD	77	Rochester	1991
Lee, Maw Lin	Prof	Missouri	C	PHD	61	Wisconsin	1968
Lee, Molly K. S.	Prof	NY Inst Tech		PHD		NYU	1970
Lee, Pong S.	Assoc	SUNY-Albany	OE	PHD		Yale	
Lee, Ronald D.	Prof	Cal-Berkeley		PHD	71	Harvard	1979
Lee, San-Sub	Asst	South Fla	H	PHD	91	N Carol	1990
Lee, Sang	Asst	Nicholls St	GF	PHD	90	N Orleans	1991
Lee, Seung-Dong	C-Ac	Alabama-Birm	CDFQ	PHD	79	So Meth	1979

Name	Rank	School	Fields	Degree	Yr	Institution	Year
Lee, Soyon	C-Pr	IL Benedict	FO	PHD	77	N Illinois	1974
Lee, Tae-Hwy	Asst	Cal-Riversid	ACG	PHD	90	Ca-SnDgo	1995
Lee, Tenpao	Prof	Niagara		PHD		Iowa St	1987
Lee, Tommy R.	Inst	NE Louisiana		MBA		NE La	
Lee, Tong Hun	Prof	Wis-Milwauke		PHD	61	Wisconsin	1967
Lee, Wei Pang	Assoc	Worcester St		PHD			
Lee, William C.	Prof	St Marys-Cal		PHD	77	Ca-SnBarb	1982
Lee, Woo Bong	C-Pr	Bloomsburg		PHD	72	Rutgers	1977
Leeds, Michael A.	Assoc	Temple	J	PHD	82	Princeton	1982
Leekley, Robert M.	Assoc	Ill Wesleyan		PHD	74	Mich St	1974
Leela, Secunderabad N.	Assoc	Millersville		PHD	65	Bombay	1969
Leeper, Eric M.	Asst	Indiana		PHD	89	Minnesota	1995
Lees, Francis A.	Prof	St John's		PHD	61	NYU	1961
Leet, Don R.	C-Pr	CS-Fresno		PHD	72	Penn	1969
Leete, Laura	Asst	Case Western	IJ	PHD	92	Harvard	1991
Leeth, John D.	Assoc	Bentley	GCJ	PHD	83	N Carol	1987
Leff, Nathaniel H.	Prof	Columbia		PHD	66	MIT	1967
Leffier, Keith B.	Assoc	U Washington		PHD	77	UCLA	1978
Leftwich, Howard M.	Prof	Cincinnati	J	PHD	65	Illinois	
Legros, Patrick A.	Asst	Cornell		PHD	89	Cal Tech	1989
Lehman, Dale E.	Assoc	Fort Lewis		PHD	81	Rochester	1983
Lehman, Eldon R.	Assoc	Bemidji St		MA		W Tx St	1967
Lehmann, Michael B.	Prof	San Francisc		PHD	69	Cornell	1966
Lehr, William H.	Asst	Columbia		ABD	91	Stanford	1991
Lehrer, Evelyn L.	Prof	Ill-Chicago	T	PHD	78	Northwes	
Leigh, Duane E.	C-Pr	Wash State		PHD	69	Mich St	1968
Leigh, J. Paul	Prof	San Jose St		PHD	79	Wisconsin	1981
Leightner, Jonathan E.	Asst	Augusta	DTOP	PHD	89	N Carol	1989
Leighton, Linda S.	Assoc	Fordham		PHD	78	Columbia	1979
Leighton, Richard I.	Assoc	SUNY-Bingham		PHD	61	Duke	1964
Leijonhufvud, Axel S. B.	Prof	UCLA		PHD			
Leitner, Keith R.	Prof	Wis-Eau Clar		PHD	74	Kansas St	1974
Lenihan, Patrick M.	Prof	E Illinois		PHD	68	Wisconsin	1967
Lenon, Mary Jane	C-As	Providence	REI	PHD	89	Conn	1986
Leon, Hyglus	Assoc	SUNY Old Wes		PHD		S Hamptn	
Leon, Jean-Claude	Asst	Catholic		PHD	87	Geo Wash	1987
Leonard, Frederick	Prof	Smith	AEG	PHD		Michigan	
Leonard, Thomas E.	Inst	Vassar	BEK	ABD		Geo Wash	1995
Leonard, William J.	Retir	St Joseph		MA	69	Notre Dm	1957
Leontief, Wassily W.	Prof	New York U		PHD	28	Berlin	
LePage, James	Assoc	Lincoln-MO		PHD		Kansas	1984
Leppel, Karen	Assoc	Widener	JCT	PHD	80	Princeton	1985
Lerman, Robert I.	Prof	American U		PHD	70	MIT	1989
LeRoy, Stephen F.	Prof	Minnesota		PHD	71	Penn	
Lesage, James P.	Prof	Toledo		PHD	83	Boston C	1988
Lester, Bijou	Assoc	Drexel		PHD	81	Penn	1988
Leube, Kurt R.	Prof	CS-Hayward		DLE	71	Salzburg	1985
Leung, Cho Kin	C-Pr	Wm Patterson		PHD	68	NYU	1974
Leung, Siu Fai	Asst	Rochester		PHD	87	Chicago	1988
Leung, Sui-ki	Asst	So Carolina		DPHI	88	UCLA	
Leuthold, Jane H.	H-Pr$	Illinois		PHD	68	Wisconsin	1967
Leveen, Serpil Sisik	C-Pr$	Montclair St	ADEG	PHD	73	NYU	1974
Leven, Bozen	Asst	Trenton St		PHD		Cornell	
Leven, Charles L.	Emer	Wash Univ		PHD	58	Northwes	1964
Levenson, Albert M.	Prof	CUNY-Queens	DFC	PHD	59	Columbia	1961
Levenstein, Margaret C.	Asst	Michigan		PHD	91	Yale	1990
Lever, Jacqueline	Asst	Albright		PHD		Pittsburgh	
Levernier, William B.	Assoc	Geo Southern		PHD	88	W Virginia	1989
Leversee, Gordon J.	Dean	Keene State		PHD		Duke	1981
Levin, Dan	Prof	Houston	MI	PHD	82	MIT	1982
on leave to Ohio State University							
Levin, Jay H.	Prof	Wayne State		PHD	68	Michigan	1976
Levin, Richard C.	Prof	Yale		PHD	74	Yale	1974
Levin, Sharon G.	C-Pr	Mo-St Louis	DJ	PHD	73	Michigan	1974
Levin, Stanford L.	Prof	S Ill-Edward		PHD	74	Michigan	1972
Levine, Aaron	C-Pr	Yeshiva		PHD		NYU	
Samson and Halina Bitensky Professor of Economics							
Levine, David K.	Prof	UCLA		PHD	81	MIT	1981
Levine, Herbert S.	Prof	Pennsylvania	P	PHD	61	Harvard	1960
Levine, Philip	Asst	Wellesley		PHD	91	Princeton	1990
Levinsohn, James A.	Assoc	Michigan		PHD	88	Princeton	1987
Levinson, Arik	Asst	Wisconsin		PHD	93	Columbia	1993
Levinson, Marshall M.	Retir	Duquesne		MA	50	Columbia	1966
Levy, Daniel	Asst	Emory	EC	PHD	90	Ca-Irvine	1992
Levy, David M.	Assoc	George Mason		PHD	79	Chicago	1983
Levy, David T.	Prof	Baltimore		PHD		N Carol	
Levy, Lester S.	Prof	No Illinois		PHD	56	Cornell	
Levy, Philip	Asst	Yale					
Lewbel, Arthur	Prof	Brandeis		PHD	84	MIT	1984
Lewis, Bradley G.	Assoc	Union	GMN	PHD	83	Chicago	1979

Lewis, Carl	Retir	Neb-Kearney		PHD		Nebraska	1969
Lewis, David P.	Emer	Alabama-Birm	CER	PHD	68	Tennessee	1969
Lewis, Eddie Miley Jr.	Prof	So Miss	F	DBA	74	Miss St	1970
Lewis, J. Patrick	Prof	Otterbein		PHD	74	Ohio St	1974
Lewis, Kenneth A.	Prof	Delaware	CE	PHD	69	Princeton	1973
Lewis, Margaret	Asst	St Benedict		PHD	89	Maryland	1989
Lewis, Stephen D.	Prof	Sonoma State		PHD	69	Ca-SnBarb	1982
Lewis, Stephen R. Jr.	Prof	Carleton		PHD	63	Stanford	1987
Lewis, Tracy R.	Prof	Florida	TDQ	PHD	75	Ca-SnDgo	1991
James Walter Eminent Scholar in Economics							
Lewis, W. Cris	Prof	Utah State	MCR	PHD	69	Iowa St	1972
Ley, Robert D.	C-Pr	Bemidji St		PHD		Wash St	1977
Leyden, Dennis P.	Assoc	N Car-Greens		PHD	87	Car Mellon	1984
Li, David	Asst	Michigan		PHD	92	Harvard	1992
Li, Elizabeth	Asst	Miami U-Ohio	AF	PHD	82	Cornell	1990
Li, Ling	Asst	Towson State		PHD	94	Pittsburgh	1994
Li, Qing	Asst	Wichita St		PHD	95	Houston	1995
Li, Tien En	Retir	Delaware St		PHD		Tx A&M	
Li, Victor	Asst	Penn State	E	PHD	92	Northwes	1992
Liang-Rong, Shiau	Prof	Norfolk St		PHD		Arkansas	1972
Liaw, K. Thomas	Assoc	St John's		PHD	88	Northwes	9-88
Libecap, Gary D.	Prof	Arizona		PHD	76	Penn	1984
Liberatore, Anthony F.	Assoc	Millikin		PHD		Conn	1984
Lichtenberg, Frank R.	Assoc	Columbia		PHD	82	Penn	1983
Lichtenstein, Larry	Assoc	Canisius		PHD		SUNY	1981
Lichtenstein, Peter M.	Prof	Boise State		PHD	74	Colorado	1975
Lichty, Richard W.	Prof	Minn-Duluth	R	PHD	71	Kansas St	1971
Liddicost, Clifton	Assoc	Wm Patterson		MA		Temple	1966
Lidman, Russell M.		Evergreen St		PHD	72	Wisconsin	1974
Lieberman, Sima	Prof	Utah		PHD	67	Berkeley	1967
Liechty, Elden E.	Retir	Weber State		PHD	72	Utah	1972
Liedholm, Carl E.	Prof	Michigan St		PHD	65	Michigan	1967
Lien, Da-Hsiang D.	Prof	Kansas		PDD	86	Cal Tech	1986
Lieu, George	Assoc	Tuskegee		PHD			
Liew, Chong K.	Deces	Oklahoma		PHD	68	Berkeley	1969
Ligeralde, Antonio	Asst	Miami U-Ohio	CE	PHD	89	Rice	1991
Liggett, Ron	Lect	Tx-Arlington		MBA	89	Tx-Arlin	1989
Light, Audrey	Asst	Ohio State		PHD	87	UCLA	1995
Lile, Stephen E.	Prof	W Kentucky	H	PHD	72	Kentucky	1973
Liles, W. Pierce	Prof	So Carolina		PHD	72	S Carol	
Lilien, David M.	Prof	Calif-Irvine		PHD	77	MIT	1984
Lill, Lloyd		SUNY-Empire	BO	PHD		Walden	1973
Lilly, Gregory A.	Asst	Elon	CDA	PHD	88	Duke	1990
Lillydahl, Jane H.	Assoc	Colorado		PHD	76	Duke	1976
Lim, Ralph	Assoc	Sacred Heart	GLM	MBA		Penn	
Lima, Anthony K.	Prof	CS-Hayward		PHD	80	Stanford	1979
Lin, An-Yhi (Steven)	Prof	S Ill-Edward	CDFO	PHD	67	Iowa St	1968
Lin, Chyi-Ing	Asst	Missouri	FO	PHD	93	Michigan	1993
Lin, Hwan-Chyang	Asst	N Car-Charl		PHD		Illinois	
Lin, Kuan-Pin	Prof	Portland St		PHD	77	SUNY-SBr	1979
Lin, Lung-Ho	Assoc	Akron		PHD	74	Notre Dm	1978
Lin, Ping	Asst	So Methodist		PHD	93	Minnesota	1993
Lin, Shuanglin	Asst	Neb-Omaha	CDEO	PHD	89	Purdue	1989
Lindauer, David	Prof	Wellesley		PHD	79	Harvard	1981
Lindeman, Bruce	Prof	Ark-Ltl Rock		PHD		Duke	1975
Lindemann, Bonnie L.	Asst	St Ambrose		PHD	93	Iowa	1984
Lindert, Peter H.	Prof	Cal-Davis	FN	PHD	67	Cornell	1978
Lindgren, Jon G.	Assoc	N Dakota St	AGH	PHD	68	Missouri	1968
Lindsay, Cotton M.	Prof	Clemson	DHJK	PHD	68	Virginia	1984
J. Wilson Newman Professor							
Lindsey, Debra A.	Asst	Howard		PHD		Howard	
Lindsey, Glenn C.	Prof	Davidson	G	MBA	56	Georgia	1957
Liner, Gaines Howard	Assoc	N Car-Charl		PHD	71	Clemson	1971
Link, Albert N.	Prof	N Car-Greens		PHD	76	Tulane	1982
Link, Charles R.	Prof	Delaware	J	PHD	71	Wisconsin	1981
Linsley, Colin A.	Assoc	St John Fshr	N	PHD	86	Essex	1987
Linster, Bruce G.	Assoc	USAF Academy		PHD	90	Michigan	1990
Linton, Oliver	Asst	Yale					
Linvill, Carl	Asst	Arkansas	DC	PHD	93	N Carol	1993
Liossatos, Panagis S.	C-Pr	Fla Internat	CODR	PHD	68	Penn	1981
Lipford, Jody W.	Asst	Presbyterian	H	PHD		Clemson	1991
Lipner, Kenneth	Assoc	Fla Internat	RJA	PHD		Rutgers	1981
Lippit, Victor D.	Prof	Cal-Riversid	AOP	PHD	71	Yale	1971
Lipsey, Robert E.	Prof	CUNY-Queens	FC	PHD	61	Columbia	1967
Liska, Terrence L.	C-Ac	Wis-Plattev		PHD	82	Wisconsin	1980
Litterst, Laurence J.	Assoc	St Benedict		PHD	81	N Illinois	1979
Little, Charles H.	Assoc	St John's		PHD		Calif	
Little, Roger D.	Prof	USN Academy		PHD	70	Houston	1970
Litwack, John M.	Asst	Stanford		PHD	88	Penn	1988
Litzinger, Patrick J.	Prof	Robt Morris		PHD	75	Pittsburgh	1977

Liu, Chao-Nan	Prof	Trenton St		PHD		Tx A&M	
Liu, Hsien-Tung	Dean	Bloomsburg					
Liu, Jung-Chao	Assoc	SUNY-Bingham		PHD	60	Michigan	1970
Liu, Peter C.	Asst	U Miami	C	PHD	89	Florida	1990
Liu, Tsung-Hua	Prof	East Wash		PHD		Toronto	1970
Liu, Tung	Asst	Ball State		PHD	90	Ca-SnDgo	1990
Liu, Yih-Wu	Prof	Youngstown		PHD	68	S Illinois	
Liveson, Avi	Asst	CUNY-Hunter		LLM	75	NYU	9-86
Livingston, Marie L.	C-Pr	No Colorado	FHOQ	PHD	84	Colo St	1985
Lizzeri, Alessandro	Asst	Princeton		PHD	95	Northwes	1995
Ljungqvist, Lars	Asst	SUNY-Buffalo	EF	PHD	88	Minnesota	1994
Lobato, Ignacio	Asst	Iowa		PHD	94	London	1994
Locay, Luis	Assoc	U Miami	DO	PHD	83	Chicago	1989
Loeb, Peter D.	C-Pr	Rutgers-Newk		PHD	73	Rutgers	1973
Loewy, Michael	Asst	Houston	EG	PHD	86	Minnesota	1991
Lofgreen, Harold A.	Prof	St Cloud St		PHD	72	Iowa	1972
Lofgren, Stephanie	Asst	USM Academy		PHD		Northwes	1995
Logan, John W. III	Asst	Rutgers-N Br	L	PHD	87	Cornell	1987
Logan, Robert	Assoc	Alaska-Fairb		PHD	86	Iowa	1986
Lokhande, Vineeta	Asst	Southern		PHD		LSU	1994
Lombard, John	Prof	Eastern Conn		PHD		Conn	
Lombard, Karen	Asst	U Miami		PHD	93	Chicago	1993
Lombardi, Waldo J.	Prof	Lg Isl-Brook	ACD	PHD		Columbia	
Lombra, Raymond E.	Prof	Penn State	E	PHD	71	Penn St	1969
Londhe, Suresh R.	Prof	So Carol St		PHD	65	LSU	1969
Long, C. Richard	Assoc	Georgia St	BE	PHD	68	Vanderbilt	1968
Long, James E.	Prof	Auburn		PHD	74	Fla St	1974
Torchmark Professor							
Long, Neal B.	Prof	Stetson	ACP	PHD	64	Indiana	1974
Long, Stanley G.	Assoc	Pitts-Johnst	ADR	PHD	69	Iowa	1973
Long, Stewart L.	Prof	CS-Fullerton		PHD	74	Illinois	1973
Long, Teresa M.	Prof	Marymount		PHD	80	Iowa St	1981
Looney, Lawrence J.	Assoc	Merrimack		MA		Boston C	
Looney, Robert	Prof	Naval Postgr		PHD	69	Berkeley	1977
Lopez, Franklin A.	Assoc	New Orleans		PHD		Tulane	
Lopomo, Giuseppe	Asst	New York U	CD	PHD	94	Stanford	1994
Lopus, Jane S.	Assoc	CS-Hayward		MA	78	Ca-Haywd	1979
Lord, William A.	Assoc	MD-Baltim Co		PHD	84	Indiana	1987
Lorenz, Edward H.	Assoc	Notre Dame	J	PHD	93	Cambridg	1986
Loschky, David J.	Prof	Missouri	TN	PHD	62	Harvard	1967
Lotspeich, Richard	Asst	Indiana St	PQ	PHD	86	New Mex	1990
Lott, William F.	Assoc	Connecticut	C	PHD	69	N Car St	1969
Loucks, Christine	Assoc	Boise State		PHD	83	Wash St	1989
Loughlin, James C.	Prof	Central Conn		PHD	65	Clark	1968
Louie, Kenneth K. T.	Assoc	Penn St-Erie	FJ	PHD	87	Penn St	1984
Loury, Glenn C.	Prof	Boston Univ	DJ	PHD	76	MIT	1991
Loury, Linda D.	Assoc	Tufts		PHD	78	MIT	1978
Love, Barry A.	C-Ac	Emory Henry		PHD		Virginia	1984
Holbert L. Harris Professorship in Free Enterprise							
Love, Jim L.	Prof	Valdosta St	R	PHD	83	Okla St	1983
Love, Thomas M.	C-Pr	No Central		PHD	67	Wisconsin	1972
Lovejoy, Robert M.	Assoc	SUNY-Bingham		PHD	63	Michigan	1965
Lovell, Hugh G.	Retir	Portland St		PHD	51	MIT	1964
Lovell, Knox	Prof	Georgia	D	PHD	66	Duke	1994
Herman & Mary Virginia Terry Professor							
Lovell, Michael C.	C-Pr	Wesleyan-CT	E	PHD	59	Harvard	1969
Chester D. Hubbard Professor of Economics & Social Science							
Lovely, Mary E.	Asst	Syracuse		PHD	89	Michigan	1988
Loviscek, Anthony	Asst	Seton Hall		PHD	80	W Virginia	
Low, Stuart A.	Prof	Arizona St		PHD	79	Illinois	1979
Lowenberg, Tony	Prof	CS-Northrdge	G	PHD	84	Simon Fr	1984
Lowengrub, Morton	Dean	Indiana		PHD			
Lowinger, Thomas C.	Prof	Wash State		PHD	70	Mich St	1978
Lowry, Darryl W.	Assoc	Roanoke		PHD	81	Berkeley	1981
Lowry, Kathleen	Inst	Wright State		MS	77	Ohio St	
Lowry, Pamela	Asst	Ill Wesleyan	F	PHD	92	Maryland	1992
Lowry, Stanley T.	Prof	Wash & Lee	BK	PHD	58	LSU	1959
Lozada, Gabriel A.	Asst	Utah		PHD	87	Stanford	1993
Lu, Laura	Asst	Lg Isl-Post		PHD	89	SUNY-SBr	
Lubell, Alfred M.	C-Pr	SUNY-Oneonta	ADF	PHD	74	NYU	1974
Lucas, Henry A. Jr.	Assoc	Salem State		JD		Suffolk	
Lucas, Robert E. B.	Prof	Boston Univ	CFJO	PHD	72	MIT	1976
Lucas, Robert E. Jr.	D-Pr	Chicago		PHD	64	Chicago	1974
John Dewey Distinguished Service Professor							
Lucchesi, Michael S.	Asst	USAF Academy		MA		U Wash	
Lucier, Richard L.	Prof	Denison		PHD	72	Claremont	1971
Luckett, Dudley G.	Prof	Iowa State	EN	PHD	58	Tx-Austin	1957
Ludke, Jerry A.	Asst	USAF Academy		MA		Stanford	
Ludolf, Gordon W.	Retir	East Tenn St		PHD	64	Ohio St	1961
Luizer, James C.	Assoc	Kutztown	JC	PHD	84	Lehigh	1984

Luksetich, William A.	C-Pr	St Cloud St		PHD	73	N Illinois	1972
Lumsdaine, Robin	Inst	Princeton					
Lund, Mark	Prof	Luther		PHD		Iowa St	1978
Lund, Peter B.	Prof	CS-Sacrament		PHD		Berkeley	1970
Lundberg, Shelly J.	Assoc	U Washington		PHD	81	Northwes	1984
Lundeen, Ardelle A.	H-Pr	So Dakota St	Q	PHD	76	Iowa St	1976
Lunn, John E.	Prof	Hope	LD	PHD	80	UCLA	1992
Lunt, William E.	Assoc	Vassar	C	PHD		Stanford	1974
Luptowski, Thomas S.	Prof	Northwood		BS			
Lusardi, Annamaria	Asst	Dartmouth		PHD	92	Princeton	1993
Lustgarten, Steven	Prof	CUNY-Baruch		PHD	71	UCLA	
Lutt, Elizabeth	Assoc	Pace		PHD		Columbia	
Lutz, Mark A.	Prof	Maine	AB	PHD	72	Berkeley	1970
Lutz, Nancy A.	Asst	Virg Tech	L	PHD	87	Stanford	1992
Lutzker, Adam	Inst	Hamilton	EB	ABD		Michigan	1995
Lwamugira, Pirudas L.	Asst	Fitchburg St		PHD	90	Temple	1991
Lyall, Katharine C.	Prof	Wisconsin		PHD	69	Cornell	1982
Lyman, R. Ashley	Assoc	Idaho	DC	PHD	72	Northwes	1976
Lynch, G.	Prof	Indiana NW	RTE	PHD	63	Wash St	1981
Lynch, Gerald J.	Assoc	Purdue		PHD	75	Kentucky	1983
Lynch, James W.	Assoc	Robt Morris		MA	72	Pittsburgh	1974
Lynch, Karla	Lect	North Texas		MS		North Tx	1993
Lynch, Lawrence K.	Prof	Transylvania		PHD	66	Kentucky	1979
Lynch, Robert	Asst	SUNY-Cortlan		PHD			
Lynch, Vernon E. Jr.	Prof	Fort Lewis		PHD	76	Arizona	1972
Lynde, Catherine	Assoc	Mass-Boston	EF	PHD	85	Ca-Davis	1983
Lynn, Billy	Assoc	St Ambrose		PHD	94	Illinois	1994
Lynn, Stuart R.	Assoc	Assumption	ABFO	PHD	71	N Carol	1987
Lyon, Andrew B.	Asst	Maryland		PHD	86	Princeton	1987
Lyon, Kenneth S.	Prof	Utah State	CDEQ	PHD	70	Chicago	1966
Lyon, William R.	Inst	Wash & Jeff		MBA		Morehead	1988
Lyons, John S.	Asst	Miami U-Ohio	NO	PHD	77	Berkeley	1985
Lyons, Patrick A.	Prof	So Dakota St	M	JD	74	S Dakota	1975
Lyons, Thomas P.	Assoc	Cornell		PHD	83	Cornell	1988
Ma, Barry K.	Asst	CUNY-Baruch		PHD	86	Stanford	1989
Ma, Ching-to Albert	Assoc	Boston Univ	JL	PHD		LondonEc	
Ma, Yulong	Asst	Alabama A&M	GO	PHD		Tx-Austin	
Maafo, E. Victor	Asst	N Carol Cen					
Maasoumi, Esfandiar	Prof	So Methodist		PHD	77	London	1989
Robert H. & Nancy Dedman Professor							
MacBeth, Thomas G.	Prof	Mass-Lowell	AC	PHD	62	S Calif	
Maccini, Louis J.	C-Pr	J Hopkins		PHD	70	Northwes	1969
MacDonald, James M.	Prof	Rensselaer		PHD	83	SUNY-Buf	1987
MacDonald, Richard A.	Asst	St Cloud St		PHD	92	SUNY-Buf	1989
Macesich, George	Prof	Florida St		PHD	58	Chicago	1959
MacEwan, Arthur	Prof	Mass-Boston	FOI	PHD	69	Harvard	1975
Machina, Mark J.	Prof	Ca-San Diego	D	PHD	79	MIT	1979
Machlis, David	Assoc	Adelphi	E	PHD	71	Rutgers	1968
Machovec, Frank M.	Asst	Wofford		PHD	86	NYU	1988
Mack, Richard Stanley	Prof	Central Wash	RQP	PHD	72	Colo St	1972
Distinguished Professor, Research (1988)							
Mackara, W. Frederick	Assoc	East Tenn St		PHD	76	Tx A&M	1975
Mackey, M. Cecil	Prof	Michigan St		PHD		Illinois	
Mackie-Mason, Jeffrey K.	Assoc	Michigan		PHD	86	MIT	1986
MacLachlan, Fiona C.	Asst	Manhattan		PHD		NYU	1992
MacLeod, W. Bentley	Prof	Boston Coll	DJ	PHD	84	Brit Col	1995
MacNair, Elizabeth	Asst	Texas-Dallas		PHD	93	Houston	
MacPhee, Craig R.	C-Pr	Nebraska	F	PHD	70	Mich St	1969
Paul C. Burnmeister College Professor							
Macpherson, David A.	Assoc	Florida St		PHD	87	Penn St	1992
MacPherson, Rod	Assoc	Montevallo		DBA		Miss St	
MacRitchie, Donald R.	Asst	Framingham		MA	85	Boston C	1987
Macunovich, Diane J.	Assoc	Williams		PHD	89	S Calif	1989
MaCurdy, Thomas E.	Prof	Stanford		PHD	78	Chicago	1983
Madan, Vibhas	Assoc	Drexel		PHD	89	Mich St	1989
Maddala, G. S.	Prof	Ohio State		PHD	63	Chicago	1975
Eminent Scholar							
Madden, John L.	Assoc	Kentucky	N	PHD	68	Kansas St	1968
Maddox, D. Pat	Assoc	Angelo State		PHD	82	Tx Tech	1982
Madhaven, Murugappa C.	Prof	San Diego St		PHD	69	Wisconsin	1968
Madresehee, Mehrdad	C-Ac	Lycoming	FHKL	PHD	85	Wash St	1986
Madsen, Ron	Prof	N Car-Charl					
Maeshiro, Asatoshi	Prof	Pittsburgh	C	PHD	65	Michigan	1979
Magaddino, Joseph P.	C-Pr	CS-Long Bch		PHD	72	Va Tech	1973
Magenau, John M. III	D-Ac	Penn St-Erie	JM	PHD	88	SUNY-Buf	1985
Magenheim, Ellen B.	Assoc	Swarthmore	DI	PHD	86	Maryland	1986
Maggs, Gary E.	Assoc	St John Fshr	E	PHD	86	W Virginia	1986
Magill, Michael J. P.	Prof	So Calif		PHD	70	Brown	1979
Magnani, Elisabetta	Asst	Fla Internat	JEFC	ABD		Yale	1995
Maguire, Margaret S.	Dean$	SUNY-Oneonta	M	PHD		Penn	1995

Name	Rank	Institution	Fields	Degree	Yr	Degree School	Year
Magura, Michael	C-Pr	Toledo		PHD	72	Boston C	1969
Mahajan, Y. Lal	Assoc	Monmouth		PHD		N Illinois	
Mahan, Gary P.	Assoc	Gannon		PHD	78	N Car St	1977
Mahdavi, Mahnaz	Assoc	Smith	FGM	PHD	86	Michigan	1985
Mahdavi, Saeid	Assoc	Tx-S Antonio	EFO	PHD	85	Ca-SnBarb	1984
Mahdi, Syed I.	Prof	Benedict Col		PHD	76	Mass	1975
Maher, William F. X.	Prof	St Peters		PHD		Boston C	1965
Mahoney, Timothy B.	Inst	So Indiana		MS	65	Illinois	1987
Mailath, George J.	Assoc	Pennsylvania	CDH	PHD	85	Princeton	1985
Main, Robert S.	C-Ac	Butler	H	PHD	73	UCLA	1981
Majestic, Paulette R.	Asst	SUNY-Oneonta	M	MBA		Pittsburgh	
Majumdar, Mukul K.	Prof	Cornell		PHD		Berkeley	
H. T. Warshow and Robert Irving Warshow Professor							
Mak, James	Prof	Hawaii-Manoa		PHD	70	Purdue	1970
Makgetla, Neva S.	Asst	Redlands		PHD		Berlin	1987
Makowski, Louis	Prof	Cal-Davis	DE	PHD	75	UCLA	1985
Malamud, Bernard	Prof	Nev-L Vegas		PHD	71	New Sch	1968
Malatesta, Paul H.	Assoc	U Washington		PHD	81	Rochester	1980
Malenbaum, Wilfred	Emer	Pennsylvania		PHD	41	Harvard	1959
Maley, Jean E.	Prof	St John Fshr		PHD	72	Rochester	1968
Maley, Leonard A.	Assoc	Nazareth		MBA	62	Cincinnati	
Malhotra, Devinder	C-Pr	Akron		PHD	79	Kansas St	1979
Malik, Arun	Assoc	George Wash	Q	PHD	84	J Hopkins	
Malixi, Margaret M.	Prof	CS-Bakersf	ACFP	PHD	88	Wisconsin	1988
Malkiel, Burton G.	Prof	Princeton		PHD	64	Princeton	1966
Mallela, Parthasaradhi	Prof	No Illinois		PHD		Rochester	
Malloy, Mary	Asst	New Rochelle	AHJO	PHD			
Malone, Laurence J.	Assoc	Hartwick	ABFJ	PHD		New Sch	1986
Maloney, Michael T.	Prof	Clemson	DGKL	PHD	78	LSU	
Maloney, Tom	Asst	Utah		PHD	93	Michigan	
Maloney, William	Asst	Illinois		PHD	90	Berkeley	1990
Malueg, David A.	Assoc	Tulane		PHD	83	Northwes	
Mamalakis, Markos J.	Prof	Wis-Milwauke		PHD	62	Berkeley	1967
Mammen, Thampy	C-Pr	St Norbert		PHD	67	Penn	1968
Mamoozadeh, G. Abbas	Assoc	Slippery Roc		PHD			
Manage, Neela D.	Assoc	Fla Atlantic		PHD	81	Geo Wash	1981
Mandle, Jay R.	Prof	Colgate	ON	PHD	69	Penn	
W. Bradford Wiley Professor of Economics							
Mandler, Michael A.	Assoc	Harvard		PHD	87	Yale	
Mandy, David M.	Assoc	Missouri	CD	PHD	87	Illinois	1994
Maneschi, Andrea	Assoc	Vanderbilt	FO	PHD	64	J Hopkins	1969
Mangiero, Susan M.	Asst	Sacred Heart	ACDG	ABD		Conn	
Mangum, Garth L.	Prof	Utah		PHD	60	Harvard	1969
Mangum, James M.	Assoc	Louisiana Te		PHD	72	Okla St	1970
Manion, Thomas A.	Prof	St Norbert		PHD		Clark	1983
Mankiw, N. Gregory	Prof	Harvard		PHD	84	MIT	1985
Mann, Bruce D.	Prof	Puget Sound	ADJK	PHD	76	Indiana	1975
Mann, Patrick C.	Prof	W Virginia	DH	PHD	67	Indiana	1967
Mann, Prem S.	Assoc	Eastern Conn		PHD	88	UCLA	1986
Manna, Rolando N.	Inst	St Peters		MA		NYU	1988
Manning, Linda M.	Assoc	Mo-Rolla		PHD	90	Il-Chicago	1989
Manning, Richard L.	Asst	Brigham Yg		PHD	89	Chicago	1990
Manove, Michael	Prof	Boston Univ	D	PHD	70	MIT	1975
Manrique, Gabriel G.	Prof	Winona State		PHD	82	Notre Dm	1989
Mansfield, Edwin	Prof	Pennsylvania		PHD	55	Duke	1963
Manski, Charles F.	Prof	Wisconsin		PHD	73	MIT	1983
Romnes & WARF Professor of Economics							
Manuel, David P.	Prof	St Marys-Tx		PHD	75	Miss	
Manuelli, Rodolfo	Assoc	Wisconsin		PHD	86	Minnesota	1993
Mao, Wen	Asst	Villanova		PHD	94	Va Tech	1995
Mar, Donald W.	Assoc	San Fran St		PHD	85	Berkeley	1987
Maran, Michael J.	Assoc	St John's		PHD		Penn	
Marburger, Daniel R.	Assoc	Arkansas St	AJMD	PHD	89	Ariz St	1989
Marcott, Craig S.	Assoc	St Thomas-MN	C	PHD		Purdue	1982
Marcouiller, Douglas	Asst	Boston Coll	FO	PHD	94	Tx-Austin	1994
Marcus, Matityahu	Prof	Rutgers-N Br	G	PHD	63	Brown	1962
Mardfin, Ward	Assoc	Hawaii Pacif		PHD		Hawaii	
Mardis, Barbara K.	Inst	No Iowa		MBA	81	N Iowa	1981
Marglin, Stephen A.	Prof	Harvard		PHD	65	Harvard	
Walter S. Barker Prof of Econ and Frank W. Taussig Research Prof of Economics							
Margo, Robert A.	Prof	Vanderbilt	NJ	PHD	82	Harvard	1989
Margolis, H. Albert	Prof	Kutztown	NC	PHD	69	Purdue	1976
Margolis, Julius	Emer	Calif-Irvine		PHD	49	Harvard	1976
Margolis, Marvin S.	Assoc	Millersville		PHD	69	Purdue	1981
Margolis, Stephen E.	Prof	N Carol St	LKD	PHD	78	UCLA	1982
Mariano, Roberto S.	Prof	Pennsylvania		PHD	70	Stanford	1971
Marin, Kenneth J.	Adj	Aquinas		MA		Michigan	1988
Marion, Nancy P.	C-Pr	Dartmouth		PHD	77	Princeton	1976
Mark, Adolph E.	Emer	DePaul		PHD	63	Illinois	
Mark, Nelson C.	Assoc	Ohio State	FG	PHD	83	Chicago	1983

Marker, William	Inst	Lewis		MA	85	N Illinois	1988
Market, Donald R.	Prof	Arkansas	E	PHD	67	LSU	1975
Marks, Denton	Assoc	Wis-Whitewat		PHD	81	Princeton	1990
Marks, Melanie B.	Asst	Longwood		PHD	93	Tx A&M	1993
Marks, Peter A.	Assoc	Rhode Isl Cl		PHD		N Carol	
Markusen, James R.	Prof	Colorado		PHD	73	Boston C	1990
Marlin, Matthew R.	Assoc	Duquesne		PHD	81	Fla St	1987
Marlow, Michael L.	Prof	Cal Poly-SLO		PHD	78	Va Tech	1988
on leave to Florida Atlantic Univ							
Marme, Christopher B.	Asst	Augustana IL	ACEO	PHD	94	Illinois	1988
Marmo, Michael	Prof	Xavier	J	PHD	71	Illinois	1970
Marquis, Milton H.	Assoc	Florida St		PHD	85	Indiana	1986
Marsh, Lawrence C.	Assoc	Notre Dame	CD	PHD	76	Mich St	1975
Marshall, James N.	Prof	Muhlenberg		PHD	82	Lehigh	1975
Marshall, Jennings B.	Prof	Samford		PHD		Kentucky	1986
Marshall, John F.	Prof	St John's		PHD		SUNY-SBr	
Marshall, John M.	Prof	Cal-Santa Br	A	PHD	69	MIT	1972
Marshall, Kathryn G.	Asst	Ohio Univ	HQ	PHD		Berkeley	
Marshall, Louise	Assoc	Marymount		PHD	89	Maryland	1976
Marshall, Robert C.	H-Pr	Penn State		PHD	83	Ca-SnDgo	1995
Marshall, Robert H.	Prof	Arizona		PHD	57	Ohio St	1957
Martel, Arthur H.	Prof	Indiana U-PA	JK	PHD	74	Mass	1970
Martellaro, Joseph A.	Emer	No Illinois		PHD		Notre Dm	
Marthinsen, John E.	C-Pr	Babson		PHD	74	Conn	1974
Martie, Charles W.	C-Ac	Quinnipiac		PHD		Conn	1991
Martin, Charles	Assoc	Ark-Ltl Rock		PHD	74	N Carol	1984
Martin, David A.	Assoc	Albright		DA	80	Lehigh	1983
Martin, David A.	Prof	SUNY-Geneseo	BA	PHD	64	Syracuse	1966
Martin, David W.	Assoc	Davidson	GQ	PHD	84	Illinois	1984
Martin, Dolores	Dean	E New Mexico		PHD	76	Va Tech	1993
Martin, Lawrence W.	Assoc	Michigan St		PHD		Maryland	
Martin, Linda R.	Assoc	Hartford		PHD	81	S Carol	1986
Martin, Randolph C.	Prof	So Carolina		PHD	71	Wash U	1970
Martin, Richard S.	Retir	Hartford		PHD		Cornell	1968
Martin, Robert E.	C-Pr	Tx-Arlington	CD	PHD	79	So Meth	1991
Martin, Thomas L.	Assoc	Cen Florida	B	PHD	81	Rice	1983
Martinez, John	Prof	Cameron		PHD		Oklahoma	1973
Martinez, Jorge L.	Prof	Georgia St	DF	PHD	78	Wash U	1977
Martins, Carlos	Asst	Oregon State	DCL	PHD	92	Tennessee	9-92
Marty, Alvin L.	Prof	CUNY-Baruch		PHD	55	Berkeley	1960
Marvasti, Akbar B.	Assoc	Houston-Down		PHD	85	LSU	1990
Marvel, Howard P.	Prof	Ohio State	L	PHD	75	Chicago	1973
Marx, Karl B.	Prof	W Illinois	ADH	PHD	61	Illinois	1961
Marxsen, Craig S.	Assoc	Neb-Kearney		PHD		Geo St	1987
Mas-Colell, Andreu	Prof	Harvard		PHD	72	Minnesota	1981
Louis Bergman Professor of Economics							
Masih, Nolin	Assoc	St Cloud St		PHD	88	Kansas	1964
Maskin, Eric S.	Prof	Harvard					
Maskus, Keith E.	Prof	Colorado		PHD	81	Michigan	1981
Mason, Andrew	Prof	Hawaii-Manoa		PHD	75	Michigan	1975
Mason, Charles F.	Assoc	Wyoming	DK	PHD	83	Berkeley	1982
Mason, Paul M.	Prof	North Fla	HE	PHD	84	Tx-Austin	1985
Mason, Timothy I.	Assoc	E Illinois		PHD	87	Indiana	1989
Mason, W. Joe Jr.	Assoc	East Tenn St		PHD	87	S Carol	1984
Mason, William J.	Prof	San Fran St		PHD	58	Iowa	1958
Masson, Robert T.	Prof	Cornell		PHD	69	Berkeley	1976
Masten, John T.	Prof	Tenn State		PHD	67	S Illinois	
Masters, Stanley H.	Prof	SUNY-Bingham		PHD	65	Princeton	1981
Mastrianna, Frank V.	Dean	Slippery Roc		PHD	68	Cincinnati	3-87
Matcheck, Dale C.	Asst	Mich-Flint		PHD	93	Cornell	1990
Mateer, Dirk	Assoc	Grove City		PHD	91	Fla St	1993
Mateer, Robert N.	C-Pr	Liberty		MBA		Tulane	1984
Matheny, Ken	Asst	Purdue		PHD	92	UCLA	1992
Mathis, Edward J.	Prof	Villanova		PHD	71	SUNY-Buf	1966
Mathis, Gilbert L.	C-Pr	Murray State	DFQ	PHD	66	Ohio St	1966
Mathis, Stephen A.	Prof	Shippensburg		PHD	79	Iowa St	1979
Mathur, Vijay K.	Prof	Cleveland St	DR	PHD	69	Wayne St	1968
Matlsev, Yuri	Assoc	Carthage	DFJP	PHD			1991
Matsui, Akihiko	Prof	Pennsylvania	CDE	PHD	90	Northwes	1990
William P. Carey Term Assistant Professor of Economics							
Matsumoto, Keishiro	Retir	So Conn St		PHD		Minnesota	
Matsuyama, Kiminori	Assoc	Northwestern		PHD		Harvard	
Matta, Benjamin N.	Assoc	New Mex St		PHD	79	Tx-Austin	1972
Mattersdorff, Guenter H.	Prof	Lewis & Clrk	GHAR	PHD	58	Harvard	1963
Matthaei, Julie Ann	Prof	Wellesley		PHD	78	Yale	1978
Matthews, John O.	Asst	Villanova		PHD	85	Temple	1986
Matthews, Peter H.	Inst	Middlebury		ABD		Yale	1995
Matthews, Steven A.	Prof	Northwestern		PHD	78	Cal Tech	1980
Matthews, Warren T.	Assoc	Houston Bapt		PHD	72	Tx A&M	1995
Mattila, John Peter	Prof	Iowa State	J	PHD	69	Wisconsin	1973

Name	Rank	Institution	Field	Degree	Yr	Degree Institution	Year
Mattox, Bruce W. Sr.	Prof	Pembroke St		PHD		Oreg St	1988
Matukonis, Michael	Asst	SUNY-Oneonta	M	MBA		Idaho	
Matusz, Steven J.	Assoc	Michigan St		PHD	83	Penn	1983
Matzkin, Rosa L.	Prof	Northwestern		PHD	86	Minnesota	
Mauney, William M.	Prof	Lenoir-Rhyne		MA	76	Appalach	1967
Centennial Professor of Economics - Director Broyhill Institute							
Maurer-Fazio, Margaret	Asst	Bates		PHD		Pittsburgh	1985
Maurice, S. Charles	Prof	Texas A&M		PHD	67	Georgia	1967
Mavros, Panagiotis	Asst	Wayne State		PHD	93	Cornell	1992
Maxwell, Don P.	Prof	Central Okla		PHD	82	Okla St	1981
Maxwell, Nan L.	Prof	CS-Hayward		PHD	83	Fla St	1985
May, Ann Mari	Assoc	Nebraska	BE	PHD	87	Colo St	1987
Mayer, Thomas	Emer	Cal-Davis	BE	PHD	53	Columbia	1962
Mayer, Walt	Assoc	Mississippi	E	PHD	86	Florida	1987
Mayer, Wolfgang	Prof	Cincinnati	FD	PHD	71	SUNY-Buf	1974
David Sinton Professor							
Mayhew, Anne	Prof	Tennessee		PHD	66	Tx-Austin	1968
Mayo, John W.	Prof	Tennessee		PHD		Wash U	
Mayor, Thomas H.	C-Pr	Houston	AK	PHD	65	Maryland	1969
Mbaku, John M.	Prof	Weber State	AHOP	PHD	85	Georgia	1991
McAfee, R. Preston	Prof	Texas	D	PHD	80	Purdue	9-90
Rex G. Baker, Jr. Professor of Political Economy							
McArthur, John R.	Asst	Wofford		PHD	91	Claremont	1990
McAuliffe, Robert E. Jr.	Assoc	Babson		PHD	82	Virginia	1982
McBearty, James C.	Assoc	Arizona		PHD	68	Illinois	1968
McBride, Howard	Retir	Cincinnati		PHD	59	Illinois	
McBride, Mark E.	Prof	Miami U-Ohio		PHD	79	Wash U	1983
McBride, Timothy	Asst	Mo-St Louis	IH	PHD	87	Wisconsin	1991
McCafferty, Stephen A.	Prof	Ohio State	EF	PHD	77	Brown	1982
McCain, Roger A. III	Prof	Drexel		PHD	71	LSU	1988
McCaleb, Thomas S.	Assoc	Florida St		PHD	75	N Carol	1980
McCall, Charles W.	C-Ac	Rider	EJ	PHD	82	Temple	1979
McCall, John B.	Assoc	Tx-Arlington	OQ	PHD	68	Okla St	1964
McCall, John J.	Prof	UCLA		PHD	59	Chicago	
McCallum, Bennett T.	Prof	Carnegie Mel		PHD	69	Rice	1981
H. J. Heinz Professor of Economics							
McCallum, George E.	Retir	St Norbert		PHD		Calif	1967
McCarl, Henry N.	Prof	Alabama-Birm	AR	PHD	69	Penn St	1969
McCarley, James F.	C-Pr	Albion	J	PHD	70	Mich St	1965
McCarthy, Patrick S.	Assoc	Purdue		PHD	76	Claremont	1978
McCarty, Cynthia S.	Asst	Jacksonvl St		PHD		N Carol	1990
McCarty, Marilu H.	Assoc	Georgia Tech	EH	PHD	72	Geo St	1972
McCarty, Therese A.	Assoc	Union	GI	PHD	87	Michigan	1987
McChesney, Fred	Prof	Emory		PHD	82	Virginia	1983
McClellan, Mark	Asst	Stanford		PHD	93	Harvard	9-95
McClelland, Patrick C.	VProf	Rockhurst		PHD	81	American	1985
McClelland, Peter D.	Prof	Cornell		PHD	67	Harvard	1968
McClintock, Brent	Asst	Carthage	EFG	PHD		Colo St	1991
McCloskey, Donald N.	Prof	Iowa		PHD	70	Harvard	1980
McClung, Bruce Alan	Asst	SW Texas St		PHD	88	Tx A&M	1988
McClure, James Edward	Assoc	Ball State		PHD	83	Purdue	1982
McCollum, James B.	Prof	Columbus		PHD	68	Tulane	1976
McComb, Robert P.	Asst	Texas Tech		PHD	89	Illinois	1991
McConnell, Virginia D.	Assoc	MD-Baltim Co		PHD	78	Maryland	
McCorkle, Gary	Asst	Tx-Brownsvil	ABM	MS	71	E Tx St	1989
McCorkle, Sarapage	Asst	Mo-St Louis	A	EDD	87	Mo-St Lo	1970
McCormack, Edward	Asst	Berea		MBA	80	E Kentuc	1985
McCormick, Amy	Asst	Mary Baldwin	J	PHD	95	Harvard	1995
McCormick, Kenneth J.	Prof	No Iowa		PHD	82	Iowa St	1982
McCormick, Robert E.	Prof	Clemson	DGKH	PHD	78	Tx A&M	
McCoy, James	Assoc	Murray State	DF	PHD	86	N Carol	1985
McCoy, Kim	Asst	Cen Missouri		PHD	94	Okla St	1990
McCrate, Elaine D.	Assoc	Vermont	JIT	PHD	85	Mass	1985
McCraw, Jessica	Lect	Tx-Arlington		MA	78	DePaul	1990
McCrickard, Donald L.	Assoc	N Car-Greens		PHD	76	N Carol	1975
McCrickard, Myra J.	Asst	Bellarmine		PHD	89	N Car St	1989
McCue, Kristen	Asst	Texas A&M		PHD	90	Chicago	1989
McCullick, Jack J.	Dean	Fort Hays St		PHD	70	Kansas St	1966
McCulloch, J. Houston	Prof	Ohio State		PHD	73	Chicago	1979
McCulloch, Laurence		Ohio State					
McCulloch, Rachel	Prof	Brandeis		PHD	73	Chicago	1987
McCutcheon, Barbara	Asst	Iowa		PHD	91	Chicago	1990
McDaniel, Bruce	Asst	No Colorado	CGMQ	PHD		Colo St	1992
McDermott, John H.	Assoc	So Carolina		PHD	79	Brown	1983
McDevitt, Catherine L.	Asst	Cen Michigan		PHD	86	Rochester	1989
McDonald, James B.	Prof	Brigham Yg		PHD	70	Purdue	1972
McDonald, John F.	Prof	Ill-Chicago	R	PHD	71	Yale	1981
McDonald, Judith Ann	Asst	Lehigh	FE	PHD	86	Princeton	1990
McDonald, Michael	Asst	Coe		MA	81	Iowa	1981

McDonald, Stephen L.	Prof	Texas	HQ	PHD	51	Tx-Austin	9-61
Addison Baker Duncan Centennial Professor in Economics							
McDonald, Vincent R.	Prof	Howard		PHD	68	Maryland	
McDonough, Carol C.	Prof	Mass-Lowell	DN	PHD	69	Boston C	1970
McDougall, Gerald S.	Dean	SE Missouri	HL	PHD	74	Claremont	1993
McDowell, John M.	Prof	Arizona St		PHD	79	UCLA	1978
McEachern, William A.	Prof	Connecticut	H	PHD	75	Virginia	1978
McEliece, James H.	Assoc	Pt Loma Naz		PHD		Co Mines	1994
McElroy, F. William	Prof	Georgetown		PHD	67	Geotown	1968
McElroy, Jerome L.	C-Pr	St Marys-Ind	AEFO	PHD	71	Colorado	8-82
McElroy, Marjorie B.	C-Pr$	Duke		PHD	69	Northwes	1976
McElroy, Michael B.	Assoc	N Carol St	E	PHD	70	Northwes	1970
McFadden, Daniel L.	Prof	Cal-Berkeley		PHD	62	Minnesota	1963
McFarland, David	Prof	No Carolina		PHD			
McFarland, Earl L. Jr.	Prof	Williams		PHD	73	Columbia	1968
McFarlin, Thomas	Asst	Westfield St		MBA		W NewEng	1978
McGahagan, Thomas A.	C-As	Pitts-Johnst	FN	PHD	76	Penn	1982
McGarrity, John P.	Asst	USAF Academy		MA		Tx-Austin	
McGarrity, Joseph	Asst	Cen Arkansas		PHD	94	Geo Mason	8-95
McGarvey, Mary G.	Assoc	Nebraska	E	PHD	83	Virginia	1992
McGee, L. Randolph	Prof	Kentucky	MG	PHD	63	Tulane	1963
McGee, M. Kevin	C-Ac	Wis-Oshkosh	H	PHD	83	Ohio St	1982
McGibany, James M.	Assoc	Marquette		PHD	83	Mich St	1983
McGill-Tillman, Patricia	Inst	Jackson St		MA	65	Atlanta	1968
McGoldrick, Kim Marie	Asst	Richmond		PHD	93	SUNY-Bin	1992
McGowan, Susan	Prof	CS-Sacrament		PHD	77	Ca-Davis	1974
McGrath, Paul T.	Assoc	Purdue-Calmu		PHD	88	N Illinois	1986
McGrath, Richard	Asst	Wm & Mary		MA		Virginia	1993
McGregor, Rob R.	Asst	N Car-Charl		PHD		S Carol	
McGuckin, J. T.	Assoc	New Mex St		PHD	90	Wisconsin	1989
McGuire, Martin C.	Prof	Calif-Irvine		PHD	64	Harvard	1992
McGuire, Robert A.	Prof	Akron		PHD	78	U Wash	1990
McGuire, Thomas G.	Prof	Boston Univ	HIL	PHD	76	Yale	1976
McHone, W. Warren	Prof	Cen Florida	R	PHD	80	Penn	1982
McIntyre, Richard	Assoc	Rhode Island		PHD	89	Mass	1989
McIntyre, Robert J.	VAsoc	Bowdoin	NP	PHD		N Carol	
McKee, David L.	Prof	Kent State	OR	PHD	66	Notre Dm	1967
McKee, Michael	Assoc	New Mexico	HKQL	PHD	85	Carleton	1991
McKenna, Edward J.	C-Ac	Conn Coll		PHD		SUNY-SBr	
McKenzie, Lionel W.	Emer	Rochester		PHD	42	Princeton	1957
McKeon, John	Asst	Fitchburg St		MS		S Illinois	1979
McKibbin, Lawrence	Dean	Washburn	L	PHD	68	Stanford	1991
McKiernan, Barbara	Asst	Ohio Univ	EGN	PHD	94	Geo Mason	1994
McKinney, Charles W.	Assoc	Whitworth		PHD		Wash St	1985
McKinney, Hannah J.	Asst	Kalamazoo	HJR	PHD	84	Penn	1988
McKinney, Joseph A.	Prof	Baylor		PHD	70	Mich St	1976
McKinney, Marie M.	Assoc	Framingham		PHD	83	SUNY-Bin	1985
McKinnon, Ronald I.	Prof	Stanford		PHD	61	Minnesota	1961
McKinnon, Thomas	Prof	Arkansas	NA	PHD		Miss	1981
McKinsey, James W.	Asst	Stonehill	A	ABD		Yale	1986
McLain, James J.	Assoc	New Orleans		PHD	72	Pittsburgh	1972
McLain, Louis P.	Assoc	Txs Wesleyan		MBA	74	So Meth	1976
McLaughlin, Francis M.	Assoc	Boston Coll	JN	PHD	64	MIT	1961
McLaughlin, Kenneth J.	Assoc	CUNY-Hunter		PHD	87	Chicago	9-94
McLaughlin, Patrick	C	NW Missouri	F	JD		Mo-Ks Cty	1978
McLean, Richard P.	Prof	Rutgers-N Br	D	PHD	79	SUNY-SBr	1986
McLean, Roy L.	Asst	SW Louisiana		PHD	94	S Calif	1995
McLean, Thomas A.	Retir	Portland St		PHD	66	Utah	1962
McLellan, Jacquelynne W.	Asst	Frostburg St		PHD	93	Wayne St	1994
McLennan, Andrew M.	Assoc	Minnesota		PHD	82	Princeton	1987
McLeod, Darryl L.	Asst	Fordham		PHD	82	Berkeley	1984
McLewin, Phillip J.	Assoc	Ramapo		PHD	70	Cornell	1974
McMahan, Ralph Stephen	Assoc	W Carolina		PHD	74	Arkansas	1970
McMahon, Marshall E.	Prof	Rhodes		PHD	72	Vanderbilt	1972
McMahon, Robert C.	Assoc	So Maine	R	PHD	70	Lehigh	1969
McMahon, Walter W.	Emer	Illinois		PHD	57	Iowa	1957
McManis, Bruce L.	H-Pr	Nicholls St	G	PHD	81	LSU	1978
McMillen, Daniel P.	Prof	Tulane		PHD	87	Northwes	1994
McMillin, W. Douglas	Prof	Louisiana St	E	PHD	79	LSU	1985
South Central Bell Business Partnership Professor							
McMinn, Jim Thomas	Prof	Austin Peay	GM	DBA		Miss St	1977
McMinn, Robert D.	C-Pr	Tx A&M-C Chr	A	PHD	73	Oklahoma	9-74
McMullen, B. Starr	Prof	Oregon State	LE	PHD	79	Berkeley	9-80
McMurry, Patrick H.	Prof	Missouri Wes	J	PHD		Arkansas	1978
McNamara, John R.	Prof	Lehigh	MO	PHD	71	Rensselae	1973
Lee Iacocca Professor of Business & Economics							
McNelis, Paul D.	Prof	Georgetown		PHD	74	J Hopkins	1977
McNertney, Edward M.	C-Ac	Tx Christian		PHD	77	Mass	1977
McNiel, Douglas W.	Prof	McNeese St		PHD	77	Okla St	1984
McNown, Robert F.	Prof	Colorado		PHD	71	Ca-SnDgo	1971

McNulty, Mark S.	Assoc	Kansas State	CD	PHD	86	Iowa St	1985
McPherson, Michael	Asst	North Texas		PHD	92	Mich St	1992
McPherson, Michael S.	Prof	Williams		PHD	74	Chicago	1974
Herbert H. Lehman Professor of Economics							
McPherson, Natalie	Asst	E Illinois		PHD	87	Maryland	1994
McPheters, Lee R.	Prof	Arizona St		PHD	72	Va Tech	1976
McQuiston, James M. Jr.	Asst	So Miss		BS	56	So Miss	1960
McRae, Larry T.	Assoc	Appalach St	M	PHD	78	N Carol	1977
McRostie, Clair	Prof	Gustavus Ado		PHD	64	Wisconsin	1957
Ogden and Elizabeth Confer Professorship in Entrepreneurship							
Mead, Arthur C.	Assoc	Rhode Island		PHD	78	Boston C	1976
Meador, Mark W.	Assoc	Loyola-Maryl	EG	PHD	80	U Wash	1980
Meadows, G. Richard	Assoc	Wis-Milwauke		PHD	72	Wash U	1971
Meadows, Tommy C.	Prof	Austin Peay	HJ	PHD		Clemson	1977
Meaney, Martha M.	C-As	Framingham		MA		Boston C	
Means, Tom S.	Assoc	San Jose St		PHD	83	UCLA	1986
Measell, Richard F.	Asst	St Marys-Ind	ADHJ	PHD	85	Maryland	8-83
Medema, Steven G.	C-Ac	Colo-Denver	HDK	PHD	89	Mich St	1989
Medley, Joseph E.	Assoc	So Maine	BO	PHD	81	Mass	1983
Medoff, James L.	Prof	Harvard					
Meyer Kestnbaum Professor of Labor & Industry							
Medoff, Marshall H.	Prof	CS-Long Bch		PHD	73	Berkeley	1979
Meehan, James P.	Asst	Edinboro		MA	61	Notre Dm	
Meehan, James W.	Prof	Colby	DM	PHD	67	Boston C	1973
Herbert E. Wadsworth Professor of Economics							
Meeks, Thomas J.	Prof	Virginia St		PHD	71	Duke	1969
Meenakshi, Rishi	Asst	Ohio Northrn		PHD	93	Mass	1993
Meepagaia, Gaminie	Asst	Howard		PHD	86	SUNY-Alb	1988
Meeropol, Michael A.	Prof	W New Eng		PHD		Wisconsin	
Mehay, Stephen L.	Prof	Naval Postgr		PHD	73	UCLA	1985
Mehdizadeh, Mostafa	Assoc	Miami U-Ohio	A	PHD	80	Oklahoma	1982
Mehra, Jadish C.	Prof	Youngstown		PHD	68	SUNY-Buf	1965
Mehra, Rajnish	Prof	Cal-Santa Br	GF	PHD	78	Car Mellon	1988
Mehrling, Perry G.	Asst	Barnard		PHD	88	Harvard	1987
Mehta, Shailendra	Asst	Purdue		PHD	90	Harvard	1990
Mehtabdin, Khalid R.	Assoc	St Rose		PHD	79	Pittsburgh	1986
Meiners, Roger E.	Prof	Tx-Arlington	KJ	PHD	76	Va Tech	1993
Meininger, Richard P.	Assoc	Ohio Northrn		PHD	87	Ohio U	1973
Meisel, John B.	Prof	S Ill-Edward		PHD	78	Boston C	1977
Meiselman, David I.	Prof	Virg Tech	D	PHD	61	Chicago	1971
Meiser, Charles W.	Assoc	Lk Superior	C	MS	66	Purdue	9-68
Meister, Charles G.	Assoc	IL Benedict	M	MBA	75	Northwes	1984
Melancon, Melissa	Asst	Grambling St		ABD		La Tech	
Melero, Francisco	Assoc	Russell Sage		PHD		Rensselae	
Melese, Francois	Assoc	Naval Postgr		PHD	82	Belgium	1987
Meltzer, Allan H.	Prof	Carnegie Mel		PHD	58	UCLA	1957
John M. Olin University Professor of Political Economy and Public Policy							
Meltzer, Yale L.	Asst	CUNY-Stn Isl	EG	MBA	66	NYU	1983
Melvin, Michael T.	Prof	Arizona St		PHD	80	UCLA	1980
Menchik, Paul L.	C-Pr	Michigan St		PHD	76	Penn	1979
Mendelsohn, Robert	Prof	Yale		PHD	78	Yale	1984
Mendes, Sergio A.	Asst	Concordia C		MA		Va Tech	1992
Mendez, Jose A.	Prof	Arizona St		PHD	80	So Meth	1980
Menezes, Carmen F.	Prof	Missouri	DF	PHD	66	Northwes	1965
Menge, John A.	Prof	Dartmouth		PHD	59	MIT	1956
Mengistu, Tadessa	Assoc	Dillard		PHD		Indiana	
Menz, Fredric C.	Prof	Clarkson	HQ	PHD	70	Virginia	1974
Mercer, Lloyd J.	Prof	Cal-Santa Br	ND	PHD	67	U Wash	1966
Mercuro, Nicholas	Prof	New Orleans		PHD	77	Mich St	1977
Merkel, Edward T.	Assoc	Troy State		PHD	74	N Illinois	1978
Merkle, Paul E.	Prof	La St-Shreve		PHD	77	La Tech	1976
Merlo, Antonio	Asst	Minnesota		PHD	92	NYU	1992
Merlo, Gary E.	Asst	Westfield St		MBA		W NewEng	1983
Merrifield, David E.	Prof	Western Wash	M	PHD	82	Claremont	1983
Merrifield, John D.	Assoc	Tx-S Antonio	HQR	PHD	84	Wyoming	1987
Merrill, William C.	Prof	Iowa State	O	PHD	64	Berkeley	1964
Merriman, David F.	Asst	Loyola-Chicg		PHD	83	Wisconsin	1987
Merva, Mary	Asst	Utah		PHD	89	Rutgers	1990
Merz, Monika	Asst	Rice		PHD	94	Northwes	1994
Merz, Thomas E.	Assoc	Mich Tech		PHD	80	Pittsburgh	1980
Mesa-Lago, Carmelo	Prof	Pittsburgh	P	PHD	68	Cornell	1968
Distinguished Service Professor of Economics and Latin American Studies							
Mescon, Timothy S.	Dean	Kennesaw St	JM	PHD	79	Georgia	1990
Messerschmidt, Daniel C.	C-Pr	Lynchburg		PHD	84	Iowa St	1985
Metcalf, Gilbert	Asst	Tufts		PHD	88	Harvard	1994
Metcalf, Gilbert E.	Asst	Princeton		PHD	88	Harvard	1988
Metrick, Andrew P.	Asst	Harvard					
Metts, Robert Lyle	Assoc	Nevada-Reno		PHD	85	Berkeley	1984
Metzger, Michael R.	C-Pr	Central Okla		PHD	78	Stanford	1991
Meurs, Mieke E.	Asst	American U		PHD	88	Mass	1989

Meyer, Bruce	Assoc	Northwestern		PHD	87	MIT	1987
Meyer, Carrie A.	Asst	George Mason		PHD	88	Illinois	1988
Meyer, Charles W.	Prof	Iowa State	G	PHD	61	J Hopkins	1961
Meyer, Christine	Asst	Bentley	EFH	PHD	95	MIT	1995
Meyer, Donald J.	Assoc	W Michigan	D	PHD	83	Tx A&M	1991
Meyer, Jack	Prof	Michigan St		PHD	74	Stanford	1983
Meyer, Laurence H.	Prof	Wash Univ		PHD	70	MIT	1969
Meyer, Paul A.	Assoc	Maryland		PHD	66	Stanford	1965
Meyer, Peter	Prof	Louisville		PHD	70	Wisconsin	
Meyer, Peter J.	Assoc	Pacific	BJL	PHD	79	Berkeley	1985
Mezzetti, Claudio	Assoc	No Carolina		PHD	88	Oxford	1990
Miceli, Thomas J.	Assoc	Connecticut	KR	PHD	88	Brown	1987
Michaels, Albert	C $	SUNY-Buffalo					
Michaels, Robert J.	Prof	CS-Fullerton		PHD	72	UCLA	1968
Michailidis, Lazaros	Assoc	Bloomfield		PHD		SUNY-Buf	1978
Michalik, Benjamin A.	Retir	St Peters	1987	PHD	57	Fordham	1947
Michalopoulos, Charles	Asst	Virg Tech	J	PHD	94	Wisconsin	1992
Michaud, Claude	Prof	INSEAD		D		Bordeaux	8-70
Michener, Ronald W.	Assoc	Virginia	EN	PHD	81	Chicago	1979
Michl, Thomas R.	Assoc	Colgate	EJ	PHD	84	New Sch	1983
Mickens, Alvin D.	Assoc	SUNY Old Wes		PHD	72	NYU	1978
Middleton, Charles R.	Dean	Colorado		PHD		Duke	
Mieczkowski, Bogdan	Prof	Ithaca	AF	PHD		Illinois	1954
Mieszkowski, Peter	Prof	Rice		PHD	63	J Hopkins	1981
Cline Professor of Economics & Finance							
Miklius, Walter	Retir	Hawaii-Manoa		PHD	64	UCLA	
Milam, Richard	Inst	Appalach St	FM	PHD	91	Va Tech	1991
Milener, Eugene D. III	Retir	Hartwick		PHD		NYU	1960
Milenkovitch, Deborah D.	Prof	Barnard		PHD	66	Columbia	1965
Milgrom, Paul R.	Prof	Stanford		PHD	79	Stanford	1987
Milkman, Martin	Assoc	Murray State	CJH	PHD	89	Oregon	1988
Miller, Carole F.	Assoc	Rhode Island		PHD	88	Syracuse	1986
Miller, Dennis D.	Assoc	Baldwin-Wal	OQ	PHD	85	Colorado	1987
Miller, Edward M.	Prof	New Orleans		PHD	70	MIT	1984
Miller, Ellen Marie	Asst	N Car-Charl		PHD	83	Florida	1982
Miller, Gerald	Assoc	Rockhurst		PHD		Notre Dm	1982
Miller, Gerald M.	SInst	Miami U-Ohio	DC	MA	73	Brown	1971
Miller, Green	Prof	Morehead St		PHD	85	Kentucky	1979
Miller, Jack	Assoc	SUNY Oswego		PHD	84	W Virginia	1981
Miller, Jeffrey B.	Prof	Delaware	EP	PHD	76	Penn	1981
Miller, John A.	Assoc	Wheaton-MA		PHD	82	Pittsburgh	1979
Miller, Jon R.	Prof	Idaho	BQ	PHD	74	Wash U	1989
Miller, Marlen F.	Prof	Pacific Luth		PHD	62	Minnesota	1970
Miller, Michael S.	Assoc	DePaul		PHD	80	Pittsburgh	1980
Miller, Norman C.	Prof	Miami U-Ohio	EF	PHD	66	Pittsburgh	1985
Julian G. Lange Professor of Economics & American Enterprise							
Miller, Oscar	Prof	Ill-Chicago	A	AM	46	Chicago	1948
Miller, Otis E.	Prof	Wm Jewell		PHD	62	Missouri	1978
Miller, Richard A.	Prof	Wesleyan-CT	L	PHD	62	Yale	1960
Andrews Professor of Economics							
Miller, Robert A.	Assoc	Carnegie Mel		PHD	82	Chicago	1982
Miller, Robert J.	Assoc	Missouri So		MA		Cen MoSt	1968
Miller, Roger F.	Prof	Tx-Arlington	K	PHD	68	Chicago	1993
Miller, Stephen M.	H-Pr	Connecticut	EF	PHD	72	SUNY-Buf	1970
Miller, Timothy I.	Prof	Denison		PHD	79	S Illinois	1978
Miller, Tracy	Assoc	Grove City		PHD		Chicago	
Milley, Donald J.	Prof	Youngstown		PHD	74	SUNY-Buf	
Milliman, Scott R.	Assoc	Jms Madison	DQ	PHD	85	Wisconsin	1986
Mills, David E.	Prof	Virginia	LD	PHD	75	Stanford	1975
Mills, Jeffrey A.	Asst	Cincinnati	C	PHD	89	Wash U	
Mills, Judith W.	Asst	So Conn St		PHD		SUNY-SBr	1991
Mills, Richard L.	Assoc	New Hampshir	CD	PHD	67	Indiana	1967
Millsaps, Steven	Prof	Appalach St	M	PHD	73	N Car St	1973
Milstein, Susan Matz	Assoc	W Maryland		MBA		MtStMary	1983
Milyo, Jeffrey	Asst	Tufts		PHD	94	Stanford	1992
Min, An-Sik	Prof	Edinboro		PHD	75	Iowa	1975
Minehart, Deborah	Asst	Boston Univ	CDL	PHD	94	Berkeley	1994
Miner, Jerry	Prof	Syracuse		PHD	58	Michigan	
Miner, Laurence A.	Assoc	Fairfield	CIJA	PHD	79	N Carol	1981
Minet, Lawrence J.	Assoc	Canisius		PHD	53	Columbia	1958
Ming, Xing	Asst	Indiana		PHD	95	Rice	1995
Mini, Peter S.	Assoc	Bryant	BN	PHD		Tulane	
Minick, Robert A.	Prof	CS-Fresno		PHD		Tx-Austin	1962
Minisian, Jora	Prof	CS-Northrdge		PHD	60	Chicago	1972
Minkler, Alanson P.	Asst	Connecticut	DK	PHD	88	Ca-Davis	1989
Minor, Frank	Assoc	St Anselm		PHD			
Minsky, Hyman P.	Retir	Wash Univ		PHD	54	Harvard	1965
Minter-Hoxby, Caroline	Asst	Harvard					
Miranne, Martha	Retir	Pace		MA		Pace	1977
Miranowski, John A.	C-Pr	Iowa State	Q	PHD	75	Harvard	1995

Mirer, Thad W.	Assoc	SUNY-Albany	H	PHD	71	Yale	1973
Mirman, Leonard J.	Prof	Virginia	ACDQ	PHD	70	Rochester	1986
Paul Goodloe McIntire Professor of Economics							
Mirmirani, Sam	C-Ac	Bryant	IMO	PHD	85	Clark	1982
Miron, Jeffrey A.	C-Pr	Boston Univ	EKN	PHD	84	MIT	1990
Mirowski, Philip E.	Prof	Notre Dame	B	PHD	79	Michigan	1990
Mirza, David B.	C-Ac	Loyola-Chicg		PHD	73	Northwes	1969
Mirza, Faisal K.	Inst	Kennesaw St	AD	MBA	76	Indiana	1981
Mischel, Kenneth M.	Asst	CUNY-Baruch		PHD	90	Columbia	
Mishkin, Frederic S.	Prof	Columbia		PHD	76	MIT	1983
Misiolek, Walter S.	Prof	Alabama		PHD	76	Cornell	1975
Mitch, David F.	Assoc	MD-Baltim Co		PHD	82	Chicago	1983
Mitchell, Douglas W.	Prof	W Virginia	E	PHD	78	Princeton	1984
Mitchell, Hadley T.	Asst	Taylor		PHD	85	Tennessee	1993
Mitchell, Janet L.	Asst	Cornell		PHD	86	Northwes	1989
Mitchell, Jeannette C.	Asst	Rochest Tech	FOB	ABD		Utah	1985
Mitchell, Mike	Asst	Nevada-Reno		PHD	88	Oregon	1988
Mitchell, Milt	Asst	Wis-Oshkosh	Q	MA	65	Wisconsin	1967
Mitchell, Shannon K.	Asst	Virg Comm		PHD	89	Virginia	1990
Mitchell, Thomas M.	Assoc	So Illinois	DC	PHD	84	Brown	1983
Mitchell, William E.	Prof	Mo-St Louis	EG	PHD	67	Duke	1965
Mitra, Tapan	C-Pr	Cornell		PHD		Rochester	
Mitsui, Toshihide	Assoc	Kansas		PHD		Minnesota	1981
Mittnik, Stefan	Assoc	SUNY-Stony B		PHD	87	Wash U	1987
Mixon, Frank	Asst	So Miss	J	PHD	92	Auburn	1994
Mixon, J. Wilson	Prof	Berry		PHD	74	U Wash	1986
Miyagiwa, Kaz	VAsoc	Louisiana St	FO	PHD	85	Tx-Austin	8-95
Miyazaki, Hajime	Prof	Ohio State	LJ	PHD	77	Berkeley	1984
Mizak, Daniel A.	Assoc	Frostburg St		PHD	84	Pittsburgh	1977
Mizrach, Bruce	Asst	Rutgers-N Br	E	PHD	87	Penn	1995
Moberly, H. Dean	Prof	Auburn-Montg	ADIQ	PHD	68	Tx A&M	1970
Mobley, Lee	Asst	Oakland	LI	PHD	89	Ca-SnBarb	1991
Mocan, Naci H.	Asst	Colo-Denver	CJI	PHD	89	CUNY	1990
Modeste, Nelson	C-Ac	So Carol St		PHD			1994
Modigliani, Franco	Emer	MIT		PHD	44	New Sch	1960
Moe, Karine S.	Asst	Macalester	AJ	ABD	95	Minnesota	1995
Moen, Jon R.	Asst	Mississippi		PHD	87	Chicago	1990
Moewes, David S.	Assoc	Concordia C		PHD		Utah	1968
Moffett, Russell E.	Prof	Ferris State		PHD		Calif	1965
Moffit, Tim	Asst	Kalamazoo	M	MBA	84	Dartmouth	1994
Moffitt, Robert A.	Prof	J Hopkins		PHD	75	Brown	1995
Mogab, John William	Assoc	SW Texas St		PHD		Tennessee	
Mogavero, Michael A.	Dean	Edinboro		PHD	79	Conn	1995
Moghadam, Fatemeh	Assoc	Hofstra	NOQ	PHD	79	Oxford	
Moghaddam, Masoud	Prof	St Cloud St		PHD	82	Iowa St	1983
Mohabbat, Khan A.	Prof	No Illinois		PHD		SUNY	
Mohaghegh, Mehdi	Assoc	Norwich		PHD	86	Clark	1986
Mohammadi, Hassan	Asst	Illinois St	E	PHD	88	Wash St	1988
Mohan, Daniel	Assoc	West Chester	GM	PHD	75	Rutgers	1980
Mohanty, Madhu	Asst	CS-L Angeles					
Mohapatra, Sarita	Lect	Utah State	ADF	PHD	95	Utah St	1995
Mohindru, Rajesh K.	Assoc	Bloomsburg		PHD		Penn	
Mohiuddin, Yasmeen	Asst	Univ South		PHD		Vanderbilt	
Mohring, Herbert D.	Emer	Minnesota		PHD	59	MIT	1961
Mohtadi, Hamid	Assoc	Wis-Milwauke		PHD	82	Michigan	1983
Mohtadi, Shahruz	Assoc	Suffolk		PHD	84	LSU	1983
Moini, Mostafa	Assoc	Okla City		PHD		Oklahoma	1965
Moite, Leonard M.	Assoc	CS-Dominguez	AEDJ	PHD	84	UCLA	1980
Mokyr, Joel	Prof	Northwestern		PHD	74	Yale	1974
Robert H. Strotz Professor of Arts & Sciences							
Molina, David Jude	Assoc	North Texas	C	PHD	83	Tx A&M	1985
Moliver, Donald M.	Assoc	Monmouth		PHD		Va Tech	
Molz, Ferdinand	Adj	York-Penn		PHD		Catholic	
Moncarz, Raul	Prof	Fla Internat	EOF	PHD	69	Fla St	1972
Moncur, James E. T.	C-Pr$	Hawaii-Manoa		PHD	71	Wash St	1969
Mondschean, Thomas H.	Assoc	DePaul		PHD	89	Wisconsin	1987
Mongell, Susan	Assoc	Calif U-Penn		PHD		Pittsburgh	1990
Monhollon, Jimmie	Prof	Hardin-Simm		PHD			
Monroe, Michael C.	Asst	Ithaca	AIR	PHD		Cornell	1988
Monsma, George N. Jr.	Prof	Calvin		PHD	69	Princeton	1969
Monson, Terry D.	Prof	Mich Tech	F	PHD	72	Minnesota	1977
Montano, Carl B.	Assoc	Lamar	OQ	PHD	82	Mich St	1981
Monteith, Chalmers A.	Retir	Kent State	N	PHD	58	Ohio St	1958
Montgomery, Edward B.	Prof	Maryland		PHD	82	Harvard	1990
Montgomery, James D.	Asst	Northwestern		PHD	89	MIT	1989
Montgomery, Mark	C-Ac	Grinnell	JQH	PHD	82	Wisconsin	1989
Montgomery, Mark	Assoc	SUNY-Stony B		PHD	82	Michigan	1988
Montgomery, Michael	Asst	Maine	AE	PHD	88	Florida	1991
Montgomery, Sarah S.	Dean	Mt Holyoke		PHD	60	Wisconsin	1956
Montias, J. Michael	Prof	Yale		PHD	58	Columbia	1963

Name	Rank	School	Field	Degree	Yr	Institution	Since
Montiel, Peter J.	Prof	Oberlin	EF	PHD	78	MIT	1990
Danforth-Lewis Professor							
Moody, Carlisle E.	Prof	Wm & Mary		PHD	70	Conn	1970
Moohr, Michael	Assoc	Bucknell		PHD		Cambridg	1975
Mookherjee, Dilip M.	Prof	Boston Univ	HLO	PHD	82	LondonEc	1995
Moomaw, Ronald L.	Prof	Oklahoma St		PHD	76	Princeton	1972
CBA Associates Chair							
Moon, Choon-Geol	Asst	Rutgers-N Br	C	PHD	87	Stanford	1987
Moore, B. C.	C-As	Delta State	AG	MBA			8-86
Moore, Bartholomew J.	Asst	Rutgers-N Br	E	PHD	90	Columbia	1990
Moore, Basil J.	Prof	Wesleyan-CT	E	PHD	58	J Hopkins	1958
Moore, Derald L.	Assoc	Tri-State		MA		Mich St	1968
Moore, Gary A.	H-Pr	SUNY-Geneseo	JK	PHD	74	Nebraska	9-74
Moore, James C.	Prof	Purdue		PHD	68	Minnesota	1969
Moore, Joseph L.	Prof	Ark Tech		PHD	75	Arkansas	1988
Moore, Mack A.	Prof	Georgia Tech	J	PHD	63	Wisconsin	1963
Moore, Margaret D.		Franklin		PHD		Ohio St	
Moore, Michael Owen	Assoc	George Wash	F	PHD	88	Wisconsin	1988
Moore, Myra	Asst	Tx Christian		PHD	94	Georgia	1994
Moore, Peter R.	Prof	Rhode Isl Cl		PHD		Illinois	
Moore, Robert E.	Asst	Georgia St	FO	PHD	88	Cornell	1989
Moore, Robert L.	Prof	Occidental	J	PHD	77	Harvard	1978
Moore, William J.	Prof	Louisiana St	IJ	PHD	70	Tx-Austin	
Gulf Coast Coca Cola Business Partnership Professor							
Moorhouse, John C.	Prof	Wake Forest		PHD	69	Northwes	1969
Mora, Marie T.	Asst	New Mex St		ABD	95	Tx A&M	8-95
Morduch, Jonathan J.	Assoc	Harvard		PHD	91	Harvard	1991
Morefield, Roger D.	Assoc	St Thomas-TX	I	PHD	77	Duke	1980
Morehouse, Thomas	Retir	Alaska-Ancho		PHD	68	Minnesota	
Moreland, Kemper W.	Prof	E Michigan		PHD	80	Wisconsin	1980
Moresi, Serge X.	Asst	Georgetown		PHD	91	MIT	1991
Morey, Edward R.	Prof	Colorado		PHD	78	Brit Col	1980
Morey, Mathew James	Assoc	Illinois St	CM	PHD		Illinois	
Morgan, Alfred D.	Prof	So Conn St		PHD		Harvard	
Morgan, Celia A.	Prof	SW Texas St		PHD	71	Houston	1971
Morgan, Daniel C. Jr.	Prof	Texas	H	PHD	62	Wisconsin	7-76
Morgan, J. Michael	C-Pr	Charleston		PHD		S Carol	1967
Morgan, John E. Jr.	Asst	N Car-Wilmin	AC	PHD		Georgia	
Morgan, Peter B.	Assoc	SUNY-Buffalo	D	PHD	78	Canterbu	1989
Morgan, W. Douglas	Prof	Cal-Santa Br	HDE	PHD	69	Berkeley	1973
Morgan, William E.	Prof	Wyoming	H	PHD	64	Colorado	1968
Morici, Peter G.	Prof	Maine	F	PHD	74	SUNY-Alb	1988
Morley, John	Asst	Marist		PHD	87	Yale	1995
Morlock, Mark J.	Prof	CS-Chico		PHD		Wash St	1980
Morman, Martin R.	Asst	Morehouse		PHD		Geo St	1990
Moroney, John R.	Prof	Texas A&M		PHD	64	Duke	1981
Morong, Cyril J.	Asst	Lyon College		PHD		Wash St	1989
Morra, Wayne A.	Asst	Beaver		PHD	84	Temple	8-81
Morrell, Stephen O.	Assoc	Barry		PHD	77	Va Tech	1990
Morris, Alpha	C-Ac	Alcorn State		PHD		Miss St	
Morris, Barry K.	C-Pr	No Alabama		PHD	74	Arkansas	1974
Morris, Clair E. Jr.	Prof	USN Academy		PHD	72	Wisconsin	1966
Morris, Clyde D.	Assoc	Youngstown		PHD	87	Case Wes	
Morris, Cynthia T.	Prof	Smith	BNOP	PHD	59	Yale	1983
Morris, John R. Jr.	Prof	Colo-Denver	D	PHD	66	Purdue	1970
Morris, Stephen	Asst	Pennsylvania	CD	PHD	91	Yale	1991
Benjamin V. Schlein Term Assistant Professor of Economics							
Morrison, Andrew R.	Asst	Tulane		PHD	89	Vanderbilt	1988
Morrison, Catherine	Prof	Tufts		PHD	82	Brit Col	1982
Morrison, Clarence C.	Prof	Indiana		PHD	64	N Carol	1970
Morrison, Rodney J.	Prof	Wellesley		PHD	65	Wisconsin	
Morrison, Steven A.	Prof	Northeastern		PHD	79	Berkeley	1982
Morrow, William R.	Prof	E Kentucky		PHD	68	Tennessee	1968
Morse, Kenneth O.	Asst	SUNY-Geneseo	FA	PHD	94	Denver	1992
Morse, Lawrence B.	Assoc	N Carol A&T		PHD	68	Minnesota	1976
Mortensen, Dale T.	Prof	Northwestern		PHD	67	Car Mellon	1965
Ida C. Cook Professor of Consumer Economics							
Mosby, James B.	Asst	Detroit Merc		MA	70	Detroit	1972
Moseldjord, Asbjorn	Assoc	St Marys-Cal		PHD		Ca-SnBarb	1991
Moseley, Fred B.	Prof	Mt Holyoke		PHD	82	Mass	1989
Moser, Ernest R.	H-Ac	NE Louisiana	BM	PHD	73	Tx A&M	1972
Moses, Anthony T.	Assoc	St Anselm		PHD			
Moses, Leon N.	Prof	Northwestern		PHD	52	Harvard	1959
Moses, Ronald P.	Asst	Ill-Chicago	F	PHD		Chicago	
Moshtagh, Ali R.	Assoc	E Illinois		PHD	88	Arkansas	1987
Moskwa, Antoni	Assoc	Allegheny	AFCP	PHD	75	Warsaw	1982
Moss, Joanna	Prof	San Fran St		PHD	78	New Sch	1981
Moss, Laurence S.	Prof	Babson		PHD	71	Columbia	1977
Moss, Richard L.	Prof	CS-San Bern		PHD	73	New Mex	1973
Mostaghimi, Mehdi	Assoc	So Conn St		PHD		Virginia	

Mostashari, Shahriar	C-Pr	Campbell		PHD		N Car St	1982
Motahar, Eshragh	Asst	Union	EFG	PHD	89	J Hopkins	1984
Motomura, Akira	Assoc	Stonehill	KN	PHD	85	Northwes	1995
Mott, Tracy L.	Asst	Denver		PHD	82	Stanford	1991
Mouhamed, Adil	Assoc	Il-Springfld	FP	PHD	85	Nebraska	1988
Moulin, Herve	Prof	Duke					
James D. Duke Professor							
Mount, Randall I.	Prof	Kent State	CD	PHD	69	Purdue	1966
Mountain, Dean C.	Prof	McMaster U	CD	PHD	79	W Ontario	1987
Mounts, William S. Jr.	Prof	Mercer-Macon		PHD	77	Georgia	1978
Mourdoukoutas, Panos	Assoc	Lg Isl-Post		PHD	83	SUNY-SBr	1984
Mourmouras, Alexandros	Assoc	Cincinnati	E	PHD	88	Minnesota	1988
Moy, Ronald L.	Asst	St John's		PHD	90	Rutgers	
Moyer, James T.	C-Pr	Albright		PHD	76	Lehigh	9-68
Mozayeni, Simin B.	Asst	SUNY-N Paltz	ALH	PHD	53	Columbia	1990
Mroz, Thomas A.	Assoc	No Carolina		PHD	84	Stanford	1989
Mrozek, Janusz R.	Asst	Georgia Tech	DQ	PHD	95	Stanford	1993
Mshomba, Richard	Asst	LaSalle	FO	PHD	92	Illinois	1991
Muehsam, Mitchell J.	Asst	Sam Houston		PHD	89	Tx A&M	1989
Mueller, Hans G.	Retir	Mid Tenn St		PHD	68	Vanderbilt	1961
Mueller, James V.	C-Ac	Alma		ABD		Ca-Irvine	1976
Mueller, Marnie	VProf	Wesleyan-CT	I	PHD	65	Yale	
Muench, Thomas	C-Pr	SUNY-Stony B		PHD	65	Purdue	1975
Mueser, Peter R.	Assoc	Missouri	DJT	PHD	83	Chicago	1985
Mui, Vai-Lam	Asst	So Calif		PHD	92	Berkeley	1992
Mukerjee, Swati	Assoc	Bentley	DFI	PHD	86	Boston U	1989
Mukherjee, Joya	VInst	Union	CO	ABD		Rice	1994
Mukheyi, Nivedita	Asst	Oakland	EF	PHD	92	Va Tech	1992
Mukhoti, Bela	Assoc	Rowan Col-NJ		PHD	64	London	1974
Mullen, John K.	C-Ac	Clarkson	GHR	PHD	78	SUNY-Bin	1977
Mullendore, Walter	Prof	Tx-Arlington	R	PHD	68	Iowa St	1969
Muller, Herman J.	Retir	Detroit Merc		PHD		Loyola	1956
Muller, Ronald E.	Prof	American U		PHD		American	1970
Mulligan, Casey	Asst	Chicago		PHD	93	Chicago	1993
Mulligan, James G.	Prof	Delaware	L	PHD	80	Minnesota	1980
Mulligan, Robert M.	Asst	Providence	EK	MA	61	Boston C	1965
Mullin, Gail	Prof	Old Dominion		PHD	83	Indiana	
Mullin, Marian V.	Assoc	West Liberty		MS	85	R Morris	1975
Mullin, Wallace P.	Asst	Michigan St		PHD	92	MIT	1992
Mullings, Llewellyn M.	Assoc	Bridgeport		PHD		Clark	
Mullins, James E.	Assoc	St Ambrose		MA	65	Marquette	1969
Mullins, Steven	Assoc	Drury		PHD	83	Okla St	1982
Multasuo, Eija	Asst	E Michigan		PHD	89	Purdue	1989
Mumy, Gene E.	Assoc	Ohio State	D	PHD	74	J Hopkins	1978
Mundell, Cyril Lee	Assoc	Loyola-N Orl	AC	PHD	76	N Carol	1981
Mundlak, Yair	Prof	Chicago		PHD	57	Berkeley	1986
on leave 1995-96; Frederick Henry Prince Professor							
Munkirs, John R.	Dean	Il-Springfld	BN	PHD	73	Oklahoma	1972
Munley, Vincent G.	C-Pr	Lehigh	HI	PHD	79	SUNY-Bin	1980
Munshi, Kaivan	Asst	Boston Univ	LO	PHD	95	MIT	1995
Munyon, Paul G.	Assoc	Grinnell	L	PHD	75	Harvard	1982
Murans, Frank				PHD	57	Mich St	
Muraoka, Dennis D.	Prof	CS-Long Bch		PHD		Ca-SnBarb	1982
Murdoch, James	Assoc	Texas-Dallas		PHD	82	Wyoming	
Murdock, E. Wayne	Prof	S F Austin		PHD	71	Oklahoma	1972
Murli, Rajan	Assoc	Scranton		PHD		Temple	1989
Murphy, Caroline	Prof	Fitchburg St		PHD		Clark	1971
Murphy, Dennis R.	Dean	Western Wash	FM	PHD	74	Indiana	1979
Murphy, Edward V.	Asst	SW Texas St		PHD		Geo Mason	1992
Murphy, George G. S.	Assoc	UCLA		PHD			
Murphy, James L.	Prof	No Carolina		PHD	64	Purdue	1964
Murphy, John J.	Retir	Catholic		PHD	61	Yale	1967
Murphy, Kevin J.	C-Ac	Oakland	JC	PHD	81	Mich St	1985
Murphy, Robert G.	Assoc	Boston Coll	EF	PHD	84	MIT	1984
Murra, Gene E.	Prof	So Dakota St	Q	PHD	63	Ohio St	1959
Murray, Charles	Asst	NE Missouri		BA		Iowa St	1991
Murray, Jack W.	Retir	Tarleton St	1995	PHD	66	Tx-Arlin	1968
Murray, James M.	Prof	WI-Green Bay		PHD	62	Oregon	1969
Murray, John E.	Asst	Toledo		PHD	92	Ohio St	1994
Murray, Matthew N.	Assoc	Tennessee		PHD	86	Syracuse	1986
Murray, Michael P.	C-Pr	Bates	R	PHD	74	Iowa St	1986
Phillips Professor of Economics							
Murray, Tracy W.	Prof	Arkansas	F	PHD	69	Mich St	1978
Distinguished Professor & Chairholder, Phillips Petroleum Company Chair/IEB							
Murrell, Peter	Prof	Maryland		PHD	77	Penn	1977
Murry, Donald A.	Prof	Oklahoma	L	PHD	66	Missouri	
Murtaugh, Frank M. Jr.	Assoc	Norwich		PHD	81	Emory	1982
Murthy, N. R. Vasudeva	Prof	Creighton	CDH	PHD	75	SUNY-Bin	1979
Murti, Vedula N.	C-As	Penn St-Harr		PHD	66	Penn	1969
Musgrave, Frank W.	C-Pr$	Ithaca	IJ	PHD	68	Rutgers	1968

Mushinski, David	Asst	Wm & Mary		MA	94	Wisconsin	1995
Musoke, Moses		SUNY-Empire	NM	PHD		Wisconsin	1985
Mustafa, Muhammad	Assoc	So Carol St		PHD	88	Wayne St	1989
Muth, Richard F.	Prof	Emory	DR	PHD	58	Chicago	1983
Fuller E. Callaway Professor of Economics							
Mutti, John	Prof	Grinnell	FHQ	PHD	74	Wisconsin	1987
Sydney Meyer Professor of International Economics							
Myatt, Sam	C	Union-TN		EDD		Memphis	
Myers, Daniel A.	Assoc	W Kentucky	R	PHD	86	Vanderbilt	1986
Myers, George G.	Retir	East Tenn St		EDD	65	Tennessee	1957
Myers, John G.	Emer	So Illinois		PHD	61	Columbia	1977
Myers, Steven	Assoc	Akron		PHD	80	Ohio St	1979
Myerson, Roger B.	Prof	Northwestern		PHD	76	Harvard	1976
N'Chu-Oguie, Charles	Assoc	San Francisc		PHD	84	Stanford	1984
Na, Jinpeng	Asst	Rutgers-Camd		PHD		SUNY-SBr	
Nachbar, John	Asst	Wash Univ		PHD	88	Harvard	1990
Nadiri, M. Ishaq	Prof	New York U		PHD	65	Berkeley	1971
Nadler, Mark A.	C-Ac	Ashland		PHD		Iowa St	1989
A. L. Garber Family Chair of Economics							
Nafziger, E. Wayne	Prof	Kansas State	OPF	PHD	67	Illinois	1966
Naggar, Tahany	Prof	West Chester	ADTN	PHD	76	Oklahoma	1977
Nahata, Babu L.	Prof	Louisville		PHD	77	N Illinois	8-78
Naish, Howard F.	Prof	CS-Fullerton		PHD		S Calif	1988
Naka, Atsuyuki	Assoc	New Orleans		PHD	89	Arizona	1989
Nalebuff, Barry J.	Prof	Yale		DPH	82	Nuffield	1989
Nam, Woo Hyun	Prof	San Diego St		PHD		U Wash	1968
Nantz, Kathryn A.	Assoc	Fairfield	JDPA	PHD	87	Purdue	1986
Naples, Michele I.	Assoc	Trenton St		PHD	82	Mass	
Naqvi, Nadeem	Assoc	Georgia	F	PHD	84	So Meth	1987
Narwold, Andrew	Assoc	San Diego		PHD	91	Ca-SnBarb	1991
Nas, Tevfik F.	Prof	Mich-Flint		PHD	77	Fla St	1982
Nash, Robert T.	Prof	Tx A&M-Kings		PHD		Tx A&M	1971
Nasser, Alan		Evergreen St					
Natke, Paul A.	Assoc	Cen Michigan		PHD	82	Notre Dm	1981
Navin, Leo J.	Retir	Bowling Gr		PHD	68	Mich St	
Navratil, Frank J.	Dean	John Carroll	G	PHD	74	Notre Dm	1973
Naya, Seiji	Prof	Hawaii-Manoa		PHD	66	Wisconsin	1961
Nazemzadah, Asghar	Assoc	Houston-Down		PHD	83	Fla St	1989
Neal, Derek A.	Asst	Chicago		PHD	92	Virginia	1991
Neal, Larry	Prof	Illinois		PHD	68	Berkeley	1967
Nechyba, Thomas	Asst	Stanford		PHD	94	Rochester	1994
Neel, Richard E.	Prof	N Car-Charl		PHD	60	Ohio St	1969
Neel, Stewart D.	Inst	USAF Academy		ABD		Rochester	
Neelakantan, P.	Asst	E Stroudsbur	D	PHD	92	SUNY-Buf	1992
Neeman, Zvika	Asst	Boston Univ	CD	PHD	95	Northwes	1995
Neenan, William B.	Prof	Boston Coll	HR	PHD	66	Michigan	1980
Nega, Berhanu	Asst	Bucknell		PHD		New Sch	1990
Negbenebor, Anthony I.	Assoc	Gardner-Webb		PHD		Miss St	1989
Negri, Donald H.	Asst	Willamette		PHD		Michigan	1988
Nehman, Gerlad	Assoc	Tx-Arlington	Q	PHD	73	Ohio St	1993
Nehring, Klaus D.	Asst	Cal-Davis	DG	PHD	91	Harvard	1992
Neill, Helen	Asst	Nev-L Vegas		PHD	92	New Mex	1992
Neill, Jon R.	Assoc	W Michigan	H	PHD	83	Pittsburgh	1980
Neils, Allan E.	Prof	East Wash		JD		Gonzaga	1969
Neilson, William S.	Assoc	Texas A&M		PHD	88	Ca-SnDgo	1988
Neimanis, George J.	Prof	Niagara		MA	65	NYU	1970
Nelson, Charles R.	Prof	U Washington		PHD	65	Wisconsin	1975
Nelson, David M.	C-Ac	Western Wash	EGI	PHD	75	Oregon	1977
Nelson, Dennis L.	Assoc	Minn-Duluth	A	PHD	70	Minnesota	1964
Nelson, Forrest D.	Prof	Iowa		PHD	75	Rochester	1980
Nelson, John P.	D-Pr	Louisville		PHD	68	Kentucky	
Nelson, Jon P.	Prof	Penn State	QD	PHD	70	Wisconsin	1969
Nelson, Julie A.	Assoc	Cal-Davis	BDH	PHD	86	Wisconsin	1988
Nelson, Michael A.	Prof	Illinois St	G	PHD	80	Purdue	1981
Nelson, Paul A.	Assoc	Mich Tech	M	PHD	74	Wisconsin	1972
Nelson, Paul S.	Assoc	NE Louisiana	DL	PHD	85	Tx A&M	1989
Nelson, Phillip J.	Prof	SUNY-Bingham		PHD	67	Columbia	1969
Nelson, Ralph L.	Prof	CUNY-Queens	MG	PHD	55	Columbia	1964
Nelson, Randy A.	Prof	Colby	GM	PHD	79	Illinois	1987
Douglas Professor of Economics							
Nelson, Richard R.	Prof	Columbia		PHD	56	Yale	1986
Henry R. Luce Professor of International Political Economy							
Nemec, Richard W.	Asst	Tx A&M-Kings		MBA		Tx A&M-Kg	1981
Neral, John A.	Assoc	Frostburg St		PHD	89	Pittsburgh	1986
Nesiba, Reynold	Asst	Augustana SD	EG	PHD	95	Notre Dm	1995
Netusil, Noelwah R.	Asst	Reed	AQDH	PHD	92	Illinois	1990
Netz, Janet	Asst	Purdue		PHD	92	Michigan	1994
Neuberger, Egon	Prof	SUNY-Stony B		PHD	58	Harvard	1967
Neuefeind, Wilhelm	C-Pr	Wash Univ		PHD	72	Bonn	1978
Neufeld, John L.	Assoc	N Car-Greens		PHD	75	Michigan	1974

Neumann, George R.	Prof	Iowa		PHD	74	Northwes	1984
Neumann, Hillar Jr.	Assoc	Northern St		PHD		Rutgers	1983
Neumark, David B.	Prof	Michigan St		PHD	87	Harvard	1995
Neumeyer, Pablo	Asst	So Calif		PHD	92	Columbia	1991
Neun, Stephen P.	C-Ac	Utica		PHD		Conn	1982
Neville, Howard R.	Deces			PHD	56	Mich St	
Newbold, Paul	Prof	Illinois		PHD	70	Wisconsin	1979
Newburger, Harriet B.	Asst	Bryn Mawr		PHD	84	Wisconsin	1987
Rosalyn R. Schwartz Lectureship							
Newell, Barbara W.	Prof	Florida St		PHD	58	Wisconsin	1987
Regents' Professor; email bnewell@mailer.fsu.edu							
Newey, Whitney K.	Prof	MIT	C	PHD			
David W. Skinner Professor of Political Economy							
Newkirk, Wayne	Prof	Drake		PHD	65	LSU	1967
Newman, Robert J.	Prof	Louisiana St	IJ	PHD	80	UCLA	1983
South Central Bell Business Partnership Professor; Director, Graduate Studies							
Newmark, Craig M.	Assoc	N Carol St	LD	PHD	84	UCLA	1984
Newsome, Bobby A.	Prof	Mid Tenn St		PHD	85	Georgia	1989
Newson, Roosevelt	Assoc	Bloomsburg					
Newton, Dahlia	Asst	Athens State	A	MBA	81	W Carol	1987
Newton, James E.	C	Franklin		MS		Wright St	
Neyman, Abraham	Prof	SUNY-Stony B		PHD	77	Hebrew U	1989
Ng, Kenneth	Assoc	CS-Northrdge	N	PHD	88	Rochester	1986
Ng, Pin T.	Asst	Houston		PHD	89	Illinois	1990
Ngoboka, Pascal	Asst	Wis-Rvr Fall		PHD	87	Wi-Milwa	1990
Nguyen, Hong V.	Assoc	Scranton		PHD	81	SUNY-Bin	1979
Nguyen, Nghiep H.	Assoc	Mid Tenn St		PHD	81	Tennessee	1981
Ni, Xiagoguang	Asst	Missouri	EH	PHD	91	Minnesota	1990
Nicholls, Grant	Inst	Centenary	ADEM	MBA		Ins Bnkg	8-91
Nichols, Archie J.	Prof	Butler	B	PHD	61	Penn	1957
Nichols, Donald A.	Prof	Wisconsin		PHD	68	Yale	1983
Nicholson, Robert H.	Assoc	Richmond		PHD	72	N Carol	1972
Nicholson, Walter E.	Prof	Amherst	ACDJ	PHD	70	MIT	1968
Ward H. Patton, Jr. Professor of Economics							
Nickerson, Peter H.	Asst	Seattle	Q	PHD	85	U Wash	1984
Nickless, Pamela J.	Assoc	N Car-Ashvil		PHD	76	Purdue	1983
Nickols, Mark W.	Asst	Univ South		PHD		Fla St	1995
Niehoff, Peter	Assoc	Denver		PHD		Nebraska	
Nielsen, Darwin B.	Prof	Utah State	Q	PHD	64	Oreg St	1965
Nielsen, Donald A.	Prof	Neb-Omaha	AR	PHD	70	Syracuse	1972
Niemi, Albert W. Jr.	Dean	Georgia	N	PHD	69	Conn	1968
Nieswiadomy, Michael L.	Assoc	North Texas		PHD	83	Tx A&M	1985
Niho, Yoshio	Assoc	Wis-Milwauke		PHD	73	Brown	1970
Nijhawan, Inder P.	Prof	Fayetteville		PHD		N Carol	
Nilsson, Eric A.	Asst	CS-San Bern		PHD	89	Mass	1989
Niman, Neil B.	Assoc	New Hampshir	BL	PHD	85	Tx-Austin	1987
Niroomand, Farhang	Assoc	So Miss	F	PHD	83	Mich St	1984
Nirro, Katsuyuki	Assoc	Gettysburg	AC	PHD		Pittsburgh	1972
Nisbet, Charles T.		Evergreen St		PHD	67	Oregon	1971
Nisbet, Mary	D	Cal-Santa Br	G	PHD	91	Glasgow	1991
Niss, James F.	Retir	W Illinois	1994	PHD		Illinois	1968
Nissan, Edward	Prof	So Miss	R	PHD	69	Tx A&M	1969
Nitsch, Thomas O.	Prof	Creighton	ENP	PHD	63	Ohio St	1969
Nix, Joan	Asst	CUNY-Queens	DG	PHD	89	NYU	1988
Njoku, Anthanasius O.	Prof	Benedict Col		PHD		Illinois	
Nnadozie, Emmanuel U.	Assoc	NE Missouri		PHD	87	Sorbonne	1989
Noam, Eli	Prof	Columbia		PHD	75	Harvard	1976
Noble, Nicholas R.	Prof	Miami U-Ohio	EC	PHD	78	Cincinnati	1976
Noel, Cuthbert	Asst	Hampton		PHD		Howard	1986
Nold-Hughes, Patricia A.	Asst	St Cloud St		PHD	91	Ca-SnBarb	1988
Noll, Roger G.	Prof	Stanford		PHD	67	Harvard	1984
Noorbakhsh, Abbas	Assoc	Slippery Roc		PHD	89	Kansas St	1990
Norberg, Robert W.	C-As	Robt Morris		MA		Ind-Penn	1968
Nord, Steven	Prof	No Illinois		PHD		Illinois	
Nordhaus, William D.	Prof	Yale		PHD	67	MIT	1967
Nordin, Harold D.	Prof	E Illinois		PHD	76	Illinois	1967
Nordquist, Gerald L.	Prof	Iowa		PHD	60	Iowa	1968
Nordstrom, Louise	Prof	Nichols Col		PHD			
Nordyke, James W.	Emer	New Mex St		PHD	59	Princeton	1964
Norman, Alfred L.	Prof	Texas	C	PHD	71	Minnesota	7-72
Norman, Emily	Asst	Mid Tenn St		PHD	94	Fla St	1993
Norman, Emlyn A.	Asst	Txs Southern		AM		Harvard	
Norman, Lee	Assoc	Idaho State		PHD	80	Utah	1981
Norrbin, Stefan C.	Asst	Florida St		PHD	86	Ariz St	1990
Norris, Hodge	Asst	Txs Southern		MS		Tx A&I	
Norsworthy, J. Randolph	Prof	Rensselaer		PHD	66	Virginia	
North, Douglass C.	Prof	Wash Univ		PHD	52	Berkeley	1983
Henry R. Luce Prof of Law & Liberty; 1993 Nobel Prize in Econ; leave 1995-96							
Northrop, Emily M.	Assoc	Southwestern	ENQR	PHD	88	Tx-Austin	1994

Norton, R. D.	Prof	Bryant	FR	PHD	77	Princeton	1985
Sarkesian Professor of Business Economics							
Norton, Seth	Assoc	Illinois St	M	PHD	82	Chicago	1992
on leave to Wheaton College, Illinois							
Norton, Virgil	Prof	W Virginia	QI	PHD	64	Oreg St	1986
Norwood, Dwight Lamar	Assoc	Campbell		PHD		Arkansas	1973
Noser, Thomas C.	Assoc	W Kentucky	CA	PHD	86	Alabama	1984
Noulas, Athanasios	Asst	Seton Hall		PHD	89	Conn	
Nourzad, Farrokh	Assoc	Marquette		PHD	82	Kansas	1981
Noussair, Charles	Asst	Purdue		PHD	93	Cal Tech	1994
Novaes, Walter	Asst	U Washington		PHD	93	MIT	1993
Novey, Donald F.	C-Pr	Saginaw Vall		MS		S Dak St	1969
Novshek, William	Assoc	Purdue		PHD	79	Northwes	1986
Novus, Ian E.	Assoc	Georgia Tech	D	PHD	85	Penn	1992
Nowell, Clifford	Assoc	Weber State	ADQ	PHD	88	Wyoming	1988
Nowka, Harry E.	Prof	SW Okla St		EDD		Okla St	1963
Nowotny, Kenneth	H-Pr	New Mex St		PHD	77	Tx-Austin	1976
Noyd, Louis E.	Assoc	No Kentucky		PHD	73	Oregon	1972
Nugent, Jeffrey B.	Prof	So Calif		PHD	65	New Sch	1973
Nugent, Rachel A.	C-As	Pacific Luth	DFQH	PHD	94	Geo Wash	1991
Nunn, Elizabeth	Asst	Puget Sound	AEN	PHD	89	Wash U	
Nunn, Geoffrey E.	Prof	San Jose St		PHD	73	Virginia	1974
Nuwer, Michael J.	Assoc	SUNY-Potsdam		PHD	85	Utah	1986
Nuxoll, Daniel A.	Asst	Virg Tech	F	PHD	92	Brown	1991
Nyamwange, Richard	Assoc	E Stroudsbur	D	MBA	82	Long Isl	1987
Nyarko, Yaw	Assoc	New York U		PHD	86	Cornell	1988
Nyatepe-Coo, Akorlie A.	Asst	Wis-La Cross	FHO	PHD	89	N Illinois	1989
Nye, John V. C.	Assoc	Wash Univ		PHD	85	Northwes	1985
Nyomba, Ajamu	Asst	Clark Atlant		PHD		Tx-Austin	
Nzeogwu, Okeleke	Assoc	Tx A&M-C Chr	AO	PHD	88	Missouri	9-93
Nziramasanga, Mudziviri T.	Assoc	Wash State		PHD	74	Stanford	1973
O'Boyle, Edward John	Assoc	Louisiana Te		PHD		St Louis	1977
O'Brien, A. Maureen	Assoc	Minn-Duluth	J	PHD	83	West Va	1982
O'Brien, Anthony P.	Assoc	Lehigh	NE	PHD	86	Berkeley	1987
O'Brien, Francis T.	C-Ac	Providence	JK	MA	57	Boston C	1958
O'Brien, J. Patrick	Dean	Loyola-N Orl	AEHR	PHD	77	Okla St	1995
O'Brien, Jamie L.	Prof	So Dakota St	K	MPA	84	S Dakota	1984
O'Brien, Kevin M.	Asst	Bradley		PHD	88	Illinois	1992
O'Brien, M. Barry	Assoc	Fran Marion		PHD		S Carol	
O'Brien, Peter A. Jr.	Assoc	Pace		MBA	57	Rutgers	1964
O'Cleiracain, Seamus	Prof	SUNY-Purchas		PHD	71	Michigan	1974
O'Connell, John F.	Prof	Holy Cross	CDIJ	PHD	70	Wisconsin	1974
O'Connell, Stephen A.	Assoc	Swarthmore	EO	PHD	86	MIT	1990
O'Connor, Dennis A.	C-Ac	Loras		PHD	84	Notre Dm	1983
O'Connor, J. Francis	C-Pr	E Kentucky		PHD	74	Minnesota	1989
O'Connor, Roy John	Inst	Va Military		MBA		Hartford	1992
O'Dea, William P.	Asst	SUNY-Oneonta	DEP	PHD	88	SUNY-Alb	1979
O'Donnell, Dennis J.	Prof	Montana	OJR	PHD		Penn St	
O'Donnell, Margaret	Prof	SW Louisiana					
O'Hara, Sabine	Asst	Rensselaer		PHD		Goetting	
O'Neil, Robert F.	Prof	San Diego		PHD	75	Fordham	
O'Neill, James B.	Prof	Delaware	A	PHD	71	Purdue	1971
O'Neill, June E.	Prof	CUNY-Baruch		PHD	70	Columbia	1987
O'Neill, Patrick B.	Assoc	North Dakota		PHD	87	Boston C	1987
O'Relly, Z. Edward	C-Pr	N Dakota St	AFOP	PHD	72	Tennessee	1969
O'Sullivan, Arthur M.	Assoc	Oregon State	DR	PHD	81	Princeton	9-92
O'Sullivan, Patrick	C-Pr	SUNY Old Wes		PHD		Fordham	
O'Toole, Dennis M.	Assoc	Virg Comm		PHD	71	Ohio U	1967
O'Toole, James K.	Prof	CS-Chico		PHD		Va Tech	1984
Oakland, William H.	C-Pr	Tulane		PHD	65	MIT	1979
Oates, Sister Mary J.	C-Pr	Regis-MA		PHD	69	Yale	1970
Oates, Wallace	Prof	Maryland		PHD	65	Stanford	1979
Oaxaca, Ronald L.	Prof	Arizona		PHD	72	Princeton	1976
Obar, Ruth I.		Hood					
Obeng, Kofi	Prof	N Carol A&T		PHD	81	Penn	1982
UPS Chair							
Oberle, Wayne H.	Prof	St Ambrose		PHD		Missouri	1977
Obst, Norman P.	Prof	Michigan St		PHD	70	Purdue	1973
Obstfeld, Maurice	Prof	Cal-Berkeley		PHD	79	MIT	
Obutelewicz, Robert S.	Assoc	Bloomsburg		PHD		Mass	
Ochoa, Eduardo M.	Prof	CS-L Angeles		PHD	84	New Sch	1984
Ochs, Jack N.	Prof	Pittsburgh	H	PHD	66	Indiana	1968
Odegaard, Thomas A.	Lect	Baylor		MA	70	Rice	1985
Odekon, Mehmet A.	Assoc	Skidmore		PHD	77	SUNY-Alb	1983
Odorzynski, Sandra J.	Assoc	St Norbert		PHD	76	Purdue	1978
Oerther, Frederick J.	Asst	Greensboro		PHD	89	Geo Mason	1990
Oettinger, Gerald	Asst	Texas	JC	PHD	93	MIT	9-92
Ofek, Haim	Assoc	SUNY-Bingham		PHD	71	Columbia	1981
Officer, Lawrence H.	Prof	Ill-Chicago	F	PHD	65	Harvard	1987
Oguledo, Victor I.	Assoc	Florida A&M	FL	PHD	89	Nebraska	1990

Ohanian, Lee E.	Asst	Pennsylvania	E	PHD	93	Rochester	1992
Lawrence R. Klein Fellow of the Institute for Econ Research; on leave U Minn							
Ohly, John H.	Assoc	Mass-Dartmou	A	PHD	76	Boston U	1977
Ohno, Yuka	Asst	Oregon State	FL	PHD	93	U Wash	9-94
Oi, Walter Y.	Prof	Rochester		PHD	61	Chicago	1967
Elmer B. Milliman Professor of Economics							
Ojemakindel, Abiodun	Assoc	Albany State		PHD	89	LSU	1989
Okello, Paul F.	Lect	Tx-Arlington		MA	89	Tx-Arlin	1990
Okonkwo, Valentine	C-Ac	Winston-Sal		PHD		Fla St	4-85
Okpala, Amon O.	Assoc	Fayetteville		PHD	84	LSU	1984
Okun, Bernard	D-Pr	CUNY-Brookly	CO	PHD	57	J Hopkins	1966
Okunade, Albert A.	Prof	Memphis		PHD	86	Arkansas	1987
Oldfather, Michael	Assoc	Kansas State	E	PHD	80	Ohio	1983
Olley, G. Steven	Asst	New York U		PHD	92	Wisconsin	1991
Olmstead, Alan L.	Prof	Cal-Davis	HN	PHD	70	Wisconsin	1969
Olmstead, Jennifer C.	Asst	Mich-Flint		PHD	94	Ca-Davis	1993
Olmsted, George M.	Asst	Indiana NW	HG	PHD	84	Northwes	1987
Olney, Martha L.	Asst	Massachusett		PHD	85	Berkeley	1984
Olowolayemo, Suryudeen	Asst	Tuskegee		PHD		Auburn	1994
Olsen, Edgar O.	C-Pr	Virginia	HI	PHD	68	Rice	1983
Olsen, Randall J.	Prof	Ohio State	J	PHD	77	Chicago	
Olsen, Reed N.	Assoc	SW Missouri		PHD	89	Illinois	1990
Olsh, John Lindsay	Prof	W Maryland		PHD		Ca-Davis	1980
Olson, Dennis D.	Asst	Ferris State		MA		Michigan	1979
Olson, Dennis O.	Assoc	Louisville		PHD	82	Wyoming	1987
Olson, Edwin G.	Assoc	Kansas State	HBM	PHD	71	U Wash	1968
Olson, Gerald W.	Prof	Mo-Kansas Ct	CGH	PHD		Rutgers	1971
Olson, John F.	Assoc	St Benedict		PHD	84	Rochester	1985
Olson, Kent W.	Prof	Oklahoma St		PHD	69	Oregon	1974
Olson, Mancur	Prof	Maryland		PHD	60	Harvard	1969
Olson, Mary K.	Asst	Wash Univ		PHD	91	Stanford	1990
Olson, Paulette I.	Assoc	Wright State		PHD	89	Utah	1988
Olson, Richard	Prof	Washburn		PHD	65	Nebraska	1980
Olson, Terry L.	Asst	NE Missouri		PHD	86	Illinois	1990
Olson, William	Assoc	Upsala	EN	PHD		Mass	1983
Omar, Hanai	Assoc	Univ of D C	AH	MS		Maryland	1976
Omarzal, Mahmood	Prof	Calif U-Penn		PHD		Indiana	1979
Omori, Yoshiaki	Asst	Connecticut	J	PHD	90	SUNY-SBr	1991
Omotoye, Richard	Asst	Hampton		PHD		Russia	1994
Onafowora, Olugbenga A.	Asst	Susquehanna	CDOQ	PHD	89	W Virginia	1989
Ondrich, Jan Ivar	Assoc	Syracuse		PHD	83	Wisconsin	
Onunkwo, Emmanuel N.	Prof	So Carol St		PHD	73	Geotown	1978
Opdahl, Roger W.	Prof	Lycoming	AENR	DED	70	Penn St	1962
Shangraw Professor of Economics							
Ophaug, John	Asst	St Olaf		JD		Minnesota	1978
Opiela, Timothy P.	Assoc	Pacific	E	PHD	87	Tx A&M	1986
Oppenheimer, Margaret M.	C-Pr	DePaul		PHD	74	Northwes	
Oppers, Stefan	Asst	Michigan		PHD	93	Harvard	1993
Orazem, Peter F.	Prof	Iowa State	J	PHD	83	Yale	1982
Orbach, Raymond L.	Prov	UCLA					
Orcutt, Bonnie	C-As	American Int	ADEI	PHD	94	Clark	1992
Ordovensky, J. Farley	Asst	Pacific	HJ	PHD	92	Duke	1993
Ordover, Janusz A.	Prof	New York U		PHD	73	Columbia	1982
Oriyomi, Abi	Asst	Morehouse		PHD			
Orlowski, Lucjan T.	Prof	Sacred Heart	EFGP	PHD	79	Poland	1983
Ormiston, Michael B.	Prof	Arizona St		PHD	77	J Hopkins	1984
Orr, Daniel	Prof	Illinois		PHD	60	Princeton	1989
Orr, John A.	Prof	CS-Chico		PHD		Wisconsin	1970
Orr, Lloyd D.	Prof	Indiana		PHD	64	Northwes	1964
Orsagh, Thomas	Assoc	No Carolina		PHD	64	Penn	1965
Ortega, Lydia	Asst	San Jose St		PHD	87	Geo Mason	1989
Ortmann, Andreas	Asst	Bowdoin	L	PHD	91	Tx A&M	1991
Orton, Eliot S.	Emer	New Mex St		PHD	71	Cornell	1970
Orvis, Charles C.	Assoc	Rhodes		PHD	75	Minnesota	1973
Osagie, Emmanuel I.	Asst	Southern		PHD		LSU	1985
Osakve, John U.	Asst	CUNY-Stn Isl	FO	PHD	80	Nebraska	1991
Osang, Thomas	Asst	So Methodist		PHD	94	Ca-SnDgo	1994
Osborne, Evan	Asst	Wright State		PHD		UCLA	1995
Osborne, Laura L.	Asst	Georgia St	C	PHD	94	Duke	1994
Oseghale, Braimoh	Assoc	F Dick-Teane		PHD	89	Temple	1994
Osei, Anthony A.	Assoc	Dillard		PHD		Howard	
Osman, Jack W.	Prof	San Fran St		PHD	66	Rutgers	1967
Ostas, James R.	Retir	Bowling Gr		PHD		Indiana	1969
Ostrosky, Anthony L. Jr.	Prof	Illinois St	ADEC	PHD	73	Pittsburgh	1973
Ostroy, Joseph M.	Prof	UCLA		PHD			
Oswald, Donald J.	Assoc	CS-Bakersf	ABKN	PHD	74	Wash St	1961
Otsuka, Yasuji	Asst	Cen Florida	D	PHD		Tennessee	1990
Ott, Attiat F.	Prof	Clark		PHD	62	Michigan	1969
Overton, Bennie	Asst	Campbell		PHD		N Car St	1995
Ovitsky, Nancy L.	Asst	N Adams St		PHD		Illinois	

Oweiss, Ibrahim M.	Assoc	Georgetown		PHD	69	Minnesota	1967
Owen, Diane	Asst	Wm & Mary		MA	86	Yale	1992
Owen, John D.	Prof	Wayne State		PHD	64	Columbia	1975
Owen, Laura J.	Asst	DePaul		PHD	91	Yale	1990
Owen, Virginia L.	Prof	Illinois St	DA	PHD	69	Illinois	1964
Owoye, Oluwole	Assoc	Western Conn		PHD	89	N Illinois	
Oyen, Duane B.	Prof	Wis-Eau Clar		PHD	73	Iowa	1976
Ozaki, Robert S.	Prof	CS-Hayward		PHD	60	Harvard	1960
Ozawa, Terutomo	Prof	Colorado St	FO	PHD	66	Columbia	1974
Ozler, Sule	Asst	UCLA		PHD	86	Stanford	1985
Ozlu, Elvan	Asst	Syracuse		PHD	93	Ariz St	
Paas, David	Assoc	Hillsdale		PHD		Nebraska	1993
Paas, Martha W.	Prof	Carleton		PHD	79	Bryn Maw	1975
Pace, Richard R.	Asst	Dayton	E	PHD	94	Rochester	1993
Pace, William	Asst	Quinnipiac		PHD		Conn	1995
Pachis, Dimitrios S.	Assoc	Eastern Conn		PHD		Mass	
Pack, Spencer J.	Prof	Conn Coll		PHD	83	N Hamp	1981
Packer, Stephen B.	Lect	St Peters		MA		Chicago	1989
Padelford, Walton M.	Prof	Union-TN	ABFO	PHD	75	LSU	1980
Padgett, Jerry H.	Dean	Winthrop		PHD	68	Purdue	9-72
Pae, Ki-Tai	C-Pr	Central Conn		PHD		Conn	1971
Page, Marianne E.	Asst	Santa Clara		PHD	95	Michigan	1995
Page, Scott	Asst	Cal Tech	H	PHD	93	Northwes	1993
Page, Talbot	Prof	Brown		PHD	72	Cornell	
Page, Walter	Prof	SUNY-Plattsb	DE	PHD	68	Kansas	1983
Paglin, Morton	Retir	Portland St		PHD	56	Berkeley	1961
Pakes, Ariel	Prof	Yale		PHD	79	Harvard	
Pal, Debashis	Asst	Cincinnati		PHD	90	Florida	
Palfrey, Thomas R.	Prof	Cal Tech		PHD	81	Cal Tech	1986
Palivos, Theodore	Asst	Louisiana St	F	PHD	92	Penn St	1992
Palm, Thomas	Prof	Portland St		PHD	67	Michigan	1967
Palmer, Charles F.	Dean	Wingate	AH	PHD			1993
Palmer, Harvey	Asst	George Mason					
Palmer, Jan S.	C-Ac	Ohio Univ	A	PHD	74	Mich St	1979
Palmer, Ransford W.	Prof	Howard		PHD	66	Clark	1973
Palmini, Dennis J.	Assoc	Wis-Stev Pt		PHD	75	Illinois	1980
Palmquist, Raymond B.	C-Pr	N Carol St	QDR	PHD	78	U Wash	1979
Palomba, Neil A.	Dean	Ball State		PHD	66	Minnesota	8-84
Palumbo, Edwin P.	Inst	Providence	RJ	MA		Boston C	
Palumbo, George M.	Prof	Canisius		PHD	77	Syracuse	1978
Palumbo, Michael G.	Asst	Houston		PHD	92	Virginia	1992
Pan, Zuohong	Asst	Western Conn		PHD		Mich St	
Panagariya, Arvind	Prof	Maryland		PHD	78	Princeton	1978
Panda, Dandeson	Asst	Delaware St		MBA		Atlanta	
Panik, Michael J.	Prof	Hartford		PHD	70	Boston C	1968
Panzar, John C.	Prof	Northwestern		PHD	75	Stanford	1983
Louis W. Menk Professor							
Papachristou, Patricia T.	Prof	Christian Br	TI	MBA	79	Memphis	1980
Papagapitos, Agapipos	Asst	St Thomas-MN	OP	PHD		Ohio St	
Papakyriazis, Artemis	Prof	Cal Poly-SLO		PHD	82	Ca-River	1982
Papakyriazis, Panagiotis A.	Prof	Cal Poly-SLO		PHD	74	Ca-SnDgo	1971
Papathanasis, Anastasios	Prof	Central Conn		PHD		Ca-Davis	1984
Papell, David H.	Assoc	Houston		PHD	81	Columbia	1984
Papke, James A.	Prof	Purdue		PHD	59	Cornell	1962
Papke, Leslie E.	Asst	Michigan St		PHD	87	MIT	1990
Pappas, Anthony	Assoc	St John's					
Paquette, Laurence R.	Prof	Westfield St		PHD	85	Mass	1987
Parai, Amar K.	Prof	SUNY-Fredoni	AF	PHD	79	So Meth	1988
Parente, Stephen	Asst	Northeastern		PHD	90	Minnesota	1991
Parigi, Bruno M.	Asst	Virg Tech		PHD	90	Rutgers	1990
Parigi, Sam F.	Prof	Lamar	J	PHD	64	Tx-Austin	1961
Regents' Professor of Economics							
Paringer, Lynn C.	Prof	CS-Hayward		PHD	78	Wisconsin	1981
Park, Chaewon	Asst	Kentucky St	ACJ	PHD		Indiana	1992
Park, David J.	Prof	CS-Pomona		PHD	62	S Calif	1965
Park, Eun-Soo	Asst	W Virginia	D	PHD	93	Northwes	1992
Park, Hong Youl	Prof	Saginaw Vall		PHD	75	Utah St	1975
Park, Jong-Heum	Assoc	Kennesaw St	ADFO	PHD	74	Okla St	1988
Park, Kang Hoon	Prof	SE Missouri	CF	PHD	81	S Illinois	1979
Park, Sang O.	Prof	Chris Newpor	DFOR	PHD		N Carol	1982
Park, Walter G.	Asst	American U		PHD	91	Yale	1991
Park, William Laird	Prof	Brigham Yg		PHD	63	Cornell	1977
Park, Young J.	Prof	Calif U-Penn		PHD	74	Temple	1977
Parke, William	Assoc	No Carolina		PHD	80	Yale	1988
Parker, Carl D.	Prof	Fort Hays St	DIJM	PHD	71	Okla St	1976
Parker, Charles	Asst	Wayne St Col	AEK	PHD	94	Ohio St	8-95
Parker, Darrell F.	Prof	Winthrop		PHD	84	Purdue	9-85
Grier Professor of Business Administration-Economics							
Parker, Elliott	Asst	Nevada-Reno		PHD	92	U Wash	1992

Parker, Jeffrey A.	C-Pr	Reed	AECF	PHD	81	Stanford	1988
George Hay Professor of Economics							
Parker, Joseph A.	Prof	New Haven		PHD		Oklahoma	
Parker, Pat		Naval Postgr					
Parker, Randall E.	Assoc	East Carol		PHD	86	Kentucky	1986
Parkin, Richard J.	Asst	Case Western	DJP	PHD	93	Mass	1992
Parkinson, Thomas L.	Prof	Moravian		PHD		Mass	1985
Parkison, Kathy	Asst	Ind-Kokomo		PHD	83	Purdue	1993
Parks, Richard	Prof	U Washington		PHD	66	Berkeley	1970
Parks, Robert P.	Assoc	Wash Univ		PHD	71	Purdue	1971
Parks, Susan	Assoc	Wis-Whitewat		PHD		Purdue	1980
Parks, Terrance C.	Prof	Indiana St	OED	PHD	74	Illinois	1966
Parsons, Donald O.	Prof	Ohio State	J	PHD	70	Chicago	1970
Parsons, George R.	Asst	Delaware	Q	PHD	85	Wisconsin	1985
Parvin, Manoucher	Prof	Akron		PHD	79	Columbia	1978
Parzych, Kenneth M.	C-Pr	Eastern Conn		PHD		Conn	
Pascal, Nina S.	Asst	Denison		PHD	79	CUNY	1995
Pasternak, Richard E.	Prof	Metro St-CO		PHD		Alabama	
Pastor, Manuel Jr.	Assoc	Occidental	O	PHD	84	Mass	1984
Patch, Elizabeth P.	Asst	Bloomsburg		PHD		Lehigh	
Pate, David S.	C-Ac	St John Fshr	J	PHD	85	Iowa St	1987
Patrick, Hugh T.	Prof	Columbia		PHD	60	Michigan	1984
Patrick, J. Michael	C-Pr	Tx A&M Intl		PHD	77	Mich St	
Patridge, Mark	Asst	St Cloud St		PHD	91	Illinois	1995
Patrono, Michael Frank	Asst	Berry		MS	88	Fla St	1989
Pattanaik, Prasanta	Prof	Cal-Riversid	AO	PHD	68	Delhi	1991
Patterson, Braxton I.	Retir	Wis-Oshkosh		PHD	61	Mich St	1967
Patterson, Debra Moore	Asst	Trinity		PHD	94	Virginia	1994
Patterson, Perry L.	Assoc	Wake Forest		PHD	86	Northwes	1986
Patterson, Seymour	Prof	NE Missouri		PHD		Oklahoma	1980
Paul, Chris W.	C-Pr	Alabama-Hunt	K	PHD	79	Tx A&M	1982
Paul, Harvey	Prof	Towson State		PHD	72	SUNY-Buf	1966
Paul, Sanjay	Asst	St Norbert		PHD	92	SUNY-Buf	1992
Paulin, Elizabeth	Asst	LaSalle	J	PHD		Tx-Austin	1988
Paus, Eva	C-Ac	Mt Holyoke		PHD	83	Pittsburgh	1987
Pauszek, Ruffin		SUNY-Empire	A	MBA		SUNY-Buf	1992
Pavsek, Daniel A.	Dean	Shenandoah		PHD	81	Case Wes	1992
Pawlak, Andrew T.	Asst	Salem State		MA		Tufts	
Paxson, Christina H.	Assoc	Princeton		PHD	86	Columbia	1986
Paxton, Donald	Prof	Jacksonvl St		PHD		Tulane	1977
Payne, James E.	Assoc	E Kentucky		PHD	89	Fla St	1992
Payne, Richard D.	Prof	Boise State		PHD	70	S Calif	1970
Peach, James T.	Prof	New Mex St		PHD	78	Tx-Austin	1980
Peake, Charles F.	Assoc	MD-Baltim Co		PHD	68	Maryland	1967
Pearce, David	Prof	Yale					
Pearce, Douglas K.	Prof	N Carol St	EG	PHD	74	Wisconsin	1985
Pearce, John F.	Prof	No Georgia		PHD		Alabama	1970
Fuller E. Callaway Professor of Economics							
Pearson, Donald W.	Prof	E Michigan		PHD	70	Tx-Austin	1969
Peart, Sandra Joan	Assoc	Baldwin-Wal	BD	PHD		Toronto	1989
Pecchenino, Rowena A.	Assoc	Michigan St		PHD	85	Wisconsin	1985
Peck, James D.	Assoc	Ohio State	D	PHD	85	Penn	1992
Peck, John E.	Prof	Ind-So Bend		PHD		Notre Dm	1969
Peck, Merton J.	Prof	Yale		PHD	54	Harvard	1978
Peck, Richard M.	Assoc	Ill-Chicago	D	PHD	83	Princeton	1981
Peckham, Brian W.	Asst	Wis-Plattev		PHD	79	Wisconsin	1987
Pecorino, Paul	Asst	Alabama		PHD	90	Duke	1994
Pedersen, William E.	Asst	SE Louisiana	AGH	PHD	95	N Orleans	1994
Pedroni, Peter	Asst	Indiana		PHD	93	Columbia	1993
Peek, Joe	Prof	Boston Coll	E	PHD	79	Northwes	1978
Peek, William A.	Assoc	Niagara		PHD	85	Syracuse	1980
Peirce, William S.	Prof	Case Western	HOQ	PHD	66	Princeton	1966
Pejovich, Svetozar	Prof	Texas A&M		PHD	63	Geotown	1975
Pellegrino, Kathleen B.	Prof	Westfield St		MBA	76	W NewEng	1978
Pelzman, Joseph	Prof	George Wash	F	PHD	76	Boston C	1980
Pemberton, Donald K.	Asst	Detroit Merc		PHD	70	Kansas	1969
Pencavel, John H.	Prof	Stanford		PHD	69	Princeton	1979
Pender, John	Asst	Brigham Yg		PHD	92	Stanford	1992
Pendse, Dilip C.	Assoc	Ind-Kokomo		PHD	71	Oreg St	
Penn, William M.	Prof	Belhaven	AM	PHD	68	Duke	1981
Pennington, Robert L.	Assoc	Cen Florida	D	PHD	77	Tx A&M	1983
Peoples, James A.	Assoc	Wis-Milwauke		PHD	84	Berkeley	1990
Pepall, Lynne	Assoc	Tufts		PHD	83	Cambridg	1987
Pepin, Raymond A.	Prof	Stonehill	AD	PHD	71	Clark	1969
Peppard, Donald M. Jr.	Prof	Conn Coll		PHD	75	Mich St	
Peppard, William	Asst	Delaware St		MS		S Eastrn	
Peppers, Larry C.	Dean	Wash & Lee		PHD		Vanderbilt	1986
Pereira, Alfredo M.	Asst	Ca-San Diego	H	PHD	88	Stanford	1987
Perelman, Michael A.	Prof	CS-Chico		PHD	71	Berkeley	1971
Peretto, Pietro	Asst	Duke					1994

Perez, Stephen J.	Asst	Virg Comm		PHD		Ca-Davis	
Perkins, Dwight H.	Prof	Harvard		PHD	64	Harvard	1963
Harold Hitchings Burbank Professor of Political Economy							
Perkins, Mary	Assoc	Howard		PHD		American	
Perli, Roberto	Asst	Pennsylvania	E	PHD	95	NYU	1995
Perline, Martin M.	Prof	Wichita St		PHD	65	Ohio St	1965
Perlman, Mark	Retir	Pittsburgh		PHD	50	Columbia	1963
Perlman, Richard W.	Prof	Wis-Milwauke		PHD	53	Columbia	1964
Perna, Francis M.	Prof	Lock Haven		PHD		Cornell	1981
Pernecky, Mark L.	Asst	St Olaf	EJA	PHD	90	Notre Dm	1990
Perri, Timothy J.	Prof	Appalach St	DJ	PHD	78	Ohio St	1980
Perry, Joseph M.	Prof	North Fla	NOR	PHD	66	Northwes	1971
Perry, Mark	Asst	Jacksonvil U		PHD	93	Geo Mason	1993
Perry, Martin K.	Prof	Rutgers-N Br	L	PHD	76	Stanford	1989
Persky, Joseph J.	Prof	Ill-Chicago	R	PHD	71	Harvard	
Pescatrice, Donn	Assoc	Iona		PHD	75	Purdue	1983
Pesek, Boris P.	Emer	Wis-Milwauke		PHD	56	Chicago	1967
Pesendorfer, Martin	Asst	Yale					
Pesendorfer, Wolfgang	Asst	Northwestern		PHD	92	UCLA	
Pesenti, Paolo	Inst	Princeton					
Petersen, Bruce C.	Assoc	Wash Univ		PHD	81	Harvard	1991
Petersen, Harold A.	Assoc	Boston Coll	G	PHD	63	Brown	1960
Petersen, Harold Craig	Prof	Utah State	GM	PHD	73	Stanford	1973
Peterson, Dean J.	Asst	Seattle	B	PHD	94	Illinois	1991
Peterson, Donald L.	Prof	So Dakota St	Q	PHD	73	Nebraska	1974
Peterson, G. Paul	VAsst	Fairfield	NB	PHD		Colo St	1992
Peterson, Janice L.	Assoc	SUNY-Fredoni	BA	PHD	87	Nebraska	1990
Peterson, Jerrold M.	Prof	Minn-Duluth	HE	PHD	70	Illinois	1969
Peterson, John	Inst	Northern St		ABD		Kansas	1992
Peterson, Kenneth D.	Asst	Furman		PHD	91	SUNY	1990
Peterson, Norris A.	Prof	Pacific Luth	J	PHD	81	Minnesota	1981
Peterson, Richard E.	Prof	Hawaii-Manoa		PHD	72	Berkeley	
Peterson, Rodney	Retir	Colorado St	1994	PHD		Nebraska	
Peterson, Steven P.	Asst	Virg Comm		PHD	89	Indiana	1989
Peterson, Thomas C.	Assoc	Cen Michigan		PHD		UCLA	1972
Petr, Jerry L.	Prof	Nebraska	P	PHD	67	Indiana	1966
C. Wheaton Battey Professor of Economics							
Petrakis, John T.	Retir	Lg Isl-Post		PHD		American	
Petratos, Vasilios	Assoc	CUNY-Stn Isl	BF	PHD	70	NYU	1974
Petree, Daniel L.	Assoc	Concordia C		PHD		Kansas	1995
Petri, Peter A.	Prof	Brandeis		PHD	76	Harvard	1974
Petruska, Dennis A.	Assoc	Youngstown		PHD	84	Ohio St	1984
Pettengill, Glenn N.	Assoc	Emporia St		PHD		Arkansas	1989
Pettit, Mary Ann	Inst	S Ill-Edward		MA	77	Tennessee	1989
Pevas, Mary Ann	Asst	Winona State		PHD		Notre Dm	1990
Pfannestiel, Maurice	Assoc	Wichita St		PHD	67	Okla St	1966
Pfeifer, Karen	C-Ac	Smith	BNOP	PHD	81	American	1979
Pflueger, Burton W.	Assoc	So Dakota St	Q	PHD	85	Illinois	1985
Pfouts, William	Emer	No Carolina		PHD	52	N Carol	1947
Pham, Chung	Prof	New Mexico	CEGO	PHD	62	Penn	1963
Phares, Donald	Prof	Mo-St Louis	HR	PHD	70	Syracuse	1969
Phares, Kathleen	Lect	Mo-St Louis	A	MA	76	Mo-St Lo	1977
Phelps, Charles E.	Prof	Rochester		PHD	73	Chicago	1984
Phelps, Charlotte D.	Assoc	Temple	TI	PHD	61	Yale	1967
Philippides, Andreas	Assoc	Teikyo Post		PHD	94	Conn	1988
Philipps, Eugene A.	Retir	Moorhead St		PHD		Illinois	1966
Philipson, Tomas J.	Asst	Chicago		PHD	89	Penn	1989
Phillips, Almarin	Emer	Pennsylvania		PHD	53	Harvard	1953
Phillips, Charles F. Jr.	Prof	Wash & Lee	L	PHD	60	Harvard	1959
Robert C. Brown Professor of Economics							
Phillips, Edward S.	Prof	Shepherd		PHD	70	Colorado	1974
Phillips, Joseph M. Jr.	Assoc	Creighton	EO	PHD	82	Notre Dm	1988
Phillips, Kerk	Asst	Brigham Yg		PHD	91	Rochester	1992
Phillips, Llad	Prof	Cal-Santa Br	JC	PHD	69	Harvard	1972
Phillips, Owen R.	C-Ac	Wyoming	DK	PHD	80	Stanford	1985
Phillips, Peter	Prof	Yale					
Phillips, Peter W.	Prof	Utah		PHD	80	Stanford	1978
Phillips, Robert F.	Assoc	George Wash	C	PHD	85	Columbia	1985
Phillips, Ronnie J.	Prof	Colorado St	GB	PHD	80	Tx-Austin	1983
Phillips, Samuel H. Jr.	Prof	George Mason		PHD	66	Virginia	
Phillips, Timothy P.	C-As	SUNY-Cortlan		MBA		Clarkson	
Phillips, William A.	Assoc	So Maine	ACDF	PHD	79	Fla St	1980
Phillips, William H.	Assoc	So Carolina		PHD	80	MIT	1979
Phipps, Tim	Assoc	W Virginia	Q	PHD	82	Berkeley	1989
Photiades, John G.	Prof	Montana	BOH	PHD		Illinois	
Pickett, John C.	Prof	Ark-Ltl Rock		PHD	70	Missouri	1986
Picone, Gabriel	Asst	South Fla	C	PHD	93	Vanderbilt	1993
Piedra, Alberto	Prof	Catholic		PHD			
Pieper, Paul J.	Assoc	Ill-Chicago	E	PHD	84	Northwes	1982
Pierce, Brooks	Asst	Texas A&M		PHD	90	Chicago	1989

Pierce, James L.	Prof	Cal-Berkeley		PHD	64	Berkeley	1976
Pierce, Thomas J.	Prof	CS-San Bern		PHD	76	Notre Dm	1976
Pierson, Lynne M.	Prof	Chapman	NE	PHD	78	Ca-River	1972
Pietra, Tito	Asst	Rutgers-N Br	D	PHD	89	Penn	1988
Pietrykowski, Bruce	Asst	Mich-Dearbor	AJPR	PHD	90	New Sch	1988
Piketty, Thomas	Asst	MIT	T				
Pillsbury, Warren A.	Retir	Lehigh		PHD	63	Virginia	1962
Pilotte, Sheree	Asst	Immaculata		PHD		Indiana	
Pinchin, Hugh M.	Prof	Colgate	F	PHD	70	Yale	1965
Pincince, Cecile M.	Lect	Assumption	AHJ	ABD		Clark	1980
Pingkaratwat, Nampeang	Assoc	Chicago St		PHD		Il-Chicago	1982
Pingle, Mark	Asst	Nevada-Reno		PHD	88	S Calif	1990
Pinto, James V.	Prof	No Arizona	DC	PHD	75	Oklahoma	1981
Piore, Michael J.	Prof	MIT	J	PHD	66	Harvard	
Pippenger, John E.	Retir	Cal-Santa Br		PHD	66	UCLA	1965
Pippenger, Michael	Asst	Alaska-Fairb		PHD	90	Purdue	1991
Pirasteh, Hassan	Prof	So Oregon St	CEG	PHD	85	Oregon	1982
Pirner, James	Lect	Rockhurst		MA	67		1983
Piron, Robert	Prof	Oberlin	BD	PHD	66	Northwes	1961
Pirouz, Kamrouz	Asst	Montclair St	ADGN	PHD		Hawaii	
Pischke, Jorn-Steffen	Asst	MIT	J	PHD	92	Princeton	1993
Pisciotta, John L.	Assoc	Baylor		PHD		Tx-Austin	1980
Pisciottoli, Louis F.	Prof	CS-Fresno		PHD	72	Duke	1967
Pitt, Mark M.	Prof	Brown		PHD	77	Berkeley	
Pizzi, Robert	Deces	Colorado Col		PHD	82	Wash	1990
Pizzigno, Gregory D.	Adj	St John's		MBA		St Johns	
Placone, Dennis L.	Assoc	Clemson	FPH	PHD	82	Pittsburgh	1976
Platt, Glenn	Asst	Miami U-Ohio	CR	PHD	93	Car Mellon	1993
Platt, Henry M.	Retir	Pace		PHD		Columbia	1966
Pledge, Michael T.	Prof	W Illinois	AEG	PHD	68	Houston	1968
Plesko, George A.	Asst	Northeastern		PHD	85	Wisconsin	1989
Pliskin, Jeffrey L.	Assoc	Hamilton	CF	PHD	85	Michigan	1982
Plosser, Charles I.	Prof	Rochester		PHD	76	Chicago	1978
John M. Olin Distinguished Professor of Economics							
Plott, Charles R.	Prof	Cal Tech		PHD	65	Virginia	1971
Edward S. Harkness Professor of Economics and Political Science							
Plumly, L. Wayne Jr.	Prof	Valdosta St	J	PHD	83	Geo St	1983
Plummer, Michael G.	Asst	Brandeis		PHD	88	Mich St	1993
Podgursky, Michael J.	C-Pr	Missouri		PHD	80	Wisconsin	1995
Pogodzinski, Joseph Michael	Assoc	San Jose St		PHD	80	SUNY-SBr	1987
Pogue, Thomas F.	Prof	Iowa		PHD	68	Yale	1965
Poirier, J. Eugene	Assoc	Georgetown		PHD		Yale	
Polachek, Solomon W.	C-Pr	SUNY-Bingham		PHD	73	Columbia	1983
Polak, Benjamin	Asst	Yale		PHD	92	Harvard	
Polavarapu, Ramana V.	Asst	Colo-Denver	IOCD	PHD	93	Ca-Davis	1993
Polkinghorn, Bette A.	Prof	CS-Sacrament		PHD	72	Ca-Davis	1971
Pollak, Robert A.	Prof	Wash Univ		PHD	64	MIT	1995
Hernreich Distinguished Professor of Economics							
Pollard, Stephen K.	Prof	CS-L Angeles		PHD	82	Ohio St	1982
Polley, Susanne M.	Asst	SUNY-Cortlan					
Pollin, Robert N.	Prof	Cal-Riversid	AE	PHD	82	New Sch	1982
Pollock, Gene Edward	C-Pr	Wooster		PHD	71	Ohio St	1961
Pollock, Richard L.	Deces	Hawaii-Manoa		PHD	67	Wisconsin	1968
Polutnik, Lidija	Asst	Babson				Geo St	1991
Pomery, John D.	Assoc	Purdue		PHD	77	Rochester	1982
Pompe, Jeffrey	Asst	Fran Marion		PHD	90	Fla St	
Pomponio, Xun	Asst	St Olaf	FP	PHD		Penn St	1991
Ponder, Henry	Prof	Fisk	Q	PHD	63	Ohio St	1984
President of the University/ Eratus Milo Cravath Professor of Economics							
Pongracic, Ivan	Asst	Indiana Wesl		MA	68	Zagreb	1987
Pontiff, Jeffrey	Asst	U Washington		PHD	94	Rochester	1992
Poole, Keith T.	Prof	Carnegie Mel		PHD		Rochester	1982
Poole, Richard W.	Retir	Oklahoma St		PHD	60	Okla St	1965
Poole, William	Prof	Brown		PHD	66	Chicago	1974
Herbert H. Goldberger Professor of Economics							
Pope, C. Arden III	Prof	Brigham Yg		PHD	81	Iowa St	1984
Pope, Clayne L.	Dean	Brigham Yg		PHD	72	Chicago	1970
Pope, Rulon D.	Prof	Brigham Yg		PHD	76	Berkeley	1982
Poplin, Toby L.	Assoc	Pfeiffer		MA	68	Appalach	1976
Popp, Anthony V.	Assoc	New Mex St		PHD	80	N Illinois	1981
Popper, Helen A.	Asst	Santa Clara		PHD	90	Berkeley	1991
Pordeli, Hassan	Dean$	Jacksonvil U		PHD	83	Nebraska	1983
Porter, Arthur L.	Assoc	So Utah		MBA	70	Stanford	1987
Porter, Philip	Prof	South Fla	H	PHD	78	Tx A&M	1985
Porter, Richard C.	Prof	Michigan		PHD	57	Yale	1964
Porter, Robert H.	Prof	Northwestern		PHD	81	Princeton	1987
William R. Kenan Jr. Professor							
Porter, Tod	Prof	Youngstown		PHD	84	Syracuse	1984
Porter-Hudak, Susan	Assoc	No Illinois		PHD		Wisconsin	
Portugal, Edwin	Asst	SUNY-Potsdam		PHD		SUNY-Alb	

Posatko, Robert C.	Prof	Shippensburg		PHD	75	Penn St	1981
Possen, Uri M.	Prof	Cornell		PHD	71	Yale	1971
Postlewaite, Andrew W.	C-Pr	Pennsylvania	DH	PHD	74	Northwes	1980
Pacific Term Professor in the Social Studies							
Potepan, Michael	Assoc	San Fran St		PHD	85	Ca-Davis	1991
Poterba, James M.	Prof	MIT	H	DPHI	83	Oxford	
Potiowsky, Thomas P.	Prof	Portland St		PHD	81	Colorado	1982
Potter, Gordon Alwyn	Retir	Pace		MDIV		Gen Theo	1969
Potter, Simon M.	Asst	UCLA		PHD	90	Wisconsin	1990
Potter, William	Assoc	Fairmont St		MA		Memphis	
Potts, Glenn T.	C-Pr	Wis-Rvr Fall		PHD	76	Iowa St	1976
Poulson, Barry W.	Prof	Colorado		PHD	65	Ohio St	1965
Powell, Irene	Assoc	Grinnell	IL	PHD	85	Wisconsin	1989
Powell, James L.	Prof	Princeton		PHD	82	Stanford	
Powelson, John P.	Retir	Colorado		PHD	51	Harvard	1966
Power, Thomas M.	C	Montana	HQR	PHD		Princeton	
Powers, John A.	Assoc	Cincinnati	C	PHD	66	Purdue	
Poznanska, Joanna K.	Assoc	Seattle Pac	F	PHD	76	Warsaw	1988
Pozo, Susan	Prof	W Michigan	F	PHD	80	Mich St	1982
Praetzel, Gary D.	Assoc	Niagara		PHD	80	SUNY-Buf	1981
Prager, Jonas	Assoc	New York U		PHD	64	Columbia	1964
Prasad, Kislaya	Asst	Florida St		PHD	88	Syracuse	1988
Prasch, Robert E.	Asst	Maine	AB	PHD	92	Berkeley	1990
Pratt, Leila J.	Prof	Tenn-Chattan	DC	PHD	75	Va Tech	1974
Hart Professor							
Pratt, Michael D.	Assoc	Virg Comm		PHD		Kansas	1979
Praveen, John	Asst	Montclair St	ADGN	PHD		Berkeley	
Premus, Robert	C-Pr	Wright State		PHD	75	Lehigh	1975
Prendergast, George A.	C-Pr	St Joseph		PHD	72	Penn	1956
Prescott, Edward C.	Prof	Minnesota		PHD	67	Car Mellon	1980
Prescott, James R.	Prof	Iowa State	R	PHD	64	Harvard	1973
Presley, Ronald W.	Dean	McMurry		PHD	75	Okla St	1994
Pressman, Steven	Prof	Monmouth		PHD	83	New Sch	1981
Price, Donald I.	Assoc	Lamar	MO	PHD	80	Arkansas	1981
Price, Edward O. III	Assoc	Oklahoma St		PHD	80	Tx A&M	1979
Price, Gregory N.	Asst	N Carol A&T		PHD		Wi-Milwa	
Price, Hollis F. Jr.	Assoc	U Miami	R	PHD	72	Colorado	1971
Primack, Martin L.	Prof	San Jose St		PHD	63	N Carol	1966
Prime, Penelope B.	Assoc	Kennesaw St	ADFO	PHD	87	Michigan	1991
Primont, Daniel A.	C-Pr	So Illinois	DC	PHD	70	Ca-SnBarb	1978
Primont, Diane F.	Asst	SE Missouri	JD	PHD	87	N Carol	1990
Prince, Steven	Asst	NW St of LA		PHD		Utah	
Prinzinger, Joseph M.	Prof	Lynchburg		PHD	74	Geo St	1984
Pritchett, Jonathan B.	Assoc	Tulane		PHD	86	Chicago	1985
Proffitt, Dennis	Prof	Grand Canyon	GD	PHD	84	St Louis	1987
Prosper, Peter A. Jr.	Prof	Union	JA	PHD	70	Cornell	1964
Prucha, Ingmar R.	Prof	Maryland		PHD	77	Viena	1981
Prus, Mark J.	Assoc	SUNY-Cortlan		PHD		Utah	
Prusa, Thomas	Assoc	Rutgers-N Br	F	PHD	88	Stanford	1994
Pryce, Priscilla	Asst	Gannon		MBA		Columbia	
Prychitko, David	Assoc	SUNY Oswego		PHD	88	Geo Mason	1989
Pryor, Frederic	Prof	Swarthmore	OP	PHD	57	Yale	1972
Pryor, Zora P.	VAsoc	St Joseph		PHD	69	Harvard	1984
Puffer, Frank W.	Prof	Clark		PHD	68	Brown	1968
Pugel, Thomas A.	Prof	New York U	DEF	PHD	78	Harvard	1978
Pulchritudoff, Nikolai	Assoc	CS-L Angeles		PHD	71	Ca-Davis	1972
Pulikonda, Naga	Assoc	Ind-Kokomo		PHD	77	Illinois	
Pulsinelli, Robert W.	Prof	W Kentucky	DK	PHD	74	Rutgers	1967
Puri, Anil K.	C-Pr	CS-Fullerton		PHD	77	Minnesota	1977
Puritz, Frederick A.	Asst	SUNY-Oneonta	M	MBA		Harvard	
Purkayastha, Dipankar	Asst	CS-Fullerton		MA	81	India	1990
Puth, Robert C.	Prof	New Hampshir	N	PHD	67	Northwes	1967
Putnam, William F.	Emer	So Carolina		MS	57	S Carol	
Putterman, Louis G.	Prof	Brown		PHD	80	Yale	1980
Pyle, Jean L.	Assoc	Mass-Lowell	JOR	PHD		Mass	
Qasmi, Bashir A.	Asst	So Dakota St	Q	PHD	86	Iowa St	1987
Qastin, Abdul Masesh	Assoc	Lakeland	DGNP	MBA		Minnesota	1985
Qayum, Abdul	Prof	Portland St		DSC	59	Netherld	1970
Qian, Yingyi	Asst	Stanford		PHD	90	Harvard	1990
Qin, Cheng-Zhong	Asst	Cal-Santa Br	D	PHD	89	Iowa	1989
Quade, Ane M.	Asst	CS-Sacrament		PHD	88	Illinois	1989
Quandt, Richard E.	Prof	Princeton		PHD	57	Harvard	1959
Quddus, Munir	Prof	So Indiana		PHD	85	Vanderbilt	1984
Quick, Lawrence	Assoc	IL Benedict	M	PHD	84	Northwes	1987
Quick, Paddy	C-Pr	St Fran-NY	ABN	PHD	75	Harvard	9-85
Quigley, Herbert G.	C-Pr	Univ of D C		DBA	77	Geo Wash	1969
Quigley, John M.	Prof	Cal-Berkeley		PHD	72	Harvard	1979
Quinlivan, Gary M.	C-Pr	St Vincent	F	PHD	83	SUNY-Alb	1981
Quinn, J. Kevin	Asst	Bowling Gr		PHD		American	1990
Quinn, Joseph F.	Prof	Boston Coll	DJ	PHD	75	MIT	1975

Quinn, Kevin G.	Asst	St Norbert		PHD		Il-Chicago	
Quinn, Stephen F.	Asst	Tx Christian		PHD	94	Illinois	1995
Quinzii, Martine	C-Pr	Cal-Davis	CDG	PHD	74	U Paris	1991
Quirmbach, Herman C.	Assoc	Iowa State	L	PHD	83	Princeton	1990
Qunjian, Daniel	Deces	Tufts		PHD		Harvard	1962
Qureski, Usman	Prof	Old Dominion		PHD	79	Houston	
Raab, Raymond L.	Prof	Minn-Duluth	L	PHD	71	Colo St	1985
Rabbitt, Michael T.	Lect	Rockhurst		MA	75	Wash U	1988
Rabin, Alan	Prof	Tenn-Chattan	E	PHD	77	Virginia	1977
UC Foundation Professor							
Rabin, Matthew	Asst	Cal-Berkeley		PHD		MIT	
Racine, Jeff	Asst	South Fla	C	PHD	91	W Ontario	1993
Radakovic, George	Assoc	Indiana U-PA	JR	PHD	79	Pittsburgh	1986
Radell, Willard W.	Prof	Indiana U-PA	NP	PHD	80	Illinois	1981
Raehsler, Rod D.	Asst	Clarion					
Rafeld, Frederick J.	Dean	Ashland		PHD	68	Ohio St	9-70
Raff, Horst	Asst	Indiana		PHD	91	W Ontario	1993
Raffa, Frederick A.	Prof	Cen Florida	E	PHD	69	Fla St	1969
Raffiee, Kambiz	Prof	Nevada-Reno		PHD	83	Oregon	1983
Ragan, James F. Jr.	H-Pr	Kansas State	JA	PHD	75	Wash U	1977
Raha, Arun	Asst	Boise State	EFO	PHD	91	Wash St	1990
Rahimian, Eric N.	C-Ac	Alabama A&M	ADOF	PHD	75	Indiana	1975
Rahman, A. K. M. Matiur	Asst	McNeese St		PHD		So Meth	1989
Rahmatian, Morteza	Prof	CS-Fullerton		PHD		Wyoming	1988
Rahsid, Salim	Prof	Illinois		PHD	76	Yale	1981
Raiklin, Ernest G.	Assoc	No Iowa		PHD	84	New Sch	1986
Railing, William F.	Prof	Gettysburg	AHP	PHD	58	Cornell	1964
Raines, Fredric Q.	Assoc	Wash Univ		PHD	67	Wisconsin	1964
Raines, J. Patrick	Assoc	Richmond		PHD		Alabama	1982
Rajanikauth, N.	Inst	Miss Vall St		MBA		Miss St	1987
Raji, Seyed	Prof	Dowling		PHD		NYU	
Rakowski, James J.	Assoc	Notre Dame	DF	PHD	68	Minnesota	1967
Ralston, Scott N.	Asst	Salisbury St		PHD	88	Tennessee	8-88
Ram, Rati	Prof	Illinois St		PHD	76	Chicago	1982
Distinguished Professor							
Ramachandran, Rama	Prof	New York U	DEH	PHD	75	Brown	1987
Ramakomud, Sriprinya	Deces	Howard		PHD		Indiana	
Ramanathan, Ramu	Prof	Ca-San Diego	CFO	PHD	67	Minnesota	1967
Ramaswamy, Sunder	Asst	Middlebury		PHD	90	Purdue	1990
Ramazani, M. Reza	Asst	St Michael's	AFEC	PHD	90	Colorado	1986
Rambeck, Charles	C-Ac	St Benedict					
Ramdas, Ganga P.	Asst	Lincoln-PA		PHD		Temple	
Ramey, Garey	Assoc	Ca-San Diego	D	PHD	87	Stanford	1987
Ramey, James	Prof	W Kentucky	GH	PHD	80	Kentucky	1992
Ramey, Valerie	Assoc	Ca-San Diego	E	PHD	87	Stanford	1987
Ramin, Taghi	Asst	Wm Patterson		PHD		NYU	1984
Ramirez, Carlos	Asst	George Mason					
Ramirez, Miguel	VAsoc	Wesleyan-CT		PHD	84	Illinois	
Ramoo, Ratha	Asst	Dickinson Cl	DQI	PHD	92	Ca-SnBarb	1994
Ramsay, Glenworth A.	Prof	Rhode Island		PHD	74	Boston C	1973
Ramsett, David E.	C-Pr	North Dakota		PHD	68	Oklahoma	1968
Ramsey, David D.	C-Ac	Illinois St	DEH	PHD	67	Minnesota	1973
Ramsey, James B.	Prof	New York U		PHD	68	Wisconsin	
Ramstad, Yngve	Prof	Rhode Island		PHD	81	Berkeley	1982
Ramstad, Yngve	Prof	Rhode Island		PHD	81	Berkeley	1982
Randall, Laura	Prof	CUNY-Hunter		PHD		Columbia	
Randolph, Susan M.	Asst	Connecticut	O	PHD	83	Cornell	1984
Ranis, Gustav	Prof	Yale		PHD	56	Yale	1960
Rankin, Carol A.	Assoc	Xavier	ADJ	PHD	80	Houston	1984
Ranlett, John G.	Prof	CS-Sacrament		PHD	56	Oregon	1957
Ransom, Michael R.	Assoc	Brigham Yg		PHD	83	Princeton	1988
Rao, J. Mohan	Assoc	Massachusett		PHD	82	Harvard	1989
Rao, Milind	Assoc	Colgate	EO	PHD	89	Columbia	1988
Rao, Polavarapu M.	VAsoc	Manhattan		PHD	72	NYU	1990
Rao, Potluri M.	Assoc	U Washington		PHD	69	Chicago	1973
Rao, Vaman	Prof	W Illinois	ACEO	PHD	73	Missouri	1979
Rao, Vijayendra	Asst	Williams		PHD	90	Penn	
Rapaport, Carol	Asst	No Carolina		PHD	89	Stanford	1988
Raper, Michael Dennis	Asst	West Georgia	AR	PHD		Geo St	
Sewell Chair of Private Enterprise							
Raphaelson, Arnold H.	Prof	Temple	H	PHD	60	Clark	1970
Rapoport, John	Prof	Mt Holyoke		PHD	70	Penn	1970
Rappi, Magdalena	Assoc	Tenn Tech		PHD	85	S Carol	1985
Rapping, Leonard A.	Deces	Massachusett		PHD	60	Chicago	1972
Rappoport, Paul N.	Assoc	Temple	C	PHD	74	Ohio St	1977
Rasche, Robert H.	Prof	Michigan St		PHD	66	Michigan	1975
Rashed, Jamal A.	Asst	Xavier	ACFO	PHD	88	So Meth	1989
Rask, Kevin N.	Asst	Colgate	QI	PHD	91	Duke	1991
Rask, Kolleen J.	Asst	Holy Cross	EFOP	PHD	89	Yale	1989
Rasmussen, Chris H.	Inst	So Dakota St	M	BA	75	SW State	1978

Rasmussen, David W.	Prof	Florida St		PHD	69	Wash U	1968
Raspen, Richard G.	C-Ac	Wilkes	M	PHD	91	Penn	7-67
Rassekh, Farhad	Asst	Hartford		PHD	83	Houston	1989
Ratajczak, Donald	Prof	Georgia St	MN	PHD	72	MIT	1973
Rath, Kali P.	Assoc	Notre Dame	CD	PHD	92	J Hopkins	1990
Ratkus, Mark	Asst	LaSalle		PHD	76	Notre Dm	1973
Ratliff, James D.	Asst	Arizona		PHD	93	Berkeley	1992
Ratowsky, Henry	Asst	CUNY-Lehman		PHD	76	CUNY	1988
Ratti, Ronald A.	Prof	Missouri	EFG	PHD	75	So Meth	1975
Rauch, James E.	Assoc	Ca-San Diego	FO	PHD	85	Yale	1986
Raut, Lakshmi K.	Asst	Ca-San Diego	CO	PHD	85	Yale	1987
Raval, Vasant H.	Assoc	Campbell		DBA		Newport	1986
Ravelle, James J.	Prof	Moravian	UB	DA		Lehigh	1978
Ravelle, Linda J.	Asst	Moravian		PHD		Lehigh	1989
Rawlins, Glenville W.	Assoc	Montclair St	AGOQ	PHD		NYU	
Rawlins, Richard	Asst	Missouri So		MS		Okla St	1988
Rawski, Thomas G.	Prof	Pittsburgh	O	PHD	72	Harvard	1985
Rawson, William S.	Assoc	So Carolina		PHD	67	Duke	1967
Ray, Cadwell L.	C-Ac	Tulsa		PHD		Tx-Austin	
Ray, Clarence G.	Prof	Nev-L Vegas		PHD	72	S Carol	1971
Ray, Debraj	Prof	Boston Univ	COD	PHD	83	Cornell	1991
Ray, Edward J.	Prof	Ohio State	F	PHD	71	Stanford	
Ray, Margaret A.	Asst	Mary Wash	LQRA	PHD	88	Tennessee	
Ray, Subhash C.	Prof	Connecticut	CD	PHD	81	Ca-SnBarb	1982
Rayack, Wendy	Assoc	Wesleyan-CT	J	PHD	84	Wisconsin	1983
Raymon, Neil A.	Assoc	Missouri	CDEF	PHD	77	Colorado	1983
Raymond, Arthur J.	Asst	Muhlenberg		PHD	90	Tufts	1991
Raymond, Jennie E.	Assoc	Auburn		PHD	89	Vanderbilt	1989
Raymond, Richard D.	Emer	Kent State	DR	PHD	63	Brown	1970
Raynold, Prosper	Assoc	Miami U-Ohio	EG	PHD	89	LSU	1989
Razzolini, Laura	Asst	Mississippi	D	PHD	94	So Meth	1994
Read, Colin	Assoc	Alaska-Fairb		PHD	88	Queen's	1989
Read, Robert A.	Lect	U Lancaster		PHD		Reading	
Reagan, Patricia B.	Assoc	Ohio State	LJ	PHD	80	MIT	
Reaves, Natalie	Asst	Mich-Dearbor	AIL	PHD	95	Wayne St	1994
Rebelo, Sergio	Assoc	Rochester	D	PHD		Rochester	
Reclam, Michael	H-Ac	Va Military		PHD	84	Ca-River	1986
Redding, Lee S.	Asst	Fordham		ABD		Princeton	1993
Reddy, Nallapu N.	C-Pr	Mich-Flint		PHD	67	Penn St	1974
Redfearn, Michael	Asst	North Texas		PHD	92	Mich St	1992
Redington, Douglas B.	Asst	Elon		PHD	89	Wyoming	1995
Redlinger, Lawrence J.	Prof	Texas-Dallas		PHD	69	Northwes	
Redmount, Esther R.	Assoc	Colorado Col		PHD	85	Virginia	1987
Reeb, Donald J.	Assoc	SUNY-Albany	RG	PHD	63	Syracuse	1965
Reece, William S.	Prof	W Virginia	CH	PHD	75	Wash U	1990
Reed, J. David	Prof	Bowling Gr		PHD	70	Kansas St	1968
Reed, Morris D.	Retir	East Central		MBA	70	Hawaii	1975
Reed, Robert	Assoc	Oklahoma	JD	PHD	85	Northwes	1992
Reeder, Danny	Asst	Okla Baptist		PHD		Okla St	1991
Rees, Daniel I.	Asst	Colo-Denver	J	PHD		Cornell	
Rees, David M.	Assoc	Mesa State		PHD		Oregon	1983
Reese, David A.	Assoc	Gustavus Ado		PHD	80	Virginia	1979
Reese, James W.	Assoc	SC-Spartanbu	AFPH	PHD		Tennessee	1982
Reeves, Silke	Asst	George Wash	E	PHD	93	UCLA	1993
Reffett, Kevin	Assoc	Arizona St		PHD	90	Purdue	1995
Register, Charles A.	C-Pr	Miss State		PHD	84	Okla St	1993
Reibman, Spencer S.	Asst	Kennesaw St	ADF	MBA	76	Chicago	1991
Reich, Michael	Prof	Cal-Berkeley		PHD	74	Harvard	1974
Reid, Clifford E.	C-Pr	Colby	DCHR	PHD	73	Princeton	1987
Reid, John Joseph	Assoc	Memphis		PHD	62	Virginia	1966
Reid, Joseph D.	Assoc	George Mason		PHD	74	Chicago	1983
Reid, Kathleen A.	C-Ac	Shepherd		PHD	86	Penn St	1983
Reifel, John W.	Prof	Grand Valley	AHOR	PHD	72	Mich St	1971
Reiland, Ralph R.	Assoc	Robt Morris		MBA		Duquesne	
Reilly, Robert J.	Assoc	Virg Comm		PHD	78	Tennessee	1978
Reiman, Mark A.	Assoc	Pacific Luth	FPQ	PHD	88	U Wash	1988
Reimer, Richard D.	Prof	Wooster		PHD	62	Mich St	1962
Hoge Professor of Economics							
Reimers, Cordella W.	Prof	CUNY-Hunter		PHD	77	Columbia	1982
Reinert, Kenneth	Asst	Kalamazoo	FDE	PHD	88	Maryland	1993
Reinganum, Jennifer F.	Prof	Vanderbilt	LK	PHD	79	Northwes	1995
Reinhardt, Nola	Assoc	Smith	OPQ	PHD	81	Berkeley	1981
Reinhardt, Uwe E.	Prof	Princeton		PHD	70	Yale	1967
Reinhart, Blaise F.	Prof	Siena		PHD		Catholic	
Reinhorn, Les	Asst	Utah State	AEH	PHD	94	Stanford	1994
Reinke, Robert W.	Assoc	South Dakota		PHD	82	Minnesota	1987
Reinwald, Thomas P.	Prof	Shippensburg		PHD	73	Illinois	1974
Reiter, Stanley	Prof	Northwestern		PHD	55	Chicago	
Charles E. and Emma H. Morrison Professor of Economics							
Reitman, David	Asst	Ohio State	L	PHD	87	Stanford	1986

Rejda, George E.	Prof	Nebraska		PHD	61	Penn	1963
V. J. Skutt Professor of Economics							
Renas, Stephen M.	Prof	Wright State		PHD	71	Geo St	
Renner, Donald E.	Prof	Mankato St	ACHR	PHD		Cincinnati	1979
Rennie, Henry	Prof	Heidelberg	AFO	PHD	73	Ohio St	1993
Renning, H. Dieter	C-Pr	CS-Stanislau		DR	61	Freiburg	1970
Renshaw, Edward F.	Prof	SUNY-Albany	H	PHD		Chicago	
Renshaw, Robert H.	Asst	No Illinois		PHD	64	Mich St	1965
Resek, Robert W.	Prof	Illinois		PHD	61	Harvard	1961
Resnick, Stephen A.	Prof	Massachusett		PHD	64	MIT	
Ressler, Rand	Asst	SW Louisiana					
Rethwisch, Kurt	Prof	Duquesne		PHD	69	Maryland	1967
Reuther, Carol	C-As	West Liberty		MS	73	Fla St	1991
Revankar, Nagesh S.	Prof	SUNY-Buffalo	DC	PHD	67	Wisconsin	1967
Revier, Charles F.	C-Pr	Colorado St	EH	PHD	78	MIT	1974
Rewerts, Glen	C-As$	Olivet Nazar		JD	87	S Illinois	1993
Reyn, Stephanie	Assoc	Western St		PHD	92		
Reynolds, Bruce L.	Prof	Union	ODP	PHD	75	Michigan	1974
Reynolds, Morgan O.	Prof	Texas A&M		PHD	71	Wisconsin	1974
Reynolds, R. Larry	Prof	Boise State	BID	PHD	77	Wash St	1979
Reynolds, Stanley	Prof	Arizona		PHD	83	Northwes	1982
Reynolds, Stephen E.	Assoc	Utah		PHD	69	Wisconsin	1969
Rezelman, John R.	Asst	SUNY-Potsdam		MA		Indiana	
Rezvani, Farahmand	Assoc	Montclair St	ACGH	PHD		CUNY	
Rhode, Paul	Asst	No Carolina		PHD	90	Stanford	1990
Rhodes, George F.	Prof	Colorado St	LC	PHD	74	Tx A&M	1978
Rhodus, W. Gregory	Prof	Bentley	ACG	MA	75	Conn	1992
Ribal, John L.	Asst	So Colorado	HF	PHD		Notre Dm	1988
Ribar, David	Asst	Penn State	J	PHD	90	Brown	1990
Ricciardi, Joseph M.	Asst	Babson		PHD	85	Tx-Austin	1985
Rice, Edward M.	Assoc	U Washington		PHD	78	UCLA	1979
Rice, G. Randolph	Prof	Louisiana St	C	PHD	70	Kentucky	1969
Rice, Walter E.	Prof	Cal Poly-SLO		PHD	73	Claremont	1964
Rich, Daniel P.	Assoc	Illinois St	DJ	PHD	87	Houston	1987
Rich, David	Inst	Capital		MA		U Wash	1990
Rich, Stuart	Prof	Wis-Whitewat		PHD		Indiana	1959
Richard, James S.	Assoc	Regis-CO		PHD	80	Tx-Austin	1979
Richard, Jean Francois	Prof	Pittsburgh	C	PHD	73	Louvain	1991
Richards, Daniel J.	Assoc	Tufts		PHD	81	Yale	1985
Richards, Donald G.	Assoc	Indiana St	FO	PHD	83	Conn	1985
Richardson, David H.	C-Pr	St Lawrence	CJEF	PHD	63	Purdue	1979
Charles A. Dana Professor of Economics							
Richardson, Harry W.	Prof	So Calif		MA	61	Manchester	1975
Richardson, J. David	Prof	Syracuse		PHD	70	Michigan	
Richardson, James A.	Prof	Louisiana St	H	PHD	71	Michigan	1970
Alumni Professor of Economics; Director Public Administration Institute							
Richer, Jerrell	Asst	CS-San Bern		PHD	91	Ca-SnBarb	1991
Richter, Donald K.	Prof	Boston Coll	DR	PHD	73	MIT	1977
Richter, Marcel K.	Prof	Minnesota		PHD	59	MIT	1959
Rickman, Bill D.	Prof	Fort Hays St	DEJ	PHD	82	Okla St	1972
Rickman, Dan S.	Assoc	Geo Southern		PHD	87	Wyoming	1993
Riddell, Thomas A.	Assoc	Smith	HNPQ	PHD	75	American	1980
Rider, Christine	Prof	St John's		PHD	79	New Sch	1976
Rider, Robert L.	Asst	CS-S Marcos		PHD	89	S Calif	1992
Ridgway, Terry R.	Assoc	Nev-L Vegas		PHD	74	Arizona	1968
Rieber, Michael	Prof	Arizona					
Rieber, William J.	Prof	Butler	F	PHD	79	Pittsburgh	1989
Riefler, Roger F.	Prof	Nebraska	R	PHD	66	U Wash	1973
Riley, John G.	C-Pr	UCLA		PHD	72	MIT	1973
Riley, Robert	Asst	St Thomas-MN	F	PHD		Wisconsin	
Riley, Teresa M.	Assoc	Youngstown		PHD	84	Syracuse	1984
Rima, Ingrid H.	Prof	Temple	B	PHD	51	Penn	1946
Rinehart, James R.	Prof	Fran Marion		PHD	62	Virginia	
Ring, David W.	Assoc	SUNY-Oneonta	DEPR	PHD	82	SUNY-SBr	1981
Ring, Raymond J. Jr.	Prof	South Dakota		PHD	73	Kansas	1978
Riordan, Michael H.	Prof	Boston Univ	DL	PHD	81	Berkeley	1988
Rios, Roberto J.	Asst	CUNY-Lehman		PHD	87	Columbia	1979
Rios-Rull, Jose-Victor	Asst	Pennsylvania	O	PHD	90	Minnesota	1992
Simon Kuznets Term Assistant Profess of Econ; email vr0j@anaga.sas.upenn.edu							
Riskin, Carl A.	Prof	CUNY-Queens	POQ	PHD	69	Berkeley	1974
Ritchey, Barry	Assoc	Anderson U	DHR	PHD		Syracuse	1991
Rittenberg, Libby T.	Assoc	Colorado Col		PHD	80	Rutgers	1989
Rittenoure, R. Lynn	Deces	Tulsa		PHD	70	Tx-Austin	1977
Rivers, Mary J.	Assoc	Seattle	CDM	PHD	82	Pittsburgh	1978
Rives, Janet M.	Prof	No Iowa		PHD	71	Duke	1984
Rivkin, Steven G.	Asst	Amherst	AIJ	PHD	91	UCLA	1993
Rizvi, Saiyid A.	Assoc	Vermont	BDF	PHD	90	New Sch	1987
Rizzo, Mario J.	Assoc	New York U		PHD	77	Chicago	1979
Roayaei, Abbas J.	Assoc	Fayetteville		PHD	84	Fla St	
Rob, Rafael	Prof	Pennsylvania		PHD	81	UCLA	1984

Rob, Rafael	Prof	INSEAD					
Roback, Jennifer A.	Assoc	George Mason		PHD	80	Rochester	1985
Robbani, Mohammad	Asst	Alabama A&M	GO	PHD		Fla Intl	
Robbins, Roy E.	C-As	St Marys-Txs		MA	75	St Marys	
Roberts, Bee-Yan	Assoc	Penn State	O	PHD	80	Wisconsin	1981
Roberts, Bruce B.	Assoc	Wm & Mary		PHD	81	Mass	1979
Roberts, Bryan	Asst	U Miami	ED	PHD	93	MIT	1993
Roberts, Charles A.	Assoc	W Kentucky	BN	PHD	79	Georgia	1969
Roberts, Judith A.	Prof	CS-Long Bch		PHD	85	Michigan	1986
Roberts, Kenneth D.	Assoc	Southwestern	GFOT	PHD	80	Wisconsin	1981
Roberts, Lloyd	Dean	Miss College		PHD	74	Miss	1982
Roberts, Mark C.	Assoc	Mich Tech		PHD	85	Arizona	1985
Roberts, Mark J.	Prof	Penn State	D	PHD	80	Wisconsin	1980
Roberts, Ray C. Jr.	Retir	Furman		PHD	61	N Carol	1969
Roberts, William W.	Prof	CS-Northrdge		PHD	74	Ca-SnDgo	1973
Robertson, Gary L.	Assoc	Aquinas		MA		Detroit	1969
Robertson, Marvin	Prof	Harding					
Robertson, Robert L. Jr.	Prof	Mt Holyoke		PHD	60	Wisconsin	1962
Robins, Philip K.	C-Pr	U Miami	IJ	PHD	72	Wisconsin	1982
Robinson, James A.	Asst	So Calif		PHD	93	Yale	1995
Robinson, Michael D.	Assoc	Mt Holyoke		PHD	87	Tx-Austin	1988
Robinson, Ned Stephen	Asst	N Car-Wilmin	A	PHD		Oklahoma	
Robinson, William J.	Asst	Nev-L Vegas		PHD	83	Colorado	1980
Robison, H. David	Assoc	LaSalle	QC	PHD	83	Maryland	1988
Robson, Denise A.	Asst	Wis-Oshkosh	AF	PHD	93	Nebraska	1994
Roca, Sergio G.	Deces	Adelphi		PHD	75	Rutgers	1971
Roche, John T.	Assoc	St John Fshr		PHD	81	Mass	1981
Rock, Charles Patrick	Prof	Rollins		PHD	86	Cornell	1984
Rock, James M.	Prof	Utah		PHD	66	Northwes	1967
Rock, Steven M.	Assoc	W Illinois	AJ	PHD	75	Northwes	1990
Rockoff, Hugh T.	Prof	Rutgers-N Br	N	PHD	72	Chicago	1971
Rockwood, Charles E.	Prof	Florida St		PHD	63	Indiana	1960
Rodgers, James D.	Prof	Penn State	HK	PHD	70	Virginia	1969
Rodgers, William	Asst	Wm & Mary		PHD	93	Harvard	1993
Rodgers, Yana	Asst	Wm & Mary		PHD	93	Harvard	1993
Rodriguez, Ada	Lect	CUNY-Lehman		MBA			
Rodriguez, Louis J.	Prof	Midwest St	EF	PHD		LSU	1981
Roe, R. David	C-Pr	Furman		PHD	78	Duke	1977
Roehl, Richard	Prof	Mich-Dearbor	ABDN	PHD	68	Berkeley	1976
Roemer, John E.	Prof	Cal-Davis	DP	PHD	74	Berkeley	1974
Roemer, Michael	SLect	Harvard		PHD	68	MIT	1974
Rogers, Augustus J.				PHD	69	Mich St	
Rogers, Carol Ann	Assoc	Georgetown		PHD	83	Princeton	1984
Rogers, Diane	Asst	Penn State	H	PHD	91	Virginia	1989
Rogers, John E.	Asst	Memphis		PHD	88	N Carol	1993
Rogers, John H.	Asst	Penn State	E	PHD	89	Virginia	1989
Rogers, Mary T.	Asst	Framingham		PHD		Mass	
Rogers, Robert	Assoc	Ashland		PHD	83	Geo Wash	1993
Rogers, Walter B.	Prof	Mid Tenn St		PHD	69	Okla St	1981
Rogerson, Richard D.	Assoc	Minnesota		PHD		Minnesota	1991
Rogerson, William P.	Prof	Northwestern		PHD		Cal Tech	
Rogoff, Kenneth S.	Prof	Cal-Berkeley		PHD	80	MIT	1989
Rohacek, Jerry K.	Prof	Alaska-Ancho	DEN	MA	69	Ca-SnBarb	1973
Rohlf, William D. Jr.	Prof	Drury		PHD	72	Kansas St	1972
Roistacher, Elizabeth A.	Prof	CUNY-Queens	RH	PHD	72	Penn	1974
Roley, V. Vance	Prof	U Washington		PHD	77	Harvard	1983
Roller, Lars-Hendrik	Assoc	INSEAD		PHD	87	Penn	9-87
Rolleston, Barbara Sherman	C-Ac	Baldwin-Wal	HR	PHD		Cornell	1983
Rollosson, Michael	Inst	Rhodes		ABD			1993
Roman, Paul D.	Assoc	St Louis		PHD	67	St Louis	1966
Romano, Richard E.	Prof	Florida	THOD	PHD	82	Pittsburgh	1982
Romans, Thomas J.	Assoc	SUNY-Buffalo	HR	PHD	63	Brown	1967
Romeo, Charles J.	Asst	Rutgers-N Br	C	PHD	89	Duke	1990
Romer, Christina D.	Assoc	Cal-Berkeley		PHD	85	MIT	1988
Romer, David H.	Assoc	Cal-Berkeley		PHD	85	MIT	1988
Romer, Paul M.	Prof	Cal-Berkeley		PHD	83	Chicago	
Romig, Rodney	Dean	Hawaii Pacif		PHD	75	Nebraska	8-87
Romps, John F.	C-Ac	St Anselm	ABEH	MA	68	Fordham	1968
Ronaghy, Hassan A.	Prof	Youngstown		PHD	69	Wisconsin	
Rook, Sarah P.	Assoc	SC-Spartanbu	ADTN	PHD		N Car St	1980
Rooney, Robert F.	Prof	CS-Long Bch		PHD		Stanford	1970
Roper, Don E.	Prof	Colorado		PHD	70	Chicago	1985
Ros, Jaime	Prof	Notre Dame	OE	PHD	78	Cambridg	1990
Rosa, Duane J.	Assoc	West Tx A&M	EOQ	PHD	89	Tx Tech	1984
Rose, David C.	Assoc	Mo-St Louis	CDIJ	PHD	87	Virginia	1985
Rose, Elaina	Asst	U Washington		PHD	93	Penn	1993
Rose, Louis	Prof	Hawaii-Manoa		PHD	70	UCLA	1969
Rose, Margarita M.	Asst	King's Col		PHD	89	Notre Dm	9-90
Rose, Mary B.	SLect	U Lancaster		PHD		Manchest	
Rose, Nancy E.	Prof	CS-San Bern		PHD	85	Mass	1985

Rosefielde, Steven	Prof	No Carolina		PHD	72	Harvard	1970
Rosegger, Gerhard	Prof	Case Western	OFND	DIUR	53	Austria	1965
Frank Tracy Carlton Professor of Economics							
Roseman, M. Richard	Prof	CS-L Angeles		PHD	69	Harvard	1970
Roseman, Robert E.	Assoc	Wash State		PHD	82	Minnesota	1983
Rosen, George	Retir	Ill-Chicago		PHD	49	Princeton	
Rosen, Harvey S.	C-Pr	Princeton		PHD	74	Harvard	1974
Rosen, Harvey S.	Retir	Cleveland St		PHD	69	Case Wes	1967
Rosen, Sherwin	Prof	Chicago		PHD	66	Chicago	1977
Edwin A. and Betty L. Bergman Professor of Economis & Social Sciences							
Rosenbaum, David I.	Assoc	Nebraska		PHD	85	Wisconsin	1985
Rosenberg, Allan B.	Assoc	West Liberty		MS	57	Illinois	1982
Coordinator of Regents BA Program							
Rosenberg, Nathan	Prof	Stanford		PHD	55	Wisconsin	
Rosenberg, Richard	Assoc	Penn State	A	PHD	69	Minnesota	1965
Rosenberg, Richard E.	Assoc	Wis-Parkside	FOP	PHD	70	Wisconsin	1970
Rosenberg, Sam	Prof	Roosevelt		PHD	75	Berkeley	1982
Rosenberry, Lisa A.	Asst	Bowling Gr		ABD		Va Tech	1995
Rosenbloom, Joshua L.	Assoc	Kansas		PHD	88	Stanford	1988
Rosendorff, Peter	Asst	So Calif		PHD	93	Columbia	1992
Rosengarth, Tom E.	Assoc	Westminst-PA		MS		Bowl Grn	1979
Rosenthal, Jean-Laurent	Asst	UCLA		PHD	88	Cal Tech	1988
Rosenthal, Robert A.	Prof	Stonehill	AL	PHD	78	Boston U	1975
Rosenthal, Robert W.	Prof	Boston Univ	CD	PHD	71	Stanford	1987
Rosenzweig, Mark R.	Prof	Pennsylvania	OJL	PHD	73	Columbia	1990
Rosovsky, Henry	Prof	Harvard		PHD	59	Harvard	1965
Lewis P. and Linda L. Geyser University Professor							
Ross, Clark G.	C-Pr	Davidson	P	PHD	76	Boston C	1979
Frontis Johnston Professor of Economics							
Ross, David R.	Asst	Bryn Mawr		PHD	84	Northwes	1992
Ross, Howard N.	Prof	CUNY-Baruch		PHD	64	Columbia	1964
Ross, Kevin L.	Asst	N Car-Wilmin	FG	PHD		Fla St	
Ross, Larry L.	Prof	Alaska-Ancho	ADE	MS	71	Oregon	1971
Ross, Leola	Asst	East Carol		PHD	94	So Meth	1994
Ross, Robert P.	Assoc	Bloomsburg		MA	58	Wash U	1967
Ross, Stephen	Asst	Connecticut	R	PHD	94	Syracuse	1994
Ross, Stephen A.	Prof	Yale		PHD	69	Harvard	1977
Sterling Professor of Economics & Finance							
Ross, Thomas A.	Assoc	Baldwin-Wal	CG	MA		Bowl Gr	
Ross, William N.	Prof	Clarion		PHD	71	Kansas St	1972
Rossana, Robert J.	Prof	Wayne State		PHD	80	J Hopkins	1991
Rosser, J. Barkley Jr.	Prof	Jms Madison	R	PHD	76	Wisconsin	1977
Rosser, Marina V.	Assoc	Jms Madison	FP	PHD	79	MoscowSt	1987
Rossetti, Jane	Asst	Frank & Mars		PHD	90	Duke	1992
Rossi, Armond A.	Asst	Frostburg St		PHD		W Virginia	
Rossiter, Rosemary D.	Assoc	Ohio Univ		PHD	80	Wi-Milw	1983
Rossman, Joseph E.	Assoc	Tx A&M-Kings		PHD		Iowa St	1976
Rotella, Elyce J.	Assoc	Indiana		PHD	77	Penn	1981
Roth, Alvin E.	Prof	Pittsburgh		PHD	74	Stanford	1982
Mellon Professor							
Roth, David	Asst	Michigan		PHD	93	Yale	1992
Roth, Margarete P.	Prof	IL Benedict	FA	PHD	67	Cologne	1970
Roth, R. Theodore	Prof	USAF Academy		PHD		MIT	
Roth, Timothy P.	C-Pr	Txs-El Paso		PHD	70	Tx A&M	1970
A.B. Templeton Professor							
Rotheim, Roy J.	Prof	Skidmore		PHD	77	Rutgers	1980
Rothenberg, Jerome	Prof	MIT	R	PHD	54	Columbia	1966
Rothenburg, Thomas J.	Prof	Cal-Berkeley		PHD	66	MIT	1966
Rothman, Philip	Asst	East Carol		PHD	90	NYU	1992
Rothschild, Robert	SLect	U Lancaster		MA		Cape Town	
Rothstein, Paul	Assoc	Wash Univ		PHD	88	Berkeley	1988
Rothstein, Sheldon H.	Asst	NE Illinois		MA		Chicago	
Rottenberg, Simon	Prof	Massachusett		PHD	50	Harvard	1971
Roubini, Nouriel	Assoc	New York U	EF	PHD	88	Harvard	1995
Roufagalas, John	Assoc	Radford		PHD	86	Florida	1985
Roumasset, James A.	Prof	Hawaii-Manoa		PHD	73	Wisconsin	1976
Rouse, Robert		Texas Tech		PHD			
Rousseau, Peter L.	Asst	Vanderbilt	EM	PHD	95	Stern Sch	1995
Rowe, John W.	C-Pr	South Fla	D	PHD	66	Illinois	1979
Rowley, Charles K.	Prof	George Mason		PHD	64	Nottnghm	1984
Roy, Raj	Prof	Toledo		PHD	68	Wayne St	1963
Roy, Tapan K.	Assoc	Eastern Conn		PHD		Temple	1977
Roy, Udayan	Asst	Lg Isl-Post		PHD		SUNY-SBr	
Royalty, Anne	Asst	Stanford		PHD	93	Yale	1993
Rubenson, Daniel L.	Prof	So Oregon St	CEK	PHD	85	Car Mellon	1986
Rubin, Jeffrey I.	Prof	Rutgers-N Br	H	PHD	75	Duke	1973
Rubin, Jonathan D.	Asst	Tennessee		PHD		Ca-Davis	1993
Rubin, Paul	Prof	Emory	K	PHD	70	Purdue	1991
Rubin, Rose M.	C-Pr	Memphis		PHD	68	Kansas St	
Rubinfeld, Daniel L.	Prof	Cal-Berkeley		PHD	72	MIT	1983

Rubinstein, Ariel	Prof	Princeton		PHD	79	Hebrew	
Ruccio, David F.	Assoc	Notre Dame	BO	PHD	84	Mass	1982
Rucker, Randal R.	Assoc	Montana St		PHD	84	U Wash	1991
Rucker, William	Asst	Ark-Pine Blf		ABD		Geo Wash	
Rudolph, Linda	Asst	St Lawrence	QKL	ABD	95	Conn	1995
Ruffin, Roy J.	Prof	Houston		PHD	67	Northwes	1976
Ruggiero, John	Asst	Dayton	R	PHD	95	Syracuse	1995
Ruhm, Christopher J.	Prof	N Car-Greens		PHD	84	Berkeley	1991
Ruiz, Nestor M.	Asst	CS-Pomona		PHD	89	Ca-Davis	1990
Rumore, Nancy C.	Inst	SW Louisiana		MS	80	LSU	
Rungeling, Brian S.	Prof	Cen Florida	J	PHD	69	Kentucky	1981
Rupert, Lyle M.	Assoc	Hendrix		MBA	85	Chicago	1987
Rupp, Daniel G.	Prof	Fort Hays St	AFH	PHD	81	Kansas St	1968
Ruprecht, Theodore K.	Retir	CS-Humboldt		PHD		Berkeley	1958
Rusek, Antonin	Assoc	Susquehanna	EFP	PHD	84	SUNY-SBr	1986
Rush, Lynda M.	Assoc	CS-Pomona		PHD	84	Ca-Davis	1986
Rush, Mark	Prof	Florida	EF	PHD	82	Rochester	1982
Rushing, Francis W.	C-Pr	Georgia St	ANP	PHD	67	N Carol	1974
Holder of the Eugenia A. and Bernard B. Ramsey Chair of Private Enterprise							
Russell, Clifford S.	Prof	Vanderbilt	HQ	PHD	68	Harvard	1986
Russell, Louise B.	Prof	Rutgers-N Br	I	PHD	71	Harvard	1987
Russell, Malcolm B.	Prof	Andrews	EN	PHD	78	J Hopkins	1979
Russell, Paul	Dean	Buena Vista		EDD	65	N Colo	9-67
Russell, R. K.	Prof	SW Okla St		PHD		Okla St	1973
Russell, R. Robert	Prof	Cal-Riversid	ADH	PHD	65	Harvard	1986
Russell, Thomas R.	Assoc	Santa Clara		PHD	73	Cambridg	1978
Russell, William R.	Prof	So Methodist		PHD		Wash	1971
Russo, Benjamin	Assoc	N Car-Charl		PHD	85	Iowa	1984
Russo, Daniel M.	Assoc	East Tenn St		BA	61	Rutgers	1967
Russo, Gerard G.	Asst	Hawaii-Manoa		PHD	89	Northwes	1987
Rust, John P.	Prof	Wisconsin		PHD	83	MIT	
Rutherford, Thomas F.	Asst	Colorado		PHD	87	Stanford	1995
Rutman, Gilbert L.	Prof	S Ill-Edward		PHD	65	Duke	1969
Rutstrom, Lisa	Asst	So Carolina					
Ruttan, Vernon W.	Prof	Minnesota		PHD	52	Chicago	1976
Regents' Professor							
Ruud, Paul A.	Assoc	Cal-Berkeley		PHD	81	MIT	1981
Ryan, Anne-Marie	Inst	Morehead St		MS	93	Wisconsin	1991
Ryan, Daniel	Asst	Temple	PL	PHD	90	Berkeley	1990
Ryan, Huldah	Asst	CUNY-Hunter					
Ryan, Peter C.	Asst	Framingham		PHD		Mass	
Ryan, Timothy P.	Dean	New Orleans		PHD	78	Ohio St	1978
Hibernia Professor of Economics							
Rychtanek, Leonard E.	Prof	No Alabama		PHD	79	Fla St	1983
Rycroft, Robert S.	Prof	Mary Wash	CHJG	PHD	78	Maryland	1977
Ryder, Harl E.	Prof	Brown		PHD	67	Stanford	1965
Ryu, Keungkwan	Asst	UCLA		PHD	90	Stanford	1990
Saari, Donald G.	Prof	Northwestern		PHD		Purdue	
Saba, Richard P.	Assoc	Auburn		PHD	74	Tx A&M	1974
Sabbarese, Donald M.	Asst	Kennesaw St	AEM	PHD	84	Geo St	1978
Sabella, Edward M.	Prof	Augsburg		PHD		Minnesota	1961
Sabi, Manijeh	Assoc	Russell Sage		PHD	86	Northeas	1988
Saboori, Farhad	Asst	Albright		PHD	85	Indiana	1986
Sabot, Richard	Prof	Williams		DPHI		Oxford	
Sachinides, Philip	Fell	Manches Inst		MA		New York	1991
Sachs, Jeffrey D.	Prof	Harvard		PHD	80	Harvard	1983
Galen L. Stone Professor of International Trade							
Sackrey, Charles Melvin	Assoc	Bucknell		PHD		Tx-Austin	1980
Sacks, Stephen R.	Prof	Connecticut	H	PHD	71	Berkeley	1971
Safarzadeh, Mohammad R.	Assoc	CS-Pomona		PHD	84	Claremont	1987
Saffer, Henry	Assoc	Kean		PHD		CUNY	9-85
Saffran, Bernard	Prof	Swarthmore	AH	PHD	63	Minnesota	1973
Franklin and Betty Barr Professor of Economics							
Saft, Lester F.	Prof	CS-Northrdge		PHD	76	UCLA	1971
Sage, Lewis C.	Assoc	Baldwin-Wal	CIJ	PHD	85	Maryland	1985
Saggi, Kamal	Asst	So Methodist		PHD	95	Penn	1995
Sahu, Anandi P.	Assoc	Oakland	EG	PHD	85	Wash U	1985
Saidi, Reza	Asst	Catholic		PHD			
Sakai, Marcia	Assoc	Hawaii-Hilo		PHD	85	Hi-Manoa	
Sakano, Ryoich	Asst	N Carol A&T		PHD	90	Alabama	1992
Sakellaris, Plutarchos	Asst	Maryland		PHD	92	Harvard	1992
Sala-i-Martin, Xavier	Assoc	Yale		PHD	90	Harvard	
Salant, Stephen W.	Prof	Michigan		PHD	73	Penn	1981
Salazar-Carrillo, Jorge	Prof	Fla Internat	OFA	PHD	67	Berkeley	
Sale, Tom S. III	H-Pr$	Louisiana Te	GE	PHD	72	LSU	1965
Salehi-Esfahani, Haideh	SLect	U Washington		PHD	85	Penn	1990
Salehi-Isfahani, Djavad	C-Ac$	Virg Tech	O	PHD	77	Harvard	1984
Salemi, Michael K.	Prof	No Carolina		PHD	76	Minnesota	1976
Zachary Smith Professor							
Salib, Anis B.	Prof	Alabama A&M	AI	PHD	72	Vanderbilt	1982

Saliba, Michael T.	Assoc	Loyola-N Orl	ADM	PHD	72	Oklahoma	1973
Saltz, Ira	Assoc	Valdosta St	F	PHD		Berkeley	1989
Saltzman, Cynthia J.	C-Ac	Widener	EFGO	PHD	86	Maryland	1980
Saltzman, Gregory M.	Assoc	Albion		PHD	82	Wisconsin	1982
Salvatore, Dominick	C-Pr	Fordham		PHD	71	CUNY	1970
Salvucci, Richard	Prof	Trinity					
Salyards, Donald M.	Prof	Winona State		PHD		Kansas St	1975
Salyer, Kevin D.	Assoc	Cal-Davis	EG	PHD	85	Ca-SnBarb	1990
Samanta, Subarna K.	C-Ac	Trenton St		PHD	85	So Meth	1987
Samhan, Muhammad	Assoc	Univ of D C	OP	PHD	76	American	1976
Samprone, Joseph C. Jr.	Prof	Georgia Col	AD	PHD		Calif	1983
Sampson, Jon	Asst	Alabama-Birm	CEI	PHD	91	CUNY	1991
Samson, Mike	Asst	Williams		PHD	94	Stanford	
Samuels, George E.	Prof	Sam Houston		PHD	72	Oregon	1975
Samuels, Warren J.	Prof	Michigan St		PHD	57	Wisconsin	1968
Samuelson, Larry W.	Prof	Wisconsin		PHD	78	Illinois	
Samuelson, Paul A.	Emer	MIT	D	PHD	41	Harvard	1940
Samwick, Andrew A.	Asst	Dartmouth		PHD	93	MIT	1994
Sanchez, Nicolas	Assoc	Holy Cross	DENO	PHD	72	S Calif	1977
Sandberg, Lars G.	Prof	Ohio State	NO	PHD	64	Harvard	
Sandberg, Michael L.	Prof	Coe		PHD	76	Iowa	1976
Sander, Larry L.	Prof	CS-Sacrament		MS		Utah	1969
Sander, William III	Assoc	DePaul		PHD	78	Cornell	1989
Sanders, Don	C-Ac	SW Texas St		JD	77	Tx-Austin	1979
Sanders, Kenneth K.	Asst	SW Okla St		PHD	90	Utah St	1990
Sanders, William V.	Prof	Clarion		PHD	81	Penn St	1981
Sanderson, Allen	SLect	Chicago		MA	70	Chicago	
Sanderson, Patricia L.	Assoc	Miss State		PHD	77	Oklahoma	1979
Sanderson, Warren	Prof	SUNY-Stony B		PHD	74	Stanford	1989
Sandler, Todd M.	Prof	Iowa State	HD	PHD	71	SUNY-Bin	1986
Sands, Barbara N.	Assoc	Arizona		PHD	85	U Wash	1985
Sandy, Jonathan G.	Assoc	San Diego		PHD	86	Ca-SnBarb	1986
Sanjak, Jolyne	Asst	SUNY-Albany	QF	PHD		Wisconsin	
Santerre, Rexford E.	Assoc	Bentley	DHI	PHD	83	Conn	1983
Santiago, Aida E.	Asst	St Fran-NY	ABJO	MA		New Sch	9-85
Santiago, Carlos E.	Prof	SUNY-Albany	OJ	PHD	82	Cornell	1988
Santoni, Gary J.	Prof	Ball State		PHD	72	New Mex	1988
Santopietro, George D.	Assoc	Radford		PHD	86	Va Tech	1987
Santos, Richard	Assoc	New Mexico	IJ	PHD	77	Mich St	1989
Sanz, Ernesto	C-Ac	Mass-Lowell	FNP	PHD		Boston C	
Saposnik, Rubin	Prof	Georgia St	D	PHD	59	Minnesota	1970
Sappington, David A.	Prof	Florida	TD	PHD	80	Princeton	1989
Lanzillotti-McKethan Eminent Scholar							
Sapra, Sunil	Asst	CS-L Angeles					
Sapsford, David	H-Pr	U Lancaster		PHD		Leeds	
Sara, Tejinder S.	H-Ac	Tuskegee		PHD		Mass	
Sardy, Hyman	Prof	CUNY-Brookly	C	PHD	63	New Sch	1957
Sargent, Thomas	Prof	Chicago		PHD	68	Harvard	1991
David Rockefeller Profesor of Econ & Social Sci							
Sarin, Rajiv	Asst	Texas A&M		PHD			9-94
Sarkar, Amin U.	Assoc	SUNY-Fredoni	OQ	PHD	88	Berkeley	1989
Sarkar, Shyamalendu S.	Prof	Saginaw Vall		PHD	69	Mich St	1969
Sarki, Ayuba J.	C-Ac	Hampton		PHD	84	Georgia	1982
Sarver, Lee	Asst	Mid Tenn St		PHD	87	Tennessee	1991
Sass, Tim R.	Asst	Florida St		PHD	84	U Wash	1990
Sasser, Sue Lynn	Asst	South Dakota		PHD	83	Tx Womans	
Sassone, Peter G.	Assoc	Georgia Tech	DH	PHD	73	Purdue	1972
Sato, Kazuo	Prof	Rutgers-N Br	E	PHD	60	Yale	1984
Sato, Ryuzo	Prof	New York U	CO	PHD	62	J Hopkins	1985
C. V. Starr Professor of Economics							
Satterthwaite, Mark A.	Prof	Northwestern		PHD	73	Wisconsin	1973
Sattinger, Michael	Prof	SUNY-Albany	J	PHD	73	Car Mellon	1981
Sattler, Edward L.	Assoc	Bradley		PHD	79	Illinois	1977
Sauer, Christine	Assoc	New Mexico	AEF	PHD	87	Brown	1985
Saunders, Lisa F.	Asst	Massachusett		PHD	87	Berkeley	1987
Saunders, Peter J.	Prof	Central Wash	EHQ	PHD	81	Colorado	1988
Saunders, Phillip	Prof	Indiana		PHD	64	MIT	1970
Saurman, David	Assoc	San Jose St		PHD	79	Tx A&M	1991
Saussy, Gordon A.	Prof	New Orleans		PHD	72	Yale	1970
Sav, Thomas G.	Prof	Wright State		PHD	81	Geo Wash	1985
Savage, Deborah A.	Asst	So Conn St		PHD		Conn	
Savage, Ian P.	SLect	Northwestern		PHD	84	Leeds	
Savage, Vernon H.	Prof	SW Texas St		PHD		Tx-Austin	
Savin, Nathan E.	Prof	Iowa		PHD	69	Berkeley	1986
Saving, Thomas R.	Prof	Texas A&M		PHD	60	Chicago	1968
Director Private Enterprise Research Center; Distinguished Prof of Economics							
Savoca, Elizabeth A.	Assoc	Smith	CEIT	PHD	82	Berekely	1982
Savoian, Roy T.	Prof	Lynchburg		PHD	79	Ca-SnBarb	1984
Savvides, Andreas	Assoc	Oklahoma St		PHD	83	Florida	1985
Sawani, Mustafa A.	Assoc	NE Missouri		PHD		Missouri	1985

Sawdy, George F.	Asst	Providence	QEH	PHD		Brown	
Sawers, Larry B.	C-Pr	American U		PHD	69	Michigan	1969
Sawhney, Bansi L.	Prof	Baltimore		PHD	75	Geo Wash	1971
Sawhney, Saroj	Assoc	Suffolk		PHD		Northeas	
Sawtelle, Barbara A.	Assoc	Simmons	E	PHD	76	MIT	
Sawyer, Juliet	Assoc	Cheyney					
Sawyer, W. Charles	Prof	So Miss	F	PHD	83	Arkansas	1983
Saxonhouse, Gary R.	Prof	Michigan		PHD	71	Yale	1970
Sazama, Gerald W.	Assoc	Connecticut	H	PHD	67	Wisconsin	1966
Scahill, Edward M.	Assoc	Scranton		PHD	83	SUNY-Bin	1989
Scalet, Kenneth G.	Assoc	York-Penn		MBA		St Johns	1970
Scaperlanda, Anthony E.	C-Pr	No Illinois		PHD	64	Tx-Austin	1964
Scarf, Herbert E.	Prof	Yale		PHD	54	Princeton	1963
Schaake, Richard A.	C-As	Pace		MBA		NYU	1966
Schachter, Gustav	Prof	Northeastern		PHD	62	NYU	1965
Schaefer, Arthur McCluny	Prof	Univ South		PHD		Penn	
Schaefer, Donald F.	Prof	Wash State		PHD	67	N Carol	1982
Schaefer, Kurt C.	Assoc	Calvin		PHD	84	Michigan	1987
Schaffer, Beverly K.	Prof	Emory	K	PHD	67	Duke	1965
Schaffer, William A.	D-Pr$	Georgia Tech	R	PHD	63	Duke	1963
Schaffner, Julie L.	Asst	Stanford		PHD	86	Yale	
Schall, Lawrence D.	C-Pr	U Washington		PHD	69	Chicago	1967
Schaniel, William C.	Assoc	West Georgia	BP	PHD	85	Tennessee	
Schansberg, D. Eric	Asst	Indiana SE	HJC	PHD	91	Tx A&M	1992
Schap, David J.	Prof	Holy Cross	CDK	PHD	82	Wash U	1981
Schapiro, Morton Owen	Dean	So Calif		PHD	79	Penn	1991
Schatz, Richard E.	Assoc	Whitworth		PHD		Hawaii	1989
Schauer, David A.	Assoc	Txs-El Paso		PHD	75	Notre Dm	1975
Scheel, Daniel Curtis	Prof	CS-Sacrament		PHD		Oregon	1969
Scheffer, Ronald E.	Assoc	Tri-State		MA		Ohio	1967
Scheinkman, Jose	C-Pr	Chicago		PHD	74	Rochester	1973
Alvin H. Baum Professor							
Schelling, Thomas	Prof	Maryland		PHD	51	Harvard	1991
Schenker, Eric	Prof	Wis-Milwauke		PHD	57	Florida	1959
Scher, Frances	Inst	Montclair St	AHIT	MA		Columbia	
Scherer, Philip M.	C-Pr	Niagara		PHD	72	Missouri	1980
Schhwalberg, Barney K.	Prof	Brandeis		PHD		Harvard	
Schiantarelli, Fabio	Assoc	Boston Coll	CEF	PHD	81	LondonEc	1992
Schibik, Timothy J.	Assoc	So Indiana		PHD	89	W Virginia	1988
Schieren, George A.	Assoc	Appalach St	M	PHD	75	N Carol	1977
Schifrin, Leonard	Prof	Wm & Mary		PHD	64	Michigan	1964
Chancellor Professor							
Schilcutt, J. Garland	C-Pr	Lakeland	M	LLD		Marian	1958
Schilling, Donald J.	Assoc	Missouri	EF	PHD	67	N Carol	1964
Schiming, Richard C.	Prof	Mankato St	AE	PHD	74	Ohio St	1981
Schlack, Robert F.	C-Pr	Carthage	FPR	PHD		Wayne St	1975
Schlee, Edward E.	Asst	Arizona St		PHD	88	Illinois	1990
Schlesinger, Harris	Prof	Alabama		PHD	80	Illinois	1987
Schlottmann, Alan M.	Prof	Tennessee		PHD	75	Wash U	1975
Schlow, David	Lect	Penn State	A	PHD	84	Penn St	1991
Schmalensee, Richard L.	Prof	MIT	O	PHD	70	MIT	1977
Goldon Y. Billard Professor Economics & Management							
Schmeidler, David	Prof	Ohio State		PHD	69	Hebrew	
Schmertmann, Carl P.	Asst	Florida St		PHD	88	Berkeley	1990
Schmidt, David R.	Prof	Indiana		PHD	94	CIT	1993
Schmidt, James R.	Prof	Nebraska		PHD	78	Rice	1977
Schmidt, Peter J.	Prof	Michigan St		PHD	70	Mich St	1977
Schmidt, Robert M.	Assoc	Richmond		PHD	81	Duke	1981
Schmidt, Shelton S.	Assoc	Union	LCA	PHD	77	Virginia	1974
Schmidt, Stephen J.	Asst	Union	LCD	PHD	95	Stanford	1994
Schmidt, Torsten	Assoc	New Hampshir	DL	PHD	90	Florida	1988
Schmitz, Suzanne	Asst	Elmhurst		PHD		Kentucky	1990
Schneider, Lynn	Asst	No Georgia		PHD	95	Houston	1995
Schnell, John F.	Assoc	Alabama-Hunt	J	PHD	84	Illinois	1990
Schodt, David W.	C-Pr	St Olaf	OAH	PHD	80	Wisconsin	1977
Schoening, Niles C.	Prof	Alabama-Hunt	R	PHD	83	Tennessee	1983
Schofield, Norman J.	Prof	Wash Univ		PHD	85	Essex	1986
William Taussig Professor							
Scholland, Ken	Assoc	Hawaii Pacif	MLFB	MSFB		Geotown	
Scholz, J. Karl	Assoc	Wisconsin		PHD	88	Stanford	1988
Schor, Juliet B.	SLect	Harvard		PHD	82	Mass	1984
Schotter, Andrew	Prof	New York U		PHD	73	NYU	1985
Schrag, Joel	Asst	Emory	DKL	PHD	93	Berkeley	1993
Schran, Peter	Prof	Illinois		PHD	61	Berkeley	1965
Schreiber, Arthur F.	Prof	Georgia St	R	DBA	69	Indiana	1969
Schreiber, Max M.	C-Ac	W Carolina		PHD	78	S Carol	1977
Schroeder, Edward A.	Assoc	Nazareth		PHD	80	UCLA	1988
Schroeter, John R.	Assoc	Iowa State	L	PHD	81	Minnesota	1983
Schuh, G. Edward	Prof	Minnesota		PHD	61	Chicago	1979
Schulman, Craig	Asst	Arkansas	F	PHD	89	Tx A&M	1989

Schultz, Brian L.	Prof	Wis-Rvr Fall		PHD	80	Notre Dm	1979
Schultz, John A.	Assoc	Shepherd		PHD	85	S Carol	1988
Schultz, T. Paul	Prof	Yale		PHD	66	MIT	1975
Schultz, Theodore	Emer	Chicago		PHD	39	Wisconsin	1943
Schulz, Eric	Asst	Williams		PHD	93	Northwes	
Schumacher, Edward	Asst	East Carol		PHD	94	Fla St	1994
Schumacher, Howard	Assoc	Kean		MA		Columbia	9-56
Schupack, Mark B.	Prof	Brown		PHD	60	Princeton	1970
Schur, Leon M.	Emer	Wis-Milwauke		PHD	55	Wisconsin	1964
Schuttler, Robert D.	Inst	Marian		MBA	80	Evansville	1985
Schutz, Eric A.	C-Ac	Rollins		PHD	82	N Carol	1987
Schwab, Robert M.	Prof	Maryland		PHD	80	J Hopkins	1980
Schwalbenberg, Henry M.	Asst	Fordham		PHD	88	Columbia	1988
Schwartz, Adina Tzur	Assoc	Lakeland	AEFG	MA		Wisc-Mil	1986
Schwartz, Carol H.	Prof	NY Inst Tech		PHD	63	Columbia	1987
Schwartz, David Lamar	Assoc	Albright		MA	64	Mich St	1965
Schwartz, Marius	Prof	Georgetown		PHD	82	UCLA	1982
Schwarz, Peter M.	Prof	N Car-Charl		PHD	80	Ohio St	1978
Schwarz, Samuel	Assoc	CUNY-Stn Isl	KC	PHD	78	Columbia	1986
Schwarz-Miller, Ann V.	Assoc	Old Dominion		PHD		Northwes	1978
Schweigert, Thomas E.	Asst	Wis-Whitewat		PHD	90	Wisconsin	1984
Schweitzer, Robert N.	C-Pr	San Fran St		PHD	63	Berkeley	1962
Schwer, Keith	Prof	Nev-L Vegas		PHD	73	Maryland	1986
Schwinn, Carl R.	Assoc	Bates	IO	PHD	78	Cornell	1975
Schydlowsky, Daniel M.	Prof	American U		PHD	66	Harvard	1990
Scoones, W. David	Asst	Texas	D	PHD	91	Queen's	9-93
Scott, Carole Elizabeth	Prof	West Georgia	NO	PHD		Geo St	
Scott, Charles E.	Prof	Loyola-Maryl	MJH	PHD	79	Vanderbilt	1985
Scott, Frank A. Jr.	Prof	Kentucky	GH	PHD	79	Virginia	1979
Scott, Gary J.	Asst	St Marys-Txs		PHD	93	Notre Dm	1994
Scott, Gerald E.	Assoc	Georgia Col		PHD	87	Maryland	1994
Scott, J. T.	Retir	Iowa State		PHD	57	Iowa St	1955
Scott, John L.	Assoc	NE Louisiana	DC	PHD	90	S Carol	1989
Scott, John T.	Prof	Dartmouth		PHD	76	Harvard	1977
Scott, Loren C.	C-Pr	Louisiana St	J	PHD	69	Okla St	1969
Thomas J. Singletary Distinguished Professor of Business Administration							
Scott, Ralph D.	Assoc	Hendrix		PHD	83	Tulane	1979
Scott, Robert C.	Prof	Bradley		PHD	75	Iowa	1975
Scribner, Barry L.	Assoc	USM Academy		PHD		Harvard	1988
Seaks, Terry G.	Prof	N Car-Greens		PHD	72	Duke	1972
Seal, James W.	Assoc	Portland	HRE	PHD	77	Illinois	1977
Seaman, Bruce A.	Assoc	Georgia St	D	PHD	78	Chicago	1978
Seater, John J.	Prof	N Carol St	EH	PHD	75	Brown	1981
Sebestyen, Zoltan H.	Assoc	SUNY-N Paltz	DFA	PHD	68	Columbia	1969
Sechtem, Everett A.	C-Pr	Neb-Kearney		PHD	86	Nebraska	1970
Sedo, Stan	Asst	New Hampshir	CJ	PHD	91	Michigan	1992
Seeborg, Michael C.	H-Pr	Ill Wesleyan	J	PHD	76	Utah	1989
Robert S. Eckley Distinguished Professor of Economics							
Seeley, Robert D.	Assoc	Wilkes	AIJ	PHD	86	Maryland	9-89
Segelhorst, Elbert W.	Retir	CS-Long Bch	1994	PHD	63	Columbia	1964
Segerson, Kathleen	Assoc	Connecticut	QD	PHD	84	Cornell	1986
Segerstrom, Paul S.	Assoc	Michigan St		PHD	84	Rochester	1984
Seguino, Stephanie	Asst	Vermont	EFOP	PHD	94	American	1995
Sehorn, Annette	Prof	SW Okla St					
Seidel, Ethan A.	Prof	W Maryland		PHD	77	J Hopkins	1969
Seidelman, James E.	Dean	Westminst-UT		PHD	86	Utah	1980
Seidenstat, Paul	Assoc	Temple	H	PHD	64	Northwes	1967
Seidenstricker, Kenneth C.	Assoc	Regis-CO		MA		Marquette	
Seidman, Laurence S.	Prof	Delaware	H	PHD	74	Berkeley	1982
Seifried, Edmond J.	Prof	Lafayette		PHD		W Virginia	1978
Seiglie, Carlos	Assoc	SUNY-Bingham		PHD	91	Chicago	1994
Seiglie, Carlos C.	Assoc	Rutgers-Newk		PHD	91	Chicago	1986
Seiver, Daniel A.	Prof	Miami U-Ohio	TG	PHD	74	Yale	1978
Seiz, Janet A.	Assoc	Grinnell	BO	PHD	85	Duke	1989
Selassie, Haile G.	Assoc	So Carol St		PHD	83	Okla St	1984
Seldon, Barry	Assoc	Texas-Dallas		PHD	85	Duke	
Selgin, George A.	Assoc	Georgia	EN	PHD	86	NYU	1989
Selim, Mohamed Ali	Assoc	St Thomas-MN	A	PHD		Minnesota	1959
Selivanoff, George A.	C-Pr	LaSierra	AF	PHD	64	American	1984
Sell, John W.	Assoc	Wooster		PHD	81	UCLA	1981
Sellers, Gary	Assoc	Akron		PHD	77	Cincinnati	1976
Sellers, John R.	Asst	Carson-Newmn	ABEO	PHD	93	Tennessee	1991
Selover, David D.	Asst	Wesleyan-CT	F	PHD	91	Ca-SnDgo	1990
Semenick Alam, Ila	Asst	Tulane		PHD	94	Rice	1994
Sen, Amartya K.	Prof	Harvard		PHD	59	Cambridg	1988
Lamont University Professor							
Sen, Arijet	Asst	Maryland		PHD	93	Princeton	1993
Seneca, Joseph J.	Prof	Rutgers-N Br	H	PHD	68	Penn	1976
Seneca, Rosalind S.	Prof	Drew	DL	PHD	71	Penn	1981
Sengupta, Jati K.	Prof	Cal-Santa Br	CO	PHD	62	Iowa St	1976

Sengupta, Kunal	Asst	Cal-Riversid	ADO	PHD	84	Cornell	1989
Sent, Esther-Mirjam	Asst	Notre Dame	BE	PHD	94	Stanford	1994
Seo, Tae Kun	Assoc	So Methodist		PHD	73	Tx A&M	1973
Seplaki, Les	C-Pr	Rutgers-Camd		PHD	70	Ca-River	
Seppi, Duane J.	Assoc	Carnegie Mel		PHD		Chicago	1986
Serow, William J.	Prof	Florida St		PHD	72	Duke	1981
Serrano, Roberto	Assoc	Brown		PHD	92	Harvard	
Seshu, Chigurupati R.	Assoc	SUNY-N Paltz	AEO	PHD	60	New Sch	1967
Sessions, Lynne	Asst	SUNY-Oneonta	M	MBA		Pittsburgh	
Sethi, Rajiv	Asst	Vermont	BCGQ	PHD	93	New Sch	1993
Settle, Russell F.	Prof	Delaware	H	PHD	74	Wisconsin	1974
Sexton, Edwin A.	Assoc	Va Military		PHD	87	Illinois	1992
Sexton, Robert L.	Prof	Pepper-Malib	ADNQ	PHD	80	Colorado	1979
Sexton, Terri A.	Prof	CS-Sacrament		PHD	81	Minnesota	1987
Seyfert, Jeff	Asst	S Nazarene		MBA	89	Tulsa	1990
Seyfried, William L.	Asst	Cen Arkansas		PHD	90	Purdue	8-90
Sfeir, Raymond	Assoc	Chapman	AC	PHD	82	Ca-SnBarb	1985
Sgontz, Larry G.	Prof	Iowa		PHD	64	Illinois	1964
Shaaf, Mohammad	Prof	Central Okla		PHD	82	Tx Tech	1980
Shaanan, Joseph	Prof	Bryant	FL	PHD	79	Cornell	
Shabahang, Homa		Chapman	F	PHD	83	Oklahoma	1991
Shaban, Radwan Ali	Assoc	Georgia Tech	DO	PHD	85	Stanford	1991
Shackelford, Jean A.	Prof	Bucknell		PHD	74	Kentucky	1975
Shadbegian, Ronald	Asst	Mass-Dartmou	HKQ	PHD	91	Clark	1993
Shadoan, Donald	Retir	E Kentucky		PHD		Kentucky	1962
Shafer, Wayne	Prof	Illinois		PHD	72	Ca-SnBarb	1990
Shaffer, Greg	Asst	Michigan		PHD	89	Princeton	
Shaffer, Linda J.	Prof	CS-Fresno		PHD	78	Northwes	1984
Shah, Parth	Asst	Mich-Dearbor	APE	PHD	90	Auburn	1991
Shah, Sudhir	Asst	Cincinnati	DC	PHD		Princeton	
Shah, Umanglal	Asst	Albany State		MS			
Shahjahan, Mirza	Assoc	Ark-Pine Blf		PHD		Bonn	
Shalishali, Kasazi	Asst	Tuskegee		PHD	93	Auburn	1993
Shandiz, Mohmood	Assoc	Okla City		PHD	81	Okla St	1985
Shane, Richard C.	Prof	So Dakota St	Q	PHD	78	Wash St	1977
Shanklin, James T.	Asst	NW Missouri	AD	MS	66	S Illinois	1966
Shannon, John C.	Assoc	Suffolk		MA		Boston C	
Shannon, Robert F.	Assoc	South Fla		PHD	66	Illinois	1966
Shannon, Russell D.	Prof	Clemson	EFOP	PHD	66	Tulane	1966
Shapiro, Aharon H.	Assoc	St John's		PHD	66	New Sch	1967
Shapiro, Edward	Retir	Toledo	1994	PHD		Harvard	1967
Shapiro, Harold T.	Prof	Princeton		PHD	64	Princeton	1988
Shapiro, Matthew D.	Prof	Michigan		PHD	84	MIT	1989
Shapiro, Perry	Prof	Cal-Santa Br	DH	PHD	67	Berkeley	1969
Shapiro, Stephen L.	Assoc	North Fla	AH	PHD	72	S Carol	1972
Shapiro, Steven J.	Assoc	New Haven		PHD	88	Geotown	1987
Shapley, Lloyd S.	Prof	UCLA		PHD			
Sharav, Itzhak	Prof	CUNY-Lehman		PHD	71	CUNY	9-67
Sharif, Mohammed	Assoc	Rhode Island		PHD	83	Boston U	1984
Shariff, Ismail	C-Pr	WI-Green Bay		PHD		Wisconsin	
Sharma, Subhash	Prof	So Illinois	C	PHD	83	Kentucky	1983
Sharma, Ved P.	Prof	Mankato St	CDT	PHD	77	Wash U	1976
Sharp, Ansel M.	Retir	Univ South		PHD	56	LSU	1985
Sharp, Robert R.	Prof	E Kentucky		PHD	69	Kentucky	1969
Sharpiro, David	Assoc	Penn State	J	PHD	72	Princeton	1980
Shatto, Gloria M.	Prof	Berry		PHD	66	Rice	1979
Shaw, John A. Jr.	Prof	CS-Fresno		PHD	69	Purdue	1965
Shaw, Kathryn L.	Assoc	Carnegie Mel		PHD	81	Harvard	1981
Shaw, Sue O.	Assoc	Longwood		PHD		Harvard	1986
Shea, John	Asst	Wisconsin		PHD	90	MIT	1990
Sheahan, John B.	Retir	Williams		PHD	54	Harvard	1954
Sheets, Doris Files	Assoc	SW Missouri		PHD	81	Missouri	1974
Sheffrin, Steven M.	Prof	Cal-Davis	EH	PHD	76	MIT	1976
Sheflin, Neil	Assoc	Rutgers-N Br	C	PHD	79	Rutgers	1975
Sheftall, Willis B.	C-Pr	Morehouse		PHD	81	Geo St	1986
Charles E. Merrill Professor of Economics							
Sheith, Kishor	Asst	Delaware St		MBA		Atlanta	
Shelburn, Marsha	Prof	So Car-Aiken		PHD	80	N Carol	1980
Shell, Karl	Prof	Cornell		PHD	65	Stanford	1986
Robert Julius Thorne Professor							
Shelley, Gary L.	Asst	Appalach St	EM	PHD	90	Va Tech	1990
Shelton, David H.	Retir	N Car-Greens		PHD	58	Ohio St	1965
Shen, Raphael	Prof	Detroit Merc		PHD	75	Mich St	1977
Shen, Ruth R.	Prof	San Fran St		PHD	61	J Hopkins	1964
Shepard, Edward M.	Assoc	LeMoyne	HJL	PHD	87	Boston C	1990
Shepherd, A. Ross	Prof	Mo-Kansas Ct	DF	PHD	63	Syracuse	1967
Shepherd, Robert J.	Lect	Ca-Santa Crz					
Shepherd, William G.	Prof	Massachusett		PHD	63	Yale	1986
Sheppard, Katharine P.	Asst	Wooster		PHD	84	Maryland	1988
Sheppard, Stephen C.	Assoc	Oberlin	CR	PHD	84	Wash U	1990

Sherer, George	Inst	Lg Isl-Brook	ABD	MPHI		Columbia	
Sheriff, Mohamed A.	Asst	Dillard		PHD		Howard	
Sherman, Howard J.	Prof	Cal-Riversid	EK	PHD	60	S Calif	1966
Sherman, Roger	Prof	Virginia	LD	PHD	66	Car Mellon	1971
Brown-Forman Professor of Economics							
Sherony, Deith R.	Prof	Wis-La Cross	ACE	PHD	82	Wi-Milw	1983
Sherry, Robert L.	Assoc	Keene State		PHD	79	Yale	1984
Shieh, John T.	Prof	CS-Pomona		DBA	81	S Calif	1967
Shieh, Yeung-Nan	Prof	San Jose St		PHD	80	Tx A&M	1989
Shields, Michael P.	C-Pr	Cen Michigan		PHD	75	Utah	
Shiers, Alden F.	Assoc	Cal Poly-SLO		PHD	77	Ca-SnBarb	1975
Shikha, Deep	Asst	St Catherine	FA	PHD	77	LSU	1985
Shiller, Robert J.	Prof	Yale		PHD	72	MIT	1982
Shiman, Daniel R.	Asst	SUNY Oswego		PHD	86	Northwes	1990
Shin, Bong Ju	Prof	Towson State		PHD	69	Ohio St	1966
Shin, Kwanho	Asst	Kansas		ABD		UCLA	1984
Shingleton, Virginia	Asst	Valparaiso	CJIA	PHD	94	Notre Dm	1992
Shinn, Earl W. III	C-Ac	Montevallo		PHD	92		1988
Shipman, William A.	Prof	Wartburg		PHD	77	Pittsburgh	1972
Shirey, Richard L.	C-Ac	Siena		PHD		SUNY-Alb	
Shirley, John	Lect	SUNY-Cortlan					
Shirvani, Hassan M.	Assoc	St Thomas-TX	FG	PHD	79	Harvard	1986
Shivakuma, Ram	Asst	N Car-Greens		PHD	92	Indiana	1993
Shleifer, Andrei	Prof	Harvard		PHD	86	MIT	1991
Shmanske, Steven	Prof	CS-Hayward		PHD	82	UCLA	1979
Shnaider, E.	Asst	Fla Inst Tec		PHD		Fla St	
Shobe, William	Asst	N Car-Greens		PHD	91	Minnesota	1989
Shockley, Frederica	C-Pr	CS-Chico	HMOR	PHD	78	Geo St	1978
Shogren, Jason F.	Prof	Wyoming	Q	PHD	86	Wyoming	1995
Shojai, Siamack	C-Ac	Manhattan		PHD		Fordham	1989
Short, Deanne M.	Asst	Bradley		PHD	89	Purdue	1989
Shoukry, Kamal	Assoc	Loyola Marym	ABCE	PHD	72	S Calif	1980
Shoven, John B.	Dean	Stanford		PHD	73	Yale	1978
Shovlain, Raymond J.	Asst	St Ambrose		MBA	80	StAmbros	1982
Showalter, Dean	Asst	SW Texas St		PHD	94	Kentucky	1995
Showalter, Mark	Asst	Brigham Yg		PHD	91	MIT	1991
Shows, E. Warren	Prof	South Fla	L	PHD	68	Geo St	1964
Shreiber, Chanoch	C-Pr	CUNY-Lehman		PHD		Columbia	
Shropshire, William O.	Prof	Ogelthorpe	EO	PHD	63	Duke	1979
Callaway Professor of Economics							
Shu, Florence P.	Assoc	SUNY-Potsdam		PHD	86	Mich St	1986
Shubik, Martin	Prof	Yale		PHD	53	Princeton	
Shughart, William F. II	Prof	Mississippi		PHD	78	Tx A&M	1988
Self Chair of Free Enterprise Holder							
Shukla, Vishwa S.	Prof	Ohio Univ		PHD	72	Wisconsin	1966
Shuklian, Steve	Asst	Marshall		PHD	88	Utah	1988
Shull, Bernard Jr.	Prof	CUNY-Hunter		PHD	57	Wisconsin	1970
Shull, Ralph	Prof	Ark-Ltl Rock		PHD	72	Arkansas	1971
Shulman, Steven J.	Prof	Colorado St	JKEI	PHD	84	Mass	1984
Shupp, Franklin R.	Prof	Illinois		PHD	59	Princeton	1960
Shute, Laurence	Assoc	CS-Pomona		PHD	73	Columbia	1988
Shwiff, Steven S.	Assoc	East Txs St	CDRO	PHD		Tx A&M	
Siberberg, Eugene	Prof	U Washington		PHD	64	Purdue	1967
Sibert, Anne C.	Assoc	Virg Tech	FE	PHD	82	Car Mellon	1993
Sibley, David S.	Prof	Texas	D	PHD	73	Yale	1-91
John Michael Stuart Centennial Professor of Ecnomics							
Sichel, Werner	C-Pr	W Michigan	D	PHD	64	Northwes	1960
Sicherman, Nachum	Assoc	Columbia		PHD	87	Columbia	1991
Sicilian, Joseph M.	C-Ac	Kansas		PHD	77	Purdue	1977
Sicilian, Paul	Asst	Grand Valley	ACDJ	PHD	91	Illinois	1987
Sickles, Robin C.	Prof	Rice		PHD	76	N Carol	1985
Siconolfi, Paolo	Asst	Columbia		PHD	87	Penn	1989
Siddiquee, Baker A.	Assoc	Il-Springfld	DEH	PHD	88	Manitoba	1987
Siden, Dorothy R.	Asst	Salem State		PHD	90	Northeas	
Sidwell, Richard J.	Prof	E Illinois		PHD	72	Utah	1970
Siebert, Calvin D.	Prof	Iowa		PHD	66	Berkeley	1965
Siegel, Abraham J.	Prof	MIT		PHD			
Howard W. Johnson Professor of Management							
Siegel, Andrew F.	Prof	U Washington		PHD	83	MIT	1990
Siegel, Rachel S.	C-Ac	Lyndon State	CGQN	MBA	89	Yale	9-90
Siegfried, John J.	Prof	Vanderbilt	LJ	PHD	72	Wisconsin	1972
Siegmund, Frederick	Assoc	Univ of D C	LI	PHD		Okla St	1976
Sievers, Allen M.	Prof	Utah		PHD	48	Columbia	1968
Sihag, Balbir S.	Prof	Mass-Lowell	CI	PHD	78	MIT	1980
Sikes, Ellen	Assoc	Campbell		MS		N Carol	1966
Silva, Donald H.	Prof	Wis-Whitewat		PHD		Missouri	1964
Silva, Emilson	Asst	Oregon	OH	PHD	93	Illinois	1993
Silver, J. Lew	Assoc	Alabama		PHD	80	Duke	1990
Silver, Stephen J.	Assoc	Citadel		PHD	83	Maryland	8-90
Silvestre, Joaquim	Prof	Cal-Davis	D	PHD	73	Minnesota	1983

Simard, Dominique	Asst	Rutgers-N Br	E	PHD	92	Queen's	1991
on leave to New York University 1995-96							
Simeone, William J.	Assoc	Providence	JEI	PHD	85	Boston C	1959
Simkins, Scott P.	Asst	N Carol A&T		PHD	88	Iowa	
Simler, Norman J.	C-Pr	Macalester	AE	PHD	59	Minnesota	1991
Simmons, Michael	C-As	N Carol A&T		PHD	79	Wash St	
Simmons, Walter O.	VAsst	John Carroll	JKNO	PHD	94	Wayne St	1995
Simms, Jonathon	Fell	Manches Inst		MSC		Southamp	1993
Simon, Alice E.	Assoc	Ohio Wesley		PHD		Ohio St	1985
Simon, Carl	Prof	Michigan					
Simon, Curtis J.	Asst	Clemson	JOR	PHD	85	SUNY-Bin	1985
Simon, Peter J.	Asst	Loras		PHD	89	N Illinois	1989
Simons, Gerald P.	Asst	Grand Valley		PHD	95	Kansas	1995
Simonson, John C.	Prof	Wis-Plattev		PHD		Wisconsin	1966
Simonson, Robert D.	Prof	Mankato St	AJ	PHD		Nebraska	1981
Simos, Evangelos O.	Prof	New Hampshir	EF	PHD	77	N Illinois	1977
Simpson, Murray S.	Asst	Davidson	O	PHD	94	Illinois	1993
Simpson, Paul	Lect	Manches Inst		MA		Newcastl	1984
Sims, Christopher A.	Prof	Yale		PHD	68	Harvard	
Simunek, Vladimir J.	Prof	St John's		PHD		Charles	
Sindt, Roger	Prof	Neb-Omaha	AR	PHD	72	Tx-Austin	1979
Singamsetti, Nageswara Rao	Assoc	Hartford		PHD		SUNY-Buf	
Singell, Larry D.	Prof	Colorado		PHD	65	Wayne St	1968
Singell, Larry D. Jr.	Assoc	Oregon	J	PHD	88	Ca-SnBarb	1988
Singer, Diana Sue	Assoc	W Maryland		MBA		Loyola	1983
Singer, L.	Prof	Indiana NW	RTE	PHD	58	Indiana	1969
Singer, Russell	Asst	King's Col		BS	58	Wilkes	9-67
Singh, Ajmer	Prof	W Oregon St		PHD	64	Oreg St	1965
Singh, Davinder	Prof	CS-Long Bch		PHD		S Carol	1983
Singh, Harinder	C-Pr	Grand Valley		PHD	85	Il-Chicago	1995
Singh, Nirvikar	Prof	Ca-Santa Crz	DLO	PHD	82	Berkeley	1982
Singh, Ram Das	Prof	Illinois St		PHD	70	N Delhi	1981
Singh, Sarjit	Retir	Clarion		PHD		Okla St	1964
Singleton, Robert	C-As	Loyola Marym	AJR	PHD	83	UCLA	1982
Singleton, Ross	Prof	Puget Sound	ADKO	PHD	77	Oregon	
Sinha, Rohini P.	Prof	Muhlenberg		PHD	65	New Sch	1965
Sink, Harry	Adj	N Carol A&T					
Siren, Raymond L.	Prof	Wash & Jeff		PHD		Pittsburgh	1975
Sisk, David E.	Prof	San Fran St		PHD	76	UCLA	1978
Sjaastad, Larry A.	Prof	Chicago		PHD	61	Chicago	1965
Sjogren, Jane O.	VAsoc	Simmons	HJ	PHD	81	Stanford	
Sjoquist, David L.	Prof	Georgia St	DR	PHD	71	Minnesota	1970
Sjostrom, J. Tomas	Assoc	Harvard					
Skaggs, Jimmy M.	Prof	Wichita St		PHD	70	Tx Tech	1970
Skaggs, Neil T.	Assoc	Illinois St	BDE	PHD	80	Duke	1979
Skaperdas, Stergios	Asst	Calif-Irvine		PHD	88	J Hopkins	1988
Skeath, Susan E.	Asst	Wellesley		PHD	89	Princeton	1989
Skeels, Jack W.	Prof	No Illinois		PHD	57	Wisconsin	1963
Skelley, A. Chris	Assoc	Rollins		PHD	85	Brown	1987
Skidmore, Mark	Asst	No Illinois		PHD	94	Colorado	1994
Skillman, Gilbert L.	Asst	Wesleyan-CT	D	PHD	85	Michigan	1993
Skillman, Richard K.	C-Ac	W New Eng		MALD		Tufts	
Skinner, Gordon S.	Retir	Cincinnati		PHD	53	Wisconsin	
Skinner, Jonathan	Prof	Dartmouth		PHD	83	UCLA	1995
Skinner, Steven P.	Prof	Western Conn		PHD		Conn	
Skogstad, Samuel J.	VProf	Georgia St	EFO	PHD	65	Wash U	1994
Skoorka, Bruce	Prof	Yeshiva		PHD	92	NYU	
Skoro, Charles L.	Prof	Boise State	JBI	PHD	77	Columbia	1982
Skorr, Arlen J.	Prof	Mankato St	AE	PHD	70	Nebraska	1965
Skov, Iva L.	Prof	CS-Long Bch		PHD	76	S Calif	1972
Skurski, Roger B.	Prof	Notre Dame	P	PHD	70	Wisconsin	1974
Slate, Stephen T.	Asst	USAF Academy		PHD		Colorado	
Slattery, Edward	Asst	Alabama St		PHD	88	Colorado	1995
Slaughter, Matthew J.	Asst	Dartmouth		PHD	94	MIT	1994
Slay, Benjamin Harlow	Asst	Middlebury		PHD	89	Indiana	1994
Sleeman, Allan G.	Assoc	Western Wash	CD	PHD	83	Simon Fr	1977
Slemrod, Joel B.	Prof	Michigan		PHD	80	Harvard	1987
Slesnick, Daniel T.	Prof	Texas	CH	PHD	82	Harvard	9-82
Slesnick, Frank	Prof	Bellarmine		PHD	72		1975
Slice, Jerry Kibler	Assoc	Presbyterian		PHD		Miss St	1989
Sliger, Bernard F.	Prof	Florida St		PHD	55	Mich St	1972
Sloan, Frank A.	Prof	Duke		PHD	69	Harvard	1993
Alexander McMahon Professor							
Slotsve, George A.	Asst	Vanderbilt	JD	PHD	89	Wisconsin	1988
Slottje, Daniel J.	Assoc	So Methodist		PHD	83	Tx A&M	1989
Slutsky, Steven M.	Prof	Florida	DH	PHD	75	Yale	1984
Smale, Stephen	Prof	Cal-Berkeley		PHD		Michigan	
Small, Kenneth A.	Prof	Calif-Irvine		PHD	76	Berkeley	1983
Smallwood, Dennis	Retir	Ca-San Diego	7-94	PHD	70	Yale	1971
Smeeding, Timothy M.	Prof	Syracuse		PHD	75	Wisconsin	

Smiley, William G.	Prof	Marquette		PHD	73	Iowa	1973
Smith, Allen W.	Prof	E Illinois		PHD	70	Indiana	1970
Smith, Barton A.	Prof	Houston	ADR	PHD	74	Chicago	1973
Smith, Bernard	Assoc	Drew	HOP	PHD	82	Yale	1986
Smith, Bruce D.	Prof	Cornell		PHD	81	MIT	
Smith, Charles L.	Asst	Txs-El Paso		PHD		Tx Tech	1991
Smith, D. Stanton	Assoc	Wash State		PHD	69	Tx-Austin	1968
Smith, David	Prof	New Mex St		PHD	71	Nebraska	1970
Smith, Dean G.	Assoc	No Arizona	RH	PHD	85	Tx A&M	1989
Smith, Evelyn K.	Asst	West Tx A&M	ABJO	PHD	75	Tx A&M	1990
Smith, Galen	Assoc	Cedarville	ABFH	MS	68	Kansas St	1981
Smith, George	Prof	New York U	N	PHD	76	Harvard	1988
Smith, Gerald A.	Prof	Mankato St	AOQ	PHD	79	LSU	1979
Smith, Gordon W.	Prof	Rice		PHD	66	Harvard	1968
Smith, Harlan	Emer	Minnesota		PHD		Chicago	
Smith, James L.	Prof	Houston	DQ	PHD	77	Harvard	1983
Smith, Janet K.	Assoc	Arizona St		PHD	80	UCLA	1981
Smith, John Z.	Asst	Vassar	J	PHD		MIT	1993
Smith, Jon L.	C-Ac	East Tenn St		PHD	82	S Carol	1980
Smith, Kenneth L.	Prof	Pittsburg St	G	PHD		Ca-River	
Smith, Kenneth R.	Dean	Arizona		PHD	68	Northwes	1980
Smith, Larry J.	Assoc	WI-Green Bay		PHD		Chicago	
Smith, Lawrence C.	Prof	Louisiana Te		PHD	68	Miss	1970
Smith, Lewis	Prof	Mississippi	E	PHD	71	Tennessee	1971
Smith, Lones A.	Asst	MIT	D	PHD	91	Chicago	1991
Smith, Lynn A.	Assoc	Clarion		PHD		Pittsburgh	1989
Smith, Mark Griffin	Assoc	Colorado Col		PHD	87	Duke	1988
Smith, Pamela	Asst	Delaware	F	PHD	92	Wisconsin	1993
Smith, Patricia	Assoc	Mich-Dearbor	ACDH	PHD	86	Va Tech	1988
Smith, Paula	Assoc	Central Okla		PHD	84	Okla St	1987
Smith, Richard S.	H-As	Ark Tech		PHD	74	Tx-Austin	1991
Smith, Rodney T.	Assoc	Claremont		PHD	76	Chicago	1983
Smith, Ronald G. E.	Prof	CUNY-Hunter		DBA		LSU	
Smith, Russell E.	Assoc	Washburn		PHD	84	Illinois	1984
Smith, Solomon S.	D-Pr	Fisk	EGM	PHD	82	S Illinois	1988
Smith, Stanley K.	Prof	Florida	J	PHD	76	Michigan	1976
Smith, Stephen C.	Assoc	George Wash	O	PHD	83	Cornell	1983
Smith, Vardaman Russell	Assoc	Jms Madison	B	PHD	80	Penn St	1979
Smith, Vernon L.	Prof	Arizona		PHD	55	Harvard	1975
Regents' Professor							
Smith, W. James	Prof	Colo-Denver	E	PHD	76	Colorado	1989
Smith, William	Asst	Memphis		PHD	87	Virginia	1993
Smith, William Doyle	Assoc	Txs-El Paso		PHD	81	Tx Tech	1981
Smith, William Robert	Assoc	Geo Southern		MBA	72	Ga South	1973
Smitka, Michael J.	Assoc	Wash & Lee	FL	PHD	89	Yale	1986
Smolowitz, Ira E.	Prof	American Int		PHD	84	Rensselae	1988
Smyser, Michael	Asst	Southern		PHD		Fla Intl	1991
Smyth, David J.	Prof	Louisiana St	E	PHD	68	Birmgham	1987
LSU Foundation Professor of Economics							
Smyth, John W.	Retir	Youngstown		PHD	73	Nebraska	
Smythe, Donald J.	Asst	Tx-Arlington	BR	PHD	93	Yale	1992
Snoonian, Paul E.	Assoc	Mass-Lowell	EQ	PHD	71	Mich St	
Snow, Arthur	Assoc	Georgia	DH	PHD	79	Wisconsin	1989
Snow, Karl N.	Asst	Brigham Yg		PHD	91	Chicago	1995
Snow, Marcellus S.	Prof	Hawaii-Manoa		PHD	74	Berkeley	1974
Snow, Sandra L.	Prof	Wis-Whitewat		PHD	76	Missouri	1981
Snowbarger, Marvin R.	Prof	San Jose St		PHD	66	Michigan	1966
Snowden, Kenneth A.	Assoc	N Car-Greens		PHD	83	Wisconsin	1983
Snowden, Peter N.	SLect	U Lancaster		PHD		Leeds	
Snyder, Christopher	Asst	George Wash	L	PHD	94	MIT	1994
Snyder, Donald	Prof	CS-L Angeles		PHD	71	Penn St	1975
Snyder, Donald L.	H-Pr	Utah State	CQ	PHD	79	Utah St	1981
Snyder, Richard S.	Asst	No Kentucky		PHD	76	Indiana	1978
Snyder, Susan	Asst	Virg Tech	H				1995
Sobel, Joel	Prof	Ca-San Diego	D	PHD	78	Berkeley	1978
Sobel, Russell S.	Asst	W Virginia	H	PHD	94	Fla St	1994
Sockwell, William D.	Assoc	Berry		PHD	89	Vanderbilt	1988
Soderlind, Steven D.	Assoc	St Olaf	RA	PHD	80	Mass	1982
Sohng, Soong Nark	Prof	Clarion		PHD	82	Wayne St	1981
Sokoloff, Joel J.	Asst	Kentucky St	ACE	MA	67	Mass	1974
Sokoloff, Kenneth L.	Assoc	UCLA		PHD	82	Harvard	1980
Solar, Donald	Prof	Lg Isl-Post		PHD	63	Columbia	1965
Solberg, Eric J.	Prof	CS-Fullerton		PHD	74	Claremont	1973
Soligo, Ronald	Prof	Rice		PHD	64	Yale	1967
Soliman, Mostafa A.	Assoc	Prairie View		PHD	67	Iowa St	1971
Sollars, David L.	Assoc	Auburn-Montg	KHAE	PHD	91	Fla St	1990
Solomon, Elinor H.	Prof	George Wash	E	PHD	48	Harvard	1982
Solomon, Hassana	Asst	Tuskegee		PHD		Auburn	1993
Solomon, Henry	Prof	George Wash	I	PHD	59	NYU	
Solomon, Lynnette K.	Retir	S F Austin		PHD	70	Arkansas	1979

Name	Rank	Institution	Fields	Degree	Yr	Degree Inst	Since
Solon, Babette S.	Assoc	CUNY-Queens	DJ	PHD	58	MIT	1961
Solon, Gary R.	Prof	Michigan		PHD	83	Princeton	1983
Solow, John L.	Assoc	Iowa		PHD	83	Stanford	1981
Solow, Robert M.	Prof	MIT	E	PHD	51	Harvard	1958
Institute Professor							
Soltow, Allen R.	Assoc	Tulsa		PHD	69	Iowa St	1973
Somanathan, E.	Asst	Emory		ABD		Harvard	1995
Sommers, Paul M.	C-Pr	Middlebury		PHD	76	Ca-SnDgo	1976
Sondey, John A.	Asst	So Dakota St	H	PHD	89	Wash St	1990
Song, E. Young	Asst	Vanderbilt	FE	PHD	90	Harvard	1990
Song, Frank M.	Asst	Cleveland St	EG	PHD	91	Ohio St	1991
Song, Inbum	Retir	Louisville		PHD		Oklahoma	
Song, Kean P.	H-As	Prairie View		PHD	93	Houston	1988
Song, Shunfeng	Asst	Nevada-Reno		PHD	92	Ca-Irvine	1992
Song, Yoon K.	Prof	Detroit Merc		PHD	69	Illinois	1969
Songha, W. A.	Assoc	Cheyney					
Sonmez, Tayfon	Asst	Michigan		PHD	95		1995
Sonnenschein, Hugo F.	Prof	Chicago		PHD	64	Purdue	
Sonny, Jacob	Assoc	Dowling		PHD		New Sch	
Sonstegaard, Miles H.	Assoc	Arkansas	H	PHD	58	Oregon	1969
Sonstelie, Jon C.	C-Pr	Cal-Santa Br	HR	PHD	75	Northwes	1977
Sontheimer, Kevin C.	Assoc	Pittsburgh	D	PHD	69	Minnesota	1979
Soofi, Abdollah S.	Assoc	Wis-Plattev		PHD	81	Ca-River	1980
Soper, John C.	Prof	John Carroll	ENA	PHD	70	Mass	1982
Sopher, Barry	Assoc	Rutgers-N Br	D	PHD	88	Iowa	1987
Sorensen, Bent	Asst	Brown		PHD	91	Copenhag	
Sorensen, Duane L.	Assoc	Indiana St	R	MS	61	Iowa St	1968
Sorensen, Phillip E.	Prof	Florida St		PHD	66	Berkeley	1971
Sorensen, Robert L.	Prof	Mo-St Louis	KMAO	PHD	71	Va Tech	1970
Sorenson, Timothy L.	Asst	Seattle	MDF	PHD	91	Harvard	1991
Soriano, Beverly	Asst	Framingham		MS		Bentley	
Sorkin, Alan L.	C-Pr	MD-Baltim Co		PHD	66	J Hopkins	1974
Sorrentino, John A. Jr.	Assoc	Temple	Q	PHD	73	Purdue	1979
Sosin, H. Kim	C-Pr	Neb-Omaha	ECO	PHD	70	Nebraska	1970
Soskin, Mark D.	Assoc	Cen Florida	C	PHD	79	Penn St	1988
Sowell, Clifford	Prof	Berea		PHD	78	Georgia	1981
Sowell, Fallaw B.	Assoc	Carnegie Mel		PHD	86	Duke	1988
Spagat, Michael	Asst	Brown		PHD	88	Harvard	
Spagnolo, John A.	Assoc	Iona	R	PHD	82	Fordham	1978
Sparks, Donald L.	Assoc	Citadel		PHD	85	London	8-86
Sparks, John A.	C-Pr	Grove City		JD		Michigan	
Spatt, Chester S.	Prof	Carnegie Mel		PHD	79	Penn	1979
Spear, Stephen E.	H-Pr	Carnegie Mel		PHD		Penn	1982
Spears, Philip V.	Prof	Berea		PHD	71	Kentucky	1968
Spector, Lee C.	Assoc	Ball State		PHD	85	Iowa	1985
Speir, Edwin G.	Prof	Georgia Col		PHD		Denver	1981
Spellman, William E.	C-Pr	Coe		PHD	70	Kansas St	1970
George R. Baker Professor of Economics and Business Administration							
Spence, James G.	Assoc	South Fla		PHD	79	Oklahoma	1975
Spencer, Austin Harvey	Prof	W Carolina		PHD	72	Indiana	1980
Spencer, David E.	Prof	Brigham Yg		PHD	74	Tx A&M	1986
Spencer, Roger W.	Prof	Trinity		PHD	69	Virginia	1980
Spencer, Theresa	Assoc	Meredith		PHD		N Car St	1987
Speros, Jonathan A.	Asst	Framingham					
Speyrer, Janet F.	Assoc	New Orleans		PHD	82	J Hopkins	1987
Spilde, Roger H.	C-Pr	Concordia C		MA	58	Iowa	1958
Spiva, G. A. Jr.	Retir	Tennessee		PHD		Tx-Austin	
Spizman, Lawrence	Prof	SUNY Oswego		PHD	77	SUNY-Alb	1977
Spraberry, Hubert O.	Prof	Howard Payne		PHD	85	Tx Tech	1986
Sprenkle, Case	Prof	Illinois		PHD	60	Yale	1960
Sprinkle, Richard L.	Assoc	Txs-El Paso		PHD	82	Arkansas	1982
Sprunger, Philip W.	Asst	Lycoming	AJQ	PHD	93	Indiana	1993
Spurr, Stephen J.	Asst	Wayne State		PHD		Chicago	1987
Sraiheen, Abdulwahab	Assoc	Kutztown	CM	PHD	86	Penn St	1990
Sridharan, K. P.	Asst	Delta State	ACFG	PHD	92	Miss	8-92
Srinivasan, T. N.	Prof	Yale		PHD	62	Yale	1980
Srivastava, Sanjay	Prof	Carnegie Mel		PHD		MIT	1982
St. Clair, David J.	Prof	CS-Hayward		PHD	79	Utah	1979
Stachetti, Ennio	Assoc	Michigan		PHD	83	Wisconsin	1992
Staelin, Charles P.	Assoc	Smith	ACDK	PHD	71	Michigan	1981
Stafford, Frank P.	Prof	Michigan		PHD	68	Chicago	1974
Stageberg, Stephen P.	Assoc	Mary Wash	CFN	PHD	84	Geotown	1982
Stahl, Dale O.	Prof	Texas	DC	PHD	81	Berkeley	7-88
Staiger, Robert W.	Assoc	Wisconsin		PHD	85	Michigan	1993
Stair, Anthony G.	Asst	Frostburg St		PHD		W Virginia	
Staley, Samuel R.	Inst	Wright State		MS	87	Wright St	
Staller, George J.	Prof	Cornell		PHD	59	Cornell	1960
Stallings, Dale G.	Retir	CS-Pomona	1994	PHD	62	Minnesota	1964
Stanfield, James Ronald	Prof	Colorado St	BA	PHD	72	Oklahoma	1976

Stanford, Richard A.	Prof	Furman		PHD	71	Georgia	1968
David C Garrett Jr. Professor of Economics							
Stanford, William G.	Assoc	Ill-Chicago	C	PHD	84	Northwes	
Stanley, Tom D.	Assoc	Hendrix		PHD	82	Purdue	1986
Stano, Miron	Prof	Oakland	IL	PHD	71	Cornell	1977
Starkey, James L.	Prof	Rhode Island		PHD	71	Boston C	1967
Starleaf, Dennis R.	Prof	Iowa State	E	PHD	67	Vanderbilt	1963
Starr, Ross	Prof	Ca-San Diego	DE	PHD	72	Stanford	1980
Starrett, David A.	C-Pr	Stanford		PHD	68	Stanford	1973
Startz, Richard	Prof	U Washington		PHD	78	MIT	1984
Stauffer, Robert F.	Assoc	Roanoke		PHD	78	Va Tech	
Steagall, Jeffrey W.	Asst	North Fla		PHD	90	Wisconsin	1990
Steckel, Richard H.	Prof	Ohio State	N	PHD	77	Chicago	1977
Stecker, Albert	Assoc	Rhode Isl Cl		DBA		Indiana	
Steele, Gerald R.	Lect	U Lancaster		MA		Sheffield	
Steele, Henry B.	Prof	Houston		PHD		MIT	
Steen, Robert C.	Assoc	Rollins	RHN	PHD	82	Princeton	1987
Steen, Todd P.	Assoc	Hope	JT	PHD	93	Harvard	1988
Steger, Eric K.	Prof	East Central		PHD	80	La Tech	1970
Stegner, Tesa	Asst	Idaho State		PHD	89	Wash St	1992
Steib, Steve B.	Prof	Tulsa		PHD	72	Iowa St	1972
Steigerwald, Douglas G.	Asst	Cal-Santa Br	C	PHD	89	Berkeley	1988
Stein, Bruno	Prof	New York U		PHD	59	NYU	1959
Stein, Howard	Assoc	Roosevelt		PHD	83	Ca-River	1983
Stein, Jerome L.	Emer	Brown		PHD	55	Yale	1956
Stein, Sheldon H.	Assoc	Cleveland St	CER	PHD	78	J Hopkins	1976
Steinberg, Danny	Assoc	San Diego St		PHD	82	Harvard	1987
Steinberg, Ivan	Asst	Jersey City	LA	MA		New Sch	
Steindl, Frank G.	Prof	Oklahoma St		PHD	63	Iowa	1962
Regents' Professor and Ardmore Chair							
Steiner, Peter	Retir	Michigan					
Steinhauer, Larry	C-Pr	Albion		PHD	74	Chicago	1968
Steinkamp, Stanley W.	Emer	Illinois		PHD	58	Michigan	1958
Steinmeier, Thomas L.	Prof	Texas Tech		PHD	75	Yale	1982
Steinnes, Donald N.	Prof	Minn-Duluth	C	PHD	72	Northwes	1981
Stellern, Michael J.	Asst	Rockhurst		PHD	83	Arizona	1979
Stephan, Paula E.	Prof	Georgia St	JO	PHD	71	Michigan	1981
Stephens, Mark A.	Assoc	Tenn Tech		PHD	85	Tennessee	1980
Stephenson, James A.	Retir	Iowa State		PHD	65	Berkeley	1964
Stephenson, Kevin M.	Asst	Middlebury		PHD	92	Cornell	1992
Stephenson, Matthew A.	C-Pr	Wofford		PHD	65	Tulane	1970
T. B. Stackhouse Professor of Economics							
Sterbenz, Frederic P.	Assoc	Wyoming	EG	PHD	81	Penn	1981
Stern, Andrew	Prof	CS-Long Bch		PHD		Columbia	1967
Stern, Louis H.	Assoc	Houston	R	PHD	64	UCLA	1967
Stern, Robert M.	Prof	Michigan		PHD	58	Columbia	1961
Stern, Steven N.	Assoc	Virginia	JCI	PHD	85	Yale	1985
Stevens, David W.	Prof	Baltimore		PHD	65	Colorado	
Stevens, Sarah Allen	Assoc	St Lawrence	FE	PHD	88	J Hopkins	1984
Stevenson, Mary H.	Assoc	Mass-Boston	JI	PHD	74	Michigan	1972
Stevenson, Thomas M. Jr.	Prof	St Louis		PHD	64	Illinois	1965
Stewart, Douglas B.	Prof	San Diego St		PHD	70	Oregon	1971
Stewart, Douglas O.	Assoc	Cleveland St	DH	PHD	74	Michigan	1972
Stewart, John F.	Prof	No Carolina		PHD	76	Wisconsin	1975
Stewart, Milton D. Jr.	Assoc	S F Austin		PHD	72	Tx-Austin	1966
Sthman, Diane L.	Assoc	NE Illinois		PHD		Il-Chicago	
Stieber, Jack	Retir	Michigan St		PHD	56	Harvard	1956
Stifflemire, Paul F. Jr.	Asst	Wash & Jeff		MBA		Suffolk	1986
Stiglitz, Joseph E.	Prof	Stanford		PHD	86	MIT	
Stillwaggon, Eileen	Asst	Gettysburg	AFQ	PHD	79	America	1995
Stinchcombe, Maxwell B.	Assoc	Texas	DC	PHD	86	Berkeley	1-94
Stine, William F.	Prof	Clarion		PHD	83	Fordham	1981
Stirling, Kathleen J.	C-Ac	Puget Sound	AEIT	PHD	87	Notre Dm	
Stiroh, Kevin	Asst	Bentley	EO	PHD	95	Harvard	1995
Stith, John	Asst	Delaware St		PHD		Union	
Stitt, Kenneth	Inst	Grove City		MA		W Virginia	
Stober, William J.	Prof	Kentucky	D	PHD	65	Duke	1965
Stockhausers, Gerard L. S.J.	Assoc	Creighton	DF	PHD	85	Michigan	1985
Stockman, Alan C.	C-Pr	Rochester		PHD	78	Chicago	1979
Wilson Professor of Economics							
Stocks, Anthony H.	C-Pr	Youngstown		PHD	63	SUNY-Buf	1968
Stodder, James P.	Asst	Rensselaer		PHD		Yale	1990
Stoker, James	Asst	Kentucky	E	PHD	95	Chicago	1995
Stokes, Houston H.	Prof	Ill-Chicago	D	PHD	69	Chicago	1968
Stokey, Nancy	Prof	Chicago		PHD	78	Harvard	1990
Stoll, John R.	Prof	WI-Green Bay		PHD	80	Kentucky	
Stollar, Andrew J.	Assoc	Bentley	CFP	PHD	73	Boston C	1976
Stoller, Michael A.	Prof	SUNY-Plattsb	MK	PHD	77	Wash U	1975
Stolnitz, George J.	Retir	Indiana		PHD	52	Princeton	
Stolte, William F.	Prof	Berea		PHD	71	Syracuse	1970

Stone, Allan D.	Prof	SW Missouri		PHD	73	Oklahoma	1972
Stone, Courtney C.	Prof	Ball State		PHD	73	UCLA	1991
Stone, Gary L.	Prof	Winthrop		PHD	80	N Carol	9-75
Stone, Gerald W. Jr.	Emer	Metro St-CO		PHD		Rice	
Stone, Irving	Prof	CUNY-Baruch		PHD	62	Columbia	1962
Stone, Joe A.	Prof	Oregon	JFE	PHD	77	Mich St	1970
W. E. Miner Professor of Economics							
Stone, Leonie L.	Asst	SUNY-Geneseo	OD	PHD	93	Ohio St	1993
Stone, Richard G.	Assoc	Elizabethtwn		PHD		Temple	1987
Stonebraker, Robert J.	Prof	Indiana U-PA	EK	PHD	73	Princeton	1971
Story, Jonathan	Prof	INSEAD		PHD	73	J Hopkins	7-74
Stradley, Scot A.	Assoc	North Dakota		PHD		Utah	
Straight, Ronald L.	Lect	Howard		DBA	79	Geo Wash	1988
Strait, Roger H.	Asst	F Dick-Teane		STB		Harvard	
Strand, Larry D.	Dean$	Biola		MBA		S Calif	1986
Strand, Stephen H.	Prof	Carleton		PHD	76	Vanderbilt	1981
Strang, Daniel R.	Prof	SUNY-Geneseo	CQ	PHD	75	Cornell	1992
Strangways, Raymond S.	Prof	Old Dominion		PHD	66	Tulane	1962
Strasma, John D.	Prof	Wisconsin		PHD	60	Harvard	1966
Strassmann, W. Paul	Emer	Michigan St		PHD	56	Maryland	
Straszheim, Mahlon R.	C-Pr	Maryland		PHD	66	Harvard	
Stratmann, Thomas	Asst	Montana St		PHD	90	Maryland	1990
Stratton, Leslie A.	Asst	Arizona		PHD	89	MIT	1988
Stratton, Peter J.	Assoc	W Illinois	AD	PHD	70	N Illinois	1970
Stratton, Richard	Assoc	Akron	ADJ	PHD	77	Conn	1978
Straub, LaVonne	Assoc	W Illinois	AIJR	PHD	83	Utah	1982
Straub, Paul	Asst	Rio Grande		PHD	91	Illinois	1995
Strauss, Jack K.	Asst	St Louis		PHD		Duke	
Strauss, John	Prof	Michigan St		PHD	81	Mich St	1992
Strausser, Clark W.	Assoc	Pitts-Johnst	CG	PHD	70	Minnesota	1973
Street, Barbara P.	Prof	Chaminade	ACEI	PHD	86	Virginia	1981
Street, Donald R.	Retir	Auburn		PHD	65	Penn St	1965
Streeter, Lanny E.	Assoc	U Miami	C	PHD	70	Illinois	1967
Strein, Charles T.	Assoc	No Iowa		PHD	77	Illinois	1970
Strickland, Thomas H.	Assoc	Mid Tenn St		PHD	79	Oklahoma	1988
Stromsdorfer, Ernst W.	Prof	Wash State		PHD	62	Wash U	1983
Strong, Jerome C.	Retir	Hartwick		PHD		Columbia	1965
Stronge, William B.	Prof	Fla Atlantic		PHD	71	Iowa St	1971
Stroup, Mike		Naval Postgr					
Stroup, Richard L.	Prof	Montana St		PHD	70	U Wash	1969
Strumpf, Koleman	Asst	No Carolina		PHD	95	MIT	1995
Stuart, Charles	Prof	Cal-Santa Br	HKD	PHD	75	Lunds	1980
Stuart, Edward F.	Assoc	NE Illinois		PHD	78	Oklahoma	1986
Stuart, Edwin	Asst	SE Okla St	AG	JD	67	Florida	1992
Stuart, Iris C.	Asst	Concordia C		PHD		Iowa	1990
Stuart, Robert C.	Prof	Rutgers-N Br	P	PHD	69	Wisconsin	1968
Stubblebine, William Craig	Prof	Claremont		PHD	63	Virginia	1966
Studenmund, A. H.	C-Pr	Occidental	C	PHD	70	Cornell	1970
Richard W. Millar Professor of Economics & Director of Institutional Research							
Stuligross, John D.	Prof	Hartwick	AEGR	PHD	71	Oklahoma	1980
Stull, William J.	Prof	Temple	IR	PHD	72	MIT	1976
Sturgeon, James I.	Assoc	Mo-Kansas Ct	BO	PHD	74	Oklahoma	1977
Sturges, David M.	Asst	Colgate	EG	PHD	94	Yale	1995
Stutsman, A. Douglas	Emer	So Alabama	AB	PHD	70	Miss	1968
Su, Vincent	Prof	CUNY-Baruch		PHD	70	Rutgers	1971
Suarez, James M.	Dean	Manhattan		PHD	72	Columbia	1984
Sublette, Werner Johann	Prof	NE Missouri		PHD		Arizona	1974
Subramanin, Shankar	Asst	Cornell		PHD		Berkeley	
Sukar, Abdul Hamid	Asst	Cameron		PHDT		Tx Tech	1987
Sukhatme, Vasant A.	Assoc	Macalester	ADO	PHD	77	Chicago	1978
Edward John Noble Associate Professor of Economics							
Sula, Laddie J.	Prof	Loras		PHD	76	Geo St	1983
Suliman, Osman	Assoc	Grambling St		PHD	84	Indiana	1988
on leave to Millersville							
Sullivan, Dennis H.	Prof	Miami U-Ohio	HI	PHD	75	Princeton	1973
Sullivan, John J.	Prof	Hartford		PHD	67	Conn	
Sullivan, Kathryn	Asst	Westfield St		PHD		Mass	1992
Sullivan, Timothy	Inst	S Ill-Edward		ABD	95	Maryland	1995
Sullivan, Timothy	Asst	Towson State		PHD	87	Illinois	1989
Sulock, Joseph M.	Prof	N Car-Ashvil		PHD	76	Virginia	1975
Sulter, Mary	Lect	Mo-St Louis	A	MIEE		Delaware	
Sum, Andrew M.	Prof	Northeastern		MA	71	MIT	1971
Summary, Rebecca M.	C-Pr	SE Missouri	FA	PHD	83	Illinois	1983
Summers, Jeffrey A.	Asst	Linfield		PHD	87	Purdue	1992
Summers, Robert	Emer	Pennsylvania		PHD	56	Stanford	1959
Sumner, Glenna L.	Asst	Birminghm So		PHD	93	Oklahoma	1993
Sumner, Scott B.	Assoc	Bentley	EN	PHD	84	Chicago	1982
Sumpta, Sister Virginia A.	Assoc	Immaculata		MA		Catholic	
Sun, Emily M.	Prof	Manhattan		PHD	57	Michigan	1964
Sun, Li-teh	Prof	Moorhead St		PHD	72	Okla St	1982

Sundar, Cuddalore S.	Asst	SE Louisiana	ADGI	PHD	93	N Orleans	1993
Sundaram, Rangarajan K.	Asst	Rochester		PHD		Cornell	
Sundstrom, William A.	Assoc	Santa Clara		PHD	86	Stanford	1987
Sung, Jane C.	Assoc	NE Missouri		PHD	85	Wayne St	1987
Sung, Simona	Asst	St Rose		PHD			
Supel, Mary R.	Asst	St Thomas-MN	L	BA		Denison	1976
Suranovic, Steven M.	Assoc	George Wash	F	PHD	87	Cornell	1988
Surdam, David	Asst	Loyola-Chicg		PHD	94	Chicago	1994
Surdyk, Lisa	Asst	Seattle Pac	G	PHD	81	U Wash	1981
Sureshwaran, S.	Asst	So Carol St		PHD	89	Clemson	1990
Surette, Gerald M.	Assoc	SUNY-Cortlan		BA			
Susa, Robert	Assoc	Gannon		MA		Catholic	
Sussman, Jeffrey		SUNY-Empire	G	PHD		CUNY	1975
Suster, Zeljan	Assoc	New Haven		PHD		Yugoslav	
Sutch, Richard C.	Prof	Cal-Berkeley		PHD	68	MIT	1967
Sutliffe, James S.	Deces	SUNY-Potsdam		PHD		Fla St	
Sutton, James E.	Prof	CS-Pomona		BS	55	Wisconsin	1964
Sutton, Terry	Prof	SE Missouri		PHD		Kansas St	1972
Suwanakul, Sontachai	Assoc	Alabama St		PHD	86	Arkansas	1989
Suzawa, Gilbert S.	Assoc	Rhode Island		PHD	73	Brown	1971
Svejnar, Jan	Prof	Pittsburgh	J	PHD	79	Princeton	1987
Svorny, Shirley V.	Assoc	CS-Northrdge	IG	PHD	79	UCLA	1978
Swaine, David W.	Assoc	Andrews	CD	PHD		Notre Dm	1978
Swaine, Howard R.	H-Pr	No Michigan	AKDH	PHD	65	UCLA	1966
Swamy, Anand V.	Asst	Maryland		PHD	93	Northwes	1993
Swan, Craig E.	C-Pr	Minnesota		PHD	70	Yale	1969
Swaney, James A.	Prof	Wright State		PHD	79	Colo St	
Swanke, Thomas A.	Asst	W Virg St	AEJO	PHD	93	Colorado	1993
Swanson, Charles	Asst	Temple	E	PHD	91	Minnesota	1993
Swanson, Gerald	Assoc	Arizona		PHD	72	Illinois	1970
Swanson, James A.	Assoc	Cen Missouri		PHD	87	Wash St	1986
Swanson, Paul	Assoc	Wm Patterson		PHD		Columbia	1982
Swartz, Thomas R.	Prof	Notre Dame	HA	PHD	65	Indiana	1965
Sweeney, George H.	Assoc	Vanderbilt	DL	PHD	77	Northwes	1976
Sweeney, Vernon E.	Prof	Sam Houston		PHD	68	Tx-Austin	1971
Sweeney, William B. Jr.	Prof	Bryant	AE	PHD	73	Sarasota	
Sweetser, Wendell E. Jr.	Asst	Marshall		PHD	79	Va Tech	1977
Swenson, Deborah	Asst	Cal-Davis	FH	PHD	91	MIT	1993
Swift, William J.	Prof	Pace		PHD	69	Wash U	1966
Swint, Kenneth J.	Asst	Wash & Jeff		PHD	89	Pittsburgh	1988
Swinton, John	Asst	South Fla	Q	ABD		Wisconsin	1995
Swofford, James L.	C-Pr	So Alabama	E	PHD	81	Florida	1984
Sylla, Richard	Prof	New York U	DN	PHD	69	Harvard	1990
Henry Kaufman Professor of the History of Financial Institutions & Markets							
Sylvester, Patrick J.	Prof	West Chester		PHD	73	Bryn Mawr	
Sylvester, Roger A.	Inst	Wright State		MS	87	Wright St	
Synn, Kyung-Hi	Prof	Liberty		PHD		Ohio St	1989
Syropoulos, C.	Asst	Penn State	F	PHD	89	Yale	1988
Tabarrok, Alexander	Asst	Ball State		PHD		Geo Mason	1994
Tabb, William K.	Prof	CUNY-Queens	RO	PHD	68	Wisconsin	1971
Taber, Alex	Asst	U Miami	CE	ABD		Chicago	1994
Taber, Christopher	Asst	Northwestern		PHD	95	Chicago	1995
Tabesh, Hamid	Asst	Wis-Rvr Fall		PHD	87	Iowa St	1988
Tabriztchi, Sireusse	Assoc	SUNY Old Wes		PHD		Columbia	
Tacker, Thomas L.		Embry-Riddle		PHD		N Carol	
Taga, Leonore S.	Assoc	Rider		PHD	79	Berkeley	1986
Tailby, Don	Assoc	New Mexico	ABNO	PHD	61	Rutgers	1967
Taira, Koji	Prof	Illinois		PHD	61	Stanford	1970
Takacs, Wendy E.	Assoc	MD-Baltim Co		PHD	76	J Hopkins	1981
Takayama, Akira	Prof	So Illinois	FEDC	PHD	62	Rochester	1983
Vandeveer Chair of Economics							
Takeyama, Lisa N.	Asst	Amherst	ADL	PHD	92	Stanford	1994
Talarico, Joseph F.	Prof	Rider	F	PHD	58	Rutgers	1967
Talbert, Lonnie E.	Prof	Arkansas St	AQMT	PHD	64	N Car St	1966
Talley, Wayne K.	Prof	Old Dominion		PHD	72	Kentucky	1972
Eminent Professor							
Talmers, William N.	Adj	Molloy		PHD	54	MIT	1979
Tam, Mo-Yin S.	Prof	Ill-Chicago	P	PHD	74	SUNY-SBr	1974
Tamura, Robert F.	Asst	Iowa		PHD	88	Chicago	1988
Tan, Chin	Assoc	Cumberland		MBA	88	Tn Tech	1988
Tandon, Kishore	Assoc	CUNY-Baruch		PHD	80	Pittsburgh	
Tandon, Pankaj	Assoc	Boston Univ	DO	PHD	79	Harvard	1978
Tang, Gloria	Assoc	Salve Regina	COT	PHD	94	Walden	1986
Tangri, Shanti S.	Prof	Rutgers-N Br	O	PHD	61	Berkeley	1970
Tank, Frederick E.	Assoc	Toledo		PHD		Wayne St	1970
Tannen, Michael B.	Prof	Univ of D C	JIEA	PHD	74	Brown	1982
Tanner, Evan C.	Asst	U Miami	FE	PHD	88	UCLA	1989
Tanner, J. Ernest	Prof	Tulane		PHD	68	Brown	1971
Tannery, Frederick J.	C-Ac	Slippery Roc		PHD	80	Pittsburgh	1981
Tansey, Francis B.	Lect	CUNY-Baruch		MBA	65	CUNY	

Tansey, Michael M.	Prof	Rockhurst		PHD	78	Wisconsin	1982
Tanski, Janet M.	Assoc	New Mex St		PHD	91	SUNY-Buf	1989
Tarascio, Vincent J.	Prof	No Carolina		PHD	66	Rice	1964
Tarhouni, Ali	SLect	U Washington		PHD	84	Mich St	1985
Tarpley, Fred A. Jr.	Prof	Georgia Tech	D	PHD	67	Tulane	1962
Tarullo, P. Ronald	Prof	Calif U-Penn		PHD		Pittsburgh	1978
Taub, Allan J.	Assoc	Cleveland St	CD	PHD	73	Northwes	1971
Taub, Bart	Assoc	Illinois		PHD	81	Chicago	1989
Taube, Paul M.	Assoc	Tx-Pan Amer		PHD	86	SUNY-Alb	1988
Tauber, Linda	Asst	CUNY-Lehman		MBA			
Tauchen, George	Prof	Duke		PHD	78	Minnesota	1977
Tauchen, Helen	Prof	No Carolina		PHD	77	Minnesota	1977
Tauman, Yair	Prof	SUNY-Stony B		PHD	79	Hebrew U	1989
Taussig, Michael K.	Prof	Rutgers-N Br	H	PHD	66	MIT	1967
Taylor, Addis C.	C-Ac	Florida A&M	JM	PHD	83	Fla St	1976
Taylor, Alan	Asst	Northwestern		PHD	93	Harvard	
Taylor, Curtis	Asst	Texas A&M		PHD	92	Yale	1992
Taylor, Donald C.	Prof	So Dakota St	O	PHD	65	Minnesota	1980
Taylor, James	Prof	U Lancaster		PHD		Lancaster	
Taylor, John B.	Prof	Stanford		PHD	73	Stanford	
Taylor, Kenna C.	Assoc	Rollins		PHD	79	Florida	1974
Taylor, Kenneth B.	C-As	Villanova		PHD	80	SUNY-SBr	1985
Taylor, Larry W.	Assoc	Lehigh	CE	PHD	84	N Carol	1984
Taylor, Leon E.	Asst	Tulane		PHD		Maryland	
Taylor, Lester D.	Prof	Arizona		PHD	63	Harvard	1972
Taylor, Millicent	Assoc	Carson-Newmn	DFC	PHD		Tennessee	8-95
Taylor, Patrick A.	C-Ac	Millsaps	AD	PHD	84	Alabama	1984
Taylor, Peter M.	Prof	USAF Academy		PHD		Maryland	
Taylor, Susan W.	Asst	Millsaps	AFH	PHD	89	LSU	1992
Taylor, Wagiha A.	Prof	Wilkes	EF	PHD	66	Clark	1969
Tchakerian, Viken	Asst	CS-Northrdge	N	PHD	91	UCLA	1991
Teeples, Ronald K.	C-Pr	Claremont		PHD		UCLA	1969
Teferra, Daniel	Prof	Ferris State		PHD	79	Wisconsin	1980
Tellew, Fuad H.	Retir	Cal Poly-SLO		PHD	59	S Calif	1960
Telmer, Chris I.	Asst	Carnegie Mel		PHD	92	Queen's	1992
Telser, Lester G.	Prof	Chicago		PHD	56	Chicago	1958
Temin, Peter	Prof	MIT	N	PHD	64	MIT	1965
Elish Gray II Professor							
Temple, Frederick C.	Retir	Southern		PHD		Wisconsin	1950
Temple, Judy A.	Asst	No Illinois		PHD	90	Mich St	
Tenenbaum, Marcel	C-Ac	Hofstra		PHD	69	Columbia	1964
Tenney, Curtis G.	Asst	USAF Academy		ABD		Okla St	
Terasawa, Katchan		Naval Postgr		PHD	72	Kansas	1972
Terkla, David G.	C-Pr	Mass-Boston	QRHL	PHD	79	Berkeley	1987
Terrebonne, Peter	Inst	Georgia St	A	PHD	92	Emory	1992
Terregrossa, Ralph A.	Asst	St John's		PHD		SUNY-Bin	
Terrell, Milton	Asst	Kansas State	CEH	PHD	91	Duke	1991
Terrell, William T.	Assoc	Wichita St		PHD	70	Vanderbilt	1967
Terry, Andy	Assoc	Ark-Ltl Rock		PHD	89	Michigan	1989
Terza, Joseph V.	Assoc	Penn State	C	PHD	81	Pittsburgh	1986
Tesar, Linda L.	Asst	Cal-Santa Br	FGE	PHD	90	Rochester	1990
Tesfatsion, Leigh S.	Prof	Iowa State	E	PHD	75	Minnesota	1990
Thakur, Rita	Prof	LaVerne		MBA		NW Mo St	1978
Thanawala, Kishor H.	Prof	Villanova		PHD	61	Bombay	1967
Thanh, Pham Chi	Prof	American U		PHD		NS Wales	1976
Tharp, Charles	Lect	Oberlin	M	MA	80	Oxford	1989
Thaver, Ranjini L.	Asst	Stetson	AHP	PHD	95	Notre Dm	1992
Thayer, Mark A.	Prof	San Diego St		PHD		New Mex	1981
Theilman, Ward	Assoc	New Haven		PHD		Illinois	
Thewell, Raphael R.	Retir	Howard		PHD		Geo Wash	
Thiagarajan, Kuttalam R.	Asst	Prairie View		MA	55	Annamali	1967
Thierfelder, Karen	Asst	USN Academy		PHD	92	Wisconsin	1992
Thilmany, Dawn	Asst	Utah State	FGOQ	PHD	94	Ca-Davis	1994
Thimester, Renate	Assoc	Loyola Marym	ABKM	PHD	67	Alabama	1971
Thistle, Paul D.	Prof	W Michigan	D	PHD	83	Tx A&M	1992
Thoma, George A. Jr.	Prof	Elmhurst		PHD	73	N Illinois	1970
Thoma, Mark A.	Assoc	Oregon	E	PHD	85	Wash St	1987
Thomadakis, Stavros B.	Prof	CUNY-Baruch		PHD	74	MIT	1974
Thomas, Christopher R.	Assoc	South Fla	L	PHD	80	Tx A&M	1982
Thomas, George		Naval Postgr					
Thomas, Hugh A.	Asst	McMaster U	G	PHD	91	NYU	1991
Thomas, Janet M.	Assoc	Bentley	DHQ	PHD	87	Boston C	1987
Thomas, Johnny	Asst	LaSierra	C	MBA	88	LomaLinda	1989
Thomas, Lloyd R. Jr.	Prof	Kansas State	EA	PHD	70	Northwes	1968
Thomas, Mark	Asst	Geneva	ABN	ABD	95	Mich St	8-94
Thomas, Oommen	Asst	Westfield St		MBA		W NewEng	1980
Thomas, Philip S.	Prof	Kalamazoo	FO	PHD	61	Michigan	1965
Thomas, Ravi	Asst	Temple	H	PHD	88	Berkeley	1989
Thomas, Regina	Inst	No Alabama		MA	92	Alabama	1992
Thomas, Robert P.	Assoc	U Washington		PHD	64	Northwes	1968

Name	Rank	Institution	Fields	Degree	Yr	Degree Institution	Year
Thomas, Robert W. Jr.	Deces	Iowa State	1994	PHD	62	Iowa St	1957
Thomas, Wade L.	Assoc	SUNY-Oneonta	DE	PHD	82	Nebraska	1989
Thomas, William	Assoc	Gustavus Ado		PHD	85	N Carol	1991
Thomas, William J.	Deces			PHD	57	Mich St	
Thomasson, Henry E.	Asst	SE Louisiana	AJ	MS		LSU	
Thompson, Alexander M.	Prof	Vassar	BH	PHD	79	Stanford	1977
Thompson, Allen R.	Assoc	New Hampshir	GM	PHD	73	Tx-Austin	1974
Thompson, Charles L.	Asst	Troy State		MS	82	Auburn	1984
Thompson, Earl A.	Prof	UCLA		PHD	61	Harvard	1965
Thompson, Frank W.	Lect	Michigan		PHD	73	Harvard	1990
Thompson, G. Richard	Prof	Clemson	HLM	PHD	72	Virginia	
Thompson, Gerald E.	Prof	Nebraska		PHD	53	Iowa	1954
Thompson, Henry L.	Prof	Auburn		PHD	81	Houston	1987
Thompson, Mark	Asst	Marshall		PHD	94	Geo St	1994
Thompson, Mary M.	Asst	Belmont		MA		Notre Dm	1983
Thompson, Paul	Prof	Jacksonvl St		PHD		Duke	1974
Thompson, Paul J.	Prof	Mankato St	AI	PHD	68	Iowa	1963
Thompson, Philip B.	VAsst	Mo-Rolla		PHD	88	Arizona	1994
Thompson, William F.	Prof	E Illinois		PHD	79	Arkansas	1981
Thomson, Ross	C-Ac	Vermont	NDB	PHD	76	Yale	1991
Thomson, William L.	Prof	Rochester		PHD		Stanford	
Thorbecke, Erik	Prof	Cornell		PHD	57	Berkeley	1974
H. Edward Babcock Professor of Economics and Food Economics							
Thorbecke, Willem	Asst	George Mason		PHD	88	Berkeley	
Thorne, Emanuel D.	Asst	CUNY-Brookly	A	PHD		Yale	1994
Thornton, James	Assoc	E Michigan		PHD	91	Oregon	1991
Thornton, James R.	Assoc	Delaware	P	PHD	74	Cornell	1973
Thornton, Judith Ann	Prof	U Washington		PHD	66	Radcliff	1961
Thornton, Mark	Asst	Auburn		PHD	89	Auburn	
Thornton, Richard M.	Emer	DePaul		PHD	76	N Illinois	1974
Thornton, Robert J.	Prof	Lehigh	JI	PHD	70	Illinois	1970
Charles W. MacFarlane Professor of Economics							
Thornton, Saranna	Asst	Colby	FEA	PHD	89	Car Mellon	1989
Thorsnes, Paul E.	Asst	Grand Valley		PHD	94	Oregon	1995
Thorson, Douglas Y.	Prof	Bradley		PHD	62	Wisconsin	1960
Thorson, James A.	Asst	So Conn St		PHD	91	Il-Chicago	1992
Throckmorton, H. Bruce	Prof	Tenn Tech		PHD	72	Arkansas	1971
Thurman, Walter N.	Prof	N Carol St	QCD	PHD	84	Chicago	1984
Thurow, Lester C.	Prof	MIT		PHD	64	Harvard	1968
Gordon Y. Billard Professor of Economics and Mgt; on leave							
Thursby, Jerry G.	H-Pr	Purdue		PHD	75	N Carol	1988
Thursby, Marie C.	Prof	Purdue		PHD	74	N Carol	1988
Burton D. Morgan Chair of Private Enterprise							
Thurston, Norman	Asst	Brigham Yg					1995
Thurston, Thom B.	Prof	CUNY-Queens	EC	PHD	70	Berkeley	1971
Thweatt, William O.	Retir	Vanderbilt		BPHI	55	Oxford	1963
Tian, Guoqiang	Prof	Texas A&M		PHD	87	Minnesota	1987
Tideman, T. Nicolaus	Prof	Virg Tech	H	PHD	69	Chicago	1975
Tiefenthaler, Jill M.	Asst	Colgate	TO	PHD	91	Duke	1991
Tiemann, Thomas K.	Prof	Elon	RC	PHD	75	Vanderbilt	1984
Tiemstra, John P.	Prof	Calvin		PHD	75	MIT	1975
Tieslau, Margie	Asst	North Texas		PHD	92	Mich St	1992
Tietenberg, Thomas H.	Prof	Colby	QK	PHD	71	Wisconsin	1977
Mitchell Family Professor of Economics							
Tiffany, Frederick G.	Asst	Wittenberg		PHD	88	Penn	1987
Timmer, C. Peter	Prof	Harvard		PHD	69	Harvard	1980
Thomas D. Cabot Professor of Development Studies							
Timmerman, Allan	Asst	Ca-San Diego	CG	PHD	92	Cambridg	1994
Timothy, Darren P.	Asst	Brigham Yg					1995
Tinari, Frank D.	Prof	Seton Hall		PHD	76	Fordham	
Tinkler, Sarah E.	Assoc	Weber State	AF	PHD	89	Oregon	1988
Tirole, Jean	VProf	MIT	O	PHD	81	MIT	1984
Tirzner, Israel M.	Prof	New York U		PHD	57	NYU	
Titus, Varkey K.	C-Ac	Emporia St		PHD	80	Wash St	8-79
Tiwari, Kashi N.	Assoc	Kennesaw St	CEG	PHD	81	So Meth	1988
Tix, Paul	Asst	Mankato St	AC	MS		N Dak St	1984
Toda, Yasushi	Assoc	Florida	RP	PHD	69	Harvard	1974
Todd, Edward		SUNY-Empire	A	PHD		Chicago	1985
Tokar, Bette L.	Assoc	Holy Family		EDD	93	Temple	
Tokle, Robert J.	Asst	Idaho State		PHD	86	Iowa St	1986
Tolin, Thomas	Asst	West Chester	JD	PHD	92	Houston	1992
Tollen, Robert D.	Assoc	Txs-El Paso		PHD		Tx-Austin	1972
Tolley, George S.	Prof	Chicago		PHD	55	Chicago	1966
Tollison, Robert	Prof	George Mason		PHD	69	Virginia	
Duncan Black Professor of Economics							
Tolliver, R. Wayne	C-Pr	Berea		DBA	87	Kentucky	1975
Tolpin, Harriet G.	Prof	Simmons	I	PHD	73	Boston C	1974
Toma, Eugenia F.	Prof	Kentucky	H	PHD	77	Va Tech	1977
Toma, Mark	Assoc	Kentucky	E	PHD	51	Va Tech	1989
Tomal, Anette	Asst	Wheaton-IL	AIM	PHD		Illinois	1995

Name	Rank	Institution	Field	Degree	Yr	Degree School	Year
Tomaska, John A.	Prof	CS-L Angeles		PHD	68	U Wash	1965
Tombe, Wani Luan	Asst	St Edwards		PHD	85	Tx-Austin	1990
Tomer, John F.	Assoc	Manhattan		PHD	73	Rutgers	1983
Tomic, Igor M.	Assoc	St John's		PHD		CUNY	
Tompkins, Daniel L.	Asst	Findlay	G	PHD		Kentucky	1994
Tonn, Victor Lux	Assoc	Salve Regina	CFGO	PHD	84	Utah St	1984
Tontar, Charles F.	Assoc	Merrimack		MA		New Sch	
Tontz, Jay L.	Dean	CS-Hayward		PHD	66	N Carol	9-69
Toporovsky, Rinaldo	Prof	F Dick-Teane		PHD	72	Columbia	1969
Topping, Elizabeth E.	Asst	SW Missouri		PHD	85	Missouri	1979
Topyan, Kudret	Asst	Manhattan		PHD		CUNY	1991
Tori, Cynthia R.	Asst	N Car-Charl		PHD	93	Kentucky	1993
Toruno, Mayo C.	C-Ac	CS-San Bern		PHD	85	Ca-River	1983
Tosh, Dennis S.	Assoc	Mississippi		PHD	80	Geo St	1980
Toumanoff, Peter	Assoc	Marquette					1995
Tourk, Khairy A.	Assoc	Illinois Tch		PHD		Berkeley	
Tower, Edward	Prof	Duke		PHD	71	Harvard	1974
Townsend, David C.	Prof	Sam Houston		PHD	53	LSU	1982
Townsend, Lizzie Waller	Asst	Delaware St		MBA		Atlanta	
Townsend, Ralph E.	Prof	Maine	CHQA	PHD	83	Wisconsin	1980
Townsend, Robert M.	Prof	Chicago		PHD	75	Minnesota	1985
Tracy, Ronald L.	Assoc	Oakland	CE	PHD	75	Mich St	1983
Tracy, William T.	Assoc	St Ambrose		EDD		Marquette	1979
Tran, Dang	Assoc	CS-L Angeles		PHD	77	Syracuse	1987
Trandel, Gregory A.	Assoc	Georgia	GK	PHD	92	Princeton	1989
Travis, Karen	Lect	Pacific Luth	CFI	ABD		U Wash	1995
Traynham, Earle C. Jr.	Dean	North Fla		PHD	73	S Carol	1973
Traynor, Thomas L.	Assoc	Wright State		PHD	88	Purdue	1988
Treacy, John J.	Retir	Wright State		PHD	64	Tulane	1967
Trebing, Harry M.	Retir	Michigan St		PHD	58	Wisconsin	1966
Trees, W. Scott	Asst	Siena		PHD		Notre Dm	
Tregarthen, Timothy D.	Prof	Colorado Spr	DEHR	PHD	72	Ca-Davis	1971
Treglia, Michael	Asst	Miami U-Ohio	CD	PHD	89	Penn St	1991
Trejo, Stephen J.	Assoc	Cal-Santa Br	J	PHD	88	Chicago	1987
Trejos, Alberto	Asst	Northwestern		PHD	94	Penn	
Tremblay, Carol	Asst	Oregon State	CJ	PHD	84	Wash St	9-92
Tremblay, Victor J.	C-Pr	Oregon State	DLC	PHD	83	Wash St	9-90
Treml, Vladimir G.	Prof	Duke		PHD	63	N Carol	1967
Trenary, Roger C.	Inst	Kansas State	A	MA	72	Wayne St	1977
Tresch, Richard W.	C-Ac	Boston Coll	H	PHD	73	MIT	1969
Trescott, Paul B.	Prof	So Illinois	EB	PHD	54	Princeton	1976
Trethewey, Richard L.	Assoc	Kenyon		PHD	71	U Wash	1969
Treyz, George I.	Retir	Massachusett	1995	PHD	67	Cornell	1969
Tribble, John A.	Assoc	Russell Sage		PHD	75	Utah St	1976
Trierweiler, John	C-Pr	Northern St		PHD	70	Nebraska	1985
Triest, Robert K.	Assoc	Cal-Davis	HI	PHD	87	Wisconsin	1988
Trimby, F. Stephen	Assoc	Worcester St		MA	69	Clark	1970
Trimm, John M.	Deces			PHD	67	Mich St	
Trivedi, Pravin K.	Prof	Indiana		PHD	70	LondonEc	1987
Trost, Alice	Asst	Mass-Boston	R	PHD	94	SUNY-Bin	1992
Trost, Robert P.	Prof	George Wash	C	PHD	77	Florida	1981
Trostle, Randolph L.	C-Ac	Elizabethtwn		PHD	83	Lehigh	9-72
Troub, Roger M.	Prof	Texas Tech		PHD	68	Oklahoma	1967
Troy, Leo	Prof	Rutgers-Newk		PHD	58	Columbia	
Troyer, Michael D.	Assoc	WI-Green Bay		PHD		Duke	
Trudeau, Gregory P.	H-Ac	Wis-Superior	Atg	MBA		StThomas	1988
Truett, Dale B.	Prof	Tx-S Antonio	DFMO	PHD	67	Tx-Austin	1973
Truitt, W. James	C-Pr	Baylor		PHD	68	Illinois	1968
Herman W. Lay Prof Private Enterprise, & Director Cntr/Priv Entrp							
Trulove, William T.	Prof	East Wash		PHD		Oregon	1969
Trumbull, William N.	C-Ac	W Virginia	HKD	PHD	85	N Carol	1983
Truscott, Michael Hugh	C-Pr	Tampa	AEF	PHD	71	LSU	1971
Trussell, T. James	Prof	Princeton					
Trussler, Susan	Assoc	Scranton		PHD		Penn St	1985
Tryon, Joseph L.	Assoc	Georgetown		PHD		Harvard	
Tsai, Mau-Sung	Prof	Evansville		PHD	66	S Illinois	1964
Tschirhart, John T.	Prof	Wyoming	DK	PHD	75	Purdue	1985
Tseng, Hui-Kuan	Assoc	N Car-Charl		PHD	88	Illinois	1988
Tseng, S. C.	Prof	Catawba		PHD		Oklahoma	
Tsiang, Grace	SLect	Chicago		PHD	91	Chicago	1990
Tsiritakes, Emmuanuel	Assoc	Miss State		PHD	87	Va Tech	1986
Tsoulouhas, Theofanis	Asst	N Carol St	CD	PHD	93	Illinois	1993
Tsurumi, Hiroki	Prof	Rutgers-N Br	C	PHD	67	Penn	1974
Tu, Yien-I	Prof	Arkansas	C	PHD	61	Iowa St	1981
Tuchscherer, Thomas H.	Prof	Portland St		PHD	73	Northwes	1966
Tuck, Bradford H.	Dean	Alaska-Ancho	CDL	PHD	73	Boston U	1977
Tucker, Dean	C-Ac	Ogelthorpe	HMQ	PHD	79	Mich St	1-88
Rikard Chaired Professor							
Tucker, Irvin Burchard III	Assoc	N Car-Charl		PHD		S Carol	1981
Tuckman, Howard P.	Dean	Virg Comm		PHD	70	Wisconsin	1993

Name	Rank	Institution	Fields	Degree	Yr	Degree Inst	Since
Tuerck, David G.	C-Pr	Suffolk		PHD	66	Virginia	1982
Tufte, David R.	Asst	New Orleans		PHD	92	SUNY-Buf	1992
Tullock, Gordon	Prof	Arizona		JD	47	Chicago	1987
Tuma, Elias H.	Emer	Cal-Davis	ANO	PHD	62	Berkeley	1967
Turay, Abdul M.	Prof	S Ill-Edward		PHD	78	Oklahoma	1995
Turchi, Boone A.	Assoc	No Carolina		PHD	73	Michigan	1971
Turek, Joseph H.	Assoc	Lynchburg		PHD	87	SUNY-Alb	1986
Turk, Michael	Assoc	Fitchburg St		PHD		Harvard	1982
Turnbull, Geoffrey K.	Prof	Louisiana St	DH	PHD	83	Wi-Milw	1984
CJ Brown Distinguished Professor of Real Estate							
Turner, Charlie G.	Assoc	Old Dominion		PHD	81	Harvard	1984
Turner, Keith K.	Prof	Neb-Omaha	EM	PHD	68	Nebraska	1969
Turner, Robert W.	C-Ac	Colgate	CH	PHD	84	MIT	1983
Turnovsky, Michelle H. L.	SLect	U Washington		PHD	78	Aust Nat	1987
Turnovsky, Stephen J.	C-Pr	U Washington		PHD	68	Harvard	1987
Turunen-Red, Arja H.	Assoc	New Orleans		PHD	85	Brit Col	1995
Tussing, A. Dale	Prof	Syracuse		PHD	64	Syracuse	1966
Tutterow, Roger C.	Asst	Kennesaw St	ACDM	PHD	90	Geo St	1991
Twedt, Ronald	Asst	Concordia C		MBT		Minnesota	1991
Twight, Charlotte	C-Pr	Boise State		PHD	83	U Wash	1986
Twomey, Michael J.	Prof	Mich-Dearbor	AEFO	PHD	73	Cornell	1977
Tybout, James R.	Prof	Georgetown		PHD	80	Wisconsin	1980
Tye, Duncan Rene	Assoc	W Carolina		PHD	74	Tulane	1977
Tyler, Thomas P.	Dean	Ark Tech		PHD	80	Arkansas	1967
Tyson, Laura D.	Prof	Cal-Berkeley		PHD	74	MIT	1977
Tzannetakis, George	C-Pr	Seton Hall		PHD	64	NYU	
Udis, Bernard	Prof	Colorado		PHD	59	Princeton	1965
Udry, Christopher R.	Asst	Northwestern		PHD	91	Yale	1990
Ukpolo, Victor	Assoc	Austin Peay	FO	PHD	85	American	1988
Ulbrich, Holley H.	Prof	Clemson	HIR	PHD	69	Conn	1967
Alumni Professor							
Ulen, Thomas	Prof	Illinois		PHD	79	Stanford	1977
Ullah, Aman	Prof	Cal-Riversid	C	PHD	71	Delhi	1989
Ullerich, Stan	Assoc	Buena Vista		PHD		Purdue	9-95
Ulveling, Edwin F.	Prof	Georgia St	AO	PHD	81	Iowa St	1967
Umbeck, John R.	Prof	Purdue		PHD	76	U Wash	1975
Unger, Kay C.	Prof	Montana	IDEC	PHD		J Hopkins	
Upadhyaya, Kamal	Lect	Salisbury St		PHD	93	Auburn	1993
Upchurch, Leo	Assoc	Tuskegee		PHD	82	Michigan	1990
Uppal, Jamshed Y.	Asst	Catholic		PHD			
Uppal, Joginder S.	Prof	SUNY-Albany	OH	PHD		Minnesota	
Upton, Charles W.	Prof	Kent State	EQ	PHD	69	Car Mellon	8-89
Ureta, Manuelita	Assoc	Texas A&M		PHD	87	Berkeley	1991
Urquhart, Robert	Asst	Denver		PHD		New Sch	
Uselding, Paul J.	Dean	Ill-Chicago	N	PHD	70	Northwes	1992
Usip, Ebenge E.	Assoc	Youngstown		PHD	84	Conn	1985
Uyar, Bulent	Assoc	No Iowa		PHD	77	Pittsburgh	1991
Uze, Barry A.		Troy State		MA	85	Miss	1989
Vachris, Michelle A.	Asst	Chris Newpor	DFHK	PHD	92	Geo Mason	1994
Vafaie, Massie	Asst	Cen St-Ohio		PHD		Cincinnati	
Vahaly, John	Assoc	Louisville		PHD	75	Vanderbilt	1975
Vahid, Farshid	Asst	Texas A&M		PHD	93		1993
Vaidya, Ashish K.	Asst	CS-L Angeles		PHD	90	Ca-Davis	1991
Vail, David Jeremiah	Prof	Bowdoin	OQ	PHD		Yale	1970
Adams-Catlin Professor of Economics							
Vaitheswaran, Ramakrishna	Prof	Coe		PHD	77	Iowa St	1973
Elnora H. and William B. Quarton Professor of Business Admin. and Economics							
Valencia, Jesus M.	Asst	Slippery Roc		PHD	88	Pittsburgh	1983
Valentine, Lloyd M.	Retir	Cincinnati		MA	51	UCLA	1954
Valentine, Martha	D-As	Regis-CO					
Valentine, Ted	Assoc	CS-Chico		PHD		Illinois	1990
Valentino, Salvatore	Retir	Creighton	A	PHD	54	Nebraska	1961
Valimaki, Juuso	Asst	Northwestern		PHD	95	Penn	1995
Valinezhad, Moosa	Assoc	W Kentucky	FE	PHD	88	Geo St	1988
Valletta, Robert G.	Asst	Calif-Irvine		PHD	87	Harvard	1989
Van Buer, Franklin D.	Asst	No Illinois		PHD	68	Illinois	1983
Van Cott, T. Norman	C-Pr	Ball State		PHD	69	U Wash	1977
Van den Berg, Hendrik F.	Asst	Nebraska	F	PHD	89	Wisconsin	1989
Van Der Heide, Evert M.	C-Pr	Calvin		PHD	82	Wayne St	1982
Van Huyck, John B.	Assoc	Texas A&M		PHD	86	Brown	1985
van Wincoop, Jan Eric	Asst	Boston Univ	EF	PHD	89	Harvard	1989
Van Zandt, Timothy	Asst	Princeton					
VanBoening, Mark V.	Asst	Mississippi		PHD		Arizona	1990
Vandegrift, Donald	Asst	Trenton St		PHD	93	Conn	
Vander Linde, Scott H.	Asst	Calvin		PHD	89	Notre Dm	
Vander Meulen, Allen Jr.	Prof	No Central		PHD	75	Brown	1978
Vanderhart, Peter G.	Asst	Bowling Gr		PHD	91	Wisconsin	1991
VanderHoff, James H.	Assoc	Rutgers-Newk		PHD	79	N Carol	1980
Vanderklaauw, H. Wilbert	Assoc	New York U		PHD	92	Brown	1992
Vanderporten, Bruce S.	Assoc	Loyola-Chicg		PHD	73	Wayne St	1978

VanderVeen, Tom	Asst	Calvin		ABD	95	Brown	1995
Vandewetering, Hylke	Prof	Iowa State	O	PHD	64	Iowa St	1964
VanEaton, Charles D.	D-Pr	Hillsdale		PHD	74	Tulane	1978
McCabe/UPS Professor							
Vanek, Jaroslav	Prof	Cornell		PHD		MIT	
Carl Marks Professor of International Studies							
VanHoose, David D.	Prof	Alabama		PHD	84	N Carol	1990
Vanscyoc, Lee	Assoc	Wis-Oshkosh	AL	PHD	87	Nebraska	1987
Vargha, Nader	Assoc	Missouri Wes	B	MA		Oklahoma	1980
Varghese, K. Thomas	Prof	Jms Madison	E	PHD	71	Wayne St	1970
Varian, Hal R.	Prof	Michigan		PHD	73	Berkeley	1977
Varma, Ranbir	C-Pr	Lg Isl-Brook	AFOP	PHD	57	New Sch	1959
Varma, Umesh C.	Inst	Campbell		MS		Jackson	1988
Vars, R. Charles Jr.	Prof	Oregon State	HO	PHD	69	Berkeley	9-66
Vasigh, Bijan		Embry-Riddle		PHD		NYU	
Vaughan, Jo Ann	Asst	Campbell		MA		N Car St	1988
Vaughan, Michael B.	Dean	Weber State	AMK	PHD	80	Nebraska	1981
Vaughn, Karen I.	Prof	George Mason		PHD	71	Duke	1978
Vedder, Richard K.	Prof	Ohio Univ		PHD	65	Illinois	1965
Distinguished Professor							
Veendorp, Emiel C.	Prof	Clark		PHD	63	Rice	1976
Veitch, John	C-Ac	San Francisc		PHD	85	Northwes	1985
Velasco, Andres	Asst	New York U		PHD	88	Columbia	
Velde, Francois R.	Asst	J Hopkins		PHD	92	Stanford	1993
Velenchik, Ann D.	Asst	Wellesley		PHD	89	Stanford	1989
Velez, Alejandro	Prof	St Marys-Txs		PHD	77	Florida	
Vella, Francis G. M.	Asst	Rice		PHD	90	Rochester	1990
Vencill, C. Daniel	Prof	San Fran St		PHD	71	Stanford	1974
Venieris, Yiannis P.	Prof	San Diego St		PHD		Oregon	1967
Venti, Steven F.	Prof	Dartmouth		PHD	82	Harvard	1982
Vento, Edward	Assoc	Tx-Pan Amer		PHD	72	Tx A&M	1982
Ventocilla, Antonio A.	Retir	Ferris State		MA		American	1967
Ventura, Jaume	Asst	MIT	E	PHD	95	Harvard	1995
Veracierto, Marcelo	Asst	Cornell		PHD		Minnesota	
Verbrugge, Randal	VAsst	Virg Tech	F				1995
Vercella, Kit J.	Prof	Alaska-Ancho	ADEO	MA	72	Ca-SnDgo	1974
Verdugo, Paul	Asst	Azusa Pacif		MA		Ca Poly	9-80
Vernarelli, Michael J.	C-Pr	Rochest Tech		PHD	78	SUNY-Bin	1976
Vernon, Jack R.	Prof	Florida	E	PHD	61	Northwes	1967
Vernon, John M.	Prof	Duke		PHD	66	MIT	1969
Vernon, Rodney G.	Asst	USAF Academy		MS		AF Inst	
Vernon, Thomas T.	Prof	Clarion		PHD	71	Kansas St	1969
Verrall, George	Assoc	Miss State		DBA	72	Miss St	1965
Versteeg, Jennie G.	C-Pr	St Michael's	ANFO	PHD	74	Clark	1980
Veseth, Michael	Prof	Puget Sound	AFH	PHD	76	Purdue	1975
Viard, Alan D.	Asst	Ohio State		PHD	90	Harvard	1990
Vickers, Douglas W.	Retir	Massachusett	1995	PHD	56	London	1977
Vijverberg, Wim P. M.	Assoc	Texas-Dallas		PHD	81	Pittsburgh	1986
Viksnins, George J.	Prof	Georgetown		PHD	64	Geotown	1968
Vilasuso, Jon	Asst	Clarkson	EFG	PHD	94	Conn	1994
Villamil, Anne P.	Assoc	Illinois		PHD	88	Minnesota	1988
Villegas, Daniel J.	Asst	Cal Poly-SLO		PHD	79	Stanford	1987
Vincent, James W.	Assoc	St Thomas-MN	Q	PHD	82	Wisconsin	1988
Vines, Timothy	Assoc	La St-Shreve		PHD		Tennessee	1989
Vinje, David L.	Prof	Pacific Luth	O	PHD	64	Wisconsin	1970
Vinod, Hrishinesh D.	Prof	Fordham		PHD	65	Harvard	1982
Virts, Nancy L.	Asst	CS-Northrdge	N	PHD	85	UCLA	1985
Viscione, Jerry A.	Dean	Seattle		PHD	73	Boston U	1988
Genevieve Albers Chair in Business Administration							
Viscusi, W. Kip	Prof	Duke		PHD	76	Harvard	1980
George C. Allen Professor							
Visgilio, Gerald R.	Prof	Conn Coll		PHD		RhodeIsl	
Vitallano, Donald F.	C-Ac	Rensselaer		PHD		CUNY	
Vittal, Mallappa	Asst	Univ of D C	A	LLB		India	1975
Vliet, Laurence C.	H-As$	USAF Academy		MA		Pittsburgh	
Vo, Han X.	Assoc	Winthrop		PHD	79	Tennessee	9-79
Voelker, Keith E.	Prof	Wis-Oshkosh	J	PHD	69	Wisconsin	1970
Vogelsang, Ingo	Prof	Boston Univ	HL	PHD	69	Heidelbe	1981
Vogelsang, Tim	Asst	Cornell		PHD		Princeton	
Vogt, Michael G.	Prof	E Michigan		PHD	76	Wisconsin	1978
Vogt, Walter H.	Retir	San Diego St		PHD		Syracuse	1974
Vohra, Rajiv	Prof	Brown		PHD	83	J Hopkins	
Vohra, Rubina A.	Asst	Jersey City	AJ	PHD		Northeas	
Von Allmen, Peter	Asst	Moravian		PHD	90	Temple	1990
Von Ende, Terry		Texas Tech		PHD		Kansas	1990
von Furstenberg, George	Prof	Indiana		PHD	66	Princeton	1970
Rudy Professor of Economics							
VonDonsel, Richard	Lect	SUNY-Cortlan					
Vonortas, Nicholas S.	Asst	George Wash	OL	PHD	89	NYU	
Voos, Paula B.	Prof	Wisconsin		PHD	82	Harvard	1981

Vora, Ashkok	Prof	CUNY-Baruch		PHD	74	Northwes	1973
Vorst, Karen S.	Assoc	Mo-Kansas Ct	EC	PHD	80	Indiana	1980
Vose, David	Assoc	Minn-Duluth	Q	PHD	66	Wisconsin	1966
Votey, Harold L. Jr.	Retir	Cal-Santa Br		PHD	68	Berkeley	1976
Vowels, Robert C.	Prof	Tenn State		PHD	64	American	
Vredeveld, George	Prof	Cincinnati		PHD	73	Indiana	1977
Vriend, Nicholas	VAsst	Virg Tech	F	PHD	93	Florence	1995
Vroman, Susan	Prof	Georgetown		PHD	77	J Hopkins	1978
Vrooman, David H. Jr.	Assoc	St Lawrence	GE	PHD	76	SUNY-Alb	1965
Vrooman, John	Asst	Idaho State		PHD	76	Tx-Austin	1995
Vuong, Quang	Prof	So Calif		PHD	82	Northwes	1982
Wachtel, Howard M.	Prof	American U		PHD	69	Michigan	1969
Wachtel, Paul A.	C-Pr	New York U	EG	PHD	71	Rochester	1972
Research Professor							
Wachter, Daniel R.	C-Ac	DePauw		PHD	82	Purdue	1979
Wachter, Michael L.	Prof	Pennsylvania	KJ	PHD	70	Harvard	1969
William B. Johnson Professor of Law & Econ; email mwachter@oyez.law.upenn.edu							
Waddoups, C. Jeffrey	Assoc	Nev-L Vegas		PHD	89	Utah	1989
Wade, John	Assoc	W Carolina		PHD	82	Purdue	1977
Wadhawan, Satish C.	Prof	Howard		PHD		Nehru	
Wadman, William Morgan	Assoc	N Car-Wilmin	CDH	PHD		Claremont	
Waggle, J. Douglas	Asst	Berry		PHD		Alabama	1994
Wagner, F. Eugene	Prof	Mo-Kansas Ct	AJO	PHD	67	Syracuse	1967
Wagner, John R.	Assoc	Westfield St		PHD	77	Temple	1986
Wagner, Richard E.	Prof	George Mason		PHD	66	Virginia	1988
Holbert I. Harris Professor of Economics							
Wah Wong, Christine Pui	Prof	Ca-Santa Crz	O	PHD	79	Berkeley	1986
Wahid, Abu	VProf	Tenn State		PHD		Manitoba	
Wahl, Jenny Bourne	Assoc	St Olaf	ADH	PHD	85	Chicago	1988
Wakeman, Douglas	Assoc	Meredith		PHD		N Carol	1987
Walbert, Mark S.	Assoc	Illinois St	CDE	PHD	84	New Mex	1984
Waldauer, Charles	Prof	Widener	DEHR	PHD	69	Syracuse	1968
Waldfogel, Joel	Assoc	Yale		PHD	90	Stanford	1990
Waldman, Don E.	Prof	Colgate	L	PHD	76	Cornell	1981
Waldman, Donald M.	Assoc	Colorado		PHD	79	Wisconsin	1984
Waldo, Douglas G.	Assoc	Florida	EFO	PHD	80	N Carol	1981
Waldron, Randall	Asst	South Dakota		PHD	94	Vanderbilt	1994
Walgreen, John A.	Prof	Wheaton-MA		PHD	65	Boston C	1967
Walgreen, Sonia	VLect	Mass-Dartmou		MA	63	Boston C	1984
Walka, Joseph J.	Dean	No Arizona	HI	PHD	69	Harvard	1986
Walker, Deborah L.	C-Ac	Loyola-N Orl	ABDJ	PHD	87	Geo Mason	1987
Walker, Donald A.	C	Indiana U-PA	BD	PHD	61	Harvard	1969
Walker, Franklin V.	Prof	SUNY-Albany	FE	PHD	58	Harvard	1966
Walker, James M.	Prof	Indiana		PHD	78	Tx A&M	1984
Walker, James R.	Assoc	Wisconsin		PHD	86	Chicago	1987
Walker, John	Asst	Wis-Rvr Fall		PHD	89	Utah	1990
Walker, John F.	Prof	Portland St		PHD	72	Utah	1966
Walker, Mark A.	Prof	Arizona		PHD	70	Purdue	1990
Walker, Mary Beth	Asst	Georgia St	D	PHD	86	Rice	1991
Walker, Roger	Deces	Hamline	J	PHD	59	Cornell	1969
Wall, Howard J.	Asst	W Virginia	FD	PHD	89	SUNY-Buf	1988
Wallace, Don	Asst	St Martin		PHD	63	U Wash	
Wallace, Frederick H.	Assoc	Appalach St	E	PHD	87	Rice	1986
Wallace, Myles S.	Prof	Clemson	EFC	PHD	76	Colorado	1980
Wallace, Neil	Prof	U Miami	E	PHD	64	Chicago	1994
Barnett Banks Chair of Money and Banking							
Wallace, Richard L.	Prof	Missouri		PHD	65	Vanderbilt	1967
Wallace, Richard M.	Assoc	Wofford		PHD	81	S Carol	1982
Wallace, Robert	Assoc	Framingham		PHD		Northwes	
Wallace, Robert	Asst	Gannon		PHD			
Wallace, Sally	Asst	Georgia St	GH	PHD	88	Syracuse	1991
Wallace, Suzanne	Assoc	Central Iowa	DJE	PHD	91	Georgia	1991
Wallace, T. Dudley	Emer	Duke					
James D. Duke Professor							
Waller, Christopher J.	Prof	Indiana		PHD	85	Wash St	1986
Wallis, John J.	Assoc	Maryland		PHD	81	U Wash	1983
Walsh, C. Gerald	Asst	Villanova		MA	60	Detroit	1960
Walsh, Carl E.	Prof	Ca-Santa Crz	E	PHD	76	Berkeley	1987
Walsh, Stephen M.	Asst	SUNY-Oneonta	M	PHD		Ca-River	
Walsh, William J.	Assoc	St Thomas-MN	E	PHD		Notre Dm	1970
Walstad, William B.	Prof	Nebraska	I	PHD	78	Minnesota	1982
State Farm Professorship							
Walter, Ingo	Prof	New York U	FG	PHD	66	NYU	1970
Charles Simon Professor of Applied Financial Economics							
Walters, Joan G.	Prof	Fairfield	EF	PHD		Radcliff	1963
Walters, Stephen J. K.	C-Pr	Loyola-Maryl	KL	PHD	82	UCLA	1981
Walther, Theodore	Prof	Bates	FG	PHD	64	New Sch	1958
Walton, Gary M.	Prof	Cal-Davis	ADN	PHD	66	U Wash	1981
Waltzman, Norman J.	Assoc	Utah		PHD	88	American	1988
Walzer, Norman C.	D-Pr	W Illinois	AHR	PHD	70	Illinois	1970

Wan, Henry Y. Jr.	Prof	Cornell		PHD		MIT	
Wan, Siaw-Peng	Asst	Elmhurst		PHD		Illinois	
Wang, Albert	Asst	Columbia					
Wang, Cheng	Asst	Carnegie Mel		PHD		W Ontario	1994
Wang, Jin	Asst	Wis-Stev Pt		PHD		Kansas St	1990
Wang, Lih-Jau	Asst	Wyoming	F	PHD	90	Ca-SnDgo	1990
Wang, Ping	Assoc	Penn State	E	PHD	87	Rochester	1987
Wang, Weiren	Asst	Kentucky	M	PHD	90	S Calif	1990
Wang, William	Inst	Ark-Pine Blf		MBA		Atlanta	
Wang, Xinghe	Asst	Missouri	CDO	PHD	90	Iowa	1990
Wang, Yong	Asst	Virg Tech	E	PHD	90	Brown	1990
Ward, Benjamin N.	Retir	Cal-Berkeley		PHD		Berkeley	
Ward, John O.	C-Pr	Mo-Kansas Ct	KIO	PHD	70	Oklahoma	1969
Ware, Stephen B.	Assoc	Indiana U-PA	BE	BA	61	Ohio Wes	1969
Warlick, Jennifer L.	Assoc	Notre Dame	HI	PHD	79	Wisconsin	1981
Warner, Elizabeth J.	Asst	Hamilton	EH	PHD	89	Michigan	1989
Warner, John T.	Prof	Clemson	DJE	PHD	76	N Car St	1980
Warner, Larkin B.	Prof	Oklahoma St		PHD	61	Indiana	1960
Regents' Professor							
Warner, Lori	Assoc	Pacific	BEN	PHD	86	Utah	1987
Warner, Rickey	Inst	Miss Vall St		MA		Atlanta	1988
Warren, J. Harold	Assoc	East Tenn St		PHD	69	Okla St	1969
Warren, Ronald S.	Assoc	Georgia	JC	PHD	76	N Carol	1985
Warren, Russell	Prof	Hardin-Simm		PHD			
Warren, Stanton A.	Prof	Niagara		PHD	73	SUNY-Buf	1981
Wasnich, Wendy	Asst	Ashland		MA		Ohio St	1985
Wasow, Bernard M.	Assoc	New York U		PHD	76	Stanford	1975
Wassall, Gregory H.	Assoc	Northeastern		PHD	78	Rutgers	1979
Wassink, Darwin	Prof	Wis-Eau Clar	FO	PHD	68	Stanford	1976
Wassmer, Robert W.	Asst	Wayne State		PHD	89	Mich St	1989
Wassom, John C.	H-Pr	W Kentucky	G	PHD	70	Indiana	1971
Wasson, E. Dale	Prof	SW Missouri		PHD	80	Okla St	1969
Wasson, Renya Reed	Asst	Villanova		PHD	92	Brown	1992
Wasylenko, Michael J.	C-Pr	Syracuse		PHD	75	Syracuse	1989
Waters, Melissa	Asst	SW Louisiana					
Waters, William	Emer	DePaul					
Watkins, John P.	Assoc	Westminst-UT	BNQ	PHD	85	Utah	1984
Watkins, Thayer H.	Prof	San Jose St		PHD	65	Colorado	1957
Watkins, Thomas G.	Assoc	E Kentucky		PHD	79	Iowa St	1984
Watkins, Todd A.	Asst	Lehigh	LO	PHD	95	Harvard	1992
Watson, Harry S.	Assoc	George Wash	H	PHD	81	Indiana	
Watson, J. Keith	Asst	SW Louisiana		PHD	83	Tx A&M	
Watson, James O.	C-Ac	Millikin		PHD	76	Purdue	1979
Watson, Joel	Asst	Ca-San Diego	CF	PHD	92	Stanford	1994
Watters, Francis M.	Retir	CS-Chico		PHD	66	Berkeley	1966
Watts, Alison	Asst	Vanderbilt	DHG	PHD	93	Duke	1993
Watts, Michael W.	Prof	Purdue		PHD	78	LSU	1981
Watts, Royce J.	Asst	W Virginia	C	MS	61	W Virginia	1955
Waud, Roger N.	Prof	No Carolina		PHD	65	Berkeley	1969
Way, Philip K.	Assoc	Cincinnati	J	PHD	86	Warwick	
Weathers, Milledge W.	Retir	Adrian		PHD	61	Munich	1968
Weaver, James H.	Retir	American U		PHD	63	Oklahoma	1963
Weaver, Janice E.	Assoc	Drake		PHD	76	Illinois	1983
Webb, Gwendolyn P.	Asst	CUNY-Baruch		PHD	88	NYU	1987
Webb, Michael A.	C-Pr	Kentucky	FO	PHD	80	Illinois	1980
Webb, Natalie J.	Asst	Naval Postgr		PHD	92	Duke	1992
Webb, Samuel C.	Prof	Wichita St		PHD	68	Kansas	1966
Webber, Douglas	Asst	INSEAD		PHD	85	Essex	1-91
Weber, Arnold R.	Retir	Northwestern	1994	PHD		MIT	
Weber, Charles T.	Assoc	Mich-Flint		PHD	77	Wayne St	1977
Weber, Christian E.	Asst	Seattle	EO	PHD	92	Duke	1993
Weber, Richard E.	Prof	Monmouth		PHD		Rutgers	
Weber, Shlomo	C-Pr	So Methodist		PHD	79	Hebrew	1993
Robert H. & Nancy Dedman Research Fellow							
Weber, William L.	Assoc	SE Missouri	GHI	PHD	86	S Illinois	1986
Weber, William V.	Assoc	E Illinois		PHD	85	Kansas	1988
Webster, Elaine	Asst	Villanova		MED	70	Rutgers	1986
Weckstein, Richard S.	Retir	Brandeis		PHD	53	Yale	1962
Weed, Norman L.	Assoc	Houston-Cl L		PHD	68	Tulane	9-94
Weeks, Gregory C.		Evergreen St		PHD	78	Wash St	1981
Wegge, Leon L.	Emer	Cal-Davis	F	PHD	63	MIT	1966
Wegge, Simone	Inst	Wm & Mary		MA	89	Northwes	1995
Weida, William J.	Prof	Colorado Col		DBA	75	Colorado	1985
Weidenbaum, Murray L.	Prof	Wash Univ		PHD	58	Princeton	1961
Edward Mallinckrodt Distinguished University Professor							
Weiher, Kenneth E.	Assoc	Tx-S Antonio	BEN	PHD	75	Indiana	1975
Weil, David	Assoc	Brown		PHD	90	Harvard	
Weil, Gordon	C-Pr	Wheaton-MA	FOP	PHD	81	Tufts	1981
Weiler, John E.	Prof	Dayton	H	PHD	73	Cincinnati	1967
Weiman, David F.	Assoc	CUNY-Queens	NOE	PHD	84	Stanford	1994

Weinberg, David R.	Assoc	Xavier	ARP	PHD	73	Berkeley	1980
Weinhold, Diana	Asst	Vanderbilt	FO	PHD	94	Ca-SnDgo	1994
Weinrobe, Maurice D.	Prof	Clark		PHD	69	Cornell	1976
Weinstein, David E.	Assoc	Harvard		PHD	92	Michigan	1991
Weinstein, Paul A.	Assoc	Maryland		PHD	61	Northwes	1965
Weinstein, Robert I.	Prof	Bradley		PHD	74	Tx-Austin	1980
Weintraub, Andrew R.	Assoc	Temple	A	PHD	66	Rutgers	1973
Weintraub, E. Roy	Dean$	Duke		PHE	69	Penn	1970
Weintraub, Irvin	Assoc	Towson State		MS	51	Columbia	1966
Weis, Charles E.	Prof	Tenn State		DBA	74	Ariz St	
Weisbrod, Burton A.	Prof	Northwestern		PHD	58	Northwes	
John Evans Professor of Economic, Director,Ctr for Urban Affairs & Policy Rec							
Weisbrot, Mark	Asst	E Illinois		PHD	93	Michigan	1990
Weise, Charles	Asst	Wm & Mary		PHD	93	Wisconsin	1993
Weisenborn, David E.	Retir	Geo Southern		PHD	68	Florida	1976
Weiser, Lawrence A.	Prof	Wis-Stev Pt		PHD	67	Wisconsin	1972
Weisman, Dennis	Asst	Kansas State	KD	PHD	93	Florida	1993
Weiss, Andrew	Assoc	So Calif		PHD	84	Sydney	1984
Weiss, Andrew M.	Prof	Boston Univ	DGJ	PHD	76	Stanford	1987
Weiss, Jeffrey		SUNY-Empire	A	PHD		Harvard	1986
Weiss, Jeffrey H.	Assoc	CUNY-Baruch		PHD	81	Wisconsin	1981
Weiss, Merle	Assoc	Temple	IJ	PHD	67	Columbia	1972
Weiss, Steven J.	Prof	Toledo		PHD	71	Colorado	1968
Weiss, Thomas J.	Prof	Kansas		PHD		N Carol	1967
Weissert, Lee J.	Asst	St Vincent		MA		Pittsburgh	1988
Weisskopf, Thomas E.	Prof	Michigan		PHD	66	MIT	1972
Weissman, Seth		Yeshiva					
Weitzman, Martin L.	Prof	Harvard		PHD	67	MIT	1989
Ernest E. Monrad Professor of Economics							
Welch, Finis R.	Prof	Texas A&M		PHD	66	Chicago	1991
Abell Professor							
Welch, Patrick J.	C-Pr	St Louis		PHD	73	Pittsburgh	1983
Welch, Robert G.	Prof	Midwest St	DG	PHD		Oreg St	1966
Welch, William P.	Assoc	Saginaw Vall		PHD	86	U Wash	1986
Welki, Andrew M.	Asst	John Carroll	HR	PHD	83	Penn St	1982
Welle, Patrick G.	Prof	Bemidji St		PHD		Wisconsin	1982
Weller, Barry R.	H-Ac	Penn St-Erie	ACE	PHD	71	Penn St	1971
Wellington, Alison J.	Asst	Davidson	J	PHD	90	Michigan	1990
Wellington, Alison J.	Asst	Naval Postgr	J	PHD	90	Michigan	1995
Wellington, Donald C.	Prof	Cincinnati	D	PHD	66	Chicago	
Wells, Arnold R.	Prof	Mankato St	ADM	PHD	66	Minnesota	1966
Wells, David R.	Asst	Denison		PHD	94	USC	1995
Wells, Donald A.	Prof	Arizona		PHD	61	Oregon	1969
Wells, Donald R.	Prof	Memphis		PHD	65	S Calif	1967
Wells, Jerome C.	Prof	Pittsburgh	O	PHD	64	Michigan	1964
Wells, John M.	Asst	Auburn		PHD	94	Tx A&M	1994
Welsh, Arthur	Prof	Penn State	A	PHD	63	Illinois	1986
Wendel, Jeanne L.	Assoc	Nevada-Reno		PHD	77	So Meth	1985
Wenders, John T.	Prof	Idaho	DL	PHD	67	Northwes	1981
Weninger, Quinn	Asst	Utah State	CQ	PHD	95	Maryland	1995
Wentworth, Donald R.	Prof	Pacific Luth	A	PHD	65	Minnesota	1972
Werner, Jan	Assoc	Minnesota		PHD		Bonn	1987
Werner, Megan	Asst	Florida	CHQ	PHD	94	Ca-SnDgo	1994
Wesolowski, Karl A.	C-Ac	Salem State		MA		Boston C	
Wessel, Robert H.	Reitr	Cincinnati		PHD	53	Cincinnati	1957
Wessels, Walter J.	Assoc	N Carol St	JD	PHD	76	Chicago	1975
West, Carol Taylor	Prof	Florida	RQC	PHD	74	Michigan	1989
West, James E.	Asst	Seattle	AD	PHD	94	Michigan	1994
West, James P.	C-Pr	Moravian		PHD		Lehigh	1989
West, Janet Mason	Asst	Neb-Omaha	AJ	MA	64	Mich St	1967
West, Kenneth D.	Prof	Wisconsin		PHD	83	MIT	1988
Westall, Oliver M.	SLect	U Lancaster		BSC		London	
Westbrook, Jilleen	Asst	Temple	FI	PHD	93	Claremont	1993
Westbrook, M. Daniel	Asst	Georgetown		PHD	78	Ohio St	1978
Westerfield, Donald	Prof	Webster	DIMC	PHD		St Louis	1984
Westfield, Fred M.	Prof	Vanderbilt	D	PHD	57	MIT	1965
Westhoff, Frank H.	Prof	Amherst	ADH	PHD	74	Yale	1973
Weston, Gerald A.	Prof	Wis-Whitewat		PHD	65	Wash St	1968
Weston, Rafael R.	Prof	Adams State		PHD	72	Harvard	1988
Weston, Samuel C.	Asst	Dallas	B	PHD	87	Pittsburgh	1987
Westphal, Larry E.	Prof	Swarthmore	DO	PHD	69	Harvard	1985
Wetchler, Sherry J.	Asst	Ithaca	AJHI	PHD	92	Maryland	1990
Wetzel, James N.	Assoc	Virg Comm		PHD	74	N Carol	1974
Wexler, Imanuel	Retir	Connecticut		PHD	59	Harvard	1961
Weymark, Diana N.	Asst	Western Wash	EF	PHD	90	Brit Col	1988
Whalen, Thaddeus J. Jr.	Prof	Santa Clara		PHD	64	Berkeley	1962
Whalley, Pamela	Lect	Western Wash	DG	ABD		Indiana	1989
Whaples, Robert M.	Asst	Wake Forest		PHD	90	Penn	1991
Whatley, Warren	Assoc	Michigan					
Wheaton, William C.	Prof	MIT	R	PHD	72	Penn	1972

Wheeler, Bert	Assoc	Cedarville	AFOP	PHD	85	Tennessee	1992
Wheeler, Clifford	Retir	NE St-Okla	1995	PHD		Missouri	1971
Wheeler, Herbert E.	Assoc	Manhattan		PHD		Fordham	1978
Wheeler, Mark V.	Assoc	W Michigan	E	PHD	85	Kentucky	1990
Whinston, Michael D.	Prof	Harvard					
Whitaker, A. Royal	Assoc	USN Academy		PHD	65	Penn	1965
Whitaker, Andrew L.	Assoc	No Central		PHD	88	Illinois	1988
Whitaker, David A.	Assoc	Richmond		PHD	71	Florida	1969
Whitaker, John K.	Prof	Virginia	BC	PHD	62	Cambridg	1969
Georgia S. Bankard Porfessor of Economics							
Whitaker, Morris D.	Prof	Utah State	FO	PHD	70	Purdue	1970
Whitaker, William M.	C-Pr	Geo Southern		PHD	68	Kentucky	1989
White, Charles	Assoc	Framingham		PHD		Chicago	
White, Charles V. A.	Assoc	New Hamp Col		PHD		Ohio St	
White, Eugene N.	C-Pr	Rutgers-N Br	N	PHD	80	Illinois	1980
White, Everett E. III	Asst	CS-Stanislau					
White, Halbert L.	Prof	Ca-San Diego	C	PHD	76	MIT	1979
White, Harry Ruff	Prof	W Carolina		PHD	66	Kentucky	1968
White, Kenneth R.	Assoc	Cen Florida	C	PHD	71	Oklahoma	1968
White, Lawrence	Prof	New York U	DGKL	PHD	69	Harvard	1976
Arthur E. Imperitore Professor of Economics							
White, Lawrence H.	Assoc	Georgia	ENB	PHD	82	UCLA	1988
White, Leonard A.	Prof	Arkansas	D	PHD	63	St Louis	1971
White, Michael D.	Prof	St Cloud St		PHD	78	Tx Tech	1978
White, Michelle J.	Prof	Michigan		PHD	73	Princeton	1984
White, Nancy E.	Assoc	Bucknell		PHD	86	Colorado	1986
White, Thomas J.	Asst	Assumption	AEGQ	PHD	89	SUNY-Bin	1994
White, William D.	Prof	Ill-Chicago	I	PHD	75	Harvard	1975
White-Means, Shelley L.	Prof	Memphis		PHD	83	Northwes	1988
Whited, Toni	Asst	Delaware	GE	PHD	90	Princeton	1994
Whitehead, John C.	Assoc	East Carol		PHD	89	Kentucky	1989
Whiteman, Charles H.	Prof	Iowa		PHD	81	Minnesota	1980
Whitesell, Frank Cook	Assoc	So Miss	A	PHD	71	Tulane	1968
Whitesell, William E.	Prof	Frank & Mars		PHD	63	Tx-Austin	1965
Henry P. & Mary B. Stager Professor of Economics							
Whitin, Thomson M.	Emer	Wesleyan-CT	C	PHD	52	Princeton	1963
Hubbard Professor							
Whiting, Cathleen L.	Assoc	Willamette		PHD	86	U Wash	1986
Whitman, Katherine	Asst	Mt St Mary's					
Whitmore, Harland W. Jr.	Prof	Cincinnati	E	PHD	69	Mich St	
Whitney, Chet	Prof	Augustana SD	C	PHD	65	Kansas	1960
Whitney, Gerald A.	Prof	New Orleans		PHD	77	Tulane	
Whitney, James D.	Prof	Occidental	F	PHD	83	Wisconsin	1982
Whittaker, Victor A.	Prof	Morgan State		PHD	71	Illinois	1974
Whitten, David O.	Prof	Auburn		PHD	70	Tulane	1968
Whyte, Charles D.	Prof	Virginia St		PHD	69	Ohio St	1974
Wible, James R.	Assoc	New Hampshir	BE	PHD	80	Penn St	1984
Wichers, C. Robert	Assoc	Pittsburgh	C	PHD	68	Amdersta	1976
Wicker, Elmus R.	Retir	Indiana		PHD	56	Duke	
Wickman, Kenneth P.	Assoc	SUNY-Cortlan		PHD	62	Syracuse	1968
Wicks, John H.	Prof	Montana	DH	PHD		Illinois	
Widener, Steven	C-Ac	New Hamp Col		PHD		N Hamp	
Wiegersma, Nancy A.	Prof	Fitchburg St		PHD	76	Maryland	1979
Wiemer, Calla J.	Asst	Hawaii-Manoa		PHD	84	Wisconsin	1984
Wier, Thomas	Asst	Alabama St		PHD	89	Tennessee	1995
Wiest, Philip Ray	Assoc	George Mason		PHD	76	Pittsburgh	
Wiggins, Steven N.	Prof	Texas A&M		PHD	79	MIT	1979
George R. Jordan Professorship							
Wight, Jonathan B.	Assoc	Richmond		PHD	82	Vanderbilt	1982
Wightman, James W.	Prof	SUNY-Potsdam		PHD		Clark	
Wihry, David F.	C-Ac	Maine	HIA	PHD	72	Syracuse	1969
Wikstrom, Joan E.	Lect	Catholic		MA			
Wilamoski, Peter R.	Asst	Seattle	F	PHD	91	Oregon	1992
Wilber, Charles K.	Prof	Notre Dame	BOP	PHD	66	Maryland	1975
Wilbratte, Barry J.	C-Pr	St Thomas-TX	FG	PHD	71	Tulane	1971
Wilcox, Nathaniel	Asst	Houston		PHD		Chicago	1991
Wilcox-Gok, Virginia L.	Asst	No Illinois		PHD	84	Wash U	1994
Wilcoxen, Peter J.	Asst	Texas	QD	PHD	89	Harvard	9-91
Wildasin, David E.	Prof	Vanderbilt	G	PHD	76	Iowa	1993
Wilde, James A.	Assoc	No Carolina		PHD	68	Princeton	1965
Wilder, Ronald P.	C-Pr	So Carolina		PHD	69	Vanderbilt	1987
Wiles, James L.	Retir	Stonehill		PHD	76	Harvard	1955
Wilford, W. Terry	Deces	New Orleans	4-94	PHD	64	So Meth	1968
Wilhelm, Mark	Asst	Penn State	I	PHD	90	NYU	1990
Wilhite, Allen W.	Prof	Alabama-Hunt	JK	PHD	81	Illinois	1988
Wilkie, Simon	Asst	Cal Tech	L	PHD	90	Rochester	1995
Wilkins, Allen J.	Assoc	Marshall		PHD	84	Wisconsin	1985
Wilkins, Bill H.	Dean	Oregon State		PHD	62	Tx-Austin	1961
Wilkins, Mira	Prof	Fla Internat	NF	PHD	57	Cambridge	1974
Wilkinson, Maurice	Prof	Columbia		PHD	65	Harvard	1965

Willard, Kristen L.	Asst	Columbia				Princeton	
Willett, Keith D.	Prof	Oklahoma St		PHD	82	New Mex	1981
Willett, Thomas D.	Prof	Claremont		PHD	67	Virginia	1977
Horton Professor of Economics							
Williams, Anne D.	Prof	Bates	O	PHD	76	Chicago	1981
Williams, Arlington W.	Prof	Indiana		PHD	78	Arizona	1979
Williams, C. Glyn	Retir	So Carolina		PHD	60	Virginia	
Williams, D. C. Jr.	Retir	So Miss		PHD		LSU	
Williams, Darrell L.	Asst	UCLA		PHD			
Williams, Donald R.	C-Pr	Kent State	J	PHD	84	Northwes	1983
Williams, E. Douglass	Asst	Carleton		PHD	89	Northwes	1989
Williams, Earl R.	Dean	NE St-Okla	DMN	PHD	68	Tennessee	1968
Williams, Eugene	Prof	McMurry		PHD	71	Arkansas	1988
Williams, Harold R.	Prof	Kent State	EF	PHD	65	Nebraska	1966
Williams, Martin	Prof	No Illinois		PHD		SUNY	
Williams, Mary L.	Assoc	Widener	BOMQ	PHD	84	Temple	1982
Williams, Mike M.	Prof	Bethune-Cook		PHD		Ohio U	1991
Williams, Nancy A.	Assoc	Loyola-Maryl	QH	PHD	84	Berkeley	1987
Williams, Nicolas	Asst	Cincinnati	J	PHD	89	Northwes	1990
Williams, Norman C.	C-Ac	Tenn Tech		PHD	72	Arkansas	1972
Williams, Raburn M.	Prof	Hawaii-Manoa		PHD	70	Chicago	1969
Williams, Robert B.	Assoc	Guilford	R	PHD	84	N Carol	1987
Williams, Robert G.	Prof	Guilford	F	PHD	78	Stanford	1978
Williams, Steven R.	Assoc	Illinois		PHD	82	Northwes	1992
Williams, Walter E.	C-Pr	George Mason		PHD	72	UCLA	1981
John M. Olin Distinguished Professor of Economics							
Williams, William V.	Retir	Hamline	1994	PHD	61	Colorado	1961
Williamson, Daniel P.	H-Pr	Cal Poly-SLO		PHD	73	Ca-SnDgo	1970
Williamson, H. F. Jr.	Assoc	Illinois		PHD	69	Yale	1964
Williamson, Jeffrey G.	Prof	Harvard		PHD	61	Stanford	1983
Laird Bell Professor of Economics							
Williamson, Joan	Asst	Delaware St		MA		NYU	
Williamson, Oliver E.	Prof	Cal-Berkeley		PHD	63	Car Mellon	1988
Williamson, Samuel H.	Prof	Miami U-Ohio	NI	PHD	68	Purdue	1983
Willig, Robert D.	Prof	Princeton		PHD	73	Stanford	1978
Willis, James F.	C-Pr	San Jose St		PHD	66	So Meth	1966
Willis, Rachel A.	Lect	No Carolina		PHD	90	Northwes	1982
Willits, Richard				PHD	76	Mich St	
Willman, Elliott	Prof	New Mex St		PHD	77	Indiana	1979
Willner, Jonathan	Asst	Okla City	FO	PHD	94	Purdue	1995
Willoughby, John A.	Assoc	American U		PHD		Berkeley	1979
Willumsen, Maria Jose	Assoc	Fla Internat	RO	PHD	84	Cornell	1984
Wilson, Charles A.	Prof	New York U		PHD	76	Rochester	1983
Wilson, Erika G.	Prof	CS-L Angeles		PHD	79	S Calif	1968
Wilson, F. Scott	C-Ac	Canisius		PHD	76	Minnesota	1977
Wilson, George W.	Prof	Cen Missouri		PHD	76	Okla St	1972
Wilson, John D.	C-Ac	Indiana		PHD	79	MIT	1985
Wilson, Linda	Lect	Tx-Arlington		MS	92	North Tx	1993
Wilson, Loretta S.	Asst	Radford		PHD	86	Mass	
Wilson, Paul W.	Assoc	Texas	RC	PHD	86	Brown	9-90
Wilson, R. Mark	Assoc	South Fla	I	PHD	77	Northwes	1978
Wilson, Richard	H-Pr	Ft Valley St		PHD	82	Missouri	9-91
Wilson, Richard C.	Asst	Tx-Arlington	AH	MA	66	Georgia	1966
Wilson, Wesley W.	Assoc	Oregon	CD	PHD	86	Wash St	1989
Wiltgen, Richard J.	Prof	DePaul		PHD	74	Illinois	1973
Wimberly, Jack Cook	Retir	So Miss		PHD		LSU	
Wimmer, Bradley	Asst	Emory Henry		PHD	92	Kentucky	1992
Wimmer, Larry T.	Prof	Brigham Yg		PHD	68	Chicago	1963
Winczewski, Greg A.	Asst	Manhattan		PHD		Fordham	1993
Winfrey, John C.	Prof	Wash & Lee	DH	PHD	65	Duke	1965
Wing, Martin M.	Asst	GMI		PHD	89	Wayne St	
Wingate, Stanley R.	Asst	St Marys-Cal		PHD		Oregon	1988
Winkelman, Richard D.	Assoc	Arizona St		PHD	66	Illinois	1965
Winkler, Anne E.	Asst	Mo-St Louis	JT	PHD	89	Illinois	1989
Winrich, J. Steven	Assoc	Centre	APN	PHD		Kentucky	1981
Winstead, Richard E.	Asst	Morehouse		BA		Fisk	1975
Winston, Barbara	C-Pr	NE Illinois		PHD		Northwes	1974
Winston, Gordon C.	C-Pr	Williams		PHD	64	Stanford	1963
Orrin Sage Professor of Political Science							
Winter, Eyal	Assoc	Wash Univ		PHD	88	Hebrew	1995
Winter, Harold	Asst	Ohio Univ	KL	PHD	90	Rochester	
Wion, Douglas A.	Assoc	Lock Haven		PHD	80	Penn St	1980
Wiseman, A. Clark	Prof	Gonzaga	AF	PHD	68	U Wash	1981
Wishart, David M.	Assoc	Wittenberg		PHD	85	Illinois	1983
Wisley, Thomas O.	Prof	W Kentucky	GHK	PHD	79	Purdue	1985
Wisman, Jon D.	Assoc	American U		PHD		American	1971
Witherspoon, James E.	Asst	Campbell		JD		Wake For	1983
Withington, Robert P.	Assoc	SUNY-Plattsb	NJ	PHD	76	Penn	1972
Witt, Tom S.	Prof	W Virginia	CR	PHD	74	Wash U	1970
Witte, Ann D.	Prof	Wellesley		PHD	71	N Car St	1985

Witte, Willard E.	Assoc	Indiana		PHD	75	Wisconsin	1981
Wittman, Donald A.	C-Pr	Ca-Santa Crz	KD	PHD	70	Berkeley	1969
Woglom, Geoffrey R.	Prof	Amherst	AEG	PHD	74	Yale	1978
Wohar, Mark	Prof	Neb-Omaha	ECGF	PHD	85	Illinois	1988
Wohl, Lawrence A.	C-Ac	Gustavus Ado		PHD	86	Wash St	1983
Wojcikewych, Raymond	C-Ac	Bradley		PHD	80	Penn St	1977
Wojick, Paul P.	Asst	St Olaf	AE	PHD	89	Colorado	1988
Wolak, Frank A.	Assoc	Stanford		PHD	85	Harvard	1986
Wolcott, Susan	Asst	Temple	FN	PHD	88	Stanford	1990
Wolf, Avner	C-Ac	CUNY-Baruch		PHD	83	Columbia	
Wolf, Holger C.	Asst	New York U	EFO	PHD	92	MIT	1992
Wolfe, Barbara L.	Prof	Wisconsin		PHD	73	Penn	1976
Wolfe, Janet C.	Lect	Michigan		MPP	80	Michigan	1987
Wolfe, Mike	Lect	Gannon		MBA		Gannon	
Wolfenbarger, J. Larry	C-Pr	Georgia Col	ABPE	PHD	74	Tennessee	1987
Wolff, Edward N.	Prof	New York U		PHD	74	Yale	1974
Wolff, Laura	Inst	S Ill-Edward		MS	88	Missouri	1990
Wolff, Richard D.	Prof	Massachusett		PHD	69		
Wolfram, Gary	Assoc	Hillsdale		PHD		Berkeley	1989
Wolfson, Martin H.	Asst	Notre Dame	EG	PHD	84	American	1990
Wolfson, Melville Z.	Assoc	New Orleans		PHD		Illinois	
Wolfson, Murray	Prof	CS-Fullerton		PHD	63	Wisconsin	1986
Wolfson, Paul J.	Asst	Wis-Milwauke		PHD		Yale	1988
Wolinsky, Asher	Prof	Northwestern		PHD		Stanford	
Wolkoff, Michael	Lect	Rochester		PHD		Michigan	
Wolnicki, Miron J.	Assoc	Villanova		PHD	80	Lodz	1984
Wolowitz, Jeffrey	SLect	Harvard					
Wolozin, Harold	Prof	Mass-Boston	B	PHD	55	Columbia	1966
Wolpin, Kenneth I.	Prof	Pennsylvania		PHD	74	CUNY	1995
Womer, N. Keith	C-Pr	Mississippi		PHD	70	Penn St	1986
Wommeldorf, Thomas		Evergreen St		PHD	89	American	1989
Wong, David C.	Assoc	CS-Fullerton		PHD		Ca-SnBarb	1981
Wong, Kar-Yiu	Assoc	U Washington		PHD	83	Columbia	1983
Wong, Kwok-Fai Matthew	Asst	St John's		PHD		Manitoba	
Wonnacott, Paul	Prof	Middlebury		PHD	59	Princeton	1994
Alan R. Holmes Visiting Professor in Monetary Economics							
Woo, Cheonsik	Asst	Clemson		PHD	94	Columbia	1992
Woo, Wing T.	Prof	Cal-Davis	EFOP	PHD	82	Harvard	1985
Wood, Clinton F.	Prof	Delta State		JD	80	Miss	8-84
Wood, Edgar	Prof	Mississippi		PHD	67	LSU	1967
Wood, J. Stuart	Assoc	Loyola-N Orl	GM	PHD	80	NYU	1984
Wood, John H.	Prof	Wake Forest		PHD	64	Purdue	1985
Reynolds Professor of Economics							
Wood, Richard H. Jr.	C-Pr	Stetson	AFO	PHD	72	Wisconsin	1970
Wood, William C.	Prof	Jms Madison	DA	PHD	80	Virginia	1989
Woodbury, Stephen A.	Prof	Michigan St		PHD	81	Wisconsin	1982
Wooders, John C.	Asst	Arizona		PHD	91	Cornell	1991
Woodford, Michael	Prof	Chicago		PHD	83	MIT	1986
Woodland, Bill M.	Prof	E Michigan		PHD	81	Purdue	1981
Woodruff, Mary Martha	C-Ac	New Haven		DED		Bridgprt	
Woodruff, Theodore S.	Prof	St Ambrose		PHD		Columbia	1995
Woodruff, William D.	Prof	Florida	N	PHD	52	Nottnghm	1966
Woods, Louis A.	Assoc	North Fla	OQR	PHD	72	N Carol	1972
Woodward, Doug P.	Asst	So Carolina		PHD	86	Tx-Austin	
Wooldridge, Jeff	Prof	Michigan St		PHD			
Wooley, Douglas C.	Prof	Radford		PHD		Conn	
Woolf, Arthur G.	Assoc	Vermont	HNR	PHD	80	Wisconsin	1980
Woolf, Linda L.	Assoc	Washburn		PHD	70	Kansas St	1969
Woolsey, W. William	Assoc	Citadel		PHD	86	Geo Mason	8-86
Word, William R.	Dean	Montevallo		PHD	70	Tennessee	1979
Workman, William	Assoc	E Oregon St		PHD	78	Utah St	
Woroby, Tamara	Assoc	Towson State		PHD	81	Queens	1978
Woudenberg, Henry W. Jr.	Assoc	Kent State	E	PHD	68	Mich St	1967
Woundy, Douglas Stanley	Inst	Va Military		ABD		Va Comm	1989
Wray, L. Randall	Asst	Denver		PHD	88	Wash U	
Wright, Arthur W.	Prof	Connecticut	KD	PHD	69	MIT	1979
Wright, Colin	Prof	Claremont		PHD		Chicago	1977
Norwood and Frances Berger Professor of Business & Soc./Director,Lincoln Inst							
Wright, Gavin	Prof	Stanford		PHD	69	Yale	1982
Wright, Jeffrey J.	Asst	Lenoir-Rhyne		PHD	87	Conn	1989
Wright, Randall	Prof	Pennsylvania	JE	PHD	86	Minnesota	1987
Wright, Virginia B.	Prof	E Kentucky		PHD	71	Geo Wash	1982
Wrightsman, Dwayne E.	Retir	New Hampshir	Fnce	PHD	64	Mich St	1964
Wrotniak, Maria	Assoc	Westminst-UT	BCO	PHD	80	Lodz	1989
Wu, De-Min	Prof	Kansas		PHD	63	Wisconsin	1964
Wu, Mickey Tai Chuen	Assoc	Coe		PHD	79	Kentucky	1979
Wu, Roland Y.	Assoc	MD-Baltim Co		PHD	71		
Wu, Shih-Yen	Prof	Iowa		PHD	60	Northwes	1964
Wu, Yangru	Asst	W Virginia	F	PHD	93	Ohio St	1995
Wu, Yeen-Kuen	Assoc	Ark-Pine Blf		MA		Atlanta	

Wuilleumier, Rudolph B.	Asst	E Kentucky		BS	67	E Kentuc	1971
Wunnava, Phanindra V.	Assoc	Middlebury		PHD	86	SUNY-Bin	1985
Wymar, Benno	Prof	South Dakota		PHD	73	Nebraska	1968
Wyplosz, Charles	Prof	INSEAD	FE	PHD	78	Harvard	9-72
Wyrick, Thomas L.	Prof	SW Missouri		PHD	79	Va Tech	1978
Wyss, Brenda	Asst	Wheaton-MA	JTO	PHD	95	Mass	1992
Xander, James A.	Assoc	Cen Florida	D	PHD	74	Georgia	1969
Xia, Feng Lei	Asst	Minot State	AF	PHD		Kansas St	1994
Xiang, Ping Qui	Asst	Northern St		PHD	93	Iowa	1993
Xu, Bin	Asst	Florida	FO	PHD	95	Columbia	1995
Xu, Peng	Asst	San Fran St		PHD	94	Iowa	1994
Xu, Xianonian	Asst	Amherst	AEO	PHD	91	Ca-Davis	1991
Xu, Zhenhui	Asst	Wm & Mary		PHD	93	Virginia	1993
Yacovissi, William A.	Prof	Mansfield		PHD	89	SUNY-Bin	1976
Yalsawarng, Suthathip	Asst	Union	CD	PHD	89	S Illinois	1989
Yamada, Tetsuji	Assoc	Rutgers-Camd		PHD	87	CUNY	1987
Yamazaki, Masato	Asst	Aquinas		PHD	84	Duke	1987
Yan, Chiou-shuang	Prof	Drexel		PHD	66	Purdue	1967
Yandell, Dirk	Prof	San Diego		PHD	81	Purdue	1981
Yang, Chin-Wei	Prof	Clarion		PHD		W Virginia	1981
Yang, Dennis	Asst	Duke		PHD	93	Chicago	1992
Yang, Wei-Hsein	Assoc	Ark-Pine Blf		PHD		Nebraska	
Yang, Yung Y.	Prof	CS-Sacrament		PHD	74	Oregon	1974
Yangru, Wu	Asst	W Virginia	F	PHD	93	Ohio St	1995
Yannelis, Nicholas C.	Prof	Illinois		PHD	83	Rochester	1988
Yarbrough, Beth V.	Prof	Amherst	ADF	PHD	83	U Wash	1982
Yaron, Amir	Asst	Carnegie Mel		PHD		Chicago	1994
Yasin, Jehad	Assoc	Ft Valley St					
Yasin, Mesghena	Asst	Morehead St		PHD	86	Cincinnati	1986
Yates, Andrew J.	Asst	Wake Forest		PHD	92	Stanford	1993
Yates, Barbara M.	C-Pr	Seattle	AEGH	PHD	69	Michigan	1970
Yates, Michael Daniel	Prof	Pitts-Johnst	JP	PHD	76	Pittsburgh	1969
Yatrakis, Pan G.	Assoc	Sacred Heart	DEFI	PHD		NYU	
Yazdi, Khalil	Assoc	St Thomas-TX	M	PHD	87	Houston	1990
Yeager, Tim	Asst	CS-Humboldt		PHD	93	Wash U	1995
Yeargan, Howard Reig	Assoc	SW Texas St		MS		Tx A&M	
Yee, Janice G.	Asst	Wartburg		PHD	90	Clark	1991
Yeh, Chiou-Nan	C-Pr	Alabama St		PHD	74	Mass	1974
Yeh, Yeong-Her	Prof	Hawaii-Manoa		PHD	66	Minnesota	1965
Yerger, David B.	Asst	Cleveland St	DF	PHD	94	Penn St	1994
Yett, Donald E.	Prof	So Calif		PHD	68	Berkeley	1966
Yezer, Anthony M.	Prof	George Wash		PHD	74	MIT	1972
Yi, Kei-Mu	Asst	Rice		PHD	89	Chicago	1990
Yi, Sang-Seung	Asst	Dartmouth		PHD	93	Harvard	1993
Yigletu, Ashagre	Assoc	Southern		PHD		Belgrade	1972
Yin, Yong	Asst	SUNY-Buffalo	CDE	PHD	95	Ohio St	1995
Ying, John S.	Assoc	Delaware	L	PHD	87	Berkeley	1987
Yinger, John M.	Prof	Syracuse		PHD	74	Princeton	1986
Yip, Chong Kee	Assoc	Georgia St	EF	PHD	88	Penn St	1988
Yochum, Gilbert R.	C-Pr	Old Dominion		PHD	74	W Virginia	1975
Yohe, Gary W.	Prof	Wesleyan-CT	D	PHD	75	Yale	1977
Yohe, William P.	Prof	Duke		PHD	59	Michigan	1958
Yoho, Devon L.	Assoc	Ball State		PHD	74	Missouri	1978
Yoon, Bong J.	Assoc	SUNY-Bingham		PHD	78	Illinois	1983
Yoon, Gawon	Asst	Wayne State		PHD	94	Ca-SnDgo	1994
Yoon, Iee	Retir	Wichita St	5-95	PHD	67	Minnesota	1968
Yoon, Mann	Asst	CS-L Angeles					
Yordon, Wesley J.	Retir	Colorado		PHD		Harvard	
Yosha, Oved	Asst	Brown		PHD	92	Harvard	
You, Jong-Il	Asst	Notre Dame	OFCE	PHD	91	Harvard	1990
Young, Alwyn	Prof	Boston Univ	O	PHD	90	Columbia	1995
Young, Ben	Lect	Mo-Kansas Ct	A	PHD	73	Oklahoma	1993
Young, Douglas J.	Prof	Montana St		PHD	78	Wisconsin	1977
Young, Edward G.	C-Pr	Wis-Eau Clar		PHD	77	Wash St	1977
Young, H. Peyton	Prof	J Hopkins		PHD	70	Michigan	1994
Young, Jeffrey T.	Prof	St Lawrence	BQ	PHD	75	Colorado	1980
Young, Linda W.	Assoc	So Oregon St	JEOF	PHD	87	Berkeley	1994
Young, Madelyn V.	Asst	Converse		PHD	91	Geo St	1991
Young, Mary E.	Assoc	Southwestern	CEJQ	PHD	89	Tx-Austin	1990
Young, Richard D.	Retir	Rice		PHD	65	Car Mellon	1965
Young, Shik C.	C-Pr	East Wash		PHD		Wash St	1966
Youngelson-Neal, Helen L.	C-Pr	Portland St		PHD	66	Columbia	1967
Yousefi, Mahmood	Prof	No Iowa		PHD	74	Ca-SnBarb	1981
Yousif, Salah A.	Asst	Alabama A&M	AJ	MA		Howard	
Yu, Ben T.	Assoc	CS-Northrdge		PHD	78	U Wash	1984
Yu, Tie-Liu	Assoc	Mercer-Atlan		PHD		Miss St	1990
Yuhn, Ky-Hyan	Assoc	Fla Atlantic					
Yun, Kwan Koo	Assoc	SUNY-Albany	CD	PHD		Stanford	
Yunker, James A.	Prof	W Illinois	ACDP	PHD	71	Northwes	1968

Name	Rank	Institution	Fields	Degree	Yr	Degree Institution	Year
Zabel, Edward	Prof	Florida	D	PHD	56	Princeton	1981
Matherly Professor							
Zabel, Jeffrey	Asst	Tufts		PHD	87	Ca-SnDgo	1989
Zadeh, Ali Haji-Mohamad	Assoc	Susquehanna	CEGO	PHD	82	Mich St	1987
Zaffke, Maurice	Prof	Liberty					
Zahka, William J.	Prof	Widener	ABNO	ABD		Bryn Maw	1959
Zahn, Frank	Prof	Neb-Omaha	E	PHD	69	Ca-SnBarb	1979
Zajac, Edward E.	Prof	Arizona		PHD	54	Stanford	1983
Zak, Gail	Asst	Eastern Conn		PHD		Tx A&M	
Zak, Thomas A.	Assoc	USN Academy		PHD	80	Vanderbilt	1981
Zaki, Mokhlis Y.	Prof	No Michigan	ACDO	PHD	69	Berkeley	1969
Zaleski, Peter A.	Assoc	Villanova		PHD	88	Maryland	1987
Zamani, Amir	Asst	Upsala	F	PHD		Columbia	1991
Zamanian, Zaman	Asst	Montclair St	ACEF	PHD		Indiana	
Zampelli, Ernest M.	C-Pr	Catholic		PHD	82	Maryland	9-85
Zampieron, Alexander Alg	Prof	Bentley	ABF	PHD	72	Fletcher	1965
Zandvakili, Sourushe	Assoc	Cincinnati	J	PHD	87	Indiana	
Zangeneh, Hamid	Assoc	Widener	EFGP	PHD	84	Missouri	1985
Zapalska, Alina	Asst	Marshall		PHD	91	Kentucky	1991
Zaporowski, Mark P.	Assoc	Canisius		PHD	85	SUNY-Alb	1983
Zappia, Gerard	C-Ac	Nazareth		MSED		Nazareth	
Zarembka, Paul	Prof	SUNY-Buffalo	BO	PHD	67	Wisconsin	1976
Zarinnia, Abdullah	Prof	Wis-Whitewat		PHD		Nebraska	1967
Zax, Jeffrey S.	Assoc	Colorado		PHD	84	Harvard	1990
Zeager, Lester A.	Assoc	East Carol		PHD	87	Pittsburgh	1986
Zech, Charles E.	Prof	Villanova		PHD	73	Notre Dm	1974
Zegeye, Abera	Assoc	Ball State		PHD	77	Indiana	1974
Zeigler, Lawrence F.	Prof	Tx-Arlington	M	PHD	69	Iowa	1969
Zein-Elabdin, Eiman	Asst	Frank & Mars		PHD	93	Tennessee	1995
Zeineldin, Aly	Assoc	Lg Isl-Post		PHD		NYU	
Zekavat, Seid M.	Assoc	Loyola Marym	ACG	PHD	64	S Calif	1964
Zelcer, Moishe	C-Ac	CUNY-Brookly	G	PHD	91	Baruch	1992
Zelleke, Girma	Assoc	Kutztown	FO	PHD	84	Colorado	1986
Zelman, Patricia G.	Assoc	Tarleton St	N	PHD	80	Ohio St	1982
Zeman, Allan H.	Assoc	Robt Morris		PHD	78	Pittsburgh	1964
Zestos, George K.	Asst	Chris Newpor	CFHO	PHD		Indiana	1993
Brauer Professor							
Zewail, Amin A.	Assoc	Lg Isl-Brook	AEHR	PHD		Fordham	
Zhang, Harold H.	Asst	Carnegie Mel		PHD		Duke	1994
Zhang, Jianbo	Asst	Kansas		PHD	90	Penn St	1990
Zhao, Anna	Asst	George Wash	O	PHD	93	Chicago	1993
Zhao, Jingang	Asst	Ohio State	CD	PHD	92	Yale	
Zheng, Buhong	Asst	Colo-Denver		PHD	93	W Virginia	1995
Zheng, Xu John	Asst	Texas	CO	PHD	92	Princeton	9-92
Zhou, Huizhong	Assoc	W Michigan	C	PHD	86	Northwes	1990
Zhou, Lin	Assoc	Yale		PHD	89	Princeton	1989
Zhou, Ruilin	Asst	Pennsylvania	FDE	PHD	93	Pittsburgh	1993
Milton C. Denbo Term Assistant Prof Econ; email ruilin@ysidro.sas.upenn.edu							
Zhou, Su	Asst	Tx-S Antonio	CEFP	PHD	91	Ariz St	1991
Ziegert, Andrea	VAsoc	Miami U-Ohio	HI	PHD	85	N Carol	1992
Ziegler, Joseph A.	H-Pr	Arkansas	R	PHD	71	Notre Dm	1980
Ziegler, William	Asst	Bethune-Cook		ABD		Nova	1991
Zietz, Joachim	Prof	Mid Tenn St		PHD	81	Gottingen	1989
Ziliak, James P.	Asst	Oregon	J	PHD	93	Indiana	1993
Zimbalist, Andrew	Prof	Smith	CJLP	PHD	74	Harvard	1974
Zimmer, Basil G.	Asst	Cen Michigan		PHD	72	Rutgers	1969
Zimmer, Donald T.	Prof	Tri-State		PHD		Indiana	1973
Zimmer, Michael A.	Prof	Evansville		PHD		Tennessee	1976
Zimmerman, David J.	Asst	Williams		PHD	92	Princeton	1991
Zimmerman, Robert O.	C-Pr	Xavier	ADEF	PHD	69	SUNY-Buf	1970
Zin, Stanley E.	Assoc	Carnegie Mel		PHD		Toronto	1988
Zinam, Oleg	Reitr	Cincinnati		PHD	63	Cincinnati	
Zinkhan, F. Christian	Assoc	Campbell		DBA		Miss St	1987
Zinser, James E.	C-Pr	Oberlin	KLO	PHD	67	Oregon	1967
Zlatoper, Thomas J.	C-Ac	John Carroll	ACD	PHD	80	Northwes	1984
Zodrow, George R.	C-Pr	Rice		PHD	80	Princeton	1979
Zomorrodian, Reza	Asst	N Adams St		EDD		Mass	
Zottola, Armand J.	Prof	Central Conn		PHD	70	Catholic	1970
Zschock, Dieter	Prof	SUNY-Stony B		PHD	67	Tufts	1966
Zuber, Richard A.	Prof	N Car-Charl		PHD	78	Kentucky	1978
Zuberi, Habib A.	Prof	Cen Michigan		PHD	71	S Illinois	1971
Zuehlke, Thomas W.	Assoc	Florida St		PHD	83	Florida	1983
Zweig, Michael	Prof	SUNY-Stony B		PHD	67	Michigan	1967
Zwerling, Harris T.	Asst	SUNY-Potsdam		PHD	79	Wisconsin	1988
Zwot, Eric W.	Asst	U Washington		PHD	92	Yale	1993
Zygmont, Zenon X.	Asst	Reed	APLF	PHD	94	Geo Mason	1993